PARALLEL COMPUTING:
ON THE ROAD TO EXASCALE

Advances in Parallel Computing

This book series publishes research and development results on all aspects of parallel computing. Topics may include one or more of the following: high-speed computing architectures (Grids, clusters, Service Oriented Architectures, etc.), network technology, performance measurement, system software, middleware, algorithm design, development tools, software engineering, services and applications.

Series Editor:
Professor Dr. Gerhard R. Joubert

Volume 27

Recently published in this series

Volumes 1–14 published by Elsevier Science.

ISSN 0927-5452 (print)
ISSN 1879-808X (online)

Parallel Computing:
On the Road to Exascale

Edited by

Gerhard R. Joubert

Technical University Clausthal, Germany

Hugh Leather

University of Edinburgh, Scotland, UK

Mark Parsons

University of Edinburgh, Scotland, UK

Frans Peters

Formerly Philips Research, Netherlands

and

Mark Sawyer

University of Edinburgh, Scotland, UK

IOS
Press

Amsterdam • Berlin • Washington, DC

ISBN 978-1-61499-620-0 (print)
ISBN 978-1-61499-621-7 (online)
Library of Congress Control Number: 2016933427

Publisher
IOS Press BV
Nieuwe Hemweg 6B
1013 BG Amsterdam
Netherlands
fax: +31 20 687 0019
e-mail: order@iospress.nl

Distributor in the USA and Canada
IOS Press, Inc.
4502 Rachael Manor Drive
Fairfax, VA 22032
USA
fax: +1 703 323 3668
e-mail: iosbooks@iospress.com

Preface

During the first decades of development of integrated circuits the performance of processors increased at an exponential rate, as was predicted by Gordon E. Moore when he published his so-called Moore's Law in 1965. It was clear, however, that the increase in compute speeds of single processor machines would eventually be curtailed by physical constraints. The ever increasing demand to solve more complex and larger problems could thus in the long run only be met by harnessing the power of multiple processors by using these in parallel fashion.

As a need arose to stimulate the development of parallel computing technologies, the biennial International Conference series on Parallel Computing (ParCo) was started in 1983. Since then this conference series has played a stimulating role in furthering the development and use of parallel machines. The success of these conferences was continued by ParCo2015, which was held from 1–4 September 2015 in Edinburgh, Scotland, UK.

As was the case with all previous events, ParCo2015 attracted many notable contributions depicting present and future developments in the parallel computing field. The contributed papers illustrate the many different trends, both established and newly emerging, that are influencing parallel computing.

The number of processors incorporated in parallel systems have rapidly increased over the last decade, raising the question of how to efficiently and effectively utilise the combined processing capabilities on a massively parallel scale. The difficulties experienced with the design of algorithms that scale well over a large number of processing elements have become increasingly apparent. The combination of the complexities encountered with parallel algorithm design, the deficiencies of the available software development tools to produce and maintain the resulting complex software and the complexity of scheduling tasks over thousands and even millions of processing nodes, represent a major challenge to constructing and using more powerful systems consisting of ever more processors. These challenges may prove to be even more difficult to overcome than the requirement to build more energy efficient systems.

To reach the goal of exascale computing, the next stage in the development of high performance systems, fundamentally new approaches are needed in order to surmount the aforesaid constraints. Exascale computing holds enormous promise in terms of increasing scientific knowledge acquisition and thus contributing to the future wellbeing and prosperity of humankind. Such powerful systems are, for example, needed for executing complex simulations and large information processing tasks resulting from large-scale scientific experiments. It is therefore vital that the parallel computing community succeeds in overcoming the associated challenges.

Innovative approaches that can assist in solving the problems encountered with the development and use of future high performance and high throughput systems were suggested by a number of conference speakers. Thus, for example, the incorporation of learning capabilities into processors may form the basis for more intelligent systems that can more readily adapt to changing processing requirements. Improved automatic scheduling of processing tasks may lead to greater efficiency and make systems easier to program. More flexible hardware designs, such as are proposed by, for example,

FPGAs offer further perspectives. Hardware could be made more reliable by improved monitoring, with automatic action taken if components fail.

This volume is a record of the stimulating exchange of information and innovative ideas to which all attendees contributed. In addition to the contributed papers, a number of mini-symposia were held, each focusing on one research theme. The topics covered by all contributors are reflected in the selection of accepted papers constituting these proceedings.

The organisers wish to thank all organisations and individuals who contributed to the success of this event. In particular the organisers wish to thank Pavlos Petoumenos for his assistance with producing this manuscript.

Gerhard Joubert
Hugh Leather
Mark Parsons
Frans Peters
Mark Sawyer

Date: 2015-12-15

Conference Organisation

Conference Committee

Gerhard Joubert (Germany/Netherlands) (Conference Chair)
Hugh Leather (UK)
Mark Parsons (UK)
Frans Peters (Netherlands)
Mark Sawyer (UK)

Organising & Exhibition Committee

Hugh Leather (UK) (Organising Chair)
Mark Sawyer (UK) (Organising Chair)

Finance Committee

Frans Peters (Netherlands) (Finance Chair)

ParCo2015 Sponsors

Cray UK Limited
DDN Storage
EPCC, Edinburgh, Scotland, UK
Seagate
Silicon Graphics Inc.
Technical University Clausthal, Germany
University of Edinburgh, Scotland, UK

Conference Program Committee

Mark Parsons (UK) (Program Committee Chair)
Mark Sawyer (UK) (Program Committee Co-Chair)

Program Committees of Mini-Symposia

Minisymposium Committee

Boris Grot (UK) (Chair)
Pavlos Petoumenos (UK) (Chair)

ParaFPGA-2015: Parallel Computing with FPGAs

Dirk Stroobandt (Belgium) (Symposium chair)
Erik H. D'Hollander (Belgium) (Programme committee chair)
Abdellah Touhafi (Belgium) (Programme committee co-chair)

Program Committee

Mike Hutton (USA)
Tsutomu Maruyama, (Japan)
Dionisios Pnevmatikatos (Greece)
Viktor Prasanna (USA)
Mazen A.R. Saghir (Qatar)
Donatella Sciuto (Italy)
Sascha Uhrig (Germany)
Sotirios G. Ziavras (USA)

Experiences of Porting and Optimising Code for Xeon Phi Processors

Adrian Jackson (UK)
Mark Parsons (UK)
Michéle Weiland (UK)
Simon McIntosh-Smith (UK)

Coordination Programming

Clemens Grelck (Netherlands)
Alex Shafarenko (UK)

Program Committee

Farhad Arbab (Netherlands)
Clemens Grelck (Netherlands)
Kath Knobe (USA)
Alex Shafarenko (UK)

WODIC: Workshop on Data Intensive Computing

Peter J Braam (UK) (Chair)

Program Committee

Andre Brinkmann (Germany)
Toni Cortes (Spain)
Nikita Danilov, Seagate (USA)
Jay Lofstead (USA)
Johann Lombardi (USA)
Christelle Piechurski (France)
Nathan Rutman (USA)

**Symposium on Parallel Solvers for Very Large PDE Based Systems
in the Earth- and Atmospheric Sciences**

Eike Müller (UK)
Chris Maynard (UK)
Graham Riley (UK)

Is the Programming Environment Ready for Hybrid Supercomputers?

Alistair Hart (UK)
Harvey Richardson (UK)

Symposium on Energy and Resilience in Parallel Programming

Dimitrios S. Nikolopoulos (UK)
Christos D. Antonopoulos (Greece)

Program Committee

Kevin Barker (USA)
Costas Bekas (Switzerland)
Nikolaos Bellas (Greece)
Kirk Cameron (USA)
Robert Clay (USA)
Rong Ge (USA)
Dimitris Gizopoulos (Greece)
Nikos Hardavellas (USA)
Georgios Karakonstantis (UK)
Spyros Lalis (Greece)
Dong Li (USA)
David Lowenthal (USA)
Naoya Maruyama (Japan)
Kathryn Mohror (USA)
Enrique S. Quintana-Orti (Spain)
Pedro Trancoso (Cyprus)
Zheng Wang (UK)

Symposium on Multi-System Application Extreme-Scaling Imperative

Dirk Brömmel (Germany)
Wolfgang Frings (Germany)
Brian J.N. Wylie (Germany)

Contents

Programming Models and Methods

Skeletons

Accelerators

Algorithms

Flow Problems

Invited Talks

Parallel Computing: On the Road to Exascale
G.R. Joubert et al. (Eds.)
IOS Press, 2016
© 2016 The authors and IOS Press. All rights reserved.
doi:10.3233/978-1-61499-621-7-3

Bio-Inspired Massively-Parallel Computation

Steve FURBER[a,1]
[a] *The University of Manchester, UK.*

Abstract. The SpiNNaker (Spiking Neural Network Architecture) project will soon deliver a machine incorporating a million ARM processor cores for real-time modeling of large-scale spiking neural networks. Although the scale of the machine is in the realms of high-performance computing, the technology used to build the machine comes very much from the mobile embedded world, using small integer cores and Network-on-Chip communications both on and between chips. The full machine will use a total of 10 square meters of active silicon area with 57,600 routers using predominantly multicast algorithms to convey real-time spike information through a lightweight asynchronous packet-switched fabric. This paper presents the philosophy behind the machine, and the future prospects for systems with increased cognitive capabilities based on an increasing understanding of how biological brains process information.

Keywords. Massively-parallel computation, neural networks, bio-inspired computing.

Introduction

Understanding the information processing mechanisms at work in the brain remains as one of the frontiers of science – how does this organ upon which we all so critically depend perform its vital functions? We know a great deal about the microscopic components – *neurons* – from which the brain is assembled, and brain imaging machines offer ever more detailed images of the macroscopic movement of activity around the brain, but the mechanisms employed to store, communicate and process information are at intermediate scales where the only available instrument to aid understanding is the computer model.

Although conventional computers may be used to support the models created by computational neuroscientists, the limitations of these machines rapidly become apparent as the modeled neural networks are scaled up. The human brain is formidably complex, comprising the order of a hundred billion neurons connected through some 10^{15} *synapses*. Communication between neurons is primarily through the propagation of asynchronous electro-chemical impulses – action potentials, or simply *spikes* – from one neuron through a synapse to the next. It is this highly-distributed asynchronous communication of very small units of information – each spike conveys of the order of one bit of information – that makes conventional computer modeling so inefficient.

---

[1] Corresponding Author, School of Computer Science, The University of Manchester, Oxford Road, Manchester M13 9PL, UK; E-mail: steve.furber@manchester.ac.uk

Communication mechanisms in conventional machines are optimized for conveying data at high rates in relatively large packets.

SpiNNaker (a compression of Spiking Neural Network Architecture) [1] is a machine that aims to overcome the communication limitations of conventional machines by supporting a brain-inspired communication architecture, the key objective of which is to convey very large numbers of small multicast packets efficiently. The machine should therefore be effective at supporting large-scale neural network models, but may also have applications in other domains – thinking about the issues surrounding efficient brain-modeling has led us to an unusual point in computer architecture space, and it remains to be seen what other problems have similar requirements.

1. History

Interest in understanding the brain as a source of inspiration for computation goes back a long way. This year (2015) is the 200th anniversary of the birth of Ada Lovelace, who assisted Charles Babbage in his pioneering work in designing mechanical computing devices. Ada is considered by some to be the first person to consider the problem of programming a computing machine. She left copious notes on her work, and among them is the following record of her thoughts on the brain:

> I have my hopes, and very distinct ones too, of one day getting cerebral phenomena such that I can put them into mathematical equations – in short, a law or laws for the mutual actions of the molecules of brain. ...I hope to bequeath to the generations a calculus of the nervous system.

Unfortunately Ada died at the tender age of 36 and did not live to fulfill the hopes expressed above. Had she done so she would have saved a lot of folk since a great deal of time, though perhaps her agenda was rather too ambitious for her time, and arguably remains so even today.

1.1. Alan Turing

Turing spent the last few years of his life in Manchester. During this time he wrote his seminal 1950 paper "Computing Machinery and Intelligence" [2], which begins with the words, "I propose to consider the question, 'can machines think?'". He then goes on to argue that this question is not well-posed as a research question, and turns it round into what he calls 'the imitation game', but which subsequent generations know simply as the Turing test for artificial intelligence.

Turing had come to Manchester because Freddie Williams and Tom Kilburn had led the development of the Manchester Small Scale Experimental Machine (the Manchester 'Baby'), which was the world's first operational electronic stored-program computer – the first electronic machine to implement Turing's big idea from the 1930s of the universal machine. Baby ran its first program on June 21st 1948, so it was just two years after this that Turing was speculating about machine intelligence. He expressed the view that all that was required for a machine to demonstrate human-like intelligence was a greater memory capacity than Baby, which had only 128 bytes of storage in its random access cathode ray rube memory. He though that about one gigabyte of storage should suffice, and machines should achieve this by the turn of the

20th century – a remarkable prediction of the development of technology, as it was around the turn of the century when a typical desktop PC would, indeed, have a gigabyte of main memory.

Today machines have many gigabytes of memory, and are perhaps a million times faster than the Baby (which Turing thought was quite fast enough), but even today no machine has convincingly passed Turing's test. This would have surprised Turing! Why is it that it has proved so difficult to deliver human-like artificial intelligence?

There are many possible explanations of why AI has proved so difficult, but my take on this issue is that we really don't understand natural intelligence yet, so we don't know what it is that we are trying to model or mimic in our machines. As a result my interest has turned to trying to accelerate our understanding of the brain, the biological platform for natural intelligence. As a computer engineer, I naturally look for ways to build machines that can contribute to this great scientific Grand Challenge.

1.2. 63 Years of Progress

Baby – the machine that attracted Turing to Manchester – consumed 3.5kW of electrical power with which it would execute 700 instructions per second, using 5 Joules per instruction. Since that time the University of Manchester has developed a series of machines, of which the latest is SpiNNaker, which was first operational in 2011 – 63 years after Baby. The nearest equivalent to Baby on SpiNNaker is one ARM processor core which, with its memory, occupies a few square millimetres of microchip area. A SpiNNaker processor core consumes 40mW of electrical power with which it executes 200 million instructions a second. These numbers make SpiNNaker about 25 *billion* times more energy efficient – measured in terms of energy per instruction – than Baby. It is this remarkable progress in just over half a century, combined with similar reductions in cost, that has enabled digital technology to become so prevalent today.

It is also worth reflecting on the fact that the unit of computation – the instruction – has changed very little over this time. Baby was a 32-bit binary machine where an instruction was something along the lines of a 32-bit binary arithmetic operation. The ARM processor used in SpiNNaker is also a 32-bit binary machine, and an ARM instruction may be a 32-bit binary arithmetic operation. True, ARM has a much richer choice of instructions than Baby's basic set of seven, but the conceptual difference is minimal.

This progress now enables us to build machines that Turing and Baby's designers could not even have dreamt of.

2. Building Brains

The availability of huge computing power today leads us to ask the question:

- Can we use the massively-parallel computing resources now available to us to accelerate our understanding of brain function?

Alongside this, there is the question of whether biology might have something to teach us about building better computers. Particularly in today's environment, where Moore's Law [3] is reaching physical limits and thermal constraints are forcing the adoption of highly parallel architectures, we can ask:

- Can our growing understanding of brain function point the way to more efficient parallel, fault-tolerant computation?

Brains demonstrate massive parallelism with massive connectivity, and they have excellent energy-efficiency compared with any form of electronic brain model. They are built from relatively modest performance components, and their internal communication speeds are very slow by electronic standards. Brains are highly tolerant of component failure – a capability that is of growing importance to today's multi-billion transistor microchips. If only we could understand how they work there would appear to be a lot we could learn about building better machines!

2.1. Neurons

Neurons – the cells from which brains are built – are somewhat like the logic gates from which computers are built. They are multiple input single output devices, and nature finds them useful across a very wide range of scales, from simple worms that have a few hundred neurons to humans with approaching a hundred billion. However, there are differences too. Logic gates typically have a few inputs, whereas neurons typically have a few thousand inputs (and some have a few hundred thousand inputs). In addition, neurons perform a much more complex assessment of their inputs than do logic gates, so the analogy should not be taken too far.

Brains also display considerable regularity in their neuronal structures. Neuroscientists talk about the six-layer cortical "microarchitecture", borrowing a term from computer engineering. This microarchitecture is very similar at the back of the brain, where low-level vision processing takes place, and at the front of the brain, where higher-level thinking and natural language processing takes place. That these very different processes run on very similar 'wetware' suggests to me that similar algorithms must be at work, but whereas low-level vision processing in the brain is at least partially understood, we have little idea what is going on in the higher-level regions.

To build an effective information processing system we must understand how to process, communicate and store information, and this applies as much to a biological system as it does to an engineered system.

- Neural *processing* can be modeled at different levels of detail, trading off biological fidelity against computational cost. Early models took a linear sum of weighted inputs, and then passed the result through a non-linear output function. Learning is achieved by adjusting the connection weights. Later models include the spiking behavior of neurons, perhaps using a leaky integrator to accumulate the inputs until a threshold is met, whereupon an output spike is generated. More complex models are available, down to multi-compartmental models with details resolving to individual ion channels.

- Neural *communication* is predominantly through spikes, which are pure asynchronous events. There are other mechanisms, such as the emission of neuromodulators such as dopamine and direct electrical connections between cells through 'gap' junctions, but spikes are the primary real-time communication mechanism. Here information is only which cell spikes and when it spikes, which can be captured using Address Event Representation

(AER) [4], where each neuron is given a unique label (address) and activity is simply a time series of such addresses.

- Neural information *storage* is more complex, and is achieved through a range of mechanisms including synaptic weight adaptation, dynamic network state, neuron dynamics, even exploiting the relatively slow propagation of signals along neuronal 'wires' as a form of delay-line storage.

All of these aspects of neuronal function can be captured in computer models of various forms, including embedding them into the hardware infrastructure in a manner that is known as *neuromorphic* computing.

3. Neuromorphic computing

Neuromorphic computing has attracted a fair amount of attention recently. The 2014 MIT Technology Review listed neuromorphic chips in its list of '10 Breakthrough Technologies', declaring that:

"microprocessors configured more like brains than traditional chips could soon make computers far more astute about what's going on around them."

In a similar vein, the 2015 World Economic Forum listed Neuromorphic technology among its 'Top 10 emerging technologies of 2015'. What is it that has encouraged these experts to view neuromorphic developments in such a positive light?

Part of the answer is that industry is taking neuromorphic technology seriously. Earlier this year IBM announced its 'TrueNorth' chip [5] – a 5.4 billion transistor chip (the largest transistor count ever made by IBM) that contains 4,096 digital neurosynaptic cores each with 256 neurons, all consuming around 70mW in total. Following a different approach, Qualcomm has developed its 'Zeroth' neuromorphic accelerator delivered on one of its Snapdragon smartphone processor chips. Large-scale academic projects include the Stanford Neurogrid [6], the Heidelberg HiCANN wafer-scale module [7], and the SpiNNaker system at Manchester.

While clear commercial applications of neuromorphic technology are still somewhat thin on the ground, there is clearly growing interest. Perhaps this is because the diminishing returns from Moore's Law mean that progress in conventional computers will inevitably slow, so alternative models of computation are attracting more interest?

Alongside this growing interest in neuromorphic technology there is also growing support world-wide for research into understanding the brain. In Europe, the ICT Flagship Human Brain Project with a headline budget of €1 billion, is developing a range of ICT platforms (including SpiNNaker and HiCANN) to support 'future neuroscience', 'future medicine' and 'future computing' agendas. In the USA, the Obama BRAIN initiative has a related agenda, and similar programmes have been announced in many other countries.

All of these factors establish an environment where there is unprecedented interest in understanding the brain and in applying that understanding to building better computers.

4. The SpiNNaker Project

SpiNNaker is a project at the University of Manchester, UK, to build a massively-parallel computer for brain-modeling applications. The project has been 15 years in conception and ten years in construction, with the goal of incorporating a million mobile phone processors into one machine. Even with a million processors, the expected capability of the machine will be to model a network of the complexity of 1% of the human brain or, if you prefer, ten whole mouse brains.

4.1. Design Principles

The principles underpinning the design of SpiNNaker are:

- *Virtualized topology*. There are many different network topologies in the brain, so the physical connectivity of the machine and the logical connectivity of the network being modeled are decoupled – in principle any neuron can be mapped onto any processor in the machine and connected to other neurons as required, though of course a sensible mapping will make the connection problem easier to solve!

- *Bounded asynchrony*. Synchronization in parallel machines is expensive in performance terms, so on SpiNNaker time models itself at every processor and there is no need for explicit synchronization.

- *Energy frugality*. Processors are free, and the real cost of computation is the energy required to carry it out.

Based on these principles, SpiNNaker was designed from the silicon upwards [8]. Each SpiNNaker package contains a custom-designed microchip incorporating 18 ARM microprocessor cores, local SRAM memories, and a multicast packet router, together with an off-the-shelf 128Mbyte low-power DDR SDRAM memory. These nodes are connected together in a regular 2D triangular mesh, which in large systems is closed to form a toroid.

4.2. Making Connections

The key innovation in SpiNNaker is in the way that the very high connectivity of the biological system is modeled [9]. We map Address Event Representation (AER) into a lightweight packet-switched network, with a multicast packet router on each SpiNNaker chip. The AER system allocates a 32-bit address to each neuron, and a typical spike packet contains just this address with an 8-bit header, 40 bits in all. There is also an optional 32-bit payload, though this is not needed for a simple spike packet.

When a packet arrives at a router an associative look-up is carried out in a ternary (3-state) content addressable memory (CAM) to see is the packet is recognized. If it is recognized, a corresponding 24-bit vector is fetched from RAM indicating to which of the 18 local cores and 6 inter-chip links the packet should be copied – it may go to 1 or any subset of the 24 destinations.

The ternary nature of the CAM allows "don't cares" to be included in the match pattern, allowing, for example, and entire population of neurons to be routed to the same destination(s) with a single entry. This, along with default routing mechanisms, enabled the router table size to be kept down to a practical 1,024 entries.

The job of mapping a neural network description, written in a standard network description language such as PyNN or Nengo, then boils down to allocating neural populations to cores and then constructing the routing tables to connect them as required by the application. The key idea here is the separation of the functionality of the neurons and synapses, which are modeled in real-time event-driven ARM code running on the cores, from the topology of the network, which is implemented entirely in the routing table hardware.

4.3. Building Machines

The scalability of the network model allows an arbitrary 2D space to be populated with SpiNNaker packages. In practice, 48 packages are mounted on a double-height extended Eurocard circuit board, and FPGAs are used to extend the network from board to board using high-speed serial links through SATA cables (Fig. 1).

We assemble 24 boards in a 19" card frame for a total of over 20,000 processors, and five card frames in a 19" rack cabinet for a total of over 100,000 processors per cabinet – the largest machine assembled to date is one such cabinet. Ten cabinets will then form the million-core machine.

Figure 1. 48-node (864-core) SpiNNaker board.

5. Conclusions

The SpiNNaker machine has been 15 years in conception and ten years in construction, but it is now ready for action and a machine with 100,000 cores is in operation. We have some 70 smaller boards and systems out with research groups around the world, making SpiNNaker the most accessible neuromorphic system currently available. In addition, a system is openly accessible through the Human Brain Project collaboratory portal, at present only to HBP partners, but from April 2016 it will be widely accessible to anyone with an appropriate application to sun on it.

Our hope is that the SpiNNaker platform will contribute to scientific progress in understanding information processing in the brain. Anyone with ideas to contribute towards this Grand Challenge is welcome to see what the platform can do for them.

6. Acknowledgements

I am grateful to Professor Ursula Martin who first drew my attention to the highly relevant extract in Section 1 from Ada Lovelace's notes when I was preparing to give the British Computer Society 2015 Lovelace Lecture.

The design and construction of the SpiNNaker machine was supported by EPSRC (the UK Engineering and Physical Sciences Research Council) under grants EP/D07908X/1 and EP/G015740/1, in collaboration with the universities of Southampton, Cambridge and Sheffield and with industry partners ARM Ltd, Silistix Ltd and Thales. Ongoing development of the software is supported by the EU ICT Flagship Human Brain Project (FP7-604102), in collaboration with many university and industry partners across the EU and beyond, and our own exploration of the capabilities of the machine is supported by the European Research Council under the European Union's Seventh Framework Programme (FP7/2007-2013) / ERC grant agreement 320689.

SpiNNaker has been 15 years in conception and 10 years in construction, and many folk in Manchester and in our various collaborating groups around the world have contributed to get the project to its current state. I gratefully acknowledge all of these contributions.

References

[1] S.B. Furber, F. Galluppi, S. Temple, L.A. Plana, The SpiNNaker project, *Proc. IEEE* **102**(5) (2014), 652-665.
[2] A.M. Turing, Computing Machinery and Intelligence, Mind **LIX**(236) (1950), 433-460.
[3] G.E. Moore, Cramming more components onto integrated circuits, *Electronics* **38**(8) (1965), 114-117.
[4] M. Mahowald, VLSI analogs of neuronal visual processing: a synthesis of form and function, Ph.D. dissertation, California Inst. Tech., Pasadena, CA., 1992.
[5] P.A. Merolla, J.V. Arthur, R. Alvarez-Icaza, A.S. Cassidy, J. Sawada, F. Akopyan, B.L. Jackson, N. Imam, C. Guo, Y. Nakamura, B. Brezzo, I. Vo, S.K. Esser, R. Appuswamy, B. Taba, A. Amir, M.D. Flickner, W.P. Risk, R. Manohar, D.S. Modha, A million spiking-neuron integrated circuit with a scalable communication network and interface, *Science* **345**(6197) (2014), 668-673.
[6] R. Silver, K. Boahen, S. Grillner, N. Kopell, K. Olsen, Neurotech for neuroscience: unifying concepts, organizing principles, and emerging tools, *J. Neurosci.* **27**(44) (2007), 11807–11819.
[7] J. Schemmel, D. Bruderle, A. Grubl, M. Hock, K. Meier, S. Millner, A wafer-scale neuromorphic hardware system for large-scale neural modeling, *Proc. Int. Symp. Circuits Syst.*, 2010, 1947–1950.
[8] E. Painkras, L.A. Plana, J.D. Garside, S. Temple, F. Galluppi, C. Patterson, D.R. Lester, A.D. Brown, S.B. Furber, SpiNNaker: A 1W 18-core System-on-Chip for massively-parallel neural network simulation, *IEEE J. Solid-State Circuits* **48**(8) (2013), 1943-1953.
[9] S.B. Furber, D.R. Lester, L.A. Plana, J.D. Garside, E. Painkras, S. Temple, A.D. Brown, Overview of the SpiNNaker system architecture, *IEEE Trans. Computers* **62**(12) (2013), 2454-2467.

Parallel Computing: On the Road to Exascale
G.R. Joubert et al. (Eds.)
IOS Press, 2016
© 2016 The authors and IOS Press. All rights reserved.
doi:10.3233/978-1-61499-621-7-11

Automatic Tuning of Task Scheduling Policies on Multicore Architectures

Akshatha Bhat [a], Andrew Lenharth [b], Donald Nguyen [c], Qing Yi [d], and
Keshav Pingali [b]

[a] *The MathWorks*
[b] *University of Texas at Austin*
[c] *Synthace Limited*
[d] *University of Colorado at Colrado Springs*

Abstract. The performance of multi-threaded applications depends on efficient
scheduling of parallel tasks. Manually selecting schedulers is difficult because the
best scheduler depends on the application, machine and input. We present a framework that automatically selects the best scheduler based on empirical tuning results.
We applied our framework to tune eleven applications parallelized using OpenMP,
TBB or the Galois system. Depending on the application and machine, we observed
up to 4X performance improvement over the default scheduler. We were also able to
prune the search space by an order of magnitude while still achieving performance
within 16% of the best scheduler.

Keywords. Autotuning, parallel programming, task parallelism, scheduling

Introduction

In multi-threaded programming, task scheduling is the assignment of tasks to available threads. In this paper, we consider the problem of scheduling tasks for algorithms
that generate new tasks dynamically. For a divide-and-conquer algorithm in which each
task is a conquer step, a strategy that processes each new task immediately in the thread
that creates it (work-first scheduling) may exploit the natural locality in the algorithm.
More general algorithms may have tasks with complex, input-dependent data dependencies, locality patterns, task duration, and task generation. In this paper, we show that a
single scheduling policy is not ideal under these conditions.

Since memory topologies and interconnects between cores, caches, packages, and
memory are becoming more complex, schedulers have to consider communication costs
in determining good scheduling policies. For example, an algorithm may prefer a strict
LIFO schedule for locality reasons, but on modern machines, strictly following a LIFO
schedule in parallel would be a significant scalability bottleneck. The diversity in machines and even the runtime characteristics of the hardware implies that a well-tuned
scheduler on one machine for an algorithm may not be ideal on another machine, even
for the same algorithm.

In this paper, we show that even for extremely dynamic and input-sensitive applications that speculatively evaluate dynamically created tasks concurrently, a stable task

---

Corresponding author: Keshav Pingali, 4.126 Peter O'Donnell Building, The University of Texas, Austin,
TX 78712. Email: pingali@cs.utexas.edu.

scheduler can typically be pre-selected for an underlying platform based on profiling results, and the pre-selected scheduler typically performs relatively well even when its execution environment changes over time. In particular, we present an empirical tuning framework that automatically finds good task schedulers from a library of tunable schedulers.

We apply this methodology to the tuning of schedulers for three parallel programming models: OpenMP [1], TBB [2] and Galois [3]. We implement a schedule tuning framework using POET [4,5], an interpreted source-to-source program transformation language designed to support fine-grained parameterization and empirical tuning of compiler optimizations. The framework is portable across different machine architectures and can be extended to support additional parallel programming models such as Cilk [6] and languages such as Java.

We evaluate eleven applications, including both regular computations and irregular graph-based applications, on different machine architectures. By automatically choosing the most suitable schedulers for iterations of parallel loops within these applications, we have observed a 1.4x-4x performance improvement over the default scheduling policies pre-selected by the parallel programming models.

Our study also reveals that while the space of schedulers is large, there are several simplifying assumptions that can be adopted to reduce the search space without sacrificing performance. We can reduce the search space by an order of magnitude compared to exhaustive search while achieving performance within 16% of the best scheduler found exhaustively. Additionally, although in principle performance of some of our applications is input-sensitive, we found that in practice there is some performance stability among schedulers with runs on different inputs. This suggests that further search space pruning can be done when optimizing programs for multiple inputs.

The rest of this paper is organized as follows. Section 1 provides background information on the Galois, TBB and OpenMP programming models and their task scheduling policies. Section 2 describes the applications we selected and our experimental design. Section 3 presents experimental results on the effectiveness of our empirical tuning approach. Section 4 discusses related work. Finally, Section 5 presents conclusions of the paper.

1. Parallel Programming Models

We consider two common parallel programming structures in this paper. The first is the parallel "do all" loop used to concurrently evaluate a fixed collection of tasks with each task independent of the others. The second is a task model in which each task may may dynamically create new tasks. This is usually modeled with dynamic work-lists. Each of the three parallel programming models, OpenMP [1] (OMP), Intel Threading Building Blocks (TBB) [2] and Galois [3], support these forms as summarized in this section.

1.1. OpenMP

OpenMP allows each parallel loops to take a schedule clause (*schedule(S,N)*) that specifies how loop iterations should be divided into contiguous non-empty sets called *chunks* and how these chunks should be distributed to different threads.

- schedule(static,N): Iterations are divided into chunks of size N which are assigned to the threads in a round-robin fashion. When N is not specified explicitly, the iterations are divided into chunks approximately equal in size so that at most one chunk is distributed to each thread.
- schedule(dynamic, N): Chunks of N iterations are dynamically assigned to each thread upon request. When a thread completes its chunk, it requests another until no work is left. When unspecified, the default value of N is 1.
- schedule(guided,N): This policy is similar to the dynamic policy except that the chunksize decreases exponentially to a minimum size of N. This policy can improve load-balance for skewed workloads.

In general, small chunk sizes and dynamic scheduling increase runtime overhead in exchange for better load balance.

OpenMP supports dynamically created tasks through the OpenMP task feature that provides the capability to spawn asynchronous tasks and wait for their completion. Schedule clauses can be specified as before, but they only apply to the iterations of the parallel for loop and not to the spawned tasks. There is no user-level method to modify task scheduling.

1.2. Intel TBB

For a fixed number of tasks, TBB provides a **parallel_for** statement that takes a range object, a function to invoke, and a partitioner object. The range object divides an iteration space into coarse units of work, analogous to chunks in OpenMP. The blocked_range object behaves the same as OpenMP static scheduling. TBB also provides other range objects which are useful for 2D and 3D work division. The range object is used recursively to divide the iteration space until chunks reach a certain "grainsize" or chunk size. Users specify the limit for chunk size using a partitioner object. The simple_partitioner lets a user explicitly choose the chunk size, while auto_partitioner picks a chunk size automatically.

For dynamically created tasks, TBB provides a **parallel_do** statement. As with OpenMP, there is no user-level method to modify task scheduling. TBB task scheduling is implemented as a "breadth-first theft and depth-first work" policy similar to the Cilk system [7].

1.3. Galois

Compared to OpenMP and TBB, Galois provides much more advanced support for dynamic creation of tasks by supporting (1) user-level control over scheduling newly created work and (2) speculatively parallelizing tasks that may have dependencies on each other. Galois ensures that, in spite of speculative parallelization, the execution appears as if all tasks are serialized in some order. Supporting this functionality adds two dimensions to scheduling:

- The behavior of Galois applications can be strongly input-dependent. The best scheduler not only varies by application but also by input to the application.
- In addition to affecting locality, runtime overhead and load balance, schedulers may also affect the cost of finding tasks that can execute in parallel at runtime (i.e.,

speculation costs). For example, a scheduler that increases locality, i.e., increases the data shared between two tasks, may also increase the frequency of conflicts (speculation failures) as those two tasks, when executed concurrently, are more likely to conflict as well.

Given the additional performance implications, Galois provides a larger set of scheduling options than TBB and OpenMP. The following is just a subset of possible scheduling options.

- FIFO, LIFO (**F/L**). Standard queues and stacks of tasks protected by a single lock. Since these data structures serialize the scheduling of tasks, they are most useful in conjunction with other strategies to build compound scheduling policies.
- ChunkedFIFO<N> and ChunkedLIFO<N> (**cF/cL**). A queue/stack of chunks of at most N tasks, protected by a single lock. Each thread maintains a private chunk from which it retrieves and places tasks until it exhausts that chunk and gets a new one from the global queue/stack.
- dChunkedFIFO<N> and dChunkedLIFO<N> (**dF/dL**). A variation of the cF/cL policies where a separate queue/stack is maintained for each last-level cache. Threads sharing a last-level cache share the same queue/stack. When it is empty, threads try stealing chunks from other last-level queues/stacks. These schedulers reduce synchronization costs on modern multicore machines by trying to limit communication between processors.
- LocalQueue<G,L> (**LQ**). A compound scheduler that creates a new scheduler from a global (G) and a local (L) base schedulers. The global scheduler manages the initial set of tasks and is shared by all threads. The local scheduler is thread-local and manages the dynamic tasks generated by the thread during execution. This scheduler reduces contention on the global scheduler because the local schedulers handle new tasks, and synchronization costs are reduced because the local schedulers are thread-local.

2. Results

To better understand the behavior and impact of task scheduling, we conducted an extensive performance study using eleven benchmarks parallelized using OpenMP, TBB and Galois, summarized in Table 1. Four of these applications are written using the Galois programming model and are taken from the Lonestar benchmark suite [8]. Delaunay triangulation (**DT**) and Delaunay mesh refinement (**DMR**) are two important computational geometry algorithms. Survey propagation (**SP**) is a heuristic SAT-solver based on Bayesian inference [9], and Asynchronous Variational Integrators (**AVI**) is a recent algorithm for performing accurate physical simulations. Eight additional benchmarks are taken from six applications of the PARSEC benchmark suite [10], which provides both TBB and OpenMP implementations for two of the applications (Blacksholes and Bodytrack). We count each distinct implementation as a different benchmark in Table 1. Our experiments used Galois library version 2.1.2 and the TBB library version 3.0.

We evaluate the performance of each benchmark in Table 1 under a large space of possible schedulers on two machines: a 40-core workstation (**M1**) with four Xeon E7-4860 CPUs and ten cores per CPU, and an SGI UltraViolet NUMA system (**M2**) with

Table 1. Benchmarks and associated default input data.

Benchmark	Model	Input
DT	Galois	triangulation of 1 M randomly selected points from a unit square
DMR	Galois	Refinement of mesh generated from triangulation of DT input
SP	Galois	Random 3-SAT with 380 K clauses and 100 K variables
AVI	Galois	166 K elem, 84 K nodes
Blackscholes	OpenMP	10 M options
BodyTrack	OpenMP	4 cameras, 261 frames, 4 K particles, 5 annealing layers
Freqmine	OpenMP	Database of 250 K documents.
Blackscholes	TBB	10 M options
Bodytrack	TBB	4 cameras, 261 frames, 4 K particles, 5 annealing layers
Swaptions	TBB	128 swaptions, 1 M simulations
StreamCluster	TBB	1 M input points

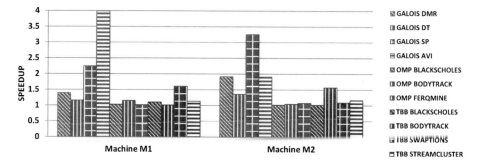

Figure 1. Performance improvement when using exhaustive search to find the best schedulers over using the default scheduler of each application

eight Xeon E7520 CPUs and four cores per CPU with 2 CPUs per NUMA node. All benchmarks are compiled using gcc 4.4.6 on **M1** and gcc 4.3.2 on **M2**, with the -O3 optimization flag. We evaluated each benchmark implementation at least five times and report the average runtime statistics of the different runs.

In this section, we show results from an exhaustive exploration of the tuning space. Using the insights gained from this search we implement a new tuning algorithm that significantly reduces tuning time without sacrificing performance (Section 3).

Figure 1 summarizes the impact of using exhaustive search to find the best task schedulers for our benchmarks compared to their performance when using the default task schedulers supplied by OpenMP, TBB, and Galois. The result shows that empirically finding the best schedulers provides a significant performance benefit for most benchmarks. Galois programs show the most improvement (average 2.2X), followed by TBB programs (average 1.2X) and OpenMP programs (average 1.06X).

The following subsections analyzes the sensitivity of the application performance to task schedulers in more depth to better understand the performance variations. In particular, we find that while the best group of task schedulers varies by application (Section 2.1) and input (Section 2.2), there are trends that can simplify the empirical search for good schedulers (Section 3): (1) the chunk size parameter common to many schedulers typically has a simple relation to performance and can be optimized independently

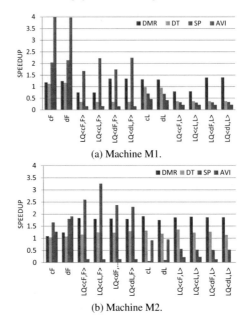

(a) Machine M1.

(b) Machine M2.

Figure 2. Performance improvement of Galois benchmarks when using different types of schedulers with their best chunk sizes over using the default Galois scheduler

of the scheduler itself, and (2) many Galois applications can be broadly characterized as preferring either LIFO or FIFO-like schedulers.

2.1. Selecting The Best Scheduler Types For Different Applications

To find the optimal scheduler for OpenMP and Galois algorithms, we search the entire scheduling space, selecting for each scheduler, the empirically found optimal chunk size for that scheduler, algorithm, machine tuple. Performance is normalized to the default scheduler for each system.

We observe that the performance of the OpenMP static scheduler can be improved (up to 15% on machine M1) by using alternative chunk sizes, but using alternative scheduler types (*e.g.*, guided or dynamic schedulers) provides limited benefit (under 5% on both machines) for all three OpenMP applications. This is because these applications contain mostly static parallel loops that do not require dynamic task scheduling

On the other hand, Galois schedulers (see Figure 2) can offer dramatically different levels of performance. Although the default scheduler (dChunkedFIFO with a chunk size of 256) offers reasonably good performance in most cases, significant speedup is possible. The *dF* bars show that improvements are possible by varying the chunk size of the default scheduler. It is also clear that specific algorithms greatly benefit from alternate schedulers. For example, while the default scheduler (dF) offers the best performance for AVI, its performance for DMR, DT, and SP is suboptimal. LQ<cL,F> is one of the best performing schedulers for SP, but one of the worst for AVI, DT and DMR. LQ trades load-balance for temporal locality, so algorithms such as DT which have little initial work suffer significant load-balance issues.

For irregular applications, algorithm characteristics play a crucial role in the choice of scheduler types, and a different scheduler type often needs to be selected for computa-

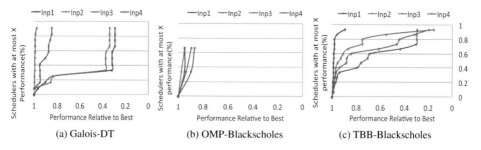

      (a) Galois-DT   (b) OMP-Blackscholes   (c) TBB-Blackscholes

Figure 3. Cumulative distribution of relative performance with different input sets.

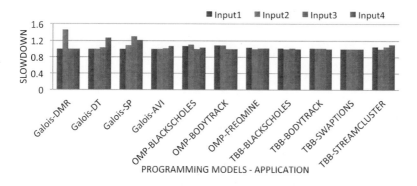

Figure 4. Performance slowdown on machine M1 when using best scheduler across inputs on a particular input.

tions with different dependence and locality properties. On the other hand, static parallel loops are relatively stable, and the same default static scheduler in OpenMP can be used for most of these loops to attain reasonably good performance.

2.2. Sensitivity Of Schedulers To Program Inputs

To study the stability of our tuning results across different application inputs, we have evaluated the performance of the best schedulers found exhaustively over multiple representative inputs.

Figure 3 shows the cumulative distribution of scheduler performance for each program input of three representative Galois, OpenMP, and TBB benchmarks. Figure 3a shows that on inputs 3 and 4 of DT, all schedulers achieved at least 0.8X of the best performance. These inputs are thus relatively insensitive to the choice of different schedulers. However, inputs 1 and 2 much more sensitive, with only about 20% of schedulers within 80% of best performance, and with a majority of schedulers achieving less than 40% of the performance of the best scheduler. Figure 3b shows that the performance of OMP-Blackscholes is largely insensitive to its schedulers, where all tested schedulers achieve more than 80% of best performance on all inputs. Interestingly, Figure 3c shows that, for most inputs, when Blackscholes is parallelized using TBB, less than half the schedulers do well, and the remaining schedulers have a wide variation in performance, unlike Figure 3a where performance is more clustered.

While the performance of different schedulers may be considerably sensitive to different application inputs for some of our benchmarks, the best scheduler for one input could perform nearly as well across a wide range of different inputs. To this end, Figure 4 quantifies the stability of the best schedulers by comparing the performance of the best scheduler for each individual input against one that performs best on the average across all program inputs. In Figure 4, the slowdowns are close to 1, indicating that a single scheduler could produce close to the best performance for all program inputs, for a majority of the benchmarks except Galois DMR, DT, and SP, where using a single scheduler for all program inputs could result in 10%-50% slowdown on some application inputs.

Overall, we find that while the selection of best schedulers could be sensitive to different application inputs for some dynamic Galois benchmarks, for a majority of the benchmarks, the best schedulers perform close to the best across different program inputs. Therefore, a best scheduler selected using a representative set of program inputs can be expected to perform well across different inputs for a majority of applications.

3. Effectiveness of Tuning

Building on the results in the previous section, we implement a tuning framework that quickly navigates a pruned search-space of schedulers using an optimized search algorithm that uses the insights from Section 2. The search space is pruned by first only comparing schedulers at their default chunk size. A gradient-based search is used to optimize the chunk size of the best found scheduler. We use the experimental design presented in Section 2 to compare the effectiveness of the optimized search with that of the much more expensive naive exhaustive search. Additionally, we evaluate the stability of the selected best schedulers across different program inputs and show that although many algorithms, especially those that perform irregular computations and dynamically spawn new tasks (e.g., the Galois benchmarks), may behave very differently when given different problems sizes and input data, a scheduler typically can be found that works well across a large class of different inputs.

Table 2 compares the search space, the tuning time required, and the selected best schedulers when naively exploring the space of schedulers versus using our optimized search algorithm to explore a pruned search space. From Table 2, we see that our optimized search is able to reduce tuning time while preserving good scheduling policies. The Galois benchmarks show the most reduction in search space and tuning time, because their scheduler space is the largest, where our optimized search is able to reduce the overall tuning space of schedulers by 24-25X while achieving performance within 10% of the scheduler found by the naive search for most benchmarks. The one outlier is DT where the best scheduler in the pruned space is 16% slower.

The best schedulers selected from the pruned space are typically the same schedulers found via naive search except that their chunk sizes differ. In particular, the naive search navigates a predetermined set of chunk sizes, while the optimized search performs a binary search of a predetermined range of chunk sizes. The binary search exploits the result of our preliminary study in that scheduling algorithms are either relatively insensitive to chunk sizes or have convex response to chunk sizes.

Model-Benchmark	Schedulers		Tuning Time		Same Best	Speedup		
	Naive	Pruned	Naive	Pruned		Naive	Pruned	Diff. (%)
Galois-DMR	588	22	13	1	No	1.39	1.34	3.9
Galois-DT	588	24	58	8	No	1.16	1.00	16.3
Galois-SP	1764	69	1114	78	Yes	2.24	2.12	5.8
Galois-AVI	588	23	1010	93	Yes	3.99	3.75	6.3
OMP-Blackscholes	54	41	144	109	Yes	1.03	1.02	3.6
OMP-Bodytrack	108	81	45	34	Yes	1.15	1.14	0.2
OMP-Freqmine	378	294	2007	1561	Yes	1.06	1.04	1.5
TBB-Blackscholes	18	12	12	8	-	1.10	1.09	0.4
TBB-Bodytrack	36	30	65	55	-	1.00	1.00	1.8
TBB-Swaptions	36	28	547	425	-	1.61	1.60	0.3
TBB-Streamcluster	72	56	120	93	-	1.13	1.08	5.1

Table 2. Comparison between naive and pruned search spaces. Tuning time is in minutes. The **Same Best** column indicates whether the same best scheduler was found in both the naive and pruned spaces although the chunk size may differ. Speedup is relative to the default scheduling policy. Difference is relative difference between naive and pruned speedups.

4. Related Work

Most parallel programming models permit developers to specify varying policies to schedule concurrent tasks. Our framework currently supports tuning of scheduling policies for applications parallelized using OpenMP [1], TBB [2], and Galois [3]. Our tuning methodology, however, is not restricted to these APIs and can be extended to support additional parallel programming interfaces.

Empirical tuning has been used in the development of many successful scientific libraries, such as ATLAS [11], OSKI [12], FFTW [13], SPIRAL [14], among others, to achieve portable high performance. More recent work on *iterative compilation* has modified the configurations of compiler optimizations based on empirical feedback from the optimized code [15,16,17,18]. Predictive modeling from machine learning has also been adopted to statically build optimization models from a representative training set of programs [19,20]. The learned models are then used to automatically determine optimization configurations for future applications without any additional tuning.

Task scheduling for homogeneous architectures has mostly focused on runtime techniques that allow applications to dynamically adapt to workload variations of the underlying platform [21,22]. Zhang et al. used runtime empirical search aided with decision trees to choose the best scheduling policy and the number of the threads to use at individual loop levels [23]. Broquedis et al. used an OpenMP compiler to generate a tree-like application parallelism structure before using the runtime to dynamically schedule and migrate threads and data among processing cores [24]. Sondag and Rajan used a phase-based tuning approach to match resource needs of code sections to asymmetric multicores at runtime [25]. Wang and Boyle used a machine learning compiler to determine the number of threads to use and scheduling policies [26].

Our work focuses on how each multi-threaded application can internally manage the scheduling of its concurrent tasks on varying platforms. It is orthogonal to the extensive studying of task scheduling policies within the operating system or the workload or performance variation studies of architectures [27], both of which focus on the interference between multiple applications instead of the needs of each individual application.

5. Conclusions

We present an automated empirical tuning framework to automatically find task scheduling policies that yield the best performance for an application on a given machine architecture and input set. The framework supports scheduling policies exposed by diverse parallel programming models such as the Galois system, Intel TBB and OpenMP. We used the framework to conduct an extensive performance study on eleven different applications and present the insights we gained in the process. Our results indicate that the performance of multi-threaded applications are sensitive to the choice of task scheduling policies, and while the best decisions often vary across different machine architecture and input data, our auto-tuning framework can be used to find the best schedulers that work well across a wide range of application inputs on each architecture.

References

[1] Dagum, L., Menon, R.: Openmp: An industry-standard api for shared-memory programming. IEEE Comput. Sci. Eng. **5**(1) (January 1998) 46–55
[2] Reinders, J.: Intel threading building blocks. First edn. O'Reilly & Associates, Inc., Sebastopol, CA, USA (2007)
[3] Pingali, K., Nguyen, D., Kulkarni, M., Burtscher, M., Hassaan, M.A., Kaleem, R., Lee, T.H., Lenharth, A., Manevich, R., Méndez-Lojo, M., Prountzos, D., Sui, X.: The tao of parallelism in algorithms. In: Proceedings of the 32nd ACM SIGPLAN conference on Programming language design and implementation. PLDI '11, New York, NY, USA, ACM (2011) 12–25
[4] Yi, Q.: POET: A scripting language for applying parameterized source-to-source program transformations. Software: Practice & Experience **42**(6) (May 2012) 675–706
[5] Yi, Q., Seymour, K., You, H., Vuduc, R., Quinlan, D.: POET: Parameterized optimizations for empirical tuning. In: POHLL'07: Workshop on Performance Optimization for High-Level Languages and Libraries. (Mar 2007)
[6] Blumofe, R.D., Joerg, C.F., Kuszmaul, B.C., Leiserson, C.E., Randall, K.H., Zhou, Y.: Cilk: an efficient multithreaded runtime system. In: Proceedings of the fifth ACM SIGPLAN symposium on Principles and practice of parallel programming. PPOPP '95, New York, NY, USA, ACM (1995) 207–216
[7] Kukanov, A., Voss, M.J.: The foundations for scalable multi-core software in intel threading building blocks. Intel Technology Journal (November 2007)
[8] Kulkarni, M., Burtscher, M., Cascaval, C., Pingali, K.: Lonestar: A suite of parallel irregular programs. In: ISPASS, IEEE (2009) 65–76
[9] Braunstein, A., MÃl'zard, M., Zecchina, R.: Survey propagation: an algorithm for satisfiability. Technical report (2002)
[10] Bienia, C., Kumar, S., Singh, J.P., Li, K.: The parsec benchmark suite: characterization and architectural implications. In: Proceedings of the 17th international conference on Parallel architectures and compilation techniques. PACT '08, New York, NY, USA, ACM (2008) 72–81
[11] Whaley, R.C., Petitet, A., Dongarra, J.: Automated empirical optimizations of software and the ATLAS project. Parallel Computing **27**(1) (2001) 3–25
[12] Vuduc, R., Demmel, J., Yelick, K.: OSKI: An interface for a self-optimizing library of sparse matrix kernels (2005)
[13] Frigo, M., Johnson, S.: FFTW: An Adaptive Software Architecture for the FFT. In: Proceedings of the International Conference on Acoustics, Speech, and Signal Processing (ICASSP). Volume 3., Seattle, WA (1998) 1381
[14] Püschel, M., Moura, J.M.F., Johnson, J., Padua, D., Veloso, M., Singer, B.W., Xiong, J., Franchetti, F., Gačić, A., Voronenko, Y., Chen, K., Johnson, R.W., Rizzolo, N.: SPIRAL: Code generation for DSP transforms. IEEE special issue on Program Generation, Optimization, and Adaptation **93**(2) (2005)
[15] Qasem, A., Kennedy, K.: Profitable loop fusion and tiling using model-driven empirical search. In: Proceedings of the 20th ACM International Conference on SuperComputing (ICS06). (June 2006)

[16] Baradaran, N., Chame, J., Chen, C., Diniz, P., Hall, M., Lee, Y.J., Liu, B., Lucas, R.: Eco: An empirical-based compilation and optimization system. In: International Parallel and Distributed Processing Symposium. (2003)

[17] Pike, G., Hilfinger, P.: Better tiling and array contraction for compiling scientific programs. In: SC, Baltimore, MD, USA (November 2002)

[18] Pan, Z., Eigenmann, R.: Fast automatic procedure-level performance tuning. In: Proc. Parallel Architectures and Compilation Techniques. (2006)

[19] Cavazos, J., Fursin, G., Agakov, F., Bonilla, E., O'Boyle, M.F.P., Temam, O.: Rapidly selecting good compiler optimizations using performance counters. In: CGO '07: Proceedings of the International Symposium on Code Generation and Optimization, Washington, DC, USA, IEEE Computer Society (2007) 185–197

[20] Dubach, C., Jones, T.M., Bonilla, E.V., Fursin, G., O'Boyle, M.F.P.: Portable compiler optimisation across embedded programs and microarchitectures using machine learning. In: MICRO 42: Proceedings of the 42nd Annual IEEE/ACM International Symposium on Microarchitecture, New York, NY, USA, ACM (2009) 78–88

[21] Hall, M.W., Martonosi, M.: Adaptive parallelism in compiler-parallelized code. Concurrency - Practice and Experience **10**(14) (1998) 1235–1250

[22] Corbalán, J., Martorell, X., Labarta, J.: Performance-driven processor allocation (2000)

[23] Zhang, Y., Voss, M.: Runtime empirical selection of loop schedulers on hyperthreaded smps. In: Proceedings of the 19th IEEE International Parallel and Distributed Processing Symposium (IPDPS'05) - Papers - Volume 01. IPDPS '05, Washington, DC, USA, IEEE Computer Society (2005) 44.2–

[24] Broquedis, F., Aumage, O., Goglin, B., Thibault, S., Wacrenier, P.A., Namyst, R.: Structuring the execution of OpenMP applications for multicore architectures. In IEEE, ed.: International Parallel and Distributed Symposium (IPDPS 2010), Atltanta, United States (April 2010)

[25] Sondag, T., Rajan, H.: Phase-based tuning for better utilization of performance-asymmetric multicore processors. In: Proceedings of the 2011 9th Annual IEEE/ACM International Symposium on Code Generation and Optimization. CGO '11, Washington, DC, USA, IEEE Computer Society (2011) 11–20

[26] Wang, Z., O'Boyle, M.F.: Mapping parallelism to multi-cores: a machine learning based approach. In: Proceedings of the 14th ACM SIGPLAN symposium on Principles and practice of parallel programming. PPoPP '09, New York, NY, USA, ACM (2009) 75–84

[27] Skinner, D., Kramer, W.: Understanding the causes of performance variability in hpc workloads. In: Workload Characterization Symposium, 2005. Proceedings of the IEEE International. (oct. 2005) 137 – 149

Architectures and Performance

Parallel Computing: On the Road to Exascale
G.R. Joubert et al. (Eds.)
IOS Press, 2016
doi:10.3233/978-1-61499-621-7-25

Algorithmic scheme for hybrid computing with CPU, Xeon-Phi/MIC and GPU devices on a single machine

Sylvain CONTASSOT-VIVIER [a] and Stephane VIALLE [b]

[a] *Loria - UMR 7503, Université de Lorraine, Nancy, France*
[b] *UMI 2958, Georgia Tech - CNRS, CentraleSupelec, University Paris-Saclay, 57070 METZ, France*

Abstract. In this paper, we address the problem of the efficient parallel exploitation of different types of computing devices inside a single machine, to solve a scientific problem. As a first step, we apply our scheme to the Jacobi relaxation. Despite its simplicity, it is a good example of iterative process for scientific simulation. Then, we evaluate and analyze the performance of our parallel implementation on two configurations of hybrid machine.

Keywords. Accelerator, Xeon-Phi/MIC, GPU, hybrid computing, heterogeneous computing, offload computing

Introduction

According to the hardware evolution in the last decades, the architecture of parallel systems becomes more and more complex. In particular, the development of many-core devices such as GPU (Graphical Processing Unit) and MIC (Many Integrated Cores) have induced an additional hierarchical level of parallelism in supercomputers. Indeed, current parallel systems are typically organized as big clusters of nodes and the many-core devices provide much larger computational power at the node level. However, the efficient programming of all that gathered power is still a major difficulty in the domain of High Performance Computing, partly due to the hierarchy in the system and to the communications between the different levels. The main issue is to design and implement efficient parallel schemes, as general as possible, that allows an efficient cooperation between all the computing units in a parallel system. The study presented in this paper is, to the best of our knowledge, one of the first attempt to solve a scientific application by using three different types of computing units inside a single node: the CPU cores, a GPU and a MIC.

After a brief review of the previous works over the programming of *hybrid* machines (containing different kinds of computing devices) in Section 1, our application and hardware testsbeds are described in Section 2. Then, Section 3 details the different algorithms designed and implemented for each kind of device (CPU, GPU, MIC). Finally, a multiple devices solution is proposed in Section 4. An experimental performance comparison and analysis, proposed in Section 5, allows us to evaluate the efficiency of our scheme and to point out the major difficulties in such cooperation.

1. Related works

In the past, we have investigated some ways to efficiently design algorithms and codes for hybrid nodes (one PC with a GPU) and clusters of hybrid nodes (cluster of multi-core nodes with GPUs) [1,2]. Overlapping of computations with communications was a key point to achieve high performance on hybrid architectures. The processing speed of each node increases when using accelerators, while interconnection networks remains unchanged, and data transfer times between CPU main memory and accelerator memory introduce new overheads.

Today, scientific computing on GPU accelerators is common, but using Xeon Phi accelerators has still to be explored, although some comparison works have been achieved. In [3], authors point out the need to optimize data storage and data accesses in different ways on GPU and Xeon Phi, but no dot attempt to use both accelerators in the same program. Another strategy is to use a generic programming model and tool to program heterogeneous architectures, like OpenCL [4]. But usually it does not hide the different architectures requirements to achieve optimal performance, and it still requires an (important) algorithmic effort to design high performance codes running concurrently on different accelerators.

2. Benchmark application and testbeds

2.1. Jacobi relaxation application

According to the scope of this paper (hybrid computing with CPU, GPU and MIC), we have chosen an application with a regular domain, that is quite representative of the scientific problems adapted to the constraints of the studied devices (especially the GPU). Indeed, the objective of this work is not to propose parallel schemes for general numerical methods but to study the best ways to make the different internal devices of a hybrid computer work together.

The Jacobi relaxation is a classical iterative process providing a simple modeling of heat transfer or electrical potential diffusion in 2D or 3D discrete domain (regular grid). The objective of this application is to compute the stable state over the entire domain for some given fixed boundary conditions. An explicit iterative 2D scheme is performed as:

$$crt[l][c] = \frac{pre[l-1][c] + pre[l][c-1] + pre[l][c] + pre[l][c+1] + pre[l+1][c]}{5} \tag{1}$$

where $crt[l][c]$ is the value of the grid point at line l and column c at the current iteration, while $pre[l][c]$ gives the value of the same grid point at the previous iteration. The other four grid points involved are the direct neighbors (in 4-connexity) of the current point.

This iterative process is performed until the termination condition is reached. As the quantities in the grid are generally coded by real numbers, the strict stabilization may not be reachable in reasonable time. Among the different solutions to get around this problem, we have chosen to fix the number of iterations. This presents the advantage of providing a complete and accurate control over the amount of computation. In fact, this parameter is essential to study some aspects of parallel algorithms, such as the scalability.

2.2. Testbeds

The machine used at CentraleSupelec (CS) is a Dell R720 server with two 6-cores Intel(R) Xeon(R) CPU E5-2620 at 2.10GHz, and two accelerators on separate PCIe buses.

One accelerator is an Intel MIC *Xeon-Phi 3120* with 57 physical cores at 1.10 GHz, supporting 4 threads each. The other one is a Nvidia GPU *GeForce GTX Titan Black* (Kepler architecture) with 2880 CUDA cores. The machine used at Loria is a Dell R720 server with two 8-cores Intel(R) Xeon(R) CPU E5-2640 at 2.00GHz, and two accelerators on separate PCIe buses. One accelerator is an Intel MIC *Xeon-Phi 5100* with 60 physical cores at 1.05 GHz supporting 4 threads each. The other one is a Nvidia GPU *Tesla K40m* (Kepler architecture) with 2880 CUDA cores. The CS machine uses CentOs 7.1.1503 and the Intel compiler v15.0.0 whereas the Loria machine uses CentOs 6.6 and the Intel compiler v14.0.3.

In this paper, we study the behavior of our parallel scheme on these two different machines, taking into account the relative computing powers of CPU, GPU and MIC.

3. Optimized kernels for single architecture and device

3.1. Multi-core CPU with OpenMP

A first version of the multi-core CPU kernel to perform the Jacobi relaxation consists in a classical domain decomposition in horizontal strips through the cores. This is achieved by inserting the parallelism at the level of the loop over the lines of the domain inside the main iterative loop. That main loop updates the current version of the grid according to the previous one. The corresponding parallel scheme is given in Listing 1.

Listing 1: Simple OpenMP scheme for the Jacobi relaxation

```
1 #pragma omp parallel num_threads(nbT) // Threads creation
2 {
3   ... // Local variables and array initializations
4   for(iter=0; iter<nbIters; ++iter){   // Main iterative loop
5     // Parallel parsing of horizontal strips of the domain
6     #pragma omp for
7     for(lig=1; lig<nLig-1; ++lig){   // Lines in each strip
8       for(col=1; col<nCol-1; ++col){ // Columns in each line
9         ind = lig * nCol + col;
10        crt[ind] = 0.2 * (prec[ind - nCol] + prec[ind-1] + ↵
                 prec[ind] + prec[ind+1] + prec[ind+nCol]);
11      }
12    }
13    #pragma omp single
14    { ... // Arrays exchange for next iteration (avoids copy) }
15  }
16 }
```

Although this simple version works quite well for small and medium sizes of grids, it is not fully scalable for grids with large lines, due to the L2 cache use that is not optimized. We remind the reader that one L2 cache is present in each core of a CPU. So, a second version has been implemented explicitly taking into account the cache management in each core. Due to the data dependencies in our application and to the cache mechanism, the modifications mainly consist in changing the update order of the elements in each horizontal strip.

In the first version, the updates are performed by following the order of the entire lines of the grid. In the second version, the horizontal strips are divided in blocks along their width and their updates are performed block by block. The height of the blocks in a given strip is the same as the height of the strip, but their width may be smaller as it is directly deduced from the cache size and the line width (lw), as illustrated in Figure 1. In fact, the optimal block width (obw) is deduced from the cache size. Then, the number

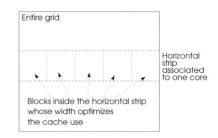

Figure 1.: Blocks in horizontal strips to optimize the cache use

of blocks (nbb) per strip is computed. Finally, the actual block width (abw) is computed in order to obtain blocks of the same width in the horizontal strip.

$$nbb = \left\lceil \frac{lw}{obw} \right\rceil, \qquad abw = \frac{lw}{nbb} \tag{2}$$

3.2. Many-core MIC with offloaded OpenMP

In order to use the MIC Xeon-Phi, Intel proposes an extension of the OpenMP library in its C/C++ compiler. It mainly consists in additional directives that allows the programmer to control the MIC directly from the CPU. It must be noticed that any classical OpenMP program can be run directly on a MIC. However, in this context, the MIC acts as an autonomous multi-core machine but it cannot cooperate (via OpenMP) with the central CPU cores. So, in the perspective of making the MIC cooperate with other devices (CPU, GPU,...), it is required to use the MIC as a co-processor of the central CPU (see [5] for an introduction to *offload* programming paradigm). One great advantage of the MIC, compared to other devices such as GPU, is that the same OpenMP code that runs on the CPU can be executed on the MIC without modification. Hence, Listing 1 can be directly executed on a MIC. However, the MIC has its own memory and can only process data in its memory. This implies the need of explicit data transfers between the central memory of the node and the memory on the MIC board.

The execution and data transfers can be expressed with the same directive, called `offload`, as depicted in Listing 2.

Listing 2: Offloading of the Jacobi relaxation on a MIC with synchronous data transfers

```
1 #pragma offload target(mic:0) inout(tabM:length(nLig*nCol) align(64))
2 { // Computes nbIters iterations of Jacobi over array tabM
3   // with nbTMic cores on the MIC
4   jacobi(tabM, nLig, nCol, nbIters, nbTMic);
5 }
```

In this example, `target` gives the identifier of the MIC device to use, and the `inout` parameter specifies that the array `tabM` (whose size must be given in number of elements) is an `in`put as well as an `out`put of the offload. That means that before the start of the computation on the MIC, the array is copied from central RAM to the MIC RAM. And once the computation is over, the array is copied back from the MIC RAM to the central RAM (at the same location). The scalar variables passed as parameters of the `jacobi` function are implicitly copied from the central RAM to the MIC RAM. Finally, the `align` parameter is optional and forces the memory allocations for the data on the MIC to be aligned at boundaries greater or equal to the specified number of bytes. Such memory alignments improve the performance of data transfers.

It is worth noticing that the offload presented in Listing 2 is blocking. So, the core CPU that executes this offload will wait for the end of the execution of `jacobi` on the MIC and for the completion of the output data transfer from the MIC memory to the central one, before resuming its execution. When the MIC is used alone, without cooperating with the CPU, this synchronous scheme is pertinent. Nevertheless, it prevents any computation by the CPU while the MIC is running. We will see in Section 4 how to perform asynchronous (non-blocking) offloads, in order to allow the CPU to work during the MIC execution. Also, we will point out the need to replace blocking data transfers by asynchronous ones, in order to overlap communication with computation.

3.3. Many-core GPU with CUDA

We designed a single CUDA kernel to process the GPU part of the Jacobi relaxation. It is called two times per iteration: to quickly and early compute the boundary of the GPU part of the Jacobi grid, and to compute the (large) rest of this grid part. We optimized our algorithm and code to make fast *coalescent* memory accesses, to use the *shared memory* of each vectorial multiprocessor of the GPU, and to *limit the divergence* of the thread of a same block (when not executing exactly the same instructions). See [6] for efficient CUDA programming rules.

Each thread of this kernel updates one point of the Jacobi Grid during one cycle, and threads are grouped in 2 dimensional blocks of a 2-dimensional grid. This kernel has been optimized using the *shared memory* of each multiprocessor of the GPU, allowing each thread to read only one data from the GPU global memory, to share this data with others threads of its block, and efficiently access the 5 input data it requires to update its Jacobi grid point. Global memory read and write are achieved in a coalescent way. Considering a block of size $BSY \times BSX$, all the threads (in the range $[0; BSY - 1] \times [0; BSX - 1]$) load data from the global memory into the shared memory, and $(BSY - 2) \times (BSX - 2)$ threads in the range $[0; BSY - 3] \times [0; BSX - 3]$ achieve computations, limiting the divergence of the threads inside a block.

Listing 3: Optimized CUDA kernel

```
1 __global__ void update(double *gpuPrec, double *gpuCrt, int ↵
     gpuLigs, int cols)
2 {
3   int idx, lig, col;
4   __shared__ double buf[BLOCKSIZEY][BLOCKSIZEX];

6   // Coordinates of the Jacobi grid to load in shared memory
7   col = blockIdx.x * (BLOCKSIZEX - 2) + threadIdx.x;
8   lig = blockIdx.y * (BLOCKSIZEY - 2) + threadIdx.y;
9   // If valid coordinates: load data and compute
10  if(col < cols + 2 && lig < gpuLigs + 2){
11    idx = lig * (cols + 2) + col;
12    buf[threadIdx.y][threadIdx.x] = gpuPrec[idx];
13    __syncthreads();
14    lig++; col++; // shift coordinates to point out element to compute
15    // if new coordinates are valid: achieve computation
```

```
16    if(col <= cols && lig <= gpuLigs && threadIdx.x < BLOCKSIZEX-2 ↩
            && threadIdx.y < BLOCKSIZEY-2){
17        idx = lig * (cols + 2) + col;
18        gpuCrt[idx] = 0.2 * (buf[threadIdx.y][threadIdx.x+1] +
19                      buf[threadIdx.y+1][threadIdx.x] +
20                      buf[threadIdx.y+1][threadIdx.x+1] +
21                      buf[threadIdx.y+1][threadIdx.x+2] +
22                      buf[threadIdx.y+2][threadIdx.x+1]);
23    }
24  }
25 }
```

Moreover, CPU memory arrays involved in the CPU-GPU data transfers have been locked in memory, using `cudaHostAlloc(...)` routine, in order to support asynchronous and faster data transfers. Finally, we used some CUDA *streams* to efficiently manage and run concurrent data transfers and kernel computations, so that we obtain a maximal overlapping.

4. Multiple architectures and devices solution

4.1. General asynchronous scheme and data distribution

In our context, the GPU is used as a scientific co-processor, and we use the MIC in *offload* mode. So, our hybrid CPU+MIC+GPU solution still uses the CPU to run the `main` function, to launch all computation steps on the GPU, on the MIC and on its own cores, and to launch the data transfers between the CPU and the accelerators. The CPU memory hosts the entire current (`crt`) and previous (`prev`) Jacobi grids, but the top part is transferred on the GPU and the bottom part on the MIC (see Figure 2). We name CPU boundaries the first and last lines computed by the CPU, GPU boundary the last line computed by the GPU, and MIC boundary the first line computed by the MIC. We name *corpus* the other lines computed by a computing device. So, each *computing device* (CPU, MIC and GPU) stores its parts of the Jacobi grids and the adjacent boundary(ies) of other device(s). In order to save memory and optimize the transfers, our

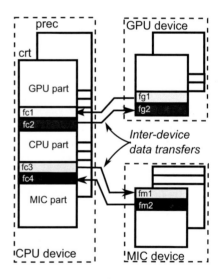

Figure 2.: Data management scheme on the three devices (CPU, MIC and GPU)

parallel algorithm is designed to allow direct transfers of the frontiers in their right place in the local arrays on the CPU and GPU. So, no intermediate array is required for the frontiers between CPU and GPU. A similar scheme would be also possible for the MIC device. However, due to a particularly slow memory allocation of offloaded data and the impossibility to transfer data from the CPU to an array that has been locally allocated on the MIC, the use of an intermediate buffer for the CPU/MIC frontiers has been necessary on the MIC side. Save for this difference, the CPU algorithm uses as symmetric

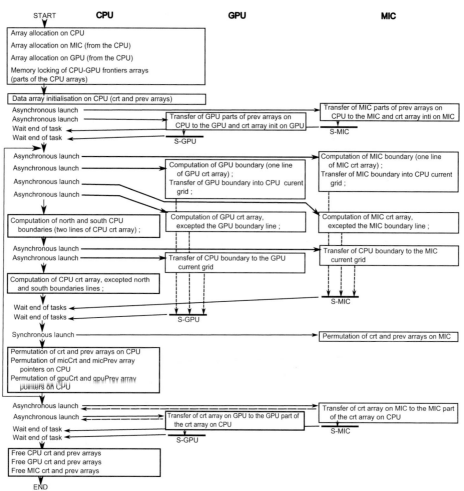

Figure 3. CPU-MIC-GPU algorithm

as possible data structures and interactions for both accelerators. Figure 3 introduces our multi-device algorithm, based on the following principles:

- Before to enter a new computation step, a processor has its previous Jacobi grid entirely updated, including the boundary of the adjacent processor. So it can compute all its part of its current grid.
- A processor sends its newly updated boundary to the adjacent processor while it receives the updated boundary of this adjacent processor.
- Boundary(ies) computation and transfer of a processor are sequentially linked, but achieved in parallel of its corpus computation. The objective is to overlap as much as possible the data transfers with large computations, as well as to avoid that a processor is underused by processing only its boundary(ies).
- The CPU launch asynchronous computations on accelerators and asynchronous data transfers from and to the accelerators. So, the two accelerators and the CPU can compute in parallel, and the different data transfers can exploit the two PCI express buses in parallel.

Obviously, two synchronization points, S-MIC and S-GPU, are mandatory to ensure that data transfers and computations are finished respectively on MIC and GPU, before to switch the arrays (current and previous grids) and to enter the next iteration.

A slight asymmetry appears between the MIC and GPU concerning the arrays switching management (pointers switching). In fact, pointers on GPU arrays are stored in the CPU memory and sent to the GPU computing kernel as parameters when launching the kernel. So, these pointers can be switched directly in the CPU memory by the CPU process. On the contrary, array pointers on MIC are stored in the MIC memory and managed by the MIC. So, the CPU needs to launch a short task on the MIC to make it switch its local array pointers.

Finally, we obtain an efficient and rather generic and symmetric parallel scheme that make cooperate CPU, MIC and GPU devices to solve the same problem.

4.2. Implementation details

To achieve asynchronous transfers between CPU and GPU, three CUDA streams are used together with two CUDA registrations of the memory banks concerned by the transfers to lock them and avoid their swapping. We recall that CUDA streams run concurrently but in each stream, data transfers and kernels are serialized. One stream is used to compute and send the *FG1* line (cf. Fig.2) to the CPU (*FC1*), another one is used to receive the *FG2* line from the CPU (*FC2*), and the last one is used to control the asynchronous computation of the GPU part. The two registrations concern the two frontier lines (*FG1* and *FG2*). The `cudaMemcpyAsync` and `cudaStreamSynchronize` functions are used to perform the asynchronous transfers and to ensure their completion before to proceed to the following computations.

Concerning the asynchronous data transfers between CPU and MIC, the `signal` clause is used in the `offload` directive computing and sending (with a `out` clause) the *FM2* line to the CPU (*FC4*). It is also used in the `offload_transfer` directive related to the reception of *FM1* from the CPU (*FC3*). There is also a signaled `offload` to asynchronously perform the computation of the MIC part. Then, the `offload_wait` directive is used to ensure the transfer completions before performing the following computations.

5. Experiments

5.1. Individual performances of the devices

Table 1 shows the absolute and relative performances of the three devices (computing units) on each testbed machine, during 5000 iterations on a grid of 20000×10000 points. The results are averages of 5 executions. On both machines, the CPU part (cores on the motherboard) is the less powerful, the MIC device is medium, and the GPU is the most powerful for this problem. The CPU and MIC units in the Loria machine are faster than the ones in the CS machine, whereas the CS machine GPU is faster than in the Loria one. This implies that the two machines have different behaviors when running the multi-device algorithm. This is detailed in the following part.

20000 × 10000 pts, 5000 iterations				
Testbed	Measure	CPU	MIC	GPU
CentraleSupelec	Computation speed	1.19E+009	3.50E+009	9.84E+009
machine	Global speed	1.19E+009	3.48E+009	9.78E+009
	Standard deviation (%)	0.51	6.18	0.04
	Speedup	1.0	2.95	8.31
Loria	Computation speed	1.60E+009	4.83E+009	7.93E+009
machine	Global speed	1.60E+009	4.69E+009	7.87E+009
	Standard deviation (%)	5.14	4.72	0.09
	Speedup	1.0	3.02	4.96
Computation speed = number of updated points / second				
Global speed includes computations, allocations and transfers				

Table 1. Absolute and relative performance of the three devices (averages of 5 executions)

20000 × 10000 pts, 5000 iterations						
Absolute speeds (in updated points / s)						
	CS machine			Loria machine		
	C = 13500, M = 15000			C = 12500, M = 14000		
C / M cutting lines	M - 500	M	M + 500	M - 500	M	M + 500
C - 500	1.15E+010	1.11E+010	8.79E+009	8.99E+009	1.01E+010	1.02E+010
C	1.12E+010	**1.22E+010**	1.12E+010	9.76E+009	**1.06E+010**	1.03E+010
C + 500	1.12E+010	1.12E+010	1.13E+010	9.64E+009	1.00E+010	9.98E+009
Speedups from GPU alone						
C - 500	1.17	1.13	0.89	1.13	1.27	1.28
C	1.14	**1.24**	1.14	1.23	**1.34**	1.29
C + 500	1.14	1.14	1.15	1.21	1.26	1.26

Table 2. Performance (speed and speedup) of heterogeneous computing with CPU, MIC and GPU

5.2. Performance of heterogeneous computing on the three devices

Table 2 shows the speeds and speedups of our heterogeneous algorithm for the same problem parameters (iterations and grid size), but with different cutting lines. As shown above, the two machines having different devices speeds, their optimal cutting lines are not the same. So, for each machine, nine measures are performed around the theoretical optimal cutting lines (based on single-device performances), using variations of ±500 lines.

First of all, we observe that our heterogeneous algorithm obtains gains with both machines, according to the fastest device alone (the GPU). However, those gains are different according to the relative powers of the devices. In the CS machine, the GPU is much more powerful than the two other devices, implying a limited potential gain of the heterogeneous version. It is worth noticing that the ideal speedup, estimated without any communication/allocation overhead is 1.43. So, with a speedup of 1.24, our algorithm obtains 87% of the ideal case. With the Loria machine, the powers of the devices are a bit closer, implying larger potential gains. However, in this case, although the ideal speedup is 1.74, the obtained one is 1.34 and the efficiency is only 77%. Moreover, it must be noticed that the cutting lines reported in Table 2 for this machine are a bit larger than the ones indicated by theory (11500 and 13500). This shifting may come from a slight overestimation of the CPU and MIC, itself due to the higher variations of performance on this machine (see *Standard deviation* in Table 1). Another possible reason of the smaller efficiency may come from the older compiler available on that machine.

Finally, those experiments confirm that our algorithmic scheme can achieve significant gains by performing a quite efficient cooperation of different kinds of computing devices inside a same machine.

6. Conclusion

A parallel scheme has been described that allows the cooperation of different computing devices inside a single hybrid machine. The major difficulty in exploiting such devices together comes from the data transfers between the central memory of the system and the local memory on each device. To obtain good efficiency, it is required to make extensive use of asynchronism between the devices as well as overlapping computations with communications by asynchronous data transfers.

Our experiments have validated our multiple-devices parallel scheme: results were qualitatively identical using one, two or three devices. Two series of asynchronous data transfers (CPU ↔ GPU and CPU ↔ MIC) have been implemented with different mechanisms and the most efficient combination has been presented.

The results show the possibility to achieve significant gains with quite good efficiencies (from 77 to 87%) according to the ideal gains without the management cost of heterogeneous devices. Our algorithm shows how to achieve them. Moreover, as it can be used inside nodes of a cluster, it represents an additional step towards a better exploitation of large parallel systems (clusters with heterogeneous accelerators).

Among many possibilities, interesting extensions of this work consist in adapting that parallel scheme to more complex scientific applications, extending it to the coupling of different solvers running on different devices, adapting it to clusters, and considering large problems that do not fit in the memory of one device alone.

References

[1] S. Vialle and S. Contassot-Vivier. *Patterns for parallel programming on GPUs*, chapter Optimization methodology for Parallel Programming of Homogeneous or Hybrid Clusters. Saxe-Coburg Publications, 2014. ISBN: 978-1-874672-57-9.

[2] S. Contassot-Vivier, S. Vialle, and J. Gustedt. *Designing Scientific Applications on GPUs*, chapter Development Methodologies for GPU and Cluster of GPUs. Chapman & Hall/CRC Numerical Analysis and Scientific Computing series. Chapman & Hall/CRC, 2013. ISBN 978-1-466571-64-8.

[3] J. Fang, A. L. Varbanescu, B. Imbernon, J. M. Cecilia, and H. Perez-Sanchez. Parallel computation of non-bonded interactions in drug discovery: Nvidia GPUs vs. Intel Xeon Phi. In *2nd International Work-Conference on Bioinformatics and Biomedical Engineering (IWBBIO 2014)*, Granada, Spain, 2014.

[4] B. Gaster, L. Howes, D. Kaeli, P. Mistry, and D. Schaa. *Heterogeneous Computing with OpenCL*. Morgan Kaufmann, 2nd edition, 2012. ISBN 9780124058941.

[5] J. Jeffers and J. Reinders. *Intel Xeon Phi coprocessor high-performance programming*. Elsevier Waltham (Mass.), 2013. ISBN 978-0-12-410414-3.

[6] J. Sanders and E. Kandrot. *CUDA by Example: An Introduction to General-Purpose GPU Programming*. Addison-Wesley Professional, 1st edition, 2010. ISBN-10 0131387685, ISBN-13 9780131387683.

Parallel Computing: On the Road to Exascale
G.R. Joubert et al. (Eds.)
IOS Press, 2016
doi:10.3233/978-1-61499-621-7-35

A Many-Core Machine Model for Designing Algorithms with Minimum Parallelism Overheads

Sardar Anisul HAQUE [a], Marc MORENO MAZA [a,b] and Ning XIE [a]

[a] *Department of Computer Science, University of Western Ontario, Canada*
[b] *ChongQing Institute for Green and Intelligent Technology, Chinese Academy of Sciences*

Abstract. We present a model of multithreaded computation with an emphasis on estimating parallelism overheads of programs written for modern many-core architectures. We establish a Graham-Brent theorem so as to estimate execution time of programs running on a given number of streaming multiprocessors. We evaluate the benefits of our model with fundamental algorithms from scientific computing. For two case studies, our model is used to minimize parallelism overheads by determining an appropriate value range for a given program parameter. For the others, our model is used to compare different algorithms solving the same problem. In each case, the studied algorithms were implemented and the results of their experimental comparison are coherent with the theoretical analysis based on our model.

Keywords. Model of computation, parallelism overhead, many-core architectures

1. Introduction

Designing efficient algorithms targeting hardware accelerators (multi-core processors, graphics processing units (GPUs), field-programmable gate arrays) creates major challenges for computer scientists. A first difficulty is to define models of computation retaining the computer hardware characteristics that have a dominant impact on program performance. That is, in addition to specify the appropriate complexity measures, those models must consider the relevant parameters characterizing the abstract machine executing the algorithms to be analyzed. A second difficulty is, for a given model of computation, to combine its complexity measures so as to determine the "best" algorithm among different possible solutions to a given algorithmic problem.

In the fork-join concurrency model [1], two complexity measures, the work T_1 and the span T_∞, and one machine parameter, the number P of processors, are combined into a running time estimate, namely the Graham-Brent theorem [1,2], which states that the running time T_P on P processors satisfies $T_P \leq T_1/P + T_\infty$. A refinement of this theorem supports the implementation (on multi-core architectures) of the parallel performance analyzer Cilkview [3]. In this context, the running time T_P is bounded in expectation by $T_1/P + 2\delta \widehat{T_\infty}$, where δ is a constant (called the *span coefficient*) and $\widehat{T_\infty}$ is the burdened span, which captures parallelism overheads due to scheduling and synchronization.

The well-known PRAM (parallel random-access machine) model [4,5] has also been enhanced [6] so as to integrate communication delay into the computation time. However, a PRAM abstract machine consists of an unbounded collection of RAM processors, whereas a many-core GPU holds a collection of streaming multiprocessors (SMs). Hence, applying the PRAM model to GPU programs fails to capture all the features (and thus the impact) of data transfer between the SMs and the global memory of the device.

Ma, Agrawal and Chamberlain [7] introduce the TMM (Threaded Many-core Memory) model which retains many important characteristics of GPU-type architectures as machine parameters, like memory access width and hardware limit on the number of threads per core. In TMM analysis, the running time of an algorithm is estimated by choosing the maximum quantity among work, span and the amount of memory accesses. Such running time estimates depend on the machine parameters. Hong and Kim [8] present an analytical model to predict the execution time of an actual GPU program. No abstract machine is defined in this case. Instead, a few metrics are used to estimate the CPI (cycles per instruction) of the considered program.

Many works, such as [9,10], targeting code optimization and performance prediction of GPU programs are related to our work. However, these papers do not define an abstract model in support of the analysis of algorithms.

In this paper, we propose a many-core machine (MCM) model with two objectives: (1) tuning program parameters to minimize parallelism overheads of algorithms targeting GPU-like architectures, and (2) comparing different algorithms independently of the targeted hardware device. In the design of this model, we insist on the following features:

1. *Two-level DAG programs.* Defined in Section 2, they capture the two levels of parallelism (fork-join and single instruction, multiple data) of heterogeneous programs (like a CilkPlus program using `#pragma simd` [11] or a CUDA program with the so-called dynamic parallelism [12]).
2. *Parallelism overhead.* We introduce this complexity measure in Section 2.3 with the objective of capturing communication and synchronization costs.
3. *A Graham-Brent theorem.* We combine three complexity measures (work, span and parallelism overhead) and one machine parameter (data transfer throughput) in order to estimate the running time of an MCM program on P streaming multiprocessors, see Theorem 1. However, as we shall see through a case study series, this machine parameter has no influence on the comparison of algorithms.

Our model extends both the fork-join concurrency and PRAM models, with an emphasis on parallelism overheads resulting from communication and synchronization.

We sketch below how, in practice, we use this model to tune a program parameter so as to minimize parallelism overheads of programs targeting many-core GPUs. Consider an MCM program $\mathscr{P}$, that is, an algorithm expressed in the MCM model. Assume that a program parameter s (like the number of threads running on an SM) can be arbitrarily chosen within some range $\mathscr{S}$ while preserving the specifications of $\mathscr{P}$. Let s_0 be a particular value of s which corresponds to an instance $\mathscr{P}_0$ of $\mathscr{P}$, which, in practice, is seen as an initial version of the algorithm to be optimized.

We consider the ratios of the work, span, and parallelism overhead given by $W_{\mathscr{P}_0}/W_{\mathscr{P}}$, $S_{\mathscr{P}_0}/S_{\mathscr{P}}$ and $O_{\mathscr{P}_0}/O_{\mathscr{P}}$. Assume that, when s varies within $\mathscr{S}$, the work ratio and span ratio stay within $O(s)$ (in fact, $\Theta(1)$ is often the case), but the ratio of the parallelism overhead reduces by a factor in $\Theta(s)$. Thereby, we determine a value $s_{\min} \in \mathscr{S}$ maximizing the parallelism overhead ratio. Next, we use our version of Graham-Brent theorem (more precisely, Corollary 1) to check whether the upper bound for the running time of $\mathscr{P}(s_{\min})$ is less than that of $\mathscr{P}(s_o)$. If this holds, we view $\mathscr{P}(s_{\min})$ as a solution of our problem of algorithm optimization (in terms of parallelism overheads).

To evaluate the benefits of our model, we applied it successfully to five fundamental algorithms [1] in scientific computing, see Sections 3 to 5. These five algorithms are the Euclidean algorithm, Cooley & Tukey and Stockham fast Fourier transform algorithms, the plain and FFT-based univariate polynomial multiplication algorithms. Other applications of our model appear in the PhD thesis [13] of the first Author as well as in [14].

Following the strategy described above for algorithm optimization, our model is used to tune a program parameter in the case of the Euclidean algorithm and the plain multiplication algorithm. Next, our model is used to compare the two fast Fourier transform algorithms and then the two univariate polynomial multiplication algorithms. In each case, work, span and parallelism overhead are evaluated so as to obtain running time estimates via our Graham-Brent theorem and then select a proper algorithm.

2. A many-core machine model

The model of parallel computations presented in this paper aims at capturing communication and synchronization overheads of programs written for modern many-core architectures. One of our objectives is to optimize algorithms by techniques like reducing redundant memory accesses. The reason for this optimization is that, on actual GPUs, global memory latency is approximately 400 to 800 clock cycles. This memory latency, when not properly taken into account, may have a dramatically negative impact on program performance. Another objective of our model is to compare different algorithms targeting implementation on GPUs without taking hardware parameters into account.

As specified in Sections 2.1 and 2.2, our many-core machine (MCM) model retains many of the characteristics of modern GPU architectures and programming models, like CUDA or OpenCL. However, in order to support algorithm analysis with an emphasis on parallelism overheads, as defined in Section 2.3 and 2.4, the MCM abstract machines admit a few simplifications and limitations with respect to actual many-core devices.

2.1. Characteristics of the abstract many-core machines

Architecture. An MCM abstract machine possesses an unbounded number of *streaming multiprocessors* (SMs) which are all identical. Each SM has a finite number of processing cores and a fixed-size private memory. An MCM machine has a two-level memory hierarchy, comprising an unbounded global memory with high latency and low throughput and fixed size private memories with low latency and high throughput.

Programs. An MCM *program* is a directed acyclic graph (DAG) whose vertices are kernels (defined hereafter) and edges indicate serial dependencies, similarly to the instruction stream DAGs of the fork-join concurrency model. A *kernel* is an SIMD (single instruction, multiple data) program capable of branches and decomposed into a number of thread-blocks. Each *thread-block* is executed by a single SM and each SM executes a single thread-block at a time. Similarly to a CUDA program, an MCM program specifies

---

[1]Our algorithms are implemented in CUDA and publicly available with benchmarking scripts from `http://www.cumodp.org/`.

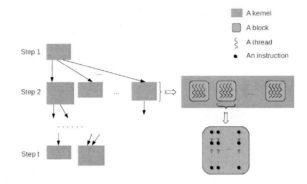

Figure 1. Overview of a many-core machine program

for each kernel the number of thread-blocks and the number of threads per thread-block. Figure 1 depicts the different types of components of an MCM program.

Scheduling and synchronization. At run time, an MCM machine schedules thread-blocks (from the same or different kernels) onto SMs, based on the dependencies specified by the edges of the DAG and the hardware resources required by each thread-block. Threads within a thread-block can cooperate with each other via the private memory of the SM running the thread-block. Meanwhile, thread-blocks interact with each other via the global memory. In addition, threads within a thread-block are executed physically in parallel by an SM. Moreover, the programmer cannot make any assumptions on the order in which thread-blocks of a given kernel are mapped to the SMs. Hence, an MCM program runs correctly on any fixed number of SMs.

Memory access policy. All threads of a given thread-block can access simultaneously any memory cell of the private memory or the global memory: read/write conflicts are handled by the CREW (concurrent read, exclusive write) policy. However, read/write requests to the global memory by two different thread-blocks cannot be executed simultaneously. In case of simultaneous requests, one thread-block is chosen randomly and served first, then the other is served.

Toward analyzing program performance, we define two *machine parameters*:

U: Time (expressed in clock cycles) to transfer one machine word between the global memory and the private memory of any SM; hence we have $U > 0$.

Z: Size (expressed in machine words) of the private memory of any SM, which sets up an upper bound on several program parameters.

The private memory size Z sets several characteristics and limitations of an SM and, thus, of a thread-block. Indeed, each of the following quantities is at most equal to Z: the number of threads of a thread-block and the number of words in a data transfer between the global memory. The quantity $1/U$ is a throughput measure and has the following property. If α and β are the maximum numbers of words respectively read and written to the global memory by one thread of a thread-block B, and ℓ is the number of threads per thread-block, then the total time T_D spent in data transfer between the global memory and the private memory of an SM executing B satisfies:

$$T_D \leq (\alpha + \beta)U, \text{ if coalesced accesses occur, or } \ell(\alpha + \beta)U, \text{ otherwise.} \qquad (1)$$

On actual GPU devices, some hardware characteristics may reduce data transfer time, for instance, fast context switching between warps executed by a SM. Other hardware characteristics, like partition camping, may increase data transfer time. As an abstract machine, the MCM aims at capturing either the best or the worst scenario for data transfer time of a thread-block, which lead us to Relation (1).

Relation (1) calls for another comment. One could expect the introduction of a third machine parameter, say V, which would be the time to execute one *local operation* (arithmetic operation, read/write in the private memory), such that, if σ is the maximum number of local operations performed by one thread of a thread-block B, then the total time T_A spent in local operations by an SM executing B would satisfy $T_A \leq \sigma V$. Therefore, for the total running time T of the thread-block B, we would have $T = T_A + T_D \leq \sigma V + \varepsilon (\alpha + \beta) U$, where ε is either 1 or ℓ. Instead of introducing this third machine parameter V, we let $V = 1$. Thus, U can be understood as the ratio of the time to transfer a machine word to the time to execute a local operation.

2.2. Many-core machine programs

Recall that each MCM program $\mathscr{P}$ is a DAG $(\mathscr{K}, \mathscr{E})$, called the *kernel DAG* of $\mathscr{P}$, where each node $K \in \mathscr{K}$ represents a kernel, and each edge $E \in \mathscr{E}$ records the fact that a kernel call must precede another kernel call. In other words, a kernel call can be executed once all its predecessors in the DAG $(\mathscr{K}, \mathscr{E})$ have completed their execution.

Synchronization costs. Recall that each kernel decomposes into thread-blocks and that all threads within a given kernel execute the same serial program, but with possibly different input data. In addition, all threads within a thread-block are executed physically in parallel by an SM. It follows that MCM kernel code needs no synchronization statement, like CUDA's `__syncthreads()`. Consequently, the only form of synchronization taking place among the threads executing a given thread-block is that implied by code divergence [15]. This latter phenomenon can be seen as parallelism overhead. Further, an MCM machine handles code divergence by eliminating the corresponding conditional branches via code replication [16], and the corresponding cost will be captured by the complexity measures (work, span and parallelism overhead) of the MCM model.

Scheduling costs. Since an MCM abstract machine has infinitely many SMs and since the kernel DAG defining an MCM program $\mathscr{P}$ is assumed to be known when $\mathscr{P}$ starts to execute, scheduling $\mathscr{P}$'s kernels onto the SMs can be done in time $O(\Gamma)$ where Γ is the total length of $\mathscr{P}$'s kernel code. Thus, we neglect those costs in comparison to the costs of data transfer between SMs' private memories and the global memory. Extending MCM machines to program DAGs unfolding dynamically at run time is work in progress.

Thread-block DAG. Since each kernel of the program $\mathscr{P}$ decomposes into finitely many thread-blocks, we map $\mathscr{P}$ to a second graph, called the *thread-block DAG* of $\mathscr{P}$, whose vertex set $\mathscr{B}(\mathscr{P})$ consists of all thread-blocks of the kernels of $\mathscr{P}$ and such that (B_1, B_2) is an edge if B_1 is a thread-block of a kernel preceding the kernel of the thread-block B_2 in $\mathscr{P}$. This second graph defines two important quantities:

$\mathrm{N}(\mathscr{P})$: number of vertices in the thread-block DAG of $\mathscr{P}$,

$\mathrm{L}(\mathscr{P})$: critical path length (where length of a path is the number of edges in that path) in the thread-block DAG of $\mathscr{P}$.

2.3. Complexity measures for the many-core machine model

Consider an MCM program $\mathscr{P}$ given by its kernel DAG $(\mathscr{K}, \mathscr{E})$. Let $K \in \mathscr{K}$ be any kernel of $\mathscr{P}$ and B be any thread-block of K. We define the *work* of B, denoted by $\mathrm{W}(B)$, as the total number of local operations performed by all threads of B. We define the *span* of B, denoted by $\mathrm{S}(B)$, as the maximum number of local operations performed by a thread of B. As before, let α and β be the maximum numbers of words read and written (from the global memory) by a thread of B, and ℓ be the number of threads per thread-block. Then, we define the *overhead* of B, denoted by $\mathrm{O}(B)$, as

$$(\alpha + \beta)U, \text{if memory accesses can be coalesced or } \ell(\alpha + \beta)U, \text{otherwise.} \qquad (2)$$

Next, the *work* (resp. *overhead*) $\mathrm{W}(K)$ (resp. $\mathrm{O}(K)$) of the kernel K is the sum of the works (resp. overheads) of its thread-blocks, while the *span* $\mathrm{S}(K)$ of the kernel K is the maximum of the spans of its thread-blocks. We consider now the entire program $\mathscr{P}$. The *work* $\mathrm{W}(\mathscr{P})$ of $\mathscr{P}$ is defined as the total work of all its kernels. Regarding the graph $(\mathscr{K}, \mathscr{E})$ as a weighted-vertex graph, where the weight of a vertex $K \in \mathscr{K}$ is its span $\mathrm{S}(K)$, we define the weight $\mathrm{S}(\gamma)$ of any path γ from the first executing kernel to a terminal kernel (that is, a kernel with no successors in $\mathscr{P}$) as $\mathrm{S}(\gamma) = \sum_{K \in \gamma} \mathrm{S}(K)$. Then, we define the *span* $\mathrm{S}(\mathscr{P})$ of $\mathscr{P}$ as the longest path, counting the weight (span) of each vertex (kernel), in the kernel DAG. Finally, we define the *overhead* $\mathrm{O}(\mathscr{P})$ of the program $\mathscr{P}$ as the total overhead of all its kernels. Observe that, according to Mirsky's theorem [17], the number π of parallel steps in $\mathscr{P}$ (which form a partition of $\mathscr{K}$ into anti-chains in the DAG $(\mathscr{K}, \mathscr{E})$ regarded as a partially ordered set) is greater or equal to the maximum length of a path in $(\mathscr{K}, \mathscr{E})$ from the first executing kernel to a terminal kernel.

2.4. A Graham-Brent theorem with parallelism overhead

Theorem 1 *The running time T_P of the program $\mathscr{P}$ executed on P SMs satisfies the inequality:* $T_{\mathrm{P}} \leq (\mathrm{N}(\mathscr{P})/\mathrm{P} + \mathrm{L}(\mathscr{P}))\mathrm{C}(\mathscr{P})$, *where* $\mathrm{C}(\mathscr{P}) = \max_{B \in \mathscr{B}(\mathscr{P})} (\mathrm{S}(B) + \mathrm{O}(B))$.

The proof is similar to that of the original result [1,2]. while the proof of the following corollary follows from Theorem 1 and from the fact that costs of scheduling thread-blocks onto SMs are neglected.

Corollary 1 *Let K be the maximum number of thread-blocks along an anti-chain of the thread-block DAG of $\mathscr{P}$. Then the running time $T_{\mathscr{P}}$ of the program $\mathscr{P}$ satisfies:*

$$T_{\mathscr{P}} \leq (\mathrm{N}(\mathscr{P})/\mathrm{K} + \mathrm{L}(\mathscr{P}))\mathrm{C}(\mathscr{P}). \qquad (3)$$

As we shall see in Sections 3 through 5, Corollary 1 allows us to estimate the running time of an MCM program as a function of the number ℓ of threads per thread-block, the single machine parameter U and the thread-block DAG of $\mathscr{P}$. Thus, the dependence on the machine parameter Z (the size of a private memory) is only through inequalities specifying upper bounds for ℓ. In addition, in each of the case studies, there is no need to make any assumptions (like inequality constraints) on the machine parameter U.

3. The Euclidean algorithm

Our first application of the MCM model deals with a multithreaded algorithm for computing the greatest common divisor (GCD) of two univariate polynomials over a the finite field $\mathbb{Z}/p\mathbb{Z}$, where p is a prime number. Our approach is based on the Euclidean algorithm, that the reader can review in Chapter 4 in [18]. Given a positive integer s, we proceed by repeatedly calling a subroutine which takes as input a pair (a,b) of polynomials in $\mathbb{Z}/p\mathbb{Z}[X]$, with $\deg(a) \geq \deg(b) > 0$, and returns another pair (a',b') of polynomials in $\mathbb{Z}/p\mathbb{Z}[X]$, such that $\gcd(a,b) = \gcd(a',b')$, and either $b' = 0$ (in which case we have $\gcd(a,b) = a'$), or we have $\deg(a') + \deg(b') \leq \deg(a) + \deg(b) - s$. Details, including pseudo-code, can be found in the long version of this paper available at http://cumodp.org/hmx2015-draft.pdf.

We will take advantage of our MCM model to tune the program parameter s in order to obtain an optimized multithreaded version of the Euclidean algorithm. Let n and m be positive integers such that the degree of the input polynomials a and b (in dense representation) satisfies $\deg(a) = n - 1$ and $\deg(b) = m - 1$, assuming $n \geq m$.

The work, span and parallelism overhead are given [2] by $W_s = 3m^2 + 6nm + 3s + \frac{3(5ms+4ns+14m+4n+3s^2+6s)}{8\ell}$, $S_s = 3n + 3m$ and $O_s = \frac{4mU(2n+m+s)}{s\ell}$, respectively.

To determine a value range for s that minimizes the parallelism overhead of our multithreaded algorithm, we choose $s = 1$ as the starting point; let W_1, S_1 and O_1 the work, span, and parallelism overhead at $s = 1$. The work ratio W_1/W_s is asymptotically equivalent to $\frac{(16\ell+8)n+(8\ell+19)m}{(16\ell+4s+4)n+(8\ell+5s+14)m}$ when m (and thus n) escapes to infinity. The span ratio S_1/S_s is 1, and the parallelism overhead ratio O_1/O_s is $\frac{(2n+m+1)s}{2n+m+s}$. We observe that when $s \in \Theta(\ell)$, the work is increased by a constant factor only meanwhile the parallelism overhead will reduce by a factor in $\Theta(s)$.

Hence, choosing $s \in \Theta(\ell)$ seems a good choice. To verify this, we apply Corollary 1. One can easily check that the quantities characterizing the thread-block DAG of the computation are $N_s = \frac{2nm+m^2+ms}{2s\ell}$, $L_s = \frac{n+m}{s}$ and $C_s = 3s + 8U$. Then, applying Corollary 1, we estimate the running time on $\Theta(\frac{m}{\ell})$ SMs as $T_s = \frac{4n+3m+s}{2s}(3s+8U)$. Denoting by T_1 the estimated running time when $s = 1$, the running time ratio $R = T_1/T_s$ on $\Theta(\frac{m}{\ell})$ SMs is given by $R = \frac{(4n+3m+1)(3+8U)s}{(4n+3m+s)(3s+8U)}$. When n and m escape to infinity, the latter ratio asymptotically becomes $\frac{(3+8U)s}{3s+8U}$, which is greater than 1 if and only if $s > 1$. Thus, the algorithm with $s = \Theta(\ell)$ performs better than that with $s = 1$, Figure 2 shows the experimental results with $s = \ell = 256$ and $s = 1$ on a NVIDIA Kepler architecture, which confirms our theoretical analysis.

4. Fast Fourier Transform

Let p be a prime number greater than 2 and let f be a vector over the prime field $\mathbb{F}_p := \mathbb{Z}/p\mathbb{Z}$. Let n be the smallest power of 2 such that the length of f is less than n, that is, $n = \min\{2^e \mid \deg(f) < 2^e \text{ and } e \in \mathbb{N}\}$. We assume that n divides $p-1$ which guarantees that the field $\mathbb{F}_p$ admits an n-th primitive root of unity. Hence, let $\omega \in \mathbb{F}_p$ such that

---

[2]See the detailed analysis in the form of executable MAPLE worksheets of three applications: http://www.csd.uwo.ca/~nxie6/projects/mcm/.

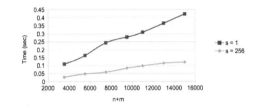

Figure 2. Running time on GeForce GTX 670 of our multithreaded Euclidean algorithm for univariate polynomials of sizes n and m over $\mathbb{Z}/p\mathbb{Z}$ where p is a 30-bit prime; the program parameter s takes 1 and 256.

$\omega^n = 1$ holds while for all $0 \leq i < n$, we have $\omega^i \neq 1$. The n-point *Discrete Fourier Transform* (DFT, for short) at ω is the linear map from the $\mathbb{F}_p$-vector space $\mathbb{F}_p{}^n$ to itself, defined by $x \longmapsto \mathrm{DFT}_n x$ with the n-th DFT matrix given by $\mathrm{DFT}_n = [\omega^{ij}]_{0 \leq i, j < n}$. A *fast Fourier transform* (FFT, for short) is an algorithm to compute the DFT. Two of the most commonly used FFTs' are that of Cooley & Tukey [19] and that of Stockham [20]. Details, including a review of those algorithms, can be found in the long version of this paper available at http://cumodp.org/hmx2015-draft.pdf. Each of these algorithms is based on a factorization of the matrix DFT_n, which translates into $\log_2(n)$ calls to a kernel performing successively three matrix-vector multiplications. In the case of Stockham's factorization, each of the corresponding matrices has a structure permitting coalesced read/write memory accesses. Unfortunately, this is not always true for the factorization of Cooley & Tukey. As we shall see, the MCM model can quantify this negative feature of this latter algorithm, thus yielding an analytical explanation to a fact which, up to our knowledge, had never measured in such precise way in the literature.

Estimates for the work, span, and parallelism overhead of each algorithm appear in http://cumodp.org/hmx2015-draft.pdf. In what follows, W_{ct}, S_{ct} and O_{ct} refer to the work, span, and parallelism overhead of the algorithm of Cooley & Tukey. Similarly, W_{sh}, S_{sh} and O_{sh} stand for the work, span, and parallelism overhead of Stockham's.

The work ratio W_{ct}/W_{sh} is asymptotically equivalent to $\frac{4n(47\log_2(n)\ell+34\log_2(n)\ell\log_2(\ell))}{172n\log_2(n)\ell+n+48\ell^2}$, when n escapes to infinity. Since $\ell \in O(Z)$, the quantity ℓ is bounded over on a given machine. Thus, the work ratio is asymptotically in $\Theta(\log_2(\ell))$ when n escapes to infinity, while the span ratio S_{ct}/S_{sh} is asymptotically equivalent to $\frac{34\log_2(n)\log_2(\ell)+47\log_2(n)}{43\log_2(n)+16\log_2(\ell)}$, which is also in $\Theta(\log_2(\ell))$. Next, we compute the parallelism overhead ratio, O_{ct}/O_{sh}, as $\frac{8n(4\log_2(n)+\ell\log_2(\ell)-\log_2(\ell)-15)}{20n\log_2(n)+5n-4\ell}$. In other words, both the work and span of the algorithm of Cooley & Tukey are increased by $\Theta(\log_2(\ell))$ factor w.r.t their counterparts in Stockham algorithm. Applying Corollary 1, we obtain the running time ratio $R = T_{ct}/T_{sh}$ on $\Theta(\frac{n}{\ell})$ SMs as $R \sim \frac{\log_2(n)(2U\ell+34\log_2(\ell)+2U)}{5\log_2(n)(U+2\log_2(\ell))}$, when n escapes to infinity. This latter ratio is greater than 1 if and only if $\ell > 1$.

Hence, Stockham algorithm outperforms Cooley & Tukey algorithm on an MCM machine. Table 1 shows the experimental results comparing both algorithms with $\ell = 128$ on a NVIDIA Kepler architecture, which confirms our theoretical analysis.

n	2^{14}	2^{15}	2^{16}	2^{17}	2^{18}	2^{19}	2^{20}
Cooley & Tukey (secs)	0.583	0.826	1.19	2.07	4.66	9.11	16.8
Stockham (secs)	0.666	0.762	0.929	1.24	1.86	3.04	5.38

Table 1. Running time of Cooley-Tukey and Stockham FFT algorithm with input size n on GeForce GTX 670.

5. Polynomial multiplication

Multithreaded algorithms for polynomial multiplication will be our third application of the MCM model in this paper. As in Section 3, we denote by a and b two univariate polynomials with coefficients in the prime field $\mathbb{F}_p$ and we write their degrees $\deg(a) = n - 1$ and $\deg(b) = m - 1$, for two positive integers $n \geq m$. We compute the product $f = a \times b$ in two ways: plain multiplication and FFT-based multiplication.

Our multithreaded algorithm for plain multiplication was introduced in [21] and is reviewed with details in `http://cumodp.org/hmx2015-draft.pdf`. This algorithm depends on a program parameter $s > 0$ which is the number of coefficients that each thread writes back to the global memory at the end of each phase (multiplication or addition). We denote by ℓ the number of threads per thread-block.

We see $s = 1$ as our initial algorithm; we denote its work, span and parallelism overhead as W_1, S_1 and O_1 respectively. The work ratio $W_1/W_s = \frac{n}{n+s-1}$, is asymptotically constant as n escapes to infinity. The span ratio $S_1/S_s = \frac{\log_2(m)+1}{s(\log_2(m/s)+2s-1)}$ shows that S_s grows asymptotically with s. The parallelism overhead ratio is $O_1/O_s = \frac{ns^2(7m-3)}{(n+s-1)(5ms+2m-3s^2)}$. We observe that, as n and m escape to infinity, this latter ratio is asymptotically in $\Theta(s)$. Applying Corollary 1, the estimated running time on $\Theta\left(\frac{(n+s-1)m}{\ell s^2}\right)$ SMs is $T_s = \left(\frac{2m-s}{m} + \log_2\left(\frac{m}{s}\right) + 1\right)(2Us+2s^2+2U-s)$. One checks that the running time estimate ratio is asymptotically equivalent to $\frac{2U\log_2(m)}{s(s+U)\log_2(m/s)}$. This latter is smaller than 1 for $s > 1$. Hence, increasing s makes the algorithm performance worse. In practice, as shown on Figure 3, setting $s = 4$ (where $\ell = 256$) performs best, while a larger s increases the running time, which is coherent with our theoretical analysis.

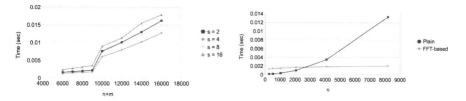

Figure 3. Running time of plain polynomial multiplication algorithm with dense polynomials of sizes n, m and parameter s on GeForce GTX 670.

Figure 4. Running time of plain and FFT-based multiplication algorithms with input size n on GeForce GTX 670.

We consider now an alternative polynomial multiplication, based on FFT, see for instance [22]. Let ℓ be the number of threads per thread-block. Based on the analysis of Stockham FFT algorithm, we obtain the work, span, and parallelism overhead of the overall FFT-based polynomial multiplication as $W_{fft} = 129n\log_2(n) - 94n$, $S_{fft} = 129\log_2(n) - 94$ and $O_{fft} = \frac{nU(15\log_2(n)-4)}{\ell}$. Applying Corollary 1, the running time estimate on $\Theta\left(\frac{n}{\ell}\right)$ SMs is $T_{fft} = \left(15\log_2(n) - \frac{13}{2}\right)(4U+25)$.

Back to plain multiplication, using $s = 4$ obtained from experimental results and setting $m = n$, we observe that the estimated running time ratio T_s/T_{fft} is essentially constant on $\Theta\left(\frac{n^2}{\ell}\right)$ SMs[3] when n escapes to infinity, although the plain multiplication performs more work and parallelism overhead.

---

[3]This is the amount of SMs required in the above estimates for the plain multiplication.

However, the estimated running time of the plain multiplication on $\Theta(\frac{n}{\ell})$ SMs becomes $T'_{plain} = \left(\frac{(n+3)(n-2)}{8n} + \log_2(n) - 1 \right)(10U + 28)$, that is, in a context of limited resource (namely SMs) w.r.t. the previous estimate. Since the running time estimate for FFT-based multiplication is also based on $\Theta(\frac{n}{\ell})$ SMs, we observe that, when n escapes to infinity, the ratio T'_{plain}/T_{fft} on $\Theta(\frac{n}{\ell})$ SMs is asymptotically equivalent to $\frac{5U(n+8\log_2(n))}{240U\log_2(n)}$, thus in $\Theta(n)$. Therefore, FFT-based multiplication outperforms plain multiplication for n large enough, when resources are limited. Figure 4 shows coherent experimental results with $\ell = 256$. In conclusion, the MCM model can take available resources into account when comparing two algorithms.

References

[1] R. D. Blumofe and C. E. Leiserson. Space-efficient scheduling of multithreaded computations. *SIAM J. Comput.*, 27(1):202–229, 1998.

[2] R. L. Graham. Bounds on multiprocessing timing anomalies. *SIAM J. on Applied Mathematics*, 17(2):416–429, 1969.

[3] Y. He, C. E. Leiserson, and W. M. Leiserson. The Cilkview scalability analyzer. In *Proc. of SPAA*, pages 145–156. ACM, 2010.

[4] L. J. Stockmeyer and U. Vishkin. Simulation of parallel random access machines by circuits. *SIAM J. Comput.*, 13(2):409–422, 1984.

[5] P. B. Gibbons. A more practical PRAM model. In *Proc. of SPAA*, pages 158–168. ACM, 1989.

[6] A. Aggarwal, A. K. Chandra, and M. Snir. Communication complexity of PRAMs. *Theoretical Computer Science*, 71(1):3–28, 1990.

[7] L. Ma, K. Agrawal, and R. D. Chamberlain. A memory access model for highly-threaded many-core architectures. *Future Generation Computer Systems*, 30:202–215, 2014.

[8] S. Hong and H. Kim. An analytical model for a GPU architecture with memory-level and thread-level parallelism awareness. *SIGARCH Comput. Archit. News*, 37(3):152–163, June 2009.

[9] L. Ma and R. D Chamberlain. A performance model for memory bandwidth constrained applications on graphics engines. In *Proc. of ASAP*, pages 24–31. IEEE, 2012.

[10] W. Liu, W. Muller-Wittig, and B. Schmidt. Performance predictions for general-purpose computation on GPUs. In *Proc. of ICPP*, page 50. IEEE, 2007.

[11] A. D. Robison. Composable parallel patterns with Intel Cilk Plus. *Computing in Science & Engineering*, 15(2):0066–71, 2013.

[12] NVIDIA. NVIDIA next generation CUDA compute architecture: Kepler GK110, 2012.

[13] S. A. Haque. *Hardware Acceleration Technologies in Computer Algebra: Challenges and Impact*. PhD thesis, University of Western Ontario, 2013.

[14] S. A. Haque, F. Mansouri, and M. Moreno Maza. On the parallelization of subproduct tree techniques targeting many-core architectures. In *Proc. of CASC 2014, LNCS 8660*, pages 171–185. Springer, 2014.

[15] T. D. Han and T. S. Abdelrahman. Reducing branch divergence in GPU programs. In *Proc. of GPGPU-4*, pages 3:1–3:8. ACM, 2011.

[16] J. Shin. Introducing control flow into vectorized code. In *Proc. of PACT*, pages 280–291. IEEE, 2007.

[17] L. Mirsky. A dual of Dilworth's decomposition theorem. *The American Math. Monthly*, 78(8):876–877, 1971.

[18] D. E. Knuth. *The Art of Computer Programming, Vol. II: Seminumerical Algorithms*. Addison-Wesley, 1969.

[19] J. Cooley and J. Tukey. An algorithm for the machine calculation of complex Fourier series. *Math. Comp.*, 19:297–301, 1965.

[20] T. G. Jr. Stockham. High-speed convolution and correlation. In *Proc. of AFIPS*, pages 229–233. ACM, 1966.

[21] S. A. Haque and M. Moreno Maza. Plain polynomial arithmetic on GPU. In *J. of Physics: Conf. Series*, volume 385, page 12014. IOP Publishing, 2012.

[22] M. Moreno Maza and W. Pan. Fast polynomial arithmetic on a GPU. *J. of Physics: Conference Series*, 256, 2010.

Parallel Computing: On the Road to Exascale
G.R. Joubert et al. (Eds.)
IOS Press, 2016
© 2016 The authors and IOS Press. All rights reserved.
doi:10.3233/978-1-61499-621-7-45

CPU performance analysis using Score-P on PRIMEHPC FX100 Supercomputer

Tomotake NAKAMURA [a]

[a] *FUJITSU LIMITED*

Abstract. Performance tuning tools are required to reach a high level of performance in a large-scale parallel system. There are many open source software (OSS) tools that can assist programmers with the performance analysis. Score-P is an efficient OSS tool for analyzing MPI communication and tuning performance. A problem is that it only uses hardware counters to analyze CPU operating states. We developed an interface between Score-P and Fujitsu's advanced profiler (FAPP), which has more functions for analyzing CPU operating states. The key benefit of our interface is that users can find the cost balance among threads in a CPU and investigate the causes of the performance problem by using there individual favorite performance tool. We demonstrated this interface's ability in tuning the CCS quantum chromodynamics (QCD) benchmark program.

Keywords. performance tuning tool, tuning

1. Introduction

There are many tools that assist programmers with the performance analysis and optimization of parallel applications. HPCToolkit [13], Scalasca [14], Score-P [5], TAU [17], and Vampir [16] are well known examples.

Score-P [5], [6] is one of the most actively developed open source software (OSS) infrastructures. Its components include an instrumentation framework that records several performance metrics including execution time, communication metrics, and optionally, hardware counters. Measurement runs can switch between tracing or profiling mode. In tracing mode, the performance events are passed to the OTF2 (successor to OTF [7] and Epilog [8]) back-end and are written to files for subsequent postmortem analysis using Scalasca or Vampir. In profiling mode, the performance events are summarized at runtime separately for each call path.

Score-P is an efficient tool for analyzing MPI communication and tuning performance, but its analysis of CPU operating states (consisting of executing instructions, waiting for memory access, waiting for an operation to complete, etc.) relies only on hardware counters. In addition, Score-P's instrumentation itself inserts special measurement calls into the application code at specific important points (events). On the other hand, although the analysis function for MPI communication of Fujitsu's advanced profiler (FAPP) is not sufficient in itself for performance analyses, it does have efficient functions for analyzing CPU operating states.

We developed an interface (an extension of Score-P) between Score-P and FAPP for efficient analysis of both MPI communication performance and CPU operating states.

2. Background

2.1. Score-P

Score-P is a performance measurement infrastructure that is being jointly developed by leading HPC performance tools groups [5], [6]. Its components consist of an instrumentation framework, several runtime libraries, and some helper tools. The instrumentation allows users to insert measurement probes into C/C++ and Fortran code that collect performance-related data when triggered during measurement runs. In order to collect relevant data, e.g., times, visits, communication metrics, or hardware counters, the applications need to link to one of several run-time libraries for serial execution, OpenMP, MPI parallelism, or hybrid combinations.

Score-P runs by default in profiling mode and produces data in the CUBE4 format [10], [9]. This data provides insights about the hot-spots in the application, and Score-P has customization options for subsequent measurement runs, for example, to select what MPI groups to record, to specify the total amount of memory the measurement is allowed to consume, to adapt trace output options, and to specify a set of hardware counters to be recorded.

Score-P experiments record by default all events during the whole execution run. If tracing is enabled, the event data on each process will be collected in buffers that must be adequately sized to store events from the entire execution.

When Score-P works together with Scalasca, it is possible to analyze the communication situation in detail. For example, together they have the ability to identify wait states in communication. Score-P and tools working with it have the ability of analyzing the communication situation of any application.

2.2. FAPP

The advanced profiler (FAPP) [2] developed by Fujitsu is used by application developers to tune applications on Fujitsu's HPC systems. FAPP has three basic functions.

- It specifies the beginning and end of a measurement interval by calling a service library from within the application in order to perform detailed analysis of a specific program location.
- It obtains detailed and accurate performance information for every measurement interval by making rigorous measurements (rather than sampling) of the times of the CPU processing, thread-parallelization processing, and process parallelization processing within the measurement interval.
- It individually analyzes the measured metrics instead of processing them as statistical averages; thereby, it can handle cases in which the performance characteristics change every time a user function is called.

FAPP collects and outputs execution performance information for a specific section of an application. One of its functions is a precision visibility function that enables data collected in any format to be analyzed using Excel Macro-enabled Workbooks in Microsoft Excel and the results to be displayed in a graph or table.

CPUs have various performance instrumentation counters that can be used to classify the total execution time of an instruction sequence in terms of CPU operating states (executing instructions, waiting for memory access, waiting for an operation to complete, etc.).

FAPP has a cycle accounting method for analyzing CPU operating states. This method is a stacked bar graph for analyzing and improving processor performance by determining where bottlenecks occur in the processor. If a performance problem is known to exist in the CPU processing, the developer can use the hardware monitor function of the detailed profiler to analyze the problem using cycle accounting.

3. Extension of Score-P and FAPP

Score-P collects hardware counter data with PAPI [4]. However, hardware counters alone are not sufficient for CPU operating states because they are raw hardware counter data and do not include precision performance analysis (PA) information, e.g., the waiting times for memory access, and delays caused by memory busy or cache busy events.

On the other hand, FAPP can collect such PA information, and we have devised a way of adding PA information from FAPP to Score-P. The resulting interface, called SP2FA, produces PA information on every function automatically by using Score-P's instrumentation.

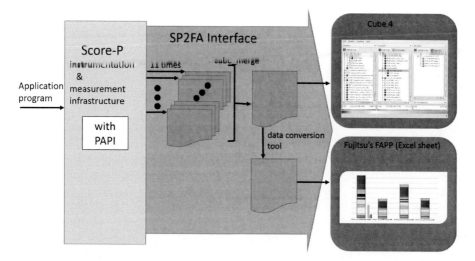

Figure 1. SP2FA: Interface between Score-P and FAPP's PA function

We implemented the SP2FA interface between the Score-P infrastructure and FAPP. SP2FA, shown in Figure 1, consisting of the following items.

- A wrapper of the Score-P measurement and cube_merge command
- A data conversion tool that converts cube data into FAPP input

The CPU of Fujitsu's new PRIMEHPC FX100 HPC system has eight performance instrumentation counters. FAPP needs 78 hardware counters for creating PA information. The performance data for an application is produced by executing the application program eleven times. Data collection is executed eleven times and causes small differences in the execution time. In order to detect these differences, one of the PA events "cycle_counts" is collected each time data is collected. The wrapper makes measurements eleven times. Cube data output from Score-P are merged into one log file by using the cube library. Next, the eleven performance measurements are merged using the cube library (cube_merge command). The merged data can be displayed and analyzed by using Cube 4. The cube data have to be converted in order for FAPP to be used to analyze the CPU operating states. The FAPP visibility function enables data collected in any format to be analyzed using Excel Macro-enabled Workbooks in Microsoft Excel and the results to be displayed in a graph or table.

We proposed a specialized SP2FA interface between Score-P and FAPP. However SP2FA can become an interface between other performance analysis tools with the function recording hardware counters and FAPP.

4. Application of the SP2FA extension interface

We evaluated SP2FA by applying it to two benchmark programs (NPB and CCS QCD) running on the FUJITSU Supercomputer PRIMEHPC FX100 [3]. The CPU of FUJITSU Supercomputer PRIMEHPC FX100, the SPARC64 XIfx processor delivers over 1 teraflops peak performance. 32 compute cores are integrated into a single processor chip. In the experiments with NPB and CCS QCD, we use a minor component (12 or 8 compute cores) of FUJITSU Supercomputer PRIMEHPC FX100 to be able to analyze the problem easier. Consequently, the performance data in subsection 4.1 and 4.2 is not peak performance of FUJITSU Supercomputer PRIMEHPC FX100.

4.1. Application to NAS parallel benchmarks

In this section, we show SP2FA can detect a load imbalance among threads in a CPU. We analyzed the NAS Parallel Benchmarks (NPB) by using Score-P, SP2FA, Cube, and FAPP. The NPB are a small set of programs designed to help evaluate the performance of parallel supercomputers. Specifically, we used MG (Class C, MPI version), one of the NPBs. MG is a memory intensive multi-grid benchmark on a sequence of meshes with long- and short-distance communication.

11 Score-P profiles of executions of 16 processes configured with different sets of hardware counters merged into a single profile. Cube's results for the MG NPB are shown in Figure 2. The metric tree includes all PA events in each function (event) for each process or thread.

Figure 3 shows FAPP's results for the MG NPB. From the cycle accounting data in the figure, we can see that these processes are balanced. For example, This is because 11 lots of hardware counter information are required. This means that differences might arise over the execution time. Minus numerical values might be output for some information due to these differences. We found out from the results that the MG NPB is balanced among the processes and is free of major problems for CPU performance.

4.2. Application to QCD

We analyzed the CCS QCD Mini program (class 2) by using Score-P, SP2FA, Cube, and FAPP. This program benchmarks the performance of a linear equation solver with a

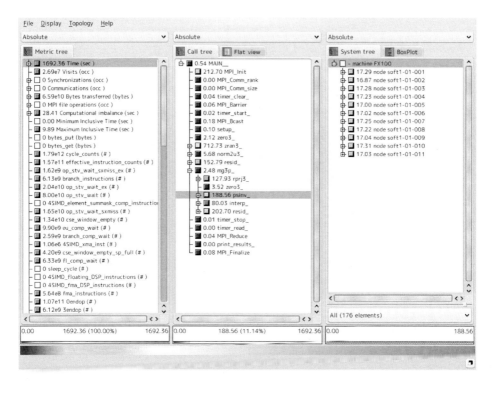

Figure 2. Cube for MG (Class C) NPB

large sparse coefficient matrix appearing in a lattice quantum chromodynamics (QCD) problem. Lattice QCD describes the properties of protons, neutrons, and nucleons in terms of more fundamental interacting elementary particles, i.e., gluons and quarks.

The key benefit of SP2FA is that users can find the cost balance among threads in a CPU and investigate the causes of the performance problem by using their individual favorite performance tool.

Figure 4 (a) shows the cycle accounting of FAPP before tuning. The execution speed was 20.5 GFLOPS. Figure 4 (a) shows that the time cost of Thread 0 in Process 0/1 is higher than other thread costs.

We identified the parts that caused imbalances by using the ability of Score-P to record each event automatically. In Figure 4 (a), "No instruction commit due to L1 cache access for an integer load instruction" and "No instruction commit waiting for an integer instruction to be completed" are imbalanced in Thread 0. We parallelized these parts by using the OpenMP directive. These parts of the code were found by CUBE to explore where the the correspoinding counts were highest on those threads. Figure 4 (a) shows that "No instruction commit due to L1/L2 cache for a floating-point load instruction" errors occur frequently as a result of indirect accesses to the elements of the array. We added a compile optimization flag "prefetch_indirect" and got the results shown in Figure 4 (b). The corresponding counts in Figure 4 (a), (b) don't appear to be noticeably imbal-

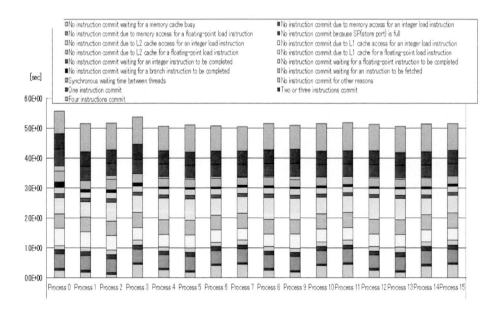

Figure 3. FAPP for MG (Class C) NPB with 16 MPI processes showing balanced execution

anced by their optimization. Execution speed increased to 29.2 GFLOPS. We achieved a 42% speed-up of the CCS QCD program by using Score-P, SP2FA, and FAPP.

5. Conclusion

We developed an interface between Score-P and Fujitsu's advanced profiler (FAPP), which has efficient functions for analyzing CPU operating states. We evaluated the interface and showed that it is useful for analyzing CPU operating states. It was possible to find load imbalance among the threads and investigate the causes of the performance problems.

References

[1] Fujitsu Limited: SPARC64 VIIIfx Extensions, 2010.
[2] Ida, K., Ohno, Y., Inoue, S., Minami, K.: Performance Profiling and Debugging on the K computer, FUJITSU Sci. Tech. J., Vol. 48, No. 3, pp. 331-339, 2012.
[3] Fujitsu   Limited: FUJITSU   Supercomputer   PRIMEHPC   FX100, http://www.fujitsu.com/global/products/computing/servers/supercomputer/primehpc-fx100, 2014.
[4] Browne, S., Dongarra, J., Garner, N., Ho, G., Mucci, P.: A Portable Programming Interface for Performance Evaluation on Modern Processors International Journal of High Performance Computing Applications, Volume 14, number 3, pp. 189–204, 2000.

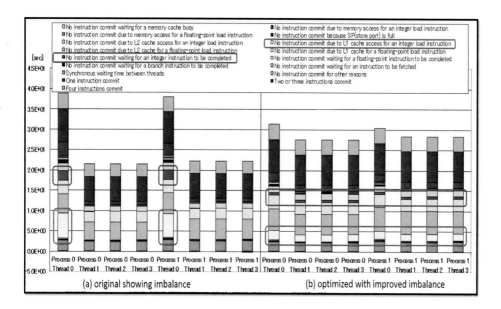

Figure 4. Cycle accounting for CCS QCD (Class 2)

[5] Knuepfer, A., Röussel, C., Mey, D., Biersdorff, S., Diethelm, K., Eschweiler, D., Geimer, M., Gerndt, M., Lorenz, D., Malony, A., Nagel, W.E., Oleynik, Y., Philippen, P., Saviankou, P., Schmidl, D., Shende, S., Tschüter, R., Wagner, M., Wesarg, B., Wolf, F.: Score-P: A Joint Performance Measurement Run-Time Infrastructure for Periscope, Scalasca, TAU, and Vampir, 2012.
[6] Score-P 1.4 user manual: https://silc.zih.tu-dresden.de/scorep-current/pdf/scorep.pdf.
[7] Knüpfer, A., Brendel, R., Brunst, H., Mix, H., Nagel, W.E.: Introducing the open trace format (OTF). In: Computational Science ICCS 2006: 6th International Conference, LNCS 3992. Springer, Reading, 2006.
[8] Wolf, F., Mohr, B.: EPILOG binary trace-data format, Technical Report FZJ-ZAM-IB-2004-06, Forschungszentrum Jülich, 2004.
[9] Cube 4.3 user guide: http://apps.fz-juelich.de/scalasca/releases/cube/4.3/docs/CubeGuide.pdf.
[10] Saviankou, P., Knobloch, M., Visser, A., Mohr, B.: Cube v4: From Performance Report Explorer to Performance Analysis Tool, In Proc. of ICCS, volume 51 of Procedia Computer Science, pp. 1343–1352, Elsevier, 2015.
[11] NASA Advanced Supercomputing Division: NAS Parallel Benchmarks, http://www.nas.nasa.gov/publications/npb.html.
[12] CCS QCD Miniapp: https://github.com/fiber-miniapp/ccs-qcd.
[13] Adhianto, L., Banerjee, S.k Fagan, M., Krentel, M., Marin, G., Mellor-Crummey, J., Tallent, N.R.: HPC-TOOLKIT: tools for performance analysis of optimized parallel programs. Concurr. Comput. Pract. Exp. 22(6), pp. 685–701, 2010.
[14] Geimer, M., Wolf, F., Wylie, B.J., Ábrahám, E., Becker, D., Mohr, B.: The scalasca performance toolset architecture. Concurr. Comput. Pract. Exp. 22(6), pp. 702–719, 2010.
[15] Scalasca 2.2 user guide: http://apps.fz-juelich.de/scalasca/releases/scalasca/2.2/docs/UserGuide.pdf
[16] Knüpfer, A., Brunst, H., Doleschal, J., Jurenz, M., Lieber, M., Mickler, H., Müller, M.S., Nagel, W.E.: The vampir performance analysis tool set. In: Resch, M., Keller, R., Himmler, V., Krammer, B., Schulz, A. (eds.) Tools for High Performance Computing, pp. 139–155, 2008.
[17] Shende, S., Malony, A.D.: The TAU parallel performance system, SAGE publications. Int. J. High Perform. Comput. 20(2), pp. 287–331, 2006.

Parallel Computing: On the Road to Exascale
G.R. Joubert et al. (Eds.)
IOS Press, 2016

doi:10.3233/978-1-61499-621-7-53

Performance improvements of polydisperse DEM simulations using a loose octree approach

G. Stein[a,1], S. Wirtz[a,2], V. Scherer[a]

[a] *Energy Plant Technology (LEAT), Ruhr-University Bochum, 44780 Bochum, Germany*

Abstract. Numerical simulations using the Discrete Element Method (DEM) are used at LEAT in the context of several important, energy related particulate flow systems. The focus of these investigations is the understanding of the heat and mass transfer processes on the micro-scale and the prediction of the related macroscopic behaviour. Most of the currently available DEM implementations, especially if the required number of particles is large, only allow for small variations in particle size if the computational effort must be kept within reasonable bounds. This is contrary to the actual requirements of many technically relevant processes where a broad size spectrum must be considered. Parallel processing helps to ease this situation to a certain degree, but the ongoing search for algorithmic improvements has not yet accomplished a definitive solution

The process of neighbourhood detection, which is required to identify the partners of the pairwise interactions determining momentum fluxes among the particles and between particles and surrounding walls is one common bottleneck. Besides the commonly used Linked-Cell method, hierarchically structured "background" meshes or octrees were proposed in the past and applied in various implementations. A new variant of the octree approach is presented and its performance with respect to particle number, particle size distribution and parallelisation is analysed and compared to conventional approaches. In order to obtain a realistic analysis, for a given code in a typical hardware environment (small engineering companies or university institutes), the benchmark addresses the technical application of particle movement in a section of a rotary drum.

Keywords. Rotary Drum, DEM, Loose Octree, MPI, Scalability

Topic Area: Applications

---

[1] Corresponding Author.
E-mail addresses: stein@leat.rub.de

[2] Corresponding Author.
E-mail addresses: wirtz@leat.rub.de

1. Introduction

Particulate flows occur in many natural and industrial processes, thus understanding the dynamical behaviour of these granular media and the associated mass and thermal energy exchange are extremely important for science and engineering. Very often experimental access is restricted to the macro scale of such flows, the internals and the microscopic action controlling the overall behaviour are typically inaccessible. The ability to simulate the mechanical interaction within the particulate solid phase, considering moving surroundings and passing fluids, is central to further understanding and description [2]. Particle based, Discrete Element Methods (DEM), which were developed during the last decades and being readily available as commercial or free software, are increasingly used in this context.

Most of the available DEM implementations [7][8] are restricted to spherical particles or to analytically defined particle shapes and allow only for small variations in particle size. These limitations arise from the computationally expensive treatment of short-range pairwise interactions among particles of complex shape and from the contact detection algorithm. This situation is contrary to the actual requirements of many relevant processes, which call for extremely large numbers of arbitrarily shaped objects [6] with a broad size spectrum where the individual particle size and shape can change over time due to physical or chemical process.

Massively parallel computing definitively is part of the solution to this big challenge, but the variety of approaches in this area (GPUs, Multi Core CPUs, Cluster, etc.) and the specific algorithmic requirements of the physical processes considered add to the complexity. Impressive results on GPUs, as obtained for specific cases [9] are not directly transferable to systems considering different complex physics.

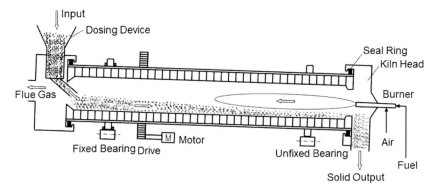

Figure 1. Sketch of a directly fired rotary kiln [5]

As a benchmark example aiming at the demands listed above and having great industrial relevance, the simulation of the bulk material movement in rotary kilns was chosen. Rotary kilns, as sketched in fig. 1, are widely used for bulk solid processing in various industries. The material transported through the kiln is heated, either directly from a flame within the kiln or indirectly through the kiln wall. The rotation of the kiln drum basically moves the material upwards on one side (exerting frictional forces on the particles at the wall), depending on the rotational speed a dynamic angle of repose is established and the particles move downhill on the surface by gravitational forces. Heat transfer occurs on these two interfaces, the kiln wall and the free surface and within the bulk. Industrial scale kilns are by far too large and the particles much too small to be simulated directly, but scaled "rotating drums" may be investigated to identify and quantify the solids flow with good transferability [2]. The macroscopic bulk movement (e. g. continuous rolling, intermittent sliding, throwing overhead), the angles of repose, the lateral mixing intensity and eventually particle segregation depend in a complex fashion on parameters like the rotational speed, the particle size (distribution), the material density, frictional properties among the particles and with the walls, the diameter of the drum, the filling degree or length and inclination of the drum.

2. Benchmark case

The numerical model of the rotating drum considered in the current work is a shorter version (diameter 300 mm, length of only 100 mm) of the device presented in [2], where a very good reproduction of corresponding monodisperse experiments could be shown. The filling degree of the drum (volume of space occupied by particles over volume of the drum), which is the parameter the kiln operator is actually interested in, increases linearly with the number of particles in case of monodisperse material.

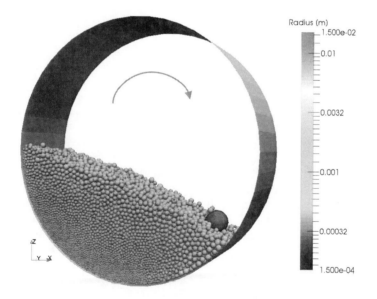

Figure 2. Snapshot of the rotary drum with polydisperse spheres rotating at 6 rpm

Although these simulations already provide deep insight and show the feasibility of DEM simulations in this context, the applicability rapidly breaks down due to the computational effort required if a material must be considered which exhibits a broad size distribution. The particle sizes of mechanically crushed materials as used in industrial applications can be nicely fit to the Rosin-Rammler-Sperling-Bennet (RRSB) [4] size distribution (also known as Weibull distribution [11])

$$D(d) = 1 - e^{-(d/\bar{d})^n}$$

where $D(d)$ is the mass fraction of particles passing through a sieve with a mesh aperture d; the two parameters of the distribution are the size parameter $\bar{d}$ (63.2%-quantile) and the spread of the distribution n. For the mechanical interaction, the resulting transport behaviour and the thermochemical processes occurring, the filling degree of the drum is of utmost importance and must be kept constant between simulation and actual operation. As shown in figure 3, the number of particles required to obtain a given filling degree steeply increases with the size ratio $\omega = d_{max}/d_{min}$. In the cases presented in figure 3. The continuous distribution defined in the interval $[0,\infty]$ was cut off at 40 mm upper size and at 0.4 mm at the lower end to obtain a defined size ratio of $\omega = 100$.

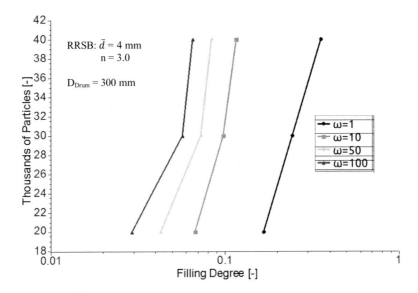

Figure 3. Number of particles and its increase with the filling degree for different size ratios

The simulation snapshot shown in figure 2 only considers one axial segment of a much longer drum. Although many aspects of the ongoing processes already can be investigated with a single segment, the obvious intention is to be able to simulate much longer domains.

3. Neighbourhood determination

One step within the overall procedure of DEM simulations requires the identification of contacts among the particles. In a brute force and most naive approach, this contact check would be performed directly between all particles in the system.

This would lead to $n \cdot (n-1) \cdot 0.5$ contact inspections, resulting in far too many needless operations since each particle obviously has only a few direct neighbours.

Several concepts and procedures were developed and applied for this next neighbour identification in order to arrive at a linear increase of operations.

3.1 Hexgrid based approaches

For monodisperse systems cartesian background meshes (we call them **"Hexgrids"**) turned out to be quite efficient. Independent of their precise implementation (lists, pointers, hash-tables), these "binning" systems group the particles being in close neighbourhood into a limited number of indexed containers covering the computational domain, thereby implicitly expressing the existing spatial "locality". Figure 4 sketches (in 2D) four particles in a domain covered by such a background mesh. Using the particle centroid, the particle index is associated with the corresponding cell. After insertion of all particles, a list of possible particle contacts is derived for each of these "cells" by forming pairs of particles from the particle indices within the cell itself and in the, at most, 26 (in 3D) "neighbouring" cells **(Hga)**. "On the fly" elimination of duplicate pairs finally results in a list of particle pairs which then must be checked for actually existing contacts.

a)   b)

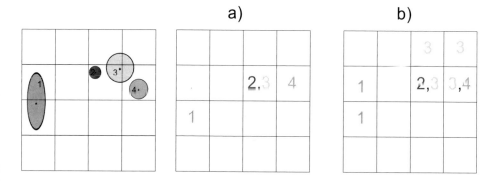

Figure 4. Particle mapping onto a Hexgrid; in a) the centroid determines the unambiguous association of a particle with a single cell, in b) multiple entries, controlled by the bounding box, occur

In the second, more efficient variant of this "Hexgrid" **(Hgb)**, the initial association of the particles with the background cells is based on a bounding box around the particles. Each particle is inserted into the index list of the cell if any spatial overlay with the bounding box exists. Thus the index of a given particle occurs, depending on its size, in multiple lists. This substantially reduces the absolute number of contact candidate lists and allows an optimisation, if the edge length of the background mesh is chosen to be in the order of the particle size. Especially for dense monodisperse material in compact domains this method often outperforms most of the other approaches.

3.2 Octree based approaches

For large domains with dynamically moving scattered polydisperse particles the methods mentioned above reach their limits with respect to memory consumption and computing times required [10]. Voronoi-meshes and tree based concepts are known to be much more suitable in this case. Especially tree based approaches [3] naturally reflect the size differences occurring in materials with wide size distributions. Again, variations of the implementation of the required tree structures (binary trees, octrees in 3D, pointer linked trees, object oriented) may be employed, which further complicates the matter but will not be discussed here.

For the case considered, a three-dimensional octree is used as the background mesh and two different approaches for insertion of the particle indices were tested. In the first variant, designated as "Ordinary Octree" **(OO)**, the particle indices are inserted according to the position of their centroids while the size decides on which tree level the insertion occurs. The level index, starting at zero, is successively increased as long as the particle (at its position) completely fits into the cell on the next level. This is similar to case a) of the "Hexgrid" and results in one entry for each particle as sketched in 2D in figure 5. The list of potential contacts is then collected by traversing the tree from the largest level index to the smallest level index as long as a particle entries exist.

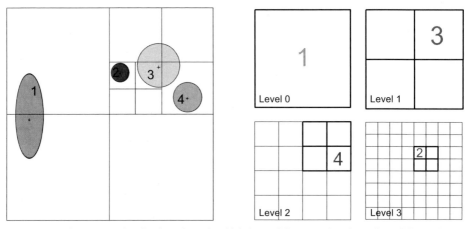

Figure 5. Ordinary Octree localisation scheme in which the particles are assigned to cells to different sizes. 1D view shows by level where particles are mapped. Particles are not allowed to straddle over multiple cells, hence the whole body must fit into one of the cells.

The disadvantage though is that the particles must fully fit into the "cell" they are associated with. This results, especially if the centroid is close to cell borders, that many small particles are inserted at level indices much smaller than their size would prescribe. This "straddling" results in considerably longer lists of potential contacts than required.

A remedy to the described "straddling" [1] is provided by a different index insertion strategy [3] termed "Loose Octree" **(LO)**. As in the case b) of the "Hexgrid" approach a bounding box is used to identify the "cells" touched by individual particles, but (and this is crucial) the index is not inserted on the level solely defined by their size. Instead the association occurs (at least [3]) one level index higher. For example, the purple particle number 4 belongs to level 2, since its size fits into the corresponding cell. Instead its spatial extent is inserted on level 3 (purple numbers).

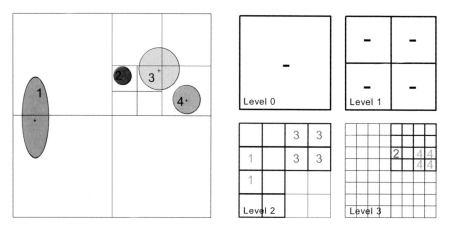

Figure 6. Loose Octree, every particle might occupy multiple cells. Different straddling rules may be considered.

At first glance this appears to be disadvantageous, but if multiple entries are removed during the collection of the final list of possible contacts, a much shorter list results. For the introductory example of the rotating drum, using 20,000 particles of the size distribution mentioned, this results in the following list lengths: Hga= 11.0, Hgb= 6.0, OO= 3.1 and LO= 1.4 millions of initial potential contacts.

4. Performance comparisons and parallelisation

DEM simulations for large numbers of particles always require to conduct the simulation on parallel computing hardware in order to obtain the results within reasonable time. Therefore the algorithm employed, in addition to being fast on single CPU (single core) systems, must also scale reasonably well on parallel systems.

The computations discussed in the following were carried out on fairly mainstream hardware consisting of a group of 4 Intel Dual Xeon E5-2600 (2 x 6 cores, NUMA activated) machines with 64 GB RAM each, which are part of a cluster interconnected with Mellanox Infiniband hardware (Mellanox MIS5023Q-1BFR InfiniScale IV QDR Switch and Mellanox MCX354A-TCBT ConnectX-3 VPI cards using PCI-E 3.0 8x). The DEM code is an inhouse code developed by LEAT.

The parallelisation is based on the domain decomposition approach which proved to be robust and efficient in the past and is implemented using OpenMPI. For this purpose the computational domain is manually decomposed into several spatially connected sections, an automated load-balancing is not provided. Particles located adjacent to the domain boundaries and the data associated with them are duplicated, they coexist in both domains and are updated every time-step. Since the connectivity between the domains is known in advance, a corresponding communication topology is set up. Although multithreading would be an additional option on multi-core CPUs, this was not pursued in order to limit the code complexity. Instead, OpenMPI automatically assigns the domains to the available CPU-cores.

To investigate the scalar performance of the different contact detection algorithms (Hgb, OO, LO) the numerical model of the rotating drum from figure 2 was employed on one of these machines. Although the code used is able to use arbitrary defined polyhedral particles [6] of any size distribution in conjunction with heat transfer and thermochemical processes, we restrict ourselves here to the mechanical behaviour of spherical particles.

As a reference case (to which all further results refer), a rotating drum at 6 rpm with 20,000 particles (material properties of glass) with Hgb variant is used. Again a RRSB size distribution, this time with a size parameter of 3 mm and a spread of 3.0 was chosen. The distribution was cut off at 30 mm upper size and 0.3 mm at the lower end, resulting in a size ratio of $\omega = 100$. This is equivalent to a filling degree of 10% of the drum, with 80,000 particles the filling degree is 30%.

Figure 7 shows the increase of computing time with the number of particles, as obtained for the three approaches considered and reveals an outstanding improvement gained by the LO approach. The reference of the relative calculation time is set to Hgb with 20,000 particles and compared to the other algorithms and particles numbers with the same hardware.

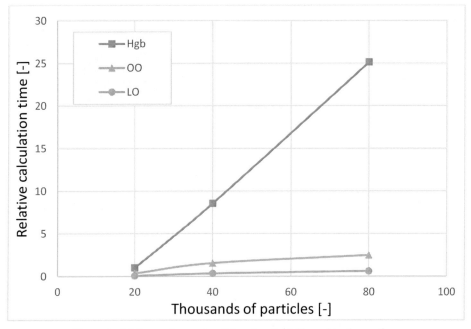

Figure 7. Relative runtimes using different next neighbour detection routines

In order to investigate the influence of the parallelisation strategy on the overall runtime of the "Loose Octree" approach, different distribution schemes of subtasks onto a number of CPU-cores were investigated. The calculation was decomposed into two, four, eight, sixteen, twenty-four and forty-eight domains, which were distributed in various ways on up to four machines (48 cores in total). In the following nomenclature the first index designates the number of machines used and the second one indicates the number of processes launched on each of the machines. The operating system always distributed these processes evenly to the available CPU cores on the individual machines.

The reference case is the same as in figure 7, using one CPU-core on one single machine (1x1 MxP at 20,000). Obviously subdividing the task into two parallel processes running on the same machine (using two Cores, 1x2 MxP) is less efficient than using two machines (2x1 MxP) instead, which nearly halves the computing time. Proceeding to two tasks on two machines (2x2 MxP) and further on to four tasks, each one on a separate machine, reflects the same expected tendencies.

Doubling the number of particles (and extending the rotary drum to a length of 200 mm) while at the same time doubling the hardware resources (4x4 MxP instead of 4x2 MxP) actually does not noticeably increase the runtime required (symbol at 160,000 particles).

Using 240,000 particles with an elongated domain, applying the same decompositions as before, shows that the 4x4 distribution only exhibits marginal performance losses. In contrast, using all available cores (4x12 MxP) results in a slight performance loss, which is due to the smaller workload of each process and the relatively larger communication overhead.

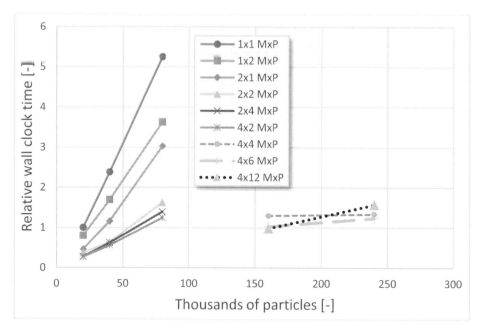

Figure 8. Relative runtime using the loose octree approach with multiple processes (ω=100)

The results show a very promising behaviour, especially as the large differences in particle size require an efficient all-to-all communication topology since the large particles potentially can span more than one domain.

5. Performance comparisons and parallelisation

Discrete element simulations will be employed more and more frequently for the investigation of increasingly complex and thus demanding physical situations. To achieve this with reasonable computing times, bottlenecks in the implementation of these codes must be removed successively. Currently the management of the particle neighbourhood, which is nothing more than the search for potential contact partners in 3D space, is one of the very time consuming steps. The work required here must be confined to a linear increase with the number of particles (and the volume of the domain considered). Running a serial process the code already improves with a ratio up to 40 using 80,000 particles compared to Hexgrid based methods when a wide particle distribution is used.

As shown for a "real world", industrially motivated example, combining the Loose Octree approach with domain decomposition for parallel computing is a promising approach.

References

[1] C., Ericson. 2005. "Real Time Collision Detection". Morgan Kaufmann.
[2] Komossa, H., S. Wirtz, V. Scherer, F. Herz, and E. Specht. 2014. "Transversal Bed Motion in Rotating Drums Using Spherical Particles: Comparison of Experiments with DEM Simulations.". Powder Technology; 264:96–104. DOI: 10.1016/j.powtec.2014.05.021
[3] Raschdorf, S., and M. Kolonko. 2011. "Loose Octree: a Data Structure for the Simulation of Polydisperse Particle Packings" International Journal for Numerical Methods in Engineering 85 (5): 625–639. DOI: 10.1002/nme.2988
[4] Vesilind, P.Aarne. 1980. "The Rosin-Rammler Particle Size Distribution." Resource Recovery and Conservation 5 (3): 275–277. DOI: 10.1016/0304-3967(80)90007-4. http://www.sciencedirect.com/science/article/pii/0304396780900074.
[5] F. Herz. 2012, Entwicklung eines mathematischen Modells zur Simulation thermischer Prozesse in Drehrohröfen, PhD Thesis, Magdeburg, docupoint Verlag
[6] Höhner, D., Wirtz, S. & Scherer, V., 2014. "A study on the influence of particle shape and shape approximation on particle mechanics in a rotating drum using the discrete element method." Powder Technology, 253, p.256-265.
[7] Kloss, C.; Goniva, C.; Hager, A.; Amberger, S.; Pirker, S. 2012. "Models, algorithms and validation for opensource DEM and CFD-DEM", Progress in Computational Fluid Dynamics, An Int. J. 2012 - Vol. 12, No.2/3 pp. 140 - 152
[8] EDEM Simulator, DEM Solutions Ltd., http://www.dem-solutions.com/software/edem-simulator/
[9] Govender, N.; Wilke, D. N.; Kok, S.; Els, R. 2014 "Development of a convex polyhedral discrete element simulation framework for NVIDIA Kepler based GPUs, Journal of Computational and Applied Mathematics", Volume 270, November 2014, Pages 386-400, ISSN 0377-0427, http://dx.doi.org/10.1016/j.cam.2013.12.032.
[10] Ogarko, V.; Luding, S. 2012, "A fast multilevel algorithm for contact detection of arbitrarily polydisperse objects." Computer Physics Communications 183(4): 931-936
[11] Stoyan, D. "Weibull, RRSB or extreme-value theorists?" Metrika, Springer, vol. 76(2), pages 153-159, February 2013.

Acknowledgements

The current work has been funded by DFG (Deutsche Forschungsgemeinschaft) within the project SCHE 322/10-1 and Energie.NRW EnEff within contract 64.65.69-EN-3005B.

Parallel Computing: On the Road to Exascale
G.R. Joubert et al. (Eds.)
IOS Press, 2016
doi:10.3233/978-1-61499-621-7-63

Execution Performance Analysis of the ABySS Genome Sequence Assembler using **Scalasca** on the K Computer

Itaru KITAYAMA [a], Brian J. N. WYLIE [a,b,1], Toshiyuki MAEDA [a]

[a] *RIKEN Advanced Institute for Computational Science, Kobe, Japan*
[b] *Jülich Supercomputing Centre, Forschungszentrum Jülich, Germany*

Abstract.

Performance analysis of the ABySS genome sequence assembler (ABYSS-P) executing on the K computer with up to 8192 compute nodes is described which identified issues that limited scalability to less than 1024 compute nodes and required prohibitive message buffer memory with 16384 or more compute nodes. The open-source Scalasca toolset was employed to analyse executions, revealing the impact of massive amounts of MPI point to point communication used particularly for master/worker process coordination, and inefficient parallel file operations that manifest as waiting time at later MPI collective synchronisations and communications. Initial remediation via use of collective communication operations and alternate strategies for parallel file handling show large performance and scalability improvements, with partial executions validated on the full 82,944 compute nodes of the K computer.

Keywords. Scalasca, Score-P, Vampir, K computer, bioinformatics.
Topic area. Software and Architectures

Introduction

Understanding the performance of the MPI library through real-life applications on petaflops machines such as the K computer and other Top500 supercomputers is key to successful transition to foreseeable Exascale computing. MPI applications developed and optimized for high-end servers often fail to take full advantage of the capability that today's supercomputers provide in part due to node-to-node communication latencies. Evaluation of the ABYSS-P [1,2] sequence assembler on the K computer demonstrated the issue in scaling; linear scaling stops early at 200 compute nodes and adding more nodes only resulted in moderate improvement until 800 nodes (only 1% use of the K computer resources). Performance decrease was observed when running with 1024 and more compute nodes, and executions with 16384 or more compute nodes were not possible since they exceeded available node memory.

---

[1] Corresponding author: b.wylie@fz-juelich.de

In the face of the very limited application performance scalability, a tool was required that best suits our needs to find performance bottlenecks. The Scalasca toolset [3] was selected as it provides profiling and tracing of MPI events to quantify bytes transferred, elapsed time in functions or distinct application call paths, and execution traces which can be viewed as timelines with Vampir [4]. Scalasca is used on many of the largest HPC systems, and was recently ported to the K computer to enable large-scale application profiling for the first time.

We discovered frequent MPI point-to-point communications used to exchange data stored in local buffers between nodes at various stages of ABYSS-P execution, and rapidly growing time for MPI point-to-point and collective communication at large scale (more than 1024 compute nodes). In the master/worker parallelisation paradigm employed by ABySS, the master needs to collect all the checkpointing messages sent from workers to transit to other processing phases. Additional serious performance and scalability inhibitors are ultimately determined to arise primarily from ineffective parallel file reading and writing.

1. Test Platform: The K Computer

A detailed description of the K computer can be found elsewhere [5]. The K computer has 82,944 compute nodes connected through the Tofu 6D mesh/torus interconnection network and attached to the Lustre-based Fujitsu Exascale Filesystem (FEFS). Each compute node has SPARC64 VIIIfx 8-core processors, 16 GB of memory, and 4 Tofu network interfaces whose maximum aggregate throughput is 20 GB/s [5–7].

A custom Linux kernel runs on each compute node and for program development Fujitsu Fortran, C, and C++ compilers and MPI library optimized for the K computer are provided [8,9].

2. Target Application: ABySS

ABySS is a parallel sequence assembler for small to large mammalian-size genomes. ABYSS-P written in C++ is the target MPI application of this paper; the program finds overlapping sequences from the distributed directed graph across the computing nodes and stitches those sequences together to obtain long sequences.

ABYSS-P uses the eager protocol for small, 4 kB messages in the master/worker programming paradigm. During execution the master process (MPI rank 0) is responsible for controlling the entire workflow and lets worker processes transit to different processing phases. The main phases studied in this paper are *LoadSequences* (each process reading data from disk and building a distributed hash table), *GenerateAdjacency* (building a distributed graph), *Erode*, *Trim*, *DiscoverBubbles* and *PopBubble* (removing bad data for quality control), and final *NetworkAssembly* (creating long sequences from the distributed graph).

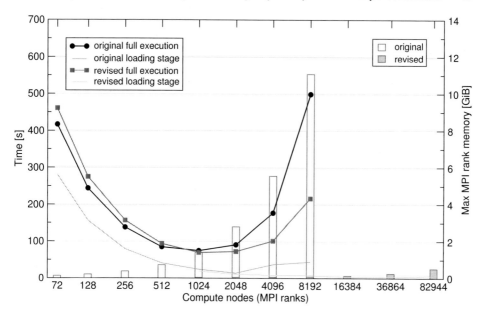

Figure 1. Original and revised ABYSS-P execution scalability on the K computer: bars of maximum MPI rank memory requirement, plot with time of best full execution and loading stage.

2.1. ABYSS-P Configuration

Configuration is done using GNU Autotools cross-compilation to build a SPARC64 binary for the K computer on the x86_64 front-ends using the Fujitsu C++ compiler FCC.

Two MCA parameters of the MPI library specific to K computer must be set prior to launching ABYSS-P: OMPI_MCA_common_tofu_fastmode_threshold=0 and OMPI_MCA_common_tofu_max_fastmode_procs=-1, the former needed to always exchange messages in eager mode to avoid deadlock, and the latter to remove the limit on the number of processes (default 1024) that can be used in eager mode. Although the K computer compute nodes have 8 cores, the job configuration is always set to allocate one process per node to allocate all the usable 14 GB of memory (i.e., excluding that required for system libraries).

Publicly-available data from the *E.coli* MG1655 laboratory strain sequenced on Illumina MiSeq system [10] is used for the experiments described in this paper. The total data read from disk is 6.1 GB, staged in to FEFS local disks.

2.2. ABYSS-P Execution Time Evaluation

Execution timings graphed as circles in Figure 1 show that the best data processing performance of the application (90 seconds) was obtained with around 768 nodes. Adding more nodes up to 1024 did not improve the performance and beyond that execution was slower. Memory required for MPI message buffers also grows rapidly and become prohibitive for executions with 16384 or more nodes. Reports of time elapsed in the key phases and user functions distinguished the most time-consuming *LoadSequences* stage but were insufficient to understand the ABYSS-P execution on the K computer, and therefore comprehensive tools for in-depth parallel performance analysis were required.

3. Profiling and Tracing with Scalasca

The open-source Scalasca toolset was developed to support scalable performance analysis of large-scale parallel applications using MPI and OpenMP on current high-performance computer systems [3]. The latest version uses the community-developed Score-P instrumentation and measurement infrastructure [11]. MPI library interposition combined with automatic instrumentation of application source routines and OpenMP parallel constructs is used to generate detailed call-path profiles or event traces from application processes and threads. Event traces are automatically analysed in parallel to identify and quantify communication and synchronization inefficiencies, and trace visualisation tools such as Vampir can be directed to show the severest instances.

These capabilities proved very valuable for the analysis of ABYSS-P, which has a complex execution structure and uses MPI extensively throughout.

3.1. Methodology

Initial measurements only of MPI events already resulted in large execution traces which hinted at distinct execution phases with very different performance characteristics. Context was provided with manual source annotations of regions (i.e., stages) of particular interest, and found to be essential to understand the complex fragmented nature of the ABYSS-P task-queuing and master-worker paradigm.

Enabling compiler instrumentation of user routines helped clarify the context for this communication, but suffered from significant measurement overheads both in execution dilation and trace buffer memory and file size requirements. To produce execution traces of managable size and reduce dilation, extensive filtering of frequently-executed short-running routines was necessary. While producing a filter for all routines coming from standard C++ libraries is straightforward, more care is required with user-level source routines. Generally those routines which are purely local computation are readily identified via scoring of analysis reports as they are not found on a call-path to MPI communication or synchronization, however, ABySS has a number of routines which have a dual nature that are used in deeply recursing call-paths. For example, `pumpNetwork` is frequently used to process outstanding communication but may also complete computations or busy-wait, so it provides valuable context but at the cost of high measurement overheads.

Following this iterative process of both augmenting and refining the instrumentation and measurement configuration, it was possible to produce rich analyses with insight into ABYSS-P parallel execution inefficiences, via summary profiles and traces. Initial summary measurements were scored to identify appropriate measurement filters that were necessary to avoid extreme measurement dilation and buffer/disk requirements for subsequent trace experiments, producing around 1 GB of event trace data per process, which were automatically analysed in parallel by Scalasca and interactively examined with Vampir.

3.2. Analysis of ABYSS-P Execution

A variety of measurements of the original version of ABYSS-P were done on the K computer with up to 8192 MPI processes.

Scalasca trace analysis of a 1024-node ABySS execution of five minutes on the K computer is concisely presented in Figure 2. Expanding and selecting nodes of the tree for metric *Time* from the left panel reveals that 8.0% of the total execution time [301,000 CPU seconds readable from the scale at the bottom] is used by MPI: 1.3% [3872s] by `MPI_Init`, 1.6% [4872s] by `MPI_Barrier` collective synchronization, 2.1% [6398s] for point-to-point communication and the remaining 3.0% [8915s] in various collective communications (mainly `MPI_Allreduce`). Selecting the *Point-to-point communication time* metric updates panels to its right identifying that it is predominantly [3832s, 60%] for `MPI_Send` in the *LoadSequences* stage shown in the centre panel, and then the right panel shows that this time is broadly distributed across (non-master) ranks: 3.74 ± 0.59 seconds.

Vampir timeline visualisation of the 1024-node ABySS trace in Figure 3 provides an overview of the execution phases for each process. The *LoadSequences* stage (in yellow) dominates the first half of the execution and reveals eight "waves" as sequence data is read from disk by each process and transferred when the local buffer is full. Although there are the same number of `MPI_Send` events and the same amount of data transferred in each stage, only those in the first wave are clearly distinguished. The *GenerateAdjacency* stage (pale blue) follows, then *Erode* dominated by `MPI_Allreduce` (orange) and *NetworkAssembly* containing a period of extensive `MPI_Barrier` (magenta) usage before the final network assembly with its huge imbalance. The `pumpNetwork` routine which polls for available messages is evident in all stages when point-to-point message transfers may occur, but is often characteristically unproductive "busy-waiting."

The Scalasca trace analysis quantified point-to-point communication *Late Sender* and *Late Receiver* blocking time sub-metrics as a negligible 3.7s, as receiving buffers are posted early by the application. Much more serious is the blocking time in `MPI_Barrier` and associated with synchronising collective communication. Figure 4 shows that `MPI_Allreduce` which is used at various points in the *Erode* stage (all of which have been selected from the call tree in the central panel) badly affects all of the processes. A popup window reports the severest single inefficiency instance on rank 271 with global severity of 1330 CPU seconds.

When Vampir is directed to zoom in to show the corresponding execution interval, as seen in Figure 5, the third `MPI_Allreduce` instance in *Erode* stands out with rank 271 waiting more than 2.0 seconds for the last of its peers to be ready to proceed. Imbalanced computation between the numerous synchronising reductions results in low efficiency and poor scaling for this ABySS-P execution stage.

3.3. Revised Instrumentation and Implementation of ABYSS-P

To avoid the measurement overhead arising from automatic instrumentation of routines by the compiler, manual annotation of ABYSS-P execution stages was employed instead, resulting in improved profiles as shown in Figure 6. Particular

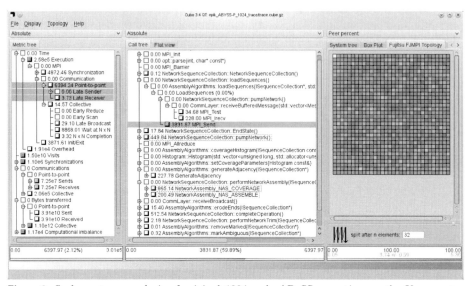

Figure 2. Scalasca trace analysis of original 1024-node ABySS execution on the K computer showing distribution of *Point-to-point communication time* metric (left pane) for the selected MPI_Send call-path in the *LoadSequences* stage (centre) for each of the processes (right pane). Values in each panel are colour-coded using the scale along the window footer, and in the various trees represent exclusive metric values for open nodes and inclusive values for closed nodes.

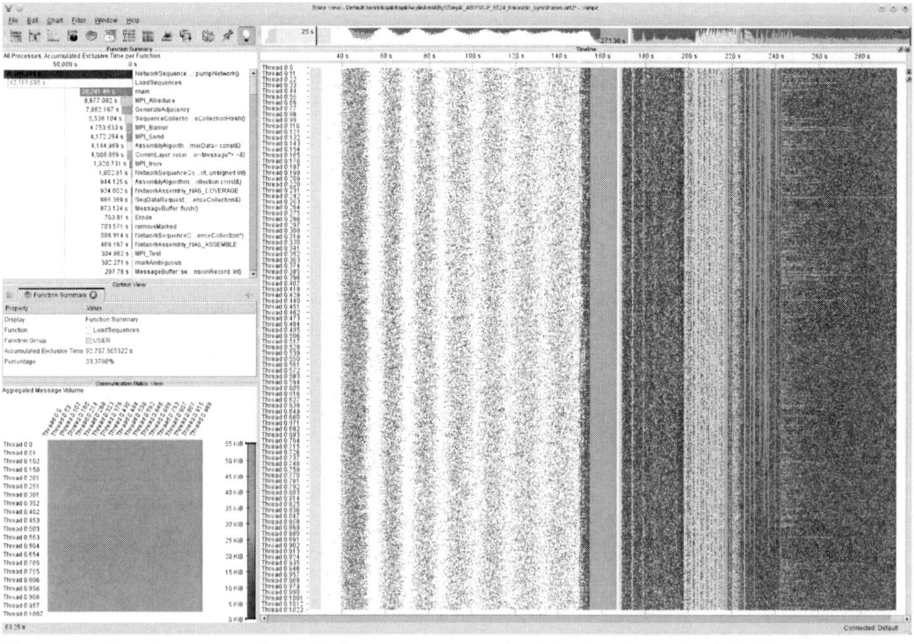

Figure 3. Vampir presentation of the same trace of original 1024-node ABySS execution on the K computer with horizontal timeline for each MPI process showing 'waves' during the *LoadSequences* stage followed by *GenerateAdjacency*, *Trim/Erode*, *PopBubble/Discover_Bubbles* and *NetworkAssembly* stages. The aggregate chart in the window head is provided for navigation when zooming, with profile of function execution times and communication matrix on left side.

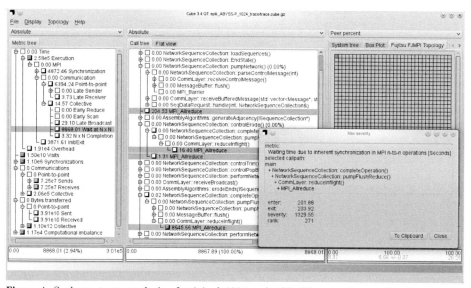

Figure 4. Scalasca trace analysis of original 1024-node ABySS execution on the K computer with severest instance of automatically identified *Wait at NxN* inefficiency in `MPI_Allreduce` during *Erode* stage detailed in popup window.

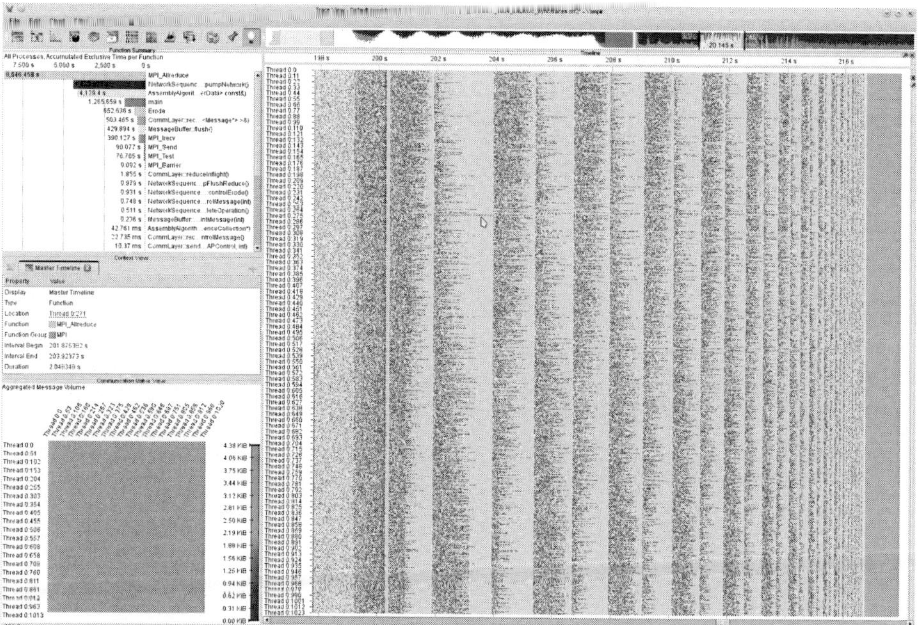

Figure 5. Vampir analysis zoomed on time interval for *Erode* stage of original 1024-node ABySS execution on the K computer with severest `MPI_Allreduce` inefficiency instance by rank 271 selected and details of selection in middle pane on left side. Dominance of sequence of reductions is evident in the (zoomed) timeline view and associated execution time profile.

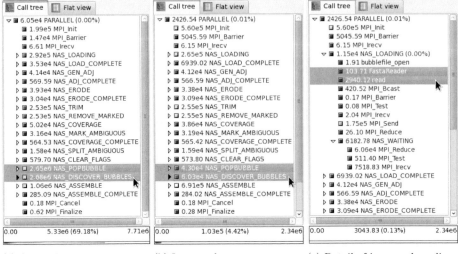

(a) Original   (b) Improved   (c) Detail of improved reading

Figure 6. Total execution time profile extracts from 8192 compute nodes of ABYSS-P with annotated execution stages and file operations.

care was required to annotate stages of master and workers consistently, such that they combine in the resulting profiles. Furthermore, the *Waiting* stage of workers between completing one computation phase and receiving direction to start the next was also distinguished and associated with the completed phase, as this helped with presenting idling arising from load imbalances.

For an execution with 8192 compute nodes shown in Figure 6(a), 69% of time (650 seconds) is attributed to coupled *PopBubble* and *Discover_Bubbles* stages which are serialised in rank order, resulting in all but one worker process idling while each rank in turn processes its local data and then creates a file. Computational load imbalances reported in ABYSS-P profiling result from the master/worker paradigm employed and associated ineffective parallelisation of file reading and writing, therefore additional manual annotations were incorporated for file operations (shown in Figure 6(c)) which helped identify that these were particularly costly and suffered from large variability.

Configuring executions on the K computer to use files in separate rank-local directories helped reduce filesystem performance variablity, while serialisation costs could be reduced by opening files in parallel, such that time for *PopBubble/Discover_Bubbles* was reduced more than fifty-fold to 12.6 seconds, only 4.4% of the much quicker overall execution time in Figure 6(b). For the *Assemble* stage, originally taking 14% of time (129 seconds), the benefit was a more modest 35% since only 4.5 MB of reconstructed contigs are written while the total length of sequences to put together varies from rank to rank, and the assignment is very imbalanced. The line with square points in Figure 1 shows how the performance of this revised version of ABYSS-P is improved at larger scale.

The MPI point-to-point communication used by ABYSS-P for coordination between master and worker processes requires an eager transfer protocol using prohibitive amounts of message buffer memory for 16,384 or more compute nodes (bars in Figure 1). A first step to avoid this substitutes Fujitsu's efficient

MPI_Reduce and MPI_Alltoall collectives in the sequence *Loading* stage, and has been validated with successful execution of *Loading* in 6.2 seconds on the full 82,944 compute nodes of the K computer. Applying similar changes to the remaining ABYSS-P stages is expected to permit complete executions at this unprecedented scale, ready for processing much larger sequence datasets.

4. Related Work

Lin [12] compared the capabilities and performance of ABySS with other *de novo* assembly tools, and found that long execution times and large memory requirements were serious constraints. ABySS execution performance with up to 128 processes has been analysed on a Dell/AMD/Mellanox cluster comparing Ethernet and Infiniband DDR networks [13], identifying that MPI communication overhead increases significantly with scale for Send/Irecv and Allreduce. Georganas et al [14] compare the performance on up to 960 cores of a Cray XC30 of their own parallel genome assembler with ABySS, where scaling parallel file reading and writing is identified as the key bottleneck that they avoided by implementing their own file format.

Call-path profiling of C++ parallel applications is often prohibitive for instrumentation-based tools [15], however, combining MPI tracing with sampling based on interrupt timers has been demonstrated to be effective in such cases [16].

5. Conclusions

ABYSS-P executions on the K computer with 1024 or more MPI processes suffered from a variety of critical performance and scalability issues, which were investigated using the Scalasca toolset. Execution traces from up to 1024 processes were collected, automatically analysed to quantify inefficiency patterns and direct Vampir timeline visualisations. Since automatic routine instrumentation by the C++ compiler and associated filtering of measurement events proved to be costly and awkward, subsequent measurements instead exploited manual source instrumentation to clearly distinguish ABYSS-P execution stages and file I/O operations, carefully matching stages executed by master and worker processes. File handling found to constitute the most serious inefficiencies was remedied by using rank-local directories on the K computer as well as code restructuring to significantly reduce serialisation costs. Scalability beyond 8192 MPI processes additionally required substituting point-to-point messages with efficient MPI collective routines for master/worker coordination, such that initial ABYSS-P execution stages (and associated Scalasca measurement experiments) have now been possible with the full 82,944 compute nodes of the K computer.

Acknowledgments

This research was made possible by using resources of the K computer at the RIKEN Advanced Institute for Computational Science. We are grateful for the dedicated effort from the Operations and Computer Technologies Division that supports the K computer and its users.

References

[1] Jared T. Simpson, Kim Wong, Shaun D. Jackman, Jacqueline E. Schein, Steven J. M. Jones, and İnanç Birol. ABySS: a parallel assembler for short read sequence data. *Genome Research*, 19(6):1117–1123, 2009.

[2] ABySS GitHub Repository, https://github.com/bcgsc/abyss.

[3] Markus Geimer, Felix Wolf, Brian J. N. Wylie, Erika Ábrahám, Daniel Becker, and Bernd Mohr. The Scalasca Performance Toolset Architecture. *Concurrency and Computation: Practice and Experience*, 22(6):702–719, April 2010.

[4] Wolfgang E. Nagel, Alfred Arnold, Michael Weber, Hans-Christian Hoppe, and Karl Solchenbach. VAMPIR: Visualization and analysis of MPI resources. *Supercomputer*, 12:69–80, 1996.

[5] Hiroyuki Miyazaki, Yoshihiro Kusano, Naoki Shinjou, Fumiyoshi Shoji, Mitsuo Yokokawa, and Tadashi Watanabe. Overview of the K computer System. *Fujitsu Sci. Tech. J.*, 48(3):255–265, 2012.

[6] Takumi Maruyama, Toshio Yoshida, Ryuji Kan, Iwao Yamazaki, Shuji Yamamura, Noriyuki Takahashi, Mikio Hondou, and Hiroshi Okano. SPARC64 VIIIfx: A New-Generation Octocore Processor for Petascale Computing. *IEEE Micro*, 30(2):30–40, 2010.

[7] Yuichiro Ajima, Tomohiro Inoue, Shinya Hiramoto, Toshiyuki Shimizu, and Yuzo Takagi. The Tofu Interconnect. *IEEE Micro.*, 32(1):21–31, 2012.

[8] Jun Moroo, Masahiko Yamada, and Takeharu Kato. Operating System for the K computer. *Fujitsu Sci. Tech. J.*, 48(3):295–301, 2012.

[9] Naoyuki Shida, Shinji Sumimoto, and Atsuya Uno. MPI Library and Low-Level Communication on the K computer. *Fujitsu Sci. Tech. J.*, 48(3):324–330, 2012.

[10] Illumina TruSeq Data Sets, http://www.illumina.com/truseq/tru_resources/datasets.ilmn.

[11] Andreas Knüpfer, Christian Rössel, Dieter an Mey, Scott Biersdorff, Kai Diethelm, Dominic Eschweiler, Markus Geimer, Michael Gerndt, Daniel Lorenz, Allen D. Malony, Wolfgang E. Nagel, Yury Oleynik, Peter Philippen, Pavel Saviankou, Dirk Schmidl, Sameer S. Shende, Ronny Tschüter, Michael Wagner, Bert Wesarg, and Felix Wolf. Score-P – A joint performance measurement run-time infrastructure for Periscope, Scalasca, TAU, and Vampir. In *Proc. 5th Parallel Tools Workshop, (Sept. 2011, Dresden, Germany)*, pages 79–91. Springer Berlin Heidelberg, 2012.

[12] Yong Lin, Jian Li, Hui Shen, Lei Zhang, Christopher J. Papasian, and HongWen Deng. Comparative studies of *de novo* assembly tools for next-generation sequencing technologies. *Bioinformatics*, 27(15):2031–2037, 2011.

[13] HPC Advisory Council. ABySS performance benchmark and profiling, May 2010.

[14] Evangelos Georganas, Aydın Buluç, Jarrod Chapman, Leonid Oliker, Daniel Rokhsar, and Katherine Yellick. Parallel de Bruijn graph construction and traversal for *de novo* genome assembly. In *Proc. ACM/IEEE Conference on Supercomputing (SC14, New Orleans, LA, USA)*, pages 437–448. IEEE Press, November 2014.

[15] Christian Iwainsky and Dieter an Mey. Comparing the usability of performance analysis tools. In *Proc. Euro-Par 2008 Workshops*, volume 5415 of *Lecture Notes in Computer Science*, pages 315–325. Springer, 2009.

[16] Zoltán Szebenyi, Todd Gamblin, Martin Schulz, Bronis R. de Supinski, Felix Wolf, and Brian J. N. Wylie. Reconciling sampling and direct instrumentation for unintrusive call-path profiling of MPI programs. In *Proc. 25th Int'l Parallel & Distributed Processing Symposium*, pages 640–648. IEEE Computer Society, May 2011.

Parallel Computing: On the Road to Exascale
G.R. Joubert et al. (Eds.)
IOS Press, 2016
© 2016 The authors and IOS Press. All rights reserved.
doi:10.3233/978-1-61499-621-7-73

Performance model based on memory footprint for OpenMP memory bound applications

César Allande [a], Josep Jorba [b], Anna Sikora [c] and Eduardo César [c]

[a] *Barcelona Supercomputing Center, Barcelona, Spain*
[b] *Universitat Oberta de Catalunya, Barcelona, Spain*
[c] *Universitat Autònoma de Barcelona, Bellaterra, Barcelona, Spain*

Abstract. Performance of memory intensive applications executed on multi-core multi-socket environments is closely related to the utilization of shared resources in the memory hierarchy. Depending on the characteristics of the application, the shared resources utilization can lead to a significant performance degradation. The exploration of different thread affinity configurations allows the selection of a proper configuration that balances the performance improvement obtained by increasing parallelism with the performance degradation due to memory contention. However, as the number of cores per processor and the number of processors per node increases, testing all possible configurations is not reasonable. We propose a performance model to estimate the execution time for a thread configuration (number and affinity distribution) for an OpenMP application parallel region based on runtime hardware counters information and the estimation of performance degradation due to memory contention generated at last level cache (LLC). The latter is estimated considering features obtained from the memory access pattern and the memory footprint. The experimental results show that the proposed methodology identifies the thread configurations which maximize the application performance by preventing memory contention on main memory.

Keywords. performance model, multi-core, multi-socket, memory contention, memory footprint, OpenMP

1. Introduction

Performance of parallel applications is expected to increase proportionally to the number of used resources. However, there are several factors that limit their scalability. On multicore architectures, the access to the memory hierarchy is possibly the most important limiting factor, specially for memory intensive applications [1]. This behaviour can be noticed significantly on the LLC (Last Level Cache) in current multicore processors, mainly because the increase on cache evictions to main memory reduces the overall data cache reuse at this level.

During a parallel program execution, its aggregated working dataset can be defined as the *memory footprint* [2] [3] [4] [5]. The continuously increasing integration of number of cores accessing shared cache levels can lead to a performance degradation [6].

One of the reasons is an imbalanced relation between the per core cache size and the per thread application footprint [7].

To minimize memory contention, it is possible to analyse the application access pattern for a concurrent execution to determine the per thread memory characteristics, such as required memory, total number of accesses, reutilization, etc. On an OpenMP parallel loop, every thread executes iterations or units of parallel work, and each unit has an associated memory footprint. This active data usage can be characterized in some applications for a set of workloads. By doing this, it is possible to expose a latent performance problem given a different workload and a thread configurations and, in many cases, to provide a configuration that minimizes the performance contention. To do that we analyse the reutilization degree of this data.

In this paper, we propose a performance model to estimate at runtime the execution time and the ideal configuration by defining a characterization of the memory footprint for small workloads to identify the degree of parallelism which can lead to a performance degradation. In our previous work, *Allande et al.*[8], the model required a dynamic exhaustive characterization in a single processor execution by analyzing all the thread configuration combination, which increases the overhead in the runtime execution.

This approach assumes the following conditions: 1) The application is iterative and all the iterations have a uniform workload; 2) Workload is evenly distributed among threads; 3) Performance degradation is mainly due to memory contention at the main memory, generated by the application memory access pattern at LLC; 4) All the cores in the processor are homogeneous. Taking into account these conditions, contributions from this work are the following:

- A methodology, based on memory trace analysis, to extract the memory footprint of parallel loop regions from an OpenMP application in order to identify memory intensive parallel regions.
- Estimation of critical configurations of the application for a specific hardware configuration.
- An execution time estimation for a configuration of a parallel region to dynamically tune the application by identifying a configuration that minimizes memory contention.

We present the methodology and the performance model in Section 2, and the validation through experimentation of two applications in Section 3, showing a maximum speedup of 2.3x. Finally, the conclusions are shown in Section 4.

2. Methodology for selecting a configuration to avoid memory contention

The memory contention problem can be generated by a large number of requests to main memory. In parallel applications, this problem can be increased at certain levels of concurrency because of the inter-relation of a shared resource utilization and the application data access patterns. In this study, we evaluate the average occupation of LLC, and the application data reutilization patterns.

To obtain the memory footprint of an application, we have developed a tracing tool, in a form of a *pintool*, using Intel's PIN framework for dynamic instrumentation [9], which extracts the memory trace in each parallel region iteration.

2.1. Trace generation and characterization of iteration footprint

We instrument the application using the *pintool* to obtain a memory trace in the format described in Equation 1. The trace is processed to obtain the memory footprint of the most reaccessed data. To do this, consecutive addresses of memory are combined, and the most significant regions are used to compute the memory footprint. Consecutive regions smaller than a cache line and reutilization degrees smaller than 4 are discarded, meaning that for the selected memory ranges, bigger than a cache line, there is an average of more than 4 accesses per each element. This criteria is defined in order to discard effects such as reutilization that can be solved at low level caches, or with no significant impact in performance. Following this, we describe the trace and profiled information.

- The minimal information unit obtained from the *pintool* is the *memOp*. Every memory operation is described by *event_id*, as the unique key identifier on the temporal access pattern, *type* refers to the memory operation (load or store), the actual virtual memory *address* and the *data_size* of the element accessed.

$$\text{memOp} = \{\text{event\_id}, \text{type}, \text{address}, \text{data\_size}\} \qquad (1)$$

- We extract the spatial access pattern by sorting the memory trace and grouping consecutive memory references. Consecutive *elements* are combined into *streams* of memory references with equal or less than *data_size* (e.g. 8 Bytes) spacing between its elements. The *stream* information (eq. 2) is composed by the different number of *elements* within the range, and the total number of references into the address space (*accesses*). Memory references from the trace, that are not aligned into sequential accesses, are discarded.

$$\text{stream} = \{\text{elements}, \text{accesses}\} \qquad (2)$$

- Streams with same properties are grouped into the same cluster (eq. 3). We extract metrics *reutil* (eq. 4) as the reutilization degree of the elements described by the cluster, and *cluster footprint* (eq. 5), which is the total size of the streams.

$$\text{cluster} = \{\text{elements}, \text{accesses}, \#\text{streams}, \text{reutil}, \text{cl\_footprint}\} \qquad (3)$$
$$\text{reutil} = \text{accesses}/\text{elements} \qquad (4)$$
$$\text{cl\_footprint} = \text{elements} \times \#\text{streams} \times \text{data\_size} \qquad (5)$$

- The iteration footprint (eq. 6) is obtained from the aggregation of all the iteraton clusters footprints. The footprint makes reference to memory elements with high reaccesses degree along the iteration execution, which must be preserved into LLC to improve locality. The ratio of the memory footprint regarding the total memory operations in the parallel region trace (eq. 7).

$$\text{footprint} = \sum_{i=1}^{\#\text{clusters}} \text{cl\_footprint}_i \qquad (6)$$
$$\text{footprint\_ratio} = \text{footprint}/\text{tot\_mem} \qquad (7)$$

2.2. Estimation of memory footprint at runtime

The memory trace generates a huge amount of information, in the order of GigaBytes. Therefore, we obtain a memory footprint from executions of the application using small workloads. Afterwards, we estimate the memory footprint from a runtime execution for a real unknown workload. To infer this value, it is possible to use runtime information provided by hardware counters, and also by the runtime library.

First, it is necessary to assume that the information on the total number of memory references obtained at runtime through hardware counters is going to be equivalent to the information given by the *pintool* trace.

Second, as the memory trace is obtained from a single iteration of the parallel region, the runtime information must be normalized as shown in eq.8. We use hardware counters to count the number of loads and stores. The number of iterations is provided by the OpenMP runtime library, which is in charge of scheduling iterations (work) among threads. This is done by a wrapper of the OpenMP runtime library which intercept OpenMP calls.

$$\text{rt\_tot\_mem} = (\text{PAPI\_LD\_INS} + \text{PAPI\_SR\_INS})/\#\text{iters} \qquad (8)$$

Third, we obtain the memory footprint per iteration by applying the representative ratio (eq.7) from the traced workloads to the *rt_tot_mem* (eq. 8).

$$\text{rt\_footprint} = \text{rt\_tot\_mem} \times \text{footprint\_ratio} \qquad (9)$$

2.3. Estimation of execution time for all configurations at runtime

After the characterization of small workloads to determine the parallel regions memory footprint, we obtain the current execution time for the first execution of the parallel region with the maximum concurrency (*maxPar_iterTime* on *maxCores* configuration). The total parallel region execution time is normalized to express iteration execution time.

Given that an iteration is the minimum work unit in an OpenMP parallel loop, the iteration execution time should be constant for any thread configuration in the absence of memory contention

We consider the iteration execution time as the minimal execution unit, and this is because parallel loops in OpenMP express an SPMD paradigm. Therefore, the computation time for this unit should be constant, and that holds true while there is no memory contention.

By using the *maxPar_iterTime* and estimating the ideal execution time, we propose a methodology to determine the execution time for all the configurations of threads in a multicore multisocket system. Additionally, this methodology allows to estimate execution times for different thread distribution policies.

First, to estimate the ideal execution time, we use the reference values obtained along the characterization of small workloads. We use serial execution times obtained from at least three traced workloads to obtain a linear regression. We consider a high correlation coefficient between memory footprint and execution time, and using this function (eq.10) we interpolate the ideal execution time for the current footprint.

$$\text{ideal\_iterationTime} = F(\text{execTime}, \text{footprint}); \qquad (10)$$

Second, we identify the iteration time (eq.12) for a number of threads configuration regarding its occupation on the LLC. To do this, we determine the level of contention at the LLC (eq.11). We assume the iteration time is constant for configurations with no contention, and iteration time is going to increase up to *maxPar_iterTime* for configurations with contention, starting from the first configuration of number of threads that overfills the LLC (*first_contention*, eq.13).

$$concurrent\_memory = footprint \times num\_threads \tag{11}$$

$$iterationTime = \begin{cases} constant & concurrent\_memory < cacheSize \\ increased & concurrent\_memory \geq cacheSize \end{cases} \tag{12}$$

$$first\_contention = min(nt) \; ; \; where \; concurrent\_memory \geq cacheSize \tag{13}$$

We use the estimation of *iterationTime* for a given thread *distribution policy*, which is the description of how threads are binded to processors for the current system. For example, a compact distribution places threads in closer cores, while a scattered policy distributes them as evenly as possible across the entire system.

Algorithm 1 shows the steps to estimate the iteration time for a given distribution policy.

Algorithm 1 Estimation of iteration time for all possible number of threads using a particular scheduling policy. *sched(x)* is a function that returns the last assigned processor id., and interpolate() is a function for a linear regression interpolation.

Data: nt=2
Result: iterationTime[maxCores]
iterTime[1] = ideal_iterTime
final_point = {maxPar_iterTime, maxCores}
while $nt \leq maxCores$ **do**
    proc_id = sched(nt)
    footprint = base_footprint * get_threads_on_proc (proc_id)

    if $footprint < cacheSize$ **then**
        iterationTime[nt] = iterTime[nt-1]
        base_point = {iterTime[nt], nt}
    else
        iterationTime[nt] = interpolate(nt, base_point, final_point)
    end
    increase nt ; increase_threads_on_proc(proc_id)
end

Finally, we determine the final execution time (eq. 15) for all thread configurations by transforming iteration times into parallel region execution times. To do this, we apply eq. 14 to determine the maximum number of iterations scheduled by the default policy in an OpenMP parallel loop (static), and use this value to multiply the iteration time for a given configuration.

$$sched\_iters_{(nt)} = RoundUp(num\_iters/nt) \tag{14}$$

$$ExectionTime_{(nt)} = sched\_iters_{(nt)} \times iterationTime_{(nt)} \tag{15}$$

The estimation for different distribution policies can be used in a multicore multisocket system to identify the configuration that minimizes the execution time.

3. Experimental Validation

In this section, we apply the proposed methodology on two applications, SP (Solver Pentadiagonal) from NAS Benchmark suite, and a version of Stream Benchmark. Both benchmarks have been selected because they are memory intensive applications which suffer from performance degradation due to memory contention at certain degree of parallelism [8], and they have been proven to benefit from tuning their configuration of number of threads and thread binding in the previous evaluation.

The benchmarks have been evaluated on the hardware architectures described in Table 1. The systems are compute nodes from Marenostrum supercomputer at BSC (Barcelona Supercomputing Center) and SuperMUC supercomputer from LRZ (Leibniz Supercomputing Center).

Table 1. Description of system architectures for performance evaluation

	MN3 node (BSC)	Fat Node (LRZ)	Thin Node (LRZ)
Proc. Name	Xeon E5-2670	Xeon E7-4870	Xeon E5-2680
Family	Sandy Bridge-EP	Westmere-EX	Sandy Bridge-EP
Frequency	2.6GHz	2.4GHz	2.7GHz
Sockets per node	2	4	2
LLC size per socket	20MB	30MB	20MB
System Memory	32GB	256GB	32GB

3.1. Obtaining memory footprint and execution time

To apply the performance model at runtime, the characterization of the memory footprint and the sequential iteration time for small workloads are required for both applications.

On the one hand, SP generates a complex memory access pattern. To obtain the memory footprint, we have traced the application using small workloads to obtain the spatial access pattern. The workloads are defined as classes and are associated to a problem size. Workloads starts at S (small), continues with W (workstation), and follows with A, B, and C (standard test problems), and finally classes D, E, and F for large test problems.

First, the benchmarks have been executed with classes S, W, and A, using the *pintool* to obtain the memory trace. A second execution with no instrumentation is required to obtain the iteration execution time. In both cases, the sequential version for each class is executed.

Next, traces have been processed to obtain the footprint. We start analyzing the spatial memory pattern by identifying *streams*, which afterwards, are combined into clusters of streams with same properties. In SP benchmark, the clustered information within the profile represents 87% of the total memory operations for class S, and 92% for classes W and A.

Finally, Table 2 shows the memory footprint (eq. 6) computed as the summation of sizes for every cluster of those with significant reutilization degree, in this case, and average of more than 4 references per memory element.

On the other hand, Stream Benchmark is a synthetic benchmark used to analyze memory bandwidth by the execution of four parallel regions performing a repetitive set of point to point operations in a vector structure. We use a version of the benchmark accessing matrix structures of 64 rows per 320K elements as described in Table 3. The benchmark is configured to repeat every vector operation 16 times, and parallelism is expressed in the outer loop of the matrix data access. That is, one iteration is going to perform 320K operations 16 times. In this case, the memory access pattern is know from

Table 2. Preprocessed information from traces of small classes. This information is required to estimate performance at runtime. The profile information of the memory intensive parallel region x_solve specifies the per cluster memory footprint for one iteration. Besides, inputs for the performance model such as the cumulative iteration footprint (*iterFootprint*) and the iteration serial execution time, are shown.

	cluster	accesses	elements	#streams	stream size	reutil	Cluster Size
SP.S	type 1	424	60	10	480	7.06	4,800B
	type 2	257	60	20	480	4.28	9,600B
	type 3	606	60	10	480	10,1	4,800B
iterFootprint							19,200B
seq.iterTime							5.66 s
SP.W	type 1	1,408	180	34	1,440	7.82	48,960B
	type 2	809	180	68	1,440	4.49	97,920B
	type 3	1,950	180	34	1,440	10.83	48,960B
iterFootprint							195,840B
seq.iterTime							67.72 s
SP.A	type 1	2,556	320	62	2,560	7.98	158,720B
	type 2	1,453	320	124	2,560	4.54	317,440B
	type 3	3,518	320	62	2,560	10.99	158,720B
iterFootprint							634,880B
seq.iterTime							240.29 s

the beginning, so we have analytically defined the memory footprint and validated it through hardware counters.

The footprints for the x_solve parallel region from SP Benchmark, and copy and add parallel regions from Stream Benchmark estimated for a concurrent execution in the experimental systems is described in Table 4. The marks show the *first_contention* configuration per processor on the validation system architectures.

Table 3. Stream Benchmark configuration, and the iteration footprint estimation per operation

N (vector elements)	320.000
Z (matrix rows)	64
D (Data Size) Bytes	8
ArraySize/ArrayFootprint	2,44 MB
MatrixSize	156,25 MB
Reaccess(repetitions)	16
copy (c=a)	4,88 MB
scalar (b=scalar*c)	4,88 MB
add (c=a+b)	7,32 MB
triad(a=b+scalar*c)	7,32 MB

Table 4. Estimation of memory footprint for a concurrent execution of x_solve parallel region, where [†] *first_contention* on MN3 and Thin nodes, and [*] *first_contention* for system Fat node

	SP Benchmark		Stream Benchmark	
	par.Reg. x_solve		par.Reg copy	par.Reg add
#threads	wkld; C	wkld; D	wkld; N=320K elements	
1	4MB	[†*]25.3MB	4.88MB	7.32MB
2	8MB	50.59MB	9.77MB	14.65MB
3	12MB	75.89MB	14.65MB	[†]21.97MB
4	16MB	101.19MB	19.53MB	29.30MB
5	[†]20MB	126.49MB	[†]24,41MB	[*]36.62MB
6	24MB	151.79MB	29.30MB	43.95MB
7	28MB	177.09MB	[*]34.18MB	51.27MB
8	[*]32MB	101.39MB	39.06MB	58.59MB

Once we have defined the memory footprint for the characterized workloads, we calculate the coefficients for a linear regression of the relation between the memory footprint and the execution time of the serial execution, in order to interpolate the ideal execution time for a new workload.

Table 5. Estimation of serial iteration time in seconds on MN3 with 20MB LLC. The highlighted cells refer to information obtained on the characterization phase. Serial Estimation time (Est.) is obtained from an interpolation of a linear regression function between footprints and measured times for classes S, W, and A

Class	Footprint	Est. (s)	Measured (s)	Rel.Error
S	19KB	3.31	5.66	41.56
W	191KB	71.02	67.72	4.88
A	620KB	239.34	240.29	0.39
B	1,638 KB	639.14	633.39	0.91
C	4,096 KB	1,605.93	1,602.95	0.06
D	25,907 KB	10,166.47	11,945.82	14.90

3.2. Estimating the best configuration at runtime

We proceed to execute the applications for a new workload using the maximum number of threads. The application is monitored at runtime to evaluate its performance. We assume the application to be iterative, and the analysis is done after the first iteration.

Firstly, we obtain memory operations rt_tot_mem (eq.8) from hardware counters (PAPI_LD_INS and PAPI_SR_INS). We apply the maximum $footprint\_ratio$ (eq. 7) from the characterized workloads to deduce the current $rt\_footprint$.

Secondly, we estimate the serial execution time for the current workload. We use a linear regression of the characterized footprint with the serial execution time. Then, this function is used to interpolate the current footprint and obtain the sequential iteration time estimation. As it can be seen in Table 5, we estimate the serial execution time with good accuracy (less than 5% error) except for class S and D. The relative error on class S is about 42% because its execution time is very small. For class D, the error estimation is generated by its memory footprint, which overpasses the LLC size limit and is expressing contention even with one thread.

We obtain the final estimation by applying Eq.15 to the iteration time estimations provided by Algorithm 1 using $first\_contention$ values as identified in Table 4. The number of iterations is provided by Eq.14.

Figure 1 shows the results of estimated execution times. Stream benchmark copy and add operations are evaluated for one processor on different architectures, *MN* on Figs. 1(a), 1(b), *ThinNode* on 1(c),1(d), and *FatNode* on 1(e),1(f). A comparison of SP on architecture *MN3* using two different thread scheduling policies: compact policy on Fig.1(g) and scatter policy on Fig.1(h).

It is important to notice that these applications express memory contention, but when the model is applied in an execution which is not expressing memory contention it provides the configuration with maximum parallelism.

The estimations for Stream Benchmark show a similar behaviour compared to the real application. On these experiments, when selecting the configuration with estimated minimum execution time, and compared with the minimum execution times for the real execution, the selected configuration differs at most by 1 thread from the best configuration, achieving a maximum speedup of 2.3x.

The different exploration of thread distribution policies on SP benchmark shows that, with the scattered distribution on 2 processors an improvement of 2.30x speedup can be achieved using 8 threads (4 threads per processor).

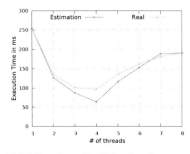

(a) MN3 system - Parallel region Copy
Config: Est. 4th = Best. 4 th (1.97x)

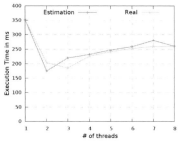

(b) MN3 system - Parallel region Add
Config: Est. 2th (1.28x)- Best. 3 th (1.41x)

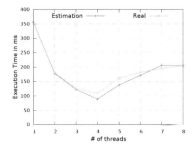

(c) Thin node system - Parallel region Copy
Config: Est. 4th = Best. 4 th (1.88x)

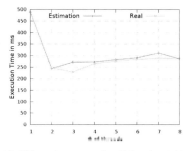

(d) Thin node system - Parallel region Add
Config: Est. 2th (1.16x) - Best. 3 th (1.25x)

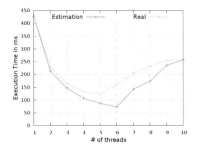

(e) Fat node system - Parallel region Copy
Config: Est. 6th (1.60x)- Best. 5 th (2.09x)

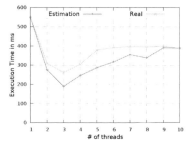

(f) Fat node system - Parallel region Add
Config: Est. 3th = Best. 3 th (1.49x)

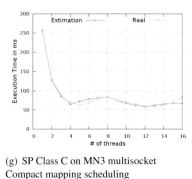

(g) SP Class C on MN3 multisocket
Compact mapping scheduling
Config: Est. 12th(1.38x) - Best. 13 th (1.39x)

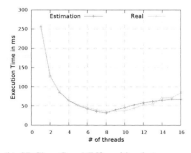

(h) SP Class C on MN3 multisocket
Scattered mapping scheduling
Config: Est. 8th = Best. 8 th (2.30x)

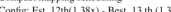

Figure 1. Comparison of model estimated execution times against real execution times. Figures from (a) to (f) are estimation on 1 processor for different architectures for parallel regions Copy and Add for the stream benchmark, and Fig. (g) and (h) comparison on SP class C on x_solve parallel region using 2 processors.

4. Conclusions

The increasing number of cores in current multicore processors causes severe scalability problems in the cache hierarchy. Memory intensive applications can experience performance degradation on parallel region execution when increasing the number of threads for some architectures. The analysis of application characteristics can expose latent performance conflicts with the memory hierarchy.

This paper proposes a methodology in order to minimize the effect of performance degradation at runtime. We obtain a characterization of the memory footprint for iterations in a parallel loop on small workloads of the application, and apply a performance model to provide a configuration of number of threads that minimizes performance degradation due to memory contention for any workload.

We characterize the SP application from the NAS Parallel Benchmarks, and a version of Stream Benchmark exposing their memory footprint characteristics. The methodology applied for different workloads of the applications provides an estimation for different configurations, which can be used to select a configuration that minimizes the effect of performance degradation. The experimental results show that the provided configuration obtains a maximum 2.3x speedup for the class C compared with the default configuration using all the available threads.

Acknowledgment

This work has been partially supported by the MICINN-Spain under contracts TIN2011-28689 and TIN2012-34557, the European Research Council under the European Union's 7th FP, and ERC Grant Agreement number 321253 . The authors thankfully acknowledge the resources and technical assistance provided by Munich Network Management Team (MNM-Team), the Leibniz Supercomputing Centre (LRZ) and the Barcelona Supercomputing Center (BSC). We would like to specially thank Karl Fuerlinger, Reinhold Bader and Sandra Mendez for the assistance, prolific discussions and feedback while preparing this manuscript.

References

[1] A. Sandberg, A. Sembrant, E. Hagersten, and D. Black-Schaffer, "Modeling performance variation due to cache sharing," in *High Performance Computer Architecture (HPCA2013), 2013 IEEE 19th International Symposium on*, Feb 2013, pp. 155–166.

[2] M. Ghosh, R. Nathuji, M. Lee, K. Schwan, and H. Lee, "Symbiotic scheduling for shared caches in multi-core systems using memory footprint signature," in *Parallel Processing (ICPP), 2011 International Conference on*, Sept 2011, pp. 11–20.

[3] S. Biswas, B. De Supinski, M. Schulz, D. Franklin, T. Sherwood, and F. Chong, "Exploiting data similarity to reduce memory footprints," in *IPDPS, 2011 IEEE International*, May 2011, pp. 152–163.

[4] S. Jana and V. Shmatikov, "Memento: Learning secrets from process footprints," in *Security and Privacy (SP), 2012 IEEE Symposium on*, May 2012, pp. 143–157.

[5] C. Ding, X. Xiang, B. Bao, H. Luo, Y.-W. Luo, and X.-L. Wang, "Performance metrics and models for shared cache," *Journal of Computer Science and Technology*, vol. 29, no. 4, pp. 692–712, 2014.

[6] B. Brett, P. Kumar, M. Kim, and H. Kim, "Chip: A profiler to measure the effect of cache contention on scalability," in *IPDPSW, 2013 IEEE 27th International*, May 2013, pp. 1565–1574.

[7] J. R. Tramm and A. R. Siegel, "Memory bottlenecks and memory contention in multi-core monte carlo transport codes," *Annals of Nuclear Energy*, 2014.

[8] C. Allande, J. Jorba, A. Sikora, and E. César, "A performance model for openmp memory bound applications in multisocket systems," *Procedia Computer Science*, vol. 29, pp. 2208 – 2218, 2014, 2014 International Conference on Computational Science.

[9] C.-K. Luk, R. Cohn, R. Muth, H. Patil, A. Klauser, G. Lowney, S. Wallace, V. J. Reddi, and K. Hazelwood, "Pin: Building customized program analysis tools with dynamic instrumentation," in *Proceedings of the 2005 ACM SIGPLAN Conference on Programming Language Design and Implementation*, ser. PLDI '05. New York, NY, USA: ACM, 2005, pp. 190–200.

Parallel Computing: On the Road to Exascale
G.R. Joubert et al. (Eds.)
IOS Press, 2016
doi:10.3233/978-1-61499-621-7-83

Evaluating OpenMP Performance on Thousands of Cores on the Numascale Architecture

Dirk Schmidl [a], Atle Vesterkjær [b], Matthias S. Müller [a]

[a] *IT Center, RWTH Aachen University*
Chair for High Performance Computing, RWTH Aachen University
Jara - High Performance Computing
{schmidl,mueller}@itc.rwth-aachen.de
[b] *Numascale AS*
av@numascale.com

Abstract. The company Numascale is one of the few companies offering shared memory systems with thousands of cores. To produce machines of such a size, a proprietary cache-coherent interconnect is used to couple standard servers into a large single system. In this work we investigate the ability of such a huge system to run OpenMP applications in an efficient way. Therefore, we use kernel benchmarks to investigate basic performance characteristics of the machine and we present a real world application from the Institute of Combustion Technology at RWTH Aachen University, called TrajSearch, which has been optimized to run efficient on such a large shared memory machine.

Introduction

Shared memory parallel programming allows all threads to access all data without the need to create copies and send data explicitly over a network. Therefore, for many applications the approach of shared memory programming is considered to be easier compared to message passing based approaches. Although Clusters, which do not offer shared memory across nodes, are by far the dominating architecture in HPC, some vendors offer large scale shared memory machines. These specialized shared memory machines are traditionally much more expensive than cluster machines. Numascale is a company offering large shared memory machines at the price of a cluster. On such a machine shared memory programs using several thousands of cores can be executed without any changes to the program. But, this does not necessarily mean that these programs run efficient. In this work we will investigate the Numascale architecture to find out if OpenMP parallel programs can be executed efficiently on this novel architecture. First, kernel benchmarks are used to investigate the machines characteristics and to highlight the strengths of the used architecture. Second, we will use a real world OpenMP application, called TrajSearch, to investigate the ability of the architecture to run such a code. TrajSearch has been optimized for large NUMA systems and was also been further tuned for the Numascale machine. Information on the required tuning will be provided before we present performance results of the code scaling to more than a thousand cores on a shared memory Numascale machine.

The rest of this work is structured as follows: First, we give an overview over related work and the Numascale architecture in section 2 before we present basic characteristics obtained by kernel benchmarks in section 3. Then we present the optimizations for the TrajSearch code and the resulting performance on the Numascale machine in section 4 before we conclude in section 5.

1. Related Work

Exploiting clusters for shared memory parallelization, e.g. done with OpenMP, has been investigated for many years. Basically, these approaches can be divided into hardware and software solutions. Nowadays, hardware solutions exist which provide large SMP systems from a few vendors (including Numascale that will be presented in the next section). SGI offers Altix UV systems with up to 2048 cores in a single system. Other vendors, like Bull offer smaller systems with up to 16 sockets based on their own interconnects, like the Bull coherent switch.

Furthermore, software approaches have been investigated which modified the Linux kernel to achieve a SSI on top of a cluster, for example MOSIX [1] or OpenMOSIX as well as Kerrighed [2] [3]. Multi-threaded applications have not been in the focus of these projects and thus they did not turn out to be very useful for OpenMP programs. MOSIX / OpenMOSIX both only allow the migration of processes and not of threads, which makes it unsuitable for OpenMP. It has been shown that Kerrighed can run OpenMP applications employing a modified threading library [4], but this project did not progress over a proof-of-concept state allowing the execution of commercial codes and the achieved performance was not suitable for productive use. The company ScaleMP offers a virtualization layer called vSMP foundation which allows to run a single Linux instance on top of an infiniband cluster. On such a machine any shared memory program can be executed, so these machines are well suited for OpenMP applications.

Specifically targeting the execution of OpenMP programs on clusters without providing a single system has also been the focus of several research projects and even commercial products. In [5] an OpenMP implementation for the TreadMarks software has been presented, which supports a subset of the OpenMP standard. In [6] an OpenMP implementation on top of the page-based distributed shared memory (DSM) system SCASH has been presented for the Omni source-to-source translator. Intel's ClusterOpenMP [7] has been the only commercial approach for OpenMP on clusters with full support for OpenMP 2.5. An examination revealed major shortcomings in the applicability and the memory management [8] for real-world applications and meanwhile Intel ceased the development of this product.

2. The Numascale Architecture

The Numascale technology enables the realization of large scale cache coherent shared memory systems from commodity servers to be built at the price of clusters. This is achieved through the use of Numascale's adapter card connected to the HyperTransport

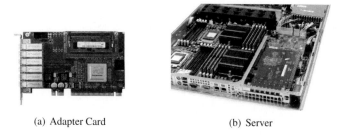

(a) Adapter Card   (b) Server

Figure 1. Numascale's adapter card (a) installed in an AMD server (b).

processor bus of standard AMD based servers. The cards are placed in servers (figure 1) where they pick up the communication between the processors on the motherboard using the native CPU communication protocol for AMD servers, Hypertransport.

The communication between the CPUs on the motherboard is routed to the next server by the Numascale Adapter Card. This way all the servers can be cabled together in racks and still be one single system running one instance of the operating system: The technology uses a low latency torus fabric between the servers, as depicted in figure 2. The resulting system is a cache coherent Non-Uniform Memory Access (ccNUMA) machine.

Shared memory is attractive to developers, as any processor can access any data in the system. So, the full memory range is available to all applications.

Performance scaling on large scale systems is generally not straightforward. The allocation of shared data can have a significant impact on the performance. On the other hand, tuning of an application may be very beneficial for performance and much less demanding than rewriting an application for a message passing model. Also, all memory and all cores will be locally available to a running process, avoiding the protocol overhead inherent in systems using a Message Passing Interface (MPI).

The Numascale system presents itself as one system with many cores and large memory for the programmer. This way Numascale provides scalable systems with a unified programming model that stays the same to the largest imaginable single system image machines that may contain thousands of processors.

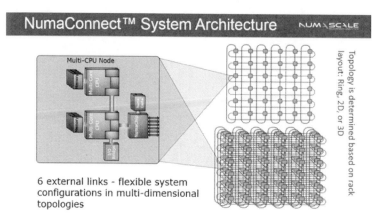

Figure 2. Illustration of the interconnect topology in a Numascale machine.

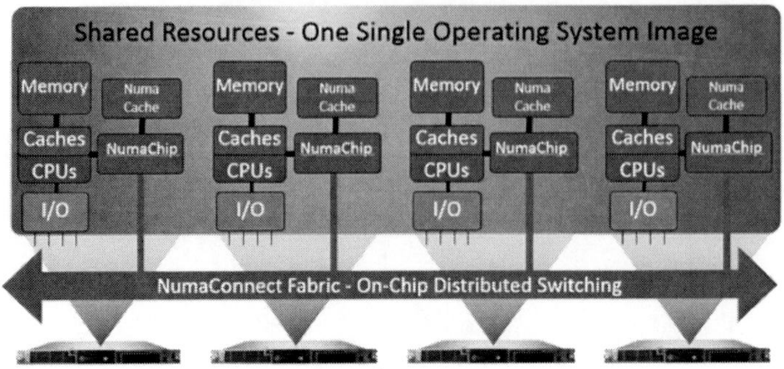

Figure 3. Illustration of the interconnect topology in a Numascale machine.

Running a single instance of the operating system simplifies the operation of the system. The Numascale adapter translates the standard server snooping cache coherency protocol to its own directory based protocol and handles all remote memory accesses system wide. All IO for the system is also aggregated, controlled and run under the single OS, see figure 3.

There are a number of pros for shared memory machines compared to clusters:

- Any processor can access any data location through direct load and store operations. This makes programming easier with less code to write and debug.
- Compilers can automatically exploit loop level parallelism providing higher efficiency with less human effort.
- With NumaConnect the system administration relates to a unified system as opposed to a large number of separate images in a cluster. This means that system administrators can spend less effort in maintaining the system.
- Resources can be mapped and used by any processor in the system enabling optimal use of resources in a single image environment Process scheduling is synchronized through a single, real-time clock that avoids serialization of scheduling associated with asynchronous operating systems in a cluster and the corresponding loss of efficiency.

All major Linux distributions are supported, i.e. Ubuntu Server, CentOS and Red Hat Enterprise Linux.

The University of Oslo's Center for Information Technology, USIT operates the Numascale installation used for this study. The systems is a PRACE prototype that it is financially supported by the PRACE-1IP project.

The Configuration of the system is as follows:

- 72 IBM x3755 M3 nodes
- 144 AMD 6174 CPUs
- 1728 Cores
- 4.6 TB Memory
- 3D Torus Interconnect (3x6x4)

3. Kernel Benchmark Results

Kernel benchmarks are designed to investigate single characteristics of a machine or software system to provide a better understanding of the hard-/software. This helps to understand the behavior of applications on these systems and sometimes it can also help to optimize applications for specific architectures.

3.1. Memory Performance

First, we investigated the memory performance for single-threaded and multi-threaded applications. Since the machine is a NUMA system, the memory performance differs when the data is located in different NUMA-nodes. Figure 4 shows the different latencies in a Numascale Shared Memory System.

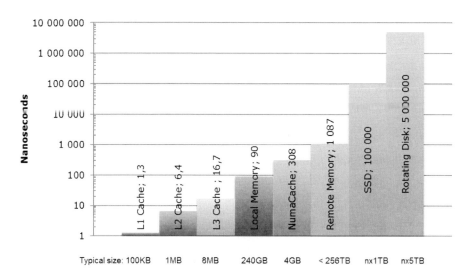

Figure 4. Access times in a Numascale Shared Memory System

The differentiator for a Numascale Shared Memory System compared to other high-speed interconnect technologies is the shared memory and cache coherency mechanisms. Data that is accessed on remote memory is cached in an 8 GB cache and can be read with a 300 nanosecond latency.

Next we investigated the bandwidth of the memory system. Our test uses the `numactl` command line tool to specify which core shall be used for the program and which NUMA node shall be used for the data. Then we measure the bandwidth reached to access this data. The test verifies, that the system comes with a considerable NUMA behavior. The memory bandwidth for a remote access can be less than 5% of the bandwidth reached for local accesses on the system. As we have shown in [9], this is typical for hierarchical NUMA-systems with multiple levels of cache coherent interconnects. So, the programmer needs to maximize the data locality as much as possible and avoid remote accesses on such a system. Also the cache can help to hide the remote latency for consecutive memory accesses.

Second, we tested the reached memory bandwidth for multithreaded applications. For such programs the total main memory bandwidth of a system is often the most important factor for performance, since many scientific applications are bound by the memory bottleneck of modern CPUs.

Because the number of memory DIMMs and memory controllers in the system rises linearly with the system size, in theory the available bandwidth could also increase linearly with the number of boards used. However, providing cache coherency becomes a very complicated task for a large number of sockets and the protocol overhead might exceed the performance gained by more memory channels in the system.

We used the stream benchmark [10] to measure the bandwidth for a different number of boards used, each board running 24 threads. Figure 5 shows the total memory bandwidth reached on the system with an increasing number of boards used. The bandwidth rises with the number of boards to the very end of the measurement to about 2 TB/s. This test shows that the system can support the need for a high memory bandwidth of many applications. For many engineering applications, as they are used at RWTH Aachen University, this is a prerequisite to potentially reach good performance on a machine.

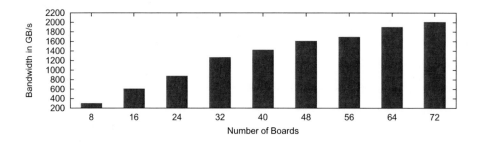

Figure 5. Achieved memory bandwidth on the Numascale machine for an increasing number of boards used.

It should be noted here, that the system reaches a memory bandwidth of 3 TB/s for a memory footprint of about 3 TB with the stream benchmark. However the scaling tests needed to be done with a smaller footprint, to allow runs also with only 8 boards of the system.

3.2. OpenMP Runtime Overhead

Besides overhead introduced by the cache coherency mechanism in the system, another potential source of overhead is the OpenMP runtime. To investigate the overhead of the OpenMP runtime, Bull et al. developed the EPCC microbenchmarks [11]. These benchmarks can be used to measure the overhead of OpenMP constructs on a given hardware. We used the benchmarks to measure the overhead for OpenMP's `parallel`, `barrier` and `for` construct on the Numascale machine for an increasing number of threads. The Intel OpenMP implementation was used.

Table 1 shows the overhead measured by our test. As expected, the overhead for a parallel region, a `barrier` or a `for` construct rises with the number of threads. The overhead to spawn and pin threads is about 80 times higher for 256 threads compared to 2 threads. For the `barrier` and `for` construct the runtime increases between 43 and

53 times. The reason is, that more threads have to be spawned or synchronized and this is much more work to be done in the runtime.

But, for a programmer this means that tuning steps like enlarging parallel regions as much as possible or avoiding synchronization when possible becomes much more important the larger the system gets. Unnecessary barrier constructs which might be avoided, e.g. with a `nowait` clause, might be acceptable if the overhead is 2 microseconds but they might limit scalability on such a large system where 53 microseconds are wasted.

Threads	PARALLEL	BARRIER	FOR
1	0.35	0.12	0.14
2	3.44	1.17	1.36
4	4.80	2.64	2.68
8	8.10	5.27	4.84
16	11.09	6.51	6.82
32	49.82	19.07	19.42
64	108.46	29.91	30.10
128	190.10	46.15	48.00
256	282.17	52.84	59.71

Table 1. Overhead in microseconds of OpenMP constructs measured with the EPCC microbenchmarks for the Intel Compiler on a Numascale test system with 256 cores.

4. TrajSearch

TrajSearch is a post-processing code for dissipation element analysis developed at the Institute of Combustion Technology[1] of RWTH Aachen University by Peters and Wang [12]. The dissipation element analysis provides a deeper understanding of turbulence and can be employed to reconstruct important statistical properties as has been shown by Gampert and Göbbert [13]. The code has been parallelized with OpenMP and optimized for large SMP machines as described in [14].

4.1. Basic Structure of the Algorithm

TrajSearch decomposes a highly resolved three dimensional turbulent flow field obtained by Direct Numerical Simulation (DNS) into non-arbitrary, space-filling and non-overlapping geometrical elements (dissipation elements). As input data the algorithm uses the 3D scalar field produced by the DNS. Then, starting from every grid point in this scalar field the search processes follow the trajectory in ascending and descending gradient direction until a maximum , respectively minimum point is found. For all points in the grid a counter is incremented to store how many trajectories crossed this point. Furthermore a list of extremal points is stored as well as the mapping of trajectories to these extremal points. All points where the trajectory ended in the same pair of minimum and maximum form a dissipation element.

All search processes can be done independently, as long as the accesses to the result arrays are synchronized. It should be mentioned here, that the compute time for the

---

[1] http://www.itv.rwth-aachen.de/

search process depends on the length of the trajectory which highly varies during the data set, resulting in a high load imbalance. Furthermore, the data needed for a search process depends on the ascending and descending gradients direction and thus is unknown a-priori. This complicates the data placement on a NUMA machine, since the data access cannot be predicted.

4.2. NUMA Optimization

Here, we will give a short overview of the optimization steps done to enable TrajSearch to run on large NUMA systems. A more detailed description of these steps has already been published in [14], where the code was optimized for a 104 core NUMA system.

Data Placement: As mentioned before, the data access pattern is unpredictable, so we cannot reach a local memory access rate close to 100 %. But, we know the starting point of every search in the scalar field. By distributing the 3D array over the machine and starting the search process on a thread where the data is local, we can achieve local accesses at least for the beginning of every search process. Furthermore, since neighboring trajectories probably run in similar directions, the caching mechanism of the Numascale machine might keep remote data in the board local cache until it is used in the next search process again.

Local Buffering: As a result the extremal points need to be stored in a global list. Locking the list for every new extremal point produced too much overhead, so every thread keeps a local list in its thread local storage during the computation and at the end these lists are merged. Some of the extremal points might be found by several threads and are thus stored in several private lists, but during the merge process this can be eliminated. The memory consumption per thread is low, so there is no need to merge double entries earlier. Furthermore, for every grid point the number of crossing trajectories is stored. To avoid extensive locking here, also thread local buffers are implemented, but the memory consumption is much higher. Potentially some GB need to be stored per thread, thus the buffers need to be flushed during computation when a certain threshold is reached into the shared result array.

NUMA-aware Scheduling: As mentioned above the workload is highly imbalanced, because of the varying length of the trajectories. Traditional OpenMP scheduling strategies to tackle load imbalance, like the `dynamic` or `guided` schedule, can be used to reduce the load imbalance, but they lead to an dynamic and thus unpredictable mapping of iterations to threads. In this case, we would loose the memory locality on the NUMA machine, even at the start of the search process. To circumvent this problem, a NUMA-aware scheduling was implemented, which works in two phases for every thread:

1. Every thread computes the iterations it had to compute with a static schedule and starts executing them.
2. When a thread finishes all its iterations, it starts to work on iterations of a different thread. This prevents threads from being idle as long as there is work to do, but it keeps them working on local data, as long as possible. The thread where iterations are taken from is determined by the remaining iterations. The thread with most iterations left gets help by the idle thread. Also, the remote thread starts to execute iterations from the end of the iteration space, whereas the local thread

works from the beginning. This helps to avoid false sharing and other interaction between the threads.

On the Numascale machine we optimized the parameters of the scheduler and we increased the size of the local buffers. Furthermore we reduced the overhead for the scheduler by using different strategies for work sharing.

4.3. Performance Results

We used the Oracle Solaris Studio 12.3 Compiler and we used a medium dataset with a memory footprint of about 45 GB to evaluate the performance on the Numascale machine.

Figure 6 shows the resulting runtime and speedup. Because a serial run would have taken about 2 weeks, we took the 24 threads run as basis for all other speedup calculations and assumed a speedup of 24 there. For an increasing number of threads the runtime declines up to 1024 threads, where a speedup of about 625 can be observed. More than 1024 threads could not be used so far, because the Oracle compiler only supports thread placement for up to 1024 threads. Without thread placement, the runtime was worse, because all the NUMA optimizations done rely on the fact that thread are evenly distributed and do not move during execution. This prerequisite is not fulfilled without binding threads to cores,

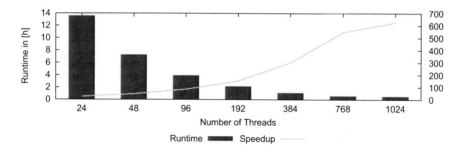

Figure 6. Runtime and Speedup of the TrajSearch application on the Numascale system with up to 1024 threads.

5. Conclusion

We investigated a Numascale system hosted at the University of Oslo with 1728 cores. Kernel benchmarks were used to investigate the memory performance and the OpenMP runtime overhead on such a huge system. One of the most remarkable results was the total memory bandwidth of about 2 TB/s reached with a shared memory program. Furthermore, we presented tuning steps done for the TrajSearch code to optimize for large NUMA systems. With these optimizations we achieved a speedup of about 625 using 1024 threads on the system. Overall, our experiments have shown that shared memory programming with OpenMP can be used on the Numascale system to achieve good performance for real world applications, but tuning these applications is needed.

Acknowledgement

Parts of this work were funded by the German Federal Ministry of Research and Education (BMBF) under grant number 01IH13001D (Score-E).

References

[1] Amnon Barak, Shai Guday, and Richard G. Wheeler. *The MOSIX Distributed Operating System: Load Balancing for UNIX*. Springer, Secaucus, NJ, USA, 1993.

[2] Christine Morin, Pascal Gallard, Renaud Lottiaux, and Geoffroy Vallée. Towards an efficient single system image cluster operating system. *Future Gener. Comput. Syst.*, 20(4):505–521, 2004.

[3] Geoffroy Vallée, Renaud Lottiaux, Louis Rilling, Jean-Yves Berthou, Ivan Dutka Malhen, and Christine Morin. A Case for Single System Image Cluster Operating Systems: The Kerrighed Approach. *Parallel Processing Letters*, 13(2):95–122, 2003.

[4] David Margery, Geoffroy Vallee, Renaud Lottiaux, Christine Morin, and Jean yves Berthou. Kerrighed: A SSI Cluster OS Running OpenMP. In *In Proc. 5th European Workshop on OpenMP (EWOMP ÂŠ03*, 2003.

[5] Honghui Lu, Y. Charlie Hu, and Willy Zwaenepoel. OpenMP on networks of workstations. In *Supercomputing '98: Proceedings of the 1998 ACM/IEEE conference on Supercomputing (CDROM)*, pages 1–15, Washington, DC, USA, 1998. IEEE Computer Society.

[6] Mitsuhisa Sato, Hiroshi Harada, Atsushi Hasegawa, and Yutaka Ishikawa. Cluster-enabled OpenMP: An OpenMP compiler for the SCASH software distributed shared memory system. *Scientific Programming*, 9(2,3):123–130, 2001.

[7] Jay P. Hoeflinger. Extending OpenMP to Clusters, 2006.

[8] Christian Terboven, Dieter an Mey, Dirk Schmidl, and Markus Wagner. First Experiences with Intel Cluster OpenMP. In *IWOMP*, pages 48–59, 2008.

[9] Dirk Schmidl, Dieter an Mey, and Matthias S. Müller. Performance characteristics of large smp machines. In Alistair P. Rendell, Barbara M. Chapman, and Matthias S. Müller, editors, *OpenMP in the Era of Low Power Devices and Accelerators*, volume 8122 of *Lecture Notes in Computer Science*, pages 58–70. Springer Berlin Heidelberg, 2013.

[10] John D. McCalpin. STREAM: Sustainable Memory Bandwidth in High Performance Computers, 1995.

[11] J. M. Bull. Measuring Synchronisation and Scheduling Overheads in OpenMP. In *In Proc. of 1st European Workshop on OpenMP (EWOMP '99)*, pages 99–105, 1999.

[12] N. Peters and L. Wang. Dissipation element analysis of scalar fields in turbulence. *C. R. Mechanique*, 334:493–506, 2006.

[13] Markus Gampert, Jens Henrik Göbbert, Michael Gauding, Philip SchÃd'fer, and Norbert Peters. Extensive strain along gradient trajectories in the turbulent kinetic energy field. *New Journal of Physics*, 2011.

[14] Nicolas Berr, Dirk Schmidl, Jens Henrik Göbbert, Stefan Lankes, Dieter an Mey, Thomas Bemmerl, and Christian Bischof. Trajectory-Search on ScaleMP's vSMP Architecture. In *Applications, Tools and Techniques on the Road to Exascale Computing : proceedings of the 14th biennial ParCo conference ; ParCo2011 ; held in Ghent, Belgium*, Advances in Parallel Computing ; 22, New York, NY, 2012. IOS Press.

Parallel Computing: On the Road to Exascale
G.R. Joubert et al. (Eds.)
IOS Press, 2016
© 2016 The authors and IOS Press. All rights reserved.
doi:10.3233/978-1-61499-621-7-93

Acceleration of Large Scale OpenFOAM Simulations on Distributed Systems with Multicore CPUs and GPUs

Boris KRASNOPOLSKY [a,b,1] and Alexey MEDVEDEV [b]

[a] *Institute of Mechanics, Lomonosov Moscow State University,
1 Michurinsky ave., Moscow, 119192, Russian Federation*
[b] *T-Services JSC, 113/1 Leninsky ave., B-405, Moscow, 117198,
Russian Federation*

Abstract.
The SparseLinSol library for solving large sparse systems of linear algebraic equations is presented in the paper. The key implementation features for multicore CPUs and GPUs are discussed. Performance characteristics are compared for "solve" part of the methods for MPI and hybrid code implementations and GPU-accelerated implementation against the hypre library for a set of matrices of 41-99 mln. unknowns on up to 128 GPU-equipped compute nodes. Preliminary results on coupling the developed library with OpenFOAM package to speedup the hydrodynamic modelling problems are discussed.

Keywords. Systems of linear algebraic equations, multigrid methods, hybrid programming models, GPU accelerators, OpenFOAM

Introduction

Solution of large sparse systems of linear algebraic equations (SLAE) remains the one of the typical problems for high performance computing (HPC) systems during the last several decades. Such a prevalence is a result of a wide range of applications finally reduced to solution of SLAEs. Computational fluid dynamics (CFD) problems for incompressible or weakly compressible flows are among them and solution time for pressure Poisson equation may exceed 90% of the total simulation time. Taking into account typical computational time costs for transient flows modelling in complex geometries of practical interest, time spent only to solve the SLAEs may be counted by weeks. An example for such an application of interest in our investigations is a problem of hydrodynamic characteristics modelling for marine propellers in OpenFOAM package. Typical grids for these problems consist of 10-100 mln. cells, whereas moving mesh regions associated with rotating propellers limit the integration time step. Ten to hundred thousand time steps must be calculated to obtain correctly averaged integral properties for the

---

[1]Corresponding Author: Boris Krasnopolsky, E-mail: krasnopolsky@imec.msu.ru.

model. Even using several hundred cores for computations, this simulation will take about a week. Thus, any attempt to speedup such simulations would be of high practical impact.

The well-known bottleneck for incompressible flows OpenFOAM simulations is caused by poor scalability of SLAE solvers [1]. The geometric-algebraic multi-grid method (GAMG), usually most efficient one to solve pressure Poisson equation, has modest scalability characteristics and provides any speedup up to hundreds of computational cores only. The OpenFOAM package is developed using MPI parallel programming model that affects the scalability of the methods.

Several attempts to implement hybrid programming models for SLAE solvers in OpenFOAM to improve the scalability are known, e.g. [2,3]. In the most thorough investigation [3] the MPI+OpenMP model was used to redesign the conjugate gradient method with DILU preconditioner. The presented results, however, were discouraging: almost all the tests demonstrated performance benefit for basic MPI implementation. One of the reasons for such a behavior is the fact that only SLAE part of the code was redesigned in terms of MPI+OpenMP model. The number of cores for non-SLAE part of the code was reduced, which leads to a significant slowdown. Due to this reason the applicability of MPI+OpenMP model for OpenFOAM simulations speedup looks very limiting and the other programming models should be considered.

Another potential option to boost the computations could be the use of accelerators or coprocessors. NVIDIA GPUs have 5-6 times higher peak performance and 3-5 times higher memory bandwidth, so GPU acceleration of CFD simulations is an attractive topic for state-of-the-art investigations. The flagship positions in development of iterative methods for multi-GPU systems are occupied by the AmgX library by NVIDIA [4]. The Culises library [5] containing self developed implementation for most common numerical methods and also compatible with AmgX library provides a unified interface to OpenFOAM package. Some benchmarking results were presented in [5], but they do not cover the multiGPU implementation scalability aspects. The AmgX library has both commercial and non-commercial academic licenses, while the Culises project is commercial. Referring to our experiments, the AmgX trial version has some functional limitations, which makes it problematic to use it even for testing for the problems of our interest.

Some other commercial and open-source libraries [6,7,8,9] are known in literature, but their functionality is limited and not sufficient for our purposes. Most of them have scalability or convergence degradation issues even on tens of nodes with GPUs.

Based on some preliminary studies [10], it was decided to start developing a new library of numerical methods SparseLinSol and a corresponding OpenFOAM solver plug-in based on it.

1. SparseLinSol Library

SparseLinSol library is developed for solving large sparse systems of linear algebraic equations. The library contains a set of popular iterative methods that could be combined as solvers, preconditioners or smoothers. Among them are the following: Krylov subspace methods, algebraic multigrid methods, Jacobi and Gauss-Seidel methods and some other. The "setup" part of multigrid methods is still partially based on hypre library [11], while "solve" part is redeveloped in terms of programming models and data structures used.

1.1. Aspects of Code Implementation for Multicore CPUs

The version of SparseLinSol library for multicore CPUs is designed in terms of MPI+Posix Shared Memory (MPI+ShM) hybrid programming model. While the use of this low-level model is highly time-consuming at the development stage, this choice has several significant advantages. All the computational processes are created at once by launching usual MPI application, while the processes sharing the same physical nodes are logically grouped inside of the library. It is assumed the only one process per node is responsible for inter-node communications. Intra-node communications for non-critical computational sections could be performed via the MPI calls and the full capabilities provided by shared memory could be utilized for the critical code sections, such as sparse matrix-vector multiplication operations (SpMV). This programming model allows us to implement simple coupling with external computational codes, including the ones based on pure MPI programming model. Thus, all the changes related to hybridization are hidden inside the library and are transparent for the main application.

The hierarchical multilevel parallelization algorithms for basic vector-vector and matrix-vector operations were developed to optimally fit the hardware architecture. Current implementation contains four-level hierarchy: node / device / NUMA node / processor core. An example of data segmentation by 16 cores with corresponding multilevel hierarchy is presented in Fig. 1. The non-empty matrix blocks are stored in CRS format with additional compression over empty rows and columns to minimize the volume of communications. The scheme of matrix segmentation and communications/computations for SpMV operation on the node level is similar to the one described in [6] (an extended scheme for GPU code implementation with additional CPU-GPU memory transfers is presented in the next subsection). The communication pattern between the nodes is built after the off-diagonal blocks compression.

A set of non-blocking synchronization primitives for each of hierarchy levels was developed to implement the matrix-vector multiplication for diagonal matrix subblock. Two implementations based on semaphores and atomics were proposed. These synchronizations were used to manage access to the non-local data over the shared memory inside the node.

1.2. Aspects of Code Implementation for GPUs

The version of algorithms for distributed systems with GPU accelerators has its own challenges. Different architecture of GPUs makes one create and implement special massively parallel algorithms for all basic operations. Two sets of algorithms for matrix-vector operations on GPU were implemented, and the combination of two matrix storage formats, CSR and ELLPACK, was used in GPU

Figure 1. Multilevel hierarchy matrix segmentation for 2 nodes, 2 devices per node, 2 NUMA nodes per device and 2 cores per NUMA node (16 cores).

code since none of well-known formats and corresponding algorithms can provide good performance in all cases. The properties of the multigrid hierarchy matrices significantly changes depending on the number of level. Usually, ELLPACK is well suitable for the finer multigrid levels in the hierarchy, while CSR is typically better for the coarser multigrid levels. The automated way to choose which format to use for a certain multigrid level matrix storage is still the problem to be finally investigated.

The special issue of GPU SpMV algorithm distributed version design is the way to achieve the best possible scalability of the algorithm keeping in mind the heterogeneous nature of GPU-accelerated HPC systems. Particularly, the asynchronous GPU-CPU memory transfers and asynchronous CUDA kernel executions must be considered.

The SpMV calculation workflow for the segmented by nodes and compressed matrix looks like this:

1. Compress the multiplier vector according to the communication pattern.
2. Copy the compressed multiplier vector from GPU memory.
3. Submit requests for asynchronous receive operations from all nodes, which are in a communication pattern.
4. Submit requests for asynchronous send operations to all nodes awaiting information form this node according to the communication pattern.
5. Do a partial SpMV calculation for a diagonal chunk with a GPU kernel launch (requires only local data).
6. Wait for receive request to finish from a node corresponding to the next matrix chunk.
7. Copy received data to GPU memory.
8. Do a partial SpMV calculation for the next chunk with a GPU kernel launch.
9. Repeat steps 6-8 for all the chunks left.

Steps 1, 5 and 8 require CUDA kernel launch, steps 2 and 7 are CUDA GPU-CPU memcopy operations, steps 3, 4, 6 are inter-node communications. Calculation/communication overlapping can be made by enabling asynchronous execution on each possible step, with the account of data dependencies between each step. Asynchronous send/receive operations can be easily implemented with MPI_Irecv/MPI_Isend/MPI_Wait functions set. CUDA kernels execution is asynchronous by default. Enabling asynchronous GPU-CPU memory copy requires some measures to carefully meet all the requirements for such operations, described in CUDA manuals. The most difficult thing is the synchronization between the end of each `MPI_Wait` operation (step 6), start of asynchronous copy to CUDA memory (step 7) and running the next calculation kernel (step 8) only after the copy is finished. Proper synchronization of these operations was successfully implemented (after several experiments having failed) only with an extensive usage of CUDA streams. The separate CUDA stream for CUDA operations related to each matrix chunk is created, and all CUDA memcopies and CUDA kernel launches implied by each step 6 and step 7 are made linked to this separate CUDA stream. The total number of CUDA streams used by a MPI-process becomes equal to the total number of neighbor nodes. Luckily, CUDA API was able to cope with such massive use of CUDA streams, and as a result full calculation/memory copy/inter-node communication overlapping was achieved.

2. Test Models and Hardware Platforms

Three test models for OpenFOAM package were considered in this paper. These models correspond to three multiblock hexahedral structured computational grids of 41, 60 and 99 mln. cells for the screw marine propellers hydrodynamic characteristics modelling problem. A set of two counter-rotating propellers coupled with a steering column was considered. The pimpleDyMFoam solver of Open-FOAM v2.3.1, supporting rotating grids and AMI interfaces for grids sub-regions coupling was used in the simulations.

In addition to complex OpenFOAM simulations, several matrices with right hand sizes were dumped from the corresponding models. These matrices were used for investigation of different implementation aspects for the chosen numerical methods in SparseLinSol library and for strong scalability benchmarking.

To solve these systems the BiCGStab [12] iterative method and algebraic multigrid preconditioner with PMIS [13] coarsening were chosen. For the GPU-related test series the 2nd-order Chebyshev polynomial smoother was used for CPU and GPU computations. For the OpenFOAM-related simulations with pure MPI model implementation one iteration of hybrid symmetric Gauss-Seidel method was applied.

In order to neglect the effects of variance in the number of iterations till convergence in scalability benchmarks the fixed number of iterations was calculated (50 iterations). This limitation, however, is not crucial: the number of iterations to reach the typical residuals of 10^{-8} was about 20 ± 2 for all the series of the tests and was generally independent on the matrix decomposition and the number of computational processes utilized.

The Lomonosov supercomputer was used for testing. GPU section of this system consists of dual-socket nodes with Intel Xeon E5630 processors and 2 NVIDIA X2070 GPUs per node connected by InfiniBand QDR interconnect. Results presented in the following sections assume utilization of all available 8 cores per node and 2 GPUs per node and provide the best performance.

3. SparseLinSol Library Performance Tests

3.1. Library Implementation Features

Several general and GPU-specific optimization features were implemented in the library. Among them are the following: the use of mixed precision computations for multigrid methods, the use of zero-vector flags indicating if the vector is identically equal to zero and the use of variable number of levels for multigrid methods, transferred to GPUs. The idea of these optimizations and their contribution on the performance boost would be discussed in the following sections.

3.1.1. Mixed Precision Computations

Every memory bound algorithm benefits from reducing the amount of memory transfers to be performed. One of the ways to do that for multigrid methods is the use of mixed precision for floating point calculations, as well as in matrix storage. Investigations were made to show that switching to 32-bit floating point precision on all matrices except the top level makes only a small influence on SLAE solution results, and this influence can be neglected. Making all matrix and vector operations 32-bit on multigrid levels besides the basic one, gives 15-25% performance boost for the whole solution process. The effect of use the mixed precision calculations on computational time reduction is demonstrated in Fig. 2 for a set of test runs with 41M matrix with GPU-accelerated version of SparseLinSol library.

3.1.2. Zero-vector Flags

The computational workflow for Krylov subspace iterative methods and multi-grid methods consists of simple basic operations such as SpMV, scalar product or linear combination of vectors. All these operations could be simplified if one of the vectors is equal to zero. Thus, knowing an argument vector consists of zero elements only, the time consuming SpMV operation could be fully avoided and replaced by a simple operation of making the resulting vector zero or even only setting the zero-flag for this vector. This is the case, for example, in multigrid cycle computations when the initial guess vector is set to zero, which is the typical situation for multigrid method used as a preconditioner. The optimization trick with introducing special zero-flags in a vector data structure made it possible to automatically eliminate unnecessary SpMV and vector operations, and helped to save 12-20% of solver time for both CPU and GPU-accelerated computations. Corresponding results for different number of computational nodes are presented in Fig. 2.

3.1.3. Variable Number of Levels on GPUs

Basic sparse matrix operations on GPU have some overhead, caused, at least, by unavoidable GPU-CPU memory copies via slow PCI-E interface and some API overhead. This fact has little impact on single-GPU implementation since all large memcopies can be made before the actual operation start, and only one CUDA kernel start API call is necessary. The multi-GPU version is affected

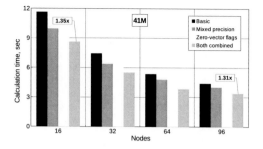

Figure 2. Effect of different optimizations on solution time for GPU-accelerated computations.

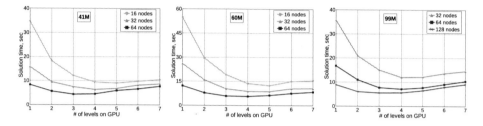

Figure 3. Dependence of solution time on the number of multigrid levels transferred to GPUs for test matrices of 41, 60 and 99 mln. unknowns

more because several GPU-CPU memcopies are required during the operation, and several CUDA kernel start API calls can't be avoided. The suggestion can be confirmed, that smaller matrix sizes are better to deal with on CPU, than on GPU, and algebraic multigrid matrix hierarchy can be moved to GPU only partially. This was proven experimentally, and best results are achieved in a combined mode with GPU algorithms used for larger matrices and CPU algorithms for smaller ones. An attempt to move all multigrid levels to GPU typically results in 30-40% higher solution time than the fastest option of GPU/CPU combination. It was noticed that when the matrix has $N_{nz} < 180000$ falling on each GPU, it is definitely better to leave it on CPU. Solution times for different number of multigrid levels transferred on GPU accelerators are presented in Fig. 3. The fastest variant in most cases is to move about a half of levels on GPU, leaving smaller levels on CPU.

3.2. Strong Scalability Results

Comparative strong scalability results for "solve" part of the methods for CPU implementation with MPI and hybrid MPI+ShM programming models as well as GPU-accelerated implementation are considered for three test matrices of 41, 60 and 99 mln. unknowns. These results incorporate mixed precision computations and zero-vector flag optimizations and assume the choice of optimal number of multigrid levels transferred to GPU. All the times are related to the ones for MPI version of CPU code from SparseLinSol library ("SLS: CPU MPI") on 32 nodes. Corresponding speedups are presented in Fig. 4.

All the curves for the matrices considered demonstrate decreasing the computation time together with increasing the number of computational nodes

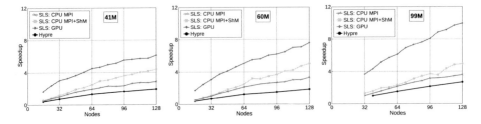

Figure 4. Scalability results for different programming models implementations and GPU-accelerated computations for test matrices of 41, 60 and 99 mln. unknowns.

used, however the parallel efficiency for MPI, MPI+ShM and GPU versions of SparseLinSol library code differs. On a 41M matrix basic MPI implementation of CPU code provides parallel efficiency of about 72% for 32 to 128 nodes with 2.9x speedup. The use of MPI+ShM model on the same matrix allows to improve the parallel efficiency up to 91% with 4.4x speedup. In these tests 1024 cores were used and the gain for hybrid model was only by a factor of 1.5, but the difference in scalability behavior for MPI and MPI+ShM models on higher scales would be dramatic [10]. GPU version of code shows 50% parallel efficiency on a 41M matrix – the lowest one, which is a consequence of GPU-CPU hybrid hardware model with some overhead on several operations like GPU-CPU memcopies and GPU compute kernel starting overhead. The use of GPUs provides 6.1x speedup on 128 nodes compared to 32 nodes CPU code results.

As it could be seen from results obtained on test runs with 60M and 99M matrices, the increase of the matrix size improves the strong scalability results for both MPI and GPU versions of code, whereas MPI+ShM parallel efficiency stays at the same highest level. The most significant improvements on speedup results are observed for GPU computations: compared to a 41M test matrix the overall speedup for a 99M matrix is increased by a factor of 1.6. This results from both a better GPU usage efficiency on 32 nodes and a better parallel efficiency increased up to 68%. Summarizing all the test runs with various matrices within a range of 32 to 128 nodes, the use of GPUs provides 1.4 to 2.8 speedups for calculations compared to an MPI+ShM model.

Reference results for hypre library, used with exactly the same numerical methods configuration, demonstrate better scalability for SparseLinSol code implementation for both MPI and MPI+ShM models. The difference in absolute time could be a result of optimizations, discussed in the previous section. Thus, using SparseLinSol library the speedup against hypre by a factor of 1.5-2.5 could be obtained for multicore CPUs or by a factor of 3.5-4.5 if GPUs are additionally used.

3.3. OpenFOAM Simulations with SparseLinSol Library

Some preliminary results on OpenFOAM modelling with developed SparseLinSol library and coupling plug-in were collected for the 60 mln. cells model. The series of simulations for the initial 60 time steps with standard OpenFOAM methods to solve pressure Poisson SLAEs and MPI version of SparseLinSol library has been done. The GAMG solver and conjugate gradient method with GAMG precon-

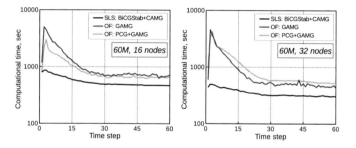

Figure 5. The dependency of the computational time on the number of time step for the model of 60 mln. cells, logarithmic scale.

ditioner in OpenFOAM were analyzed. The computational times for 40-60 time steps are close to the ones observed in the following unsteady simulations, that allow us to estimate the impact on the overall modelling process speedup.

The experiments demonstrated similar behavior of the computational time on the number of time step for both OpenFOAM methods configurations (fig. 5). Initial time steps require much higher number of iterations for linear solver, that lead to a significant increase for computational time. The BiCGStab method with classical algebraic multigrid preconditioner from the SparseLinSol library provides results, less sensitive on the number of time step. The convergence rates for SparseLinSol library significantly exceed the ones for OpenFOAM methods for initial time steps and somewhat better for 40-60 time steps. Even the use of MPI implementation for SparseLinSol library methods improves the parallel efficiency for OpenFOAM simulations considered, whereas for 16 nodes (128 cores) the computational time reduction, provided by the use of SparseLinSol library, was about 27%, for 32 nodes configuration the time was reduced by 35%.

4. Future work

Several directions of further work are planned. While the current GPU implementation for the "solve" part of the methods demonstrate good scalability results, some further improvements could be made. Among them are the choice of more relevant GPU matrix format and use of P2P communications between 2 or more GPUs inside a node. The investigation of RDMA-style inter-node interactions via NVIDIA GPUDirect technology advantages for these algorithms is also an important part of the future work. Implementation of multigrid methods "setup" part in terms of hybrid model for CPUs and for GPUs is challengcable question, and is a focus of current work. It promises significant improvement of the OpenFOAM plug-in performance.

5. Conclusion

The SparseLinSol library, containing a set of numerical methods for solving large sparse SLAEs, implemented in terms of MPI and hybrid MPI+ShM programming models for multicore CPUs with additional option to use GPU accelerators is presented and some implementation aspects are discussed. The efficiency of this library is demonstrated up to 128 GPU-equipped compute nodes for a set 41-99 mln. unknowns test matrices, obtained from the OpenFOAM simulations for screw marine propellers hydrodynamic characteristics modelling problem. Significant improvement against hypre library is shown, very good utilization of multicore CPU hardware and rather good GPU hardware utilization even on a maximum scale is noted for "solve" part of the methods.

OpenFOAM coupling plug-in for solving SLAEs is tested on practical CFD modelling problem with a significant improvement against the OpenFOAM built-in GAMG SLAE solver.

Acknowledgments

The reported study was supported by the Supercomputing Center of Lomonosov Moscow State University [14].

References

[1] C. Zannoni, PRACE Second Implementation Phase (PRACE-2IP) project. D9.1.1: Support for Industrial Applications Year 1. Tech.report. 2012.
[2] M. Culpo, Current Bottlenecks in the Scalability of OpenFOAM on Massively Parallel Clusters. PRACE-2IP Whitepaper. 2012. http://www.prace-ri.eu/IMG/pdf/Current_Bottlenecks_in_the_Scalability_of_OpenFOAM_on_Massively_Parallel_Clusters.pdf.
[3] P. Dagna and J. Hertzer, Evaluation of Multi-threaded OpenFOAM Hybridization for Massively Parallel Architectures, PRACE-2IP Whitepaper. 2013. http://www.prace-project.eu/IMG/pdf/wp98.pdf.
[4] AmgX   V1.0:   Enabling   reservoir   simulation   with   classical   AMG.   http://devblogs.nvidia.com/parallelforall/amgx-v1-0-enabling-reservoir-simulation-with-classical-amg/.
[5] B. Landmann, AeroFluidX: A Next Generation GPU-Based CFD Solver for Engineering Applications. GTC Technology conference, 2015. http://on-demand.gputechconf.com/gtc/2015/presentation/S5189-Bjoern-Landmann.pdf.
[6] J. Kraus, M. Foester, T. Brandes and T. Soddemann, Using LAMA for Efficient AMG on Hybrid Clusters, *Computer Science - Research and Development* **28** (2013), 211–220.
[7] SpeedIT. http://speedit.vratis.com/.
[8] Ofgpu: GPU v1.1 linear solver library for OpenFOAM. 2014. http://www.symscape.com/gpu-1-1-openfoam.
[9] D. Combest and J. Day, Cufflink: a library for linking numerical methods based on CUDA C/C++ with OpenFOAM. http://cufflink-library.googlecode.com.
[10] B. Krasnopolsky, The Reordered BiCGStab Method for Distributed Memory Computer Systems, *Procedia Computer Science* **1** (2010), 213–218.
[11] R. Falgout and U.M. Yang. Hypre: a Library of High Performance Preconditioners, *Computational Science – ICCS 2002, Lecture Notes in Computer Science* **2331** (2002), 632–641.
[12] H.A. Van der Vorst, Bi-CGSTAB: A Fast and Smoothly Converging Variant of Bi-CG for the Solution of Nonsymmetric Linear Systems, *SIAM J. Sci. and Stat. Comput.* **13** (1992), 631–644.
[13] H. De Sterck, U.M. Yang and J.J. Heys, Reducing Complexity in Parallel Algebraic Multigrid Preconditioners, *SIAM J. Matrix Anal. Appl.* **27** (2006), 1019–1039.
[14] V. Sadovnichy, A. Tikhonravov, Vl. Voevodin and V. Opanasenko. "Lomonosov": Supercomputing at Moscow State University, *Contemporary High Performance Computing: From Petascale toward Exascale* (2013), 283–307.

Parallel Computing: On the Road to Exascale
G.R. Joubert et al. (Eds.)
IOS Press, 2016
doi:10.3233/978-1-61499-621-7-103

Optimized variant-selection code generation for loops on heterogeneous multicore systems

Erik HANSSON [a] and Christoph KESSLER [a]

[a] *Linköpings Universitet, 58183 Linköping, Sweden*

Abstract. We consider the general problem of generating code for the automated selection of the expected best implementation variants for multiple subcomputations on a heterogeneous multicore system, where the program's control flow between the subcomputations is structured by sequencing and loops. A naive greedy approach as applied in previous works on multi-variant selection code generation would determine the locally best variant for each subcomputation instance but might miss globally better solutions. We present a formulation and a fast algorithm for the global variant selection problem for loop-based programs. We also show that loop unrolling can additionally improve performance, and prove an upper bound of the unroll factor which allows to keep the run-time space overhead for the variant-dispatch data structure low. We evaluate our method in case studies using an ARM big.LITTLE based system and a GPU based system where we consider optimization for both energy and performance.

Keywords. Code generation, variant selection, heterogenous systems, GPU-based System

Introduction

To keep up with the demand of more and more computational power, processor manufacturers have turned to heterogenous general purpose multicore and accelerator based systems to avoid the problems that increased clock speed and limited level instruction parallelism bring. Today heterogenous architectures are a reality, and range from server and desktop computer systems to architectures for embedded devices such as smart phones. A typical example of a heterogenous system is a server having multicore CPUs and GPUs. Another more specific example is the big.LITTLE architecture by ARM which has, on the same chip, small cores for power efficiency and larger cores for high performance.

The main drawback of heterogenous systems is in programmability, both when high performance or power efficiency is required. It is not obvious when to use what resource in a heterogeneous system, especially when data sizes are not known until runtime and the software consists of several combined algorithms. One specific example is the case study of ARM big.LITTLE by Kim et al. who show that the smaller core types (LITTLE) can in some cases be faster than the larger ones (big) and that the larger cores can in some cases be more power efficient [1]. They also state that performance should be *predicted* based on the application's properties (memory access patterns, instruction level parallelism etc.). This brings us to the problem of optimized software composition. A software component performs a particular computation or task and can have one or several implementation variants targeting possibly different available hardware such as GPU or CPU. *Composition* is the binding of a specific implementation variant (callee) to a call instance. Usually there is an additional cost for changing execution mode (e.g. the type of execution unit) which is not neglectable, and that of course has to be taken into account. When optimizing composition of different components we want to optimize for a particular target goal, for example minimize total execution time or total energy use. We also distinguish between different scopes of optimizations, a) Greedy (local) optimization, b) Sequence optimization and c) Global optimization.

In greedy (local) optimization only one component invocation is considered at a time and its best variant is selected for each invocation is selected given the cost relevant state, consisting of the call context (operand properties and locations), and machine state such as resources loads. An example can be found in our earlier work, see [2]. In sequence optimization, a sequence of invocations are considered together. One example is the bulk scheduling scheme described in [3,4], which decides if to run all component invocations on either CPU or GPU. Another, more sophisticated solution is shortest path computation where switching between the different execution modes is allowed. One example can be found in [5]. In this paper we will consider global optimization of sequences and loops.

Optimized composition from multivariant annotated parallel software components has been a way tackle the problem how to best utilize the performance of heterogenous systems, see for example [6,7,3]

Another example is our own, earlier, work [2] where we showed how to select at runtime which execution mode to use for parameterized components to best utilize the hardware. The predictors were derived using machine learning. In [5] we combined for sequences of subcomputations their machine-learning based predictors with shortest path calculation to select the best execution sequence of components where the cost of switching execution mode was taken into account.

In this paper we give a new formalization of the problem, we extend our method to loops and give a fast algorithm for global composition of loop-based programs. We also consider loop unrolling for further optimization and give an upper bound on the unroll factor of loops to achieve optimal selection code. We give some experimental results for big.LITTLE platform and a GPU based system.

1. Formulation using Min-Plus Algebra

Now we will formulate costs for component execution, switching, sequences of components and loops over components, using operators in min-plus algebra. Min-Plus Algebra is a nice way to formulate shortest path problems, see for example [8]. In min-plus algebra, the matrix-matrix multiplication operation $A \otimes B$ is defined for $A, B \in \mathbb{R}^{n \times n}$[8] as

$$A \otimes B = \min_{k \in N}(a_{ik} + b_{kj}) \quad \forall i, j = 1, \ldots, n \qquad (1)$$

For example, this means that the elements of $A^2 = A \otimes A$ are the weights of the shortest path between i and j of at most 2 hops for all $i, j \in N$ where N is the set $1, \ldots, n$ and n is a given integer $n \geq 1$ [8].

Given a $n \times n$ matrix A of direct distances between places, the (length of the) shortest path between any two places can be found simply by repeatedly squaring A as in
Equation 1 until a power A^h is found whith $h \geq n$ [8].
    We refer to [8] for further information on min-plus algebra.

1.1. Model

Assume that we have a heterogeneous computer system which has n execution modes.
For example, we can model the ARM big.LITTLE multicore processor as having two
execution modes, big (B) and LITTLE (L) if we enforce to execute on either big or
LITTLE cores only at any time. Also assume that we have software components which
have one implementation variant per execution mode[1]. We model a software component
C as a black box component. When executing a call of the component on big.LITTLE
we can enter the component in either L or B. Independently of what actually happens
inside the component we can exit it either in mode L or B. We can assume that there is
(at least) one shortest path between each entry and exit point. This is illustrated in Figure
1. There we also show the artificial component S which models the switching costs
between the modes before entering C. In the case of a GPU-based system, switching cost
also includes transfer of operands required for C that are not yet available in the device
memory to be used by C in the corresponding (GPU) mode or vice versa.
    The execution cost of a software component C can be expressed as the $n \times n$ matrix
C where n is the number of execution modes. In the same way we have a $n \times n$ switching
cost matrix S. The composition of S and C as shown in Figure 1a into A can be expressed
as $A = S \otimes C$.

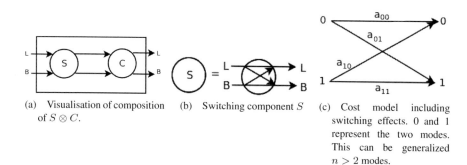

(a) Visualisation of composition   (b) Switching component S (c) Cost model including
     of $S \otimes C$.   switching effects. 0 and 1
                                                                        represent the two modes.
                                                                        This can be generalized
                                                                        $n > 2$ modes.

Figure 1. Composition, switching component and cost model.

In Figure 2, we visualize the notation for loops, shown as back-edges in the figure. The two back-edges represent that we can exit and enter the loop body in different
modes. In Figure 2, it is sufficient to only add two back-edges. Additional switches are
not necessary because we have switching nodes contained within all component nodes.
    By sequencing and loops we can further compose several component calls to new
components in a hierarchical manner.

---

[1]If there are several variants (e.g. different parallel or sequential algorithms) per core type, these can be
selected separately for each core type, thus reducing the problem to n pre-composed variants.

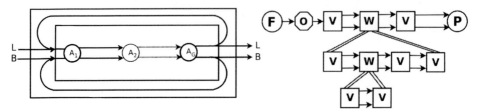

Figure 2. Example: Loop over a sequence of component calls.

Figure 3. Example of a region tree of a function.

K iterations over a loop body A, where A possibly is a composition itself, can be written as A^K if we assume that cost parameters in the loop body (cost matrix A) are loop-invariant. By definition the cost function of the body components(s) in the loop's *steady state* has to be loop invariant. In our algebraic formulation this means that the matrix entries do not change with loop iterations and are know upon entry of the loop. Where this is not the the case for the first loop iteration (e.g. for transfers of data reused in subsequent iterations),it can be achieved by peeling off the first iteration.

Loop peeling can also be described using min-plus algebra. For example $A \otimes A^{K-2} \otimes A$ expresses that the first and last iteration is peeled off. (Virtual) loop peeling allows to express different switching and selection behavior (shortest path cycles) for the first iterations (e.g more cache misses/transfers) and the steady state of the loop. Unrolling the loop with a factor two can be written $(A \otimes A)^{\frac{K}{2}}$, assuming K is even.

Consider the case where we have a loop body consisting of a sequence of G components component calls as in Figure 2 and K loop iterations.

We can express R-way unrolling together with peeling off the first iteration:

$$\underbrace{(A_1 \otimes \cdots \otimes A_G)}_{\text{prologue}} \otimes \underbrace{\left[(A_1 \otimes \cdots \otimes A_G)^R\right]}_{\text{unrolled kernel for steady state}}^{\frac{K-1}{R}} \tag{2}$$

The steady state denotes the case where we reenter the (possibly, unrolled) kernel in the same mode as we exit, and is recurring.

The condition $R \leq n$ also gives an upper bound on the unroll factor; if we unroll n times (number of modes/states), we will be on the safe side to get an optimal execution path for the steady state of the loop. Since there are n possible states a loop body state will be repeated after at most n iterations.

An interesting side note is that our formalization allows us to describe different optimizations levels. For example, bulk scheduling [4] can be expressed by not allowing any switching between execution modes in the switching matrices. In Figure 2 the upper (L) or lower (B) paths must be followed.

2. Optimization Principle

Here we will give an overview of how our model can be applied in a structural manner for optimized selection code generation in a compiler or in a runtime system.

A *region* encapsulates a contiguous subgraph of the control flow (graphs) that has only one point of entry so that a (structured) program can be viewed as a hierarchy or tree of regions which enclose each other [9]. In the region tree example of Figure 3, F

represents the start node of a contiguous program region [2] and P the end. W represents a loop-header and V a normal base level component call. The arrows denote control flow. We call a region cost-invariant if all cost vector and matrix elements for the region are know at entry of program control to the region, and do not vary during the execution of the region.

Between any two nodes there are two edges, representing control flow with the two execution modes. O is the optimization computation, to be performed at run time, at the entry to a cost-invariant region, i.e., we know all parameters for O to calculate the shortest execution time. For the cost-invariant region, O calculates the least cost path (cycle for steady state of loops) starting from the current state of O by doing the matrix calculations (in min-plus algebra) as described in Section 1.1 bottom up through the cost-invariant region tree.

O determines and stores for each component call in the region which mode it should be executed in. The optimization done in O can be considered overhead, as it is part of the total execution time. In the general case we need a dispatch table to store the solution information. The table should contain which component variant should be invoked for each component call in the region. Before each call is executed a lookup in the dispatch table is done to check which mode to execute it in. Doing this lookup is fast but also considered overhead.

If we apply our upper bound for of unrolling the loop n times from the previous section instead of unrolling the loop fully[3], we do not need to have an entry for each loop iteration in the table; only for the prologue and the steady state. In the simplest form, the actual transformation of the loop into prologue-steady-state form can be done at compile time. The size of the dispatch table will be linear in the number of nodes in the region tree, since the maximal unroll factor to consider is a constant, n, and the prologue size is also constant per loop. The dispatch table size thus depends on n^l where l is the maximal nesting depth of the loops in a cost-invariant region, which also is a constant. The total size of the table will be $\mathcal{O}(qn^l)$ where q is the number of nodes in the tree.

Instead of peeling and unrolling the loop into prologue and steady-state in the code we can achieve the same effect by leaving the code structure intact and doing the peeling/unrolling in the dispatch table only. An advantage is that code size will not grow as in the case of code unrolling. To support unrolling of loops in the dispatch table, the table can be implemented as a tree, representing the region tree. In this case the dispatch table size will also be $\mathcal{O}(qn^l)$ where l is the depth of the tree. Hence, from the point of dispatch table size and code size there is no gain by unrolling the code itself.

We have in this section given an overview how we can calculate the shortest path for a sequence of components, including nested loops over components, and achieve optimized structural composition at runtime.

3. Implementation

In order to support and conduct experiments we have implemented a lightweight C/C++ based run-time system prototype for optimized software composition. It supports the concept of components, multiple implementation variants calls and smart data contain-

---

[2]Usually a program starts in a given fixed execution mode.
[3]However, it might not be feasible , e.g. if K is statically unknown.

ers. At the moment it can handle control flow involving component calls, sequences, and loops. Data flow is defined by the the input and output operands of each call. The smart data containers keep track of where data is residing (host or device memory) to avoid unnecessary data transfers. The run-time system supports global optimization as well as greedy and bulk optimization schemes. We can also use it to calculate the worst case execution schedule. There is functionality for loop unrolling.

Each component can have multiple implementation variants (for example using CUDA or OpenMP) for which the user can provide cost predictor functions parametrized in data size and data locality (and possibly further cost relevant properties). The user can also provide switching cost predictors which estimate the mode switching and data transfer cost. These predictors are essential for the different optimization schemes.

The runtime system provides an API function for connecting the model representations of the two component calls A and B in sequence by control flow.

In this way, a sequence of calls is linked together [4]. Likewise, an API function exits fo construct model representations of loops. In order to globally optimize which implementations variants to use for a cost-invariant contiguous program region A of interest, we call `optimize(A)` before the actual invocations in the program flow. The `optimize` call evaluates the cost predictors for both execution costs and the switching costs and creates a dispatch data structure from the tree-like internal representation pointed to by its argument.

In order to limit the combinatorial explosion of the possible number of states for many different operand data, we currently consider array operands only at the granularity of whole array accesses, and do not consider scalar operands for the optimization as their impact on transfer cost is negligible.

As `optimize` can, in some cases, be slow, we also provide a variant of `optimize` which does the same as `optimize` but progresses faster since it cuts off branches in the solution space that can not be optimal. [5] Finally we provide the `run` function for executing the program region with the selection dispatch table created by the preceding `optimize` call.

4. Evaluation

We implemented and evaluated our approach for two heterogenous systems: (a) the big.LITTLE development board Odroid-XU3 from Hardkernel [10] and (b) a GPU based system. The Odroid-XU3 has a Samsung Exynos5422 Cortex-A15 2.0GHz quad core and Cortex-A7 quad core CPU with 2GB on-chip memory [10] running Linux kernel 3.10.69 (armv7l). The GPU based system has an Intel Xeon E5-2630L CPU and Nvidia Kepler K20c GPU and runs Linux kernel 3.13.0-43-generic. For big.LITTLE our implementation variants are parallelized using standard pthreads, where we pin the threads to the cores by setting their affinity. For the GPU based system, CPU variants are written in OpenMP and GPU variants in CUDA.

---

[4]Note that these calls to the runtime system API are intended to be generated automatically from high-level annotations of the programs components and of the calls by a source-to-source compiler in future work, similarly as in Dastgeer et al. [4].

[5]This pruning cannot be used when searching for the worst-case solution.

4.1. Synthetic Benchmark

We implemented synthetic benchmarks based on five basic parallel components: *copy*, *axpy*, *randpow*, *randcube* and *scale*. *copy* performs a simple array copy from a source to a destination. *axpy* is the classical BLAS routine axpy. *randpow* picks, for each element position in the input array x a random position p_i, calculates the power of the input element x_{p_i} to itself and stores it in position p_i of the output array. *randcube* is similar but calculates the cube $x_{p_i}^3$. *scale* scales the source array with a constant and produces an output array.

In contrast to *copy*, *scale* and *axpy*, *randpow* and *randcube* introduce a high number of cache misses. We also observed that randpow has both better performance and uses less energy when running on the LITTLE cores.

4.2. Libsolve

We used an ODE solver application based on the Libsolve software by Korch and Rauber [11]. Libsolve basically consists of calls of the components *copy*, *absaxpy*, *axpy*, *scale* and *absquotMax* inside a loop. We have adopted the source code of Libsolve used in [4], which has six component calls (copy is called twice in the loop body). Hence, there are, with no unrolling, 64 different execution possibilites for the the body of the loop if there are two available execution modes (implementation variants).

4.3. Results for big.LITTLE

Libsolve   On big.LITTLE we experimented with problem sizes 2K, 4K... 6400K elements for Libsolve. As stated above there are 64 different possibilites of how (on big or LITTLE) to execute the calls in the loop body. In the case of problem size 200K elements, the optimal way, both considering energy and time, is to execute the component instances on the following cores: LITTLE → big → big → big → big → LITTLE. This is 1.09 times more energy efficient and 1.04 times faster than the best bulk solution (big only). However, on the largest problem size (6400K elements) the bulk solution on big is the most energy efficient one.

Synthetic benchmark   In the cases below we used calls to the three components *copy*, *axpy* and *randpow* described above in sequence in the body of a loop and unrolled the loop with a cyclic data dependency chain two times, hence we have 64 different possible execution combinations and we executed them all for different problem sizes[6]. We will discuss some interesting observations.

In one particular case we get, for problem size 100000 elements, both the lowest execution time (0.1202 s) and minimum energy use (0.4298 J) if we execute the components on big → LITTLE → big in a loop. In this particular case a period of one was enough. However, executing the same problem using bulk scheduling on LITTLE would have taken 0.194 s and used 0.44 J and on big 0.147 s and 0.50 J.

We have some cases where a period of one (i.e. unroll factor) is not enough. For example for a problem size 1600000 elements we use the minimal energy when we

---

[6]Each combination was executed 15 times for each problem size to reduce variations of execution times and energy.

execute on LITTLE → big → LITTLE → big → LITTLE → LITTLE in a loop and total energy consumption is 7.397 J. In contrast, bulk scheduling would give 7.66 J for running on LITTLE only and 11.16 J on big only. If we only would allow unroll factor one, the most energy efficient case is where we have big → LITTLE → big in a loop which has an energy consumption of 11.21 J.

4.4. Results for GPU based System

Synthetic benchmark For our GPU based system we experimented with the synthetic benchmarks *scale*, *copy* and *randcube* with implementation variants for both for CPU and GPU that can be used with our runtime system. We derived predictors both for the communication cost for our smart data containers and the predictors for the actual computation using the tool Eureqa Pro which is using symbolic regression [12]. For measuring total system energy on our GPU system we used the MeterPU library [13].

In Figure 4 we show predicted energy divided by the actual used energy for a 16 iteration loop over cyclically dependent *scale*, *copy* and *axpy* component calls when doing different amounts of loop unrolling (2, 4 and 8). The figure shows that the prediction can be relatively accurate; it ranges from less than 1.009 to up to 1.06 times of the actual consumed energy. It also shows that the more unrolling is done the more accurate the prediction gets.

Libsolve However, an important observation when experimenting with Libsolve on GPU based systems is that accurate predictors are the key for optimization. Our experiments show that for a particular setup (problem size and number of iterations) the consumed measured energy for GPU execution fluctuates within a factor of 2.3 which makes it really hard to create predictors. We see similar fluctuations when considering time instead. Another contributing reason might be that the predictor values are accumulated and due to the global minimization we can not expect that prediction errors will even out in the end. However, the predicted energy optimal solution for the same setup is correct (bulk-CUDA) and the predicted worst solution alternates between CPU and GPU creating additional switching costs. If we compare the actual measured average consumed energy, the worst (predicted) solution uses around 10.5 times more energy than a bulk-CUDA execution. This shows that ranking different paths still works quite well even with noisy predictors.

5. Related Work

Optimized software composition is in general a very broad area of research and has many applications. Examples range from composing web services for quality of service [14] to composing scientific computations on GPU based systems for performance [3,4,7].

The PEPPHER composition tool [7] by Dastgeer et al. targets heterogenous multi-core and GPU based systems and the software components are written in C/C++. The components can be annotated with metadata using XML descriptors. The framework has three parts; one for composition and one for optimization, and a StarPU based runtime system [7]. At the moment, one drawback with PEPPHER is that it only performs greedy local optimization instead of global optimization.

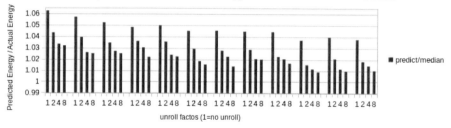

Figure 4. Predicted energy divided by actually used energy for a 16 iteration loop over *scale*, *copy* and *axpy* calls with different unroll factors. Smallest problem size 6M elements (left most) to 8.75 M elements (right most) executed on a GPU based system. Shown measured energy is the median value of five executions.

The Global Composition Framework (GCF) by Dastgeer [3,4] optimizes sequences of component calls using a bulk selection scheme. Basically GCF estimates the runtimes executing all components either on CPU or GPU in bulk. No switching between CPU and GPU is considered and could (at least theoretically) lead to sub-optimal solutions, but estimating the runtimes and using such a simplistic heuristic is fast.

Similarly to PEPPHER, the Elastic computing framework [15] allows the user to run the same application code on different targets by separating functionality and implementation. It also supports different implementations of the same functionality and can also help optimize the selection by trying to explore different combinations [15].

Kessler and Löwe [16] propose global optimized composition for simple recursive components on a single-mode (homogeneous parallel) system using lookup tables compiled off-line for selected problem sizes from user-provided predictor functions.

The general idea of calculating the shortest path to minimize total execution time of a dependency graph where "parallel nodes" represent different variants of the same components has briefly been discussed by Ericsson[17]. However, he does not go into detail and there is no implementation or evaluation.

Lifa [18] presents methods to map and schedule tasks in a control flow graph on the fly for heterogenous systems consisting of multicore GPUs, CPUs and reconfigurable FPGAs, to minimize energy while meeting the deadlines of the tasks.

6. Conclusion

We have given a formalization of the global selection problem for sequences and loops and derived an upper bound on the unroll factor for loops when having a fixed number of execution modes on a heterogenous system.

We have also given an overview how to implement our model in a compiler or runtime system. We have shown how to find the best variant combinations of components for unrolled loops. We also showed that it is possible to use off-the-shelf machine learning tools such as Eureqa Pro to derive sufficiently accurate predictor functions, both for computations and data communications.

Our results for synthetic benchmark and the Libsolve benchmark show that in some cases the bulk selection algorithm delivers suboptimal solutions in both energy and performance optimization. Measurements also show that unrolling the loop in some cases can improve the energy use on the ARM big.LITTLE architecture.

Future work will extend this work to cover additional control flow constructs such as if-then-else constructs. Pruning techniques to limit the runtime overhead of optimization is also important to investigate. Another interesting key problem that has to be tackled is how to generate accurate predictor functions in a systematic way, including how to quantify and limit their global accumulated misprediction error when using them to minimize costs.

Acknowledgments   This work was supported by SeRC and EU FP7 EXCESS. Thanks to Nutonian for providing a free academic licence of Eureqa Pro.

References

[1]   J. M. Kim, S. K. Seo, and S. W Chung. Looking into heterogeneity: when simple is faster. In *The 2nd International Workshop on Parallelism in Mobile Platforms*, June 2014.

[2]   Erik Hansson and Christoph Kessler. Optimized selection of runtime mode for the reconfigurable PRAM-NUMA architecture REPLICA using machine-learning. In *Proc. of 7th Int. Workshop on Multi-/Many-Core Computing Systems (MuCoCoS'14) at Euro-par 2014*, Springer LNCS, Aug 2014.

[3]   Usman Dastgeer. *Performance-aware Component Composition for GPU-based systems*. PhD thesis, Linköping University, Software and Systems, The Institute of Technology, 2014.

[4]   Usman Dastgeer and Christoph Kessler. Performance-aware composition framework for GPU-based systems. *The Journal of Supercomputing*, pages 1–17, 2014.

[5]   Erik Hansson and Christoph Kessler. Global optimization of execution mode selection for the reconfigurable PRAM-NUMA multicore architecture REPLICA. In *Proc. 6th Int. Workshop on Parallel and Distributed Algorithms and Applications (PDAA'14) in conjunction with CANDAR'14*, December 2014.

[6]   Christoph W. Kessler and Welf Löwe. A framework for performance-aware composition of explicitly parallel components. In Christian H. Bischof, H. Martin Bücker, Paul Gibbon, Gerhard R. Joubert, Thomas Lippert, Bernd Mohr, and Frans J. Peters, editors, *PARCO*, volume 15 of *Advances in Parallel Computing*. IOS Press, 2007.

[7]   Usman Dastgeer, Lu Li, and Christoph Kessler. The PEPPHER Composition Tool: Performance-Aware Composition for GPU-based Systems. *Computing*, 96(12):1195–1211, 2014.

[8]   Peter Butkovič. *Max-linear systems: theory and algorithms*. Springer monographs in mathematics. Springer, London, Dordrecht, Heidelberg, 2010.

[9]   Alfred V. Aho, Monica S. Lam, Ravi Sethi, and Jeffrey D. Ullman. *Compilers: Principles, Techniques, and Tools (2Nd Edition)*. Addison-Wesley Longman Publishing Co., Inc., Boston, MA, USA, 2006.

[10] Hardkernel. Odroid-xu3. http://www.hardkernel.com/. [Online; accessed March 2015].

[11] Matthias Korch and Thomas Rauber. Optimizing locality and scalability of embedded runge–kutta solvers using block-based pipelining. *J. Parallel Distrib. Comput.*, 66(3):444–468, March 2006.

[12] M. Schmidt and H. Lipson. Distilling Free-Form Natural Laws from Experimental Data. *Science*, 324(5923):81–85, 2009.

[13] Lu Li, Christoph Kessler. MeterPU: A Generic Measurement Abstraction API Enabling Energy-tuned Skeleton Backend Selection. In *Proc. International Workshop on Reengineering for Parallelism in Heterogeneous Parallel Platforms (REPARA-2015) at ISPA-2015 (to appear)*, 2015.

[14] D.A Menasce. Composing Web services: a QoS view. *Internet Computing, IEEE*, 8(6):80–90, Nov 2004.

[15] John Robert Wernsing and Greg Stitt. Elastic computing: A framework for transparent, portable, and adaptive multi-core heterogeneous computing. *SIGPLAN Not.*, 45(4):115–124, April 2010.

[16] C. Kessler and W. Löwe. Optimized composition of performance-aware parallel components. *Concurrency and Computation: Practice and Experience*, 24(5):481–498, 2012.

[17] Morgan Ericsson. *Composition and Optimization*. PhD thesis, Växjö University, School of Mathematics and Systems Engineering, 2008.

[18] Adrian Alin Lifa. *Hardware/Software Codesign of Embedded Systems with Reconfigurable and Heterogeneous Platforms*. PhD thesis, Linköping University, The Institute of Technology, 2015.

Parallel Computing: On the Road to Exascale
G.R. Joubert et al. (Eds.)
IOS Press, 2016

113

doi:10.3233/978-1-61499-621-7-113

MPI communication on MPPA Many-core NoC: design, modeling and performance issues

Minh Quan HO [a,c], Bernard TOURANCHEAU [a], Christian OBRECHT [b],
Benoît DUPONT DE DINECHIN [c], Jérôme REYBERT [c]

[a] *Grenoble Informatics Laboratory (LIG) - University Grenoble Alpes, France*
[b] *INSA-Lyon, CETHIL UMR 5008 Villeurbanne, France*
[c] *Kalray Inc. S.A. - Montbonnot, France*

Abstract. Keeping up with the performance trend of the last decades cannot be achieved anymore by stepping up the clock speed of processors. The usual strategy is nowadays to use lower frequency and to increase the number of cores, where data communication and memory bandwidth can become the main barrier. In this paper, we introduce an MPI design and its implementation on the MPPA-256 (Multi Purpose Processor Array) processor from Kalray Inc., one of the first worldwide actors in the many-core architecture field. A model was developed to evaluate the communication performance and bottlenecks on MPPA. Our achieved result of 1.2 GB/s, e.g. 75% of peak throughput, for on-chip communication shows that the MPPA is a promising architecture for next-generation HPC systems, with its high performance-to-power ratio and high-bandwidth network-on-chip.

Keywords. Many-core, NUMA, Distributed memory, Network-on-Chip, MPI, Performance modeling, MPPA.

Introduction

In this paper, we propose the design of an MPI Message-Passing library [1] for the intra communication on many-core processors, using the vendor support library (MPPAIPC [2]) as the transfer-fabric to build MPI protocols from scratch, while porting any of existing MPI implementations such as MPICH or OpenMPI is not be possible due to limited on-chip memory of most recent many-core processors.

Based on studied MPPA hardware specifications presented in [3,2], this paper does a brief hardware summary and focuses on an MPI design over (but not limited to) the MPPA architecture, with detailed implementation algorithms and formulated models following vendor-hardware characteristics (K, h) and different optimizing approaches (Lazy, Eager). These studies is generic enough to be compared/ported to other very-similar architectures, on which doing/optimizing MPI communication over Network-on-chip is still a challenging or never-posed question.

The remainder of this paper is organized as follows: Section 1 briefly introduces the MPPA architecture and the MPPAIPC components used in our implementation. Section 2 describes our MPI architecture design. Section 3 resumes
our MPI implementation in pseudo-codes of blocking and non-blocking communication (`MPI_Send` and `MPI_Isend`). Some optimization ideas are then proposed
and developed in this section such as (1) synchronization-free "eager send" and
(2) implicit local-buffered "lazy send" for short and medium sized messages respectively. A throughput estimation model based on the data transmission time
is also introduced in section 4 to evaluate the communication performance. Section 5 presents our results for the ping-pong test following two scenarios, either
symmetric ranks (MPI compute node - MPI compute node) or asymmetric ranks
(MPI compute node - MPI I/O), corresponding on MPPA to CC-CC and CC-
I/O subsystem respectively. Different optimization approaches are also tested and
compared. Finally, conclusions are given in section 6.

1. MPPA-256 Andey Hardware and Software

1.1. Architecture overview

The MPPA-256 Andey [3] embeds 256 VLIW compute cores grouped into 16 compute clusters (CC) and four I/O subsystems (IOS). Each compute cluster operates 2MB of shared memory and 16+1 VLIW cores running at 400 MHz. These
cores are divided into 16 user cores referred to as Processing Elements (PEs) and
one system-reserved core known as Resource Manager (RM). The four I/O subsystems (North, South, East, West), each containing four cores, integrate DRAM
controllers managing the off-chip DDR memory. CCs and IOS are connected by
two network-on-chip: Data NoC (D-NoC) and Control NoC (C-NoC) [2], both ensuring reliable delivery by the credit-based flow control mechanism [4] also FIFO
arrival using static NoC routing [5]. No acknowledgment is needed at the packet
reception. As a result, there is no need to consider a TCP layer implementation
when building any communication library above these NoCs (e.g MPI).

1.2. MPPA Inter-Process-Communication (MPPAIPC)

A programming model available on MPPA matching our working scope in this
paper is MPPAIPC - an specific POSIX-like library [2] following the distributed
memory model, where communication and synchronization between CCs and IOS
are achieved using IPC primitives through connecting objects :

Sync object provides light-weight and low-latency synchronization barriers by
exchanging 64-bits messages on CNoC.

Portal object supports data transfer on DNoC using one-sided communication
with zero-copy transfer. The sender (Tx) can write to the receiver's buffer (Rx)
via a known `dnoc_tag` number, with an optional offset.

RQueue object implements FIFO 120-byte-message queues with user-defined
receive buffer length ($120 \times nb\_slot$). The inbound flow is controlled by a credit
mechanism that ensures available buffer space to store incoming messages before
being handled by the Rx rank. Callback function on message arrival can be defined
to implement an Active Message Server [6].

2. MPPA-MPI design

2.1. Global design

In the MPPA context, each CC is referred to as an MPI rank. Each MPI rank owns a private memory space of 2MB. A hybrid MPI I/O rank is introduced running on the North IOS and manages the off-chip DDR memory. This MPI I/O rank is started from the host via the `k1-mpirun` command and is responsible for spawning MPI compute ranks on CCs subsequently. To keep the portability of any MPI legacy code, this extra MPI I/O rank is not listed in the `MPI_COMM_WORLD`. Any communication with this rank can be achieved through a "local communicator" (`MPI_COMM_LOCAL`) that groups all MPI ranks within an MPPA processor (i.e 17 ranks). Fig. 1 illustrates the structure of our MPPA-MPI implementation.

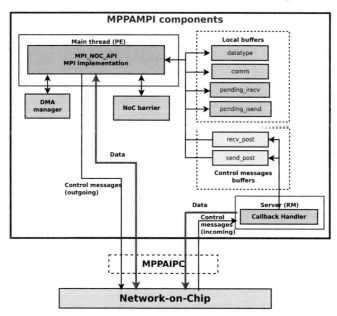

Figure 1. MPPA-MPI components and interaction with Network-on-chip through MPPAIPC.

2.2. MPI-inter-process Control (MPIC)

Each MPI transaction begins by exchanging control messages at the MPIC layer between MPI ranks. Control messages are used for exchanging information about MPI transaction type and synchronization point in case of rendez-vous protocol. An RQueue-based active message server [6] running on each MPI rank (CC and IOS) handles incoming control messages from all other ranks (including itself on loop-back). In an MPI send/receive, The Tx rank posts a *Request-To-Send* (`send_post_t`) to the Rx rank; idem, the Rx rank sends back a *Clear-To-Send* (`recv_post_t`) containing its allocated `dnoc_tag`, to which the Tx rank will send data. Beforehand, this `dnoc_tag` needs to be configured and linked to the receive buffer to enable remote writing. Control messages exchanged in the MPIC layer contain either one of the structures defined in Fig. 2.

```
typedef struct send_post_s { /* Tx to Rx (Request-To-Send) */
   mppa_pid_t    sender_id;     /* ID of Tx process */
   int           mpi_tag;       /* MPI message tag */
   ...
} send_post_t;

typedef struct recv_post_s { /* Rx to Tx (Clear-To-Send) */
   int           dnoc_tag;      /* DNoc allocated on Rx */
   mppa_pid_t    reader_id;     /* ID of Rx process */
   int           mpi_tag;       /* MPI message tag */
   ...
} recv_post_t;
```

Figure 2. Control message structures

2.3. MPI-inter-process Data-Transfer (MPIDT)

MPIDT is a light-weight wrapper of MPPAIPC *Portal* primitives. From received information (e.g. dnoc_tag), data are sent in either blocking or non-blocking mode dependent on the calling MPI function (see Tab. 1 for detailed function mapping).

Mode	Portal primitives	MPPA-MPI
Blocking send	mppa_pwrite() mppa_pwrites()	MPI_Send, MPI_Ssend
Non-blocking send	mppa_aio_write() (DMA engine)	MPI_Isend, MPI_Issend
Receive	mppa_aio_read()	MPI_Recv, MPI_Irecv
Termination	mppa_aio_wait()	MPI_Wait

Table 1. Portal primitives and their associating MPI functions.

3. MPPA-MPI implementation

3.1. MPI_Send - MPI_Recv

Most well-known and optimized MPI libraries contain many (combined) techniques to perform the MPI_Send call. In the first time, we chose to implement this function with rendez-vous blocking behavior, in order to avoid extra buffer space and minimize memory usage. This choice certainly adds more synchronization cost but does not change the functionality of the send/receive transaction. Some optimization approaches will be presented in the coming sections.

3.2. MPI_Isend - MPI_Recv

The implementation of MPI_Isend uses non-blocking *Portal* primitives on both PE and RM on the Tx side. When the Tx rank (PE0) reaches MPI_Isend in its execution *without* having received any matching `recv_post`, it creates a "non-started" `pending_isend` request containing related information (buffer pointer, dest, count, tag etc.) and returns. On arrival of the matching `recv_post`, the RM core (callback handler) reads the previous `pending_isend` request and triggers a non-blocking data send (to the `recv_post.dnoc_tag` of the Rx rank). The request is then set to "started" state to be distinguished from other "non-started" requests. This propriety ensures that the transfer is performed only once for each transaction, either by the PE core (in `MPI_Isend`) or by the RM core (in callback handler). At the end, "started" requests will be finished and cleaned by `MPI_Wait`. Algorithms 1 and 2 present in more details the implementation of `MPI_Isend` and of the callback handler.

Algorithm 1 MPI_Isend(buf, count, datatype, dest, tag, comm, request)

1: my_rank ← get_rank(comm);
2: /* *send send_post to dest* */
3: send_send_post(my_rank, dest, tag, comm, ...);
4: req ← new_request(buf, count, ..., PENDING_ISEND);
5: /* *look for a matching recv_post (MPIC layer)* */
6: recv_post ← find_recv_post(count, datatype, tag, ...);
7: **if** recv_post ≠ NULL **then**
8:    /* *configure/start a non-blocking write (MPIDT layer)* */
9:    aio_request ← configure_aio_write (buf, recv_post.dnoc_tag, ...);
10:    req→status := STARTED;
11:    req→aio_request := aio_request;
12: **else**
13:    /* *Do nothing (request initialized NON_STARTED)* */
14: **end if**
15: request ← req;
16: **return** MPI_SUCCESS;

Algorithm 2 callback_recv_post(recv_post)

1: /* *look for a matching pending_isend* */
2: req ← find_pending_isend(recv_post);
3: **if** req ≠ NULL **then**
4:    /* *configure/start a non-blocking write (MPIDT layer)* */
5:    aio_request ← configure_aio_write (req→buf, recv_post.dnoc_tag, ...);
6:    req→status := STARTED;
7:    req→aio_request := aio_request;
8: **else**
9:    save_recv_post(recv_post);
10: **end if**
11: **return** ;

3.3. Optimization

3.3.1. Eager send optimization

Our idea is to pack any MPI message which can fit into a 120-byte space, as a control-message and send it directly to the Rx's active server. In reality, the maximum data payload is about 96 bytes (24 bytes is used for control header). This approach is synchronization-free when the MPI_Send call can return before a matching receive is posted (non-local). For longer messages, using several "eager sends" introduces segmentation and reassembly costs. We implemented a test case where messages are splitted into "eager" pieces in order to determine the best communication trade-off in Fig. 4. Such segmentation however consumes memory for buffers and therefore puts more pressure on RM's resources and limits its usage in practice.

3.3.2. Lazy send optimization

Lazy send consists in copying medium-size message into a local buffer and returns. The RM is then responsible for sending it to the destination. Unlike eager_buffer on the Rx side, lazy_buffer is allocated on the Tx side. This approach must be used with care because bad communication scheduling may lead to buffer wasting and lazy messages remaining for too long. Inversely, a dense communication scheme should neither be set to "lazy" mode in order to be able to send data directly rather than spending time doing memcpy in local memory.

3.3.3. DMA thread usage

MPI_Isend uses *Portal* non-blocking primitive to configure a Tx DMA thread for data sending. The DMA engine implements a fetch instruction that loads the next cache line while pushing the current line into the NoC. This fetch is nowadays not available on PE cores, meaning that outbound throughput using PE is 4 times lower than using DMA engine (1 B/cycle vs. 4 B/cycle). Thus, tuning to use non-blocking DMA on MPI_Send for messages of size greater or equal to DMA_THRESHOLD will maximize the transfer performance.

4. MPPA-MPI Throughput modeling

The MPPA-256 Network-on-chip [7] is designed so that any path linking two CCs always contains less than eight hops (including two local hops - one at sender and one at receiver). The average switching time on a NoC router is 7 cycles, then it takes the packet at most 8 cycles to reach the next hop. In the worst case, the link distance (time a packet spends on NoC to reach its destination) is 112 cycles ($7 \times 8 + 8 \times (8 - 1)$). However, the necessary time to send a buffer (transmission time - t) is about $O(N)$ cycles [8] (where N the buffer size in bytes), which is much longer than the link distance [9].

As a result, we describe the transmission time t as a function of the buffer size N, a constant transfer ratio K and a default overhead h (aka. the cost of sending an empty buffer). This default overhead presents the initial cost of MPI implementation management (ID mapping, metadata setup, synchronization, error checking ...) and/or configuring the peripherals (cache, DMA) to prepare for data sending. This cost is paid on each MPI call and is independant to the subsequent data-sending process (which is presented by a data-transfer factor K). The ping-pong round-trip time (RTT) is approximately the sum of the transmission time on both sides, as the propagation time is negligible.

$$TransmissionTime: \quad t = K \times N + h \; (cycles) \tag{1}$$

$$RTT \simeq 2 \times t = 2 \times (K \times N + h) \; (cycles) \tag{2}$$

$$Throughput: T = \frac{2 \times N}{RTT} \simeq \frac{N}{K \times N + h} = \frac{1}{K + \frac{h}{N}} \; (bytes/cycle) \tag{3}$$

$$\lim_{N \to \infty} T \simeq \lim_{N \to \infty} \frac{1}{K + \frac{h}{N}} = \frac{1}{K} \; (bytes/cycle) = 400 \times K^{-1} \; (MB/s) \tag{4}$$

$$(at \; frequency \; 400 \; MHz)$$

The constant K is a value specific to each send function with its own underlying transport primitive. For example, the `MPI_Isend` which uses the DMA engine with peak throughput of 4 B/cycle, would have its transfer ratio K of about 0.25. The `MPI_Send`, with default peak throughput of 1 B/cycle (no DMA engine), should obtain a transfer ratio K around 1.

5. Results and Discussion

5.1. Experimental platform

Using the MPPA Developer platform [10] with AB01 board and MPPA-256 Andey processor integrated, we set up ping-pong tests between:
(1) MPI rank 0 (CC_0) - MPI rank 15 (CC_15) and
(2) MPI I/O 128 (IOS_128) - MPI rank 15 (CC_15).
All MPI cluster ranks run at the same clock frequency of 400 MHz. The North IOS running the MPI I/O rank is configured to use the DDR controller at the default frequency of 600 MHz.

In each case, the same MPI send function is used on both sides (`MPI_Send` or `MPI_Isend`). At the first time, all tests are run without any optimization in order to calibrate the proper throughput of each context (Fig. 3). At the second time, we enable all optimization on the `MPI_Send` test and compare our optimization approaches in term of latency, throughput and messages sent per second (Fig. 4). Each ping-pong is repeated 50 times. We assume that there is no waiting time inside the MPI send function, since all ranks start at the same time and run at the same clock speed. Hence, the duration of the MPI send function can be considered as the transmission time. Depending on the send context, the measured transmission time is fitted into a linear correlation $K \times N + h$ presented in Tab. 2. The ratio of standard error over mean value from all obtained results is always less than 0.2%.

5.2. Compute cluster ↔ Compute cluster

Communication links between CCs are bi-directionally symmetric. According to our model and the K values from Tab. 2, the estimated maximum throughput

From	To	MPI_Send	MPI_Isend
CC_0	CC_15	$t = 0.98 \times N + 31430$	$t = 0.27 \times N + 33690$
CC_15	CC_0	$t = 0.98 \times N + 30240$	$t = 0.27 \times N + 32850$
IOS_128	CC_15	$t = 13.52 \times N + 159544$	$t = 0.84 \times N + 181300$
CC_15	IOS_128	$t = 0.98 \times N + 129200$	$t = 0.26 \times N + 144500$

Table 2. Transmission time (cycles).

(given by $400 \times K^{-1}$ MB/s) should be around 408 MB/s and 1481 MB/s for MPI_Send and MPI_Isend respectively. The ratio $\frac{h}{N}$ can be ignored in this case. Fig. 3a shows obtained results that match with our estimation model.

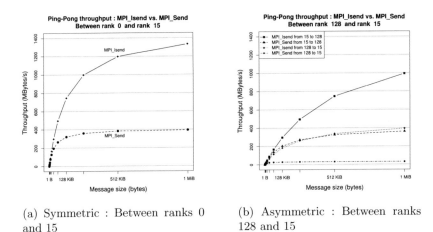

(a) Symmetric : Between ranks 0 and 15

(b) Asymmetric : Between ranks 128 and 15

Figure 3. Ping-pong throughput MPI_Send (PE core) vs. MPI_Isend (DMA).

5.3. Compute cluster ↔ I/O subsystem

Contrary to the symmetric communication performance between CCs, the transmission rate on I/O subsystem relies on the DDR bandwidth, which is much lower than the on-chip memory on CCs. We observed higher K values and much more considerable overhead h on the IOS_128, showing that the communication link from IOS to CCs might be the bottleneck on the MPPA. It is then difficult ignoring $\frac{h}{N}$ in this case. Keeping on our throughput estimation by $400 \times (K + \frac{h}{N})^{-1}$ now matches with experiment results on Fig. 3b, where the performance gap between the CC_15 and the IOS_128 is also illustrated.

5.4. Optimization comparison

We focus now on finding, on a given message size, the best send method among the four (Normal, Eager, Lazy and DMA) to use on MPI_Send, in order to obtain lowest latency (round-trip-time) and/or highest ping-pong throughput, by enabling all optimizations and re-running our experiments between CCs. We also evaluate the number of messages sent per second in each approach by dividing

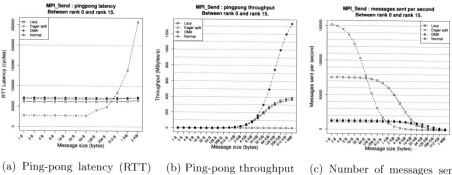

(a) Ping-pong latency (RTT)   (b) Ping-pong throughput   (c) Number of messages sent
on short buffers   per second

Figure 4. Optimization approaches comparison.

the clock frequency (400 MHz) by the duration of the MPI_Send call (in cycles). As the message will now be "eagerly" sent or "lazily" buffered and MPI_Send returns right afterward, this duration on Eager(-splitting) or Lazy could no longer be evaluated as the transmission time in the Tab. 2, but respectively by :

$$E \times (floor(\frac{N}{96}) + 1) \ (cycles, E \approx 3800) \tag{5}$$

$$O_{memcpy}(N) = 1.28 \times N + 5300 \ (cycles) \tag{6}$$

where E is the constant necessary cost to send 1 eager-split and O_{memcpy} is a linear function of memcpy cost. Note that in the Lazy approach, the message is sent in background by the RM. Hence, Eager and Lazy methods provide lower latency and higher message rate on short buffers, since they were designed to get rid of two-sided synchronization and the buffer size is still small enough not to be outperformed by the DMA's high-throughput capacity. Fig. 4a shows that the ping-pong latency for [1 .. 256 B] using eager-splitting is reduced by half compared to DMA or Normal. Otherwise, this latency increases radically as soon as its transmission time, despite being smaller at the beginning, getting repeated as many times as split segmentation $(floor(\frac{N}{96}) + 1)$. On the other hand, using DMA on large buffers optimizes bandwidth utilization compared to Normal (using PE) or Lazy (using RM) methods. (Fig. 4b). Fig. 4c illustrates the message-rate of the four send methods. Not only this kind of measure gives user a high-level point of view about the implementation's capacity to support communication load, but it shows interesting advantages of Eager and Lazy methods in tuning MPI applications, thanks to their fast sending time for short messages and synchronization-free algorithm.

6. Conclusions

In this paper, we have introduced the design and performance issues of an MPI implementation on the Kalray MPPA-256. The MPPA-MPI library provides 1.2 GB/s of throughput for any inter compute-cluster point-to-point communication and this performance depends on the underlaying MPPAIPC library. Optimization ideas such as eager send and lazy message are proposed, implemented and compared to determine the best approach based on threshold. A synthetic model is also presented for each approach to evaluate their communication latency and throughput. The HPL benchmark is also successfully ported on MPPA as a validation test of our MPI library.

The next-generation MPPA processor aims at supporting global addressable DDR off-chip memory (Distributed Shared Memory) on clusters and will be more energy efficient. Our future work aims studying the performance gain and detailed power consumption of this new MPPA processor.

References

[1]   William D Gropp, Ewing L Lusk, and Anthony Skjellum. *Using MPI: portable parallel programming with the message-passing interface*, volume 1. MIT Press, 1999.

[2]   Benoît Dupont de Dinechin, Pierre Guironnet de Massas, Guillaume Lager, Clément Léger, Benjamin Orgogozo, Jérôme Reybert, and Thierry Strudel. A Distributed Run-Time Environment for the Kalray MPPA®-256 Integrated Manycore Processor. *Procedia Computer Science*, 18:1654–1663, 2013.

[3]   Benoît Dupont de Dinechin, Renaud Ayrignac, P-E Beaucamps, Patrice Couvert, Benoît Ganne, Pierre Guironnet de Massas, François Jacquet, Samuel Jones, Nicolas Morey Chaisemartin, Frédéric Riss, et al. A clustered manycore processor architecture for embedded and accelerated applications. In *High Performance Extreme Computing Conference (HPEC), 2013 IEEE*, pages 1–6. IEEE, 2013.

[4]   Siavash Khorsandi and Alberto Leon-Garcia. Robust non-probabilistic bounds for delay and throughput in credit-based flow control. In *INFOCOM'96. Fifteenth Annual Joint Conference of the IEEE Computer Societies. Networking the Next Generation. Proceedings IEEE*, volume 2, pages 577–584. IEEE, 1996.

[5]   Davide Bertozzi, Antoine Jalabert, Srinivasan Murali, Rutuparna Tamhankar, Stergios Stergiou, Luca Benini, and Giovanni De Micheli. NoC synthesis flow for customized domain specific multiprocessor systems-on-chip. *Parallel and Distributed Systems, IEEE Transactions on*, 16(2):113–129, 2005.

[6]   Thorsten Von Eicken, David E Culler, Seth Copen Goldstein, and Klaus Erik Schauser. *Active messages: a mechanism for integrated communication and computation*, volume 20. ACM, 1992.

[7]   Kalray Inc. MPPA-256 Cluster and I/O Subsystem Architecture, 2015. Specification documentation.

[8]   Kalray Inc. MPPAIPC Performance, 2013. Benchmark report.

[9]   Shashi Kumar, Axel Jantsch, Juha-Pekka Soininen, Martti Forsell, Mikael Millberg, Johny Öberg, Kari Tiensyrjä, and Ahmed Hemani. A network on chip architecture and design methodology. In *VLSI, 2002. Proceedings. IEEE Computer Society Annual Symposium on*, pages 105–112. IEEE, 2002.

[10] Kalray Inc. Kalray platforms and boards. Accessed March 30, 2015.

Parallel Computing: On the Road to Exascale
G.R. Joubert et al. (Eds.)
IOS Press, 2016
© 2016 The authors and IOS Press. All rights reserved.
doi:10.3233/978-1-61499-621-7-123

Drivers for Device to Device Streaming

Dominic ESCHWEILER [a], Volker LINDENSTRUTH [a]

[a] *Frankfurt Institute for Advanced Studies, Frankfurt am Main, Germany*

Abstract. PCIe is the common way for integrating high-speed interconnects and manycore accelerators into cluster nodes. In this paper we describe a zero copy approach for communicating between two PCIe devices involving shared DMA memory buffers. Furthermore, we show the requirements for transferring data directly between two PCIe devices without using the main memory of the host computer. We included the support for direct device communication into our **PDA** (**P**ortable **D**river **A**rchitecture) which is a library for implementing user-space drivers.

Keywords. GPU, Interconnect, Microdriver, DMA, Architecture

Introduction

Heterogeneous manycore accelerators such as GPUs are highly integrated co-processors which achieve a much higher compute performance than traditional CPUs. The compute cores of such devices often do not support the execution of an operating system and implement only a small instruction set. Furthermore, they usually have a limited I/O capability in terms of storage and networking. The saved silicon is then used for implementing many more compute cores than it is possible at the main CPU which executes the operating system. Heterogeneous manycore accelerators are therefore able to execute up to thousands of threads in parallel but need a "real" CPU as platform. Such accelerators also have fast main memory which is separate from the main memory of the hosting computer. The high packaging density and therefore massive parallelism makes heterogeneous accelerators interesting for HPC applications. A cluster node equipped with such co-processors achieves much more compute power. Additionally, heterogeneous computing has proven to be the currently most energy-efficient paradigm in HPC [1][2].

   In an HPC environment the most performed I/O operation is the communication between the compute nodes. The data to be processed must be moved to the accelerator memory before computation. After processing, the results must be moved to a different location, which may be a remote compute node or even another accelerator at the same host. Sending data to another remote host is done with a high speed interconnect device. Heterogeneous manycore devices and high-speed interconnects are separate devices, which means that the data needs to be copied between these two entities. Copying is also needed if data has to be exchanged between two accelerators at the same node. Therefore, it is preferable to stream the data directly, or at least without unnecessary copy steps, between the devices. Direct streaming, which is called DDMA (**D**irect **D**evice **M**emory **A**ccess) in this paper, has some advantages over the unnecessary copying from and into a host DMA-buffer. Direct streaming achieves higher data rates and reduces latencies and it reduces the host memory usage, which leaves much more memory bandwidth for the applications running at the host.

1. Contributions of This Paper

The zero copy approaches shown in this paper support the data transfer to and from devices used for communication between nodes. This paper therefore deals with operating system support for inter-node communication in large HPC systems. We extended the PDA library to support this use case.

Figure 1 shows the traditional datapath of two communicating DMA devices. Modern operating systems forbid programming device drivers with side effects to ensure that only one instance can access the hardware. Sharing resources such as DMA memory buffers is therefore strictly prohibited in classical driver programming. Therefore, both manycore and interconnect device have their own DMA memory buffers. The CPU must copy the content of these buffers on each external data transfer.

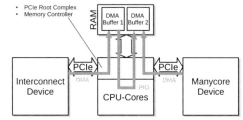

Figure 1. Traditional streaming pattern between two DMA devices. Each driver has its own DMA memory buffers.

A first step towards improving the situation is to have shared DMA buffers between both devices. This paper shows how to extend the PDA library for supporting such DMA buffer sharing across multiple devices. We propose a way of achieving this which is easily adaptable to almost all other drivers. Figure 2 depicts a data path which includes a shared buffer scheme. This is considered to be a zero-copy approach because it does not require

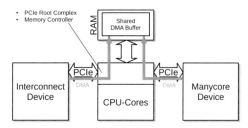

Figure 2. A shared DMA buffer does not require the CPU to copy data between two memory locations.

the expensive memory copy performed by the CPU. Interconnect and manycore device copy the data from and into the main memory by themselves, which is the point of the original DMA idea. Driver libraries still need to support this scenario, even if it would be better to stream the data directly, because direct streaming requires special hardware support by at least one of the two devices.

The optimal data path between manycore accelerator and interconnect is the direct transfer between the devices. Figure 3 shows such a direct communication which saves as many resources as possible because it does not involve CPU or the host memory. We describe how DDMA works in general and outline the related requirements to the hardware design. We also describe in this paper how we transparently extended the PDA for DDMA. Device drivers which use our microdriver li-

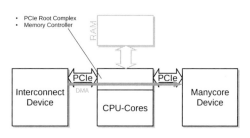

Figure 3. DDMA between two devices.

brary can participate in a DDMA interaction with only little modification. We tested the described extensions with INTEL Xeon Phi hardware but they should also work with DDMA extensions such as AMD DirectGMA [3] and NVIDIA GPUDirect [4]. NVIDIA already showed [5] that DDMA improves data throughput and latencies by one order of magnitude.

The remainder of this paper is organized as follows. The next section gives an overview of the related work. Section 3 gives an overview of the PDA DDMA implementation. An evaluation is presented in Section 4 which shows how we tested our approach. Finally, Section 5 concludes the work.

2. Related Work

NVIDIA provides GPUDirect [4] as an extension to its CUDA library. AMD provides a similar API called DirectGMA [3]. The first version [6] of GPUDirect provided DMA buffer sharing of two devices. Later versions [7] brought support for direct device-to-device communication. This approach requires modifications in both drivers and Linux kernel. Furthermore, the authors of both cited publications got the support for DDMA from a closed vendor library. In fact there is little published knowledge about the technology behind such work. In contrast, this paper has a focus on the issues which arise on the lowest layer of interconnect and manycore devices. It therefore describes a new approach for DDMA which is called "OS-bypassing". The paper also describes details of a DMA buffer sharing scheme which works with a wide range of fast interconnect devices.

The PDA is a microdriver library which targets HPC use cases. Microdriver means that the whole device driver executes in user space providing all the advantages of the user space to system programming. In our previous work [8] we proved that this approach works for high throughput and low latency use cases. Furthermore, in Eschweiler et al. [9] we showed fast microdriver extensions for intra-node communication such as shared memory. In contrast, this paper mostly deals with inter-node communication by accelerating the data transfer from and to an interconnect device. However, the work shown in this paper also extends the intra-node capabilities of our library because modern compute nodes can have more than one manycore device. The techniques shown in this paper make it possible to transfer data directly between such devices inside a node.

3. Implementation

This section outlines details of our implementation for the DMA scenarios described above. It also gives an overview of hardware requirements and underlying hardware mechanisms.

3.1. DMA Buffer Sharing

Traditionally, the device driver allocates a DMA buffer in kernel space. The PDA, even though it is a microdriver library, also allocates DMA memory in its kernel adapter and maps it into the user-space process of the requesting driver. We call this approach "kmem-allocation".

Another approach is to take a user-space buffer (usually allocated with `malloc`) and translate it back into physical addresses in the kernel adapter ("vmem-allocation"). In this case the user-space process owns the memory, which it deallocates by issuing `free` or by termination of the process. This imposes the issue that the hardware might still access the related memory while the operating system releases it. The DMA device could then corrupt data of other software processes if the operating system reassigns the freed pages. Even an IOMMU (**I/O M**emory **M**anagement **U**nit) will not contain this fault because the user-space process will not automatically remove the IOMMU mapping when it frees the buffer. Especially a crash of the user-space driver might unpredictably deallocate the DMA memory. There is no safe way for stopping the device in such a situation before the operating system frees the memory. For instance, the kernel adapter could monitor a virtual file which is opened when the driver starts and closed if the user-space process terminates. It seems reasonable that the kernel adapter stops the device on a close call of the monitored file. The operating system closes all opened file descriptors in case the related process crashes. However, this approach will not work in all cases because there is no guarantee that the operating system will release the resources sequentially. Furthermore, the virtual file systems in Linux usually do not offer internal callbacks for file closing. It is therefore not possible to monitor a virtual file in sysfs which is used for implementing the PDA.

The PDA kernel adapter deals with this issue by translating a process ID and related virtual memory addresses into physical addresses. Afterwards, it increments the reference counter of each physical page in the virtual memory system. This means that the pages are not returned into the memory pool if the user-space process crashes. The PDA kernel adapter does not return the pages in question until the user-space explicitly signals to release the buffer. Therefore, a device can still perform DMA operations even if the device driver crashed. In this case the unreturned pages bridge the time between a crash and the device reset issued by the re-spawning device driver.

Currently there are only limited ways for sharing DMA memory buffers inside the Linux kernel space. A kernel driver could expose its buffers by providing a function which returns a pointer to a DMA region. The importing kernel driver could simply call this function and use the provided memory. However, the Linux maintainers do not recommend this and drivers which expose memory in this way are unlikely to become a part of the Linux mainline. The issue with this approach is that there is no instance keeping track of who is accessing the resource. The dma_buf extension of Linux deals with this, but needs extensive modifications of all participating kernel drivers. Almost no developer started integrating dma_buf, because there are no other drivers supporting it (chicken or the egg dilemma). Therefore, most device drivers in Linux do not support the dma_buf API.

A second conceivable way for achieving DMA memory sharing between two devices seems to be the resource sharing at the user-space library. Figure 4 shows a related scheme. Two device drivers could interact if the first driver passes a pointer to a kmem-allocation to the second driver. Afterwards, the second driver could translate the passed pointer into a vmem-allocation in its context. However, this approach does not work be-

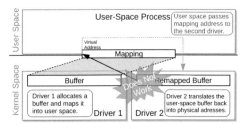

Figure 4. Mapping a kmem-buffer into user space and translating it back does not work.

cause Linux does not provide mechanisms for translating kmem-mappings into physical addresses. The reason is that the only way in Linux for manually mapping memory into user space is to use the system call `mmap`. `mmap` is responsible for mapping file contents into the virtual memory of a process. Therefore, the semantics of such memory regions are different from normal virtual memory. For example, a file memory mapping does not necessarily map the same physical memory on each access because the kernel can remap it on the fly. In addition, pinning is impossible which makes a back translation of such buffers even harder. Furthermore, mapped kernel memory does not come from the same memory pool as virtual memory does. A back translation to a page frame is therefore not possible (please see Section 3.2.3 for further details).

The conclusion is that all drivers which have to share a DMA buffer need to support back translation from virtual memory. Figure 5 depicts a scheme in which the user-space process allocates virtual memory and passes it to both drivers. The drivers translate the virtual addresses back into physical ones. Afterwards, the drivers can pass the physical addresses to each related device which then share the same buffer for DMA. This approach works with a large range of de-

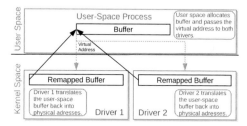

Figure 5. Two devices can share a DMA buffer if both device drivers translate a user-space buffer into physical addresses.

vice drivers out of the box, because drivers of latency- and throughput-optimized hardware often support buffer translation for zero copy. For example, the InfiniBand API IB-Verbs [10] features the function `ibv_reg_mr` for translating user-space buffers. OpenCL provides the function `clCreateBuffer` with the flag `CL_MEM_USE_HOST_PTR` for this purpose.

3.2. Direct Device DMA

Besides software support, DDMA requires dedicated hardware support of at least one of the two devices. Also the host infrastructure needs to be configured for DDMA. This paper outlines the concept, hardware-, and software-requirements for DDMA. We also show how the PDA supports DDMA with a technique which we call OS-bypassing.

3.2.1. Concept

Figure 6 depicts a possible tree structure of a PCIe interface. A DDMA communication needs an actor and a server. The actor can be a device with a common DMA engine, it does not require the implementation of dedicated hardware for DDMA. The server must map DMA-capable memory to one of its device memory regions. This means that the device memory region should be backed with real memory and the related controller needs to be able to handle read and write requests with arbitrary length up to 4 KiB. Fortunately most GPUs already have a fast main memory which they can expose to a device memory region. The way DDMA works in PCIe is that the device driver configures the DMA engine of the actor to read and write into a memory region of the server device instead into a DMA buffer at the main memory of the host. However, this approach has some hardware limitations which are described in the next subsection.

3.2.2. Hardware Constraints

Transferring data directly between PCIe devices places certain demands on the hardware. Figure 6 also shows three possible data paths for DDMA. A fast interconnect connects the two CPU sockets. In this case we used an INTEL-based system in which QPI (**Q**uick **P**ath **I**nterconnect) connects the sockets. Todays CPUs integrate the PCIe root complex directly on the die. Each socket connects PCIe bridges which connect the devices. PCIe is a packet-based protocol and all connections are point to point. The PCIe specification only requires that memory-mapped device regions must be visible to all CPUs. Furthermore, the specification also only requires that host main memory must be addressable from the device. Whether or not other device regions are addressable from a device depends on the mainboard, chipset, and CPU used.

The data path between Device 0 and 1 (red line) works in most cases with maximum data rate. DDMA between devices which connect to the same socket but to different bridges (blue path) works on newer platforms (e.g. INTEL Sandy Bridge) with full performance, but with degraded performance at early QPI-based systems. A DDMA involving QPI (gray path) does not work on older systems (e.g. INTEL Nehalem) and with severely degraded performance ($< 1\mathrm{GiB/s}$) on current platforms. In any case address resolution and performance depends on the related platform and requires manual testing before productive use.

X86 CPUs also feature IOMMUs since the introduction of virtualization extensions [9]. IOMMU support must be turned off on all currently available platforms because all DDMA participants must have the same view to the memory. Some X86 servers provide a related option in the BIOS/UEFI setup. The Linux kernel deactivates all IOMMUs if it gets the boot options `intel_iommu=off amd_iommu=off iommu=noforce`. The server device should expose its whole main memory to a BAR-addressed device memory region at

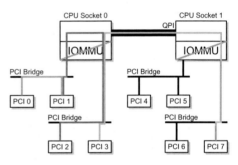

Figure 6. Bus tree of a modern two socket server system with eight PCIe devices attached.

once. A BAR (**B**asic **A**ddress **R**egister) is a device register pointing to a memory region which is mapped to the CPU address space and also handled by the device. Some GPUs only expose a window of their main memory. Non-server environments require this because BAR sizes are often limited to 32 bit and less at such platforms. Mainboards which do not support large BAR sizes often refuse booting. This is the main reason why the majority of gaming GPUs are not DDMA-capable. However, modern computing GPUs often have more than 4 GiB of memory requiring support for 64 bit addressable BARs. Even some newer server mainboards do not support this.

3.2.3. Why Generic Approaches Do Not Work

The most performance- and latency-critical device drivers already implement user-space address translation. Furthermore, the PDA supports mapping of device memory into a user-space process since it is a library for programming user-space device drivers. Therefore, it would be convenient if such mappings could be translated back into physical addresses as already described in Section 3.1. This would have the advantage of leaving the driver of the actor device untouched. Also only the driver of the server device would require code adjustments for supporting DDMA. Most Linux driver implementations use the internal kernel function `get_user_pages` for translating virtual into physical addresses. This function looks up the physical addresses in the page table of the calling process.

Figure 7 depicts the structure of such a table. Virtual addresses consist of two pieces. The first piece determines an entry in the page table containing a page frame number which references a page frame in the physical memory. The second part of the virtual address determines the page offset inside the referenced page frame. This page translation system only manages pages of the virtual memory system. Such pages can for example be swapped out, which is not possible with device memory. The Linux kernel therefore marks related mappings into a virtual address space as "I/O memory". These mappings do not

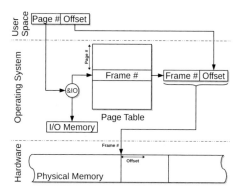

Figure 7. Paging in Linux. The memory system does not manage I/O memory, which makes a back translation with `get_user_pages` impossible.

have an entry in the page table and `get_user_pages` fails to work in this case. This implies that actor drivers need to be modified for DDMA since there is no way of getting device memory mappings through the kernel internal translation routines.

3.2.4. A User-Space Centric Approach

PDA-based drivers get DMA-buffer objects from the PDA allocation routines. Such objects provide a mapping of the related memory and an SGL (**S**catter **G**ather **L**ist) which stores the physical addresses of the DMA-buffer. A device driver typically programs the SGL into the device for passing the location of the DMA buffer. Therefore, such a device driver also accepts device memory if the related DMA-buffer object generated by the PDA library actually delivers valid data.

The PDA already provides user-space mappings of device memory. Drivers of server devices which are not PDA-based can simply pass a pointer to the PDA API. The PDA stores this pointer into a DMA-buffer object. Generating an SGL from an address stored in a BAR is straightforward. A BAR is a register which stores a physical address of the memory region in question. The PDA can already retrieve this physical address in user space. On the other hand the SGL is a data-structure meant to be programmed into the actor device which requires physical addresses anyway. It is necessary to be aware that, even though a device memory region can be accessed like usual memory, it is managed by the device and not by the operating system. Therefore there is no reason for handling such addresses with the operating system. The PDA reads the BAR address and its length directly from the register and generates an SGL with a single entry because the related device memory is naturally consecutive. We call that approach "OS-bypassing" because the operating system only provides the register mapping and the PDA bypasses the complete memory management system.

Drivers which are PDA-based do not need much modification in order to become DDMA-capable. The server device drivers only needs to pass a BAR object and an offset to the actor driver if both drivers are PDA-based. A PDA BAR object has functions for exposing the physical BAR address to external drivers. This means that the actor driver needs modifications if only the server driver is PDA-based. The PDA is also capable of generating a DMA buffer object from a physical address. Therefore, the server driver needs modification if it is not PDA-based and does not already expose the required BAR addresses. However, APIs like the DDMA extension of AMD for OpenCL [3] already provide these addresses in user space.

4. Evaluation

We evaluated the DDMA enhancements of the PDA with an INTEL Xeon Phi and a detector readout device called CRORC (**R**ead **O**ut **R**eceiver **C**ard). The CRORC is used at the CERN-experiment ALICE for reading out detector data into the central HPC-system for realtime analysis. It is a DMA-device similar to high-speed interconnects such as InfiniBand. A CRORC is well suited to be the actor device for our tests, because its device driver is PDA-based. The Xeon Phi is a manycore device which exposes its whole memory (8 GiB GDDR5) to a device memory region. Therefore, it acts as the server device in the following tests. We implemented a PDA-based stub driver for this device, which exposes the device memory to other drivers.

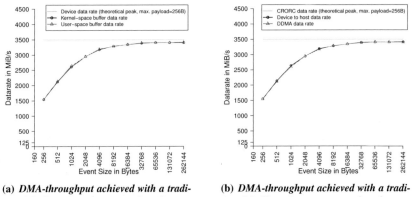

(a) *DMA-throughput achieved with a traditional buffer scheme, compared to the performance achieved with buffer sharing.*

(b) *DMA-throughput achieved with a traditional buffer scheme, compared to the performance achieved with DDMA.*

Figure 8. *Benchmark results for both zero-copy approaches.*

Figure 8 shows the performance of a CRORC driven with the zero-copy approaches introduced in Section 1 compared to the performance achieved with a traditional buffer scheme which requires extra copy steps. The x-axis shows marks for each measurement for a specific event size (packet size). We took measurements for event sizes of a power of two between 256 B and 256 KiB. The y-axis outlines the achieved data rate for each event size. A larger event size means more payload data throughput caused by less management overhead. The CRORC constantly achieves a throughput of $\approx 3.5\text{GiB/s}$. However, the device needs to transfer one management descriptor for each event. Therefore, the payload data rate drops for smaller event sizes. The results depicted in Figure 8(a) and Figure 8(b) show that both buffer sharing and DDMA do not perform worse than the kernel buffer. The results also show that the maximum payload throughput for the CRORC in this case ranges at $\approx 3.5\mathrm{GiB/s}$. This fact is important for the next observations.

Figure 9 depicts measurements regarding the resource usage while a CRORC is receiving data. Figure 9(a) shows the results of a memory throughput benchmark (ramspeed) which ran on an idle system, while a CRORC was forwarding data with a traditional separated buffer scheme, and while the CRORC was performing DDMA. A DMA device has a higher memory access priority than a software process. Therefore, a memory benchmark executed while a DMA device is active shows the remaining memory bandwidth available for software applications. The test system was an Intel Xeon E5-2640 with four channels of DDR3 1333 memory, which provides a theoretical peak throughput of $42.4\,\mathrm{GiB/s}$. The benchmark achieves almost peak performance ($\approx 39\,\mathrm{GiB/s}$) if the CRORC is not active. An active CRORC driven with separate buffers reduces the remaining memory bandwidth to $\approx 25\,\mathrm{GiB/s}$, even though the achieved payload data rate is much smaller. Therefore, the readout with two buffers reduces the available bandwidth by $\approx 14\,\mathrm{GiB/s}$. In this case the data stream causes four memory accesses: the DMA access which streams into the memory, two accesses for reading and writing during the `memcpy` between the DMA buffers, and for the DMA access from the memory. None of these memory accesses are cached, which reduces the available bandwidth by four times the data rate produced by the CRORC ($4 \cdot 3.5\,\mathrm{GiB/s} = 14\,\mathrm{GiB/s}$). Compared to this the remaining memory bandwidth is much higher ($\approx 37\,\mathrm{GiB/s}$) if the CRORC performs DDMA. The available bandwidth is reduced by only $\approx 2\,\mathrm{GiB/s}$, because the management descriptors must still be copied to main memory in this case.

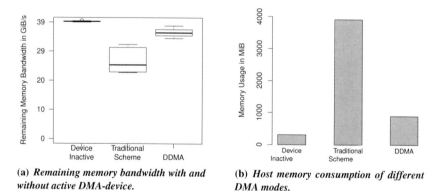

(a) *Remaining memory bandwidth with and without active DMA-device.*

(b) *Host memory consumption of different DMA modes.*

Figure 9. *Resource usage of different DMA modes.*

Figure 9(b) depicts the memory usage related to all three access patterns introduced in Figure 9(a). A CRORC operated with kernel buffers uses three times more main memory than with DDMA. The DDMA scheme still requires $\approx 700\,\mathrm{MiB}$ of main memory for storing management descriptors. The CRORC buffer sizes are flexible and can be chosen by the user. We have chosen buffer sizes which fit into host- and accelerator memory for a fair comparison.

5. Conclusion

Techniques like DMA buffer sharing and DDMA improve latencies, data rates, and reduce the overall resource usage. This also reduces costs if less memory bars are needed in each compute node. Both paradigms require a sophisticated memory management, which is not addressed by the most operating systems. For example, current operating systems are not able to manage accelerator memory at all, caused by the device-defined behavior of PCIe memory resources. It is therefore impossible to integrate such memory regions into the current memory management system of Linux even though they map into the same address space as usual main memory. In this paper we presented a generic operating system interface for allocating and managing such resources. The extensions for the PDA shown in this paper are a proposal for a standardized interface.

Furthermore, DDMA introduces some disadvantages which the hardware vendors need to resolve. It would be beneficial to be able to use the IOMMU with DDMA. Another issue is that the end-user cannot be sure whether all PCIe memory regions are visible for all other devices in the system. This is often not documented, relies on the CPU or mainboard, and requires manual testing before productive use. The reduction of data rates between devices if the communication involves the interconnect between CPU sockets is also an issue.

References

[1]   Matthias Bach, Jan de Cuveland, Heiko Ebermann, Dominic Eschweiler, Jochen Gerhard, Sebastian Kalcher, Matthias Kretz, Volker Lindenstruth, Hans-Jürgen Lüdde, Manfred Pollok, and David Rohr. A Comprehensive Approach for a Power Efficient General Purpose Supercomputer. In *Proc. of the 21th Euromicro International Conference on Parallel, Distributed and Network-Based Processing (PDP), Belfast, Northern Ireland*. IEEE Computer Society, 2 2013.

[2]   David Rohr, Sebastian Kalcher, Matthias Bach, Abdulqadir Alaqeeli, Hani Alzaid, Dominic Eschweiler, Volker Lindenstruth, Alkhereyf Sakhar, Ahmad Alharthi, Abdulelah Almubarak, Ibraheem Alqwaiz, and Riman Bin Suliman. An Energy-Efficient Multi-GPU Supercomputer. In *Proceedings of the 16th IEEE International Conference on High Performance Computing and Communications, HPCC 2014*. IEEE, IEEE, 8 2014.

[3]   Pierre   Boudier,   Graham   Sellers,   Benedikt   Kessler,   and   Ofer   Rosenberg. cl_amd_bus_addressable_memory.

[4]   NVIDIA. *Developing a Linux Kernel Module Using RDMA for GPUDirect*. NVIDIA Corporation, 2701 San Tomas Expressway Santa Clara, CA 95050, july 2012.

[5]   Davide Rossetti. Benchmarking GPUDirect RDMA on Modern Server Platforms, October 2014.

[6]   Gilad Shainer, Ali Ayoub, Pak Lui, Tong Liu, Michael Kagan, Christian Trott, Greg Scantlen, and Paul Crozier. The development of Mellanox/NVIDIA GPUDirect over InfiniBand –a new model for GPU to GPU communications. *Computer Science - Research and Development*, 26(3-4):267–273, 2011.

[7]   Sreeram Potluri, Khaled Hamidouche, Akshay Venkatesh, Devendar Bureddy, and Dhabaleswar Panda. Efficient Inter-node MPI Communication Using GPUDirect RDMA for InfiniBand Clusters with NVIDIA GPUs. In *42nd International Conference on Parallel Processing (ICPP)*, pages 80–89, October 2013.

[8]   Dominic Eschweiler and Volker Lindenstruth. The Portable Driver Architecture. In *Proceedings of the 16th Real-Time Linux Workshop*, Duesseldorf, Germany, October 2014. Open Source Automation Development Lab (OSADL).

[9]   Dominic Eschweiler and Volker Lindenstruth. Efficient Management of Large DMA Memory Buffers in Microdrivers. In *Proceedings of the 20th IEEE International Conference on Parallel and Distributed Systems, ICPADS 2014*. IEEE, IEEE, 12 2014.

[10] Mellanox. *RDMA Aware Networks Programming User Manual*. Mellanox Technologies, Mellanox Technologies, Ltd., Beit Mellanox, PO Box 586 Yokneam 20692, Israel, rev 1.6 edition, 2014.

Programming Models and Methods

Parallel Computing: On the Road to Exascale
G.R. Joubert et al. (Eds.)
IOS Press, 2016
doi:10.3233/978-1-61499-621-7-135

Portable Parallelization of the EDGE CFD Application for GPU-based Systems using the SkePU Skeleton Programming Library

Oskar SJÖSTRÖM [a], Soon-Heum KO [b], Usman DASTGEER [a], Lu LI [a] and
Christoph W. KESSLER [a,1]

[a] *Linköpings Universitet, 58183 Linköping, Sweden*
[b] *National Supercomputing Centre (NSC), 58183 Linköping, Sweden*

Abstract. EDGE is a complex application for computational fluid dynamics used
e.g. for aerodynamic simulations in avionics industry. In this work we present
the portable, high-level parallelization of EDGE for execution on multicore CPU
and GPU based systems by using the multi-backend skeleton programming library
SkePU. We first expose the challenges of applying portable high-level parallelization to a complex scientific application for a heterogeneous (GPU-based) system
using (SkePU) skeletons and discuss the encountered flexibility problems that usually do not show up in skeleton toy programs. We then identify and implement necessary improvements in SkePU to become applicable for applications containing
computations on complex data structures and with irregular data access. In particular, we improve the *MapArray* skeleton and provide a new *MultiVector* container
for operand data that can be used with unstructured grid data structures. Although
there is no SkePU skeleton specifically dedicated to handling computations on unstructured grids and its data structures, we still obtain portable speedup of EDGE
with both multicore CPU and GPU execution by using the improved MapArray
skeleton of SkePU.

Keywords. Computational Fluid Dynamics, EDGE, Unstructured Mesh, Skeleton
Programming, SkePU Library, GPU-Based System

Introduction

In this paper we report on the portable parallelization of parts of the inner, sequential solver core in the computational fluid dynamics (CFD) flow simulation application
EDGE using the SkePU skeleton programming library for GPU-based systems. At the
outer level, EDGE already supports MPI parallelism by domain decomposition. Our
work allows to leverage additional parallelism on top of the original EDGE MPI code for
a convenient and portable exploitation of heterogeneous node architectures. The (node-
level) sequential CFD flow solver in EDGE was selected as a challenging case study to
stress-test the applicability and performance of general-purpose skeleton programming
frameworks with a complex HPC application with a large code base and irregular data
access patterns. By profiling the sequential (node) EDGE code, we identified two core

---

[1] Corresponding Author. E-mail: firstname.lastname@liu.se

functions in the solver that dominate the overall performance of the application. These functions were ported from Fortran to C++ and then refactored using SkePU skeletons. We found that the SkePU version with code generated for OpenMP and CUDA gained in both cases up to 40% speedup over the sequential C++ code, even though the irregular data access pattern of the EDGE solver does not perfectly match the more general *MapArray* skeleton in SkePU. — It was expected already at the start of the project that modifications to SkePU might be necessary in order to be able to support the types of computations present in EDGE. A specific issue to be solved was the need to instantiate MapArray for more than 3 operands (resp., more than 1 read-only operand), which is due to a limitation in the current SkePU API design. This was finally solved by adding a new container type, *MultiVector*, to SkePU and extending MapArray to work with MultiVector operands. Other problems experienced during the evaluation was hitting the device memory limit for huge operands with very large test cases.

We first give a short introduction to SkePU and to the EDGE application. We summarize the process of profiling and porting to SkePU, introduce the new MultiVector container, and present experimental results. We also discuss related work and conclude with suggestions for future work. Further details can be found in [1].

1. SkePU

Skeleton programming is a high-level parallel programming approach where an application is written with the help of skeletons. A *skeleton* is a pre-defined, generic building block such as map, reduce, scan, farm, pipeline etc. that implements a common specific pattern of computation and data dependence, and that can be customized with (sequential) user-defined code parameters (*user functions*) to instantiate executable functions. Skeletons provide a high degree of abstraction and portability with a quasi-sequential programming interface, as their implementations encapsulate all low-level and platform-specific details such as parallelization, synchronization, communication, memory management, accelerator usage and other optimizations.

SkePU[2] [2] is an open-source skeleton programming framework for multicore CPUs and multi-GPU systems. It is a C++ template library with currently seven data-parallel skeletons (Map, Reduce, Scan, MapOverlap/Stencil, MapArray, ...) and one task-parallel skeleton (Farm). All SkePU skeletons have backends (implementation variants) for sequential C++, OpenMP, CUDA and OpenCL, and SkePU also supports execution on multiple GPUs both with CUDA and OpenCL. Portable user functions are specified with a macro language; from the macros, platform specific versions are generated. SkePU also supports auto-tunable selection of the expected fastest backend at skeleton calls, based on the current problem size and operand location [3].

SkePU provides currently two generic container types (`Vector`, `Matrix`) for passing operands to and from skeleton calls. These are *smart containers* in that they implement software caching of accessed elements and track valid copies of elements in various memory modules to automatically eliminate unnecessary data transfers at runtime [4].

SkePU skeletons are polymorphic in the operand container type. As an example, the *MapArray* skeleton of SkePU applies the user function elementwise to each element of one or two input vectors or matrices, and allows in each elemental computation to

---

[2]SkePU: http://www.ida.liu.se/labs/pelab/skepu

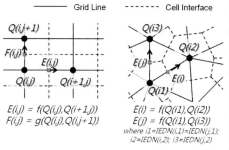

Figure 1. Vertex-centered finite volume description of structured (left) and unstructured (right) grid, along with the data format. Since indices of edges and connecting nodes are identical in the structured format, looping over edge counts for computing the flux (E and F) satisfy the contiguous access of the array of flow properties (Q) which is defined in the node. On the other hand, an extra array ($IEDN$) is needed to specify the connectivity between edges and nodes in unstructured data, and the stride (distance between two referential elements in the memory address) between connecting nodes is highly irregular.

read-only access any element(s) of a third vector or matrix operand. This dependence pattern is essential to be able to express many common computations, e.g. dense and sparse matrix-vector multiplication. Interestingly, MapArray is not supported in some other skeleton frameworks.

2. EDGE Application and Needs for Hybrid Programming

Computational Fluid Dynamics (CFD) numerically solves a system of governing equations to describe the fluid flow in space and time. CFD codes are classified as either structured or unstructured ones, depending on the tessellation of the geometry, which is the so-called *grid*. As illustrated in Figure 1, the structured grid discretizes the space into quadrilateral elements with contiguity, while the unstructured one consists of arbitraty polygons to represent the geometry. The capability of using any polygons makes the unstructured grid easier to model the complex geometry. On the other hand, the computation performance is worse on the unstructured code due to the less spatial locality of data, which leads to more fetching of referential dataset to the cache.

EDGE [3] is a CFD solver mainly developed by the Swedish Defense Research Agency (FOI). The code solves the Reynolds-averaged Navier-Stokes equations to simulate the complex flow field involving the shock and flow separation around aerial vehicles. In the numerical aspect, the EDGE code adopts a node-centered finite-volume technique to compute the unstructured domain. The flow solver is written in Fortran 95 and incorporates Message Passing Interface (MPI) parallelism. A domain partitioning technique is adopted to achieve data parallelism. The entire grid is split to the number of MPI ranks at the pre-processing step by the help of the METIS library.

We point out that this work intends to add the thread parallelism on top of the original EDGE MPI code for the smarter exploitation of modern and upcoming HPC architectures. As observed by OVERFLOW [5] and SP-MZ NAS benchmark [6] experiments, the hybrid MPI-OpenMP code is unable to outperform the pure MPI counterpart in a fair competition (i.e., MPI partitions are also perfectly load-balanced) at small CPU core counts. Nevertheless, we argue that the deployment of thread parallelism through SkePU framework contributes to achieving the better performance (1) by enabling the use of accelerator devices on the system, and (2) at massive core counts where the MPI code ceases to accelerate. Regarding the second argument, the computational gain by using

---

[3]EDGE documentation: http://www.foi.se/en/Customer–Partners/Projects/Edge1/

more MPI cores is finally cancelled out by the increased cost in collective operations above a certain MPI size. Hybrid MPI+OpenMP simulation at those core counts will be effective as a means of reducing the communication overhead.

3. Preparing EDGE for Use with SkePU

Profiling   The experimented test case is the unstructured domain covering the *wing-body* configuration which consists of 4 million nodes with 15.9 million edges to capture the complex flow field around this geometry. The serial run allocates 1.6 Gigabyte memory for this inviscid simulation.

As is demonstrated in [1], the two heaviest subroutines are *Artvis* and *Convflux* that take 29% and 19% of total simulation time, respectively. The latter computes the convective flux which is the product of the flow properties (density, velocity and temperature) in the middle of connecting nodes. The former adds the artificial diffusion from the flow gradient between connecting nodes to ensure the numerical stability. Since both functions contribute to computing the flux, they look almost the same in the code structure and the data access pattern. With regard to the number of calls to these two functions, the Convflux function is called substantially more often than the Artvis function. That leads to the expectation that the performance gain by thread parallelism will be higher for the more computationally-intensive Artvis function. As the two functions together account for 48% of total simulation time, Amdahl's Law yields an upper bound for overall speed-up of 1.92 (if all code in both functions could be accelerated infinitely).

Porting to C++   The porting of heavy subroutines (*Artvis* and *ConvFlux*) and associated kernels from Fortran to C++ was mandatory to make use of the C++ based SkePU framework. Ported functions are given a C interface in order to avoid the name mangling in C++ and to enable the call from Fortran caller routines. These functions are compiled separately and compiled with parental Fortran objects at linking stage. With regard to the performance, the C++ implementation of Artvis is about 30% slower than the Fortran implementation, while there is almost no slowdown or even slight speedup for the C++ Convflux calls. Overall, the C++ port of EDGE is about 20% slower. Frequent calls of intrinsic mathematical functions (*pow*, *sqrt*, *abs*) in Artvis lead to this overhead.

Need for SkePU Extensions   Extra change is necessary to apply data parallelism by SkePU skeletons on the EDGE code due to the characteristics of the unstructured data format. As we addressed, ported hot-spots loop over edges and they store resulting flux contributions in node-based arrays. This eventually leads to the race condition, as we can identify from the unstructured data description in Figure 1. Neighbouring edges (*i* and *j*) can often be assigned to different threads and they independently write the result in $i1^{th}$ element of the node-based array. As the use of critical section or locks to avoid this collision leads to the substantial overhead between threads, we separate this update operation from the computation loop and run it sequentially.

As most skeletons (Map, MapOverlap, Reduce, Scan) in SkePU are designed for the structured data format, we employ SkePU's very general MapArray skeleton, which uses the `ARRAY_FUNC` [1] construct for specifying the user function and generating its platform-specific variants:

```
#define ARRAY_FUNC( userfnname, rettype, fparam1, fparam2, calc )\
  struct userfnname { ... }
```

MapArray takes a single input array processed elementwise and another input array for random access, and returns an output array of the same datatype. However, use of this skeleton necessitates the packing of multiple flow property arrays, along with the connectivity map array (*IEDN* in Fig. 1) which is of different datatype, due to the constraint on the number of input arguments. This results in a substantial overhead for data packing.

An alternative to using MapArray is using the Map skeleton, after reordering and duplicating some data and breaking up the calculation in many lightweight Map calls with temporary containers [1]. Overhead associated with data processing and large amount of skeleton calls lead to very poor performance with this implementation. It gives us a clear motivation for adding new functionality within SkePU to handle unstructured datasets.

4. Extending MapArray in SkePU

The goal in modifying SkePU was to create a variant of the MapArray skeleton that allows for an arbitrary number of read-only inputs. This allows the parts of the EDGE flow solver that we consider for parallelization to be implemented with a single skeleton call per function, causing minimal call overhead.

Different ways of solving the issues were considered (see [1] for details). The most elegant solution would be to allow for a parameter with a dynamic size. This could be implemented as list of lists or with variadic templates. The main issue with these types of constructs is that they are not compatible with CUDA. It is possible to pass a class object such as an STL vector to a device function, but it is not possible to use its member functions, unless those member functions are also declared as device functions which would break the portability of the code. C++11 features such as variadic templates that could elegantly solve the problem are also not currently supported by CUDA. As one of the main features of SkePU is to have code that is highly portable and works across different platforms, it was desirable to have a solution that maintains this.

Another way to approach the problem is to attempt to pack the input data into a single vector. This vector could then be passed into the existing MapArray implementation. Unfortunately this causes high overhead. If the entire application was made from scratch, the data structures could be adapted to suit SkePU. However, since we are only modifying a small portion of a large existing application, it is not feasible to alter the data structures used by the rest of the program. This would mean that the data needs to be packed each time before a SkePU skeleton is used, creating overhead that grows in proportion to the problem size.

Ultimately the decision was made between two different types of implementations. One option was to set a cap to the amount of inputs that the skeleton would be able to handle. An implementation with a set number of inputs would be made where each individual input would be handled the same way as a single input was in the previous implementations. The user would then fill any extraneous inputs with dummy data that would be ignored by SkePU. There are two main drawbacks to this approach: (1) A maximum number of accepted inputs would have to be set rather than allowing an arbitrary number of inputs, and (2) it would potentially create very messy user code.

The second option was to use a struct encapsulating arrays of an arbitrary size. The individual elements of this struct can then be accessed inside a device function. The main drawback of this approach is that the user has to access data directly rather than via an accessor method and the implementation is not as easily integrated into the existing SkePU framework. The latter approach was chosen in order to have an implementation supporting any number of inputs. Implementation details are described in the following.

MultiVector   The new implementation of MapArray was designed with the goal to allow an arbitrary number of read-only inputs. To make this possible a new data structure needed to be added. The purpose of this data structure (henceforth referred to as MultiVector) is to encapsulate all the input vectors that are required by the user function. For compatibility with CUDA the MultiVector was implemented as a basic struct. This allows it to be passed as an input when invoking a CUDA device function and the struct members can be accessed from within such a device function.

A MultiVector consists of two structs: one struct to hold arrays of input data, and a second one to hold pointers to such arrays. Both structs consist of three members: two array pointers to store the location of the input data on the host and on the device, and one scalar value containing the size of the arrays. The interface to the structure consists of a number of member functions that can be used on the host side when creating the MultiVector structure. Inside the user function, an interface like this is not possible while keeping compatibility with CUDA. Instead, the user needs to access each data element directly inside the struct. A nice feature of this kind of implementation is that it can encapsulate data of any type without restrictions. The example below shows how user code would use the MultiVector, in the main code:

```
int *input1 = {2,3,8,4};    double *input2 = {1.3,5.2};
MultiVector C;
C.allocData( 2 );
C.addData( 0, 4*sizeof(int), input1 );
C.addData( 1, 2*sizeof(double), input2 );
```

and within a user function (using the *subvector* construct to address subvectors):

```
int *input1 = subvector( C, 0, int * );    // {2,3,8,4}
double *input2 = subvector( C, 1, double * );    // {1.3,5.2}
return input2[0] + input1[2];    // 1.3 + 8
```

When calling the CUDA backend of the extended MapArray skeleton, a deep copy of the multi-vector structure is performed to transfer all the input parameters to the GPU. The GPU addresses are stored in the device portion of the multi-vector which is then used inside the user function. This is followed by a call to the MapArray kernel where the multi-vector is passed as an input to each invocation of the user function. When calling a backend that does not make use of the GPU, the pointer to the device portion of the multi-vector is set to the value of the host pointer. This allows the code within the user function to run on any backend without modification. The template parameters used by MapArray have also been modified to allow for the input and output parameters to be of different types. The full source code of the MultiVector implementation and the revised MapArray implementation is available in [1] and integrated in SkePU v1.2.

5. Results and Discussion

We measured the speed-ups for overall execution and for the individual SkePU-ported parts of the EDGE implementation on a Linux x86 server with two Xeon processors (16

Table 1. Data transfer times. The second and third rightmost columns show the shares of the total execution time of EDGE. "DTP" refers to the data transfer time divided by the parallel part's execution time.

Test case	Size	Multigrid	Host-to-Device (s)	Device-to-Host (s)	Data transfer	Ported section	DTP
Static mixer	2786	ON (4)	0.311	0.229	2.35%	49.90%	30.84%
		OFF	0.064	0.048	2.80%	85.85%	53.06%
RAE 2822 airfoil	22088	ON (4)	1.908	1.004	3.55%	45.12%	27.88%
		OFF	0.229	0.124	7.06%	53.98%	33.36%
Heating coil	29826	ON (4)	3.014	2.53	5.23%	43.35%	26.79%
		OFF	0.698	0.57	7.93%	65.11%	40.24%
yf17	97104	ON (4)	13.764	12.481	8.36%	40.15%	24.81%
		OFF	0.23	0.124	0.77%	61.53%	38.03%
DPW4 wing-body	4074967	ON (3)	18.882	17.824	11.06%	47.29%	29.23%
		OFF	9.13	8.588	11.66%	55.81%	34.49%

cores) and an NVIDIA Fermi GPU. We also collected the cost for offloading (data transfer time between host and device memories) to better evaluate the benefits and drawbacks of GPU-assisted execution. We experimented over five different geometric configurations (*grid*), whose sizes range from O(1K) to O(1M) nodal points, as listed in Table 1. We point out that O(1M) is a hard limit on the available problem size due to the limit on GPU device memory.

Data transfer   Table 1 shows costs for offloading and execution of the SkePU-ported section. One CPU core is utilized for computation on the host and the offloading cost to the GPU device is collected through the NVIDIA-distributed profiler. SkePU-ported hot-spots (2nd column from the right) consist of the parallel section which updates flux components in edges, and the sequential section where SkePU schedules execution and converts the edge-based solution into the node-based global array. They spend 54—65% of total EDGE simulation runtime except a very small test case of static mixer for default simulations and this relative cost reduces to 40—50% by applying multigrid technique. It is because of the extra computation for restriction/prolongation between different levels of grids in the multigrid technique, which are non-ported subroutines.

The cost for offloading (3rd column from the right) increases substantially as the problem size increases, and it is independent of the direction of data flow. Looking at the ratio between data transfer time and parallel execution time (the rightmost column), it takes 25—40 % of the runtime on the device. One common technique for circumventing such an overhead in CUDA is to overlap data transfer with computations by use of streams [7]. However, this approach is not feasible in our case because each hot-spot consists of one loop operation where all input variables are simultaneously accessed. An idea to mitigate the offloading overhead with the help of SkePU would be to integrate the MultiVector structure introduced in this paper with the existing smart containers [4]. This would reduce the cost for offloading by skipping transfer of data that are not updated between device accesses. Such an implementation is left for future work.

Absolute and Relative Speedup   Figure 2 shows execution times at different implementations with different hardware usage. To start from the comparison between the baseline C++ code and the SkePU implementation running at one CPU core, we see the significant overhead in SkePU version. It is even larger than previous SkePU applications which

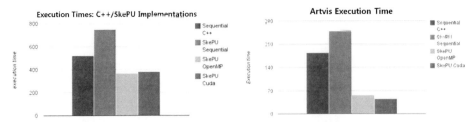

Figure 2. Execution times of overall EDGE (left) and the Artvis calls (right) using the Wing-body test case.

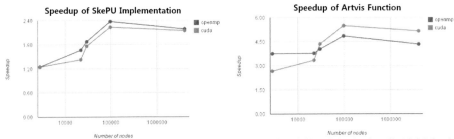

Figure 3. Relative speedups over the single-threaded SkePU version (left) and the Artvis calls (right) for the considered test cases without multigrid technique.

solved the structured dataset. We identified that multiple sources synthetically worsen the performance of the SkePU implementation in unstructured data. Apart from the cost for creating the multi-vector structure, each MapArray skeleton shows the worse performance than the baseline code because it does not perfectly match the memory access and computation pattern, and results in more data transfer than actually accessed by the user function invocations. Additionally, the necessity of separating the flux update operation from main computation body and operating it sequentially (remarked in Section 4) leads to a decrease in the temporal locality of the array.

Despite the performance degradation at a serial run, the SkePU implementation can achieve the performance gain by the better exploitation of hardware without explicit change on the code. We gain 1.35—1.40 times speedup in comparison to the baseline code by enabling the OpenMP or the CUDA backend. The speedup by thread parallelism is mainly contributed by the significant speedup in Artvis subroutine.

Comparisons of the performance of the SkePUized version for calls to Artvis and for entire porting, using OpenMP and CUDA backends, can be seen in Figure 3. Looking at these graphs, we find the general trend of improved speedup as the problem size increases. For the Artvis calls, we reach roughly 5 times speedup in wing-body simulation (the biggest case) using CUDA. According to our measurement in the wing-body case using Amdahl's Law [1], the parallelized part of ported code is 61.8% and the speedup bound is 2.61. The parallelized fraction in Artvis subroutine is 82.8%, thus the ideal speedup is 5.8. We affirm that the speedup of 5 in Artvis function is rather reasonable.

The scaling of the SkePU code with OpenMP backend with the available number of cores can be seen in Figure 4 (left). Also, the difference in the speedup depending on multigrid technique is presented in Figure 4 (right). We find a little more than two times speedup by fully exploiting 16 cores in our testbed, which is natural if we remind the speedup limit is 2.61. Regarding multigrid, we see more speedup without this technique due to prescribed reason (extra computation in non-ported part). This difference in

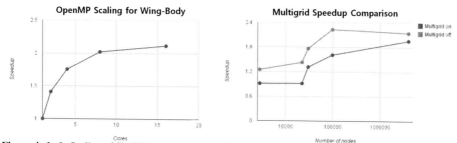

Figure 4. Left: Scaling of SkePU implementation using the OpenMP backend. Multigrid disabled. — Right: Relative speedups (with OpenMP backend) over the single-threaded SkePU execution, without vs. with multigrid for considered test cases.

speedup does however decrease as the problem size grows, which is due to the coarser grids becoming larger where the disparity in speedups between problem sizes becomes smaller.

6. Related Work

Specific multithreaded CPU or GPU solutions for handling unstructured mesh computations and indirect addressing can apply customized techniques for optimizing computation structure, communication and memory accesses and are not constrained by a limited set of predefined computation and dependence patterns provided by general-purpose high-level programming constructs such as the SkePU skeletons, but require generally more implementation effort.

Ferenbaugh [8] presents a GPU version of an unstructured mesh kernel in CUDA. To minimize the cost of data movement between the CPU and GPU, the data movement is overlapped with computations by streaming. Such an optimiziation could also be considered for future work on EDGE. To overcome data locality issues, three different strategies are investigated in [8]: (a) Reordering of data on the CPU and moving it to the GPU, (b) moving data to the GPU and then reordering it, and (c) moving data to the GPU and relying on hardware caches to enhance performance.

A different GPU solution is presented by Waltz [9], where an unstructured mesh compressible flow solver is deployed on a GPU. To improve its performance the calculations are refactored to minimize the number of memory accesses and increase the number of floating point operations.

7. Conclusions and Future Work

The two subroutines that use the largest portion of the EDGE application's total execution time have been ported from Fortran to C++. These functions were then parallelized in a portable, high-level form with the help of SkePU.

This work spotted some of the potential weaknesses of the current SkePU framework. One of them is the lacking flexibility of the macros used to define the user functions of SkePU. In order to overcome the limit in the number of read-only operands in the SkePU API, a modification of the MapArray skeleton was required, leading to a general solution with a new container type called MultiVector.

In spite of MapArray not being a perfect fit, we still achieved an absolute speedup of the portable high-level code over C++ of up to 40%.

The main drawback of skeleton programming is that many computations in applications and algorithms do not fit well into the available set of skeletons. In SkePU there is also a problem with the flexibility of many of the skeleton implementations due to the portability requirements. During the work described here, both of these issues became apparent as several attempted solutions proved to not be feasible. Algorithmic skeletons rely on the regularity and structure that regular programs such as dense linear system solvers often have. When working on an unstructured grid, as is the case with EDGE, it becomes harder to find efficient ways to map computations to available skeletons.

Despite these issues, there is a substantial gain in execution time achieved by the SkePU implementations, and as the library is further developed these types of applications can be a viable target for parallelization with SkePU.

Future work on the SkePU port of EDGE will include tests on multi-GPU systems and applying autotuned backend selection (for performance and energy optimization) for the SkePU port. Also, further general improvements to SkePU could help here, such as support in MapArray for very large operands that exceed device memory size. It might even be worthwile to define specific container types in SkePU to represent unstructured grids, and skeletons operating on these. Another area for future research would be to parallelize other applications working on the unstructured grid model with the help of the MultiVector.

Acknowledgments   We thank SNIC for providing access to HPC resources. This work was partly funded by EU FP7 EXCESS and by SeRC (www.e-science.se). We thank Peter Eliasson, Dmitry Khabi and Vi Tran for commenting on an earlier version of this work. The second author would like to acknowledge the financial support from SAAB for the performance analysis of the EDGE code and the associated advice from Per Weinerfelt at SAAB and Peter Eliasson at FOI.

References

[1]   O. Sjöström. Parallelizing the EDGE application for GPU-based systems using the SkePU skeleton programming library. Master thesis LIU-IDA/LITH-EX-A-15/001-SE, Linköping University, Feb. 2015.

[2]   J. Enmyren and C. Kessler. SkePU: A multi-backend skeleton programming library for multi-GPU systems. In *Proc. 4th Int. Workshop on High-Level Parallel Programming and Applications (HLPP-2010), Baltimore, Maryland, USA*. ACM, Sep. 2010.

[3]   U. Dastgeer, L. Li, and C. Kessler. Adaptive implementation selection in a skeleton programming library. In *Proc. Adv. Par. Processing Techn. Conf. (APPT)*, LNCS vol. 8299, pp. 170–183. Springer, Aug. 2013.

[4]   U. Dastgeer and C. Kessler. Smart containers and skeleton programming for GPU-based systems. *International Journal of Parallel Programming*, 2015. DOI: 10.1007/s10766-015-0357-6.

[5]   H. Jin, D. Jespersen, P. Mehrotra, R. Biswas, and L. Huang. High performance computing using MPI and OpenMP on multi-core parallel systems. *Parallel Computing*, pages 562–575, 2011.

[6]   E. Ayguade, M. Gonzalez, X. Martorell, and G. Jost. Employing nested OpenMP for the parallelization of multi-zone computational fluid dynamics applications. *J. Par. and Distr. Comput.*, pp. 686–697, 2006.

[7]   M. Harris: How to Overlap Data Transfers in CUDA C/C++. Nvidia, devblogs.nvidia.com/parallelforall/how-overlap-data-transfers-cuda-cc, Dec. 2012 (acc. Feb. 2015).

[8]   C. Ferenbaugh. A comparison of GPU strategies for unstructured mesh physics. *Concurrency and Computation: Practice and Experience*, 25:1547–1558, 2012.

[9]   J. Waltz. Performance of a three-dimensional unstructured mesh compressible flow solver on NVIDIA Fermi-class graphics processing unit hardware. *Int. J. f. numer. methods in fluids*, 72:259–268, Oct. 2012.

Parallel Computing: On the Road to Exascale
G.R. Joubert et al. (Eds.)
IOS Press, 2016
doi:10.3233/978-1-61499-621-7-145

Structured parallel implementation of Tree Echo State Network model selection

Marco DANELUTTO, Claudio GALLICCHIO, Alessio MICHELI,
Massimo TORQUATI and Daniele VIRGILIO

Dept. Computer Science Univ. of Pisa

Abstract. In this work we discuss the parallelization of the model selection process for Tree Echo State Networks. We consider two different "structured" parallelization strategies: one based on functional replication of the computations needed to evaluate the different steps in the model selection process, and the other one exposing and exploiting the dependency graph in the aggregate selection process computations. Both parallelizations have been implemented using FastFlow. Experimental results on state-of-the-art multicore architectures are discussed in detail that demonstrate the feasibility and the efficiency of the parallelizations.

Keywords. algorithmic skeletons, macro-dataflow, FastFlow, tree echo state network, reservoir computing

1. Introduction

Structured parallel programming models have been developed to support the design and implementation of parallel applications. These programming models provide the parallel application programmers with a set of pre-defined, ready to use parallel pattern abstractions that may be directly instantiated, alone or in composition, to model the whole parallel behaviour of the application at hand. This raises the level of abstraction for the parallel application programmers. While the application programmer is developing the application, he/she must not take care of the architectural and parallel exploitation issues. These issues are dealt efficiently using the state-of-art techniques by the framework programmers. Algorithmic skeletons, developed since early '90s in the field of High Performance Computing (HPC) [1] led to the development of several structured parallel programming frameworks including Muesli [2], SKEPU [3] and FastFlow [4]. In the meanwhile, the software engineering community further developed the design pattern concept [5] into the *parallel design pattern* concept [6]. Although not directly providing the programmer with ready-to-use programming abstractions (e.g. library calls, objects, high order functions) modelling the parallel design patterns, this approach enforced the idea that parallelism has to be expressed through composition of well known, efficient and parametric parallelism exploitation patterns rather than through *ad-hoc* composition of lower level mechanisms. The advantages deriving from structured parallel programming approaches have been clearly identified as a viable solution to the development of efficient parallel application is the well known Berkeley report [7].

The challenge of developing learning models able to directly deal with complex data structures has gained an increasing interest in the machine learning research area. Indeed, while traditional machine learning techniques are naturally suitable for dealing with flat input domains, the emerging necessity to perform learning on input data naturally representable by means of sequences, trees or graphs led to the development of many research approaches for structured domains. For the case of sequence processing, in the neuro-computing area the class of *recurrent* neural networks [8] is considered widely useful since it can be used to approach an heterogeneity of problems in application domains like signal processing, time-series forecasting, speech recognition, computer vision, natural language processing and bioinformatics. However, training of recurrent neural networks typically involves some known drawbacks, among which one of the most relevant is related to the high computational training costs (though already in general inferior to those required by other machine learning approaches e.g. involving support vector machines with kernels, hidden Markov models or inductive logic programming). Within the class of recurrent neural networks, the *reservoir computing* (RC) paradigm has recently been proposed. Based on fixed contractive settings of the state dynamics, RC networks are able to discriminate among samples in the input structured sequential domain even without an intensive learning process [9]. One of the most representative neural network models developed according to the RC paradigm is the *echo state network* (ESN) [10]. In the ESN model, the dynamical reservoir component is characterized by an high number of randomly connected artificial neurons (units) and it is able to create an high dimensional echo state response to the provided input. Such state can then be used to produce the desired output via a simple linear regression tool. More recently, a generalization of the ESN model, called *tree echo state network* (TreeESN) [11], has been proposed in order to directly deal with tree structured input data with the desirable efficient learning characterization of the RC approach. The TreeESN model has found successful applications in interdisciplinary fields such as for instance XML Document Processing, Cheminformatics and Bioinformatics structured data analysis [11].

In this paper we take into consideration the parallelization of the learning procedure for TreeESNs, and in particular we focus on the model selection process. When creating a new predictive task, this is the most computationally expensive phase. Reducing its completion time helps to analyse more extensively the different neural network instances in the model selection process. Furthermore, it can help to respect a temporal strict deadline if a specific quality of service should be guaranteed. The problem of the parallelization is faced by using the *algorithmic skeletons*.

Two different parallel solutions addressing the described problem has been developed using FastFlow [4,12]. FastFlow is a C++ skeleton framework that grants both programmability and efficiency. The parallel patterns are built on top of an efficient communication mechanisms that provides lock-free and memory fence free synchronization mechanisms. The library targets cache coherent shared memory multicore architectures. The programmability of the framework derives from the number of different parallel patterns implemented–and provided as primitive objects to the application programmers–mainly exploiting stream parallelism. Furthermore, the possibility to use the efficient lower level mechanisms makes possible to build from scratch a missing parallel pattern as well as to adapt/tune the already existing ones. The presented parallelization methods can be utilized also for ESNs (as a specific case of TreeESNs) and, with some refinements, also for all the reservoir neural networks.

2. Tree Echo State Network model

The TreeESN [11] is a neural network model designed to deal with tree input structured domain exhibiting an efficient training with respect to the class of recursive neural networks. The TreeESN is able to build a predictive model employing a dataset composed by $k-$ary trees. In a $k-$ary tree, a set of nodes are arranged in a hierarchical way composing a tree structure with a fixed arity. A label is associated to each tree node, specifying the values of the properties that characterize the information available at that node. The TreeESN training phase aims at finding an hypothesis fitting the target values of the tree samples contained in the dataset.

The TreeESN is composed by three fundamental components: the input layer, the reservoir and the readout. The input layer simply feeds the reservoir network with the node labels information. The reservoir network is a recurrent neural network that computes a state for each tree node. The reservoir is composed by an high number of sparsely and randomly connected artificial neurons. The reservoir and the input layer constitute the TreeESN encoding network. The readout component is fed by the state information coming from the reservoir network. Once trained, it is able to produce the output value of the TreeESN model.

The strength of the TreeESN model is the efficiency in the training phase, since only the readout component needs to be trained. Indeed, the encoding network is typically initialized according to conditions ensuring contractivity of the state dynamics, and then is left untrained. The readout component is usually implemented as a standard linear regression tool, and it is trained using efficient linear methods, e.g. least mean squares by pseudo-inverse or ridge regression. A trained TreeESN is able to map an input tree into a non structured (vectorial) output. In the TreeESN model, the prediction phase, i.e. the whole process of output computation, is implemented by applying the following three sequential steps:

1. The input tree is recursively encoded by reservoir component in an encoded tree, with the same topology of the input one. In particular, the reservoir encodes each node of the input tree by using the label associated to that node and the states already computed for its children.
2. The encoded tree is mapped into a single vector using a state mapping function, in order to represent it in a compact way. Usually, a function that selects the state of the root node is used.
3. After the application of the state mapping function, the output can be computed by the readout for non structured data, as explained above.

Further information on the TreeESN model, including details on the initialization condition, the properties of the state dynamics and the training process can be found in [11].

3. The model selection

3.1. The Problem

In the model selection process, which is part of the validation process, several neural networks instances are analyzed to select the best performing one. The networks instances are provided by specifying the values of some tunable parameters called *hyper-parameters*. Different hyper-parameters describe different aspects either of the neural network or of the learning process. They are selected within a limited number of user defined values. All the possible combinations of the hyper-parameters are evaluated in the model selection process.

In order to perform the model selection, the dataset is partitioned in two different sets: the training and the validation set. The neural network model, characterized by the hyper-parametrization values needed to be examined, is trained on the training set. After the training process, the accuracy achieved by the trained model is evaluated on the validation set. The learning model with the best accuracy on the validation set is then chosen by the model selection process.

3.2. The parallel implementations

The basic assumption of the parallel implementations we introduce in this work is the "streamization" of the model selection process basing on the hyper-parameters values. However, different parallel techniques can be applied at finest grain parallelizing each one of the steps involved in the neural network setup, training and evaluation. The efficient parallelization of each phase requires a non-trivial effort even as the parallel solution should take into account the numerical errors introduced by the parallel computation. The proposed solutions aim at emphasizing the programmability easiness by using the algorithmic skeleton methodology. They support the production of efficient multi-core implementation for the model selection task by reusing the sequential code of the TreeESN implementation. Furthermore, the presented solutions produce an implementation flexible enough to support experiments with different types of algorithms in the reservoir computing fields without requiring to reimplement in parallel each new component/algorithm.

Two different versions of the model selection process have been developed using the FastFlow framework. In both the cases, it has been decided to use a streaming parallelization exploiting the sequential code already available. Both versions use a highly optimized implementation of the BLAS/LAPACK libraries: the Intel MKL library. The first naive solution is based on the well known task farm parallel pattern [13]. In this implementation, realized as a master-worker (Fig. 1a), the tasks dispatched by the farm emitter (Master in the figure) are the hyper-parameters values describing a characterization of the TreeESN instances. Once the tasks have been received by the workers, the sequential computation is executed by building from scratch a new TreeESN model. The fundamental steps executed by the workers are: the initialization of the reservoir input neurons, the state computation for both the training and the validation set, the learning phase and, finally, the performance estimation achieved by the predictive learning model.

The second implementation is based on a macro-dataflow pattern [14,15]. This solution has been derived by the data dependencies emerging from the learning procedure for a single TreeESN instance hyper-parametrization. Furthermore, some objects (see Fig. 2 and corresponding description in the text below) created by evaluating a network characterization (i.e. neural network components and computed states) can be re-utilized

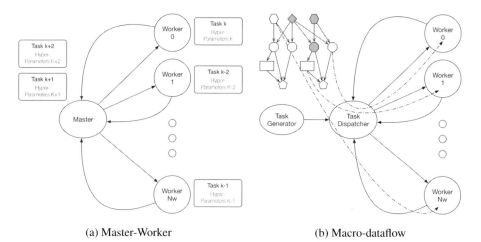

(a) Master-Worker   (b) Macro-dataflow

Figure 1. The figures show the architectures of the two parallel pattern implementations in FastFlow. The circles represent the entities involved in the computations. The workers are delegated to compute the serial part of the computation. The master and dispatcher distribute to the workers the tasks to be computed through communication channels (identified by the arrows between nodes). In the master-worker, the sent tasks are the neural network hyper-parameters, while for the macro-dataflow implementation they are the fireable dataflow tasks associated with the different hyper-parametrization values.

as long as they share the same subset of hyper-parameters. Since these objects are reused in a read-only way, there are no coherence issues. Fig. 2 shows how the previously described learning and testing processes can be modelled using a data-flow graph. As shown, the initialization of the input layer and the reservoir are necessary to compute the states of the tree samples. These states are computed independently for the training and the validation set. As soon as the computation of the training set state is completed, the readout component can be trained. In order to evaluate the accuracy of trained TreeESN model the state computations and the readout training operations must be ended.

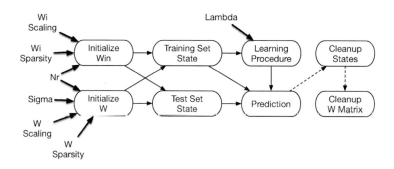

Figure 2. The learning and testing dataflow for a TreeESN model

In the macro-dataflow implementation, the shared data are: the input layer, the reservoir network (as neural network components) and the sample states (both for the training and the validation set samples). The result of a macro-dataflow instruction can be shared across different TreeESN instances only when that task depends entirely on the same subset of the hyper-parameters values. For instance, the states computed on one training set does not change holding the same hyper-parameters values. Therefore, the TreeESN instances sharing the same hyper-parameters values for the encoding network can reuse the already computed data in order to avoid multiple useless computations.

Fig. 1b shows the implementation of the macro-dataflow in FastFlow. In the developed parallelization, the task generator produces the tasks building the dataflow graph for all the hyper-parameters to be examined. A task is created specifying the sequential function to be executed and, when it is possible, exploiting the proper data dependencies. In the Fig. 2, the cleanup tasks are not based truly on a data dependency but instead they are based on task dependencies. They are called when an object is no more useful for the global computation and it can be deallocated from the memory. The task dispatcher module receives all the generated tasks and manages their executions on the workers preserving the explicit data/task dependencies. The task scheduling policy has been set to prioritize least recently generated task in order to make significant the generation task order. The tasks have been generated to guarantee the locality of the overall computation.

3.3. General applicability

Our parallelization methods can also be applied to other machine learning models. Since the model selection is based on the evaluation of all the combinations of the hyper-parameters, the farm parallelization can be applied independently of the adopted machine learning model. The macro-dataflow parallelization, instead, has a more limited applicability. Firstly, the used dataflow schema can be directly applied also to the ESN model, since it can be considered as a particular case of TreeESN. However, it can be used for all the reservoir based neural networks making simple changes in the data dependencies description (dataflow) of the learning procedure. In general, the parts that need to be modified are related to the reservoir initialization and the cleanup procedures.

Finally, the proposed parallel implementations may be also used to produce an ensemble [16] of TreeESNs. Such ensemble can be built using TreeESN models with different random reservoir initialization. Machine learning theory provides a ground to explain the advantage of this approach for the improvement of the resulting accuracy of prediction [16].

4. Experimental validation

We present experimental results on the two parallel implementations concerning the model selection procedure on the TreeESN. The experiments have been run on a Intel Sandy Bridge and on an Intel PHI processors. In particular, all the versions have been evaluated in terms of the exhibited performance (i.e. completion time and scalability) on an dual processor *Intel Xeon E5-2650* (2×8 core, two way hyperthreading) architecture. The tests have been executed on an dataset composed by 893 tree samples that have been partitioned in a training and a validation set. The partition ratios associated to each set are respectively of 2/3 and 1/3. In the dataset every tree has 5 labels per node and an arity degree equal to 2. The trees are characterized by having a maximum height equal to 4 and an average nodes number of 8.406. The hyper-parameters values used for the model selection are shown in Tab. 1.

Name	Values	Description
Trials	{0, 1, 2, 3, 4}	The number of random initializations for each network instance to be independent from statistical fluctuations.
Nr	{100, 250, 500, 750}	The number of the reservoir recurrent neurons.
Sigma	{0.1, 0.4, 0.7, 1, 3, 6, 9}	The contractivity factor associated to the reservoir network.
W_scaling	{0.01, 0.1, 1}	The scaling factor associated to the connection among neurons in the reservoir network.
W_connectivity	{0.05, 0.1, 0.2}	The connectivity ratio among the neurons in the reservoir network.
Win_scaling	{0.01, 0.1, 1}	The scaling factor associated to the connection between input and reservoir neurons.
Win_connectivity	{1}	The connectivity ratio between the input node label and the reservoir neurons.
Lambda	{0.05, 0.1, 0.15, 0.2, 0.25}	The regularization factor used for *Ridge regression* learning method [17].

Table 1. The TreeESN hyper-parameters values used for testing the completion time and the scalability.

In order to evaluate the computational grain, a profiling of the completion time between the training and the testing phase on a single hyper-parametrization has been performed. Taking in account the best hyper-parametrization selected by the model selection carried on the examined dataset, the time spent in the training and test phase is respectively 15.542 and 7.102 seconds.

Fig. 3 and Fig. 4 show the completion time and the scalability exhibited respectively by the farm and the macro-dataflow parallel implementation w.r.t. their parallelism degree. The completion time of the macro-dataflow parallel version outperforms the farm version. It must be noticed that in the master-worker implementation the different phases involved in the building of a TreeESN model are computed every time from scratch. While in the macro-dataflow implementation, the data are reused when the same intermediate data are shared among different TreeESN hyper-parametrizations. However, both versions obtain a good scalability limited by the number of physical cores. The intensive usage of double precision operations limits the obtained scalability values, since the execution unit is unable to sustain the floating point operation load. The scalability results are further reduced by heavy vectorization optimizations introduced by the compiler and the MKL library on the TreeESN sequential code.

Since the performance of the macro-dataflow parallelization has been demonstrated to be very good both in terms of completion time and scalability, a further test on a different architecture has been performed only for this version. The platform considered is an Intel Xeon PHI 5100 coprocessor with 60 4-way multithreading cores. The obtained results (Fig. 5) show a behaviour similar to the one observed onto the Intel Xeon Sandy Bridge architecture, scaling up to 64 multithreading contexts.

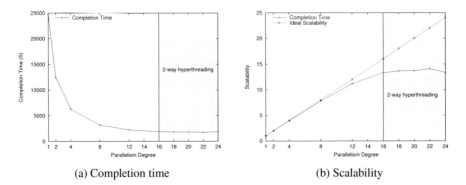

(a) Completion time   (b) Scalability

Figure 3. Analysis of the master-worker parallelization on an Intel Xeon Sandy Bridge 2x8cores, 2-way hyperthreading.

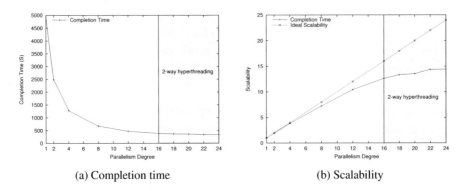

(a) Completion time   (b) Scalability

Figure 4. Analysis of the macro-dataflow parallelization on an Intel Xeon Sandy Bridge 2x8cores, 2-way hyperthreading.

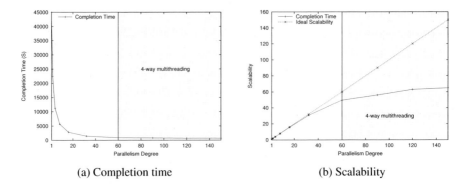

(a) Completion time   (b) Scalability

Figure 5. Analysis of the macro-dataflow parallelization on the Intel PHI 5100

Eventually, the memory consumption has been evaluated in order to understand if a trade-off between performance and memory usage exists. The occupancy of memory in the farm implementation is limited by the number of the workers involved in the computation. Each worker allocates the whole data structure needed for the training of a

TreeESN model. Conversely, the macro-dataflow implementation does not have a clear memory upper bound. Some experimental results has shown that the memory usage is comparable with the one used in the farm implementation. This is due mainly to the data locality exploited by the task dispatcher module that limits the usage of the memory.

5. Related Work

At the best of knowledge, a few works in literature deal with model selection paralleliza-tion methods. A couple of works [18,19] analyse respectively the model selection and the cross-validation process for the support vector machine (SVM) using the efficient train-ing SMO algorithms. The work in [18] faces the problem for the GP-GPU architecture, while the work in [19] approaches the same problem for a multicore cluster architecture. Both the works based their increased performance on the sharing of the kernel matrix across multiple hyper-parametrization and exploiting the underlying system architecture efficiently. In our work, we follow the same principle trying to reuse, as much as pos-sible, the neural network components and states among different hyper-parameters. The number of shared objects is bigger compared to the one in the SVM method. The sharing of the objects has been managed using a dataflow graph describing the data dependencies and using the macro-dataflow parallel pattern to schedule the tasks among the workers.

6. Conclusion and future work

In this paper, two different parallel implementations for the model selection process of the TreeESN networks have been presented. They exploit respectively the farm and a macro-dataflow parallelization patterns. Both of them achieve a good scalability lim-ited by the execution unit unable to maintain the double precision operations load. The TreeESN model selection code expresses a set of data dependencies (across different hyper-parametrizations). Usually, they cannot be exploited by the skeleton framework, conversely FastFlow offers to the programmers a macro dataflow parallel pattern that can be used to take advantage of the dependencies exploiting when it is possible the already computed data. The benefits arising from the usage of the macro-dataflow parallel pat-tern are reflected in a smaller time completion and in a better speed-up compared to the master-worker parallel implementation. Finally, the presented parallelization techniques can be applied also to other machine learning models. We are considering the possibil-ity to analyse a hybrid solution exploiting our parallel implementations to target "clus-ter of multicores" architectures. Furthermore, we will possibly consider other machine learning models for parallelization.

Acknowledgments

This work has been partially supported by EU FP7-ICT-2013-10 project REPARA (No. 609666) "Reengineering and Enabling Performance And poweR of Applications" and EU H2020-ICT-2014-1 project RePhrase (No. 644235) "REfactoring Parallel Heteroge-neous Resource-Aware Applications - a Software Engineering Approach".

References

[1] M. Cole. Bringing skeletons out of the closet: A pragmatic manifesto for skeletal parallel programming. *Parallel Comput.*, 30(3):389–406, March 2004.

[2] Steffen Ernsting and Herbert Kuchen. Algorithmic skeletons for multi-core, multi-gpu systems and clusters. *Int. J. High Perform. Comput. Netw.*, 7(2):129–138, April 2012.

[3] Johan Enmyren and Christoph W. Kessler. Skepu: A multi-backend skeleton programming library for multi-gpu systems. In *Proceedings of the Fourth International Workshop on High-level Parallel Programming and Applications*, HLPP '10, pages 5–14, New York, NY, USA, 2010. ACM.

[4] Marco Danelutto and Massimo Torquati. Structured parallel programming with core fastflow. In Viktria Zsk, Zoltn Horvth, and Lehel Csat, editors, *Central European Functional Programming School*, volume 8606 of *Lecture Notes in Computer Science*, pages 29–75. Springer International Publishing, 2015.

[5] Erich Gamma, Richard Helm, Ralph Johnson, and John Vlissides. *Design Patterns: Elements of Reusable Object-oriented Software*. Addison-Wesley Longman Publishing Co., Inc., Boston, MA, USA, 1995.

[6] Timothy Mattson, Beverly Sanders, and Berna Massingill. *Patterns for Parallel Programming*. Addison-Wesley Professional, first edition, 2004.

[7] Krste Asanovic, Rastislav Bodik, James Demmel, Tony Keaveny, Kurt Keutzer, John Kubiatowicz, Nelson Morgan, David Patterson, Koushik Sen, John Wawrzynek, David Wessel, and Katherine Yelick. A view of the parallel computing landscape. *Commun. ACM*, 52(10):56–67, October 2009.

[8] J.F. Kolen and S.C. Kremer. *A field guide to dynamical recurrent networks*. IEEE Press, 2001.

[9] C. Gallicchio and A. Micheli. Architectural and markovian factors of echo state networks. *Neural Networks*, 24(5):440–456, 2011.

[10] H. Jaeger and H. Haas. Harnessing nonlinearity: Predicting chaotic systems and saving energy in wireless communication. *Science*, 304(5667):78–80, 2004.

[11] C. Gallicchio and A. Micheli. Tree echo state networks. *Neurocomputing*, 101:319–337, 2013.

[12] FastFlow home page, 2015. http://calvados.di.unipi.it.

[13] Horacio González-Vélez and Mario Leyton. A survey of algorithmic skeleton frameworks: High-level structured parallel programming enablers. *Softw. Pract. Exper.*, 40(12):1135–1160, November 2010.

[14] M. Aldinucci, M. Danelutto, L. Anardu, M. Torquati, and P. Kilpatrick. Parallel patterns + macro data flow for multi-core programming. In *Proc. of Intl. Euromicro PDP 2012: Parallel Distributed and network-based Processing*, pages 27–36, Garching, Germany, February 2012. IEEE.

[15] D. Buono, M. Danelutto, T. De Matteis, G. Mencagli, and M. Torquati. A lightweight run-time support for fast dense linear algebra on multi-core. In *Proc. of the 12th International Conference on Parallel and Distributed Computing and Networks (PDCN 2014)*. IASTED, ACTA press, February 2014.

[16] Christopher M Bishop. *Pattern recognition and machine learning*. springer, 2006.

[17] H. D. Vinod. A survey of ridge regression and related techniques for improvements over ordinary least squares. *The Review of Economics and Statistics*, pages 121–131, 1978.

[18] Q. Li, R. Salman, E. Test, R. Strack, and V. Kecman. Parallel multitask cross validation for support vector machine using GPU. *J. Parallel Distrib. Comput.*, 73(3):293–302, 2013.

[19] G. Ripepi, A. Clematis, and D. D'Agostino. A hybrid parallel implementation of model selection for support vector machines. In *23rd Euromicro International Conference on Parallel, Distributed, and Network-Based Processing, PDP 2015, Turku, Finland, March 4-6, 2015*, pages 145–149, 2015.

[20] M. Lukosevicius. A practical guide to applying echo state networks. In *Neural Networks: Tricks of the Trade - Second Edition*, pages 659–686. 2012.

Parallel Computing: On the Road to Exascale
G.R. Joubert et al. (Eds.)
IOS Press, 2016
© *2016 The authors and IOS Press. All rights reserved.*
doi:10.3233/978-1-61499-621-7-155

Java Implementation of Data Parallel Skeletons on GPUs

Steffen ERNSTING and Herbert KUCHEN [a,1]

[a] *University of Muenster, Department of Information Systems, Germany*

Abstract. Multi-core processors with up to 8 cores and more as well as GPUs with thousands of cores are omnipresent. In order to fully exploit their parallel computing capability, programmers have to deal with low-level concepts of parallel programming. These low-level concepts constitute a high barrier to efficient development of parallel applications. A higher level of abstraction would be desirable.

In order to assist programmers in developing parallel applications *Algorithmic Skeletons* have been proposed. They encapsulate well-defined, frequently recurring parallel programming patterns, thereby shielding programmers from low-level aspects of parallel programming.

The main contribution of this paper is the design and implementation of data parallel skeletons with GPU support in Java. Additionally, on the basis of three benchmark applications, including Matrix multiplication, N-Body calculations, and Shortest paths, we evaluate the performance of the presented implementation on a GPU cluster.

Keywords. High-level parallel programming, Algorithmic skeletons, Java, GPGPU

Introduction

Nowadays, Multi-core and many-core processors are ubiquitous. Both the growing complexity of applications and the growing amount of data lead to high demand for high performance. In the last few years we can observe a trend towards hardware accelerators, especially graphics processing units (GPUs). Fully exploiting the resources provided by multi-core processors and GPUs still requires programmers to deal with intrinsic low-level concepts of parallel programming. These low-level concepts constitute a high barrier to efficient development of parallel applications and also make it a tedious and error-prone task.

With algorithmic skeletons [1,2] Cole has proposed an approach to structured high-level parallel programming. Algorithmic skeletons can be considered as high-level tools that encapsulate well-defined, frequently recurring parallel and distributed programming patterns, thereby hiding low-level details and also encouraging a structured way of parallel programming.

In this paper, we present an approach to implementing data parallel skeletons with GPU support in Java. Because of the lack of native GPU support in Java, we make use

---

[1]Corresponding Author: Steffen Ernsting, University of Muenster, Leonardo-Campus 3, 48149 Muenster, Germany; E-mail: s.ernsting@uni-muenster.de.

of Aparapi (A parallel API) [3,4], an API that translates suitable Java (byte)code into OpenCL code that can be executed on GPUs. With MPJ Express [5] there is a quality MPI implementation needed for internode communication in distributed systems.

The remainder of this paper is structured as follows. Section 1 introduces the *Muenster Skeleton Library* (Muesli), briefly pointing out its concepts and benefits. Section 2 gives a short overview of current advances in GPGPU programming in Java. The implementation of data parallel skeletons with GPU support is presented in Section 3 and evaluated in Section 4. Related work is discussed in Section 5 and finally, Section 6 concludes the paper and gives a short outlook to future work.

1. The Muenster Skeleton Library Muesli

The C++ library Muesli provides algorithmic skeletons as well as distributed data structures for shared and distributed memory parallel programming. It is built on top of MPI and OpenMP. Thus it provides efficient support for multi- and many-core computer architectures as well as clusters of both. For the data parallel part of Muesli there are also skeletons with GPU support (using CUDA) available [6,7]. Additionally, there is a Java implementation of Muesli's data parallel part (CPU only). [8]

Conceptually, we distinguish between data parallel and task parallel skeletons. Data parallel skeletons such as `map`, `zip`, and `fold` are provided as member functions of distributed data structures, including a one-dimensional array, a two-dimensional matrix, and a two-dimensional sparse matrix [9].[2] Communication skeletons such as, for example, `permutePartition` assist the programmer in dealing with data that is distributed among several MPI processes. Task parallel skeletons represent well-known process topologies, such as *Farm, Pipeline* (Pipe), *Divide and Conquer* (D&C) [10] and *Branch and Bound* (B&B) [11]. They can be arbitrarily nested to create a process topology that defines the overall structure of a parallel application. The algorithm-specific behavior of such a process topology is defined by some particular user functions that describe the algorithm-specific details.

In Muesli, a user function is either an ordinary C++ function or a functor, i.e. a class that overrides the function call operator. Due to memory restrictions, GPU-enabled skeletons must be provided with functors as arguments, CPU skeletons take both functions and functors as arguments. As a key feature of Muesli, the well-known concept of *Currying* is used to enable partial application of user functions [12]. A user function requiring more arguments than provided by a particular skeleton can be partially applied to a given number of arguments, thereby yielding a "curried" function of smaller arity, which can be passed to the desired skeleton. On the functor side, additional arguments are provided as data members of the corresponding functor.

2. GPGPU in Java

Since their introduction in 2007 and 2009, respectively, CUDA [13] and OpenCL [14] have enabled C++ programmers to use GPUs as general purpose accelerators in order to

---

[2]In this paper, we focus on the data structures array and matrix. The sparse matrix currently does not support GPU skeletons.

speed up their (massively parallel) programs. With their C language extensions, CUDA C [15] and OpenCL fit in seamlessly with C++. In contrast, Java has built-in features such as multi-threading and networking, but there is no native support for general purpose computing on graphics processing units (GPGPU). In recent years various projects set about introducing GPGPU into the Java world.

On the one hand there are approaches that provide Java bindings to an underlying CUDA or OpenCL implementation through Java Native Interface (JNI) [16]. Here, the programmer certainly must have some experience with CUDA or OpenCL in order to effectively call the corresponding Java bindings. On the other hand there are frameworks that translate Java bytecode into CUDA C or OpenCL. In this case, the programmer does not necessarily know anything at all about CUDA C or OpenCL as she writes Java code, which gets translated to native code. A runtime system handles data transfer and kernel launches.

In [17] Jorge Docampo et al. evaluated the most relevant projects: JCUDA [18], jCuda [19], JOCL [20], JogAmp's JOCL [21] (Java bindings) and Java-GPU [22], Root-beer [23], and Aparapi [3,4] (bytecode translation). They found that Java bindings provide better performance, certainly at the cost of usability when compared to the approaches that make use of source-to-source translation.

For our Java implementation of data parallel skeletons with GPU support we opted for Aparapi. Aparapi is an API for data parallel Java that translates at runtime suitable Java (byte)code into OpenCL code that can be executed on GPUs. It does not deliver the performance of Java bindings such as jCuda, but instead provides good programmability, which is ideal for high-level approaches such as algorithmic skeletons.

2.1. Aparapi

In Aparapi, Java code that is desired to be translated into OpenCL code in order to be run on a GPU has to be implemented in terms of a so-called kernel. Just as its counterparts in CUDA and OpenCL, a kernel is executed by many GPU threads in parallel. Data is accessed and processed depending on the *thread id*. A simple kernel that maps a function (add1(**int**)) to a range of values is shown in listing 1.

```
1  int add1(int value) {
2      return value+1;
3  }
4  Kernel myMapKernel = new Kernel(){
5      public void run(){
6          int i = getGlobalId();
7          out[i]=add1(in[i]);
8      }
9  };
10 myMapKernel.execute(in.length);
```

Listing 1: A simple map kernel.

Similarly to creating and starting threads in Java, the programmer has to implement the kernel's behavior within the run()-method that is called when the kernel is launched by the execute(Range)-method. Range identifies the number of data parallel work items to be processed (in this case 0,...,in.length-1).

Prior to launching a kernel, the programmer may choose an appropriate execution mode. The supported execution modes in Aparapi are: *GPU*, *CPU*, *JTP*, and *SEQ*. For the *GPU* and *CPU* modes Java code is translated into OpenCL code and is then run on the corresponding OpenCL device. *JTP* and *SEQ* stands for Java thread pool and sequential execution, respectively. In this case, pure Java code is executed.

Generally, kernels are restricted to use only arrays of primitive data types. At present Aparapi provides only limited support for simple Java objects. However, because of incompatible memory layouts between Java and OpenCL the performance will be poor. Future releases may address this issue.

3. Implementation of Data Parallel Skeletons on GPUs

As already mentioned in section 1, data parallel skeletons in Muesli are provided as member functions of distributed data structures. As the name suggests, distributed data structures are distributed among several MPI processes, each maintaining a partition of the entire data structure. We distinguish between the *global view* that considers the entire

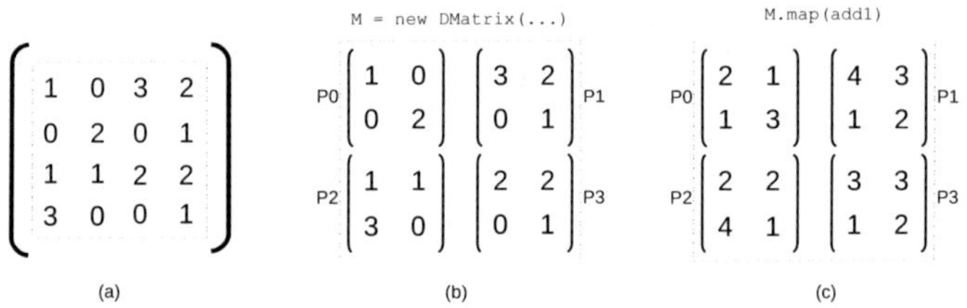

Figure 1. (a) Global view of a distributed matrix. (b) Local view of a distributed matrix. (c) Local view after applying the Map skeleton.

data structure, and the *local view* that considers the decomposition into local partitions (see Figure 1 (a) and (b)). Programmers may concentrate on the *global view* because all data parallel skeletons process the entire data structure, meaning all elements of a data structure (see Figure 1 (c)). However, when designing their programs/algorithms, they must keep in mind that data is physically separated in distributed memory.

Parallelism is achieved through a two-tier approach. Intra-node parallelization (i.e. parallelization on the CPU or GPU) is handled by Aparapi. Thus, a skeleton takes as argument a kernel implemented by the user. Listing 2 and 3 show the application of the map skeleton.

```java
1 public abstract class MapKernel extends Kernel {
2     protected final int[] in, out; // set by constructor
3     // To be implemented by the user.
4     public abstract int mapFunction(int value);
5     public void run() {
6         int gid = getGlobalId();
7         out[gid] = mapFunction(in[gid]);
8     }
9 }
```

Listing 2: Abstract class `MapKernel` to be extended by the user.

The user must extend the class `MapKernel` by implementing the abstract method `mapFunction` (Listing 3, lines 1-5). This method represents the actual map function that is applied to each element of the data structure (Listing 2, line 7). In this case, the map function just increments each element by 1. Finally, the map skeleton is called with an instance of class `Add1` as argument (Listing 3, line 7).[3]

```
1  public class Add1 extends MapKernel {
2      public int mapFunction(int value) {
3          return value+1;
4      }
5  }
6  ...
7  DIMatrix M = new DIMatrix(...);
8  ...
9  M.map(new Add1());
```

Listing 3: Application of the the predefined Muesli map skeleton.

Int this data parallel setting, in some cases it is necessary that processes are able to communicate with each other. This inter-node communication is handled by MPJ Express (MPJE) [5]. MPJE is a Java implementation of the MPI standard, which uses for message passing either pure Java socket communications or native MPI through JNI. In order to give an example of inter-node communication, Listing 4 schematically presents the `fold` skeleton. According to the two-tier parallelization, first each process calculates a local result by folding its local partition of the data structure (line 2). This is done in parallel by CPU or GPU threads, depending on the execution mode. In the next step all local results are shared among the processes (lines 4-5) in order to finally calculate a global result which is then returned by the skeleton (line 7).

```
1  public int fold(FoldKernel k) {
2      int localResult = localFold(k, localPartition);
3
4      int[] localResults = new int[numProcs];
5      allgather(localResult, localResults); // simplified
6
7      return localFold(k, localResults);
8  }
```

Listing 4: Scheme of the `fold` skeleton.

Being able to pass additional arguments to a kernel is crucial for most algorithms. Consider the class `Add1` in Listing 3. If we wanted to have another kernel that adds 2 instead of 1, we could implement another class `Add2`. The more convenient way to achieve this would be to just add an additional argument to the kernel (see Listing 5). The additional argument is represented by an attribute that is initialized e.g. by the constructor. The type of kernel arguments is restricted to primitive data types and arrays of primitive data types. Java objects are currently not supported due to Aparapi restrictions.

---

[3]Note that the `I` in `DIMatrix` denotes the data type **int**.

```
1  public class AddN extends MapKernel {
2      protected int N;
3      public AddN(int N) {
4          this.N = N;
5      }
6      public double mapFunction(double value) {
7          return value+N;
8      }
9  }
10 DIMatrix M = new DIMatrix(...);
11 M.map(new AddN(2));
```

Listing 5: Adding additional arguments to a kernel.

4. Experimental Results

In order to demonstrate how the presented data parallel skeletons with GPU support perform, we have implemented three benchmarks: Matrix multiplication, N-Body, and Shortest paths. Due to lack of space, only the matrix multiplication benchmark and its implementation is described in detail. Performance results are presented for all benchmarks. The test system for the benchmarks is a multi-node GPU cluster. Each node is equipped with two Intel E5-2450 (Sandy Bridge) CPUs with a total of 16 cores and two NVidia Tesla K20x GPUs. For each benchmark, we considered two configurations: *CPU* and *GPU*. For the *CPU* configuration, 16 threads per node are employed. For the *GPU* configuration a single GPU per node has been used. Each configuration was run on multiple nodes, ranging from 1 to 16 nodes.

4.1. Matrix multiplication

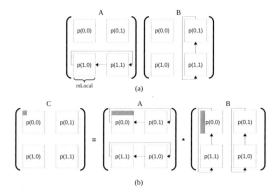

Figure 2. Cannon's algorithm: (a) Initial shifting of submatrices. (b) Intermediate result of first submatrix multiplication and stepwise shifting of submatrices.

For the matrix multiplication benchmark, we implemented Cannon's algorithm [24] for multiplying two $n \times n$-matrices. It is based upon a checkerboard block decomposition and assumes the matrices to be split into p submatrices (local partitions) of size $m \times m$, where p denotes the number of processes and $m = n/\sqrt{p}$. Initially the submatrices of A and B are shifted cyclically in horizontal and vertical direction, respectively (see Figure 2 (a)). Submatrices of row i (column j) are shifted i (j) positions to the west (north). After the initial shifting, the first submatrix multiplication takes place (see Figure 2 (b)). The grey boxes indicate one pair of row and column to calculate the dot product from. This is done in parallel by all processes for each element of C. Within each step, a submatrix multiplication takes place followed by a row and column shift of A and B, respectively. In total, $\sqrt{p}$ steps are required until each process has calculated one submatrix of the result matrix C.

```
1  public DFMatrix matmult(DFMatrix A, DFMatrix B, DFMatrix C) {
2      A.rotateRows(negate);
3      B.rotateCols(negate);
4
5      Dotproduct dp = new Dotproduct(A, B)
6      for (int i = 0; i < A.getBlocksInRow(); i++) {
7          C.mapIndexInPlace(dp);
8          A.rotateRows(-1);
9          B.rotateCols(-1);
10     }
11     return C;
12 }
```

Listing 6: Implementation of Cannon's algorithm using data parallel skeletons.

```
1  class Dotproduct extends MapIndexInPlaceKernel {
2      protected float[] A, B;
3      public Dotproduct(DFMatrix A, DFMatrix B) {
4          super();
5          this.A = A.getLocalPartition();
6          this.B = B.getLocalPartition();
7      }
8      public float mapIndexFunction(float Cij, int row, int col) {
9          float sum = Cij;
10         for (int k = 0; k < mLocal; k++) {
11             sum += A[row * mLocal + k] * B[k * mLocal + col];
12         }
13         return sum;
14     }
15 }
```

Listing 7: Map kernel that calculates the dot product.

The implementation of the algorithm is presented in Listing 6. The initial shifting is performed by the communication skeletons `rotateRows` and `rotateCols`, respectively, in lines 2-3. When called with a functor as argument, these skeletons calculate the number of positions each submatrix has to be shifted by applying the functor to the row and column indices of the submatrices, respectively. According to the functor `negate`, a submatrix of row i (column j) is shifted i (j) positions to the west (north). When called with the argument -1 (lines 8-9), submatrices of row i (column j) are shifted one position to the west (north). In line 7 the submatrix multiplication is performed by the `mapIndexInPlace` skeleton. It is called with an instance of the dot product kernel presented in Listing 7 as argument. The suffix `Index` indicates that amongst the element itself also the indices of that element are passed to the user function (Listing 7, line 8). Indices passed to the user function by the skeleton are always global indices. Local indices can be calculated with help of the provided attributes `mLocal` (see line 10) and `nLocal` (not used in this example). The suffix `InPlace` denotes that the skeleton works in-place, i.e. elements are overwritten. The dot product of corresponding rows of matrix A and columns of matrix B is calculated in lines 10-12.

Performance results are reported in Figure 3. GPU speedups (w.r.t the *CPU* config.) range from about 5x (16 nodes) to about 90x (1 node). Worse (GPU) speedups on higher node counts is due to CPU cache effects that result in super-linear speedups (about 42x on 16 nodes compared to a single node) for the *CPU* configuration.

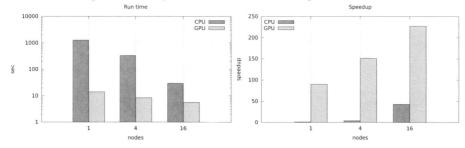

Figure 3. Results of the Matrix multiplication benchmark. Left: Run time on a logarithmic scale. Right: Speedups w.r.t to a single node in *CPU* configuration.

4.2. N-Body

Performance results for the N-Body benchmark are reported in Figure 4. The GPU speedups (w.r.t the *CPU* config.) range from about 3.5 (16 nodes) to about 13 (1 node). In this case, the speedup drop for higher node counts is likely due to a smaller computation to communication time ratio. Whereas inter-node speedups are close to ideal for the *CPU* configuration, for the *GPU* configuration the speedups decrease with increasing node counts.

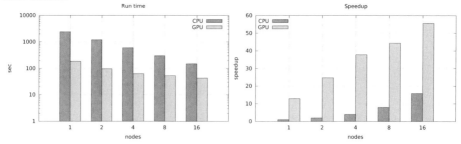

Figure 4. Results of the N-Body benchmark. Left: Run time on a logarithmic scale. Right: Speedups w.r.t to a single node in *CPU* configuration.

4.3. Shortest Paths

Performance results for the Shortest paths benchmark are reported in Figure 5. For the *CPU* configuration the results are similar to the Matrix multiplication benchmark. For higher node counts super-linear speedups are noticeable. Again, this is very likely due to cache effects. For the *GPU* configuration, however, higher node counts result in strongly decreasing speedups. The speedup when shifting from 4 to 16 nodes is only about 1.06, which is very close to no speedup at all.

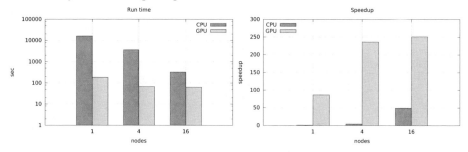

Figure 5. Results of the Shortest paths benchmark. Left: Run time on a logarithmic scale. Right: Speedups w.r.t to a single node in *CPU* configuration.

5. Related Work

SkelCL [25] and SkePU [26] are C++ skeleton frameworks targeting multi-core, multi-GPU systems. While SkelCL is exclusively built on top of OpenCL, SkePU provides support for both CUDA and OpenCL. Additionally, SkePU allows for heterogeneous execution as well as performance-aware dynamic scheduling and load balancing. Fast-Flow [27] is a C++ framework providing high-level parallel programming patterns. It supports heterogeneous shared memory platforms equipped with hardware accelerators such as GPUs, Xeon Phi, and Tilera TILE64 as well as clusters of such platforms. However, as of this writing all three frameworks are limited to the C++ programming language and do not provide a Java implementation of their skeletons.

6. Conclusion

We have presented an implementation of data parallel skeletons with GPU support in Java. It provides a high-level approach for simplifying parallel and distributed programming. Applications developed with these skeletons are portable across a variety of platforms, including CPUs and GPUs. The programmer may specify whether she wants to run a program either on CPUs only or with GPU support. The use of Java, with features such as e.g. its huge standard library, garbage collection, and reflection also contributes to making (parallel) programming more comfortable. However, it also carries some disadvantages: because of the restriction to primitive data types there is no opportunity to implement generic data structures, which results in code bloat. This problem could solve itself in the future, if the restriction to primitive data types falls. Also, the use of JNI results in an additional performance overhead. In order to evaluate that overhead, we plan to make a comparison of Java and the C++ implementations of our data parallel skeletons in a forthcoming paper. For future work, we plan to provide support for multi-GPU and Xeon Phi hardware configurations.

References

[1] M. Cole. *Algorithmic Skeletons: Structured Management of Parallel Computation.* MIT Press, 1989.
[2] M. Cole. Bringing skeletons out of the closet: a pragmatic manifesto for skeletal parallel programming. *Parallel computing*, 30(3):389–406, 2004.
[3] G. Frost. A parallel API, 2011.
[4] Aparapi Github pages. https://github.com/aparapi/aparapi. Accessed Feb. 2015.
[5] A. Shafi, B. Carpenter, and M. Baker. Nested parallelism for multi-core HPC systems using Java. *J. Parallel Distrib. Comput.*, 69(6):532–545, 2009.
[6] S. Ernsting and H. Kuchen. Algorithmic Skeletons for Multi–Core, Multi–GPU Systems and Clusters. *International Journal of High Performance Computing and Networking*, 7(2):129–138, 2012.
[7] S. Ernsting and H. Kuchen. A Scalable Farm Skeleton for Heterogeneous Parallel Programming. In *Parallel Computing: Accelerating Computational Science and Engineering (CSE), Proceedings of the International Conference on Parallel Computing, ParCo 2013, Garching, Germany*, pages 72–81, 2013.
[8] S. Ernsting and H. Kuchen. Data Parallel Skeletons in Java. In *Proceedings of the International Conference on Computational Science (ICCS), Omaha, Nebraska, USA, 2012*, pages 1817–1826, 2012.
[9] P. Ciechanowicz. Algorithmic Skeletons for General Sparse Matrices on Multi-Core Processors. In *Proceedings of the 20th IASTED International Conference on Parallel and Distributed Computing and Systems (PDCS)*, pages 188–197, 2008.
[10] M. Poldner and H. Kuchen. Skeletons for Divide and Conquer Algorithms. In *Proceedings of the IASTED International Conference on Parallel and Distributed Computing and Networks (PDCN)*. ACTA Press, 2008.
[11] M. Poldner and H. Kuchen. Algorithmic Skeletons for Branch and Bound. In *Proceedings of the 1st International Conference on Software and Data Technology (ICSOFT)*, volume 1, pages 291–300, 2006.
[12] H. Kuchen and J. Striegnitz. Higher-Order Functions and Partial Applications for a C++ Skeleton Library. In *Proceedings of the 2002 joint ACM-ISCOPE Conference on Java Grande*, pages 122–130. ACM, 2002.
[13] J. Nickolls, I. Buck, M. Garland, and K. Skadron. Scalable Parallel Programming with CUDA. *Queue*, 6(2):40–53, March 2008.
[14] OpenCL Working Group. The OpenCL specification, Version 1.2, 2011.
[15] Nvidia Corp. *NVIDIA CUDA C Programming Guide 6.0.* Nvidia Corporation, 2014.
[16] JNI-related APIs and Developer Guides. http://docs.oracle.com/javase/7/docs/technotes/guides/jni/index.html. Accessed Feb. 2015.
[17] J. Docampo, S. Ramos, G. L. Taboada, R. R. Expósito, J. Touriño, and R. Doallo. Evaluation of Java for General Purpose GPU Computing. In *27th International Conference on Advanced Information Networking and Applications Workshops, Barcelona, Spain, 2013*, pages 1398–1404, 2013.
[18] Y. Yan, M. Grossman, and V. Sarkar. JCUDA: A Programmer-Friendly Interface for Accelerating Java Programs with Cuda. In H. Sips, D. Epema, and H.-X. Lin, editors, *Euro-Par 2009 Parallel Processing*, volume 5704 of *Lecture Notes in Computer Science*, pages 887–899. Springer Berlin Heidelberg, 2009.
[19] jCuda Website. http://jcuda.org. Accessed Apr. 2015.
[20] jOCL Website. http://jocl.org. Accessed Apr. 2015.
[21] JogAmp Website. http://jogamp.org. Accessed Apr. 2015.
[22] P. Calvert. Parallelisation of Java for Graphics Processors. *Part II Dissertation, Computer Science Tripos, University of Cambridge*, 2010.
[23] P. C. Pratt-Szeliga, J. W. Fawcett, and R. D. Welch. Rootbeer: Seamlessly using GPUs from Java. In *HPCC 2012*, 2012.
[24] M. J. Quinn. *Parallel computing (2nd ed.): theory and practice.* McGraw-Hill, Inc., New York, NY, USA, 1994.
[25] M. Steuwer, P. Kegel, and S. Gorlatch. SkelCL – A Portable Skeleton Library for High-Level GPU Programming. In *HIPS '11: Proceedings of the 16th IEEE Workshop on High-Level Parallel Programming Models and Supportive Environments*, Anchorage, AK, USA, May 2011.
[26] J. Enmyren and C. W. Kessler. SkePU: a Multi-Backend Skeleton Programming Library for Multi-GPU Systems. In *Proceedings of the fourth international workshop on High-level parallel programming and applications*, HLPP '10, pages 5–14, New York, NY, USA, 2010. ACM.
[27] M. Aldinucci, M. Torquati, M. Drocco, G. Peretti Pezzi, and C. Spampinato. An Overview of FastFlow: Combining Pattern-Level Abstraction and Efficiency in GPGPUs. In *GPU Technology Conference (GTC 2014)*, San Jose, CA, USA, March 2014.

Parallel Computing: On the Road to Exascale
G.R. Joubert et al. (Eds.)
IOS Press, 2016

doi:10.3233/978-1-61499-621-7-165

Data parallel patterns in Erlang/OpenCL

Ugo ALBANESE, Marco DANELUTTO

Dept. of Computer Science, Univ. of Pisa

Abstract. We introduce a library supporting execution of data parallel kernels on GPUs from Erlang. The library provides calls with the same semantics of the map and fold functions of the lists Erlang library, where the functions to be computed on the input list(s) are actually provided as OpenCL C kernels. The map and reduce (fold) higher order functions are provided in such a way that subsequent calls may leave temporary data (partial results) on the GPU memory while computing complex, possibly composed data parallel patterns. In addition, data transfers to and from the GPU, from and to the Erlang subsystem, are overlapped with Erlang to C and C to Erlang marshaling, such that the cost of the overall type conversion is minimized. We assess the performances of the data parallel library via simple synthetic benchmarks and real application kernels showing substantial speedups with respect to pure Erlang implementation of the same synthetic benchmarks/application kernels.

Keywords. Erlang, GPU, OpenCL, data parallelism, parallel patterns, algorithmic skeletons

1. Introduction

Erlang [7,1] is a general-purpose functional programming language and run time environment developed by Ericsson since the 1980s with built-in support for concurrency, distribution and fault tolerance. Erlang is licensed as open source and it has been adopted by many leading telecom and IT companies. Nowadays it is successfully being used in other industries including banking, finance and e-commerce. Erlang is distributed with a large collection of libraries called OTP (Open Telecom platform) [8] allowing the user to easily develop applications using anything from telecommunication protocols to HTTP servers. It also provides implementations of several patterns that have proven useful, over the years, in the development of massively concurrent software. Most production Erlang applications are actually Erlang/OTP applications. OTP is also open source and distributed with Erlang.

Erlang is a general-purpose language especially well suited for the application domain for which it was designed. This is a niche domain mostly consisting of distributed, reliable, soft real-time concurrent systems. Erlang demonstrates less efficiency in other common domains, such as image processing or, more in general, numerical applications, where high performance in iterative computations is a prime requirement. In this perspective, it is evident how much Erlang could benefit from GPU raw processing power in solving problems in this latter class of applications. Unfortunately, Erlang does not provide any primitive and integrated way to access GPU computing facilities. Furthermore, GP-GPUs require specification of the computations to be offloaded to the GP-GPU as *kernels* coded in C either using OpenCL C [11] (AMD, Intel and nVidia devices) or CUDA C [4] (nVidia devices only), which also represents a problem when considering the possibility to target GPUs from Erlang.

In this work we introduce a library (Skel0CL) aimed at providing some kind of GPU support within Erlang. The library ensures that the Erlang programmer has the possibility to develop code (modeled after the classical collective operations of the Erlang lists library) processing lists of floating point numbers on GPUs. Skel0CL provides different, extremely efficient implementations of map and reduce (fold) collective operations fully respecting the signatures of the corresponding higher order functions in the Erlang lists module at the price of obliging the programmer to provide the parameter functions to be executed on the GPU as OpenCL C code.

The whole work has been developed in the framework of the activities of the EU funded FP7 STREP project ParaPhrase [12]. The ParaPhrase project aims to produce a new structured design and implementation process for heterogeneous parallel architectures, where developers exploit a variety of parallel patterns to develop component based applications that can be mapped to the available hardware resources, and which may then be dynamically re-mapped to meet application needs and hardware availability. The whole ParaPhrase approach is based on a methodology introducing parallel design patterns into sequential code through program re-factoring (source to source rewriting) [10]. The set of parallel patterns object of the re-factoring include stream parallel *and* data parallel patterns. Data parallel patterns, in turn, include the map and reduce patterns considered in this work. Last but not least, ParaPhrase methodology is demonstrated in two different programming frameworks: C++ and Erlang. In C++, the re-factoring introducing the parallel patterns directly targets FastFlow [5,9], that is sequential C++ code is re-factored to C++ code hosting calls to the FastFlow structured parallel programming library. In Erlang, CPU cores are targeted by re-factoring sequential Erlang code to Erlang code with calls to the **skel** parallel pattern library [14,2].

The main contribution of this paper may be summarized as follows:

- We provide a seamless integration of GPU data parallel patterns in Erlang
- We provide an efficient implementation of the map, mapzip and reduce patterns on the GPU, including efficient data transfer from Erlang run time to GPU memory and vice versa
- We report the results of experiments that validate the library design.

The rest of the paper details the approach (Sec. 2), the implementation of the proposed library (Sec. 3) and the experimental results validating the approach (Sec. 4). Sec. 5 eventually summarizes our achievements and concludes the paper.

2. Skel0CL: seamless integration of GPU data parallel patterns in Erlang

Following the "minimal disruption" principle stated in Murray Cole's algorithmic skeleton manifesto [3], Skel0CL provides the data parallel patterns targeting GPU as higher order functions. The library basically provides two patterns:

Map pattern, applying a function f to all the items x_i of an input list and providing as result the list of the $f(x_i)$ results. A *map2* pattern is also provided, accepting two lists as input along with a function f and providing the list of the values obtained applying f on the two corresponding elements of the two lists (this is also known as the **mapzip** pattern).

Reduce pattern, "summing up" all the items x_i in a list by means of a commutative[1] and associative operator $\oplus$ and providing as result the scalar value $x_1 \oplus x_2 \oplus \ldots \oplus x_n$

Both kind of patterns are provided in an "LL" version (input from Erlang lists, output to Erlang lists), an "LD" version (input from Erlang lists, output in a device (GPU) buffer, a "DL" version (input from device buffer, output to Erlang lists, and a "DD" version (input from a device buffer, output to a device buffer). All functions are named after the name of the pattern and the kind of I/O data; they take two parameters, the function to be used (f or $\oplus$) and the list (or buffer) to be processed. Therefore, to map a function F onto all the items of a list L, a programmer will simply call:

```
skel_ocl:mapLL(F,L).
```

But how will F be provided? In a sequential library call such as:

```
lists:map(F,L).
```

F may be defined as a normal Erlang unary function, e.g.

```
F(X) -> X + 1.0.
```

However, being directed to the GPU, the F parameter of the skel_ocl:map has to be provided through some OpenCL C code. SkelOCL provides two Erlang functions CreateMapKernel/2 and CreateReduceKernel/2 taking two parameters: the first one denotes the name of the file where the OpenCL code definition for F may be found. The second one is the name of the kernel function. These two functions return an Erlang *resource object* that can be passed through different actual calls. As a result, the complete specification of the map_ocl call above could be:

```
Fk  = skel_ocl:createMapKernel("f.c","f").
Res = skel_ocl:mapLL(Fk, L).
```

where the file f.c hosts the OpenCL C code for the f map parameter:

```
double f(double x) { return (x+1.0); }
```

Despite the fact this is actual C code, there is no other way to support GPU kernel specification. We took into account the possibility of providing a subset of Erlang expressions as GPU kernels and automatically compiling on-the-fly the Erlang kernel function expressions to OpenCL C. However, we do not have OpenCL versions of the Erlang standard libraries and therefore we should have added the limitation not to use Erlang libraries in the kernel expressions. At that point the effort required to the Erlang kernel function programmer could be considered equivalent to the effort of learning the minimum of C necessary to write the kernel functions.

---

[1] commutativity is required to ensure correctness in case of "misordered" updates

In case of repeated (or combined) usage of data parallel patterns on the GPU, buffers on GPU may be conveniently used to keep intermediate results. This saves significant percentages of the overall CPU-GPU memory transfers (as well as a number of marshaling/un-marshaling operations). As an example, consider a program where the result is computed as a *reduce*(*g*, *map*(*f*, *L*)). This may be simply written in SkelOCL as:

```
Fk = skel_ocl:createMapKernel("f.c","f").
Gk = skel_ocl:createReduceKernel("g.c", "g").
L = ... .
Intermediate = skel_ocl:mapLL(Fk,L).
Result = skel_ocl:reduceLL(Gk,Intermediate).
```

This, however, turns out to be rather inefficient; several of the steps required, are in fact unnecessary:

1. Marshaling L from the Erlang run-time to the C run-time and then transferring the result to the GPU memory

2. Computing the map data parallel pattern on the GPU

3. Transferring back the data from GPU memory and marshaling it back to the Erlang run time

4. Marshal back the intermediate result to the C run-time and then transferring it to the GPU

5. Compute the reduce data parallel patterns on the GPU

6. Transfer back the results on the CPU and marshal them back to the Erlang run-time.

A much better solution would be to leave the intermediate results on the GPU. This may be programmed quite simply in SkelOCL by declaring a buffer on the GPU and then using it for the intermediate array storage. The following code may be eventually used:

```
Buf = skel_ocl:allocDeviceBuffer(Size,read_write).
skel_ocl:mapLD(Fk, InputList, Buf, ListLen).
Res = skel:ocl:reduceDL(Gk,Buf).
```

The execution of the code only requires the marshaling of the initial data from Erlang run time to the C/GPU memory and the marshaling of the final result from C/GPU to Erlang. All in all (see also the code shown in Sec. 4), we think the library interface satisfies the "minimum disruption" principle stated by Cole.

It's worth pointing out that we could have provided an even higher level formalism to expressed composition of map and reduce patterns, such that the allocation of the buffers and the choice of the correct LL/DL/DD versions could have been completely automatized and hidden to the final user (the application programmer).

This is, indeed, something we will consider in the near future.

3. Implementation

The implementation of `SkelOCL` functions exploits Erlang NIFs (Native Interface Functions) [6]. Erlang, from version R14B onwards, provides an API to implement native functions, in C/C++, that are called in the same way as the Erlang implemented ones. Such functions are called NIF (Native Implemented Functions) and, to interact with Erlang's VM, they use the API provided in the `erl_nif` module [6]. A NIF library contains native implementations of some functions of an Erlang module. Each NIF must also have an implementation in Erlang that will be invoked if the function is called before the NIF library has been successfully loaded, so to throw an exception or, perhaps, provide a fallback implementation if the NIF library is not implemented for some architecture.

Since a native function is executed as a direct extension of the native code of the VM, its execution is not made in a safe environment. That is, if the native function misbehaves, so the whole VM will. In particular, quoting the module's documentation [6]:

- A native function that crashes will crash the whole VM. An erroneously implemented native function might cause a VM internal state inconsistency, which may cause a crash of the VM, or miscellaneous misbehavior of the VM at any point after the call to the native function.
- A native function that does lengthy work (more than 1ms long) before returning will degrade responsiveness of the VM, and may cause miscellaneous strange behaviors. Such strange behaviors include, but are not limited to, extreme memory usage, and bad load balancing between schedulers. Strange behaviors that might occur due to lengthy work may also vary between OTP releases.

As workarounds for the last limitation, several methods are suggested in the documentation, depending on the ability to fully control the code to execute in the native function. If that is the case, the best approach is to divide the work into multiple chunks of work and call the native function multiple times. If full control of the code is not possible (e.g. when calling third-party libraries) then is recommended to dispatch the work to another thread, return from the native function, and wait for the result. The thread can send the result back to the calling thread using message passing. In version R17B a new kind of experimental schedulers have been introduced for dealing with long running functions.

A dirty NIF is a NIF that cannot be split and cannot execute in a millisecond or less and therefore it performs work that the Erlang run-time cannot handle cleanly. Although the usage of dirty NIFs is generally discouraged, for some applications it may be considered acceptable. For example, if the only work done by an Erlang program is carried out by the NIF, scheduling interferences are not a problem. Despite all these issues and limitations, the `SkelOCL` functions are implemented by NIFs, as we are targeting computations that, once they offload something to be computed on the GPU, should simply (actively) wait for the termination of the offloading call. This means we can neglect the negative effects of long lasting NIF calls on the Erlang scheduler.

When using NIFs, data comes to the C environment as Erlang run time data structures that can be accessed (read and written) through proper NIF library calls. As we decided to process lists, when we call a map or reduce GPU pattern we first need to transform Erlang lists to C `double[]` vectors. This is made using a simple recursive scan of the Erlang lists whose code may be summarized as follows:

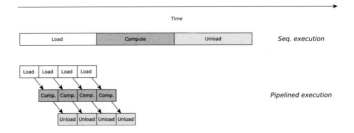

Figure 1. Unrolling of mapLL phases in time: *Load* comprises un-marshaling and copying data from host to device; *Unload* is the opposite process, covering copying from device to host and marshaling the output. *comp* are the phases computing on the GPU. The upper diagram refers to sequential NIF function implementation, the lower diagram refers to our pipelined implementation.

```
if(enif_is_list(env,list)) {
  enif_get_list_length(env,list,&len);
  x=(double*)enif_alloc(len*sizeof(double));
  ERL_NIF_TERM curr_list=list;
  for(int i=0; i<len; i++){
    ERL_NIF_TERM hd, tl;
    enif_get_list_cell(env, curr_list, &hd,&tl);
    if(!(enif_get_double(env, hd, &(x[i])))){
      ...
    }
    curr_list = tl;
  } else { ... }
```

This is a time-consuming process, due to the internal complexities of the enif_xx functions. We measured total times in the range of milliseconds for lists with hundreds of thousands of items. In order to reduce the impact of this time, we adopted a *pipeline* approach:

- we decide a chunk size and we start translating lists in chunks of that size
- at the steady state, we translate chunk $i + 1$ while chunk i is being computed on the GPU and the result of chunk $i - 1$ is being marshaled back to the Erlang run time.

Overall this guarantees a *quasi* complete overlap of the marshaling times with the kernel computation times for decently long lists. The only problem is the determination of the parameter chunk size, which at the moment is devised according to heuristics[2].

With this implementation, the computation of a

```
skel_ocl:mapLL(KernelF,List,ListLength).
```

happens as depicted in Fig. 1.

In order to further improve SkelOCL implementation, we also exploited the GPU DMA to copy data asynchronously between device and host in such a way we succeed

---

[2]the programmer may supply the chunk size modifying a #define statement in the code. Chunk size is defined in such a way the overall computation/communication ratio is optimized, e.g. in such a way the computation time is as close as possible to the time needed to transfer the chunk data

in overlapping data transfers to computation phases. The DMA exploitation uses two (in-order) OpenCL command queues to issue kernel execution and data transfer commands independently. Last but not least, several heuristics have been used to identify different parameters of interest in the GPU implementation of the high level patterns provided by SkelOCL. The number of threads used, the chunk size picked up to split list marshalling/unmarshalling and therefore overlap marshalling/unmarshalling with GPU data transfers and kernel computation, etc. are all derived by simple heuristic functions applied to known parameters from the GPU at hand.

4. Experimental results

We performed a full set of tests to validate the performance of the library. The experiments have been run on two distinct architectures: *pianosa.di.unipi.it*, a dual 8 core, 2-way hyper-threading Intel Xeon E5-2650 CPU machine equipped with an NVIDIA GeForce GTX 660 GPU with 5 Streaming Processors (192 CUDA cores each) and a single copy engine (DMA), and *titanic.di.unipi.it*, a dual 12 core AMD Magny Cours equipped with a NVIDIA Tesla C2050 GPU with 14 Streaming Processors (32 core each) and a double copy engine. Erlang R15 and R16 have been both used successfully. For the sake of simplicity, in the following we only discuss the results of the experiments run on *pianosa*, the more modern architecture among the two, the results on *titanic* being completely similar.

We run two different kind of experiments, to validate SkelOCL: a) some synthetic benchmarks have been used to stress the different high level patterns provided by the library, and b) some small, real use cases have been used to show actual performance advantages achieved with the library even in case of "fine grain" map/reduce computations.

4.1. Synthetic benchmarks

First, we run some synthetic benchmarks, one for each skeleton; we implemented them in three different ways: using Erlang lists module functions, using SkelOCL and in C++/OpenCL. By comparing their completion time we can measure the relative speedup: pure Erlang vs. SkelOCL shows the advantage in using our library, instead SkelOCL vs. C++/OpenCL shows how much inefficient our skeletons are in respect to the baseline C++/OpenCL implementation. Having the need to simulate various arithmetic intensities in our test applications, we added to user-functions (computing a single arithmetic operation on the single list element to compute the result) a delay loop that computes the sin function a specified number of times. In this way we can easily vary the computation grain and therefore highlight the effect of (un-)marshaling on the total cost of the computation.

Fig. 2, 3 and 4 plot the results we achieved when different SkelOCL patterns are used. Fig. 2 is relative to the execution of a synthetic mapLL benchmark, Fig. 3 and 4 plot the results achieved when computing a map+reduce pattern and a mapzip+reduce pattern, instead. In all the cases, the average of the results on 10 different runs of the same program are shown. The performance improvement over pure Erlang implementation is significant (up to 400x). At the same time the loss with respect to the pure C++/OpenCL reference implementation is acceptable (less than 20% when "significant" (in terms of elapsed time) kernels are executed on the GPU).

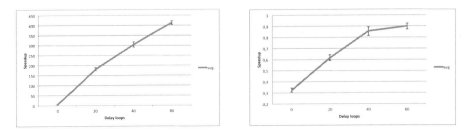

Figure 2. mapLL test: speedup vs. pure Erlang and vs. C++/OpenCL

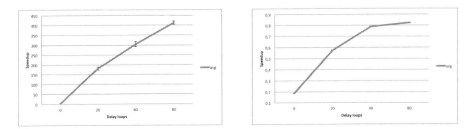

Figure 3. mapLD+reduceDL test: speedup vs. pure Erlang and vs. C++/OpenCL.

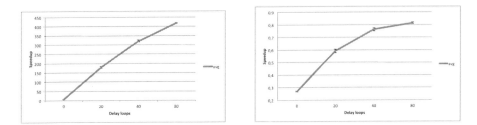

Figure 4. mapzipLD+reduceDL test: speedup vs. pure Erlang and vs. C++/OpenCL.

4.2. Application kernels

The results discussed in Sec. 4.1 evidence that good speedups may be achieved in case of "long lasting" functions used as parameters of our SkelOCL calls. We made another set of experiments aimed at evaluating the kind of improvements achieved in the completion time of real application kernels with no additional computations.

For the first experiment we a) computed the approximation of the integral of a given function (using a map and a reduce pattern), and b) we computed a simple vector product (using a mapzip and a reduce pattern). The function we considered for the integral is a 5th degree polynomial. On *pianosa* the speedup achieved in the two cases with different amount of points is shown in Fig. 5.

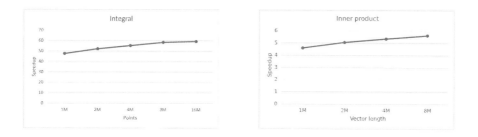

Figure 5. Integral and inner product: speedup GPU vs. pure Erlang.

While, in the case of integration, the computation of the single point requires a number of floating point operations in the range of tens, in case of the dot product, each point contributes with just two FP operations: a product (for the map) and a sum (for the reduce). It is worth pointing out that these speedups, although not impressive, are relevant as they related to the speedup of computations performed on data that before and after are fully accessible as Erlang lists to the Erlang code. Other solutions, providing access to GPU facilities in Erlang [13] actually allocate the data to be processed on the GPU directly in Erlang *binaries*, which makes the interface with C/OpenCL something more efficient, but does not provide full access to the processed data to Erlang programmers unless binary to Erlang conversion is performed in a completely serial way.

The second experiment was related to the computation of π through the classical MonteCarlo method (and therefore exploiting again a map+reduce pattern). In this case, we also achieved a speedup close to 7 w.r.t. Erlang execution of the computation. The generation of the random points was performed in Erlang, then the list was passed to the OpenCL kernel to compute the approximated π value. In case we also generated the random point on the GPU, better speedups could have been achieved.

5. Related work & Conclusions

We outlined the implementation of an Erlang library providing the Erlang programmer the ability to use GPUs through classic high order list processing functions. The library has been developed in the framework of the FP7 EU project ParaPhrase. To the best of our knowledge, the only other framework providing some GPU access from Erlang is the *skel* library developed by our colleagues at the Univ. of St. Andrews [14,13]. SkelOCL differs from **skel** in three main respects: a) it succeeds overlapping memory transfers to/from GPU memory with data marshalling/unmarshalling from Erlang, which gives some advantages on "short" GPU computations, b) does not use Erlang binaries to store data to be processed on the GPU, which provides better accessibility to Erlang programmers, and c) includes all the OpenCL peculiar code in the library, rather than providing the access to OpenCL functions (buffer allocation, data transfer, kernel computation, and the alike) directly in Erlang in such a way they can be directly used by the programmer/introduced through proper re-factoring. We have, actually, plans to merge the two implementations in the **skel** library, which is one of the official products of the (already terminated) ParaPhrase project. Besides describing the main features of SkelOCL and some of the principal implementation techniques used, we also provided experimental results on *state-of-the-art* multicore CPU with GP-GPU architectures validating the whole approach. In particular, the experimental results show that with long running kernels (synthetic benchmarks) noteworthy speedups may be achieved (2 orders of magnitude), while with short kernels speedups in the order of units or tens may be achieved w.r.t. sequential CPU execution.

Acknowledgments

This work has been partially supported by EU FP7-ICT-2013-10 project REPARA (No. 609666) "Reengineering and Enabling Performance And poweR of Applications" and EU H2020-ICT-2014-1 project RePhrase (No. 644235) "REfactoring Parallel Heterogeneous Resource-Aware Applications - a Software Engineering Approach".

References

[1]   Joe Armstrong. *Programming Erlang: Software for a Concurrent World*. Pragmatic Bookshelf, 2007.
[2]   Christopher Brown, Marco Danelutto, Kevin Hammond, Peter Kilpatrick, and Archibald Elliott. Cost-directed refactoring for parallel erlang programs. *International Journal of Parallel Programming*, 42(4):564–582, 2014.
[3]   Murray Cole. Bringing skeletons out of the closet: a pragmatic manifesto for skeletal parallel programming. *Parallel Computing*, 30(3):389–406, 2004.
[4]   Shane Cook. *CUDA Programming: A Developer's Guide to Parallel Computing with GPUs*. Morgan Kaufmann Publishers Inc., San Francisco, CA, USA, 1st edition, 2013.
[5]   Marco Danelutto and Massimo Torquati. Structured parallel programming with core FastFlow. In *Central European Functional Programming School, 5th Summer School, CEFP 2013, Cluj-Napioca, Revised Selected Papers*, number 8606 in LNCS, pages 28–74. Springer Verlag, 2014.
[6]   Erlang NIF module documentation. http://www.erlang.org/doc/man/erl_nif.html.
[7]   Erlang Platform Home Page. http://www.erlang.org.
[8]   Erlang/OTP Documentation. http://www.erlang.org/doc/.
[9]   The FastFlow parallel programming framework. http://calvados.di.unipi.it/dokuwiki/doku.php/ffnamespace:about.
[10] Kevin Hammond, Marco Aldinucci, Christopher Brown, Francesco Cesarini, Marco Danelutto, Horacio González-Vélez, Peter Kilpatrick, Rainer Keller, Michael Rossbory, and Gilad Shainer. The paraphrase project: Parallel patterns for adaptive heterogeneous multicore systems. In Bernhard Beckert, Ferruccio Damiani, Frank S. de Boer, and Marcello M. Bonsangue, editors, *Formal Methods for Components and Objects, 10th International Symposium, FMCO 2011, Turin, Italy, October 3-5, 2011, Revised Selected Papers*, volume 7542 of *Lecture Notes in Computer Science*, pages 218–236. Springer, 2011.
[11] Aaftab Munshi, Benedict Gaster, Timothy G. Mattson, James Fung, and Dan Ginsburg. *OpenCL Programming Guide*. Addison-Wesley Professional, 1st edition, 2011.
[12] The Paraphrase project. http://www.paraphrase-ict.eu/.
[13] ParaPhrase. Final Pattern Transformation System, D4.4, 2015. Deliverable 4.4, available http://paraphrase-enlarged.elte.hu/downloads/D4-4.pdf.
[14] A Streaming Process-based Skeleton Library for Erlang. https://github.com/ParaPhrase/skel.

Parallel Computing: On the Road to Exascale
G.R. Joubert et al. (Eds.)
IOS Press, 2016
doi:10.3233/978-1-61499-621-7-175

Hybrid Coarrays: a PGAS Feature for Many-Core Architectures

Valeria CARDELLINI [a] and Alessandro FANFARILLO [a] and Salvatore FILIPPONE [a]
and Damian ROUSON [b]

[a] *Dipartimento di Ingegneria Civile e Ingegneria Informatica*
Università di Roma "Tor Vergata", Roma, Italy
[b] *Sourcery, Inc.*
Berkeley, California, USA

Abstract. Accelerators such as NVIDIA GPUs and Intel MICs are currently provided as co-processor devices, usable only through a CPU host. For Intel MICs it is planned that this constraint will be lifted in the near future: CPU and accelerator(s) will then form a single, many-core, processor capable of peak performance of several Teraflops with high energy efficiency. In order to exploit the available computational power, the user will be compelled to write a code more "hardware-aware", in contrast to the common philosophy of hiding hardware details as much as possible. The simple two-sided communication approach often used in message-passing applications introduces synchronization costs that may limit the performance on the next generation machines. PGAS languages, like coarray Fortran and UPC, propose a one-sided approach where a process accesses directly the remote memory of another process without interrupting its execution. In this paper, we propose a CUDA-aware coarray implementation, capable of merging the expressive syntax of coarrays with the computational power of GPUs. We propose a new keyword for the Fortran language, which allows the user to map with a high-level syntax some hardware features of the many-core machines. Our hybrid coarray implementation is based on OpenCoarrays, the coarray transport layer currently adopted by the GNU Fortran compiler.

Keywords. PGAS, Coarrays, CUDA, Fortran, Accelerators

Introduction

In order to reach challenging performance goals, computer architecture will change significantly in the near future. A large amount of research about exascale challenges has been published and the main limitations to performance growth have been identified as: 1) energy consumption; 2) degree of parallelism; 3) fault resilience; 4) memory size and speed [1].

The HPC community (software/hardware vendors, academia, and government agencies) is designing the architecture for the next generation machines. In [2] the authors use an abstract machine model in order to represent a possible exascale node architecture (Fig. 1, reprinted with permission from [2])

This representation depicts a heterogeneous node composed by two types of computational units: 1) *fat cores* (traditional CPU cores) suitable for algorithms with low level

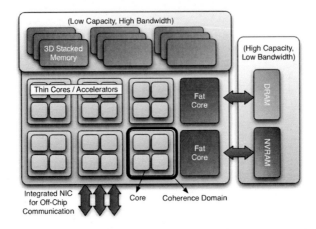

Figure 1. Model of exascale node architecture

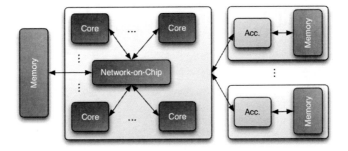

Figure 2. Current heterogeneous node with discrete accelerators

of parallelism and 2) *thin cores*, providing high aggregate performance and high energy efficiency. Another difference from today's architectures is the presence of a low capacity on-chip memory with high bandwidth. This new memory will likely be a multi channel DRAM (MCDRAM), a variant of the Hybrid Memory Cube (HMC) technology [3,4]. The idea is to create a DRAM stack and couple it with a logic process for buffering and routing tasks. This buffer layer makes the problem of data routing easier to solve.

The heterogeneous nature of the compute nodes (with fat and thin cores involved in the computation), the frequency scaling performed for energy reasons, and the possible fault of a compute node tend to break the assumption of homogeneous hardware considered by the bulk-synchronous model (BSP). In this model, each thread/process goes through a computational phase, and then waits until all reach a full barrier; this is a very regular pattern. The Partitioned Global Address Space (PGAS) parallel programming model, implemented for example by coarray Fortran and Unified Parallel C (UPC), is better suited for irregular and dynamic communication patterns and, in our opinion, is a valid alternative to the common MPI two-sided approach.

In this work, we combine the ease of programming provided by coarray Fortran with the power of NVIDIA GPUs; as far as we know, this is the first attempt to combine these two technologies. The most common heterogeneous architecture currently in use is represented in Fig. 2, where a multi-core CPU is connected with discrete accelerator devices through a PCIe bus. In this paper we explore the use of hybrid coarrays on this reference architecture to demonstrate the suitability of the coarray programming model for the next generation of HPC platforms.

To account for the various memory layers present in the accelerators (in this case the GPU), we propose a new variable attribute called "accelerated". This attribute suggests the compiler to store/treat the variable in a "fast" way on the heterogeneous node, thereby delegating the memory management to the runtime environment. Work on heterogeneous (MCDRAM and external DRAM) memory management systems has already appeared in literature [5]; our proposal of an explicit keyword makes it possible to use such systems in a very convenient way.

1. Background on Accelerators

In the HPC world, many-core co-processors are referred to as "accelerators". Currently, the most common accelerator cards available on the market are GPUs (mainly provided by NVIDIA) and Intel Xeon Phi coprocessors, based on Intel Many Integrated Cores (MIC) architecture. These devices are provided as a separate card to be plugged on the PCI Express channel. Any such accelerator needs a CPU (called *host*), which actively interacts with the accelerator in order to send/receive data and/or invoke computational kernels. Accelerators are throughput-oriented, energy-efficient devices; since one of the main challenges for exascale computing is power consumption, accelerators currently represent the best option for breaking the "power wall".

In 2014, the National Energy Research Scientific Computing Center (NERSC) announced that its next supercomputer, named "Cori", will be a Cray system based on a next-generation Intel MIC architecture; this machine will be a self-hosted architecture, neither a co-processor nor an accelerator. In other words, the concept of accelerator as a separate co-processor will disappear in the foreseeable future; such a deep change in the processor architecture will require writing much more hardware-aware code in order to exploit all the available computational power.

1.1. Architectural Changes - Intel Xeon Phi

Table 1 provides a comparison between an Intel Ivy-Bridge processor and an Intel Xeon Phi Knights-Landing (KNL), thus illustrating the change between the current and future generations of HPC platforms[1].

There are two major changes when moving from a "classic" CPU to a KNL:

- More cores per node with longer vector registers;
- Two levels of memory with a small amount of very fast memory.

1.2. Architectural Changes - NVIDIA GPUs

The architectural changes proposed by NVIDIA for its next generation GPU (named Pascal) are similar to those proposed by the Intel Xeon Phi:

- More (and slower) cores;
- Fast 3D (stacked) memory for high bandwidth and energy efficiency;

---

[1]Edison and Cori are the names of the systems installed or planned at NERSC.

Features	Edison (Ivy-Bridge)	Cori (Knights-Landing)
Num. physical cores	12 cores per CPU	60+ physical cores per CPU
Num. virtual cores	24 virtual cores per CPU	240+ virtual cores per CPU
Processor frequency	2.4-3.2 GHz	Much slower than 1 GHz
Num. OPs per cycle	4 double precision	8 double precision
Memory per core	2.5 GB	Less than 0.3 GB of fast memory per core and less than 2 GB of slow memory per core
Memory bandwidth	≈ 100 GB/s	Fast memory has $\approx 5\times$ DDR4

Table 1. Architectural changes (source: NERSC)

- A new high-speed CPU-GPU interconnect called NVLink from 5 to 12 times faster than the current PCIe.

With CUDA 6.0, NVIDIA accomplished one of the most important goals outlined in CUDA 2.0: to provide a Unified Memory, that is shared between the CPU and GPU, bridging the CPU-GPU divide.

Before CUDA 2.0, the only way to use memory on CUDA was to explicitly allocate a segment and manually copy the data from the CPU to the GPU using the cudaMemcpy() function. CUDA 2.0 introduced the zero-copy memory (also known as *mapped memory*); this feature allows to declare a portion of memory on the CPU to be directly accessible by the GPU. With this scheme the data movement is not directly coordinated by the user. CUDA 4.0 witnessed the introduction of the Unified Virtual Address (UVA) space: the CUDA runtime can identify where the data is stored based on the pointer value. UVA support makes it possible to directly access a portion of memory owned by a GPU from another GPU installed on the same node. In CUDA 6.0, NVIDIA introduced the concept of *managed memory*: data can be stored and migrated in a user-transparent way and the resulting code is thus much cleaner and less error-prone. At a first glance, zero-copy memory and managed memory look the same: both relieve the user from explicitly making copies from/to the GPU memory. The difference between the two is in *when* the memory access is done: for zero-copy, the transfer is started when the memory is accessed, whereas for managed memory the transfer is initiated immediately before the launch and after the kernel termination.

1.3. Clusters of GPUs

On hybrid clusters equipped with CPUs and GPUs, the most common way to exploit parallelism is through MPI for the inter-node communication, and CUDA for the GPU computation. This approach requires explicit data movement from/to GPU/CPU in order to send and receive data. In the latest evolution of both hardware and runtime libraries, this task has been either included in the MPI GPU-aware implementations [6,7] or performed with proprietary technologies, like GPUDirect. In [8] we compared the performance of various manual data exchange strategies with a CUDA-aware MPI implementation using PSBLAS [9]; we concluded that the MPI CUDA-aware implementation is largely sensitive to data imbalance.

2. Parallel Programming Models for Next Generation Architectures

The next computer architectures will expose hundreds of cores per single compute node; this will require adaptations of the commonly used programming models. Most importantly, to feed the cores with enough data, the memory hierarchy will have to expand, introducing additional layers between the cores and the main memory.

2.1. Hybrid MPI/OpenMP Approach

A common strategy to exploit the computational power provided by the many-core devices is to use a hybrid approach, combining MPI and OpenMP (or a similar directive-based language) for inter- and intra-node communication, respectively. This approach is common in GPU clusters, where the inter-node communication is performed with MPI and the actual computation is performed with CUDA or OpenCL on the local GPU(s) [8].

2.2. The PGAS Approach

An alternative to the MPI/OpenMP hybrid approach is to use a Partitioned Global Address Space (PGAS) model, as implemented for example by coarray Fortran (CAF) [10, 11] and Unified Parallel C (UPC). The PGAS parallel programming model attempts to combine the Single Program Multiple Data (SPMD) model commonly used in distributed memory systems with the semantics of shared memory systems. In the PGAS model, every process has its own memory address space but can expose a portion of its memory to other processes. At this time there are already publications [12,13] on the usage of PGAS languages on Intel Xeon Phi (KNC architecture); even though the evidence is not conclusive, it is our feeling that PGAS languages will play an important role for the next generation of architectures. This is especially because, as already mentioned, on an exascale machine equipped with billions of computing elements, the bulk-synchronous execution model adopted in many current scientific codes will be inadequate.

3. Introduction to Coarrays

Coarray Fortran (also known as CAF) began as a syntactic extension of Fortran 95 proposed in the early 1990s by Numrich and Reid [10]; it is now part of the Fortran 2008 standard (ISO/IEC 1539-1:2010) [11]. The main goal of coarrays is to allow language users to create parallel programs without the burden of explicitly invoking communication functions or directives such as with MPI and OpenMP.

A program that uses coarrays is treated as if it were replicated at the start of execution; each replication is called an *image*. Images execute asynchronously and explicit synchronization statements are used to maintain program correctness; a typical synchronization statement is `sync all`, acting as a barrier for all images. Each image has an integer image index varying between one and the number of images (inclusive); the run time environment provides the `this_image()` and `num_images()` functions to identify the executing image and the total number of them.

Variables can be declared as *coarrays*: they can be scalars or arrays, static or dynamic, and of intrinsic or derived type. All images can reference coarray variables located on other images, thereby providing data communications; the Fortran standard further provides other facilities such as locks, critical sections and atomic intrinsics.

3.1. GNU Fortran and LIBCAF

GNU Fortran (GFortran) is a free, efficient and widely used compiler; in 2012, GFortran started supporting the coarray syntax but only provided single-image execution, i.e., no actual communication. The main design point was to delegate the communication effort to an external library (LIBCAF) so that the compiler remains agnostic about the actual transport layer employed in the communication. Therefore, GFortran translates coarray operations into calls to an external library: OpenCoarrays. In [14] we presented two OpenCoarrays LIBCAF implementations, one based on MPI and the other based on GASNet [15]. Here we focus on LIBCAF_MPI, which assumes an underlying MPI implementation compliant with version 3.0. The following example shows how GFortran uses LIBCAF_MPI for a coarray allocation.

Coarray Fortran declaration of an array coarray with a dimension of 100 and an unspecified co dimension.

```
program alloc
implicit none
integer , dimension(100)  ::  x[*]
! More code here
```

Actual GNU Fortran call to OpenCoarrays function (C code)

```
x = (integer(kind=4)[100] * restrict) _gfortran_caf_register
(400, 0, (void * *) &caf_token.0, 0B, 0B, 0);
```

Actual memory and window allocation inside LIBCAF_MPI

```
MPI_Win_allocate(actual_size , 1, mpi_info_same_size ,
                 CAF_COMM_WORLD, &mem, *token);
```

In the example, the total amount of memory requested is 400 bytes (100 elements of 4 bytes each). The local memory will be returned by the function and stored inside the x variable, whereas the variable used for remote memory access will be stored in the *caf_token.0* variable. In the case of LIBCAF_MPI, such token represents the MPI_Window used by the one-sided functions.

4. Hybrid Coarray Fortran

In this paper, we propose to merge the expressivity of coarray Fortran with the computational power of accelerators. As far as we know, this is the very first attempt to use coarray Fortran with accelerators. The idea is to exploit the Unified Memory provided by CUDA 6.0 to make a coarray variable accessible from either the CPU or the GPU in a completely transparent way. The only changes required in OpenCoarrays are: (1) to separate the MPI window allocation and creation, and (2) to synchronize the CUDA device before using the memory. In MPI-2, the only way to create a window is to locally allocate the memory (via `malloc` or `MPI_Alloc_mem`) and then use the `MPI_Win_create` for the actual window creation, whereas with MPI-3 there is the option of a single call to `MPI_Win_allocate`. Our approach is to allocate the local memory using the cudaMallocManaged function in order to make that portion of memory "CUDA manageable", then call the cudaSyncDevice function, and finally create the window with MPI_Win_create. This approach is easy and general to implement, although it is not necessarily guaranteed to be the most efficient. A reasonable alternative would be either to delegate all communications to a CUDA-aware MPI implementation or to use a mapped memory approach, at the price of introducing a strong dependency on the quality of the MPI implementation. However, in our preliminary tests we found that the managed memory (Unified Memory) provided by CUDA 6.5 does not work too well with RDMA protocols (provided for example on Cray machines); we are fairly confident that such issue will be addressed in future CUDA implementations.

4.1. "ACCELERATED" Fortran Variables

With the approach introduced in the previous section, each coarray declared in the program requires interfacing with CUDA. What we suggest is a new variable attribute we call "accelerated". The meaning of this keyword is to mark a Fortran variable as "special", with faster access than a regular variable and suitable for accelerated computations.

In our current implementation an "accelerated" variable is CUDA-accessible; note that it is not necessarily also a coarray variable. The keyword is not meant to replace openACC statements for CUDA allocations, it just suggests the compiler to treat the variable differently than usual variables. We believe that such a keyword can play a significant role in the next generation architectures, where each processor will be an accelerator itself. As explained in Sec. 1.1, the Intel Knights-Landing will expose two types of memory: the first small and fast, the latter big and slow. Declaring a variable as "accelerated" would suggest the compiler that it could reside in the faster memory; in this case, the "accelerated" keyword assumes almost the same meaning as the "shared" keyword on CUDA. To test these ideas, we modified GFortran by adding this new keyword as an extension, currently affecting only allocatable variables. For coarray variables, we modify the _gfortran_caf_register by adding one more argument representing the accelerated attribute. For non-coarray variables, we force the allocation through cudaMallocManaged using a new function called _gfortran_caf_register_nc implemented in LIBCAF_MPI.

5. Experimental Results

To show the benefits of hybrid coarrays, we analyze in this section the performance of a matrix-matrix multiplication kernel based on the SUMMA algorithm [16]. We run the tests on Eurora, a heterogeneous cluster provided by CINECA, equipped with Tesla K20 and Intel Xeon Eight-Core E5-2658. We used the pre-release GCC-6.0, with OpenCoarrays 0.9.0 and IntelMPI-5. This unusual combination is because IntelMPI is the best MPI implementation provided on Eurora; however, OpenCoarrays can be linked with any MPI-3 compliant implementation.

5.1. MPI/CUDA vs. Hybrid CAF

On a cluster of GPUs, the most commonly used approach consists of employing MPI for the communication among GPUs, assuming that each process uses only one GPU, and then calling the CUDA kernel on each process. This simple approach allows to use several GPUs on the cluster but it may suffer from the synchronization imposed by the two-sided functions (MPI_Send, MPI_Recv) provided by MPI. In order to invoke the CUDA kernels from Fortran using GNU Fortran, we make extensive use of the C-interoperability capabilities introduced in Fortran 2003. A typical example of C interoperability for the dot product $a \cdot b$ performed with CUDA is the following:

```
interface
  subroutine memory_mapping(a,b,a_d,b_d,n,img) &
                  &bind(C, name="memory_mapping")
    use iso_c_binding
    real(c_float) :: a(*),b(*)
    type(c_ptr) :: a_d, b_d
    integer(c_int),value :: n
    integer(c_int),value :: img
  end subroutine memory_mapping
  subroutine manual_mapped_cudaDot(a,b,partial_dot,n) &
                  & bind(C, name="manual_mapped_cudaDot")
    use iso_c_binding , only : c_float ,c_int ,c_ptr
    type(c_ptr),value :: a,b
    real(c_float) :: partial_dot
    integer(c_int),value :: n
  end subroutine
end interface
```

The two subroutines are interfaces for the C functions called memory_mapping and manual_mapped_cudadot. The first is used to map the memory previously allocated on the CPU for *a* and *b* onto the GPU; the function returns two C pointers called a_d and b_d which represent pointers usable on the GPU. The latter is the wrapper for the actual computational kernel. It takes as input arguments the GPU pointers returned by the memory_mapping function. NVIDIA claims that Unified Memory, besides reducing code complexity, could also improve the performance by transferring data on demand between CPU and GPU. There are already some studies [17] on Unified Memory performance, that shows the advantages to be strongly problem-dependent.

5.2. SUMMA Algorithm

SUMMA stands for Scalable Universal Matrix Multiplication Algorithm and is currently used in ScaLAPACK. The SUMMA algorithm is particularly suitable for PGAS languages because of the one-sided nature of the involved transfers.

Listing 1: Usual matrix product	Listing 2: SUMMA approach

```
do i=1,n1
  do j=1,n2
    do k=1,n3
      C(i,j) = C(i,j) &
             + A(i,k)*B(k,j)
    end do
  end do
end do
```

```
do k=1,n3
  do i=1,n1
    do j=1,n2
      C(i,j) = C(i,j) &
             + A(i,k)*B(k,j)
    end do
  end do
end do
```

Listings 1 and 2 allow to compare the pseudo-code for the usual matrix product to that of the SUMMA algorithm when we wan to multiply matrices *A* and *B*, resulting in matrix *C*. SUMMA performs *n* partial outer products (column vector by row vector). This formulation allows to parallelize the two innermost loops on *i* and *j*. Using MPI two-sided, each process has to post a send/receive in order to exchange the data needed for the computation; with coarrays, because of the one-sided semantics, each image can take the data without interfering with the remote image flow.

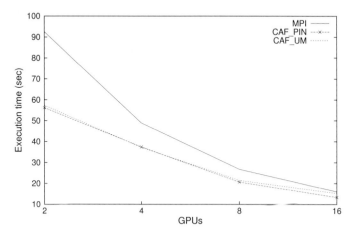

Figure 3. Performance of SUMMA: MPI-based vs. coarray Fortran implementations on Eurora cluster

Figure 3 compares the performance achieved by the coarray Fortran and MPI based implementations of the SUMMA algorithm. The chart shows the mean execution time on 10 runs using a matrix of size 4096x4096. We also report the performance of LIB-CAF_MPI with the CUDA support based on CUDA mapped memory as well as on Unified Memory, labeled with CAF_PIN and CAF_UM respectively. We observe that the performance achieved with Unified Memory is equal or worse than that achieved with the usual pinned memory, as already noted in [17].

6. Conclusions

In this paper, we show how PGAS languages, and in particular coarray Fortran, can provide significant speedup in a hybrid CPU+Accelerator context. We show that using coarray Fortran, besides simplifying the code, improves the performance because of the one-sided semantic which characterizes PGAS languages. We also propose a new variable attribute called "accelerated" for the Fortran language. Such attribute instructs the compiler to treat the variable as suitable for acceleration. Based on what we currently know about future architectures, we think that such keyword can play a significant role in the post-petascale era, where heterogeneous code will be a must for exploiting all the computational power provided by complex and energy efficient architectures.

Acknowledgments

We gratefully acknowledge the support received from: CINECA for the access on Galileo/Eurora for the project OpenCAF under the ISCRA grant program for 2015; National Energy Research Scientific Computing Center, which is supported by the Office of Science of the U.S. Department of Energy under Contract No. DE-AC02-05CH11231, for the access on Hopper/Edison under the OpenCoarrays grant.

References

[1] J. Shalf, S. Dosanjh, and J. Morrison. Exascale computing technology challenges. In *Proc. of 9th Int'l Conf. on High Performance Computing for Computational Science*, VECPAR '10, pages 1–25. Springer-Verlag, 2011.

[2] J. A. Ang et al. Abstract machine models and proxy architectures for exascale computing. In *Proc. of 1st Int'l Workshop on Hardware-Software Co-Design for High Performance Computing*, Co-HPC '14, pages 25–32. IEEE, 2014.

[3] J. Jeddeloh and B. Keeth. Hybrid memory cube new DRAM architecture increases density and performance. In *Proc. of 2012 Symp. on VLSI Technology*, VLSIT, pages 87–88, June 2012.

[4] HMC Consortium. Hybrid memory cube, 2015. http://www.hybridmemorycube.org/.

[5] L.-N. Tran, F.J. Kurdahi, A.M. Eltawil, and H. Homayoun. Heterogeneous memory management for 3D-DRAM and external DRAM with QoS. In *Proc. of 18th Asia and South Pacific Design Automation Conf.*, ASP-DAC '13, pages 663–668, January 2013.

[6] H. Wang, S. Potluri, D. Bureddy, C. Rosales, and D.K. Panda. GPU-aware MPI on RDMA-enabled clusters: Design, implementation and evaluation. *IEEE Trans. Parallel Distrib. Syst.*, 25(10), 2014.

[7] A.M. Aji, J. Dinan, D. Buntinas, P. Balaji, W.-C. Feng, K.R. Bisset, and R. Thakur. MPI-ACC: An integrated and extensible approach to data movement in accelerator-based systems. In *Proc. of IEEE 14th Int'l Conf. on High Performance Computing and Communication*, HPCC '12, 2012.

[8] V. Cardellini, A. Fanfarillo, and S. Filippone. Sparse matrix computations on clusters with GPGPUs. In *Proc. of 2014 Int'l Conf. on High Performance Computing Simulation*, HPCS '14, pages 23–30, 2014.

[9] S. Filippone and Buttari A. Object-oriented techniques for sparse matrix computations in Fortran 2003. *ACM Trans. Math. Softw.*, 38(4), 2012.

[10] R. W. Numrich and J. Reid. Co-array Fortran for parallel programming. *SIGPLAN Fortran Forum*, 17(2):1–31, August 1998.

[11] R. W. Numrich and J. Reid. Co-arrays in the next Fortran standard. *SIGPLAN Fortran Forum*, 24(2):4–17, August 2005.

[12] M. Luo, M. Li, M. Venkatesh, X. Lu, and Panda D. UPC on MIC: Early experiences with native and symmetric modes. In *Proc. of Int'l Conf. on Partitioned Global Address Space Programming Models*, PGAS '13, October 2013.

[13] N. Namashivayam, S. Ghosh, D. Khaldi, D. Eachempati, and B. Chapman. Native mode-based optimizations of remote memory accesses in OpenSHMEM for Intel Xeon Phi. In *Proc. of 8th Int'l Conf. on Partitioned Global Address Space Programming Models*, PGAS '14, pages 12:1–12:11. ACM, 2014.

[14] A. Fanfarillo, T. Burnus, V. Cardellini, S. Filippone, D. Nagle, and D. Rouson. OpenCoarrays: Open-source transport layers supporting coarray fortran compilers. In *Proc. of 8th Int'l Conf. on Partitioned Global Address Space Programming Models*, PGAS '14, pages 4:1–4:11. ACM, 2014.

[15] D. Bonachea. GASNet Specification, v1.1. Technical Report UCB/CSD-02-1207, Univ. of California Berkeley, 2002.

[16] R. A. van de Geijn and J. Watts. SUMMA: Scalable universal matrix multiplication algorithm. *Concurr. Comput.: Pract. Exper.*, 9:255–274, 1997.

[17] R. Landaverde, Z. Tiansheng, A.K. Coskun, and M. Herbordt. An investigation of unified memory access performance in CUDA. In *Proc. of IEEE High Performance Extreme Computing Conf.*, HPEC '14, pages 1–6, September 2014.

Parallel Computing: On the Road to Exascale
G.R. Joubert et al. (Eds.)
IOS Press, 2016

185

doi:10.3233/978-1-61499-621-7-185

Lapedo: Hybrid Skeletons for Programming Heterogeneous Multicore Machines in Erlang

Vladimir JANJIC, Christopher BROWN, Kevin HAMMOND

School of Computer Science, University of St Andrews, UK.

$\{vj32,\ cmb21,\ kh8\}$@st-andrews.ac.uk

Abstract. We describe *Lapedo*, a novel library of *hybrid* parallel skeletons for programming *heterogeneous* multi-core/many-core CPU/GPU systems in Erlang. Lapedo's skeletons comprise a mixture of CPU and GPU components, allowing skeletons to be flexibly and dynamically mapped to available resources, with all of the low-level tedious code to divide work between CPUs and GPUs, transfer the data between the main and GPU memory and offload computations to the GPUs provided by the library. We evaluate the effectiveness of *Lapedo* on three realistic use cases from different domains, demonstrating significant improvements in speedups compared to CPU-only and GPU-only executions.

Keywords. Parallel skeletons, Hybrid skeletons, Heterogeneous multi-core systems, GPU offloading

1. Introduction

Following the initial stages of the multi-core revolution, further major changes in computer hardware are now ongoing. Hardware is getting increasingly heterogeneous, integrating *accelerators*, such as graphic processing units (GPUs), field programmable gate arrays (FPGAs) and even lightweight many-core CPU accelerators, with traditional multi-core processors. These *heterogeneous* systems have a potential to deliver orders of magnitude more performance than traditional CPU-only based systems, and are increasingly found in high-performance architectures. In order to fully exploit the potential that these systems offer, programmers needs to combine several different low-level programming models, e.g. OpenCL for GPUs, VHDL or Verilog for FPGAs and OpenMP for CPUs. They must also explicitly manage data transfers between main memory and accelerator memory, schedule computations, fetch results, etc. Moreover, the solutions that perform optimally are usually tied to a specific heterogeneous architecture and cannot easily be ported, yielding problems in terms of e.g. increased maintenance costs and lack of longevity. This makes programming heterogeneous multi-core/many-core systems *extremely difficult and complex* compared with programming multi-core CPUs. What is needed are high-level programming abstractions, hiding the hardware complexity of such systems by abstracting over the varying low-level models, while still achieving (near-)optimal accelerated performance.

This paper presents *Lapedo*[1], a novel system of parallel *skeletons* for programming heterogeneous multi-core/many-core systems in the functional language Erlang. Functional programming approaches naturally provide high-level abstractions through e.g. higher-order functions. In *Lapedo*, we exploit this to build skeletons: parameterised parallelism templates that abstract over low-level parallelism details and parallel structures of a program. Hybrid skeletons contain alternative implementations of their components for different processor types, automatically providing tedious and error-prone code for transferring data to/from processor types, scheduling, fetching results, etc. *Lapedo* also provides mechanisms for dividing work between different processor types, ensuring load balancing and eliminating the need for extensive profiling and performance tuning. This allows skeletons to be flexibly deployed on an arbitrary combination of CPUs and GPUs, allowing us to achieve performance results that are better than either CPU or GPU execution alone, while still keeping a very high-level of abstraction. Although in this paper we focus only on GPU accelerators, our low-level implementation is based on OpenCL and our work can, therefore, be easily extended to a wide range of other accelerators, including Intel Xeon PHIs, FPGAs and DSPs. The general hybrid skeleton approach can also be applied to other language frameworks, such as C++, Java, Haskell, etc. This paper makes the following research contributions:

1. we describe the *Lapedo* Erlang library of *hybrid skeletons* that allow CPU and accelerator components to be combined within the same skeleton;
2. we describe the current *Lapedo* implementation on heterogeneous CPU/ GPU combinations; and,
3. we demonstrate that *Lapedo* allows us to produce efficient and scalable code for heterogeneous systems, achieving real speedups of up to 21.2 over sequential Erlang programs on a 24-core machine with a GPU.

2. Heterogeneous Parallelism and Skeletons

Compared to traditional CPUs, accelerators usually offer higher-performance (in terms of e.g. FLOPS) at lower clock speeds and with reduced energy usage per unit of performance. However, they are usually restricted in terms of the parallelism model that is offered (often only data-parallel) and can be much more difficult to program than traditional CPU-only systems. This creates a significant barrier for applications programmers. In this paper, we will restrict our attention to CPU/GPU combinations, representing the current most widely-used class of heterogeneous multicores. However, since our implementations target the OpenCL programming model, which is supported by other types of accelerators (such as FPGAs), our work is also applicable in wider settings.

---

[1]Named after the hybrid *Lapedo* or *Lagar Velho* Neanderthal/Homo Sapiens skeleton.

Conventional Approaches to GPU Programming The two most widely-used approaches to GPU programming, CUDA and OpenCL provide similar portable, but low-level SIMD programming interfaces. Unfortunately, *programmability* is still generally lacking with these models: the programmer needs to take care of a number of very low-level programming aspects, including the number of threads and thread blocks, data transfers between CPUs and GPUs and scheduling of computations on the GPUs. Some newer standards, such as SyCL[2], aim to further simplify GPU programming by offering further abstractions. In addition, there are several algorithmic skeleton libraries (see Section 2.2) for programming GPUs, such as SkePU [7] and SkeCL [15]. However, these models are either restricted to GPUs only or require the programmer to have a deep understanding not only of the problem that is being solved, but also of the underlying hardware architecture. This usually results in a solution that is heavily optimised for a particular hardware system and which, therefore, lacks *performance portability*. The GPU-specific code is also often highly fragile and likely to be error-prone.

Hybrid Programming Approaches There are several models that support combining CPUs and GPUs for the same computation, including mapping of work to different devices, and thus allowing proper "hybrid" programming. StarPU [5] is a runtime system that supports CPU/GPU systems and is used as one of the backends for SkePU. It maps the SkePU skeleton calls to one or more *tasks* that can be mapped to different devices. It was shown to give good performance for simple benchmarks on CPU/GPU configurations [10]. Compared to this approach, the library that we present in this paper is higher level, thanks to the use of functional programming technology (see below). Grewe and O'Boyle proposed a purely static partitioning scheme for OpenCL [9], based on predictive modelling and program features. While this enables deriving good mappings, the programming model is still OpenCL, making it too low-level for non-experts. Qilin [11] is a heterogeneous programming system that includes an automatic adaptive mapping technique to map computations processing elements on CPU/GPU machines. We use a very similar mechanism for deriving a division of work between CPUs and GPUs in Section 3.1.

2.1. (Heterogeneous) Parallel Programming in Erlang

Erlang [1] is a strict, impure, functional programming language. It is widely used in the telecommunications industry, but is also beginning to be used more widely for high-reliability/highly-concurrent systems, e.g. databases [12], AOL's *Marketplace by Adtech* [16], and WhatsApp [13]. It has excellent support for concurrency and distribution, including built-in fault-tolerance. Erlang supports a threading model, where *processes* model small units of computation. The scheduling of processes is handled automatically by the Erlang Virtual Machine, providing basic load balancing mechanisms. We build on these lower-level mechanisms to provide higher-level parallelism abstractions, using *algorithmic skeletons*. We exploit all the usual Erlang distribution mechanisms to build highly-distributed scalable systems, where individual nodes can exploit accelerators using *Lapedo*.

---

[2]https://www.khronos.org/sycl

Accelerator Programming in Erlang   Erlang has no native support for programming accelerators. However, a library containing OpenCL bindings is available [14], which provides an Erlang interface to low-level OpenCL functions to set up accelerator computations, transfer data to/from the accelerators, and launch kernels implemented in OpenCL, plus basic marshalling mechanisms between *binary* data structures in Erlang and C arrays. While enabling programmers to write their code in Erlang, this library does not simplify GPU programming, since the programmer is still required to write code that is equivalent to programming directly in OpenCL. In the *Lapedo* library, we build on this library to provide higher-level skeletons that encapsulate most of the required OpenCL code.

2.2. Skeletons

Algorithmic skeletons abstract commonly-used patterns of parallel computation, communication, and interaction [4] into parameterised templates. For example, we might define a *parallel map* skeleton, whose functionality is identical to a standard *map* function, but which creates a number of Erlang processes (*worker processes*) to execute each element of the map in parallel. Using a skeleton approach allows the programmer to adopt a top-down *structured* approach to parallel programming, where skeletons are composed to give the overall parallel structure of the program. Details such as communication, task creation, task or data migration, scheduling, etc. are embedded within the skeleton implementation, which may be tailored to a specific architecture or class of architectures. This offers an improved level of portability over typical low-level approaches. A recent survey of algorithmic skeleton approaches can be found in [8].

2.3. The Skel Library for Erlang

Lapedo is integrated into the *Skel* [3,2] library, which defines a small set of classical skeletons for Erlang. Each skeleton operates over a stream of input values, producing a corresponding stream of results. Skel also allows simple composition and nesting of skeletons. We consider the following skeletons:

- `func` is a simple wrapper skeleton that encapsulates a sequential function as a streaming skeleton. For example, in Skel `{func, fun f/1}` denotes a `func` skeleton wrapping the Erlang function, `f`, with `f/1` denoting the arity of `f`. In this paper, we denote `func` skeleton simply by `{func, fun f}`. When *func* is instantiated, a new Erlang process is created and mapped to a single OS thread, which executes the function sequentially without any parallelism.
- `pipe` models a composition of skeletons $s_1, s_2, \ldots, s_n$ over a stream of inputs. Within the pipeline, each of the s_i is applied in parallel to the result of the s_{i-1}. For example, in Skel: `{pipe, [{func, fun f}, {func, fun g}, {func, fun h}]}` denotes a parallel pipeline with three stages. Each pipeline stage is a `func` skeleton, wrapping the Erlang functions, `f`, `g`, and `h`.
- `farm` models application of the same operation over a stream of inputs. Each of the n farm *workers* is a skeleton that operates in parallel over independent values of the input stream. For example, in Skel: `{farm, 10, {pipe, [{func, fun f}, {func, fun g}]}}` denotes a `farm` where

the worker is a parallel pipeline with two stages (each the `func` skeleton wrapper for the functions `f` and `g`, respectively). This example `farm` has 10 workers, as specified by the second parameter, therefore running 10 independent copies of the pipeline skeleton.

- `cluster` is a data parallel skeleton, where each independent input, x_i can be partitioned into a number of sub parts, $x_1, x_2, \ldots, x_n$, that can be worked upon in parallel. A skeleton, s, is then applied to each element of the sub-stream in parallel. Finally the result is combined into a single result for each input. An example, in Skel: {cluster, {func, fun f}, fun dec, fun rec} denotes a `cluster` skeleton with each worker a simple sequential function, where the `dec` function is used to decompose each input list into chunks, and the `rec` function is used to recompose the list of result from the chunks of results. This is similar to the `farm` skeleton example above, except the number of workers is not specified for the `map` skeleton but rather implicitly computed by the `dec` function. Note that `decom` and `recom` can be identity functions, in which case we get the usual `map` skeleton applied to each element of input stream, where the `func` skeleton is applied to each element of an input list in parallel.

- `feedback` wraps a skeleton s, feeding the results of applying s back as new inputs to s, provided they match a filter function, f.

3. The Lapedo System for Hybrid Skeletons

Lapedo extends the Skel library described in Section 2.3 with hybrid versions of the *farm* and *cluster* skeletons that combine CPU and GPU *components*, which are expressed by wrapping operations using the `func` skeleton. This ensures that operations written for a CPU will be mapped to single sequential OS thread, and GPU operations will be mapped to a GPU device. In general, a programmer is required to provide these components which, in the case of the GPU, contain all the code for creating buffers, transferring data to and from the GPU and scheduling the kernel that implements the actual operation. *Lapedo* provides a mechanism for automatically generating this boilerplate code, and, in order to use the hybrid skeletons, a programmer is only required only to write Erlang CPU components and relatively simple problem-specific GPU kernels in OpenCL.

Hybrid Farm. Similarly to the CPU-only farm skeleton (Section 2.2), hybrid farm applies the same operation to a stream of inputs in parallel. It requires two skeleton instances that provide implementations of the operation for a sequential CPU thread and a GPU. Each element of the input stream is tagged with either cpu or gpu tag[3] and, depending on this tag, sent to one of the two inner skeletons. In this way, different processor types process input elements in parallel. The syntax of the hybrid farm skeleton is

{hyb_farm, CPUSkeleton, GPUSkeleton, NCPUWorkers, NGPUWorkers}

---

[3]In the future, additional tags will be supported to accommodate additional accelerator types.

where NCPUWorkers and NGPUWorkers are the number of instances of the CPUSkeleton and GPUSkeleton that are created. These determine how many input elements will be tagged with the cpu and gpu tags. For example, if there are 20 input tasks, and NCPUWorkers is 4 and NGPUWorkers is 1, then 16 tasks will be tagged with the cpu tag and 4 will be tagged with the gpu tag. For example

{hyb_farm, {func, fun f_CPU/1}, {func, fun f_GPU/1}, 4, 1}

defines a hybrid farm skeleton, where the operation is a simple function, f_CPU being a sequential CPU operation and f_GPU for a GPU operation. As mentioned above, the code for f_GPU can be generated automatically, based on a programmer-provided OpenCL kernel that implements a function equivalent to f_CPU.

Hybrid Cluster.   Similarly to the Section 2.2, we focus on a list version of the hybrid cluster skeleton, where each element in an input stream is a list, and each of these lists is decomposed into sublists that are processed in parallel. *Lapedo* also provides a more general version of this skeleton, that works on arbitrary data structures. The syntax of the hybrid cluster skeleton is

{hyb_cluster, CPUSk, GPUSk, DecompFun, RecompFun, NCPUW, NGPUW}

As in the case of the hybrid farm, CPUSk and GPUSk provide CPU and GPU implementations of the operation that is to be applied to the sublists (generated by DecompFun) of each list of an input stream. Decomposing an input list appropriately in the case of the hybrid cluster is usually non-trivial, due to a difference in performance of a CPU thread over a GPU for a given problem. For this reason, we provide two variants of the hybrid cluster skeleton that automatically find a good decomposition of work:

- {hyb_cluster, CPUSk, GPUSk, ChunkSizeMult, TimeRatio, NCPUW, NGPUW}, where ChunkSizeMult is a minimal length of each sublist, with the length of each sublist after decomposition being its multiplier. TimeRatio is a ratio between the processing time of a single sublist of size ChunkSizeMult on a CPU and on a GPU (which can be obtained using profiling). This parameter determines how much faster the GPU is in processing work than a CPU thread (or vice versa). NCPUW and NGPUW determine how many sublists will be processed by sequential CPU threads and how many by GPUs. These two parameters also determine the total number of chunks that each task is decomposed into (NCPUW+NGPUW) and, together with TimeRatio, determine the length of each sublist. For more details about how lengths of sublists are calculated, see Section 3.1
- {hyb_cluster, CPUSk, GPUSk, ProfChunk, NCPUW, NGPUW}, which is similar to the above version, with the difference that ChunkSizeMult and TimeRatio parameters are here automatically calculated by doing profiling on a user provided example sublist ProfChunk, which needs to be representative of the sublists that will be processed by CPUSk and GPUSk.

3.1. Division of Work Between CPUs and GPUs.

The `hyb_cluster` skeleton requires the numbers of CPU and GPU workers to be specified explicitly (`NCPUW` and `NGPUW` parameters). Where there is no nesting of skeletons, i.e. where there is only a `hyb_cluster` skeleton at the top level, and the `CPUSk` and `GPUSk` skeletons are simple `func` skeletons, we can simply set `NCPUW` and `NGPUW` to be the number of CPU cores and GPU devices in the system, respectively. The problem with this, however, is that for suitable problems, GPUs are much faster in processing tasks than CPU cores. Therefore, if we divide input lists into equally-sized sublists, the same amount of work will be assigned to each CPU and GPU worker, in which case GPUs will finish much faster than CPU cores, resulting in load imbalance.

The aforementioned problem can be avoided if we do a smarter decomposition of input lists. Assuming that a given problem is regular (i.e. that it takes the same amount of time to process each element of an input list) and that we can obtain timing information (e.g. using profiling) to determine how much faster can a GPU process a set of list items than a CPU core (including time to transfer the data to/from the GPU memory), we can, using some simple formulae, derive how many list items should be processed by the GPUs and how much by each CPU core in order to get the best execution time. For example, assume that we have g GPUs and c CPU cores in a system, and that the ratio between processing time for k items between a CPU and a GPU is ratio. If an input list has n items (where n is divisible by k), then we can estimate the time it takes to process all of the items in the list if n_c items are processed by CPU cores by

$$T(n_c) = \max\left\{\left\lceil\frac{\left\lceil\frac{n_c}{k}\cdot\text{ratio}\right\rceil}{c}\right\rceil, \left\lceil\frac{\frac{n-n_c}{k}}{g}\right\rceil\right\},$$

where the first argument of the max is the time it takes to process n_c items on CPU cores, and the second argument is the time it takes to process the remaining items by the GPUs. The best time we can obtain is then $\min\{T(n_c)|n_c \in \{0, k, 2k, ..., n\}\}$, and the optimal number of items to process on CPU cores is such n_c for which this minimum is obtained. In this way, we calculate a pair $(n_c, n - n_c)$ for the number of list items to be processed by CPU cores and the GPUs, respectively. Sublists lengths sizes for CPU cores are then

$$\left\{\underbrace{\left\lfloor\frac{n_c}{c}\right\rfloor, \left\lfloor\frac{n_c}{c}\right\rfloor, \cdots \left\lfloor\frac{n_c}{c}\right\rfloor}_{c-(n_c \bmod c) \text{ times}}, \underbrace{\left\lceil\frac{n_c}{c}\right\rceil, \left\lceil\frac{n_c}{c}\right\rceil, \cdots, \left\lceil\frac{n_c}{c}\right\rceil}_{n_c \bmod c \text{ times}}\right\}.$$

We can similarly calculate the chunk sizes for the GPUs. The parameter k above should be chosen so that it gives the best parallelism on the GPU, i.e. it should be maximum number of list items that the GPU can process in parallel (parameter `ChunkSizeMult` in the description of `hyb_cluster` skeleton).

4. Evaluation

We evaluate *Lapedo* on three realistic use cases: *Ant Colony Optimisation*, *Football Simulation* and *Image Merging*. The experiments were conducted on a system that comprises two 12-core 2.3GHz AMD Opteron 6176 processors, 32GB RAM and NVidia Tesla C2050 GPU with 448 CUDA cores. We evaluate the speedups relative to the sequential Erlang versions. To eliminate the effect of variation of the execution times for CPU components on the same configuration (i.e. with the same number of cores used), each data point is averaged over 10 application runs with the same input data.

4.1. Ant Colony Optimisation

Ant Colony Optimisation (ACO) [6] is a heuristic for solving NP-complete optimisation problems. We apply ACO to the Single Machine Total Weighted Tardiness Problem (SMTWTP) optimisation problem, where we are given n jobs and each job, i, is characterised by its processing time, p_i deadline, d_i, and weight, w_i. The goal is to find the schedule of jobs that minimises the total weighted *tardiness*, defined as $\sum w_i \cdot \max\{0, C_i - d_i\}$, where C_i is the completion time of the job, i. The ACO solution consists of a number of iterations, where in each iteration each ant independently tries to improve the current best schedule, and is biased by a *pheromone trail*.The top-level skeleton structure is:

Pipe = {pipe, [{hyb_cluster, [{func, fun ant_c/1}], [{func, fun ant_g/1}]}],
        TimeRatio, fun struct_size /1, fun make_chunk/2,
        fun lists : flatten /1, NrCPUW, NrGPUW},
          [{func, fun update_and_spawn/1}]]},
Feedback = {feedback, [Pipe], fun ant_feedback/1},

A speedup graph is given in Figure 1(a). We can see that the CPU-only version shows modest speedups, up to 5.13 on 22 cores, degrading slightly when all 24 cores are used (this is probably the result of a saturation/scheduling conflict with other applications). The GPU-only version (where the number of CPU cores is 0) shows a better speedup of 7.52 than any CPU-only version. Combining CPU threads with a GPU gives clear benefits over either processor type alone, delivering speedups of up to 12.2 when 20 CPU threads and a GPU are used. The graph shows some anomalies, e.g. at 2 CPU threads plus a GPU, the performance is less than one CPU thread plus a GPU; at 18 CPU threads, there is a slight dip in speedup; and beyond 20 threads, performance plateaus. This can probably be mostly explained by the effects of work division described in Section 3.1. In the case of 1 CPU thread plus a GPU, our algorithm derives good work division where the CPU threads and GPU finish the execution at approximately the same time. Adding 1 thread, more work is given to the CPU threads, and in this case it may happen that the GPU finishes its portion of work earlier, resulting in imbalance.

4.2. Football Simulation

Football Simulation predicts the outcomes of football games, and is used by betting companies to calculate the winning odds for matches. Each simulation ac-

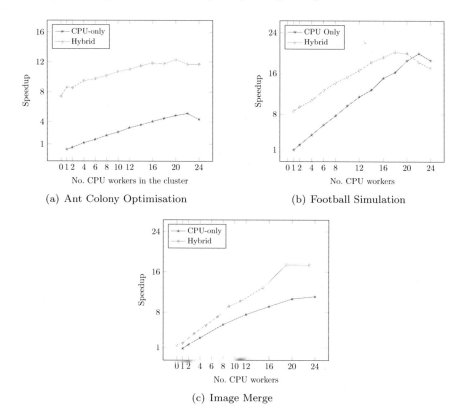

Figure 1. Speedups for Ant Colony, Football Simulation and Image Merge

cepts information about the teams involved in a match (e.g. attack and defence strength), and uses a randomised routine to predict the end result of the match. The final prediction for each match is averaged over multiple simulations. The top-level skeleton structure is

Cluster = {hyb_cluster, {func, fun(P) −> sim_match_cpu(P, NrSims) **end**},
            {func, fun(P) −> sim_match_gpu(P, NrSims) **end**},
            ChunkSizeMult, TimeRatio, NCPUW, NGPUW},
AllRes = skel:do(Cluster, AllPairs),
Results = [get_average_score(OnePairRes) || OnePairRes <− AllRes].

P is a pair of tuples that contains the necessary information about one match, i.e. information about one pair of teams. In the simplest case, we provide just two floating point numbers for each team, attack and defence strength. For each pair of teams, `sim_match_cpu` or `sim_match_gpu` is called `NrSimulations` times, and then the average score is computed using the `get_average_score` function. The speedups of *Football Simulation* are given in 1(b). Both CPU-only and hybrid version show improved speedups (from 1 and 8.3) when more CPU workers (and, therefore, CPU threads) are used, up to the point where the best speedup is obtained (20.2 with 18 CPU workers for hybrid version and 20 with 22 workers for CPU-only version). After this point, when more CPU workers are added, the performance starts to drop. This is due to unpredictability of performance of workers as the total number of Erlang processes approaches the number of cores, due to scheduling issues. This also has the effect that the division of work between CPU and GPU workers in the hybrid case is sub optimal when more than 18 CPU workers are used, explaining the earlier dip in performance for the hybrid case. Altogether, we can observe that when a smaller number of CPU threads are used, the hybrid version significantly outperforms the CPU-only version.

4.3. Image Merge

Image Merge is an application from the computer graphics domain. It reads a stream of pairs of images from files, and merges images from each pair. The top-level skeleton structure is

Farm = {hyb_farm, {func, fun merge_cpu/1}, {func, fun merge_gpu/1}},
FinalImages = skel:do(Farm, Images).

The speedups for Image Merge are given in Figure 1(c). We can observe that the hybrid version significantly outperforms the CPU-only version regardless of the number of CPU workers used, with the best speedups of 17 and 10 for hybrid and CPU-only version. We also observe an increase in speedup as the number of CPU workers increases. As usual, when the number of CPU workers approaches the number of CPU threads, we observe a drop in performance.

5. Conclusions and Future Work

This paper describes *Lapedo*, a system of hybrid skeletons for Erlang. Skeletons abstract commonly-used patterns of parallel computation, communication, and interaction into parameterised templates. Hybrid skeletons combine components that are specialised for different processor types , thus allowing efficient exploitation of heterogeneous multi-core/many-core systems while still offering a very high-level programming model. We have focused purely on CPU/GPU combinations, but since our library is built on top of OpenCL, it can also be used with other accelerators. We have also described a simple mechanism for dividing work between processor types. Finally, we have demonstrated *Lapedo* on three realistic Erlang applications. Our results show clear benefits of using hybrid skeletons, giving significantly better speedups compared to CPU-only skeletons with only a modest increase in programming effort, programmers are only required to write relatively-simple OpenCL kernels. In the future work, we plan to extend the *Lapedo* library with additional, domain-specific skeletons (e.g. orbit skeleton) and to adapt it to support emerging accelerator classes.

Acknowledgements

This work was funded by European Union FP7 grant "ParaPhrase: Parallel Patterns for Adaptive Heterogeneous Multicore Systems" (code 288570) and H2020 grant "RePhrase: Refactoring Parallel Heterogeneous Resource-Aware Applications – a Software Engineering Approach" (code 644235). We would like to thank Christoph Kessler for very useful suggestions on improving the paper.

References

[1]   J. Armstrong, S. Virding, and M. Williams. *Concurrent Programming in Erlang.* Prentice-Hall, 1993.

[2]   I. Bozó, V. Fordós, Z. Horvath, M. Tóth, D. Horpácsi, T. Kozsik, J. Köszegi, A. Barwell, C. Brown, and K. Hammond. Discovering Parallel Pattern Candidates in Erlang. In *Proc. 13th Erlang Workshop*, Erlang '14, pages 13–23. ACM, 2014.

[3]   C. Brown, M. Danelutto, K. Hammond, P. Kilpatrick, and A. Elliott. Cost-Directed Refactoring for Parallel Erlang Programs. *IJPP*, 42(4):564–582, 2014.

[4]   M. I. Cole. *Algorithmic Skeletons: A Structured Approach to the Management of Parallel Computation.* PhD thesis, 1988. AAID-85022.

[5]   U. Dastgeer, C. Kessler, and S. Thibault. Flexible Runtime Support for Efficient Skeleton Programming. In K. de Bosschere, E. H. D'Hollander, G. R. Joubert, D. Padua, F. Peters, and M. Sawyer, editors, *Advances in Parallel Computing, vol. 22: Applications, Tools and Techniques on the Road to Exascale Computing*, pages 159–166. IOS Press, 2012. Proc. ParCo conference, Ghent, Belgium, Sep. 2011.

[6]   M. den Besten, T. Sttzle, and M. Dorigo. Ant Colony Optimization for the Total Weighted Tardiness Problem. In *PPSN VI*, volume 1917 of *Lecture Notes in Computer Science*, pages 611–620. 2000.

[7]   J. Enmyren and C. W. Kessler SkePU. A Multi-backend Skeleton Programming Library for multi-GPU Systems. In *Proc. HLPP '10*, pages 5–14. ACM, 2010.

[8]   H. González-Vélez and M. Leyton. A Survey of Algorithmic Skeleton Frameworks: High-level Structured Parallel Programming Enablers. *Softw. Pract. Exper.*, 40(12):1135–1160, Nov. 2010.

[9]   D. Grewe and M. F. OBoyle. A Static Task Partitioning Approach for Heterogeneous Systems Using OpenCL. In J. Knoop, editor, *Compiler Construction*, volume 6601 of *Lecture Notes in Computer Science*, pages 286–305. Springer Berlin Heidelberg, 2011.

[10] C. Kessler, U. Dastgeer, S. Thibault, R. Namyst, A. Richards, U. Dolinsky, S. Benkner, J. L. Träff, and S. Pllana. Programmability and Performance Portability Aspects of Heterogeneous Multi-/Manycore Systems. In *Proc. DATE-2012 conference on Design, Automation and Test in Europe, Dresden, Germany*, Mar. 2012.

[11] C.-K. Luk, S. Hong, and H. Kim. Qilin: Exploiting parallelism on heterogeneous multiprocessors with adaptive mapping. In *42nd Annual IEEE/ACM International Symposium on Microarchitecture*, MICRO 42, pages 45–55, New York, NY, USA, 2009. ACM.

[12] Rashkovskii, Yurii. Genomu: A Concurrency-Oriented Database. In *Erlang Factory SF*, 2013.

[13] Reed, Rick. Scaling to Milions of Simultaneous Connections. In *Erlang Factory SF*, 2012.

[14] T. Rogvall. OpenCL Binding for Erlang. https://github.com/tonyrog/cl.

[15] M. Steuwer and S. Gorlatch. SkelCL: Enhancing OpenCL for High-Level Programming of Multi-GPU Systems. In *Par. Comp. Tech.*, Springer LNCS vol. 7979, pp. 258–272. 2013.

[16] Wilson, Ken. Migrating a C++ Team to Using Erlang to Deliver a Real-Time Bidding Ad System In *Erlang Factory SF*, 2012.

Parallel Computing: On the Road to Exascale
G.R. Joubert et al. (Eds.)
IOS Press, 2016
doi:10.3233/978-1-61499-621-7-197

Evaluation of 3-D Stencil Codes on the Intel Xeon Phi Coprocessor

Mario HERNÁNDEZ [a,c,1], Juan M. CEBRIÁN [a] José M. CECILIA [b] and
José M. GARCÍA [a]

[a] *Dept. of Computer Engineering, University of Murcia, 30100, Murcia, Spain*
[b] *Computer Science Department, Universidad Católica San Antonio de Murcia, Spain*
[c] *Academic Unit of Engineering, Autonomous University of Guerrero, Chilpancingo, Gro., México*

Abstract. Accelerators like the Intel Xeon Phi aim to fulfill the computational requirements of modern applications, including stencil computations. Stencils are finite-difference algorithms used in many scientific and engineering applications for solving large-scale and high-dimension partial differential equations. However, programmability on such massively parallel architectures is still a challenge for inexperienced developers.

This paper provides the evaluation of the Intel Xeon Phi (Knights Corner) for 3-D Stencil Codes using different optimization strategies. Our evaluation is based on three kernels that are widely applied to simulate heat, acoustic diffusion as well as isotropic seismic wave equations. Our experimental results yield performance gains over 25x when compared to high-level sequential implementations (e.g., Matlab). Energy measurements show a similar trend to that of performance. Vectorization is the key strategy from our results, from both performance and energy points of view.

In addition, we propose a set of tips to optimize stencil codes based on a C/C++ OpenMP implementation. We guide developers in maximizing the benefits of hardware-software co-design for computing 3-D stencil codes running on the this architecture.

Keywords. 3-D stencil codes, Xeon Phi, performance optimizations, 3-D finite difference

Introduction

In the last decade, there has been a technological shift for both hardware and software towards massively parallel architectures (accelerators). Intel Many Integrated Core (MIC) [1] [2] and Graphics Processing Units (GPUs) [3] clearly show the potential of these architectures, especially in terms of performance and energy efficiency. The most powerful supercomputers in the world are currently based on accelerators [4]. Concurrently, there has been a quick evolution on programming models for co-processors and GPUs. However, porting applications to these systems is still not a straight-forward task. In order to maximize performance and energy efficiency of their systems, software developers need to use the latest breakthroughs in both high performance computing and the specific field of interest (e.g., image processing, modeling of acoustic or heat diffusion, etc). This vertical approach enables remarkable advances in computer-driven scientific simulations (the so-called hardware-software co-design).

As stated in [5], many applications are developed using an algorithmic method that captures a pattern of computation and communication (so-called *Dwarf*). These patterns are repeated in different applications and thus, hardware-software solutions can be extrapolated to many scientific areas. This is actually the case of stencils. Stencil codes comprise a family of iterative kernels that operate over an N-dimensional data structure

---

[1] Corresponding Author: Department of Computer Engineering, University of Murcia, 30100, Murcia, Spain; E-mail: mario.hernandez4@um.es

that changes over time, given a fixed computational pattern (stencil). Given the high level of abstraction and the wide variety of stakeholders that can benefit from stencil computations, the implementation is usually developed using high level programming languages such as Matlab [6].

In this paper, we compile and evaluate a set of optimization guidelines using three 3-D stencil kernels from different fields of research: 1) 3-D heat diffusion stencil (11-point), 2) 3-D acoustic diffusion stencil (7-point) and 3) 3-D isotropic seismic wave stencil (25-point). We start from a simple sequential implementation of the code in Matlab. The first step is to port the code to C/C++ using OpenMP. This version will be the starting point of our evaluation. Our results show substantial performance gains (over 25x) compared to a sequential high-level scientific programming language implementation (e.g., Matlab), while at the same time we experience a reduction in the energy consumption at a board level. The aim of this paper is to give some useful tips to inexperienced software developers to optimize stencil computations for the Intel Xeon Phi architecture.

The paper is structured as follows. The next section gives some fundamentals and related work about stencil computations and the MIC architecture. Some tips for improving the parallel performance for 3-D stencil codes are introduced in Section 2. Section 3 shows our evaluation results. Finally, we summarize our conclusions in Section 4.

1. Background and Related Work

1.1. 3-D Stencil Computations

Stencil codes [7,8,9] are a type of iterative kernels which update data elements according to some fixed predetermined set or pattern. The stencil can be used to compute the value of several elements in an array at a given time-step based on its neighbour values. This may include values computed in previous time-steps (including the element itself). Stencils are the base of finite-difference algorithms used for solving large-scale and high-dimension partial differential equations (PDEs). PDEs provide numerical approximations to computational expensive problems, being widely used in many scientific and engineering fields. This allows scientists to accurately model phenomena such as scalar-wave propagation, heat conduction, acoustic diffusion, etc.

Algorithm 1 shows the pseudo-code of a generic three-dimension (3-D) stencil solver kernel. It is implemented as a triple nested loop traversing the complete data structure while updating each grid point. The computation of every output element usually requires: a) the weighted contribution of some near neighbors in each direction defined by the physics of the problem, b) the previous value of that element in a time *t-1* (for second order in-time stencils) and, c) a single corresponding point from other input arrays. The code normally uses two copies of the spatial grid swapping their roles as source and destination on alternate time steps as shown in the Algorithm 1.

Algorithm 1 The 3-D stencil solver kernel. *width, height, depth* are the dimensions of the data set including border (*halo*) points.

```
 1: for time = 0; time < TimeMax; time + + do
 2:   for z = 1; z < depth − BorderSize; z + + do
 3:     for y = 1; y < height − BorderSize; y + + do
 4:       for x = 1; x < width − BorderSize; x + + do
 5:         stencil_solver_kernel();
 6:       end for
 7:     end for
 8:   end for
 9:   tmp = Input_Grid; Input_Grid = Output_Grid; Output_Grid = tmp;
10: end for
```

An important feature of these algorithms is that 3-D stencil kernels usually suffer from a high cache miss rate and poor data locality [7]. The reason is that, for input sizes that exceed the cache capacity, by the time we reuse an entry from the dataset it has already been replaced from the cache. Moreover, the non-linear memory access pattern of 3D based implementations creates additional memory stalls. As a result, standard implementations of the 3D stencil solvers typically reach a small fraction of the hardware's peak performance [10].

1.2. Intel Xeon Phi Architecture

The Intel Xeon Phi (Knights Corner) coprocessor [1,2] is the first commercial product of the Intel MIC family. The design is purely throughput oriented, featuring a high number of simple cores (60+) with support for 512-bit wide vector processing units (VPU). The VPU can be used to process 16 single-precision or 8 double-precision elements per instruction. To keep power dissipation per unit area under control, these cores execute instructions in-order and run at a low frequency (<1.2Ghz). The architecture is backed by large caches and high memory bandwidth. Xeon Phi is based on the x86 ISA, allowing a certain degree of compatibility with conventional x86 processors (but not binary).

The architecture is tailored to run four independent threads per core, where each in-order core can execute up to two instructions per cycle. Unlike latency oriented architectures, the MIC architecture assumes that applications running on the system will be highly parallel and scalable. In order to hide the cache/memory latency caused by the in-order nature of the cores, the scheduling policy swaps threads on each cycle. When an application runs a single thread per core, the scheduler switches to a special *null thread* before going back to the application thread. Suffice it to say, Intel recommends at least two threads per core, although the optimal may range from 2 to 4. Running a single thread per core will reduce the peak capacity of the system by half.

1.3. Related Work

Multi-core architectures provide good opportunities for parallelizing stencil applications. Authors in [11] present a thorough methodology to evaluate and predict stencil code performance on complex HPC architectures. The authors in [12] introduce a methodology that directs programmer efforts toward the regions of code most likely to benefit from porting to the Xeon Phi as well as providing speedup estimates. Other researchers [13,14] investigate the porting and optimization of the test problem basic N-body simulation for the Intel Xeon Phi coprocessor, which is too the foundation of a number of applications in computational astrophysics and biophysics.

Many proposals have been focused on improving cache reuse. Tiling is a program transformation that can be applied to capture this data reuse when data does not fit in cache. In [15,16] authors focus on exploiting data locality applying tiling techniques. On the other hand, several works like [17,18] consider locality and parallelism issues. Kamil *et al.* [17] examine several optimizations targeted to improve cache reuse across stencil sweeps. Their work includes both an implicit cache oblivious approach and a cache-aware algorithm blocked to match the cache structure. This enables multiple iterations of the stencil to be performed on each cache-resident portion of the grid. Authors in [18] develop an approach for automatic parallelization of stencil codes that explicitly addresses the issue of load-balanced execution of tiles.

2. Optimizing Stencil Codes for the Xeon Phi

This section focuses on key design decisions that should be considered to exploit massively parallel architectures at maximum. The main tradeoffs between the different optimization strategies are discussed to help designers in making an informed decision. We pay our attention to the following performance aspects: parallelization, memory issues (cache blocking and data structure optimizations), vectorization, and other easy-to-use low level hardware mechanisms for maximizing the performance. Performance evaluation and energy results are shown in the Section 3.

2.1. Parallelization Strategies

The parallelization process consists of dividing an application in different "threads" or "tasks" that run in parallel on the target architecture. Libraries like *Boost* or *OpenMP* allow software developers to easily write parallel applications and orchestrate a parallel run. OpenMP development is based on *#pragma* statements that are captured by the compiler, validated and translated to the appropriate function calls to the OpenMP library and runtime system. For instance, the directive *#pragma omp parallel for private(i)* before a for loop instructs the compiler to parallelize the *for* loop using all available cores and that each core holds a private instance of variable *i*. Additional requirements for using OpenMP include the declaration of the OMP header file in the source code, and the compiler flag *-openmp* to link with the OpenMP libraries. The *collapse* clause is useful in stencils to merge loop iterations, increasing the total work units that will be partitioned across the available threads.

In this paper, we have parallelized the outer two loops using the *OMP parallel for* pragma with the *collapse* construct, as shown in Figure 2. The inner loop is left unchanged to be vectorized (described in Section 2.3). We have set the KMP_AFFINITY to *scatter* to distribute the threads across the Xeon Phi cores, maximizing the usage of the cache storage space.

Algorithm 2 The 3-D stencil solver kernel parallelized with OpenMP.

1: **for** $time = 0; time < TimeMax; time + +$ **do**
2:      #pragma omp for collapse (2);
3:      **for** $z = 1; z < depth - BorderSize; z + +$ **do**
4:          **for** $y = 1; y < height - BorderSize; y + +$ **do**
5:              **for** $x = 1; x < width - BorderSize; x + +$ **do**
6:                  $stencil\_solver\_kernel()$;
7:              **end for**
8:          **end for**
9:      **end for**
10:     $tmp = Input\_Grid; Input\_Grid = Output\_Grid; Output\_Grid = tmp$;
11: **end for**

2.2. Memory issues

3-D stencils operate over an input data represented as a three-dimensional array of elements (single/double floating point precision). Next we summarize the best practices we have followed to improve the performance related to memory allocation and usage.

Data Allocation. Our first recommendation is related to the way data is allocated in memory. We advise to allocate all rows of the 3-D arrays consecutively in memory (i.e., row major order). This way of allocating memory follows the convention for n-dimensional arrays in C/C++, meaning that the right-most index of the array has an access pattern of stride one. Therefore, mapping the unit stride dimension to the inner loop in nested loop iterations produces a better use of cache lines. The dataset is thus accessed in order of planes (layers), columns, and rows from outer to inner level.

Data Alignment. Another key factor that can limit performance in the Xeon Phi architecture is the use of unaligned loads and stores. To perform data alignment correctly, the traditional memory allocation function calls in C/C++ (i.e. *malloc()* and *free()*) are replaced by an alternative implementations that support data alignment (i.e. _mm_malloc() and _mm_free()).

For the Xeon Phi we select an alignment factor of 64 bytes, which is passed as a parameter to the _mm_malloc() routine. For example, to allocate the *Input_Grid* float data structure aligned to 64-bytes we can use float Input_Grid = _mm_malloc(Input_Grid_Size, 64). Additionally, we have used the clause _assume_aligned (*Input_Grid, 64*) to provide the compiler with additional information regarding the alignment of the *Input_Grid* in vectorized loops. Without this information, the compiler may not be able to correctly identify the alignment used by the data structure.

Padding. Padding is an interesting technique that rearranges data in cache memory by allocating extra unused "dummy" information in data structures. In our case, padding has been a very convenient technique to be applied in stencil codes for two main reasons:

1. To avoid the misalignment among rows. As the dataset structure is allocated in memory as a whole, i.e. by using a single _mm_malloc() instruction, this may lead to a misalignment of the data between rows depending on the width of the *x* dimension. Thus, we use a new *width* adding some elements (if needed) to ensure that the first element of each row is on the desired address boundary (64 bytes in Xeon Phi). The new *width* with padding is calculated as $width\_PADD = ((((width * sizeof(REAL)) + 63)/64) * (64/sizeof(REAL)))$. REAL stands for the data type used (float or double) in the kernel.

2. Avoiding pathological conflict misses. Conflict misses[2] may appear under certain combinations of blocking size, input size, etc. In some unlikely scenarios, several cache lines mapping to the same cache set may cause a low cache hit rate. For the Xeon Phi this happens when a kernel accesses data with a *4KB* stride (*L1*) or a *64KB* stride (*L2*). In our kernels, we have experienced this problem in the seismic kernel when accessing data in the Z dimension in some specific input grid sizes. Our recommendation is to use *padding* in the problematic dimension to change the access stride.

Blocking. Stencil codes with an input size that does not fit on the higher cache levels of the processor will experience a significant performance degradation due to cache capacity misses. Code transformations that improve data locality can be useful to hide the complexities of the memory hierarchy, improving overall performance of 3-D stencil codes. Basic transformations include loop transformations[3] and data transformations[4] (e.g., blocking).

Blocking is a transformation which groups loop iterations into subsets (or tiles) of size N. The size of the tiles needs to be adjusted to fit in the cache in order to obtain maximum performance gains by exploiting data locality. In this way, cache misses can be minimized by bringing a data block into cache once for all necessary accesses.

In 3-D stencil codes our goal is to exploit data locality, focusing on increasing the reuse of the elements of the plane (X-Y) for some layers. The first step is to create tiles of size *bz*, *by* and *bx*. Next, three additional loops are created over the three existing loops to traverse the dataset in tiles of the selected sizes. A blocking version of a generic 3-D stencil is shown in algorithm 3. After an analysis of different block sizes we empirically found that *width_TBlock=width*, *height_TBlock=4* and *depth_TBlock=4* offer good results for all the evaluated kernels, that is, blocking four rows over four Z planes while keeping all columns.

---

[2]Misses caused by cache lines that map to the same cache set.
[3]Loop rearrange.
[4]Changing the layout of data.

Algorithm 3 Blocking technique applied to the 3-D stencil solver.

```
 1:  for bz = 1; bz < depth − BorderSize; bz+ = depth_Tblock do
 2:      for by = 1; by < height − BorderSize; by+ = height_Tblock do
 3:          for bx = 1; bx < width − BorderSize; bx+ = width_Tblock do
 4:              for z = bz; z < MIN(bz + depth_Tblock, depth − BorderSize); z + + do
 5:                  for y = by; y < MIN(by + height_Tblock, height − BorderSize); y + + do
 6:                      for x = 1; x < MIN(width_Tblock, width − BorderSize − bx); x + + do
 7:                          stencil_solver_kernel();
 8:                      end for
 9:                  end for
10:              end for
11:          end for
12:      end for
13:  end for
```

2.3. Vectorization

One of the key design features of the Xeon Phi architecture is the use of wide SIMD registers and vector functional units to improve performance. The MIC Knights Corner (KNC) architecture implements a subset of the AVX512 instruction set that operates over 512-bit wide registers. It is crucial to make use of SIMD features in order to get the best performance out of this architecture.

There are several issues that need to be addressed to achieve the automatic vectorization of the code. The first one is data alignment. Unaligned loads are not available on the KNC architecture, but will be in the upcoming Knights Landing (KNL). Therefore, data accesses must start with an address aligned to 64 bytes (as discussed previously). The second issue is remainders. Vectorizing a loop requires to handle the remainder data items when the number of iterations is not a multiple of the vector length (peeling the loop). Nevertheless, this is handled automatically by the compiler in our evaluation.

The ICC compiler checks for vectorization opportunities whenever the code is compiled using *-O2* or higher. Developers can help the compiler to face loop dependencies by providing additional information to guide the vectorization process. By using the `#pragma simd` sentence before the inner most loop the programmer instructs the compiler to vectorize without performing any dependency, aliasing or performance analysis. This *pragma* is designed to minimize the amount of source code changes required to vectorize the code. In addition, the *restrict* keyword before a pointer variable informs ICC that the memory referenced by that pointer is not accessed in any other way (avoiding pointer aliasing), and may be necessary in the vectorization process (requires the `-restrict` compiler flag). Alternatively, the `-fargumentnoalias` compiler flag would instruct the compiler that function arguments cannot alias each other along the whole program.

2.4. Other Easy-to-Use Low-Level Optimizations

We have restricted ourselves to easy-to-use low level hardware optimizations that can be used by non-experienced programmers. Other optimization techniques, such as the use of intrinsics, FMA instructions, or prefetching are therefore out of scope of this paper.

Streaming stores. When an application writes its output in a memory location, the destination data block is loaded from memory and moved along the memory hierarchy until it reaches the L1 and thus it can be written. However, if the data block is not required for any computation other than storing the output, this operation can seriously pollute the memory hierarchy. Streaming stores address this problem by storing a continuous stream of output data without gaps between data items directly into memory, skipping the intermediate levels of the memory hierarchy. This method stores data using a non temporal buffer, improving memory bandwidth utilization and potentially performance. We have used non-temporal stores in the 3-D stencils by putting a *#pragma vector non temporal* directive before the inner-most loop. Alternatively, the developer can use the compiler flag *-opt-streaming-stores* to control the generation of streaming stores.

Huge page size. The Xeon Phi architecture can be configured to run using either 4KB or 2MB page sizes (*aka* huge pages). This configuration allows the Xeon Phi architecture TLB to map 128 MB of memory, as compared to the 256KB mapped by default. This might reduce page faults significantly (up to 15%) in certain applications. The allocation of huge pages is done by replacing the *_mm_malloc()* calls with the *mmap()* function.

ECC Memory and Turbo. Error-Correcting Code (ECC) is used to provide error detection and correction in case of hardware memory errors. On Xeon Phi, it is possible to enable/disable ECC, slightly increasing performance. Turbo mode is another feature of the Xeon Phi KNC to allow overclocking based on the current power usage and temperature. ECC can be enabled/disabled using the command *micsmc –ecc disable/enable mic0*, whereas *micsmc –turbo enable/disable mic0* can be used to enable/disable the Turbo mode.

3. Evaluation

In this Section, we evaluate experimental results for the optimization carving previously presented on the Xeon Phi architecture. Regarding performance comparison between Intel Xeon Phi and other computing platforms such as Nvidia GPUs, we refer the interested reader to our previous work [19].

3.1. Target Platforms

Our evaluation uses the Intel's ICC compiler (version 14.0.2), running on CentOS 6.5 with kernel 2.6.32 and Intel's MPSS 3.4.3. The target system contains two Ivy Bridge-EP Intel Xeon E5-2650v2 CPUs (2x8 cores in total) running at 2.6 GHz and 32GB of DDR3-1600 main memory. The evaluated Intel Xeon Phi coprocessor is the 7120P model. The 7120P has 61 cores working at 1.238 GHz, 32KB of the L1 data and instruction caches and 512 KB of L2 cache per core. The architecture provides a theoretical peak computation of 2420 gigaflop per second (GFlop/s) for single precision variables (32 bits). In addition, another important feature of Intel Xeon Phi coprocessors is the high memory bandwidth. The 7120P has 16 memory channels, each 32-bits wide, adding up to a theoretical bandwidth of 352 GB/s (transfer speeds of 5.5 GT/s).

With these features, the theoretical arithmetic intensity[5] (AI) to exploit the full performance of the Xeon Phi 7120P is around 10.9 Flop/Byte. Considering the true achievable maximum memory bandwidth is limited to 50-60% of the peak memory bandwidth, the feasible AI is around 6.8 Flop/Byte. This means that, for this architecture, we can characterize a given compute kernel as compute bounded if its AI is greater that 6.8 Flop/Byte, or memory bounded in the opposite case.

3.2. Target Codes

We have evaluated three different stencil solvers to test our approach. These solves cover a wide research area and have distinct computational features. The most common stencil code is represented by the 3-D acoustic diffusion stencil, which uses a stencil of 7-point spatial neighbors and second order in time. It uses three different matrices of the same size for the kernel calculation and has a low AI (slightly more than 1). Our second kernel is the 3-D isotropic seismic wave stencil of 25-point spatial neighbors and also second

---

[5]Number of floating point operations per byte of data [10].

order in time. This solver has greater AI than the previous one (slightly greater than 2), although it uses an additional matrix for storing physical characteristics (four matrices in total). Finally, we have evaluated our simplest solver, the 3-D heat diffusion stencil of 11-point spatial neighbors and first order in time, which only uses two matrices for the stencil calculation and has an AI close to 3. As we can observe, all codes are memory-bounded and thus, they could only achieve a small fraction of the peak performance of the Xeon Phi.

Related the shape of the grid, as it dictates the memory access patterns, rectangular cuboid shapes of *width x height x depth* have been chosen for the experiments. Finally, two sizes of the input grid of the kernels have been considered: small one (grid of 400x300x200 and 92 MB of size) and large one (400x600x1000 grid, 916 MB size). Note that these sizes are referred as to the size of only one of the input matrices of the kernels.

3.3. Experimental Performance Evaluation

The base implementations of our kernels are developed using C and OpenMP. The C versions outperform the equivalent Matlab codes by a factor of $\sim 5\times$ when running on a single thread. Additionally, we validate our results by performing a performance profile using both Intel VTune Amplifier XE 2015 (for detailed code analysis) and PAPI (for power measurements and L1 cache analysis).

Figure 1 shows the performance and speedup (secondary Y axis) for the two analyzed matrix sizes and for the different optimizations we have presented along the paper. We have set four threads per core and the KMP_AFFINITY to *scatter*, and the block size used in the graphs are *width_TBlock=width, height_TBlock=4* and *depth_TBlock=4*. The labels of the plots mean the following: *base*) stands for unvectorized code, *B-Block*) for unvectorized code with blocking, *Vectoriz*) for vectorized code, *V-Block*) for vectorized code with blocking, *V-H-Block*) for vectorized code with blocking and huge pages, *V-S-Block*) for vectorized code with blocking and sstores and, finally, *oth(t-ECC)*) for vectorized code with blocking, sstores, turbo and ECC disabled.

The use of blocking on the parallel base code offers little to none performance improvement in both sizes and for all kernels. This suggests that the Xeon Phi is able to significantly hide the memory latency by switching threads during cache misses. On the other hand, when vectorization is enabled, data elements from matrices are consumed much faster by the VPU, and blocking mechanisms start to pay off. Vectorization shows a substantial performance improvement for all kernels and sizes, but is far from the ideal $16\times$ speedup expected from the 512-bit registers. Checking at the VTune profile we notice that the memory-boundedness nature of the kernels is severely limiting the performance of the vector units. As a consequence, blocking obtains a clear improvement when applied to the vectorized version.

We have also tested our kernels using *huge pages* and *sstores* but found no performance improvement but for heat stencil kernel, specially for big matrix sizes. Again, we

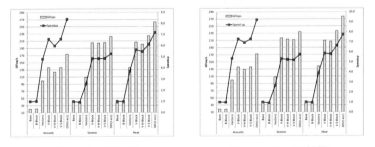

(a) Small size (92 MB)   (b) Large size (916 MB)

Figure 1. Performance (Gflops) and speedup (secondary Y) of different optimization strategies for the 7120P.

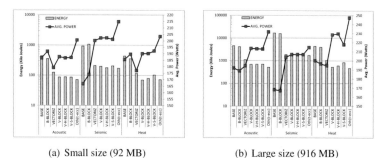

(a) Small size (92 MB)   (b) Large size (916 MB)

Figure 2. Energy and average power (secondary Y) of different optimization strategies for the 7120P.

attribute this behavior to the low AI of the kernels and the way that the Xeon Phi hides latency by constantly context switching between execution threads. Finally, disabling ECC and overclocking the board yields substantial performance improvements for all kernels (although most of the performance benefit comes from disabling ECC).

Figure 2 shows the energy profile and the average power (secondary Y axis) for the two analyzed matrix sizes. Energy measurements show a similar trend to that of performance. The greatest energy saving comes from vectorization, showing a slight increase in the average power consumed by the board for big matrix sizes. This gives an idea on how beneficial is this technique to improve energy efficiency. Moreover, for small matrix sizes, both acoustic and heat kernels show a reduction on the average power dissipated by the board. This can only mean that the cores spend more time idle waiting for data, and power saving mechanisms remain active for longer periods of time.

The average power remains barely unchanged for both acoustic and seismic kernels when using other optimizations rather than vectorization. This suggests that the core activity remains relatively unchanged, something that does not happen with the heat kernel. This could be attributed to its higher AI, meaning that code changes have a greater impact on the computations performed by this kernel, even if they do not translate into a noticeable speedup. Finally, when ECC is disabled and the cores are overclocked, we see a substantial increment on the average power dissipated by the board. There is a direct relationship between power and frequency, when overclocking the cores the power dissipated by the board increases accordingly.

4. Conclusions and Future Work

Programmability on massively parallel architectures can be a challenge for inexperienced developers. Real world applications based on Stencil computations can take great advantage of the proposed Intel Xeon Phi architecture, not only providing faster results, but also improving accuracy by allowing more detailed simulations of different phenomena. This has a real impact on the society enabling scientists to overcome emerging challenges.

This paper presents an evaluation of 3-D stencil codes running on the Intel Xeon Phi (Knights Corner) architecture. We have used the C/C++ language with OpenMP extensions to code the three stencils kernels evaluated in this work. Experimental results show the performance evolution for different kernels through the optimization process. Vectorization is the key strategy from our results, from both performance and energy points of view. In addition, the application of blocking techniques improves memory locality for these kernels, and thus performance and energy. Finally, the use of overclocking and non-ECC memory improves the performance but expending more energy at the board level.

Additionally, we have provided a set of guidelines to help developers in maximizing the benefits of hardware-software co-design for computing our three 3-D stencil codes, but the proposed advise will ease the porting of any stencil-based application to this architecture.

As for future work, we are interesting to extend our evaluation to larger datasets using also double data types. To properly handle big sizes, we plan to split input data among different Xeon Phi cards, analyzing the communication effects on the performance.

Acknowledgements

This work is jointly supported by the Fundación Séneca under grant 15290/PI/2010, and the Spanish MINECO as well as EC FEDER funds under grant TIN2012-31345 and CAPAP-H5 NoE (TIN2014-53522-REDT). In addition, to Nils Coordinated Mobility under grant 012-ABEL-CM-2014A (partly financed by the ERDF). Mario Hernández was supported by the PROMEP under the Teacher Improvement Program (UAGro-197) - México.

References

[1] Jim Jeffers and James Reinders. *Intel Xeon Phi coprocessor high-performance programming*. Elsevier Waltham (Mass.), Amsterdam, Boston, 2013.

[2] Rezaur Rahman. *Intel Xeon Phi Coprocessor Architecture and Tools: The Guide for Application Developers*. Apress, Berkely, CA, USA, 1st edition, 2013.

[3] M. Garland, S. Le Grand, J. Nickolls, J. Anderson, J. Hardwick, S. Morton, E. Phillips, Yao Zhang, and V. Volkov. Parallel Computing Experiences with CUDA. *IEEE, Micro*, 28(4):13–27, July 2008.

[4] Top 500 supercomputer site, [last access 15 June 2015]. http://www.top500.org/.

[5] Krste Asanovic and et al. The landscape of parallel computing research: A view from berkeley. Technical Report UCB/EECS-2006-183, Berkeley, Dec 2006.

[6] Timmy Siauw and A. M. Bayen. *An introduction to MATLAB programming and numerical methods*. Elsevier, 2015.

[7] Ulrich Trottenberg, Cornelius W Oosterlee, and Anton Schuller. *Multigrid*. Academic press, 2000.

[8] Matteo Frigo and Volker Strumpen. Cache Oblivious Stencil Computations. In *Proc. of the 19th Annual International Conference on Supercomputing*, ICS '05, pages 361–366, New York, USA, 2005. ACM.

[9] V.T. Zhukov, M.M. Krasnov, N.D. Novikova, and O.B. Feodoritova. Multigrid effectiveness on modern computing architectures. *Programming and Computer Software*, 41(1):14–22, 2015.

[10] Jim Reinders and James Jeffers. *High Performance Parallelism Pearls, Multicore and Many-core Programming Approaches*, chapter Characterization and Auto-tuning of 3DFD, pages 377–396. Morgan Kaufmann, 2014.

[11] Raúl de la Cruz and Mauricio Araya-Polo. Modeling stencil computations on modern HPC architectures. In *5th Int. Workshop (PMBS14) held as part of SC14*. Springer, 2014.

[12] J. Peraza, A. Tiwari, M. Laurenzano, L. Carrington, W.A. Ward, and R. Campbell. Understanding the performance of stencil computations on Intel's Xeon Phi. In *Int. Conf. on Cluster Computing (CLUSTER)*, pages 1–5, Sept 2013.

[13] Jianbin Fang, Henk Sips, LiLun Zhang, Chuanfu Xu, Yonggang Che, and Ana Lucia Varbanescu. Test-driving Intel Xeon Phi. In *Proc. of the 5th ACM/SPEC Int. Conf. on Performance Engineering*, pages 137–148. ACM, 2014.

[14] Karpusenko Vadim Vladimirov Andrey. Test-driving Intel Xeon Phi coprocessors with a basic N-body simulation. *Coflax International*, 2013.

[15] G. Rivera and Chau-Wen Tseng. Tiling Optimizations for 3D Scientific Computations. In *Supercomputing, ACM/IEEE Conference*, pages 32–32, Nov 2000.

[16] Yonghong Song, Rong Xu, Cheng Wang, and Zhiyuan Li. Data locality enhancement by memory reduction. In *Proc. of the 15th int. conf. on Supercomputing*, pages 50–64. ACM, 2001.

[17] Shoaib Kamil, Kaushik Datta, Samuel Williams, Leonid Oliker, John Shalf, and Katherine Yelick. Implicit and Explicit Optimizations for Stencil Computations. In *Proc. of the Workshop on Memory System Performance and Correctness*, MSPC '06, pages 51–60, New York, USA, 2006. ACM.

[18] Sriram Krishnamoorthy and Muthu *et al.* Baskaran. Effective Automatic Parallelization of Stencil Computations. In *Proc. of the Conf. on Programming Language Design and Implementation*, pages 235–244, New York, USA, 2007.

[19] Mario Hernández, Baldomero Imbernón, Juan M Navarro, José M García, Juan M Cebrián, and José M Cecilia. Evaluation of the 3-d finite difference implementation of the acoustic diffusion equation model on massively parallel architectures. *Computers & Electrical Engineering*, Published online: 18 July 2015. Doi: 10.1016/j.compeleceng.2015.07.001.

Parallel Computing: On the Road to Exascale
G.R. Joubert et al. (Eds.)
IOS Press, 2016
doi:10.3233/978-1-61499-621-7-207

Hierarchical Parallelism in a Physical Modelling Synthesis Code

James PERRY, Stefan BILBAO and Alberto TORIN
The University of Edinburgh

Abstract

Modern computer hardware provides parallelism at various different levels - most obviously, multiple multicore processors allow many independent threads to execute at once. At a finer-grained level, each core contains a vector unit allowing multiple integer or floating point calculations to be performed with a single instruction. Additionally, GPU hardware is highly parallel and performs best when processing large numbers of independent threads. At the same time, tools such as CUDA have become steadily more abundant and mature, allowing more of this parallelism to be exploited.

In this paper we describe the process of optimising a physical modelling sound synthesis code, the Multiplate 3D code, which models the acoustic response of a number of metal plates embedded within a box of air. This code presented a number of challenges and no single optimisation technique was applicable to all of these. However, by exploiting parallelism at several different levels (multithreading, GPU acceleration, and vectorisation), as well as applying other optimisations, it was possible to speed up the simulation very significantly.

1. Background

1.1. Digital Sound Synthesis

Digital sound synthesis has a long history, dating back at least as far as work at Bell Labs in the 1950s; the earliest techniques employed simple computational structures, such as circular reading from waveforms stored in buffers (wavetable synthesis), or the summation of sinusoidal tones [1]. Later refinements to such sound-producing algorithms, such as frequency modulation synthesis (FM) [2] and waveshaping methods [3] have led to the widespread use of such synthesis techniques. The main advantage of such methods is that, computationally speaking, they are extremely cheap. On the other hand, they are also not well-suited to producing sounds of a natural acoustic character; one way of addressing the synthetic character of sounds produced in this way is through the use of recorded audio fragments, or sampling, however this is very inflexible. Another is through simulation-based approaches, whereby the equations of motion describing a vibrating system are simulated in their entirety. Such methods are referred to as physical modeling synthesis.

Many approaches to physical modeling synthesis have emerged - perhaps the best known are digital waveguides, based on the use of efficient delay line structures to simulate wave motion in 1D objects [4]; and modal methods, whereby the dynamics of a vibrating object are decomposed into modal contributions [5]. More recently, approaches based on direct time-stepping methods such as the finite difference time domain methods (FDTD) [6] have been employed - while more computationally intensive, such methods allow for the simulation of more complex instrument configurations, involving the coupling of multiple disparate components, which are often nonlinear, and also the immersion of the instrument in the 3D acoustic field [7]. NESS (Next Generation Sound Synthesis) is a project currently under way at the University of Edinburgh which is devoted to the exploration of such synthesis methods on a large scale, and for a great variety of instrument types: percussion, string, brass, electromechanical, and also 3D room simulations. As computational requirements are heavy, implementation in parallel hardware is necessary, and this forms the basis of the NESS project.

1.2. Physical model

The Multiplate 3D code [8] is a physical modelling synthesis code that simulates multiple rectangular plates, aligned horizontally within a finite box of air. The plate simulations are performed using a non-linear model based on the von Kármán equations for thin plate vibration [9]. The displacement $w(x, y, t)$ of one plate at position (x, y) and time $t \in \mathbb{R}^+$ is governed by the following partial differential equations:

$$\ddot{w} = -\kappa_1 \Delta^2 w + \mathcal{N}(w, F) + f_+ + f_- \tag{1a}$$

$$\Delta^2 F = -\kappa_2 \mathcal{N}(w, w), \tag{1b}$$

where F is an auxiliary variable called Airy's stress function, Δ^2 represents the biharmonic operator and the double dot notation indicates the second derivative with respect to time. The operator $\mathcal{N}$ is a bilinear mapping that for any two functions f, g is defined as

$$\mathcal{N}(f, g) = \partial_{xx} f \partial_{yy} g + \partial_{yy} f \partial_{xx} g - 2\partial_{xy} f \partial_{xy} g, \tag{2}$$

which introduces the nonlinearity in the model. The quantities κ_1 and κ_2 are constants defined by the physical parameters of the model, while f_+ and f_- represent the pressure exerted on the plate by the acoustic field from above and from below. Loss terms can be added to the first of (1), as well.

The acoustic field surrounding the plates can be described by the 3D wave equation [10]. Suitable boundary and coupling conditions must be imposed at the walls of the airbox and at the interfaces with the plates, respectively. More details can be found in [8].

1.3. Numerical implementation

The behaviour of the physical model described above can be calculated by discretising the underlying physical equations with the finite difference method [6]. Despite the considerable mathematical complexity of the model, the numerical implementation has a very simple structure, see Section 1.4.

When viewed as a sound synthesis tool, the code is flexible enough to accomodate the wishes of a composer. The dimensions of the airbox, as well as the sizes and positions of the plates can be specified by the user, together with all the physical parameters characterising the model. The plates and the airbox have separate co-ordinate systems, allowing the optimal grid spacing to be used for each element of the simulation, interpolations being performed between the various grids when necessary. Input to the model is provided in the form of simulated strikes on the plates, and audio outputs are taken both from points on the plate surfaces and points within the airbox. The nonlinear equations (1) produce more realistic sounds than a simple linear model, especially when higher amplitude strikes are introduced. A finite difference scheme for their solution has been presented in [11].

For the purposes of comparing the speeds of different versions of the code, we will focus on one particular test problem that is fairly typical of the problems users want to simulate: a set of three plates of different sizes (specifically, 0.81x0.87m, 0.39x0.42m, and 0.05x0.61m) embedded in an airbox measuring 1.37x1.32x1.32m. For most of the tests, the time taken to run the simulation for 50 timesteps (representing just over 1 millisecond of real time at 44.1kHz) was used to quickly compare different versions of the code.

The code was initially written in Matlab, making extensive use of sparse matrix operations for almost every operation. However, the Matlab version is extremely slow: simulating the test problem for one second takes over an hour and a half (specifically, 5877 seconds) on a typical machine, and so an optimised version is highly desirable.

For examples of sounds generated using the code, please see [12].

1.4. Code Structure

Each simulation timestep generates a single audio sample, so to run a one second simulation at CD quality (44.1kHz), 44100 timesteps must be run; rendering a four minute long composition would require over 10 million timesteps. The high number of timesteps required for practical runs makes the code quite computationally intensive despite its relatively small domain size, and limits the amount of parallelism available in the code since dependencies prevent parallelisation in the time dimension.

The main loop of the code can be divided into the following three major categories:

1. the linear system solve for each plate
2. the airbox simulation
3. the remainder

Solver	Remainder	Airbox	Total
2.40s	0.81s	2.26s	5.47s

Table 1. Profile of original Matlab implementation

The remainder mostly consists of building a system matrix for each plate that is then used in the linear system solve, but also includes other operations, such as interpolating between the plate co-ordinate system and the airbox co-ordinate system.

In the Matlab version of the code, the time spent in each of these sections for a 50 iteration run of the test problem is shown in Table 1. No single part of the code dominates the run time, so all must be optimised in order to improve the performance significantly.

The airbox simulation is an excellent candidate for GPU acceleration, being a simple linear stencil update where all points can be run in parallel. Because it is coupled to the plate simulations, it would be advantageous to also simulate the plates on the GPU to minimise the amount of data transfered across the PCI bus. However, the linear system solve operation required at each timestep for each plate - or more specifically, the preconditioner for this solver - proved extremely difficult to parallelise effectively.

2. Optimisation and Parallelisation

2.1. Solver

The original Matlab version of the code used the preconditioned conjugate gradient solver algorithm [13] with a Cholesky preconditioner. Instead of generating the preconditioner from the system matrix, which would have to be redone at every timestep, the Cholesky decomposition [14] of the biharmonic operator [15] is computed once for each plate at startup and stored for later use. This preconditioner is extremely effective for the systems in Multiplate, often allowing them to be solved in fewer than 5 iterations of the conjugate gradient solver.

For each iteration of the conjugate gradient algorithm, the preconditioner step computes two triangular solves using the Cholesky decomposition. Unfortunately the triangular solve is an inherently serial operation: every value being solved for is dependent on the value computed in the previous row, making this algorithm unsuitable for GPU acceleration or domain decomposition. While there have been attempts [16] to optimise triangular solves using CUDA, these are highly dependent on there being potential for parallelism within the matrix structure; matrices without this potential are unlikely to run well in CUDA as serial GPU performance is very poor. This was the case for our test problem, for which this method was many times slower than simply running the algorithm on a single CPU core. It was clear that this phase of the code was likely to become a bottleneck.

We initially sought an alternative preconditioner that was more easily parallelisable. However, when we tested several preconditioners provided by the

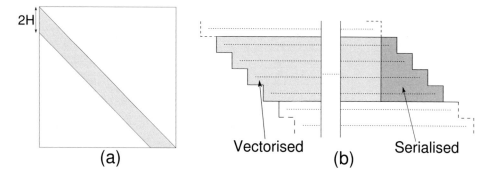

Figure 1. (a) Sparsity of Cholesky decomposition; (b) vectorising the triangular solve

PETSc library, only the ones that used triangular solves (Cholesky, LU and the incomplete variants thereof) were effective, with the other algorithms requiring hundreds of solver iterations in order to converge, and taking much more time.

We then ported the code to C and tested two further preconditioning methods: dense inverses, and sparse approximate inverses. Although for many systems a dense matrix would be too large to work with, our plates are relatively small systems so it is feasible to compute a dense inverse for the biharmonic matrix. This allows the triangular solves to be replaced with a simple dense-matrix-by-vector multiplication - a highly parallel operation that is well suited to GPU acceleration. However, due to the sheer number of operations required, it is much slower than the triangular solve, even when run on a GPU. For our test matrix, an optimised CUDA matrix-by-vector multiplication took $393\mu S$, slower than even the unoptimised C triangular solve ($220\mu S$ for both forward and back solves), although still faster than running the triangular solves in CUDA ($890\mu S$).

We also tried using a sparse approximation to the inverse of the matrix, generated by MSPAI [17], to reduce the number of operations required. Unfortunately the matrices generated this way were poor approximations and were not usable as an effective preconditioner.

There appeared to be no good alternative to the triangular solves, and so our only option was to make them run as fast as possible. It had also become clear that they were not going to run well on a GPU and would have to be kept on the CPU. Although they are unsuitable for most traditional parallelisation techniques due to dependencies between the rows, they can be sped up to some degree using SIMD (single instruction multiple data) instructions. The Cholesky decomposition of the biharmonic operator results in a banded matrix with a fully populated band extending 2H points below the diagonal (where H is the height of the plate's grid in points), but no non-zero values outside this band - see Figure 1(a). It is possible to vectorise the triangular solve, running several rows at once, with a relatively small amount of serialisation at the diagonal end - see Figure 1(b). (In practice, the ratio of vectorised time to serialised time is much greater than in the diagram, which is exaggerated for clarity).

The vast majority of Intel and AMD processors now support SSE (Streaming SIMD Extensions) and SSE2. These are 128-bit wide vector instruction sets:

Code version	Run time (μS)
Original C	110
Banded C	94
Unrolled C	72
SSE	26

Table 2. Run times of triangular solver implementations

the original SSE supported 4-way parallelism on single precision floating point numbers, with SSE2 adding 2-way parallelism for double precision numbers. The original version of the multiplate code uses double precision exclusively; although single precision would be more than adequate for the audio outputs generated by the code, using single precision for the simulation itself has been found to cause numerical instability in similar codes. However, our tests showed that single precision was adequate for the preconditioner and so 4-way SSE instructions can be used.

Before turning to SSE, the C version of the triangular solve was optimised as much as possible. The generic compressed sparse row matrix format used to store the Cholesky decomposition was replaced by a banded format, eliminating an indexing step from the inner loop. The inner loop was also unrolled to reduce loop overheads. Both of these optimisations improved the performance slightly. However the C compiler (gcc) was still not able to vectorise this routine automatically, so a hand coded implementation using SSE intrinsics was created. This version of the triangular solve is around 4.2x faster than the original C version and 2.8x faster than the optimised C version. The time taken (in microseconds) for a triangular solve of a 1155x1155 matrix (band size 70) from the test problem is shown in Table 2. The SSE triangular solve increased the speed of the entire linear system solver by 1.6x.

Newer processors also support AVX (Advanced Vector Extensions), a 256-bit wide vector instruction set supporting 4-way double precision and 8-way single precision. This has the potential to speed up some codes even more, but unfortunately it is a bad fit for the triangular solve, which is quite reliant on being able to permute the vector elements arbitrarily. Although SSE can permute vector elements without limitation, this is not the case for AVX: the 256-bit AVX vector is divided into two 128-bit "lanes". Only four instructions can move values between lanes and there is often a performance penalty for doing this, which in the case of the triangular solve negates the benefit of using AVX.

2.2. System Matrix Builder

Building the system matrix requires a complex sequence of algebraic operations which must be performed for each plate at each iteration of the timestep loop. The original Matlab version of the code uses generic sparse matrix operations to implement this, as does the subsequent unoptimised C port. However, many of the steps can be done more efficiently by taking into account the matrix structures, which stay the same even when the numbers within them change. The majority of the matrices used in the code represent some kind of stencil applied to a 2D grid of points; square 3x3 and 5x5 stencils are the most common. These translate into diagonally banded matrices. The 3x3 stencil matrices have 3 bands (one on the diagonal and one either side), each 3 elements wide, and the 5x5 matrices have 5 bands (one on the diagonal and two either side), each 5 elements wide. There are no non-zero elements outside the bands.

Rather than storing these as generic sparse matrices, they can be stored much more efficiently by taking into account their structure: only their overall size, the distance between the bands and an array of values need to be stored, saving memory and freeing the CPU from having to work with index arrays when manipulating them. We supplemented our generic sparse matrix library with a banded matrix library, capable of storing matrices representing 3x3 and 5x5 stencils as described. The most critical and frequently used functions (banded-matrix-by-vector multiplications) were implemented as optimised SSE2 kernels. For even greater performance, some sequences of operations required for building the system matrix were rolled together into custom functions, merging loops and avoiding the need to write intermediate results back to memory. Overall, these optimisations sped up the "remainder" part of the code by 9.2x.

2.3. Airbox Update

The airbox update phase is, in isolation, a good candidate for GPU acceleration, consisting of the same operation performed many times across a large number of data elements with no dependencies between them. Its integration with the plate simulations (which must run on the CPU for good performance, as described above) makes it somewhat less suitable, due to the need to transfer data across the bus to and from the GPU during the timestep loop. However, this data transfer time proved to be an insignificant part of the overall simulation time.

A CUDA kernel was written to perform the airbox stencil update. Additionally, the interpolations between airbox and plate grids were offloaded to the GPU using the CuSparse library [18] - as these were already implemented as sparse-matrix-by-vector multiplications, this was straightforward. For the test problem, the CUDA version of the airbox update runs around 6 times faster than the single core C version, including the data transfer overheads.

It is advantageous to overlap the airbox computations on the GPU with the plate updates on the CPU and run them concurrently; this is non-trivial because the plate updates require the latest values from the airbox before they can run, but it was achieved using the following scheme. The airbox update for timestep t+1 is run concurrently with the plate updates for timestep t. This means that the values from the airbox computation are always ready when the plates require them. However, airbox elements adjacent to the plates will be computed incorrectly because they depend on the plate updates for the previous timestep which have not yet completed, so these elements must be recalculated after the plate updates finish. This recalculation only affects a small fraction of the whole airbox so it does not have a significant impact on overall performance, compared with the benefit from the overlap. (Due to the handling of the domain in CUDA it is faster to simply compute these elements and then overwrite them later with the correct values, rather than omit them from the first computation). The data transfer between CPU and GPU was not overlapped with the computation.

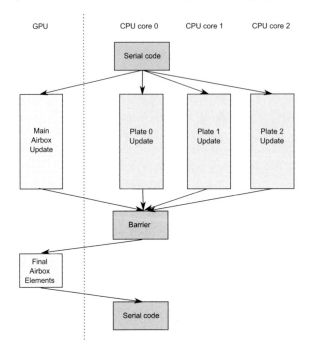

Figure 2. Execution timeline for optimised code

2.4. Parallelising the Plates

Whilst there are dependencies between each plate and the airbox, no direct dependencies exist between the individual plates. The triangular solve algorithm prevents us from running them on the GPU as described above, but they are a good candidate for running in parallel using multithreading, taking advantage of modern multicore CPUs. This was initially attempted using OpenMP, however performance was very poor due to the worker threads yielding the CPU when idle, resulting in up to 23ms being wasted every timestep on waiting for the threads to be scheduled again. There did not appear to be any portable way to force OpenMP to keep the threads running constantly, so a lower level approach using Pthreads was used instead.

The end result is that, given enough CPU cores, the plate updates all run in parallel, while most of the airbox update runs concurrently on the GPU. Typically, this results in the whole system running as fast as the largest plate simulation, with the other plates and the airbox being effectively "for free". See Figure 2.

3. Conclusion

The final optimised version of Multiplate 3D runs approximately 60-80x faster than the original Matlab version for typical problem sizes, making it much more practical for use by researchers and composers - runs which previously took hours to complete can now be done in minutes. This demonstrates that where

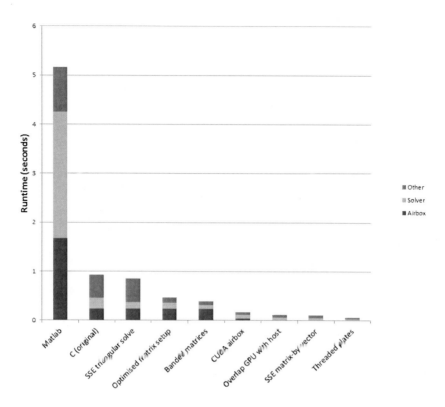

Figure 3. speeds and profiles of different versions of code

no single optimisation technique can deliver useful performance gains by itself, a combination of multiple techniques can potentially be more effective.

The overall speeds and profiles of the different versions of the code are broken down in Figure 3. It shows that the airbox simulation was sped up dramatically when switching from the sparse matrix-based version in Matlab to a simple loop in the C port, and then sped up again when porting to CUDA. Overlapping the airbox computation on the GPU with the plates on the CPU effectively hides the time spent on the airbox completely. The solver portion of the code was sped up in stages, gaining a lot of speed with the move from Matlab to custom C code, and even more when the generic C sparse matrix routines for triangular solves and matrix-vector multiplies were replaced with optimised SSE kernels operating on custom banded data structures. The remainder of the code was also markedly sped up by replacing generic sparse matrix operations with custom optimised code. Finally, running the plate simulations in parallel gave another boost to both these sections of the code.

The performance figures given in this paper relate to the `fermi1` system at EPCC. This system comprises 4 6-core Intel Xeon X5650 CPUs running at 2.67GHz, and 4 NVidia Tesla C2050 GPUs. Unless otherwise noted, CPU performance numbers are for single threaded code. GPU performance numbers are always for a single GPU as no attempt was made to take advantage of multiple

GPUs. The Matlab version of the code could not be run on the `fermi1` system, so the Matlab timings have been adjusted by multiplying them by a scaling factor to reflect the difference in performance between `fermi1` and the system they were actually run on.

4. Acknowledgements

This work was supported by the European Research Council, under grant number StG-2011-279068-NESS.

References

[1]   C. Roads and J. Strawn, editors. *Foundations of Computer Music.* MIT Press, Cambridge, Massachusetts, 1985.

[2]   J. Chowning. The synthesis of complex audio spectra by means of frequency modulation. *Journal of the Audio Engineering Society*, 21(7):526–534, 1973.

[3]   M. LeBrun. Digital waveshaping synthesis. *Journal of the Audio Engineering Society*, 27(4):250–266, 1979.

[4]   J. O. Smith III. *Physical Audio Signal Processing.* Stanford, CA, 2004. Draft version. Available online at `http://ccrma.stanford.edu/~jos/pasp04/`.

[5]   D. Morrison and J.-M. Adrien. Mosaic: A framework for modal synthesis. *Computer Music Journal*, 17(1):45–56, 1993.

[6]   B. Gustafsson, H.-O. Kreiss, and J. Oliger. *Time Dependent Problems and Difference Methods.* John Wiley and Sons, New York, New York, 1995.

[7]   S. Bilbao. *Numerical Sound Synthesis.* John Wiley and Sons, Chichester, UK, 2009.

[8]   A. Torin and S. Bilbao. A 3D multi-plate environment for sound synthesis. *Proc. of the 16th Int. Conference on Digital Audio Effects (DAFx-13), Maynooth, Ireland*, 2013.

[9]   A. Nayfeh and D. Mook. *Nonlinear oscillations.* John Wiley and Sons, New York, 1979.

[10] P. M. Morse and K. U. Ingard. *Theoretical acoustics.* McGraw-Hill Inc., USA, 1986.

[11] S. Bilbao. A family of conservative finite difference schemes for the dynamical von krmn plate equations. *Numerical Methods for Partial Differential Equations*, 24(1):193–216, 2008.

[12] A. Torin. 3D multi-plate environment web page. `http://edin.ac/1TavajV`, 2013.

[13] J. R. Shewchuk. An introduction to the conjugate gradient method without the agonizing pain. `http://www.cs.cmu.edu/ ./quake-papers/painless-conjugate-gradient.pdf`, 1994.

[14] N. J. Higham. Cholesky factorization. *Wiley Interdisciplinary Reviews: Computational Statistics*, 1(2):251–254, 2009.

[15] Dr. A. P. S. Selvadurai. *Partial Differential Equations in Mechanics 2.* Springer, 2000.

[16] M. Naumov. Parallel solution of sparse triangular linear systems in the preconditioned iterative methods on the gpu. *NVIDIA Corp., Westford, MA, USA, Tech. Rep. NVR-2011-001*, 2011.

[17] A. Kallischko. *Modified Sparse Approximate Inverses (MSPAI) for Parallel Preconditioning.* Dissertation, Fakultät für Mathematik, Technische Universität München, mar 2008.

[18] NVIDIA. Cusparse library. *NVIDIA Corporation, Santa Clara, California*, 2011.

Parallel Computing: On the Road to Exascale
G.R. Joubert et al. (Eds.)
IOS Press, 2016
© 2016 The authors and IOS Press. All rights reserved.
doi:10.3233/978-1-61499-621-7-217

Harnessing CUDA Dynamic Parallelism for the Solution of Sparse Linear Systems

José ALIAGA , [a,1] Davor DAVIDOVIĆ [b], Joaquín PÉREZ [a], and
Enrique S. QUINTANA-ORTÍ [a]

[a] *Dpto. Ingeniería Ciencia de Computadores, Universidad Jaume I, Castellón (Spain)*
[b] *Institut Ruđer Bošković, Centar za Informatiku i Računarstvo - CIR, Zagreb (Croatia)*

Abstract. We leverage CUDA dynamic parallelism to reduce execution time while significantly reducing energy consumption of the Conjugate Gradient (CG) method for the iterative solution of sparse linear systems on graphics processing units (GPUs). Our new implementation of this solver is launched from the CPU in the form of a single "parent" CUDA kernel, which invokes other "child" CUDA kernels. The CPU can then continue with other work while the execution of the solver proceeds asynchronously on the GPU, or block until the execution is completed. Our experiments on a server equipped with an Intel Core i7-3770K CPU and an NVIDIA "Kepler" K20c GPU illustrate the benefits of the new CG solver.

Keywords. Graphics processing units (GPUs), CUDA dynamic parallelism, sparse linear systems, iterative solvers, high performance, energy efficiency

Introduction

The discretization of partial differential equations (PDEs) often leads to large-scale linear systems of the form $Ax = b$, where the coefficient matrix $A \in \mathbb{R}^{n \times n}$ is *sparse*, $b \in \mathbb{R}^n$ contains the independent terms, and $x \in \mathbb{R}^n$ is the sought-after solution. For many problems (especially those associated with 3-D models), the size and complexity of these systems have turned iterative projection methods, based on Krylov subspaces, into a highly competitive approach compared with direct methods [1].

The Conjugate Gradient (CG) method is one of the most efficient Krylov subspace-based algorithms for the solution of sparse linear systems when the coefficient matrix is symmetric positive definite (s.p.d.) [1]. Furthermore, the structure and numerical kernels arising in this iterative solver are representative of a wide variety of efficient solvers for other specialized types of sparse linear systems.

When the target platform is a heterogeneous server consisting of a multicore processor plus a graphics processing unit (GPU), a conventional implementation of the CG method completely relies on the GPU for the computations, and leaves the general-purpose multicore processor (CPU) in charge of controlling the GPU only. The reason is that this type of iterative solvers is composed of fine-grain kernels, which exhibit a low ratio between computation and data accesses (in general, O(1)). In this scenario, com-

---

[1] Corresponding Author: Dpto. de Ingeniería y Ciencia de Computadores, Universidad Jaume I, 12.071– Castellón (Spain); E-mail: aliaga@icc.uji.es.

municating data via a slow PCI-e bus mostly blurs the benefits of a CPU-GPU collaboration. In addition, in [2] we demonstrated the negative effect of CPU-GPU synchronization when the body of the iterative loop in the CG solver is implemented via calls to the GPU kernels, e.g. in CUBLAS/cuSPARSE. The cause is that, in such implementation, the CPU thread in control of the GPU repeatedly invokes fine-grain CUDA kernels of low cost and short duration, resulting in continuous stream of kernel calls that prevents the CPU from entering an energy-efficient C-state.

Our solution to alleviate these performance and energy overheads in [2] was to *fuse* (i.e. *merge*) CUDA kernels in order to decrease their number, thus reducing the volume of CPU-GPU synchronizations. The main contribution of this paper lies in the investigation of *dynamic parallelism* (DP) [3], as a complementary/alternative technique to achieve the same effect with a more reduced programming effort. Concretely, this work provides a practical demonstration of the benefits of DP on a solver like the CG method, representative of many other sparse linear system solvers as well as, in general, fine-grain computations. Our experimental evaluation of this algorithm on a platform equipped with an Intel Xeon processor and an NVIDIA "Kepler" GPU reports savings in both execution time and energy consumption, respectively of 3.65% and 14.23% on average, for a collection of problems.

DP is a recent technology introduced recently in the CUDA programming model, and is available for NVIDIA devices with compute capability 3.5 or higher. With DP, a child CUDA kernel can be called from within a parent CUDA kernel and then optionally synchronized on the completion of that child CUDA kernel. Some research on DP pursue the implementation of clustering and graph algorithms on GPUs [4,5,6], and a more complete analysis of unstructured applications on GPUs appears in [7]. This technology is also included as a compiler technique [8] to handle nested parallelism in GPU applications. DP is also used to avoid deadlocks in intra-GPU synchronization, reducing the energy consumption of the system [9].

The rest of the paper is structured as follows. In section 1 we briefly review the CG method and the fusion-based approach proposed in our earlier work. In section 2 we present the changes required to a standard implementation of the CG solver in order to efficiently exploit DP. In section 3 we evaluate the dynamic(-parallel) implementation of the new solver, and in section 4 we summarize the insights gained from our study.

1. Fusions in the CG method

1.1. Overview

Figure 1 offers an algorithmic description of the CG solver. Concerning the computational effort of the method, in practice the cost of the iteration loop is dominated by the sparse matrix-vector multiplication (SpMV) involving A. In particular, given a sparse matrix A with n_z nonzero entries, the cost of the SpMV in O1 is roughly $2n_z$ floating-point arithmetic operations (flops), while the vector operations in the loop body (O2, O3, O4, O5 and O8) require $O(n)$ flops each.

The dependencies between the operations in the body of the iterative loop of the CG method dictate a partial order for their execution. Specifically, at the $(j+1)$-th iteration,

Initialize $r_0, p_0, x_0, \sigma_0, \tau_0; j := 0$	
while $(\tau_j > \tau_{max})$	Loop for iterative CG solver
$\quad v_j := Ap_j$	O1. SPMV
$\quad \alpha_j := \sigma_j / p_j^T v_j$	O2. DOT
$\quad x_{j+1} := x_j + \alpha_j p_j$	O3. AXPY
$\quad r_{j+1} := r_j - \alpha_j v_j$	O4. AXPY
$\quad \zeta_j := r_{j+1}^T r_{j+1}$	O5. DOT product
$\quad \beta_j := \zeta_j / \sigma_j$	O6. Scalar op
$\quad \sigma_{j+1} := \zeta_j$	O7. Scalar op
$\quad p_{j+1} := z_j + \beta_j p_j$	O8. XPAY (AXPY-like)
$\quad \tau_{j+1} := \| r_{j+1} \|_2 = \sqrt{\zeta_j}$	O9. Vector 2-norm (in practice, sqrt)
$\quad j := j + 1$	
endwhile	

Figure 1. Algorithmic formulation of the CG method. In general, we use Greek letters for scalars, lowercase for vectors and uppercase for matrices. Here, τ_{max} is an upper bound on the relative residual for the computed approximation to the solution.

$$(j+1)\text{-th iteration}$$
$$\ldots \to O8 \to \overline{O1 \to O2 \to O4 \to O5 \to O6 \to O7 \to O9} \to O1 \to \ldots$$

must be computed in that order, but O3 and O8 can be computed any time once O2 and O6 are respectively available.

1.2. Merging kernels in CG

In [2], we exploited that two CUDA kernels related by a RAW (read-after-write) dependency [10], dictated by a vector v that is an output of/input to the first/second kernel, can be merged if *(i)* both kernels apply the same mapping of threads to the elements of v shared (exchanged) via registers; *(ii)* both kernels apply the same mapping of thread blocks to the vector elements shared (exchanged) via shared memory; and *(iii)* a global barrier is not necessary between the two kernels.

In addition, in [2] we developed a tailored implementation of the kernel DOT that consisted of two stages, say DOT_{ini}^M and DOT_{fin}^M, so that the first stage can be efficiently merged with a prior dependent kernel. In particular, the first stage was implemented as a GPU kernel which performs the costly element-wise products and subsequent reduction within a thread block, producing a partial result in the form of a temporary vector with one entry per block. This was followed by a *routine* DOT_{fin}^M which completed the operation by repeatedly reducing the contents of this vector into a single scalar via a sequence of calls to GPU kernels; see [2] for details.

Figure 2 illustrates the fusions that were derived in our previous work for the CG solver when SPMV is based on the CSR scalar or ELL formats [11]. The node colors distinguish between three different operation types: SPMV, DOT and AXPY-like (AXPY/XPAY). As argued earlier, each DOT operation (O2 and O5) is divided into two stages (a or b, corresponding respectively to kernel DOT_{ini}^M and routine DOT_{fin}^M) in order to facilitate the fusion of the first one with a previous kernel. The fusions are encircled by thick lines and designate three macro-kernels: {O1-O2a}, {O3-O4-O5a}, {O5b-O6-O7-O9}; plus two single-node (macro-)kernels: {O2b} and {O8}. The arrowless lines connect independent kernels (e.g., O3 and O4) and the arrows identify dependencies inside macro-kernels (e.g., from O1 to O2a) and between them (e.g., from {O1-O2a}

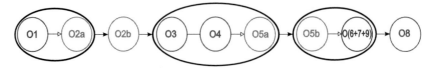

Figure 2. Fusions for the CG solver with SpMV based on the scalar CSR or ELL format.

to {O2b}). When SpMV employs the CSR vector format [11] the fusion graph differs
from that in Figure 2 in that O1 and O2a cannot be merged.

This specialized formulation of the CG solver merged multiple numerical operations, reducing the number of synchronizations and data transfers, in turn yielding a more
efficient hardware utilization. The experimental evaluation with a varied benchmark of
linear systems from the University of Florida Matrix Collection and the 3D Laplace problem, using a server equipped with an Intel Core i7-3770K processor and an NVIDIA
GeForce GTX480 GPU, revealed remarkable CPU energy savings and minor improvements on runtime, with respect to a plain implementation of the CG method based on the
use of CUBLAS kernels and the CUDA polling synchronization mode.

2. Exploiting DP to Enhance CG

In principle, kernel fusion and DP are orthogonal techniques that can be applied independently or in combination. As described next, our *dynamic version* of CG integrates
specialized implementations of DOT, AXPY and XPAY, which are more efficient than their
"fusible" counterparts previously developed for the *merge version*.

2.1. Two-stage dynamic DOT

Our previous implementation of DOT divided this operation into two stages, $\text{DOT}_{\text{ini}}^{\text{M}}$ and
$\text{DOT}_{\text{fin}}^{\text{M}}$, with the former one implemented as a CUDA kernel and the second being a routine that consists of a loop which invoked a CUDA kernel per iteration. The problem
with this approach is that, if integrated with DP, $\text{DOT}_{\text{fin}}^{\text{M}}$ involves a sequence of nested
calls to CUDA kernels from inside the GPU and, in practice, incurs a large overhead. In
order to avoid this negative effect, we redesigned DOT as a two-stage procedure, $\text{DOT}_{\text{ini}}^{\text{D}}$
and $\text{DOT}_{\text{fin}}^{\text{D}}$, but with each stage implemented as a single CUDA kernel. One main difference between $\text{DOT}_{\text{ini}}^{\text{D}}$ and $\text{DOT}_{\text{ini}}^{\text{M}}$ is that the former cannot be merged with other kernels.
However, we note that the "dynamic" version of the first stage is intended to be used in
combination with DP and, therefore, reducing the number of kernels is no longer a strong
urge (though it may still be convenient).

Figures 3 and 4 illustrate the implementation of the GPU kernels $\text{DOT}_{\text{ini}}^{\text{D}}$ and $\text{DOT}_{\text{fin}}^{\text{D}}$,
respectively. There, n specifies the length of the vectors, x and y are the vectors involved
in the reduction. The first kernel is invoked as

```
DOT_D_ini <<NumBlk, BlkSize, sizeof(float)*BlkSize>> (n, x, y, valpha);
```

and reduces the two vectors into NumBlk=256 partial results, stored upon completion in
valpha. We note that, for performance reasons, this kernel spawns GrdSize = NumBlk
· BlkSize= 256 · 192 threads, and each thread, processes two entries (one at threadId
and a second at threadId+BlkSize) per iteration and per chunk of 2·GrdSize elements

```
 1  __global__ void DOT_D_ini(int n, float *x, float *y, float *valpha) {
 2  extern __shared__ float vtmp[];
 3
 4  // Each thread loads two elements from each chunk
 5  // from global to shared memory
 6  unsigned int   tid      = threadIdx.x;
 7  unsigned int   NumBlk   = gridDim.x;    // = 256
 8  unsigned int   BlkSize  = blockDim.x;   // = 192
 9  unsigned int   Chunk    = 2 * NumBlk * BlkSize;
10  unsigned int   i        = blockIdx.x * (2 * BlkSize) + tid;
11  volatile float *vtmp2   = vtmp;
12
13  // Reduce from n to NumBlk * BlkSize elements. Each thread
14  // operates with two elements of each chunk
15  vtmp[tid] = 0;
16  while (i < n) {
17     vtmp[tid] += x[i] * y[i];
18     vtmp[tid] += (i+BlkSize < n) ? (x[i+BlkSize] * y[i+BlkSize]): 0;
19     i          += Chunk;
20  }
21  __syncthreads();
22
23  // Reduce from BlkSize=192 elements to 96, 48, 24, 12, 6, 3 and 1
24  if (tid < 96) { vtmp[tid] += vtmp[tid + 96]; } __syncthreads();
25  if (tid < 48) { vtmp[tid] += vtmp[tid + 48]; } __syncthreads();
26  if (tid < 24) {
27     vtmp2[tid] += vtmp2[tid + 24]; vtmp2[tid] += vtmp2[tid + 12];
28     vtmp2[tid] += vtmp2[tid + 6 ]; vtmp2[tid] += vtmp2[tid + 3 ];
29  }
30
31  // Write result for this block to global mem
32  if (tid == 0) valpha[blockIdx.x] = vtmp[0] + vtmp[1] + vtmp[2];
33  }
```

Figure 3. Implementation of kernel DOT$_{ini}^{D}$.

of the vectors, yielding a coalesced access to their entries; see Figure 5. The subsequent invocation to kernel

```
DOT_D_fin <<NumBlk2, BlkSize2, sizeof(float)*BlkSize2>> (valpha);
```

then produces the sought-after scalar result into the first component of this vector. The grid and block dimensions NumBlk = 256, BlkSize = 192, NumBlk2 = 1, BlkSize2 = NumBlk = 256 passed for the kernel launches were experimentally determined, except for BlkSize which was set to the number of CUDA cores per SMX (streaming multiprocessor).

2.2. Two-stage dynamic AXPY/XPAY

For performance reasons, the AXPY and XPAY have been also reorganized in the dynamic version of CG so that each CUDA thread operates with a pair of elements of each vectors. Figure 6 offers the code for the former, with the second operation being implemented in an analogous manner. There, n specifies the length of the vectors, x and y are the vectors involved in the operation, and alpha is the scalar. The call to this kernel is done as

```
 1  __global__  void DOT_D_fin(float *valpha) {
 2    extern __shared__ float vtmp[];
 3
 4    // Each thread loads one element from global to shared mem
 5    unsigned int   tid = threadIdx.x;
 6    volatile float *vtmp2 = vtmp;
 7
 8    vtmp[tid] = valpha[tid]; __syncthreads();
 9
10    // Reduce from 256 elements to 128, 64, 32, 16, 8, 2 and 1
11    if (tid < 128) { vtmp[tid] += vtmp[tid + 128]; } __syncthreads();
12    if (tid < 64)  { vtmp[tid] += vtmp[tid + 64 ]; } __syncthreads();
13    if (tid < 32)  {
14      vtmp2[tid] += vtmp2[tid + 32]; vtmp2[tid] += vtmp2[tid + 16];
15      vtmp2[tid] += vtmp2[tid + 8 ]; vtmp2[tid] += vtmp2[tid + 4 ];
16      vtmp2[tid] += vtmp2[tid + 2 ]; vtmp2[tid] += vtmp2[tid + 1 ];
17    }
18
19    // Write result for this block to global mem
20    if (tid == 0) valpha[blockIdx.x] = *vtmp;
21  }
```

Figure 4. Implementation of kernel DOT^{D}_{fin}.

```
AXPY_D <<NumBlk3, BlkSize3/2>> (n, alpha, x, y);
```

with $\text{NumBlk3}=\lceil n/\text{BlkSize3} \rceil$ and $\text{BlkSize3} = 256$. The same values are also used for the dynamic implementation of XPAY.

Finally, our dynamic CG solver merges O3 and O4 into a single macro-kernel. creating another macro-kernel with the scalar operations (O6, O7 and O9) and the second stage of the last DOT (O5b)

3. Experimental Evaluation

We next expose the performance and energy of the dynamic CG solver compared with our previous implementations [2]. For this purpose, we employ several sparse matrices from the University of Florida Matrix Collection (UFMC)[2] and a difference discretization of the 3D Laplace problem; see Table 1. For all cases, the solution vector was chosen to have all entries equal 1, and the independent vector was set to $b = Ax$. The iterative solvers were initialized with the starting guess $x_0 = 0$. All experiments were done using IEEE single precision arithmetic. While the use of double precision arithmetic is in general mandatory for the solution of sparse linear systems, the use of mixed single/double-precision in combination with iterative refinement leads to improved execution time and energy consumption when the target platform is a GPU accelerator.

The target architecture is a Linux server (CentOS release 6.2 with kernel 2.6.32 with CUDA v5.5.0) equipped with a single Intel Core i7-3770K CPU (3.5 GHz, four cores) and 16 Gbytes of DDR3 RAM, connected via a PCI-e 2.0 bus to an NVIDIA "Kepler"

---

[2]http://www.cise.ufl.edu/research/sparse/matrices/

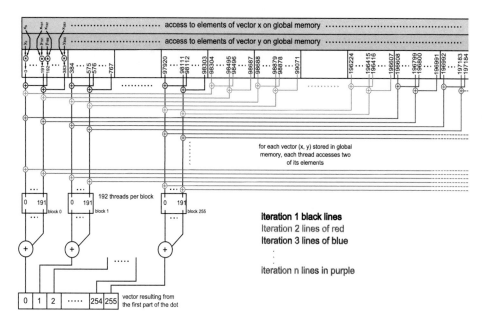

Figure 5. Implementation of DOT_{ini}^{D}.

```
 1  __global__ void AXPY_D(int n, float *alpha, float *x, float *y) {
 2    unsigned int NumBlk   = gridDim.x;
 3    unsigned int BlkSize  = blockDim.x;
 4    unsigned int i        = blockIdx.x * (2 * BlkSize) + threadIdx.x;
 5    unsigned int Chunk    = 2 * NumBlk * BlkSize;
 6
 7    while (i < n) {
 8      y[i] += *alfa * x[i];
 9      if (i + BlkSize < n) y[i + BlkSize] += *alfa * x[i + BlkSize];
10      i += Chunk;
11    }
12  }
```

Figure 6. Implementation of kernel AXPY^{D}.

K20c GPU (compute capability 3.5, 706 MHz, 2,496 CUDA cores) with 5 GB of DDR5 RAM integrated into the accelerator board. Power was collected using a *National Instruments* data acquisition system, composed of the NI9205 module and the NIcDAQ-9178 chassis, and plugged to the lines that connect the power supply unit with motherboard and GPU.

Our experimental evaluation included four implementations of the CG solver:

- CUBLASL is a plain version that relies on CUBLAS kernels from the legacy programming interface of this library, combined with *ad-hoc* implementations of SPMV. In this version, one or more scalars may be transferred between the main memory and the GPU memory address space each time a kernel is invoked and/or

Matrix	Acronym	n_z	n	n_z/n
BMWCRA1_1	bmw	10,641,602	148,770	71.53
CRANKSEG_2	crank	14,148,858	63,838	221.63
F1	F1	26,837,113	343,791	78.06
INLINE_1	inline	38,816,170	503,712	77.06
LDOOR	ldoor	42,493,817	952,203	44.62
AUDIKW_1	audi	77,651,847	943,645	82.28
A252	A252	111,640,032	16,003,001	6.94

Table 1. Description and properties of the test matrices from the UFMC and the 3D Laplace problem.

CUDA mode	Implementation	Time			Energy		
		Min	Max	Avg.	Min	Max	Avg.
Polling	CUBLASL	0.00	0.00	0.00	0.00	0.00	0.00
	CUDA	0.08	0.41	0.21	0.23	7.94	1.79
	MERGE	-0.89	-3.07	-1.71	-1.42	5.03	0.62
	DYNAMIC	-1.54	-4.76	-3.65	-1.17	-3.32	-2.58
Blocking	CUBLASL	0.62	12.88	7.15	-3.30	-13.48	-10.85
	CUDA	0.78	9.39	4.74	-4.45	-12.62	-10.70
	MERGE	-0.59	-1.70	-1.06	-8.31	-13.96	-12.47
	DYNAMIC	-1.54	-4.71	-3.65	-13.73	-14.50	-14.23

Table 2. Minimum, maximum and average variations (in %) of execution time and energy consumption for CG with respect to the baseline.

its execution is completed.

- CUDA replaces the CUBLAS (vector) kernels in the previous version by our *ad-hoc* implementations.
- MERGE applies the fusions described in Section 1, including the two-stage $\text{DOT}_{\text{ini}}^{M}$ $+\text{DOT}_{\text{fin}}^{M}$.
- DYNAMIC exploits DP including the two-stage dynamic implementations of DOT, AXPY and XPAY introduced in Section 2 and merging O3 and O4 into a single macro-kernel.

Furthermore, we execute these configurations under the CUDA polling and blocking synchronization modes. We evaluated three different implementations of SPMV, scalar CSR, vector CSR and ELL [11], but only report results for the second one (vector CSR) which was experimentally determined to be the best option for most of the matrix cases.

Figure 7 reports the time and energy variations of the CUDA, MERGE and DYNAMIC versions of the CG solver with respect to CUBLASL executed in the CUDA polling synchronization mode (*baseline case*) for each matrix case. Table 2 summarizes these results via minimum, maximum and average numbers (with the former two corresponding to the largest and smallest in absolute value).

Let us analyze first the CUBLASL implementation executed in blocking mode. Compared with the same routine executed in polling mode (i.e, the baseline case), we observe an appealing reduction of the energy consumption, -10.85% on average, though it comes at the cost of a noticeable increase in the execution time, around 7.15% on average. The CUDA version of the solver executed in polling mode incurs a very small overhead in execution time with respect to the baseline (0.21% on average) and a slightly larger one in

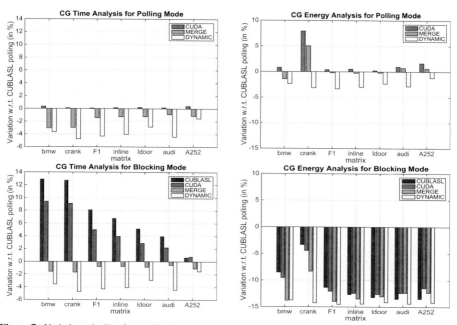

Figure 7. Variations (in %) of execution time and energy consumption of the CG solver (left and right, respectively) with respect to the baseline.

energy (1.79% on average). Moreover, when executed in blocking mode, the CUBLASL and CUDA implementations offer a close behavior, with a considerable increase in execution time that neutralizes the benefits of the notable reduction in energy. The MERGE variant of the solver combines the speed of a polling execution with the energy efficiency of a blocking one. In particular, this variant executed in blocking mode slightly reduces the average execution time (by -1.06%) while extracting much of the energy advantages of this mode (reduction of -12.47% on average). Finally, the DYNAMIC implementation outperforms all other variants, including MERGE, obtaining the largest reduction in both time and energy (respectively, -3.65% and -14.23% on average). In addition, the DYNAMIC version of the solver does not require the complex reorganization of the code entailed by the MERGE case.

4. Concluding Remarks

We have presented a CUDA implementation of the CG method for the solution of sparse linear systems that exploits DP as means to produce a more energy efficient solution. With this new implementation, the CPU invokes a single "parent" CUDA kernel in order to launch the CG solver on the GPU, and can then proceed asynchronously to perform other work or be simply put to sleep via the CUDA blocking synchronization mode and the CPU C-states. The GPU is then in charge of executing the complete solver, with the parent kernel calling other "child" CUDA kernels to perform specific parts of the job. In order to improve efficiency, we have redesigned the implementation of the key vector operations arising in CG, concretely the dot product and axpy-like operations, into two-stage CUDA kernels. This is particular important for the former operation in order to avoid that the exploitation of DP results in a hierarchy of "nested" invocations to other CUDA kernels (i.e., a multilevel structure of parents and children).

The experimentation on a platform with a recent Intel Core i7-3770K CPU and an NVIDIA "Kepler" K20c GPU reports the superiority of the dynamic CG solver, which outperforms our previous fusion-based implementation, in both execution time and energy consumption. From the programming point of view, the dynamic version also presents the important advantage of being more modular, as it does not require the major reorganization of CG, via kernel fusions, that were entailed by the fusion-based implementation.

We have applied similar techniques to iterative solvers based on BiCG and BiCGStab, as well as variants of these and CG that include a simple, Jacobi-based preconditioner, with similar benefits on performance and energy efficiency. The gains that can be obtained with DP heavily depend on the granularity of the CUDA kernels and, as the complexity of the preconditioner grows, we can expect that the positive impact of DP decreases.

Acknowledgments

This research has been supported by EU under projects EU FP7 318793 (Exa2Green), EU FEDER, the COST Program Action IC1305: Network for Sustainable Ultrascale Computing (NESUS), and the project TIN2011-23283 of the *Ministerio de Economía y Competitividad*.

References

[1]   Yousef Saad. *Iterative Methods for Sparse Linear Systems*. SIAM, 2nd edition, 2003.

[2]   J. I. Aliaga, J. Pérez, E. S. Quintana-Ortí, and H. Anzt. Reformulated Conjugate Gradient for the Energy-Aware Solution of Linear Systems on GPUs. In *42nd Int. Conference on Parallel Processing (ICPP)*, pages 320–329, 2013.

[3]   NVIDIA Coorporation. Dynamic parallelism in CUDA. http://developer.download.nvidia. com/assets/cuda/files/CUDADownloads/TechBrief_Dynamic_Parallelism_in\ _CUDA.pdf, February 2015.

[4]   Jeffrey DiMarco and Michela Taufer. Performance impact of dynamic parallelism on different clustering algorithms. volume 8752, pages 87520E–87520E–8, 2013.

[5]   Fei Wang, Jianqiang Dong, and Bo Yuan. Graph-based substructure pattern mining using cuda dynamic parallelism. In *IDEAL-2013*, volume 8206 of *Lecture Notes in Computer Science*, pages 342–349. Springer Berlin Heidelberg, 2013.

[6]   Jianqiang Dong, Fei Wang, and Bo Yuan. Accelerating birch for clustering large scale streaming data using cuda dynamic parallelism. In *IDEAL-2013*, volume 8206 of *Lecture Notes in Computer Science*, pages 409–416. Springer Berlin Heidelberg, 2013.

[7]   Jin Wang and Sudhakar Yalamanchili. Characterization and analysis of dynamic parallelism in unstructured gpu applications. In *2014 IEEE International Symposium on Workload Characterization*, 2014.

[8]   Yi Yang, Chao Li, and Huiyang Zhou. Cuda-np: Realizing nested thread-level parallelism in gpgpu applications. *Journal of Computer Science and Technology*, 30(1):3–19, 2015.

[9]   L. Oden, B. Klenk, and H. Froning. Energy-efficient stencil computations on distributed gpus using dynamic parallelism and gpu-controlled communication. In *Energy Efficient Supercomputing Workshop (E2SC), 2014*, pages 31–40, 2014.

[10] J. L. Hennessy and D. A. Patterson. *Computer Architecture: A Quantitative Approach*. Morgan Kaufmann Pub., San Francisco, 2003.

[11] Nathan Bell and Michael Garland. Efficient sparse matrix-vector multiplication on CUDA. NVIDIA Technical Report NVR-2008-004, NVIDIA Corp., December 2008.

Parallel Computing: On the Road to Exascale
G.R. Joubert et al. (Eds.)
IOS Press, 2016
doi:10.3233/978-1-61499-621-7-227

Model-Driven Development of GPU Applications

Christoph WINTER [a] and Jan DÜNNWEBER [a,1]

[a] *Ostbayerische Technische Hochschule Regensburg, Germany*

Abstract Programming GPUs with low-level libraries like CUDA and OpenCL is a tedious and error-prone task. Fortunately, algorithmic skeletons can shield developers from the complexity of parallel programming by encapsulating common parallel computing patterns. However, this simplification typically constrains programmers to write their applications using the GPU library employed by the skeleton implementation. In this work, we combine skeletal programming with model-driven software development (MDSD) to increase the freedom of choice regarding the employed GPU library instead of leaving all technical decisions to the skeleton implementation. We present a code-generator that transforms models comprising skeletons, their input data and input functions to parallel C++ code while taking care of data offset calculations. The generator has been tested using different GPU and multi-GPU communication libraries such as Thrust and CUDA-MPI. We demonstrate our novel approach to GPU programming with two example applications: affinity propagation and n-body simulation.

Keywords. GPU Computing, CUDA, MDSD, Algorithmic Skeletons

Introduction

Recently, the use of graphical processing units for general processing (GPGPU) has become almost as popular as using GPUs in computer graphics. In the scientific community, a variety of skeleton libraries has been developed for GPU platforms [1,2]. These libraries can shield developers from low-level details of GPU programming. However, they either lack support for programming multiple GPUs or they depend on built-in distributed data structures (DDSs). Using skeletons and DDSs can eliminate the need for explicit message passing and simplify the programming of multiple GPUs. But compared with lower-level libraries such as CUDA MPI, a skeleton application may suffer from performance penalties on multi-GPU platforms. Moreover, when a DDS is used in the skeleton code that is built on top of a particular communication library, any application using this skeleton must use exactly this library for handling the CPU/GPU and inter-GPU communication. We, in contrast, propose that developers using algorithmic skeletons for GPU programming should retain control over both, computation and communication.

---

[1]Corresponding Author: Jan Dünnweber, Ostbayerische Technische Hochschule Regensburg, Fakultät für Informatik und Mathematik, UniversitätsstraÃŸe 31, 93053 Regensburg, Germany; E-mail: jan.duennweber@oth-regensburg.de

Most skeleton libraries let application programmers choose among many different skeleton implementations such as task farm, pipeline, etc. since different parallel programs typically make use of different, application-specific communication patterns. However, the platform-aware decomposition of data can impact the performance of a parallel program considerably and, thus, we present a set of tools that leave this task to the application programmer as well. To reduce the emerging complexity when dealing with explicit data exchange via message passing, we propose to utilize model-driven software development (MDSD) for GPGPU programming.

Model-driven software development is a collective term for techniques that automatically generate compilable source code from formal models. Applications are incrementally developed on the basis of such models, which are translated into source code by MDSD tools [3]. We extend this strategy for programming GPUs by combining it with algorithmic skeletons as follows: Our MDSD tool generates extensible or rather partial programs including generic function bodies which developers can supplement with their own implementations. This approach to GPU programming improves the efficiency of application development since many repetitive tasks are delegated to the MDSD tool.

Section 1 of this paper presents our novel graphical user interface that allows programmers to compose skeleton applications based on graphical diagrams, i. e., on a very high level of abstraction. Section 2 describes in more detail the different domains of the metamodel underlying our automatic model-to-code transformation. Here, we discuss to what extent programmers can fine-tune the runtime and communication behavior of the generated CUDA C++ code particularly with regard to communication libraries. Section 3 explains how the code generator internally works and the tools we employed to implement it. Section 4 reports on our experimental results for our example applications affinity propagation and n-body simulation. Section 5 concludes this paper with a discussion of related work.

1. Our Model Editor for Graphical Parallel Programming

Figure 1 shows the graphical user interface of our model editor.

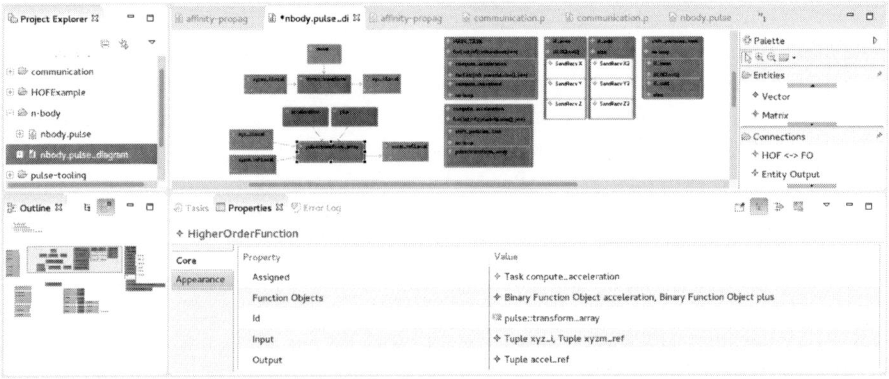

Figure 1. Building GPGPU C++ Applications Using Graphical Diagrams

The multi-window layout looks similar to the popular Eclipse IDE for C/C++ and Java Programming.

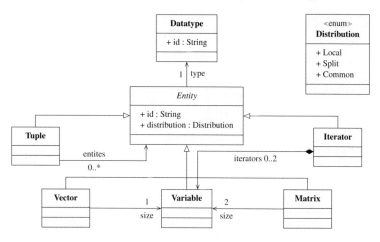

Figure 2. The metamodel's data domain with the strongly typed abstract `Entity` and its derived data structures like `Variable` and `Vector` or `Matrix` which can be distributed among several GPUs via pre-defined `Distribution` properties

We built this interface using the Eclipse Graphical Modeling Framework (GMF) [4] to provide programmers with a familiar interface. GMF is intended to impose restrictions on models, e.g., a workflow model which can informally be seen as an arbitrary sequence of operations.

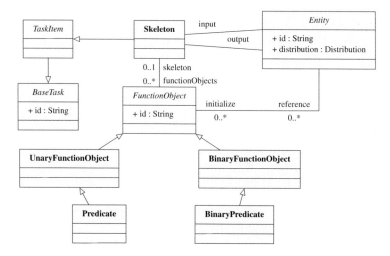

Figure 3. The metamodel's computation domain

Using GMF, one can formalize the workflow into a well-defined model with input and output elements for all operations, which must all have certain types, chosen from a selection of available types, such that only operations with matching types can be chained. Once, such a metamodel is specified (via a freely available Eclipse plugin) and stored in XML-format, GMF can provide a graphical editor for models that adhere to this specification. Our metamodel is depicted by the UML-diagrams in Figure 2–5 and is explained in more detail in Section 2.

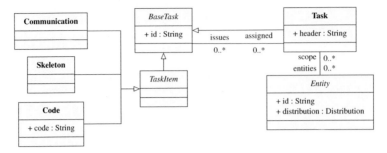

Figure 4. The metamodel's program structure

Even without a lot of Eclipse experience, users will intuitively understand the project explorer subwindow in the upper left corner, the outline subwindow in the lower left corner and the palette window in the upper right corner of Figure 1. Here, one can switch among projects, view a model's outline - i. e., a map of all its elements - or extend a model by dragging new elements from the palette into a diagram.

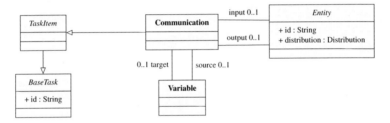

Figure 5. The metamodel's domain of communication

The main window of Figure 1 contains one such diagram. Below this window is an editable property table for diagram elements. The screenshot in Figure 1 captures all editor windows and, therefore, the subwindows are pretty small. However, it is visible that a diagram is a directed graph which assigns parameters, depicted as boxes with different shades (depending on whether they carry data or code), to different skeletons which are depicted using shaded boxes as well. Thus, an understanding of algorithmic skeletons [5] is sufficient to build, e. g., the model of a task farm application. The fine-tuning for a specific GPU platform can then be done by a customization in the property editor, where, e. g., the segment size can be adjusted for data that is distributed over the available GPUs in segment-wise manner. Thus, programmers who know about the composition of their target platform can take advantage from features like data locality when multiple GPUs are available without going into the low-level details of cudaMemcpy()-calls themselves.

2. Our GPU Programming Metamodel for MDSD

Metamodels for MDSD define components and relationships among these components. We identified four domains that a metamodel must cover in order to build applications that may run on GPU clusters: data, computation, communication and program structure.

1. The *data domain*, as illustrated in the class diagram in Figure 2, covers strongly typed abstract entities. Variables, vectors and matrices are concrete subclasses of such entities which may be distributed among several GPUs using three different distribution properties: Local, Split and Common.
2. The *computation domain*, shown in Figure 3, comprises the algorithmic skeletons in our approach. Skeletons are parameterized with user-defined functions which are either unary or binary and may reference to arbitrary data entities.
3. The *program structure domain*, shown in Figure 4, defines the scope of the data being processed and the sequence of the processing steps in the form of *tasks*. Each task has an id and a header that makes it possible to process it always, conditionally or multiple times.
4. The *communication domain* is used to exchange partial results between GPUs and is shown in Figure 5. Entities from the data domain are associated with source and target GPUs in the communication domain, which allows programmers to take advantage of data locality, when, e. g., recurring tasks should always be processed on the same GPU.

On the basis of this flexible domain model, we set up a template library (called *Pulse*) that lets users of our model editor (described in Section 1) combine entities like functions, input and output freely, i. e., with less restrictions than that of a strongly typed programming language. The more of these entities are readily provided by our *Pulse* library, the less programming has to be done manually, after our code generator (described in Section 3) has processed the model. Currently, especially numerical applications (like the ones described in Section 4) can benefit from our template library, since *Pulse* contains primarily matrices, vector-to-vector mappings etc. However, our model-driven approach to GPU development can easily be extended to applications from other scientific fields, e. g., computational biology, by including new templates for the entities these applications work on into our template library.

3. Our Code Generator for GPGPU programs

The most important MDSD tool that we use to demonstrate our approach is a model-to-text transformer that we have implemented using the modular generator framework openArchitectureWare (oAW) and its languages Xpand and Xtend [2]. The Eclipse IDE supports these technologies via plugins and, thus, we could integrate our code generator into the IDE like our graphical model editor from Section 1. The code generator produces artifacts of parallel programs from models which are compliant to the metamodel described above. Note that these artifacts are not necessarily fully executable programs, like the result of compiling a program in a graphical programming language, e. g., a " virtual instrument" in LabVIEW [6]. The output is rather a collection of source code files that makes use of algorithmic skeletons, i. e., except for trivial tests, the generated code must still be extended by user-defined parameter functions, before it can be used to process data. The advantage over alternative means for simplifying the programming of GPGPU applications, such as generating all the code or using a particular skeleton library, lies in the combination of simplicity with flexibility: Programmers only need to

---

[2]http://www.openarchitectureware.org

write very few lines of C++ code manually, since the generated artifacts cover all the necessary algorithmic logic of skeletons, such as the coordination of parallel tasks according to their dependencies. However, the communication behavior of the final executable can be optimized for different target platforms, including multi-GPU clusters, by customizing communication properties in the model editor.

The model-to-text transformation can be partitioned into three major steps:
1. Import the formal model and create an instance of the model.
2. Code generation on the basis of templates and their extensions.
3. Post-process generated textual artifacts.

The final output is CUDA C++ source code and our code generator includes all required headers and starts to define the main program by initializing the MPI library. After each process is associated to one particular GPU, the automatic setup is completed and the generator continues to transform the actual application model: At first, all entities of the model are defined.

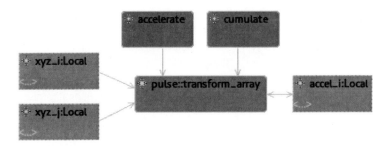

Figure 6. A Functional Model for Computing the Acceleration

Figure 6 shows that for one of our example applications (n-body simulation) the data entities are two input elements (xyz_i, xyz_j) and one output element for intermediate and final results (accel_i), which are all customized to be stored locally on one GPU. The processing is done by the transform_array skeleton defined in our template library *Pulse* which takes two user-defined functions as parameters: the accelerate function and the cumulate function for accumulating the per-particle acceleration.

Once the model is defined, the generator traverses all tasks beginning with the root task. If the header field of a task is set, the field is copied to the output file. The generator continues to produce the code for all sub-tasks issued by the root task. For each specialization of a task, a particular template is used, such that the code generation is a modular process which developers may manipulate.

4. Experimental Results

The first application that we implemented using our model-driven approach to GPU-programming was affinity propagation: A data clustering technique that searches through large data sets to find representative subsets, called exemplars, using a similarity function [7].

Figure 7 shows the speedup for running this application in single-precision mode (SP) and in double-precision mode (DP) for data sets of an increasing size. The use of a single GPU (K20) leads to a performance improvement close to factor 5.

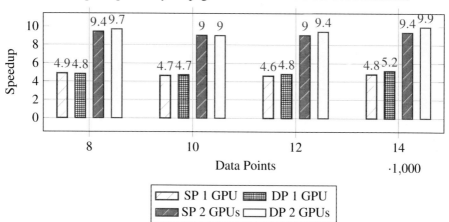

Figure 7. Speedup Comparison for the Affinity Propagation Experiment

A second K20-GPU makes the application almost 10 times faster as compared to the runtime of the same experiment using an OpenMP-based parallel implementation that we have written and tested on our Intel Xeon E5-Server (2.5Ghz, 15 MB Cache). Obviously neither the problem size nor the computation accuracy impairs the enhancements we gained.

The absolute runtimes that we measured on our GPU server are shown in Figure 8. When we compare these results with runtimes reported for the original implementation [7] our parallel version identified the same clusters 18 times faster. Other researchers who also employed multi-GPU Servers for affinity propagation have reported similar runtimes [8]. This proves that our model-driven approach to GPU-programming can be used to build competitive software, while programmers work on a very high level of abstraction: We used our graphical editor (see Section 1) to specify the affinity propagation algorithm as an iterative process wherein two matrices that rate how adequate the assignment of the data to the different exemplars is, according to the original specification [7].

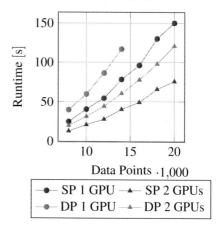

Figure 8.: Absolute Runtimes

From that model, our code generator (see Section 3) produced CUDA C++ code that we had to extend by only 31 lines of hand-written code for the user-defined functions (plus some initialization code for loading the input data). Moreover, all hand-written parts are concerned with application-specific tasks like initializing the matrices, computing similarities etc. The distribution of the data is handled by the generated code, appropriate to the property adjustments we made in our graphical model editor.

As a second experiment, we implemented an n-body simulation, i. e., the evolution of a system of bodies such as stars attracting each other through gravitation. Figure 9 sums up our results using the brute-force technique where all pair-wise interactions are evaluated. This is actually not the most efficient algorithm, however it is quite popular for demonstrating the potential of GPUs, since all pairs can be processed independently and the GPUs can work at full capacity [9].

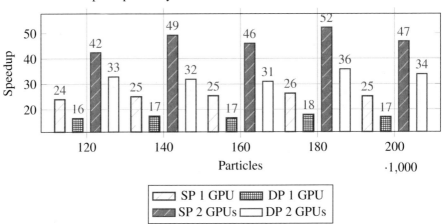

Figure 9. Speedup n-body Simulation

Like in Figure 7, the relative speedup values were computed using the runtime for the same simulation on the CPU of the same server. Again, the reference measurements for the CPU where obtained using an OpenMP-based parallel implementation of the same application that we have written to achieve a fair comparison, since we focus on the speedup gained by using GPUs instead of analyzing the speedup over a sequential version, which could have been gained using an arbitrary skeleton library. Considering a parallel reference implementation, the performance gains around factor 50 make our MDSD approach to parallel programming particularly favorable when the target platform is a GPU server. The notable difference between the double and the single-precision version, which gained by factor 36 at most in our second experiment, can be explained as an effect of non-uniform memory access: With a computation accuracy that is 3 times lower than DP on a K20, the threads of the OpenMP version can work on cached, i. e., thread-local particle data and, thus, deliver a better performance in this computationally intensive application (AP, in contrast, is rather a data-heavy application which cannot benefit from thread-local caching in this manner). For the n-body simulation, we extended the automatically generated code by only 16 lines: more or less the same loop nest that we declared as a parallel omp for-loop in the OpenMP version.

We have chosen affinity propagation and n-body simulation as our experimental applications since they are quite different: Affinity propagation has little communication costs, since only vector segments have to be exchanged among the GPUs. The all-pairs algorithm for the n-body simulation, in contrast, requires that all GPUs see all particle updates in every iteration. The positive results for both experiments encourage us to promote our model-driven approach to GPU programming as a software development technique that is not restricted to a certain class of applications.

5. Conclusion and Related Work

The n-body simulation is an often-used application for performance experiments with CUDA C++. However, our implementation does not require that the input size is 2^N and can, therefore, not directly be compared with the demonstration code from NVIDIA [9]. Our kernel-code includes a check allowing it to process input of different sizes as well, resulting in an around 20% slower absolute runtime. For certain input (especially with a small number of data points) our parallel affinity propagation software is also around 15% slower than other multi-GPU implementations [8]. However, it was not our goal to implement a clustering software that is faster than a domain-specific implementation that makes use of explicit message passing via low-level MPI.

Our work is closer related to former approaches to graphical programming with algorithmic skeletons, like SkIE [10] and CO2P3S [11]. Model-driven development widens the fundamental idea of using a graphical model to that effect that not all the technical decisions are taken away from the programmer. The selection of skeletons and the customization of their communication properties using our graphical model editor has been demonstrated as a novel development technique for GPU applications which have significant performance advantages over programs based on a classical library. Although programming with algorithmic skeletons is similar to using a functional language, to the extent that many functions in a program serve as arguments and results to other functions, GPU-programmers, who most likely have more background in object-oriented languages like C++, are not required to learn a new programming language, like, e. g. , NOVA [12]. However, our metamodel treats computations as evaluations of functions and avoids state and mutable data such that users of our model editor will benefit from these features when they are designing a new parallel program, while they can still write the application-specific, sequential parts of their programs in C++. Therefore, we propose to consider the use of MDSD in more performance-critical areas and expect an adequate growth of our *Pulse* library accompanied by more applications in the future.

We gratefully acknowledge NVIDIA's support of this work by the donation of two Tesla GPUs within the scope of NVIDIA's *academic partnership program*. Sincerely, we also thank the anonymous reviewers who helped us to improve the clarity and completeness of this publication.

References

[1] Bell N. and Hoberock J.: Thrust: A Productivity-Oriented Library for CUDA. GPU Computing Gems: Jade Edition, Pages 359–373, Morgan Kaufmann, USA 2011

[2] MarquÃ©s R., Paulino H., Alexandre F. and Medeiros P.D.: Algorithmic Skeleton Framework for the Orchestration of GPU Computations. In: Proceedings of the Euro-Par. Conference on Parallel and Distributed Computing, Lecture Notes in Computer Science, Vol. 8097, Pages 874–885. Springer, Berlin 2013

[3] Beydeda S., Book M. and Gruhn V. (ed.): Model-Driven Software Development. Springer, Berlin 2005

[4] Dean D., Moore W., Gerber A., Wagenknecht G. and Vanderheyden P.: Eclipse Development Using the Graphical Editing Framework and the Eclipse Modeling Framework, IBM RedBooks, IBM Corp., USA 2004

[5] Cole M.I.: Algorithmic Skeletons: Structured Management of Parallel Computation. Pitman, London 1989

[6] Johnson G., Jennings R.: LabVIEW Graphical Programming: Practical Applications in Instrumentation and Control. 2nd edn., McGraw-Hill Education, Boston, USA 1997

[7] Frey B.J., Dueck D.: Clustering by Passing Messages Between Data Points, Science 315, Pages 972–976, AAAS Washington, USA 2007

[8] Kurdziel, M., Boryczko, K.: Finding Exemplars in Dense Data with Affinity Propagation on Clusters of GPUs. In: Concurrency and Computation: Practice and Experience 25(8), Pages 1137–1152, Wiley, USA 2013

[9] Nguyen H.: GPU Gems 3: Programming Techniques for High-Performance Graphics and General-Purpose Computation. Addison-Wesley, USA 2007

[10] Bacci B., Danelutto M., Pelagatti S. and Vanneschi M.: SkIE: a Heterogeneous Environment for HPC Applications. Parallel Computing Journal, Volume 25, Issue 13-14, Pages 1827–1852, Elsevier Science, Amsterdam 1999

[11] Tan K., Szafron D., Schaeffer J., Anvik K. and MacDonald S.: Using Generative Design Patterns to Generate Parallel Code for a Distributed Memory Environment. In: Proceedings of the Ninth Symposium on Principles and Practice of Parallel Programming, Volume 38 Issue 10, Pages 203–215, ACM New York, USA 2003

[12] Collins, A., Grewe, D., Grover, V., Lee, S. and Susnea, A.: Nova: A Functional Language for Data Parallelism. In: Proceedings of the International Workshop on Libraries, Languages, and Compilers for Array Programming, Pages 8:8–8:13., ACM New York, USA 2014

Parallel Computing: On the Road to Exascale
G.R. Joubert et al. (Eds.)
IOS Press, 2016
© 2016 The authors and IOS Press. All rights reserved.
doi:10.3233/978-1-61499-621-7-237

Exploring the Offload Execution Model in the Intel Xeon Phi via Matrix Inversion

Peter BENNER [a], Pablo EZZATTI [b], Enrique S. QUINTANA-ORTÍ [c], and
Alfredo REMÓN [a,1]

[a] *Max Planck Institute for Dynamics of Complex Technical Systems, Magdeburg,
Germany*
[b] *Instituto de Computación, Universidad de la República, Montevideo, Uruguay*
[c] *Dept. de Ingeniería y Ciencia de los Computadores, Universidad Jaime I, Castellón,
Spain*

Abstract. The explicit inversion of dense matrices appears in a numerous key scientific and engineering applications such as model reduction or optimal control,
asking for the exploitation of high performance computing techniques and architectures when the problem dimension is large. Gauss-Jordan elimination (GJE) is an
efficient in-place method for matrix inversion that exposes large amounts of data-
parallelism, making it very convenient for hardware accelerators such as graphics processors (GPUs) or the Intel Xeon Phi. In this paper, we present and evaluate several practical implementations of GJE, with partial row pivoting, that especially exploit the off-load execution model available on the Intel Xeon Phi to carry
out a significant fraction of the computations on the accelerator. Numerical experiments on a system with two Intel Xeon E5-2640v3 processors and an Intel Xeon
Phi 7120P compare the efficiency of these implementations, with the most efficient
case delivering about 700 billions double-precision floating-point operations per
second.

Keywords. Matrix inversion, Gauss-Jordan elimination, heterogeneous systems,
Intel Xeon Phi, high performance.

Introduction

The end of Dennard scaling [1], in the middle of the past decade, discontinued the "GHz
race" and marked the shift towards the design of multicore computer architectures. Since
then, the steady increase of transistors dictated by Moore's law [2] has promoted the
power wall into a major constraint [3,4,5]. As a result, we have moved into the era of
"dark silicon" [6], and high performance computing (HPC) facilities are rapidly deploying *heterogeneous* systems in an attempt to benefit from their more favourable flops-per-
Watt ratios [7].

Most of today's heterogeneous HPC servers are equipped with one ore more general
purpose multicore processors (i.e., conventional CPUs) plus a many-core accelerator,
such as an AMD or NVIDIA graphics processing unit (GPUs) or an Intel Xeon Phi [8].

---

[1]Corresponding author: Sandtorstr. 1, 39106 Magdeburg, Germany; E-mail: remon@mpi-
magdeburg.mpg.de.

Programming these heterogeneous platforms is a considerable challenge, though the development of programming tools such as CUDA [9], OpenACC [10], and OpenCL [11] has contributed to the adoption of accelerator technologies.

The Intel Xeon Phi (Knights Corner product line) is a coprocessor built at 22 nm process size, with 60(+1) hardware cores capable of running 4 threads per core, for an impressive total of 240 threads. Compared with GPU technologies, the Intel Xeon Phi presents the advantage of being an x86-based system, for which there exist a considerable amount of legacy software as well as a number of standard parallelization tools and libraries. In particular, Intel offers two execution models on its accelerators: in the *native model*, the coprocessor is regarded a stand-alone platform, in charge of executing the complete application. In the alternative *offload model*, the CPU in the server hosting the Intel Xeon Phi board (device) is in control, off-loading certain parts of the computation to the coprocessor.

In this paper we explore the Intel Xeon Phi and its mainstream execution models as a hardware/software technology to boost compute-intensive dense linear algebra operations. Concretely, our analysis targets matrix inversion via Gauss-Jordan elimination (GJE) [12]. While we recognize that the calculation of the explicit inverse is only required in a reduced number of scientific applications (e.g., model reduction, polar decomposition, optimal control and prediction, statistics,...), the procedure underlying GJE is representative of many other matrix factorizations for the solution of linear systems and linear least-squares problems [12]. In this sense, we believe that the results from our study can be applied to a considerable part of the contents of dense linear algebra libraries such as LAPACK [13]. In more detail, our paper makes the following contributions:

- We present and evaluate several parallel routines for matrix inversion via GJE that include partial (row) pivoting for numerical stability [12] and operate under Intel's native or offload execution models.
- Our *hybrid* implementations for the offload model aim to minimize the volume of data communicated between host and device, reducing it to the transfers of two panels (narrow column blocks) per iteration of the algorithm.
- Our advanced implementations accommodate high performance techniques such as look-ahead [14] for the factorization of the panel that stands in the algorithm's critical path and double blocking (use of BLAS-3 for the panel factorization). Furthermore, these routines merge certain suboperations of the algorithm in order to increase their granularity and take advantage of the ample hardware concurrency in Intel's accelerator.
- Our experimental results on a server comprising two 8-core Intel Xeon E5-2640 v3 processors and an Intel Xeon Phi 7120P board report around 700 GFLOPS (billions of floating-point arithmetic operations, or flops, per second).

The rest of the paper is structured as follows. In Section 1, we introduce the GJE algorithm for matrix inversion. Next, in Section 2, we present several implementations of the algorithm that leverage the Intel Xeon Phi architecture to accelerate this operation. This is followed by the experimental evaluation of the new routines in Section 3, and a few conclusions and remarks in Section 4.

1. Matrix inversion via GJE

GJE is an efficient in-place method for matrix inversion, with a computational cost and numerical properties analogous to those of traditional approaches based, e.g., on the LU factorization [15], but superior performance on a varied range of architectures, from clusters [16] to general-purpose multicore processors and hybrid CPU-GPU systems [17].

Figure 1 shows a blocked version of the GJE algorithm for matrix inversion using the FLAME notation. There, $m(A)$ stands for the number of rows of matrix A. For details on the notation, we refer the reader to [18,19]. A description of the unblocked version of GJE, called from inside the blocked routine, can be found in [16]; for simplicity, we do not include the application of pivoting in the algorithm, but details can be found there as well. Furthermore, all the actual implementations include this technique. Given a square (non-singular) matrix of size $n = m(A)$, the cost of matrix inversion using this algorithm is $2n^3$ flops, performing the inversion in-place so that, upon completion, the entries of A are overwritten with those of its inverse.

Algorithm: $[A] := \text{GJE\_BLK}(A)$

Partition $A \rightarrow \left(\begin{array}{c|c} A_{TL} & A_{TR} \\ \hline A_{BL} & A_{BR} \end{array} \right)$

   where A_{TL} is 0×0

while $m(A_{TL}) < m(A)$ **do**

   Determine block size b

   Repartition

$$\left(\begin{array}{c|c} A_{TL} & A_{TR} \\ \hline A_{BL} & A_{BR} \end{array} \right) \rightarrow \left(\begin{array}{c|c|c} A_{00} & A_{01} & A_{02} \\ \hline A_{10} & A_{11} & A_{12} \\ \hline A_{20} & A_{21} & A_{22} \end{array} \right)$$

   where A_{11} is $b \times b$

$\begin{bmatrix} A_{01} \\ A_{11} \\ A_{21} \end{bmatrix} := \text{GJE\_UNB}\left(\begin{bmatrix} A_{01} \\ A_{11} \\ A_{21} \end{bmatrix} \right)$	Unblocked Gauss-Jordan
$A_{00} := A_{00} + A_{01}A_{10}$	Matrix-matrix product
$A_{20} := A_{20} + A_{21}A_{10}$	Matrix-matrix product
$A_{10} := A_{11}A_{10}$	Matrix-matrix product
$A_{02} := A_{02} + A_{01}A_{12}$	Matrix-matrix product
$A_{22} := A_{22} + A_{21}A_{12}$	Matrix-matrix product
$A_{12} := A_{11}A_{12}$	Matrix-matrix product

Continue with

$$\left(\begin{array}{c|c} A_{TL} & A_{TR} \\ \hline A_{BL} & A_{BR} \end{array} \right) \leftarrow \left(\begin{array}{c|c|c} A_{00} & A_{01} & A_{02} \\ \hline A_{10} & A_{11} & A_{12} \\ \hline A_{20} & A_{21} & A_{22} \end{array} \right)$$

endwhile

Figure 1. Blocked algorithm for matrix inversion via GJE without pivoting.

From the implementation point of view, the loop body in the blocked algorithm consists of two types of operations: the factorization of the "current" panel, referred to hereafter as A^C, is composed of the three blocks A_{01}, A_{11} and A_{21}, with b columns each; and 6 matrix multiplications, of different dimensions, that update the remaining blocks of the matrix. In a practical implementation, the algorithmic block size b needs to be carefully tuned for the target architecture because the factorization of the panel lies on the critical path and that particular operation is considerably slower than the matrix multiplications. Furthermore, in a platform with separate memory address spaces (e.g., a conventional CPU-GPU or a CPU-Xeon Phi server), the width of this panel impacts the granularity of communication between host and device.

2. High Performance Implementations for the Intel Xeon Phi

In this section we present a series of implementations of matrix inversion via GJE that leverage either the native or the offload execution models in the Intel Xeon Phi, and progressively integrate increasingly complex strategies to improve performance.

2.1. Native Phi implementation

This version mimics the blocked algorithm in Figure 1 performing all the computations (panel factorization and matrix multiplications) in the accelerator via calls to the numerical kernels in a native implementation of the Intel MKL library. As argued in Section 1, despite the high performance that can be expected for the matrix-matrix products, the factorization of the current panel strongly constrains the global efficiency of this "naive" solution.

2.2. Hybrid CPU-Phi implementation with concurrent execution

The initial hybrid version exploits both the CPU and Xeon Phi coprocessor present in the platform. In order to do so, we split the computations between both types of resources by performing the panel factorization on the CPU while off-loading all the matrix multiplications to the accelerator. This is an ideal workload distribution for CPU-GPU platforms, as the GPU cannot efficiently deal with the intricacies entailed by the application of partial pivoting. It is also an appealing choice when the computational power of the CPU is much lower than that of the accelerator. (However, we recognize that this is not the case for the target platform, where the 16 Intel Xeon cores in the host feature a theoretical peak of about 332 double-precision (DP) GFLOPS which is not negligible compared with the 1,208 DP GFLOPS for the Intel Xeon Phi 7120P.)

The plain version proceeds as follows. Consider that the matrix initially resides in the host's main memory, and let us assume hereafter that the matrix dimension n is an integer multiple of the block size b. At the beginning of the procedure, the CPU factorizes the first (current) panel of b columns $A^C = \left[A_{01}^T, A_{11}^T, A_{21}^T \right]^T$, while the rest of the matrix is concurrently copied to the accelerator's memory. Upon completion of this initial panel factorization, A^C is sent to the accelerator's memory.

The following steps are next executed for each iteration of the main loop (see the left plot in Figure 2 for the block naming convention):

    1. The accelerator updates the blocks to the right of the current panel (i.e., those in A^N and A^{R1}) with respect to A^C.

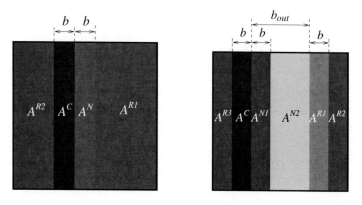

Figure 2. Partition of the matrices in the hybrid GJE versions.

2. The b columns to the right of the current panel, in A^N, are sent back to the host. (These columns will become the "current" panel in the next iteration.)
3. The accelerator updates the blocks to the left of the current panel (in A^{R2}) with respect to A^C, while the factorization of A^N concurrently proceeds in the CPU.
4. The contents of A^N are transferred to the accelerator.

The computations ocurring during one iteration of the loop can be thus summarized as:

$$\text{Update}\left(A^N, A^{R1}\right) \rightarrow \text{Transfer}\left(A^N\right) \rightarrow \left\{\text{Update}\left(A^{R2}\right) \mid\mid \underline{\text{Factor}\left(A^N\right)}\right\} \rightarrow \text{Transfer}\left(A^N\right),$$

where the arrows indicate a strict order while the parallel lines "$\mid\mid$" are used to indicate an overlapped execution, and the colors distinguish between the operations performed by the CPU (in blue and underlined) and the accelerator (in brown).

At the end of the main loop, to complete this process, the accelerator updates the rightmost $n - b$ columns, and the complete matrix contents except the last panel are sent back to the CPU.

The performance of this concurrent version of GJE strongly depends on the parameter b. In particular, the computation of the matrix-matrix products on the Intel Xeon Phi accelerator benefits from the adoption of a large value of b, while the fact that the panel factorization lies in the critical path in principle favours the selection of smaller values for b. To partly alleviate this drawback, we replaced the (unblocked) factorization kernel by a blocked variant (with double blocking) that operates with an independent block size, say $b_{in} < b$, in order to accelerate the panel factorization.

2.3. Hybrid CPU-Phi implementation with look-ahead

This implementation introduces a few relevant optimizations to further leverage concurrency and improve the workload balance between the CPU and the Intel Xeon Phi. The major difference is the reorganization of the computations exposed next.

Let us assume again that, before the computation commences, the original matrix resides in the host main memory. In the first step, the CPU factorizes A^C while the rest of the matrix is concurrently transferred to the accelerator.

The following process then is executed at each iteration of the main loop (see the left plot in Figure 2):

1. The contents of A^C are transferred to the accelerator.
2. The accelerator updates A^N with respect to A^C, and the contents of the former panel are next sent to the CPU.
3. The accelerator updates all columns of A except those in A^C and A^N, (i.e., those in A^{R1} plus A^{R2},) with respect to A^C; and, in parallel, the CPU factorizes A^N.

The computations ocurring during one iteration can be thus summarized as:

$$\text{Transfer}\left(A^C\right) \rightarrow \text{Update}\left(A^N\right) \rightarrow \text{Transfer}\left(A^N\right) \rightarrow \{\text{Update}\left(A^{R1}, A^{R2}\right)\} \parallel \text{Factor}\left(A^N\right)\}.$$

Compared with the previous variant, now the two large updates are performed by the accelerator while the CPU proceeds with the factorization.

To complete the procedure, the accelerator then performs the last update, involving all the matrix contents except the last b columns, and all but these last b columns are copied back to the CPU. This reordering of the computations in practice introduces look-ahead into the algorithm, improving load balancing and further decreasing the negative impact of the high cost of panel factorization on the algorithm's performance.

To further increase the performance of this GJE version, we merged the six matrix multiplications involved in the updates into two kernels. For example, the update of the columns to the right of the current panel in the blocked GJE algorithm (see Figure 1) requires the following matrix-matrix products:

$$\begin{aligned} A_{02} &:= A_{02} + A_{01}A_{12}, \\ A_{22} &:= A_{22} + A_{21}A_{12} \quad \text{and} \\ A_{12} &:= A_{11}A_{12}, \end{aligned} \tag{1}$$

which can be transformed into the following sequence of operations:

$$\begin{aligned} W &:= A_{12}, \\ A_{12} &:= 0 \quad \text{and} \\ \begin{bmatrix} A_{02} \\ A_{12} \\ A_{22} \end{bmatrix} &:= \begin{bmatrix} A_{02} \\ A_{12} \\ A_{22} \end{bmatrix} + \begin{bmatrix} A_{01} \\ A_{11} \\ A_{21} \end{bmatrix} \cdot W. \end{aligned} \tag{2}$$

An analogous transform is possible with the matrix multiplications that update the columns to the left of A^C.

The initial implementation in (1) comprises three matrix-matrix products of smaller dimension than the single coarser-grain multiplication in (2). We can thus expect the latter approach to be more efficient given the large amount of hardware concurrency featured by Intel's coprocessor. On the other hand, the new strategy requires some data copies and an extra memory workspace (for W). To reduce the overhead introduced by the copy and initialization, these operations are performed via the appropriate kernels in Intel MKL. Moreover, W is allocated only once, and reused for all the matrix-matrix products, after which this workspace is released.

The block size is a critical optimization parameter for this algorithm as the value chosen for b has to balance three objectives:

- From equation (2), we note that the updates are performed in terms of matrix multiplications, where one of the dimensions of the operands is b. In order to attain high performance from this kernel, we need that this parameter is large enough to amortize the cost of the transfers with enough computation in the multiplication.

- The block size must equilibrate the costs of Factor (A^N) and Update (A^{R1}, A^{R2}). In our target platform, where the CPU offers a performance peak that is similar to that of the accelerator, this will ask for large values of b.
- The block size cannot become too large as, otherwise, the cost of the transfers and Update (A^N) become no longer negligible, constraining performance. We note that the communication can be considered as pure overhead; furthermore, the CPU is idle while the computation of Update (A^N) proceeds in the accelerator, waisting computational resources.

2.4. Sliding window

The previous discussion on the block size exposes some of the optimization difficulties of the version that employs look-ahead. We next introduce a fourth version of the GJE algorithm that tackles this problem by introducing a "sliding window". The idea is that the factorization still operates on a panel of width b, but the updates on A are distributed between CPU and accelerator using a sliding window of dimension b_{out} around the current panel. In this variant the CPU is in charge of the columns inside the window and the accelerator performs the remaining computations.

Again, in the first step, the CPU factorizes A^C while the columns that lie out of the window (the last $n - (b + b_{out})$ of the matrix) are concurrently transferred to the accelerator. The following process is then executed at each iteration of the main loop (see the right plot in Figure 2):

1. The current panel A^C is transferred to the accelerator.
2. The CPU updates panels A^{N1} and A^{N2} with respect to A^C, and then factorizes A^{N1}. Simultaneously, the accelerator updates A^{R1}, A^{R2} and A^{R3}.
3. The accelerator transfers A^{R1} to the CPU to preserve the width of the sliding window (and, therefore, the workload distribution).

These computations can be summarized as follows:

$$\text{Transfer}\left(A^C\right) \rightarrow \{\text{Update}\left(A^{R1}, A^{R2}, A^{R3}\right) \,\|\, \{\underline{\text{Update}\left(A^{N1}, A^{N2}\right) \rightarrow \text{Factor}\left(A^{N1}\right)}\}\}$$
$$\rightarrow \text{Transfer}\left(A^{R1}\right).$$

By introducing this additional level of blocking, this variant effectively decouples the algorithmic block size, determined by b, from the workload distribution between CPU and accelerator.

3. Experimental Evaluation

In this section we evaluate the four GJE versions introduced in Section 2. In particular, we refer to the native, hybrid CPU-Phi with concurrent execution, hybrid CPU-Phi with look-ahead and hybrid CPU-Phi with sliding window versions as GJE_{PHI}, GJE_{HYB}, GJE_{LA} and GJE_{SW}, respectively. While we also developed several other implementations, in or-

Processor	#Cores	Freq. (GHz)	RAM size	Compiler
Intel Xeon E5-2640v3	16	2.6	16 GB	icc
Intel Xeon Phi 7120P	61	1.4	16 GB	v15.0.1

Table 1. Architectures and compilers for the experimental evaluation.

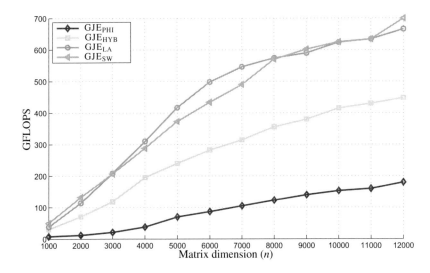

Figure 3. Performance of the implementations of GJE with partial pivoting for the inversion of matrices in the Intel Xeon Phi.

der to isolate the effect of the individual optimization techniques that were described, for simplicity we only include these four in the comparison.

The target platform is equipped with two multi-core Intel Xeon E5-2640v3 processors and an Intel Xeon Phi 7120P board; see Table 1 for details on the hardware and compilers. All the routines employ IEEE DP arithmetic and the linear-algebra kernels in Intel MKL (version v11.2.1). The codes were compiled with the −O3 optimization flag. All the matrices and vectors were conveniently aligned in memory in order to exploit the SIMD capabilities of the processors. The environments variables KMP_AFFINITY and OMP_NUM_THREADS were set, for the Intel Xeon Phi accelerator, to compact and 240, respectively.

In order to optimize the optimal block sizes (b, b_{in} and b_{out}), we follow an empirical approach based on iterative optimization. For this purpose, we proceed in multiple optimization passes. Concretely, an initial sampling run is performed while a monitoring tool captures specific performance information such as the cost of the different stages or the number of cache misses. Using the captured information and the application of some heuristics, the search space is trimmed/refined, for further exploration in subsequent passes via sampling runs. Table 2 shows the optimal block sizes for two problem sizes and the two most advanced versions of GJE. As could be expected, the version with look-ahead requires a much larger block size to obtain an even distribution of the

n	Variant	b_{in}	b	b_{out}
7,000	GJE$_{LA}$	96	480	–
	GJE$_{SW}$	48	160	1,280
11,000	GJE$_{LA}$	128	704	–
	GJE$_{SW}$	64	224	2,016

Table 2. Optimal block sizes.

workload but, as we will illustrate next, for the largest problem size this constrains the performance.

Figure 3 reports the performance, in terms of DP GFLOPS rates, obtained by the four GJE versions introduced in Section 2, operating on matrices of dimension n between 1,000 and 12,000. Looking at the performance curves in the figure, the implementation that performs all the computations in the Intel Xeon Phi accelerator, GJE$_{PHI}$, clearly attains the lowest GFLOPS rates. The reason is that, when b is large, its performance is constrained by the factorization stage while, on the other hand, when b is small, the matrix-matrix products become the bottleneck. The GJE$_{HYB}$ implementation notably increases performance with respect to the native version. Concretely, the overlapped execution of the factorization and updates combined with the use of two independent block dimensions yields an acceleration factor of up to 4. Our version GJE$_{LA}$ outperforms the previous two, delivering a peak close to 700 DP GFLOPS for the largest matrix, thanks to improvement in overlapping between CPU and accelerator as well as the aggregation of kernels. Finally, the version that operates with a sliding window attains the highest GFLOPS rates for the largest matrix, and points in the direction that higher performance differences might be obtained for the inversion of larger problems with this variant.

4. Concluding Remarks and Future Work

We have evaluated several implementations (versions) of GJE with partial pivoting for matrix inversion on a heterogeneous server equipped with conventional multicore CPUs and an Intel Xeon Phi coprocessor with 60(+1) cores. Our plain version based on the native model for the accelerator only exploits the parallelism within the matrix multiplications present in the algorithm attaining quite low performance, though this drawback is not intrinsic to the execution model. Indeed, we believe that the application of optimization techniques such as look-ahead, double blocking and the fusion of certain matrix multiplications can significantly improve the performance of this solution. On the other hand, a problem of this execution model is that the system's memory is then limited to that of the accelerator board, which in general is smaller than the capacity of the host's memory. Our hybrid versions operate under the offload model and exploit both the CPU and coprocessor to deliver more efficient inversion procedures. Concretely, the first hybrid version combines an overlapped execution using both computational resources with double blocking. The second hybrid version also features an overlapped execution, combined in this case with look-ahead. In addition, this code integrates double blocking and the fusion of matrix multiplications. Finally, the third hybrid version effectively decouples the algorithmic block size from the workload distribution, yielding the best performance results for the largest problems.

Acknowledgments

Enrique S. Quintana-Ortí was supported by project TIN2011-23283 of the Ministry of Science and Competitiveness and FEDER, and project P1-1B2013-20 of the Fundació Caixa Castelló-Bancaixa and UJI. Peter Benner, Pablo Ezzatti and Alfredo Remón were supported by the EHFARS project funded by the German Ministry of Education and Research BMBF.

References

[1]   R.H. Dennard, F.H. Gaensslen, V.L. Rideout, E. Bassous, and A.R. LeBlanc. Design of ion-implanted MOSFET's with very small physical dimensions. *IEEE J. of Solid-State Circuits*, 9(5):256–268, 1974.

[2]   G.E. Moore. Cramming more components onto integrated circuits. *Electronics*, 38(8):114–117, 1965.

[3]   M. Duranton, K. De Bosschere, A. Cohen, J. Maebe, and H. Munk. HiPEAC vision 2015, 2015. https://www.hipeac.org/assets/public/publications/vision/hipeac-vision-2015_DqOboL8.pdf.

[4]   J. F. Lavignon *et al.* ETP4HPC strategic research agenda achieving HPC leadership in Europe.

[5]   R. Lucas *et al.* Top ten Exascale research challenges, 2014. http://science.energy.gov/~/media/ascr/ascac/pdf/meetings/20140210/Top10reportFEB14.pdf.

[6]   H. Esmaeilzadeh, E. Blem, R. St. Amant, K. Sankaralingam, and D. Burger. Dark silicon and the end of multicore scaling. In *Proc. 38th Annual Int. Symp. on Computer architecture*, ISCA'11, pages 365–376, 2011.

[7]   The green500 list, 2015. http://www.green500.org.

[8]   The top500 list, 2015. http://www.top500.org.

[9]   NVIDIA Corporation. *CUDA C programming guide v6.5*, 2015. http://docs.nvidia.com/cuda/cuda-c-programming-guide/.

[10] Project home page for OpenACC - directives for accelerators. http://www.openacc-standard.org/.

[11] Project home page for OpenCL - the open standard for parallel programming of heterogeneous systems. project home page. http://www.khronos.org/opencl/.

[12] G.H. Golub and C.F. Van Loan. *Matrix Computations*. The Johns Hopkins University Press, Baltimore, 3rd edition, 1996.

[13] E. Anderson, Z. Bai, J. Demmel, J. E. Dongarra, J. DuCroz, A. Greenbaum, S. Hammarling, A. E. McKenney, S. Ostrouchov, and D. Sorensen. *LAPACK Users' Guide*. SIAM, Philadelphia, PA, USA, 1992.

[14] P. Strazdins. A comparison of lookahead and algorithmic blocking techniques for parallel matrix factorization. Technical Report TR-CS-98-07, Department of Computer Science, The Australian National University, Canberra 0200 ACT, Australia, 1998.

[15] N.J. Higham. *Accuracy and Stability of Numerical Algorithms*. SIAM, Philadelphia, PA, USA, second edition, 2002.

[16] E.S. Quintana-Ortí, G. Quintana-Ortí, X. Sun, and R.A. van de Geijn. A note on parallel matrix inversion. *SIAM J. Sci. Comput.*, 22:1762–1771, 2001.

[17] P. Benner, P. Ezzatti, E. S. Quintana-Ortí, and A. Remón. Matrix inversion on CPU-GPU platforms with applications in control theory. *Concurrency and Computation: Practice & Experience*, 25(8):1170–1182, 2013.

[18] P. Bientinesi, J. A. Gunnels, M. E. Myers, E. S. Quintana-Ortí, and R. A. van de Geijn. The science of deriving dense linear algebra algorithms. *ACM Trans. Math. Soft.*, 31(1):1–26, March 2005.

[19] J. A. Gunnels, F. G. Gustavson, G. M. Henry, and R. A. van de Geijn. FLAME: Formal linear algebra methods environment. *ACM Trans. Math. Soft.*, 27(4):422–455, 2001.

Parallel Computing: On the Road to Exascale
G.R. Joubert et al. (Eds.)
IOS Press, 2016
doi:10.3233/978-1-61499-621-7-247

Programming GPUs with C++14 and Just-In-Time Compilation

Michael HAIDL [1], Bastian HAGEDORN , and Sergei GORLATCH

University of Muenster, Germany

Abstract. Systems that comprise accelerators (e.g., GPUs) promise high performance, but their programming is still a challenge, mainly because of two reasons:
1) two distinct programming models have to be used within an application: one for
the host CPU (e.g., C++), and one for the accelerator (e.g., OpenCL or CUDA);
2) using Just-In-Time (JIT) compilation and its optimization opportunities in both
OpenCL and CUDA requires a cumbersome preparation of the source code. These
two aspects currently lead to long, poorly structured, and error-prone GPU codes.
Our PACXX programming approach addresses both aspects: 1) parallel programs
are written using exclusively the C++ programming language, with modern C++14
features including variadic templates, generic lambda expressions, as well as STL
containers and algorithms, 2) a simple yet powerful API (PACXX-Reflect) is offered for enabling JIT in GPU kernels; it uses lightweight runtime reflection to
modify the kernel's behaviour during runtime. We show that PACXX codes using
the PACXX-Reflect are about 60% shorter than their OpenCL and CUDA Toolkit
equivalents and outperform them by 5% on average.

Keywords. GPUs, C++14, Parallel Programming, JIT, Runtime Reflection

1. Introduction

Accelerators such as Graphics Processing Units (GPUs) are increasingly used in today's
high-performance systems. However, programming such systems remains complicated,
because it requires the use of two distinct programming models: one for the host CPU
(e.g., C or C++) and one for the GPU (e.g., OpenCL or CUDA). The codes for GPUs
(so-called kernels) are written using limited subsets of the C/C++ language which miss
many advanced features of the current standards like C++14 [1]. Furthermore, specific
language constructs of CUDA and OpenCL for parallelization and synchronization have
to be additionally mastered by the GPU software developers. Last but not least, the Just-
In-Time (JIT) compilation which is a proven technique for simplifying and optimizing
the programming process is provided for GPUs on a very restricted scale.

This paper aims at simplifying and improving the programming process for systems
with GPUs and other accelerators by making two main contributions:

1. We present and implement *PACXX (Programming Accelerators with C++)* - a
   unified programming model based on the newest C++14 standard that uniformly
   covers both host and kernel programming without any language extensions.

---

[1] Corresponding Author: Michael Haidl, E-mail:michael.haidl@uni-muenster.de.

2. We develop *PACXX-Reflect* – a simple yet powerful API to enable lightweight JIT compilation of PACXX programs in order to optimize the kernel code during program execution by using values that become known at runtime.

While our previous paper [2] focuses on the implementation of PACXX this paper introduces the JIT approach for PACXX, puts our approach in the broad context of related work, and provides an extensive comparison with the programming process in CUDA.

We evaluate our programming approach for GPUs with C++14 and JIT compilation using two case studies – matrix multiplication and Black-Scholes model for the option market – and demonstrate that PACXX codes are about 60% shorter than their manually optimized OpenCL and CUDA Toolkit equivalents and outperform them 5% on average.

The structure of the paper is as follows. Section 2 provides an overview of the state of the art and related work in programming for systems with accelerators in general and the JIT compilation approaches for such systems in particular. In Section 3, we explain the PACXX programming approach and compare it to CUDA by way of example. We present our approach to JIT compilation using the PACXX-Reflect API in Section 4. In Section 5, we briefly describe the implementation of PACXX and we evaluate our approach on two case studies by comparing the size and performance of PACXX codes to the corresponding CUDA and OpenCL programs. Finally, we conclude in Section 6.

2. State of the Art and Related Work

In current programming approaches like CUDA and OpenCL, the code for a GPU (so-called kernel) is written using a limited subset of the C/C++ language, e.g., CUDA C++ [3] which misses many advanced features of the current standards like C++14 [1]. Memory management for the GPU memory has to be performed by the developer explicitly, because C++ has no language support for distinct memories. Memory is explicitly allocated twice - first in the host memory and then again in the GPU's memory. The developer is also responsible for performing explicit synchronization (copying) between the two distinct memories. This implies a significantly longer boilerplate (host-)code for memory management as compared to C++ where allocation and initialization are performed together through the RAII (Resource Acquisition Is Initialization) idiom [4].

Although CUDA and OpenCL (in a provisional version of the OpenCL 2.1 standard [5]) have been recently extended with static C++11 language features, these C++ extensions define new, for C++ developer unfamiliar, language elements (e.g., cast operators), while dynamic language features of C++ such as the Standard Template Library are still not provided by neither CUDA nor OpenCL.

Several recent approaches aim at integrating the accelerator programming into C++. The C++ AMP approach [6] extends C++ by an explicit data-parallel construct (`parallel_for_each`), and so-called `array_views` provide functions for memory transfers. The developer still needs to use a wrapper (i.e., write an additional line of code) for each memory allocation and use the C++ AMP views instead of the original C++ data types in order to achieve that memory synchronization is done transparently by the system. SYCL [7] is a high-level interface that integrates the OpenCL programming model into C++ by using the lambda features of the C++11 standard, but it still demands multiple memory allocations for so-called `Buffers` both in the host and kernel code. Nvidia Thrust [8] and AMD Bolt [9] are libraries implementing the functionality of the

C++ Standard Template Library (STL) in a data-parallel way, but they are restricted to accelerators from the corresponding vendor and do not support modern C++14 language features. Annotation-based approaches OpenMP [10] and OpenACC [11] expect the user to use parallelism-specifying directives in addition to C++. STAPL [12] offers STL functionality which is executed in parallel by the underlying runtime system, but it targets distributed-memory systems rather than systems with GPUs.

None of the described programming models offers the possibility to transform and optimize the kernel code during execution, i.e., in a Just-In-Time (JIT) manner. For example, writing a kernel for a particular size of input data provides usually better performance than a generic kernel, due to additional optimizations performed by the compiler. However, writing separate kernels for different data sizes would lead to a poorly structured, hardly maintainable codes. Just-in-time compilation can be used to optimize code by taking into account values which become known during the execution of the program: thereby, compilers can additionally optimize code when performance-critical variables (e.g., exit conditions of loops) are resolved.

OpenCL and the newest releases of CUDA support JIT compilation of kernel code. However, both approaches demand that the kernel code is provided as human-readable code which has a security drawback: the source code may be disclosed to non-authorized parties. The NVRTC [13] library supports all C++ features available in CUDA for JIT compilation. Unfortunately, a complicated problem arises using NVRTC. to allow function overloading and template functions as kernels, CUDA C++ follows the C++ standard regarding function name mangling while kernel names are machine generated and unknown to the developer. Without knowing the mangled name of a kernel, the function pointer for invoking the kernel cannot be retrieved and the kernel cannot be called. Additionally, template kernels must be explicitly instantiated prior to their use by the developer. The current solution is to enforce the C naming policy using `extern "C"`, but this completely disables function overloading and templates for kernels, because function names are no longer unique and the right kernel cannot be resolved by its name. Another solution could be an additional library providing function name de-mangling, but this would introduce more development overhead and unnecessary boilerplate code, because function names would have to be combined with the actual data types used in the templates. Another recent JIT approach is LambdaJIT [14] that automatically parallelizes the lambda functions used in STL algorithms. Through different back-ends, LambdaJIT is capable of offloading computations to a GPU.

This paper describes a novel approach to programming systems with GPUs and other accelerators: our PACXX model relies exclusively on the newest C++14 standard without any extensions, and we use lightweight runtime reflection to provide JIT compilation and optimization of PACXX programs. PACXX provides the programmer with all advanced features of C++14, e.g., variadic templates, generic lambda expressions, as well as STL containers and algorithms. Reflection enables a program to modify its behaviour and is well known in languages like Java and Scala [15] but is unavailable in C++. In contrast to other approaches like Reflex [16] and XCppRefl [17] which aim to integrate full runtime reflection of the type system into C++, PACXX-Reflect follows a lightweight approach: we do not perform any type analysis or introspection.

3. The PACXX Programming Model

To explain our C++-based approach to GPU programming, we consider a popular example in parallel computing: vector addition. We start with a C++ program and then compare how this program is parallelized for GPU using CUDA vs. our PACXX approach.

```
1 int main(){
2   vector<int> a{N}, b{N}, c{N};
3   for (int i = 0; i < N; ++i)
4     c[i] = a[i] + b[i];
5 }
```

Listing 1: Sequential vector addition in C++.

Listing 1 shows the sequential C++ source code for the vector addition. The memory is allocated and initialized with the default constructor of the vector's element type, here with 0 – following the RAII (Resource Acquisition Is Initialization) idiom – during the construction of the three STL containers of type std::vector in line 2. The calculation is performed by the for-loop in line 3.

```
1 __global__ void vadd (int* a,        int main(){
2     int* b, int* c, size_t size){       vector<int> a{N}, b{N}, c{n};
3   auto i = threadIdx.x                  auto vadd = kernel([](
4       + blockIdx.x * blockDim.x;          const auto& a, const auto& b
5   if (i < size)                           auto& c){
6     c[i] = a[i] + b{i];                     auto i = Thread::get().global;
7 }                                           if (i < a.size())
8 int main(){                                   c[i.x] = a[i.x] + b[i.x];
9   vector<int> a{N}, b{N}, c{N};          }, {{N/1024 + 1}, {1024}});
10  int* da, db, dc;                       auto F = async(launch::kernel,
11  cudaMalloc(da, N*sizeof(int));                      vadd, a, b);
12  cudaMemcpy(da,&a[0],sizeof(int)        F.wait();
13    * N, cudaMemcpyHostToDevice); }
14  : // 5 additional lines
15    // for vectors b and c
16  vadd<<<N/1024 + 1, 1024>>>
17            (da, db, dc, N);
18  cudaDeviceSynchronice();
19 }
```

Listing 2: Two versions of parallel vector addition: in CUDA (left) and PACXX (right).

Listing 2 (left) shows how the vector addition is parallelized using CUDA. The CUDA kernel replaces the sequential for-loop of the C++ version with an implicitly data-parallel version of the vector addition. The vadd kernel is annotated with the global keyword (line 1) and is, according to the CUDA standard, a free function with void as return type. In CUDA, functions called by a kernel have to be annotated with the device keyword to explicitly mark them as GPU functions. This restriction prohibits the use of the C++ Standard Template Library (STL) in the kernel code because the functions provided in the STL are not annotated and, therefore, callable only from the host code. The parameters of the vadd kernel are raw integer pointers. Memory accessed by the kernel must be managed by the developer explicitly (line 11). To use the kernel, memory is allocated on the GPU and the data is synchronized between both memories (line 12). On the host side, three instances of std::vector are used for the computation. Since STL features cannot be used in CUDA, three raw integer pointers are defined in line 10 to represent the memory of the GPU. Memory is allocated using the CUDA Runtime API; for brevity, the calls to this API are only shown for one vector. For each allocation and synchronization, an additional line of code is necessary (e.g., line 11). Passing arguments to a kernel by reference which is common in C++, is not possible in CUDA, so we have to use the pointers defined in line 10 and pass them by value. To launch the kernel, a launch configuration must be specified within <<< >>> in each kernel call (line 16), i.e., a CUDA-specific, non-C++ syntax is used. CUDA threads are organized in a grid of blocks with up to three dimensions. In our example, 1024 threads are the maximal number of threads in one block, and $N/1024 + 1$ blocks (N is the size of the vectors) form the so-called launch grid. While all threads execute the same kernel code, the work is partitioned using the index ranges; in our example, each thread computes a single addition depending on its absolute index in the x-dimension (line 3). The identifier of the thread within the grid and the block are obtained using variables threadIdx, blockIdx, blockDim and gridDim (not shown in the code). To prevent an out-of-bounds access of threads with $i >= N$, a so-called *if guard* (line 5) is used. However, the size of the vector has to be known in the kernel code and is passed as additional parameter to the kernel (line 2). The GPU works asynchronously to the host, therefore, the host execution must be explicitly synchronized with the GPU using the CUDA Runtime API (line 18).

Summarizing, the CUDA code is very different from the original C++ version. A complete restructuring and new language constructes are necessary, and the size of code increases significantly.

Listing 2 (right) shows the PACXX source code that performs the same computation. It is a pure C++14 code without any extensions (e.g., new keywords or special syntax), with the kernel code inside of the host code, that uses std::async and std::future from the STL concurrency library [1] to express parallelism on the GPU. In PACXX, there are no restrictions which functions can be called from kernel code, however, the code must be available at compile-time, i.e., functions from pre-compiled libraries cannot be called. As in CUDA, a PACXX kernel is implicitly data parallel: it is defined with a C++ lambda function (lines 5-9). PACXX provides the C++ template class kernel (line 4) to identify kernels: instances of kernel will be executed in parallel on the GPU. The launch configuration (the second parameter in line 9) is defined analogous to CUDA. As in CUDA, threads are identified with up to three-dimensional index ranges which are used to partition the work amongst the GPU's threads. The thread's index can be obtained through the Thread class (line 6). To retrieve values from the thread's block, the class Block is available. The kernel instance created in line 3 is passed to the STL-function std::async (line 10) that invokes the kernel's execution on the GPU. PACXX provides an STL implementation based on libc++ [18] where an additional launch policy (launch::kernel) for std::async is defined to identify kernel launches besides the standard policies of the C++ standard (launch::async and launch::deferred). Passing the launch::kernel policy to std::async (line 10) implies that the kernel should be executed on the GPU, rather than by another host thread. The additional parameters passed to std::async (line 11) are forwarded to the kernel. As a significant advantage over CUDA, parameters of a kernel in PACXX can be passed by reference, as with any other C++ function. PACXX manages the GPU memory implicitly [2], i.e., no additional API for memory management (as in CUDA and OpenCL) has to be used by the developer. Non-array parameters passed by reference are copied to the GPU prior to the kernel launch and are automatically synchronized back to the host when the kernel has finished. For arrays, the `std::vector` and `std::array` classes are used. As in the original C++ version, memory is allocated using the `std::vector` class (line 2). PACXX extends the STL containers `std::vector` and `std::array` with the lazy copying strategy: synchronization of the two distinct memories happens only when a data access really occurs, either on the GPU or on the host. This happens transparently for the developer and reduces the programming effort significantly. As compared, to the CUDA version, the PACXX code only needs 13 LoC, i.e., it is almost 50% shorter. The PACXX kernel also requires an *if guard* to prevent out-of-bounds access, but there is no need to pass the size of the vectors to the kernel as an additional parameter, because each instance of `std::vector` knows the number of contained elements which can be obtained by the vector's `size` function (line 7). The `std::async` function used to execute the kernel on the GPU returns an `std::future` object associated with the kernel launch (line 10); this object is used to synchronize the host execution with the asynchronous kernel more flexibly than in CUDA: the `wait` member function (line 12) blocks the host execution if the associated kernel has not finished yet.

Due to the exclusive usage of the C++14 syntax and implicit memory management of kernel parameters and STL containers, GPU programming using PACXX is shorter and easier for C++ developers than when using CUDA.

4. The PACXX-Reflect API

To exploit JIT compilation in CUDA or OpenCL, the source code must be prepared manually by the developer; it is commonly represented as a string, either in the executable itself or loaded from a source file.

Listing 3 compares the JIT-compilable version of vector addition in CUDA (left) and PACXX (right). In CUDA, a placeholder (`"#VSIZE#"`) is introduced into the kernel code. During program execution this placeholder is replaced by the string with the actual size of vector a (line 12– 19). However, changing the kernel code at runtime requires additional programming effort in the host code and, therefore, increases the program length. Furthermore, during the JIT compilation the kernel code passes all compiler stages including parsing, lexing and the generation of an abstract syntax tree (AST). Since the AST for the kernel code is created at runtime of the program, errors in the kernel code are found first at program execution which makes debugging more difficult. With the vector's size hard-coded into the kernel code, the additional parameter for the vector size as in Listing 2 becomes unnecessary, but this is only a minor optimization since kernel parameters are stored in the very fast constant memory of the GPU.

On the right-hand side of Listing 3, the same modification to the *if guard* is made using PACXX-Reflect: the dynamic part of the *if guard* condition is replaced by a constant value using the Reflect API. This is accomplished using the `reflect` function which is defined as a variadic template function that takes a lambda expression and an arbitrary number of additional parameters. The `reflect` function forwards the return value of the lambda expression passed to it (line 8); the expression is evaluated in the host's context,

```
 1  vector<int> a{N}, b{N}, c{N};          vector<int> a{N}, b{N}, c{N};
 2  string str{ R"(
 3  extern "C"                              auto vadd = [](const auto& a,
 4  __global__ void vadd(int* a,                              const auto& b,
 5                   int* b, int* c){                         auto& c){
 6    auto i = threadIdx.x                  auto i = Thread::get().global.x;
 7         + blockIdx.x * blockDim.x;       auto size =
 8    int size = #VSIZE#;                   reflect([&]{return a.size();});
 9    if (i < size)                         if (i < size)
10      c[i] = a[i] + b[i];                   c[i] = a[i] + b[i];
11  })" };                                  };
12  string v{to_string(a.size())};
13  string p{"#VSIZE#"};
14  string vadd{str};
15  auto npos = string::npos;
16  for(size_t i = 0;
17    (i = vadd.find(p, i))!= npos;
18     i += v.size())
19    vadd.replace(i, p.size(), v);
```

Listing 3: JIT-compilable vector addition in CUDA (left) and PACXX (right).

i.e., the instances of the `reflect` template function are JIT-compiled for the host architecture and executed on the host prior to the kernel's launch. Only constant values and
kernel parameters are allowed as arguments or captured values by the lambda expression, because they are, from the kernel's point of view, compile-time constant values.
In Listing 3 (right), a direct call to the `size` function of the `std::vector` requires two
loads (of the `begin` and the end iterator) from the GPUs memory which might introduce
overhead on some architectures. To avoid this, a lambda expression which wraps the call
to the `size` function of vector a is passed to the `reflect` function; the returned value
from `reflect` is considered static for the kernel execution and the function call is replaced by the computed value, such that no loads are necessary to retrieve the vector's
size. Summarizing, the replacement of the function call with the constant value happens
transparently for the developer.

5. Implementation and Evaluation

PACXX is implemented using LLVM [19] and uses its code generation libraries to generate PTX code [20] for Nvidia GPUs and SPIR code [21] for other architectures (e.g.,
Intel Xeon Phi accelerators). PACXX-Reflect operates on the LLVM IR (intermediate
representation) generated by the PACXX offline compiler (implemented in Clang [22]),
rather than on the source code itself, thus reducing the overhead of JIT compilation as
compared to the current solutions for OpenCL and CUDA and avoids the name mangling
problem by design.

 For evaluation, two case studies programmed in C++14 and implemented using
PACXX are compared to the reference implementations from the CUDA Toolkit [23]:
1) Black-Scholes computation [24] used in high-frequency stock trading, and 2) matrix
multiplication [25].

To evaluate the performance of PACXX codes on other architectures than GPUs, the programs from the CUDA Toolkit were also manually re-written in OpenCL. The PACXX and CUDA implementations are compiled at runtime for CUDA Compute Capability 3.5 with standard optimizations enabled (no additional floating point optimizations), using the latest CUDA Toolkit (release 7.0). The CUDA PTX code is generated by the Nvidia NVRTC library; the host code is compiled by Clang 3.6 with standard O3 optimizations.

For evaluation we use the state-of-the-art accelerator hardware: an Nvidia Tesla K20c GPU controlled by an Intel Xeon E5-1620 v2 at 3.7 GHz, and an Intel Xeon Phi 5110p hosted in a dual-socket HPC-node equipped with two Intel Xeon E5-2695 v2 CPUs at 2.4 GHz. For the Intel Xeon Phi and Intel Xeon, we used the Intel OpenCL SDK 2014. We employed the Nvidia profiler (nvprof) and the OpenCL internal facilities for performance measurements.

5.1. Black-Scholes computation

Our first example is the Black-Scholes (BS) model which describes the financial option market and its price evolution. Both programs, from CUDA Toolkit and the PACXX implementation, compute the Black-Scholes equation on randomly generated input data seeded with the same value to achieve reproducible and comparable results. Input data are generated for $81.92 \cdot 10^6$ options.

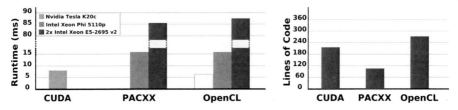

Figure 1. Runtime (left) and lines of code (right) for the Black-Scholes application.

Figure 1 shows the measured runtime and the program size in Lines of Code (LoC); the latter is calculated for the source codes formatted by the Clang-format tool using the LLVM coding style. We observe that the OpenCL version (273 LoC) is about 3 times longer and the CUDA version (217 LoC) about 2 times longer than the PACXX code in pure C++ (107 LoC). The advantages of PACXX regarding the code size arise from the tasks performed transparently by the PACXX runtime: device initialization, memory management and JIT compilation, whereas in CUDA and OpenCL these tasks have to be performed explicitly.

The PACXX code has also advantages regarding runtime on the Nvidia K20c GPU (about 4.3%) and on the dual socket cluster node (about 6.7%). On the Intel Xeon Phi, the PACXX code is only about 0.1% slower than the OpenCL version. On the Nvidia Tesla K20c, since the OpenCL implementation from Nvidia is still for the OpenCL 1.1 standard where floating point division are not IEEE 754 compliant, the higher speed of the OpenCL version (16.1% faster than PACXX) is achieved for the lower accuracy.

5.2. Matrix Multiplication

Our second case study is the multiplication of dense, square matrices. The PACXX code uses the Reflect API to compute the sizes of the matrices: the `reflect` function retrieves the input vector's size and computes its square root to get the number of rows/columns in the matrix. The `reflect` call is evaluated during the runtime compilation and the value (our matrices are of size 4096×4096) is automatically embedded into the kernel's intermediate representation. For the OpenCL and CUDA codes, the values are introduced into the kernel code by string replacement before it is JIT compiled.

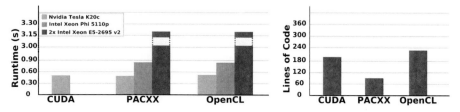

Figure 2. Runtime (left) and lines of code (right) for matrix multiplication.

Figure 2 shows the runtime and size of the PACXX code as compared to the CUDA code (compiled with NVRTC) and the OpenCL code on the three evaluation platforms. The PACXX program is again much shorter than its CUDA and OpenCL counterparts. We observe that the kernel becomes 2.7% faster on the K20c GPU when using PACXX-Reflect and its JIT capabilities. The PACXX code is about 0.2% slower on the Intel architectures as compared to the OpenCL implementation. On the Nvidia Tesla K20c, PACXX code outperforms CUDA NVRTC and OpenCL codes by 2.6% and 3.3%, correspondingly.

6. Conclusion

We presented PACXX – a programming model for GPU-based systems using C++14 and JIT compilation. We demonstrated that on modern accelerators (GPUs and Intel Xeon Phi) PACXX provides competitive performance and reduces the programming effort by more than 60% of LoCs as compared to CUDA or OpenCL. The code size reduction is achieved through JIT compilation and memory management tasks performed by PACXX implicitly in contrast to CUDA and OpenCL where they must be programmed explicitly. Additionally, PACXX enables application developers to program OpenCL and CUDA capable accelerators (e.g., Nvidia GPU and Intel Xeon Phi) in a modern object-oriented way using all advanced features of C++14 and the STL.

Acknowledgements

We would like to thank Nvidia for their generous hardware donation used in our experiments. We are grateful to Michel Steuwer for many hours of fruitful discussions, and to Tim Humernbrum for valuable input.

References

[1] isocpp.org. *Programming Languages - C++ (Committee Draft)*, 2014.

[2] Michael Haidl and Sergei Gorlatch. PACXX: Towards a Unified Programming Model for Programming Accelerators Using C++14. In *Proceedings of LLVM Compiler Infrastructure in HPC (LLVM-HPC) at Supercomputing 14*, pages 1–11. IEEE, 2014.

[3] Nvidia. *CUDA C Programming Guide*, 2015. Version 7.0.

[4] Herb Sutter and Andrei Alexandrescu. *C++ Coding Standards: 101 Rules, Guidelines, and Best Practices*. Pearson Education, 2004.

[5] Khronos OpenCL Working Group. *The OpenCL C++ Specification*, 2015. Version 1.0.

[6] Microsoft. *C++ AMP : Language and Programming Model*, 2012. Version 1.0.

[7] Khronos OpenCL Working Group. *SYCL Specifcation*, 2015. Version 1.2.

[8] Nathan Bell and Jared Hoberock. Thrust: A Parallel Template Library. *GPU Computing Gems Jade Edition*, page 359, 2011.

[9] AMD. *Bolt C++ Template Library*, 2014. Version 1.2.

[10] James C. Beyer et al. OpenMP for Accelerators. In *OpenMP in the Petascale Era*, pages 108–121. Springer, 2011.

[11] openacc-standard.org. *The OpenACC Application Programming Interface*, 2013. Version 2.0a.

[12] Ping An et al. STAPL: An Adaptive, Generic Parallel C++ Library. In *Languages and Compilers for Parallel Computing*, pages 193–208. Springer, 2003.

[13] Nvidia. *NVRTC - CUDA Runtime Compilation - User Guide*, 2015.

[14] Thibaut Lutz and Vinod Grover. LambdaJIT: A Dynamic Compiler for Heterogeneous Optimizations of STL Algorithms. In *Proceedings of the 3rd ACM SIGPLAN Workshop on Functional High-Performance Computing*, pages 99–108. ACM, 2014.

[15] Martin Odersky et al. The Scala Programming Language. *URL http://www.scala-lang.org*, 2008.

[16] S. Roiser. Reflex - Reflection in C++. In *Proceedings of Computing in High Energy and Nuclear Physics*, 2006.

[17] Tharaka Devadithya, Kenneth Chiu, and Wei Lu. C++ Reflection for High Performance Problem Solving Environments. In *Proceedings of the 2007 Spring Simulation Multiconference*, volume 2, pages 435–440. International Society for Computer Simulation, 2007.

[18] The LLVM Compiler Infrastructure. *libc++ C++ Standard Library*, 2014.

[19] Chris Lattner and Vikram Adve. LLVM: A Compilation Framework for Lifelong Program Analysis & Transformation. In *Proceedings of International Symposium on Code Generation and Optimization, 2004. CGO 2004*, pages 75–86. IEEE, 2004.

[20] Nvidia. *PTX:Parallel Thread Execution ISA*, 2010. Version 4.2.

[21] Khronos OpenCL Working Group. *The SPIR Specification*, 2014. Version 1.2.

[22] Chris Lattner. LLVM and Clang: Next Generation Compiler Technology. In *Proceedings of the BSD Conference*, pages 1–2, 2008.

[23] Nvidia. *CUDA Toolkit 7.0*, 2015.

[24] Victor Podlozhnyuk. Black-Scholes Option Pricing. *CUDA Toolkit Documentation*, 2007.

[25] Vasily Volkov and James W Demmel. Benchmarking GPUs to Tune Dense Linear Algebra. In *Proceedings of International Conference for High Performance Computing, Networking, Storage and Analysis, SC'08.*, pages 1–11. IEEE, 2008.

Parallel Computing: On the Road to Exascale
G.R. Joubert et al. (Eds.)
IOS Press, 2016
© 2016 The authors and IOS Press. All rights reserved.
doi:10.3233/978-1-61499-621-7-257

Active Packet Pacing
as a Congestion Avoidance Technique
in Interconnection Network

Hidetomo SHIBAMURA

Institute of Systems, Information Technologies and Nanotechnologies
CREST, Japan Science and Technology Agency
2-1-22 Momochihama, Sawara-ku, Fukuoka 814-0001, Japan

Abstract. A congestion avoidance technique using active packet pacing for inter-connection network is presented. In this technique, communication packets are sent intermittently by adjusting the inter-packet gap in order to match up packet flows precisely. Therefore the network congestion is avoided. The gap is pre-calculated for each communication according to the communication hop, and the value is explicitly passed to a sending function. Performance evaluations for some collective communications were performed by using an interconnect simulator and a benchmark program was executed on an actual machine. Finally, the scalability and effectiveness of packet pacing in interconnection network were confirmed.

Keywords. packet pacing, congestion avoidance, interconnection network, HPC, network simulation

Introduction

In most of HPC systems, a communication message is split into some packets and they are continuously injected into the interconnection network. When two or more different packet flows merge into a same direction link on a router, each throughput of flows is reduced and trailing packets are often blocked by packet conflict. These blocked packets are buffered on the router; however network latency increases because it must wait restart of transmission of preceding packets. In addition, the latency grows in accordance with communication hops because the situation of packet blocking propagates upstream. In such crammed packet transmission, heavy traffic communication (e.g. All-to-all communication) puts considerable workload on interconnect and may cause a slowdown of the program execution. Thus, in order to relax suppressed communication, this paper proposes aggressive use of packet pacing in interconnection network as a congestion avoidance technique.

The aim of this study is to clarify effectiveness of packet pacing in interconnection network. Communication performances of various algorithms which use packet pacing were evaluated by using an interconnect simulator. In addition, a benchmark program was executed on a supercomputer to show a possibility of packet pacing on an actual machine.

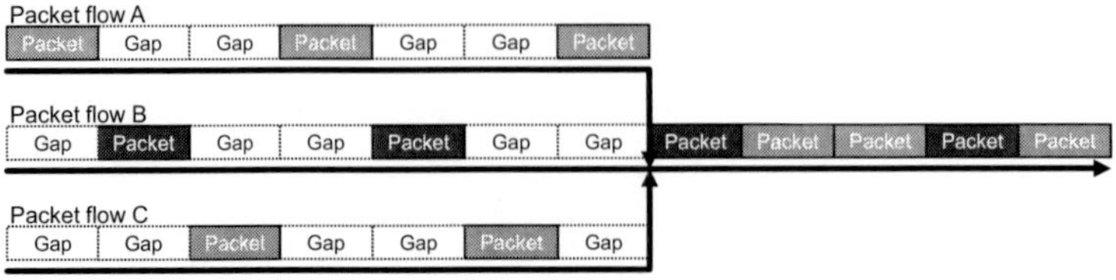

Figure 1. Merging three packet flows on a router using packet pacing.

In the following, Section 1 describes active packet pacing and Section 2 introduces an interconnect simulator NSIM. Section 3 examines the effectiveness of packet pacing by simulation, and then Section 4 also examines the effectiveness by real execution on an actual supercomputer. The concluding remarks and future directions of research are cited in Section 5.

1. Active Packet Pacing

A wide variety of congestion avoidance techniques are proposed and applied in networking. Packet pacing (or packet spacing) is one of the techniques, which throttles packet injection by inserting non-sending period (inter-packet gap) between sending packets. Since interleaved packet flows having appropriate inter-packet gap can be merged smoothly on a router as show in Figure 1, the packet blocking is resolved and network latency is also decreased.

There are many studies on packet pacing for global networking, but very few for interconnection network in contrast. Most of packet pacing are observation-based and throttle packet injection according to RTTs (Round Trip Time) [1] or ECNs (Explicit Congestion Notification) [2]. Thus, they can be defined as a category of *passive* packet pacing. In such pacing, source node takes time to detect any occurrence of network congestion because there is a delay until receiving a packet for RTT or ECN which returns from destination node. Since this delay retards the timing of packet pacing, there is a possibility to aggravate the congestion.

On the other hand, this study proposes using *active* packet pacing which controls the packet injection aggressively. In this packet pacing, inter-packet gap is pre-calculated per a route before packet injection in accordance with *m*essage overlap degree which is the number of messages across the link at the same time. In other words, optimum gap values are definitely found in every communication. Various communication patterns of major collective communications are simple and easily understandable, and the cost for the calculation of the gap is not so high.

2. NSIM: An Interconnect Simulator

Interconnection network, one of the important components in constructing parallel computer, is characterized by link bandwidth, topology, routing, flow control, and so on. Furthermore, the network must have a high affinity for parallel application. Designing an interconnection network with inappropriate parameters will lead to degradation of network performance and jeopardize high performance gained by parallelization. Since it

Table 1. Specification of an evaluation system

Parameter	Value
Topology	2D-torus / 3D-torus
Routing	Dimension Ordered Routing (DOR) + dateline
Flow control	Virtual cut-through, Credit base
Link bandwidth	4GB/s (unidirection)
Routing computation (RC)	4ns
Virtual-channel allocation (VA)	4ns
Switch allocation (SA)	4ns
Switch traversal (ST)	4ns
Switch latency	78ns
Cable latency	10ns
MTU	2KiB
Packet size	32B - 2KiB (MTU)
Packet header size	32B
Number of virtual channel	2
Virtual-channel buffer size	8KiB (MTU×4)
Flit size	16B
Number of NIC	4(enables simaltaneous send/receive)
DMA rate	16GB/s
Memory bandwidth	16GB/s
MPI overheads	200μs

is indeed important to select the most effective parameters, interconnect simulation is indispensable to evaluate performance of interconnection network before proceeding to major steps [3].

NSIM is an interconnect simulator, which is developed to assist in various performance evaluation of exascale interconnection network [4]. Since NSIM is based on parallel discrete event simulation (PDSE) and implemented with MPI, it works on various platforms. The most recent version of NSIM supports Remote Direct Memory Access (RDMA) style communication [5]. NSIM generates communication events internally in response to actual execution of MPI-like C program without using communication log files obtained from a real machine or artificially generated. Very fine interconnect configuration and mapping of rank to node are given by dedicated files. Mesh, torus (up to 6-dimension), Tofu (K computer, FX10), and FatTree are supported. NSIM could simulate a random ring communication (HPCC) on 128K-node 3D-torus in 18 minutes by using real 128-core system for example.

3. Performance Evaluation by Simulation

In this section, some collective communications are simulated to show a possibility of packet pacing and are evaluated from the point of view of performance indexes. A target evaluation system in these simulations is assumed to have mechanisms and performance roughly correspond to recent supercomputers. The specification of the system is given in Table 1.Note that each parameter is decided from mainstream technology, and performance and the system is nonexistent.

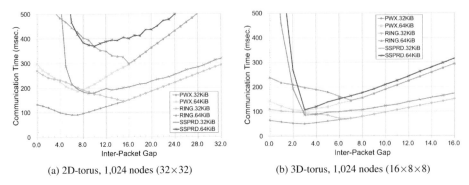

(a) 2D-torus, 1,024 nodes (32×32)   (b) 3D-torus, 1,024 nodes (16×8×8)

Figure 2. Communication time with various inte-packet gap value.

3.1. Simple Packet Pacing

Three alltoall communications were simulated by using NSIM in order to examine basic potential of packet pacing. The alltoall algorithms are pair-wise exchange (PWX), ring (RING), and simple spread (SSPRD). The simulation is performed by changing topology, node size, alltoall algorithm, message size, and inter-packet gap. The gap value is fixed in each simulation, i.e. same gap value is always used for packet injection in a simulation. Here, gap=0.0 means that there is no space between packets; therefore, the packets are continuously injected. On the other hand, gap=2.0 means that twice the time of a packet transmission time is inserted as illustrated in Figure1.

Figure 2(a) shows the communication time for each inter-packet gap on a 2D-torus system having 1,024 nodes. From the figure, the communication time of every algorithm is decreased by increasing the inter-packet gap from 0.0. However, too big gap value causes performance degradation. Figure 2(b) shows similar results on a 3D-torus.

From these figures, it is clear that each algorithm has an optimum pacing point which minimizes the communication time.

3.2. MOD Packet Pacing

Five alltoall communications were simulated in order to examine the effectiveness of MOD pacing. MOD is message overlap degree described in Section 2. The inter-packet gap is defined as $hopcount - 1$ because each link is shared by messages of the number of hop-count at most. Moreover, the gap is calculated repeatedly for each communication step in each algorithm. Two alltoall communications, bruck's algorithm (bruck)[6], and butterfly (btfly), were added to the simulation.

Figure 3(a) shows the communication time with several message sizes on a 2D-torus system and Figure 3(b) shows one on a 3D-torus. Every communication time is reduced drastically by using MOD pacing. Furthermore, the effectiveness of packet pacing also improves as the message size increases because long-term packet blocking caused by large-size message is suppressed.

From these results, it is confirmed that MOD pacing decreases communication time of every alltoall algorithm and works well for larger message size.

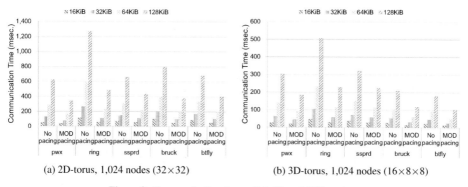

(a) 2D-torus, 1,024 nodes (32×32) (b) 3D-torus, 1,024 nodes (16×8×8)

Figure 3. Communication time with/without MOD pacing.

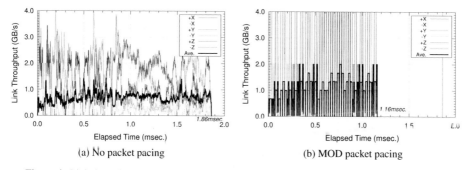

(a) No packet pacing (b) MOD packet pacing

Figure 4. Link throughput transitions of pairwise exchange (3D-torus 4×4×4, 40KiB message size).

3.3. Link Throughput

This subsection focuses on link throughput. A simulation of pairwise exchange algorithm was performed with 40KiB message size on a 64-node 3D-torus system. Link throughput of each elapsed time was recorded by NSIM and Figure 4 shows the transitions. Note that the link bandwidht is 4GB/s.

Figure 4(a) is the outcome without packet pacing, and Figure 4(b) is one with MOD pacing. By using packet pacing, some link throughput become maximum and the execution performance becomes 1.62 times faster (from 1.86 to 1.16 msec.).

A similar evaluation on A2AT, a novel alltoall algorithm for mesh/torus [7], was also performed with 1MiB message size on an 81-node 2D-torus system. Figure 5(a) is the result without packet pacing and Figure 5(b) is one with MOD pacing on a 2D-torus. Every link throughput is remarkably improved and the execution performance also becomes 3.2 times faster (from 84.0 to 25.8 msec.) and 107.5% of ideal execution time (24.0msec.) is achieved.

From these results, it is clear that packet pacing can improve utilization of network resources.

3.4. Scalability

In this subsection, speed-up ratios for each node size were investigated in order to investigate whether packet pacing has an affinity with future exascale system. Six 2D-torus

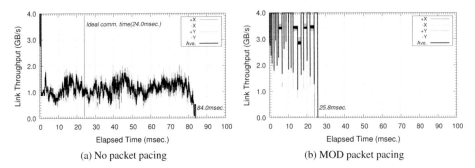

Figure 5. Link throughput transition of A2AT (2D-torus 9×9, 1MiB message size).

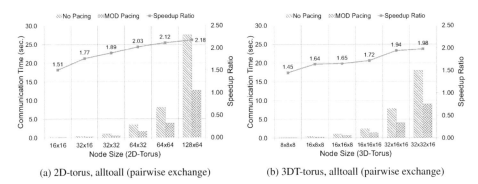

Figure 6. Communication time and speedup ratio on various node size.

systems up to 8K nodes and six 3D-torus systems up to 16K nodes were simulated with pairwise exchange algorithm. Message size was 200KiB.

Figure 6(a) shows the results of 2D-torus systems and Figure 6(b) shows one of 3D-torus systems. As the number of nodes increases, the speedup ratio also grows by approximately doubled.

These results indicate that packet pacing has a good affinity with large-scale interconnection network.

4. Performance Evaluation on Actual Machine

This section demonstrates the effectiveness of packet pacing on an actual machine. A random ring communication program which is one of the benchmark programs in HPCC (HPC Challenge) [8] was executed on Fujitsu FX10 supercomputer system at Kyushu University in Japan. On FX10, users can adjust the inter-packet gap value via an environment variable at time of submitting job. The program was executed while varying inter-packet gap, message size, and the number of node up to 768 nodes.

Figure 7 demonstrates the results. Every graph surely represents that as the gap increases, the speedup ratio also grows. Similarly, as the message size increases, the speedup ratio also grows. Besides, good pacing point area (top of arch) can be found.

Consequently, active packet pacing may be one of effective congestion avoidance techniques for interconnection network toward future exascale system.

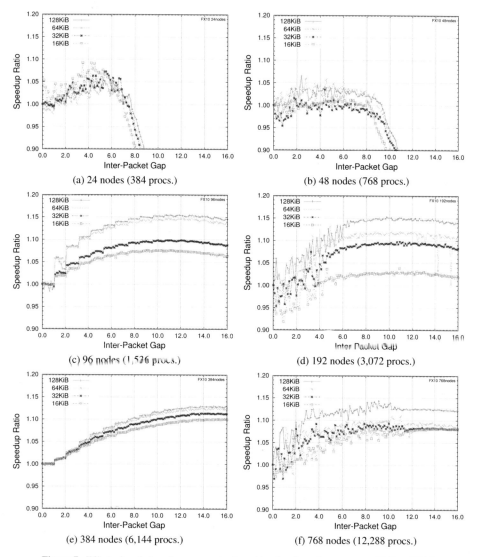

Figure 7. Effect of packet pacing on an actual machine (random ring comm. on Fujitsu FX10).

5. Conclusion

This paper presented active packet pacing which controls the packet injection aggressively as a congestion avoidance technique. Performance evaluation by interconnect simulation was performed and it was clear that proper setting of inter-packet gap greatly improves communication performance. Furthermore, the scalability and the effectiveness of packet pacing were verified on an actual supercomputer.

Future work includes applying packet pacing to not only collective communication but also practical parallel application. Performance evaluations of a few applications are in progress.

Acknowledgements

This research was supported by JST, CREST. The computational resources were provided by RIIT in the Kyushu University.

References

[1] A. Aggarwal, A. Savage, and T. Anderson: Under-standing the Performance of TCP Pacing, INFOCOM 2000 Nineteenth Annual Joint Conference of the IEEE Computer and Communications Societies, pp.1157–1165, 2000.

[2] G. Pfister, M. Gusat, W. Denzel, D. Craddock, N. Ni, W. Rooney, T. Engbersen, R. Luijten, R. Krishnamurthy, and J. Duato: Solving Hot Spot Contention Using InfiniBand Architecture Congestion, Proceedings HP-IPC 2005, 2005.

[3] R. Susukita, H. Ando, M. Aoyagi, H. Honda, Y. Inadomi, K. Inoue, S. Ishizuki, Y. Kimura, H. Komatsu, M. Kurokawa, K. Murakami, H. Shibamura, S. Yamamura, and Y. Yu: Performance Prediction of Large-scale Parallel System and Application using Macro-level Simulation, International Conference for High Performance Computing, Networking, Storage and Analysis (SCf08), 2008.

[4] H. Miwa, R. Susukita, H. Shibamura, T. Hirao, J. Maki, M. Yoshida, T. Kando, Y. Ajima, I. Miyoshi, T. Shimizu, Y. Oinaga, H. Ando, Y. Inadomi, K. Inoue, M. Aoyagi, and K. Murakami: NSIM: An Interconnection Network Simulator for Extreme-Scale Parallel Computers, IEICE Trans. Inf. & Syst., Vol. E94-D, No.12, pp.2298–2308, 2011.

[5] H. Shibamura: NSIM-ACE: Network Simulator for Global Memory Access, JST/CREST International Symposium on Post Petascale System Software (ISP2S2), Poster session, 2014.

[6] J. Bruck, C.T. Ho, S. Kipnis, E. Upfal, D. Weathersby: Efficient algorithms for all-to-all communications in multiport message-passing systems, Parallel and Distributed Systems, IEEE Trans. 8(11), pp.1143-1156, 1997.

[7] S. Yazaki, H. Takaue, Y. Ajima, T. Shimizu, and H. Ishihata: An Efficient All-to-all Communication Algorithm for Mesh/Torus Networks, Proc. 10th IEEE Intl. Symp. on Parallel and Distributed Processing with Applications (ISPA2012), pp.277–284, 2012.

[8] P.R. Luszczek, D.H. Bailey, J.J. Dongarra, J. Kepner, R.F. Lucas, R. Rabenseifner, and D. Takahashi: The HPC Challenge (HPCC) benchmark suite, Proc. 2006 ACM/IEEE Conference on Supercomputing, SC'06, 2006.

Parallel Computing: On the Road to Exascale
G.R. Joubert et al. (Eds.)
IOS Press, 2016
doi:10.3233/978-1-61499-621-7-265

Hybrid Parallelization of Hyper-Dimensional Vlasov Code with OpenMP Loop Collapse Directive

Takayuki UMEDA [a,1] and Keiichiro FUKAZAWA [b]

[a] *Solar-Terrestrial Environment Laboratory, Nagoya University, Japan*
[b] *Academic Center for Computing and Media Studies, Kyoto University, Japan*

Abstract. Space plasma is a collisionless, multi-scale, and highly nonlinear medium. Computer simulations with the first-principle kinetic equation are essential for space plasma studies. In the present study, a hyper-dimensional Vlasov (collisionless Boltzmann) simulation code, which is a first-principle method for collisionless space plasma, is parallelized with two-level hybrid MPI and OpenMP and is benchmarked on massively-parallel supercomputer systems. The benchmark result shows that the loop "collapse" directive option of the OpenMP reduces threading overhead of multiple loops. It is also shown that the hybrid parallelism with MPI and OpenMP is useful to reduce the communication time of MPI collective communication subroutines.

Keywords. high performance computing, kinetic simulation, hybrid parallelization, loop collapse, performance evaluation

Introduction

Massively-parallel computation has now become an essential approach in various scientific fields. Recent high-end supercomputer systems have much more than 10^4 compute nodes. However, due to the installation space and network capability, the number of compute nodes may saturate at $\sim 10^5$, while the performance per node, that is, the number of compute cores per node may increase in future. On massively-parallel cluster systems with many-core processors, there arises an issue on the performance of the multi-level hybrid (with MPI and OpenMP) parallelism against the single-level flat MPI parallelism. In scientific computing with Eulerian-grid-based methods, such as fluid simulations, the MPI-OpenMP hybrid parallelism sometimes does not outperform the flat-MPI parallelism on 64bit-x86-processor-based PC clusters together with the Intel compiler environment. On the other hand, the hybrid parallelism empirically outperforms the flat-MPI parallelism on high-end supercomputer systems with compilers developed by hardware vendors, such as the Fujitsu FX10 and the K computer [1,2], possibly due to the capability of OpenMP thread parallelism of compilers.

---

[1]Corresponding Author: Solar-Terrestrial Environment Laboratory, Nagoya University, Nagoya 464-8601, Japan; E-mail: umeda@stelab.nagoya-u.ac.jp.

The present study deals with the MPI-OpenMP hybrid parallelism of the Vlasov simulation method, which is a first-principle method in space plasma science. Since no less than 99.9% of the matter in the visible Universe is in the plasma state, which is considered to be the "fourth state" of the matter, studies of space plasma are important for understanding our Universe as well as space exploration of human beings. Here, the Boltzmann equation with the Coulomb-Lorentz force but without collision terms is called the Vlasov equation. It is known that the (magneto) hydro dynamic equations, i.e., the conservation laws for mass, momentum and energy are derived from the kinetic (Vlasov) Boltzmann equation by using the method of moments. In the framework of the (magneto) hydro dynamic approximations, first-principle kinetic processes are artificially given in a form of various diffusion coefficients. For full understanding of space plasma, on the other hand, it is important to self-consistently include first-principle kinetic processes, such as the generation of plasma waves, particle acceleration and heating, into magneto hydro dynamics (MHD). However, first-principle kinetic simulations require enormous computing resources.

In the Vlasov simulation method, distribution functions of plasma particles are defined on the grid cells in "hyper"-dimensional (>three-dimensional) position-velocity phase space. The Vlasov simulation treats up to six dimensions with three dimensions for position coordinate and three dimensions for velocity coordinate. Let us consider a six-dimensional simulation on high-end supercomputer systems. A computation with 30^6 grid cells requires ~ 30 GB memory. The size of memory per compute node in typical high-end systems is 16–64 GB but may not increase in future. This means that the number of grid cells per compute node in six-dimensional simulation ($\sim 10^9$) is not likely to increase in future. On the other hand, the number of compute core per node has already exceeded 30 and may increase in future. This means that the number of compute core per node is larger than the number of iterations per single loop, which is an issue in thread parallelism.

In the present study, we use the "COLLAPSE" directive option(clause) of the OpenMP to collapse multiple loops with a small number of iterations in thread parallelism with a large number of threads for future Exa-scale computing. Unfortunately, there are a limited number of supercomputer systems that allow six-dimensional simulation. Thus, we use a five-dimensional code with two dimensions for position coordinate and three dimensions for velocity coordinate. We conduct a performance measurement study of our parallel Vlasov code on scalar-type systems with large number of cores. Note that five-dimensional simulations are commonly performed in plasma science [3,4,5].

1. Overviews of Basic Equations and Numerical Schemes

Our solar system is filled with plasma particles ejected from the Sun, which is called the solar wind. Since the density of plasma particles in space is low and the mean-free path (average distance between collisions of plasma particles) is large, the word "space plasma" is generally equivalent to collisionless plasma. The plasma behaves as a dielectric medium with strong nonlinear interactions between plasma particles and electromagnetic fields. That is, electric currents are caused by the motion of charged particle, electromagnetic fields are caused by electric currents, and charged particles are accelerated/decelerated by electromagnetic fields. Thus, it is essential to use computer simulation for understanding of space plasma.

The Vlasov simulation method solves the kinetics equations of space plasma, i.e., the Maxwell equations (1) and the Vlasov (collisionless Boltzmann) equation (2),

$$
\left.
\begin{aligned}
\nabla \times \mathbf{B} &= \mu_0 \mathbf{J} + \frac{1}{c^2} \frac{\partial \mathbf{E}}{\partial t} \\
\nabla \times \mathbf{E} &= -\frac{\partial \mathbf{B}}{\partial t} \\
\nabla \cdot \mathbf{E} &= \frac{\rho}{\epsilon_0} \\
\nabla \cdot \mathbf{B} &= 0
\end{aligned}
\right\}
\tag{1}
$$

$$
\frac{\partial f_s}{\partial t} + \mathbf{v} \cdot \frac{\partial f_s}{\partial \mathbf{r}} + \frac{q_s}{m_s} \left[\mathbf{E} + \mathbf{v} \times \mathbf{B} \right] \cdot \frac{\partial f_s}{\partial \mathbf{v}} = 0
\tag{2}
$$

where $\mathbf{E}$, $\mathbf{B}$, $\mathbf{J}$, ρ, μ_0, ϵ_0 and c represent electric field, magnetic field, current density, charge density, magnetic permeability, dielectric constant and light speed, respectively. The Vlasov equation (2) describes the development of the distribution functions by the electromagnetic (Coulomb-Lorentz) force, with the collision term in the right hand side set to be zero. The distribution function $f_s(\mathbf{r}, \mathbf{v}, t)$ is defined in position-velocity phase space with the subscript s being the species of singly-charged particles (e.g., $s = i$ and e for ions and electrons, respectively). The Maxwell equations and the Vlasov equation are coupled with each other via the current density $\mathbf{J}$ that satisfies the continuity equation for charge

$$
\frac{\partial \rho}{\partial t} + \nabla \cdot \mathbf{J} = 0
\tag{3}
$$

These equations are regarded as the "first principle" of the collisionless plasma.

It is not easy to solve the hyper-dimensional Vlasov equation numerically, in terms of both computational resources and computational accuracy. The Vlasov equation (2) consists of two advection equations with a constant advection velocity and a rotation equation by a centripetal force but without diffusion terms. To simplify the numerical time-integration of the Vlasov equation, we split the advection and rotation operators into three parts [6],

$$
\frac{\partial f_s}{\partial t} + \mathbf{v} \cdot \frac{\partial f_s}{\partial \mathbf{r}} = 0
\tag{4}
$$

$$
\frac{\partial f_s}{\partial t} + \frac{q_s}{m_s} \mathbf{E} \cdot \frac{\partial f_s}{\partial \mathbf{v}} = 0
\tag{5}
$$

$$
\frac{\partial f_s}{\partial t} + \frac{q_s}{m_s} \left[\mathbf{v} \times \mathbf{B} \right] \cdot \frac{\partial f_s}{\partial \mathbf{v}} = 0
\tag{6}
$$

Equations (4) and (5) are scalar (linear) advection equations in which $\mathbf{v}$ and $\mathbf{E}$ are independent of $\mathbf{r}$ and $\mathbf{v}$, respectively. For solving the multidimensional advection equations, we adopt a multidimensional conservative semi-Lagrangian scheme [6] together with a positive, non-oscillatory and conservative limiter [7,8]. Note that the continuity equation for charge (3) is exactly satisfied by using the conservative multidimensional advection scheme [6]. Equation (6), on the other hand, is a multidimensional rotation equation which follows a circular motion of a profile at constant speed by a centripetal force. For stable rotation of the profile on the Cartesian grid system, the "back-substitution" scheme

[9] is applied. In addition, the Maxwell equations are solved by the implicit Finite Difference Time Domain (FDTD) method [10], which uses the Conjugate Gradient (CG) method for checking convergence.

2. Hybrid parallelization

Since hyper-dimensional simulations require huge memory, massively parallel computation is necessary. The velocity distribution functions in the Vlasov code is defined as a hyper-dimensional array on a fixed grid system. Thus it is easy to parallelize the Vlasov code with the "domain decomposition" as the first-level process parallelism, but only in the position coordinate [11]. The velocity space is not parallelized because there arise some additional communications overhead due to a reduction operation in the computation of the charge and current densities (i.e., the zeroth and first moments) at a given position. It is well-known that the domain decomposition involves the exchange of halo layers for the distribution function and electromagnetic field data at boundaries of each computational sub-domain. The present non-oscillatory and conservative scheme [7,8] used in the "Velocity" and "Position" subroutines uses six grid cells for numerical interpolation, and three halo grids are exchanged by using the "MPI_Sendrecv" subroutine in the standard message passing interface (MPI) library for simplicity, portability and stability [11]. Here, the "Velocity" subroutine solves both Eqs.(5) and (6) for the advection and rotation in the velocity space, respectively, and the "Position" subroutine solves Eq.(4) for the advection in the configuration space. In the "Maxwell" subroutine which solves Eq.(1) with the CG method, one halo grid is exchanged by using the "MPI_Sendrecv" subroutine at every iteration step of the CG method. The "MPI_Allreduce" subroutine is also used for checking convergence at every iteration step.

Figure 1 shows an overview of Fortran program of our five-dimensional Vlasov code. For computing numerical fluxes in the conservative scheme in advection and rotation equations (4-5), quintuple loops are used where the loop counter variables "i," "j," "l," "m" and "n" correspond to the coordinates in the x, y, v_x, v_y and v_z directions, respectively. The distribution function is defined as "f(Nvx,Nvy,Nvz,Nx,Ny)" to speed up the computation of the charge and current densities. Note that the sextuple loops with the loop counter variable "k" for the coordinate in the z direction should be used in six-dimensional code.

As a second-level thread parallelism, we use OpenMP. The "OMP(PARALLEL)DO" directive parallelizes the most outer loop to reduce the threading overhead. In the present study, we add a clause "COLLAPSE" to parallelize multiple loops. Note that the argument of the "COLLAPSE" clause depends on the structure of the inner loops and the attribute (shared/private) of the work arrays used inside the loops. In the present study, the number "2" is chosen as the argument of the "COLLAPSE" clause since the private work arrays inside the three inner loops have dependence on "l," "m" and "n." Note that the number "3" should be use as the argument of the "COLLAPSE" clause in six-dimensional code.

It should also be noted that the "Maxwell" subroutine does not use the "COLLAPSE" clause since the electromagnetic fields have two dimensions in the present five-dimensional code. In six-dimensional code, however, the "COLLAPSE" clause should be used with the argument number "2."

```
 0!*** Overveiw of Program ***
 1!$OMP PARALLEL PRIVATE(dfx,dfy,dfz)
 2!$OMP DO COLLAPSE(2)
 3   do j=1,Ny
 4     do i=1,Nx
 5       do n=1,Nvz
 6         do m=1,Nvy
 7           do l=1,Nvx
 8!             computation of numerical fluxes.
 9             dfx(l,m,n)= ...
10             dfy(l,m,n)= ...
11             dfz(l,m,n)= ...
12           end do
13         end do
14       end do
15       do n=1,Nvz
16         do m=1,Nvy
17           do l=1,Nvx
18             f(l,m,n,i,j)=f(l,m,n,i,j)+dfx(l,m,n) &
                            +dfy(l,m,n)+dfz(l,m,n)
19           end do
20         end do
21       end do
22     end do
23   end do
24!$OMP END DO
25!$OMP END PARALLEL
```

Figure 1. Overview of program for the five-dimensional code with three velocity and two spatial dimensions.

3. Performance Evaluation

In the present study, we compare the performance of a code with the "COLLAPSE" clause (Figure 1, labeled as "loop-collapsed" code) and without "COLLAPSE" clause (labeled as "as-is" code [12]). We measure the elapsed (computational and communication) time of each subroutine of these codes by using the "MPI_Wtime" function.

3.1. System descriptions

We used the following two supercomputer systems for the performance evaluation.

The Fujitsu PRIMERGY CX400 at Research Institute for Information Technology, Kyushu University is a typical PC-cluster-type supercomputer system. Two Xeon E5-2680 (SandyBridge, 2.7 GHz and 8 cores) processors with 128 GB memory are installed on each compute node. The inter-node network topology of the system is not uniform, i.e., a non-fat tree where five groups of 256 compute nodes and one group of 196 compute nodes are connected each other. All the compute nodes in each group are connected each other with the fat-tree full bisection bandwidth by the FDR Infiniband. Thus, the system has a total of 1476 compute nodes (23,616 compute cores) with a theoretical peak performance of 510 TFlops. Intel(R) 64 Fortran Compiler XE Version 14.0.2 and MPI Library Version 4.1.3 are installed on this system. The compiler options are as follows:

```
-mcmodel=large -i-dynamic -ipo -ip -O3 -xAVX -openmp
```

The K computer at the RIKEN Advanced Institute for Computational Science is a national-flagship supercomputer in Japan. A single SPARC64 VIIIfx (2.0 GHz and 8 cores) processor and 16 GB memory are installed on each node. The inter-node network topology of the K computer is the six-dimensional mesh/torus called "Tofu." The K computer has a total of 82,944 compute nodes with a theoretical peak performance of 10 PFlops. In the present benchmark study, we use 32,768 compute nodes (262,144 compute cores) with a theoretical peak performance of 4.2 PFlops. Fujitsu Fortran Driver and MPI Library Version 1.2.0 are installed on this system. The compiler options are as follows:

```
-Kvisimact,simd=2,ocl,preex,openmp
```

3.2. Result

3.2.1. CX400

Figure 2 shows the average elapsed time of each subroutine for one time step on the CX400 system. Here, the "Total" elapsed time corresponds to the entire elapsed time ("Velocity"+"Position"+"Maxwell") for one time step.

The left panels of Figure 2 show the result with a single compute node. In this performance measurement, we use $N_{v_x} \times N_{v_y} \times N_{v_z} \times N_x \times N_y = 30 \times 30 \times 30 \times 160 \times 80$ grid points which correspond to $\sim$16 GB memory for entire computation. We change the number of threads as 1, 2, 4, 8, and 16 by the "OMP_NUM_THREADS" environment variables. For the as-is code on a single compute node, the flat MPI parallelism (one thread case) is fastest, and the elapsed time increases as the number of threads increases. The computational speed for the flat MPI case is 81.19 GFlops, which corresponds to 23.49% computational efficiency to the theoretical peak performance.

In contrast to the as-is code, the hybrid parallelism is faster than the flat MPI parallelism (one thread case) for the loop-collapsed code. It is surprising that the loop-collapsed code runs faster than the as-is code even for the cases with one thread and two threads, although the order of iteration should be same. A reason for this is not clear but may be because of the difference in optimization by the compiler. The hybrid parallelism with two threads is fastest for the loop-collapsed code on a single compute node. The computational speed for this case is 83.59 GFlops, which corresponds to 24.19% computational efficiency to the theoretical peak performance.

The right panels in Figure 2 show the result with the entire (i.e., 1476) compute nodes. In this performance measurement, we use $N_{v_x} \times N_{v_y} \times N_{v_z} \times N_x \times N_y = 30 \times 30 \times 30 \times 5760 \times 3280$ grid points which correspond to $\sim$23.6 TB memory for entire computation. The comparison between the single node case and the entire compute node case shows the weak scaling. In contrast to the single node case, the elapsed time decreases as the number of threads increases except for the case with sixteen threads. This is because the elapsed time of the "Maxwell" subroutine is not negligible to the total elapsed time for the cases with one and two threads, while its elapsed time for the

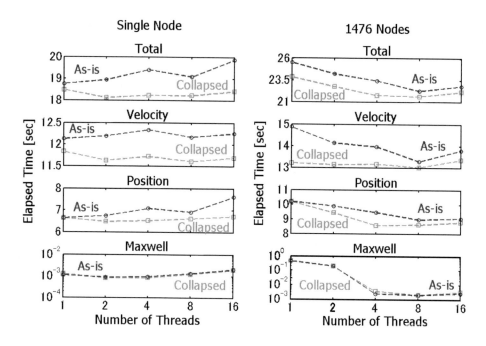

Figure 2. Average elapsed time of each subroutine for one time step on the CX400. Results with a single compute node and 1476 compute nodes are shown in the left and right panels, respectively. Results with as-is and loop-collapsed codes are shown by the circle and square marks, respectively.

cases with four, eight and sixteen threads is two orders of magnitude less than that for one and two threads. A reason for the performance loss of the "Maxwell" subroutine is the increase in the communication time for the "MPI_Allreduce" subroutine used for checking convergence at every iteration step of the CG method. The performance loss with sixteen threads is due to the communication time of the "MPI_Sendrecv" subroutine, which becomes larger as the number of threads increases. The best performance of the as-is code and the loop-collapsed code on 1476 compute nodes is given with eight threads as 100.94 TFlops and 103.87 TFlops, respectively, which corresponds to 19.79% and 20.36% computational efficiency, respectively, to the theoretical peak performance. The weak scaling measurement suggest that the scalability of the entire (i.e., 1476) compute nodes from a single compute node is 0.84 for the loop-collapsed code. A reason of the performance loss is the non-flat network topology of the CX400 system.

3.2.2. K computer

Figure 3 shows the average elapsed time of each subroutine for one time step on the K computer, with the same format as Figure 2. The left panels show the result with a single compute node. In this performance measurement, we use $N_{v_x} \times N_{v_y} \times N_{v_z} \times N_x \times N_y = 30 \times 30 \times 30 \times 80 \times 80$ grid points which correspond to ~ 8 GB memory for entire computation. We change the number of threads as 1, 2, 4, and 8 by the "OMP_NUM_THREADS" environment variables. In contrast to the CX400 system, the hybrid parallelism is faster than the flat MPI parallelism (one thread case) even for the as-is code on a single compute node [12]. The hybrid parallelism with four threads is fastest, with the computa-

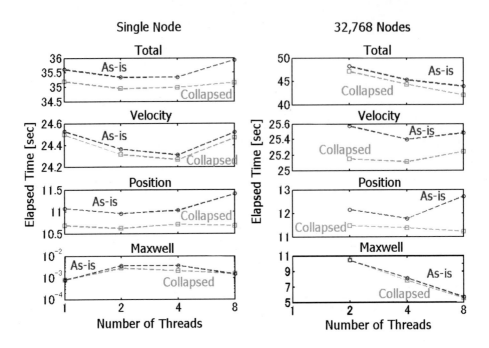

Figure 3. Average elapsed time of each subroutine for one time step on the K computer. Results with a single compute node and 32,768 compute nodes are shown in the left and right panels, respectively. Results with as-is and loop-collapsed codes are shown by the circle and square marks.

tional speed of 2.86 GFlops which corresponds to 17.8% computational real efficiency to the theoretical peak performance.

A small improvement is seen in the computational performance by loop-collapsing from the as-is code. The hybrid parallelism with two threads is fastest for the loop-collapsed code on a single compute node. In this case, the computational speed is 2.90 GFlops which corresponds to 18.1% computational efficiency to the theoretical peak performance. The elapsed time of each subroutine for both as-is and loop-collapsed codes does not change so much with different number of threads. The elapsed time of the "Maxwell" subroutine is negligible to the total elapsed time.

The right panels of Figure 3 show the result with 32,768 compute nodes. In this performance measurement, we use $N_{v_x} \times N_{v_y} \times N_{v_z} \times N_x \times N_y = 30 \times 30 \times 30 \times 20, 480 \times 10, 240$ grid points which correspond to ~ 262.1 TB memory for entire computation. The computational speed becomes faster as the number of threads becomes larger for both as-is and loop-collapsed codes. Note that the results for the flat MPI parallelism (one thread case) for both as-is and loop-collapsed codes are not available since the jobs exceeded the wall time limit of the system.

The elapsed times of the "Velocity" and "Position" subroutines increase by less than 10% from a single node to 32,768 compute nodes for both codes. On the other hand, the elapsed time of the "Maxwell" subroutine occupies a large part of the total elapsed time. This is due to the communication time for the "MPI_Allreduce" subroutine. The computational speed of the "Velocity" and "Position" subroutines does not change so much with different number of threads, while the computational speed of the "Maxwell" subroutine becomes substantially faster with larger number of threads for both codes. The best performance of the as-is code and the loop-collapsed code on 32,768 compute nodes is given with eight threads as 606.53 TFlops and 633.76TFlops, respectively, which corresponds to 14.66% and 15.11% computational efficiency, respectively, to the theoretical peak performance. The weak scaling measurement suggests that the scalability of 32,768 compute nodes from a single node is 0.85 for the loop-collapsed code. One may think that this value is not so large. The reason of this small scalability is because MPI collective communication functions installed on the K computer are optimized only for $96 \times N$ nodes (with N being integer). In fact, the elapsed time of the "Maxwell" subroutine on 36,864 compute nodes is of the order of 10^{-3} sec. We have obtained best performance of the as-is code and the loop-collapsed code on 36,864 compute nodes as 804.54 TFlops with four threads and 817.73TFlops with eight threads, respectively, which corresponds to 17.05% and 17.33% computational efficiency, respectively, to the theoretical peak performance. The scalability of 36,864 compute nodes is more than 0.95 [12].

4. Conclusion

In this paper, we compared the performance between the flat MPI parallelism and the hybrid parallelism with MPI and OpenMP by using a five-dimensional Vlasov code which is a first-principle simulation method for space plasma science. In hyper-dimensional simulations, the number of iterations in each loop is small ($\ll 100$). Therefore, we use the "COLLAPSE" clause of the OpenMP to collapse multiple loops. It is shown that the performance increase by loop collapsing is large on the CX400 system with the Intel compiler, but is small on the K computer with the Fujitsu compiler. However, the result clearly suggests that the loop collapsing with the "COLLAPSE" clause of the OpenMP reduces the threading overhead of multiple loops, which is important for many-core CPU/GPU/co-processors (e.g., Ref.[13,14]).

It is also shown that the communication time of MPI collective communication functions increases as the number of processes increases, which is not negligible with 10^4 computing processes and substantially affects the computational (elapsed) times with 10^5 computing processes. The multi-level hybrid parallelism is important for reducing the communication time of MPI collective communication functions on a system with a large number of compute nodes (e.g., Ref.[15]). This is important especially for future a massively-parallel system with many-core processors to reduce the number of computing processes.

Acknowledgements

One of the authors (TU) thanks Dr. Keigo Nitadori for his helpful advice on the loop collapse clause of OpenMP. This study is supported by MEXT/JSPS Grant-In-Aid (KAK-ENHI) for Challenging Exploratory Research No.25610144 and No.15K13572. The benchmark runs were performed on the Fujitsu CX400 system at Research Institute for Information Technology, Kyushu University as an Advanced Computational Scientific Program, and the K computer at the RIKEN Advanced Institute for Computational

Science as HPCI Systems Research Projects (ID: hp120092, hp140064, hp140081 and hp150069).

References

[1]   K. Fukazawa, T. Nanri, and T. Umeda, Performance evaluation of magnetohydrodynamics simulation for magnetosphere on K computer, *Commun. Comput. Inf. Sci.*, **402** (2013) 570–576.

[2]   T. Umeda and K. Fukazawa, Performance measurement of parallel Vlasov code for space plasma on scalar-type supercomputer systems with large number of cores, *Commun. Comput. Inf. Sci.*, **402** (2013) 561–569.

[3]   A. Ghizzo, F. Huot, and P. Bertrand, A non-periodic 2D semi-Lagrangian Vlasov code for aser-plasma interaction on parallel computer, *J. Comput. Phys.*, **186** (2003) 47–69.

[4]   H. Schmitz and R. Grauer, Kinetic Vlasov simulations of collisionless magnetic reconnection, *Phys. Plasmas*, **13** (2006) 092309.

[5]   Y. Idomura, M. Ida, T. Kano, N. Aiba, and S. Tokuda, Conservative global gyrokinetic toroidal full-f five-dimensional Vlasov simulation, *Comput. Phys. Commun.*, **179** (2008) 391–403.

[6]   T. Umeda, K. Togano, and T. Ogino, Two-dimensional full-electromagnetic Vlasov code with conservative scheme and its application to magnetic reconnection, *Comput. Phys. Commun.*, **180** (2009), 365–374.

[7]   T. Umeda, A conservative and non-oscillatory scheme for Vlasov code simulations, *Earth Planets Space*, **60** (2008), 773–779.

[8]   T. Umeda, Y. Nariyuki, and D. Kariya, A non-oscillatory and conservative semi-Lagrangian scheme with fourth-degree polynomial interpolation for solving the Vlasov equation, *Comput. Phys. Commun.*, **183** (2012), 1094–1100.

[9]   H. Schmitz and R. Grauer, Comparison of time splitting and backsubstitution methods for integrating Vlasov's equation with magnetic fields, *Comput. Phys. Commun.*, **175** (2006), 86–92.

[10] K. S. Yee, Numerical solution of initial boundary value problems involving Maxwell's equations in isotropic media, *IEEE Trans. Antenn. Propagat.*, **AP-14** (1966), 302–307.

[11] T. Umeda, K. Fukazawa, Y. Nariyuki, and T. Ogino, A scalable full electromagnetic Vlasov solver for cross-scale coupling in space plasma, *IEEE Trans. Plasma Sci.*, **40** (2012), 1421–1428.

[12] T. Umeda and K. Fukazawa, Performance tuning of Vlasov code for space plasma on the K computer, *Commun. Comput. Inf. Sci.*, **447** (2014) 127–138.

[13] C. Liao, Y. Yan, B. R. de Supinski, D. J. Quinlan, B. Chapman, Early experiences with the Openmp accelerator model, *Lect. Notes Comput. Sci.*, **8122** (2013) 84–98.

[14] S. Ghosh, T. Liao, H. Calandra, and B. M. Chapman, Performance of CPU/GPU compiler directives on ISO/TTI kernels, *Computing*, **96** (2014) 1149–1162.

[15] K. Nakajima, Flat MPI vs. hybrid: Evaluation of parallel programming models for preconditioned iterative solvers on "T2K Open Supercomputer," *Int. Conf. Parallel Proc. Workshops, 2009*, (2009) 73–80.

Parallel Computing: On the Road to Exascale
G.R. Joubert et al. (Eds.)
IOS Press, 2016
doi:10.3233/978-1-61499-621-7-275

Active Resource Management for Multi-Core Runtime Systems Serving Malleable Applications

Clemens GRELCK

System and Network Engineering Lab
University of Amsterdam
Amsterdam, Netherlands

Abstract. Malleable applications are programs that may run with varying numbers of threads and thus on varying numbers of cores because the exact number of threads/cores used is irrelevant for the program logic and typically determined at program startup.

We argue that any fixed choice of kernel threads is suboptimal for both performance and energy consumption. Firstly, an application may temporarily expose less concurrency than the underlying hardware offers, leading to waste of energy. Secondly, the number of hardware cores effectively available to an application may dynamically change in multi-application and/or multi-user environments. This leads to an over-subscription of the available hardware by individual applications, costly time scheduling by the operating system and, as a consequence, to both waste of energy and loss of performance.

We propose an active resource management service that continuously mediates betwen dynamically changing intra-application requirements as well as on dynamically changing system load characteristics in a near-optimal way.

Keywords. resource management, multicore computing, runtime systems

Introduction

Malleable applications are programs that may run with varying numbers of threads and thus on varying numbers of cores without recompilation. Malleability is characteristic for many programming models from data-parallel to divide-and-conquer and streaming data flow. The actual amount of concurrency is application and data dependent and may vary over time. It is the runtime system's task to map the actual concurrency to a fixed number of kernel threads / cores.

For example, in data-parallel applications the number of iterations of a parallelised loop and thus the available concurrency typically exceeds the total number of cores in a system by several if not many orders of magnitude. Consequently, data-parallel applications typically scale down the structurally available concurrency in the application to the actually available concurrency of the execution platform. This is done by applying one of several available loop scheduling techniques, such as block scheduling, cyclic scheduling or (guided) self scheduling.

The same compiled binary application can within certain limits run on any number of cores. Typically, the number of threads used is provided at application start through a command line parameter or an environment variable and then remains as set throughout the entire application life time. Dynamic malleability is not exploited. Common examples of such data-parallel runtime systems are OPENMP[4] or our own functional data-parallel array programming language Single Assignment C [9,7].

Malleable applications can also be found in the domain of divide-and-conquer applications, for instance written in modern versions of OPENMP[1] using explicit task parallelism or in CILK[2]. In either case the divide-and-conquer style parallelism, in beneficial scenarios, just like the data parallel approach exposes much higher levels of concurrency than general-purpose multi-core systems can exploit. The solution here in one way or another is to employ a fixed number of worker threads and work stealing techniques to balance the intra-application workload.

As a last example we mention streaming applications as for instance written in the declarative coordination language S-NET [10,8]. S-NET defines the coordination behaviour of networks of asynchronous, stateless components and their orderly interconnection via typed streams. S-NET achieves a near-complete separation of concerns between the engineering of sequential application building blocks (i.e. *application engineering)* and the composition or orchestration of these building blocks to form a parallel application (i.e. *concurrency engineering)*. S-NET effectively implements a macro data flow model where components represent non-trivial computations. Again the level of concurrency is not determined by the S-NET streaming application, but instead by characteristics of individual program runs. The S-NET runtime system [5] effectively maps the available concurrency to a number of threads that is determined upon program startup by the user and then remains fixed throughout the application's runtime.

All these examples share the common property that a generally high degree of concurrency is mapped down to a much smaller and per application run fixed number of kernel threads and thus execution units. We argue that any fixed number of kernel threads used throughout a program run is suboptimal for two reasons. Firstly, we waste energy for operating all computing resources whenever the application effectively exposes less concurrency than the execution architecture provides. Secondly, in typical multi-application or even multi-user environments we cannot expect any single application to have exclusive access to the hardware resources. Consequently, applications compete for resources in an uncontrolled and non-cooperative way. This leads to time slicing in the operating system and thus to suboptimal performance of each application (assuming non-interactive, compute-oriented applications as they prevail in parallel computing). In this work we propose active resource management for malleable applications.

1. Malleable runtime system model

In order to have a wider impact we do not look into individual applications, but rather into common runtime system scenarios for parallel execution. For practical reasons we do not focus our work on any specific programming language, compiler or runtime system, but instead look at a simple, idealised task-oriented, work-stealing runtime system. Our model runtime system consists of a number of kernel worker threads. Each worker thread has a double ended task queue. If the task queue is not empty, a worker thread removes the first task from the head of the queue and executes it. Task execution may lead to the creation of further tasks that are would be added at the end of the local task queue. If a worker thread completes execution of a task, it continues with the following task from the queue. Should the queue become empty, the worker thread switches into work stealing mode and systematically checks other worker thread's task queues for work. If successful, the worker steals the work and continues as above. If the workers fails to find stealable tasks, it waits a while and tries again.

This model runtime system matches a large variety of concrete existing runtime system for a diversity of programming languages and models. While the ways tasks are spawned and synchronised, etc, may be very different, the relevant properties as far as our current work is concerned are surprisingly homogeneous. Further common characteristics are that the runtime system works with any number of worker threads. With a single worker thread we produce overhead due to the internal parallel organisation of the application program without having any any benefits from parallel execution, but the program logic itself is not compromised. Should the number of worker threads exceed the actual concurrency exposed by an application program that does not create sufficiently many independent tasks, worker threads unsuccessfully search for work. Again, we waste resources and produce overhead, but the correct execution of the application is not challenged.

This observation already sets the margins of our current work. Neither too few nor too many worker threads make good use of execution resources and thus do not lead to favourable relationship between computing resources invested and performance obtained. Typically, concrete runtime systems either greedily grab all computing resources provided by the hardware or rely on a fixed number of cores to be assigned at application start via a command line parameter or an environment variable or possibly some user input.

2. Active resource management

We argue that any fixed choice of kernel threads is suboptimal for both performance and energy consumption. Firstly, an application may temporarily expose less concurrency than the underlying hardware offers, leading to waste of energy. Secondly, the number of hardware cores effectively available to an application may dynamically change in multi-application and/or multi-user environments. This leads to an over-subscription of the available hardware by individual applications, costly time scheduling by the operating system and, as a consequence, to both waste of energy and loss of performance.

In our proposed solution a *resource management server* dynamically allocates execution resources to a running application program and continuously monitors the adequacy of the resources both with respect to application demands as well as with respect to system load characteristics. The (fine-grained) tasks managed by

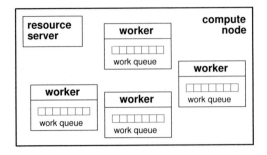

Figure 1. Resource server architecture for malleable runtime systems

the runtime system are automatically mapped to the dynamically varying number of effectively available worker threads (or cores).

In this way, we actively control the energy consumption of a system and reduce the overall energy footprint. Unused computing resources and entire areas of silicon may first run on a reduced clock frequency assuming new work becomes available shortly. After some while of inactivity individual cores and entire sockets may reduce their voltage and could eventually be powered down entirely.

Furthermore, we create the means to simultaneously run multiple independent and mutually unaware resource management enabled applications on the same set of resources by continuously negotiating resource distribution proportional to demands. In contrast to an application-unaware operating system our approach has the advantage that the resource management server understands both sides: the available resources in the computing system **and** the parallel behaviour of the resource management aware running applications. This is why we expect to achieve better performance and less energy consumption compared to today's multi-core operating systems.

3. Resource management server

The *resource management server* is a system service that dynamically allocates execution resources to running programs on demand. A dedicated resource server (thread) is responsible for dynamically spawning and terminating worker threads as well as for binding worker threads to execution resources like processor cores, hyperthreads or hardware thread contexts, depending on the platform being used. We illustrate our system architecture in Fig. 1.

Upon program startup only the resource server thread is active; this is the master thread of the process. The resource server thread identifies the hardware architecture the process is running on by means of the `hwloc` utility [3,6]. Optionally, the number of cores or generally hardware resources can be restricted by the user. This option is primarily meant as a means for experimentation, not for production use. Next, the resource server initialises the runtime system, creates a work queue, adds the initial task into the queue and turns into a worker thread. We assume here that the application somewhat specifies an initial task. As in the case of S-NET this could likewise mean to read data from standard input or the like.

The worker thread executes its standard work stealing procedure and begins execution of the initial task. Creation (and termination) of worker threads is controlled by the resource server making use of two counters, or better *resource level indicators*. The first one is the obvious number of currently active worker threads. This is initially zero. The second resource level indicator is a measure of *demand for compute power*. This reflects the number of work queues in the process. Thus, the demand indicator is initially set to one. Both resource level indicators are restricted to the range between zero and the total number of hardware execution units in the system.

If the demand for computing resources is greater than the number of workers (i.e. the number of currently employed computing resources), the resource server spawns an additional worker thread. Initially, this condition holds trivially. The creation of an additional worker thread temporarily brings the (numerical) demand for resources into an equilibrium with the number of actively used resources. Before increasing the demand the new worker thread must actually find some work to do. In general, the new thread could alternatively steal existing work from other threads. In any case, once doing productive work, the worker signals this to the resource server, and the resource server increments the demand level indicator, unless demand (and hence resource use) has already reached the maximum for the given architecture. This procedure guarantees a smooth and efficient organisation of the ramp up phase.

Worker threads may reach states of unemployment when all local work is exhausted (empty task queue) and no tasks are ready to be stolen from other workers. The worker signals this state to the resource server, which in turn reduces the demand level indicator by one. The worker thread does not immediately terminate because we would like to avoid costly repeated termination and re-creation of worker threads in not uncommon scenarios of oscillating resource demand. At first, the kernel thread is put to sleep effectively reducing its resource overhead to near zero, before effectively terminating the thread with a configurable delay following an extended period of inactivity.

4. Multiple independent applications

The next step in advancing the concept of resource management servers is to address multiple independent and mutually unaware applications (or instances thereof) running at overlapping intervals of time on the same set of execution resources. Fig. 2 illustrates our approach with two applications. The role of the resource management server as introduced in the previous section is split into two disjoint parts: a local resource server per application (process) manages the worker threads of the S-NET runtime system and adapts the number and core-binding of the workers as described before.

The second part of multi-application resource management servers lies with a separate process that we coined *meta resource server*. This meta resource server is started prior to any resource management enabled application process. It is in exclusive control of all hardware execution resources of the given system. We deliberately ignore the underlying operating system here as well as potentially running further applications unaware of our resource management model.

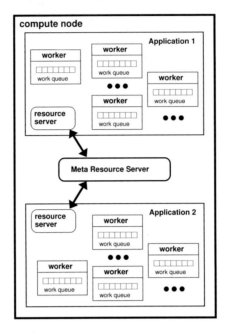

Figure 2. Resource server architecture for multiple independent applications

Whenever a local resource server has reason to spawn another worker thread, in the current multi-application scenario, it first must contact the meta resource server to obtain another execution resource. The meta server either replies with a concrete core identifier or it does not reply at all. In the former case the local resource server of the corresponding application spawns another worker thread and binds it to the given core. In the latter case the local resource server simply does nothing, which means that the number of execution resources currently occupied by this application remains unmodified.

As said before, the meta resource server is in control of all execution resources and decides which application can make use of which cores. With a single application (instance) the system behaves almost exactly as described in the previous section. The local resource server, assuming that the application exposes ample concurrency, incrementally obtains all available resources on the compute node. Only the additional inter-process communication marginally slows down this process.

Let us look at the more interesting scenario of two applications that both expose sufficient concurrency to make use of the entire compute server by themselves. One is started first and obtains one core after the other until it occupies the entire system.

Now, we start the other application. To do this we must first admit that the meta resource server as well as the local resource servers are scheduled preemptively by the operating system. In other words they are not in possession of an exclusive core. And neither are the worker threads. While we guarantee that no two worker threads are bound to the same core at the same time, resource management servers may well interfere with worker execution. With large numbers of cores it may prove more suitable in the future to reserve particular cores for resource management, but the still fairly low core counts representative today, we choose the above solution in order to avoid wasting considerable computing resources. Our general underlying assumption here is that time spent on any form of resource management is negligible compared with the actual computing.

Coming back to our example, all cores are in "exclusive" use by the first application when we start the second application. Hence, we effectively only start the second application's local resource server, which in turn contacts the meta resource server via inter-process communication to ask for a computing core. Since the meta resource server has no such core at hand, it first needs to get one back from another application. To determine the relative need for computing resources the meta resource server compares two numbers for each application:

a) the number of currently allocated cores;
b) the demand for cores, i.e. how many cores the application has asked for.

The quotient between the latter and the former determines the relative need for cores.

In our running example and assuming an 8-core system, the first application has a demand quotient of $\frac{9}{8}$ because it currently occupies all eight cores but asked for one more core (we assume ample internal concurrency). The second application has a demand quotient of $\frac{1}{0}$ which we interpret as infinitely high. Thus, a new application that has been started but does not yet have any execution resources has a very high relative demand. The meta resource server goes back to the first application and withdraws one the cores previously allocated to it. The local resource server decides which worker thread to terminate and empties that threads work queue, which is simply appended to another work queue. The worker thread is not preemptively terminated but we wait until it finishes its current box computation. After that the worker thread tries to retrieve the next read license from its work queue, but finds its work queue removed. The thread, thus, signals the local resource server its end and terminates. The local resource server immediately communicates the availability of the corresponding core back to the meta resource server. The meta resource server allocated that core to the second application, which now starts to ramp up its execution.

Assuming that the second application likewise exposes ample concurrency, it will soon ask the meta resource server for another threads. The meta resource server, by means of the demand quotients, step-by-step takes execution resources away from the first application and gives them to the second application until an equilibrium is reached. In order to avoid moving resources back and forth uselessly, the meta resource server makes sure that moving one execution resource from one application to another does not invert relative demands.

If the first application terminates at some point in time while the second is still running, all vacated resources will be moved over to the second application.

In our work we focus on long running, compute-intensive applications. Conseqently, adaptations of resources allocated to one or another application are rather infrequent. Furthermore, the number of independent such applications running simultaenously on the same system naturally remains limited. Thus, we do not expect the meta resource server to become anything like a performance bottleneck, despite its central role in the proposed software architecture.

5. Managing Energy Consumption

Intel's Single Chip Cloud Computer (SCC) [12,11] pioneered application-level control of energy consumption by organising its 48 cores into 24 pairs, whose clock frequency can be adjusted, and into 8 voltage islands of 6 cores each, for which the voltage can be adjusted. In other cases, the operating system may adjust voltage and frequency based on load. What the example of the Intel SCC architecture teaches us is that changing the voltage is fairly time-consuming and that voltage and frequency cannot efficiently be controlled on the finest level of execution units, but rather in groups of units of varying size.

We make use of such facilities by creating worker threads step-wise in a demand-driven manner and bind these threads to run on hardware resources as concentrated as possible. For example, on a dual-processor, quad-core, twice hyperthreaded system we would start at most 16 worker threads. While ramping up the number of active worker threads we first fill the hyperthreads of one core, then the cores of one processor, and only when the number of workers exceeds eight, we make use of the second processor. This policy allows the operating system to keep the second processor at the lowest possible clock frequency or even to keep it off completely until we can indeed make efficient use of it.

While we only ramp up the number of worker threads on-demand as computational needs grow, we also reduce the number of workers when computational needs decrease. This fits well with our work stealing based runtime system organisation. If a worker runs out of private work, i.e. its work queue becomes empty, it turns into a thief and tries to obtain work from other workers' work queues. If that also fails, it must be concluded that there is at least currently no useful work to do and the worker terminates. By doing so the worker releases the corresponding hardware resource and, thus, gives the operating system the opportunity to reduce its energy consumption by reducing clock frequency and/or voltage or by shutting it down entirely.

While it is fairly straightforward during worker thread creation to incrementally invade the available hierarchical execution resources, worker thread termination as described above is bound to result in a patchwork distribution of active workers over hardware resources over time. This would render the energy-saving capacities of the operating system largely ineffective. To overcome this shortcoming, the resource server continuously monitors the allocation of worker threads to hardware resources and rebinds the workers as needed.

6. Related work

The work closest to our's is the concept of *invasive computing*, advocated by Teich et al [13,14]. Here, application programs execute a cycle of four steps:

1. explore resources,
2. invade resources,
3. compute,
4. retreat / vacate resources.

Whereas these steps in one way or another can also be found in our proposal, the fundamental difference between their work and our's is the following: Teich et al demand every application to explicitly implement the above steps and provide an API to do so. In contrast, we develop a runtime system that automatically mediates between malleable but otherwise resource-unaware applications and a set of hardware resources that only become known at application start and are typically shared by multiple applications.

Other related work can be found in the general area of operating system process/thread scheduling. Operating systems have long had the ability to map dynamically changing numbers of processes (or kernel threads) to a fixed set of computing resources. However, operating systems do this in an application-agnostic way as they cannot affect the number of processes or threads created. They can merely admister them. As long as the number of processes is less than the number of resources, various mapping policies can be thought of like in our solution. As soon as the number of processes exceeds the number of resources, an operating system resorts to preemptive time slicing.

This all makes sense as long as one takes the resource demands of applications as fixed, but exactly that assumption does not hold for malleable applications. More precisely, malleable applications do have the freedom to adjust resources internally. Trouble is that the application programmer effectively can hardly make use of this opportunity as she or he has no indication of what a good policy could be at application runtime. The operating system, on the other hand, can only react on applications' demands, but not control or affect them in any way. This is exactly where our runtime system support kicks in.

7. Conclusion and future work

We presented active resource management for malleable applications. Instead of running an application on all available resources (or some explicitly defined subset thereof), our runtime system service dynamically adjusts the actually employed resources to the continuously varying demand of the application as well as the continuously varying system-wide demand for resources in the presence of multiple independent applications running on the same system.

Our motivation for this extension is essentially twofold. Firstly, we aim at reducing the energy footprint of streaming applications by shutting down system resources that at times we cannot make effective use of due to limitations in the concurrency exposed. Secondly, we aim at efficiently mediating the available resources among several S-NET streaming applications, that are independent and unaware of each other.

We are currently busy implementing the proposed runtime system techniques within the FRONT runtime system of S-NET, which is one of many variants of the model runtime system described earlier in the paper. As future work we plan to run extensive experiments demonstrating the positive effect on system-level performance of multiple applications as well as their accumulated energy footprint.

References

[1] E. Ayguade, N. Copty, A. Duran, J. Hoeflinger, Y. Lin, F. Massaioli, X. Teruel, P. Unnikrishnan, and G. Zhang. The Design of OpenMP Tasks. *IEEE Transactions on Parallel and Distributed Systems*, 20(13):404–418, 2009.

[2] R. Blumofe, C. Joerg, B. Kuszmaul, C. Leiserson, K. Randall, and Y. Zhou. Cilk: An Efficient Multithreaded Runtime System. *Journal of Parallel and Distributed Computing*, 37(1):55–69, 1996.

[3] F. Broquedis, J. Clet Ortega, S. Moreaud, N. Furmento, B. Goglin, G. Mercier, S. Thibault, and R. Namyst. hwloc: a Generic Framework for Managing Hardware Affinities in HPC Applications. In IEEE, editor, *PDP 2010 - The 18th Euromicro International Conference on Parallel, Distributed and Network-Based Computing*, Pisa Italie, 02 2010.

[4] L. Dagum and R. Menon. OpenMP: An Industry-Standard API for Shared-Memory Programming. *IEEE Transactions on Computational Science and Engineering*, 5(1), 1998.

[5] B. Gijsbers and C. Grelck. An efficient scalable runtime system for macro data flow processing using s-net. *International Journal of Parallel Programming*, 42(6):988–1011, 2014.

[6] B. Goglin. Managing the Topology of Heterogeneous Cluster Nodes with Hardware Locality (hwloc). In *International Conference on High Performance Computing & Simulation (HPCS 2014)*, Bologna, Italy, July 2014. IEEE.

[7] C. Grelck. Shared memory multiprocessor support for functional array processing in SAC. *Journal of Functional Programming*, 15(3):353–401, 2005.

[8] C. Grelck, S. Scholz, and A. Shafarenko. Asynchronous Stream Processing with S-Net. *International Journal of Parallel Programming*, 38(1):38–67, 2010.

[9] C. Grelck and S.-B. Scholz. SAC: A functional array language for efficient multithreaded execution. *International Journal of Parallel Programming*, 34(4):383–427, 2006.

[10] C. Grelck, S.-B. Scholz, and A. Shafarenko. A Gentle Introduction to S-Net: Typed Stream Processing and Declarative Coordination of Asynchronous Components. *Parallel Processing Letters*, 18(2):221–237, 2008.

[11] J. Howard, S. Dighe, Y. Hoskote, S. Vangal, et al. A 48-core ia-32 message-passing processor with dvfs in 45nm cmos. In *IEEE International Solid-State Circuits Conference (ISSCC'10), San Francisco, USA*, pages 108–109. IEEE, 2010.

[12] T. Mattson, R. van der Wijngaart, M. Riepen, T. Lehnig, P. Brett, W. Haas, P. Kennedy, J. Howard, S. Vangal, N. Borkar, G. Ruhl, and S. Dighe. The 48-core scc processor: the programmers view. In *Conference on High Performance Computing Networking, Storage and Analysis (SC'10), New Orleans, USA 2010*. IEEE, 2010.

[13] J. Teich, J. Henkel, A. Herkersdorf, D. Schmitt-Landsiedel, W. Schröder-Preikschat, and G. Snelting. Invasive computing: An overview. In M. Hübner and J. Becker, editors, *Multiprocessor System-on-Chip*, pages 241–268. Springer, 2011.

[14] J. Teich, A. Weichslgartner, B. Oechslein, and W. Schröder-Preikschat. Invasive computing — concepts and overheads. In *Forum on Specification and Design Languages (FDL 2012)*, number 217–224. IEEE, 2012.

Parallel Computing: On the Road to Exascale
G.R. Joubert et al. (Eds.)
IOS Press, 2016
© *2016 The authors and IOS Press. All rights reserved.*
doi:10.3233/978-1-61499-621-7-285

Improving Energy-Efficiency of Static Schedules by Core Consolidation and Switching Off Unused Cores

Nicolas MELOT [a], Christoph KESSLER [a] and Jörg KELLER [b,1]

[a] *Linköpings Universitet, 58183 Linköping, Sweden*
[b] *FernUniversität, 58084 Hagen, Germany*

Abstract. We demonstrate how static, energy-efficient schedules for independent, parallelizable tasks on parallel machines can be improved by modeling idle power if the static power consumption of a core comprises a notable fraction of the core's total power, which more and more often is the case. The improvement is achieved by optimally packing cores when deciding about core allocation, mapping and DVFS for each task so that all unused cores can be switched off and overall energy usage is minimized. We evaluate our proposal with a benchmark suite of task collections, and compare the resulting schedules with an optimal scheduler that does however not take idle power and core switch-off into account. We find that we can reduce energy consumption by 66% for mostly sequential tasks on many cores and by up to 91% for a realistic multicore processor model.

Keywords. Energy-efficiency, static scheduling, moldable tasks, core power model

Introduction

Frequency scaling of cores has for several years been the method of choice to minimize energy consumption when executing multiple tasks on a parallel machine till a fixed deadline, cf. e.g. [6]. In recent VLSI generations however, the static power consumption in a processor core slowly starts to dominate the dynamic power consumption, so that frequency scaling loses its importance. Running with higher frequency and switching off idle cores might be an alternative, but the overhead for putting a core to sleep, and waking it up again later is considerable and much higher than the overhead for changing the frequency. This hurts especially if a streaming application is processed, where the same scheduling round occurs repeatedly, i.e. many times.

This overhead might be avoided if one packs the tasks onto fewer cores and have the remaining cores switched off all the time. This requires knowledge about the hardware, operating system and the application behavior; consequently, a solution must lie in a form of a user-level, application-specific scheduler. In order to achieve this in a scheduler, the underlying energy model of the cores must reflect this and distinguish between an idle

---

[1]Corresponding Author: J. Keller, FernUniversität in Hagen, Faculty of Mathematics and Computer Science, Parallelism and VLSI Group, Postfach 940, 58084 Hagen, Germany; E-mail: joerg.keller@fernuni-hagen.de.

core and a core that is switched off. However, this is typically not the case, as the idle power of a core often is much smaller than the power when the core is under full load and processing a compute-intensive task.

In order to test our hypothesis, we have extended an energy-optimal scheduler for independent, parallelizable tasks with deadline [5] so that its processor model incorporates idle power, which in turn necessitates to clearly distinguish between static and dynamic power consumption in the core model. We schedule a benchmark suite of task sets with the new scheduler, and compare the resulting schedules with the corresponding schedules from the scheduler without taking idle time into account. We find that the energy consumption of the schedules is improved by 66% for mostly sequential tasks on many cores and by up to 91% for a realistic multicore processor model.

The remainder of this article is organized as follows. In Section 1, we briefly summarize basics about power consumption of processor cores. In Section 2, we briefly explain the scheduler from [5] and extend it to include idle power consumption. In Section 3, we present the results of our experiments. In Section 4, we give conclusions and an outlook onto future work.

1. Power Consumption in Multicore Processors

The power consumption of a processor core can be roughly split into dynamic power and static power. Dynamic power P_d is consumed because transistors are switching. This is influenced by the energy needed for a switch, which depends quadratically on the supply voltage (as long as this voltage is far enough from the threshold voltage), how often the switch occurs, i.e. the frequency f within set F of applicable discrete frequency levels, and how many transistors are switching, i.e. on the code executed [3]. There are more influence factors such as temperature, but for simplification we assume that minimum possible voltage for a given frequency (and vice versa) are linearly related, and that for compute intensive tasks, the instruction mix is such that we know the average number of transistors switching. Therefore, ignoring the constants, we get

$$P_d(f) = f^3 .$$

Static power is consumed because of leakage current due to imperfect realization of transistors and due to momentary shortcuts when switching both transistor parts of CMOS circuits. Static power is both dependent on frequency and on a device-specific constant κ [1]. For simplification, we express it as

$$P_s(f) = f + \kappa \cdot \min F .$$

For simplification, we assume a proportionality factor of 1 and get:

$$P_t(f) = \zeta \cdot P_d(f) + (1 - \zeta) \cdot P_s(f) ,$$

where $\zeta \in [0; 1]$ expresses the relative importance of dynamic and static power consumption.

The energy consumed by a processor core while processing a load can be computed as the product of power consumption and time, while the power consumption is fix, or by summing over sub-intervals in which power consumption is fix. The total energy consumed by a multicore is the sum of the core energy consumptions.

We consider a processor set P and a task set T. If a processor core runs idle, it consumes power as well. However, as long as idle power is sufficiently lower than the power under load, it might be ignored. Moreover, consider the situation that n tasks $i \in T$ with workloads of τ_i cycles each are processed at frequencies f_i on p cores before a deadline M. Then the runtime r_i of task[2] i is $r_i = \tau_i / f_i$, and the total energy can be computed as

$$E = \sum_{i \in T} r_i \cdot P_t(f_i) + \sum_{j \in P} t_j \cdot P_{idle} , \qquad (1)$$

where t_j is the sum of the lengths of all idle periods on core j, and P_{idle} is the idle power. We ignore the overhead in time and energy to scale frequencies between tasks, as we assume that the task workloads are much larger than the scaling time.

If the power under load is modified to

$$\tilde{P}_t(f) = P_t(f) - P_{idle} ,$$

then the formula for the total energy changes to

$$E = \sum_{i \in T} r_i \cdot \tilde{P}_t(f_i) + \sum_{i \in T} r_i \cdot P_{idle} + \sum_{j \in P} t_j \cdot P_{idle} \qquad (2)$$

$$= \sum_{i \in T} r_i \cdot \tilde{P}_t(f_i) + M \cdot p \cdot P_{idle} , \qquad (3)$$

because the sum of the task runtimes and the idle periods is the total runtime of all cores. The latter part is fixed for given p and M and hence not relevant when energy is to be optimized.

Please note that even if we specify the idle periods explicitly and optimize with Eq. (1), energy consumption remains the same for different placements of tasks as long as the frequencies are not changed. For example, both schedules in Fig. 1 consume the same amount of energy, as each task is run at the same frequency in both schedules. In the following, we will assume $P_{idle} = \eta P_t(f_{min})$, where f_{min} is the minimum possible operating frequency. This is a simplification, as even in idle mode, some transistors are used and thus $P_d > 0$, but it gives a good lower bound.

Another possible view on idle periods is that cores might enter a sleep-mode during such periods, and hence the energy consumption of idle phases might be neglected. However, the times to bring an idle core into a sleep-mode and to wake it up again are much larger than frequency scaling times, and hence cannot be ignored or is not even feasible in many applications. Yet, one possibility to take advantage of sleep-modes is core consolidation, where tasks are packed onto fewer cores, and unused cores are not switched on at all. E.g. in the schedules of Fig. 1, one core could remain switched off in the right schedule, while all cores would be used in the left schedule. Thus, if idle power is counted and if core consolidation is possible, the energy consumption would be

---

[2]The formula is for a sequential task. For a parallel task on q processors, the runtime is $\tau_i/(f_i q e(q))$, where $e(q)$ is the parallel efficiency of that task on q processors.

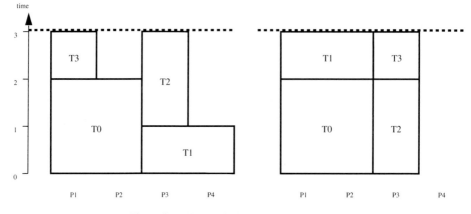

Figure 1. Different schedules for identical task set.

lower in the right case: Eq. (3) would change in the sense that p in the last term would be replaced by $p - u$, where u is the number of switched-off cores.

2. Energy-efficient Static Schedules of Parallelizable Tasks

We presented a new static scheduling algorithm called crown scheduling for task sets with parallelizable tasks and a deadline, where the energy consumption is to be minimized [5]. Such a task set models a streaming application with throughput requirements or real-time constraints, where all tasks are active simultaneously, and forward intermediate results directly to follow-up tasks, which avoids costly off-chip memory accesses. Multiple tasks on one core are scheduled round-robin up to a scheduling point, i.e. the production of the next intermediate result. If task communications go from one scheduling round to the next, then the tasks are independent within one round, where the deadline M of the round is derived from the throughput requirements, and the workloads τ_i of the tasks within one round are derived from the tasks' computational requirements. Thus the scheduling round is executed repeatedly, as indicated in Fig. 2(b). Tasks are assumed to be possibly parallelizable, i.e. we assume moldable tasks that are assigned widths w_i with $1 \leq w_i \leq \min\{W_i, p\}$, where W_i is the task-specific maximum width. A task uses w_i cores from beginning to end. With a task-specific parallel efficiency function $e_i(q)$, the runtime of a task running with q cores at frequency f_i can be given as $r_i = \tau_i/(f_i \cdot q \cdot e_i(q))$.

We assume a parallel machine with p cores, where each core can be independently scaled to a frequency from a finite set $F = \{F_1, \ldots, F_s\}$ of frequencies, and where the core power consumptions under load, i.e. $P_t(F_k)$, and idle power P_{idle} is known.

Then the scheduling consists of allocating w_i cores to each task, determine the operating frequency for each task, and arranging the parallel tasks such that all tasks are completed before the deadline, and that energy consumption is minimized.

In crown scheduling, we impose the following restrictions (assume p is a power of 2): Each task width must be a power of 2, and for each width w, there are p/w groups of that width. For example, for $w = p/2$, there are 2 groups, one comprising cores 1 to $p/2$, the other comprising the remaining cores. This reduces the number of possible

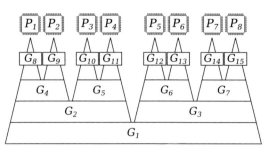
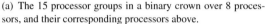

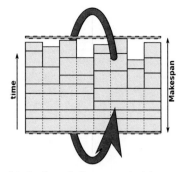

(a) The 15 processor groups in a binary crown over 8 processors, and their corresponding processors above.

(b) An (unscaled) crown schedule running in Round-Robin fashion.

Figure 2. A group hierarchy and a possible corresponding unscaled crown schedule for 8 processors.

allocations from p to $\log p$ and the number of possible mappings from 2^p to $2p - 1$. The groups are executed in order of decreasing width, so that a structure like in Fig. 2(a) arises, which also gives rise to the name "crown". As the rounds are executed over and over, a conceptual barrier is necessary at the beginning of a round (Fig. 2(b)), however, in practice, the parallel algorithm in the first task of group 1 (for width p) ensures an implicit synchronization of the cores.

In order to compute an optimal crown schedule, an integer linear program is used. The program uses $n \cdot p \cdot s$ binary variables $x_{i,j,k}$ with $x_{i,j,k} = 1$ if and only if task i is mapped to group j and run at frequency F_k. The width of group j is $w(j) = p/2^{\lfloor \log_2 j \rfloor}$, ie. group 1 has width p, groups 2 and 3 have width $p/2$, etc. The runtime of a task i can then be expressed as

$$r_i = \sum_{j,k} x_{i,j,k} \cdot \frac{\tau_i}{w(j) \cdot F_k \cdot e_i(w(j))}$$

and thus the target function, i.e. the energy to be minimized, is

$$E = \sum_{i} \sum_{j,k} x_{i,j,k} \cdot \frac{\tau_i \cdot P_t(F_k)}{w(j) \cdot F_k \cdot e_i(w(j))} \ . \tag{4}$$

In order to obtain feasible schedules, we formulate the constraint

$$\forall i \ : \ \sum_{j,k} x_{i,j,k} = 1 \ ,$$

i.e. each task is mapped exactly once. Furthermore, let C_m be all groups that comprise core m. Then

$$\sum_{i} \sum_{j \in C_m} \sum_{k} x_{i,j,k} \cdot \frac{\tau_i}{w(j) \cdot F_k \cdot e_i(w(j))} \leq M \ ,$$

i.e. the sum of the runtimes of all tasks mapped onto core m does not supersede the deadline. Finally, we forbid allocating more cores to a task than its maximum width allows:

$$\forall i \ : \ \sum_{j,w(j)>W_i} \sum_k x_{i,j,k} = 0 \ .$$

In the form stated above, idle power is treated as described in the previous section. To explore whether core consolidation is helpful, we additionally use p binary variables u_m where $u_m = 1$ if and only if core m is not used at all. Then the target function can be derived from Eq. (3) by adding idle power as in Eq. (4) but subtracting from p all unused cores:

$$E_{cons} = \sum_i \sum_{j,k} x_{i,j,k} \cdot \frac{\tau_i \cdot (P_t(F_k) - P_{idle})}{w(j) \cdot F_k \cdot e_i(w(j))} + \left(p - \sum_m u_m\right) \cdot P_{idle} \ . \qquad (5)$$

In order to set the u_m variables correctly, we need further constraints. If a core m is used, then u_m must be forced to 0:

$$\forall m \ : \ u_m \leq 1 - (1/n) \cdot \left(\sum_{j \in C_m, i, k} x_{i,j,k} \right) \ .$$

If any task i is mapped (at any frequency) to a processor group that uses m, then the sum is larger than zero, and hence the right-hand side is less than 1. Multiplying by $1/n$ ensures that the right-hand side can never be less than 0.

Forcing u_m to 1 if core m is not used is not strictly necessary, as an optimal solution will set as many u_m as possible to 1 to minimize energy. Yet, to also have feasible non-optimal schedules (e.g. in case of time-out), one can set

$$u_m \geq 1 - \sum_{j \in C_m, i, k} x_{i,j,k} \ .$$

3. Experiments

In this section, we compare schedules computed with target function (4) and schedules computed with target function (5), both for the same task sets. Then we evaluate corresponding schedules for their energy consumption if unused cores can be switched off.

To do this, we implement the ILP models from the previous section in AMPL and an analytical schedule energy evaluator in C++. We use the benchmark suite of task collections that already served to evaluate the crown scheduler heuristics [5].

We model the Intel i5 4690k Haswell processor with 2, 4, 8, 16 and 32 identical cores. We assume that each core's frequency can be set independently to one discrete value in the set $F=\{1.2, 1.4, 1.5, 1.6, 1.7, 1.9, 2, 2.1, 2.2, 2.3, 2.5, 2.7, 2.9, 3, 3.2, 3.3, 3.5\}$. For small and medium problems and machine sizes, several categories of synthetic task collections are defined by the number of cores ($p \in \{1, 2, 4, 8, 16, 32\}$), the number of tasks (10, 20, 40 and 80 tasks), and tasks' maximum widths W_t: sequential ($W_t = 1$ for all t), low ($1 \leq W_t \leq p/2$), average ($p/4 \leq W_t \leq 3p/4$), high ($p/2 \leq W_t \leq p$) and random ($1 \leq W_t \leq p$). Tasks' maximum widths are distributed uniformly. The target makespan of each synthetic task collection is the mean value between the runtime of an ideally load balanced task collection running at lowest frequency and at highest frequency.

We also use task collections of real-world streaming algorithms: parallel FFT, parallel-reduction and parallel mergesort. FFT comprises $2 \cdot p - 1$ parallel tasks in a balanced binary tree. In level $l \in [0; \log_2 p]$ of the tree, there are 2^l data-parallel tasks of width $p/2^l$ and work $p/2^l$ so all tasks could run in constant time. The mergesort task collection is similar to FFT, but all its tasks are sequential. Parallel reduction involves $\log_2 p + 1$ tasks of maximum width 2^l and work 2^l for $l \in [1; \log_2 p + 1]$; they can also run in constant time. For these regular task collections, we use more constraining target makespan M.

Finally, we use the technique of [2] to extract tasks' workload and parallel efficiency from the Streamit benchmark suite [7]. We schedule all variants of the applications *audiobeam, beamformer, channelvocoder, fir, nokia, vocoder, BubbleSort, filterbank, perfectest* and *tconvolve* from the Streamit compile source package. We use their compiler to obtain each task's estimated workload, parallel degree and its communication rate that we use to compute the task's parallel efficiency.

We use ψ_j to compute tasks j's parallel efficiency $e_j(q)$ (Eq. 6).

$$
e_j(q) = \begin{cases} 1 & \text{if } q = 1 \\ \tau_j/(\tau_j + q \cdot \psi_j) & \text{if } q > 1 \text{ and } q \le W_j \\ 10^{-6} & \text{otherwise} \end{cases} \tag{6}
$$

We measure the overall scheduling quality (energy consumption) using our integrated crown scheduler [5] and the enhanced version of this paper. We use the energy model as described by Eq. 5 with $\zeta = 0.649$, $\kappa = 52.64$ and $\eta = 0.5$. These parameters are derived from power values of an Intel Haswell processor. We only left out a constant factor, because that does not show when comparing energy values of schedules, and we weakened the term κ, because a high value might favor switching off cores too much. We run the ILP solver on a quad-core i7 Sandy Bridge processor at 3GHz and 8GB of main memory. We use Gurobi 6.0.0 and ILOG AMPL 10.100 with 5 minutes timeout to solve both ILP models, on Ubuntu 14.04.

Figures 3, 4 and 5 shows that our core consolidation technique benefits mainly to task collections whose tasks' parallel degree is low. This is not surprising as parallelization of tasks already balances load, so that re-arranging the tasks is difficult [4]. The benefits increase with the number of tasks and the number or cores. The energy consumption of classic task collections is reduced by 12% on average for 63 tasks, 16% on average with mergesort and 63% on average with 32 cores. The energy consumption of the synthetic task collection is reduced by 41% on average for 80 tasks, 53% on average with sequential or tasks of low parallel degree and 63% on average with 32 cores. Fig. 6 indicates this results also apply to our Streamit Task collections. The energy consumption of the Streamit task collection is reduced by 74% on average for 127 tasks, 61% on average with the application *FIR* and 74% on average with 32 cores.

The consolidation technique can lead to energy savings only if schedules yield enough idle time to move tasks from a core to another. If there is no room to move a task to a processor, then all tasks already mapped to this processor as well as the task to be moved need to be run at a higher frequency. Because of the rapid growth of the dynamic power function (f^3), this can lead to the consumption of more energy than the

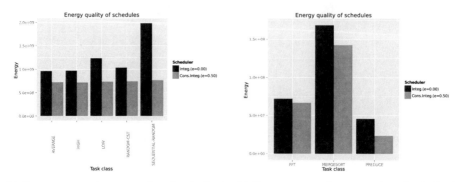

(a) Energy consumption per number of tasks for the synthetic task collection.

(b) Energy consumption per number of tasks for the class task collection.

Figure 3. Our technique performs better on sequential task collections.

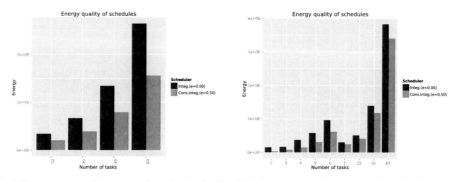

(a) Energy consumption per number of tasks for the synthetic task collection.

(b) Energy consumption per number of tasks for the classic task collection.

Figure 4. Our technique performs better on task collections with many tasks.

energy saved by switching one or several cores off. The more tasks are sequential, the more difficult it is for schedulers to eliminate idle time and the more energy saving can our technique provide. Also, the more cores are available to switch off, the more energy saving opportunities. This happens in our experimental setup and that more loose target makespan values can result in greater differences in schedules quality. In extreme cases, core consolidation reduces the energy consumption to 91% of the one by our crown scheduler without consolidation for the classic task collection, 81% for the Streamit task collection and 81% for the synthetic collection, while both schedulers could find an optimal solution withing the 5 minutes timeout.

Finally, Fig. 7 shows that the core consolidation technique does not influence the optimization time of our crown scheduler.

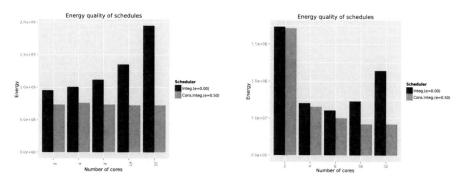

(a) Energy consumption per number of tasks for the synthetic task collection.

(b) Energy consumption per number of tasks for the classic task collection.

Figure 5. Our technique performs better on many cores.

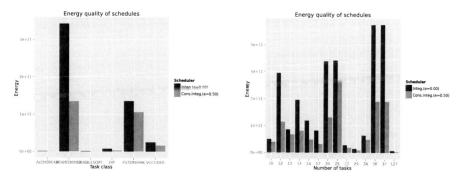

(a) Energy consumption per number of tasks for the Streamit task collection.

(b) Energy consumption per number of tasks for the class task collection.

Figure 6. The Streamit task collection is mostly insensitive to our technique.

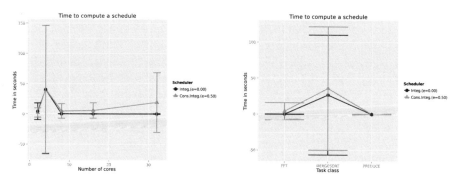

(a) Optimization time by number of cores for the classic task collection.

(b) Optimization time by number of cores for the classic task collection.

Figure 7. The additional packing constraint over our integrated crown scheduler does not affect significantly the optimization time.

4. Conclusions and Future Work

We have presented a study on how core consolidation, i.e. switching off unused cores, can be integrated in the integer linear program of a static, energy-efficient scheduler for moldable tasks. We have evaluated with a benchmark suite of synthetic and real-world task graphs that on a generic multicore architecture, about 66% of energy consumption can be saved on average and up to 91% in the most extreme case. The experiments also show that the core consolidation doesn't affect significantly the optimization of our integrated ILP crown scheduler.

In the future, we would like to integrate the overhead for frequency scaling and core switch-off/wake-up into our models, in order to explore at which level of task granularity it becomes worthwhile switch off idle cores temporarily. Also, our consolidation technique could be integrated into other schedulers not restricted by the crown constraints.

Acknowledgements

C. Kessler acknowledges partial funding by EU FP7 EXCESS and SeRC. N. Melot acknowledges partial funding by SeRC, EU FP7 EXCESS and the CUGS graduate school at Linköping University. The authors would like to thank Denis Trystram's group at IN-RIA Grenoble for fruitful discussions that inspired our work on this paper.

References

[1] A. P. Chandrasakaran and R. W. Brodersen. Minimizing power consumption in digital CMOS circuits. *Proc. IEEE*, 83(4):498–523, Apr. 1995.

[2] M. I. Gordon, W. Thies, and S. Amarasinghe. Exploiting coarse-grained task, data, and pipeline parallelism in stream programs. In *Proc. 12th Int. Conf. on Architectural Support for Programming Languages and Operating Systems*, ASPLOS XII, pages 151–162. ACM, 2006.

[3] D. Helms, E. Schmidt, and W. Nebel. Leakage in CMOS circuits — an introduction. In *Proc. PATMOS 2004*, LNCS 3254, pages 17–35. Springer, 2004.

[4] C. Kessler, P. Eitschberger, and J. Keller. Energy-efficient static scheduling of streaming task collections with malleable tasks. In *Proc. 25th PARS-Workshop*, number 30 in PARS-Mitteilungen, pages 37–46, 2013.

[5] N. Melot, C. Kessler, J. Keller, and P. Eitschberger. Fast Crown Scheduling Heuristics for Energy-Efficient Mapping and Scaling of Moldable Streaming Tasks on Manycore Systems. *ACM Trans. Archit. Code Optim.*, 11(4):62:1–62:24, Jan. 2015. ISSN 1544-3566.

[6] K. Pruhs, R. van Stee, and P. Uthaisombut. Speed Scaling of Tasks with Precedence Constraints. *Theory of Computing Systems*, 43(1):67–80, July 2008.

[7] W. Thies, M. Karczmarek, and S. Amarasinghe. Streamit: A language for streaming applications. In *Compiler Construction*, volume 2304 of *Lecture Notes in Computer Science*, pages 179–196. Springer Berlin Heidelberg, 2002. doi: 10.1007/3-540-45937-5_14.

Parallel Computing: On the Road to Exascale
G.R. Joubert et al. (Eds.)
IOS Press, 2016
doi:10.3233/978-1-61499-621-7-295

Efficient Parallel Linked List Processing

Ashkan TOUSIMOJARAD and Wim VANDERBAUWHEDE

School of Computing Science, University of Glasgow, UK

Abstract. OpenMP is a very popular and successful parallel programming API, but efficient parallel traversal of a list (of possibly unknown size) of items linked by pointers is a challenging task: solving the problem with OpenMP workshar-ing constructs requires either transforming the list into an array for the traversal or for all threads to traverse each of the elements and compete to execute them. Both techniques are inefficient. OpenMP 3.0 allows to addresses the problem using pointer chasing by a master thread and creating a task for each element of the list. These tasks can be processed by any thread in the team. In this study, we propose a more efficient cutoff-based linked list traversal using our task-based parallel programming model, GPRM. We compare the performance of this technique in both GPRM and OpenMP implementations with the conventional OpenMP implementation, which we call Task-Per-Element (TPE).

Keywords. Task Stealing, Parallel Linked List, GPRM, OpenMP, Manycore

Introduction

The concept of *task* already exists in OpenMP and other fork-join models. In this study, we explore the efficiency of task parallelism for an important class of algorithms: Linked List Processing. We first introduce our parallel programming framework, GPRM, and explain the task stealing technique it employs. We then demonstrate an efficient method-ology for parallel list processing implemented in both OpenMP and GPRM. We compare the performance of this method with a common method of list processing using OpenMP tasks per list element (TPE) on a modern manycore platform, the Intel Xeon Phi.

Pointer chasing or list traversal are the names that have been used for this problem [1] [2]. The problem is defined in [1] as traversing a linked list computing a sequence of Fibonacci numbers at each node. As another example, we consider traversing a linked list and sorting a small array of integer numbers (up to a thousand numbers) at each node by a Quicksort algorithm.

Authors in [3] have investigated the performance of up to 32 OpenMP threads for processing dynamic lists managed by pointers in a simulator of financial markets. They have concluded that if the overhead is not dominant, meaning that the unit of work is not too small, using `omp single nowait` directive appears to be suitable. Also in [1], the performance of the TPE method has been evaluated on a multicore CPU. In this paper, however, we focus on the challenges arising in a manycore system such as the Intel Xeon Phi with 240 logical cores. We will demonstrate that when the tasks are tiny and/or the lists are large, the overhead of the TPE method becomes significant.

1. The Intel Xeon Phi Manycore System

The Intel Xeon Phi coprocessor 5110P used in this study is an SMP (Symmetric Multi-processor) on-a-chip which is connected to a host Xeon processor via a PCI Express bus interface. The Intel Many Integrated Core (MIC) architecture used by the Intel Xeon Phi coprocessors gives developers the advantage of using standard, existing programming tools and methods. Our Xeon Phi comprises 60 cores (240 logical cores) connected by a bidirectional ring interconnect.

The Xeon Phi provides four hardware threads sharing the same physical core and its cache subsystem in order to hide the latency inherent in in-order execution. As a result, using at least two threads per core is almost always beneficial [4]. The Xeon Phi has eight memory controllers supporting 2 GDDR5 memory channels each. The clock speed of the cores is 1.053GHz. Each core has an associated 512KB L2 cache. Data and instruction L1 caches of 32KB are also integrated on each core. Another important feature of the Xeon Phi is that each core includes a SIMD 512-bit wide VPU (Vector Processing Unit).

All the benchmarks are implemented as C++ programs, and all speedup ratios are computed against the running time of the sequential code implemented in C++ (which means they are directly proportional to the absolute running times). The benchmarks have been executed natively on the Intel Xeon Phi. For that purpose, the executables are copied to the Xeon Phi, and we connect to it from the host machine using ssh. The Intel compiler icpc (ICC) 14.0.2 is used with the -mmic and -O2 flags for compilation.

2. Programming Models

2.1. OpenMP

OpenMP is the de-facto standard for shared-memory programming, and is based on a set of compiler directives or pragmas, combined with a thread management API. OpenMP has been historically used for loop-level and regular parallelism through its compiler directives. Since the release of OpenMP 3.0, OpenMP also supports task parallelism [5]. It is now widely used in both task and data parallel scenarios.

The Intel OpenMP runtime library (as opposed to the GNU implementation) allocates a task list per thread for every OpenMP team. Whenever a thread creates a task that cannot not be executed immediately, that task is placed into the thread's deque (double-ended queue). A random stealing strategy balances the load [6].

2.2. The Glasgow Parallel Reduction Machine (GPRM)

The Glasgow Parallel Reduction Machine (GPRM) [7] provides a pure task-based approach to manycore programming by structuring programs into *task code*, written as C++ classes, and *communication code*, written in GPC, a restricted subset of C++. The communication code describes how the *tasks* interact. GPC is a simple functional language with parallel evaluation with a fully C++ compatible syntax. What this means is that it is possible to compile task code and GPC communication code with a C++ compiler and get correct functionality, but without the parallelism.

The GPC compiler compiles the communication code into the Glasgow Parallel Intermediate Representation (GPIR) (the *task description* code), which is an S-expression based, bare-bones functional languages inspired by Scheme [8], e.g. $(S_1 (S_2 10) 20)$ represents a task S_1 taking two arguments, the first argument is the task S_2 which takes as argument the numeric constant 10, and the second argument is the numeric constant 20. The GPIR code is further compiled into lists of *bytecodes*, which the GPRM virtual machine executes with concurrent evaluation of function arguments – in other words the VM is a coarse-grained parallel reduction machine where the methods provided by the *task code* constitute the instructions.

The number of threads in GPRM is set to the number of logical cores of the underlying hardware. Each thread runs a *tile*, which consists of a *task manager* and a *task kernel*. The *task kernel* is typically a self-contained entity offering a specific functionality to the system, and on its own is not aware of the rest of the system. The task kernel has run-to-completion semantics. The corresponding *task manager* provides an interface between the kernel and other *tiles* in the system. Since threads in GPRM correspond to execution resources, for each processing core there is a thread with its own *task manager*. The GPRM system is conceptually built as a network of communicating sequential *tiles* that exchange packets to request computations and deliver results. At first glance, the GPRM model may seem static and intolerant to runtime changes. However, in this paper, we discuss how it can efficiently balance the load and thrive in dynamic environments. For load balancing, compile-time information about the task dependencies is combined with an efficient task-stealing mechanism.

3. Task Stealing

In GPRM, *Task stealing* is the process of stealing *tasks* from the *ready* tasks queues of other threads. If enabled, it allows threads to steal *tasks* from each other when they become idle. This can balance the load if there are enough tasks in the ready queues.

Superficially, the stealing mechanism may seem quite similar to the classical work-stealing approaches [9] [10] [11], but there are fundamental differences, due to the nature of our parallel programming model. In a fork-join model like OpenMP, when control flow forks, the master thread executes one branch and the other branch can be stolen by other threads (thieves). Multiple branches can be generated as the program is executed. This classical approach needs double-ended queues (deques), such that the workers work at the back of their own deques, while thieves can steal from the front of the others' deques. *Steal child* (used by TBB) –the newly created child becomes available to the thieves– and *steal continuation* (used by Cilk Plus) –the continuation of the function that spawned new task becomes available to the thieves– are two variations of the conventional work-stealing approach. The stealing semantics for OpenMP are implementation dependent. The OpenMP rules imply that *steal child* must be the default but steal-continuation is permitted if a `task` is annotated with as `untied` [12].

In GPRM, we do not use a fork-join model for task creation, hence there is no concept such as task spawning: the C++ methods used in the GPC code are compiled into tasks. At compile-time, the compiler specifies the initial mapping between tasks and threads (even if the creation of a task is conditional, its initial host thread is specified). The parent tasks in the GPRM model are not the same as the parents in the Directed Acyclic Graph (DAG). Rather, the parent tasks are the ones that request computations from their children, hence will depend on their children, e.g. t3 is the parent of the t1 and

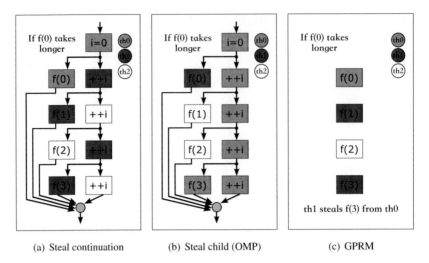

(a) Steal continuation   (b) Steal child (OMP)   (c) GPRM

Figure 1. (a) Steal Continuation: 4 steals, (b) Steal Child: 3 steals, (c) GPRM-Steal: 1 steal

t2 tasks, following the order of the function calls: B.t3(B.t1(x), B.t2(y));.

With this background information, it is more clear what we mean by *task stealing*. Our stealing mechanism is about stealing the individual tasks, rather than the whole branch. In the conventional work-stealing approaches, the stolen branch could create more tasks during the execution of the program, and they would be executed by the thief (unless other workers become free and steal from that thief). The GPRM-specific task stealing mechanism is useful because all the tasks are initially allocated to threads (*tiles*). The stealing mechanism only tunes the initial allocation set by the compiler. Therefore, assuming that all the tasks are exactly the same and the number of them is a multiple of the number of the processing cores in the system, most probably no stealing occurs. In order to illustrate the differences between the stealing techniques in details, consider Fig. 1 and the example in List. 1.

```
1 /* GPRM Implementation. Trivial to implement using OpenMP tasks */
2 #pragma gprm unroll
3 for(int i=0; i < N; ++i)
4   f(i);
```

Listing 1: Micro-benchmark to illustrate the differences between the stealing techniques

Suppose we have only 3 threads (specified with 3 colours: white, light blue, and dark blue), N = 4, and f(0) takes more time to complete.

- The number of steals for the *steal continuation* becomes 4, as th1 and th2 can steal continuations before th0 finishes its first job.
- The number of steals is 3 for the *steal child* technique. th1 steals the first child and th2 the second. Since newly spawned tasks are put at the back of the deque and each worker thread takes the tasks from the back of its own deque, therefore after all iterations, th0 executes f(3). Assuming that th2 has started executing f(1) an epsilon before th0 reaches f(3), f(2) becomes available for th2 (note

that th1 is still busy executing f(0)).

- GPC compiler unrolls the task creation loop and assigns the tasks to the worker threads. In the *GPRM-Steal* technique in Fig. 1(c), assuming that th1 has started its work an epsilon before th2, it can steal f(3) from the *ready* queue of the busy thread (*tile*), th0.

4. An Efficient Linked List Processing Technique

```
 1 /* TPE (Task-Per-Element) */
 2 #pragma omp parallel
 3 {
 4   #pragma omp single
 5   {
 6     p = mylist->begin();
 7     while(p!=mylist->end()) {
 8       #pragma omp task
 9       {
10         process(p);
11       }
12       p++;
13     } // of while
14   } // of single
15 }
16 /* ----------------------------------------------------- */
17 /* OpenMP implementation of the method with cutoff */
18 #pragma omp parallel private(p) //p must be private
19 {
20   #pragma omp single
21   {
22   p = mylist->begin();
23   for(int i=0; i < CUTOFF; i++) {
24     process(p);
25     #pragma omp task // tied
26     {
27       while(p!=mylist->end()) {
28         int j=0;
29         while(j < CUTOFF && p!=mylist->end()) {
30           j++; p++;}
31         if(p!=mylist->end()) {
32           process(p);}
33       } // of while
34     } // of task
35     p++;}
36   } // of single
37 }
38 /* ----------------------------------------------------- */
39 /* GPRM implementation of the method with cutoff */
40 #pragma gprm unroll
41 for(int i=0; i < CUTOFF; i++) {
42   par_list(i, CUTOFF, &MyProcess::process, mylist);}
```

Listing 2: TPE v.s. cutoff-based linked list processing

The cutoff methods and their role to reduce the overhead of task creation are discussed in [13] and [14]. We use this concept to propose an efficient pointer chasing technique.

To traverse a list (of unknown size) similar to the problem discussed in [5], we propose to limit the number of tasks to a cutoff value. Assuming there are CUTOFF chunks of work, the chunk with id k, gets the head of list, goes k steps further to its starting point, processes the element, and then goes CUTOFF steps further to process its next element. It continues to jump CUTOFF steps until the end of the list. The implementation of the TPE processing (creating one task per element) of linked lists as well as the implementations of the proposed method in both OpenMP and GPRM is shown in Listing. 2.

The GPRM implementation of the par_list is similar to a single-threaded version of the OpenMP code (i.e. without pragmas). Wherever the size of the list is known, a GPRM par_cont_list with a similar implementation to a par_cont_for [15] can also be used.

5. Experiments

As stated earlier, the problem we are targeting is defined as traversing a linked list sorting a small array of integers at each node. The purpose is to parallelise this problem on a manycore system. All speedups are computed against the sequential codes in C++.

We have considered two types of workloads: Balanced and Unbalanced, described in Listing. 3. Two different array sizes to sort are chosen: 240 and 1000. 240 is used to create a completely unbalanced workload on 240 cores using the formula in Listing. 3. By using *p % N as the size of array to be sorted at each node, where *p is the linked list node ID, different nodes gets different arrays to sort. The maximum difference with the balanced workload can be seen for the initial configuration with NTH=240 and CUTOFF=240. For example th1 gets all arrays with size 1 to sort, while th239 gets all arrays with size 239. Obviously, by changing the cutoff value to other numbers, the pattern changes, but still different elements of the list have different array sizes to sort (240 different sizes).

```
1 /* Balanced Workload */
2 //N is the size of the array
3 for(int i=0; i < N; i++) {
4   A->push_back(i);}
5 quickSort(*A, 0, N);
6 /* ------------------------------------------------------ */
7 /* Unbalanced Workload */
8 //p is the pointer to the L-L node ID, thus *p is a unique integer
9 for(int i=0; i < *p % N; i++) {
10   A->push_back(i);}
11 quickSort(*A, 0, *p % N);
```

Listing 3: Creation of balanced and unbalanced workloads.

For both balanced and unbalanced workloads, the exact amount of work to be accomplished by each thread depends on the size of the list, and the cutoff value. Therefore, the balanced workload does not necessarily mean that all threads get exactly the same

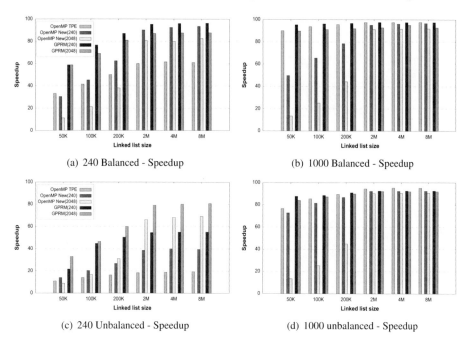

(a) 240 Balanced - Speedup

(b) 1000 Balanced - Speedup

(c) 240 Unbalanced - Speedup

(d) 1000 unbalanced - Speedup

Figure 2. Speedup charts for different cases. Cutoff-based approaches have been tested with cutoffs: 240, 2048

work, but at least the amount of work to do at each node is the same. Instead of finding the optimal cutoff value that has the minimal overhead that leads to a fair distribution of work, we focus on the efficiency of runtime load balancing in GPRM versus OpenMP using different cutoffs.

6. Results

We first compare the three approaches. For the cutoff-based OpenMP and GPRM implementations, we have used the cutoff 240, and a large power of 2 number (2048) to allow for better distribution of tasks as well as more opportunities for task stealing. Although the bests results are not necessarily obtained with these cutoff values (as shown in Fig. 3), we aim to show that they are sufficient to outperform the TPE approach for both balanced (with cutoff 240) and unbalanced (with cutoff 2048) workloads.

6.1. Comparing all implementations

The reason why the Task-Per-Element (TPE) approach is inefficient is evident from Fig. 2. It shows that for small tasks (of size 240), its best performance is about 65% of the peak for balanced workload and about 25% of the peak for the unbalanced one. For the larger tasks (of size 1000) and the linked list sizes greater than 100K, its performance is comparable with the GPRM implementation of the proposed method.

The cutoff-based OpenMP approach has also shown unexpected behaviours when the list itself is small. In all cases, the performance for the 50K list with cutoff 2048 is poor.

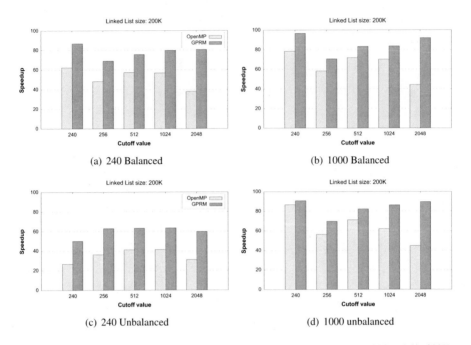

Figure 3. OpenMP v.s. GPRM implementation of the proposed method for Linked List of size 200K

6.2. *Comparing the effect of cutoff in OpenMP vs. GPRM*

For the next round of comparison, we compare the cutoff-based implementations. For that purpose, we use a medium-sized list to skip the poor performance of the OpenMP version for small lists. Figure 3 shows that in all cases, GPRM has a better performance. Below is what happens in the background using the GPRM approach:

For the balanced workloads, we expect to see the best performance with cutoff 240. Cutoff 256 changes the fair distribution, as 16 threads have to handle the chunks 240 to 256. As the cutoff number becomes larger, more tasks will be created and hence the load can be balanced more efficiently, helping the runtime system to reach near the performance of the initial case (with cutoff 240).

For the unbalanced workloads, we need to distinguish between the 240 and 1000 cases. In the case of 240, initially the workload is completely unbalanced with no chance of stealing. As the cutoff becomes larger, more opportunities for load balancing become available. Apparently the cutoff of 2048 in this case results in very fine-grained tasks, and imposes a small overhead to the system. As 1000 different array sizes are distributed between only 240 different workers, this situation is different from the case of 240 and the workload is not as imbalanced as we expect. In order to have a similar situation, we have tested the same experiment with a value of 960 (which is a multiple of 240). Therefore, for the cutoff 240, thread k receives arrays with sizes k, k+240, k+480, and k+720, and the load is again unbalanced. In that case, the cutoff of 2048 has a visible performance improvement over the cutoff of 240 (10-15%) [1].

---

[1]We have intentionally not used the number 960 for the large arrays to show that our results are independent of the regular distribution of tasks on threads

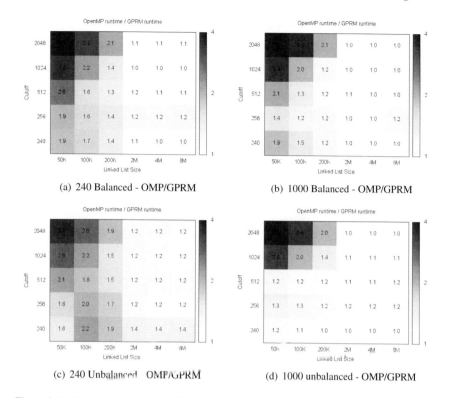

(a) 240 Balanced - OMP/GPRM

(b) 1000 Balanced - OMP/GPRM

(c) 240 Unbalanced - OMP/GPRM

(d) 1000 unbalanced - OMP/GPRM

Figure 4. Performance comparison of the OpenMP and GPRM implementations of the proposed method

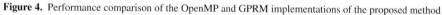

6.3. Comparing the performance of the proposed method in OpenMP vs. GPRM

For a detailed comparison between GPRM ad OpenMP, we consider heat maps where the value for each cell is calculated as (`OpenMP runtime / GPRM runtime`). It can be observed that a large cutoff for small lists in the OpenMP implementation results in poor performance. It is true that the range of optimal cutoff values depends on the task granularity and the input data set [16], but at least for different cases of both balanced/unbalanced workloads here and for cutoff values up to 2048, we did not see a drastic slowdown with GPRM, as opposed to what we observed with OpenMP.

One reason why the same implementation in OpenMP does not have consistent performance is that in OpenMP the tasks are not pre-assigned to threads, while in GPRM they are assigned to threads almost evenly at compile-time. Another reason is the differences between the stealing mechanisms, which themselves come from the differences between the parallel execution models.

It is worth mentioning that we have also measured the speedup results for the balanced workloads against the sequential runtime on an E5-2620 (2.00GHz) Xeon processor. The best speedup results for the 240 and 1000 balanced cases using 12 threads (one per logical core) were 6.4× and 5.8× respectively. The parallel performance for these cases could only be improved up to 7.7× and 7.2× using the Xeon Phi (over the sequential runtime on the E5-2620 Xeon system). However, our main goal in this study was to compare the performance of GPRM and OpenMP on a system with many cores, and propose an efficient methodology for linked list processing in such a system.

7. Conclusion

In this paper we have proposed an efficient cutoff-based parallel linked list traversal method and demonstrated its advantages over the conventional implementation using OpenMP tasks, which we call Task-Per-Element (TPE).

Furthermore, we have shown that our task-based parallel programming model, GPRM, makes it easier to traverse the elements of a linked list in parallel (even if the size of the list changes at runtime). The cutoff-based implementation in GPRM also results in superior performance compared to the both OpenMP implementations (TPE and cutoff-based) in almost all cases, but most dramatically in the case of smaller lists.

The performance of the proposed method in GPRM demonstrates how controlling the number of tasks combined with a low-overhead load balancing technique can lead to efficient parallel linked list processing on a manycore system, such as the Xeon Phi.

References

[1] Tim Mattson and Larry Meadows. A hands-on introduction to openmp. *Intel Corporation*, 2014.
[2] Eduard Ayguadé, Nawal Copty, Alejandro Duran, Jay Hoeflinger, Yuan Lin, Federico Massaioli, Ernesto Su, Priya Unnikrishnan, and Guansong Zhang. A proposal for task parallelism in openmp. In *A Practical Programming Model for the Multi-Core Era*, pages 1–12. Springer, 2008.
[3] Federico Massaioli, Filippo Castiglione, and Massimo Bernaschi. Openmp parallelization of agent-based models. *Parallel Computing*, 31(10):1066–1081, 2005.
[4] James Jeffers and James Reinders. *Intel Xeon Phi Coprocessor High Performance Programming*. Newnes, 2013.
[5] Eduard Ayguadé, Nawal Copty, Alejandro Duran, Jay Hoeflinger, Yuan Lin, Federico Massaioli, Xavier Teruel, Priya Unnikrishnan, and Guansong Zhang. The design of openmp tasks. *Parallel and Distributed Systems, IEEE Transactions on*, 20(3):404–418, 2009.
[6] Jérôme Clet-Ortega, Patrick Carribault, and Marc Pérache. Evaluation of openmp task scheduling algorithms for large numa architectures. In *Euro-Par 2014 Parallel Processing*. Springer, 2014.
[7] Ashkan Tousimojarad and Wim Vanderbauwhede. The Glasgow Parallel Reduction Machine: Programming shared-memory many-core systems using parallel task composition. *EPTCS*, 137:79–94, 2013.
[8] Gerald Jay Sussman and Guy L Steele Jr. Scheme: An interpreter for extended lambda calculus. In *MEMO 349, MIT AI LAB*, 1975.
[9] Robert D Blumofe, Christopher F Joerg, Bradley C Kuszmaul, Charles E Leiserson, Keith H Randall, and Yuli Zhou. Cilk: An efficient multithreaded runtime system. *Journal of parallel and distributed computing*, 37(1):55–69, 1996.
[10] Robert D Blumofe and Charles E Leiserson. Scheduling multithreaded computations by work stealing. *Journal of the ACM (JACM)*, 46(5):720–748, 1999.
[11] Nimar S Arora, Robert D Blumofe, and C Greg Plaxton. Thread scheduling for multiprogrammed multiprocessors. *Theory of Computing Systems*, 34(2):115–144, 2001.
[12] Michael McCool, James Reinders, and Arch Robison. *Structured parallel programming: patterns for efficient computation*. Elsevier, 2012.
[13] Alejandro Duran, Julita Corbalán, and Eduard Ayguadé. Evaluation of openmp task scheduling strategies. In *OpenMP in a new era of parallelism*, pages 100–110. Springer, 2008.
[14] Ashkan Tousimojarad and Wim Vanderbauwhede. Comparison of three popular parallel programming models on the Intel Xeon Phi. In *Euro-Par 2014: Parallel Processing Workshops*, pages 314–325. Springer, 2014.
[15] Ashkan Tousimojarad and Wim Vanderbauwhede. A parallel task-based approach to linear algebra. In *Parallel and Distributed Computing (ISPDC), 2014 IEEE 13th International Symposium on*, pages 59–66. IEEE, 2014.
[16] Alejandro Duran, Xavier Teruel, Roger Ferrer, Xavier Martorell, and Eduard Ayguade. Barcelona openmp tasks suite: A set of benchmarks targeting the exploitation of task parallelism in openmp. In *Parallel Processing, 2009. ICPP'09. International Conference on*, pages 124–131. IEEE, 2009.

Parallel Computing: On the Road to Exascale
G.R. Joubert et al. (Eds.)
IOS Press, 2016
© 2016 The authors and IOS Press. All rights reserved.
doi:10.3233/978-1-61499-621-7-305

Streams as an alternative to halo exchange

Daniel J. HOLMES [a,1], Caoimhín LAOIDE-KEMP [a]

[a] *EPCC, The University of Edinburgh, UK*

Abstract.
Many scientific problems can be solved computationally by using linear algebra to calculate numerical solutions. The data dependencies in linear algebra operations are often expressed in a stencil structure. The ubiquitous parallelisation technique for stencil codes, to enable the solution of large problems on parallel architectures, is domain decomposition.

One of the limitations of domain decomposition, affecting the scalability and overall performance of any stencil code, is the necessity to transmit information from neighbouring stencil grid points between the domains, and in particular between processes, known as halo exchange. The necessity of halo exchange limits the size of problems that can be solved numerically as the performance often scales poorly, in particular in poorly load balanced systems. Extensive work has been done to improve the performance of such codes, such as multi-depth halos and dynamic load balancing by changing the domain size, however, these methods all use the concept of halos for the basic communication pattern.

In this paper we propose an alternative to the traditional halo exchange method of transmitting data between processes. In our model inter-process communication becomes a uni-directional stream, and not an exchange, in that it is transmitted in one direction only. This removes the pair-wise synchronisation between neighbouring processes inherent in the halo exchange pattern. As all communication is uni-directional, data can be updated in place, rather than double-buffered, resulting in half the memory usage of the traditional approach. In this paper we also present our preliminary findings which show that for a one-dimensional implementation of this model using a Jacobi-stencil code, that the streaming method is consistently faster than the exchange pattern. At 16,000 processes, for both strong and weak scaling, streaming is over ten times faster than halo exchange.

We are currently investigating further optimisation strategies and extending to multi-dimensional domain decomposition.

Keywords. Halo exchange, streams, MPI, domain-decomposition, stencil codes

1. Introduction

One of the most significant challenges faced by parallel computing is that of efficient communication between processors. Using large numbers of processors can increase performance via parallelism, but this also increases the computational cost and complexity of communication in the network. As the HPC community strives towards Exascale computers, this will present a greater barrier to performance on high-end machines. It will be necessary to search for improvement in all areas of processor communication;

---

[1]Corresponding Author: *dholmes@epcc.ed.ac.uk*

including the physical interconnects, network topologies, communication patterns, and application algorithms. This work investigates the viability and scalability of an alternative stream-based approach to one of the most commonly used communication patterns, namely halo exchange for stencil based domain decomposition codes.

Numerical linear algebra is an essential tool in computational science applications, primarily because matrices are central to many computational discretisation methods (e.g. finite difference method and finite element method). These discretisation methods are used to provide numerical solutions to differential equations, which cannot be solved analytically.

Linear algebra problems can be solved via standard methods, such as Gaussian elimination, LU factorisation, Jacobi iterative, Conjugate Gradient, and Krylov Subspace. These standard methods are provided by numerical libraries, such as BLAS/LINPACK/LAPACK/ScaLAPACK and PETSc [1,2,3,4,5,6]. Both the current metric for measuring the performance of Top500 [7] machines (LINPACK) and the main contender for its replacement (HPCG [8]) implement standard linear algebra solution algorithms. In all these methods, each step requires the values of neighbouring domain locations from one or more previous steps. This pattern of data-requirements is called a stencil.

Domain decomposition is a common parallelisation technique for stencil codes whereby the data for the entire problem domain is partitioned and each process calculates a particular domain partition in parallel. Applying the stencil at the edge of a domain partition requires information from the edges of neighbouring domain partitions. Typically, halo (or ghost) regions are created by each process to store a copy of neighbouring edges. The halo/ghost regions are updated each time-step of the algorithm by exchanging information calculated locally with information calculated by neighbouring processes.

The exchanging of halo information at every step means that no process can become more than one step ahead or behind its immediate neighbours. Consequently, this can be modelled as a bulk synchronous parallel (BSP) algorithm [9] where an application consists of many super-steps with each super-step involving local computation, global communication and barrier synchronisation. In this model, barrier synchronisation commonly comes from global reductions of data that allow important properties of the system (e.g. total chemical energy of a molecular dynamics system) to be computed and monitored. Typically, much of the communication is overlapped with computation using asynchronous transfers, and barrier synchronisations are reduced in frequency to minimise their effect on performance. Therefore, the cost of each super-step in a BSP model of the halo exchange algorithm depends on the time taken for the slowest local calculation. Delays in one process propagate to neighbouring processes and delays in multiple processes tend to accumulate rather than cancel each other out.

Delays can occur for many reasons including load-imbalance, heterogeneous or adaptive hardware resources (e.g. CPU frequency boost/energy-saving modes), and interrupts from the operating system and other system software. Although the majority of these sources can be mitigated or eliminated on well-managed supercomputers, it has been shown that the effects of even small amounts of system noise can be dramatically negative even on current large scale machines [10,11]. It is expected that these negative effects will be even worse on future Exascale machines.

1.1. Related work

Time-parallel algorithms, in particular Parareal [12], interleave calculations from multiple time-steps. The Parareal time-parallel time-integration method can be used to solve several time-segments of an integration problem in parallel. It uses a 'shooting' method to estimate the initial values for each time segment before sufficient data is available to perform a fully accurate calculation. These segments can be solved in parallel and then refined by comparing boundary values. This algorithm is supported by proofs of the necessary theorems and examples of convergence. The halo exchange communication pattern requires that each time-step be completed before the next one can begin. Both the Parareal algorithm and the proposed streaming algorithm permit calculation of different time-steps concurrently. However, whereas Parareal *estimates* the values of future data points, the proposed streaming algorithm uses knowledge of the data dependencies to calculate *exact* future values. The streaming algorithm presented in this work calculates accurate but incomplete information for multiple time-steps. In contrast, Parareal calculates estimated but complete information for multiple time-steps.

Systolic architectures can be thought of as a hardware analogue to the software pattern that is proposed in this paper. Systolic architectures are characterised by an "assembly-line" construction, in which data is passed from memory, through an array of processing elements, and finally back to memory. Each processing element executes a fixed set of instructions on the data before passing it on. This is in contrast to von Neumann architectures, where instructions are passed to the data elements. Computers with systolic architectures gained popularity in the 1970s and 80s, but have since fallen out of favour. This is primarily because the machines must be designed with a specific task in mind in order to achieve the maximum performance. This is not ideal in the present day when large computers are designed with the aim of performing well for all HPC applications.

The theory behind systolic machines, as well as their potential benefits, are well known [13]. Von Neumann machines often have significant bottlenecks due to expensive memory accesses. Systolic architectures avoid this by using data elements multiple times for a single memory access. Kung [13] gives examples of systolic arrays that would be suitable for a variety of common computational tasks. However, this does not directly address the problem of the expense associated with requiring a separate machine for each application. A key difference of the streaming algorithm is that it is entirely implemented in software. Since software is far easier and cheaper to modify than hardware, it is hoped that the algorithm will not suffer from being overly specialised.

A project was undertaken to propose the introduction of an extension to OpenMP 3.0 that would allow the streaming of data between parallel tasks [14]. The extension would add two optional clauses to the OpenMP task construct: input and output. These clauses would take a list of items as arguments, with each item describing data to be streamed and the behaviour of the stream. The project demonstrated how this syntax can be used to effectively parallelise a number of common OpenMP patterns (e.g. pipelines and filters), as well as indicating in detail how the model implements an FFT algorithm.

This extension to OpenMP shows both that there is an interest in parallelising using streaming models, and that there is scope for significant performance benefits, with a speedup of up to 18.8 achieved in certain cases. It is relevant to this work in that it demonstrates an attempt to combine the use of streams with standard parallelisation libraries. However, it proposes an extension to OpenMP, while this work uses the tools that are already available in the existing MPI library to create a new algorithm. Additionally, it focuses on OpenMP, which is suited for parallelisation on smaller machines.

2. Modifying the halo exchange algorithm

In practice, the domain-decomposition parallelisation technique must use a multi-dimensional decomposition, such as a 2D or 3D torus, in order to take advantage of more processes. For example, a 3D problem domain containing 1000x1000x1000 cells cannot use more than 1000 processes if limited to a 1D decomposition, whereas a 2D decomposition could use up to 1,000,000 processes. Larger problem domains are often not necessary to obtain valid scientific simulations but reducing the time-to-solution via strong scaling is highly desirable. However, this work so far focuses on 1D decomposition in order to prove the concepts involved are valid and useful before tackling the complexities of generalising the approach to multi-dimensional decompositions. Whilst the figures and text in this paper refer to a 1D sub-domain of cells, those cells may consist of multi-dimension problem data. For a 2D problem, a 1D decomposition would mean that each cell is a whole row or a whole column. For a 3D problem, each cell in a 1D decomposition would be a slab or plane through the entire domain.

2.1. The limitations of halo exchange

The data dependencies for a typical halo exchange code are represented schematically in Figure 1. The figure shows the local sub-domain for one processor (10 contiguous cells with solid lines on the bottom row) with the halo or ghost cells at each edge of this sub-domain (single cell with dashed lines). Also shown are parts of the two neighbouring processors, one to the left and one to the right. The bottom row represents the completely-computed last iteration and the top row represents the partially-computed next iteration. Two types of data dependency are included in the figure: communication from edge cells to neighbouring halo cells and computation from the completely-computed iteration to the partially-computed iteration. The halo cells are copies of the edge cells from neighbouring sub-domains. Their values are needed to compute the values of the local edge cells in the next iteration, which will in turn be communicated into the neighbouring halo cell copies needed for the following iteration.

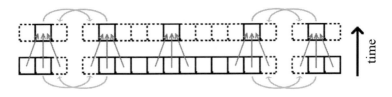

Figure 1. Schematic of data dependencies for a 1-D decomposition with a 3-point stencil using the halo exchange communication pattern

In terms of data-dependencies, the critical path in this communication pattern is as follows:

1. the particular processor updates a cell at the edge of its sub-domain
2. the value of that edge-cell is sent to a neighbouring processor
3. the neighbouring processor receives the value into a ghost cell
4. the neighbouring processor updates a cell at the edge of its sub-domain
5. the value of that edge-cell is sent to the particular processor
6. the particular processor receives the value into a ghost cell

This communication pattern requires one full round-trip between alternate updates to edge-cells. Using blocking MPI routines means that processors are idle while waiting for the communication to take place. Using non-blocking MPI routines allows for the possibility of overlapping communication with computation. Typically, a halo exchange code will issue a non-blocking send and a non-blocking receive for each neighbouring process, compute all of the non-edge cells, wait for the non-blocking communications to complete, and then compute the edge-cells. This procedure can then be repeated as many times as necessary. Overlap can only realistically occur if the MPI library supports asynchronous progress, e.g. via a progress thread.

Figure 2 shows how a single process can calculate some data from multiple future iterations without any communication with its neighbours. The 3-point stencil used in this example results in each processor being able to calculate a triangular temporal sub-domain of data, starting from the base and working upwards towards the tip. Data outside the triangle cannot be computed without communication, as it depends on data from neighbouring processes.

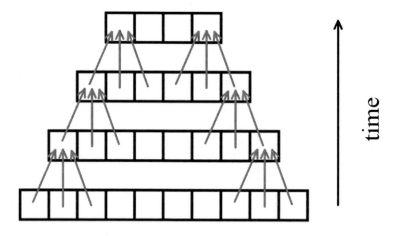

Figure 2. Schematic of data dependencies for a 1-D decomposition with a 3-point stencil partial computation of future iterations without communication

Another common refinement of halo exchange communication pattern is to increase the depth of the halo region. Having more cells communicated in each exchange is likely to improve usage of the network but requires that some cells are calculated by both the local process and its neighbouring process. If we consider a one-dimensional problem with a 3-point stencil, decomposed in 1D with a halo region of depth d, there is a duplication of the calculation in $d * (d - 1)$ cells every d iterations per process. If the time per message is modelled as $L + size/B$, where L is the latency and B is the bandwidth, then a halo-region of depth d will save $(d-1)*L$ message time every d iterations. The average cost per iteration for this case is therefore $(d-1)*(U-L/d)$, which suggests that a halo depth of $d = 1$ is optimal in this example. If non-blocking MPI routines are used and the MPI library supports asynchronous progress, then the message latency is entirely hidden by overlapping with computation, whatever the depth of the halo. This cost function also assumes that the processors are precisely load-balanced and execute instructions at identical rates. In practice, these assumptions are likely to be false and so there are situations where a halo-depth greater than 1 cell does improve the overall performance of the code.

2.2. An alternative to halo exchange: first steps

Conceptually, each process could calculate the entire triangular temporal sub-domain, discarding the inner portion of that triangle when no further data-dependencies require those cells. All processes could then shift data in a ring topology, i.e. send the left edge of their triangle to their left neighbouring process and receive the left edge being sent from their right neighbouring process. Each process would then have sufficient data to calculate another triangular temporal sub-domain, this time starting from the tip and working upwards towards the base. This algorithm could be repeated until some global property of the system meets a criterion for stopping. It breaks the bi-lateral communication dependency between neighbouring processes, only requiring communication in one direction. However, it still assumes a BSP model in that, to be efficient, all processes must finish their local calculations and communication at the same time to avoid propagating delays that are likely to accumulate with delays elsewhere rather than dissipate or overlap with other delays.

The key refinement to this communication pattern involves using an output data stream to transmit the lefthand edge to the left neighbour process and an input data stream to receive the righthand edge from the right neighbour process. Refer to section 2.3 for a definition and some implementation options using MPI. Processes send data values into their output stream as they become available and receive data values from the input stream only when they are needed to perform calculations.

The primary advantage of this method is that processes do not rely on data from their neighbour processes relating to iteration n until they reach iteration $n+k$ (where k is the number of iterations a process can calculate on its own before it runs out of data to compute). Hence, if a process is delayed it will not cause any delay in other processes unless the delay is such that its neighbours are now k iterations ahead. For comparison, in halo exchange neighbouring processes will be delayed if they get more than one iteration ahead).

The data layout for the streaming communication pattern is shown schematically in Figure 3. In this algorithm, the intention is to produce new data at left edge of the triangular sub-domain (now labelled the send buffer) as early as possible and to immediately and asynchronously initiate the transfer of that data to the left neighbouring process.

Typical operation of this algorithm (after an initial start-up phase) will consist of reading data from the receive buffer, using that data to calculate all future iteration cell values that depend, directly or indirectly, on that data until new data has been produced in the send buffer, whereupon new data must be read from the receive buffer.

At the point in the algorithm depicted in the snapshot represented by Figure 3, the process has data for eighteen cells: eight retained from previous calculations, two re-

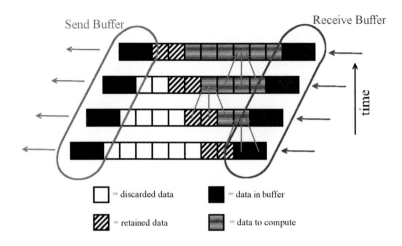

Figure 3. Schematic of data dependencies for a 1-D decomposition with a 3-point stencil using the proposed streaming communication pattern

ceived from its right neighbouring process (with receive buffer space for six more that could be in transit but are not yet needed). In addition, there are eight cells of previously calculated data in the send buffer space that is being asynchronously transmitted to the left neighbouring process. Some or all of the data in the send buffer may have already arrived at the left neighbour process (and may have even been used in calculations there), but verification of this has not yet been performed locally because it is not necessary until this process produces more data that must be sent.

It can be seen that the sub-domain for each process shifts one cell per time-step in the opposite direction to the data-flow in the streams. This means that each process has a different sub-domain than it would if using halo exchange, but the global dataset will be identical and the two calculations will produce exactly the same results for each cell at each time-step.

This algorithm enables all receive streams to be at a position significantly behind the corresponding sending stream. If the process shown in Figure 3 stopped processing for a considerable time, its left neighbouring process could continue until it had emptied both this process send buffer and its own receive buffer and the right neighbouring process could continue until it had filled both this process receive buffer and its own send buffer. This observation indicates that this algorithm should be able to tolerate very significant delays in individual processes as long as no process fails completely and the delays average out over the very long term.

2.3. What is a stream?

Commonly the stream interface allows writing (if it is an output stream) and reading (if it is an input stream). Obtaining the position within the stream is not relevant for this algorithm so has not been implemented.

The implementation used in this work uses a pool of MPI persistent point-to-point operations each one referencing a chunk of a circular buffer. Each chunk consists of cells from the same calculation iteration. In Figure 3, each 2 cell wide block coloured in solid black is a single chunk and each of the horizontal arrows represents a single persistent point-to-point communication operation.

Writing to the output stream is implemented as follows:

1. Ensure that the oldest persistent send operation is complete (MPI_WAIT)
2. Copy the new data to the chunk of the send buffer referenced by that persistent send operation
3. Start that persistent send operation (MPI_START)

Reading from the input stream is implemented as follows:

1. Ensure that the oldest persistent receive operation is complete (MPI_WAIT)
2. Copy the new data from the chunk of the receive buffer referenced by that persistent receive operation
3. Start that persistent receive operation (MPI_START)

A variant on this simple implementation of stream functionality using existing MPI calls involves increasing the size of the MPI messages by grouping together multiple chunks into a single message. In this variant, an integer index for each buffer indicates which chunks are readable (for the receive buffer) or writeable (for the send buffer). For the send buffer, the persistent send operation is only started when the current buffer chunk is full (i.e. written completely). For the receive buffer, the persistent receive operation is only started when the current buffer chunk is empty (i.e. read completely).

It is also possible to implement stream functionality using single-sided MPI calls. Either the producer process can use MPI_PUT (or a derived function, such as MPI_RPUT) to send the data to the consumer process or the consumer process can use MPI_GET (or a derived function, such as MPI_RGET) to receive the data from the producer process. In either case, the remote buffer is a first-in-first-out queue with a circular buffer for which well-known implementations exist [15,16] involving atomic operations on index counters that can be provided by MPI operations, e.g. MPI_COMPARE_AND_SWAP. This type of implementation has not been attempted as part of this work because it is known that MPI point-to-point out-performs MPI single-sided for producer-consumer patterns [17] if MPI adopts a notified access mode for single-sided communication then it is anticipated that a stream implementation with higher performance than the point-to-point one presently considered should be possible.

3. Preliminary findings

For this work, a simple Jacobi iterative solver application using 1-D domain decomposition for the diffusion equation was used. A reference application using the halo exchange communication pattern with MPI persistent point-to-point functions was created. The stream implementation based on MPI persistent point-to-point functions, described in section 2.3, was used to form a comparison application. Several design decisions for the stream implementation (such as the total buffer size, the number of chunks per MPI message, and the maximum number of in-flight messages) were left as tunable parameters to assist with debugging and optimisation.

All performance measurements were performed on ARCHER, the UK National Supercomputer service, a Cray XC30 machine with two 12-core 2.7 GHz Intel Ivy Bridge CPUs per node and an Aries interconnect network connecting a total of 4920 compute nodes.

3.1. Results

Figure 4 shows the results of investigating whether varying the halo depth makes any significant difference for this example problem. We varied the halo depth from 1 to 5000 cells. All other parameters were kept at the same representative values (512 processes, 1.92 million data cells per process, 10,000 iterations per timed batch and 10 timed batches per data point). No significant difference in wall clock time-to-solution was observed, as highlighted by the horizontal "trend-line" showing the average of all the data points in the plot. This is expected behaviour because the simple Jacobi calculation is very well load-balanced, the MPI library on ARCHER supports asynchronous progress and the cost of duplicated calculation, even for 5,000 cells, is small when compared to the time taken to calculate the other 1.92 million cells. For all other tests involving the halo exchange code we used a halo depth of 1.

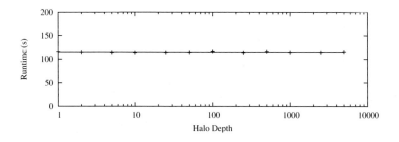

Figure 4. Investigation of the effect of halo-depth on halo exchange algorithm. All tests use 512 processors and 1,920,000 data cells per processor. Each data value is the average of 10 timed batches of 10,000 iterations. The "trend-line" is the average of all data points. Error bars showing the standard error of the sample mean are present but too small to be visible.

Figures 5 and 6 show the results of investigating the scalability of both the halo exchange and the stream communication patterns. Figure 5 shows speed-up relative to a serial version of the Jacobi code achieved when strong scaling a problem size of 1 billion cells (i.e. the nearest equivalent in 1D to a representative 3D problem of 1000x1000x1000 cells). The data points begin with a 512-process experiment, which demonstrates super-linear speed-up because a single core cannot use all available memory channels when reading main memory. A further region of super-linear speed-up is apparent at larger process counts when the problem size per process fits into the L3 cache available to each processor core. This second region occurs earlier for the stream pattern because the stream code can do in-place updates to the data and so only requires one working copy of the sub-domain data whereas the halo exchange code uses double-buffering.

Figure 6 shows strong and weak scaling for a smaller problem size of 1.92 million cells for all the strong scaling tests (i.e. 100 cells per process for 16k processes) and 100

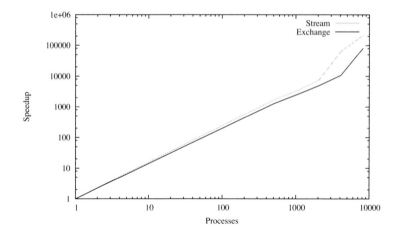

Figure 5. Investigation of strong scaling for both the halo exchange and the stream communication patterns using a problem size that just fits into the memory accessible by one process on ARCHER. Each data value is the average of 10 timed batches of 100,000 iterations divided by 10 to aid comparison by estimating times for batches of 10,000 iterations. Error bars showing the standard error of the sample mean are present but too small to be visible.

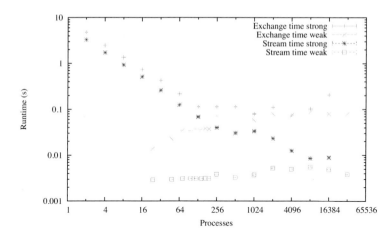

Figure 6. Investigation of strong and weak scaling for both the halo exchange and the stream communication patterns using a small problem size. The problem size for the strong scaling experiments is 100*16k cells in total for all tests. The problem size for the weak scaling experiments is 100 cells per process for all tests. Each data value is the average of 10 timed batches of 10,000 iterations (for strong scaling) or 1,000,000 iterations (for weak scaling). The times for weak scaling values are divided by 100 to aid comparison by estimating times for batches of 10,000 iterations. Error bars showing the standard error of the sample mean are present but too small to be visible.

cells per process for all the weak scaling tests. The very small problem sizes were chosen as an attempt to simulate part of a job where a larger problem size is scaled to many more processes. Both codes strong scale well from 2 processes to 128 processes with the streaming code slightly faster than the exchange code. However, with 256 processes or more, the exchange code stops strong scaling but the streaming code continues to strong scale well up to 16k processes. The weak scaling data for the stream code shows very consistent times up to 128 processes and a small variability for 256 or more processes. The exchange code shows poor weak scaling up to 128 processes but consistent times for 256 or more processes. The stream code is faster for all comparable data points; at 16k processes it is over 10x faster than the exchange code.

4. Conclusions and future work

We propose a new parallelisation technique that will be relevant to many HPC applications. Our preliminary findings indicate that it is likely to provide significant performance improvements for applications that currently use the halo exchange communication pattern. This new communication pattern should allow many applications to increase in scale without the need for improved hardware, as well as alleviating communications bottlenecks on larger systems. This new technique should be able to reduce the effect of system noise on domain decomposition codes and allow the linear algebra computations that underpin most scientific programming to scale efficiently beyond the limitations of the popular halo exchange technique. We believe, therefore, that this stream communication pattern warrants further research and we set out below our intended research topics.

The stream communication pattern must be extended to multi-dimensional domain decomposition, i.e. at least 2D, and the efficacy of higher dimensional decompositions should also be investigated. The 2D case could be treated as two 1D cases perpendicular to each other, one that defined its cells to be rows of data and the other that defines its cells to be columns of data. Each process could calculate a square-based pyramid of data without needing communication, then shift a triangular face of data leftwards around a left-right ring (exactly as the 1D case presented here), calculate a tetrahedron of data to fill in the gap between it and its rightwards neighbour process, then shift a parallelogram shaped face of data downwards around a down-up ring (another 1D case), and finally calculate the missing data needed to fill in the trough between it and the upwards neighbour process. The complexities and opportunities for optimisation have not yet been fully explored.

Both applications could be modified to inject simulated load-imbalance and system noise at runtime. Load-imbalance could be simulated by forcing one or more processes to re-calculate data by performing some, or all, cell updates more than once. If no kernel-level noise injection option is available on a particular test system, noise can instead be simulated with additional user processes running on the same CPU cores as the main application. The noise processes use an interrupt-driven timer to alternate between busy-wait for a short time period and idle-sleep for a longer time period, resulting in a customisable noise overhead, e.g. 2.5%, and a controllable noise signature, e.g. 2.5 milliseconds at 10Hz or 25 microseconds at 1000Hz (as used in [2]).

A stream is a well-defined, self-contained concept that can be implemented in many different ways. This work implements streams using MPI point-to-point routines because this is convenient and portable. An implementation of streams using single-sided communication with notified access semantics, e.g. via DMAPP or GPI-2, may perform better due to more appropriate synchronisation semantics and elimination of the MPI point-to-point message matching logic, which is unnecessary for this situation.

A theoretical performance model would support the design decisions and direct the potential optimisations both for implementations of the stream concept and for expressions of the streaming communication pattern. We plan to publish our theoretical model in a future paper.

There is currently no concept of stream in the MPI Standard. Although, as we have shown, a stream can be implemented using existing MPI routines, there are advantages and disadvantages to adding "MPI Stream" to the MPI Standard. Advantages include the potential for lower software overhead, more efficient resource usage, and avoidance of full point-to-point matching for each unit of transmitted data. Disadvantages include increased complexity of the MPI Standard and additional implementation effort for MPI library writers.

References

[1] C. L. Lawson, R. J. Hanson, D. R. Kincaid, and F. T. Krogh. Basic linear algebra subprograms for fortran usage. *ACM Trans. Math. Softw.*, 5(3):308–323, September 1979.

[2] An updated set of basic linear algebra subprograms (blas). *ACM Trans. Math. Softw.*, 28(2):135–151, June 2002.

[3] J. J. Dongarra, Jeremy Du Croz, Sven Hammarling, and I. S. Duff. A set of level 3 basic linear algebra subprograms. *ACM Trans. Math. Softw.*, 16(1):1–17, March 1990.

[4] Jack Dongarra. Performance of various computers using standard linear equations software.

[5] E. Anderson, Z. Bai, C. Bischof, S. Blackford, J. Demmel, J. Dongarra, J. Du Croz, A. Greenbaum, S. Hammarling, A. McKenney, and D. Sorensen. *LAPACK Users' Guide*. Society for Industrial and Applied Mathematics, Philadelphia, PA, third edition, 1999.

[6] Satish Balay, Shrirang Abhyankar, Mark F. Adams, Jed Brown, Peter Brune, Kris Buschelman, Lisandro Dalcin, Victor Eijkhout, William D. Gropp, Dinesh Kaushik, Matthew G. Knepley, Lois Curfman McInnes, Karl Rupp, Barry F. Smith, Stefano Zampini, and Hong Zhang. PETSc Web page. http://www.mcs.anl.gov/petsc, 2015.

[7] The top 500 supercomputer sites. Top500.org. http://www.top500.org.

[8] J Dongarra. High performance conjugate gradients benchmark. http://www.hpcg-benchmark.org/.

[9] Leslie G. Valiant. A bridging model for parallel computation. *Communications of the ACM*, 33(8):103–111, August 1990.

[10] Kurt B. Ferreira, Patrick G. Bridges, Ron Brightwell, and Kevin T. Pedretti. The impact of system design parameters on application noise sensitivity. *Cluster Computing*, 16(1):117–129, 2013.

[11] Kurt B. Ferreira, Patrick G. Bridges, and Ron Brightwell. Characterizing application sensitivity to os interference using kernel-level noise injection. In *SC*, page 19. IEEE/ACM, 2008.

[12] Martin J. Gander and Stefan Vandewalle. Analysis of the parareal time-parallel time-integration method. *SIAM J. Scientific Computing*, 29(2):556–578, 2007.

[13] Sun-Yuan Kung. On supercomputing with systolic/wavefront array processors. *Proceedings of the IEEE*, 72(7):867–884, Jul 1984.

[14] Antoniu Pop and Albert Cohen. A stream-computing extension to openmp. In Manolis Katevenis, Margaret Martonosi, Christos Kozyrakis, and Olivier Temam, editors, *HiPEAC*, pages 5–14. ACM, 2011.

[15] Maged M. Michael and Michael L. Scott. Simple, fast, and practical non-blocking and blocking concurrent queue algorithms. In James E. Burns and Yoram Moses, editors, *PODC*, pages 267–275. ACM, 1996.

[16] Edya Ladan-Mozes and Nir Shavit. An optimistic approach to lock-free fifo queues. *Distributed Computing*, 20(5):323–341, 2008.

[17] Roberto Belli and Torsten Hoefler. Notified access: Extending remote memory access programming models for producer-consumer synchronization. In *IPDPS*, pages 871–881. IEEE Computer Society, 2015.

Parallel Computing: On the Road to Exascale
G.R. Joubert et al. (Eds.)
IOS Press, 2016
doi:10.3233/978-1-61499-621-7-317

An Embedded C++ Domain-Specific Language for Stream Parallelism

Dalvan Griebler [a,b], Marco Danelutto [b], Massimo Torquati [b], Luiz Gustavo Fernandes [a]

[a] *Faculty of Informatics, Computer Science Graduate Program,*
Pontifical Catholic University of Rio Grande do Sul, Porto Alegre, Brazil
[b] *Computer Science Department, University of Pisa, Italy*

Abstract. This paper proposes a new C++ embedded Domain-Specific Language (DSL) for expressing stream parallelism by using standard C++11 attributes annotations. The main goal is to introduce high-level parallel abstractions for developing stream based parallel programs as well as reducing sequential source code rewriting. We demonstrated that by using a small set of attributes it is possible to produce different parallel versions depending on the way the source code is annotated. The performances of the parallel code produced are comparable with those obtained by manual parallelization.

Keywords. Parallel Programming, Domain-Specific Language, Stream Parallelism, Multi-Core, Parallel Patterns, C++11 Attributes.

Introduction

Stream processing is used in many domains for solving problems such as image, data, and network processing. Almost all of these algorithms have the same pattern of behavior: they process continuous input and produce continuous output [1]. Moreover, stream-based applications require high throughput and low latency for real-time data analysis, quality of image processing, and efficient network traffic.

To achieve high-performance in streaming applications on multi-core architectures, developers have to deal with low-level parallel programming for taking advantage of the platform features. This can be a complex and time consuming task for software engineers that are not familiar with fine tuning and optimization of parallel code.

Our primary design goal is to allow C++ developers to express stream parallelism by using the standard syntax grammar of the host language. Secondly, we aim to enable minimal sequential code rewriting thus reducing the efforts needed to program the parallel application. Additionally, we aim to provide enough flexibility for annotating the C++ sequential code in different ways. The objective is to quickly obtain several different parallel versions to perform fast parallel code prototyping.

This research builds on DSL-POPP [2,3]. It is a Domain-Specific Language (DSL) designed for pattern-oriented parallel programming aimed at providing suitable building blocks (that are filled with sequential C code), and simplifying the implementation of Master/Slave and Pipeline patterns on shared memory systems. Its interface relies on the availability of a set of user mumble and intrusive annotations, parsed and processed by a dedicated compiler. This paper presents a new DSL to address limitations imposed by the DSL-POPP's interface when expressing stream parallelism, parallel code generation, and different domain design goals.

Due to sustained contact with the REPARA project[1] team during the development of our current research, we have integrated the REPARA principles with those developed in DSL-POPP. We preserve the DSL-POPP principles of reducing significant sequential code rewriting by annotating the code. We have adopted the REPARA annotation mechanisms that allow us to be fully compliant with the standard C++11 language features (the host language syntax is embedded in the DSL) and reuse some techniques (like the GCC plugins to register custom attributes) to avoid rebuilding existing compiler tools. While DSL-POPP annotations are designed for novice parallel programming developers, REPARA's annotations are intermediate attribute annotations for parallelizing sequential code which are not directly exposed to end users [4], instead they are automatically inserted by appropriate tools. The main contributions of this paper are as follows:

- A domain-specific language for expressing stateless stream parallelism.
- An annotation-based programing interface that preserves the semantics of DSL-POPP's principles and adopts REPARA's C++ attribute style, avoiding significant code rewriting in sequential programs.

The paper is organized as follows. Section 1 highlights the contributions in comparison with the related work. Sec. 2 presents the proposed attributes for stream parallelism. Sec. 3 demonstrates the design implementation to introduce the proposed C++ attributes and parallel code transformation. Sec. 4 describes how to use our DSL in two applications as well as performance experiments. Finally, Sec. 5 discuss our paper contributions and future works.

1. Related Work

Standard parallel programming interfaces for High Performance Computing (HPC) such as OpenMP [5] and Cilk [6] were not designed for stream parallelism. Also, they are not provided by C++11 standard host language syntax, requiring the user to learn a new syntax. TBB [7] and FastFlow [8] are frameworks for structured parallel programming using algorithmic skeletons. They both preserve the host language syntax but require many changes in the source code to express parallelism. Finally, StreamIt[2] is a language specifically designed for stream parallelism [9]. To use it, C++ developers have to rewrite the source code, learn a new syntax and programming language. In contrast to the previously mentioned frameworks, our DSL only requires developers to find the stream parallelism regions and annotate them with the appropriate attributes. In addition, it also avoids rewriting the source code (like in FastFlow and TBB) and learning of a non-standard C++ syntax (like in Cilk and OpenMP).

Even though OpenMP and Cilk are designed to exploit loop-based parallelism, recent research ([10] and [11]) have tried to use the concept of stream parallelism in their interfaces. Authors of [10] proposed to add input and output pragma primitives for OpenMP tasks, which is like describing the data-flow graph in a sequential code and has now been adopted by the OpenMP-4.0. On the other hand, researchers proposed to in-

---

[1] http://parrot.arcos.inf.uc3m.es/wordpress/
[2] http://groups.csail.mit.edu/cag/streamit

clude pipeline parallelism using Cilk based implementation [11]. In their concept, "while loops" are used to implement pipelines assisted by language extension keywords. Even if both initiatives target stream parallelism, the drawback of these solutions remain source code rewriting, low-level parallel programming, and non-standard C++ programming. Building on these approaches is against our design goals. However, all related work offers potential environments to implement the parallel code for our domain-specific language. We have chosen FastFlow because it provides suitable building blocks for pipeline and farm skeletons, and it is efficient enough on multi-core architectures due to its lock-free implementation [12,13].

2. Attributes for Stream Parallelism

This section introduces the domain-specific language keywords to meet the design goals. We do not change the standard C++ attributes' syntax [14] for annotating codes. However, we determine how the attributes should be declared, ensuring the correct parallel code transformation. Table 1 describes the proposed keywords. All attributes are part of the stream parallelism namespace (named as `spar`), and they are placed inside of double brackets (`[[attr-list]]`). The first one on the list must be the attribute identifier (ID), which is one of the two first attributes from Table 1.

Attributes	Description
`ToStream()`	it annotates a loop or block for implementing a stream parallelism region
`Stage()`	it annotates a potential block stages that computes the stream inside of `ToStream`
`Input()`	used to indicate input streams for the ID attributes
`Output()`	used to indicate output streams for the ID attributes
`Replicate()`	it is an auxiliary attribute to indicate a stage replication

Table 1. The generalized C++ attributes for the domain-specific language.

As described in the introduction, almost all streaming applications have the same pattern of behavior when processing input and output streams. Therefore, we provide two keywords (`Input()` and `Output()`), which are optional arguments for the ID attributes. Basically, they are used to indicate the input and output stream that can be any variable's data type used as an argument. Consequently, a stream declaration in our context is viewed as singular or a list of the same or different data types. Also, we provide the auxiliary replicate attribute (`Replicate()`), which is associated with a stage block (`Stage()`). When necessary, this attribute will allow programmers to build non-linear computations for scaling the performance, where its argument is a constant value delimiting the number of workers for the stage.

```
1  auto b;
2  [[ToStream(Input(b))]] loop(...){
3    b = read(b);
4    [[Stage(Input(b),Output(b))]]
5    { b = proc(b); }
6    [[Stage(Input(b))]]
7    { b = write(b); }
8  }
```

Listing 1 Bounded/Unbounded streams in loops.

```
1  [[ToStream(Input(u))]]{
2    u = read(u);
3    [[Stage(Input(u),Output(u)),Replicate(N)]]
4    { u = proc(u); }
5    [[Stage(Input(u))]]
6    { u = write(u); }
7  }
```

Listing 2 Unbounded streams with replication.

A stream flow can be bound or unbound and can come from internal or external sources. The possibility of annotating loops is advantageous because the block declaration can be reused and the end of the stream can be determined based on the loop statement. However, the end of the stream may never be known or difficult to handle when coming from external sources. In this case, it is possible to annotate the parallel region as a code block, where the end of the stream has to be programed inside the `ToStream` by using a break. Listing 1 and 2 illustrate the usage of all attributes for two scenarios.

Using the `ToStream()` is like saying: *"execute this block of code for each instance of the input"*. Once it is declared, at least one stage block has to be annotated inside of its declaration. Grammar 1 describes the semantic rules for annotating the code. We do not allow any intermediary code between stage blocks. This limitation is needed to ensure correct code transformation and maintain the source code semantics. `ToStream()` structure declaration nesting is not allowed in the current implementation.

⟨*tostream*⟩ ::= '[[' 'ToStream' '('[',']|⟨*input*⟩|[',']|⟨*output*⟩|[',']')' ']]' [⟨*loop-stmt*⟩] '{' {⟨*cmds*⟩}* {⟨*stage*⟩}+ {⟨*cmds*⟩}* '}'
        ⟨*stage*⟩ ::= '[[' 'Stage' '('[',']|⟨*input*⟩|[',']|⟨*output*⟩|[',']')' [',' ⟨*replicate*⟩] ']]' [⟨*loop-stmt*⟩] '{' {⟨*cmds*⟩}* '}'
        ⟨*input*⟩ ::= 'Input' '(' ⟨*args*⟩ ')'
        ⟨*output*⟩ ::= 'Output' '(' ⟨*args*⟩ ')'
        ⟨*replicate*⟩ ::= 'Replicate' '(' ⟨*consts*⟩ ')'

Grammar 1: DSL's grammar using EBNF notation.

Once the stream parallel region is known, programmers have to identify the stream consuming activities and their input and output dependency for annotating one or more `Stage()` blocks. This activity can analyze network packets, apply a filter over images/videos, discover relevant information in a data set, among other kinds of computations. Depending on the application, it is possible to have a sequence of activities computing over the same stream and data dependent on the result of the previous activity. This is the same as the pipeline parallel pattern, which is composed of stages. Note that we are not able to manage statefull pipeline parallelism implementation. Therefore, when adding the replicate attribute to the stage block, our DSL assumes that the computations inside the stage can compute independently. It is up to the user to deal with the statefull pipeline activities, since this can not always be avoided [15].

3. Implementation

This section describes the design implementation of the proposed attributes using the GCC plugins technique and some parallel code transformation rules.

3.1. Introducing C++ Attributes with GCC plugin technique

C++ attributes originated from GNU C attributes (`__attribute__((<name>))`). Since C++11 up to the most recent version, a new way to annotate was included in the standard C++ language (`[[attr-list]]`) [14,16]. The syntax of the attributes was improved as well as the interface to support C++ features. A great advantage over the pragma-based annotation is the possibility of declaring almost everywhere in a program. However, each attribute implementation will determine where it can be annotated (*e.g.*, types, classes, code blocks, etc.). Also, the compiler is able to fully recognize the new standard mechanism, even if an attribute is not implemented by the language. This means that when adding customized attributes in the source code, the compiler attaches them in the Abstract Syntax Tree (AST) and simply ignores them in the code generation.

There are different techniques for taking advantage of this annotation mechanism such as adapting the source code of the GCC compiler, using an external parser, and creating a plugin. We propose using GCC plugins[3] because it avoids changing the internal structure of the compiler and gives us access to AST for parsing the arguments and source code tree. Therefore, it is possible to intercept the compiler during the program compilation for performing source-to-source parallel code generation, based on the the transformation rules that will be present in the next section.

3.2. Parallel Code Transformation

Our DSL provides high-level abstractions that are simple for the user, but have a complex system design for efficient code transformation. With only five keywords, we aim to provide several ways for annotating code to introduce stream parallelism without significant source code changes, which will be demonstrated in the experiment section (Section 4). To address this flexibility in code transformation, the system integrates algorithm skeleton principles such as the interacting and nesting mode [17]. These are mapped by the annotation of the computation activities (identify by using the `ToStream` and Stage ID attributes), spatial constrains (identify by using input and output attributes), temporal constrains (defined by the order of the declarations and their spatial constrains), and interaction (based on the users' stream dependency specification and using lock-free queues of FastFlow[4] runtime to communicate). Finally, we implement persistent nesting when the replicate attribute is declared in a stage activity.

We use a functional notation for representing our transformation rules, dividing in two phases: first we built our skeleton tree and after the FastFlow ones. S is a sequential code block and R is a replication function used to replicate S for a number of times. In FastFlow, we used their functional skeleton notation that includes Farm and Pipeline patterns [13]. Therefore, S can be a `ToStream` or `Stage` block type, where our syntax allows only add `Replicate` on the stages. It means that R only calls S for a stage type.

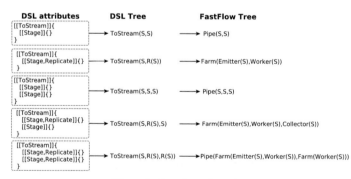

Figure 1. Transformation rules.

Figure 1 presents the main transformation rules. The data graph dependency is build when analysing the input and output so that the communication is implement. Note that in our stream parallelism region, the first block always will be no more than S, and

---

[3] https://gcc.gnu.org/onlinedocs/gccint/Plugins.html
[4] http://mc-fastflow.sourceforge.net/

everything that is left out the stage is part of the `ToStream` *S*. Consequently, it is also responsible for producing and coordinate the stream.

Figure 2 sketches the pseudo parallel code transformation to give an overview of the transformation sequence. The source code example is implemented in a simple pipeline, whereas in our interface the first stage is always the `ToStream` annotation, and the subsequent `Stage` annotations follow. Therefore, our example is a pipeline with three stages. To transform this source into a parallel FastFlow code, first we analyze all data dependencies declared as input and output attributes. Because AST access is possible, we can recognize the data types to create a single stream "struct" (label 1), which is the communication channel between stages. Secondly, we transformed the annotated blocks in stages by using the FastFlow building block interface (labels 2, 3, and 4). Lastly, we built the pipeline to run accordingly (label 5).

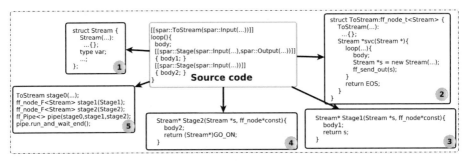

Figure 2. Example of the peseudo parallel code transformation using FastFlow runtime.

Declaring the `Replicate` for a `Stage` attribute, means that this stage will replicate as many times as specified using the FastFlow farm skeleton. Since the computation is structured, the plugin only needs to change the code for the last step (label 5). Although we did not illustrate all of the code in detail, this example also shows why it is important for us to use FastFlow for our runtime instead of other libraries in the code transformation. In addition, it avoids having to rebuild the synchronization and communication that FastFlow has already implemented on top of POSIX Threads.

4. Experiments

This section presents the DSL usage on an image processing and a numerical application. Whenever possible, we compare the performance of the transformed code with an equivalent code annotated with OpenMP pragmas, which is the reference standard for parallel programming on multi-core platforms. We reported the best execution time obtained for each tests. The performance value reported is the average value obtained over 40 runs. We used a dual-socket NUMA Intel multi-core Xeon E5-2695 Ivy Bridge micro-architecture running at 2.40GHz featuring 24 cores (12+12) each with 2-way Hyperthreading. Each core had 32KB L1 and 256KB L2 private, and 30MB L3 shared. The operating system was Linux 2.6.32 x86_64 shipped with CentOS 6.5. We compiled our tests using GNU GCC 4.9.2 with the –O3 flag. Since we are in the process of completing the implementation of the tools, results of the parallel code generation are inserted manually based on the rules of Section 3.2.

4.1. Sobel Application

This program applies the Sobel filter over bitmap images contained in a directory and writes the filtered images in a separate directory. Looking at Listing 3 and 4, the stream computation starts with the "while loop", where it is getting the file's information from the directory. Inside the loop, each file is preprocessed to get its name and extension. If it is a bitmap file, image's information is stored (e.g., image size, height, and width), as well as its buffers. Only after this has been completed, the program reads the image bytes from the disk to apply the filter. When this phase is concluded, the program writes the image to the disk. Finally (outside the loop), the program prints how many images were filter and how many files were ignored (non bitmap files).

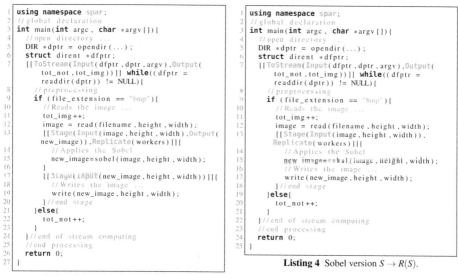

Listing 3 Sobel version $S \rightarrow R(S) \rightarrow S$.

Listing 4 Sobel version $S \rightarrow R(S)$.

Using the proposed attributes, different ways for annotating this application are possible. We can observe that there are three potential stages (read, filter, and write). Therefore, the first strategy is to annotate the stage as presented in Listing 3, introducing the ToStream block in order to read images from the disk. After this, we can replicate the filtering phase because it is a costly computation and each image can be computed in parallel. The last stage just writes the images on the disk. Note that it is very important that input and output dependencies are properly declared[5]. This annotated code will be transformed as sketched in the worker model of Figure 3(a) (label $[S \rightarrow R(S) \rightarrow S]$).

It is up to the developer to choose the best code annotation schema for scaling performance. However, the expressiveness of our model allows developers to perform minimal changes on the sequential code with different annotation scheme and degree of parallelism. For example, in order to merge the two stages, it is sufficient to comment out lines 16 and 17 of Listing 3. Consequently, we have the code of Listing 4, producing the worker model sketched in Figure 3(a) (label $[S \rightarrow R(S)]$). Moreover, in respect to the first version of this application (Listing 3), we can produce a different worker model labelled as $S \rightarrow R(S) \rightarrow R(S)]$ (Figure 3(a)) by only adding the replicate attribute in the last stage.

---

[5]This is because our system assumes that the user's specification is correct. Wrong specifications may produce non-sequential code equivalence.

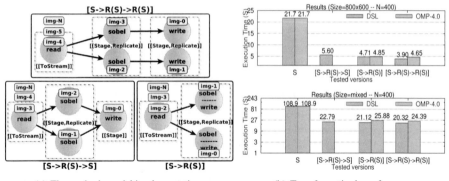

(a) The worker's model implementation.   (b) Transformation's performance.

Figure 3. Implementation of the sobel application.

OpenMP-4.0 provides task parallelism pragma annotations for implementing computations that are not "for loop-based". However, non-linear pipelines such as the solution of the worker model of Figure 3(a) (label $[S \rightarrow R(S) \rightarrow S]$) can not be implemented (unless the original code is properly changed). This is because once a parallel region is annotated, all threads will go through the entire code block. Recently, OpenMP-4.0 added the new "depend" clauses, where the user can specify dependencies of the task group. This allows us to implement a comparable implementation of the $[S \rightarrow R(S) \rightarrow S]$ version. Yet, the worker model behavior is different. While in our solution each stage is always processing its input stream, in OpenMP, the end of each task region is a barrier for the group of tasks and all threads go through each phase. Furthermore, in both OpenMP implementations ($S \rightarrow R(S) \rightarrow R(S)$ and $S \rightarrow R(S)$) it was necessary to annotate two critical sections, where the program sums the total of the images read and ignored. On the other hand, using our solution this may be avoided.

We executed two experiments for this application. The graph on top of Figure 3(b) uses a balanced workload that has 400 images with the same size and 40 files that are not bitmap extensions. On the other hand, the graph at the bottom uses an unbalanced workload. As can be observed, our solution achieves the best executions times.

4.2. Prime Numbers Application

This application is the naïve algorithm for finding primer numbers. Basically, our implementation receives a number as input and checks by simply dividing it, and adding up every prime that is found. Listing 5 and 6 demonstrate the two ways for introducing stream parallelism for this application by using our DSL. In Listing 5 we annotate as stage the part of number checking using the auxiliary replicate attribute. A critical point in this program is the sum of the prime number already found (line 16). For this version we let the ToStream block perform this operation because it is sequentially executed. Another key point is to declare the output dependency so that when a number is checked it will be sent back.

In the second version we simply annotated the sum operation as a normal stage (Listing 6 on line 16). Consequently, we can accelerate our program because the stream flowed naturally and the ToStream does not pay with extra control of the multiple inputs. This communication difference can be visualized in Figure 4(a). In OpenMP version, the only way for implementing this application was using the "parallel for" annotation, and specifying the following clauses: reduction(+:total), schedule(auto), shared(n), and num_threads(workers).

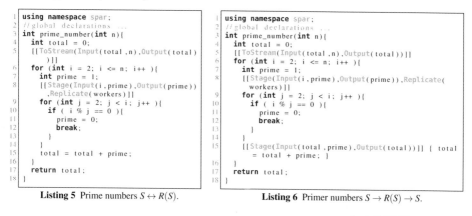

Listing 5 Prime numbers $S \leftrightarrow R(S)$.   **Listing 6** Primer numbers $S \to R(S) \to S$.

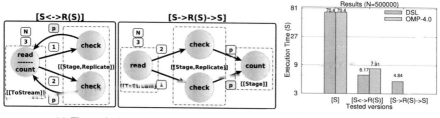

(a) The worker's model implementation.   (b) Transformation's performance.

Figure 4. Implementation of the primer numbers application.

The results of the experiments are sketched in the graph of Figure 4(b). Our workload was to find the prime numbers in [1:500000]. As can be observed, we achieved better execution times than OpenMP in the $[S \leftrightarrow R(S)]$ version and even better results in the $[S \to R(S) \to S]$ transformation.

5. Conclusions

In this paper we presented a new embedded DSL for expressing simple stream-based parallelism. We used C++11 attributes as annotation mechanism and proposed GCC plugins technique for their implementation. We achieved all desired goals, demonstrating through simple examples that our standard annotation-based interface is flexible enough by only providing five attributes.

In the experiment section, the proposed DSL demonstrated good flexibility by supporting different ways for annotating programs to obtain different stream parallel implementations of the same application. The experiments shown efficient parallel code transformations by using FastFlow as runtime framework. The obtained performance are comparable with those obtained by parallelizing the code (when possible) using OpenMP. The DSL interface proposed increased code productivity (measured by SLOCCount[6])

---

[6]http://www.dwheeler.com/sloccount/

when compared directly with the FastFlow code: by 23.4% for the sobel application and by 27.5% for the prime number application. As a future work, we plan to implement automatic source-to-source transformation and to perform more experiments to evaluate our DSL with other stream-based applications.

Acknowledgements. This work has been partially supported by FAPERGS, CAPES, FACIN (Faculty of Informatics of PUCRS), and EU projects REPARA (No. 609666) and RePhrase (No. 644235).

References

[1]   Henrique C. M. Andrade, Bugra Gedik, and Deepak S. Turaga. *Fundamentals of Stream Processing*. Cambridge University Press, New York, USA, 2014.

[2]   Dalvan Griebler and Luiz G. Fernandes. Towards a Domain-Specific Language for Patterns-Oriented Parallel Programming. In *Programming Languages - 17th Brazilian Symposium - SBLP*, volume 8129 of *LNCS*, pages 105–119, Brasilia, Brazil, October 2013. Springer.

[3]   Dalvan Griebler, Daniel Adornes, and Luiz G. Fernandes. Performance and Usability Evaluation of a Pattern-Oriented Parallel Programming Interface for Multi-Core Architectures. In *International Conference on Software Engineering & Knowledge Engineering*, pages 25–30, Canada, July 2014. SEKE.

[4]   REPARA Project. D6.2: Dynamic Runtimes for Heterogeneous Platforms. Technical report, University of Pisa, Pisa, Italy, November 2014.

[5]   Barbara Chapman, Gabriele Jost, and Ruud van der Pas. *Using OpenMP: Portable Shared Memory Parallel Programming (Scientific and Engineering Computation)*. MIT Press, London, UK, 2007.

[6]   Robert D. Blumofe, Christopher F. Joerg, Bradley C. Kuszmaul, Charles E. Leiserson, Keith H. Randall, and Yuli Zhou. Cilk: An Efficient Multithreaded Runtime System. In *Symposium on Principles and Practice of Parallel Programming*, volume 30 of *PPOPP '95*, pages 207–216, USA, August 1995. ACM.

[7]   James Reinders. *Intel Threading Building Blocks*. O'Reilly, Sebastopol, CA, USA, 2007.

[8]   Marco Aldinucci, Sonia Campa, Peter Kilpatrick, and Massimo Torquati. Structured Data Access Annotations for Massively Parallel Computations. In *Euro-Par 2012: Parallel Processing Workshops*, volume 7640 of *LNCS*, pages 381–390, Greece, August 2012. Springer.

[9]   William Thies, Michal Karczmarek, and Saman P. Amarasinghe. StreamIt: A Language for Streaming Applications. In *Proceedings of the 11th International Conference on Compiler Construction*, CC '02, pages 179–196, Grenoble, France, April 2002. Springer-Verlag.

[10] Antoniu Pop and Albert Cohen. A Stream-Computing Extension to OpenMP. In *Proceedings of the 6th International Conference on High Performance and Embedded Architectures and Compilers*, HiPEAC '11, pages 5–14, Heraklion, Greece, January 2011. ACM.

[11] I-Ting Angelina Lee, Charles E. Leiserson, Tao B. Schardl, Jim Sukha, and Zhunping Zhang. On-the-fly Pipeline Parallelism. In *ACM Symposium on Parallelism in Algorithms and Architectures*, SPAA '13, pages 140–151, Portland, Oregon, USA, June 2013. ACM.

[12] Marco Aldinucci, Marco Danelutto, Peter Kilpatrick, Massimiliano Meneghin, and Massimo Torquati. An Efficient Unbounded Lock-Free Queue for Multi-core Systems. In *Euro-Par 2012 Parallel Processing*, volume 7484 of *LNCS*, pages 662–673, Greece, August 2012. Springer.

[13] Marco Aldinucci, Sonia Campa, Fabio Tordini, Massimo Torquati, and Peter Kilpatrick. An Abstract Annotation Model for Skeletons. In *Formal Methods for Components and Objects*, volume 7542 of *Lecture Notes in Computer Science*, pages 257–276, Turin, Italy, October 2011. Springer Berlin Heidelberg.

[14] Jens Maurer and Michael Wong. Towards Support for Attributes in C++ (Revision 6). Technical report, The C++ Standards Committee, September 2008.

[15] William Thies and Saman Amarasinghe. An Empirical Characterization of Stream Programs and Its Implications for Language and Compiler Design. In *International Conference on Parallel Architectures and Compilation Techniques*, PACT '10, pages 365–376, Austria, September 2010. ACM.

[16] ISO/IEC. Information Technology - Programming Languages - C++. Technical report, International Standard, Geneva, Switzerland, August 2011.

[17] Anne Benoit and Murray Cole. Two Fundamental Concepts in Skeletal Parallel Programming. In *International Conference on Computational Science (ICCS)*, volume 3515 of *LNCS*, pages 764–771, USA, May 2005. Springer.

Parallel Computing: On the Road to Exascale
G.R. Joubert et al. (Eds.)
IOS Press, 2016
© 2016 The authors and IOS Press. All rights reserved.
doi:10.3233/978-1-61499-621-7-327

Pipeline Template for Streaming Applications on Heterogeneous Chips

Andrés RODRÍGUEZ [a], Angeles NAVARRO [a], Rafael ASENJO [a,1],
Francisco CORBERA [a], Antonio VILCHES [a], and María GARZARÁN [b]

[a] *Universidad de Málaga, Andalucía Tech, Spain*
[b] *University of Illinois at Urbana-Champaign, USA*

Abstract. We address the problem of providing support for executing single streaming applications implemented as a pipeline of stages that run on heterogeneous chips comprised of several cores and one on-chip GPU. In this paper, we mainly focus on the API that allows the user to specify the type of parallelism exploited by each pipeline stage running on the multicore CPU, the mapping of the pipeline stages to the devices (GPU or CPU), and the number of active threads. We use a real streaming application as a case of study to illustrate the experimental results that can be obtained with this API. With this example, we evaluate how the different parameter values affect the performance and energy efficiency of a heterogenous on-chip processor (Exynos 5 Octa) that has three different computational cores: a GPU, an ARM Cortex-A15 quad-core, and an ARM Cortex-A7 quad-core.

Keywords. Parallel Pipeline, Heterogenous chips, On-chip GPU, Performance-Energy efficiency

Introduction

Streaming applications are very common in today's computing systems, in particular mobile devices [1] where heterogeneous chips (comprising several cores and a GPU) are the dominant platforms. Our approach extends the parallel pipeline template provided in TBB [2] to make the most out of these heterogeneous on-chip architectures.

As study case to demonstrate the use of our template, we introduce ViVid[2], an application that implements an object (e.g., face) detection algorithm [3] using a "sliding window object detection" approach [4]. ViVid consists of 5 pipeline stages as we depict in Fig. 1. The first and the last one are the Input and Output stages (serial), whereas the three middle stages are parallel (stateless[3]) stages.

There is a certain degree of leeway when it comes to map applications like ViVid onto a heterogeneous architecture. For instance, one needs to consider the granularity or number of items that should be simultaneously processed on each

---

[1]Corresponding Author: E.T.S.I. Informática. Complejo Tecnológico, E-29071 Málaga, Spain; E-mail: asenjo@uma.es

[2]http://www.github.com/mertdikmen/vivid

[3]A stage is parallel or stateless when the computation of an item on a stage does not depend on other items.

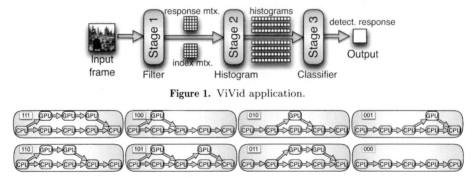

Figure 1. ViVid application.

Figure 2. All possible mappings of stages to GPU and/or CPU for ViVid.

stage, the device where each stage should be mapped, and the number of active CPU cores that minimize the execution time, the energy consumption, or both (depending on the metric of interest). The *granularity* determines the level at which the parallelism is exploited on the CPU. In our approach, the user can specify two levels of granularity: Coarse Grain (CG) and Medium Grain (MG). If different items can be processed simultaneously on the same stateless stage on the CPU, then CG granularity can be exploited. On the other hand, if the stage exhibits nested parallelism (which can be exploited by using OpenCL, OpenMP or TBB), then a single item can be processed in parallel by several cores on the CPU, and in that case MG granularity is exploited. In our approach, CG granularity implies as many items in flight as number of threads the user sets, while MG granularity entails two items in flight (i.e., simultaneously traversing the pipeline) at most: one being processed on the GPU device and another one processed in parallel on the multicore CPU.

The *pipeline mapping* determines the device where the different stages of the pipeline can execute. Fig. 2 graphically depicts the possible mappings for the three middle parallel stages of ViVid. Let's assume that a pipeline consists of S_1, S_2, ... S_n parallel stages. We use a n-tuple to specify all possible stage mappings to the GPU and the CPU devices: $\{m_1, m_2, ..., m_n\}$. The i-th element of the tuple, m_i, will specify if stage S_i can be mapped to the GPU and CPU, $(m_i = 1)$, or if it can be mapped only to the CPU $(m_i = 0)$. If $m_i = 1$, the item that enters stage S_i will check if the GPU is available, in which case it will execute on the GPU; otherwise, it will execute on the CPU. For instance, the ViVid examples of Fig. 2 correspond to the tuples (row major order): $\{1,1,1\}$, $\{1,0,0\}$, $\{0,1,0\}$, $\{0,0,1\}$, $\{1,1,0\}$, $\{1,0,1\}$, $\{0,1,1\}$, $\{0,0,0\}$. In our implementation, mapping $\{1,1,1\}$ represents a special case: if the GPU is available when a new item enters the pipeline, then all the stages that process it will be mapped to the GPU.

There are two main contributions in this paper. First, section 2 introduces the API of our framework, aimed at easing the implementation of an heterogeneous pipeline application while allowing the user to specify the parameters of interest: i) the granularity level at which the parallelism of each stage can be exploited (Coarse or Medium grain), ii) the mapping of the pipeline stages to the different devices; and iii) the number of threads to control the number of active computational cores. Second, in section 3 we present ViVid results when executing on a big.LITTLE heterogeneous on-chip architecture, analyzing how the granularity level, the mapping, and the number of active threads affects the performance and energy consumption of our study case.

1. Related work

One approach for coding streaming applications is to use a programming language with support for streams, such as StreamIt [5]. However, these languages do not provide support for heterogenous CPU-GPU executions. Concurrent execution on the CPU and GPU of the heterogenous platforms delivers higher performance than CPU-only or GPU-only executions [6], but programming frameworks that provide support for computing on a heterogeneous architecture such as Qilin [7], OmpSs [8] or StarPU [9] just consider performance when deciding task distribution among CPU cores and GPU accelerators. An additional difference between these related works and ours is that they mainly focus on data parallel patterns, while we focus on streaming applications. Moreover, we also study energy efficiency, and as we show in [10], we can consider energy in the scheduling decisions. FastFlow [11] provides a good framework for programming pipelines. Our proposal offers added values as the dynamic mapping of stages to processing devices takes into account not only performance but also energy efficiency or the data buffer self-management. Anyway, we could have used FastFlow instead of TBB as the base to implement our pipeline framework.

2. Programming interface for the pipeline template

In this section, we introduce the API of our pipeline library. It provides a programming environment for C++ that facilitates the configuration of a pipeline, hiding the underlying TBB implementation and automatically managing the necessary memory data management and transfers between devices.

Fig. 3 shows all the components involved in the pipeline operation and the software stack. The Item is the object that traverses the pipeline. It contains the references to the data buffers that the different processing stages of the pipeline use as input and output. To create a new pipeline instance, the user has to declare a new Item class (extended from a provided Item base class) that contains the references to data buffers used by the pipeline stages. For data buffer management, there is a data buffer class already defined, that hides all the important operations like allocation, deallocation, data movements, zero-copy buffer mappings, etc. The aim of this data buffer class is to offer an abstraction layer that automatically manages and makes data accessible to the device (CPU or GPU) where the item has to be processed.

The programmer can provide up to three different functions for every processing stage of the pipeline: one to implement the processing stage on the GPU device using OpenCL, a second one to implement the stage on a single CPU core (CG granularity), and the third one to implement the stage on multiple CPU cores (MG granularity). The implementations not provided will not be considered when searching for the best pipeline configuration.

The interface has four main components:

- Items: objects that traverse the pipeline carrying the data buffers.

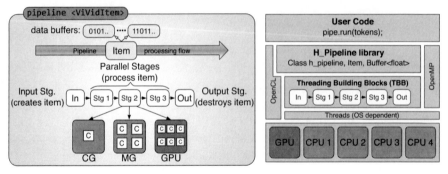

Figure 3. ViVid application and software stack.

- Pipelines: the pipeline itself composed of n stages. The pipelines can be configured statically by the user or run in an auto-configuration mode. This auto-configuration model uses an analytical model [10] to dynamically compute and use the best configuration.
- Stage functions: each processing stage needs to be implemented for CPU and/or GPU. The pipeline uses the appropriate function for each stage.
- Buffers: n-dimensional arrays that can be used both in the host code and in the OpenCL kernels.

Due to space constraints, we will only show here some details of the pipeline specification and usage. The interested reader can find more details in [12].

2.1. Item class

Fig. 4 shows a code snippet for the `Item` class declaration used in the ViVid pipeline. First, our pipeline interface is made available by including the `h_pipeline.h` header file (line 1). It also defines the `h_pipeline` namespace which contains all the classes of the interface. As previously mentioned, before creating the pipeline, the programmer must define an `Item` subclass (line 6). Objects of this class will traverse the stages of the pipeline. The item class must extend from `h_pipeline::Item` and declare as many `DataBuffers<T>` members as needed for the pipeline execution. The class constructor and destructor methods must hold the buffers creation and deletion, respectively. Alternatively and to avoid too many operations of buffer allocation/deallocation, a pool of buffers can be used. In that case, acquire and release methods can be invoked so that the same buffers are reused by different items. The Input and Output stages (i.e. the first and last serial stages of the pipeline, *In* and *Out*) automatically call the constructor and destructor of the `Item` class, respectively.

2.2. Pipeline

Fig. 5 shows a pipeline definition and usage example. After declaring the `ViVidItem` as shown in Fig. 4, we can create a new pipeline using that class (line 6) passing as constructors arguments the number of threads, `numThreads`, that will run the pipeline in parallel. In this study we set as maximun number of threads $nC + 1$, being nC the number of CPU cores. Notice also that the CPU (CG and MG granularity) and the GPU functions of the three stages for the ViVid example need to be set up before the pipeline can run (see lines 9

```
 1  #include "h_pipeline.h"          // Required classes defined here
 2
 3  /***********************************************************
 4   * 1.- ITEM Class (holds the data that traverse the pipeline stages)
 5   ***********************************************************/
 6  class ViVidItem : public h_pipeline::Item {
 7  public:
 8      //Buffer definitions
 9      DataBuffer<float> *frame;    // Input buffer
10      ...
11      DataBuffer<float> *out;   // Output buffer
12
13      //Constructor definition. Allocation or buffer acquire
14      ViVidItem() {
15          //Data Buffer allocation
16          ...
17      }
18      //Destructor definition. Deallocation or buffer release
19      ~ViVidItem() { ... }
20  };
```

Figure 4. Using the Item Class.

to 11). In case we want to run the pipeline using a static configuration, we use specific methods to configure some aspects of the pipeline, such as the stages that should map to the GPU or the granularity (MG or CG) that should be used on the CPU (line 14). In our example, in line 14, parameter $\{1,0,1\}$ represents the n-tuple defined in the Introduction, and the last argument, **true**, indicates that MG granularity will be exploited when an item is processed on the CPU.

Once the pipeline is configured for a static configuration, it can be run (line 15) by setting the maximum number of items that are allowed to be simultaneously traversing the pipeline. Another option to run the pipeline is to use the adaptive configuration mode (line 18) (see [10]). Under this mode, our framework dynamically finds the best configuration. In this case, the user has to select the optimization criterion (**THROUGHPUT, ENERGY, THROUGHPUT_ENERGY**) and the maximum overhead allowed due to the training step required when running in the adaptive mode explained in [10].

```
 1  /***********************************************
 2   * 2.- Pipeline declaration and usage
 3   ***********************************************/
 4  int main(int argc, char* argv[]){
 5      int numThreads = nC+1;    // number of threads = nC+1
 6      h_pipeline::pipeline<ViVidItem> pipe(numThreads);
 7
 8      // Set CG, MG and GPU functions for each stage
 9      pipe.add_stage(cg_f1, mg_f1, gpu_f1);
10      pipe.add_stage(cg_f2, mg_f2, gpu_f2);
11      pipe.add_stage(cg_f3, mg_f3, gpu_f3);
12
13      //Setting a static pipeline configuration: mapping '101' and MG
14      pipe.set_configuration({1,0,1}, true);
15      pipe.run(numTokens);   // maximum number of items in flight
16
17      //Dispatch of the adaptive configuration mode for the pipeline
18      //pipe.run(numTokens, ENERGY, maxoverhead);
19  }
```

Figure 5. Pipeline declaration and usage.

2.3. Pipeline stage functions

An important part of the pipeline definition is the configuration of the pipeline stages. In the interface, the **add_stage()** method (Fig 5, lines 9 to 11) is used

to add each one of the stages while identifying the possible functions that may
be called to process the items. Fig. 6 shows an example of these stage functions
definition.

```
 1  /*********************************************
 2   * 3.- Functions definition example
 3   *********************************************/
 4  // Example for filter 3 of ViVid
 5  void cg_f3(ViVidItem *item) // Coarse grain CPU version
 6  {
 7      float * out, cla, his;
 8      out = item->out->get_HOST_PTR(BUF_WRITE);    // get buffer on host for writing
 9      cla = item->cla->get_HOST_PTR(BUF_READ);     // get buffer on host for reading
10      his = item->his->get_HOST_PTR(BUF_READ);     // get buffer on host for reading
11      // do cpu things like  out[XXX] = his[XXX] + cla[XXX];
12  }
13  void mg_f3(ViVidItem *item) // Medium grain CPU version
14  {
15      float * out, cla, his;
16      out = item->out->get_HOST_PTR(BUF_WRITE);    // get buffer on host for writing
17      cla = item->cla->get_HOST_PTR(BUF_READ);     // get buffer on host for reading
18      his = item->his->get_HOST_PTR(BUF_READ);     // get buffer on host for reading
19
20      tbb::parallel_for( 0, aheight, 1, [&] (size_t i) {
21          // do cpu things like  out[i] = his[i] + cla[i];
22      });
23
24      // #pragma omp parallel for
25      // for (size_t i=0; i<aheight; i++) {
26          // do cpu things like  out[i] = his[i] + cla[i];
27      // }
28  }
29  void gpu_f3(ViVidItem *item)    // GPU OpenCL version
30  {
31      cl_mem out,cla,his;
32      out = item->out->get_CL_BUFFER(BUF_WRITE);   // get buffer on device for
                writing
33      cla = item->cla->get_CL_BUFFER(BUF_READ);    // get buffer on device for
                reading
34      his = item->his->get_CL_BUFFER(BUF_READ);    // get buffer on device for
                reading
35
36      // Setting kernel parameters
37      // Launching kernel
38      //...
39  }
```

Figure 6. Functions for pipeline stages operations (CG, MG, GPU).

The programmer can provide three different versions of the same function.
The pipeline will use the appropriate version of the function to map the stage to
one CPU core, several CPU cores, or the GPU device. Each function receives as
argument a pointer to the item to be processed. From such item we can obtain the
pointers to the input/output data buffers by using the method get_HOST_PTR()
to obtain a host pointer, or get_CL_BUFFER() to obtain an OpenCL buffer object usable at the GPU device. In both cases, the access type to that buffer inside the function must be indicated by the programmer (options are: BUF_READ,
BUF_WRITE, BUF_READWRITE).

Fig. 6 shows the definition of two functions that can be invoked on the CPU
and a third one to process an item on the GPU. First, in line 5 we have the CPU
function for CG granularity, that is basically a serial code to process an item
on the CPU. For this granularity, parallelism is exploited at the task level since
several cores may be running this function at the same time for different items.
Next in line 13, we have the definition for MG granularity, were all the cores
will collaborate in processing a single item. Now, data parallelism is exploited,

and to that end in this example we rely on `tbb::parallel_for()` (line 20). MG granularity can be also exploited using OpenMP as shown in commented line 24. Finally we have the GPU code defined in the `gpu_f3` function (line 29). Note also that pipeline parallelism is exploited because concurrent items traverse the stages of a pipeline at their own pace.

3. Experimental results

We run our experiments on an Odroid XU3 bare-board. The Odroid has a Samsung Exynos 5 Octa (5422) featuring a Cortex-A15 2.0Ghz quad-core and a Cortex-A7 quad-core CPUs (ARM's big.LITTLE architecture). The Cortex-A15 quad-core contains 32 KB (Instruction)/32 KB (Data) private caches and a 2 MB L2 shared cache, while the Cortex-A7 quad-core has 32 KB (Instruction)/32 KB (Data) private caches and a 512 KB L2 shared cache. This platform features current/power monitors based on TI INA231 chips that enable readouts of instant power consumed on the A15 cores, A7 cores, main memory and GPU. The Exynos 5 includes the GPU Mali-T628 MP6. We have chosen this heterogenous on-chip processor because it presents one interesting feature that we consider in our study. In particular, it allows two levels of heterogeneity: two devices with different ISA: a GPU and a multicore CPU, plus two different processor technologies inside the multicore CPU. Thus, in this system we have three type of cores with different computational capabilities sharing the main memory.

The board runs Linux Ubuntu 14.04.1 LTS, and an in-house library measures energy consumption [13]. On this platform, the compiler used is gcc 4.8 with -O3 flag. The OpenCL SDK v1.1.0 is used for the Mali GPU. The code for the CPU functions is vectorized using NEON intrinsics. For the MG granularity versions, the `omp parallel for` pragma was used on each stage. Intel TBB 4.2 provides the core template of the `pipeline` pattern. For each experiment, we measured time and energy in 5 runs of our application and report the median value. The input data consists of 100 low-definition frames (600 × 416 pixels).

Next, we explore how the level of granularity of the stages (MG and CG), the mapping of stages to the different devices, and the number of threads affects the energy-performance efficiency. We have explored all the pipeline mappings for the different granularities, but Fig. 7 shows a comparison between Medium-Grain (MG) and Coarse-Grain (CG) granularities only for the mapping that achieves the highest frame rate (i.e. the highest pipeline throughput). The pipeline mapping is {1,0,1} in both cases (101 in the labels), which means that stages 1 and 3 can potentially be mapped to the GPU and CPU, but stage 2 is only mapped to the CPU. For reference, results when only the CPU is exploited are also shown for each granularity (CPU-only CG, CPU-only MG).

Fig. 7(a) shows the energy per frame (Joules) vs. the frame rate (i.e. throughput measured in frames per second of fps) for each experiment. In other words, it depicts energy efficiency vs. performance efficiency. On each line, we show 9 points: each one represents the energy per frame vs. fps when the experiment runs from 1 thread (the leftmost point) to 9 threads (the last point in the line). In the CPU experiments (CPU-only CG and MG) the first 4 points (from 1 to 4 threads) represent the contribution due to the A15 cores, the next 4 points (from 5 to 8 threads) the contribution due to the A7 cores, and the last point

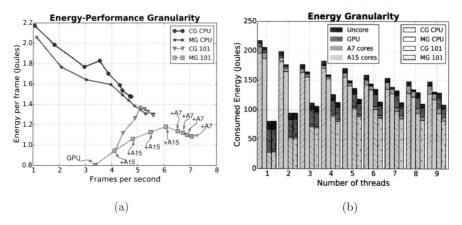

Figure 7. Study of the impact of the granularity on ViVid.

represents a situation of oversubscription. When the GPU is incorporated, i.e. the MG 101 and CG 101 experiments, the first point represents the contribution due to only the GPU (1 thread), the next 4 points with the label "+A15" (from 2 to 5 threads) the contribution due to the A15 cores, and the last 4 points with the label "+A7" (from 6 to 9 threads) the contribution due to the A7 cores. Note that while increasing the number of threads, the Linux scheduler first occupies the A15 cores. Once these are busy, the A7 cores are exploited.

Fig. 7(a) shows that for CPU-only the energy efficiency and the frame rate improve as the number of threads increases. It also shows that incorporating the GPU (CG 101 and MG 101) reduces the energy consumption. The minimum energy consumption is achieved with 1 thread (just the GPU), which is 2.7x and 2.6x more energy efficient than the 1 thread CPU-only CG and CPU-only MG granularities, respectively. However, both CG 101 and MG 101 experiments tend to increase the energy consumption when adding more threads (specially when the A15 cores are incorporated, as shown for the 2nd to the 5th point in both lines). Both CG and MG granularities improve the frame rate as the number of threads increases, but CG consumes more energy and achieves lower performance than MG. Interestingly, when we add the A7 cores in the CG 101 and MG 101 experiments (threads 6 to 9, or 6th to 9th point), both granularities improve the performance while slightly reducing the energy consumption. In any case, for this application, MG 101 delivers the highest frame rate (for 9 threads) with just a degradation of 35% of the energy consumption when compared to the minimum consumption (1 thread, just the GPU).

Fig. 7(b) shows the breakdown of the energy consumption as we increase the number of threads: it shows the contribution due to the A15 and A7 cores, the GPU, and the Uncore units of the chip. The first bar represents the CPU-only CG experiment, the second one the CPU-only MG experiment, while the third and fourth the CG 101 and MG 101 experiments, respectively. The figure shows that, for the CPU-only experiments, the A15 energy component reduces significantly (while slightly increasing the A7 component) as the number of threads increases. Also for any number of threads, the A15 energy component is always smaller in CPU-only MG than in CPU-only CG: this is due to a better cache locality exploitation of MG (where only one frame is processed at a time) versus CG (where the number of frames being processed at a given time is equal to the number of active threads). On the other hand, for the `CG 101` and `MG 101` experiments, the A15 energy component increases from 1 to 5 threads. However, it reduces the GPU energy component since the cores are now taking some of the iterations that were previously processed on the GPU. The overall result is an increment in the total energy consumption because the A15 are less energy efficient than the GPU. Adding more threads in these experiments means that we incorporate the A7 cores, which slightly reduces or stabilizes the A15 energy component, while marginally increasing the A7 component. The figure also shows that the GPU and Uncore energy components are correlated: both decrease from 1 to 5 threads (A15 cores), and from there they stabilize. The `MG 101` experiment shows smaller energy consumption in the A15 component, due to a better cache exploitation under this granularity, as commented before. In any case, for 9 threads, `MG 101` is 16.2% more energy efficient than `CG 101`.

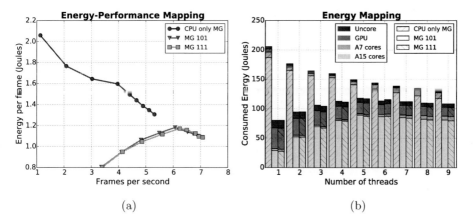

Figure 8. Study of the impact of the mapping on ViVid.

Since we have identified that the best granularity for this code is MG, we study the impact that mapping has for this granularity. We compare the case that obtains the best throughput (the mapping 101) with the case in which we minimize communications between the GPU and the CPU (mapping $\{1,1,1\}$ where all the stages can be mapped to the GPU if the item entering the pipeline finds the GPU available). Fig. 8(a) shows a comparison between `MG 101` and `MG 111`. Again, for reference, we show the results when only the CPU is exploited (`CPU-only MG`). Fig. 8(b) shows the breakdown of the energy consumption for these experiments.

In this case, both mappings have a similar behavior: adding the A15 cores (from 2 to 5 threads) increases the throughput at the cost of increasing the energy consumption (due to the A15 energy component as shown in Fig. 8(b)). Adding the A7 cores improves the frame rate and reduces (slightly) the energy consumption. Anyway, for 9 threads the `MG 101` mapping gives a slightly higher frame rate (not apparent in the figure) and lower energy consumption than `MG 111`. The differences between both mappings are small because stage 2 (the stage with a different mapping on each experiment) has a small computational load: it takes less than 5% of the computation of an item in the pipeline.

4. Conclusions

In this work, we present a framework API to specify pipeline applications that can run on heterogenous on-chip processors. Our template allows the configuration of three parameters: the granularity exploited by each stage in the multicore CPU (CG or MG), the mapping of the stages to the devices (GPU or CPU cores), and the number of active threads. We use this framework to study how these parameters affect performance and energy efficiency in a heterogenous on-chip processor (Exynos 5 Octa) that has three different computational cores: a GPU, an A15 quad-core and an A7 quad-core. Our results show that although heterogenous executions are the ones that achieve higher performance, it does so by increasing the energy consumption in the system when the A15 cores are incorporated. By incorporating the energy efficient A7 cores we can still increase a little the performance, while slightly reducing the energy consumption. Our experiments also show that MG granularity tends to demand less consumption in the A15 energy component due to a better locality exploitation.

References

[1] J. Clemons, Haishan Zhu, S. Savarese, and T. Austin. Mevbench: A mobile computer vision benchmarking suite. In *IISWC*, pages 91–102, Nov 2011.

[2] James Reinders. *Intel Threading Building Blocks: Outfitting C++ for Multi-Core Processor Parallelism*. O'Reilly Media, 2007.

[3] Mert Dikmen, Derek Hoiem, and Thomas S Huang. A data driven method for feature transformation. In *Proc. of CVPR*, pages 3314–3321, 2012.

[4] Michael Jones and Paul Viola. Fast multi-view face detection. *Mitsubishi Electric Research Lab TR-20003-96*, 3, 2003.

[5] Robert Soule, Michael I. Gordon, Saman Amarasinghe, Robert Grimm, and Martin Hirzel. Dynamic expressivity with static optimization for streaming languages. In *The 7th ACM International Conference on Distributed Event-Based Systems*, Arlington, TX, June 2013.

[6] Canqun Yang et al. Adaptive optimization for petascale heterogeneous CPU/GPU computing. In *CLUSTER*, pages 19–28, 2010.

[7] Chi-Keung Luk, Sunpyo Hong, and Hyesoon Kim. Qilin: Exploiting parallelism on heterogeneous multiprocessors with adaptive mapping. In *MICRO 42*, pages 45–55, 2009.

[8] J. Planas, R.M. Badia, E. Ayguade, and J. Labarta. Self-adaptive ompss tasks in heterogeneous environments. In *Parallel Distributed Processing (IPDPS), 2013 IEEE 27th International Symposium on*, pages 138–149, May 2013.

[9] C. Augonnet, S. Thibault, R. Namyst, and P. Wacrenier. StarPU: a unified platform for task scheduling on heterogeneous multicore architectures. *Concurr. Comput. : Pract. Exper.*, 23(2):187–198, February 2011.

[10] A. Vilches, A. Navarro, R. Asenjo, F. Corbera, R. Gran, and M. Garzaran. Mapping streaming applications on commodity multi-CPU and GPU on-chip processors. *IEEE Tran. on Parallel and Distributed Systems*, 2015. doi:10.1109/TPDS.2015.2432809.

[11] Marco Aldinucci, Marco Danelutto, Peter Kilpatrick, and Massimo Torquati. Fastflow: high-level and efficient streaming on multi-core. In *Programming Multi-core and Many-core Computing Systems*. October 2014.

[12] A. Rodriguez, A. Vilches, A. Navarro, R. Asenjo, F. Corbera, R. Asenjo, R. Gran, and M. Garzaran. Productive interface to map streaming applications on heterogeneous processors. Technical report, Comput. Architecture Dept., 2015. http://www.ac.uma.es/~asenjo/research/.

[13] F. Corbera, A. Rodriguez, R. Asenjo, A. Navarro, A. Vilches, and M. J. Garzaran. Reducing overheads of dynamic scheduling on heterogeneous chips. In *Workshop on High Performance Energy Efficient Embedded Systems (HIP3ES)*, 2015.

Applications

Parallel Computing: On the Road to Exascale
G.R. Joubert et al. (Eds.)
IOS Press, 2016
doi:10.3233/978-1-61499-621-7-339

Efficient and scalable distributed-memory hierarchization algorithms for the sparse grid combination technique

Mario HEENE [a,1] and Dirk PFLÜGER [a,1]

[a] *Institute for Parallel and Distributed Systems, University of Stuttgart, Germany*

Abstract. Finding solutions to higher dimensional problems, such as the simulation of plasma turbulence in a fusion device as described by the five-dimensional gyrokinetic equations, is a grand challenge facing current and future high performance computing (HPC). The sparse grid combination technique is a promising approach to the solution of these problems on large scale distributed memory systems. The combination technique numerically decomposes a single large problem into multiple moderately sized partial problems that can be computed in parallel, independently and asynchronously of each other. The ability to efficiently combine the individual partial solutions to a common sparse grid solution is a key consideration to the overall performance of large scale computations with the combination technique. This requires a transfer of each partial solution from the nodal basis representation into the hierarchical basis representation by hierarchization. In this work we will present a new, efficient and scalable algorithm for the hierarchization of partial solutions that are distributed over multiple process groups of an HPC system.

Keywords. higher-dimensional problems, sparse grids, combination technique, distributed memory parallelization, exascale computing

Introduction

The solution of higher-dimensional problems, especially higher-dimensional partial differential equations (PDEs), that require the joint discretization of more than the usual three spatial dimensions plus time, is one of the grand challenges in current and future high performance computing. Resolving the simulation domain as fine as required by the physical problem, is, in many cases, not feasible due to the exponential growth of the number of unknowns – the so-called curse of dimensionality. This can be observed, for example, for the simulation of plasma turbulence in a fusion reactor with the code GENE [1] and is the driving motivation for the SPPEXA project EXAHD [2]. The five-dimensional gyrokinetic equations are the underlying physical model. Fully resolved simulations of a large fusion reactor like the world's flagship fusion experiment ITER would require computational grids with 10^{12} to 10^{15} grid points. As a result such simu-

---

[1] Supported by the German Research Foundation (DFG) through the Priority Programme 1648 Software for Exascale Computing (SPPEXA) and the Cluster of Excellence in Simulation Technology (EXC 310/1) at the University of Stuttgart.

lations are currently not feasible, even on today's largest HPC systems. Due to the large quantity of unknowns, they are expected to be infeasible with classical discretization techniques even on future exascale systems.

Sparse grids are a hierarchical approach to mitigate the curse of dimensionality by drastically reducing the number of unknowns, while preserving a similar accuracy as classical discretization techniques that work on regular grids [3]. However, due to their recursive and hierarchical structure, and the resulting global coupling of basis functions, the direct sparse grid approach is not feasible for large-scale distributed-memory parallelization.

A great approach to the solution of high-dimensional problems is the sparse grid combination technique [4]. It is based on an extrapolation scheme and decomposes a single large problem (i.e. discretized with a high resolution) into multiple moderately-sized partial problems. This introduces a second level of parallelism, enabling one to compute the partial problems in parallel, independently and asynchronously of each other. This breaks the demand for full global communication and synchronisation, which is expected to be one of the limiting factors with classical discretization techniques to achieve scalability on future exascale systems. Furthermore, by mitigating the curse of dimensionality, it offers the means to tackle problem sizes that would be out of scope for the classical discretization approaches. This allows us to significantly push the computational limits of plasma turbulence simulations and other higher-dimensional problems.

The sparse grid combination technique computes the sparse grid approximation of a function f by a weighted sum of partial solutions $f_{\vec{l}}$ on coarse and anisotropic Cartesian component grids $\Omega_{\vec{l}}$. The discretization of each d-dimensional component grid $\Omega_{\vec{l}}$ is defined by the level vector $\vec{l} = (l_1, \cdots, l_d)^T$, which determines the uniform mesh width 2^{-l_i} in dimension i. The number of grid points of a component grid is $|\Omega_{\vec{l}}| = \prod_{i=1}^d 2^{l_i} \pm 1$ (+1 if the grid has boundary points in dimension i and -1 if not).

In order to retrieve a sparse grid approximation $f_{\vec{n}}^{(c)} \approx f$ one can combine the partial solutions $f_{\vec{l}}(\vec{x})$ as

$$f_{\vec{n}}^{(c)}(\vec{x}) = \sum_{\vec{l} \in \mathscr{I}} c_{\vec{l}} f_{\vec{l}}(\vec{x}), \tag{1}$$

where $c_{\vec{l}}$ are the combination coefficients and $\mathscr{I}$ is the set of level vectors used for the combination. $\vec{n}$ denotes the maximum discretization level in each dimension. It also defines the discretization of the corresponding full grid solution $f_{\vec{n}}$ on $\Omega_{\vec{n}}$. Fig. 1 (left) shows a two-dimensional example.

For problems involving time-dependent initial-value computations, as is the case in GENE, recombination has to be performed after every time step, or at least every few time steps, to guarantee convergence and stability of the combined solution. Recombination means to combine the partial solutions according to Eq. (1) and to set new initial values for each partial problem based on the result. After that, the independent computations are continued until the next recombination point. In our scenario it is necessary to compute the combined solution every few time steps, even if convergence or stability are not an issue, to trace certain physical properties of the solution field over time. Being the only remaining step that involves global communication, an efficient implementation is crucial for the overall performance of computations with the combination technique.

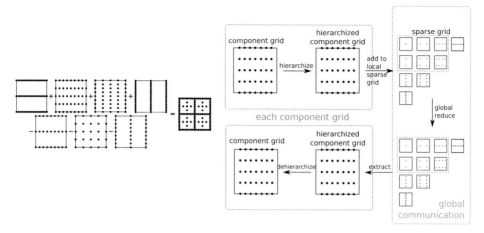

Figure 1. Left: Component grids in two dimensions with $\vec{n} = (4,4)^T$ and the resulting sparse grid. **Right:** The key parts of the recombination step: hierarchization, global communication, dehierarchization.

The naive way to perform the (re)combination would be to interpolate each partial solution onto the full grid $\Omega_{\vec{n}}$ and obtain the combined solution by "simply" adding up grid point by grid point weighted by the combination coefficients. However, for the large-scale computations with GENE that we aim for, this is not feasible. The size of the full grid would be so large that even just storing it would be out of scope.

The only efficient (or even feasible) way is to (re)combine the partial solutions in the corresponding sparse grid's hierarchical space. The right hand side of Fig. 1 depicts the three substeps of the recombination: hierarchization, global communication, and de-hierarchization. In the first step, each partial solution is transferred from the nodal basis of its component grid to the hierarchical basis of the sparse grid by hierarchization. The global communication step reduces the individual partial solutions to the combined solution. Afterwards, the combined solution is transferred back to the original nodal basis of each component grid by dehierarchization.

The first large-scale initial value computations with the combination technique and GENE that we aim for will use up to 90000 cores on Germany's Tier-0/1 supercomputer Hornet. A possible setup could consist of 425 component grids, where each of the 165 largest component grids would have more than 60 GB. Each of them can efficiently be computed on 2048 to 16392 cores (GENE scales very well in that range). Note that the corresponding full grid $\Omega_{\vec{n}}$ would have more than 10^{15} grid points. For our computations we divide the computational resources, i.e. the available MPI processes, into groups. For our setup this could be, for example, 44 groups of 2048 processes. A dedicated central manager process distributes the component grids to the process groups, where they are computed one after each other. The manager also coordinates the recombination step.

For such large-scale setups, where the component grids are distributed onto several thousand processes, an efficient and scalable implementation of the hierarchization (and dehierarchization), as well as the global communication step, is crucial for the overall duration of the recombination. In [5,6] we already presented efficient implementations of the global communication step. In this work, we focus on hierarchization and dehier-archization as the remaining two steps of the recombination. Since dehierarchization is just the inverse operation of hierarchization and yields an almost identical algorithm, we only address hierarchization here.

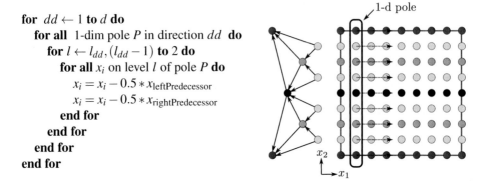

for $dd \leftarrow 1$ **to** d **do**
  for all 1-dim pole P in direction dd **do**
    for $l \leftarrow l_{dd}, (l_{dd} - 1)$ **to** 2 **do**
      for all x_i on level l of pole P **do**
        $x_i = x_i - 0.5 * x_{\text{leftPredecessor}}$
        $x_i = x_i - 0.5 * x_{\text{rightPredecessor}}$
      end for
    end for
  end for
end for

Figure 2. Left: Unidirectional hierarchization principle (from [7]). **Right:** Hierarchization of the x_2-dimension. The graph shows the dependencies for the hierarchization of each 1-dimensional pole.

1. Hierarchization algorithms for shared-memory parallelization

The most common approach to hierarchize is the so-called unidirectional principle. The d dimensions of the component grid are hierarchized one after each other, exploiting the underlying tensor structure. A well optimized implementation of the unidirectional algorithm is presented in [7] (also see Fig. 2). For the hierarchization of each dimension, the algorithm traverses the grid in 1-dimensional poles. For each pole, 1-dimensional hierarchization in direction of the current dimension is performed. Here the grid points are updated level by level, starting on the highest level. The graph in Fig. 2 illustrates the dependencies for the 1-dimensional hierarchization. Independent of the current dimension and the dimensionality of the problem, the poles always traverse the grid in direction of the innermost dimension (indicated by the arrows in Fig. 2). This way, optimal cache use is granted even if each grid point in the pole is in a different cache-line. For our higher-dimensional application it is safe to assume that the grids have a discretization level per dimension not much higher than 10. Assuming double precision and a grid with boundary, we would obtain a maximum cache use of approximately 1025 grid points $\times$ 64 Bytes per cache line, thus $\approx$ 64 KByte. Thus, even for very large grids, it should be possible to perform the hierarchization of each pole at least in the L2 cache of a modern processor.

In [7], the lower bound for the runtime of the unidirectional hierarchization of a componente grids that is significantly larger than the cache is found to be

$$2d \cdot (\#\text{gridpoints}) \cdot (\text{size of datatype}) / (\text{memory bandwidth}). \qquad (2)$$

The implementation in [7] applies shared-memory parallelization (OpenMP), vectorization and blocking techniques, and achieves a performance close to this bound.

In [8], the same authors present a cache-oblivious hierarchization algorithm that avoids the d global sweeps over the component grid of the uni-directional principle. It recursively divides the component grid into smaller subproblems that completely fit into the cache. Unidirectional hierarchization is then applied to each of the subproblems. In almost all cases their approach was faster than their implementation of the unidirectional principle. Again, their algorithm is only intended for shared-memory parallelization.

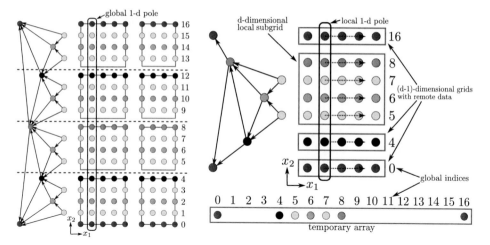

Figure 3. Left: Component grid distributed onto eight processes. **Right:** Distributed hierarchization with remote data from the local view of one process.

2. A new hierarchization algorithm for distributed-memory parallelization

---

Algorithm 1 Distributed unidirectional hierarchization.

---

for $dd \leftarrow 1$ **to** d **do**
    calculate dependencies and exchange values (via MPI) in direction dd
    hierarchize local subdomain in direction dd
end for

Large-scale parallel applications in science and engineering, like GENE, typically use MPI parallelization and computational grids that are distributed onto a large numbers of nodes of an HPC system. Our new distributed unidirectional hierarchization algorithm is able to hierarchize such distributed grids in a scalable and distributed way.

The approaches presented in Sec. 1 use shared-memory parallelization, i.e., the whole component grid is available in the main memory of a node and can be directly accessed by all its processes. This is not possible any more with distributed grids. Whenever a process needs data from the subgrid of another process, this data cannot be directly accessed any more, but instead has to be exchanged using the MPI interface. Fig. 3 shows a component grid distributed onto eight different MPI processes. The dependency graph for the hierarchization in x_2-direction illustrates that the update of many points requires data which are in the subgrids of other processes.

We do the hierarchization of each dimension in two steps (see Alg. 1). First, each process determines from the dependency graph which values it has to exchange with other processes. The dependency graph can be deduced from the discretization and the domain partitioning and is known to each process without additional communication. The data is exchanged using non-blocking MPI calls. Each process stores the received remote data in form of $(d-1)$-dimensional grids.

After the communication step, each process locally performs the hierarchization in a similar fashion as presented in Sec. 1: The local subgrid is traversed with 1-dimensional poles (see Fig. 3). If we would decide for the update of each grid point whether its dependencies are contained in the local or the remote data, we would obtain bad performance due to branching and address calculations. In order to avoid this, we copy the local and the remote data to a temporary 1-d array which has the full global extent of the current dimension. We then perform the hierarchization of the current pole in the temporary array using an efficient 1-d hierarchization kernel. Afterwards, the updated values are copied back to the subgrid. Considering our assumption on the maximum extent per dimension not being much more than level 10, the temporary array will easily fit into the cache, even for very large grids. The poles traverse the local subgrid and the remote data in the same cache-optimal order as in the serial case (see Sec. 1). Thus, no additional main memory transfers are required.

3. Results

We investigated the scalability of our distributed hierarchization algorithm on Germany's Tier-0/1 supercomputer Hornet. It currently consists of 3944 dual-socket nodes, which have 24 cores of Intel Xeon E5-2680 v3 (Haswell) and 128 GByte of main memory.

We measured the runtime for the distributed hierarchization of component grids of dimensionality d with discretization levels $\vec{l}$ and a domain decomposition of $\vec{p}$ processes per dimension. The entries in $\vec{p}$ were always powers of two. Although this is not necessary for our distributed hierarchization algorithm, it is a natural choice considering the relation of the number of grid points and $\vec{l}$. Furthermore, it simplified the setup of our experiments, as the total number of processes for every possible domain decomposition is a power of two as well. We performed strong and weak scaling experiments with 32, 64, 128, 256, 512, 1024, 2048, 4096, 8192, 16384 and 32768 cores on Hornet using all 24 cores per node. Strong scaling means the problem size stays constant with increasing processor count; the number of grid points per process decreases. For weak scaling the problem size is increased proportionally to the processor count; the number of grid points per process stays (roughly) constant. The grids had boundary points in all dimensions. This represents the worst-case scenario in terms of runtime: The use of boundary points results in more data to be exchanged over the network and more main memory accesses than without boundary points.

In the following experiments, we present the average time per process, unless otherwise stated. The time per process for the global data exchange as well as for the local hierarchization step fluctuates. For the hierarchization, on the one hand, the processes have (slightly) different numbers of grid points. On the other hand, 24 processes have to share the memory bandwidth of the node. Also, some processes have to exchange more data than other processes. Furthermore, communication is externally influenced by the overall load on the network at the time the measurements were done. Nevertheless, we have observed that the maximum times scale in the same fashion as the average ones.

Our main focus is on 5-dimensional grids, the dimensionality of our target application GENE, but Fig. 4 also shows measurements for the dimensionalities 3, 4, and 6. Note that our combination technique software framework can handle problems of arbitrary dimensionality. The grids used here have isotropic discretization and isotropic domain decomposition. We speak of an anisotropic domain decomposition if the number of processes per dimension is not proportional to the number of grid points per dimension. To be precise, neither discretization nor domain decomposition were always completely

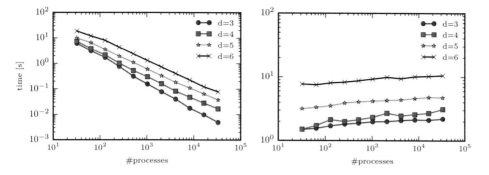

Figure 4. Strong (left) and weak (right) scaling results for grids of different dimensionalities.

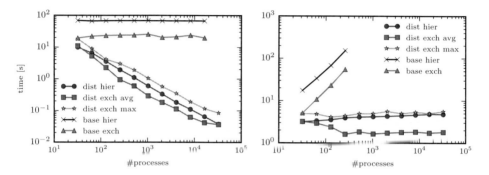

Figure 5. Strong (left) and weak (right) scaling results for a 5-dimensional grid. Individual times for data exchange and hierarchization for the distributed hierarchization algorithm (dist) and for a straightforward implementation using serial hierarchization (base).

isotropic, but the entries of $\vec{l}$ did not differ by more than one, or a factor of two in $\vec{p}$ respectively. When increasing the number of processes we doubled $\vec{p}$ in the dimension where it had the smallest entry.

For strong scaling the grids were $\vec{l} = (11,11,10)^T$ (34.4 GB), $\vec{l} = (8,8,8,8)^T$ (34.9 GB), $\vec{l} = (7,7,6,6,6)^T$ (36.5 GB) and $\vec{l} = (6,6,5,5,5,5)^T$ (40.08 GB). The algorithm scales well independent of the dimensionality. Going from 32 to 32768 cores we still obtain a speedup of 265 for $d = 5$. For weak scaling we started with grids of $\vec{l} = (10,10,10)^T$ (8.6 GB), $\vec{l} = (8,8,7,7)^T$ (8.7 GB), $\vec{l} = (6,6,6,6,6)^T$ (9.2 GB) and $\vec{l} = (5,5,5,5,5,5)^T$ (10.3 GB). We increased the grid size proportionally to the number of processes, incrementing the entry in $\vec{l}$ with the smallest value. For $d = 5$ the runtime slightly increases from 3.17s (32 cores) to 4.75s (32768 cores), which corresponds to a parallel efficiency of 66%.

Fig. 5 shows the individual aggregated times (sum over all dimensions) of the communication step and the hierarchization step for our $d = 5$ setting. Here, we additionally present the maximum time for the communication step. All three times scale well for both strong and weak scaling. For larger processor counts, the average and maximum time for the communication differ by a constant factor. The time for the hierarchization has the same complexity as the communication time.

Fig. 5 also presents the individual communication and hierarchization time of a straightforward implementation based on the serial implementation of the unidirectional

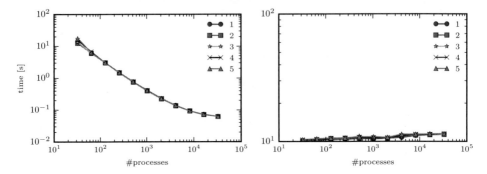

Figure 6. Strong (left) and weak (right) scaling results for the distributed hierarchization of an anisotropic 5-dimensional grid. For each case the number denotes the anisotropic dimension.

principle as presented in Sec. 1. Here the whole grid is gathered in the memory of a single node and (serial) hierarchization is performed. We included this test to demonstrate that such an approach cannot scale up to large process counts, neither in a strong nor in a weak fashion. For strong scaling the time it takes to gather the grid on one node and to hierarchize the grid is nearly constant, independent of the number of processes. For weak scaling the runtime of this approach will necessarily increase proportionally to the problem size. The grid size is limited by the size of the main memory of a node (128 GB on Hornet).

Component grids of the combination technique can have very anisotropic discretizations. While it is theoretically possible to obtain discretizations with level 1 in all but one dimension, such extremely anisotropic grids need to be frequently excluded in practice due to numerical or physical constraints. As a compromise, we used discretization level 16 for one and level 4 for all other dimensions for strong scaling. For weak scaling we started with an isotropic grid with $\vec{l} = 6,6,6,6,6$ and only increased the level in one dimension. We started with 32 processes in one dimension and only increased $\vec{p}$ in this dimension. Fig. 6 shows that it does not matter in which dimension the anisotropy is. More importantly, the speedup when going from 32 to 32768 cores is 196 for strong scaling, which is worse than in the isotropic case. The time per grid point is 40% higher than for the isotropic grid (32768 cores).

In our combination technique scenario the domain decomposition would be chosen so that it is optimal for the application, either by the user or automatically by the application. Therefore, we have to assume that anisotropic domain decompositions can occur. In Fig. 7 we show the influence of extremely anisotropic domain decompositions on the runtime by increasing the number of processes only in one dimension. Considering the symmetry in the above results, we only performed the experiments in dimension 1 and 5. For strong scaling the grid was $\vec{l} = (7,7,6,6,6)^T$ (36.6 GB). We started with 32 processes in one dimension and only increased $\vec{p}$ in this dimension. However, in every dimension there must be at least one grid point per process. When this number was reached we continued to increase the next dimension. This point was reached with 128 cores, note the kink in the plot. After this point the scalability improved. However, it was significantly worse than in the above cases having isotropic domain decomposition. Unlike for isotropic decompositions where the data to be exchanged with other processes decreases with increasing process count, in case of very anisotropic decompositions the data to be exchanged remains constant.

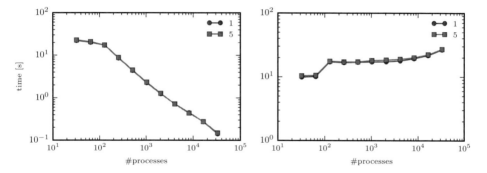

Figure 7. Strong (left) and weak (right) scaling results for the distributed hierarchization of a 5-dimensional grid which has an anisotropic domain decomposition either in dimension 1 or dimension 5.

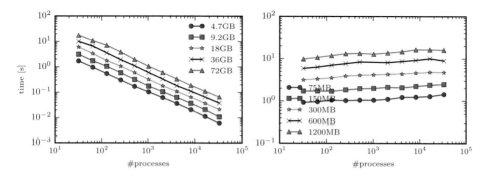

Figure 8. Strong (left) and weak (right) scaling results for the distributed hierarchization of 5-dimensional grids with different grid sizes.

For weak scaling we started with $\vec{l} = (6,6,6,6,6)^T$ and always increased the smallest entry in order to maintain an isotropic discretization. We started with 32 processes in one dimension and only increased $\vec{p}$ in this dimension. Going from 32 to 64 cores there is no real increase in the anisotropy of the domain decomposition as the discretization level in the same dimension is increased, too. Anisotropy in the domain decomposition starts to exist from 128 cores on, which explains the jump in the plot. Unlike for isotropic decompositions where the data to be exchanged with other processes remains (almost) constant, in case of extremely anisotropic decompositions the data to be exchanged grows with the problem size. Thus, weak scaling is not possible in these cases.

In Fig. 8 we finally investigate to which extent the actual size of the grid has impact on the scalability. The discretization and the domain decomposition of the grids were kept as isotropic as possible (increasing $\vec{l}$ and $\vec{p}$ where they have the lowest entry). For strong scaling we used grids with $\vec{l} = (6,6,6,6,5)^T$ (4.7 GB), $\vec{l} = (6,6,6,6,6)^T$ (9.2 GB), $\vec{l} = (7,6,6,6,6)^T$ (18 GB), $\vec{l} = (7,7,6,6,6)^T$ (36 GB), $\vec{l} = (7,7,6,6,6)^T$ (72 GB). For weak scaling we started with $\vec{l} = (6,6,6,5,5)^T$ (roughly 75 MB per core), $\vec{l} = (6,6,6,6,5)^T$ (150 MB), $\vec{l} = 6,6,6,6,6$ (300 MB), $\vec{l} = (7,6,6,6,6)^T$ (600 MB) and $\vec{l} = (7,6,6,6,6)^T$ (1200 MB) on and $\vec{p} = (2,2,2,2,2)^T$ cores. The largest grid had a total size of almost 36 TByte distributed onto 32768 cores. The results nicely show that the actual size of the grids does not influence strong or weak scaling noticeably.

4. Future Work

Future work could include further optimization of the distributed hierarchization algorithm. For the communication algorithm itself, there is not much room for improvement, as it is not possible to reduce the amount of data to be exchanged. However, there are processes which have to send the same block of data to many recipients. This might be improved by using collective MPI calls, e.g. *MPI_Bcast*. We expect larger optimization potential by hiding some of the hierarchization computations behind data transfers. The idea would be to not exchange all the data at once in a single big block during the communication step, but in small blocks instead. After the first block has been exchanged, the hierarchization of this block can already begin while the next block is being exchanged.

Another possible topic could be to use the cache-oblivous hierarchization algorithm (Sec. 1 or [8]) in a distributed fashion. Although it might be possible to reduce the time for the hierarchization step, the same lower bound for the data exchange as for the unidirectional principle is present (the amount of data to be exchanged is the same). In Fig. 5 it can be seen that the (maximum) time for the data exchange was higher than for the hierarchization. Thus, even a reduction of the hierarchization time by a factor d, which would be the lower bound for this algorithm, would not bring a huge performance benefit. Furthermore, the algorithm is only applicable for the special case where powers of two are used for the domain decomposition.

5. Conclusion

In this article we presented a new distributed hierarchization algorithm for higher-dimensional component grids with optimal communication complexity. Being a substep in the recombination, a scalable implementation of distributed hierarchization is crucial to enable large-scale computations with the combination technique. We demonstrated the strong and weak scalability of this algorithm on up to 32768 cores. We investigated different dimensionalities and grid sizes, as well as the influence of anisotropy in both discretization and domain decomposition. We showed that the new distributed hierarchization scales well, while the standard implementation cannot scale to large core counts.

References

[1] T. Görler, X. Lapillonne, S. Brunner, T. Dannert, F. Jenko, F. Merz, and D. Told. The global version of the gyrokinetic turbulence code GENE. *Journal of Computational Physics*, 230(18):7053 – 7071, 2011.

[2] Dirk Pflüger, Hans-Joachim Bungartz, Michael Griebel, et al. Exahd: An exa-scalable two-level sparse grid approach for higher-dimensional problems in plasma physics and beyond. In *Euro-Par 2014: Parallel Processing Workshops*, LNCSE, pages 565–576. 2014.

[3] Hans-Joachim Bungartz and Michael Griebel. Sparse Grids. *Acta Numerica*, 13:147–269, 2004.

[4] M. Griebel, M. Schneider, and Zenger. A comb. technique for the solution of sparse grid problems, 1992.

[5] Philipp Hupp, Riko Jacob, Mario Heene, et al. Global communication schemes for the sparse grid combination technique. In *Par. Comp.: Accelerating Comp. Science and Eng.*, pages 564 – 573, 2014.

[6] Philipp Hupp, Mario Heene, Riko Jacob, and Dirk Pflüger. Global communication schemes for the numerical solution of high-dimensional PDEs. *Parallel Computing*, submitted.

[7] Philipp Hupp. Performance of unidirectional hierarchization for component grids virtually maximized. *Procedia Computer Science*, 29:2272–2283, 2014.

[8] P. Hupp and R. Jacob. A cache-optimal alternative to the unidirectional hierarchization algorithm. *Proceedings of the Workshop Sparse Grids and Algorithms 2014*, submitted.

Parallel Computing: On the Road to Exascale
G.R. Joubert et al. (Eds.)
IOS Press, 2016
doi:10.3233/978-1-61499-621-7-349

Adapting a Finite-Element Type Solver for Bioelectromagnetics to the DEEP-ER Platform

Raphaël LÉGER [a,1], Damian A. MALLÓN [b], Alejandro DURAN [c] and
Stéphane LANTERI [a]

[a] INRIA Sophia-Antipolis Méditerranée, France
[b] Jülich Supercomputing Centre, Germany
[c] Intel Corporation Iberia, Spain

Abstract. In this paper, we report on our recent efforts towards adapting a Discontinuous Galerkin Time-Domain solver for computational bioelectromagnetics to the novel, heterogeneous architecture proposed in the DEEP-ER european project on exascale computing. This architecture is based on the Cluster/Booster division concept which will be recalled. As a first step, we summarize the key features of the application and present the outcomes of a profiling of the code using the tools developed by DEEP-ER partners. We then go through the subsequent general improvements of the application as well as specific developments aimed at exploiting efficiently the DEEP-ER platform. This particularly includes porting the application to the Intel® Many Integrated Core Architecture. We conclude with an outlook on next steps, including the different Cluster/Booster division strategies.

Keywords. discontinuous galerkin time-domain, heterogeneous computing, exascale computing, Intel xeon phi, numerical dosimetry

Introduction

Exascale computing will inevitably rely on manycore technology. In the current top 10 systems of the top 500 list, traditionally dominated by proprietary Massively Parallel Processing (MPP) systems, 40% use coprocessors/accelerators. These highly parallel coprocessors give new opportunities to application developers to speed up their simulations. However, they come at a price, as programming them requires extra effort to deal with massive amounts of threads, wide vector units, new levels in the memory hierarchy, and the need of user managed memory transfers.

Intel® Xeon Phi™ products aim at improving the management of this complexity by using a processor architecture which is more familiar to application developers than GPGPU cards are. This architecture enables applications to run in different modes: they can be programmed using the *offload mode* – where the application runs in the normal processors and offloads specific kernels to be executed in the coprocessors – the so called

---

[1] Corresponding Author: Raphaël Léger, INRIA Sophia-Antipolis Méditerranée, 2004 route des Lucioles, 06902 Sophia-Antipolis CEDEX, France; E-mail: raphael.leger@inria.fr.

native mode – using exclusively the Intel Xeon Phi coprocessors without normal processors being part of the application execution – and *symmetric mode* – where an application can use simultaneously both the processors and coprocessors using MPI communication between them. The next generation of Intel Xeon Phi products will also be available as stand-alone processors. It is worth noting that the Intel®Many Integrated Core Architecture (Intel MIC Architecture) facilitates the programmers job, but a manual effort to improve the threading parallelization, the use of the memory hierarchy or the efficient exploitation of the vector units is generally required to significantly improve the delivered performance.

Exascale requires to expose as much parallelism as possible, and a wise use of resources to keep the power budget under constraints while improving the performance of the applications. To this aim, the DEEP project [1] leverages the first generation of Intel Xeon Phi coprocessor capabilities to decouple the coprocessors from the Cluster nodes (which are otherwise tied to each other, imposing some constraints). The set of coprocessor nodes constitute the so called Booster nodes, which is a separate part of the system with a different fabric enabling autonomous operation of the coprocessors. This allows a dynamic combination of Cluster nodes and Booster nodes in every job. This way, applications can use the coprocessors in two different ways: (1) as dynamically allocated discrete offload destinations, allowing to overcome load imbalance issues, since Cluster nodes with extra work can use more Booster nodes if necessary; and (2) as a set of coprocessors with direct communication, separating different parts of the application according to their scalability. Thus, low scalable parts run on the Cluster, and highly scalable parts – with communication among them – run on the Booster. Following a co-design effort, the OmpSs programming model [2] has been extended to enable both use models.

The DEEP-ER project addresses two issues that were not addressed by its older sibling: scalable I/O and resiliency. Using the DEEP project as foundation, the DEEP-ER project will use the more capable second generation Intel Xeon Phi processor (code-named Knights Landing), and will integrate Booster nodes and Cluster nodes in the same fabric. Together with the Intel Xeon Phi processors, the Booster nodes will include Non Volatile Memory (NVM), to enable very high bandwidth for I/O intensive applications. Taking into account applications requirements, the BeeGFS filesystem [3,4] is being extended to make an efficient use of NVM, where data in the global filesystem will use NVM as cache, prefetching and flushing data as necessary. Additionally, SIONlib [5] is used in the project to alleviate the problem of "small I/O", where hundreds of thousands of small files are written simultaneously by each process in a large job. It does that by aggregating all these files in a reduced set of files, putting less pressure on the metadata servers. Exascale 10 (E10) [6] libraries are also being developed to mitigate this problem when using the MPI-IO interfaces. Efficient I/O enable efficient resiliency. In DEEP-ER resiliency is implemented in two different ways: Scalable Checkpoint-Restart (SCR), and task-based resiliency. The SCR API is being extended to support a number of features, namely "buddy checkpointing" where most of the checkpoints are written to a neighbors' NVM, instead of the global filesystem, allowing an even more scalable approach. The task-based resiliency approach restarts a given OmpSs task using its saved input data, when a transient error has being detected in a memory page that contained data used by the tasks. Moreover, Network Attached Memory (NAM) will be an experimental part of the project, being used to assist in book keeping for I/O and resiliency libraries. An overview of the DEEP-ER hardware architecture is sketched on Figure 1. In a co-design

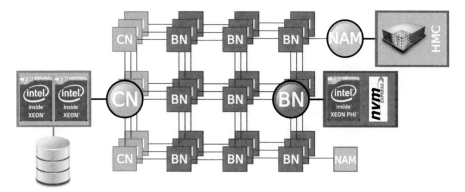

Figure 1. DEEP-ER hardware architecture sketch. The distribution of Cluster Nodes, Booster Nodes and NAM is not yet decided. Cluster nodes and the parallel filesystem storage nodes are merged in the prototype.

effort, the DEEP-ER project involves the adaptation of applications from different areas of science and engineering to its architecture, leveraging its software stack. In this context, the objective of this paper is to give an overview of the steps taken so far in approaching the DEEP-ER hardware and software environment with the application we describe in the following sections.

1. Application Background

In this work, we consider a simulation tool for the numerical assessment of the exposure of human tissues to electromagnetic waves. MAXW-DGTD solves the 3D Maxwell-Debye PDE system [7] in which the unknowns are an electric field **E**, a magnetic field **H** and an electric polarization **P**. The solver is based on a Discontinuous Galerkin Time-Domain (DGTD) method [8], which is a form of finite-element method. It is based on a cellwise local variational formulation and a weak coupling of a given cell to its direct neighbours through a numerical flux (like finite-volume methods). We use a centered numerical flux and nodal Lagrange polynomials basis functions of order k [9]. The family of kth order polynomials is denoted P_k throughout the paper. The value of k impacts the accuracy of the numerical solution through the local amount of discretization points per cell N_k. Lagrange basis functions P_k are such that $N_k = (k+1)(k+2)(k+3)/6$. Equipped with a second order explicit leap-frog time stepping method, the fully discretized scheme for each cell i reads:

$$
\begin{cases}
\dfrac{\mathbb{M}_i^{\mu}}{\Delta t}\left(\overline{\mathbf{H}}_i^{n+\frac{3}{2}} - \overline{\mathbf{H}}_i^{n+\frac{1}{2}}\right) = \displaystyle\sum_{k=1}^{3} \mathbb{K}_i^{x_p}\overline{\mathbf{E}}_i^{n+1} + \sum_{a_{ij}\in\mathscr{T}_d^i} \mathbb{F}_{ij}\overline{\mathbf{E}}_j^{n+1}, \\[4mm]
\dfrac{\mathbb{M}_i^{\varepsilon}}{\Delta t}\left(\overline{\mathbf{E}}_i^{n+1} - \overline{\mathbf{E}}_i^{n}\right) = -\displaystyle\sum_{k=1}^{3} \mathbb{K}_i^{x_p}\overline{\mathbf{H}}_i^{n+\frac{1}{2}} - \sum_{a_{ij}\in\mathscr{T}_d^i} \mathbb{F}_{ij}\overline{\mathbf{H}}_j^{n+\frac{1}{2}} \\[4mm]
\qquad\qquad + \dfrac{\mathbb{M}_i}{\Delta t}\left(\overline{\mathbf{P}}_i^{n+1} - \overline{\mathbf{P}}_i^{n}\right) + \mathbb{M}_i^{\sigma}\dfrac{\left(\overline{\mathbf{E}}_i^{n+1} + \overline{\mathbf{E}}_i^{n}\right)}{2}, \\[4mm]
\dfrac{2\tau_r^i}{\Delta t}\left(\overline{\mathbf{P}}_i^{n+1} - \overline{\mathbf{P}}_i^{n}\right) = \varepsilon_0\left(\varepsilon_s^i - \varepsilon_\infty^i\right)\left(\overline{\mathbf{E}}_i^{n+1} + \overline{\mathbf{E}}_i^{n}\right) - \left(\overline{\mathbf{P}}_i^{n+1} + \overline{\mathbf{P}}_i^{n}\right).
\end{cases}
\tag{1}
$$

In (1), $\overline{\mathbf{X}}_i^m$ are the vectors (of size $3 \times N_k$) of discrete unknowns at cell i and time-step m. Cell-local matrices $\mathbb{K}_i^{x_{p=1\dots 3}}$ and $\mathbb{F}_{ij}$ are stiffness and interface (with cell j) matrices. Also, we define $\mathbb{M}_i^{\alpha=\varepsilon,\mu} := \alpha\mathbb{M}_i$ where $\mathbb{M}_i$ are mass matrices. All these matrices are block diagonal, of size $(3 \times N_k)^2$. While the three blocks of mass and stiffness matrices are dense, the blocks of interface matrices are sparse. Finally, n is the time step, and $\varepsilon, \mu, \sigma, \tau_r$ are space-dependent physical input parameters. Spatial discretization of the biological media and surrounding air is based on an unstructured tetrahedral mesh. The traditional approach for exposing parallelism with such a solver is based on mesh partitioning. Each submesh is assigned to a given computing unit, and neighboring sub-meshes are coupled by exchanging values of unknown fields located at the boundary be-tween subdomains through point-to-point (p2p) MPI messages, once per time step [10]. In [11], Cabel et al. present the adaptation of MAXW-DGTD to a cluster of GPU ac-celeration cards. For this, they rely on a hybrid coarse-grain SPMD programming model (for inter-GPU communication) / fine-grain SIMD programming model (for intra-GPU parallelization), clearly showing the potential of the DGTD method for leveraging hybrid SIMD/MIMD computing.

2. Analysis and general optimizations

Figure 2 outlines the workflow of the solver and shows the mesh of a human head, to-gether with its partitioning. This mesh is composed of 1.8×10^6 cells for 5 different materials and will be used for all further experiments in this paper. In most simulations, the time loop represents roughly 90% of the total simulation time. While significant I/O activity is mostly concentrated in pre- and post- processing phases – in which we re-spectively read geometrical data (the mesh and its partitioning), and write the physical

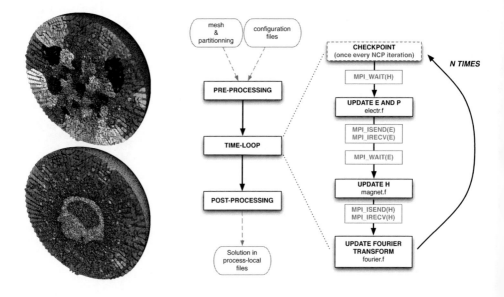

Figure 2. Mesh and partitioning - MAXW-DGTD workflow chart

512 proc. (32 nodes)	$k=1$	$k=2$	$k=3$	$k=4$
Parallel eff. - Block / Non-Block	0.56 / 1.01	0.60 / 0.94	0.67 / 0.96	0.76 / 0.97
Speedup due to NB Comms	1.96	1.56	1.44	1.28

Table 1. Performance improvement due to non-blocking communications. Parallel efficiency is computed taking as a reference the walltime observed on 16 processes of the DEEP cluster (i.e. one node).

solution in the Fourier space to process-local files – it may also impact the time-loop when application-level checkpointing is activated. The specific topic of I/O is addressed in section 4. Set aside these periodical checkpoints, the time-loop is dominated by the computational operations characterizing the DGTD scheme (1), and, to a lesser extent, constructing on the fly a Fourier-transformed solution.

In the rest of this section, we report on our efforts – driven by trace analysis of MAXW-DGTD with the help of Extræ and Paraver [12] – aiming to study and improve communications (in subsection 2.1) as well as data locality (in subsection 2.2) .

2.1. Processing and communications

In the baseline version of the solver, the approach to p2p communications was based on looping over neighbouring subdomains and relying on blocking MPI_SENDRECV calls in a pipeline fashion. This leads to a pattern represented in figure 3-(a), in which one can see the pipeline approach through the tilted aspect of the MPI events. The late-senders issue which results from this strategy has been solved by implementing non-blocking communications allowing to drastically reduce the amount of time spent within MPI routines (partly by enabling the update of the Fourier transform to be overlapped by communication operations for exchanging the values of $\overline{\mathbf{H}}$). Table 1 shows some of the observed performance improvements which result from upgrading communications, allowing to reach very satisfying efficiency values lying close to 1.00. Trace analysis of the baseline version also shows that the portion of runtime spent within communications decreases with the increase of order k. Consequently, upgrading to non-blocking communications leads to a speedup (for a fixed number of MPI ranks) which is higher for lower values of k. Latest strong scaling results for the time loop on the DEEP Cluster[2], based on Intel®Xeon®processor E5-2680, using 16 processes per node up to 64 nodes are represented on figure 3 - (b).

2.2. Improving data locality

In the application, load balance (which is for an important part a result of the mesh partitioning with the help of the MeTiS [13] tool) is already satisfying with a typical amount of only a few percent of instruction imbalance between processes. This is however not so clear for performance-related metrics such as instructions per cycle (IPC) or typical cache-miss rate. This phenomenon is an effect of an imbalance of data locality. Such an imbalance takes place in the phase which consists in retrieving values of the unknown fields at the neighbouring cells j of a given cell i (i.e. $\overline{\mathbf{E}}_j$ and $\overline{\mathbf{H}}_j$) in order to compute the contribution of the interface-matrix term to the scheme (1). First, one should keep in mind that the $\mathbb{F}_{ij}$ matrices are sparse. Therefore, this phase holds complex gather-scatter access patterns. Second, as the underlying mesh is unstructured, we neither have a priori

---

[2]Hardware configuration is described in section 6.

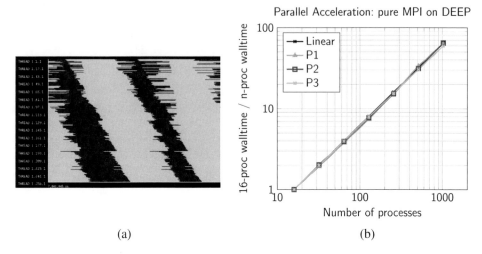

(a)   (b)

Figure 3. (a): Paraver visualization of processing events (blue) and MPI_SENDRECV events (brown) in the case of blocking p2p communications involving 256 processes. (b): Scalability results - 20 time loop iterations for a 1.8 million cells human head mesh - pure MPI speedup on the DEEP Cluster using 16 processes per node, from one to 64 nodes.

control on the typical difference of index between one cell and its neighbour (i.e. the memory locality of the concerned data) nor on its balancing among processes. One way

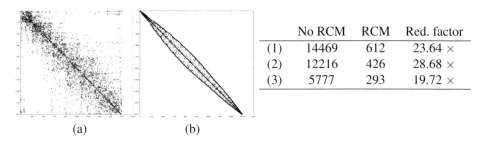

	No RCM	RCM	Red. factor
(1)	14469	612	23.64 ×
(2)	12216	426	28.68 ×
(3)	5777	293	19.72 ×

(a)   (b)

Figure 4. Example of profile of the cell affinity matrix before (a) and after (b) renumbering - Over 128 processes: (1): worst bandwidth, (2): average bandwidth, (3): best bandwidth.

to cope with this is to apply a cell-index renumbering scheme – at the pre-processing stage – aiming to minimizing the bandwidth of the mesh connectivity matrix[3]. For this, we rely on the so-called Reverse Cuthill-McKee [14] algorithm. Figure 4 shows the effect of such renumbering on the connectivity matrix of one subdomain over 128. For this setting and $k = 1...4$, the observed speedups due to RCM renumbering are respectively: 1.26, 1.19, 1.11, 1.05.

---

[3]We recall the bandwidth of matrix $A = (a_{i,j})$ is the sum of integers $k_{min} + k_{max}$ such that $a_{i,j} = 0$ if $j < i - k_{min}$ or $j > i + k_{max}$.

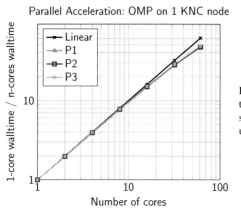

Figure 5. Scalability results - 20 time loop iterations for a 1.8×10^6 cells human head mesh. OpenMP speedup at the level of one Intel Xeon Phi coprocessor, using 4 threads per core, from 1 to 61 cores.

3. Approaching the DEEP-ER Booster: porting to the Intel MIC Architecture

In this section, we report on two specific improvements that have been specifically undertaken in order to approach the booster side of the DEEP-ER architecture: threading and vectorization.

3.1. Threading

Exploiting efficiently the many-core architecture of the Intel Xeon Phi leads to depart from the initial parallelization approach towards a hybrid MPI/OpenMP programming model. This modification is aiming to minimize the amount of MPI processes required to exploit a given amount of Xeon Phi nodes. The idea is not only in order to limit MPI-overhead but also to alleviate stress on the mesh partitioning phase. An important feature of DGTD methods is the cell-local structure of their formulation, which naturally appears in (1). A direct outcome of (1) is that most of the processing in the application is essentially structured around loops on cells i, which are intrinsically parallel and well load-balanced. Consequently, they lend themselves well to the classical OpenMP parallel loop construct with a static scheduling policy. Applying this strategy leads to an amount of processing left outside any parallel region of the code which represents about only 0.2% of CPU time in the sequential case. NUMA awareness has been implemented by ensuring each thread realizes the first memory access its concerned data. This step is not mandatory to approach the first generation of Intel Xeon Phi coprocessors (codenamed Knights Corner) of the DEEP Booster, but lays the foundation to exploit the NUMA structure of the next generation of Intel Xeon Phi processors (codenamed Knights Landing) which will enable the DEEP-ER Booster. Figure 5 shows strong scaling results of the OpenMP parallelization strategy executed in a node with an Intel Xeon Phi coprocessor. For these experiments, with an affinity policy set to "compact", we use 4 threads per core and increase the number of cores from 1 to 61. The observed parallel efficiency for the full 244 available threads on the coprocessor are respectively for $k = 1...4$: 81%, 79%, 82% and 94%.

3.2. Vectorization

Achieving good performance on the Intel MIC architecture requires the ability of efficiently exploiting their 512 bits-wide registers. Using Intel® VTune™ tools to investigate the baseline version of the application (with $k = 3$) using 240 threads of the coprocessor shows that 84% of CPU time in the time-loop is spent in what can be identified as vectorizable kernels. These kernels consist for the most part in applying the cell-local mass, stiffness and interface matrices introduced in (1). A first step towards vectorization

```
DO k=1,ndl                              DO ic=1,3
  flx(k) = 0.0d0                          DO k=1,ndl
  fly(k) = 0.0d0                            temp1=flux(k,ic,jt)
  flz(k) = 0.0d0                          !$OMP SIMD
  DO j=1,ndl                               DO j=1,ndl
    flx(k) = flx(k) + amat(k,j)*flux(1,j,jt)    fl(j,ic) = fl(j,ic) + amat(j,k)*temp1
    fly(k) = fly(k) + amat(k,j)*flux(2,j,jt)  ENDDO
    flz(k) = flz(k) + amat(k,j)*flux(3,j,jt)  ENDDO
  ENDDO                                  ENDDO
ENDDO

          OLD                                    NEW
```

Figure 6. Cell-local Inverted Mass Matrix/Vector product kernel rewriting. Here, jt is the index of the local cell, ndl is N_k, and ic=1...3 describes the 3 blocks of $\mathbb{M}_i^{-1}$ of which coefficients are stored in amat.

improvement consists in upgrading the matrix-vector products to a more efficient syntax, as exemplified in figure 6. This step includes loop reordering and data rearranging (e.g. inverting the two first dimensions of the flux array), as well as relying on OpenMP SIMD constructs to enforce vectorization in innermost loops. A second crucial step is to make sure that concerned data is well-aligned is these rewritten kernels. This is not a priori the case given the values of N_k (renamed ndl in the algorithm of figure 6). The most lightweight solution to this issue is to add padding bytes to the first dimension of concerned double precision arrays in order to reach the next multiple of 64 Bytes, that is to say in the case of amat: amat(1:ndl,1:ndl) becomes amat(1:ndl+MOD(ndl,8),1:ndl). Of course, the same treatment should be applied to intermediate arrays such as the fl array of previous example. It is interesting to remark that first, these modifications come at a very moderate memory cost. The few concerned matrices are indeed shared by all threads of a given process. Second, data alignment almost comes for free on the DEEP cluster nodes based on Intel® microarchitecture code name Sandy Bridge. On these, registers can hold 2 double precision real numbers and N_k happens to be an even number for moderate orders – except for $k = 4$ where $N_k = 35$ and should be padded to 36. Table 2 summarizes the speedup resulting from vectorization enhancement for different values of k, taking the baseline multithreaded version of the code as the reference. One will notice that higher order computations involving larger matrix/vector operations naturally take a better advantage of vectorization optimizations. It is worth noting that the speedup for $k = 4$ is remarkably nearly twice as important as for $k = 1$. Table 3 shows the compared

Speedup with respect to Baseline (OpenMP threading)	$k = 1$	$k = 2$	$k = 3$	$k = 4$
Optimized Linear Algebra + OpenMP SIMD + RCM	1.07	1.33	1.32	1.40
... + Padding bytes	1.13	1.63	1.72	2.18

Table 2. Vectorization speedup (full time-loop) - 244 threads on an Intel Xeon Phi coprocessor

performance of the tuned application between the Intel Xeon processors of the DEEP cluster nodes and the Intel Xeon Phi coprocessor for different values of k. For these experiments, the application is run using one process and multiple OpenMP threads on one (out of two) socket of a DEEP cluster node (with 8 cores) and one Booster node using all available 244 threads. It is worth noting that also in that case, the higher the order k is, the greater is the improvement met by the application. In particular, vectorization-oriented optimizations have a decisive impact on the 4th order solver, for which the node to node comparison leans toward the MIC architecture. It is interesting to remark that, first, the larger local problems are, the higher is the reached percentage of peak performance and second, this tendency is more pronounced on the Intel MIC architecture than DEEP cluster nodes.

Intel Xeon Phi coprocessor speedup v.s...	$k = 1$	$k = 2$	$k = 3$	$k = 4$
...DEEP cluster node (one socket, 8 cores)	1.13	1.61	1.55	2.16
... full DEEP cluster node (16 cores)	0.60	0.89	0.87	1.16
%Pperf	$k = 1$	$k = 2$	$k = 3$	$k = 4$
Full Intel Xeon Phi coprocessor (61 cores)	2%	5%	7%	12%
Full DEEP cluster node (16 cores)	14%	21%	32%	38%

Table 3. Performance comparison of the tuned application: Intel Xeon Phi coprocessor speedup with respect to a DEEP cluster node, reached percentage of Peak Performance (%Pperf).

4. I/O Scalability

In the application, most of the I/O activity resides in application-level checkpointing and writing the final solution to disk. In both cases the output operations – which involve a total amount of data that is independent from amount of sub-meshes – are performed to process-local files. In the DEEP-ER software stack, SIONlib [5] is an adequate tool to alleviate the stress on the filesystem which occurs when increasing significantly the amount of parallel file access. As such, it has been integrated to the application. Figure 7 shows the improvement in terms of output time due to the use of the SIONlib library, for two different problem sizes corresponding to $k = 1$ and $k = 3$. The number of processes is increased up to 1024 on the DEEP cluster, which we recall is equipped with the BeeGFS filesystem. It is interesting to remark how SIONlib allows to maintain to an almost constant level the output time as the number of processes is increased. This is not the case when the baseline methodology is used. In that situation, the output time grows almost linearly with the number of processes, which is an effect of the filesystem overhead being the vast majority of the time spent in the output routines.

5. Concluding remarks and outlook

The outcome of recent efforts in porting the application to the Intel MIC architecture should allow to reach the best performance out of the DEEP-ER prototype by running at least the time loop in its Booster side based on the next generation of the Intel Xeon Phi processors. The Cluster side might still be leveraged for running some parts of the pre- and post-processing phases which do not lend themselves well to multithreading, as well as I/O intensive routines. One possibility to achieve this is to consider a model in which these less scalable and I/O phases would be reverse-offloaded from Booster processes to Cluster processes in a one-to-one mapping. This will be achieved by exploiting the

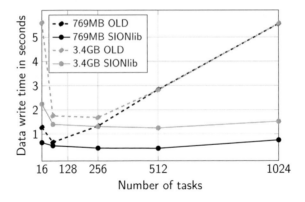

Figure 7. I/O scalability with SIONlib: comparison of outpit times (w/ & w/o SIONlib - DEEP cluster)

OmpSs DEEP offload functionality, developed at Barcelona Supercomputing Center for the DEEP-ER platform. In future work, the OmpSs framework will also be leveraged to expose task-based parallelism and exploit task-based resilience.

6. Acknowledgments

This work has been funded by the DEEP-ER (Dynamical Exascale Entry Platform - Extended Reach) FP7 project of European Commission (grant agreement no. 610476). The authors would also like to acknowledge the work of the Exascale Cluster Laboratory behind the DEEP-ER project.

Intel, Xeon, Xeon Phi, VTune and Many Integrated Core are trademarks or registered trademarks of Intel Corporation or its subsidiaries in the United States and other countries.

* Other brands and names are the property of their respective owners.

Hardware configuration used throughout this work is described in table 4.

	Processor model	Memory	Network	Compiler	OS
(1)	2 x Intel Xeon E5-2680	32GB	Infiniband	Intel15.2.164	CentOS 6.3
(2)	Intel Xeon Phi Coprocessor 7120A	16GB	-	Intel15.1.133	2.6.38.8+MPSS3.2.1

Table 4. Hardware and software configuration - (1) DEEP cluster nodes, (2) Intel Xeon Phi

References

[1] Damian A. Mallon, Norbert Eicker, Maria Elena Innocenti, Giovanni Lapenta, Thomas Lippert, and Estela Suarez. On the scalability of the clusters-booster concept: a critical assessment of the DEEP architecture. In *Proceedings of the Future HPC Systems: The Challenges of Power-Constrained Performance*, FutureHPC '12, pages 3:1–3:10, New York, NY, USA, 2012. ACM.

[2] Alejandro Duran, Eduard Ayguadé, Rosa M Badia, Jesús Labarta, Luis Martinell, Xavier Martorell, and Judit Planas. OmpSs: a proposal for programming heterogeneous multi-core architectures. *Parallel Processing Letters*, 21(02):173–193, 2011.

[3] http://www.beegfs.com. BeeGFS/FhGFS, 07 2015. Accessed: 2015-07-09.

[4] Jan Heichler. Picking the right number of targets per server for BeeGFS®. Technical report, ThinkParQ, March 2015.

[5] Wolfgang Frings, Felix Wolf, and Ventsislav Petkov. Scalable massively parallel I/O to task-local files. In *Proceedings of the Conference on High Performance Computing Networking, Storage and Analysis, SC '09*, pages 17:1–17:11, Portland, Oregon, 2009.

[6] André Brinkmann, Toni Cortes, Hugo Falter, Julian Kunkel, and Sai Narasimhamurthy. E10 – Exascale IO. White paper, Exascale10 Workgroup, http://www.eiow.org/home/E10-Architecture.pdf, May 2014.

[7] Jonathan Viquerat, Maciej Klemm, Stéphane Lanteri, and Claire Scheid. Theoretical and numerical analysis of local dispersion models coupled to a Discontinuous Galerkin Time-Domain method for Maxwell's equations. Research Report RR-8298, INRIA Sophia-Antipolis Méditerrannée, May 2013.

[8] Loula Fezoui, Stéphane Lanteri, Stéphanie Lohrengel, and Serge Piperno. Convergence and stability of a Discontinuous Galerkin Time-Domain method for the 3D heterogeneous Maxwell equations on unstructured meshes. *ESAIM: Mathematical Modelling and Numerical Analysis*, 39:1149–1176, 11 2005.

[9] Jan S Hesthaven and Tim Warburton. *Nodal Discontinuous Galerkin methods: algorithms, analysis, and applications*, volume 54. Springer-Verlag New York Inc, 2008.

[10] Clément Durochat, Stéphane Lanteri, and Raphaël Léger. A non-conforming multi-element DGTD method for the simulation of human exposure to electromagnetic waves. *International Journal of Numerical Modelling: Electronic Networks, Devices and Fields*, 27(3):614–625, 2014.

[11] Tristan Cabel, Joseph Charles, and Stéphane Lanteri. Performance evaluation of a multi-gpu enabled finite element method for computational electromagnetics. In Michael Alexander et al., editor, *Euro-Par 2011: Parallel Processing Workshops - CCPI, CGWS, HeteroPar, HiBB, HPCVirt, HPPC, HPSS, MDGS, ProPer, Resilience, UCHPC, VHPC, Bordeaux, France, August 29 - September 2, 2011, Revised Selected Papers, Part II*, volume 7156 of *Lecture Notes in Computer Science*, pages 355–364. Springer, 2011.

[12] Vincent Pillet, Jesús Labarta, Toni Cortes, and Sergi Girona. Paraver: A tool to visualize and analyze parallel code. In *Proceedings of WoTUG-18: Transputer and occam Developments*, volume 44, pages 17–31. mar, 1995.

[13] George Karypis and Vipin Kumar. A fast and high quality multilevel scheme for partitioning irregular graphs. *SIAM Journal on scientific Computing*, 20(1):359–392, 1998.

[14] W. Liu and A. Sherman. Comparative analysis of the Cuthill–McKee and the Reverse Cuthill–McKee Ordering Algorithms for Sparse Matrices. *SIAM Journal on Numerical Analysis*, 13(2):198–213, 1976.

Parallel Computing: On the Road to Exascale
G.R. Joubert et al. (Eds.)
IOS Press, 2016
doi:10.3233/978-1-61499-621-7-361

361

High Performance Eigenvalue Solver in Exact-diagonalization Method for Hubbard Model on CUDA GPU

Susumu YAMADA [a,c,1], Toshiyuki IMAMURA [b,c] and Masahiko MACHIDA [a,c]

[a] *Center for Computational Science & e-Systems, Japan Atomic Energy Agency*
[b] *Advanced Institute for Computational Science, RIKEN*
[c] *CREST (JST)*

Abstract. The graphics processing unit (GPU) is an excellent accelerator and it can realize speedup with appropriate tuning. In this paper, we present a tuning technique for the exact diagonalization method, which is widely used as a numerical tool to obtain the ground state (the smallest eigenvalue and the corresponding eigenvector) of the Hamiltonian derived from the Hubbard model, on the GPU architecture. Since the Hamiltonian is a sparse matrix, an iteration method is used for solving the eigenvalue problems. We mainly tune the code for the multiplication of the Hamiltonian and a vector, which is the most time-consuming operation in the iteration method. The numerical test shows that the tuned code is faster than the one with using the routine "cusparseDcsrmm" of cuSPARSE library. Moreover, the tuned method on NVIDIA Tesla M2075 achieves about $3\times$ speedup as compared with the thread-parallelized code on six threads of Intel Xeon 5650 for the multiplication.

Keywords. matrix-vector multiplication, CUDA GPU, exact diagonalization method, eigenvalue problem, quantum lattice systems

Introduction

The Hubbard model[1,2] has attracted a tremendous number of physicists since the model exhibits a lot of interesting phenomena such as High-T_c superconductivity. They have proposed many computational approaches to reveal the properties of the model. The most accurate approach is the exact diagonalization method which solves the ground state (the smallest eigenvalue and the corresponding eigenvector) of the Hamiltonian derived exactly from the models. Since the Hamiltonian is a huge sparse matrix, we usually solve the eigenvalue problem by an iteration method whose most time-consuming operation is a matrix-vector multiplication. We have previously parallelized the exact diagonalization method on a parallel vector supercomputer system, such as the Earth Simulator, in consideration of the physical properties of the model and obtained some novel physical results[3,4,5,6]. However, the proposed algorithm is specialized for a vector

---

[1] Corresponding Author: Susumu Yamada, Japan Atomic Energy Agency, 178-4 Wakashiba, Kashiwa, Chiba, 277-0871, Japan; E-mail: yamada.susumu@jaea.go.jp

processor and the algorithm is not suitable for scalar multi-core CPUs, which are nowa-days the mainstream processors. Actually, the algorithm achieves only a few percent of the theoretical peak performance of the CPU.

The graphics processing unit (GPU), which is the other mainstream processor, can achieve an excellent performance with regular data access pattern. Therefore, efficient matrix storage formats have been discussed for the high performance multiplication of a sparse matrix and a vector for the GPU[7,8] . On the other hand, T. Siro et al. have proposed a high performance algorithm for the Hamiltonian-vector multiplication on the NVIDIA GPU by partitioning the vector into one-dimensional blocks in consideration of the physical properties of the Hubbard model[9].

In this research, we transform the vector into a two-dimensional array using the property of the Hubbard model and propose a multiplication algorithm that partitions the above array into two-dimensional blocks, in order to execute the exact diagonalization code on a GPU. Moreover, we will investigate the relationship between the performance and the shape of the block in order to find the optimal shape.

The rest of the paper of structured as follows. In Section 2, we briefly introduce the Hubbard model and the storing data for high performance computing, and we propose a tuning strategy of the multiplication on the GPU. Moreover, Section 3 presents the result of the numerical experiment on Fermi GPU. A summary and conclusion are given in Section 4.

1. Storing Hamiltonian and vector for High performance Exact diagonalization of Hubbard model

The Hamiltonian of the Hubbard model (Figure 1) is

$$H = - \sum_{i,j,\sigma} t_{i,j}(c_{j\sigma}^{\dagger}c_{i\sigma} + c_{j\sigma}c_{i\sigma}^{\dagger}) + \sum_{i} U_{i}n_{i\uparrow}n_{i\downarrow}, \qquad (1)$$

where $t_{i,j}$ is the hopping parameter from the i-th site to the j-th one and U_i is the repulsive energy for on-site double occupation of two fermions on the i-th site. Quantities $c_{i,\sigma}$, $c_{i,\sigma}^{\dagger}$ and $n_{i,\sigma}$ are the annihilation, the creation, and the number operator of a fermion with pseudo-spin σ on the i-th site, respectively. Here, each state of the spins in the model corresponds to each index of the Hamiltonian. The hopping parameter causes the element $t_{i,j}$ with the column-index corresponding to the original state and the row-index corresponding to the state after hopping (see Figure 2). Moreover, each diagonal element derives from the repulsive energy U_i on each state (see Figure 2). When we solve the ground state of the Hamiltonian, we can understand the properties of the Hubbard model.

In the exact diagonalization method, we usually solve the ground state of the Hamiltonian utilizing an iteration method, such as the Lanczos method [10], the CG method [11,12], and so on, because the Hamiltonian is a huge sparse matrix. It is crucial to tune the Hamiltonian matrix-vector multiplication, since the multiplication is the most time-consuming operation of the solvers. Therefore, the storage formats for the Hamiltonian and the vector are critical for high performance computing. Here, we notice that the multiplication Hv can be split as

$$Hv = Dv + (I_{\downarrow} \otimes A_{\uparrow})v + (A_{\downarrow} \otimes I_{\uparrow})v, \qquad (2)$$

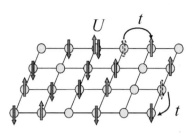

Figure 1. The schematic figure of the Hubbard model, where t and U are the hopping parameter and the repulsive energy in the double occupation on a site, respectively. The up-arrow and the down-arrow stand for fermion with up-spin and down-spin, respectively.

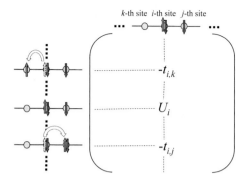

Figure 2. How to construct the Hamiltonian of the Hubbard model. Each state of the spins corresponds to each index of the Hamiltonian. The hopping parameter $t_{i,j}$ derived from hopping an up-spin from the i-th site to the j-th one is allocated in off-diagonal. The element from the repulsive energy U_i is allocated in the main diagonal. Here, it is noted that i, j, and k are the site numbers, not the indexes of the matrix.

where $I_{\uparrow(\downarrow)}$, $A_{\uparrow(\downarrow)}$, and D are the identity matrix, a sparse symmetric matrix derived from the hopping of an up-spin (a down-spin), and a diagonal matrix from the repulsive energy, respectively. This formula (2) shows that we can execute the multiplication by storing the nonzero elements of the three matrices $A_\uparrow$, $A_\downarrow$, and D, not those of the Hamiltonian. Moreover, we can see that the last two multiplications of (2) can be transformed into $A_\uparrow V$ and $VA_\downarrow^T$ utilizing the property of the direct product with the identity matrix, where the matrix V is constructed by decomposing the vector v into n blocks and ordering them in the two-dimensional manner as follows

$$v = (\underbrace{v_{1,1}, v_{2,1}, \ldots, v_{m,1}}_{\text{the first block}}, \underbrace{v_{1,2}, v_{2,2}, \ldots, v_{m,2}}_{\text{the second block}}, \cdots, \underbrace{v_{1,n}, v_{2,n}, \ldots, v_{m,n}}_{\text{the }n\text{-th block}})^T. \tag{3}$$

Here, m and n are the dimensions of the $A_\uparrow$ and $A_\downarrow$, and a pair of subscripts of each element indicates an index on the matrix V. In the following section, we will tune the multiplications by using the property in which the matrix V is dense.

2. Exact diagonalization for Hubbard model on GPU

2.1. Algorithm of Hamiltonian-vector multiplication

The multiplication (2) can be represented as

$$V_{i,j}^{new} = \bar{D}_{i,j}V_{i,j} \tag{4}$$

$$+ \sum_{k=1}^{m} A_{\uparrow i,k}V_{k,j} \tag{5}$$

$$+ \sum_{k=1}^{n} V_{i,k}A_{\downarrow k,j}, \tag{6}$$

Table 1. Details of GPU Server.

Processor	Intel Xeon X5650 (2.66GHz)
Number of cores per processor	6
GPU	NVIDIA Tesla M2075
Fortran Compiler	pgfortran 12.3-0
CUDA Driver Version	4000
Compile option (GPU)	`-fast -Mcuda:4.0 -lcublas -llapack -lblas`
Compile option (CPU)	`-fast -llapack -lblas`

where the subscript i, j of the matrix is represented as the (i, j)-th element and $\bar{D}$ is constructed from the diagonal elements of the matrix D by the same manner as to (3). Here, each element of V^{new} can be executed in parallel for all value of i and j. Therefore, we implement the multiplication on CUDA GPU using the parallelism.

2.2. Implementation of multiplication on CUDA GPU

In this subsection, we propose an implementation strategy for the multiplications (4), (5), and (6) on a CUDA GPU. The multiplications are realized with the CUDA Fortran codes shown in Figure 3. Here, the data of the matrix V for AV and VA^T have to be stored in row-major order and column-major one, respectively, so that the contiguous memory access can be realized. Therefore, the transpose operation for V is required as an additional one. Our proposed algorithm is as follows:

1. $V^{new} \leftarrow$ Elementwise product of $\bar{D}$ and V (Figure 3 (a)),
2. $V_t \leftarrow V^T$ (transpose),
3. $V^{new} \leftarrow V^{new} + A_{\uparrow}V$ using V_t (Figure 3 (b)),
4. $V^{new} \leftarrow V^{new} + VA_{\downarrow}^T$ (Figure 3 (c)).

On the other hand, the algorithm for AV proposed in [9] uses the matrix V stored in column-major order. Therefore, it does not need the transpose operation, however, it can not realize the contiguous memory access.

When we execute a code on the GPU, we divide tasks and data of the code, and we assign each divided them into each GPU thread. The thread block shape, that is, the thread layout, can be chosen arbitrarily. For example, the algorithm proposed in [9] is essentially the same as the algorithms on `blockDim%y=1`. However, the shape has a strong influence over the performance on the GPU and the appropriate shape has to be chosen for high performance computing. Therefore, we examine the elapsed times for the multiplications of the Hamiltonians derived from the 16-site one-dimensional and 4×4-site two-dimensional Hubbard models with the open boundary condition using double precision in several thread block shapes with 128, 256, 512, and 1024 threads on the GPU server with NVIDIA Tesla M2075 (its details are shown in Table 1). Here, the number of spins and the dimension of the model have influence on the size of the Hamiltonian matrix and the distribution of non-zero elements of the matrix, respectively.

Table 2 shows the optimal shape and its elapsed time for each operation. The result shows as follows:

- In (4), the case of `blockDim%x=128` and `blockDim%y=1`, i.e, the matrix is subdivided into colunmwise strip-shaped blocks, is optimal, because the multiplication is equivalent to the elementwise product of 1-dimensional vectors.

```
i=(blockIdx%x-1)*blockDim%x+threadIdx%x
j=(blockIdx%y-1)*blockDim%y+threadIdx%y
!!
  V_new(i,j)=D̄(i,j)*V(i,j)
```

(a)Elementwise product of $\bar{D}$ and V

```
j=(blockIdx%x-1)*blockDim%x+threadIdx%x
i=(blockIdx%y-1)*blockDim%y+threadIdx%y
!!
  do k=iru(i), iru(i+1)-1
    V_new(i,j)=V_new(i,j)+Au(k)*Vt(j,icu(k))
  enddo
```

(b) $A_\uparrow V$

```
i=(blockIdx%x-1)*blockDim%x+threadIdx%x
j=(blockIdx%y-1)*blockDim%y+threadIdx%y
!!
  do k=ird(j), ird(j+1)-1
    V_new(i,j)=V_new(i,j)+V(i,icd(k))*Ad(k)
  enddo
```

(c) $VA_\downarrow^T$

Figure 3. Hamiltonian (matrix)-vector multiplication in CUDA Fortran. V_t in $A_\uparrow V$ is the transpose of V. The contiguous memory access can be realized by using V_t. Here, the non-zero elements of the matrices $A_\uparrow$ and $A_\downarrow$ are stored in the CRS format, that is, the vectors A*, ic*, and ir* store the the value of non-zero elements, the column indexes of the elements, and the indexes where each row starts.

- In (5) and (6), the optimal blockDim%x is 32. The reasons are as follows: For the coalesced memory access on the CUDA GPU, blockDim%x should be a multiple of 16. Moreover, since our method uses the CRS format for storing the non-zero elements of the matrices $A_\uparrow$ and $A_\downarrow$, the number of the elements in each low is not the same. Accordingly, only when blockDim%x is a multiple of 32, the same instruction with 32 contiguous threads in one warp can be executed. On the other hand, in order to realize the effective reuse of data, we should use small blockDim%x and large blockDim%y. However, when blockDim%y is too large, all data can not be stored in cache memory. Consequently, the optimal blockDim%x is 32, and the optimal blockDim%y depends on the distribution of non-zero elements of the matrix.

We implement the multiplication in CUDA Fortran in consideration of these results in the following numerical examinations.

2.3. Performance comparison with cuSPARSE

Since $A_\uparrow V$ and $VA_\downarrow^T$ are multiplications of a sparse matrix and a dense matrix, we can realize the multiplications with using the NVIDIA CUDA Sparse Matrix Library (cuS-PARSE) [13]. The multiplication $A_\uparrow V$ can be executed using "cusparseDcsrmm" routine straightforwardly. On the other hand, when we execute the multiplication $VA_\downarrow^T$ using "cusparseDcsrmm", we have to transform $VA_\downarrow^T$ into $(A_\downarrow V^T)^T$. Therefore, this multiplication requires the transpose of the matrix and its algorithm is as follows:

Table 2. Optimal shape and elapsed time for Hamiltonian-vector multiplication on GPU.

a) 1-D model with 5 up-spins and 5 down-spins

	Transpose	$\bar{D}_{i,j}V_{i,j}$	AV	VA^T
blockDim%x	4	128	32	32
blockDim%y	64	1	8	16
Elapsed time (sec)	3.94×10^{-3}	4.29×10^{-3}	1.70×10^{-2}	1.23×10^{-2}

Dimension of $A_{\uparrow}(A_{\downarrow})$: 4368,   Number of non-zero elements of $A_{\uparrow}(A_{\downarrow})$: 30030
Dimension of Hamiltonian H: 19079424,   Number of non-zero elements of H: 281421504

b) 2-D model with 5 up-spins and 5 down-spins

	Transpose	$\bar{D}_{i,j}V_{i,j}$	AV	VA^T
blockDim%x	4	128	32	32
blockDim%y	64	1	16	16
Elapsed time (sec)	3.94×10^{-3}	4.29×10^{-3}	2.17×10^{-2}	1.78×10^{-2}

Dimension of $A_{\uparrow}(A_{\downarrow})$: 4368,   Number of non-zero elements of $A_{\uparrow}(A_{\downarrow})$: 48048
Dimension of Hamiltonian H: 19079424,   Number of non-zero elements of H: 438826752

c) 1-D model with 6 up-spins and 6 down-spins

	Transpose	$\bar{D}_{i,j}V_{i,j}$	AV	VA^T
blockDim%x	4	128	32	32
blockDim%y	32	1	16	16
Elapsed time (sec)	1.34×10^{-2}	1.49×10^{-2}	6.30×10^{-2}	4.73×10^{-2}

Dimension of $A_{\uparrow}(A_{\downarrow})$: 8008,   Number of non-zero elements of $A_{\uparrow}(A_{\downarrow})$: 60060
Dimension of Hamiltonian H: 64128064,   Number of non-zero elements of H: 1026049024

d) 2-D model with 6 up-spins and 6 down-spins

	Transpose	$\bar{D}_{i,j}V_{i,j}$	AV	VA^T
blockDim%x	4	128	32	32
blockDim%y	32	1	16	16
Elapsed time (sec)	1.34×10^{-2}	1.49×10^{-2}	8.59×10^{-2}	6.93×10^{-2}

Dimension of $A_{\uparrow}(A_{\downarrow})$: 8008,   Number of non-zero elements of $A_{\uparrow}(A_{\downarrow})$: 96096
Dimension of Hamiltonian H: 64128064,   Number of non-zero elements of H: 1603201600

1. $V_1 \leftarrow Dv$ (elementwise product),
2. $V_1 \leftarrow V_1 + A_{\uparrow}V$ (using "cusparseDcsrmm"),
3. $V_{tmp} \leftarrow V^T$ (transpose),
4. $V_2 \leftarrow A_{\downarrow}V_{tmp}$ (using "cusparseDcsrmm"),
5. $V^{new} \leftarrow V_1 + (V_2)^T$ (transpose and addition).

Since step 3 (transpose) is independent of step 1 and 2 in this algorithm, it is a possible to execute the transpose (step 3) on the CPU in parallel with step 1 and 2 on the GPU. However, the parallel calculation requires extra data transfer between CPU and GPU, because all data in this numerical experiment can be stored in GPU memory. Therefore, we execute all calculations on the GPU in this research. Figure 4 shows the elapsed time of the multiplication using "cusparseDcsrmm" and our method. The result indicates that our method is 1.7-2.7 times faster than "cusparseDcsrmm". There are two reasons why "cusparseDcsrmm" is slower. One is that the routine "cusparseDcsrmm" assumes that the dense matrix is tall. The other is that although it is desirable to store the data of the dense

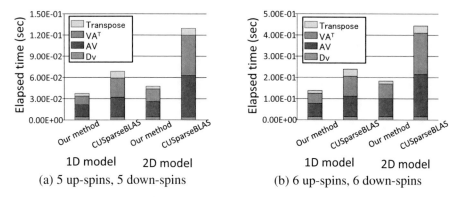

(a) 5 up-spins, 5 down-spins   (b) 6 up-spins, 6 down-spins

Figure 4. Elapsed time of the multiplication using "cusparseDcsrmm" and our method.

Table 3. Elapsed time and performance for exact diagonalization on GPU and CPU (6 cores). In GPU, the elapsed time for AV includes that of transposing V into V_t. In CPU, since $\bar{D}_{i,j}V_{i,j}$ and AV are merged to reduce the load/store operations from memory, the total elapsed time of them is shown.

Dim. of Model		Number of iterations	Elapsed time (sec)					GFLOPS	
			Overall	Multiplication				Overall	multi-plication
				Total	$\bar{D}_{i,j}V_{i,j}$	AV	VA^T		
1D	GPU	88	39.44	13.04	1.34	7.32	4.38	11.16	13.72
	CPU	86	72.13	36.30	25.22		11.08	5.95	4.82
2D	GPU	102	50.00	19.57	1.55	10.62	7.40	12.59	16.70
	CPU	99	95.48	54.44	33.80		20.64	6.39	5.83

matrix in the row-major order for the contiguous data access, the column-major order has to be used for using "cusparseDcsrmm". Therefore, we conclude that our method is more suitable for the Hamiltonian-vector multiplication than the routine "cusparseDcsrmm" on the GPU.

3. Numerical experiment

We examine the performance of the exact diagonalization code using double precision on GPU and CPU (6 cores) on the server shown in Table 1. We use the LOBPCG method [11,12] as the exact diagonalization code and solve the same Hubbard models with 6 up-spins and 6 down-spins in the previous section. The thread-parallelized code for the multiplication for CPU is shown in Figure 5. Moreover, we implement the linear oper ations in the GPU code using CUBLAS. Table 3 shows the elapsed time and the per- formance (GFLOPS). The result demonstrates that the GPU gains a about 2× speedup for the whole code compared to CPU (6 cores). Moreover, we notice that the perfor- mance for the 2D model is superior to that for the 1D one for the GPU. The reason is that there is more non-zero elements of Hamiltonian derived from the 2D model and the increase in cache hit rate is expected. Especially, an about 3× speedup is achieved only for the multiplication operation. Therefore, we conclude that our tuning strategy of the Hamiltonian-vector multiplication is very effective for the GPU.

```
!$omp parallel do
   do ii=1,nnp        !! nnp is the number of OpenMP threads
   ndim0=(ndim-1)/nnp+1
   !!
   !! Elementwise product of D̄ and V   (D̄ᵢ,ⱼVᵢ,ⱼ)
      do j=1,mdim
         do i=max(1,(ii-1)*ndim0+1),min(ndim,ii*ndim0)
            V_new(i,j)=D̄(i,j)*V(i,j)
         enddo
      enddo
   !!
   !! A↑V
      do j=1,mdim,32
         do i=max(1,(ii-1)*ndim0+1),min(ndim,ii*ndim0)
            do k=iru(i), iru(i+1)-1
               do jj=j,min(j+31,ndim)
                  V_new(i,jj)=V_new(i,jj)+Au(k)*V(icu(k),jj)
               enddo
            enddo
         enddo
      enddo
   !!
   !! VA↓ᵀ
      do j=1,mdim
         do k=ird(j), ird(j+1)-1
            do i=max(1,(ii-1)*ndim0+1),min(ndim,ii*ndim0)
               V_new(i,j)=V_new(i,j)+V(i,icd(k))*Ad(k)
            enddo
         enddo
      enddo
   !!
   enddo
!$omp end parallel do
```

Figure 5. Hamiltonian-vector multiplication in Fortran code for multi-threads (OpenMP). In $A_\uparrow V$, the loop tiling with block size 32 is used for improving the cache memory use. Here, `ndim` and `mdim` are the dimensions of $A_\uparrow$ and $A_\downarrow$, respectively.

4. Conclusion

We have proposed the tuning strategy for the Hamiltonian-vector multiplication on the exact diagonalization method for the Hubbard model on the CUDA GPU. The strategy is realized in consideration of the property of the Hubbard model, not the storage format of a sparse matrix. We examined the performance of our strategy by changing the thread block shape, that is, `blockDim%x` and `blockDim%y`, and we specified the optimal one. We compared the performance for solving the Hubbard model with our strategy on the GPU to that on 6 cores. The result demonstrated that the GPU gains about $2\times$ speedup compared to the 6 cores. Especially, an about $3\times$ speedup has been achieved only for the Hamiltonian-vector multiplication.

In future work, we aim to realize the high performance exact diagonalization for larger Hubbard models on large computer systems with multi-GPUs. In order to achieve this, we will investigate the strategy for data communication between CPU and GPU, and between nodes. Then, we will examine the physical property of larger Hubbard models with executing the method on the multi-GPUs.

Acknowledgment

This research was partially supported by CREST (JST) and JSPS KAKENHI Grant Number 15K00178.

References

[1]   M. Rasett, editor. *The Hubbard Model: Recent Results*. World Scientific, Singapore, 1991.
[2]   A. Montorsi, editor. *The Hubbard Model*. World Scientific, Singapore, 1992.
[3]   The Earth Simulator Center. http://www.jamstec.go.jp/esc/index.en.html.
[4]   M. Machida, S. Yamada, Y. Ohashi, and H. Matsumoto. Novel superfluidity in a trapped gas of fermi atoms with repulsive interaction loaded on an optical lattice. *Phys. Rev. Lett.*, 93:200402, 2004.
[5]   S. Yamada, T. Imamura, and M. Machida.   16.447 tflops and 159-billion-dimensional exact-diagonalization for trapped fermion-hubbard model on the earth simulator. In *Proc. of SC05*, 2005.
[6]   S. Yamada, T. Imamura, T. Kano, and M. Machida. High-performance computing for exact numerical approaches to quantum many-body problems on the earth simulator. In *Proc. of SC06*, 2006.
[7]   N. Bell and M. Garland. Efficient sparse matrix-vector multiplication on cuda. Technical report, NVIDIA Technical Report NVR-2080994, 2008.
[8]   N. Bell and M. Garland. Implementing sparse matrix vector multiplication on throughput-oriented processor. In *Proc. of SC09*, 2009.
[9]   T. Siro and A. Harju. Exact diagonalization of the hubbard model on graphics processing units. *Comp. Phy. Comm.*, 183:1884–1889, 2012.
[10] J.K. Cullum and R.A. Willoughby. *Lanczos Algorithms for Large Symmetric Eigenvalue Computations, Vol.1: Theory*. SIAM, Philadelphia, 2002.
[11] A. V. Knyazev. Preconditioned eigensolvers - an oxymoron? *Electronic Transactions on Numerical analysis*, 7:104–123, 1998.
[12] A. V. Knyazev. Toward the optimal eigensolver: Locally optimal block preconditioned conjugate gradient method. *SIAM J. Sci. Comput.*, 23:517–541, 2001.
[13] cuSPARSE. URL: https://developer.nvidia.com/cusparse.

Parallel Computing: On the Road to Exascale
G.R. Joubert et al. (Eds.)
IOS Press, 2016
doi:10.3233/978-1-61499-621-7-371

A general tridiagonal solver for coprocessors: Adapting g-Spike for the Intel Xeon Phi

Ioannis E. VENETIS, Alexandros SOBCZYK, Alexandros KOURIS,
Alexandros NAKOS, Nikolaos NIKOLOUTSAKOS and
Efstratios GALLOPOULOS
HPCLab, Computer Engineering and Informatics Department
University of Patras, Greece

Abstract. Manycores like the Intel Xeon Phi and graphics processing units like the NVIDIA Tesla series are prime examples of systems for accelerating applications that run on current CPU multicores. It is therefore of interest to build fast, reliable linear system solvers targeting these architectures. Moreover, it is of interest to conduct cross comparisons between algorithmic implementations in order to organize the types of optimizations and transformations that are necessary when porting in order to succeed in obtaining performance portability. In this work we aim to present a detailed study of the adaptation and implementation of g-Spike for the Xeon Phi. g-Spike was originally developed to solve general tridiagonal systems on GPUs, on which it returns high performance while also solving systems for which other state-of-the-art general tridiagonal GPU solvers do not succeed. The solver is based on the Spike framework, using QR factorization without pivoting implemented via Givens rotations. We show the necessary adaptations on the Xeon Phi because of the significant differences in the programming models and the underlying architectures as well as the relative performance differences for data access and processing operations.

Keywords. parallel tridiagonal solvers, Givens rotations-based QR, Intel Xeon Phi, Spike framework, singular matrix

Introduction

Manycores like the Intel Xeon Phi and graphics processing units like the NVIDIA Tesla series are prime examples of commercially available systems for accelerating applications that run on current CPU multicores. Nowadays, it is common for HPC systems to be built as clusters of multicores, with each node being enhanced by coprocessor accelerators. It becomes, therefore, of interest to build fast, reliable linear system solvers targeting these coprocessors and to conduct cross comparisons between algorithmic implementations in order to define and organize the types of optimizations and transformations that are necessary when porting in order to succeed in obtaining performance portability. One major category of

solvers targets banded and in particular, tridiagonal matrices. In fact, surveying the research literature ([1]) leads to the conclusion that tridiagonal solvers
have been designed for practically every newcomer HPC system. For example, we
now find several descriptions of tridiagonal solvers for GPUs [2–14] that build on
previous work on parallel solvers; see e.g. [15–18].

In this work in progress we aim to present a study of the adaptation and
implementation of the g-Spike solver for the Xeon Phi. The solver, based on a
method proposed in [19], was recently redesigned, implemented, and shown ([20])
to return high performance on GPUs while also solving systems for which other
state-of-the-art general tridiagonal solvers for the GPU do not succeed. The solver
is based on the Spike framework ([21–23]) and can be applied even when the partitioning creates singular submatrices along the diagonal; this is a key advantage
of g-Spike over existing methods. We show the adaptations that are necessary
on the Xeon Phi because of the significant differences in the programming models
and the underlying architectures as well as the relative performance differences for
data access and data processing operations. Our interest is in performance, scalability and a systematic comparison with the optimizations applied and achieved
performance relative to an NVIDIA Tesla system.

1. Motivation and previous work

The recently introduced Intel Xeon Phi is a coprocessor that has drawn the attention for speeding up computationally intensive parts of applications; [24]. Therefore, we are interested in effective tridiagonal solvers on this coprocessor.

Fast tridiagonal solvers of parallel complexity $\mathcal{O}(\log n)$ have long been known,
but require special matrices (e.g. diagonally dominant or symmetric positive definite) in order to work reliably; cf. [25]. Otherwise, if Gaussian elimination is
used, it is prudent to apply pivoting so as to reduce the risk of instability. Partial
pivoting might perturb the tridiagonal structure, however, and cause additional
overhead in their implementation. One recent important finding ([3]) was the very
high performance that can be achieved for tridiagonal solvers on GPUs based
on the Spike approach and a special block diagonal pivoting approach [26]. The
algorithm of [3] was carefully mapped on the GPU architecture and was shown
to be fast for very large problems, also solving systems that could not be solved
by existing methods in NVIDIA's cuSPARSE library (these methods are based
on cyclic reduction and its variants and thus require special properties from the
matrix.) Following these developments, the main outstanding issues were on the
topic of stability of the methods; see e.g. related comments in [27]. In particular,
one issue is related to the overall stability because of the "small support pivoting"
in Spike, the other because of the ad-hoc partitioning that may lead to singular
subproblems and failure. Regarding the former, it is worth noting that experiments in [3] demonstrated that the Spike approach introduced in that paper is
not only fast but has forward stable behavior (cf. [25]), that is the results returned are commensurate with those of a backward stable method. The latter issue was recognized (cf. [28]) but not addressed in [3]. The question arises because,
even after accepting the overhead of an effective pivoting strategy, a partitioned

non-singular matrix can have one or more blocks along the diagonal be singular. Without safeguards, a method attempting to solve these blocks would fail.

To address this issue, we recently introduced `g-Spike`, a scheme competitive with [3] in performance and returning solutions with acceptable forward error when current direct tridiagonal solvers on GPUs deliver inaccurate results; cf. [20]. In particular, the partitioning and divide-and-conquer strategies that are commonly used not only in cuSPARSE but also in SCALAPACK[1], are not designed to work if any of the generated sub-systems is detected to be singular. In order to improve on this issue, we revisited the first version of the Spike algorithm as it was proposed in [19] and considered a CUDA implementation and its performance. The algorithm uses Givens-based QR factorization of the tridiagonal submatrices along the diagonal. Not only pivoting is unnecessary, but in addition we showed that the scheme contains a "singularity detection and modification" procedure. We also showed that this is equivalent with a special low rank update of the matrix that boosts unwanted zero values making possible the computation of partial solutions that are then used to construct the solution of the entire (nonsingular) tridiagonal system. `g-Spike` differs in several aspects from the theoretical description in [19]. The method does not require from the system to be similar to a symmetric one and the formulation of the treatment of any singularities is different. Moreover, there are differences in the treatment of the reduced system. Like [19], however, it allows the user to partition without worrying about the occurrence of singular blocks, since these are handled automatically. As our experiments indicate, despite the higher cost of QR relative to LU, `g-Spike` exploits the high performance of elementary CUDA kernels and it has performance similar or better than the block diagonal pivoting approach of [3].

2. Porting `Spike` to the Intel Xeon Phi

A number of recently built supercomputers utilize the Xeon Phi in order to achieve performance that puts these systems in the Top500 list of the most powerful computers, turning the Xeon Phi into a top-notch solution for accelerating large applications. Considering this fact, in addition to the previously described properties of `g-Spike`, we aim towards an implementation of our algorithm for the Xeon Phi. The Xeon Phi is a recently introduced coprocessor and aims to provide functionality similar to GPUs that support CUDA and OpenCL, i.e., provide to applications the opportunity to offload computationally intensive parts to it for faster execution. However, both the architecture and the programming models used on the Xeon Phi are radically different than that of a GPU. Whereas a GPU provides even thousands of computational cores, the Xeon Phi provides only up to 61 cores, although each one supports 4-way Hyper-Threading, i.e., it supports execution of four threads in hardware that share the resources of a single core. Furthermore, the architecture of each core is completely different among the two coprocessors. Long latency memory accesses are handled in the GPU by simply switching to another thread that is ready for execution. No special hardware is used to minimize memory access times. As long as there are enough threads, each

---

[1]See for example http://icl.cs.utk.edu/lapack-forum/viewtopic.php?t=24

core can continue executing instructions of the application. On the other hand, the Xeon Phi follows a more traditional approach, since large data caches are employed for this purpose. Furthermore, an important source of execution speed improvement, in addition to the multiple cores and threads per core, is the employment of vectorization. With 512-bit wide SIMD registers, a single instruction can be applied on a larger number of operands than previous processors support.

CUDA and OpenCL are the primary programming models employed to offload computations to a GPU. Both are based on the C programming language, either as an extension (CUDA) or a library (OpenCL). However, the fact that they are relatively new programming models means that there is a small number of programmers that use them. On the other hand, one of the main programming models for the Xeon Phi is OpenMP, which is already well established, well known and widely used. The addition of directives to exploit the SIMD capabilities of the coprocessor, instead of using intrinsics until recently, further simplifies programming. Hence, one advantage of the Xeon Phi is that it provides an attractive programming environment that is more familiar to a wider range of programmers.

Having as a starting point the implementation for the GPU, several adaptations had to be made, due to the different architecture of the coprocessors, taking a number of key points into account. A first decision had to be made about the execution model that would be used. The *native* mode allows building an application for the Xeon Phi, copying the relevant executable file to the coprocessor and starting execution from the coprocessor itself. On the other hand, the *offload* mode allows inclusion of appropriate directives in the source code of the application, which denote which parts of the code and data are copied to the coprocessor for processing. Execution starts at the system that hosts the coprocessor. As soon as execution reaches a point where directives have been added, the relevant code and the necessary data are copied to the coprocessor. Finally, when calculations are completed the annotated data is copied back to the host and execution continues there. Since the GPU supports only the *offload* mode of execution, we also opted towards this mode for the Xeon Phi in order to make fair comparisons, which requires the time for data transfers to be accounted for in both cases.

2.1. High level parallelization strategy

With respect to the parallelization strategy for the algorithm, we decided to follow a two-level approach that fits the architecture of the Xeon Phi. At the first level OpenMP is used to distribute work among hardware threads. At the second level, each thread takes advantage of vectorization. Recall that mapping calculations on execution units in a GPU is performed by defining a grid of blocks, with each block consisting of a grid of threads. Each level of this hierarchy can have up to 3 dimensions. Hence, blocks within the grid and threads within each block are identified through a set of coordinates, which are assigned by the system software of the GPU. A rather complicated, but automated procedure was followed in [20] for g-Spike to determine the best combination on the number of blocks and threads for a given GPU, so as to create an optimal number of sub-blocks in the initial matrix. Porting g-Spike to the Xeon Phi required replacement of this procedure. The number of sub-blocks in this case is determined by the number of hardware threads requested during execution. A by-product of this change has been a large simplification of indexing elements of the matrix, thus increasing the overall percentage of executing useful floating-point calculations in the application. Finally, the embarrassingly parallel nature of calculations allows for a straightforward parallelization of the modified code using OpenMP. More specifically, calculations within a sub-block do not depend on data of other sub-blocks. Hence, a simple #omp parallel for directive at a few, selected points in the code is enough to assign each sub-block to a hardware thread of the Xeon Phi. Overall, leveraging this level of parallelism in the case of g-Spike has been far easier for the Xeon Phi than for the GPU.

2.2. Vectorization aspects

Using vectorization in g-Spike, which is the main source of achieving high levels of performance on the Phi, proved to be not as straightforward. The implementation of g-Spike on the GPU can be split into two distinct operations, (i) reorganization of data within the initial matrix and (ii) performing actual calculations. We analyze separately the possibility of vectorizing each of these operations.

The purpose of the first set of operations is to move into adjacent memory locations the elements of the matrix that are accessed together when performing calculations and at the end bring the elements back to their original position. As far as the GPU is concerned, this allows exploitation of coalesced memory accesses from the memory of the GPU (DRAM). This has a significant impact on the total execution time, since it reduces overall data transfer time. When porting the application to the Xeon Phi, we decided to keep these operations due to the existence of data caches. Accessing an element brings now into the cache the rest of the elements required for an operation. Since there are no data dependencies when reorganizing elements, vectorization is straightforward. In order, however, for elements in their original position to be collected and moved to adjacent memory locations a "gather" like vectorization instruction is exploited. This implies that the solution might be architecture specific and will probably cost more on other architectures. Even on the Xeon Phi, these instructions do not have the same performance compared to vectorization instructions where data is already on adjacent memory locations.

Process (ii) above can be further decomposed into three steps, (a) *Givens QR* decomposition, (b) a *rank correction* step and (c) *backward substitution* for the formation of the spikes. For the rest of the paragraph we focus on (a) and (c). From an algorithmic perspective, these two steps are inherently sequential, since they consist of loops with *Read-After-Write* (RAW or "flow") dependencies (e.g. Figure 1). Such loops cannot be vectorized, thus preventing a straightforward mapping of the corresponding code on the Xeon Phi. It is worthy of note that when the subsystems have additional structure, e.g. positive definiteness or diagonally dominance, one can use methods such as cyclic reduction or recursive doubling to take advantage of hierachical parallelism or vectorization; see e.g. Algorithm SPIKE-CR in [5] and references therein. In the literature, however, there do not seem to be implementations for general tridiagonal systems that use parallel algorithms to solve the subsystems resulting from the partitioning. We are

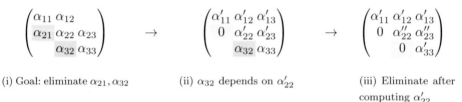

(i) Goal: eliminate α_{21}, α_{32} (ii) α_{32} depends on α'_{22} (iii) Eliminate after computing α'_{22}

Figure 1.: *Read-After-Write* data dependencies for the Givens QR step.

currently investigating this issue and plan to consider the use of further levels of parallelism taking advantage of the hierarchical structure of the Spike algorithm in order to use Spike within each subsystem as well as vector processing to handle multiple right-hand sides.

3. Numerical experiments

In order to evaluate our approach, we conducted experiments on a single Xeon Phi accelerator. The host system used is an 8x Intel(R) Core(TM) i7-3770K CPU @ 3.40GHz running CentOS 6.6 (x86_64). The Xeon Phi accelerator of the system is the 3120A with 57 cores @ 1.1GHz, each core supporting 4-way HyperThreading and a total of 6GB main memory. The compiler used is the Intel Compiler 15.0.1.

The first experiment evaluates the impact of automatic vectorization and hand-tuning vectorization by adding directives in our code. Results are shown in Figure 2. The size of the system to be solved is $N = 2^{20}$ and the time measured includes transferring code and data to the Xeon Phi, performing calculations on the Phi and returning data back to the host (cf. Figure 2a). Even without adding vectorization directives, the compiler was able to vectorize some loops in the code. We use this version of the code as a baseline ("No vectorization" in Figure 2a). Adding vectorization directives to loops that had not been automatically vectorized, as described in Subsection 2.2, yields an improvement ranging from 3% in the case of 128 threads to 19% in the case of 8 threads. Best performance is achieved when 16 threads are created. However, the speedup achieved in this case is a rather modest 2.33. We attribute this low speedup to the short execution time of g-Spike and the overhead to create and handle large numbers of threads

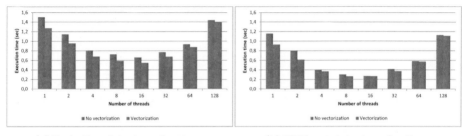

(a) Including data transfer time.   (b) Without data transfer time.

Figure 2.: Performance improvement after hand-tuning vectorization.

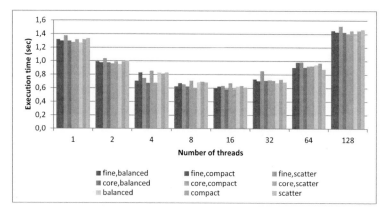

Figure 3.: Effect of different OpenMP thread mapping strategies.

in the run-time system of the Xeon Phi. Similar conclusions can be drawn from Figure 2b, where time to transfer data is not accounted for.

Another possibility to improve performance is to define the mapping of software threads on the hardware threads of the Phi. Different mappings affect the exploitation of the cache hierarchy and the required bandwidth to main memory. Results with this strategy are shown in Figure 3. When *fine* granularity is defined, each OpenMP thread is bound to a single hardware thread. In the case of *core* granularity, all OpenMP threads bound to a core are allowed to float between the different hardware threads of that core. These granularity options can be combined with affinity types. With *compact*, an OpenMP thread is assigned to a free hardware thread that is as close as possible to the hardware thread where the previous OpenMP thread has been assigned. Specifying *scatter* distributes OpenMP threads as evenly as possible across the entire system. The type *balanced* is similar to *scatter* with the difference that when multiple hardware threads have to be used on the same core it ensures that the OpenMP thread numbers are close to each other. The combinations of the above options correspond to the first six bars in Figure 3. However, with the above definitions no upper limit in the number of used cores is set. The last three bars correspond to the case when we further restrict the number of used cores to the minimum necessary, e.g., for 32 OpenMP threads we request usage of 8 cores. It can be observed that these options can have a significant effect on performance. For example, when the *core* granularity is specified and 4 OpenMP threads are created, the difference between the best and worst case for different affinity types reaches 21%. It is also worth noting that in most cases the best performance was achieved when restricting the total number of cores to use (last three bars) and exploiting the *balanced* affinity type.

We also compared our results with solvers from the SCALAPACK library[2] designed for general banded systems and in particular routine pdgbsv [29]. It is worth noting that the LAPACK routine dgtsv which solves a general tridiagonal system is not threaded in the Intel Math Kernel Library (MKL) and therefore we did not use it in our experiments. The results are presented in Figure 4. SCALAPACK requires MPI to run its routines in parallel. In order to simplify

---

[2]See http://www.netlib.org/scalapack/index.html.

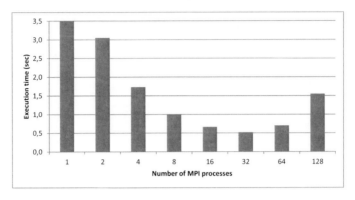

Figure 4.: Execution time of SCALAPACK routine `pdgbsv` using different numbers of cores on the Xeon Phi.

implementation and data collection, we used the *native* mode for running `pdgbsv` on the Xeon Phi, i.e., the host does not participate in the computations and no data is transferred between the host and the coprocessor. Hence, the results of Figure 4 should be compared to Figure 2b, which also does not include time for data transfers. `g-Spike` is up to 5 times faster than `pdgbsv` when 2 and 4 threads and processes are used respectively. The Intel MPI implementation used in our experiments exploits shared memory to exchange data among processes that reside on a shared memory system, like the Intel Xeon Phi. Hence, the difference in execution time is mainly due to the different algorithmic approaches. It is worth noting that both algorithms have a similar behavior as more cores are used, e.g., execution time increases as more cores are used.

4. Conclusions and future work

In this paper we presented our effort to port the `g-Spike` algorithm, a general tridiagonal solver developed for the GPU, to the Intel Xeon Phi coprocessor. A two-level parallelization approach has been utilized for this purpose. OpenMP directives have been used at the first level to distribute work among execution units on the Xeon Phi. Vectorization directives have then been used as the second level of parallelism. Our experience from porting our algorithm from one coprocessor architecture to another was that OpenMP was significantly easier to use for distributing work, in contrast to mapping the algorithm on the grid of blocks and threads on a GPU. On the other hand, exploiting vectorization throughout our implementation has been more difficult. We intend, however, to further investigate the possible solutions at this level. Since this difficulty shows up in other tridiagonal solvers, an efficient solution would be of general interest. Our experimental results indicate that the low computational load of our algorithm does not allow effective use of all available cores of the Xeon Phi. Other solvers, like the one from SCALAPACK used herein, also suffer from the same issue. Fortunately, appropriately mapping software to hardware threads might improve performance significantly. Finally, we intend to further investigate other relevant solvers and compare their performance to `g-Spike` on the Xeon Phi.

Acknowledgments

The present work was financially supported by the "Andreas Mentzelopoulos Scholarships, University of Patras". We would like to thank the reviewers for their valuable comments and suggestions that improved the final version of our paper.

References

[1] E. Gallopoulos, B. Philippe, and A.H. Sameh. *Parallelism in Matrix Computations*. Springer, 2016.

[2] D. Goeddeke and R. Strzodka. Cyclic reduction tridiagonal solvers on GPUs applied to mixed-precision multigrid. *Parallel and Distributed Systems, IEEE Transactions on*, 22(1):22–32, 2011.

[3] L.-W. Chang, J.A. Stratton, H.S. Kim, and W.-M.W. Hwu. A scalable, numerically stable, high-performance tridiagonal solver using GPUs. In *Proc. Int'l. Conf. High Performance Computing, Networking Storage and Analysis*, SC '12, pages 27:1–27:11, Los Alamitos, CA, USA, 2012. IEEE Computer Society Press.

[4] L.-W. Chang. *Scalable Parallel Tridiagonal Algorithms with Diagonal Pivoting and Their Optimization for Many-core Architectures*. PhD thesis, Dept. of Electrical and Computer Eng., University of Illinois at Urbana-Champaign, 2014.

[5] L.-W. Chang and W.-M.W. Hwu. A guide for implementing tridiagonal solvers on GPUs. In V. Kindratenko, editor, *Numerical Computations with GPUs*, pages 29–44. Springer, 2014.

[6] H.-S. Kim, S. Wu, L.-w. Chang, and W-m.W. Hwu. A scalable tridiagonal solver for GPUs. In *Proc. 2011 Int'l. Conf. Paral. Proc.*, ICPP '11, pages 444–453, Washington, DC, USA, 2011. IEEE Computer Society.

[7] I-J. Sung, J.A. Stratton, and W.-M.W. Hwu. Data layout transformation exploiting memory-level parallelism in structured grid many-core applications. In *Proc. 19th Int'l. Conf. Parallel Arch. Compil. Tech. (PACT)*, PACT '10, pages 513–522, New York, NY, USA, 2010. ACM.

[8] NVIDIA. *CUDA Toolkit Documentation v. 6.5: cuSPARSE*, Accessed Oct. 28, 2014. http://docs.nvidia.com/cuda/cusparse.

[9] A. Davidson, Y. Zhang, and J.D. Owens. An auto-tuned method for solving large tridiagonal systems on the GPU. In *In Proc. of 2011 IPDPS*, 2011.

[10] J. Lamas-Rodriguez, F. Argüello, D.B. Heras, and M. Bóo. Memory hierarchy optimization for large tridiagonal system solvers on GPU. In *10th IEEE Int'l. Symposium on Parallel and Distributed Processing with Applications*, pages 87–94. IEEE, July 2012.

[11] B.J. Murphy. Solving tridiagonal systems on a GPU. In *20th Annual Int'l. Conf. High Perf. Comput., HiPC 2013, Bengaluru (Bangalore), Karnataka, India, December 18-21, 2013*, pages 159–168. IEEE Computer Society, 2013.

[12] P. Quesada-Barriuso, J. Lamas-Rodríguez, D.B. Heras, M. Bóo, and F. Argüello. Selecting the best tridiagonal system solver projected on multi-core CPU and GPU platforms. In H.R. Arabnia, editor, *Proc. PDPTA'11*, pages 839–845, 2011.

[13] Y. Zhang, J. Cohen, and J.D. Owens. Fast tridiagonal solvers on the GPU. *ACM SIGPLAN Notices*, 45(5):127–136, 2010.

[14] D. Zhao and J. Yu. Efficiently solving tri-diagonal system by chunked cyclic reduction and single-GPU shared memory. *J. Supercomput.*, pages 1–22, 2014.

[15] P. Arbenz. On ScaLAPACK's banded system solvers. In M. Deville and R. Owens, editors, *Proc. 16th IMACS World Congress 2000 on Scientific Computation, Applied Mathematics and Simulation (IMACS2000)*, page 6 pages (CD). IMACS, 2000.

[16] P. Arbenz, A. Cleary, J. Dongarra, and M. Hegland. A comparison of parallel solvers for general narrow banded linear systems. *Parallel and Distributed Computing Practices*, 2(4):385–400, 1999.

[17] P. Arbenz and M. Hegland. Scalable stable solvers for non-symmetric narrow-banded linear systems. In P. Mackerras, editor, *Seventh International Parallel Computing Workshop (PCW'97), Australian National University*, 1997.

[18] J.J. Dongarra and L. Johnsson. Solving banded systems on a parallel processor. *Parallel Comput.*, 5(1-2):219–246, 1987.

[19] A.H. Sameh and D.J. Kuck. On stable parallel linear system solvers. *J. Assoc. Comput. Mach.*, 25(1):81–91, January 1978.

[20] I. E. Venetis and A. Kouris and A. Sobczyk and E. Gallopoulos and A. H. Sameh. A direct tridiagonal solver based on Givens rotations for GPU architectures. *Parallel Computing*, 2015.

[21] E. Polizzi and A.H. Sameh. A parallel hybrid banded system solver: The SPIKE algorithm. *Parallel Computing*, 32:177–194, 2006.

[22] M. Manguoglu, F. Saied, A. Sameh, and A. Grama. Performance models for the Spike banded linear system solver. *Sci. Program.*, 19(1):13–25, Jan. 2011.

[23] H. Gabb, D.J. Kuck, P. Tang, D. Wong, A.H. Sameh, M. Manguoglu, and E. Polizzi. Intel Adaptive Spike-Based Solver, Submitted Oct. 2010, accessed Mar. 1, 2015. https://goo.gl/HZA2ra.

[24] J. Jeffers and J. Reinders. *Intel Xeon Phi Coprocessor High Performance Programming*. Morgan Kaufmann Publishers Inc., San Francisco, CA, USA, 1st edition, 2013.

[25] N.J. Higham. *Accuracy and Stability of Numerical Algorithms*. SIAM, Philadelphia, 2nd edition, 2002.

[26] J.B. Erway and R.F. Marcia. A backward stability analysis of diagonal pivoting methods for solving unsymmetric tridiagonal systems without interchanges. *Numerical Linear Algebra with Applications*, 18:41–54, Jan. 2011.

[27] W.-M. Hwu. What is ahead for parallel computing. *JPDC*, 74(7):2574–2581, 2014. Special Issue on Perspectives on Parallel and Distributed Processing.

[28] L.-W. Chang. Scalable parallel tridiagonal algorithms with diagonal pivoting and their optimization for many-core architectures. Master's thesis, Electrical and Computer Engineering of the Graduate College of the University of Illinois at Urbana-Champaign, 2014.

[29] L. S. Blackford, J. Choi, A. Cleary, E. D'Azevedo, J. Demmel, I. Dhillon, J. Dongarra, S. Hammarling, G. Henry, A. Petitet, K. Stanley, D. Walker, and R. C. Whaley. *ScaLAPACK Users' Guide*. Society for Industrial and Applied Mathematics, Philadelphia, PA, 1997.

Parallel Computing: On the Road to Exascale
G.R. Joubert et al. (Eds.)
IOS Press, 2016
© 2016 The authors and IOS Press. All rights reserved.
doi:10.3233/978-1-61499-621-7-381

CAHTR: Communication-Avoiding Householder TRidiagonalization

Toshiyuki IMAMURA [a,c,1], Takeshi FUKAYA [a,c], Yusuke HIROTA [a,c],
Susumu YAMADA [b,c], and Masahiko MACHIDA [b,c]

[a] *RIKEN, Advanced Institute for Computational Science*
[b] *CCSE Japan Atomic Energy Agency*
[c] *CREST Japan Science and Technology agency*

Abstract. The present paper describes an efficient communication optimization technique for Householder tridiagonalization called CAHTR and evaluates its parallel performance. CAHTR is intended to reduce the number of problems in collective communication, especially MPI_Allreduce operations. We demonstrate the optimal version of CAHTR(3) compared with a naive implementation CAHTR(0). The CAHTR algorithms are evaluated on the K supercomputer system, and speed-up exceeds x1.4 for the case of $N = 5000$ and $P = 1024$.

Keywords. communication avoidance, massively parallel eigenvalue solver, Householder tridiagonalization, MPI_Allreduce, parallel DSYMV

Introduction

Narrow memory bandwidth and slow interconnects of modern parallel computers have been reported to result in serious problems by developer teams of state-of-the-art numerical libraries, especially eigensolvers such as ScaLAPACK [1,2], ELPA [3,4], and EigenExa [5,6]. Due to a memory bottleneck, the Householder tridiagonalization is the most time-consuming part of the eigen-decomposition of a dense real symmetric matrix. The memory bottleneck in the Householder tridiagonalization is encountered by two types of operations, symmetric-matrix vector multiplication (SYMV) and rank2 update of a matrix (SYR2), which are categorized as Level2 BLAS. The Dongarra–Sorensen block algorithm [7] resolves the problem in SYR2 by replacing SYR2 with SYR2K, which is the block version of SYR2. Successive Band Reduction or multi-stage tridiagonalization by Bischof et al. [8,9] has resolved the problem in SYMV by replacing SYMV with SYMM or GEMM. Both algorithms contribute to refining the memory bottleneck on parallel eigenvalue solvers. The network bottleneck in parallel computer systems is another matter entirely. Even if the computational cost can be reduced by introducing interconnected processing nodes, the network latency increases according to the number of nodes. Thus, parallel computing must be considered as a trade-off problem between computation and communication.

---

[1] 7-1-26 Minatojima-minami-machi, Chuo-ku, Kobe, Hyogo 650-0047, Japan;
E-mail: imamura.toshiyuki@riken.jp

(01) **for** $j = N \ldots 1$ **step** $-M$
(02) $U \leftarrow \emptyset$ and $V \leftarrow \emptyset$.
(03)   **for** $k = M \ldots 1$ **step** -1
(04)   Compute a Householder reflector (β, u) from $W(:,k)$.
(05) $v := Au$.
(06) $v := v - (UV^\top + VU^\top)u$.
(07) $v := (v - u(u,v)/2\beta)/\beta$.
(08) $U \leftarrow [U,u], V \leftarrow [V,v]$.
(09) $W \leftarrow W - (UV^\top + VU^\top)$.
(10)   **endfor**
(11) $A \leftarrow A - (UV^\top + VU^\top)$.
(12) **endfor**

Figure 1. Dongarra–Sorensen block Householder algorithm

Communication avoidance (CA) is thought to be a key technology for overcoming the above-mentioned drawbacks. CA is based on several programming techniques, such as data replication, exchange of calculation order, and improvement of locality. Typical examples of CA are the Tall Skinny QR decomposition (TSQR) algorithm [10] and the matrix power kernel (MPK) algorithm [11]. These algorithms contribute to reducing communication overhead for the orthonormalization operation and the Krylov subspace iteration method, respectively. Also, block algorithms such as [7] and [12] have a property of reducing communications naturally. However, it is quite hard to exchange a non-block algorithm into a block algorithm due to the data dependency. Even though flops count increases, the CA algorithms tend to reduce the number of communication in order to reduce the total computational time.

In the present study, the authors propose a novel algorithm for the Householder tridiagonalization called Communication-Avoiding Householder TRidiagonalization (CAHTR) by two simple procedures; exchanging execution order, and combining multiple communications. We confirm the effect of the CA-based Householder tridiagonalization on a massively parallel computer.

1. Implementation of parallel Householder tridiagonalization

Let us review a naive implementation of the Householder tridiagonalization. Figure 1 shows the Dongarra–Sorensen block algorithm, a typical sequential algorithm, which is adopted in LAPACK and ScaLAPACK as dsytrd and pdsytrd, respectively.

For distributed parallel implementation, we herein assume a 2D block-or-cyclic parallel data distribution in most eigenvalue libraries, such as ScaLAPACK, ELPA, and EigenExa. In the algorithm, the collective operations broadcast by MPI_Bcast and allreduce by MPI_Allreduce are indispensable for both holding the Householder reflector 'u' by all processes and computing an inner product, respectively. Parallel SYmmetric Matrix-Vector multiplication (SYMV) corresponding to line (05) is a special case of matrix-vector multiplication and can be performed by multiple inner products with column vectors and row vectors. Figure 2 shows two SYMV algorithms, a simple kernel and an extended kernel that take symmetry into account.

(01) **for** $i \in \{1 \ldots n\}$ && $i \in \Pi$
(02) $\quad \sigma := 0;\ \gamma := x_\Pi[i]$.
(03) $\quad$ **for** $j \in \{1 \ldots n\}$ && $j \in \Gamma$
(04) $\quad\quad$ **if** ($j < i$) **then**
(05) $\quad\quad\quad \sigma += (\alpha := A(j,i)) \cdot x_\Gamma[j]$.
(06) $\quad\quad\quad y_\Gamma[j] += \alpha\gamma$.
(07) $\quad\quad$ **endif**
(08) $\quad$ **endfor**
(09) $\quad w_\Pi[i] := \sigma$.
(10) $\quad$ **if** ($i \in \Gamma$) $y_\Gamma[i] += A(i,i) \cdot x_\Gamma[i]$.
(11) **endfor**
(12) **allreduce** $w[i \in \Pi]$ **over** Π on each column
(13) **for** $i \in \{1 \ldots n\}$ && $i \in \Gamma$ && $i \in \Pi$
(14) $\quad y_\Gamma[i] += w_\Pi[i]$
(15) **endfor**
(16) **allreduce** $y[j \in \Gamma]$ **over** Γ on each row

(01) $\tau := 0$.
(02) **for** $i \in \{1 \ldots n\}$ && $i \in \Pi$
(03) $\quad \sigma := 0;\ \gamma := x_\Pi[i]$.
(04) $\quad$ **for** $j \in \{1 \ldots n\}$ && $j \in \Gamma$
(05) $\quad\quad$ **if** ($j < i$) **then**
(06) $\quad\quad\quad \sigma += (\alpha := A(j,i)) \cdot x_\Gamma[j]$.
(07) $\quad\quad\quad y_\Gamma[j] += \alpha\gamma$.
(08) $\quad\quad$ **endif**
(09) $\quad$ **endfor**
(10) $\quad \tau += (w_\Pi[i] := \sigma) \cdot \gamma$.
(11) $\quad$ **if** ($i \in \Gamma$) **then**
(12) $\quad\quad y_\Gamma[i] += (\alpha := A(i,i) \cdot \gamma);\ \tau += \alpha\gamma$
(13) $\quad$ **endif**
(14) **endfor**
(15) **for** $j \in \{1 \ldots n\}$ && $j \in \Gamma$
(16) $\quad \tau += y_\Gamma[j] \cdot x_\Gamma[j]$.
(17) **endfor**
(18) **allreduce** $w[i \in \Pi]$ and τ **over** Π on each column
(19) **for** $i \in \{1 \ldots n\}$ && $i \in \Gamma$ && $i \in \Pi$
(20) $\quad y_\Gamma[i] += w_\Pi[i]$
(21) **endfor**
(22) **allreduce** $y[j \in \Gamma]$ and τ **over** Γ on each row

Figure 2. Parallel SYMV ($y := Ax$) and the extended kernel $[y; \tau] := [Ax; x^\top A x] = [I, x]^\top A x$.

In Figure 2, the notation rules for data distribution refer to Katagiri's study [13]. The rules are summarized as follows:

1. A variable represented by a Greek letter is scalar.
2. A capital letter refers to a matrix.
3. A small letter with a subscript (Γ or Π) refers to a distributed vector, the indices of which are available if the indices are in the set (Γ or Π).
4. Γ and Π represent available row and column index groups, respectively. For example, the process, the id of which is (I, J), has $\Gamma := \{I, I + P_{row}, I + 2P_{row}, \ldots\}$ and $\Pi := \{J, J + P_{column}, J + 2P_{column}, \ldots\}$, when data distribution is in a cyclic-cyclic fashion and the process grid is $P_{row} \times P_{column}$.
5. All other terms are local scalar variables or constants.
6. An index with a bracket '[ ]' or parenthesis '()' is defined in a global view.

The parallel SYMV algorithm (Figure 2) must be designed so as to reduce the total amount of memory access to matrix $A(j,i)$ by taking advantage of row-wise and column-wise communication. On the other hand, this parallel SYMV algorithm requires two expensive allreduce operations in order to sum each element of distributed vectors 'w' and 'y' along the row or column process groups. Furthermore, lines (04), (06) and (07) in Figure 1 need norm of a vector and inner products. Thus, at least five allreduce operations are required in a single issue of the two-sided Householder transformation for a naive parallel implementation.

2. Reduction of the overhead of allreduce

The startup cost for collective operations such as allreduce is relatively large on a standard parallel computer system. Figure 3 presents the benchmark results for multi-

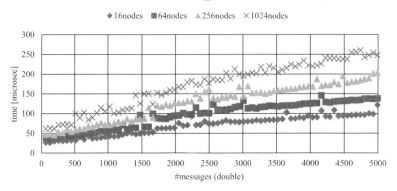

Figure 3. Cost of multi-`MPI_Allreduce` on the K computer.

Allreduce collective communication on the K computer. For practical purposes, the multi-Allreduce operation is defined by simultaneous collective operations along multiple row or column groups, which appears in parallel matrix calculation.[2] The startup penalty is observed to be 25 microseconds, which is the time required to perform 3.84×10^6 floating point calculations on a single node of the K computer, whose peak performance per node is 128 GFLOPS. The result also indicates that a single allreduce operation for a few words and an aggregated allreduce operation consisting of several allreduce operations complete in a similar time. Thus, we are concerned primarily with the number of allreduce operations.

As shown in the previous section, each iteration of the Householder tridiagonalization requires five allreduce operations. In the ELPA library [3,4], Au and $[U,V]^\top u$ are calculated at the same time as $[A;U^\top;V^\top]u$. Then, a single allreduce operation is eliminated without any additional calculations. Consequently, ELPA requires four allreduce operations. Let us refer to the original Householder tridiagonalization and the ELPA's algorithm as CAHTR(0) and CAHTR(1), respectively, in terms of the number of allreduce operations eliminated.

2.1. Three-operation version (CAHTR(2))

Figure 4 shows CAHTR(2), which eliminates **two** allreduce operations in the innermost iteration of the Householder tridiagonalization. The key concept is to extend the form of matrix A and the Householder reflector vector u. Multiplying 'u' and 'e' (a unit vector) by the extended matrix yields $v := Au, d := Ae, \rho = \|u\|^2$, and $\tau := (u,e) = u_1$, simultaneously [14]. Step (5) overtakes step (1) through (4), and step (8) overtakes step (7). Moreover, correction terms are added to steps (4)' and (7)'. The correctness of step (7)' is confirmed by the following equations:

$$\phi := (v^1, u^1) = (v^0, u^1) - (Uc_V + Vc_U)^\top u^1 = (v^0, u^1) - c_V^\top c_U - c_U^\top c_V. \qquad (1)$$

[2] In the benchmark, the process grid is supposed to $\sqrt{P} \times \sqrt{P}$. $\sqrt{P}$ processes are employed in each allreduce operation, and multiple $\sqrt{P}$ allreduce's are run along $\sqrt{P}$ row or $\sqrt{P}$ column process groups, simultaneously.

$$(1)\ \tau := u^\top e, \rho = u^\top u$$
$$(2)\ \sigma := -\text{sign}(\sqrt{\rho}, \tau)$$
$$(3)\ \beta := \sqrt{\rho}(\sqrt{\rho} + |\tau|)$$
$$(4)\ u := u - \sigma e$$
$$(5)\ v := Au$$
$$(6)\ [c_U; c_V] := [U, V]^T u$$
$$(7)\ v := v - (U c_V + V c_U)$$
$$(8)\ \phi := v^\top u$$
$$(9)\ v := (v - u(\phi/2\beta))/\beta$$

$$(1)'\ \begin{bmatrix} v & d \\ \rho & \tau \end{bmatrix} := \begin{bmatrix} A & u \\ u^\top & 0 \end{bmatrix} \begin{bmatrix} u & e \\ 0 & 0 \end{bmatrix}$$
$$(2)'\ \sigma := -\text{sign}(\sqrt{\rho}, \tau)$$
$$(3)'\ \beta := \sqrt{\rho}(\sqrt{\rho} + |\tau|)$$
$$(4)'\ [u, v] := [u, v] - \sigma[e, d]$$
$$(5)'\ [c_U; c_V; \phi] := [U, V, v]^T u$$
$$(6)'\ v := v - (U c_V + V c_U)$$
$$(7)'\ \phi := \phi - 2c_U^\top c_V$$
$$(8)'\ v := (v - u(\phi/2\beta))/\beta$$

Figure 4. Three-operation version (CAHTR(0) [left] and CAHTR(2) [right]).

$$(1)''\ \begin{bmatrix} v & d \\ \hline \rho & \tau \\ \hline c_U & g_U \\ c_V & g_V \\ \hline \phi & v_1 \\ v_1 & a_{11} \end{bmatrix} := \begin{bmatrix} I & 0 & 0 & 0 \\ \hline 0 & 1 & 0 & 0 \\ \hline 0 & 0 & I & 0 \\ 0 & 0 & 0 & I \\ \hline u^\top & 0 & 0 & 0 \\ e^\top & 0 & 0 & 0 \end{bmatrix} \begin{bmatrix} A & u & U & V \\ u^\top & 0 & 0 & 0 \\ U^\top & 0 & 0 & 0 \\ V^\top & 0 & 0 & 0 \end{bmatrix} \begin{bmatrix} u & e \\ 0 & 0 \\ 0 & 0 \\ 0 & 0 \end{bmatrix}$$
$$(2)''\ \sigma := -\text{sign}(\sqrt{\rho}, \tau)$$
$$(3)''\ \beta := \sqrt{\rho}(\sqrt{\rho} + |\tau|)$$
$$(4)''\ \begin{bmatrix} u & v \\ c_U & c_V \end{bmatrix} := \begin{bmatrix} u & v \\ c_U & c_V \end{bmatrix} - \sigma \begin{bmatrix} e & d \\ g_U & g_V \end{bmatrix}$$
$$(5)''\ v := v - (U c_V + V c_U)$$
$$(6)''\ \phi := \phi - 2c_U^\top c_V + \sigma(\sigma a_{11} - 2v_1)$$
$$(7)''\ v := (v - u(\phi/2\beta))/\beta$$

Figure 5. CAHTR(3): two-operation version.

2.2. Two-operation version (CAHTR(3), minimal version)

We propose a more advanced, two-operation version of the CAHTR algorithm, CAHTR(3), which eliminates **three** out of the five required allreduce operations. Step (5)' in Figure 4 overtakes steps (2)' through (4)' and it is combined with step (1)'. This requires an additional multiplication of vectors from the left of the extended matrix in step (1)''. This operation yields several terms required in order to correctly update u and v. Equation 2 shows the derivation of the correction term of ϕ from CAHTR(2).

$$\phi := (v^0 - \sigma d, u^0 - \sigma e) - 2c_V^\top c_U$$
$$= (v^0 . u^0) - \sigma(v^0, e) - \sigma(d, u^0) + \sigma^2(d, e) - 2c_V^\top c_U$$
$$= (v^0, u^0) - 2c_V^\top c_U + \sigma(\sigma a_{11} - 2v_1). \quad (\because (d, u^0) = (Ae, u^0) = (e, v^0) = v_1) \quad (2)$$

In CAHTR(3), we completely divide the algorithm into global and local parts. Only step (1)'' includes two allreduce operations, and all other steps proceed locally. The extended kernel requires two allreduce operations, which is minimal in terms of the number of allreduce operations.

Table 1. Additional parallel calculations per iteration compared to CAHTR(0) and the Allreduce operations required per iteration. Here, n and k refer to the matrix dimension and the block factor (semi-bandwidth-1), respectively. For simplicity, the number of processes is assumed to be a squared number, and the process gird is $\sqrt{P} \times \sqrt{P}$.

	CAHTR(0)	CAHTR(1)	CAHTR(2)	CAHTR(3)
additional calculation per itr.	—	—	(4)' $\frac{2n}{\sqrt{P}}$	(4)" $\frac{2n}{\sqrt{P}} + 4k$
(step) parallel complexity	—	—	(7)' $2k$	(6)" 5
	(1) 1	(1) 1	(1)' $\frac{n}{\sqrt{P}} + 1$	(1)" $\frac{n}{\sqrt{P}} + 1$
	(5) $\frac{n}{\sqrt{P}}$	(5) $\frac{n}{\sqrt{P}}$	(1)' $\frac{n}{\sqrt{P}}$	(1)" $\frac{n}{\sqrt{P}} + 2k + 1$
Allreduce operation per itr.	(5) $\frac{n}{\sqrt{P}}$	(6) $\frac{n}{\sqrt{P}} + 2k$	(5)' $2k + 1$	—
(step) message size	(6) $2k$	(8) 1	—	—
	(8) 1	—	—	—

2.3. Complexity analysis

The main calculation of CAHTR(2) appears in step (4)' of Figure 4. Its complexity is $O(n)$, and its cost is equivalent to $2n/$(sustained daxpy FLOPS) by the time. In the case of the K computer, the sustained daxpy performance is 14.3 GFLOPS (= 43 GB/s [15]). On the other hand, the reduction in the allreduce startup time is expected to be 2*25=50 microseconds as described in Section 2. Since 14.3×10^9 [flop/s] * 50×10^{-6}[s] = $2 * 356 \times 10^3$ [flop] , 50 microseconds is a time equivalent to performing a DAXPY with $n = 356K$. Therefore, the cost increment of CAHTR(2) is negligible. Similar arguments hold for CAHTR(3). Table 1 summarizes the additional parallel calculations per iteration compared with CAHTR(0). Moreover, the required allreduce operations are presented. Here, n and k refer to the size of the intermediate matrix to be transformed and the intermediate block width (corresponding to the loop counter at step (03) in Figure 1), respectively. In addition, Table 1 suggests that CA does not affect the total message size and simplifies the following explanation of the total cost.

Let us use the following simple cost model to interpret the parallel performance:

$$T = \alpha \cdot \#\text{messages} + \beta \cdot \#\text{words} + \gamma \cdot \#\text{flops}.$$

Three coefficients α, β, γ are the communication startup time, the reciprocal of the network throughput, and the reciprocal of FLOPS, respectively. In general, the terms of α and β are represented by functions of P. In the discussion, we fix P, and treat α and β as constants. The differences between CAHTR(k) and CAHTR(0) ($\Delta_k \equiv T_k - T_0$, $k = 1, 2, 3$) are obtained as follows:

$$\Delta T_1 \equiv T_1 - T_0 \sim -\alpha N \tag{3}$$

$$\Delta T_2 \equiv T_2 - T_0 \sim -2\alpha N + \gamma \sum_{l=0}^{N/M-1} \sum_{k=0}^{M-1} (2(lM+k)/\sqrt{P} + 2k)$$

$$\sim \{-2\alpha + \gamma(N/\sqrt{P} + (1+1/\sqrt{P})M)\}N \tag{4}$$

$$\Delta T_3 \equiv T_3 - T_0 \sim -3\alpha N + \gamma \sum_{l=0}^{N/M-1} \sum_{k=0}^{M-1} (2(lM+k)/\sqrt{P} + 4k + 5)$$

$$\sim \{-3\alpha + \gamma(N/\sqrt{P} + (1+1/\sqrt{P})2M + 5)\}N \tag{5}$$

The complexity of the whole process of the naive Householder tridiagonalization is $O(\alpha N + \beta N^2/\sqrt{P} + \gamma N^3/P)$ [16], where α and β are monotonically increasing functions with respect to P, and $O(\beta/\alpha) \sim O(1)$. In this case, the ratio of communication overhead to the total cost is obtained as follows:

$$O(\alpha N)/O(\alpha N + \beta N^2/\sqrt{P} + \gamma N^3/P) \sim 1/O(1 + (\beta/\alpha)N/\sqrt{P} + (\gamma/\alpha)N^2/P). \quad (6)$$

As explained in the previous paragraph, the startup overhead α is 25×10^{-6} [s] when $P = 16$. The term γ is obtained by $1/14.3\text{GFLOPS} = 70 \times 10^{-12}$ [s/word]. Typical parallel eigenvalue computation is performed with parameters such as $N = 10000$ and $P = 1024$. In this case, $\alpha \gg \gamma N/\sqrt{P}$ clearly holds. These parameters yield $\Delta T_3 < \Delta T_2 < \Delta T_1$, and decrement of the communication cost is effective, especially when P is large or when N is not huge. Equation (6) supports this tendency, and it is reasonable for parallel computer systems other than the K computer, because the ratio of α to γ does not differ significantly. Therefore, taking advantage of the proposed communication avoidance technology is a worthy strategy for improving the Householder tridiagonalization.

3. Numerical experiments

In this section, we examine the performance improvements provided by CAHTR(1), CAHTR(2), and CAHTR(3) as compared with CAHTR(0) using the K computer at RIKEN AICS [17].

Figure 6 demonstrates the performance improvement obtained by the implementation of CAHTR(*), when the matrix size N is small or when the number of nodes is large. Communication takes up a relatively large portion of the total computational time. The startup cost of allreduce is 25 microseconds on the K computer when 16 nodes are used. Optimistically, a reduction of 25 microseconds $\times 3 \times 1000 = 75$ milliseconds is expected. Figure 6 shows a 50 millisecond reduction. This value increases when the number of nodes increases because the startup cost of the collective communication also increases (see the case of 1024 nodes in Figures 6 and 3).

Figures 7 and 8 show the elapsed time ratio for CAHTR(0)/CAHTR(x). Most of the values plotted in the contour profiles exceed 1.0, except at the bottom-right corner in Figure 8. These two figures also suggest that CAHTR(3) performs faster when the matrix size is smaller because the communication overhead becomes drastically smaller than CAHTR(0) in such a situation. The best performance improvement is at $N=5000$ (matrix size) and $P=1024$ (number of nodes). The most outstanding result is a x1.4 improvement in CAHTR(3)/CAHTR(0). The observation is reasonable and acceptable considering the cost analysis presented in the previous section.

Several benchmark reports [18,16] summarize the performance of the EigenExa library, in which the proposed algorithms are used. These reports indicate that the Householder tridiagonalization or reduction to a banded matrix is the most time-consuming part, which greatly influences the full-diagonalization performance. The communication time for CAHTR(3) is approximately 85 percent of the total time when $P = 1K$ and $N = 1000$, which is not a suitable for a massively parallel system. Figure 6 also shows that the communication time of CAHTR(3) with $N = 30000$ and $P = 1K$ is 75 percent or less of the total time, whereas that of CAHTR(0) for the same configuration is approxi-

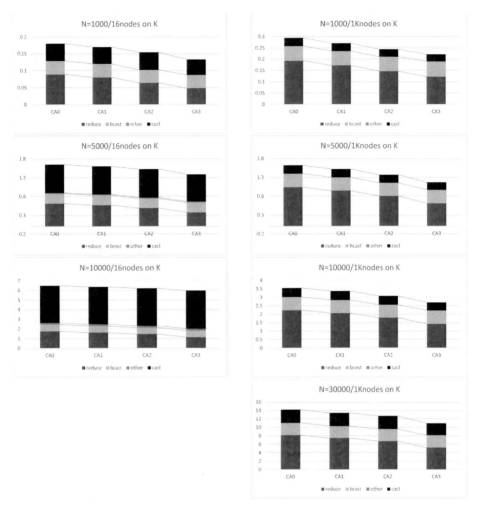

Figure 6. Time breakdown for the CAHTR(x) benchmark (denoted by 'CAx' with $x = 0,1,2,3$) for several parameter configurations, N = 1000 (top), 5000 and 10000 (middle), and 30000 (bottom), and #nodes=16 (left) and 1024 (right). The unit of the vertical axis is seconds.

mately 80 percent or more of the total time. The CAHTR algorithms refine workability and scalability when the number of processes is large but the matrix dimension is small.

4. Conclusion

We have proposed a new type of communication-avoiding algorithm for the Householder tridiagonalization, namely, CAHTR(3). The proposed algorithm has an extended matrix form and divides computation into global and local components. The global computation consists of $(y;t) = [I,u]^\top Ax$, and the number of allreduce operations is limited to two. Numerical experiments revealed a good improvement in performance. We confirmed that the algorithm works effectively when the matrix size is small or when the

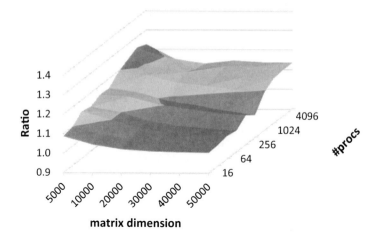

Figure 7. Elapsed time ratio for CAHTR(0)/CAHTR(2).

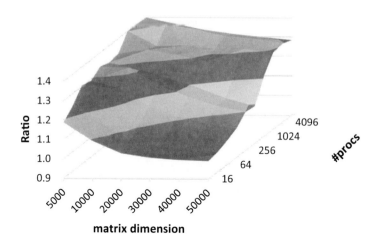

Figure 8. Elapsed time ratio for CAHTR(0)/CAHTR(3).

number of nodes is large. In other words, CAHTR performs effectively when the communication overhead is dominant. A x1.4 improvement in performance was obtained using CAHTR(3). The proposed CAHTR(3) algorithm refines the network bottleneck of the Householder tridiagonalization.

Generally, the network bottleneck will become more significant in emerging supercomputer systems. However, the network bottleneck is too large to be insignificant compared to calculations and other operations. The introduction of CAHTR is very simple and straightforward and involves the distributive law, exchange of execution order, merging of multiple collective communications, and the introduction of correction terms. Since the concept of communication avoidance is applicable to other numerical linear algebra routines, the application of CA to present and future parallel processing is inevitable.

Acknowledgments

The CAHTR(3) algorithm has been included in EigenExa (Version 2.3 later) and is available from the EigenExa homepage [6]. The authors would like to thank RIKEN, JAEA, and JST for their support. The results of the present study were obtained in part using the K computer at RIKEN Advanced Institute for Computational Science. The present study was supported in part by JSPS KAKENHI through a Grant-in-Aid for Scientific Research (B), Number 15H02709.

References

[1] L. Blackford, J. Choi, A. Cleary, E. D' Azevedo, J. Demmel, I. Dhillon, S. Hammarling J. Dongarra, G. Henry, A. Petitet, K. Stanley, D. Walker, and R. Whaley. *ScaLAPACK Users' Guide*. SIAM, 1997.
[2] ScaLAPACK. http://www.netlib.org/scalapack/.
[3] T. Auckenthaler, V. Blum, H. J. Bungartz, T. Huckle, R. Johnny, L. Kramer, B. Lang, H. Lederer, and P. R. Willems. Parallel solution of partial symmetric eigenvalue problems from electronic structure calculations. *Parallel Computing*, 27:783–794, 2011.
[4] ELPA. http://elpa.rzg.mpg.de/.
[5] T. Imamura, S. Yamada, and M. Machida. Development of a high performance eigensolver on the peta-scale next generation supercomputer system. *Progress in Nuclear Science and Technology*, 2:643–650, 2011.
[6] EigenExa. http://www.aics.riken.jp/labs/lpnctrt/EigenExa_e.html.
[7] S. Hammarling, D. Sorensen, and J. Dongarra. Block reduction of matrices to condensed forms for eigenvalue computations. *J. Comput. Appl. Math.*, 27:215–227, 1987.
[8] C. Bischof, M. Marques, and X. Sun. Parallel bandreduction and tridiagonalization. In *Proc. the 6th SIAM Conf. on Parallel Processing for Scientific Computing*, pages 22–24, 1993.
[9] C. Bischof, B. Lang, and X. Sun. Parallel tridiagonalization through two-step band reduction. In *Proc. the Scalable Performance Computing Conference*, pages 23–27, 2014.
[10] James Demmel, Laura Grigori, Mark Hoemmen, and Julien Langou. Communication-optimal parallel and sequential qr and lu factorizations. *SIAM J. Scientific Computing*, 34:206–239, 2012.
[11] M. Hoemmen. Communication-avoiding krylov subspace methods. *PhD Thesis*, 2010.
[12] E. Carson, N. Knight, and J. Demmel. An efficient deflation technique for the communication avoiding conjugate gradient method. *ETNA*, 43:125–141, 2014.
[13] T. Katagiri and Y. Kanada. An efficient implementation of parallel eigenvalue computation for massively parallel processing. *Parallel Computing*, 27(14):1831–1845, 2001.
[14] H. Kondo, T. Yoshida, R. Tamura, and T. Imamura. About development of eigenvalue solver optimized communication by auto tuning *(in Japanese)*. *IPSJ-SIG-Notes*, 2012-HPC-133(24), 2012.
[15] HPC challenge, result. http://icl.cs.utk.edu/hpcc/hpcc_results.cgi?display=combo and http://icl.cs.utk.edu/hpcc/hpcc_record.cgi?id=492.
[16] T. Fukaya and T. Imamura. Performance evaluation of the EigenExa eigensolver on Oakleaf-FX: tridiagonalization versus pentadiagonalization. In *Proc. the 16th IEEE International Workshop on Parallel and Distributed Scientific and Engineering Computing (PDSEC2015)*, 2015.
[17] RIKEN AICS. What is K computer? http://www.aics.riken.jp/en/k-computer/about/.
[18] H. Imachi and T. Hoshi. Hybrid numerical solvers for massively parallel eigenvalue computation and their benchmark with electronic structure calculations. *IPSJ Transactions on Advanced Computing Systems (accepted and in print)*, 52, 2015 (see http://arxiv.org/abs/1504.06443v1).

Parallel Computing: On the Road to Exascale
G.R. Joubert et al. (Eds.)
IOS Press, 2016
© 2016 The authors and IOS Press. All rights reserved.
doi:10.3233/978-1-61499-621-7-391

Simulation of external aerodynamics of the DrivAer model with the LBM on GPGPUs

Andrea PASQUALI [a,1], Martin SCHÖNHERR [a], Martin GEIER [a], and
Manfred KRAFCZYK [a]

[a] *Institut für Rechnergestützte Modellierung im Bauingenieurwesen (iRMB), Technische Universität Braunschweig, Germany*

Abstract. We studied the external aerodynamics of a car employing CFD numerical simulations with the cumulant LBM on GPUs. We performed the analysis for different grid resolutions and for single- and multi-GPU simulations. In order to evaluate the performance of our implementation, we also carried out numerical simulations with the FVM on a CPU cluster using OpenFOAM®. The results showed a good agreement to experimental data and the cumulant LBM computation was substantially faster than the FVM. The cumulant LBM multi-GPU implementation demonstrated also high parallel efficiency. Our work shows that the cumulant LBM on GPU is a valid alternative to FVM on CPUs to perform accurate and efficient CFD simulations of complex engineering problems.

Keywords. Computational Fluid Dynamics (CFD), cumulant lattice Boltzmann method (cumulant LBM), General-Purpose computing on Graphics Processing Units (GPGPU), DrivAer, Engineering

Introduction

The optimization of the external aerodynamics of a car is an important field of investigation for engineers. In order to predict and to study the interaction between the car and the air, experimental tests have been established in wind tunnel setups. They are very expensive and also difficult to set up, implement and manage over the years. To overcome these problems, mathematical models have been developed in order to perform numerical simulations on computers. Nowadays, Computational Fluid Dynamics (CFD) is a standard approach to investigate the behaviour of flow around objects such as cars. Alongside the standard CFD methods, such as the finite volume method (FVM) that solves the Navier-Stokes (N-S) equations, over the last three decades the lattice Boltzmann method (LBM) has emerged as a new effective modelling and simulation approach to CFD. With the development of these mathematical models, there has also been continuous improvement in the hardware and computational resources. High performance computing (HPC) for parallel computations on central processing unit (CPU) clusters is the reference for

---

[1]Corresponding Author: Andrea Pasquali, Technische Universität Braunschweig, Pockelstr. 3, 38106 Braunschweig, Germany; E-mail: pasquali@irmb.tu-bs.de.

CFD numerical simulations. However, in recent years a new architecture has been introduced as a valid alternative to CPU clusters, the general-purpose computing on graphics processing units (GPGPU or simply GPU).

We continue this section giving some background and information regarding the cumulant LBM and the GPU, showing why the LBM is suitable for GPUs and what has been done to date regarding LBM on GPUs. We describe the car model chosen for the analysis and the simulation setup in Section 2, while results, comparison, and performance of the numerical simulations are presented in Section 3. Finally in Section 4 we draw conclusions and give an outlook to future work.

Cumulant lattice Boltzmann method

The lattice Boltzmann method is a numerical method for solving the weakly compressible N-S equations. It is motivated by the Boltzmann transport equation [1] and deals with a discrete local distribution function in momentum space, f. The discrete lattice Boltzmann equation in three dimensions is written as:

$$f_{ijk(x+i\xi\Delta t)(y+j\xi\Delta t)(z+k\xi\Delta t)(t+\Delta t)} = f_{ijkxyzt} + \Omega_{ijkxyzt} \tag{1}$$

where $i\xi$, $j\xi$, and $k\xi$ are the variables in momentum space, ξ is the discrete speed and $i, j, k \in \mathbb{Z}$ and x, y, and z are the variables in space, t is the time variable, and Ω is the collision operator. The evolution of the flow field is split into two steps: the streaming step propagates the distributions according to their respective momentum direction from node to node (lhs of Eq. (1)) and the collision step rearranges the local distributions on each node (rhs of Eq. (1)). The hydrodynamic quantities such as density, velocity and pressure are the moments of f and are computed locally. Hence, to recover these quantities interpolation is never required in the standard LBM and finite differences are never explicitly computed. In order for the streaming to be exact, the discretization of the momentum space is chosen to match exactly with the discretization of the grid. This means that the grid has to be Cartesian and f streams from node to node on a lattice with aspect ratio equal to one, and the speeds are chosen such that all the neighbouring and the source point are reached in a single time step. Due to this duality of the spacial discretization and the discretization of the momentum space the LBM fullfills exactly all chosen conservation laws, i.e. conservation of mass, momentum and angular momentum.

However, this simple modelling of the evolution of the flow does not free us from the difficulty to solve the collision operator Ω that is a convolution of integrals. Our latest solution to Ω is termed cumulant LBM [2]. The cumulant LBM uses cumulants as observable quantities which are both Galilean invariant and statistically independent of each other:

$$c_{\alpha\beta\gamma} = \xi^{-\alpha-\beta-\gamma} \frac{\partial^\alpha \partial^\beta \partial^\gamma}{\partial \Xi^\alpha \partial \Upsilon^\beta \partial Z^\gamma} \ln(\mathscr{L}\{f_{ijk}(i\xi, j\xi, k\xi)\}) \Big|_{\Xi=\Upsilon=Z=0} \tag{2}$$

where Ξ, Υ and Z are the coordinates of the frequency-momentum-space. Cumulants are used only in the collision step where each cumulant is relaxed towards its equilibrium with an individual rate $\omega_{\alpha\beta\gamma}$. While $\omega_{\alpha\beta\gamma}$ for the second moments ($\alpha+\beta+\gamma=2$) fixes the viscosity of the fluid, those for the third and higher moments can be set between 0 and 2. It is demonstrated that the cumulant LBM has very good accuracy and stability of the results and even smaller error than other known LBM methods also for high Reynolds numbers.

Graphics processing units

GPGPUs are graphics processing units for performing computations usually done by CPUs. With the addition of floating-point support, and increased performance of floating-point operations per second and memory bandwidth in combination with the introduction of the unified programmable architecture (the Nvidia® Compute Unified Device Architecture - CUDA), it is straightforward to write applications for computations on the GPU. Because of its highly parallel nature, graphics cards can operate on graphics data (like images) very fast: the same program is executed on many data elements in parallel with an high ratio of arithmetic operations to memory operations. Managing large volumes of data on the GPUs has the enormous advantage to drastically reduce the computational time and to speed up computations. The first application running faster on the GPU than with an optimized implementation on the CPU was an LU factorization in 2005 [3]. However, in these operations with data sharing between the host (CPU) and the device (GPU), the movement of data from the host to the device and vice-versa can still be a bottleneck in the process.

LBM on GPU

One of the first applications of LBM on GPUs was done by Li et al. in 2003 [4]. Li accelerated the LBM computations on the GPU by storing distribution functions into 2D textures and mapping the Boltzmann equations completely to rendering operations. In [5,6] it has been shown (taking into account optimized data structures) how LBM implementations on GPUs can achieve better performance compared to CPU applications. The LBM performance is given by the number of nodal updates per second (NUPS) while the raw performance of a GPU can be estimated as the number of floating point operation per second (FLOPS). Giving some numbers, a well implemented LBM kernel using a uniform grid without any boundary conditions has a performance of app. 1840 FLOPS per grid node with app. 700 MNUPS [7]. The graphics card Nvidia® *Tesla K40c* has a theoretical peak performance of circa 4290 GFLOPS in single precision. Thus the LBM kernel performance is 1840 FLOPS · 700 MNUPS = 1288 GFLOPS with an efficiency of 1288 GFLOPS / 4290 GFLOPS = app. 30%.

1. Cumulant LBM implementation on GPU

We implemented the cumulant LBM on the GPU minimizing the amount of data required to define the grid and perform the stream and collision operations.

1.1. Eso-Twist, pointer chasing, and node updating

The data structure used in the cumulant LBM consists in a sparse matrix called Eso-Twist [8]. Early implementations of the lattice Boltzmann method use two data arrays for streaming, one for reading and one for writing, and streaming and collision are separated steps. The Eso-Twist data structure allows to combine streaming and collision into a single step and requires only one data array for both reading and writing. The notation of the distributions for a three-dimensional lattice with 27 discrete speeds is shown in Figure 1a. The node in the middle (in dark grey) is the source point from which the distributions

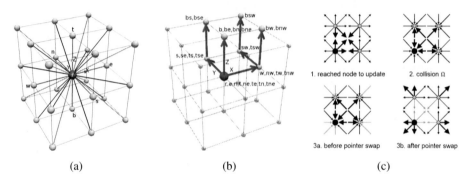

(a)   (b)   (c)

Figure 1. The D3Q27 lattice (a), location of the distributions and pointer chasing (b), and node updating (c).

stream to the 26 neighbours (in light grey). Distributions moving in positive directions (east, north, top, north-east, top-east, top-north, top-north-east) are stored at the index of the respective source node (rest), while distributions moving in negative directions are stored in the respective neighbour in opposite direction. In this way all the distributions are stored only at the nodes in positive directions and only links to seven neighbours have to be provided for each source point (Figure 1b). This number is further reduced to three by the application of a pointer chasing algorithm. The arrows in Figure 1b indicate the pointer chasing paths to reach the neighbours starting form the source point. Hence, the entire connectivity of the D3Q27 lattice is completely defined only by three neighbours in positive X-, Y- and Z-direction.

While collision is performed as usual, streaming is carried out by swapping pairs of distributions with anti-parallel directions after the collision step (Figure 1c). All distributions are written back to the place where the distribution moving in opposite direction has been read. After the procedure is completed for all the nodes, the pointers to the arrays of distributions moving in positive and negative directions are exchanged such that the original ordering of the distributions is restored. The computational time for the swap process is negligible.

1.2. Grid refinement

When solving complex CFD engineering problems, we have to adapt the resolution of the grid in order to have a fine mesh only where necessary. In order to keep the physical quantities, such as the speed of sound, Mach number, and Reynolds number, constant in all the grid resolutions, we have to provide different time step lengths for each grid resolution. For this reason, we should interpolate between the grid resolutions both in space and time. We adopt the approach of overlapping grids presented in [9] and implemented in [10]: only interpolation in space and not in time is required and a quadratic interpolation, that is required for recovering the velocity, is achieved by using compact quadratic interpolations. This approach requires non-aligned grids. Figure 2a shows an example of a grid with two different resolutions. There, the position of a coarse and fine node does not coincide spatially with an offset of $(\Delta x/4, \Delta x/4, \Delta x/4)$ with Δx being the distance between two adjacent coarse nodes. In addition, the two grids have an overlapping region for the interpolation in space in both directions, from the coarse to fine grid (CF) and from the fine to coarse grid (FC). The interpolation zones are shown in grey in Figure 2a. Due to the symmetry of the interpolation zones, the technique is indepen-

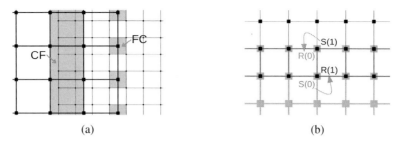

Figure 2. Grid refinement interface (a), and multi-GPU implementation (b).

dent of the orientation of the interface and does not require any special treatment for corners. Moreover, the use of an overlapping region occupies less memory on GPU than an interpolation in time without overlapping region.

1.3. Multi-GPU

When we want to solve large systems and speed up the simulation, we have to parallelize our kernel. In order to perform parallel computations on multiple GPUs, we have to transfer the node distribution function and we have to know which node sends and which node receives it. Figure 2b shows the communication between two GPUs. There, the first GPU has index 0 (bottom) while the second GPU has index 1 (top). The parts of the grid that are allocated on each GPU have duplicated nodes called "receive" (R). The "receive" nodes have the same position as the "send" nodes (S) on different GPUs and they are located at the boundary of the grid. These nodes are required to ensure the correct operation of the LBM kernel in order to avoid bounce-back effects from the boundary interface. In fact, considering for example GPU(0), the distribution functions of the nodes R(0) are updated by the communication operation, and the correct values come from the nodes S(1). The same holds accordingly for GPU(1). The communication among GPUs is performed by using MPICH [11] and the operation is ordered: we perform communication first in X-, then in Y- and finally in Z-direction.

2. Model description

The model selected for the analysis is the DrivAer car presented in [12]. We focused on the rear end fastback configuration of the car with side mirrors, wheels and detailed underbody. We discretized the model provided in CAD format with triangular mesh, and exported in STL format by using the pre-processing software ANSA® [13]. We used the cumulant LBM grid generator LBMHexMesh [14] to generate the unstructured multi-level three-dimensional LBM grid with second order accurate boundary definition (cut cell approach). Three different grid resolutions were tested: coarse mesh, medium mesh and fine mesh. The coarse mesh, with 17.9 M points, and the medium mesh, with 46.7 M points, were generated to run on one single GPU. The fine mesh, with more than 100 M points, was built to run on two GPUs as the number of points did not fit on one single GPU. The grid refinement ratio, defined as the ratio between the grid spacing of two different grids, was 1.5 between the coarse / medium grids and the medium / fine grids. To evaluate the performance of the cumulant LBM multi-GPU implementation, we

Grid name	Min Δx	# points	Hardware	Comp. time	Ave. C_d	Dev. C_d
coarse	7.03125 mm	17.9 M	1x GPU	8.7 h	0.325	18.2%
medium	4.6875 mm	46.7 M	1x GPU	31.9 h	0.290	5.5%
fine	3.125 mm	125.6 M	2x GPUs	63.4 h	0.274	-0.4%
coarse-par	7.03125 mm	18.2 M	2x GPUs	5.5 h	0.325	18.2%
medium-par	4.6875 mm	47.1 M	2x GPUs	19.4 h	0.290	5.5%
coarse-FVM	7.03125 mm	13.3 M	128x CPUs	147.5 h	0.300	9.1%

Table 1. Summary of the grids used in this work and results.

created another two meshes to run on two GPUs: a fourth coarse grid like the first one, and a fifth medium grid like the second one. In addition, for comparing LBM on GPU to FVM on CPU, a sixth coarse grid like the first one was created for running in parallel with OpenFOAM®. All the grids had seven grid refinement levels and we created the FVM grid with the same settings as the LBM grid. A summary of the different grids is given in Table 1.

The simulation settings were the same for all the computations. The fluid was air with kinematic viscosity of $15.11 \cdot 10^{-6}$ m^2/s, and density of 1.204 kg/m^3 at 20°C. The Reynolds number was $4.87 \cdot 10^6$ with the car length as reference length. We set the following boundary conditions: uniform velocity at the inlet, the ground, the top and the side faces of the domain, and no-slip for the car body. At the outlet we used the uniform static pressure for the FVM, while we set the velocity extrapolation for the cumulant LBM. At the car wheels we set the rotating velocity boundary condition for the cumulant LBM, while the rotation of the wheels is ensured by the multiple reference frame (MRF) control volume for the FVM. Moreover, the cumulant LBM solves the weakly compressible N-S equations and we used the relaxation parameters $\omega_{\alpha\beta\gamma} = 0.5$ for the third moments, while the FVM solves the incompressible N-S equations. The physical time simulated is 5 s. We performed all the simulations as implicit large eddy simulation (I-LES), without any explicit turbulence modelling and wall functions, and with an initialized velocity field at the beginning of the simulation.

We computed the entire cumulant LBM simulation in single precision by using the Nvidia® *Tesla K40c* graphics card. For computing the FVM simulation, we used the cluster at the department for Architecture, Civil Engineering and Environmental Sciences of the Technische Universität Braunschweig. We decided to use 16 nodes for the total number of 128 cores with the standard PT-Scotch decomposition method compiled in OpenFOAM®, since we tested that by increasing or decreasing the number of nodes, the FVM simulation did not speed up for this particular case. A summary of the different hardware used is also given in Table 1.

3. Results

We present the numerical results, comparison to the experimental measurement, and performance achieved in terms of computational time, speed-up, and parallel efficiency for all the simulations. Table 1 reports the computational time, and the averaged numerical drag coefficient (C_d) with its deviation from the experimental measurement.

3.1. Drag and pressure coefficients

The experimental value for the drag coefficient is 0.275. The minimum deviation of C_d for the cumulant LBM simulations was -0.4% for the grid *fine*, while the FVM simulation gave a deviation of 9.1%. We achieved a very good result for the cumulant LBM simulation by using a grid with minimum resolution at the car surface of 3.125 mm, and a value of 0.5 for the relaxation parameters $\omega_{\alpha\beta\gamma}$ for the third moments ($\alpha+\beta+\gamma=3$). This value for $\omega_{\alpha\beta\gamma}$ was chosen by performing different simulations.

The pressure coefficient (C_p) is experimentally measured at the symmetry plane of the car and reported separately for the top and the bottom part. In order to compare it with our numerical results, we also probed the pressure acting on the body of the car in its symmetry plane, and computed C_p separately for the top part (above Z = 100 mm) and the bottom part (below Z = 100 mm). Figure 3a and Figure 3b show the C_p along the longitudinal car axis X for the top and bottom part of the car, respectively. The numerical pressure coefficient C_p generally showed good agreement compared to the experimental measurements, especially when refining the grid. For all the grids, the C_p at the top of the car differed from the experimental data at the location of the roof just after the windscreen (from X = 1.25 m to X = 2 m circa, in Figure 3a). The explanation can be due to the setup of the wind tunnel test where the car model was fixed on the roof with an arm that was big compared to the car size (Figure 6 in [12]). This probably disturbed the flow around the car affecting the accuracy of the measurements on the car body. The C_p at the bottom of the car was noisier than the experimental data. The reason can be due to the big number of points used for plotting the curve as a result of the detailed discretization of the underbody.

3.2. LBM grid convergence study

Since the grids had the same grid refinement ratio of 1.5, the order of the convergence q of the cumulant LBM grids was calculated as [15]:

$$q = ln\left(\frac{f_3 - f_2}{f_2 - f_1}\right) / ln(r) \qquad (3)$$

where r is the grid refinement ratio, and f_3, f_2 and f_1 are the numerical solutions for the grid *coarse*, *medium* and *fine*, respectively. Using Eq. (3) q was 1.93, thus showing

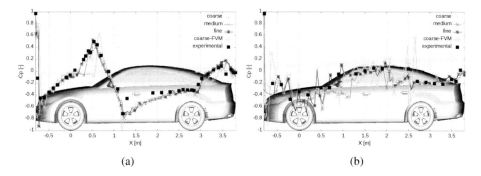

(a)   (b)

Figure 3. Pressure coefficient C_p along the longitudinal car axis X for the top part (a) and the bottom part (b).

a second order of the convergence. Using Eq. (3) the order of the convergence was not depending on the exact solution $C_d = 0.275$.

3.3. LBM and FVM comparison and performance

In order to compare LBM on GPU to FVM on CPU, we used a FVM grid (*coarse-FVM*) with a comparable number of points to the mesh for LBM (*coarse*). We generated the meshes with the same settings and we performed the simulations without any turbulence model and wall functions. The FVM simulation gave a deviation of C_d of 9.1% while the cumulant LBM simulation gave 18.2%. The FVM simulation gave better results compared to the cumulant LBM for the same grid resolution. However, the FVM took 147.5 hours (6.15 days) for running in parallel on 128 CPUs while the cumulant LBM took only 8.7 hours for running on a single GPU, thus showing that the cumulant LBM on GPU was 17 times faster. Moreover, computing the LBM simulation by using a finer grid the deviation of C_d decreased to only -0.4% and the simulation was still faster than the FVM. The advantage to use a fine mesh resides in the possibility to better resolve the flow structures and to capture eddies of different scales which is not possible to be resolved by the coarse grid. Figure 4 shows the contour plot of the velocity of the flow at the back of the car in its symmetry plane for the LBM grid *fine* (Figure 4a) and the FVM grid *coarse-FVM* (Figure 4b). We had a clear picture of the eddy structures resolved in the wake regions of the car by using different grid resolutions: with the fine grid it was possible to resolve a greater number of length scales of the turbulence, while with the coarse grid this was not possible. Fine grid means a large system to be solved and consequently the necessity to speed up the simulation. The LBM grid *fine* consisting of 125.6 M points computed even faster than the FVM grid *coarse-FVM*: the computational time for the cumulant LBM on two GPUs was of 63.4 hours while for the FVM on a 128 CPUs cluster was of 147.5 hours. Thus, the computational time for fine mesh with LBM on GPU would certainly outperform the FVM on CPU with finer meshes.

   We checked the raw performance of the cumulant LBM evaluating the number of nodal updates per second (NUPS). The cumulant LBM GPU implementation performed at 189.1, 197.0, and 191.1 MNUPS for the grid *coarse*, *medium*, and *fine*, respectively. The NUPS highly depends on the number of grid refinements levels used. With many grid refinement levels (seven in this case), the largest part of the computational time was consumed for the interpolation between grids. However, by using an LES approach, many grid refinement levels were necessary in order to have a fine grid to resolve correctly the boundary layer. Moreover, the choice of the collision operator played an important role in the performance. The cumulant collision operator is for example more expensive

(a)   (b)

Figure 4. Velocity contour plot for the LBM grid *fine* (a) and the FVM grid *coarse-FVM* (b).

than others. However, simulating a car in a free-stream with high Reynolds number, the use of a more advanced collision operator such as the cumulant LBM was mandatory for stability reasons. The efficiency of the cumulant LBM on GPU is given by the ratio $(P_1 \cdot P_n)/P_T$, where P_1 is the number of FLOPS per grid node, P_n is the NUPS, and P_T is the theoretical peak performance of the GPU. While P_T depends on the GPU chosen and P_n can be evaluated checking the time for updating all the grid nodes, for calculating P_1 we should count all the multiplications and additions not only for the kernel, but also for the operations of boundary conditions and grid refinement interface. Although we did not calculate P_1 due to the complexity of the cumulant LBM kernel composed of more than thousand lines, we expect an efficiency similar (app. 30%) to that one showed by us in [7].

3.4. LBM multi-GPU performance

In order to compare the performance of the cumulant LBM multi-GPU to the single GPU implementation, we carried out cumulant LBM simulations for the coarse and the medium grid resolution also in parallel by using two GPUs. We used the same graphics cards and we computed the same physical time. The simulation of the coarse resolution grid took 8.7 hours in serial (coarse) and 5.5 hours in parallel (coarse-par), and the simulation of the medium resolution grid lasted 31.9 hours in serial (medium) and 19.4 hours in parallel (medium-par). We evaluated the efficiency E of the parallel implementation as:

$$E = \frac{T_{ser}}{n \cdot T_{par}} \tag{4}$$

where n is the number of graphics cards used ($n = 2$ in this case), and T_{ser} and T_{par} are the computational time for the serial and parallel simulation, respectively. The parallel efficiency was 80.0% for the coarse resolution grid and it slightly increased to 82.3% by using a bigger number of points with the medium resolution grid. This app. -20% leak in efficiency can be due to the absence of communication hiding in our implementation. Indeed, the cumulant LBM kernel works on each GPU separately and only when all the nodes are processed the exchange between GPUs is performed through MPICH communication. We expect an improvement of the efficiency by taking into account communication hiding among GPUs. Moreover, different MPI protocols can be tested in order to get even better performance. However, the efficiency was evaluated by using parallel simulations on only two GPUs and we can expect a reduction of the efficiency using more than two GPUs, due to the bigger number of communications necessary with many graphics cards.

4. Conclusion and outlook

In this work we showed that the lattice Boltzmann method on graphics processing units is a valid approach to perform CFD simulations of a complex engineering problem, such as the external aerodynamics of a car, and thus a valid alternative to standard FVM on CPU cluster.

Indeed, the cumulant LBM gave a low deviation of the drag coefficient C_d for the fine grid and a good agreement of the pressure coefficient C_p with the experimental data. The accuracy of the results depends on the value chosen for the relaxation parameters $\omega_{\alpha\beta\gamma}$ for the third moments ($\alpha+\beta+\gamma=3$). The function of this parameter is not well known yet. We should further investigate the importance of $\omega_{\alpha\beta\gamma}$, studying some correlation with the Reynolds number, the grid resolution and the turbulence intensity.

Furthermore, the very low computational time compared to a standard FVM on CPUs was among the advantages of our LBM approach on GPU, especially when using a fine mesh. The importance to use a fine grid consists in the possibility to resolve a bigger number of length scales of the turbulence. Fine grid means large system and therefore we have the necessity to speed up the simulations. The cumulant LBM on GPUs shows to address this request.

Regarding the parallel efficiency of the cumulant LBM on multiple GPUs, more work has to be done in order to allow simulations with more than two GPUs, test different MPI protocols, and implement communication hiding.

References

[1] R. Benzi, S. Succi, M. Vergassola, The lattice Boltzmann equation: theory and applications, Physics Reports (1992)
[2] M. Geier, M. Schönherr , A. Pasquali, M. Krafczyk, The cumulant lattice Boltzmann equation in three dimensions: theory and validation, Computers and Mathematics with Applications (2015)
[3] N. Galoppo, N.K. Govindaraju, M. Henson, D. Manocha, LU-GPU: efficient algorithms for solving dense linear systems on graphics hardware, in: Proceedings of Supercomputing 2005, Seattle WA (2005)
[4] W. Li, X. Wei, A. Kaufman, Implementing lattice Boltzmann computation on graphics hardware, The Visual Computer (2003)
[5] J. Tölke, Implementation of a Lattice Boltzmann kernel using the Compute Unified Device Architecture developed by nVIDIA, Computing and Visualization in Science (2008)
[6] J. Tölke, M. Krafczyk, TeraFLOP computing on a desktop PC with GPUs for 3D CFD, International Journal of Computational Fluid Dynamics (2008)
[7] M. Schönherr, A second-order accurate mesh refinement implementation for a D3Q27 Cumulant-LBM on GPGPUs, 12th International Conference for Mesoscopic Methods in Engineering and Science (2014)
[8] J. Linxweiler, Ein integrierter Softwareansatz zur interaktiven Exploration und Steuerung von Strömungssimulationen auf Many-Core-Architekturen, Ph.D. thesis, Fakultät Architektur, Bauingenieurwesen und Umweltwissenschaften, TU-Braunschweig, 2011
[9] M. Geier, A. Greiner, J.G. Korvink, Bubble functions for the lattice Boltzmann method and their application to grid refinement, European Physical Journal Special Topics 171 (2009)
[10] M. Schönherr, K. Kucher, M. Geier, M. Stiebler, S. Freudiger, M. Krafczyk, Multi-thread implementations of the lattice Boltzmann method on non-uniform grids for CPUs and GPUs, Computers and Mathematics with Applications (2011)
[11] MPICH, High-Performance Portable MPI, https://www.mpich.org/
[12] A.I. Heft, T. Indinger, N.A. Adams, Introduction of a New Realistic Generic Car Model for Aerodynamic Investigations, SAE (2012)
[13] BETA CAE System SA, ANSA, http://www.beta-cae.gr/ansa.htm
[14] A. Pasquali, M. Schönherr , M. Geier, M. Krafczyk, LBMHexMesh: an OpenFOAM based grid generator for the Lattice Boltzmann Method, 7th Open Source CFD International Conference (2013)
[15] Examining Spatial (Grid) Convergence, NASA, http://www.grc.nasa.gov/WWW/wind/valid/tutorial/spatconv.html

Parallel Computing: On the Road to Exascale
G.R. Joubert et al. (Eds.)
IOS Press, 2016
© *2016 The authors and IOS Press. All rights reserved.*
doi:10.3233/978-1-61499-621-7-401

A Parallel Algorithm for Decomposition of Finite Languages

Tomasz JASTRZĄB [a,1], Zbigniew J. CZECH [a], Wojciech WIECZOREK [b]

[a] *Institute of Informatics, Silesian University of Technology, Poland*
[b] *Institute of Informatics, University of Silesia, Poland*

Abstract. The paper deals with the problem of finite languages decomposition, which is believed to be computationally hard. Our objective is to propose an improved parallel algorithm finding all non-trivial decompositions of a finite language L, provided that they exist. The paper introduces a novel method of pruning a solution space by defining locally significant states of an automaton A accepting language L. It also proposes an adaptive way for adjusting the algorithm parameters, which has not been studied yet in the past. The performance of the algorithm is experimentally verified on a set of large languages and the results are reported. The algorithm proves to be successful in finding the decompositions of selected languages in a reasonable amount of time.

Keywords. parallel algorithms, languages and automata, decomposition of finite languages

Introduction

The study of regular and, in particular, finite languages is well motivated by a wide range of their applications, including text processing [1], pattern matching, lexical analysis in compilers and many others. Advances in this area are also of importance for various tasks of grammatical inference [2,3] and bioinformatics. In the latter field the process of decomposition of finite languages may lead to the discovery of new knowledge related to similarities and mutations in amino-acid sequences. The results of decomposition can be also applied as a way of obtaining a space-minimal representation of finite languages, provided that they are decomposable.

The problem of finite languages decomposition is known to be intractable, yet decidable. However, its NP-completeness has not be proved [4]. The theoretical aspects of finite languages decomposition, including its nonuniqueness and noncommutitivity, were studied for instance in [4,5]. There exist sequential and heuristic algorithms proposals discussed in [6,7], that are focused on finding the first decomposition of a finite language, provided that the language is not prime. According to the results reported in [7] the metaheuristics do not perform well in

---

[1]Corresponding author: Institute of Informatics, Silesian University of Technology, ul. Akademicka 16, 44-100 Gliwice, Poland; Email: Tomasz.Jastrzab@polsl.pl

solving the problem of finite languages decomposition. Moreover, since a universal algorithm capable of decomposing languages of arbitrary length is not known, the exhaustive search methods usually have to be applied. However, as mentioned in [6] the size of solution space, even for relatively small languages, can be significant thus the need for parallel algorithms arises. The work by Wieczorek [6] became the basis for the design of parallel versions of the algorithm seeking all available decompositions, that were presented in [8,9,10] by the authors of this paper. The algorithms and results presented here constitute the continuation of our works on the subject.

We propose an improved parallel algorithm exploring the solution space efficiently. The algorithm traverses the states of the finite automaton accepting language L in a recursive manner until the threshold level is reached, at which further computation is distributed among processors. However, unlike the previously devised algorithms, discussed in [8,9,10], in case of the improved version proposed in this paper, the threshold level is computed dynamically in each of the processors instead of being set beforehand. The advantages of such approach are as follows. First of all, the algorithm is able to adjust itself to the new, previously unseen languages easily, without the need for performing random guesses about the optimal value of the threshold level. Secondly, it is more reliable since it makes the decisions based on the actual processed data at a given point of algorithm execution. And finally, making the threshold level vary allows for faster exploration of the solution space. The thorough investigation of the optimal threshold level is motivated by the fact that it is highly influential in terms of the efficiency of the parallel part of the algorithm, as stated in [9]. Given that the parallel part is a dominating phase of the algorithm the speedup values obtained for its execution in multiprocessor environment are close to linear.

The performance of the parallel algorithm is further improved by reducing the solution space based on the definitions of globally and locally significant states of a finite automaton A. The latter notion is a novelty in the context of finite languages decomposition. A theorem related to language decomposability, based on the definition of locally significant states is given and formally proved in the paper. Provided that the language possesses certain structure the application of the aforementioned theorem may lead to fast determination of language primality. Hence it can be viewed as an important step towards finding a universal method for deciding upon language decomposability. It is also noteworthy that the definition can be applied concurrently to independent parts of the automaton. Consequently, large languages composed of tens of thousands of words, represented by automata containing hundreds of states can be decomposed efficiently.

The paper is organized as follows. Section 1 introduces the notions of globally and locally significant states. Section 2 proposes an improved parallel algorithm for finite languages decomposition. An algorithm for solution space reduction based on definitions from section 1 and an adaptive method for the threshold level adjustment, is also discussed in Section 2. Section 3 reports the experimental results obtained for the decomposition of large finite languages. The last section contains conclusions.

1. Definitions

A language L is said to be *finite* if it consists of a finite number of words (strings) over an alphabet Σ. Typically the size (length) of language L is measured in terms of the number of words of the language and is denoted by $|L|$. Since every finite language is also regular [11] it can be represented in the form of a finite automaton $A = \{Q, \Sigma, \delta, q_0, Q_F\}$, where Q is the set of states of the automaton, Σ is the alphabet, δ is the transition function, q_0 is the starting state and $Q_F \subseteq Q$ is the set of accepting states. For the purpose of this paper we consider the analyzed language large if either $|L|$ or $|Q|$ is considerable. The value of $|Q|$ is computed for a minimal acyclic deterministic finite automaton (MADFA) accepting language L, for which we extend the transition function according to the following rules: (i) $\delta(q, \lambda) = \lambda$ and (ii) $\delta(q, xa) = \delta(\delta(q, x), a)$, where $a \in \Sigma$, $x \in \Sigma^*$, $q \in Q$.

The problem of finite languages decomposition can be defined as follows. Given finite language L, find two non-empty languages L_1, L_2 such that $L = L_1 \times L_2$, where '$\times$' denotes the catenation of the input sets [5]. The *catenation* in this context can be viewed as a Cartesian product of input sets with duplicates removed. A finite language L is said to be indecomposable (or prime) if either L_1 or L_2 consists exclusively of the empty word λ, for all existing decompositions. In terms of automata theory the problem of finite languages decomposition is given in the following way. Let $A = \{Q, \Sigma, \delta, q_0, Q_F\}$ be a finite automaton accepting language L, i.e. $\mathcal{L}(A) = L$. Then the task is to find a subset of the states of automaton A, $Q_D \subseteq Q$ such that the union of all subwords generated on the paths between q_0 and the members of set Q_D (the union of *left* languages), catenated with the intersection of all subwords generated on the paths between members of Q_D and the final states of A (the intersection of *right* languages) produces language L [6], i.e.:

$$L_1 \subseteq \bigcup_{q \in Q_D} \overleftarrow{q} \tag{1}$$

$$L_2 \subseteq \bigcap_{q \in Q_D} \overrightarrow{q} \tag{2}$$

Let L be a decomposable finite language and $A = \{Q, \Sigma, \delta, q_0, Q_F\}$ be the minimal acyclic deterministic finite automaton accepting language L. Then it was proved in [6] that there exists a non-trivial decomposition of L that is based on the *significant* states of automaton A. We recall in definition 1 the notion of a significant state, calling it a *globally* significant state as opposed to the locally significant state introduced later on. The reason for naming those states as globally significant is that they affect the whole automaton, not just particular words.

Definition 1. *Let L and A be defined as previously. Then a globally significant state of automaton A is the state possessing the following properties: (i) if $q \notin Q_F$ then $|\delta(q, a)| \geq 2$, (ii) if $q \in Q_F$ then $|\delta(q, a)| \geq 1$, where $a \in \Sigma, q \in Q$.*

Let $L = L_1 \times L_2$. Then $|L_1 \times L_2|$, before duplicates removal, has to be at least equal to $|L|$. Let also $w \in L$ be a word that is split by a certain state q, such that $w = xy$ and $x \in \overleftarrow{q}$, $y \in \overrightarrow{q}$, where $\overleftarrow{q}$ and $\overrightarrow{q}$ denote the left and right languages of state q, respectively. Then introducing the state q into set Q_D has the following implications:

1. the size of L_1 is increased by $|\overleftarrow{q}|$, since L_1 is the union of left languages (Eq. (1)),
2. the suffix y becomes the member of L_2 (Eq. (2)).

Finally, let a *locally* significant state be defined as follows.

Definition 2. *A state $q \in Q$ of a minimal acyclic deterministic finite automaton accepting language L is said to be locally significant if for a word $w = xy, w \in L$ the following holds:*

$$count(y) * |\overrightarrow{q}| \geq |L| \tag{3}$$

where count *returns the number of occurences of suffix y in all words $w \in L$.*

Given the definition 2, the following theorem holds.

Theorem 1. *Let L be a decomposable finite language and Q_D denote the decomposition set of L. Then all members of Q_D have to be locally significant.*

Proof. To prove the property stated in Theorem 1 let us assume the contrary, namely that $\exists_{q \in Q_D} count(y) * |\overrightarrow{q}| < |L|$ (by definition 2). Let $w = xy$, $x \in \overleftarrow{q}$, $y \in \overrightarrow{q}$. Let also $L = L_1 \times L_2$, where L_1, L_2 are as defined in Eqs. (1) and (2). By Eq. (2), $|\overrightarrow{q}|$ is the upper bound on $|L_2|$. Thus, for L to be decomposable $|L_1| > count(y)$ has to be satisifed. However, since $count(y)$ is the upper bound on the number of valid prefixes of word w, then $|L_1| <= count(y)$ should hold. This contradicts the previous assumption and ends the proof. $\qquad \square$

As an immediate corollary of Theorem 1 it follows that given an automaton A accepting language L the determination of locally significant states of this automaton may lead to stating language primality. Namely, the language is prime, if either (i) there exists a word with no locally significant states defined, or (ii) there exists a word whose only locally significant state is q_0 and the word does not appear as a suffix of any other word.

2. Algorithms

The parallel algorithm performing language decomposition is shown in Figure 1. It uses procedure ADJUSTK (line 2), which modifies the threshold parameter K visible in line 3. Parameter K is modified if the number of additional states complementing the current decomposition set does not change for the predefined number of recursive calls. Such a situation may suggest that the states constituting the correct decomposition set were possibly found and consequently the phase in lines 4–9 should be entered soon. However, to avoid excessive increase of K (resulting in a large number of permutations to be generated and verified) an upper limit is also imposed, which postpones further threshold value increase by modifying the recursive calls count. By controlling the dynamics of K parameter change we are able to keep the balance between the amount of time spent in both phases of the algorithm.

The algorithm in Figure 1 assumes that the minimal acyclic deterministic finite automaton accepting input language L was already built and reduced by means of definitions 1 and 2. By reduction of the automaton we mean that only those states of the automaton which are both globally and locally significant are taken into account, since as shown in Theorem 1 the decomposition is always based on these states. The procedure takes as input arguments the set of pairs composed of a word and its corresponding globally and locally significant states (parameter X) and the current decomposition set (parameter Y).

The algorithm proceeds as follows. At the beginning of each recursive call the value of parameter K may be modified basing on the outcomes of the previous step, as discussed before (line 2). In line 3 the number of additional states, i.e. states not yet present in the decomposition set and not removed by the pruning procedures in lines 18–29, is computed and compared to threshold K. If the threshold level is reached the power set of the additional states is generated and distributed among processors basing on their ranks. Generated permutations of states are then used to compute languages L_1, L_2 according to Eqs. (1) and (2) and their catenation is later compared with input language L (lines 4–9). However, by the virtue of assumptions related to definition 2 only if $|L_1| * |L_2| > |L|$ holds, the actual comparison with L occurs. If the condition in line 3 is not satisfied the word with minimal number of states is selected (line 11) and its states are analyzed (lines 16–31). Two pruning steps are applied in lines 18–29, prior to re-entering the decomposition procedure with an augmented decomposition set (line 30). The pruning in lines 18–22 follows directly from Eq. (2). Namely, since L_2 is an intersection of right languages, then a state whose right language does not contain currently analyzed suffix cannot be a part of L_2. On the other hand, the solution space reduction in lines 23–29 is motivated by the following fact. Provided that some states were removed in lines 18–22, the count of suffixes resulting from right languages of these pruned states was decreased and consequently some other states could have become locally insignificant.

The algorithm applies parallelism to *computation*, replicating data structures in each processor. The replication is conducted in two ways, namely through communication or directly as a result of algorithm execution. The communication is related to initial step of language data transmission as well as to local states significance determination (lines 23–29), as discussed in section 3. Except for the phase in lines 4–9 each processor proceeds according to the same execution path, thus automatically keeping the data copy synchronized with other processors. Finally, assuming that consecutive numbers are assigned to each permutation in the power set (line 4), a permutation is verified by the processor if the permutation number, taken modulo the number of processors, matches processor rank.

In the actual implementation, the algorithm from Figure 1 was also optimized in terms of memory in the following ways. Firstly, all texts were treated as immutable elements, thus the memory pointer was just shared. Secondly, when memory allocation was required instead of allocating large, mostly unused blocks of memory an on-demand approach was applied. The approach was based on keep-

1: **procedure** PARALLELDECOMPOSE(X, Y)
2:     ADJUSTK()   ▷ K modification
3:     **if** $|(\text{states} \in X) - Y| \leq K$ **then**
4:         **for all** $S \subseteq ((\text{states} \in X) - Y)$ **do**   ▷ power set generation
5:             $D \leftarrow Y \cup S$, $L_1 = \bigcup_{q \in D} \overleftarrow{q}$, $L_2 = \bigcap_{q \in D} \overrightarrow{q}$
6:             **if** $L_1 \times L_2 = L$ **then**
7:                 print D ▷ decomposition found
8:             **end if**
9:         **end for**
10:     **else**
11:         find $x_1 \in X$ with min. number of states
12:         **if** x_1 has no states **then**
13:             **return**
14:         **end if**
15:         remove x_1 from X
16:         **for all** $q_1 \in (\text{states of } x_1)$ **do**   ▷ traverse states
17:             $s \leftarrow$ suffix of x_1 in q_1
18:             **for all** $q_2 \in (\text{states} \in X)$ **do**   ▷ suffix-based pruning, Eq. (2)
19:                 **if** $s \notin \overrightarrow{q_2}$ **then**
20:                     remove q_2
21:                 **end if**
22:             **end for**
23:             **for all** $x_2 \in X$ **do**
24:                 **for all** $q_2 \in (\text{states of } x_2)$ **do**   ▷ locality-based pruning
25:                     **if** COUNT(suffix of x_2 in q_2) $* |\overrightarrow{q_2}| < |L|$ **then**
26:                       remove q_2 from x_2
27:                   **end if**
28:                 **end for**
29:             **end for**
30:             PARALLELDECOMPOSE(X, $Y \cup q_1$)
31:         **end for**
32:     **end if**
33: **end procedure**

Figure 1. The parallel algorithm

ing track of the amount of elements already allocated in given block and resizing the block by an additional amount of memory when necessary. The resize quantity was experimentally selected to balance the overhead incurred by frequent memory reallocations and excessive memory usage. Thanks to these two improvements, the total amount of memory used, was significantly decreased, which made it possible to decompose analyzed large languages.

3. Experiments

The experiments were conducted using C language implementation of the parallel algorithm combined with Message Passing Interface (MPI) library used for inter-

Table 1. The characteristics of analyzed languages

Name	$|\Sigma|$	$|L|$	$|Q_{ini}|$	$|Q_{gss}|$	$|Q_{lss}|$
RG_{1_1}	5	75881	124	116	107
RG_{1_2}	5	83639	154	144	129
RG_{1_3}	5	84378	133	124	109
RG_{2_1}	4	32520	151	144	134
RG_{2_2}	5	61995	160	150	138
RG_{2_3}	5	53941	167	160	148
ST_1	10	42440	145	100	93
ST_2	10	36769	214	152	143
ST_3	10	27177	230	173	168

processor communication. The major part of the experiments has been carried out in two computer centers located in Gdańsk and Gliwice.

Two groups of languages were considered in the experimental setup. The first group (RG) was generated using random grammars, according to the rules discussed in [6]. All the languages belonging to this group were decomposable, due to the structure of the grammar production rules. In particular, the fact that the starting rule was always a catenation of two other rules of the grammar guaranteed that the languages were decomposable. Half of the languages proposed in this set (RG_1) was considered large in terms of the number of words, while the other half (RG_2) was perceived large in terms of finite automata sizes. The second group (ST) was produced as a combination of selected training and test languages presented during the StaMinA competition [12] modified slightly for the purpose of this assessment. The modification involved mainly the removal of metainformation in the form of word classification in the positive or negative set, since such information is not relevant to the decomposition problem at hand. The languages belonging to this group were also selected in a way ensuring their decomposability.

The overview of selected languages is given in Table 1. The columns denote respectively: **Name** – the name of the language, $|\Sigma|$ – the size of alphabet, $|L|$ – the size of language, i.e. number of words, $|Q_{ini}|$ – the size of the automaton A accepting language L, i.e. initial number of states, $|Q_{gss}|$ – the number of globally significant states, $|Q_{lss}|$ – the number of states after initial local significance determination. It can be observed that the selected languages provide a wide range of different features, which allows us to show the universality of the proposed parallel algorithm. It is also worth noticing that although the local significance of states is applied on the level of particular words it may also lead to the complete removal of a state from the automaton A. Such a situation is confirmed by the experimental results visible in the last column of Table 1.

Prior to the evaluation of the main parallel decomposition procedure, the evaluation of three cooperation schemes was performed, in order to choose the most efficient approach for the locally significant states determination. The cooperation schemes were as follows: *no-cooperation, star-based cooperation* and *ring-based co-operation* (MPI_Allgather was also considered, providing results comparable to star-based cooperation). In every scheme the size of the search space was bounded from above by the the total length of all words belonging to the language L. The

Table 2. The execution times of the cooperation schemes (in seconds)

Category	N = 8	N = 16	N = 32
	No-cooperation		
30-60k	0.42	0.43	0.43
60-90k	1.18	1.20	1.21
	Star-based cooperation		
30-60k	0.33	0.36	0.47
60-90k	0.53	0.51	0.59
	Ring-based cooperation		
30-60k	0.73	1.18	2.13
60-90k	1.18	1.83	3.23

first scheme searched the whole space in each of the processors building the set of locally significant states. The remaining two schemes splitted the space between processors, computed partial results, gathered them to produce the final result and redistributed the final result to all processors. The difference between the last two schemes was in the way the processors communicated with each other during results gathering and redistribution. In star-based topology every processor was communicating directly with the 0th processor, while with ring-based topology the communication occurred between processors with neighbouring ranks. The execution times, measured using MPI_Wtime() function, obtained for all three schemes are shown in Table 2. It presents the values obtained for the experiments performed for 8, 16 and 32 processors. However, instead of presenting individual results for every language, two categories based on language cardinalities were created. Category **30-60k** includes languages RG_{2_1}, RG_{2_3}, ST_1, ST_2 and ST_3, with the remaining languages belonging to the category labelled **60-90k**. Such a division was motivated by the fact that individual differences in execution times for languages in the same category were negligible.

From the results shown in Table 2 it can be concluded that for the first category of languages, i.e. **30-60k**, the no-cooperation and star-based cooperation schemes perform in a similar manner, regardless of the number of processors used. This means that for the first group the benefits of distributed computation are diminished by the overhead of communication. With the increase of language cardinality, the star-based cooperation starts to prevail over the other two schemes. It is approximately two times faster than the no-cooperation approach and up to six times faster than ring-based cooperation. The ring-based cooperation is certainly the worst approach out of the three analyzed schemes, being usually much slower than the other cooperation methods. To sum up, let us state that especially in case of large languages it may be worthwhile to split the local state significance computation between processors.

The execution times for the parallel decomposition algorithm, expressed in seconds, are shown in Table 3. The algorithm was able to find decompositions of all analyzed languages, which confirms the validity of the proposed approach. Table 3 presents the results obtained for 32 processors used. The last column shows the maximum value of the threshold level that was reached during dynamic K parameter adjustment. In all cases the number of recursive calls for which the count of additional states is allowed to remain unchanged without triggering

Table 3. The execution times of the parallel algorithm (in seconds)

Name	N	Execution time	Max. K
RG_{1_1}	32	69.43	18
RG_{1_2}	32	127.74	22
RG_{1_3}	32	79.20	18
RG_{2_1}	32	24.31	18
RG_{2_2}	32	79.02	21
RG_{2_3}	32	742.86	28
ST_1	32	42.16	17
ST_2	32	21.23	21
ST_3	32	4.75	10

modification of K was set to 250. The initial value of K was set to 10 for all languages.

As can be observed from the results presented in Table 3 the performance of the algorithm is satisfactory in all cases. Language RG_{2_3} turned out to be the hardest out of analyzed languages, neverthless the execution time is still acceptable. These results should be considered important since our previous attempts at decomposing even much smaller languages sometimes required several hours to find the solution. A thing worth observing is also that, although the decomposition of all languages was started with the exact same set of parameters (initial K, the count of recursive calls triggering change) the maximum value of K differs between languages. This clearly shows that the adjustment of the threshold level is really dynamic and based on the currently processed data. Furthermore it should be expected that keeping the value of K unchanged would make the computation last much longer in most cases. Let us also notice that the proposed pruning methods allow to move to the phase of decomposition sets generation quite quickly. Combining this fact with the well-balanced parallelism in the generation phase produces an efficient method for large finite languages decomposition.

4. Conclusions

The paper introduces an improved version of the parallel algorithm for the decomposition of large finite languages. It discusses an adaptive method for adjusting algorithm parameters and proposes a notion of locally significant states. A theorem based on the definition of local significance is formulated and proved. The local significance of states is also used to prune the solution space during algorithm execution. The reported results of several experiments performed on languages of tens of thousands of words show that the proposed enhancements have practical importance.

We believe that the algorithm is a significant contribution to the field of parallel algorithms applications. A distinguishing feature of the proposal is that it is equally well applicable in the distributed as well as shared memory architectures since the interprocessor communication is kept at the minimum. The introduced time and memory optimizations and successful experimental results stand for this hypothesis.

In the future we plan to further explore the idea of locally significant states by proposing a method for language primality determination. We are also going to apply the results of the decomposition of finite languages in the field of bioinformatics to analyze amino-acid sequences.

Acknowledgments

The work was supported by the Polish National Science Center upon decision DEC-2011/03/B/ST6/01588, PL-Grid Infrastructure and the infrastructure supported by POIG.02.03.01-24-099/13 grant: "GeCONiI—Upper Silesian Center for Computational Science and Engineering". We thank the following computing centers where the computations of our project were carried out: Academic Computer Centre in Gdańsk TASK, Academic Computer Centre CYFRONET AGH, Kraków (computing grant 027/2004), Poznań Supercomputing and Networking Center, Interdisciplinary Centre for Mathematical and Computational Modeling, Warsaw University (computing grant G27-9), Wrocław Centre for Networking and Supercomputing (computing grant 30).

References

[1]   Ciura, M., and Deorowicz, S. (1999). *Experimental Study of Finite Automata Storing Static Lexicons.* Technical Report, Silesian Technical University, Gliwice, 1999.

[2]   de la Higuera, C. (2005). A bibliographical study of grammatical inference. *Pattern Recognition*, 38 (9), pp. 1332–1348.

[3]   Wieczorek, W. (2010). A Local Search Algorithm for Grammatical Inference. In: Sempere, J.M., and García, P. (Eds.), *Grammatical Inference: Theoretical Results and Applications.* LNCS 6339, Springer-Berlin, pp. 217–229.

[4]   Salomaa, A., and Yu, S. (2000). *On the Decomposition of Finite Languages.* In: Rozenberg, G., and Thomas, W. (Eds.). Developments in Language Theory: Foundations, Applications and Perspectives, World Scientific Publishing, Singapore, pp. 22–31.

[5]   Mateescu, A., Salomaa, A., and Yu, S. (1998). *On the Decomposition of Finite Languages.* In: Technical Report, Turku Centre for Computer Science.

[6]   Wieczorek, W. (2009). *An algorithm for the decomposition of finite languages.* Logic Journal of the IGPL, 18 (3), pp. 355–366.

[7]   Wieczorek, W. (2009). *Metaheuristics for the Decomposition of Finite Languages.* In: Kłopotek ,M.A., Przepiórkowski ,A., Wierzchoń ,S.T., and Trojanowski ,K. (Eds.). Recent Advances in Intelligent Information Systems, Akademicka Oficyna Wydawnicza EXIT, pp. 495–505.

[8]   Czech, Z.J. (2010). *A parallel algorithm for finite languages decomposition.* In: Wakulicz-Deja, A. (Ed.): Systemy wspomagania decyzji. Instytut Informatyki Uniwersytetu Śląskiego, Sosnowiec, pp. 289–295 (in Polish).

[9]   Jastrząb, T. (2014). *A comparative analysis of two parallel algorithms for finite languages decomposition,* Pomiary Automatyka Kontrola, 60 (6), pp. 350–354.

[10]   Jastrząb, T., and Czech, Z.J. (2014). *A parallel algorithm for the decomposition of finite languages,* Studia Informatica, 35 (4), pp. 5–16.

[11]   Yu, S. (1997). *Regular languages.* In: Rozenberg, G., and Salomaa, A. (Eds.), Handbook of Formal Languages: Volume 1. Word, Language, Grammar. Springer, pp. 41–111.

[12]   Walkinshaw, N., Lambeau, B., Damas, C., Bogdanov, K., and Dupont, P. (2013). *STAMINA: a competition to encourage the development and assessment of software model inference techniques,* Empirical Software Engineering, 18 (4), pp. 791–824.

Parallel Computing: On the Road to Exascale
G.R. Joubert et al. (Eds.)
IOS Press, 2016
doi:10.3233/978-1-61499-621-7-411

Exploiting the Space Filling Curve Ordering of Particles in the Neighbour Search of Gadget3

Antonio RAGAGNIN [a,d], Nikola TCHIPEV [c], Michael BADER [c], Klaus DOLAG [b] and
Nicolay HAMMER [d]

[a] *Universität-Sternwarte-München, (ragagnin@lrz.de)*
[b] *Universität-Sternwarte-München*
[c] *Department of Informatics, Technische Universität München*
[d] *Leibniz Supercomputing Centre, München*

Abstract.

Gadget3 is nowadays one of the most frequently used high performing parallel codes for cosmological hydrodynamical simulations. Recent analyses have shown that the Neighbour Search process of Gadget3 is one of the most time-consuming parts. Thus, a considerable speedup can be expected from improvements of the underlying algorithms.

In this work we propose a novel approach for speeding up the Neighbour Search which takes advantage of the space-filling-curve particle ordering. Instead of performing Neighbour Search for all particles individually, nearby active particles can be grouped and one single Neighbour Search can be performed to obtain a common superset of neighbours.

Thus, with this approach we reduce the number of searches. On the other hand, tree walks are performed within a larger searching radius. There is an optimal size of grouping that maximize the speedup, which we found by numerical experiments.

We tested the algorithm within the boxes of the *Magneticum* large scale simulation project. As a result we obtained a speedup of 1.65 in the Density and of 1.30 in the Hydrodynamics computation, respectively, and a total speedup of 1.34.

Gadget3 (GAlaxies with Dark matter and Gas intEracT) simulates the evolution of interacting Dark Matter, gas and stars in cosmological volumes [1,2]. While Dark Matter is simulated so it interacts only through gravity, gas obeys the laws of hydrodynamics. Both Dark Matter and gas are simulated by a particle approach. Gadget3 uses a Tree-PM (see, e.g. [3]) algorithm for the gravitational interactions between both Dark Matter and gas particles. Smoothed Particle Hydrodynamics (SPH) is used for the hydrodynamic interaction, as described in [4].

Gadget3 employs a variety of physical processes, e.g. gravitational interactions, density calculation, hydrodynamic forces, transport processes, sub-grid models for star formation and black hole evolution. All these algorithms need to process a list of active particles and find the list of nearby particles ("neighbours"). These neighbours are typically selected within a given searching sphere, defined by a given searching radius, defined by local conditions of the active particles (see, e.g. [5]). This problem is called Neighbour Search and is one of the most important algorithms to compute the physics implemented in Gadget3.

1. Neighbour Search in Gadget3

Simulations of gravitational or electromagnetic interactions deal with potentials having, ideally, an infinite range. There are several known techniques (e.g. Barnes-Hut [6], Fast Multipole Expansion[7]) that can deal with this problem. These techniques subdivide the interaction in short-range and long-range interactions. The long-range interactions are resolved by subdividing the simulated volume in cubes, and assigning to each of them a multipole expansion of the potential. The short-range potential is usually evaluated directly. This leads to the problem of efficiently finding neighbours for a given target particle, within a given searching radius. Finding neighbours by looping over all particles in memory is only suitable when dealing with a limited number of particles. Short-distance neighbour finding can be easily implemented by a Linked-Cell approach. Since long-distance computation is implemented subdividing the volume in a tree (an octree if the space is three-dimensional), this tree structure is commonly used for short-distance computations too. This is also a more generic approach, since Linked-Cell is more suitable for homogeneous particle distributions.

1.1. Phases of Neighbour Search

In Gadget3, the Neighbour Search is divided into two phases. The first phase searches for neighbours on the local MPI process and for boundary particles with possible neighbours of other MPI processes. The second phase searches for neighbours in the current MPI process, of boundary particles coming from others MPI processes. In more detail, the two phases of the Neighbour Search can be summarized in the following steps:

- First phase:
  * for each internal active particle P_i: walk the tree and find all neighbouring particles closer than the searching distance h_i;
  * when walking the tree: for every node belonging to a different MPI process, particle and external node are added to an export buffer;
  * if the export buffer is too small to fit a single particle and its external nodes: interrupt simulation.
  * if the export buffer is full: end of first phase.
  * physical quantities of P_i are updated according to the list of neighbours obtained above.

- Particles are exported.
- Second phase:
  * for each guest particle P_i: walk the tree and search its neighbours;
  * update properties of P_i according to the neighbours list;
  * send updated guest particles back to the original MPI process.

- Current MPI process receives back the particles previously exported and updates the physical quantities merging all results from the various MPI processes.
- Particles that have been updated are removed from the list of active particles.
- If there are still active particles: start from the beginning.

Hydrodynamics Routines	Time $[s]$	Hydrodynamics Parts	Time $[s]$
First Phase	$3.21 \cdot 10^5$	Physics	$1.55 \cdot 10^5$
First Phase Neighbour Search	$1.89 \cdot 10^5$	Neighbour Search	$2.63 \cdot 10^5$
Second Phase	$9.81 \cdot 10^4$	Communication	$7.17 \cdot 10^4$
Second Phase Neighbour Search	$7.36 \cdot 10^4$		

Figure 1. Left: Scalasca timing of the most expensive routines of the Hydrodynamics module in Gadget3. Right: Aggregate timing of the Hydrodynamics parts.

The definition of neighbouring particles is slightly different between the Gadget3 modules. In the Density module, neighbours of the particle P_i are all the particles closer than its searching radius h_i. In the Hydrodynamics module, neighbours are all particles P_j closer than $max(h_i, h_j)$ to P_i.

1.2. Impact of the Neighbour Search in the Gadget3 Performance

Tree algorithms are suitable for studying a wide range of astrophysical phenomena [8,9]. To perform the Neighbour Search in Gadget3, an octree is used to divide the three dimensional space. Further optimization is obtained by ordering the particles according to a space-filling curve. In particular, Gadget3 uses the Hilbert space-filling curve to perform the domain decomposition and to distribute the work among the different processors.

We analysed the code with the profiling tool Scalasca [10]. In Figure 1 (left table) we show the profiling results for the Hydrodynamics module, which is the most expensive in terms of time.

The Hydrodynamics module is called once every time step. It calls the First Phase and the Second Phase routines multiple times. While the First Phase updates the physical properties of local particles, the Second Phase deals with external particles with neighbours in the current MPI process. Particles are processed in chunks because of limited exporting buffers, so the number of times those functions are called depends on the buffer and data sizes. Between the First Phase and Second Phase calls there are MPI communications that send guest particles to others MPI processes. First Phase and Second Phase routines are the most expensive calls inside Hydrodynamics, Density and Gravity. Both the First Phase and the Second Phase perform a Neighbour Search for every active particle.

In Figure 1 (right table), the Hydrodynamics part has been split into three logical groups: Physics, Neighbour Search and Communication. Communication between MPI processes has been estimated a posteriori as the difference between the time spent in Hydrodynamics and the sum of the time spent in the First Phase and Second Phase. This is well justified because no communications between MPI processes are implemented inside First Phase and Second Phase. The time spent in Physics has been computed as the difference between the First (or Second) Phase and the Neighbour Search CPU time. From this profiling, it turns out that for the Hydrodynamics module, Communication and Physics take less time than the Neighbour Search. This was already suggested by a recent profiling [11]. Both results highlight the interest in speeding-up the Gadget3 Neighbour Search.

The three most time consuming modules in Gadget3 are Hydrodynamics, Density and Gravity. In this work we only improved Density and Hydrodynamics modules. There are two main reasons for excluding the Gravity module from this improvement. First,

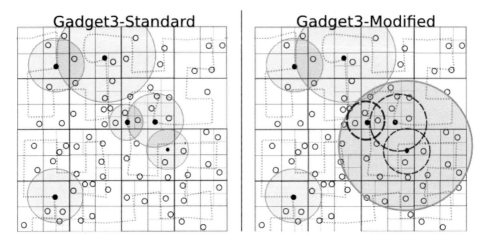

Figure 2. Difference between the standard method of Neighbour Search and the new one. Left panel contains the standard method, where for each active particle a new Neighbour Search is performed from scratch within a given searching radius h_i. Right panel contains the modified version, where particles are grouped within a certain radius R and the Tree Walk is performed only once for a group of particles, within a searching radius of $R + max(h_i)$. In both panels, the octree is represented by square subdivisions, red circles represent the Neighbour Search radius, full dots represent active particles and empty dots represent inactive particles. The dashed line indicates the Hilbert curve.

Gravity module implements a Tree-PM algorithm [12]. Unlike in Density and Hydrodynamics, particles do not have a defined searching radius. In fact the criterion whether or not a node of the tree must be opened take into account the subtended angle of this node by the particle. Also, for the way it is implemented in Gadget3, the Gravity module does not makes a clear distinction between the Neighbour Search and the physics computations, making it difficult to modify the Neighbour Search without a major rewriting of the module.

2. Neighbour Recycling in Gadget3

We now show a novel approach to speed up the Neighbour Search. It takes advantage of the space-filling-curve particle ordering in Gadget3. As the locality of particles in memory maps to the locality of particles in the three dimensional space, consecutive active particles share a significant part of their neighbours. Therefore, nearby active particles are grouped and one single Tree Walk is performed to obtain a common superset of neighbours. By that we reduce the number of tree walks. On the other hand, tree walks are performed within a larger searching radius. A sketch of the algorithm change is shown in Figure 2.

In addition, the speedup gained by reducing the number of tree walks is lowered by the extra work to filter the true neighbours of each active particle from the superset of neighbours. Thus, we may expect that there is an optimal grouping size to maximize the speedup, which can be determined by numerical experiments.

A common Molecular Dynamics technique to recycle neighbours is the Verlet-List algorithm [13]. In the Verlet-List approach, a superset of neighbours is associated to each particle which is used within multiple time steps. In our approach we associate a superset of neighbours to multiple particles, within a single time step. This technique takes into account that two target particles which are close together will also share part of the neighbours.

Neighbour Recycling groups can be built by using the underlying octree structure. Each group can be defined as the set of leaves inside nodes which are of a certain tree depth. Then, a superset of neighbours is built by searching all particles close to that mentioned node. For each previously grouped particle, this superset of neighbours is finally refined. An advantage of this technique is that the number of tree walks is reduced, though at the expense of a larger searching radius.

The level of the tree at which the algorithm will group particles determines both the number of tree walks and the size of the superset of neighbours. This superset must be refined to find the true neighbours of a particle. Thus, increasing its size will lead to a more expensive refinement.

2.1. Implementation of Neighbour Recycling using a Space Filling Curve

Many parallel codes for numerical simulations order their particles by a space-filling curve, mainly because this supports the domain decomposition [14,15,16]. In this work we will benefit from the presence of a space-filling curve to implement a Neighbour Recycling algorithm. Due to the nature of space-filling curves, particles processed consecutively are also close by in space. Those particles will then share neighbours.

Given a simulation for N particles, our algorithm proceeds as follows. A new group of particles is created, and the first particle is inserted into it. A while loop over the remaining particles is executed. As long as these particles are closer than a given distance R to the first particle of the group, they are added to the same set of grouped particles. Once a particle is found, which is farther than R, the group is closed and a new group is created with this particle as first element. The loop above mentioned is repeated until there are no more particles. We call N_{group} the number of particles in a given group; h_i the searching radius of the i-th particle of the group. Then, a superset of neighbours is obtained by searching the neighbours of the first particle of the group, within a radius of $R + max(h_i)$. This radius ensure that all neighbours of all grouped particles are included in the searching sphere. For each grouped particle, the superset of neighbours is refined to its real list of neighbours. The refined list of neighbours is then used to compute the actual physics quantities of the target particle. Thus, the number of tree walks is reduced by a factor equal to the average number of particles in a group, $\langle N_{\text{group}} \rangle$.

It is clear that a too low value of R will group too few particles and lead to $\langle N_{\text{group}} \rangle \simeq 1$, thus leading to no noticeable performance increase. On the other hand, if R is too large, the superset of neighbours will be too large with respect to the real number of neighbours, producing too much overhead.

2.2. Adaptive Neighbour Recycling

In typical cosmological hydrodynamical simulations performed by Gadget3, a fixed R will group fewer particles in low-density regions and more particles in high density regions. Therefore a more reasonable approach is to reset R before every Neighbour Search and choose it as a fraction of the searching radius h_i, which itself is proportional to the local density. In this way, low density regions will have a larger R than high density re-

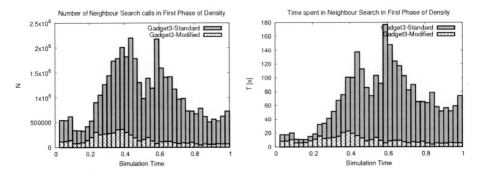

Figure 3. Left panel: every bin contains the number of Neighbour Search calls performed in that bin. Right panel: every bin contains the CPU time spent by the Neighbour Search. In both panels the orange (dark) histogram represents the standard version, light blue (light) histogram represents the modified version.

gions. This is obtained by imposing the following relation between R and the searching radius h of the grouped particles:

$$R = f \cdot h_0,$$

where f is a constant defined at the beginning of the simulation.

In a typical Gadget3 simulation, the number of particles N_{ngb} within the searching radius h_i is a fixed quantity. Locally it varies only within a few percent. In the approximation that every particle has the same number of neighbours N_{ngb}, we can write it as $N_{ngb} = 4\pi \rho h_i^3 / 3$, where ρ is the local number density. Furthermore, if the grouping radius is small enough, the density does not vary too much and we can set $h_i = h$. With those two approximations, the superset of neighbours is $N_{candidates} = 4\pi \rho (R + h)^3 / 3$ and the number of particles in a group is $N_{group} = 4\pi \rho R^3 / 3$. Combining those relations we obtain the following relation:

$$f = \left(\frac{N_{candidates}}{N_{ngb}} \right)^{\frac{1}{3}} - 1 = \left(\frac{N_{group}}{N_{ngb}} \right)^{\frac{1}{3}} \tag{1}$$

2.3. Side Effects of Neighbour Recycling

The Neighbour Recycling algorithm will increase the communication. Because tree walks are performed within a larger radius, the number of opened nodes increases. As a direct consequence, nodes of the tree belonging to other MPI processes will be opened more times than the original version. In the standard approach, the export buffer is filled only with particles whose searching sphere intersect that node. Since the new approach walks the tree for a group of particles, all particles belonging to the group are added to the export buffer. This leads to a greater amount of communications.

3. Speedup of the Recycling Neighbours Approach on Gadget3

We now investigate quantitatively how the new algorithm affected the performances of the code with respect to the old version. To show in details the effect of this new al-

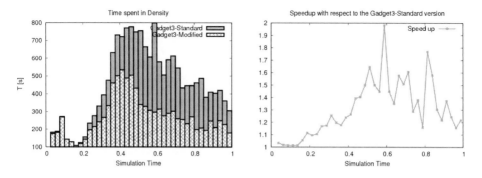

Figure 4. Left panel: every bin contains the time spent in executing the Density module. The orange (dark) histogram represents the standard version, light blue (light) histogram represents the modified version. Right panel: speedup of the modified version with respect to the standard version, as a function of the simulation time.

gorithm, we gradually implemented it in various parts of Gadget3 seeing the partial speedups. First we added the Neighbour Recycling in the First Phase of the Density computations. Then it has been added on both phases of Density computation, and finally it has been added in both the Hydrodynamics and Density computations.

3.1. The Test Case

We test the algorithm in a cosmological hydrodynamical environment. We use initial conditions from the *Magneticum* project [17]. To test our algorithm we chosen the simulation box5hr. This setup has a box size of 18 Mpc/h and $2 \cdot 81^3$ particles. The simulation run on 8 MPI processes, each with 2 threads. The average number of neighbours is set to $\langle N_{ngb} \rangle = 291$.

We have chosen a value of $f = 0.5$. Using Equation 1, we obtain $\langle N_{candidates} \rangle = 3.375\langle N_{ngb} \rangle$. This means that a Tree Walk will now search for 3.375 more particles compared to the old of Gadget3. On the other hand such a high theoretical number of particles in a group will definitely justify the overhead of the Neighbour Recycling. In fact it is inversely proportional to the number of times the tree walk is executed. Still, such a low ratio between the size of superset of neighbours and the true number of neighbours will not produce a noticeable overhead in the refining of the superset of neighbours.

3.2. Results

The algorithm has been first implemented in the first phase of Density module computation of Gadget3. Figure 3 (left panel) shows the number of Neighbour Search calls performed during the simulation. The Neighbour Recycling version of the code has roughly the same amount of searches throughout the whole simulation, whereas the old version has a huge peak of Neighbour Search calls around a simulation time of 0.4. There, the number of Neighbour Search calls from the standard to the modified version, drops of a factor of 10. Compared to the old version, this also means that in this part of the simulation, the average number of particles in a group is 10.

Theoretically, if all particles within the same sphere were put into the same group, the number of Neighbour Search calls should drop by a factor of $\langle N_{group} \rangle \simeq 230$. There

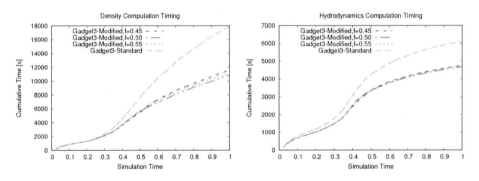

Figure 5. Wall time (in seconds) as a function of the simulation time for different runs: standard version and the new version with $f = 0.45, 0.50, 0.55$. Left panel: Density computation timings. Right panel: Hydrodynamics computation timings.

may be two main reasons why this value is not reached: some time steps do not involve all particles, thus the density of active particles is lower than the density of all particles (which is used to calibrate the radius of the grouping sphere); moreover, the space-filling-curve ordering will leads to particles outside the grouping sphere before the sphere is completely filled. Those two effects contribute in reducing the number of particles within a grouping sphere, thus increasing the number of Neighbour Search calls.

Figure 3 (right panel) shows the time (in seconds) spent to execute tree walks before and after the modification. Because the simulation runs on a multi core and using multiple threads, the total time corresponds to the sum of CPU times of all threads. This plot shows a speedup that reaches the order of 10 when the simulation time is approximately 0.4. Although the average time of a single Neighbour Search is supposed to be higher, the total time spent for doing the Neighbour Search in the new version is smaller.

The time spent in the density module is shown in Figure 4 (left panel). Here the Neighbour Recycling is implemented in both the first and the second phases of the density computation. Unlike previous plots, in this plot the time is the cumulative wall time spent by the code. As already pointed out, this new version increases the communications between MPI processes. The density module also has very expensive physics computations. The maximum speedup on the whole density module is larger than a factor of 2.

Figure 6 shows the projected gas distribution in three different phases of the simulation. At the beginning of the simulation gas is distributed homogeneously; this means that the majority of particles are in the same level of the tree. In the middle panel, voids and clusters can be seen. Particles in clusters require smaller time steps, and thus a larger number of Neighbour Search calls. This is in agreement with the peak of Neighbour Search calls around a simulation time of 0.4 in Figure 4. This explains why density computations became more intensive for a value of the simulation time greater than 0.4 (see Figure 5).

Now we check the impact of the Neighbour Recycling on the whole simulation. Figure 4 (right panel) shows the speedup obtained by implementing the Neighbour Recycling in both the Density and Hydrodynamics module (the two numerically most expensive modules). The total speedup reaches a peak of 2.2.

In Figure 5 (left panel), using the new approach we see a total cumulative execution time of the Density module of $1.0 \cdot 10^4 s$, while the standard version has $1.7 \cdot 10^4 s$, which

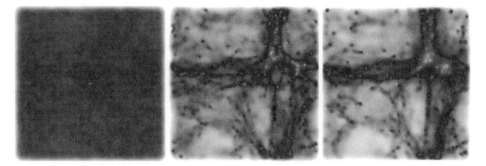

Figure 6. Gas distribution of the cosmological simulation `box5hr`. Left panel shows the gas distribution of nearly the initial conditions of the simulation; central panel at the middle of the simulation, where clusters start forming; right panel at the end of the simulation. The simulation contains also Dark Matter and stars that have been removed from those plots.

correspond to a speedup of 1.64. Figure 5 (right panel) shows the same for the Hydrodynamics module. The old version spent a cumulative time of $6.0 \cdot 10^3 s$, whereas the new version has $4.6 \cdot 10^3 s$. Leading to a speedup in the hydrodynamics of 1.30. The Hydrodynamics module achieved a speedup of 1.30. Besides the Density module, a speedup can be seen also at the beginning of the simulation.

Figure 5 shows the wall time of the simulation when varying the parameter f. Since we do not knew a priori which value of f will have maximized the speedup, we found it by numerical experiments. We tried several values of it; values of f near zero gives no speedup, while values of f much greater than one slow down the whole simulation. In Figure 5 there are the timings for the setups with $f = 0.45, 0.50, 0.55$. The maximum speedup is obtained for $f = 0.50$ in both the Density and Hydrodynamics computations.

4. Conclusions

We developed and implemented a way to recycle neighbours to accelerate the Neighbour Search in order to fasten Gadget3. Our technique should work, in principle, for any N-Body code with a space-filling-curve ordering of particles.

This technique groups particles that will be processed one after the other and that are close enough, and makes a single neighbour search for them . We presented a version of the algorithm that scales the grouping radius with the local density. This version depends on a constant factor f. We found the value of f that gives the maximum speedup. In case of the simulation `box5hr` of the *Magneticum* project, corresponds to one half of the searching radius of the single particles. This radius, of course, depends on the way particles are grouped together. In this approach we opted for a grouping that depends on the distance from the first particle of the group. This decision is arbitrary and dictated by the simplicity of the implementation.

This configuration leads to a speedup of the density computation of 1.64, which is known to be one of the most expensive modules in Gadget3. Implementing this technique in the hydro-force computation too gives a speedup of the whole simulation of 1.34.

References

[1]   M. Allalen, G. Bazin, C. Bernau, A. Bode, D. Brayford, M. Brehm, J. Diemand, K. Dolag, J. Engels, N. Hammer, H. Huber, F. Jamitzky, A. Kamakar, C. Kutzner, A. Marek, C. B. Navarrete, H. Satzger, W. Schmidt, and P. Trisjono, "Extreme scaling workshop at the LRZ," in *Parallel Computing: Accelerating Computational Science and Engineering (CSE), Proceedings of the International Conference on Parallel Computing, ParCo 2013*, vol. 25 of *Advances in Parallel Computing*, pp. 691–697, IOS Press, 2013.

[2]   V. Springel, "The cosmological simulation code GADGET-2," *Monthly Notices of the Royal Astronomical Society*, vol. 364, pp. 1105–1134, Dec. 2005.

[3]   G. Xu, "A new parallel N-Body gravity solver: TPM," *Astrophysical Journal Supplement Series*, vol. 98, p. 355, May 1995.

[4]   A. Beck, G. Murante, A. Arth, R.-S. Remus, A. Teklu, J. Donnert, S. Planelles, M. Beck, P. Foerster, M. Imgrund, *et al.*, "An improved SPH scheme for cosmological simulations," *arXiv preprint arXiv:1502.07358*, 2015.

[5]   L. Hernquist and N. Katz, "TREESPH - a unification of SPH with the hierarchical tree method," *Astrophysical Journal Supplement Series*, vol. 70, pp. 419–446, June 1989.

[6]   J. Barnes and P. Hut, "A hierarchical O(N log N) force-calculation algorithm," *Nature*, vol. 324, pp. 446–449, Dec. 1986.

[7]   L. Greengard and V. Rokhlin, "A new version of the fast multipole method for the Laplace equation in three dimensions," *Acta numerica*, vol. 6, pp. 229–269, 1997.

[8]   L. Hernquist, "Performance characteristics of tree codes," *Astrophysical Journal Supplement Series*, vol. 64, pp. 715–734, Aug. 1987.

[9]   M. S. Warren and J. K. Salmon, "A portable parallel particle program," *Computer Physics Communications*, vol. 87, no. 1, pp. 266–290, 1995.

[10] M. Geimer, F. Wolf, B. J. Wylie, E. Ábrahám, D. Becker, and B. Mohr, "The Scalasca performance toolset architecture," *Concurrency and Computation: Practice and Experience*, vol. 22, no. 6, pp. 702–719, 2010.

[11] V. Karakasis et al. EMEA IPCC user form meeting, Dublin, 2015.

[12] J. S. Bagla, "TreePM: A code for cosmological n-body simulations," *Journal of Astrophysics and Astronomy*, vol. 23, no. 3-4, pp. 185–196, 2002.

[13] L. Verlet, "Computer "experiments" on classical fluids. i. thermodynamical properties of Lennard-Jones molecules," *Phys. Rev.*, vol. 159, pp. 98–103, Jul 1967.

[14] H.-J. Bungartz, M. Mehl, T. Neckel, and T. Weinzierl, "The PDE framework Peano applied to fluid dynamics: an efficient implementation of a parallel multiscale fluid dynamics solver on octree-like adaptive Cartesian grids," *Computational Mechanics*, vol. 46, no. 1, pp. 103–114, 2010.

[15] P. Gibbon, W. Frings, and B. Mohr, "Performance analysis and visualization of the n-body tree code PEPC on massively parallel computers.," in *PARCO*, pp. 367–374, 2005.

[16] P. Liu and S. N. Bhatt, "Experiences with parallel n-body simulation," *Parallel and Distributed Systems, IEEE Transactions on*, vol. 11, no. 12, pp. 1306–1323, 2000.

[17] M. Project, "Simulations." http://magneticum.org/simulations.html, Feb. 2015.

Parallel Computing: On the Road to Exascale
G.R. Joubert et al. (Eds.)
IOS Press, 2016
doi:10.3233/978-1-61499-621-7-421

On-the-fly memory compression for multibody algorithms

Wolfgang ECKHARDT [a] , Robert GLAS [b] , Denys KORZH [a] , Stefan WALLNER [b] and
Tobias WEINZIERL [c,1]

[a] *Department of Informatics, Technische Universität München, Germany*
[b] *Physics Department, Technische Universität München, Germany*
[c] *School of Engineering and Computing Sciences, Durham University, Great Britain*

Abstract. Memory and bandwidth demands challenge developers of particle-based codes that have to scale on new architectures, as the growth of concurrency outperforms improvements in memory access facilities, as the memory per core tends to stagnate, and as communication networks cannot increase bandwidth arbitrary. We propose to analyse each particle of such a code to find out whether a hierarchical data representation storing data with reduced precision caps the memory demands without exceeding given error bounds. For admissible candidates, we perform this compression and thus reduce the pressure on the memory subsystem, lower the total memory footprint and reduce the data to be exchanged via MPI. Notably, our analysis and transformation changes the data compression dynamically, i.e. the choice of data format follows the solution characteristics, and it does not require us to alter the core simulation code.

Keywords. n-body simulation, data compression, communication-reducing algorithms

Introduction

Widening memory gaps between compute units and the main memory, stagnating main memory per core as well as network bandwidth restrictions [1] lead into a dilemma in supercomputing: scientific interest and weak scaling laws require codes to increase the problem size, while strong scaling tells us that scaling is limited; but upscaling that keeps pace with the growth of concurrency misfits the aforementioned architectural trends. This problem can be studied at hands of multibody problems such as smoothed particle hydrodynamics (SPH) where upscaling translates into an increase of particle counts.

Facing memory and bandwidth constraints, it is convenient to switch from double to single precision. This allows to run twice as many computations for the same memory access characteristics, twice as many particles can be studied with the same memory footprint, and the bandwidth requirements for a given setup are halved. Where the rigorous switch from the C datatype `double` to `float` is not feasible for accuracy and stability constraints, some codes switch from one representation into the other in differ-

---

[1]Corresponding Author: Tobias Weinzierl, School of Engineering and Computing Sciences, Durham University, Lower Mountjoy South Road, DH1 3LE Durham, United Kingdom; E-mail: tobias.weinzierl@durham.ac.uk.

ent application phases. Notably in linear algebra algorithms such techniques have been applied successfully—though mainly due to speed reasons rather than concerns about the memory footprint [2]. Yet it remains a problem-specific, sometimes tricky and often even experiment-dependent decision whether to work with reduced accuracy. Furthermore, mixed precision algorithms require the modification of core compute functions (kernels). They are not minimally invasive in terms of coding, while the best-case savings are limited to a factor of two.

We study SPH's memory footprint challenge at hands of the Sedov blast Sod shock benchmark (see [3,4], e.g.) realised with a C++ merger of the AMR framework Peano and its particle administration [5,6,7] with the SPH kernels from SWIFT [8] using double precision. To lower the memory demands without kernel modifications, we propose to generalise concepts from [9]. Control volumes cluster the computational domain. Cells of linked-cell or modified linked lists algorithms [10] act as such volumes. Within each volume, we analyse all particles located inside as soon as all computational work such as force computations or particle position and velocity updates for these particles have terminated. We determine the average value and deviation of the particles' attributes such as position, speed or density from the average, and we switch into a hierarchical attribute representation, i.e. to hold the derivations from the means. Basically, one reference particle is chosen per cell and all values are stored relative to this particle's properties. These hierarchical values are stored with only few bytes where global accuracy constraints allow us to do so. Before their next usage, all particle data is back-transformed into plain C++ data types. We compress and uncompress the particles on-the-fly. The same technique is applied to the MPI data exchange.

To the best of our knowledge, our realisation of this simple idea goes significantly beyond other work: First, we are able to offer precision formats with down to two bytes per floating point value. This allows us to introduce savings beyond the magic factor of two experienced for `double` vs. `float`. Second, our approach is completely dynamic, i.e. it anticipates the solution behaviour. It compresses data only where compression is beneficial and preserves a prescribed accuracy. In SPH, it anticipates the smoothness of the solution. Third, our compressing is deployed to separate threads and runs parallel to the original code. Fourth, it does not require any alterations of the original compute kernels. It is minimally invasive. Finally, the idea also can be applied straightforwardly to MPI data exchange.

We study the proposed ideas on a cluster equipped with Xeon Phi accelerators. Memory constraints here play an important role. While we focus on a benchmark setup, our methodological contributions apply to other application areas and real-world setups as well. The remainder is organised as follows: We start from a description of our benchmark code (Section 1) before we introduce our idea of on-the-fly compression in Section 2. Some remarks how this compression embeds into the simulation life cycle precede numerical results in Section 4. A brief outlook and remarks on future work (Section 5) close the discussion.

1. Case study

As the present paper studies data layout considerations at hands of SPH, it studies a continuous medium represented by particles (Figure 1). Each particle carries a unique

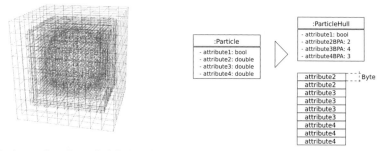

Figure 1. Left: A snapshot of a typical Sedov blast simulation. Right: `tearApart` decomposes a particle object into its hull and a byte stream.

smoothing length and interacts with any other particle closer than the smoothing length. We restrict to short-range interactions modelled with finite smoothing lengths. The extension of the present ideas to long-range interactions is technically straightforward.

Figure 2. Pseudo-code of overall case study algorithm.

```
 1:  while time<terminal time do
 2:      // 1st sweep: calculate density
 3:      for all cells c in grid do
 4:          for all cells c' that share at least one face with c do              ▷ Includes cell c
 5:              Load c' if not loaded before throughout this sweep
 6:              for all particles p in c do                                      ▷ Outer loop
 7:                  for all particles p' in c' do                               ▷ Inner loop
 8:                      If p ≠ p', update attributes of p such as density dermining smoothing length
 9:                  end for
10:                  Newton iteration: re-evaluate inner loop if smoothing length computation not converged
11:              end for
12:              Store away c' if not required anymore throughout traversal
13:              Adopt the AMR structure if smoothing lenghts permit/require
14:          end for
15:      end for
16:      // 2nd sweep: calculate forces                      ▷ Same loop structure as density calculation
17:      // 3rd sweep: half kick and drift, i.e. increase time by Δt/2        ▷ Same loop structure as density
18:                    ▷ calculation without particle-particle interaction; might change admissible Δt
19:      // 4th sweep: recalculate density                   ▷ Same code as density calculation before
20:      // 5th sweep: calculate forces                      ▷ Same loop structure as density calculation
21:      // 6th sweep: half kick, i.e. increase time by Δt/2      ▷ Same loop structure as previous half kick
22:  end while
```

Our simulation workflow comprises a sequence of nested loops (Figure 2). An outer loop steps through the simulation time. We rely on a global time stepping where each particle advances in time by the same delta. Local time stepping has no impact on the data flow. Yet, it changes the memory access characteristics. The time stepping itself is realised in leap frog form. It splits up the particles' position updates into two updates corresponding to half the time step size each. Each update comprises a force calculation, a position update (and an update of other quantities) as well as a recomputation of the particles' smoothing lengths. Such a scheme is in $\mathcal{O}(|\mathbb{P}|^2)$ for $|\mathbb{P}|$ particles. It would be inefficient to compare all particles with all particles because of the finite smoothing length. We thus rely on a grid and linked cell lists [11,12]:

We split up the computational domain into cells—in our case cubes due to a space-tree/octree formalism—track for each cell all adjacent cells, embed the particles into the cells, i.e. make each cell hold its particles, and check only particles from one cell vs. particles of its own or neighbouring cells. Adaptive mesh refinement (AMR) is directly introduced by nonuniform smoothing lengths. To keep the computational work as small as possible, our dynamic refinement criterion tries to introduce as small cells as possible. To allow us to realise the plain linked cell idea where only direct neighbour cells are checked, this minimum mesh size is constrained by the maximum of the smoothing lengths of all particles held within a cell. It may never underrun. Such an AMR-based linked cell strategy is popular in various other application areas such as molecular dynamics, too. Different to the latter codes, our smoothing length is a non-linear, time-dependent function of the particle properties.

The Sedov blast Sod shock setup acts as test bed for the introduced algorithmic ingredients (Figure 1). Cubic splines dominate the particle-particle interaction, and boundary treatment effects are neglected as we simulate only few time steps. For the realisation of the AMR, we rely on our meshing framework Peano [5,7]. All physics code fragments stem from SWIFT [8]. For the assignment of particles to the grid and vice versa, i.e. for gluing particles and grid together, we rely on the PIDT technique [6].

Several application characteristics guide our considerations: All reasonable and accurate simulations depend on the ability to handle as many particles as possible. If the total memory available is small, this memory has to be used carefully. All particle-particle interactions are computationally intense—one reason for the growing popularity of particle formalisms in supercomputing (see for example [13] for other application areas)—and thus natural vectorisation candidates given a proper data layout. All time steps move particles (twice) and the data structures thus have to be well-suited to reorder particle sets and to exchange particles between ranks and cores.

Such a melange of characteristics poses an interesting challenge for clusters with Xeon Phi accelerators. The arithmetic intensity and the localised operations make it promising with respect to the wide vector registers and high core counts. Its memory requirements, the Phi's strict alignment rules and the comparably small memory per core as well as the interconnect heterogeneity (core to core, accelerator to accelerator on same host, accelerator to accelerator on different hosts, ...) however render efficient coding challenging. Proper data structure choices play a major role. In this context, we furthermore note that SPH-type codes are complex. Changes of the data layout thus are problematic both economically and with respect to bugs. A minimally invasive approach to memory footprint tuning that keeps computational kernels unaltered is desirable. Our approach is minimally invasive and relies on a simple smoothness assumption similar to [9]: As the particles represent a continuum, spatially close particles often hold similar physical properties.

2. On-the-fly data compression

Each cell in the grid holds an set of particles. Since particles change their position only in two out of six sweeps, since only few particles travel from one cell into another cell per position update, and since we have to obtain high vectorisation efficiency, we hold them continuously rather than in linked lists or maps. For the majority of steps, the particle sequences remain invariant. Each particle carries eleven scalar floating point quantities plus three vector quantities being the curl, the velocity and the position in space. Traditionally, two storage paradigms for such a setup do exist: array of structs (AoS) and struct of arrays (SoA). Hybrids are possible.

There are pros and cons coming along with each variant. SoA is advantageous for vectorisation. Its memory access characteristics are better than AoS if individual steps require subsets of the particles' attributes. The former property might loose importance due to gather and scatter instructions in future AVX versions as long as particle sets fit into the caches. AoS makes the particles' reassignment to cells and distributed memory parallelisation easier as particles are collocated in memory. Challenges however arise if particles are augmented with non-double attributes on hardware such as the Xeon Phi that require strict alignment. Compilers can reduce memory fill-ins (padding) due to attribute reordering—attributes are held in a struct with decreasing size—but some memory is 'lost'. As no scheme is always superior to the other, some codes change representations on-the-fly. For simplicity, our case study code is based upon AoS only, and we neglect tuning techniques transforming AoS into SoA temporarily to exploit vector units. AoS also integrates directly into our particle handling [6] triggering MPI calls.

We observe that the information density for a particular attribute within a cell is limited. Let $a(p)$ be a generic attribute of particle $a \in \mathbb{P}$. It is held in double precision.

$$A(c) = \frac{1}{|\mathbb{P}(c)|} \sum_{p \in \mathbb{P}(c)} a(p)$$

is the standard mean for all particle attributes within a cell. Then,

$$\hat{a}(p) = a(p) - A(c)$$

is a hierarchical attribute representation, i.e. the attribute value relative to the mean value. We use the term hierarchical as our idea is geometrically inspired [9]. It introduces a two-scale notion of attributes, as the nodal (read real) attribute content results from a coarse/generalised mean value plus a surplus. We assume that for many particles within one cell, the number of significant bits in $\hat{a}$ is small. Significant bits are those that are required to reconstruct the original value a up to sufficient/machine precision. Though there might be escapees, most particle attributes cluster around their respective mean value as the particles represent a continuum. If represented in hierarchical form, double precision of these attributes is luxury.

We hence introduce `tearApart` and `glueTogether`. `glueTogether` is the inverse of `tearApart` subject to precision considerations as detailed below. Both require a reference particle defining the mean values $A(p)$. `tearApart` furthermore is passed an error threshold ε. It removes all double precision arguments from the particle and returns a particle hull—an object with all the non-double attributes such as `bool`s plus one number per double attribute with values from one to six—as well as a stream of bytes (Figure 1). The hull can be stored with techniques from [9] efficiently and does not require any alignment. Efficiently means that all the integer numbers are squeezed into one long integer. The byte stream is a linearisation of all the attributes. They first are converted into their hierarchical representation. Second, we rewrite them as $\hat{s} \cdot 2^{\hat{e}}$, $\hat{s} \in \mathbb{N}$, i.e. we explicitly break up IEEE double precision. The exponent $\hat{e}$ third is stored as one byte on the stream. Finally, we store $\hat{s}$ as an integer value with a fixed number of bytes such that the whole attribute needs $bpa \geq 2$ bytes. *bpa* (bytes per attribute) is held within the hull. Let $f_{bpa}(a(p))$ encode the storage of an attribute. tearApart chooses bpa minimal subject to $|f_{bpa}(a(p)) - a(p)| \leq \varepsilon$. For $bpa > 7$, no memory is saved. In this case, tearApart skips any particle transformation and returns the unaltered particle. For $bpa \leq 7$, tearApart reduces the memory requirements. A combination of the two operations and their byte stream idea with SoA is straightforward but not followed up here. If we apply tearApart on a sequence of particles, we note that we obtain a heterogeneous sequence of objects regarding their memory footprint. Depending on the particles' properties and the precision threshold, tearApart decides for each particle how many bytes are sufficient to encode the data or whether tearing them apart pays off at all. Obviously, the inverse glueTogether does not require a threshold.

3. Integration into simulation workflow and parallelisation

We do not use our decomposition into hierarchical, compressed attributes plus hull as one and only data representation. Instead, we apply tearApart after a cell's data has been used for the last time throughout a grid traversal. Its counterpart glueTogether acts as preamble to any computation after the first load of a cell. Particles are compressed in-between two grid traversals and are held with double values as long as they are required for computations. The two data conversations plug into all algorithm phases.

To facilitate this life-cycle, we rewrite $A(c)$ per cell into a tuple $(A,\tilde{A})(c)$. tearApart relies on $A(c)$ input to decompose the particles. In parallel, it determines the average value of attribute a in $\tilde{A}(c)$. glueTogether reconstructs all particle structs at hands of $A(c)$. Afterwards, it sets $A(c) \leftarrow \hat{A}(c)$. This tuple-based scheme allows for a single pass realisation. Each compression works with an average from the previous grid traversal. Though $A(c)$s' lagging behind by one traversal probably yields non-optimal compression factors, it does not harm the correctness.

As compression and reconstruction of the particles plug into the first usage or the last usage of a cell as a preamble or epilogue respectively, no alterations of the compute kernels are necessary. The approach is minimally invasive. As we stick to AoS throughout the computations, memory movements due to particle moves/reordering are minimised and the transfer of whole particles through MPI is straightforward. As we analyse the average attribute values on-the-fly on a per-cell basis, our approach is lo-calised. It yields high compression rates where the particle attributes are homogeneous. Yet it is robust in regions where they differ significantly from each other. As we decide per particle whether compression pays off, iterations end up with data structures where some particles are compressed and others not. Since we hold the particles per cell in an array that obviously has to be able to grow due to glueTogether, tearApart and glueTogether implicitly sort the particles according to their derivation from the mean values: We make tearApart run through a cell's particle sequence reversely, and we make glueTogether append particles at the end of a sequence. A plain C++ vector suffices. The later the particle within a cell's particle sequence the higher the probability that it is compressed. This sorting that implicitly kicks in after the first iteration ensures that no frequent particle reordering due compression is necessary.

With the uncompress-compute-compress life-cycle, the effective memory demands of the code depend on the fact how long particles have to remain uncompressed; how long they are 'active', i.e. in-use. In-between grid sweeps, the memory footprint is smaller than or equal to the original scheme besides the average value tuples per cell. As cells are by an order of magnitude fewer than particles, this impact can be neglected. For regular Cartesian grids, an estimate on the upper number of active cells is straightforward. Assuming homogeneous particle counts per cell then yields statements on the maximum memory footprint. Such bounds are, to the best of our knowledge, unknown for AMR in general. Empirically known however is the fact that a traversal of the adaptive grid by a space-filling curve (SFC) is advantageous. SFCs yield localised traversals due to their underlying Hölder continuity. Subdomains induced by a segment of an SFC have a small surface relative to their volume, i.e. their contained cells [14]. This property translates into the subdomain of active cells. The total memory footprint of uncompressed particles thus is relatively small. However, quantitative bound exist only for regular tessellations. We use the Peano SFC.

While the particle moving and, thus, the exchange of whole particles via MPI rely on plain structs, all other application phases in Algorithm 2 do not exchange all particle data such as particle positions. They exchange attribute subsets. Our code transfers these quantities in Jacobi-style, i.e. they are computed and sent out at the end of the traversal. Prior to the subsequent grid sweep we then merge them into the data on the receiver side. We therefore may either send out data prior to the compression epilogue or exchange compressed quantities. The latter reduces the bandwidth requirements.

Our grid decomposition is non-overlapping [7]: Cells are uniquely assigned to ranks while the vertices in-between are replicated along domain decomposition boundaries. We propose—in accordance with the PIDT scheme from [6]—to hold particles within the dual grid. Technically, the particle lists $\mathbb{P}(c)$ are split 2^d times, assigned to vertices, and all particles are stored within those lists whose vertices whose vertices are closest to their particle positions. As vertices along subdomain boundaries are replicated among all adjacent ranks, also the mean values are available on each rank; a payoff of the tuple storage. MPI data exchange thus can use the average tuples. No modifications become necessary. The compressed MPI exchange is minimally invasive.

tearApart is an operation that delays the program execution. We model it as task. Once all particles within a cell are not used anymore, their memory location remains invariant. We spawn a tearApart task compressing data while the original SPH algorithm continues. The compression runs parallel to computations. In return, we introduce a flag per particle list that is secured by a semaphore. It is set once tearApart finishes and checked by the load process triggering glueTogether prior to any uncompression.

glueTogether introduces overhead as well. As grid traversals are deterministic, this phase can be deployed to a prefetching task, too. While this is, in principle, straightforward, we do not follow-up it here. tearApart/glueTogether tasks are not visible to the original code and do not increase its complexity. However, estimates on the total memory footprint have to be validated carefully for the concurrent particle handling. Conversions might be delayed, and thus the total memory footprint might increase.

4. Results

All experiments were conducted on the Beacon system's Xeon Phi 5110P accelerators. Each accelerator hosts 8 GByte of memory, and four accelerators are plugged into one Xeon E5-2670 host. The Phis are programmed in native mode, and we do not use the

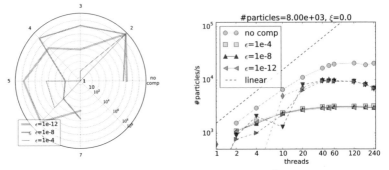

Figure 3. Left: Number of attribute compressions with different *bpa* for $\xi = 0.8, h = 0.008$. Right: TBB scaling on one Xeon Phi for different compression rates (solid lines) and scaling if `tearApart` is deployed to separate tasks (dotted lines).

host. All codes were translated with the Intel 2015 compiler, all results are given in particle updates per second, i.e. the timings are normalised by the total particle count. The shared memory parallelisation relies on Intel's Threading Building Blocks (TBB).

Our setup starts from particles aligned in a Cartesian grid with spacing h. Each particle experiences a slight random perturbation $\xi \cdot h$ of its position with $\xi \in (0,1)$, i.e. the setup is not perfectly symmetric. The AMR criterion is chosen initially such that the smoothing length corresponds to $1.1255h$. The particles' mass is set to h^3, and their internal energy equals $\frac{3}{2} \cdot 10^{-5}$ everywhere besides in a sphere of radius 0.1 around the centre of the cubic computational domain. Within the sphere, the particles' internal energy is increased by $\frac{10^3}{33} \cdot h^3$. This additional energy component triggers the blast (Figure 1). An increase in time is to some degree equivalent to increasing ξ.

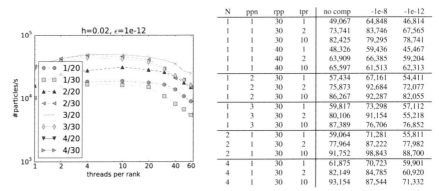

N	ppn	rpp	tpr	no comp	-1e-8	-1e-12
1	1	30	1	49,067	64,848	46,814
1	1	30	2	73,741	83,746	67,565
1	1	30	10	82,425	79,295	78,741
1	1	40	1	48,326	59,436	45,467
1	1	40	2	63,909	66,385	59,204
1	1	40	10	65,597	61,513	62,313
1	2	30	1	57,434	67,161	54,411
1	2	30	2	75,873	92,684	72,077
1	2	30	10	86,267	92,287	82,055
1	3	30	1	59,817	73,298	57,112
1	3	30	2	80,106	91,154	55,218
1	3	30	10	87,389	76,706	76,852
2	1	30	1	59,064	71,281	55,811
2	1	30	2	77,964	87,222	77,982
2	1	30	10	91,752	98,843	88,700
4	1	30	1	61,875	70,723	59,901
4	1	30	2	82,149	84,785	60,920
4	1	30	10	93,154	87,544	71,332

Figure 4. Left: Throughput for different combinations of accelerator count/MPI ranks per Xeon Phi ($\xi = 0$). The compression is not applied on MPI messages. Right: Throughput of hybrid code where compression is always applied to the MPI message sizes. If compression inside the domain is switched off, the domain boundary applies $\varepsilon = 10^{-12}$. N=number of nodes, ppn=phis used per node, rpp=ranks per phi, tpr=threads per rank. Results are strong scaling measurements with $h = 0.01$.

While small ε increase the number of particles that are not or almost not compressed ($bpa = 6$), $bpa = 2$ is sufficient for the majority of particles for all ε (Figure 3). The original memory footprint stems from particles with 176 bytes each plus the memory required for the AMR grid. For both, bit optimisations from [9] have been applied. The hull of the particle including the bpa flags in contrast is 40 bytes. As such, we compress the memory footprint to 0.25 ($\varepsilon = 10^{-12}$), 0.21 ($\varepsilon = 10^{-8}$) or 0.17 ($\varepsilon = 10^{-4}$). These measurements comprise overheads required for dynamic data structures.

We observe reasonable scaling of the code (Figure 3), but the code can not exploit more than one hardware thread per floating point unit. While the compression allows us to upscale the problem per node, it reduces the code's throughput. However, we note that the compression can be ran in the background of the actual solve. With the compression in the background, we flood the Phi with tasks [15] and thus start to make up for the compression's runtime penalty. It remains open whether task-based glueTogether could close the gap completely.

If we use more than one Xeon Phi with compression only applied within the domain, we obtain the best throughput for three Xeon Phis running 20 MPI ranks with 4 TBB threads each: with a hybrid code, slight overbooking of the floating point units pays off. If we use more than one node, the performance deteriorates. If we study the best-case throughputs and apply the compression on data exchanged via MPI (Figure 4), we observe that more signficiant overbooking (30 ranks with 10 threads, e.g.) starts to pay off. We also are faster than TBB-only codes on one accelerator. Up to three Xeon Phis per node yield a performance improvement—though far from linear—while the compression with background tasks allows the hybrid code now to offer the memory compression for free in terms of runtime. Multithreading has closed the compression's runtime gap. We furthermore observe that four accelerators distributed among four nodes yield higher throughput than four accelerators plugged into one node. Reasons for this have to be some kind of resource competition. All in all, the compression of the MPI messages speeds up the code by a factor of five compared to an uncompressed data exchange, while the basic performance characteristics remain preserved. See [6] for a discussion of the code's scaling behaviour—the present figures study soley strong scaling.

5. Outlook and conclusion

The present work introduces techniques that help us to squeeze more simulation into given memory and communication bandwidth allowance. This will become mandatory for the exascale era [1]. Picking up the seminal fourth recipe of [16], our approach might fall into a class of techniques that help us to deliver *more science per byte*. An important advantage of the present work compared to classic mixed precision is that the original compute kernels remain unaltered.

While our algorithmic setting is flexible, we find that basically either aggressive compression with two bytes per floating point numbers or (almost) no compression at all are used. Reasons for this might be a result of the chosen use case, but the effect deserves further studies. If only few *bpa* choices are sufficient, the particle hull footprint can be reduced further. In the context of data compression, we reiterate that our technique is well-suited to equip codes with higher than double precision without making the memory footprint explode. Also, we suggest that a reduction of memory footprint and, thus, data moves reduces the energy consumption of codes. This deserves further investigation.

Acknowledgements

We appreciate the support from Intel through Durham's Intel Parallel Computing Centre (IPCC) which gave us access to latest Intel software. Special thanks are due to Matthieu Schaller for his support and advise on the SWIFT code [8]. All underlying software is open source and available at [5]. This material is based upon experimental work supported by the National Science Foundation under Grant Number 1137097 and by the University of Tennessee through the Beacon Project. Any opinions, findings, conclusions, or recommendations expressed in this material are those of the authors and do not necessarily reflect the views of the National Science Foundation or the University of Tennessee. The project has received funding from the European Union's Horizon 2020 research and innovation programme under grant agreement No 671698 (ExaHyPE).

References

[1]   J. Dongarra, P. H. Beckman, et al. The International Exascale Software Project Roadmap. *IJHPCA*, 25(1):3–60, 2011.

[2]   M. Baboulin, A. Buttari, J. Dongarra, J. Kurzak, J. Langou, J. Langou, P. Luszczek, and S. Tomov. Accelerating scientific computations with mixed precision algorithms. *Computer Physics Communications*, 180:2526–2533, 2009.

[3]   P. Gonnet.   Efficient and scalable algorithms for smoothed particle hydrodynamics on hybrid shared/distributed-memory architectures. *SISC*, 37(1):C95–C121, 2015.

[4]   V. Springel. E pur si muove: Galilean-invariant cosmological hydrodynamical simulations on a moving mesh. arxiv e-prints, 0901.4107, mnras. *Mon. Not. of the R. Astron. Soc.*, 2009.

[5]   T. Weinzierl et al. Peano—a Framework for PDE Solvers on Spacetree Grids, 2015. www.peano-framework.org.

[6]   T. Weinzierl, B. Verleye, P. Henri, and D. Roose. Two particle-in-grid realisations on spacetrees. *Parallel Computing*, 2015. (submitted, arXiv, 1508.02435).

[7]   T. Weinzierl. The Peano software—parallel, automaton-based, dynamically adaptive grid traversals. Technical Report arXiv150604496W, eprint arXiv:1506.04496, Durham University, 2015.

[8]   P. Gonnet, M. Schaller, et al. Swift—shared-memory parallel smoothed particle hydrodynamics (sph) code for large-scale cosmological simulations, 2015. http://www.swiftsim.com.

[9]   H.-J. Bungartz, W. Eckhardt, T. Weinzierl, and C. Zenger. A precompiler to reduce the memory footprint of multiscale pde solvers in c++. *Future Generation Computer Systems*, 26(1):175–182, January 2010.

[10]   W. Mattson and B. M. Rice. Near-neighbor calculations using a modified cell-linked list method. *Computer Physics Communications*, 119(2-3):135–148, 1999.

[11]   B. Quentrec and C. Brot. New method for searching for neighbors in molecular dynamics computations. *Journal of Computational Physics*, 13(3):430 – 432, 1973.

[12]   R. Hockney and J. Eastwood. *Computer Simulation Using Particles*. Academic Press, 1988.

[13]   R. Yokota, G. Turkiyyah, and D. Keyes. Communication complexity of the fast multipole method and its algebraic variants. *Supercomputing frontiers and innovations*, 1(1), 2014.

[14]   H.-J. Bungartz, M. Mehl, and T. Weinzierl. *Euro-Par 2006, Parallel Processing, 12th International Euro-Par Conference*, volume 4128 of *LNCS*, chapter A Parallel Adaptive Cartesian PDE Solver Using Space–Filling Curves, pages 1064–1074. Springer-Verlag, Berlin, Heidelberg, 2006.

[15]   M. Schreiber, T. Weinzierl, and H.-J. Bungartz. Cluster optimization and parallelization of simulations with dynamically adaptive grids. In F. Wolf, B. Mohr, and D. an Mey, editors, *Euro-Par 2013*, volume 8097 of *Lecture Notes in Computer Science*, pages 484–496, Berlin Heidelberg, 2013. Springer-Verlag. preprint.

[16]   D. E. Keyes. Four Horizons for Enhancing the Performance of Parallel Simulations Based on Partial Differential Equations. In A. Bode, T. Ludwig, W. Karl, and R. Wismüller, editors, *Euro-Par '00: Proceedings from the 6th International Euro-Par Conference on Parallel Processing*, volume 1900 of *Lecture Notes in Computer Science*, pages 1–17. Springer-Verlag, 2000.

Parallel Computing: On the Road to Exascale
G.R. Joubert et al. (Eds.)
IOS Press, 2016
doi:10.3233/978-1-61499-621-7-431

Flexible and Generic Workflow Management

Sebastian LÜHRS [a], Daniel ROHE [a], Alexander SCHNURPFEIL [a],
Kay THUST [a] and Wolfgang FRINGS [a]

[a] *Jülich Supercomputing Centre, Forschungszentrum Jülich GmbH, Germany*

Abstract. Running and combining HPC applications often leads to complex scientific workflows, even more when code is to be executed in several different computing platforms. We present a flexible and platform independent framework for workflow definition and execution based on a redesigned version of the benchmarking environment JUBE. By means of a generalised configuration method this new version of JUBE can now be applied to more complex production, development and testing scenarios. It provides user-defined parameter substitution at all workflow stages, automated job submission, extensive directory and result handling and customisable analysis steps. In this report we demonstrate how it can be used to implement a given workflow representation and how it relates to and differs from other generic workflow management systems.

Keywords. workflow management, parameter handling, automatic job submission, platform independent

Introduction

Developing and executing scientific applications, in particular on High Performance Computing (HPC) architectures, typically results in a complex workflow structure of compilation, pre- and post-processing steps and platform-dependent job submission. Managing these scientific workflows, be it manually or by user-generated scripting, can be a tedious and error-prone task. Moreover, it often results in significant amounts of work that needs to be repeated for every single use case. Application parameters may for instance change at several stages in these workflows and are then difficult to monitor. Furthermore, reproducibility and documentation of raw results is highly important yet difficult to handle if sources, configuration files and input data change multiple times during the application development process.

Script based solutions help automating the workflow creation and monitoring, but are typically adapted to one specific application and to one or a few platforms. In contrast to a script based solution, multiple workflow management tools are available which allow the creation of complex workflow structures using a Graphical User Interface (GUI). These tools follow a very generic approach of handling scientific workflows and are quite user friendly due to their intuitive usage model, in particular when using remote computational resources. On the downside, these tools can be very complex to set up or complicated to extend, and testing new workflow approaches can take quite some time.

Here we describe a third approach by modifying the benchmarking environment JUBE [1] to allow for a more generic, lightweight workflow creation, which mostly focuses on parametrisation of all kinds of steps needed in a complete workflow. It does not target to access widely distributed remote services. The main purpose is to help users parametrising their job runs, monitor the workflow processing and create reproducible data on their specific HPC system(s).

Related Work

We first reviewed the existing benchmarking environment JUBE, which provides a solid HPC workflow management environment allowing compilation, job submission and analysis [2]. JUBE was developed in 2008 to handle typical benchmark execution steps and was used in projects like DEISA or PRACE. It is implemented using the Perl scripting language and can be configured using predefined XML (Extensible Markup Language) based configuration files. It became evident that the JUBE runtime environment can in principle be configured using program specific configuration files, so that in addition to its usability for benchmarking, the creation of production, development and testing scenarios is also possible [3].

Compared to other workflow management systems like Taverna [4] or Kepler [5], JUBE handles workflows in a more lightweight manner. Workflow steps are based on shell commands such that existing script solutions can easily be included. In particular, when using a workflow management system for the first time or during the adaptation of a new workflow, this helps to produce results very fast. Similar to Taverna, JUBE uses a data-driven orchestration, which means that JUBE will start executing all steps with no additional dependencies and will add more steps to the execution queue as soon as the steps they depend on are resolved [6]. In addition to local execution Taverna and Kepler also provide a set of services to access remote computational resources e.g. by using WSDL [7] definitions which describe the remotely accessible web service. However, for scientific HPC workflow handling users mostly need access to a platform specific job management system. For this purpose JUBE provides a very simple access by using standardised job file templates which will be submitted using the platform specific command line tools. On top of that we focus on local workflow execution and therefore decided not to establish an additional web-service based structure. This restriction helps shortening the setup process of the scientific workflow management environment when accessing a new platform for the first time.

Workflows in JUBE are defined by means of XML configuration files with a simple structure that can be created or modified using any text editor. This approach allows to easily modify configuration files in a remotely accessed HPC environment. In addition we provide an XML schema [8] and a DTD [9] file to help users writing the configuration files.

The original JUBE workflow is however rather strict due to its focus on benchmarks and a mostly predefined input file layout. Multiple job submissions, multiple compile steps or complex pre- and post-processing steps are tedious to implement using the existing configuration options. Due to these and other restrictions we developed a new Python-based version of JUBE (JUBE2) which now provides a configuration interface for more flexible workflow creation as well as other additional features. In the following we describe the new release only.

Workflow Creation and Execution

In contrast to previous JUBE versions the new release now uses a dependency driven step structure similar to make [10]. Inside a single step the predecessors it depends on must be defined. This allows for more complex workflow execution graphs with multiple predecessors. Closed loops are not allowed inside this structure. In addition to the execution order given by the dependencies, JUBE2 uses parametrisation to determine the number of unique step runs. Parameters are defined by simple comma-separated lists of values and each value will result in a separate step execution. Each specific step and parameter combination creates a unique execution unit, called work package. The workflow management system automatically creates the cross-product of the parameter sets in case multiple are available. Dependent steps are executed at least once for each existing predecessor parameter combination.

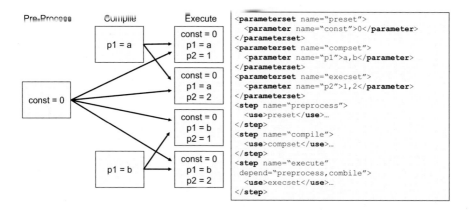

Figure 1. A sample workflow and the corresponding JUBE2 configuration representation.

Figure 1 shows the combination of a given step order and the automatic parameter expansion. By default JUBE2 keeps separate parameter combinations physically apart from each other to prevent interference between them. If this behaviour is not desired it is also possible to use a shared operation which is executed only once and collectively in a shared folder and can be used to collect data from different parameter combinations.

Independent work packages are collected in an internal execution queue and can thus be immediately executed. New elements are added to the queue as soon as the work packages they depend on are finalised.

In HPC workflows users often invoke asynchronously executed commands like the job submission to an HPC job management system, e.g. SLURM [11], or to execute a program as a background or batch process. Workflow management systems often use an additional service like UNICORE [12] to monitor these jobs and block the running workflow execution until the specific command is executed [13]. Beyond synchronous commands the previous versions of JUBE and also JUBE2 allow the use of non-blocking techniques to wait until a specific asynchronous command finishes. JUBE2 starts the given asynchronous commands and marks the corresponding step as running. It uses a user triggered pull behaviour to update its internal command status, this means that JUBE2 will stop after all asynchronous commands were submitted and the work package queue is empty. The user can restart JUBE2 to check if one of the running commands has been finished by checking if a user defined file was created, which marks the completion of the command. All dependent commands and steps will then be continued automatically.

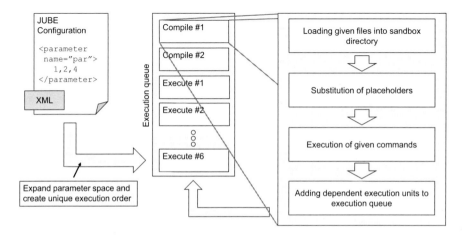

Figure 2. JUBE2 work package execution order.

Within one work package there are four main tasks to be handled by JUBE2. The structure is shown in figure 2. First, external files will be linked or copied into the workflow environment. Next, placeholders inside of these files will be replaced by using the available parameters. After this, the given commands will be executed and finally new dependent work packages will be added to the internal queue.

Due to its original usage for creating easily adjustable benchmark configurations, the parameter handling in JUBE2 is very flexible. Parameters can be used in command expressions, in file names or for replacing placeholders within input or source files. Even parameters within other parameters or parameters which are calculated by using another parameter values are possible. Within a generic scientific workflow this enables users to parameterise their applications using *one single* point of definition without keeping track of all files or commands which have to be modified.

The last step of a workflow execution in JUBE2 can be a customised analysis step. For benchmarking this step is used to scan the output files for relevant timing or scaling information which can be used to create a final result representation.

More generally, in particular when applied to numerical experiments, it can be used to create an overview of all executed application runs, including a customised view of the parameters used along with a custom analysis.

Directory and Data Handling

Each workflow execution uses its own directory structure. Inside this structure, JUBE2 handles its metadata and it creates a sandbox directory for each separate work package. This avoids interference between different runs and creates a reproducible structure. External files like source files or input files can be copied or linked to be accessible within the sandbox directories.

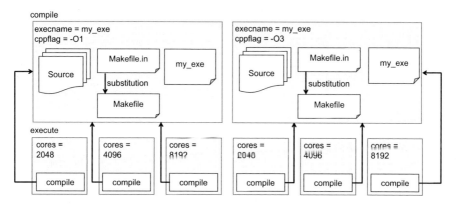

Figure 3. Directory and file access between different work packages.

To access files from another work package JUBE2 automatically creates symbolic links between dependent steps. Figure 3 shows an example of this structure between execute and compile steps. The link name points to the dependent step name and automatically provides a parameter consistent file access. It is also possible to change the directory to a user defined directory name.

Compared to previous versions the directory management was changed. Directories used to be specified by a single branch of the possible parameter tree and were specified by a fixed set of parameters. Now, by separating each step's directory, the workflow structure becomes more flexible allowing to reproduce specific steps more easily.

Platform Independency

Porting an existing scientific workflow to a new computing platform can be very time consuming. The HPC job submission or the computing environment may differ significantly. To allow for the creation of platform independent workflows JUBE2 provides a set of several different inclusion techniques. This means platform dependent and independent data can be stored separately and a generic workflow can include additional platform specific parameters. Thereby the user can create a platform specific JUBE2 definition, which provides the most important parameters, substitutions or system files. Once prepared, this definition can be reused without any further changes. Inside the generic part of the workflow these definitions can be included as a whole or they can be used as a template with selected minor changes imposed by the user. To switch between different platform definitions the user can choose a directory to search for those definitions.

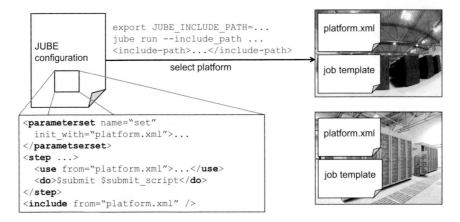

Figure 4. Available include options within a JUBE2 configuration file and the different possibilities to specify the include file directory.

Figure 4 gives an overview of the different ways to include configuration details specifying the local HPC environment, e.g. `platform.xml` will hold all platform specific parameters and the `job template` will provide a generic job submission script. The external data can be used to initialise local datasets or they can directly be added to a step-specific environment. JUBE2 also provides a generic `include` which only copies XML-data into the local XML structure without parsing any JUBE2 semantics.

The new version of JUBE does not require or impose a fixed layout of the platform definition files. We tried to avoid such a layout because it is hard to maintain and special platforms often cannot be mapped properly into this structure. Hence parameter names can be selected e.g. either by computing site or in a community-specific manner.

Use Case

We tested the new implementation of JUBE to handle some typical HPC workflows which mostly contain a parameter driven compilation, job submission and an optional post processing step on local HPC systems. Of course applications which are still used for benchmarking like HPL [14], IOR [15] or mdtest [16] could be adapted to the new configuration file layout to be able to use the new workflow environment.

We also tested JUBE2 during the development phase of new applications to provide monitoring during the testing stage and to find the sweet spot concerning a specified set of parameters. In an application from condensed matter physics we can substitute model parameters in source files, code parameters during compilation and system parameters in the job submission process, and we can inject complex shell scripting if needed, e.g. to access special hardware instances. The completed runs are stored separately and results can easily be compared. This allows for an efficient execution of numerical experiments since it fully automates the execution of batches and at the same time ensures maximum documentation and reproducibility by storing source code, runtime parameters and results separately for each run. Subsequent analysis procedures can be predefined and also added or altered even after the experiment to automate data processing. This can highly facilitate numerical experiments not only concerning the effort needed for execution, but maybe even more importantly concerning documentation, analysis and long-time storage.

All these examples were executed on different HPC infrastructures. The flexible layout of defining the workflow structure allows us to easily add new or replace existing options in the platform definitions without rewriting the complete workflow definition. This is a crucial property in order to easily port the framework to new HPC systems.

Outlook

Due to its generic approach the new JUBE allows to implement additional script based features without changing the core workflow environment. Nevertheless we monitor the usage of JUBE2 with the help of users' feature requests, especially from the HPC community. New features and commonly used configuration structures will be added to the core environment to allow for a more user friendly usage.

We plan to implement additional support to reuse data of old workflow runs, e.g. to avoid unnecessary long compilation steps. Also the possible HPC job management system interactions will be extended to allow JUBE2 to exploit more of the features which are specific to different job management environments. Last but not least it is planned to allow workflow modifications at runtime. Currently the workflow bases on the parameters which are defined in the configuration. Runtime results cannot change this structure at the moment, because they are only visible during the separate analysis step.

Conclusion

Scientific workflow handling is an important task to provide a reproducible and user friendly application environment. Application specific solutions can help to automate the workflow process and are very flexible but are also difficult to maintain and similar structures need to be implemented repeatedly if a new application should be adapted. Generic workflow management systems create an environment to specify most common workflow steps and structures.

In this paper we described how to use the latest, restructured version of the benchmarking environment JUBE to be used also as a general generic workflow management system for production or test scenarios. It is very lightweight and still provides a flexible configuration model. The parameter driven model inside of JUBE2 helps to easily change application parameters without having to change multiple files by hand. Important aspects of typical HPC workflow steps like job submission, runtime specific sandbox directories or platform independency can be provided using JUBE2.

References

[1]   *JUBE Benchmarking Environment*: `http://www.fz-juelich.de/jsc/jube`, July 2015
[2]   A. Galonska, W. Frings, P. Gibbon, D. Borodin, A. Kirschner: *JuBE-based Automatic Testing and Performance Measurement System for Fusion Codes*, Parallel Computing: Applications, Tools and Techniques on the Road to Exascale Computing, IOS Press, Advances in Parallel Computing Volume 22, 2012, doi: 10.3233/978-1-61499-041-3-465
[3]   W. Frings, A. Schnurpfeil, S. Meier, F. Janetzko, L. Arnold: *A Flexible, Application- and Platform-Independent Environment for Benchmarking*, Parallel Computing: From Multicores and GPU's to Petascale, IOS Press, Advances in Parallel Computing Volume 19, 2010, doi: 10.3233/978-1-60750-530-3-423
[4]   Katherine Wolstencroft, Robert Haines, Donal Fellows, Alan Williams, David Withers, Stuart Owen, Stian Soiland-Reyes, Ian Dunlop, Aleksandra Nenadic, Paul Fisher, Jiten Bhagat, Khalid Belhajjame, Finn Bacall, Alex Hardisty, Abraham Nieva de la Hidalga, Maria P. Balcazar Vargas, Shoaib Sufi, and Carole Goble: *The Taverna workflow suite: designing and executing workflows of Web Services on the desktop, web or in the cloud*, Nucleic Acids Research, 41(W1): W557-W561, 2013, doi: 10.1093/nar/gkt328
[5]   B. Ludaescher, I. Altintas, C. Berkley, D. Higgins, E.Jaeger, M.Jones, E. A. Lee, J. Tao, Y. Zhao: *Scientific Workflow Management and the Kepler System, Concurrency and Computation: Practice & Experience*, vol. 18, no. 10, pp. 1039-1065, 2006, doi: 10.1002/cpe.994
[6]   V. Curcin, M. Ghanem: *Scientific workflow systems - can one size fit all?*, Biomedical Engineering Conference, 2008. CIBEC 2008. Cairo International, vol. 1, no. 9, pp. 18-20 Dec. 2008, doi: 10.1109/CIBEC.2008.478607
[7]   *Web Service Description Language (WSDL)*: `http://www.w3.org/tr/wsdl20`, July 2015
[8]   *XML Schema*: `http://www.w3.org/XML/Schema`, July 2015
[9]   *Document Type Definition (DTD)*: `http://www.w3schools.com/xml/xml_dtd_intro.asp`, July 2015
[10] *GNU Make*: `https://www.gnu.org/software/make`, July 2015
[11] A. Yoo, M. Jette, and M. Grondona: *Slurm: Simple Linux Utility for Resource Management*, Job Scheduling Strategies for Parallel Processing, volume 2862 of Lecture Notes in Computer Science, pages 44-60, Springer-Verlag, 2003, doi: 10.1.1.10.6834
[12] *Uniform Interface to Computing Resources (UNICORE)*: `https://www.unicore.eu`, July 2015
[13] S. Holl, O. Zimmermann, M. Hofmann-Apitius: *A UNICORE Plugin for HPC-Enabled Scientific Workflows in Taverna 2.2*, Services (SERVICES), 2011 IEEE World Congress, pp. 220,223, 4-9 July 2011, doi: 10.1109/SERVICES.2011.46
[14] *Portable Implementation of the High-Performance Linpack Benchmark for Distributed-Memory Computers (HPL)*: `http://www.netlib.org/benchmark/hpl`, July 2015
[15] *IOR HPC Benchmark*: `http://sourceforge.net/projects/ior-sio`, July 2015
[16] *mdtest HPC Benchmark*: `http://sourceforge.net/projects/mdtest`, July 2015

Parallel Computing: On the Road to Exascale
G.R. Joubert et al. (Eds.)
IOS Press, 2016

doi:10.3233/978-1-61499-621-7-439

A Massively Parallel Barnes-Hut Tree Code with Dual Tree Traversal

Benedikt STEINBUSCH [a,1], Marvin-Lucas HENKEL [b], Mathias WINKEL [a] and Paul GIBBON [a,c]

[a] *Institute for Advanced Simulation, Jülich Supercomputing Centre, Forschungszentrum Jülich GmbH, 52425 Jülich, Germany*
[b] *Faculty of Physics, University of Duisburg-Essen, 47048 Duisburg, Germany*
[c] *Centre for mathematical Plasma Astrophysics, Department of Mathematics, KU Leuven, Celestijnenlaan 200B, 3001 Heverlee, Belgium*

Abstract. Hierarchical methods like the Barnes-Hut (BH) tree code and the Fast Multipole Method (FMM) are important tools to decrease the algorithmic complexity of solving the N-body problem. We report on recent efforts to achieve massive scalability on IBM Blue Gene/Q and other highly concurrent supercomputers with our BH tree code PEPC by replacing a thread synchronization strategy based on traditional lock data structures with atomic operations. We also describe the integration of the Dual Tree Traversal a more recent algorithm that combines advantages of both BH tree code and FMM into PEPC. We explain how the scalability of this algorithm is influenced by the existing communication scheme and we propose a modification to achieve better distributed memory scalability.

Keywords. N-body problem, hierarchical methods, hybrid parallelism

Introduction

Solving the N-body problem is an important component of many applications in the field of computational science. A naive implementation can quickly become a bottleneck however, due to the $\mathcal{O}\left(N^2\right)$ complexity of calculating all pair-wise mutual interactions:

$$\Phi_i = \sum_{j\neq i} \phi(x_i,q_i,x_j,q_j) \quad i \in 1\ldots N \tag{1}$$

While the computation of short-ranged interactions can usually be accelerated using e.g. spatial cutoff techniques, long-ranged interactions require a different approach. One possibility is to discretise the spatial domain in the form of a computational grid on which a partial differential equation for the interaction force field can be solved numerically (e.g. the particle-in-cell scheme). This solution strategy can readily benefit from

---

[1] Corresponding Author: Benedikt Steinbusch, Forschungszentrum Jülich GmbH, IAS - JSC, 52425 Jülich, Germany; E-mail: b.steinbusch@fz-juelich.de

the significant advances made in the field of numerical linear algebra to accelerate the computation. Grid-based techniques however favour certain forms of (typically closed) boundary conditions and require adaptive grid management in order to efficiently deal with strongly inhomogeneous densities.

Another possibility to solve the N-body problem efficiently is the family of mesh-free, hierarchical techniques which have first been proposed in the 1980s. Among the members of this family are the Barnes-Hut (BH) tree code [1] and the Fast Multipole Method (FMM) [2]. Common to these methods is a hierarchical decomposition of space into sub-regions containing fewer and fewer bodies.

The BH tree code computes interaction results for each individual body by selecting appropriate regions to interact with from the hierarchy via an acceptance criterion (AC) that can be based on both geometric and physical quantities (x and q in (1)). On average, the number of interaction partners for each body is typically $\mathcal{O}(\log N)$ and thus the total time complexity of the tree code algorithm is $\mathcal{O}(N \log N)$. BH tree codes to this day are the subject of active research [3,4].

The FMM makes more rigorous use of the hierarchical decomposition by also considering pair-wise interactions between regions and passing the results on to the multiple bodies contained therein. Interaction partners are selected based on an AC that is based primarily on the topology of the decomposition and that can be evaluated statically. The dual use of the decomposition allows the FMM to reach a time complexity of $\mathcal{O}(N)$.

Both methods usually apply a series expansion to the interaction law in order to retain the desired amount of accuracy when computing results of aggregate interactions in a single step. Mirroring the one sided use of the spatial decomposition, the BH tree code expands the interaction law in a single parameter (the source coordinate x_j), while the FMM applies expansions in two parameters (source coordinate x_j and destination coordinate x_i).

More recently a novel hybrid algorithm, the Dual Tree Traversal (DTT), has been proposed [5,6]. Like the FMM it maximises the benefits of the spatial decomposition and employs series expansion in both spatial parameters. The DTT combines this with the flexibility offered by the AC of the BH tree code. It has been shown empirically to also have a time complexity of $\mathcal{O}(N)$.

In this paper, we present our work on PEPC, the **P**retty **E**fficient **P**arallel **C**oulomb-solver. PEPC was conceived in 2003 as a distributed memory parallel BH tree code for electrostatic interactions. It has since evolved to include different laws of interaction and successfully makes use of a hybrid parallelisation scheme [7].

First we report on recent efforts to achieve massive scalability on IBM Blue Gene/Q and other highly concurrent supercomputers by replacing a thread synchronisation strategy based on traditional lock data structures with atomic operations. We show results for intra node scaling utilising all 64 hardware threads of the A2 compute chip and inter node scaling utilising all 458752 cores of the JUQUEEN supercomputer at JSC.

Then we describe the integration of the DTT algorithm into PEPC. We explain how the scalability of this algorithm is influenced by the existing communication scheme and we propose a modification to achieve better distributed memory scalability.

1. Massively Parallel Barnes-Hut Tree Code

1.1. The Barnes-Hut Algorithm

The Barnes-Hut algorithm proceeds in two phases. Phase 1 builds a tree decomposition of the source bodies $b_j, j \in 1, \ldots, N$. PEPC follows the Hashed Oct-Tree scheme proposed in [8], repeated here as algorithm 1. The algorithm rearranges the distribution of the bodies among parallel processes according to their spatial position making use of a space-filling curve. It builds a local part of the tree bottom-up on every process using only the information of the bodies assigned to that process. This local part spans from the leaves containing individual bodies to the "branch nodes". Branch nodes are those nodes that are farthest up the tree from the leaves yet still only contain bodies assigned to a single process. The set of all branch nodes of all processes contains all bodies. Next, all branch nodes are made available on every process and the global part of the tree is built bottom-up from all branch nodes on every process. Finally, all processes have a tree that contains the same global part (between root node and branch nodes) everywhere and a local part below the branch nodes with information about the local bodies. Figure 1 shows a simple distributed tree right after its construction as seen by one of the processes. In general, both global and local parts are deeper than one level, local parts end in more than one branch node and branch nodes are not all at the same level.

Algorithm 1 Phase 1 of the BH algorithm: distributed tree construction
---
1: **function** TREE(b)   ▷ Construct tree from bodies b
2:     calculate integer coordinates k along space-filling curve
3:     sort bodies b among processes according to k
4:     construct tree bottom-up until branch nodes
5:     distribute branch nodes
6:     finish construction bottom up from branch nodes to root
7:     **return** root
8: **end function**

Phase 2 of the algorithm (see algorithm 2) calculates the forces on all local bodies due to the ensemble of all bodies as described by the tree decomposition. Calculating the force on one particular body involves a top-down traversal of the tree (function FORCE)

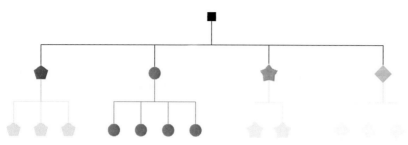

Figure 1. A distributed tree after tree construction as seen by process 1; information from different processes is distinguished by colour and shape (process 0: blue pentagons, 1: red circles, 2: green stars, 3: yellow diamonds). The global part of the tree is in black rectangles. Information that is not available locally on process 1 is half transparent.

Algorithm 2 Phase 2 of the BH algorithm: force computation

 1: **function** FORCEALL(t)   ▷ forces on all bodies b
 2:    **for** $i \leftarrow 1, \ldots, N$ **do**
 3:        $\Phi_i \leftarrow$ FORCE($root, b_i$)
 4:    **end for**
 5:    **return** Φ
 6: **end function**
 7: **function** FORCE(t, b)   ▷ force on body b due to tree t
 8:    **if** ISLEAF(t) **or** AC(t, b) **then**
 9:        **return** $\phi(t, b)$
10:    **else**
11:        **return** $\sum_{c \in t}$ FORCE(c, b)
12:    **end if**
13: **end function**

---

starting at the root node. The force on a body due to a node in the tree (and all the bodies contained therein) can be calculated in a single application of ϕ (or its series expansion) if the node is found to be suitable – either by being a leaf or by fulfilling the acceptance criterion (AC). Otherwise the force is calculated as the sum of forces due to the children of the node. Applications of function FORCE for different bodies b_i are independent and can be performed in parallel by multiple processes and threads. The next section describes how this parallelism is exploited and how it interacts with the non-locality of certain parts of the tree.

1.2. A Hybrid Parallelisation for the Barnes-Hut Algorithm

PEPC uses a heterogeneous hybrid parallelisation for the BH force computation phase, i.e. it assigns structurally different tasks to different POSIX threads [7]. While most threads contribute to the computation of body-region and body-body interactions (worker threads), at least one thread on each distributed memory process is responsible for handling communication with other processes (communicator thread).

The loop that starts the tree traversal for different bodies on line 2 of algorithm 2 is parallelised among the worker threads. If the children of a node have to be visited by a traversal (line 11 in algorithm 2), but are not available locally, the worker thread enqueues a request for the children of that node to be processed by the local communicator thread and defer the remainder of the traversal until later, starting a new traversal for a different body in the meantime. The communicator thread asynchronously sends requests from the queue to other processes on behalf of the worker threads. It also receives and acts upon messages from other processes.

This latency-hiding scheme helps to achieve an overlap of computation and communication [8]. The dependency between the two kinds of threads necessitates an inter-thread synchronisation mechanism.

1.3. Concurrent Access to Shared Resources

The acquisition of bodies from the list by the worker threads (loop in line 2 of algorithm 2) is coordinated via a shared counter. Access to this shared resource from multi-

---

Algorithm 3 Concurrent access to a shared counter, synchronised via a lock

    function ACQUIREBODY(c)   ▷ acquire a body by incrementing a counter
        LOCK(c)
        $i \leftarrow c$
        $c \leftarrow c + 1$
        UNLOCK(c)
        return i
    end function

---

ple worker threads was originally synchronised using the read/write lock facilities of the POSIX threads API as described in algorithm 3.

While this solution scaled well to a moderate number of threads as found e.g. on IBM Blue Gene/P systems, it could not efficiently handle the 64 hardware threads that are available on the A2 compute chip of the Blue Gene/Q system. It is possible to keep the number of concurrent threads low by splitting the 16 cores available on each compute node among multiple distributed memory processes. In practice however, it is desirable to utilise all cores on a single compute node in a shared-memory parallel fashion since a larger number of processes leads to unnecessary fragmentation of the tree data structure which in turn leads to increased need for communication.

As an alternative to the read/write locks, we investigated atomic operations, which enable consistent (atomic) manipulation of primitive types by multiple concurrent threads. One such operation performs an addition on a variable and returns its value before or after the addition. We change the algorithm to acquire a body for force computation to manipulate the shared counter via atomic operations only and remove the lock as illustrated in algorithm 4.

Algorithm 4 Concurrent access to a shared counter, synchronised via atomic operations

    function ACQUIREBODY(c)   ▷ acquire a body by incrementing a counter
        atomic
            $i \leftarrow c$
            $c \leftarrow c + 1$
        end atomic
        return i
    end function

Communication between worker threads and communicator threads is performed by enqueueing requests in a single-consumer multi-producer ring buffer. The buffer is filled with valid entries between a head and a tail pointer that are incremented using modulo arithmetic. These operations were previously also protected from data races using locks.

Algorithm 5 Atomic modulo arithmetic using *compare-and-swap*

    function ATOMICMODINCREMENT(x, mod)
        repeat
            $y \leftarrow x$
        until CAS(x, y, (y + 1) % mod)
    end function

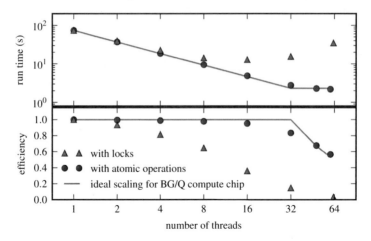

Figure 2. A strong scaling of PEPC on a single node of the IBM Blue Gene/Q installation JUQUEEN from 1 to 64 threads.

Since modulo arithmetic is not available as an atomic primitive itself, we implement it using another primitive, the *compare-and-swap* CAS(x, old, new). CAS atomically replaces the value of a variable x with a new value and returns true, if the variable is currently holding a certain old value, otherwise it leaves the value untouched, returning false. The atomic modular arithmetic operation is given in algorithm 5.

Figure 2 shows a strong scaling of PEPC utilising 1 to 64 threads. It compares two versions, one using read/write locks and one using atomic operations. Note that for more than 32 threads, the theoretically available SMP concurrency is saturated due to hardware restrictions.

With these changes in place, the worker threads and the communicator threads cooperate efficiently and allow PEPC to achieve high parallel efficiency on the whole of JUQUEEN, see figure 3. PEPC is thus also a member of the High-Q club established at the Jülich Supercomputing Centre in 2013 [9].

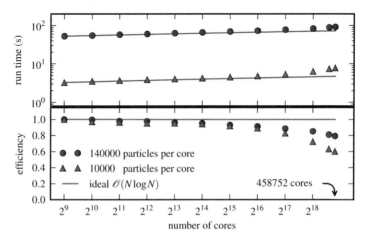

Figure 3. A weak scaling of PEPC on the IBM Blue Gene/Q installation JUQUEEN from a single node board to the whole machine.

2. Dual Tree Traversal

2.1. The Dual Tree Traversal Algorithm

Despite the remarkable scalability achieved with PEPC demonstrated in figure 3, the fact remains that the algorithm is fundamentally $\mathcal{O}(N \log N)$: many more operations are being performed than would be computed by an equivalent fast multipole method for the same precision in the force calculation. To improve the original BH tree code algorithm to $\mathcal{O}(N)$ therefore, we extend it to use the DTT algorithm as described in [6]. Due to the similarities between the two algorithms, this enhancement does not require a full rewrite of the application, but can be accomplished with a few self-contained changes that take advantage of the existing parallel framework. These changes are:

1. Introducing additional objects and operators in the mathematical back-ends.
2. Constructing the DTT algorithm on top of the existing implementation of the tree data structure and the newly added mathematical tools.

In particular, the tree construction phase as shown for the BH algorithm (algorithm 1) can be re-used almost completely unchanged, save for the initialisation of the aforementioned additional mathematical objects. Phase 2 of the BH algorithm is replaced

---

Algorithm 6 Phase 2 of Dual Tree Traversal: Sow procedure
```
 1: procedure SOW(s, t)
 2:     if (ISLEAF(s) and ISLEAF(t)) or AC(s, t) then
 3:         Φ_t ← Φ_t + φ(s,t)
 4:     else if ISLEAF(t) then
 5:         SPLITSOURCE(s, t)
 6:     else if ISLEAF(s) then
 7:         SPLITTARGET(s, t)
 8:     else if DIAMETER(s) > DIAMETER(t) then
 9:         SPLITSOURCE(s, t)
10:     else
11:         SPLITTARGET(s, t)
12:     end if
13: end procedure
14: procedure SPLITSOURCE(s, t)
15:     for all children c of source do
16:         SOW(c, t)
17:     end for
18: end procedure
19: procedure SPLITTARGET(s, t)
20:     for all children c of target do
21:         task
22:             SOW(s, c)
23:         end task
24:     end for
25:     taskwait
26: end procedure
```

$$\Phi_t \leftarrow \Phi_t + \phi(s,t)$$

by two distinct phases in the DTT algorithm. The first, called SOW, is given in algorithm 6.

The SOW phase traverses two trees which may be identical in a mutually recursive fashion, using them for information about the source and target body distribution. It calculates interactions between pairs of nodes that either fulfil the acceptance criterion AC or cannot be split further. Otherwise it tries to split the bigger of the two nodes under consideration (keeping the potential interaction partners at a similar level) or split the node that is not a leaf. Figure 4 illustrates the evolution of this algorithm. Parallelism is exploited during this phase by performing traversals for distinct target nodes in separate tasks using OpenMP (lines 21 and 25 in algorithm 6).

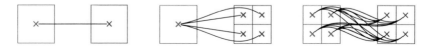

Figure 4. Evolution of the SOW phase of the DTT algorithm: starting at the root nodes of both source and target trees (left) the algorithm first splits the target tree root (middle) and then the source tree root (right)

The last phase of the DTT algorithm, called REAP, translates the results of interactions between pairs of nodes to results for the bodies contained therein. It operates in a top-down manner on the local part of the tree only.

Algorithm 7 Phase 2 of Dual Tree Traversal: Reap procedure

1: **procedure** REAP(n)
2:     **if** ISLEAF(n) **then**
3:         $\Phi_{body} \leftarrow \Phi_n$
4:     **else**
5:         **for all** children c of n **do**
6:             $\Phi_c \leftarrow \Phi_n$
7:             REAP(c)
8:         **end for**
9:     **end if**
10: **end procedure**

2.2. Request/Response Communication in the DTT Algorithm

The DTT algorithm re-uses the request/response communication scheme presented in the BH section of this paper. However, while the DTT works as intended in combination with this scheme, it does not scale as well to large distributed memory partitions. This deficiency stems from the fact that the latency-hiding scheme employed in the BH algorithm does not easily translate to the DTT. Specifically, in the BH algorithm, a series of independent traversals of the input tree data structure is performed for every element of the output data structure, a flat list of bodies. Each one of these traversals can be suspended and another one can be performed in its place while waiting for remote information. In the DTT algorithm, both input and output are hierarchical data structures (the spatial tree decomposition) which are traversed in a mutually recursive manner. If the traversal tries to split a source node in line 15 of algorithm 6 and the children are not available locally it has to stop and wait for the remote information to be fetched by the communicator thread. In the meantime, other tasks might progress, but, typically, the need for remote information first arises at the level of the branch nodes (all information above is available locally after tree construction). Consequently, the number of tasks spawned at that point is equal to the number of branch nodes owned by the encountering process, which is comparable to the amount of hardware threads offered by current processors, so there is no remaining work to replace the waiting traversal.

To remedy this problem we evaluate an eager request/response mechanism. Along with the request for the missing children of a source node, the requesting process sends the target node that is currently being considered as an interaction partner. This allows the communicator thread on the process receiving the request to perform a traversal of its local tree. Starting at the requested nodes, it evaluates the AC for those nodes and their descendants and the target node sent along with the request. All nodes up to and including those that finally meet the AC are collected and sent as part of the response. This procedure anticipates all future communications due to the target node and its descendants based on a worst-case estimate, i.e. the nodes sent along in the response fulfil the AC for the original target node (by definition) and all its descendants (under the reasonable assumption that $AC(t,s) \Rightarrow AC(c,s) \, \forall \, c \in t$).

In practice, however, the eager mechanism lead to a significant decrease in performance. The decrease in request/response round trips won by anticipating multiple levels of communication is not enough to offset the increased work load put on the communicator threads by the collecting tree traversal. Additionally, for larger problem sizes, the increased size of the response messages is often enough to overflow the buffers allocated for MPI buffered communication. We therefore revert to the unmodified request/response scheme.

Figure 5 shows a weak scaling of the DTT algorithm as implemented in PEPC on top of the unmodified request/response communication scheme. Compared to the scaling behaviour of the BH algorithm in figure 3, the DTT shows a more pronounced fall-off of efficiency for the medium sized problem. However, in terms of efficiency, it performs similarly for large problem sizes, where both algorithms achieve a parallel efficiency of about 0.8 on the whole machine. In terms of total wall time, the DTT outperforms the BH algorithm for large problem sizes, due to its $\mathcal{O}(N)$ complexity.

3. Conclusion

In this paper, we have discussed aspects of parallel implementations of both the Barnes-Hut algorithm and the Dual Tree Traversal algorithm.

We have demonstrated how atomic operations can be used to replace more general locking mechanisms in order to prevent multi-threading bottlenecks on processors offering a high degree of parallelism. Our implementation of the BH algorithm in PEPC based on a general request/response communication scheme scales well on distributed memory machines at medium and large problem sizes.

Furthermore, we have shown results for the scaling behaviour of our implementation of the DTT algorithm in PEPC utilizing up to nearly 0.5 million cores on JUQUEEN. It achieves a parallel efficiency similar to that of the BH algorithm at large problem sizes and offers a better time to solution due to the $\mathcal{O}(N)$ complexity. At medium and small

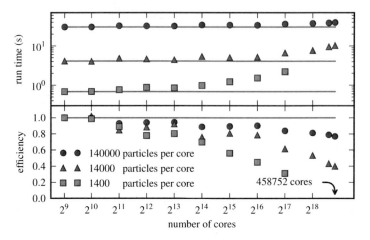

Figure 5. A weak scaling of the dual tree traversal algorithm in PEPC on the IBM Blue Gene/Q installation JUQUEEN from a single node board to the whole machine.

problem sizes the DTT does not yet reach the efficiency of the BH algorithm. We plan to investigate this issue further in the future.

Acknowledgements

Computing time for this work has been granted through the JARA-HPC partition. M. Henkel's contribution to this work has been funded by the Jülich Supercomputing Centre guest student programme.

References

[1]   Josh Barnes and Piet Hut. A hierarchical O(N log N) force-calculation algorithm. *Nature*, 324(6096):446–449, December 1986.

[2]   L Greengard and V Rokhlin. A fast algorithm for particle simulations. *Journal of Computational Physics*, 73(2):325–348, 1987.

[3]   Michael S. Warren. 2HOT: An improved parallel hashed oct-tree N-body algorithm for cosmological simulation. *Scientific Programming*, 22:109–124, 2014.

[4]   Jeroen Bedorf, Evghenii Gaburov, Michiko S. Fujii, Keigo Nitadori, Tomoaki Ishiyama, and Simon Portegies Zwart. 24.77 Pflops on a Gravitational Tree-Code to Simulate the Milky Way Galaxy with 18600 GPUs. In *SC14: International Conference for High Performance Computing, Networking, Storage and Analysis*, pages 54–65, 2014.

[5]   Michael S. Warren and John K. Salmon. A portable parallel particle program. *Computer Physics Communications*, 87(1-2):266–290, May 1995.

[6]   Walter Dehnen. A Very Fast and Momentum-conserving Tree Code. *The Astrophysical Journal*, 536(1):L39–L42, June 2000.

[7]   Mathias Winkel, Robert Speck, Helge Hübner, Lukas Arnold, Rolf Krause, and Paul Gibbon. A massively parallel, multi-disciplinary BarnesHut tree code for extreme-scale N-body simulations. *Computer Physics Communications*, 183(4):880–889, April 2012.

[8]   M. S. Warren and J. K. Salmon. A parallel hashed Oct-Tree N-body algorithm. *Proceedings of the 1993 ACM/IEEE conference on Supercomputing - Supercomputing '93*, pages 12–21, 1993.

[9]   Forschungszentrum Jülich – JSC – High-Q Club. http://www.fz-juelich.de/ias/jsc/EN/Expertise/High-Q-Club/_node.html. [Online; accessed 31-July-2015].

Parallel Computing: On the Road to Exascale
G.R. Joubert et al. (Eds.)
IOS Press, 2016
doi:10.3233/978-1-61499-621-7-449

Performance modeling of a compressible hydrodynamics solver on multicore CPUs

Raphaël PONCET [a,1], Mathieu PEYBERNES [b], Thibault GASC [c,d] and
Florian DE VUYST [d]

[a] *CGG, 27 Avenue Carnot, 91300 Massy FRANCE*
[b] *CEA, centre de Saclay, DEN/SAC/DANS/STMF/LMSF, F-91191, Gif-sur-Yvette Cedex,*
FRANCE
[c] *Maison de la Simulation, CEA Saclay, F-91191, Gif-sur-Yvette Cedex, FRANCE*
[d] *CMLA, ENS Cachan et CNRS UMR 8536, 61 av. du Président Wilson, F-94235*
Cachan, FRANCE

Abstract. This work is devoted to the performance modeling of a vectorized multi-
threaded implementation of a compressible hydrodynamics solver on current multicore CPUs. The underlying explicit time-advance scheme is based on a La-
grange+remap discretization. The algorithm consists in nine elementary kernels
that exhibit, for most of them, a stencil update pattern. Using the Execution Cache
Memory (ECM) model — a refinement of the Roofline model —, we devise a high
fidelity performance model, allowing us to finely understand and overcome bottlenecks of the algorithm and accurately predict global code performance.

Keywords. performance modeling, performance engineering, performance metric,
memory-bound, compute-bound, compressible hydrodynamics, Roofline model,
Execution Cache Memory model

Introduction

Compressible hydrodynamics solvers of Lagrange+remap type (see figure 1) are very
relevant to industrial applications including defense, automotive, naval and manufacturing industries as they are the basic building blocks for a class of simulation programs
called "hydrocodes" ([1]) which are widely used in these fields. Despite this fact, up to
our knowledge, there are no comprehensive quantitative works in the literature studying
the single node performance of such algorithms.

Hereafter, we focus on the performance modeling and optimization of an archetypal
vectorized and multithreaded 2D Lagrange+remap solver on cartesian meshes on a current multicore CPU. This is not an trivial task, as this solver consists in 9 kernels that are
very different, ranging from memory-bound kernels resembling a Jacobi stencil update,
to compute-bound kernels that make a heavy usage of transcendental functions (mainly
`sqrt` and `div`) to compute fluid equations of state. We tested two performance models: a refined Roofline model ([2]) using static analysis to compute effective peak arith-

---

[1]Corresponding Author: raphael.poncet@cgg.com

Figure 1. Density field (in_rho) for the reference triple-point test case — see [6] for a description — solved by our Lagrange+remap solver.

metic throughput, and the recently published Execution Cache Memory (ECM) model ([3], [4], [5]), that improves the Roofline model by taking into account the cache hierarchy. We find out that while both models are equivalent and quantitatively accurate for compute-bound kernels, the ECM model is more precise for bandwidth bound kernels. Moreover, it can accurately predict multicore scalability. Let us also emphasize that we chose *CPU cycles per cache line worth of data* (hereafter denoted as cy/CL) as a performance metric for our ECM model, instead of the commonly used *floating point operation per seconds* (Flop/s). This choice allows us to overcome the main limitation of the Flop/s performance metric: the unavailability of reliable Flop/s hardware performance counters on recent multicore CPUs. See section 3 for a more thorough discussion.

The paper is organized as follows: in section 1, we present the Lagrange+remap algorithm and implementation details. The systems we used for benchmarking purposes are detailed in section 2. In section 3, we describe the two performance models used, Roofline and ECM. Finally, we present the results of our performance modeling methodology to the Lagrange+remap algorithm in the main section of the paper, section 4.

1. Lagrange+remap solver implementation

In our Lagrange+remap solver, three main hydrodynamical variables, namely the mass, the internal energy and the velocity are computed on a 2D cartesian grid (with directions x and y). To this end, the algorithm is organized into nine kernels, computing also temporary variables introduced by the Lagrange+remap numerical scheme (see figure 2).

In industrial multiphysics hydrocodes, discrete thermodynamic variables are usually located at grid cell centers, while discrete velocity variables are located at grid nodes (staggered discretization). For variables defined on grid cell centers, the corresponding arrays are accessed using imbricated FOR loops iterating over all grid cells. For our 2D solver, each cell is logically addressed in memory by the inner x-loop and the outer y-loop as follows:

```
#pragma omp parallel for
```

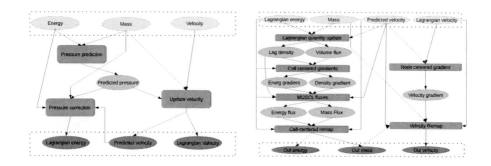

Figure 2. Dataflow diagrams of the Lagrange (left) and remap (right) parts of the algorithm. Kernels are represented in blue, input data in light green, output data in dark green, and temporary data in khaki green.

Table 1. Number and type of CPU instructions for two Lagrange+remap kernels.

Kernel name	Load	Store	Add	Mul	Div	Sqrt
Pressure prediction	10	2	18	16	2	1
Pressure correction	11	1	8	8	1	0

```
for (int iy = 0; iy < ny; ++iy) {
  for (int ix = 0; ix < nx; ++ix) {
    const int cell = (nx * iy) + ix;
    energy[cell] = ...
    mass[cell] = ...
    ...
```

In the above code snippet, nx (resp. ny) is the number of cells in the x-horizontal direction (resp. y-vertical direction) of the grid. Thus nx · ny is the total number of grid cells. In order to apply the performance models presented in the following sections, the starting point is to determine, for each kernel, the number and type of CPU instructions of a single core kernel call, regardless of SIMD vectorization. We give in table 1 two examples. Our kernels have different memory access patterns, which has important consequences for performance: while stores are always streaming stores, loads can be streaming loads or stencil-like loads. For instance, for the Pressure prediction kernel, the ten loads correspond to two streaming loads and two *Jacobi-like 2D nodal stencil* loads, and for the Pressure correction kernel, the eleven loads correspond to three streaming loads and two Jacobi-like 2D nodal stencil loads. A Jacobi-like 2D nodal stencil load consists in loading the velocities defined in the four nodes belonging to a given cell (see figure 3):

```
#pragma omp parallel for
  for (int iy = 0; iy < ny; ++iy) {
    for (int ix = 0; ix < nx; ++ix) {
      //cell: cell index
      const int cell = (nx * iy) + ix;
      //cell+iy: index of the node located southwest of cell
      const double velocity_SW = velocity[cell + iy];
```

Table 2. Characteristics of the CPU hardware used.

Micro Architecture	Intel SandyBridge	Intel Haswell
Model	E5-2670	i5-4590T
Number of cores	8	4
Clock (GHz)	2.6	2.0
Peak Flops DP (GFlop/s) (full socket)	168	64.0
Cache sizes (L1 — L2 — L3)	8x32kB — 8x256kB — 20MB	4x32kB — 4x256kB — 6MB
Theoretical Bandwidth (GBytes/s)	51.2	25.6
Measured triad Bandwidth B_{max} (GBytes/s)	38.4	22.2
L1 $\leftrightarrow$ L2 bandwidth (cy/CL)	2	1
L2 $\leftrightarrow$ L3 bandwidth (cy/CL)	2	2

```
const double velocity_SE = velocity[cell + iy + 1];
const double velocity_NW = velocity[cell + iy + nx + 1];
const double velocity_NE = velocity[cell + iy + nx + 2];
...
```

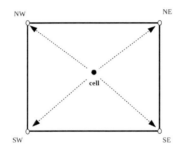

Figure 3. Jacobi-like 2D nodal stencil velocity. A quantity (for instance the pressure) defined at the center of the cell is computed from velocities defined at the four nodes belonging to the cell: the nodes are located in the southwest (SW), southeast (SE), northwest (NW) and northeast (NE) corners.

2. Experimental testbed

We tested our implementation on two multicore CPUs, an octo-core Intel Sandy Bridge desktop processor, and a quad-core Intel Haswell desktop processor, whose characteristics are detailed in table 2. This allows us to validate our methodology for two different CPU microarchitectures, for a various number of cores. The main improvements of the Haswell microarchitecture over the Sandy Bridge microarchitecture relevant for our study are the doubling of the L1 cache memory bandwidth, the improvement of the DIV port throughput, and the introduction of a hardware level *fused multiply add* (FMA) arithmetic instruction. The practical impacts of these hardware evolutions for our algorithm are discussed in section 4.

As we will see in the next section, the maximum memory bandwidth that can be reached by our streaming kernels is an input parameter for our analytical models. The theoretical bandwidth reported by CPU manufacturers can never be attained in practice, so, following [3], we take from now on as an effective sustainable peak bandwidth B_{max} (see table 2) the result of a McCalpin STREAM triad benchmark ([7]).

3. Performance modeling

Our main objective is to be able to quantitatively predict and understand code performance, using simple analytical models. For this, we build upon previous works, since the rise of processor complexity in the last ten years has prompted a renewed interest in theoretical models that allow application developers to make sense of program performance. The seminal Roofline model ([2]) has been subsequently refined by the ECM — Execution Cache Memory —model ([3], [4]). A recent paper ([5]) has shown that this model can quantitatively predict performance of individual stencil kernels. Following the methodology of these works, we have built both Roofline and ECM models for all kernels of our algorithm. This allows us to test and compare the predictive capabilities of both models on a statistically relevant set of kernels.

Performance metric

We use the *floating point operations per second* (Flop/s) metric for reporting roofline performance, as is commonly done. The advantage of this metric is that it is easy to directly compare sustainable kernel performance with peak CPU arithmetic throughput, and thus get an insight on kernel efficiency on a given machine. However, it has two main limitations: first, it is not directly correlated with a meaningful performance metric for application developers (who are generally interested in the number of loop iterations done per unit of time). Moreover, in some cases, the Flop/s hardware counters on recent multicore CPUs — such as the Sandy Bridge processor — are known to possibly return unreliable data. For these reasons, we use the *cycles per cache line worth of data* (cy/CL) metric for our ECM model. Indeed, on the one hand, it is directly correlated with the number of loop iterations per unit of time, and on the other hand, it is a reliable metric that can be measured on any CPU (because it can be derived directly from CPU runtime).

Roofline model

The Roofline model has been initially defined as a conceptual qualtitative model ([2]) to explain differences of behaviour between compute-bound and memory-bound algorithms, and can be adapted to become more quantitative. The Roofline model models the performance with the following single formula:

$$P = \min(P_{max}, AI * B_{max}), \tag{1}$$

where P_{max} is the kernel peak arithmetic throughput (in GFlop / s), AI is the kernel arithmetic intensity (in Flop / Byte), and B_{max} is the peak bandwidth (in GByte /s). While parameter AI is uniquely defined by the algorithm, several choices are possible for B_{max} and P_{max}. We use a refined version of the Roofline model, where B_{max} is chosen to be the measured triad bandwidth on the full CPU system (see table 2), and P_{max} is determined using static analysis, using the Intel IACA[2] tool. The subsequent peak arith-

---

[2]Intel Architecture Code Analyzer

metic throughput takes into account add/mul imbalance, transcendental functions such as div and sqrt, and floating point pipeline bubbles.

Execution Cache Memory ECM model

The ECM model pioneered by Treibig and Hager ([3]) is a refinement of the Roofline model that still neglects any latency effect, but takes into account the cache hierarchy. As in [3], [4], [5], we assume that STORE and floating point arithmetic instructions are overlapped with the data transfers between different levels of the memory system, whereas LOAD operations do not overlap. The data transfer rates between the L1 and L2 caches, and between the L2 and L3 caches, depend on the architecture and are given in table 2. The data transfer rate $B_{L3\to mem}$ (in cy/CL) between the L3 cache and memory subsystem depends on the CPU frequency f (in GCycles/s) and the sustainable bandwidth B_{max} (in GBytes/sec), and is given by the following formula:

$$B_{L3\to mem} = \frac{64f}{B_{max}}, \tag{2}$$

since a cache line is 64 Bytes large on both the processors we used. We refer to [3], [4], [5] for a more precise description of the ECM model.

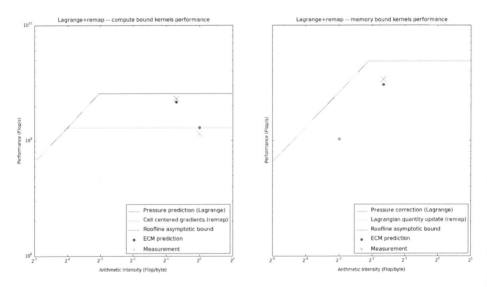

Figure 4. Comparison between measurements and performance models for two Lagrange+remap compute-bound kernels (left), and two Lagrange-remap memory-bound kernels (right), on an Intel Sandy Bridge multicore CPU. The ECM model is more precise than the Roofline model for memory-bound kernels (see table 3 for an exhaustive summary of ECM accuracy). In both models, the Intel IACA tool was used to statically predict maximum kernel arithmetic throughput.

4. Experimental results

Experimental protocol

We compared our models with measurements made on a parallel single node implementation of our algorithm: it is vectorized using AVX SIMD intrinsics, and multithreaded using the OpenMP library. We use the `likwid-perfctr` tool (from the open source `likwid` suite — [8]) to measure Flop/s, and a high precision RDTSC timer to accurately compute kernel runtime.

ECM in practice

Hereafter, we detail the application of the ECM model to our kernels. an ECM prediction time T_{ECM} is given by $T_{ECM} = \max(T_{OL}, T_{nOL} + T_{data})$ ([3], [4]), where T_{data} is the transfer time through the memory hierarchy (L1 upwards), T_{nOL} the time taken by the load instructions (we assume that these instructions can not overlap with any memory transfer) and T_{OL} the time for all other instructions (store and arithmetic instructions). The times T_{OL} and T_{nOL} are determined using `Intel IACA`. For data in memory, the time T_{data} is given by $T_{data} = T_{L1L2} + T_{L2L3} + T_{L3Mem}$, where T_{L1L2}, T_{L2L3} and T_{L3Mem} are respectively the transfer times between L1 and L2, L2 and L3 and L3 and memory. For small datasets residing in L3 memory, T_{data} is given by $T_{data} = T_{L1L2} + T_{L2L3}$. Transfer times for streaming loads and stores can be computed readily using micro architecture knowledge (see table 2). For stencil memory load access patterns, we also have to estimate the number of cachelines needed for a 2D stencil load. This number can be 1 or 2, depending on the size nx of the cartesian grid in the fastest dimension x, and the size of the considered cache: for nx sufficiently small, two successive rows of the velocity array fit in this cache, and the velocity elements SW, SE and NW are supposed to be loaded some inner iterations before. For instance, for the `Pressure correction` kernel (see table 1), there are 11 loads and 1 store between L1 cache and registers. But only 7 cache lines are transfered from memory to L1 cache: 5 for the loads and 2 for the stores (including write allocate). For this kernel on the Haswell architecture, the ECM prediction is given by the load instructions (10 cy/CL) plus the transfers between L1 and L2 (7 cy/CL), L2 and L3 (14 cy/CL) and L3 and memory (40 cy/CL) which is the value 71 cy/CL given in table 3. In contrast, the other kernel `Pressure predicted` of table 1 is compute-bound, and its bottleneck is the DIV/SQRT unit, corresponding to an ECM prediction of 168 cy/CL.

Comparison between performance models and measurements

First, we compare the Roofline and ECM models, for single core performance. Figure 4 present typical results: while the models are equivalent for compute-bound kernels, they are not for memory-bound kernels. Indeed, the Roofline model assumes that one single core can saturate the memory bandwidth, which is not the case for recent multicore CPUs. On the contrary, the ECM model, by adding basic knowledge about the cache bandwidths and organization, can estimate the fraction of the memory bandwidth that can actually be used by a single core. Since, except for the memory interface, all the processor resources scale with the number of cores, we can deduce multicore scalability: for our Haswell machine for instance, in the memory-bound regime, we expect scalability until the bandwidth limit of 5.8 cy/CL, corresponding to the triad benchmark, is reached. For each kernel, we can estimate the bandwidth consumption (by counting the number of cache line loads and stores, including write allocate), and express it in cy/CL. From this we deduce the fraction of bandwidth used by the kernel on one core, and then the maximum speedup until bandwidth saturation. In the compute-bound regime, we expect scalability to be ideal. Table 4 shows that these theoretical values match well with measurements.

Table 3. Comparison between our single core ECM performance model and measurements for the Haswell architecture. Performance is expressed in cycle per cache line worth of data (cy/CL), and kernel type can be CB — Compute Bound — or MB — Memory Bound. In general, our analytical model, despite its simplicity, gives an accurate performance prediction, especially when the data resides in L3 and/or the kernel is compute-bound.

Kernel name		data in L3				data in memory		
	type	prediction	measure	error	type	prediction	measure	error
Lagrange kernels								
Pressure prediction	CB	168 cy/CL	173 cy/CL	3%	CB	168 cy/CL	173 cy/CL	3%
Update velocity	CB	56 cy/CL	59 cy/CL	5%	MB	80 cy/CL	78 cy/CL	3%
Pressure correction	CB	56 cy/CL	58 cy/CL	3%	MB	71 cy/CL	65 cy/CL	8%
Remap kernels								
Lagrangian q. update	CB	56 cy/CL	58 cy/CL	3%	MB	57 cy/CL	58 cy/CL	2%
Cell centered gradient	CB	168 cy/CL	170 cy/CL	1%	CB	168 cy/CL	170 cy/CL	1%
MUSCL fluxes	MB	21 cy/CL	25 cy/CL	16 %	MB	44 cy/CL	42 cy/CL	5%
Cell centered remap	CB	56 cy/CL	57 cy/CL	2%	MB	76 cy/CL	65 cy/CL	17%
Node centered gradient	CB	168 cy/CL	170 cy/CL	1%	CB	168 cy/CL	170 cy/CL	1%
Velocity remap	MB	13 cy/CL	14 cy/CL	7%	MB	30 cy/CL	25 cy/CL	17%

Table 4. Multicore scalability for all Lagrange+remap kernels, for data in memory. While speedup is almost ideal for all compute-bound kernels, performance saturates for memory bound kernels, because memory bandwidth is shared between the cores.

Kernel name	Speedup on 8-core Intel Sandy Bridge			Speedup on 4-core Intel Haswell		
	type	predicted	measured	type	predicted	measured
Lagrange kernels						
Pressure prediction	CB	8	7.45	CB	4	3.5
Update velocity	MB	2.6	3.0	MB	1.4	1.6
Pressure correction	MB	2.8	3.0	MB	1.5	1.5
Remap kernels						
Lagrangian q. update	MB	3.2	3.4	MB	1.6	1.6
Cell centered gradient	CB	8	7.9	CB	4	3.9
MUSCL fluxes	MB	2.3	2.6	MB	1.3	1.4
Cell centered remap	MB	2.5	2.7	MB	1.2	1.6
Node centered gradient	CB	8	7.9	CB	4	3.9
Velocity remap	MB	2.3	2.7	MB	1.5	1.5

Then, in table 3, we compare measurements and ECM predictions for all kernels on our Haswell system, and show that this model gives a very accurate prediction of single core performance, with a mean/median error of 4.5%/3% for data in L3, and 6.3%/3% for data in memory. Results on Sandy Bridge are qualitatively and quantitatively similar with a mean/median error of 7.3%/6.6% for data in L3 and 8.1%/6.9% for data in memory. Still, one can notice a few outliers, which are probably due to phenomena not taken into account by the ECM model (such as register pressure, or overlaps between load/store and arithmetic instructions more complex than the simple rules used in this paper).

Performance models as a tool for hardware extrapolation and code optimization

Table 5. Predicted and measured speedups of cache blocking optimization, for two selected Lagrange+remap memory bound kernels.

Kernel name	Predicted speedup	Measured speedup
Pressure correction	1.25	1.24
Update velocity	1.16	1.13

Performance models are useful not only as predictive tools, but also as investigation tools. For each kernel, they exhibit the bottleneck that limits its performance: memory bandwidth for memory-bound kernels, or the relevant arithmetic port for compute-bound kernels (regular arithmetic port or `div`/`sqrt` unit). To demonstrate the usefulness of our methodology, we give two examples of applying the ECM model.

Cache blocking. This very classical optimization can improve performance of bandwidth-limited kernels having a stencil-like pattern by splitting the loops to improve spatial locality. To study the impact of cache blocking we consider a very fine mesh ($nx > 10^6$) in order to make sure that of two successive grid rows can not be stored in any cache, and consider a new version of our kernels with cache blocking. The goal is to rearrange some loops including 2D stencil loads in order to avoid as many cache misses as possible. To do that, we transform the memory domain into smaller chuncks. Each chunck is chosen small enough to fit a 2D stencil into a given cache (L1 cache in this work), thereby maximizing data reuse. Each loop containing a 2D stencil load is typically rewritten as:

```
// Assume nx is multiple of block_size
for ( num_block = 0; num_block < nx; num_block += block_size) {
  for (int iy = 0; iy < ny; ++iy) {
    for (int ix = num_block; ix < num_block + block_size; ++ix) {
      const int cell = (nx * iy) + ix;
      const double velocity_SW = velocity[cell + iy];
      const double velocity_SE = velocity[cell + iy + 1];
      const double velocity_NW = velocity[cell + iy + nx + 1];
      const double velocity_NE = velocity[cell + iy + nx + 2];
      ...
```

The ECM model is able to predict with a good accuracy the speedup obtained with the cache blocking version of our kernels as we see in table 5, for two typical examples.

Algorithm performance prediction on new hardware. Another use for performance models is to be able of extrapolate the performance of a given algorithm on a given CPU design, using only known informations about micro-architectures, e.g. get the real sustained performance improvements of the algorithm, instead of the peak performance improvements. For instance, for our *pressure prediction* kernel — the kernel of our Lagrange+remap solver with the largest runtime —, the ECM model predicts 252 cy/CL for SNB, and 168 cy/CL for HSW (e.g. a 50% performance increase). For our experimental machines, this translates to a 1.15 predicted speedup (because our Haswell system as a frequency of 2.0 GHz compared to 2.6 GHz for our Sandy Bridge system), which is very close to the 1.16 measured speedup. Besides an accurate quantitative prediction, our methodology allows us to correlate micro-architecture improvments with sustained performance improvments : for this kernel for instance, the performance increase is mainly due to the improved DIV port throughput on Haswell. Notice that our methodology uses a *measured* effective bandwidth B_{max}. In the case where such measurement is not possible, B_{max} can alternatively be extrapolated from the theoretical bandwidth.

The two previous examples showed practical applications of performance models for a given algorithm. However, performance models can also be used as a guide to design numerical methods that can efficiently exploit current and future computer hardware. We refer to [9] for an in-depth discussion on codesign for Lagrange+remap hydrocodes algorithms such as the one studied in this work.

Concluding remarks

In conclusion, we believe that our methodology of performance modeling and analysis provides a rather generic and reusable approach for understanding performance of complex (by structure and by task) solvers. This paper has shown a successful application of this methodology to hydrodynamics problems. It allows for accurate runtime prediction, and can efficiently guide optimization efforts. In future works, we will build on this methodology to detail the code optimization strategies that can be employed to improve hydrodynamics solvers.

Acknowledgments

We are indebted to Intel and Thomas Guillet for providing us access to the Sandy Bridge test system used for benchmarking. We would like to thank Philippe Thierry for interesting discussions related to performance modeling.

References

[1] D.J. Benson: Computational methods in Lagrangian and Eulerian hydrocodes, *Computer methods in Applied mechanics and Engineering* **99**, 2, pp 235–394, 1992
[2] S. Williams, A. Waterman, and D. Patterson: Roofline: An Insightful Visual Performance Model for Multicore Architectures, *Commun. ACM*, 2009, **52**, pp 65–76
[3] J. Treibig and G. Hager: Introducing a Performance Model for Bandwidth-Limited Loop Kernels, *Lecture Notes in Computer Science Volume 6067*, 2010, pp 615–624.
[4] G. Hager, J. Treibig, J. Habich, and G. Wellein: Exploring performance and power properties of modern multi-core chips via simple machine models, *Concurrency and Computation: Practice and Experience*, 2013.
[5] H. Stengel, J. Treibig, G. Hager, and G. Wellein: Quantifying performance bottlenecks of stencil computations using the Execution-Cache-Memory model, 2015, *submitted*. Preprint: arXiv:1410.5010
[6] J.R. Kamm, J.S. Brock, S.T. Brandon, D.L. Cotrell, B. Johnson, P. Knupp, et al.: Enhanced verification test suite for physics simulation codes. *LANL report no. LA-14379, Los Alamos National Laboratory*, 2008
[7] JD. McCalpin, STREAM: Sustainable memory bandwidth in high performance computers, *Technical Report*, University of Virginia, continuously updated.
[8] J. Treibig, G. Hager, and G. Wellein: LIKWID: A lightweight performance-oriented tool suite for x86 multicore environments, *Proceedings of PSTI 2010*, 2010.
[9] F. De Vuyst, T. Gasc, R. Motte, M. Peybernes, and R. Poncet: Performance study of industrial hydrocodes: modeling, analysis and aftermaths on innovative computational methods, ISC High Performance 2015, Frankfurt, HPCSET 2015, 2nd International Workshop on High Performance Computing Simulation in Energy/Transport Domains, DOI:10.13140/RG.2.1.3178.2240.

Parallel Computing: On the Road to Exascale
G.R. Joubert et al. (Eds.)
IOS Press, 2016
© 2016 The authors and IOS Press. All rights reserved.
doi:10.3233/978-1-61499-621-7-459

Developing a scalable and flexible high-resolution DNS code for two-phase flows

Iain BETHUNE [a,1], Antonia B K COLLIS [a], Lennon Ó NÁRAIGH [b], David SCOTT [b]
and Prashant VALLURI [c]

[a] *EPCC, The University of Edinburgh, UK*
[b] *School of Mathematical Sciences and CASL, University College Dublin, Ireland*
[c] *Institute for Materials and Processes, School of Engineering, The University of Edinburgh, UK*

Abstract. We introduce TPLS (Two-Phase Level Set), an MPI-parallel Direct Numerical Simulation code for two-phase flows in channel geometries. Recent developments to the code are discussed which improve the performance of the solver and I/O by using the PETSc and NetCDF libraries respectively. Usability and functionality improvements enabled by code refactoring and merging of a separate OpenMP-parallelized version are also outlined. The overall scaling behaviour of the code is measured, and good strong scaling up to 1152 cores is observed for a 5.6 million element grid. A comparison is made between the legacy serial text-formatted I/O and new NetCDF implementations, showing speedups of up to 17x. Finally, we explore the effects of output file striping on the Lustre parallel file system on ARCHER, a Cray XC30 supercomputer, finding performance gains of up to 12% over the default striping settings.

Keywords. Computational Fluid Dynamics, Direct Numerical Simulation, PETSc, NetCDF, Parallel I/O

Introduction

TPLS (Two-Phase Level Set) is an open-source program for simulation of two-phase flows in 3D channel geometries using high resolution Direct Numerical Simulation. Due to the high computational cost of these calculations, parallelization is essential, and scaling has now been demonstrated to several thousand CPU cores. To achieve this, the code has been developed by a collaboration of experts in HPC applications development, applied mathematics and algorithms, and the physics of multiphase flows.

TPLS is unique in several aspects. Unlike other programs such as OpenFOAM, the TPLS solver has been purpose-built for supercomputing architectures like ARCHER and keeping large scale simulations of two-phase interfacial flows (coupled with complex transport phenomena) in mind. Most open source solvers like OpenFOAM, Gerris, Fluidity and commercial solvers like ANSYS-Fluent/CFX offer only one interface-capturing

---

[1]Corresponding Author: *ibethune@epcc.ed.ac.uk*

method (the volume-of-fluid method) thereby limiting the applicability of these solvers to either free-surface, stratified, or wavy-stratified flows. TPLS offers the users a choice of two types of interface-capturing methods: the diffuse-interface method and the level-set method. This enables the solver to accurately simulate not only the aforementioned flows but also a wide variety of physics (currently unavailable in all of the above solvers) including stratified-slug flow transitions, interfacial turbulence [1], counter-current flows [2], contact-line motion, phase change and heat transfer [3].

1. TPLS Overview

TPLS solves the incompressible Navier-Stokes equations. The interface is captured using either a choice of levelset [4] or diffuse-interface [5] methodologies (the latter is referred to hereafter as DIM). Detailed equations for the implementation of the levelset framework are presented below; the reader is referred to Reference [5] for the details concerning the implementation of the DIM methodology.

In the levelset formulation, a continuous surface tension model [4] is employed as a model for the two-phase Navier–Stokes equations with the sharp interfacial matching conditions. The model equations for the velocity $\boldsymbol{u}$ and the pressure p read

$$\rho(\phi)\left(\frac{\partial \boldsymbol{u}}{\partial t}+\boldsymbol{u}\cdot\nabla\boldsymbol{u}\right)=-\nabla p+\frac{1}{\text{Re}}\nabla\cdot\left[\mu\left(\nabla\boldsymbol{u}+\nabla\boldsymbol{u}^{T}\right)\right]+\frac{1}{\text{We}}\delta_{\varepsilon}(\phi)\hat{\boldsymbol{n}}\nabla\cdot\hat{\boldsymbol{n}}+\mathscr{G}\rho(\phi)\hat{\boldsymbol{z}},$$
(1a)

$$\nabla\cdot\boldsymbol{u}=0,$$
(1b)

$$\hat{\boldsymbol{n}}=\frac{\nabla\phi}{|\nabla\phi|}, \qquad \frac{\partial\phi}{\partial t}+\boldsymbol{u}\cdot\nabla\phi=0,$$
(1c)

where $\hat{\boldsymbol{z}}$ is the unit vector prescribing the downward-direction of the acceleration due to gravity. Here also, $\phi(\boldsymbol{x},t)$ is the levelset function indicating in which phase the point $\boldsymbol{x}$ lies ($\phi < 0$ in the bottom layer, $\phi > 0$ in the top layer). The (possibly multivalued) interface $\eta(\boldsymbol{x},t)$ is therefore the zero level set, $\phi(\boldsymbol{x},t)=0 \implies \boldsymbol{x}=(x,y,\eta(x,y,t))$. Moreover, the levelset function determines the unit vector normal to the interface ($\hat{\boldsymbol{n}}$) as well as the density and viscosity, via the relations $\rho = r(1-H_{\varepsilon}(\phi))+H_{\varepsilon}(\phi)$ and $\mu = \text{Re}^{-1}[m(1-H_{\varepsilon}(\phi))+H_{\varepsilon}(\phi)]$ respectively. The function $H_{\varepsilon}(\phi)$ is a regularized Heaviside function, which is smoothed across a width $\varepsilon = 1.5\Delta x$ (Δx is the grid spacing, see below). Finally, $\delta_{\varepsilon}(s) = dH_{\varepsilon}(s)/ds$ is a regularized delta function supported on an interval $[-\varepsilon,\varepsilon]$. Note that the model is presented in non-dimensional form, such that Re is the Reynolds number, $1/\text{We}$ is a dimensionless measure of surface tension (We is the Weber number), and $\mathscr{G}$ is a dimensionless version of the gravitational constant.

Equations (1) are solved numerically on a regular 3D grid of grid spacing Δx in each Cartesian direction. A finite-volume discretization is employed based on an idealised channel geometry with a range of different inlet conditions that can be prescribed by the user (Figure 1). The code evolves the physical variables (pressure, fluid velocities, and interface configuration) through discrete time steps. The pressure is treated using a projection method and the time marching is carried out using a combination of third-order

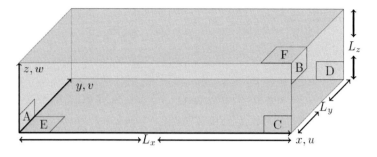

Figure 1. (Picture thanks to James Fannon). Computational domain $[0, L_x] \times [0, L_y] \times [0, L_z = 1]$. Periodic boundary conditions (PBC) or Neuman conditions are used in the streamwise (faces AB). PBC are used in the spanwise (faces CD) directions. Finally, no-slip boundary conditions are used on faces E and F.

Adams-Bashforth and second-order Crank-Nicholson methodologies. At each time step, the key computational tasks performed amount to the solution of large systems of sparse linear equations with tens of millions of unknowns, for the key physical variables. In addition regular I/O is required to save the system state for later analysis and visualization, or restart in the case of hardware failure.

The code is implemented in Fortran 90, initially with MPI parallelization using a 2D domain decomposition (in x and y dimensions) and bespoke Jacobi / SOR iterative solvers. Over the last two years, we have improved the TPLS code in several respects to give better performance, scalability and usability, moving from an in-house code specialised for use by the original developers, to a open-source, flexible program which can be easily be used by others, including academic and industrial users.

1.1. Linear solvers from PETSc

TPLS was first released in June 2013 on Sourceforge [6] under the open-source BSD licence. With support from the HECToR Distributed Computational Science and Engineering (dCSE) scheme, we re-implemented the most expensive part of the calculation – the pressure solver [7] – in PETSc [8].

We make use of two main features of PETSc. A Distributed Array (DA) object is used to represent the distributed regular 3D grid described in Figure 1, holding a scalar value (the pressure) at each grid point. At present, for compatibility with the rest of the code which does not yet use PETSc, we retain the same 2D domain decomposition to avoid an expensive data redistribution before and after the pressure solve, requiring only a local copy-in/copy-out operation on each process. In general PETSc permits all three dimensions to be decomposed and eventually once all solvers in TPLS have been migrated to use PETSc this could be used to give additional scalability since for the same number of processors, a 3D decomposition results in more compact domains with smaller surface area resulting in reduced communication. The DA also provides the periodic boundary conditions in the spanwise direction, without the need for adding explicit halo swapping code.

To compute the pressure at a given time step we construct a PETSc distributed sparse matrix A, representing the discretized equation in a canonical $Ax = b$ matrix-vector equation form. PETSc provides a KSP (Krylov SubsPace) object, which implements various iterative algorithms for solving linear equations of this form, abstracting away the details of the solution algorithm including the implementation of communication and periodic boundary conditions, and allows access to a wide variety of different Krylov solvers and preconditioners. Initial tests using the GMRES method with a Block Jacobi preconditioner, showed a speedup of 54% in the pressure solve on 1024 cores, using a grid with 11 million points, and 80% on 2048 cores, compared with the legacy Jacobi/SOR iteration (see [7] for timing data). This is due to improved strong scaling, rising from 60% efficiency from 1024 to 2048 cores with the Jacobi/SOR method, to linear scaling (100% efficiency) with the PETSc implementation. At this stage, the major remaining bottleneck was output, which on 1024 cores could take around 50% of the total runtime.

1.2. NetCDF I/O

In TPLS version 2.0, we have re-implemented the original serial output routines using the NetCDF library [9]. All of the state variables in TPLS are stored on distributed 3D grids. For ease of post-processing, this distributed data must be reconstructed in canonical Cartesian order and written to a single file, which initially contained the data in a text format. TPLS version 1.0 used a 'single file, single writer' or 'master IO' I/O approach, that is, a 'master' process coordinated the I/O, receiving multiple MPI messages from all other processes, rearranged the data to reconstruct the global data set, and then performed the file write. Despite being reasonably straightforward to implement, this method has several disadvantages; other processes will be idle while the master performs I/O (or will idle after arriving early at the next synchronization point), the I/O time is a constant so will inhibit strong scaling due to Amdahl's law, and the need to store the global data limits the size of problem which can be studied to that which fits in memory on a single process. With this master I/O structure, each MPI process, sends 105 messages to the master process, which adds significant overhead.

Three types of output files were generated by TPLS 1.0: `phi-channel`, `uvw-channel` and a backup file. The file `uvw-channel` contains four variables — `U`, `V`, `W`, `Pressure` — each labelled by grid coordinates, which are then separated during post-processing. The backup or checkpoint file contains all 14 state variables amalgamated into one single file. In the new I/O strategy, these files were split up so that one variable is stored per file. This was found to improve performance as although many small files will limit the optimal use of bandwidth, one large file results in excessive synchronization between processes.

NetCDF provides various routines for parallel I/O, allowing all processes to write simultaneously to a single file, and stores data in a binary file format with optional compression using the HDF5 library [10]. While HDF5 does not support writing to compressed files in general, when using HDF5 behind the NetCDF interface data is written with a defined 'chunk size' enabling the HDF5 compression algorithm to work correctly in parallel.

TPLS uses the following command from the NetCDF Fortran 90 interface to create the new I/O files:

```
nf90\_create(filename, cmode, ncid,
    comm=PETSC\_COMM\_WORLD, info=MPI\_INFO\_NULL)
```

The use of the comm and info parameters ensure that parallel I/O is enabled. The variable cmode is set to:

```
cmode = IOR(NF90\_NETCDF4, NF90\_MPIIO)
```

which results in the creation of a parallel HDF5/NetCDF-4 file, which will be accessing using MPI-IO.

By default parallel file access using NetCDF is 'independent', in that any process may access the file without waiting for others, also known as 'single file, multiple writers'. In this mode, files are created by each process individually writing the appropriate section of a file, according to the defined data distribution (see below). In this setup data is not transferred between processes, but synchronization is required. The alternative is a 'collective' file access pattern where each process must communicate with all other processes to receive and rearrange data but the data is written all at once. The 'independent' I/O model results in file locking when each process writes and therefore it is expected that this method does not scale. With the 'collective' method, i.e. the I/O system knows that all processes are writing, enabling optimization of the I/O operation specific to the I/O pattern and potentially increasing bandwidth. This pattern of I/O should result in the best scaling for file writes and is the choice implemented in TPLS.

For convenience, we have retained the original I/O routines as an option which can be selected through the use of input file parameters to enable the use of TPLS on machines where NetCDF is not installed and/or not desired. We also implemented full control of the I/O frequency for each file type independently and also the frequency of the restart checkpointing which was previously tied to the hard-coded frequency of regular file writing. Removing the need to provide checkpoint files at each data output step in itself can provide significant speedups for users.

As a result, we have obtained an order-of-magnitude reduction in I/O time, a compression factor of 6.7 compared to the TPLS 1.0 text files and removed the memory bottleneck of requiring rank 0 to gather the entire domain. We have also refactored the original routines which wrote periodic backups of the simulation state for restarting a crashed simulation to use the same file format as the output produced for analysis, reducing code complexity significantly.

We provide convenient post-processing tools to convert between the text and NetCDF file format, to aid data analysis. However, we note that NetCDF can be read natively by many visualization and analysis tools, including ParaView, which can easily produce iso-surfaces (e.g. Figure 2), volume renderings, and movies from TPLS output.

1.3. Diffuse Interface Method

In addition to the Level Set method, we have added an MPI-parallel implementation of the Diffuse Interface Method (DIM), which is available as an option to users. The DIM is based on the Cahn-Hilliard equation [11] which describes phase separation. The DIM was originally developed by Pedro Sáenz [3] in a separate code which was used to study droplets. This code featured only OpenMP parallelism and so could not scale to the large core counts needed for physically relevant system sizes of the channel geometries supported by TPLS. Importing this code into TPLS involved establishing the relationships between the variables (and the way they are indexed) in the two codes and changing the boundary conditions to match those in Figure 1. One particular point to note is that

Figure 2. Sample output from TPLS using Paraview visualization software, showing the isosurface $\phi = 0$, coloured by the vertical elevation

the value of order parameter ϕ used to characterize the phase lies between 0 and 1 in the levelset implementation but between -1 and +1 in DIM. The Cahn-Hilliard equation is a fourth order equation. It was implemented as two coupled second order equations each of which has a stencil size of one. This helped the integration of the DIM code as TPLS already used halo swaps appropriate to this stencil size. Distributing the loops over the indices of the variables across multiple MPI processes, when before they had been confined to one process (because of the use of OpenMP) was straightfoward within this framework.

1.4. Usability Improvements

Finally, with the support Mike Jackson of the Software Sustainability Institute, we have completely redesigned the user interface to TPLS. All simulation parameters can now be configured through input files or command-line arguments, obviating the need for users to modify and recompile the code for every application. A separate tool for creating initial flow conditions needed to start a new simulation is also provided, making use of NetCDF as the file format, again removing the need to modify the hard-coded initialization routines. The code has also been refactored to improve extensibility, and we used this to allow the DIM method to be provided as an option to the user. In future, this will allow for features such as different simulation geometries (e.g. counter-current flows) and new physics (e.g. phase change) which are currently implemented in separate programs to be included in the main TPLS version.

2. Benchmark results

To demonstrate the performance characteristics of TPLS, we have carried out strong scaling benchmark calculations using a grid size of 256x144x152, or 5.6 million elements. This is smaller than previous studies [7], but serves to expose the strong scaling behaviour at smaller numbers of cores than would be apparent with a larger grid. To be representative of production calculations we have executed 5,000 time steps, with parallel output every 1,000 steps. The timings reported were measured on ARCHER, a Cray XC30 supercomputer with two 12-core 2.7 GHz Intel Ivy Bridge CPUs per node, and an Aries interconnect network connecting the total of 4920 compute nodes.

Table 1. Scaling of TPLS using Levelset method

Nodes	Cores	Wallclock time (min)	Speedup
1	24	675	1.00
6	144	82	8.23
12	288	38	17.8
48	1152	17	39.7

Table 1 shows superlinear scaling up to 288 cores, due to the local sections of the distributed 3D grids becoming small enough to fit fully within the processor cache hierarchy. At 1152 cores communication overhead becomes evident although the scaling efficiency is still over 80%. Because of the 2D decomposition, each process has a long, narrow domain of size 8x4x152 and so the communication to computation ratio is high since the quantity of halo data to be exchanged scales with the surface area of the domain rather than the interior volume. Complete conversion of the code to use PETSc, enabling use of a 3D domain decomposition will improve this as the domains will become more compact, reducing the impact of communication for a fixed number of processes.

For this grid size on 1152 cores, TPLS has around 5000 elements per core. This is similar to or slightly better than other open-source codes such as OpenFOAM, where the optimal number of cores for similar problem sizes was found to be range from 128 to 1024 depending on which physics and geometry were employed (see [12], table 6). By contrast, the commercial CFD code HyperWorks Virtual Wind Tunnel, achieves only 80% scaling efficiency on 576 cores, using a much larger mesh (22 million elements, 38000 per core) [13].

3. Parallel I/O

As discussed in section 1.2, the changes to the I/O routines improve performance, decrease the total file size by use of HDF5 compression and facilitate ease of use by providing the user more controls over types and frequency of output. This section discusses in more detail the performance improvements observed.

3.1. Performance of the NetCDF I/O Implementation

Table 2 shows the performance improvement in the total execution (wallclock) time of the TPLS code from the old text formatted 'single file, single writer' mode to the 'single file, collective write' mode enabled by the use of parallel NetCDF. The times reported are means from 3 runs of a 100 time step simulation on a 512x144x152 grid, writing output and backup files every 10 time steps. These are more frequent than would be typical for a production calculation (as in Section 2), and the large grid size is designed to increase the cost of I/O. This comparison was performed after the code refactoring that whilst

Table 2. Performance of TPLS using NetCDF and text I/O routines

Number of nodes	1	3	24	128	256
Number of processors	24	72	576	3072	6144
Text time (s)	10211	7589	7347	7530	11879
NetCDF time (s)	3998	1838	428	689	1635
Relative Speedup	2.6	4.1	17.1	10.9	7.3

leaving the original I/O routines intact, improved control of the routines so that a like-for-like comparison could be made using the same frequency of file output for both text and NetCDF modes. These results show that for an 11 million grid point simulation the NetCDF implementation improves the runtime of TPLS by a factor of between 2.6 and 17.1 depending on the number of cores used. The best relative speedup between the two I/O methods is obtained on 24 nodes (576 cores) of ARCHER. Some of the speedup may be attributed to the reduction in the total amount of data to be written (a factor of 6.7), however this clearly does not explain the total improvement on core counts above 72 is greater than 6.7.

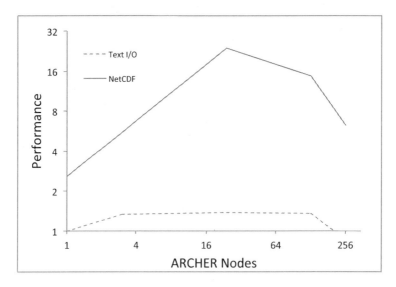

Figure 3. Performance of TPLS between 24 and 6144 cores on ARCHER comparing the NetCDF and text I/O implementations

Figure 3 shows the performance of TPLS using both I/O methods up to 6144 processors. The performance metric shown is a speedup relative to the time taken using the original text I/O method on 1 node. Here we demonstrate that when using the original I/O routines, performance is limited to 1.4 on 24 nodes (576 cores), compared to 23.9 using the NetCDF enabled I/O routines. Scaling of the NetCDF I/O is also significantly better, showing a speedup of 9.3 on 24 nodes over the single-node performance. This will greatly facilitate the simulation of larger systems in the future which has currently been

Table 3. Time in seconds of NetCDF I/O with different stripe settings

Number of cores	Number of OSTs			
	1	**4**	**8**	**48**
24	151.30	134.27	131.60	165.54
72	126.83	94.38	93.03	158.92
576	232.48	170.86	150.95	264.42
3072	401.76	243.55	227.66	348.36
6144	606.76	453.25	417.56	804.07

restricted by the I/O overhead, memory bottleneck and the limited control over write frequency.

3.2. The effects of using striping in I/O

A further aspect of investigation in this work was to assess the optimal 'data striping' for use in TPLS. The Lustre parallel file system available on ARCHER is accessed via a set of IO servers — Object Storage Servers (OSSs) — which access data provided by Object Storage Targets (OSTs). A file is 'striped' when it is spread over multiple OSTs and read or write operation on such a file access multiple OSTs concurrently. File striping thus provides a simple way to potentially increase I/O performance in many applications but is often not investigated. Thus for the final part of our work we assessed the optimal striping for TPLS, and whether striping would have a significant impact on performance.

Given the architecture of the ARCHER Lustre parallel file system, the 'single file, collective write' model used in the new NetCDF I/O implementation should benefit from striping each file across multiple OSTs. We compared the performance of the file write operations using the same simulation set up as in Section 3.1, striping the output files across 1, 4, 8 and 48 OSTs per file. By default on ARCHER all files are striped across 4 OSTs, unless otherwise specified by the user and the maximum striping possible is 48 due to the number of OSTs per file system. Lustre stripes files in a block-cyclic fashion with a fixed block size of 1 MiB.

The data presented in section 3.1 used the ARCHER default data striping (4 stripes). Table 3 shows that additional performance improvements (up to 12% on 576 cores) can be gained by striping over 8 OSTs although the effect is small compared to the minimum (1) and the maximum (48) stripes. For simulations using even larger grid sizes, we expect that further improvement may be gained by striping the data across more than 8 OSTs.

4. Conclusion

Due to the use of established scientific libraries such as PETSc and NetCDF over bespoke solutions, we have shown TPLS to be a better performing and more scalable code. In addition, refactoring the code structure to remove the need for editing code in order to set up different simulations makes TPLS much more usable and enables it to be provided as a precompiled package on ARCHER.

Two major challenges remain unsolved in the current released version: firstly, to take full advantage of the scalability provided by PETSc, in particular the ability to use a 3D domain decomposition, requires porting all of the solvers in the code to use this framework. Once this is complete the additional overhead of copying data to/from PETSc data structures at each time step can also be avoided. Secondly, development of additional physics, boundary conditions, and geometries takes place to date in separate branch versions of the TPLS code. To take full advantage of the performance improvements which are implemented in the trunk, these must be merged.

Nevertheless, TPLS usage is already growing, and as well as being used for research applications [1,2] has also attracted the interest of industrial users such as Shell R&D.

Acknowledgement

This work was funded by the embedded CSE programme of the ARCHER UK National Supercomputing Service (http://www.archer.ac.uk) and the HECToR Distributed Computational Science and Engineering (CSE) Service operated by NAG Ltd. HECToR – A Research Councils UK High End Computing Service — was the UK's national supercomputing service, managed by EPSRC on behalf of the participating Research Councils. Its mission was to support capability science and engineering in UK academia. The HECToR supercomputers were managed by UoE HPCx Ltd and the CSE Support Service was provided by NAG Ltd (http://www.hector.ac.uk). Additional support was provided by the EPSRC Grant EP/K00963X/1 "Boiling in Microchannels".

References

[1]   Lennon Ó Náraigh, Prashant Valluri, David M. Scott, Iain Bethune, and Peter D. M. Spelt. Linear instability, nonlinear instability and ligament dynamics in three-dimensional laminar two-layer liquidliquid flows. *Journal of Fluid Mechanics*, 750:464–506, 7 2014.

[2]   Patrick Schmidt, Lennon Ó Náraigh, Mathieu Lucquiaud, and Prashant Valluri. Linear and nonlinear instability in vertical counter-current laminar gas-liquid flows. *arXiv preprint arXiv:1507.04504*, 2015.

[3]   P. J. Sáenz, K. Sefiane, J. Kim, O. K. Matar, and P. Valluri. Evaporation of sessile drops: a three-dimensional approach. *Journal of Fluid Mechanics*, 772:705–739, 6 2015.

[4]   Mark Sussman and Emad Fatemi. An efficient, interface-preserving level set redistancing algorithm and its application to interfacial incompressible fluid flow. *SIAM Journal on scientific computing*, 20(4):1165–1191, 1999.

[5]   Hang Ding, Peter DM Spelt, and Chang Shu. Diffuse interface model for incompressible two-phase flows with large density ratios. *Journal of Computational Physics*, 226(2):2078–2095, 2007.

[6]   TPLS: High Resolution Direct Numerical Simulation of Two-Phase Flows. http://sourceforge.net/projects/tpls/.

[7]   David Scott, Lennon Ó Náraigh, Iain Bethune, Prashant Valluri, and Peter D. M. Spelt. Performance Enhancement and Optimization of the TPLS and DIM Two-Phase Flow Solvers. *HECToR dCSE Report*, 2013.

[8]   Satish Balay, Shrirang Abhyankar, Mark F. Adams, Jed Brown, Peter Brune, Kris Buschelman, Lisandro Dalcin, Victor Eijkhout, William D. Gropp, Dinesh Kaushik, Matthew G. Knepley, Lois Curfman McInnes, Karl Rupp, Barry F. Smith, Stefano Zampini, and Hong Zhang. PETSc Web page. http://www.mcs.anl.gov/petsc, 2015.

[9]   NetCDF web page. http://www.unidata.ucar.edu/software/netcdf.

[10]   The HDF Group. Hierarchical Data Format, version 5. http://www.hdfgroup.org/HDF5/, 1997-2015.

[11]   John W. Cahn and John E. Hilliard. Free energy of a nonuniform system. i. interfacial free energy. *The Journal of Chemical Physics*, 28(2):258–267, 1958.

[12]   Gavin Pringle. Porting OpenFOAM to HECToR. *HECToR dCSE Report*, 2010.

[13]   Greg Clifford and Scott Suchyta. Staying Out of the Wind Tunnel with Virtual Aerodynamics. *Proceedings of the Cray User Group (CUG), 2015*, 2015.

Parallel Computing: On the Road to Exascale
G.R. Joubert et al. (Eds.)
IOS Press, 2016
© 2016 The authors and IOS Press. All rights reserved.
doi:10.3233/978-1-61499-621-7-469

FPGA Port of a Large Scientific Model from Legacy Code: The Emanuel Convection Scheme

Kristian Thorin HENTSCHEL [a], Wim VANDERBAUWHEDE [a] and
Syed Waqar NABI [a,1]

[a] *School of Computing Science, University of Glasgow*

Abstract. The potential of FPGAs for High-Performance Computing is increasingly recognized, but most work focuses on acceleration of small, isolated kernels. We present a parallel FPGA implementation of a legacy algorithm, the seminal scheme for cumulus convection in large-scale models developed by Emanuel [1]. Our design makes use of pipelines both at the arithmetic and at the logical stage level, keeping the entire algorithm on the FPGA. We assert that modern FPGAs have the resources to support this type of large algorithms. Through a practical and theoretical evaluation of our design we show how such an FPGA implementation compares to GPU implementations or multi-core approaches such as OpenMP.

Keywords. FPGA, Pipeline Parallelism, High-Level Synthesis, MaxJ

Introduction

Scientific applications, such as weather models, often use computationally intensive iterative floating point algorithms. The need for parallelisation and use of High-Performance Computing (HPC) architectures, multi-core CPU, GPU, and FPGA, to achieve the best possible performance and power efficiency, has now largely been recognised. However, there is still a large body of legacy code for algorithms that do not lend themselves to straight-forward parallelisation and porting to such systems. These original algorithms need to be tackled for parallelisation to continue providing performance and efficiency gains. When comparing HPC architectures and performance, most benchmarking approaches use small, well-isolated algorithms that operate uniformly on a large amount of data. These kernels are carefully selected and extracted to explicitly target execution-time hotspots in a larger application. For some applications this is a sound approach given the large amount of work required to manually craft and optimise efficient FPGA implementations. By contrast, in this work we tackle a realistic kernel from the domain of numerical weather modelling, where acceleration of one or very few targeted kernels does not work well, and a more nuanced approach is needed.

---

[1]Corresponding Author. E-mail: syed.nabi@glasgow.ac.uk

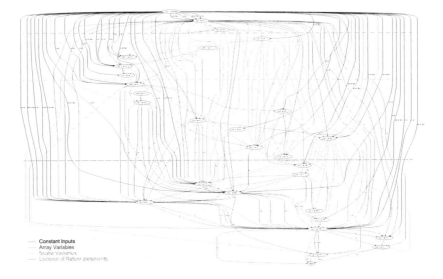

Figure 1. This dense dataflow graph gives an overview of the complexity of array and scalar dependencies between the loops of the original algorithm. A dependency is assumed where the same variable is written in one loop and read in another. The algorithm consists of 24 top-level DO-loops, some of which contain nested loops up to three levels deep.

1. Porting a real-life Convection Kernel to FPGA

We report the porting of a widely used convection algorithm [1] from single-threaded Fortran code to a pipelined FPGA architecture using a high-level synthesis (HLS) tool. Making use of a streaming paradigm and targeting fine and coarse grained pipeline parallelism, we analyse and port the convection algorithm. We argue that modern FPGAs have the capacity and performance required for dealing with such considerably more complex floating point algorithms, and explore options for optimization of our design. The convection kernel is part of the FLEXPART lagrangian particle dispersion simulator [2] used a.o. to predict the spread of the ash cloud from the Icelandic volcano in 2010 and the radio-active fall-out from the Fukushima reactor incident in 2011. We have ported the rest of the simulator to OpenCL in [3], but the aim of this work is to explore issues in porting a large and complex kernel to FPGAs. Figure 1 illustrates the complexity of dependencies in this kernel, showing the results as a graph of the top-level loops.

2. Prior Work

At least two separate efforts have been made to port the Flexpart simulator to HPC systems: Zeng describes a C++ port of the Fortran application, FlexCPP [4,5], making use of general purpose GPU processing (using CUDA[6]) and multi-core CPUs (using OpenMP[7]). The convection scheme is left largely untouched. Another implementation, FlexOCL by Harvey et al. [3], extends this to work with the more widely supported OpenCL standard [8]. Their work does not attempt to parallelise the convection scheme. The authors note that while convect is computationally intensive, it does not map well to the mostly data-parallel OpenCL model.

In more general FPGA, GPU, and CPU performance surveys such as that by Vestias et al [9] show that FPGAs are competitive for certain workloads, such as some map-reduce applications and custom state-machines. More importantly, the flexible architecture allows for custom pipeline depths and has more efficient support for branches and loops when implemented as a high-throughput streaming design. In analysing performance of these architectures, or when demonstrating HLS tools, most work focuses on relatively small examples, which can be efficiently mapped as custom state-machines or data-parallel designs: Hussain describes a k-means ranking algorithm [10] implemented as a parametrized and showing the FPGA's capability's for saving space and energy through custom number representations. Lienhart show an implementation of the n-body simulation [11], aiming for high throughput. Our work, in contrast, while not yet claiming optimal performance, shows that complete, significantly larger (in terms of lines of code) and more complex (in terms of control flow) floating point algorithms can also be implemented within the resource limits of modern FPGAs. Our approach, based on pipelining at a coarse level (streaming multiple data sets), and a fine-grained arithmetic level (streaming individual layers through a loop), faces similar considerations to those described by Gordon [12]. They apply coarse software pipelining to a multi-core CPU system and develop optimization strategies for determining the best mapping of a set of streaming computations to data-parallel or task-parallel sections.

3. Approach

We analysed the original Fortran code for dataflow dependencies between blocks, restructured it following the original top-level do-loops, and informally expressed the parallelism in each block as a set of map and reduce operations. Some of the nested loops were merged or split into multiple kernels. For an initial exploration, we dealt with the set of loops towards the end of the algorithm, representing about 60% of execution time and over 30% of the total lines of legacy code. The analysed loops are split into smaller kernels based on the parallelism patterns we have identified. The current implementation splits these nine do-loops into about 25 kernels. They are detailed in Table 1. The dependencies between the kernels are shown in Figure 2, with the constant inputs, distributed to many kernels, and the output streams omitted for clarity.

The Maxeler HLS tools [13] provide a Java meta-programming model for describing computation kernels and connecting data streams between them. This description is compiled to a VHDL design making use of deeply pipelined floating point cores at the lowest level. Pipeline parallelism is used at all levels: The floating point operations within each kernel are deeply pipelined by the Maxeler compiler and, at a higher level, the kernels are interconnected by streams for the relevant data arrays, creating a coarse pipeline of kernels. The algorithm operates on many independent columns (coarse pipeline) of air defined by the atmospheric conditions at a number of layers which are traversed in multiple stages (fine pipeline). We intend to balance and selectively duplicate the stages as multiple data-parallel lanes for optimal throughput of a steady stream of columns and also pipeline the reductions in the stream using a tree-based approach.

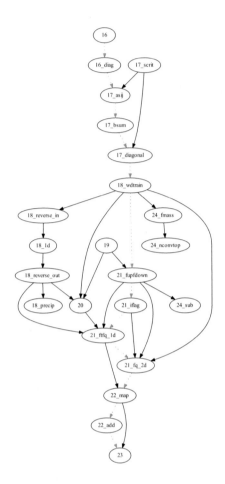

Figure 2. The targeted loops have been split into 23 kernels with these dependencies, the critical path of the coarse pipeline is highlighted. The dependencies on the input kernels, the output streams, and corresponding utility kernels are not shown to maintain clarity.

3.1. Kernel Implementation

The kernels can roughly be described as following a small set of design patterns, as many show similarities in the pattern of parallelism. These are detailed in Table 1: There are nine *map* or *diagonal map* kernels and five trivial *reduction* kernels. The remaining kernels require more complicated *fold* operations and it is harder to extract useful parallelism from them due to the dependency on earlier iterations, or complicated nested loops. Finally, a few utility kernels are used to mitigate limitations of the streaming paradigm, such as providing scalar output streams or reversing streams.

Map. The simplest pattern of parallelism is used in seven kernels. These kernels consume their input streams one element at a time, apply the computation, and produce an output element. There is no dependency between iterations, so the pipeline can be started whenever an input is available, in the best case on every clock tick.

Loop	Kernels	Ticks	Pattern
16	16	n^2	Map
	16_diag	$2 \cdot n^2$	Diagonal Map
17	17_scrit	n	Map
	17_asij/17_bsum	$2 \cdot n^2$	Row Reduce/Map
	17_diag	$3 \cdot n^2$	Diagonal Map
18	18_wdtrain	$15 \cdot n^2$	Fold*
	18_reverse_in/out	$2 \cdot n$	Reverse
	18	$440 \cdot n$	Fold*
	18_precip	1	Scalar
19	19	$12 \cdot n$	Reduce
20	20	$31 \cdot n$	Reduce
21	21_fupfdown	n^3	Fold*
	21_iflag	$2 \cdot n$	Reduce/Map
	21_ftfq_1D	n	Map
	21_fq_2D	$2 \cdot n^2$	Col Reduce/Map
22	22_map	n	Map
	22_add	$15 \cdot n$	Reduce
23	23	n	Map
24	24_fmass	n^2	Map
	24_nconvtop	$2 \cdot n^2$	Reduce
	24_sub	n	Map

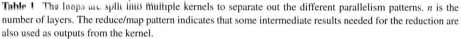

Table 1 The loops are split into multiple kernels to separate out the different parallelism patterns. n is the number of layers. The reduce/map pattern indicates that some intermediate results needed for the reduction are also used as outputs from the kernel.

Diagonal map. In a variation on the simple map, these kernels consume and produce two-dimensional inputs, but only apply the computation or assignment to the elements on the diagonals. Again, there are no dependencies between loop iterations, but a large stream has to be traversed in order to get to the correct position where the computation results are actually used.

Reduction. Simple reductions produce a scalar result from a long input stream. These are implemented as a pipeline, where a new input element is only consumed after the previous processing has completed, thus decreasing the pipeline utilisation. In most cases, this reduced throughput is not a problem, as for example an addition takes 15 cycles, and a comparison for finding a maximum value only takes two cycles. Except for 22_add, these reductions are not part of the critical path.

Row or column reduction. A few kernels produce one-dimensional arrays from 2D inputs. If this reduction happens along a row, the array is stored in column-major order, and the latency of the reduction operator is less than the width of the array, the pipeline can still be fully utilised. In this case, useful work can be dispatched and an input element consumed at every cycle.

Combined Reduction/Map. In some cases, a reduction kernel also doubles to perform a map operation. In this case, an intermediate result used for the reduction is also output as an independent result stream. An example is the 21_iflag kernel, which also produces some values at each iteration, which are then used by later kernels. This puts

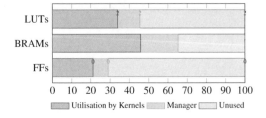

Figure 3. FPGA Resource Utilisation

the kernel on the critical path, although the reduction result is only required for the final output. Such kernels could also be split into two separate pure map and reduce stages.

Specialised folds. A few kernels have slightly more complicated inner dependencies. For example, in 18 each element depends on the previously computed element, causing a very deep pipeline dependency of 440 empty cycles. This greatly increases the kernel's number of required ticks, although it only operates on a one-dimensional array. In 21_fupfdown there are three levels of nested loops, with the inner-most loop performing a reduction along the row of another 2D array. Finally, while 18_wdtrain is close to a row reduction, the computation of the initial value is different, and specialised pipeline delays have been inserted to ensure correctness without greatly increasing the delay caused by the reduction itself.

Scalar. The single-tick kernel 18_precip simply generates an output scalar from a stream of length one emitted from a previous kernel. It has been split out of 18 to avoid increasing that kernel's latency further.

Array reversal and transposition. Kernel 18 traverses its inputs from the top level towards the bottom level, such that level i depends on the results obtained for level $i+1$. Its inputs and outputs are all one-dimensional, and can be reversed by first writing them into a memory, and then reading from there in reverse order. The same approach is used in 21_fq_2d where a 2D input matrix is transposed in order to reduce it along a column, and generate a 2D result such that output (i, j) depends on the input at (j, i).

Input array processing. The input arrays are all one-dimensional, and are stored in the FPGA card's on-board DDR memory as an array of structs. This makes consuming them in order, as they will be streamed to the kernels, more efficient as the DDR memory operates in bursts larger than the struct size. A small amount of padding is used at the end of each struct, to ensure that the struct size exactly divides into the burst size. This makes scheduling of the input kernel and buffering of the structs more efficient. An input-processing kernel consumes these structs one at a time, and produces an independent stream for each individual array.

4. Performance and Optimizations

Throughout the discussion of our performance and power efficiency results we refer to the theoretically estimated performance numbers as *est-single*, *est-pipeline*, *est-balanced* and to the actually measured results as *fpga-single* for the single-column baseline implementation. Our base implementation (non-optimized, single-column, single instance) occupies about two-thirds of the logic and block RAM resources on our FPGA (Figure 3). The kernel clock frequency is 200MHz, and at this speed the design achieves a

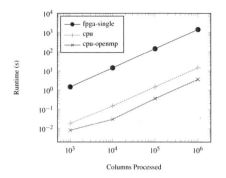

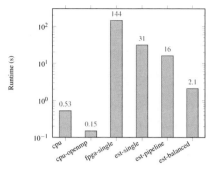

(a) Measured run time for different input sizes.

(b) Measured and estimated run times for 100K columns.

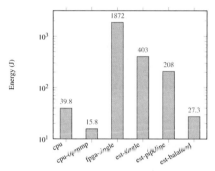

(c) Energy usage, derived from 100K columns run time and measured power.

Figure 4. Performance results.

Implementation	Power (W)	Runtime (s)	Energy (J)
System Idle	56.3	–	–
cpu	75.5	0.53	39.8
cpu-openmp	104.9	0.15	15.8
fpga-single	68.6	144	1872
est-single	68.6	31.0	403
est-pipeline	68.6	16.0	208
est-balanced	68.6	2.1	27.3

Table 2. Measured power figures, with measured and estimated runtimes and the resulting energy usage for processing 100,000 columns.

throughput of 0.7columns/ms on a single column of atmosphere. The performance is limited by the very high latency of the overall pipeline, which has to be flushed for every new column. By processing a steady stream of successive columns in-flight in a coarse pipeline (*est-pipeline*) the design should be capable of achieving a throughput of at least 47.6columns/ms, with room for further improvement when reducing the delay of the current slowest outlier stage. For comparison, a single-threaded CPU implementation (running on Intel core i7) achieves a throughput of 68columns/ms.

As the kernels have different throughput and latency figures, further optimization work will focus on balancing the coarse pipeline stages to alleviate stalling and buffering requirements (*est-balanced*). The most straight-forward balancing can be achieved by replicating the slowest kernels as multiple lanes, each working on different columns. There is also potential for improving the algorithmic mapping from legacy code to the stream model, which currently closely follows the sequential implementation with loops of up to $(n_{layers})^3$ iterations. In most of these cases only a small number of elements in a large stream is actually accessed. We could be read into a local cache and access in a random-access fashion, in a much lower number of total cycles. The flow of input and intermediate data arrays also still has potential for optimization to avoid buffering and stalling. There are enough resources available on the FPGA to support all these methods, as the current bottleneck stages only consume a very small part of the overall resources.

We measured two CPU versions of the algorithm for comparison: a single-threaded version *cpu*, and an OpenMP multi-core CPU version *cpu-openmp*, both compiled with gcc -O2 on CentOS/Linux 2.6.32. The only modification from *cpu* is that here the loop over all columns is annotated with the OpenMP #pragma omp parallel for. For all CPU benchmarking we use our C port of the same subset of loops currently included in the *fpga-single* port.

Our test system – Maxeler's "Maia Desktop" workstation – consists of an Intel i7-3770S quad-core CPU clocked up to 3.10GHz, connected to an FPGA board based on the Altera Stratix V FPGA by the PCI Express bus. The overall power usage of the system (CPU + FPGA + peripherals) was measured using a Watt meter. The performance results of our tests are summarized in Figure 4 and Table 2.

Note that the throughput estimate is a worst-case estimate and assumes that there is no overlap between the stages of the coarse pipeline. This case of no overlap, shown in Figure 5a, only occurs for reductions on the critical path. In the best case, which would occur for adjacent maps of the same number of elements, illustrated in Figure 5b, the second kernel's fill latency could be hidden completely by the overlap: It can start executing immediately after the first element has been produced in the preceding kernel. Where additional buffering is required, stages process different numbers of elements, or where there is a mismatch between the production and consumption rate, as shown in Figure 5c, one of the kernels might stall waiting for input. This additional execution time for one of the kernels however is always hidden by the time taken by the longer-running kernel which has already been taken into account.

5. Discussion

In our analysis of individual nested loops for parallelism contained therein, we found that a small number of patterns repeatedly occur in the legacy code, and sometimes are combined or only slightly modified. Very rarely did a loop warrant a completely different approach. Not all of these combinations of higher-level constructs can be efficiently parallelised. Our chosen approach interprets all patterns as pipelines, and treats the arrays and matrices as one-dimensional streams. This simplifies the implementation, but sometimes requires extra steps, such as buffers to reverse or transpose an input stream. More efficient and varied implementations of these standard patterns could be devised, such as many parallel lanes for map operations, or tree-based reductions.

The currently available HLS tools already greatly simplify the implementation of FPGA based algorithms, yet the effort is still significant. While it offers a great deal of

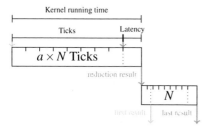

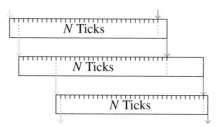

(a) Worst case, a reduction on the critical path: No overlap as the reduction result is needed for the next kernel to start processing its first layer.

(b) Best case, e.g. equally sized maps with equal processing rates. Overlap only slightly limited by latencies.

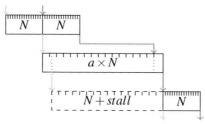

(c) Buffers and different processing rates. Overlap limited by different phases, stalling may occur but is hidden by overlap with previous kernel.

Figure 5. Pipeline interactions. In most cases, the pipeline stages can usefully overlap at the layer-levels.

control, efficient deep pipelines of the arithmetic operations, and takes away much of the 'plumbing' complexity and synchronisation between kernels, the programmer has to be familiar with FPGA-specific architecture traits, such as flip flops, buffers, multiplexers, counters, memory controllers and burst sizes, and working around pipeline data hazards.

Our performance evaluation and estimates have shown that it should be possible to obtain performance comparable to a CPU, and better power efficiency, from an FPGA with reasonable area requirements. There are many ways the performance and efficiency could be further improved, with different machine configurations and future FPGA chips: Firstly, on an only slightly larger FPGA the entire design can be duplicated, to provide twice the throughput at essentially the same power usage. As we found memories and logic resources to be the main limiting factors, future FPGAs could provide a different mix of resources to better suit this kind of design: With more memories, and integrated floating point units, saving on logic resources to implement arithmetic operations, even FPGAs of a similar size could likely host multiple copies of the entire algorithm without a significant power usage overhead. Different machine configurations could also help, by adding multiple FPGAs to one host CPU, or using lower power host CPUs, a large gain in efficiency can be achieved. The host CPU and peripherals account for a much larger share of power usage than the FPGA card itself in our desktop machine. Once the completed, optimised FPGA version has been integrated with a CPU or OpenCL host application, the convection calculations could even proceed in parallel with other work. Convection is largely independent from the rest of the Flexpart simulator. In this case, all devices could be doing useful work at all times, rather than wasting power on waiting for input data or results.

6. Conclusions and Future Work

In conclusion, we have implemented a state-of-the-art convection algorithm on FPGA. The algorithm is considerably larger and more complex than most prior examples, and its irregular control flow poses challenges to traditional parallelization. We described an analysis process for the legacy code and a process for mapping it to parallelizable abstractions. We use a recent set of commercial HLS tools to create a complete synthesizable baseline implementation of the algorithm and have shown that FPGAs can indeed represent large, sequentially structured algorithm with dense dependency graphs efficiently, within the resource limits. Beyond our proof-of-concept single-column implementation we have designed and analysed straight-forward performance enhancements, such as creating a balanced coarse pipeline. Our analysis shows that performance comparable to a single-core CPU is achievable, at better power efficiency. Finally, in terms of the implementation process itself, we have found high-level synthesis tools to be very useful in cutting down the required implementation effort. With some additional controls, such as over the automatically generated stream buffers, and more optional higher-level abstractions, these tools could make FPGAs much more accessible to a general audience.

References

[1] Kerry A Emanuel. A scheme for representing cumulus convection in large-scale models. *Journal of the Atmospheric Sciences*, 48(21):2313–2329, 1991.
[2] A Stohl, H Sodemann, S Eckhardt, A Frank, P Seibert, and G Wotawa. The lagrangian particle dispersion model flexpart version 8.2. *FLEXPART user guide*, 2011. Accessed November 02, 2014.
[3] Paul Harvey, Wim Vanderbauwhede, and Saji Hameed. Accelerating lagrangian particle dispersion modelling with opencl. In *IWOCL*, 2014. Workshop Paper.
[4] Jiye Zeng, Tsuneo Matsunaga, and Hitoshi Mukai. Using nvidia gpu for modelling the lagrangian particle dispersion in the atmosphere. In *International Congress on Environmental Modelling and Software*. iEMSs, 2010.
[5] Jiye Zeng. Lagrangian particle dispersion program (flexcpp). 2012. Accessed November 09, 2014.
[6] CUDA Nvidia. Programming guide, 2008.
[7] Leonardo Dagum and Ramesh Menon. Openmp: an industry standard api for shared-memory programming. *Computational Science & Engineering, IEEE*, 5(1):46–55, 1998.
[8] John E Stone, David Gohara, and Guochun Shi. Opencl: A parallel programming standard for heterogeneous computing systems. *Computing in science & engineering*, 12(1-3):66–73, 2010.
[9] Mario Vestias and Horacio Neto. Trends of cpu, gpu and fpga for high-performance computing. In *Field Programmable Logic and Applications (FPL), 2014 24th International Conference on*, pages 1–6. IEEE, 2014.
[10] Hanaa M Hussain, Khaled Benkrid, Ahmet T Erdogan, and Huseyin Seker. Highly parameterized k-means clustering on fpgas: Comparative results with gpps and gpus. In *Reconfigurable Computing and FPGAs (ReConFig), 2011 International Conference on*, pages 475–480. IEEE, 2011.
[11] Gerhard Lienhart, Andreas Kugel, and Reinhard Manner. Using floating-point arithmetic on fpgas to accelerate scientific n-body simulations. In *Field-Programmable Custom Computing Machines, 2002. Proceedings. 10th Annual IEEE Symposium on*, pages 182–191. IEEE, 2002.
[12] Michael I Gordon, William Thies, and Saman Amarasinghe. Exploiting coarse-grained task, data, and pipeline parallelism in stream programs. In *ACM SIGOPS Operating Systems Review*, volume 40, pages 151–162. ACM, 2006.
[13] Maxeler Technologies. Programming MPC systems white paper. 2013. Accessed December 01, 2014.

Parallel Computing: On the Road to Exascale
G.R. Joubert et al. (Eds.)
IOS Press, 2016
© 2016 The authors and IOS Press. All rights reserved.
doi:10.3233/978-1-61499-621-7-479

How to Keep a Geographic Map Up-To-Date

Marco GREBE [a,b], Tilman LACKO [a] and Rita LOOGEN [b]

[a] *Volkswagen AG, Wolfsburg, Germany*
[b] *Philipps-Universität Marburg, Germany*

Abstract. Nowadays, data for digital maps are collected using a small fleet of specialised expensive vehicles. This approach is not sufficient for daily updates of all roads. Daily or even faster updates, needed for modern driver assistance systems, can be made by combining the, individually less accurate, sensor data of standard cars. In this paper we propose a framework which comprises a parallel system to apply use case specific iterative algorithms to incoming data. Fast adaptation to changed situations is achieved by using a graph structure for representing sequences of groups of detected objects. A case study on maintaining a map of traffic signs has been performed to prove the capabilities of the framework.

Keywords. Geographic Maps, Parallel Computing, Message Passing

Introduction

This paper introduces the architecture of *PAGSI*[1] and the graph structure *ASG*[2]. Together, *PAGSI* and *ASG* provide a framework to use simple iterative algorithms to generate and maintain a distributed map of objects based on data provided by many imperfect and moving sensors. The interface for those iterative algorithms was designed to support many different types of geographic objects, allowing scalable parallelization with a low communication overhead and minimising the number of error-prone corner cases. An algorithm to maintain a map of traffic signs is used as proof of concept.

The context of this research are digital maps used in modern cars. Driver assistance systems are fast increasing in numbers and complexity [1]. Without a reliable map, the systems have a limited foresight like a human driver who uses a route for the very first time. An up-to-date map enables the systems to anticipate situations. For example, the speed can be adapted when knowing about a speed limit behind the next hill.

Another example is the display of traffic signs on the car's main screen. The information for this is derived from the car's camera and a static map for navigation. If the map was reliable, signs could be shown before the car passes them, which enabled the driver to drive more comfortably and economically. However, nowadays, such static maps are not reliable and do not always reflect the current situation.

---

[1] Parallel Aggregation of Geographic data using Scala with Iterative algorithms. See section 1
[2] Adapting Subset Graph. See section 3

The reason is that today's maps are compiled using data collected with a small single purpose fleet. Those fleets have advanced sensors but are very expensive and not capable of traversing the whole network of streets in a short period of time. The maps in cars are therefore mostly outdated and error-prone which reduces drivers trust in them.

To achieve a sufficient up-to-dateness and data timeliness, the rate, at which traffic signs are recorded, has to be increased. To achieve this, we consider any car equipped with a camera for traffic sign recognition as a sensor and combine their detections in a centralised map of signs. The single measurements are not as good as those of a specialised fleet, but this disadvantage will be made up by the very high number of sensors [2]. Using this approach other problems based on geographic objects detectable by car sensors can be solved, like a map of speed bumps or pot-holes in the road.

Our framework *PAGSI* has been designed as a general platform to generate maps using a large amount of data collected by vehicles. It gets a stream of detections from each active car, analyses these and maintains a map of objects deduced from the obtained data. The logic needed to handle a new use case consists of an algorithm for including one single data point into the map. The framework lifts this algorithm to handle streams of data from a fleet of cars. Apart from creating new objects, the map has to be maintained and objects no longer present in reality have to be erased from the map. Detecting those objects is difficult, since we do not expect sensors to send a message if they detect nothing. *ASG* helps to determine which objects were not detected, but should have been.

The first part of our paper introduces the frameworks purpose, architecture and work partitioning. The second part shows a sample plugin for maintaining maps of traffic signs using the *PAGSI* framework. In the third section a short explanation of *ASG* is given. Afterwards some related work is shown. The last section is a conclusion of this paper and a description of our future work.

1. The *PAGSI* Framework

PAGSI is a framework to keep a digital map up-to-date by continuously collecting and analysing observations of geographic objects from various moving cars. The name symbolises a framework which uses **P**arallel Computing to **a**ggregate streams of **g**eographic data. The framework is implemented using **S**cala and updates a set of objects using an **i**terative algorithm.

1.1. Scenarios

Most modern cars are equipped with a range of sensors and have therefore the possibility to detect different objects. If such a car passes a real object r the sensors make one or more observations $o_r^0, o_r^1, \cdots, o_r^k$. These observations are sent from the car to a server. The aim is to build and maintain a consistent, accurate, and up-to-date map of all real objects. For each object a kind, a position, and a set of attributes are stored. It is important to ensure that there is exactly one entry for each real object in the map. This requirement is difficult because the information sent by the cars is not perfect, due to inaccuracy of sensors. The following three scenarios must be handled:

- An object is in the map and it is observed.

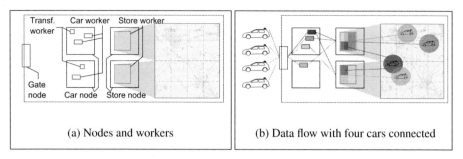

(a) Nodes and workers (b) Data flow with four cars connected

Figure 1. Structure of the *PAGSI*Framework

The observation (type, position, attributes) of the object corresponds with the data in the map. This should be the most common case.

It might however also be the case that not all the observed information corresponds with the data in the map. A speed limit 80 could e.g. be observed as 60 or vice versa, or the GPS position may be inaccurate, which might be the case in forests, due to a disturbed connectivity to GPS satellites.

- An object is in the map, but not observed.

  In this case, there are two possible reasons: Either the object has been removed and thus cannot be observed any more, or the object is still there, but the car did not observe it, e.g. due to a parking truck.

- An object which is not in the map is observed.

  If the observation is correct, the newly installed object must be entered into the map. However, it may also be the case that the observation is wrong, because the observed object is not real, but just a picture, e.g. on a truck or on a large poster.

As we will explain later, our framework is capable of dealing with all these scenarios.

1.2. Architecture

Each machine in a cluster is called a node and has exactly one role which defines the node's behaviour. Figure 1(a) shows the 3 different roles of nodes: a single gate node, several car nodes and several store nodes. Each node hosts a set of workers with different tasks.

We use the Actor Abstraction, which was first described in [3], as implemented in akka actors [4]. Actors are organised in a tree structure with a single distinguished root actor per node. If an actor starts another actor, it becomes the parent of the new actor. Actors work asynchronously and communicate via Message Passing. Each worker is identified with exactly one actor, which may manage a set of child actors for subtasks.

The Gate Node The gate node exists to keep the number of entry points into the framework small and enable active load balancing strategies. It is the interface between cars and the framework. When node waits for a TCP connection which is used to receive data from a set of cars. For each connected car, the address of a car worker is maintained. All messages from the car are forwarded to the corresponding car worker. If a new car connects, a new car worker is requested from one of the car nodes, if the car is not known. When a car does not send a message for a defined time its car worker is shut down.

Car Nodes   Each car node hosts a set of car workers. For every continuous connection of one car to the framework there is exactly one car worker. This worker receives all messages sent by its corresponding car. In order to analyse the input from the car, the car worker requests a limited region of the digital map containing the position of its car from the associated store worker. These snapshots of regions of the digital map only contain the needed information and are cached within the car node. The reloading of cached parts is triggered after a fixed time. Between two reloads of the same part this part of the map used by a car worker may be outdated.

Another responsibility of the car node is to start a transformation worker if this is requested by a store node. Transformation workers are started at store nodes because they normally need data of multiple store workers. The transformation worker produces messages which delete, create or modify objects. For this, it requests a more detailed map of an area than the car workers. The extended map includes observations which could not be matched to an object. All results of car and transformation workes are sent to the matching store worker and are called *events*.

Store Nodes   Each store node hosts a fixed number of store workers. Each store worker is responsible for a range of tiles[3][5] and is the only one with the right to change objects inside these tiles. The tiles are serialised and arranged similar to the distributed storage system of Laksham and Malik [6] to minimise the work needed to find the store worker responsible for each tile.

Every incoming *event* is included into the map. As car workers may have outdated tiles, not every *event* leads to a change of the map. There a three cases for incoming *events*: (1) If an *event* carries a reference to an existing object the *event* is combined with the object using a function called *p.insert* and provided by a plugin. (2) If the *event* denotes the creation or deletion of an object a new object is created or an old one deleted. (3) Otherwise the *event* carries an unmatched detection and is stored aside. The following transformation cycles determine what to do with *events* stored aside. Messages starting a transformation interval are sent to a car node in regular intervals. The store workers are responsible to log incoming events and store snapshots into a distributed file system in regular intervals to minimise data loss if a store worker crashes.

Figure 1(b) shows the flow of data from four cars over their individual car workers to the location specific store workers.

Plugins   The specific logic for each use case, for example the map of traffic signs, is encapsulated in a plugin. Each plugin *p* consists of three main functions:

- *p.work* is applied by a car worker. It takes a message sent by a car and a simplified snapshot of a tile of the current map and computes the resulting *events*, which are passed to the corresponding store worker.
- *p.transform* is applied by a car node to repeatedly transform the current map in fixed time steps, which includes generating objects from observations which could not be matched to an existing object. When a new object should be created a corresponding *event* is sent to the store worker. There a new object is created and all stored aside observations the object is based on are deleted. The object

---

[3]A tile is a geographic area. We use Google's tile definition: There is only one level 0 tile: the whole surface of the earth. Each following tile level $i \in [1,..21]$ has 4^i tiles and is defined by dividing each level $i-1$ tile into 4 pieces.

is only created if observations were not used in the meantime for the creation of other objects. When an existing object should be deleted, a special *event* is sent to the store worker which then deletes the object. All effects which are not directly triggered by a single car are enabled using *p.transform*.

- *p.insert* is called by a store worker to insert an *event* into an existing object stored in the map like described in case (1). If the object was deleted in the mean time the *event* is handled as in case (3).

p.transform and *p.insert* are separated because they work on different views of the map. *p.insert* needs the up-to-date view of an object and changes the state of this single object in the map. *p.transform* needs the information of a whole area and generates *events* which create new objects or delete outdated objects.

1.3. Behaviour of PAGSI

The three scenarios defined in section 1.1 are handled by a car worker in the following way:

- An object is in the map and it is observed.
  If a car worker can match an observation to an object already in the map, an ESK (**E**vent: **s**een **k**nown object) *event* will be generated and sent to the store worker holding this object. There the function *p.insert* is called to insert the new observation into the object's state.
- An object is in the map, but not observed.
  This is not directly observable, but deduced from information about the car's position. If an object in the map was not observed but should have been, an ENK (**E**vent: **n**ot seen **k**nown object) *event* will be generated, sent, and inserted like an ESK from above.
- An object which is not in the map is observed.
  If a car worker cannot match an observation with an existing object, an ESU (**E**vent: **s**een **u**nknown object) *event* is generated and sent to the store worker which manages the area of the observation. There it is stored in a separated structure but provided to each transformation of the area. Different transformation instances can initiate the creation of different objects whose existence is derived from an overlapping set of ESUs. To prevent this, the store node ensures, that all needed ESUs are still unused before creating a new object.

1.4. Amount of communication between nodes

A main goal designing *PAGSI* was to reduce the amount of communication needed when the number of nodes increases. After explaining which data has to be exchanged between nodes in *PAGSI* we will compare this to an approach using geographic partitioning only.

Our main focus lies on the communication between car nodes and store nodes. A car node sends generated *events* to different store nodes. To generate those *events* the store nodes provide a simplified view of the world for *p.work* and the separately stored unmatched observations to the car nodes. The number and size of all this data is determined by the used plugins and independent from the number of nodes. Figure 2(a) shows that if a new store node or car node is added some new routes for communication are created, but the amount of data sent does not increase.

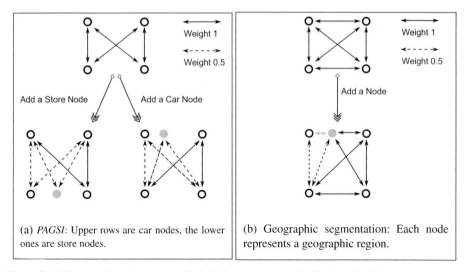

(a) *PAGSI*: Upper rows are car nodes, the lower ones are store nodes.

(b) Geographic segmentation: Each node represents a geographic region.

Figure 2. Adding a node to the structure. Each circle represents a node. Each two headed arrow represents a communication route. The weight of an arrow shows the amount of communication following this route.

An alternative approach would be not to distinguish between car nodes and store nodes. Then only one type of node does everything with one node per geographic region. Communication then is needed if one car crosses the border between two nodes and the state of this car has to be moved from one node to the other. If objects near a border are detected the known data from the other side of the border has to be requested, because each observation has a geographic uncertainty. Figure 2(b) shows that the introduction of a new node results in a new border and therefore route of communication. This is represented by the red arrow. All other routes stay the same or are split.

As complexity and number of plugins increases the number of nodes needed to handle the computation will also increase. Therefore new borders arise and the total length of borders, which defines the amount of communication, increases. The more plugins are used and the more complex the used algorithms become the bigger the size of each car's state gets. This effect would increase the amount of communication needed if only geographic segmentation is used. This is prevented using a layered model like *PAGSI*.

2. Proof of Concept

We implemented a proof of concept in order to evaluate the accuracy and precision of an algorithm using *PAGSI*. The first goal was to test if the measurements of camera and GPS sensor of a standard car are sufficient to generate a map of traffic signs. The second goal was to test if an iterative algorithm using *PAGSI*'s architecture is capable of generating results as good as those produced by a repeated hierarchical clustering, which does not run in a distributed environment.

We implemented a TSR (Traffic Sign Recognition) plugin, which is used to maintain a map of traffic signs based on the results of the traffic sign recognition software and camera of modern cars. The cars store position and attributes of all traffic signs which can be identified by their local software and camera. The data were collected using a small fleet of cars equipped to collect all detections of traffic signs by the camera along with periodically sampled GPS positions. These cars were driven in the area of germany for more than two month and allowed us to tune the algorithms using realistic data.

A small test track of around 16 km with a high number of traffic signs[4] and changing landscapes was used as ground truth to verify our system. After recording each sign's position and meaning it was classified as in a forest, in a town or with free line of sight to GPS satellites. Then the track was driven more than 20 times on a single day.

2.1. System setup

First a hierarchical cluster algorithm [7] was implemented and used as reference. This algorithm runs on a single machine and returns one map which can only be updated, if the complete algorithm is started from scratch again. The single measurements were sorted by their location. Then each single tile t was clustered along with the data of adjacent tiles, while storing only those objects, whose position was inside tile t. This was to prevent problems in regions near a tile's border. The clustering was stopped when a minimal distance was reached. The distance function d was based on a p-norm [8], but took into account the direction t from which a traffic sign was seen. $d((x_1,y_1),(x_2,y_2)) :=$ $||(x_1-x_2,(y_1-y_2)*c)||_4$, where (x_i,y_i) is the position of sign i and the y-axis is parallel to the direction from which sign 1 was seen. c is a factor which depends on the camera and was set to 0.2 during our tests. The p-norm was adapted, because it's much easier to determine the angle of an object then its distance.

Second an early version of *PAGSI* was used. The system was implemented in Scala using Akka actors and some Java packages for geographic representation and computations. Four actors were used to read the data files and pass them to the system. The used distance function was the same as above.

2.2. The Plugin

Each car sends the position and attributes of all traffic signs its camera identifies. The three functions of a *PAGSI* plugin had the following tasks:

p.work: Each incoming traffic sign recognition is compared to the set of known traffic signs. If a match is found, an ESK is generated. If none is found an ESU is sent.

p.transform: The transform function takes all ESUs and all known objects ($\hat{=}$traffic signs) in an area. After filtering those ESUs, which now can be matched to an object, the remaining ESUs are grouped by similarity. For each group of similar ESUs which is big enough an *event* for creating a new object and dropping the related ESUs is created. Last all traffic signs which were not observed for a defined time are deleted.

p.insert: Incoming ESKs are combined with the referenced object. ESUs are stored aside and used in *p.transform* steps. These are the only tasks performed by *p.insert*, which keeps the number of needed store nodes small.

2.3. Results

The tests showed good results and produced a correct map of the test track. Every traffic sign which was detected by the camera was present in the map, and no non existent signs

---

[4]more than 40 signposts with one or two signs

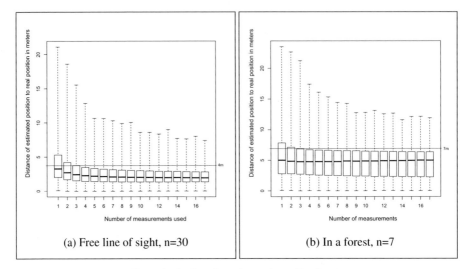

Figure 3. Quality of positions estimated by *PAGSI*

were shown. The results using *PAGSI* were equal to those using hierarchical clustering. Also the number of measurements needed to get a stable good result was not different.

Figure 3 shows the quality of the results using *PAGSI* separated by the type of situation. With a free line of sight 75% of all estimated signs were less than 4 m away from the signs' true position. Only 4 measurements were sufficient to achieve this precision. No sign was more than 11 m away. Inside a forest the results converged acceptable fast, but kept a bigger distance to the reference measurements. This may happen due to systematic disturbances in the GPS signal, signal problems while measuring the ground truth and the low number of signs.

A major problem was to decide if a sign was no longer present in the real world. A simple ageing of signs which have not been seen for a time span needs much time to delete a sign. Instead we used a directed weighted graph similar to *ASG* to track the order in which signs were detected. Each sign in the map is a vertex in this graph. And if sign s was detected after sign s' was detected the weight of the edge (s', s) was incremented by one, or set to one if it didn't already exist. Based on this graph the signs which could be seen next were determined and if the car passed one of them without detecting it, an ENK was sent. The promising results of this approach led to *ASG* which is an elaborated version of this idea and will be described in the next section.

3. *ASG*

ASG is used to predict the set of objects which should be detected next. This section gives an introduction to the aims and mechanisms of *ASG*.

3.1. Motivation

There are two problems motivating the usage of *ASG*. First sending new map data to car workers is one of the main parts of communication needed in *PAGSI*. If each car worker loads whole tiles based on the geographic position of the car there is a high number of unnecessarily loaded objects, which may not even be reachable. The number of objects can be reduced, if only objects with a high probability of detection are loaded. Second the most crucial part of *PAGSI* is to detect and remove vanished objects. To identify those objects, the car's position has to be checked against positions from which those objects were detected. *ASG* can help to minimize the number of objects which have to be tested.

3.2. Construction and Maintenance

ASG is a simple directed weighted graph. It can address these needs without relying on an external up-to-date map of streets. The **vertices** are sets of IDs of objects. Each object can be referenced by none, one or many vertices. Each set represents a set of objects which is highly likely to be seen together by a subset of cars. An **edge** (V, V') with weight $w > 0$ means that if all objects referenced by V are detected by one car the probability of all objects associated to V' being detected next is w. The vertices themselves do not have a position. Edges and vertices are maintained using a stream of IDs of detected objects, which is generated by the car workers.

3.3. Using ASG

Each car worker tracks the position of its car and requests Tiles based on this geographic position. After some objects were detected and matched the tracker knows the car's position in the graph. Then no complete Tiles are requested, but single objects determined by the graph edges. If the best match to a vertex is a partial match with some objects missing each missing one becomes a candidate for an object that should have been seen. For each of the candidates the car's positions are compared to the object's position. If they are close enough and no ESK for this object arrives an ENK is generated. The ENK's weight is computed using the weight of the edge which lead to this vertex and the number of missing objects.

4. Related Work

XFCD   Extended Floating Car Data (XFCD) means data recorded by cars driving in normal traffic. A car's position, the state of the rain sensors, the lights, or friction monitoring[9] can be used to get further information about the roads state and possibly dangerous situations. The data used by *PAGSI* can be classified as XFCD.

MapReduce   MapReduce [10] is a programming model used to batch process large amounts of data in a distributed way. One important characteristic is the usage of two independent layers: map and reduce. The map level is similar to *p.work* and the reduce level is similar to *p.insert*. But MapReduce is not designed to maintain a big state per reduce or a dataflow like needed by *p.transform*.

CEP   Complex event processing (CEP) systems are descendants of databases and their language is related to database queries. These queries are extended to support a notation of time and patterns in data over time. CEP systems, like Spark[11] and Esper[12] are designed to handle incoming event streams. Each event matches one of a fixed of patterns, for example a stream of numbers representing the measurements of a temperature sensor over time. Queries can be placed to be executed continuously on one or more streams and set them in relation. The results of a query is again an eventstream and can be used as input for other queries, which allows complex constructions. *PAGSI* is not implemented using a CEP system, because CEP systems are not made to maintain a complex state like a map of all traffic signs.

5. Conclusion and Futurework

The aim of *PAGSI* is to generate and maintain geographic maps from data collected by a big number of independent and error-prone sensors. Parallelization of work is not only achieved by strict geographic segmentation, but by using a layered approach segmenting by car and by geographic region. This keeps the amount of communication independent of the number of nodes. Furthermore iterative algorithms are used to include single new data points into the model without the complexity of a complete hierarchical clustering every *n* steps. A test using real data showed good results in quality of the resulting map and number of observations needed to determine changes. *ASG* was introduced to identify objects which should have been observed but were not. It allows much shorter response times as simple ageing mechanisms when objects have to be deleted from the map. Further improvements of *ASG* are possible, but can not be reliably validated until a higher number of plugins and live data are available.

Our future work aims towards reducing the number of messages needed by *PAGSI*. Therefore we develop a method for estimating the number of messages an actor based algorithm produces in a fixed time. The estimations can then be used to identify which optimisation has the highest influence on the bandwidth the algorithm needs.

References

[1]   Joachim Mathes and Harald Barth. Weiterentwicklung der Assistenzsysteme aus Endkundensicht. *Automobiltechnische Zeitschrift*, 2:12–17, 2014.

[2]   Marco Grebe. Iterative, funktionale Berechnung einer Verkehrszeichenkarte aus realen Fahrzeug ottendaten unter Verwendung von Akka Actors. Master's thesis, Philipps-Universität Marburg, 2013.

[3]   Gul Agha. *Actors: A Model of Concurrent Computation in Distributed Systems*. MIT Press, Cambridge, MA, USA, 1986.

[4]   Typesafe Inc. Akka actors. *http://www.akka.io/*, 2015.

[5]   Google Inc. Google maps documentation: Tiles. *https://developers.google.com/maps/documentation/javascript/maptypes?#TileCoordinates*, 2015.

[6]   Avinash Lakshman and Prashant Malik. Cassandra: A decentralized structured storage system. *SIGOPS Oper. Syst. Rev.*, 44(2):35–40, April 2010.

[7]   Ethem Alpaydin. *Introduction to Machine Learning*. The MIT Press, 2nd edition, 2010.

[8]   A. Deitmar. *Analysis*. Springer-Lehrbuch. Springer Berlin Heidelberg, 2014.

[9]   Werner Huber, Michael Lädke, and Rainer Ogger. Extended floating-car data for the acquisition of traffic information. In *6th World Congress on Intelligent Transport Systems*, 1999.

[10] Jeffrey Dean and Sanjay Ghemawat. Mapreduce: Simplified data processing on large clusters. *Commun. ACM*, 51(1):107–113, January 2008.

[11] Matei Zaharia, Mosharaf Chowdhury, Michael J. Franklin, Scott Shenker, and Ion Stoica. Spark: Cluster computing with working sets. In *Proceedings of the 2Nd USENIX Conference on Hot Topics in Cloud Computing*, HotCloud'10, pages 10–10, Berkeley, CA, USA, 2010. USENIX Association.

[12] EsperTech Inc. Esper. *http://www.espertech.com/esper/*.

Parallel Computing: On the Road to Exascale
G.R. Joubert et al. (Eds.)
IOS Press, 2016
doi:10.3233/978-1-61499-621-7-489

489

Static and Dynamic Big Data Partitioning on Apache Spark

Massimiliano Bertolucci [b] Emanuele Carlini [a] Patrizio Dazzi [a] Alessandro Lulli [a,b]
Laura Ricci [a,b,1]

[a] *Istituto di Scienze e Tecnologie dell'Informazione, CNR, Pisa, Italy*
[b] *Department of Computer Science, University of Pisa, Pisa, Italy*

Abstract. Many of today's large datasets are organized as a graph. Due to their size it is often infeasible to process these graphs using a single machine. Therefore, many software frameworks and tools have been proposed to process graph on top of distributed infrastructures. This software is often bundled with generic data decomposition strategies that are not optimised for specific algorithms. In this paper we study how a specific data partitioning strategy affects the performances of graph algorithms executing on Apache Spark. To this end, we implemented different graph algorithms and we compared their performances using a naive partitioning solution against more elaborate strategies, both static and dynamic.

Keywords. BigData, Graph algorithms, Data partitioning, Apache Spark

Introduction

In the last years the amount of data produced worldwide has been constantly increasing. For example, in 2012 were created every day 2.5 exabytes (2.5×10^{18}) of data [1], which comes from multiple and heterogeneous sources, ranging from scientific devices to business transactions. Often, data is modelled as a graph in order to organize and extract knowledge from it. Due to its size, it is often infeasible to process this data by exploiting the computational and memory capacity of a single machine. To overcome this limitation, it is common to adopt distributed computing environments. Many approaches of this kind have been designed so far. In this context, approaches based on the MapReduce [2] paradigm are very popular and are able to efficiently exploit large set of computing resources based on commodity hardware. The MapReduce paradigm belongs to the wider family of structured parallel programming approaches, which originated from the proposal of Cole [3] in the late '80s and, across the years, have been implemented by several tools and frameworks [4,5,6,7,8]. However, despite their wide adoption, these frameworks are not the best choices for any purpose. As a consequence, alternative paradigms have been proposed. Some of them have been based on the BSP bridging model [9]. A common trait shared by these frameworks [10] is that they provide the possibility to describe graph processing applications from the point of view of a vertex in the graph. These frameworks are often referred as Think Like a Vertex frameworks

---

[1]Corresponding Author. E-mail: laura.ricci@di.unipi.it

(TLAV). Each vertex processes the same function independently, accessing only its local context (usually its neighbourhood), therefore without having a global view on the graph. As discussed by Gonzalez *et al.* in their GraphX paper [11], the development of efficient algorithms through these frameworks requires to solve several non-functional issues and, among these, the definition of proper graph partitioning strategies is of paramount importance. In fact, the authors show how the assignment of vertices to machines minimising the number of edges crossing partitions leads to good performance with a large class of graphs.

The findings of Gonzalez *et al.* are based on a static partitioning, i.e. the partitioning is computed before starting the execution of the graph algorithm. This solution performs well when the computation on the vertices of the input graph happens to be uniform (e.g. the computation performs at the same rate on different vertices) or according to a communication pattern that can be statically predicted. However, in many graph algorithms the computation is not uniform and neither has a static communication pattern. To evaluate the role of partitioning in these kind of algorithms, in this paper we consider a set of different vertex-centric algorithms, characterised by different communication/computational patterns. The algorithms we studied in this paper belongs to two main families. The first kind of algorithms assumes a static structure of the graph, i.e. it does not change along the computation. A well known algorithm belonging to this class is the PAGERANK [12]. We also consider two further algorithms of this class: TRIANGLE COUNTING [13] and the KCORE decomposition [14]. The other class of algorithms we examined are those in which the topology of the communication graph changes during the computation. Both the algorithms belonging to this class that we studied are aimed at the detection of Connected Components [15,16]. We analysed the behaviour of all these algorithms when adopting different partitioning approaches, both static and dynamic. In conclusion, the main contribution of this paper is the presentation, the analysis and the comparison of a set of vertex-centric problems using different partitioning strategies. We have considered the following algorithms and partitioning approaches:

- *algorithms:* PAGERANK, TRIANGLE COUNTING, KCORE Decompositions, Connected Components
- *partitioner:* Spark Hash, BKW, SWAP, DESC

Each algorithm has been implemented on top of Apache Spark[17] and executed on a cluster composed by 3 machines, each composed by 32 cores and 128 Gbytes of RAM.

1. Related Work

The problem of graph partitioning has been extensively studied. Recently, due to the increasing size of the datasets, many solutions have been proposed targeting large graphs and suitable to the current TLAV frameworks. Among many, some target distributed implementations [18,19] or adopt the streaming model [20,21]. However, the METIS family of graph partitioning software [22] is still often considered the de facto standard for near-optimal partitioning in TLAV frameworks [10]. An extensive analysis of all the methods is beyond the scope of this work and we concentrate in particular on the effects of a good partitioning strategy in TLAV frameworks. As far of our knowledge, this is the first work evaluating the impact of different graph partitioning strategy in Apache Spark.

Other works evaluate the impact of graph partitioning on different TLAV framework. The outcome of such evaluation is not always the same, suggesting that extensive work must be done in order to understand the benefits of a good balanced partitioner. For what concern static partitioner evaluation, Salihoglu et al. [23] propose GPS, a Pregel-like graph processing system, and evaluates static partitioning on it. The framework uses a BSP model of computation and the graph can remain in memory during the computation. Their claim is that, using a balanced k-way partitioning, GPS is able to reduce run time of the PAGERANK algorithm between 2.1x and 2.5x with respect to a random partitioner. Instead, Connected Components and Single Source Shortest Path get less benefits. They perform some tests also using Giraph, another Pregel-like framework, and found that a k-way partitioning gets only marginal improvements. They tested the system also with a dynamic relabelling technique and found marginal improvement in time limited to the PAGERANK algorithm. For what concern Hadoop MapReduce, Ibrahim et al. [24] describe LEEN, a locality-aware and fairness-aware key partitioning to save the network bandwidth dissipation during the shuffle phase of MapReduce. Experimental evaluation shows that this approach is up to 40% better with respect to the default Hash partitioner. However they test their optimization just with a word count algorithm and they do not perform evaluation of algorithms exploiting different communication patterns. Different results have been obtained by Shao et al. [25]. Using Giraph, they found that the performance over well partitioned graph might be worse than Hash partitioner in some cases. The cause is that the local message processing cost in graph computing systems may surpass the communication cost in several cases. Due to this, they propose a partition aware module in Giraph to balance the load between local and remote communication. One work starting an evaluation of the partition strategy with Apache Spark has been presented recently by Amos et al. [26]. The focus of the work is a system to answer queries using Spark but, in the evaluation, they consider the problem of choosing the proper dimension for the partitions. If the size is too small, the system suffers an overhead for the management of the partitions. If the size is too large, data are sequentially processed. They empirically find a good trade-off for their specific application domain but an analysis of the impact of different partition strategies on other domains and algorithms is not presented.

Spark [17] is a distributed framework providing in memory computation making use of Resilient Distributed Datasets (RDD) [27]. RDDs are distributed data structures where it is possible to apply multiple operators such as Map, Reduce and Join. In Spark, the RDDs are partitioned by default using an Hash partitioner. The framework provides also the possibility to use a custom partitioner for data. However in the original and successive works an evaluation regarding the use of different partitioners is not presented.

2. Data Partitioning

In this paper we consider a set of different vertex-centric algorithms characterised by different communication/computational patterns targeting distributed computations. For each of them we evaluate how, even simple partitioning strategies can enhance their performances. The algorithms tested can be grouped into two main families. The algorithms belonging to the first family keep every vertex of the graph always active during the whole computation, and it communicates with its neighbours at each iteration. The second family of algorithms that we consider in our study selectively deactivate a subset of vertices during the computation. A detailed description of all the algorithms we implemented and exploited in our study is presented in Section 3. To develop all the algorithms considered in our study, we exploited the standard API of Apache Spark. Even if the Spark environment currently offers the GraphX library [11] for graph analysis we developed our own vertex-centric abstraction, in fact, when we started our work, GraphX was not stable yet, especially when used with massively iterative algorithms. To conduct our study, we embodied in Spark the different partitioning strategies we decided to apply. We can describe a partitioner as an entity that takes in input the identifier of a vertex id_V and gives as output the identifier of a partition id_P.

2.1. Spark embedded partitioners

Plain Spark already provides two different partitioners *hash* and *range*. The first one is based on a hashing function that takes in input id_V and returns the id_P of the partition depending on the behavior of the hashing function adopted. The standard function used by Spark is based on the module function. Basically, it aims at distributing all the identifier of the graph in a uniform way. Conversely, the *range* function aims at distributing the vertices of the graph on the basis of user provided ranges, e.g., all the nodes whose identifier is in the range $100 - 200$ are assigned to partition 2. In our study we exploited the first one of these two strategies, which we used as a baseline in our comparisons.

2.2. Balanced k-way partitioners

The first class of data decomposition strategies we embodied in Spark is based on the balanced k-way partitioning. It consists in a static partitioning strategy that decomposes the graph in k parts each one composed by the same amount of nodes, approximately. This approach is interesting because, by accepting a certain degree of approximation, it admits a polynomial time verification of its results (NP-complete). In fact, graph partition problems usually fall under the category of NP-hard problems. Solutions to these problems are generally derived using heuristics and approximation algorithms. However, balanced graph partition problem can be shown to be NP-complete to approximate within any finite factor. To conduct our study, we decided to use the suite of algorithms for partitioning provided by Metis. It provides solutions for partitioning a graph into a configurable amount of parts using either the multilevel recursive bisection or the multilevel k-way partitioning paradigms. As we mentioned, we used the latter approach, indeed, the multilevel k-way partitioning algorithm provides additional capabilities (e.g., minimize the resulting subdomain connectivity graph, enforce contiguous partitions, minimize alternative objectives, etc.). To exploit the features provided by Metis in Spark we decided to organise the computations in two steps instead of embedding the Metis library directly in the Spark framework. Basically, we give the graph in input to the multilevel balanced k-way partitioning provided by Metis, then we exploit the result to re-label the vertices of the graph accordingly to the partitions returned by Metis so that the Spark hash partitioner will be able to assign the vertices belonging to the same partition to the same machine.

2.3. *Dynamic partitioners*

The other kind of partitioning strategies that we have studied in our work falls in the class of dynamic partitioners. These approaches do not rely on a pre-computed decomposition of data, instead, they aim at adjusting the distribution of vertices to the machines that are more suited to compute them, depending on the behavior of the actual computation. In particular, we are interested in adjusting the distribution of the computation workload when the amount of active nodes decreases. To this end, in our study we investigated two different approaches of dynamic partitioning. The first one is based on a reduction of the partitions that is merely proportional to the number of active nodes. This strategy can be applied to any algorithm because it does not require any additional information about the nodes except the number of nodes that are active at a certain stage of the computation. We called this strategy "DESC". The other strategy we studied can be applied only to the algorithms that during their computation label the nodes of the graph in a way such that the nodes that communicate more one each others share the same label. In this case the dynamic partitioning strategy "clusters" the nodes sharing the same label in the same partition, when possible. The name of this strategy is "SWAP".

3. Case studies

As we mentioned above, we evaluated the impact of different partitioning strategies with several algorithms This section briefly presents such algorithms.

3.1. PAGERANK

PAGERANK [12] is one of the most popular algorithms to determine the relevance of a node in a graph. It is measured by means of an iterative algorithm characterised by a neighbour-to-neighbour communication pattern. Basically, every node is characterised by a value, representing its relevance. For each iterative step of the computation, every node redistributes its value among its neighbours. At the end of the iterative step each node sums up the "contributions" received, the resulting value represents its updated relevance.

3.2. TRIANGLE COUNTING

TRIANGLE COUNTING is a well known technique for computing the clustering coefficient of a graph. More in detail, a *triangle* exists when a vertex has two adjacent vertices that are also adjacent to each other. Several sequential and parallel solutions have been proposed for this problem. The algorithm we adopted in this paper is a vertex-centric version of the solution proposed by Suri and Vassilvitskii [13]. In the first step of the algorithm each vertex, in parallel, detects all the triples it belongs to that have two neighbours having a higher node degree. In the second step each vertex, in parallel, gathers all the messages received and, for each of them, checks the existence of a third edge closing the triple. The algorithm is characterized by a neighbour-to-neighbour communication pattern. The neighbourhood of each node is fixed, i.e. does not change during the computation steps. In the first step all the vertices are performing computation, whereas in the second step only the nodes which have received a message actually compute.

3.3. KCORE *Decomposition*

In many cases the study of the structure of a large graph can be eased by partitioning it into smaller sub-graph, which are easier to handle. To this aim, the concept of the KCORE decomposition of a graph results very useful. A KCORE of a graph G is a maximal connected subgraph of G in which all vertices have degree at least k. K-coreness is exploited to identify cohesive group of nodes in social networks, i.e. subset of nodes among which there are strong, frequent ties or to identify the most suitable nodes to spread a piece of information in epidemic protocols. Our algorithm is based on the solution proposed by Montresor *et al.* [14], which computes the K-coreness of each node using an iterative epidemic algorithm. Each node maintains an estimation of the coreness of its neighbours, which is initialized to infinity, whereas the local coreness of each node is initialized to its degree. At each step, each node sends the current value of its local coreness to its neighbours. When a node is updated about the coreness of one of its neighbours, if it is lower than its current local estimation, it records the new estimated value and checks if its local coreness has been changed by this update. In case, it sends its new coreness to its neighbours. The algorithm terminates when messages are no longer sent. As in PAGERANK, the communication pattern characterizing the algorithm is a fixed neighbour-to-neighbour pattern. However, differently from PAGERANK, nodes not participate to the message exchange at each iteration because only nodes that updates their coreness send messages in that iteration.

3.4. HASH-TO-MIN

Rastogi *et al.* [15] surveyed several algorithms for computing the connected components of a graph. All of them are characterized by associating a unique identifier to each node of the graph and by identifying each connected component through the minimum identifier of the nodes belonging to that component. In HASH-TO-MIN, each node initializes its own cluster to a set including itself and its neighbours. During the computation each node selects the node v_{min} with the minimum identifier in its cluster and sends its cluster to v_{min} and v_{min} to all other nodes of the cluster. In the receive phase, each node updates its cluster by merging all the received clusters. If the resulting cluster is unchanged from the previous iteration, the node do not exchange messages in the following steps, but it may receive a message which re-activates its computation. At the end of the computation, each node of a connected component is tagged with the minimum identifier, whereas this latter node has gathered all the identifiers of its connected component. In the HASH-TO-MIN algorithm, the communication pattern is not fixed, since each node may choose a different set of recipients at each iteration (the set of recipients is defined by the nodes in its cluster). Furthermore, as happens in KCORE, a node may be de-activated at some iteration.

3.5. CRACKER

CRACKER [16] is an algorithm that aims at optimizing HASH-TO-MIN. Each node checks its own neighbourhood and autonomously decides if its participation to the computation of the connected components shall be stopped. In any case, the node maintains the connectivity with its own neighbours. Like it happens with HASH-TO-MIN, the com-

Table 1. Completion time with synthetic graphs (best times are in bold)

	size	KCORE		PAGERANK		TRI COUNT		HASHTOMIN		CRACKER	
		HASH	BKW	HASH	BKW	HASH	BKW	HASH	BKW	HASH	BKW
NEWMAN	1M	44	**42**	111	**100**	43	**42**	160	**118**	65	**63**
	2M	60	**58**	162	**137**	65	65	331	**188**	95	**82**
	4M	90	**87**	274	**217**	110	**109**	633	**347**	153	**128**
POWERLAW	1M	**109**	110	149	**135**	**83**	88	125	**90**	66	**58**
	2M	182	**180**	235	**207**	**156**	167	**147**	152	85	**81**
	4M	327	**275**	431	**358**	**340**	358	276	**273**	138	**134**
WATTZ	1M	111	**107**	107	**82**	41	**40**	137	**97**	73	**58**
	2M	171	**167**	150	**123**	62	**61**	172	**149**	101	**80**
	4M	286	**275**	253	**196**	103	**101**	326	**270**	160	**130**

munication pattern is not fixed, but, with respect to HASH-TO-MIN when a node decides to stop its participation to the computation of the connected components, it may not be reactivated.

4. Experimental evaluation

The experimental evaluation has been conducted on 96 cores of a cluster of 3 machines, each composed by 32 cores and 128 GB of RAM. The evaluation has considered both the static partitioning, in which the partition is statically created before the computation, and the dynamic partitioning in which the partitioning is performed during the computation. Experiments measured the completion time without considering the time needed to compute the partitioning, i.e. the partitioning of the nodes is supposed to be given at the start of the computation.

4.1. Static Partitioning, Synthetic Graphs

These experiments measured the completion time of KCORE, PAGERANK, CRACKER, TRIANGLE COUNTING and HASH-TO-MIN with three different dataset sizes (number of nodes) in the set $\{1000000, 2000000, 4000000\}$. The graphs type considered are the Watts-Strogartz (WATTZ), Newman-Watts-Strogartz (NEWMAN) and Power-law (POWERLAW) and have been generated by means of the Snap library [28]. The results are shown in Table 1. We can observe that a BKW partitioning of the graph yields better completion times in almost all cases, with the exception being the TRIANGLE COUNTING algorithm, when applied to the powerlaw graph. The TRIANGLE COUNTING is not an iterative algorithm like the others and consists of just two steps of computation. As a consequence it performs communication only one time, hence the advantages of a BKW partitioner are not evident.

4.2. Static Partitioning, Real Graphs

This experiment measured the completion time of three algorithms: CRACKER, PAGER-ANK and KCORE. For conducting the experiment we considered two real graphs: the Youtube social network and the road of Texas[2]. All the values are computed considering the average of six independent runs. From the results shown in Figure 1, we can conclude what follows. First, using HASH the completion time is almost always greater than when

---

[2]both graphs have been taken from `snap.standford.edu`

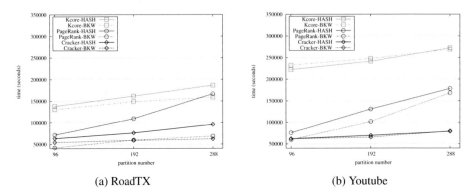

(a) RoadTX   (b) Youtube

Figure 1. Execution time with various static partitioning strategies

using BKW for all the algorithms considered. Interestingly, the difference is smaller for the Youtube social network. In the road network dataset by nature a lot of nodes have degree equals to 1 or 2 and also the maximum vertex degree is in the order of tens. Due to this a BKW partitioner is able to cut a smaller amount of edges with respect to a social network graph. This results in the majority of the computation not requiring communication between different partitions. Second, the biggest improvement from HASH to BKW is obtained with PAGERANK, due to its communication pattern. In PAGERANK all the nodes communicate with their neighbours at every iteration. Therefore, a partitioning of the nodes according to the topology of the graph reduces the inter-partition communications, which in turns reduces the completion time. The third aspect worth noticing is the fact that an increased number of partitions leads to worse the performances. In principle, an higher number of partitions is beneficial as it would allow the scheduler for a better allocation of the load on the workers. However, the increased costs in term of inter-partition communications is dominant and, as a consequence it leads to a longer completion time.

4.3. Dynamic Partitioning

In order to evaluate the performances that the dynamic partitioning could achieve, we set up an experiment in which we compare the performance of the CRACKER algorithm when adopting the HASH strategy against the performance it achieves with DESC and SWAP dynamic partitioners. The experiment has been conducted using the graph representing the road of California, taken from the SNAP repository maintained by the Stanford University[3]. This graph consists of around 2 million nodes and 2.7 million edges, with a large connected component that includes almost all the nodes of the whole graph. The results are presented in Figure 2. The SWAP strategy yields slightly better results than the HASH dynamic partitioner, as it successfully reallocates active nodes among the workers. However, we believe that this behaviour is only beneficial when executing algorithms that do not reactivate previously deactivated nodes and in which the rate of deactivation is relatively steady. Both characteristics match with the behaviour of CRACKER. By comparisons, the DESC strategy has basically the same performances that HASH, as

---

[3]snap.stanford.edu

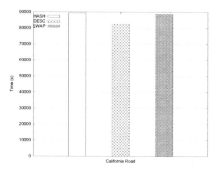

Figure 2. Comparison of the dynamic partitioners when executing CRACKER

it takes a longer time to reallocate, as in CRACKER the label of the nodes change continuously.

5. Conclusion

In this paper we conducted an analysis focusing on the adoption of partitioning strategies supporting BigData graph computations. The analysis was conducted by measuring the impact of both static and dynamic partitioning approaches on several different algorithms, working on data structured as a graph. Our work especially focused on the impact of different partitioning strategies when applied to BSP-like computational frameworks. In particular our investigation focused on Apache Spark, one of the most widely used distributed framework targeting BigData computations. From the result obtained, we observed that a carefully chosen partitioning strategy can lead to an improvement in the computational performances, both with static and dynamic partitioning. As a future work, we plan to implement more elaborate strategy dynamic partitioning, and to experiment with them in larger graphs.

References

[1] Andrew McAfee, Erik Brynjolfsson, Thomas H Davenport, DJ Patil, and Dominic Barton. Big data. *The management revolution. Harvard Bus Rev*, 90(10):61–67, 2012.
[2] Dean Jeffrey and Ghemawat Sanjay. Mapreduce: Simplified data processing on large clusters. *Communication ACM*, 1, 2008.
[3] Murray Cole. *Algorithmic skeletons.* Springer, 1999.
[4] Marco Aldinucci, Marco Danelutto, and Patrizio Dazzi. Muskel: an expandable skeleton environment. *Scalable Computing: Practice and Experience*, 8(4), 2007.
[5] Marco Danelutto and Patrizio Dazzi. A java/jini framework supporting stream parallel computations. 2005.
[6] M. Leyton and J.M. Piquer. Skandium: Multi-core programming with algorithmic skeletons. In *Parallel, Distributed and Network-Based Processing (PDP), 2010 18th Euromicro International Conference on*, pages 289–296, Feb 2010.
[7] Herbert Kuchen. *A skeleton library.* Springer, 2002.
[8] Marco Danelutto, Marcelo Pasin, Marco Vanneschi, Patrizio Dazzi, Domenico Laforenza, and Luigi Presti. Pal: exploiting java annotations for parallelism. In *Achievements in European Research on Grid Systems*, pages 83–96. Springer US, 2008.

[9]   Leslie G Valiant. A bridging model for parallel computation. *Communications of the ACM*, 33(8):103–111, 1990.

[10] Robert Ryan McCune, Tim Weninger, and Greg Madey. Thinking like a vertex: a survey of vertex-centric frameworks for large-scale distributed graph processing.

[11] Joseph E. Gonzalez, Reynold S. Xin, Ankur Dave, Daniel Crankshaw, Michael J. Franklin, and Ion Stoica. Graphx: Graph processing in a distributed dataflow framework. In *11th USENIX Symposium on Operating Systems Design and Implementation, OSDI '14, Broomfield, CO, USA, October 6-8, 2014.*, pages 599–613, 2014.

[12] Lawrence Page, Sergey Brin, Rajeev Motwani, and Terry Winograd. The pagerank citation ranking: bringing order to the web. 1999.

[13] Siddharth Suri and Sergei Vassilvitskii. Counting triangles and the curse of the last reducer. In *Proceedings of the 20th International Conference on World Wide Web, WWW 2011, Hyderabad, India, March 28 - April 1, 2011*, pages 607–614, 2011.

[14] Alberto Montresor, Franscesco De Pellegrini, and Daniele Miorandi. Distributed k-core decomposition. *IEEE Trans. Parallel Distrib. Syst.*, 24(2):288–300, 2013.

[15] Vibhor Rastogi, Ashwin Machanavajjhala, Laukik Chitnis, and Akash Das Sarma. Finding connected components in map-reduce in logarithmic rounds. In *Data Engineering (ICDE), 2013 IEEE 29th International Conference on*, pages 50–61. IEEE, 2013.

[16] Alessandro Lulli, Laura Ricci, Emanuele Carlini, Patrizio Dazzi, and Claudio Lucchese. Cracker: Crumbling large graphs into connected components. In *20th IEEE Symposium on Computers and Communication (ISCC) (ISCC2015)*, Larnaca, Cyprus, July 2015.

[17] Matei Zaharia, Mosharaf Chowdhury, Michael J Franklin, Scott Shenker, and Ion Stoica. Spark: cluster computing with working sets. In *Proceedings of the 2nd USENIX conference on Hot topics in cloud computing*, volume 10, page 10, 2010.

[18] Fatemeh Rahimian, Amir H Payberah, Sarunas Girdzijauskas, Mark Jelasity, and Seif Haridi. Ja-be-ja: A distributed algorithm for balanced graph partitioning. In *Self-Adaptive and Self-Organizing Systems (SASO), 2013 IEEE 7th International Conference on*, pages 51–60. IEEE, 2013.

[19] Emanuele Carlini, Patrizio Dazzi, Andrea Esposito, Alessandro Lulli, and Laura Ricci. Balanced graph partitioning with apache spark. In *Euro-Par 2014: Parallel Processing Workshops*, pages 129–140. Springer, 2014.

[20] Charalampos Tsourakakis, Christos Gkantsidis, Bozidar Radunovic, and Milan Vojnovic. Fennel: Streaming graph partitioning for massive scale graphs. In *Proceedings of the 7th ACM international conference on Web search and data mining*, pages 333–342. ACM, 2014.

[21] Isabelle Stanton and Gabriel Kliot. Streaming graph partitioning for large distributed graphs. In *Proceedings of the 18th ACM SIGKDD international conference on Knowledge discovery and data mining*, pages 1222–1230. ACM, 2012.

[22] George Karypis and Vipin Kumar. Multilevel graph partitioning schemes. In *ICPP (3)*, pages 113–122, 1995.

[23] Semih Salihoglu and Jennifer Widom. Gps: A graph processing system. In *Proceedings of the 25th International Conference on Scientific and Statistical Database Management*, page 22. ACM, 2013.

[24] Shadi Ibrahim, Hai Jin, Lu Lu, Song Wu, Bingsheng He, and Li Qi. Leen: Locality/fairness-aware key partitioning for mapreduce in the cloud. In *Cloud Computing Technology and Science (CloudCom), 2010 IEEE Second International Conference on*, pages 17–24. IEEE, 2010.

[25] Yingxia Shao, Junjie Yao, Bin Cui, and Lin Ma. Page: A partition aware graph computation engine. In *Proceedings of the 22nd ACM international conference on Conference on information & knowledge management*, pages 823–828. ACM, 2013.

[26] Brandon Amos and David Tompkins. Performance study of spindle, a web analytics query engine implemented in spark. In *Cloud Computing Technology and Science (CloudCom), 2014 IEEE 6th International Conference on*, pages 505–510. IEEE, 2014.

[27] Matei Zaharia, Mosharaf Chowdhury, Tathagata Das, Ankur Dave, Justin Ma, Murphy McCauley, Michael J Franklin, Scott Shenker, and Ion Stoica. Resilient distributed datasets: A fault-tolerant abstraction for in-memory cluster computing. In *Proceedings of the 9th USENIX conference on Networked Systems Design and Implementation*, pages 2–2. USENIX Association, 2012.

[28] Jure Leskovec and Rok Sosič. SNAP: A general purpose network analysis and graph mining library in C++. http://snap.stanford.edu/snap, June 2014.

Mini-Symposium:
ParaFPGA-2015: Parallel Computing with FPGAs

Parallel Computing: On the Road to Exascale
G.R. Joubert et al. (Eds.)
IOS Press, 2016
doi:10.3233/978-1-61499-621-7-501

ParaFPGA15: Exploring threads and trends in programmable hardware

Erik H. D'Hollander[a,1] , Dirk Stroobandt[a] and Abdellah Touhafi[b]

[a] *ELIS department, Ghent University, Belgium*
[b] *ETRO department, Vrije Universiteit Brussel, Belgium*

Abstract. The symposium ParaFPGA focuses on parallel techniques using FPGAs as accelerator in high performance computing. The green computing aspects of low power consumption at high performance were somewhat tempered by long design cycles and hard programmability issues. However, in recent years FPGAs have become new contenders as versatile compute accelerators because of a growing market interest, extended application domains and maturing high-level synthesis tools. The keynote paper highlights the historical and modern approaches to high-level FPGA programming and the contributions cover applications such as NP-complete satisfiability problems and convex hull image processing as well as performance evaluation, partial reconfiguration and systematic design exploration.

Keywords. FPGA performance, high-level synthesis, OpenCL, functional programming, satisfiability problem, image processing

Introduction

After hyping expectations on the role of FPGAs in high performance and low power computing, data centers, internet of things, streaming applications, accelerators and extensions, there is a general consensus that a lot of work needs to be done. FPGAs in SoC and datacenters are on the downward slide in Gartner's hype cycle but the same company hints that a significant research effort is underway to optimize the productivity and acceptance in promising application domains [1]. At the same time, FPGAs evolve in speed and complexity to programmable processing systems with an integrated logic fabric and specialized IP cores. In addition, the major vendors have gone long strides to accelerate the design cycle with high level synthesis tools and standardized languages such as OpenCL. This makes the FPGA arena a prosperous playfield for research and innovation. The fifth edition of ParaFPGA, Parallel Computing with FPGAs, follows this trend with papers covering NP-hard problems, image processing, high-level synthesis and heterogeneous computing.

1. Contributions

The keynote paper "*FPGAs as Components in Heterogeneous High-Performance Computing Systems: Raising the Abstraction Level*" [2] discusses the historical

---

[1] Corresponding Author. E-mail: erik.dhollander@elis.ugent.be

initiatives and trends in high level synthesis over the three ages of FPGAs. In order to maintain correctness and productivity, HLS languages should have an affine mapping onto the hardware components. The author advocates a functional language paradigm to express parallel and pipelining operations in an implicit and effective way. While OpenCL is a viable alternative because of its cross platform compatibility, the compute model behind this language foregoes the inherent coarse-grain pipelining capabilities of FPGAs [3].

FPGAs are well fit for 7 non-numerical problems defined in the 13 dwarfs prototype paradigms for parallel computing — a dwarf is an algorithmic method that captures a pattern of computation and communication [4]. Two symposium papers deal with the NP-complete Boolean satisfiability (SAT) problem of the branch and bound dwarf. The first paper "*FPGA Acceleration of SAT Preprocessor*" [5] implements a new branch and bound technique, "unhiding", to reduce the search space and to simplify the Boolean SAT-formula. To this end a binary implication graph (BIG) is generated from the dependencies between the literals. The literals visited during the graph traversal receive several "time stamps" to identify their ordering with respect to several characteristics. Using time stamps it is possible to find tautologies between the clauses. "Unhiding" means detecting and removing these tautologies. The implementation of the unhiding-algorithm on a Kintex FPGA is discussed. Ample parallelism is available in huge formulas with $O(10^6)$ clauses and variables, however due to marginal benefits, the parallelism deployed is limited to 16.

In the second paper on satisfiability, "*Leveraging FPGA clusters for SAT computations*" [6], a cluster of 200 FPGAs is used to find van der Waerden numbers. A van der Waerden number $W(K,L)$ is the smallest integer n such that if the positive consecutive integers $\{1,2,...,n\}$ are partitioned into K classes, then at least one class contains an arithmetic progression of length L, i.e. sequence $\{a, a + d, a + 2d, ..., a + (L - 1)d\}$ for some integers a and d. Earlier development was done on a Beowulf cluster [7]. In order to speed up the computation, a Beowulf cluster is replaced by a cluster of FPGA boards, containing 4 FPGAs, each capable to solve 2 computation tasks. Using dynamic task assignment on 400 solvers, new van der Waerden numbers have been identified in a time frame from 6 to 9 months. The paper describes the hardware and software setup of this application.

Image processing tends to be suited for GPU acceleration. Nevertheless, for applications with a streamlined data access pattern and irregular computations, FPGAs may be an interesting alternative. A case in point is the paper "*High-Speed Calculation of Convex Hull in 2D Images Using FPGA*" [8] where a fast bounding box calculation algorithm is described for 640x480 as well as 1920x1080 monochrome images. Andrew's monotone chain algorithm [9] operates on a stream of sorted input pixels, by repeatedly evaluating the convexity using he incoming points and incrementally building the convex hull. In the FPGA, a "trimming step" calculator eliminates redundant pixels. Next, left- and right half-hull are calculated in parallel and merged into the complete convex hull. The algorithm is I/O bound for small images and compute bound for large images. In the GPU implementation the trimming and partial convex hull calculations do not overlap. As a consequence the FPGA implementation yields a speedup boost of up to 23 times with respect to the GPU implementation. The validity of the technique is shown in a surface-mounted device detection application.

Accelerators are commonplace in today's HPC environment. Still, providing a common programming language to efficiently use architecturally different accelerators such as FPGAs and GPUs is quite a challenge. In "*Workload Distribution and*

Balancing in FPGAs and CPUs with OpenCL and TBB" [10] different accelerator topologies are used to compute the components of a sliding window object detection algorithm (filter, histogram, classifier). Interestingly, all accelerators are programmed with the same OpenCL source code. In the application test case, the accelerators show comparable performance, but the FPGAs have substantially lower power consumption. The results of this experiment demonstrate that one standard parallel programming language may be able to close the semantic gap between accelerators, hindering unbridled use of heterogeneous computing.

The time to load FPGA designs remains expensive. This can be alleviated by partial reconfiguration, which allows sharing computing resources between related tasks. Still a framework is needed to operate dynamic task switching from the connected CPU. The paper *"A Run-Time System for Partially Reconfigurable FPGAs: The case of STMicroelectronics SPEAr board"*[11] describes the experience gained with a development board connecting a Virtex-5 FPGA accelerator daughter board and an ARM Cortex A9 dual-core processor. A run-time system manager is presented which schedules software and hardware tasks, including dynamic reconfiguration of the FPGA. The benefits and possible improvements of the architecture are explored with a hardware Ray Tracer application running on the accelerator in parallel with a software edge detection application running on the processor.

In contrast with accelerators having a fixed architecture, the performance of an FPGA largely depends on the way the hardware is used. This entails exploring the reconfigurable design landscape to maximize the performance and minimize the resource usage. In the paper *"Exploring Automatically Generated Platforms in High Performance FPGAs"* [12] a number of heuristics are presented to guide the selection of memories, bus structures and interfaces. These guidelines are then applied to an image processing and a Monte Carlo simulation application. Experimental results show that employing these rules allows to systematically improve the design.

2. Acknowledgement

The organizers of ParaFPGA15 thank the members of the program committee who provided timely and elaborated reviews helping to maintain the scope and quality of this symposium.

References

[1] M. Reitz, "Competitive Landscape: FPGA Vendors Closing in on ASICs, ASSPs, the IoT and Security as Chip Costs Rise, 2014," Gartner, G00263185, Oct. 2014.

[2] W. Vanderbauwhede, "FPGAs as Components in Heterogeneous High-Performance Computing Systems: Raising the Abstraction Level," in *Proceedings of the conference Parallel Computing 2015, Edinburgh, Series Advances in Parallel Computing, Vol. 27, IOS Press*, 2015.

[3] H.-S. Kim, M. Ahn, J. A. Stratton, and W. W. Hwu, "Design evaluation of OpenCL compiler framework for Coarse-Grained Reconfigurable Arrays," in *Field-Programmable Technology (FPT), 2012 International Conference on*, 2012, pp. 313–320.

[4] K. Asanovic, R. Bodik, B. C. Catanzaro, J. J. Gebis, P. Husbands, K. Keutzer, D. A. Patterson, W. L. Plishker, J. Shalf, S. W. Williams, and others, "The landscape of parallel computing research: A view from Berkeley," Technical Report UCB/EECS-2006-183, EECS Department, University of California, Berkeley, 2006.

[5]   M. Suzuki and T. Maruyama, "FPGA Acceleration of SAT Preprocessor," in *Proceedings of the conference Parallel Computing 2015, Edinburgh, Series Advances in Parallel Computing, Vol. 27, IOS Press.*

[6]   M. Kouril, "Leveraging FPGA clusters for SAT computations," in *Proceedings of the conference Parallel Computing 2015, Edinburgh, Series Advances in Parallel Computing, Vol. 27, IOS Press,* 2015.

[7]   M. Kouril, "A Backtracking Framework for Beowulf Clusters with an Extension to Multi-cluster Computation and Sat Benchmark Problem Implementation," University of Cincinnati, Cincinnati, OH, USA, 2006.

[8]   K. Kanazawa, K. Kemmotsu, Y. Mori, N. Aibe, and M. Yasuanga, "High-Speed Calculation of Convex Hull in 2D Images Using FPGA," in *Proceedings of the conference Parallel Computing 2015, Edinburgh, Series Advances in Parallel Computing, Vol. 27, IOS Press,* 2015.

[9]   A. M. Andrew, "Another efficient algorithm for convex hulls in two dimensions," *Inf. Process. Lett.,* vol. 9, no. 5, pp. 216–219, 1979.

[10]   R. Asenjo, A. Navarro, A. Rodriguez, and J. Nunez-Yanez, "Workload distribution and balancing in FPGAs and CPUs with OpenCL and TBB," in *Proceedings of the conference Parallel Computing 2015, Edinburgh, Series Advances in Parallel Computing, Vol. 27, IOS Press,* 2015.

[11]   G. Charitopoulos, D. Pnevmatikos, M. D. Santambrogio, K. Papadimitriou, and D. Pau, "A Run-Time System for Partially Reconfigurable FPGAs: The case of STMicroelectronics SPEAr board," in *Proceedings of the conference Parallel Computing 2015, Edinburgh, Series Advances in Parallel Computing, Vol. 27, IOS Press,* 2015.

[12]   P. Skrimponis, G. Zindros, I. Parnassos, M. Owaida, N. Bellas, and P. Ienne, "Exploring Automatically Generated   Platforms in High Performance FPGAs," in *Proceedings of the conference Parallel Computing 2015, Edinburgh, Series Advances in Parallel Computing, Vol. 27, IOS Press,* 2015.

Parallel Computing: On the Road to Exascale
G.R. Joubert et al. (Eds.)
IOS Press, 2016
doi:10.3233/978-1-61499-621-7-505

FPGAs as Components in Heterogeneous High-Performance Computing Systems: Raising the Abstraction Level

Wim VANDERBAUWHEDE [a,1] and Syed Waqar NABI [a]

[a] School of Computing Science, University of Glasgow

Abstract. We present an overview of the evolution of programming techniques for Field-Programmable Gate Arrays (FPGAs), with a particular focus on High-Level Synthesis (HLS) and Heterogeneous Computing (HC), and we argue that, in the context of High-Performance Computing (HPC), FPGAs should be treated as components of a larger heterogeneous compute platform. Consequently, HLS and HC tools become compilation targets rather than high-level development tools. Compiler technology has to evolve to automatically create the best compiled program variant by transforming a given original program. We describe our methodology based on type transformations and cost models, which allows to automatically generate correct-by-construction program variants and accurately estimate their performance, so that an optimal program can be constructed by the compilation system.

Keywords. High-level Programming for FPGAs, Functional Programming, High Performance Computing, Scientific Computing, Compiler Techniques.

Introduction

FPGAs have come an long way from their inception in the early 1980s as an alternative to ASICs without the high upfront non-recurring engineering (NRE) costs, to their current stature and status as a distinct platform with its own unique properties and selling points. We trace this journey from a programming perspective, with a particular focus on the application of FPGAs in High-Performance Computing and data centres. For a more generic and technology-focused review of FPGA history we refer the reader to the excellent overview paper "Three Ages of FPGAs" by Stephen Trimberger [1].

We argue that what could effectively be called a Fourth Age of FPGAs has already started: FPGAs have become components in heterogeneous compute platforms, and that this new stage requires another radical evolution in the programming approach – we are no longer programming FPGAs but heterogeneous systems. The complexity of both the systems and the applications is such that it is no longer realistic to expect the programmer to achieve optimal performance by manually partitioning the program and handcraft an optimal version of each sub-program for its target component in the heterogeneous system. Instead, the compilation tools and runtime systems must perform this task for us. To do so they build on the developments in High-Level Synthesis and Heterogeneous

---

[1]Corresponding Author. E-mail: wim.vanderbauwhede@glasgow.ac.uk

Programming: effectively, the languages that are the high-level input languages for these tools become the compilation targets.

In this paper we present our work on automatic, correct-by-construction program transformation using a novel approach based on type transformations, and its application to FPGA programming. We show that through a combination of automatic generation of program variants and an accurate FPGA cost model, it is possible to generate and select the optimal version of a given program for the target architecture.

1. A Trip Down Memory Lane

In this section we trace the historic evolution of FPGA computing starting from the theoretical basis of computation, through the foundations of computers and ICs, the advent of FPGAs and the advance in their technology and programming techniques, up to the current state of the art.

1.1. The Theory

In the 1930 a lot of fundamental research was carried out on the nature of computation, resulting from the challenge posed in 1928 by David Hilbert, known as the *Entscheidungsproblem* (German for 'decision problem'). The Entscheidungsproblem asks for an algorithm to decide whether a given statement is provable from the basic axioms using the given rules of logic. In 1936, Alan Turing published his Universal Machine [2] (which can be considered as an abstract stored-program machine) and showed that a general solution to the Entscheidungsproblem is impossible. In that same year, Alonzo Church came to the same conclusion via a very different route, the lambda calculus, a formal system for expressing computation based on function abstraction and application [3]. Also in 1936, Kondrad Zuse introduced what was essentially the stored-program computer in the patents for his Z3 machine [4]. In 1937, Turing showed that the Universal Machine and the lambda calculus are equivalent, a result known as the "Church-Turing thesis". In 1945, John Von Neumann proposed his eponymous architecture. The stored-program architecture led to a long line of imperative, memory-based programming languages intended for sequential execution. The interesting observation is that the lambda calculus originated at the same time, but the functional languages for which it forms the basis have been mostly ignored, at least in industry – until recently.

1.1.1. The Foundations

The decades after the second world war saw the invention and rapid evolution of many of the crucial foundations of today's computer technologies. In 1958, Jack Kilby prototyped the first integrated circuit and only a few years later, in 1965, Gordon Moore made the observation now know generally as "Moore's Law" [5].[2]

Meanwhile, the first real programming languages had appeared. In 1957, before the first IC or microprocessor, John Backus created Fortran, and in 1958, John McCarthy designed LISP; in 1972, Dennis Ritchie created C. In 1977, the Fortran-77 standard was

---

[2]It is interesting to note that today, Moore's Law is usually illustrated using the evolution of microprocessors, but the first microprocessor was only developed in 1971.

released; in 1978, Kernighan and Ritchie published "The C Programming Language" which became the de-facto standard until the ANSI C standard appeared.

Also in 1977, the same John Backus warned during his famous Turing Award lecture [6] about the "von Neumann bottleneck", and advocated a functional style of programming. In 1973 Robin Milner at Edinburgh University had created ML, a functional programming language based on the lambda calculus, and Backus indeed referred to this work in his speech.

However, C and Fortran became popular, and as processor speed and memory capacity grew steadily, there appeared to be no need to heed Backus's warning: with every new generation, single-threaded, imperative programs ran faster without any additional effort.

1.1.2. Hardware Description Languages and FPGAs

With the growth in complexity of ICs, by the 1980s the need for better design tools became acute. In 1981, the US DoD initiated a programme to address the issue, resulting in the development of VHDL. In 1984, Prabhu Goel and Phil Moorby developed the Verilog HDL; in 1987, the VHDL Standard IEEE 1076-1987 was released, followed by the Verilog HDL Standard IEEE 1364-1995. It is interesting to look at the motivation for these languages: the expressed rationale for VHDL was to create a language with a wide range of descriptive capability that was independent of technology or design methodology [7]. Over the next two decades these HDLs grew in popularity but unfortunately not in capability, while the size and complexity made possible by each new generation of CMOS technology grew according to the diktat of Moore's law.

The 1980s also saw the advent of the first reprogrammable logic devices and FPGAs, originally intended as rapid prototyping platforms for ASIC design. The first commercial FPGA (Xilinx XC2064) had 1200 logic cells. Following the same trend as the rest of the semiconductor industry, FPGA grew steadily in size and complexity, incorporating other components besides LUTs, such as memory units and DSP or ALU blocks.

Because of this growth in complexity and size, by the end of the 20th century, both ASIC and FPGA design was about to reach a new impasse: the design productivity gap.

1.1.3. High-Level Synthesis

In his paper "Why the design productivity gap never happened" [8], HD Foster writes

> "In 1997, SEMATECH set off an alarm in the industry when it warned that productivity gains related to IC manufacturing capabilities (which increased at about 40% per year) outpaced the productivity gains in IC design capabilities (which increased at about 20% per year).

This observation, which became known as the design productivity gap, was the main motivation behind High-Level Synthesis, colloquially known as "C-to-Gates". Already in 1996, Oxford University had developed Handel-C , and its release was followed by a spate of new High-Level Synthesis languages in the past 15 years. Without being exhaustive we mention Mitrion-C, Bluespec, MaxJ, Impulse-C, Catapult C, AutoPilot (now Vivado), DIME-C and more recently University of Toronto's LegUp and Microsoft's Catapult. A more comprehensive list can be found in our book [9]; the list simply serves to illustrate the need for these languages, but also the fact that they result in a way in a return to the situation before HDLs were standardised: a very wide variety of incompatible approaches. We will discuss High-Level Synthesis in more detail in Section 2.

1.1.4. Heterogeneous Computing

Meanwhile, another trend in technology evolution was about to end: processor frequency scaling. In 2005, Herb Sutter wrote his now famous article that coined the phrase "The Free Lunch Is Over" [10]. In this article he pointed out that with the end of frequency scaling, processor manufacturers were turing to multicore architectures, an observation that was of course already widely recognised in academia.

Around the same time, the technology until then known as "graphics cards" achieved sufficient maturity to become Graphics Processing Units, and with that came the start of a new trend, Heterogeneous Computing. In 2007, Nvidia released CUDA to allow C-based programming of their GPUs, and in 2009 Apple developed OpenCL, an open-standard framework for writing programs that execute across heterogeneous platforms. Since then, a wide variety of architectures such as GPUs, Intel's Many Integrated Cores and indeed FPGAs, support the OpenCL standard.

2. Approaches to High-Level FPGA Programming

Despite being known usually as "C-to-Gates", there is a wide variety of HLS approaches, both in terms of syntax and their programming model. The following discussion aims to illustrate commonalities and differences, and to discuss the suitability of HLS tools for High-Performance Computing.

2.1. Handel-C and Bluespec SystemVerilog

Handel-C [11] is a synchronous programming language, it builds synchronous circuits using global clocks. Its abstractions operate at the level of simple transformations on data and movement of data between variables that map to registers. Parallelism can be explicitly defined using the *par* construct. The language has C-like syntax but the semantics follow Hoare's Communicating sequential processes (CSP) paradigm [12].

Bluespec SystemVerilog (BSV) [13] specifies a modules behaviour using a collection of rules, which describe the conditions to take an action and the effects of the action on the state. In other words, BSV provides a high-abstraction-level FSM design mechanism incorporated into SystemVerilog.

Both languages are actually low-level languages, quite close to HDLs, and in terms of their abstraction level better suited for embedded systems design than High-Performance Computing.

2.2. Impulse-C, DIME-C, Vivado and LegUp

There are many approaches that are a closer fit to the "C-to-Gates" than the previous ones, in the sense that they actually aim to provide synthesis from a restricted subset of C. In the case of Impulse-C, this is augmented using a CSP-based stream API; both approaches provides pragmas to control the synthesis behaviour, but unlike Handel-C they do not provide an explicit *par* construct. DIME-C and Impulse-C were designed with embedded systems design in mind, but the streaming paradigm of Impulse-C makes it suitable for higher-level applications programming, DIME-C has actually been used to program the Maxwell FPGA supercomputer [14] and Impulse-C does support a wide range of HPC platforms. From an HPC perspective, both approaches are suitable but mainly lack convenient constructs for parallelisation across multiple instances.

Vivado HLS started out as AutoPilot in 2006. Its main distinctive feature is that it supports compilation from C/C++. It claims to have very few restrictions on the code, however, similar to e.g. DIME-C and Impulse-C, it provides specific pragma's and API calls without which it is not possible to achieve good performance. Vivado now supports OpenCL but in fact Xilinx targets Vivado more at embedded systems design than High-Performance Computing, because it has a separate OpenCL solution, SDAccel.

LegUp [15] is an open source HLS tool that "allows software techniques to be used for hardware design". LegUp accepts a standard C program as input and automatically compiles the program to a hybrid architecture containing an FPGA-based MIPS soft processor and custom hardware accelerators that communicate through a standard bus interface. As a consequence of this approach, which prioritises easy of use over performance, LegUp is not primarily intended for HPC applications.

2.3. MaxJ

Maxeler's MaxJ [16] language is a Java-based dataflow programming language. The FPGA design is built up using Java objects such as streams, kernels, multiplexers, etc which allow to build coarse-grain dataflow pipelines. It is relatively high level but still offers sufficient level of control over the implementation. The compiler automatically addresses fine pipelining of the floating point arithmetic units, and the resulting implementation includes auto generated flow control and buffering on the streams interconnecting kernels as well as interfaces to the host CPU and on-board memory. As such, this approach is much more suited to HPC applications than any of the previous ones.

2.4. Mitrion-C

Like MaxJ, Mitrion-C [17] is a dataflow programming language, but it is strongly influenced by functional programming languages such as Haskell [18] or Single-Assignment C (SAC) [19]. Mitrion-C provides streams as first-class language objects; its semantics are based on single assignment and its stream processing is similar to the *map/fold* list operations in Haskell or SAC's *with*-loop array operations. Because of its functional semantics, Mitrion-C did not acquire the same popularity as other C-to-Gates languages, but it is of interest as the language that comes closest to the approach we advocate in Section 5.

3. Heterogeneous Programming and FPGAs

Accelerators attached to host systems (GPUs, manycores such as Intel's Xeon Phi and FPGAs) are becoming increasingly popular. A number of languages and frameworks are available to program these *heterogeneous* platforms, i.e. platforms consisting of a host processor and one or more accelerators, e.g. CUDA, OpenCL, C++ AMP, MaxJ. Of these, only OpenCL is an open standard.

The starting point for all these approaches is that the programmer must decide which part of the host program to offload to the accelerator, then writes the host code for data movement and control of the accelerator using a dedicated API and the actual accelerator code using a dedicated language. In that sense they are actually similar to many of the HLS languages, especially those used for HPC. Consequently, HLS tool developers have been able to leverage their considerable expertise to support OpenCL.[3]

Typically, heterogeneous programming frameworks assume data parallelism for the accelerator workload: each kernel is single-threaded and works on a portion of the data. The programmer must identify these portions and the amount of parallelism. This model is not ideal for FPGAs because it does not allow to express coarse-grained dataflow pipelines. As a result of their adoption for FPGA programming, recent OpenCL specifications have kernel pipes allowing construction such pipelines.

The main advantage of OpenCL in particular is that it allows the same code to be deployed on different platforms. This has allowed researchers to demonstrate the advantage of FPGAs in terms of energy efficiency for a wide range of HPC applications.

4. FPGAs as Components in Heterogeneous Systems

Modern HPC clusters have heterogeneous nodes with GPUs, MICs and increasingly FPGAs. However, HPC workloads typically have a very complex codebase, frequently developed for clusters of single-core systems or – at best – homogeneous multicore systems. For example, the Weather Research and Forecasting Model, the most popular open source model used in weather and climate research, is written in Fortran-90 with support for MPI and OpenMP, and counts over one million lines of code. Parts of the codebase (a few thousands of lines) have been accelerated manually on GPUs. Changing the entire codebase for a GPU/MIC/FPGA system would be a huge task, and the result would not be portable.

Apart from the complexity of manually porting a weather simulator to FPGAs, there is also the question of the optimal partitioning of the code: FPGAs are good at some tasks, e.g. bit level, integer and string operations, pipeline parallelism rather than data parallelism, streaming dataflow computations; but not so good at others, e.g. double-precision floating point computations and random memory access computations, for which resp. GPUs and modern manycores are much better suited. For complex HPC applications, no single device will be optimal for the whole codebase. So we need to be able to split the codebase *automatically* over the different components in the heterogeneous system.

Therefore, it has become necessary to once again raise the abstraction level, this time beyond heterogeneous programming and high-level synthesis. Device-specific high-level abstraction is no longer appropriate. And although OpenCL is relatively high-level and in principle device-independent, it is far from performance-portable, requiring effectively different code for different devices. Therefore, we argue that high-level synthesis languages and heterogeneous programming frameworks should become compilation targets, just as assembly languages and HDLs have become compilation targets.

5. Automatic Program Transformations and Cost models

Our proposed flow (Figure 1) raises the programming abstraction for FPGAs such that we can express the design in a functional language like Idris [20] or Haskell. This func-

---

[3]The restrictions on the OpenCL kernel language were originally motivated by GPU architectures, but they are essentially the same as those of the HLS tools.

tional abstraction enables *type transformation* that reshape the data and allows to derive a new program variant that is *correct-by-construction*. This transformation effectively creates a new design variant. A light-weight cost-model allows evaluation of multiple design variants, opening the route to a fully automated compiler that can generate variants, evaluate them, choose the best option, and generate HDL code for FPGA targets.

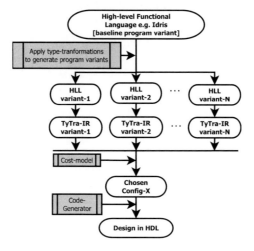

Figure 1. The TyTra design flow. Design entry can be in a functional language like Idris, variants can be generated using type transformations and converted to the TyTra IR. Our prototype back-end compiler automatically costs the variants and emits HDL code.

5.1. Exemplar: Successive Over-Relaxation

We consider an SOR kernel, taken from the code for the Large Eddy Simulator, an experimental weather simulator [21]. The kernel iteratively solves the Poisson equation for the pressure. The main computation is a stencil over the neighbouring cells (which is inherently parallel), and a reduction to compute the remaining error (not shown).

We express the algorithm in a functional language (Idris) using higher order functions to describe array operations. The baseline implementation will be:

```
ps = map  p_sor  pps
```

where *pps* is a function that will take the original vectors *p, rhs, cn** and return a single new vector of size *im.jm.km*, where each elements is a tuple consisting of all terms required to compute the SOR. *p_sor* computes the new value for the pressure for a given input tuple from *pps*:

```
p_sor pt = reltmp + p_c
where
(p_i_p1,...,p_c,rhs_c) = pt
reltmp = omega * (cn1 * (
    cn2l_x * p_i_p1 + cn2s_x * p_i_m1
  + cn3l_x * p_j_p1 + cn3s_x * p_j_m1
  + cn4l_x * p_k_p1 + cn4s_x * p_k_m1 )
  - rhs_c) - p_c
```

Our main purpose is to generate variants by transforming the *type* of the functions making up the program and *inferring* the program transformations from the type transformation. The details and proofs of the type transformations are available in [22]. In brief, we reshape the vector in an order-preserving manner and infer the corresponding program that produces the same result. Each reshaped vector in a variant translates to a different arrangement of streams. We then use our cost-model to choose the best design.

As an illustration, assume that the type of the 1D-vector is *t* and its size *im.jm.km*, which we can *transform* into e.g. a 2-D vector with sizes *im.jm* and *km*:

```
pps : Vect  (im*jm*km)  t        --1D vector
ppst: Vect  km  (Vect  im*jm  t) --transformed 2D vector
```

Resulting in a corresponding change in the program:

```
ps = map  p_sor  pps            --original program

ppst = reshapeTo  km  pps       --reshaping data
pst  = map  (map  p_sor)  ppst --new program
```

where *map p_sor* is an example of partial application. Because *ppst* is a vector of vectors, the outer map takes a vector and applies the function *map p_sor* to this vector. This transformation results in a reshaping of the original streams into parallel lanes of streams, implying a configuration of parallel kernel pipelines in the FPGA.

5.2. Design Variant Evaluation using a Cost Model

The target IR language for our compiler, the TyTra-IR, has been designed specifically to allow generation of estimates of reasonable accuracy to evaluate trade-offs of design variants. We have discussed the IR and the cost-model in [23].

The TyTra Back-end Compiler (TyBEC) calculates these estimates from the IR without any further synthesis: the throughput estimate, the host/memory bandwidth, and the resource utilisation for a specific FPGA device. Our throughput performance measure is *EWGT (Effective Work-Group Throughput)*, defined as the number of times an entire work-group (the loop over index-space) of a kernel is executed every second.

Figure 2 shows evaluation of variants generated by reshaping the input streams and costing the corresponding IR description. For maximum performance, we would like as many lanes of execution as the resources on the FPGA allow, or until we saturate the IO bandwidth. If data is transported between the host and device, then beyond 4 lanes, we encounter the *host communication wall*; further replication of kernel-pipeline will not improve performance unless the communication-to-computation ratio decreases by having more kernel iterations per invocation of SOR. If the all the data is made available in the device's global (on-board) memory then the communication wall moves to about 16 lanes. We encounter the *computation-wall* at six lanes, where we run out of LUTs on the FPGA. However, we can see other resources are under-utilised, and some sort of resource-balancing can lead to further performance improvement.

Our cost-model is very light-weight, and e.g. the evaluation of five variants takes a few seconds. That is orders-of-magnitude faster than e.g. the Maxeler flow that takes tens of minutes to generate preliminary estimates for one variant. A light-weight cost-

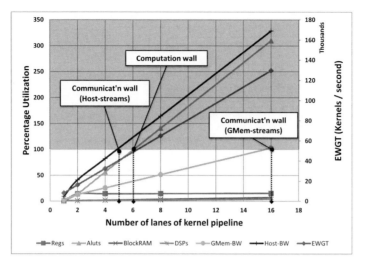

Figure 2. Evaluation of variants for the SOR kernel based on our cost-model. In this illustration, the variants are generated by changing the number of kernel-pipelines. (There are 16 data points for pressure along each dimension. We assume the kernel repeats 10 times to converge.)

model is essential for our proposed approach of automatically evaluating many design variants as part of the TyTra compiler flow. Our preliminary results show that there is some trade-off in the accuracy of our cost model, though it already gives useful information for an informed choice from the variants, as we can see from Figure 2. Our prototype backend compiler generates synthesizeable HDL code from our IR, and we are working on creating a front-end that can automatically generate design variants through type transformations of a baseline version of the kernel.

6. Conclusions

In this paper we intended to give an overview of the evolution of FPGAs as HPC platforms, and discuss the road ahead. High-Level Synthesis and Heterogeneous Programming have both been very important steps forward, and the performance that can be achieved using FPGAs is already impressive. However, we need to raise the abstraction level even more, above the current single-architecture abstractions for high-level programming. The growing complexity of both HPC applications and future HPC (exascale) platforms requires full-system compilers for heterogeneous systems, where FPGAs are merely components.

We have presented our proposed approach, based on functional languages, *type transformations* and cost models, as one possible way to achieve this goal. We have shown that we can automatically generate different correct-by-construction program variants from a given program and that our FPGA cost model is accurate enough to allow us to select the best variant of the program for our architecture. Our next steps are to use an optimisation algorithm to guide the creation and selection of the program variants, and to create cost models for other components in heterogeneous systems.

Acknowledgments   The TyTra project is funded by the UK EPSRC (EP/L00058X/1).

References

[1]   S. M. Trimberger, "Three ages of fpgas: A retrospective on the first thirty years of fpga technology," *Proceedings of the IEEE*, vol. 103, no. 3, pp. 318–331, 2015.

[2]   A. M. Turing, "On computable numbers, with an application to the entscheidungsproblem," *J. of Math*, vol. 58, no. 345-363, p. 5, 1936.

[3]   A. Church, "A set of postulates for the foundation of logic," *Annals of mathematics*, pp. 346–366, 1932.

[4]   R. Rojas, "Konrad zuse's legacy: the architecture of the z1 and z3," *Annals of the History of Computing, IEEE*, vol. 19, no. 2, pp. 5–16, 1997.

[5]   G. E. Moore *et al.*, "Cramming more components onto integrated circuits," *Proceedings of the IEEE*, vol. 86, no. 1, pp. 82–85, 1998.

[6]   J. Backus, "Can programming be liberated from the von neumann style?: A functional style and its algebra of programs," *Commun. ACM*, vol. 21, no. 8, pp. 613–641, Aug. 1978. [Online]. Available: http://doi.acm.org/10.1145/359576.359579

[7]   R. Lipsett, C. F. Schaefer, and C. Ussery, *VHDL: Hardware description and design.*   Springer Science & Business Media, 2012.

[8]   H. Foster, "Why the design productivity gap never happened," in *Computer-Aided Design (ICCAD), 2013 IEEE/ACM International Conference on*, Nov 2013, pp. 581–584.

[9]   W. Vanderbauwhede and K. Benkrid, *High-Performance Computing Using FPGAs.*   Springer, 2013.

[10] H. Sutter, "The free lunch is over: A fundamental turn toward concurrency in software," *Dr. Dobbs journal*, vol. 30, no. 3, pp. 202–210, 2005.

[11] C. Sullivan, A. Wilson, and S. Chappell, "Using c based logic synthesis to bridge the productivity gap," in *Proceedings of the 2004 Asia and South Pacific Design Automation Conference.*   IEEE Press, 2004, pp. 349–354.

[12] C. A. R. Hoare, "Communicating sequential processes," *Communications of the ACM*, vol. 21, no. 8, pp. 666–677, 1978.

[13] R. Nikhil, "Bluespec system verilog: efficient, correct rtl from high level specifications," in *Formal Methods and Models for Co-Design, 2004. MEMOCODE '04. Proceedings. Second ACM and IEEE International Conference on*, June 2004, pp. 69–70.

[14] G. Genest, R. Chamberlain, and R. Bruce, "Programming an fpga-based super computer using a c-to-vhdl compiler: Dime-c," in *Adaptive Hardware and Systems, 2007. AHS 2007. Second NASA/ESA Conference on.*   IEEE, 2007, pp. 280–286.

[15] A. Canis, J. Choi, M. Aldham, V. Zhang, A. Kammoona, J. H. Anderson, S. Brown, and T. Czajkowski, "Legup: High-level synthesis for fpga-based processor/accelerator systems," in *Proceedings of the 19th ACM/SIGDA International Symposium on Field Programmable Gate Arrays*, ser. FPGA '11.   New York, NY, USA: ACM, 2011, pp. 33–36.

[16] O. Pell and V. Averbukh, "Maximum performance computing with dataflow engines," *Computing in Science Engineering*, vol. 14, no. 4, pp. 98–103, July 2012.

[17] W. Vanderbauwhede, L. Azzopardi, and M. Moadeli, "Fpga-accelerated information retrieval: High-efficiency document filtering," in *Field Programmable Logic and Applications, 2009. FPL 2009. International Conference on.*   IEEE, 2009, pp. 417–422.

[18] P. Hudak, S. Peyton Jones, P. Wadler, B. Boutel, J. Fairbairn, J. Fasel, M. M. Guzmán, K. Hammond, J. Hughes, T. Johnsson *et al.*, "Report on the programming language haskell: a non-strict, purely functional language version 1.2," *ACM SigPlan notices*, vol. 27, no. 5, pp. 1–164, 1992.

[19] S.-B. Scholz, "Single assignment c: efficient support for high-level array operations in a functional setting," *Journal of functional programming*, vol. 13, no. 06, pp. 1005–1059, 2003.

[20] E. Brady, "Idris, a general-purpose dependently typed programming language: Design and implementation," *Journal of Functional Programming*, vol. 23, pp. 552–593, 2013.

[21] C.-H. Moeng, "A large-eddy-simulation model for the study of planetary boundary-layer turbulence," *J. Atmos. Sci.*, vol. 41, pp. 2052–2062, 1984.

[22] W. Vanderbauwhede, "Inferring Program Transformations from Type Transformations for Partitioning of Ordered Sets," 2015. [Online]. Available: http://arxiv.org/abs/1504.05372

[23] S. W. Nabi and W. Vanderbauwhede, "An intermediate language and estimator for automated design space exploration on fpgas," in *International symposium on Highly Efficient Accelerators and Reconfigurable Technologies (HEART2015), Boston, USA*, 2015. [Online]. Available: http://arxiv.org/abs/1504.045791

Parallel Computing: On the Road to Exascale
G.R. Joubert et al. (Eds.)
IOS Press, 2016

515

doi:10.3233/978-1-61499-621-7-515

FPGA Acceleration of SAT Preprocessor

Masayuki Suzuki [a,1] and Tsutomu Maruyama [a]

[a] *Systems and Information Engineering, University of Tsukuba*
1-1-1 Ten-ou-dai Tsukuba Ibaraki 305-8573 JAPAN

Abstract. The satisfiability (SAT) problem is to find an assignment of binary values to the variables which satisfy a given formula. Many practical application problems can be transformed to SAT problems and many SAT solvers have been developed. In many SAT solvers, preprocessors are widely used to reduce the computational cost. In this paper, we describe an approach for implementing a preprocessor (Unhiding) on FPGA. In the Unhiding, literals and clauses are eliminated to reduce the search space by finding the redundancies in the formula. The data size of the formula is very large in general, and the acceleration is limited by the throughput of the off-chip DRAM banks. In our approach, N clauses are processed in parallel, and the literals in them are sorted into K shift registers so that K banks in the external DRAMs can be accessed in round robin order to achieve higher memory throughout.

Keywords. Satisfiability problems, Preprocessor

Introduction

Given a set of variables and a set of clauses which are disjunctions of the variables and their negations, the goal of the satisfiability (SAT) problem is to find a truth assignment to the variables which satisfies all clauses. Many kinds of problems such as formal verification of hardware systems can be transformed to k-SAT, and many SAT solvers have been researched in order to solve them efficiently[1]. The size of the SAT problems is very large in general, and it is desired to solve these large problems efficiently. In many SAT solvers, preprocessors are widely used [2][3][4]. The main purpose of the preprocessors is to reduce the search space by eliminating literals and clauses by finding the redundancies in a given formula. The preprocessors work especially well for the formal verification of real circuits, because many redundancies are involved in them.

FPGAs are very promising devices for accelerating SAT solvers, because the hardware resources can be fully utilized by the reconfiguration; a preprocessor can be configured first, and then a SAT solver can be reconfigured. However, the data size of the SAT problems is very large, and external DRAM banks are required. As the result, the performance of an FPGA accelerator is limited by the access delay and the throughput of the DRAM banks, though the inherent parallelism in the SAT problems are very high. We have reported that it is nevertheless possible to achieve considerable speedup by an FPGA SAT solver and preprocessor[5][6][7].

---

[1]Corresponding Author: A Doctoral Student, University of Tsukuba 1-1-1 Ten-ou-dai Tsukuba Ibaraki 305-8573 JAPAN, E-mail: suzuki@darwin.esys.tsukuba.ac.jp

Table 1. The number of variables($\times 10^6$), literals($\times 10^6$) and clauses($\times 10^6$) in the benchmark sets and the elimination ratio by the Unhiding (1.00 means no reduction)

benchmark	original			preprocessed(ratio)			
	#v	#c	#l	#v	#c (u.c.))	#l	t(sec)
SAT_dat.k95-24_1_rule_2	1.54	6.04	15.2	0.95	0.97(49%)	0.60	5.03
9vliw_m_9stages_iq3_C1_bug9	0.52	13.4	39.2	0.99	1.00(54%)	0.50	7.98
blocks-blocks-36-0.120-NOTKNOWN	0.49	8.78	19.1	1.00	1.00(51%)	0.68	5.75
SAT_dat.k90.debugged	1.46	5.72	14.3	0.95	0.97(50%)	0.60	4.77
grid-strips-grid-y-3.065-SAT	0.48	3.97	9.59	1.00	0.99(23%)	0.73	2.99

't': measured on Core i7-2600 3.4GHz with 8GB main memory using 8 thread execution.

In this paper, we describe an FPGA implementation of the Unhiding[4], a newer and more powerful preprocessor than previous ones. In this implementation, N clauses are processed in parallel, and the memory accesses generated by them are sorted into K shift registers. Then, K DRAM banks are accessed in round robin order to achieve higher memory throughput.

1. SAT problems and solvers

The satisfiability (SAT) problem is a very well-known combinatorial problem. An *instance* of the problem can be defined by a given boolean formula $F(x_1, x_2, ..., x_n)$, and the question is to find an assignment of binary values to the *variables* $(x_1, x_2, ..., x_n)$ which makes the formula true. Typically, F is presented in conjunctive normal form (CNF), which is a conjunction of a number of *clauses*, where a clause is a disjunction of a number of *literals*. Each literal represents either a boolean variable or its negation. For example, in the following formula in CNF (C_i are clauses: C_1, C_2 and C_4 have two literals, and C_3 has three literals), $\{x_1, x_2, x_3\} = \{1, 1, 0\}$ satisfies all clauses, namely the formula F.

$$F(x_1, x_2, x_3) = C_1(x_1, x_2, x_3) \wedge C_2(x_1, x_2, x_3) \wedge C_3(x_1, x_2, x_3) \wedge C_4(x_1, x_2, x_3)$$
$$C_1(x_1, x_2, x_3) = \overline{x}_1 \vee x_2 \qquad C_2(x_1, x_2, x_3) = \overline{x}_2 \vee \overline{x}_3$$
$$C_3(x_1, x_2, x_3) = x_1 \vee \overline{x}_2 \vee x_3 \qquad C_4(x_1, x_2, x_3) = x_1 \vee \overline{x}_3$$

Many hardware SAT solvers have been proposed to date ([8][9]; here, we only refer two of them), but as for the preprocessor, our previous work[7] is the only one example to our best knowledge. In this paper, we show an FPGA implementation of a newer and more powerful preprocessor Unhiding[4].

2. Unhiding

The Unhiding is a preprocessor used in a SAT solver, Lingeling[10]. The Unhiding eliminates the redundant literals and clauses by analyzing data dependencies among them. Table 1 shows the number of variables (#v), clauses (#c) and literals (#l) in five problems in SAT benchmark 2014[11] and the elimination ratio by the Unhiding. '#u.c.' shows the ratio of the unit clauses after Unhiding is applied. A unit clause has only one literal in it, and it has to be true. Thus, every unit clause can be easily eliminated, but the Unhiding leaves its elimination to SAT solvers. In the Unhiding, first, the data dependencies among literals are analyzed, and the binary implication graph (BIG) is generated (this step is called 'stamping'). Then, using the BIG, literals and clauses are eliminated by applying the algorithms described below.

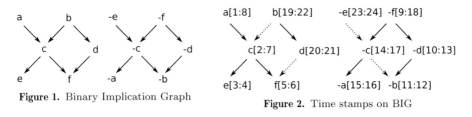

Figure 1. Binary Implication Graph

Figure 2. Time stamps on BIG

2.1. Stamping

First, we define the data dependency between two literals, 'if a is true, then b is true ($\{a \rightarrow b\}$)' as follows.

$$\{a \rightarrow b\} \equiv (\overline{a} \vee b)$$

In the formula generated from real circuits, many clauses of this form are included. From a formula $F = \{\overline{a} \vee c\}, \{\overline{b} \vee c\}, \{\overline{b} \vee d\}, \{\overline{c} \vee e\}, \{\overline{c} \vee f\}, \{\overline{d} \vee f\}$, a BIG of the literals shown in Fig.1 can be obtained. To construct this BIG, the Unhiding performs the depth first search (DFS) of the literals, and assigns 'time stamps' to each of them (called 'stamping').

A literal l has the following time stamps.

1. *discovered* ($dsc(l)$): given when l is first visited.
2. *finished* ($fin(l)$): given before returning to its parent literal.
3. *observed* ($obs(l)$): given when l is accessed (when l has more than one parent, the above stamps are given on the first visit, but not on the later visits from other parents. this time stamp is updated on both visits).
4. *parent* ($prt(l)$): the parent literal of l.

Fig.2 shows an example of two time stamps, $[dsc(l), fin(l)]$, of the BIG in Fig.1. In Fig.2, literal a is visited first by the DFS. Then c and e are visited. e has no child, so the DFS goes back to c, and moves to f, the next child of c. Then, the DFS goes back to a. One of the root literals is selected at random, and $-f$ (negation of f) is chosen as the next root. When the DFS started from b, c is visited first, but it has already been visited, and no stamps are given (except for $obs(c)$) on this visit.

In the Unhiding, the five following algorithms are applied to eliminate literals and clauses; (1) failed literal elimination (FLE), (2) transitive reduction (TRD), (3) equivalent literal substitution (ELS), (4) unhiding tautology elimination ($UHTE$), and (5) unhiding literal elimination ($UHLE$). The first three are applied while giving the time stamps to the literals, and the last two are applied afterward.

2.2. Failed literal elimination

A literal x is called 'failed literal' if the given formula F becomes false when a unit clause $\{x\}$ is added to F. For a clause $\{l \rightarrow l'\}$, if there exists a common parent of l' and $\overline{l'}$, their parent, x, is the failed literal. Such parent literal exists when $dsc(root(l)) \leq obs(\overline{l'})$. This means that there is a dependency such that $\{root(l) \rightarrow x\}, \{x \rightarrow \overline{l'}\}, \{x \rightarrow l\}, \{l \rightarrow l'\}$.

When the above condition becomes true, the Unhiding goes back the stack generated by the DFS to find the common parent, and finds the literal x that satisfies $dsc(x) \leq obs(\overline{l'})$. Then, the Unhiding adds $\{\overline{x}\}$ to F to teach the value of x to SAT solvers.

2.3. Transitive reduction

For a directed graph G that has node u and v, G' is called 'transitive reduction (*TRD*)' of G if G' satisfies (1) G has a direct edge from u to v, and G' has a path from u to v and (2) G' is the minimum set that satisfies (1). For example, the transitive reduction of $F = \{u \to a\}, \{a \to v\}, \{u \to v\}$ is $F' = \{u \to a\}, \{a \to v\}$. The truth of F and F' is equivalent. Thus, by using F' instead of F, the clause $\{u \to v\}$ can be eliminated. This clause eliminated is called 'transitive reduction', and a clause $\{u \to v\}$ is a transitive edge if $dsc(u) < obs(v)$.

2.4. Equivalent literal substitution

For a clause $\{l \to l'\}$, if $fin(l') = 0$ (this means that no $fin(l')$ is given to l' yet) and $dsc(l') < dsc(l)$, there exists a cyclic relation $\{l \to l'\}, \{l' \to l\}$. By assigning the same time stamps to l and l', it becomes possible to detect the dependencies among the literals more efficiently. This process is called 'equivalent literal substitution (*ELS*)'.

2.5. Unhiding tautology elimination

For a formula $F = \{a \lor b \lor c\}, \{\bar{a} \to x\}, \{x \to b\}$, the clause $\{a \lor b \lor c\}$ can be eliminated as follows.

$$\{a \lor b \lor c\} \land \{\bar{a} \to x\} \land \{x \to b\} \equiv (\{a \lor b \lor c\} \land \{\bar{a} \to b\}) \land \{\bar{a} \to x\} \land \{x \to b\}$$

$$\equiv \{\bar{a} \to x\} \land \{x \to b\} \tag{1}$$

In this example, $\{a \lor b \lor c\}$ is called 'hidden tautology', and the operation to eliminate the hidden tautology is called 'unhiding tautology elimination (*UHTE*)'.

By using the time stamps, it is possible to know whether a clause C is a hidden tautology or not. C is a hidden tautology if a literal l_{pos} in C and its negation l_{neg} (this negation is not included in C) satisfies $dsc(l_{neg}) < dsc(l_{pos})$ and $fin(l_{neg}) > fin(l_{pos})$.

2.6. Unhiding literal elimination

For a formula $F = \{a \lor b \lor c \lor d\}, \{a \to b\}, \{b \to c\}$, two literals, a and b in $\{a \lor b \lor c \lor d\}$ can be eliminated as follows.

$$\{a \lor b \lor c \lor d\} \land \{a \to b\} \land \{b \to c\} \equiv (\{a \lor b \lor c \lor d\} \land \{\bar{a} \lor b\}) \land \{b \to c\}$$

$$\equiv (\{b \lor c \lor d\} \land \{\bar{b} \lor c\}) \land \{a \to b\} \equiv \{c \lor d\} \land \{a \to b\}, \{b \to c\} \tag{2}$$

This procedure is called 'unhiding literal elimination (*UHLE*)', and the eliminated literals are called 'hidden literals'. By using time stamps, hidden literals can be found. If two literals l and l' in a clause C satisfies (1) $dsc(l) < dsc(l')$ and $fin(l) > fin(l')$, or (2) $dsc(\bar{l}) > dsc(\bar{l'})$ and $fin(\bar{l}) < fin(\bar{l'})$. l is the hidden literal, and can be eliminated.

3. Implementation on an FPGA

Fig.3 shows a block diagram of our system. Stamping unit executes the DFS, and gives the time stamps to literals. This unit also executes *TRD*, *ELS* and *FLE*. Simplification unit executes *UHTE* and *UHLE* using the time stamps, and eliminates literals and clauses. Time stamp cache is a cache memory especially designed for time stamps.

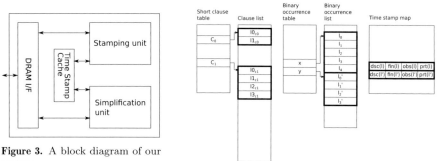

Figure 3. A block diagram of our system

Figure 4. Data structure

3.1. Data Structure in DRAM banks

Fig.4 shows the data structure used in our system. In the short clause table, the starting addresses of the clauses whose length are not longer than 32, and their lengths are stored. The clause list stores the literals in each clause. Binary occurrence table stores the starting addresses of the binary occurrence lists, and their last addresses. Binary occurrence list stores the other literals in the binary clauses that contains the literal. Time stamp map is an associative array to look up the time stamps from the variable number. These data are stored in the off-chip DRAM banks.

3.2. Processing sequences and memory accesses

The procedures executed by our system is the same as the software program. First, the time stamps are given to the literals by the stamping unit (in this unit, *TRD*, *ELS* and *FLE* are also executed), and then, literals and clauses are eliminated by the simplification unit (by *UHTE* and *UHLE*) using the BIGs generated by the stamping unit. There are three types of memory access sequences in our system.

1. Binary occurrence table are scanned, and the root literals are listed up. This memory access sequence can be efficiently executed by burst-read.
2. Starting from the root literals, literals are accessed by the DFS. This memory access sequence is random, and the access delay is the main bottleneck of this stage. In our system, a specialized cache memory for the time stamps is used to improve the memory access delay.
3. Time stamps of the literals in a clause are read, and *UHTE* and *UHLE* are applied to them. This access sequence is also random. In our implementation, *N* clauses are processed in parallel, and the literals in them are sorted into *K* block RAMs in FPGA according to the *K* external DRAM banks that store the literal data. Then, the *K* DRAM banks are accessed in round robin order to hide the random access delay. If *N* is large enough, the access delay can be almost hidden. The specialized cache memory for the time stamps is also used here to further improve the memory access delay.

3.3. Time stamping unit

Fig.5 shows a block diagram of the stamping unit. The stamping unit, first, looks up the root literals using the root literal finder. A literal *l* can be a root if *l* is not

---

Algorithm 1 Stamping sequence part1

1: List root literals (RTS)
2: stamp := 0
3: **while** $root \in RTS$ **do**
4:      Push root to Stack
5:      **while** Stack is not empty **do**
6:          l is the head of Stack
7:          **if** l does not have children **then**
8:              Processed on Stack
9:              **if** observed != 0 **then**   ▷ FLE
10:                  **if** $dsc(l_{failed}) > observed$ **then**
11:                      $l_{failed} := l$
12:                  **else**
13:                      **parallel**
14:                          Write $\{\bar{l}_{failed}\}$; observed := 0
15:                      **end**
16:                  **end if**
17:              **end if**
18:
19:              Processed on S
20:              **if** $is\_equivalent(l)$ == false **then**   ▷ ELS
21:                  stamp := stamp + 1
22:                  **repeat**
23:                      **parallel**
24:                          $l' := S.pop()$
25:                          $dsc(l') := dsc(l)$
26:                          $fin(l') := stamp$
27:                      **end**
28:                      Write l' time stamp to DRAM and Time stamp cache
29:                  **until** $l'! = l$
30:              **end if**
31:

---

included in any clause (note that $\bar{l}$ is included in several clauses). This means that there exists no literals such as $\{x \to l\}$. This can be easily detected by scanning binary occurrence list. Then, a stack is used to assign the time stamps by the DFS. This stack stores (1) literal l, (2) the time stamps of l and $\bar{l}$, (3) the address of binary occurrence list of $\bar{l}$, (4) $is\_visited(l)$, a flag that shows whether *FLE* and *TRD* have already applied or not, and (5) $is\_equivalent(l)$, a flag that shows if l is a equivalent literal. S is a buffer to hold the literals to which $fin()$ should be attached when the DFS returns from the literals. In our current implementation, their depths are fixed to 256.

Algorithm 1 and 2 show the details of the time stamping procedure in our system. In the algorithm, **parallel, parallel if** and **parallel else if** blocks are executed in parallel.

In our system, the four units, the failed literal detector, transitive edge detector, equivalent literal detector, and child node checker, run in parallel (line 34,39,44 and 56 in the algorithm 2). The first three units execute *FLE*, *TRD* and *ELS* respectively. The child node checker checks if each child literal has been already visited. Their results are sent to the controller, and the stack and buffer S are updated.

Algorithm 2 Stamping sequence part2

32:	**else**	▷ l has children
33:	Read a time stamp of l' (one of a l child) from DRAM or Time stamp cache	
34:	**parallel if** $is\_visited == false$ && $dsc(root(l)) \leq obs(\overline{l'})$	
35:	**parallel**	▷ FLE
36:	$l_{failed} := l$; $observed := obs(\overline{l'})$	
37:	$is\_visited(l) := true$	
38:	**end**	
39:	**parallel else if** $is\_visited(l) == false$ && $dsc(l) < obs(l')$	
40:	**parallel**	▷ TRD
41:	Remove $\{\overline{l} \vee l'\}$ from Clause table	
42:	$is\_visited(l) := true$	
43:	**end**	
44:	**parallel else if** $is\_visited(l) == false$ && $dsc(l) == 0$	
45:	**parallel**	
46:	Processed on Stack	▷ Visit l'
47:	$stamp := stamp + 1$	
48:	$dsc(l') := stamp$; $obs(l') := stamp$	
49:	$is\_visited(l') := false$	
50:	$is\_equivalent(l') := false$	
51:	Read l' children	
		▷ Update l time stamp
52:	$is\_visited(l) := true$	
53:		
54:	Push l' to S	
55:	**end**	
56:	**parallel else if** $fin(l') == 0$ && $dsc(l') < dsc(l)$	
57:	**parallel**	▷ ELS
58:	$dsc(l) := dsc(l')$	
59:	$is\_equivalent(l) := true$	
60:	**end**	
61:	**end if**	
62:	$obs(l') := stamp$	
63:	**end if**	
64:	**end while**	
65:	**end while**	

3.4. Simplification Unit

Fig.6 shows a block diagram of the simplification unit. After the time stamps were given to the literals, *UHTE* and *UHLE* are applied by the simplification unit. *UHTE* and *UHLE* are operations to find a literal in a clause that satisfies $dsc(l_{neg}) < dsc(l_{pos})$ and $fin(l_{neg}) > fin(l_{pos})$, or $dsc(l) < dsc(l')$ and $fin(l) > fin(l')$. For these two operations, only the time stamps of the literals in a clause are required. Thus, theoretically, we can apply *UHTE* and *UHLE* in parallel to all clauses in the formula at the same time. In our system, 16 clauses of up to $L_s = 32$ literals are processed in parallel, and for each clause, *UHTE* and *UHLE* are applied in parallel. The simplification unit works as follows.

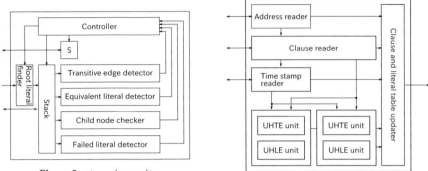

Figure 5. stamping unit

Figure 6. simplification unit

1. The address reader reads the starting address of $N = 16$ clauses of up to $L_s = 32$ literals, and their length from the short clause table.
2. The clause reader reads all literals of the N clauses from the clause list.
3. The time stamp reader reads the time stamp of the literals from the time stamp map.
4. *UHTE* and *UHLE* units apply *UHTE* and *UHLE* to N clauses in parallel using the time stamps.
5. The clause and literal table updater updates clause list when the literals or clauses are eliminated.
6. 1) to 5) are repeated until all clauses of up to 32 literals are processed.

In this sequence, the access delay to read the time stamps becomes the bottleneck of the performance, because they are random accesses to the off-chip DRAM banks To hide the access delay, the accesses to the time stamps are interleaved. By interleaving these accesses, and processing N clauses in parallel, we can issue the next access without idle time, and hide the access delay. For example, the time stamps of $F = \{a, b, c\}, \{b, c, d\}, \{c, d, e\}$ are accessed as follows when the number of DRAM banks is $K = 2$. The literals in F are sorted into K block RAMs on FPGA, $B0$ and $B1$. $B0$ is the block RAM for the literals stored in DRAM bank 0, and $B1$ is that in DRAM bank 1. In this case, $B0 = \{a, c, c, c, e\}$ and $B1 = \{b, b, d, d\}$. Then, time stamps of literals in $B0$ and $B1$ is read from each DRAM bank alternately (the sequence is $\{a, b, c, b, c, d, c, d, e\}$). When the time stamps are already cached, they are used, and the DRAM bank is not accessed. With this approach, all DRAM access cannot be interleaved, but this approach is very simple, and is powerful enough to hide the delay when 16 clauses are processed in parallel. As shown in this example, the literals are not fetched in the order of the literals in the clauses. Therefore, the time stamps are rearranged in that order in the time stamp reader.

4. Experimental Results

We have implemented the circuit on Xilinx Kintex-7 XC7VLX325T. The circuit size except of DRAM I/F is 32K LUTs and 340 block RAMs. The operational frequency is 200 MHz (it is depend on DRAM I/F). In this implementation, up to 8192 time stamps can be cached in the cache memory, and *UHLE* and *UHTE* are applied to 16 clauses of up to 32 literals in parallel. In the following discussion, a

Table 2. The performance of our system

| | literal elimination rate | | | execution time | |
| | our system (L_s) | | SW | | |
benchmark	16	**32**	64	ratio	t(sec)	speedup
SAT_dat.k95-24_1_rule_2	0.39	**0.40**	0.40	1.00	3.91	1.29 (0.69/3.68)
9vliw_m_9stages_iq3_C1_bug9	0.34	**0.41**	0.44	0.86	3.52	2.27 (1.30/3.49)
blocks-blocks-36-0.120-NOTKNOWN	0.25	**0.25**	0.27	0.91	2.96	1.94 (1.21/3.37)
SAT_dat.k90.debugged	0.39	**0.40**	0.40	1.00	3.70	1.29 (0.69/3.68)
grid-strips-grid-y-3.065-SAT	0.19	**0.19**	0.19	0.89	1.81	1.65 (0.91/3.74)

hardware simulator is used to evaluate the performance of the system by changing the parameters.

Table 2 compares the literal elimination rate and the execution time with the software program. In our system, *UHTE* and *UHLE* are applied to only the clauses with up to 32 literals ($L_s = 32$), because with $L_s = 64$, the elimination rate cannot be improved significantly. In Table.2, 0.41 means that 41% of the literals could be eliminated, and 0.86 (v.s. software) means that our elimination rate is 0.86 times of the software program. The slight decrease of the elimination rate is caused by the clauses with many literals (more than 64). The ratio of those clauses is less than 1%, but they affect the elimination rate. In our next implementation, it is necessary to implement a special unit for those long clauses. However, as shown in this table, the elimination rate by our system is still high. The speedup is compared with the software program on Intel Core i7-2600 3.4GHz with 8GB main memory and 8 thread execution. The total speedup by our system is 1.3 to 2.3 times. This acceleration rate is not so high. This is caused by the following three reasons. First, the software program uses 4 cores (8 threads). Second, the performance of our system and CPU is limited by the memory bandwidth, but the CPU has a larger cache memory (8MB). Last, in our current implementation, the time stamping phase is not accelerated because of its complexity, though it is possible to apply the same memory access optimization used for *UHTE* and *UHLE*. In Table 2, the two values in the parentheses show the speedup in the time stamping and other phases respectively. The speedup in other phases (for them, our memory access optimization is applied) is 3.4 to 3.7, and it is high enough when we consider that the CPU is running using 4 cores. The acceleration of the time stamping phase is the most important issue to be challenged in our next implementation.

Fig.7 shows the processing speed when we change the number of clauses that are processed in parallel in the simplification unit. As shown in this graph, by increasing the parallelism, we can expect more speedup, but the improvement becomes slower as the parallelism becomes higher. From this graph, the parallelism is fixed to 16 in our current implementation.

Fig.8 shows the execution time when we change the DRAM access time. In this figure, the performance is normalized by that when the delay is 50 FPGA clock cycles (100 nsec). The change of the performance against the DRAM access delay is small, and it seems that our approach to hide the DRAM access delay is working well.

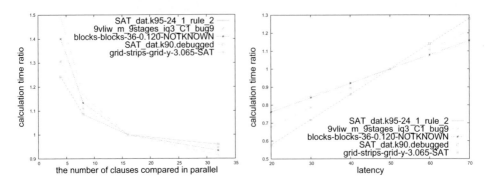

Figure 7. Parallelism in the simplification unit and the processing speed

Figure 8. The execution time for different DRAM access time

5. Conclusions and Future work

In this paper, we proposed an implementation method of the Unhiding, a preprocessor for SAT solvers. In our implementation, to achieve the high performance
for very large problems, N clauses are processed in parallel, and the literals in
the N clauses are sorted into K block RAMs according to K memory banks that
store the literals. Then, K memory banks are accessed in the round robin order to
maximize the memory throughput, and hide the access delay. After fetching the
literals, they are resorted and given to each clauses. Experimental result shows a
good performance, and shows that this approach works well for very large problems. In our current implementation, the time stamping phase is not accelerated.
Using the same approach, it is possible to accelerate the phase. This is one of
our main future work. We also need to evaluate the performance of this system
combined with SAT solvers.

References

[1] http://www.satisfiability.org/
[2] Niklas Eén, Armin Biere: Effective Preprocessing in SAT Through Variable and Clause
     Elimination. SAT 2005: 61-75
[3] Cédric Piette, Youssef Hamadi, Lakhdar Sais: Vivifying Propositional Clausal Formulae.
     ECAI 2008: 525-529
[4] Marijn Heule, Matti Järvisalo, Armin Biere: Efficient CNF Simplification Based on Binary
     Implication Graphs. SAT 2011: 201-215
[5] Kenji Kanazawa, Tsutomu. Maruyama: An FPGA Solver for SAT-encoded Formal Verifi-
     cation Problems, FPL2014: 38-43
[6] Kenji Kanazawa, Tsutomu. Maruyama: FPGA Acceleration of SAT/Max-SAT Solving us-
     ing Variable-way Associative Cache, FPL2014: 1-4
[7] Masayuki Suzuki, Tsutomu Maruyama: Variable and clause elimination in SAT problems
     using an FPGA. FPT 2011: 1-8
[8] K.Gulati, S.Paul, et.al, "FPGA-based hardware acceleration for Boolean satisfiability"
     Trans. ACM TODAES Vol.14, 2009
[9] K.Kanazawa, T.Maruyama, "An Approach for Solving Large SAT Problems on FPGA",
     Trans. ACM TRETS Vol.4, No.1, 2010
[10] Lingeling, Plingeling and Treengeling http://fmv.jku.at/lingeling/
[11] SAT Competitions http://www.satcompetition.org

Parallel Computing: On the Road to Exascale
G.R. Joubert et al. (Eds.)
IOS Press, 2016
© 2016 The authors and IOS Press. All rights reserved.
doi:10.3233/978-1-61499-621-7-525

Leveraging FPGA clusters for SAT computations

Michal Kouril, PhD [1]

Cincinnati Children's Hospital Medical Center
University of Cincinnati, USA

Abstract. Field Programmable Gate Arrays (FPGAs) can be an important computational tool for increasing the efficiency of SAT solvers. We have developed an efficient SAT solver for computing van der Waerden numbers using a cluster of over 200 Xilinx Spartan XC6SLX150 FPGAs that were originally dedicated to Bitcoin mining. This cluster should compute $W(5,3)$ in 6-9 months with modest power and cooling requirements. We discuss the challenges of building and operating this computational system. Finally, we report the values of four new off-diagonal van der Waerden numbers.

Keywords. FPGA, SAT, Van der Waerden numbers

Introduction

We present an innovative infrastructure for SAT computation based on repurposed Bitcoin mining[10] FPGA hardware. As the Bitcoin mining difficulty increases, the cost of electricity to run FPGA miners exceeds potential rewards. Consequently, there has recently been a sell-off of FPGA-based hardware that Bitcoin miners can no longer operate profitably. The hardware is often sold for a fraction of the list price, making it a viable option for alternative purposes such as combinatorics computation (Ramsey numbers, van der Waerden numbers, Schur numbers, etc.), cryptology, including brute-force search, as well as Monte Carlo simulations, to name a few. In this paper we will focus on Xilinx Spartan FPGA based boards – specifically ZTEX 1.15y with four Xilinx Spartan XC6SLX150 devices. We show how they can be efficiently repurposed for computing van der Waerden numbers, and potentially for other similarly complex SAT problems.

Given positive integers K, L, the van der Waerden number[13] $W(K,L)$ is the smallest integer n such that if the positive consecutive integers $\{1, 2, ..., n\}$ are partitioned into K classes, then at least one class contains an arithmetic progression (a.p.) of length L. The off-diagonal numbers $W(K; L_1, L_2, ..., L_m)$ are defined similarly by requiring that for every partition into K classes there is at least one class containing an a.p. of length L_i, for some $i \in \{1, 2, ..., m\}$.

The majority of research into finding on- and off-diagonal van der Waerden numbers or their lower bounds has used general-purpose SAT solvers on standard

---

[1]Corresponding Author: Cincinnati Children's Hospital Medical Center, University of Cincinnati, 3333 Burnet Ave, Cincinnati, OH 45229, USA; E-mail: Michal.Kouril@cchmc.org.

PCs[3][9][12][1][2][4]. In our earlier work we computed several off-diagonal van der Waerden numbers on Beowulf clusters. In an effort to obtain larger van der Waerden numbers we moved from a high performance computational cluster[5] to one enhanced by FPGA–based computations. We were then able to verify all known on- and off-diagonal van der Waerden numbers using an FPGA–based computations on 5x Xilinx Virtex-6 boards[6]. We also determined the hardest to compute numbers to-date: $W(2,6) = 1132$[8] and $W(3,4) = 293$[6], in the span of several months.

To progress beyond the current limits we anticipate either significant computational advances in the solver algorithm, larger numbers of computational resources, or a combination of both. In our recent work, we initially focused on the second element by tying together hundreds of FPGAs to contribute to a single computation. However, we had to overcome associated challenges on the algorithmic level as well. This integration of algorithm and computational hardware resources poses challenges not only for software development, but also in terms of power, cooling, etc. The recent availability of new resources from Bitcoin mining, which can be repurposed for SAT computation, therefore represents a significant new development.

Bitcoin mining started in 2008[10] as a research project. Bitcoin is a widely distributed virtual currency with great appeal for people skeptical of state controlled monetary systems. The process of mining new Bitcoins involves a SHA-256 hash algorithm as well as a global block difficulty, which increases with the increasing hash rate of the Bitcoin mining network. As the difficulty increases, more powerful computer hardware is required to sustain profitability. Thus, whereas Bitcoin mining was originally implemented on regular PCs, then GPUs, followed by FPGAs, it now largely takes place on ASICs based single purpose hardware.

In this paper we focus on FPGAs. Many boards have appeared on the market for example the ZTEX 1.15x (1x FPGA) and 1.15y (4x FPGAs), Lancelot, Icarus, X6500, etc. Each board typically contains one or more FPGA devices and necessary I/O communication circuitry to program the FPGA and send/receive data between the FPGA and a computer. With the increasing difficulty of Bitcoin mining these boards are no longer cost effective and are therefore becoming available on the secondary markets.

We will detail how we repurposed ZTEX 1.15y boards, originally employed in Bitcoin mining, for the SAT computation. We focus on the van der Waerden number $W(5,3)$ computation, but discuss the reusability of FPGA clusters for other problems as well.

1. Architecture

Our FPGA computational cluster involves several components (outlined in Figure 1). Each FPGA board contains four independent FPGA devices connected to a Cypress EZ-USB FX2 microcontroller. All boards are connected to a host computer via USB ports. Multiple cluster units are then connected to the network, which facilitates the distribution of the tasks to the solvers.

A repository of unassigned tasks is maintained by a dedicated server. When a solver completes its assigned task, then its state becomes idle. The software running on each FPGA cluster periodically checks the status of the connected FPGA-based solvers. Upon encountering an idle solver, a new task is then requested from the task-repository server (using simple web service), and when this new task is received it is assigned to the previously idle server. All solvers run independently.

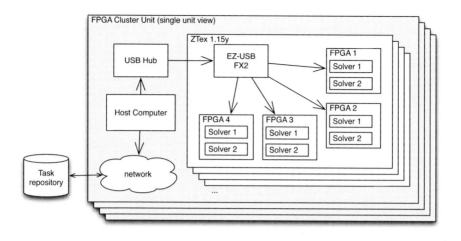

Figure 1. FPGA cluster system architecture.

As part of the design process we considered power, cooling, and connectivity requirements. Power consumption is dependent on the design uploaded into the FPGAs. We anticipated somewhat lower power consumption than was required by the same hardware for Bitcoin mining due to the differences between the highly tuned mining software and our SAT implementation. The same logic holds for cooling where each FPGA device used in Bitcoin mining not only requires a heat sink but also well maintained active cooling. Instead of cooling each FPGA device separately, as originally designed, we removed all small fans and replaced them with whole case cooling using 120mm fans to limit the number of potential failure points.

We targeted a design with over 50 connected boards split into multiple independent systems of 15-22 boards built into server cases. Each system is equipped with an off-the-shelf 750Watt or larger ATX power supply targetting 50W/board. The host systems run Linux on pico-ITX VIA EPIA PX10000 motherboards. This motherboard provides a minimal footprint, Ethernet connectivity, USB flash drive booting, ATX PSU control, etc.

Given the large number of boards per system the cost of the system is dominated by the price of the boards (new costs 349EUR[2] in 2015). The costs of the remainder of the infrastructure including high wattage power supply (750W/15 boards), USB infrastructure, sufficiently large computer case, 150mm fans, etc. are nominal.

1.1. FPGA design

We enhanced the FPGA solver software (see Figure 3) used for computing $W(2,6)$ and $W(3,4)$. Additional optimizations included CRC checks for incoming data, a reworked host data transfer logic to implement the ZTEX board FX2 device interface (see Section 1.3) as well as a memory interface to store all satisfiable assignments. In the $W(5,3)$ solver for $n = 120$ configuration (see Section 2), the FPGA device, Xilinx Spartan LX150, only hosts two solvers per device, however we believe that with further optimization incorporating three or four instances per device might be possible.

---

[2]http://shop.ztex.de

Targetted van der Waerden number	FPGA resources	Time	Number of solvers	Frequency
W(2,6)[8]	4x Xilinx Virtex 4 LX60	3 months	4	100MHz
W(2,6) verification[6]	5x Xilinx Virtex 5 LX110	12 days	20	200MHz
W(3,4)[6]	5x Xilinx Virtex 6 LX240T	36 days	20	150MHz
W(5,3)	200x Xilinx Spartan 6 LX150	6-9 months	400	96MHz

Table 1. Comparison with the previous efforts.

Our previous solvers [8][6] utilized Virtex 4, 5 and 6 (see Table 1). The combinatorial logic within the SAT solver takes significant advantage of the high-speed carry chains to improve performance and simplify design. Porting the design to the Spartan 6 architecture, which has significantly fewer high-speed carry chain logic components, limits the number of solvers one can fit on a single device of equivalent size.

The FPGAs on the ZTEX 1.15y board are clocked by 48 MHz. Using DCM/PLL we chose to target 96 MHz under which we were able to place-and-route design with 2 solvers per single FPGA.

The design is fully pipelined with 15-stage combinatorial block (see Figure 3). We experimented with increasing the number of stages which put pressure on the carry chain logic availability and did not lead to significant improvement in speed. Reducing the number of stages lead to missed timing goals.

We used the standard development tools Xilinx ISE 14.7 with no special parameters to synthesize and place-and-route the design. The synthesis of the solver block took 144s, the synthesis and place-and-route, including the generation of the final bit file, took 1 hour on a 4-core i7 system with 16GB RAM. For the resulting design report see Figure 2.

1.2. FPGA design to collect all solutions

In the past [8][6] we leveraged PC based solvers to gather all solutions given an initial assignment for a particular n. When computing $W(5,3)$ for $n = 120$ the difficulty is significantly higher and the gap between the performance of an FPGA and PC based solver is wider. Thus gathering all satisfiable assignments on a PC became infeasible. Therefore, we developed an FPGA version of the solver that also returned all satisfiable assignments in addition to reporting a judgement whether a particular initial assignment is satisfiable or unsatisfiable.

FPGAs are limited in size, and the amount of memory that can be allocated directly on the device is relatively small. We were able to work within this constraint using an asymmetrical dual port FIFO component, which stores the current assignment every time the solver encounters a satisfiable assignment. Due to the design size increase we were limited to one solver per device, storing up to 4096 assignments. To save valuable FPGA space the content of the FIFO is then reported out to the host by repurposing the wires for the counter status.

1.3. EZ-USB FX2 interface

In our previous setups we utilized serial interface RS232, or data-over-JTAG, as a communication interface between FPGA boards and a host computer. Leveraging open

```
Slice Logic Utilization:
  Number of Slice Registers:                40,344 out of 184,304   21%
    Number used as Flip Flops:              40,344
    Number used as Latches:                      0
    Number used as Latch-thrus:                  0
    Number used as AND/OR logics:                0
  Number of Slice LUTs:                     43,730 out of  92,152   47%
    Number used as logic:                   37,821 out of  92,152   41%
      Number using O6 output only:          25,112
      Number using O5 output only:           7,264
      Number using O5 and O6:                5,445
      Number used as ROM:                        0
    Number used as Memory:                     452 out of  21,680    2%
      Number used as Dual Port RAM:              0
      Number used as Single Port RAM:            0
      Number used as Shift Register:           452
        Number using O6 output only:          40
        Number using O5 output only:           0
        Number using O5 and O6:              412
    Number used exclusively as route-thrus:  5,457
      Number with same-slice register load:  5,453
      Number with same-slice carry load:         4
      Number with other load:                    0

Slice Logic Distribution:
  Number of occupied Slices:                15,560 out of  23,038   67%
  Number of MUXCYs used:                    34,240 out of  46,076   74%
  Number of LUT Flip Flop pairs used:       51,936
    Number with an unused Flip Flop:        18,379 out of  51,936   35%
    Number with an unused LUT:               8,206 out of  51,936   15%
    Number of fully used LUT-FF pairs:      25,351 out of  51,936   48%
    Number of unique control sets:              18
    Number of slice register sites lost
      to control set restrictions:              40 out of 184,304    1%
```

Figure 2. Xilinx Spartan 6 LX150 FPGA device utilization with two solvers for W(5,3).

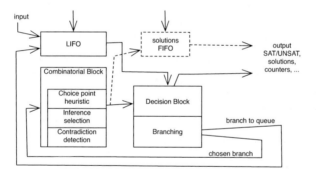

Figure 3. FPGA solver architecture.

source libraries from ZTEX we amended the sample code for the Cypress EZ-USB FX2 controller and redeveloped our FPGA solver data transfer functions. This basic functionality utilizes 26 wires across four 8-bit interfaces *PA*, *PB*, *PC* and *PD*. *PB* and *PD* are used to transfer data to and from the FPGAs. *PA* and *PC* serve as control signals including FPGA and solver selection, read and write clocking, etc.

To address the interface between the host computer and EZ-USB FX2, as well as the EZ-USB FX2 and FPGA we developed C code for the EZ-USB FX2 to translate USB endpoint data transfers with the help of ZTEX libraries. This programming provides basic functions such as FPGA selection, solver selection, data transfers between the host and individual FPGAs. The EZ-USB FX2 controller only facilitates communication and does not actually contribute to computation.

1.4. The PC interface

The host computer interface was developed using Java examples from ZTEX and code adapted from previous versions of the van der Waerden solvers. The code starts by enumerating all connected FPGA boards, uploads the programs into the EZ-USB FX2 microcontroller and the FPGAs, and initiates computation by reading the list of initial paths and uploading them into each solver. The code then continues checking the status of the computation on each solver and if a change is encountered (e.g., solver completed, solution or exception found) it notes the result and uploads the next initial path.

2. Van der Waerden numbers

When building the FPGA cluster we initially targeted the van der Waerden number $W(5,3)$. The best lower bound known to date is $W(5,3) > 170$, discovered by Marijn Heule[4]. Therefore, we built a solver with $n = 120$: smaller than the anticipated van der Waerden number but large enough to overcome the computational barrier[7]. By building a smaller solver we saved FPGA space and increased the computational speed. When considering $n = 120$ it is obvious, given the existence of the lower bound, that we find some assignments (solutions) for which the solver returns true (or satisfiable). Then we collect all the solutions and try to extend them to the maximum n in order to find $W(5,3)$.

In order to prepartition the search space we followed the methodology used to compute $W(2,6)$[8] and $W(3,4)$[6]. We created $4,249,508$ individual subtasks that are given one-by-one to the solvers. The prepartitioning was done on a PC by starting with a middle-placed unavoidable pattern $\{112\}$ (i.e. a pattern that has to occur in any satisfiable assignment for $n > n_0$) and expanding it while eliminating redundant recolored patterns in the minimal representation (see the discussion in [8] and [6] for details of the process). We stop expanding while the number of subtasks is still manageable generating initial assignments of length 15. Initial adhoc testing indicated that determining on satisfiability of a single task, using $W(5,3)$ solver for $n = 120$, requires less than an hour on average although a single task can take anywhere between seconds and hours.

3. Results

Our FPGA cluster consisted of four separate units with a total of 57 ZTEX 1.15y boards (recall that each board has four FPGAs). The maximum number of participating solvers was 456. The initial phase processed 10% of $W(5,3)$ tasks at $n = 120$ and was completed in 26 days. Results showed that out of 424,950 initial paths there are 199 for which satisfiable assignments exist. The average time to complete one task was 34 minutes yielding an estimate of six to nine months to complete the search.

After collecting complete results for all 199 satisfiable tasks for $n = 120$ using a modified FPGA solver (see discussion in Section 1.1), and extending them to the maximum n for which none of the five colors contains an arithmetic progression of length three, we found that this maximum n is 170. This result matches the bound found by Heule[4]. After processing the remaining 90% tasks we will be able to establish $W(5,3)$.

$W(r; k_1, k_2, ..., k_r)$	Result
$W(2; 3, 20)$	389
$W(4; 2, 3, 3, 6)$	115
$W(4; 2, 2, 3, 12)$	163
$W(5; 2, 2, 3, 3, 5)$	95

Table 2. Newly discovered off-diagonal van der Waerden numbers

3.1. Bottlenecks

Due to the average time to complete one task (34 minutes) the computation is dominated by the FPGA-based work. The communication (the time it takes to assign the work as well as collect the results) is negligible.

As discussed earlier, the current design doesn't allow for more than 2 solvers per FPGA. Further design improvements, and taking full advantage of the Xilinx tools' capabilities, should overcome this bottleneck to increase the number of solvers to at least 3 while maintaining the same frequency. Obviously, with increased utilization and/or frequency the power demands tend to grow and the current power supplies might pose an additional bottleneck.

3.2. Additional off-diagonal van der Waerden numbers found using FPGAs

We leveraged FPGAs to verify that $W(2; 3, 19) = 349$ published by Ahmed, Kullmann and Snevily[2] and also confirmed their conjecture that $W(2; 3, 20) = 389$. Additional newly discovered van der Waerden numbers are listed in Table 2.

3.3. Challenges and Limitations

During the course of building and running the system we encountered numerous challenges similar to those previously experienced by the Bitcoin mining community. USB hub stability varies greatly by manufacturer and some of the cheaper models tend to either fail entirely or cause frequent disconnects and reconnects of the FPGA boards. Recall that the USB network in a single system has anywhere between 15 and 22 connections which are constantly polled for the latest status. To partially mitigate this, the software should periodically scan the USB bus and re-engage reconnected FPGA boards.

There may also be issues with power supply quality, although not as pronounced as with Bitcoin mining. It is imperative that when building the system the user is careful to match the maximum power each power supply rail can provide with an appropriate number of boards.

High heat dissipation and the need to ensure adequate cooling is another challenge. Per the earlier discussion we tried to minimize possible points of failure and removed the individual FPGA fans in favor of all system 120mm fans which are easier to monitor and replace.

3.4. Extension to Schur numbers

We also implemented a Schur numbers[11] solver to compute $S(5)$, which showed similar potential to $W(5, 3)$. Unfortunately the computational difficulty proved to be too great even for this FPGA cluster. To evaluate the computational difficulty of $S(5)$ we kept expanding the initial paths while checking the runtime of a few random initial paths on the FPGA cluster with the goal of a single initial path (task) to complete within 1 hour using $S(5) = 140$ solver. We reached the goal for the initial path length of 24 at which point the estimated number of initial paths is 10^{11} yielding runtime of many thousands of years.

3.5. Other applications and reusability

The increased availability of FPGAs and their demonstrated effectiveness in support of SAT solvers shows that this computational paradigm has great potential for solving combinatorial problems related to computing van der Waerden numbers, such as computing Ramsey and Schur numbers. Moreover, cryptology and other computationally challenging problems seem suitable for this approach as well. With further research and build out of the successful implementations on similar hardware we expect that significant progress will be made in solving problems in this area.

Acknowledgements

We would like to thank Miroslaw Truszczynski and Victor Marek for ideas about Schur and Ramsey numbers as potential extensions of this computational paradigm.

References

[1] Tanbir Ahmed. Some new Van der Waerden numbers and some Van der Waerden-type numbers. *INTEGERS*, 9:65–76, March 2009.

[2] Tanbir Ahmed, Oliver Kullmann, and Hunter Snevily. On the van der waerden numbers. *Discrete Applied Mathematics*, 174:27–51, 2014.

[3] Michael R Dransfield, Victor W Marek, and Mirosaw Truszczyski. Satisfiability and computing van der waerden numbers. In Enrico Giunchiglia and Armando Tacchella, editors, *Theory and Applications of Satisfiability Testing*, volume 2919 of *Lecture Notes in Computer Science*, pages 1–13. Springer Berlin Heidelberg, 2004.

[4] Marijn Heule and Toby Walsh. Internal symmetry. *The 10th International Workshop on Symmetry in Constraint Satisfaction Problems (SymCon'10)*, pages 19–33, 2010.

[5] Michal Kouril. A Backtracking framework for beowulf clusters with an extension to multi-cluster computation and sat benchmark problem implementation. *Dissertation*, November 2006.

[6] Michal Kouril. Computing the van der Waerden number W(3,4)=293. *INTEGERS*, 12:A46, September 2012.

[7] Michal Kouril and John Franco. Resolution tunnels for improved sat solver performance. In Fahiem Bacchus and Toby Walsh, editors, *Theory and Applications of Satisfiability Testing*, volume 3569 of *Lecture Notes in Computer Science*, pages 143–157. Springer Berlin Heidelberg, 2005.

[8] Michal Kouril and Jerome L Paul. The van der Waerden number W (2, 6) is 1132. *Experimental Mathematics*, 17(1):53–61, 2008.

[9] Bruce Landman, Aaron Robertson, and Clay Culver. Some new exact van der waerden numbers. *Integers: Electronic J. Combinatorial Number Theory*, 5(2):A10, 2005.

[10] Satoshi Nakamoto. Bitcoin: A peer-to-peer electronic cash system. *Consulted*, 1(2012):28, 2008.

[11] Issai Schur. Über die Kongruenz $x^m + y^m = z^m (mod\ p)$. *Jahresber. Deutsche Math.-Verein.*, 15:114–116, 1916.

[12] Pascal Schweitzer. Problems of unknown complexity: graph isomorphism and Ramsey theoretic numbers. *Dissertation zur Erlangung des Grades des Doktors der Naturwissenschaften*, 2009.

[13] Bartel Leendert Van der Waerden. Beweis einer Baudetschen Veermutung. *Nieuw Archief voor Wiskunde*, 15:212–216, 1927.

Parallel Computing: On the Road to Exascale
G.R. Joubert et al. (Eds.)
IOS Press, 2016
© *2016 The authors and IOS Press. All rights reserved.*
doi:10.3233/978-1-61499-621-7-533

High-Speed Calculation of Convex Hull in 2D Images Using FPGA

Kenji KANAZAWA [a,1], Kahori KEMMOTSU [a], Yamato MORI [a], Noriyuki AIBE [b] and
Moritoshi YASUANGA [a]

[a] *Integrated Systems Laboratory, University of Tsukuba*
[b] *SUSUBOX, Co., ltd.*

Abstract. Given a set of points, a convex hull is the smallest convex polygon containing all the points. In this paper, we describe a high-speed method for calculating the convex hull of 2D images based on Andrew's monotone chain algorithm using FPGA. This algorithm arranges input points in ascending order, according to their y-coordinates, and repeatedly checks for convexity using every group of three subsequent points by calculating the cross product of the vectors they generate. In order to arrange the points in ascending order, they must be sorted by their y coordinates, which tends to significantly increase the total execution time when calculating the convex hull in larger images. In our method, (1) all the points on a row in a given image are acquired in parallel, (2) only the points that can compose the convex hull are selected, and (3) the convex hull is concurrently built from the selected points during the previous steps. These three steps are successively executed until all rows in the image have been processed. The FPGA implementation of our method produces throughput 23.2 times faster than the GPU implementation.

Keywords. FPGA, GPU, Convex hull, Image processing

Introduction

Given a set of finite points, $P(p_1, p_2, ..., p_n)$, the convex hull of P is the smallest convex polygon that contains all points in P. Calculating convex hulls is a central problem in computational geometry and has many applications, such as image processing, computer vision, and design automation [1]. Several algorithms [2,3,5,6] and their accelerators have been proposed [4,7]. In terms of computational geometry, these algorithms are evaluated under conditions in which the coordinates of all points are previously known. In real-world problems, however, we must first detect the coordinates of points in order to calculate their convex hull. Therefore, detecting coordinates should be included in the calculation of the convex hull in order to apply the algorithm to real-world problems. Our work includes the development of a computer vision system for a chip mounter, a machine that mounts surface-mount devices onto a printed circuit board. Our system captures the image of the device that is to be mounted, calculates its convex hull, and detects the device's rotation using the convex hull.

In this paper, we describe a method for the high-speed calculation of the convex hull in 2D images based on Andrew's monotone chain algorithm [2] using an FPGA. Andrew's monotone chain is one of the best-performing algorithms used to calculate 2D

---

[1]Corresponding Author: Assistant Professor, Faculty of Engineering, Information and Systems, University of Tsukuba, 1-1-1 Ten-ou-dai Tsukuba, Ibaraki, Japan; E-mail: kanazawa@cs.tsukuba.ac.jp

convex hulls, and it is well suited to hardware acceleration because of its simple control structure. This algorithm consists of the following three main steps. (i) All given points are sorted in the ascending order of their y-coordinates. (ii) The top and bottom extreme points, t and b, respectively, are determined, and the other points are partitioned into two subsets, depending on whether they lie to the left or right of line $\overline{tb}$. (iii) The half-hulls in the subsets (left and right hulls) are calculated and merged in order to construct the full convex hull. When applying these steps to a point set in a given image, we must first scan the entire image in order to acquire all the points. This tends to increase the total execution time for larger images. In our method, the following steps are successively executed for each row in the image until all the rows have been processed. (1) All points in a row in the image are acquired. (2) Only points that can form the convex hull are selected. (3) Two half-hulls are simultaneously constructed from the selected points, concurrent with the previous two steps.

We demonstrate the GPU and FPGA implementations of our method, compare their performances using the size of the input image and the number of points in the image as parameters, and show the FPGA implementation outperforms the GPU implementation.

1. Andrew's Monotone Chain Algorithm

Fig. 1 shows the procedure of Andrew's monotone chain algorithm. Before calculating the convex hull, all points in the given point set, S[N], are sorted according to their y-coordinates. In the case of equal y-coordinates, the points are then sorted by their x-coordinates. Subsequently, the top and bottom extreme points (t and b, respectively) are determined, and the other points are partitioned into two subsets by line $\overline{tb}$: points on the left and right sides of $\overline{tb}$ (Steps 1 through 4).

In each subset, all points are successively scanned (the scan begins with t), and their inclusion in the convex hull is determined, i.e., we determine whether they are vertices of the (half) convex hull (Steps 5 and 6). Let us consider the construction of the right-side hull (Step 5) . Here, $S_R[0]$ equals t and is unconditionally pushed onto the stack, H_R, because t is clearly a vertex of the convex hull. The remaining points are then processed as follows.

i.   Point sets $S_R[1]$ and $S_R[2]$ are read out, and the cross product of $\overrightarrow{S_R[0]S_R[1]}$ and $\overrightarrow{S_R[0]S_R[2]}$ is calculated in order to determine whether $S_R[0]$, $S_R[1]$, and $S_R[2]$ create a clockwise turn. If the cross product is greater than zero, these three points make a clockwise turn. If it is less than zero, they make a counter-clockwise turn.

ii. If the points turn clockwise, $S_R[1]$ and $S_R[2]$ are pushed onto H_R in this sequence. Otherwise, $S_R[1]$ is discarded and $S_R[2]$ is pushed onto H_R.

iii. The next point in S_R ($S_R[3]$) is read out, and the top two points in H_R and $S_R[3]$ are considered in the same manner used in Step 1 in order to determine whether they create a clockwise turn.

iv. If a clockwise turn is produced, $S_R[3]$ is pushed onto H_R. Otherwise, the top point in H_R is popped, and then $S_R[3]$ is pushed onto H_R.

v.   Steps 3 and 4 are sequentially repeated for $S_R[i]$ ($i \geq 4$), as well as for $S_R[3]$.

The left-side hull is also constructed in an analogous manner, substituting S_R and H_R with S_L and H_L, respectively (Step 6). Unlike with the right side, points in $S_L[i]$ are stacked onto H_L if the top two points in H_L and $S_L[i]$ ($i \geq 3$) create a counterclockwise turn in Steps 2 and 4. Finally, H_R and H_L are merged in order to construct the full convex hull (Step 7).

Input point set S[N].

Step 1. Arrange points in S[N] into ascending order according to their y-coordinates.

Step 2. Determine the top and bottom extreme points (t and b, respectively).

Step 3. Construct line $\overline{tb}$.

Step 4. Partition the points into two subsets ($S_R[N_R]$ and $S_L[N_L]$) depending on whether they lie on the respective right or left side of $\overline{tb}$.

Step 5. Construct the right-side hull.

begin
```
   for (i = 0, j = 0; i < N_R; i++) {
      while (j >= 2 && cross(H_R[j-2], H_R[j-1], S_R[i])† < 0) j -= 1;
      H_R[j++] = S_R[i];
   }
```
end

Step 6. Construct the left-side hull.

begin
```
   for (i = 0, j = 0; i < N_L; i++) {
      while (j >= 2 && cross(H_L[j-2], H_L[j-1], S_L[i]) > 0) j -= 1;
      H_L[j++] = S_L[i];
   }
```
end

Step 7. Join H_R and H_L in order to construct the full convex hull.

† **cross**(P_0,P_1,P_2) calculates the cross product of $\overrightarrow{P_0P_1}$ and $\overrightarrow{P_0P_2}$.

Figure 1. Andrew's monotone chain

2. Related Work

In [4], the quickhull algorithm [3] was implemented on the GPU. This algorithm incor porates the divide-and-conquer approach, which is analogous to the quicksort method. Unlike Andrew's Monotone chain, this algorithm does not require sorting all points in advance. Using point sets including 10 million points that were randomly generated in 2D space as benchmarks, the implementation of [4] on NVIDIA GTX280 was 14 times faster than that of the Intel Core i7-920. In this approach, however, the coordinates of all points are assumed to be previously known. When applying this method to image pro-cessing, we must first scan the entire image and obtain the coordinates of the points, and the time required to do this must be taken into consideration.

An algorithm for convex hull extraction in 2D binary images was proposed in [5]. First, this algorithm scans the given image in four directions (top to bottom, right to left, bottom to top, and left to right), extracting the vertices of the polygon that contain the point set in the given image. Second, the convexity of the polygon is checked in order to extract a convex hull. This method is similar to Andrew's monotone chain method, in which three consecutive points in the vertices are read out and the cross product is calculated in order to determine whether the points turn clockwise or counterclockwise. In [6], another convex hull algorithm for 2D images was proposed. This algorithm first detects top, bottom, leftmost and rightmost extreme points of the polygon in the image. It then scans the region surrounded by the horizontal and vertical lines that pass through each extreme point respectively in order to extract the other vertices of the polygon, and determine the convex hull of the polygon in the same manner used in [5]. The computa-tion time of these methods varies depending on the size of the convex hulls. For larger convex hulls, significant regions of the image can be omitted, consequentially reducing the total computation time. However, this is not true for smaller convex hulls.

In [7], a parallel algorithm for $n \times n$ images on a reconfigurable mesh computer was proposed. However, the details of its implementation and a performance evaluation were not presented.

Input pixel stream P[H × W].

Step 1. Raster scan P[H × W] and construct two half-hulls.

begin
```
  for (y = 0; y < H; y++) {
    for (x = 0; x < W; x++) {
      /*Acquiring coordinates of valid points*/
      P_tmp = thresholding(P[x + y*H]);
      if (P_tmp = exceeds threshold) {

        /* Construct right-side hull. */
        while (j >= 2 && cross(H_R[j-2], H_R[j-1], P_tmp) < 0) j -= 1;
        H_R[j++] = P_tmp;

        /* Construct left-side hull. */
        while (k >= 2 && cross(H_L[k-2], H_L[k-1], P_tmp) > 0) k -= 1;
        H_L[k++] = P_tmp;
      }
    }
  }
```
end

Step 2. Join H_R and H_L in order to construct the full convex hull.

Figure 2. Outline of our approach

3. Basics of Our Approach

In the following discussion, "*candidates*" denotes the pixels that are not classified as background. As was mentioned in 1, Sorting (Step 1 in Fig. 1) is executed and a total of $3 \times N$ *candidates* are scanned (Steps 2, 4, 5 and 6 in Fig. 1). In addition, we must first scan all pixels in order to acquire the coordinates of the *candidates* in the image before calculating the convex hull, where H is the height of the image and W is the width. This can be dominant of total calculation time. In order to reduce the total execution time, we modify the procedure presented in Fig. 1 as follows.

1. Scan the pixel stream and acquire the coordinates of the *candidates* in raster scan order.
2. Remove Steps 1 through 4, which eliminates the partitioning of the *candidates* into two subsets.
3. Execute Steps 5 and 6 for *all candidates*, respectively, to construct each half-hull.

Fig. 2 shows the procedure used in our modified monotone chain. In this procedure, we do not need to explicitly sort all *candidates* because acquiring the coordinates of the *candidates* in raster scan order is equivalent to sorting the *candidates*. Furthermore, removing the partitioning of the points into two subsets allows us to simultaneously obtain the coordinates of the *candidates* and construct each half-hull. While the apparent computation time required to construct the two half-hulls is $2 \times \mathcal{O}(N)$, its actual computation time decreases to $\mathcal{O}(N)$ by constructing the two half-hulls in parallel. Consequently, we can calculate the convex hull of an image within the time needed to scan the pixel stream.

4. Implementation

4.1. FPGA Implementation

Fig. 3 displays a block diagram of our approach. In this diagram, input pixels are binarized during the thresholding stage, and then delivered to the trimming unit. In each row of the image, the trimming unit selects the *candidates* that are located in the outermost sides in each row and provides them to the subsequent circuits in raster scan order. This is because only the *candidates* that are located in the outermost sides in each row can

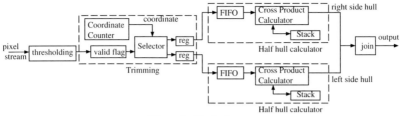

Figure 3. Block diagram

be the vertices of the convex hull. Thus, we can drastically reduce the number of the *candidates* that must be analyzed to at most twice the height of the image. Then, two half-hulls are constructed using the half-hull calculators and merged in order to create the full convex hull.

4.1.1. Trimming Unit

Fig. 4 displays details of the trimming unit. This circuit generates the coordinates of the input pixels using the x- and y-coordinate counter. The x-coordinate counter is incremented each time a pixel is inputted, and the y-coordinate counter is incremented each time all pixels in a row are inputted. The data widths of the x and y-coordinates are 10b and 9b, respectively, for images of size 640×480, and 11b and 10b, respectively, for images of size 1920×1080.

When the first *candidate* in a row is inputted, 'valid flag', which indicates the existence of a *candidate* in the row, is asserted and the values of the coordinate counters, namely, the coordinates of the *candidate* are stored in both 'l-coordinate register' and 'r-coordinate register'. Each time another *candidate* in the row is inputted, the r-coordinate register is overwritten by the values of the coordinate counters at that time. After inputting all the pixels in a row, the values of l- and r-coordinate registers are stored in the FIFOs in the half-hull calculators using the valid flag as the write enables for the FIFOs.

4.1.2. Half-Hull Calculator

Fig. 5 presents details of the half-hull calculator. The half-hull calculator determines if the *candidates* are contained in the half-hull. In this circuit, coordinates of the first two *candidates* are unconditionally stacked. After this, the method repeatedly determines if the subsequent *candidates* are contained in the half-hull.

In order to construct the right-side hull, the top two entries in the stack and the coordinates of the subsequent *candidate*, p_n, are first set to the registers. The coordinates of p_n are also stored in a temporal buffer. The cross product calculator determines the cross product of the two vectors that are generated using these three *candidates*, as in section 1, in order to determine whether the triple produces a clockwise or counterclockwise turn (clockwise if the result is positive, counterclockwise when negative). If a clockwise turn

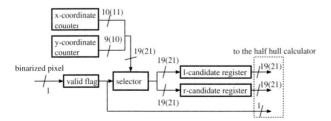

Figure 4. Trimming unit

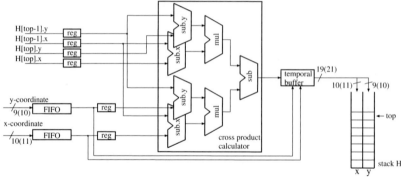

Figure 5. Half-hull calculator

is determined, the coordinates stored in the temporal buffer are pushed onto the stack. Otherwise, the top of the stack is replaced with p_n. The same process is repeated until all inputs have been processed. Simultaneously, the left-side hull is also constructed using the second half-hull calculator in a similar manner, except when accessing the stack. For the left-side hull, an input in the temporal buffer is pushed onto the stack if the input and the top two entries of the stack create a counterclockwise turn. Otherwise, it replaces the information stored at the top of the stack.

After processing all input *candidates*, only the vertices of each half-hull are stored in the stacks, and the full convex hull can straightforwardly be constructed by reading out and joining the *candidates* in each stack.

4.1.3. Parallelizing Trimming Unit

The performance of our approach is limited by the following factors: (1) speed of choosing the *candidates* in the trimming unit, (2) transferring speed of the input pixel stream, and (3) speed of half-hull calculation. In this section, we describe the parallelization of the selecting process of outermost *candidates*.

Fig. 6 illustrates the parallelized trimming unit. All pixels in a row are transferred from the host computer via high-speed I/O (i.e., PCI-express (PCIe)) to a line buffer (a serial-in parallel-out shift register). Then, these pixels are simultaneously read out, binarized and inputted into the parallelized trimming unit. In the following discussion, we assume that the value of the *candidates* is *true* and the value of background pixels is *false*.

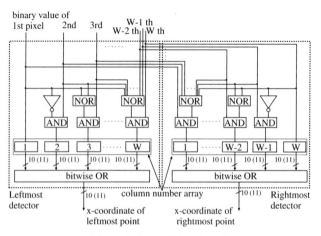

Figure 6. Parallel trimming unit

The left block outputs the x-coordinate of the leftmost *candidate*, and the right block outputs that of the rightmost *candidate*. The column number array is a set of ROMs that contain the column numbers of the image. Each ROM outputs its own column number only if its input is *true*.

In the left block, the i-th ROM ($i > 1$) takes the AND of the i-th pixel's value and the NOR of the pixels' values in the lower columns as its input, although the 1st ROM has only the 1st pixel as its input. Thus, each ROM outputs its own column number if the input pixel for the corresponding column is a *candidate* and those in the lower columns are not. The right block has a similar structure. However, in this case, each ROM outputs its own column number if the input pixel for the corresponding column is a *candidate* and those in the *upper* columns are not.

This circuit can simultaneously evaluate all the pixels in a row, but its actual performance is limited by the processing speed of the half-hull calculators or the data transferring speed of the input pixel stream from the host computer. We discuss these issues in section 5.

4.2. GPU Implementation

In this section, we briefly describe GPU implementation using CUDA in order to create a performance comparison. Our target GPU is NVIDIA GTX780Ti (ELSA GeForce GTX 780 Ti S. A. C). This GPU has 15 streaming multiprocessors (MPs), and each MP can execute up to 2048 threads by assigning two blocks.

Our GPU implementation consists of the following steps like the FPGA implementation: (1) scanning pixels and acquiring *candidates*, (2) calculating two half-hulls, and (3) constructing the full convex hull. Unlike the FPGA implementation, the GPU implementation does not overlap Steps (1) and (2), facilitating its SIMD processing. However, the parallelism in Step (1) is maximized by assigning as many threads as possible.

In Step (1), the target image is partitioned into 30 subimages and each subimage is assigned to one block, given an image whose width is 1024 or less, i.e., size 640×480, which can be seen in Fig. 7. In each block, every pixels in a row in the subimage are assigned to the individual threads, and each block searches the leftmost and rightmost

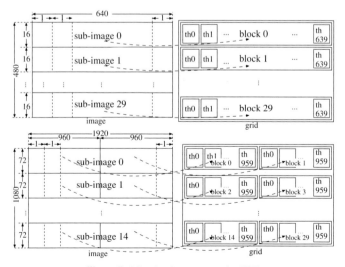

Figure 7. Mapping images onto the GPU

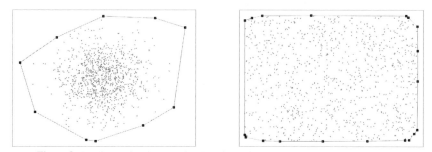

Figure 8. Random points in normal and uniform distributions and their convex hulls

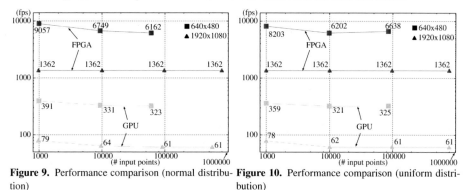

Figure 9. Performance comparison (normal distribution)

Figure 10. Performance comparison (uniform distribution)

candidates in the row using parallel reduction [8], and the selected *candidates* are stored in global memory. This process is applied to all rows in the subimage. Two half-hulls are then constructed in parallel, and the full convex hull is consequentially calculated.

Given an image whose width is more than 1024, i.e., size 1920×1080, the target image is partitioned into 15 subimages. Each subimage is assigned to two blocks because the maximum number for each block is less than the width of the image. The left half of the subimage is assigned to the first block, and the right half is assigned to the second block. As with the 640×480 image, each block independently applies the parallel reduction. Therefore, up to four *candidates* are selected in each row, and their interior *candidates* are deleted in order to reduce the calculation time of the half-hulls. After scanning the entire image, two half-hulls are constructed from the selected *candidates* and joined in order to form the full convex hull.

5. Performance Evaluation

We implemented our method on images up to a size of 1920×1080 pixels on Xilinx XC7V485T. The circuit with a parallel trimming unit occupied 23.0K LUTs, four block RAMs, and four DSPs, which is significantly smaller than current FPGAs. (In addition, we need to implement the PCIe interface circuit. Consequently, total utilization of the resources will be slightly increased.)

We evaluated the performance of our FPGA implementation with a parallel trimming unit and the GPU implementation. In this evaluation, we estimated the performance of the FPGA implementation using logic simulation. The operation frequency was assumed to be 100 MHz. Fig. 8 displays examples of the images we used for the evaluation. The left image represents a point (*candidate*) set, which was randomly generated using a normal distribution, and the right one was generated using a uniform distribution. In these images, dots and rectangles indicate *candidates*, and the rectangles and edges signify

Table 1. Number of clock cycles required to process one row

Image size	Distribution	
	Normal	Uniform
640×480	$21 \sim 34$	$26 \sim 34$
1920×1080	$35 \sim 36$	$35 \sim 36$

the vertices and edges, respectively, of the convex hulls. In the following evaluations, performances of GPU and FPGA are the average of 10 runs, respectively.

Figs. 9 and 10 exhibit the performances of the FPGA and GPU implementations. In each figure, the horizontal axis represents the number of *candidates*, and the vertical axis measures the throughput in frames per second (fps) of the FPGA and GPU implementations. Rectangles indicate throughput for 640×480 images, whereas triangles signify 1920×1080 images. The number of *candidates* in the images increased from one thousand to ten thousand for the 640×480 image and from one thousand to one million for the 1920×1080 image. It should be noted that duplicate *candidates*, which are located on the same pixel, were omitted from the images. Therefore, the actual number of *candidates* has been decreased by 0.1 to 44.1%. The value adjacent to each symbol represents the throughput for the corresponding test case.

As was mentioned in section 4.1.3, the actual performance is limited by the processing speed of the half-hull calculators or by the data-transferring speed of the input pixel stream from the host computer. The effective data transferring rate of the PCIe using the Xilinx KC705 Connectivity Kit is 22.8 Gbps [9] although this value can vary according to the performance of the chipset in the host computer. When the operation frequency of the circuit is 100 MHz, width of the images is W pixels, and data size per pixel is eight bits (our method uses only brightness ('Y signals') of the images encoded by YUV color space, which can be represented by eight bits), the number of clock cycles required to provide one row in images using KC705 is $8 \times W \times 100 \times 10^6/(22.8 \times 10^9)$, which is 23 for 640×480 images and 68 for 1920×1080 images, respectively. Table 1 shows the average number of clock cycles needed to process one row of an image in our experiment. When processing 1920×1080 images, the circuit's performance is limited by the data transferring speed. In another case, the processing speed of the half-hull calculators is the limiting factor when examining the performance of the circuit, excluding some of the 640×480 images that were generated using a normal distribution and the number of the *candidates* is 1000.

As can be seen in Figs. 9 and 10, the FPGA implementation results exceeds those of the GPU implementation in all test cases, and the speedup ratio of the FPGA implementation to the GPU implementation is as large as 23.2.

6. Application to Surface-Mount Device Detection

As was mentioned in the Introduction, our work includes the development of a computer vision system for a chip mounter. In general, pins of an electric device have higher brightness than the other region of the device. Thus, we can extract the pins of an electric device by binarizing the device's image. From the binarized image, we can estimate the mechanical features of the device such as the form, the central position, and the rotation.

Our system calculates a convex hull from the binarized image of a device, detects the minimum bounding rectangle (MBR) for the convex hull, and estimates the rotation of the device using the rotation of the MBR in order to correct the device's rotation on the mounting position of the printed circuit board. Fig. 11 exhibits the detection of MBR of a chip capacitor. The leftmost image displays a chip capacitor, the second from the left is

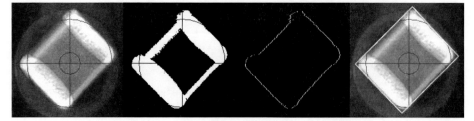

Figure 11. Detection of the minimum bounding rectangle

the binarized image of the chip capacitor, the third from the left is the result of extraction of the *candidates* for the convex hull vertices, and the rectangle to the rightmost shows the result of the detection of the MBR. After detecting the MBR, our system estimates the rotation of the device from the rotation of the MBR, and then the chip mounter corrects the rotation of the device on the mounting position of the printed circuit board.

In our current implementation, we separate the object and background in a given image using simple binarization and a static threshold value. Therefore, the accuracy of the detection is influenced by disturbances such as the variation in illuminance of external light from outside of the chip mounter. The introduction of a more sophisticated thresholding method will be included in future work.

7. Conclusions

In this paper, we proposed a high-speed method for calculating the convex hull of 2D images using FPGA. Our method calculates the convex hull in a given image at a rate as high as 9057 fps and 1362 fps for images of size 640×480 and 1920×1080 pixels, respectively, and requires less hardware resource. In many applications, convex hull calculation is used as a preliminary task for more sophisticated work. In our method, large amounts of hardware resource are still available, and we can execute more sophisticated work using the same FPGA. Furthermore, we applied our proposed method to a computer vision system in a chip mounter in order to estimate the rotation of an electric device. As part of our ongoing research, we aim to improve the robustness of the rotation estimation using the remaining hardware resources.

References

[1] F. P. Preparata and M. I. Shamos, "Computational Geometry: An Introduction", Springer-Verlag, 1985.

[2] A. M. Andrew, "Another efficient algorithm for determining the convex hull in two dimensions", Information Processing Letters, vol. 9, pp. 216–219, 1979.

[3] W .Eddy, "A New Convex Hull Algorithm for Planar Sets", ACM Transactions on Mathematical Software, Vol. 3, No. 4, pp. 398–403, 1977.

[4] S. Srungarapyu, D. P .Reddy, K. Kothapalli and P. J. Narayanan, "Fast Two Dimensional Convex Hull on the GPU", AINA-2011, pp.7–12, 2011.

[5] Q. Ye, "A fast algorithm for convex hull extraction in 2D images", Pattern Recognition Letters 16, pp.531–537, 1995

[6] X. Zhang, Z. Tang, J. Yu and M. Guo, "A Fast Convex Hull Algorithm for Binary Image", Informatica (Slovenia) 34. 3, pp.369–376, 2010

[7] A. Errami, M. Khaldoun, J. Elmesabahi and O.Bouattane, "$\Theta(1)$ Time Algorithm for Structural Characterization of Multi-Leveled Images and its Applications on Reconfigurable Mesh Computer", Journal of Intelligent and Robotics Systems 44(4), pp.277–290, 2005

[8] G. E. Belloch, "Prefix sums and their applications", Technical report, CMU-CS-90-190, 1990

[9] Xilinx Inc., "Kintex-7 FPGA Connectivity Targeted Reference Design User Guide", 2014

Parallel Computing: On the Road to Exascale
G.R. Joubert et al. (Eds.)
IOS Press, 2016
© 2016 The authors and IOS Press. All rights reserved.
doi:10.3233/978-1-61499-621-7-543

Workload distribution and balancing in FPGAs and CPUs with OpenCL and TBB

Rafael Asenjo[a] , Angeles Navarro[a] , Andres Rodriguez[a] and Jose Nunez-Yanez[b]

[a] *Universidad de Málaga, Andalucía Tech, Spain*
[b] *University of Bristol, UK*

Abstract. In this paper we evaluate the performance and energy effectiveness of FPGA and CPU devices for a kind of parallel computing applications in which the workload can be distributed in a way that enables simultaneous computing in addition to simple off loading. The FPGA device is programmed via OpenCL using the recent availability of commercial tools and hardware while Threading Building Blocks (TBB) is used to orchestrate the load distribution and balancing between FPGA and the multicore CPU. We focus on streaming applications that can be implemented as a pipeline of stages. We present an approach that allows the user to specify the mapping of the pipeline stages to the devices (FPGA, GPU or CPU) and the number of active threads. Using as a case study a real streaming application, we evaluate how these parameters affect the performance and energy efficiency using as reference a heterogeneous system that includes four different types of computational resources: a quad-core Intel Haswell CPU, an embedded Intel HD6000 GPU, a discrete NVIDIA GPU and an Altera FPGA.

Keywords. FPGA, OpenCL, heterogeneous scheduling, streaming application.

Introduction

Energy efficiency is a fundamental consideration in both embedded and High Performance Computing (HPC). In HPC computational complexity means that power requirements of server racks have reached the level of megawatts and electricity bills continue to increase. Additionally, device power density is limiting the option of using more logic to solve problems in parallel. Confronted with this energy challenge designers are moving towards heterogeneous architectures in which specialized hardware units accelerate complex tasks. A good example of this trend is the introduction of GPUs (Graphics Processing Units) for general purpose computing with the help of parallel programming framework such as OpenCL (Open Computing Language). OpenCL is a cross-platform parallel programming model designed to facilitate effective use of heterogeneous processing platforms. FPGAs (Field Programmable Gate Arrays) are an alternative high performance technology that offers bit-level parallel computing in contrast with the word-level parallelism deployed in GPUs and CPUs. Bit-level parallel computing fits certain algorithms that cannot be parallelized easily with traditional methods. FPGAs also excel in tasks that require very low latency such as financial computing thanks to its ability to establish direct wired connections between streaming processing pipelines customized for the input data without intermediate memory transfers. Recently, FPGAs manufacturers have been pioneering OpenCL for FPGAs aiming to overcome their low-level programming models. In this paper we consider an accelerated system that combines FPGAs and GPUs with OpenCL support together with a multi-core CPU that can act as host or actively participate in the computation. We evaluate different approaches to distribute the workload between host and accelerator in order to exploit processing threads mapped to the host in addition to the accelerator. The objective is to measure if simultaneous computing among these devices could be more favorable from and energy and/or performance points of view compared with off-loading and CPU idling. As a case study, we introduce ViVid, an application that implements an object (e.g., face) detection algorithm [1] using a "sliding window object detection" approach [2]. ViVid consists of 5 pipeline stages as we depict in Fig. 1. The first and the last one are the Input and Output stages (serial), whereas the three middle stages are parallel (or stateless).

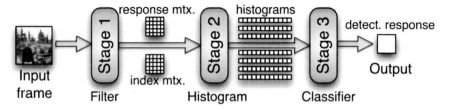

Figure 1. Vivid application

The main contribution of this paper is the study of the performance portability that a realistic OpenCL application can obtain in FPGA devices compared with GPU and CPU devices. We also propose a mechanism to simultaneously compute the OpenCL kernels with FPGA (GPU) and a multicore CPU, and explore its effects on performance and energy.

The rest of the paper is organized as follows. Section 1 reviews background and related work that uses FPGAs with OpenCL for processing intensive applications. Section 2 presents details of our test system that also considers discrete and embedded GPU devices as comparison points. Section 3 evaluates the performance, power and energy characteristics of each of these devices individually to asses their suitability. Section 4 explores the possibility of using the FPGA or GPU device simultaneously with the multicore CPU to further accelerate the system and reduce overall processing time. Section 5 presents the conclusions and proposes future work.

1. Background and Related work

There are significant efforts at using FPGAs as an acceleration technology based on the same programming model as the one used for other accelerators in the system. One of the objectives is to make FPGAs more attractive devices for software engineers by raising the level of abstraction and significantly increasing the level of productivity [3]. FPGAs are hardware configurable after manufacturing so custom circuits can be created to match the application requirements. Modern FPGAs are formed by a 2-dimensional array of basic logic cells that are used to form logic and also include additional embedded memory, DSP blocks, high speed transceivers and I/Os, CPU cores (e.g. ARM/Intel) and routing which wire together all these elements to create custom circuits. FPGAs have been traditionally programmed using a RTL flow (e.g. VHDL/Verilog) but this has started to change over the last few years. Altera, for example, has introduced the Software Development Kit (SDK) for OpenCL (AOCL) which is an OpenCL-based heterogeneous parallel programming environment for their devices. There are two steps to program a FPGA with an OpenCL application using the AOCL tool. Firstly, the Altera Offline Compiler (AOC) compiles the OpenCL kernels and secondly, the host-side C compiler compiles the host application and then links the compiled OpenCL kernels to it [4]. Each OpenCL kernel is compiled to a custom pipelined-style parallel circuit consuming FPGA resources. AOCL favours a single but very deep pipeline in which multiple work-items execute in parallel. It is possible to replicate pipelines for even more parallelism creating multiple compute units. The custom FPGAs circuits can provide better performance per watt compared to GPUs for certain applications [5] according to the Altera literature.

The more common approach of using these devices consists of offloading complex kernels to the accelerator by selecting the best execution resource at compile time. It is also possible to do run-time selection by including different versions of the same kernel as long as enough hardware resources are available to implement all the kernel versions simultaneously. The idea of run-time has been explored previously in the literature mainly around systems that combine GPUs and CPUs. For example, selection for performance with desktop CPUs and GPUs has been done in [6] that assigns percentages of work to both targets before making a selection based on heuristics. Energy aware decisions also involving CPUs and GPUs have been considered in [7] which requires proprietary code. A more related work in the context of streaming applications [8] considers performance and energy when looking for the optimal mapping of pipeline stages to CPU and on-chip GPU, although FPGAs are not studied. Recently, IBM has proposed a new programming language called Lime and the Liquid Metal [9] system that combines GPUs, FPGAs and CPUs. This approach uses a proprietary language and cannot leverage the extended efforts invested in creating high-level compilers by the different vendors. SnuCL also proposes [10] an OpenCL framework for heterogeneous CPU/GPU clusters, considering how to combine clusters with different GPU and CPU hardware under a single OS image. In this paper we extend previous research around the idea of run-time selection by considering the efficiency of OpenCL-supported FPGAs compared with GPUs and CPUs and also the possibility of deploying CPUs and FPGAs simultaneously.

2. Test system specifications

In order to perform a fair comparison a single test system is considered in which all the computational resources are installed. This test system is formed by a desktop environment running Windows 7 64-bit and equipped with the different OpenCL targets which are the Terasic DE5-net board that includes an Altera Stratix V A7 FPGA, a Core i7 4770k 3.5 GHz Haswell CPU with a HD6000 embedded GPU and a Nvidia Quadro K600 GPU. We have selected the K600 GPU as an example of low-power device with comparable thermal power dissipations rated at 25 W for the FPGA and 40 W for the GPU.

Currently the larger FPGA available in the Altera OpenCL program is the Stratix V D8. Our device is the Stratix V A7 FPGA that is comparable in size to the D8 in all the parameters except in embedded DSP blocks. The Altera Stratix V A7 FPGA contains 622,000 logic elements comparable to the 695,000 available in the Stratix V D8 FPGA. The embedded memory in both FPGAs is rated at 52 Mbit for both devices, which can be used as private or local memory in OpenCL. The main difference is that the A7 device contains 256 27x27 DSP blocks, which is much lower than the 1963 DSP blocks present in the D8. The device memory is formed by 4GB DDR3 at 800 MHz installed in the DE5-net board with a max bandwidth of 25 GB/s.

 The Nvidia Quadro K600 has 192 CUDA cores, 1 GB DDR3 memory, the max bandwidth is equivalent to the DE5-net and the top floating point performance is indicated as 336 GFLOPs. This top performance is much more difficult to determine in the FPGA device since the amount of floating point hardware that can be implemented depends on the type of operations and the logic that is required by the rest of the algorithm. One of the strengths of the FPGA is its abundant and flexible local memory that can be used to buffer data reducing the need for off-chip memory accesses. The K600 and the Stratix V are both manufactured using a 28 nm process and were introduced in 2012 and 2011 respectively.

Table 1 shows the measurements taken to evaluate the (idle) power of the system when no benchmarks are running and only OS background activity is present. With this data it is possible to estimate that the idle power of the GPU card is around 8 Watts while the idle power of the FPGA card is approximately 22 Watts. Note that this is the power of the whole card including device memory and not just the GPU or FPGA devices. The system without accelerators shows the idle power without any cards installed. As a reference the idle power of the CPU socket that includes the quad-core and the embedded GPU has been measured at 9 Watts using the Intel energy counters available on chip. We can consider these values estimations that should be further refine with proper instrumentation in future work.

Table 1. Analysis of idle power for whole system

	Idle Power (Watts)
No accelerator	44
GPU in	52
FPGA in	66
GPU-FPGA in	74

3. Performance and energy evaluation of individual devices

 Table 2 shows the results of running the Vivid application accelerated by a single device for the configuration that includes the three processing kernels that correspond to the parallel stages: filter (F1), histogram (F2) and classifier (F3). A stream of 100 LD (416x600) images was used in our experiments. The power has been estimated by measuring the wall plug power with the benchmark running and then subtracting the idle power reported in section 3. The host code, accelerator code for the CPUs and accelerator code for the GPUs have been compiled with Visual studio 2013, TBB 4.3 and Nvidia OpenCL 6.0 respectively. The GPUs' OpenCL kernels were compiled using -03. The FPGA code is compiled offline with version 14.1 of the Altera AOC tools with the addition of the -fpc pragma that instructs the compiler to remove floating-point rounding operations and conversions whenever possible and carry additional mantissa bits to maintain precision during internal operations. The utilization ratios of the different logic resources and resulting kernel frequency for the FPGA are shown in Table 3 depending in which stage is implemented in the device.

Table 2. Power and performance analysis

Device	Time (sec.)	Throughput (fps)	Power (Watts)	Energy (Joules)
CPU (1 core)	167.610	0.596	37	6201
CPU (4 cores)	50.310	1.987	92	4628
FPGA	13.480	7.418	5	67
On-chip GPU	7.855	12.730	16	125
Discrete GPU	13.941	7.173	47	655

Table 3. FPGA kernels resource utilization and frequency

Kernel	Logic resources (Altera Logic Modules)	DSP blocks	Memory (bits)	Freq (Mhz)
F1	77,425 (32%)	44/256	6,896,354 (13%)	283
F3	163,733 (69%)	106/256	18,693,257 (35%)	225
F1+F2+F3	209,848 (89%)	162/256	24,679,220 (47%)	186

Table 2 shows that the power used by the FPGA card when it is active is significantly lower than the other resources. This is surprising since its TDP is comparable to the discrete GPU. An analysis of the profiling reports shows that the FPGA pipeline stalls waiting for memory around 10% of the time which could have an implication in power but in any case this result indicates a good power efficiency of the FPGA card with this application.

Fig. 2 shows the breakdown of the average time per frame (in ms.) for each stage of ViVid and on each device. Labels onGPU and disGPU represent de on-chip and discrete GPUs, respectively. Interestingly, stages 1 and 2 map better on the on-chip GPU, whereas stage 3 behaves best on the FPGA. We also show the times that data transfers (host-to-device and device-to-host) require in each case. Clearly, these times are lower for the integrated GPU because it does not require PCIe bus transactions, as the others devices do. For instance, data transfer times on the FPGA are 1.7x higher than those on the on-chip GPU. Fig. 2 suggest that the most effective configuration should combine the embedded GPU and FPGA simultanously.

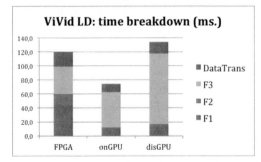

Figure 2. Breakdown of times for each stage and on each device.

4. Simultaneous computing experimental results

When an application like ViVid runs on a heterogeneous architecture, it is possible to distribute the workload so that more than one device is active simultaneously. In this case many possible configurations are possible. In this section we focus on combining CPU and GPU or FPGA devices and leave an extension that uses all the accelerator resources simultaneously (i.e. CPU and GPU and FPGA) as future work. Fig. 3 graphically depicts the possible mappings for the three parallel stages to the CPU cores and the accelerator (GPU or FPGA). In addition, it is possible to control the number of active CPU cores that compute together with the accelerator to minimize the execution time, the energy consumption, or both (depending on the metric of interest). The pipeline mapping determines the device where the different stages of the pipeline can execute. Let's assume that a pipeline consists of S1, S2, ... Sn stages. We use a n-tuple to specify a static stage mapping to the accelerator and the CPU devices: {m1, m2, ..., mn}. The i-th element of the tuple, mi, will specify if stage Si can be mapped to the accelerator and CPU, (mi= 1), or if it can only be mapped to the CPU (mi= 0). If mi= 1, the item that enters stage Si will check if the accelerator is available, in which case it will execute on it; otherwise, it will execute on the CPU. For instance, for the ViVid example of Fig. 3 we represent the tuples (row major order): {1,1,1}, {1,0,0}, {0,1,0}, {0,0,1}, {1,1,0}, {1,0,1}, {0,1,1}, {0,0,0}. In our implementation, mapping {1,1,1} represents a special case: if the accelerator is available when a new item enters the pipeline, then all the stages that process it will be mapped to it.

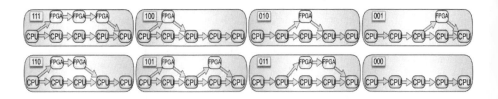

Figure 3. Possible stage mappings of stages to the accelerator and/or CPU for ViVid.

Fig. 4 shows the performance (fps or frames per second) and energy usage (Joules) after using configuration {100} that maps the first Vivid filter (F1) to the accelerator. The x-axis represents the number of threads that goes from 1 to 8, to evaluate the hiper-threading feature of the Haswell CPU. Note that the energy is represented in log scale. In the figure we see that if the number of threads is limited to one then only the FPGA or GPU accelerator are used, but if the number of threads is higher the scheduler uses the cores as additional computing resources. It is possible to observe in Fig. 4 that when only one thread is active the performance of all the accelerators is comparable but the FPGA configuration is much more energy efficient. In this case, the FPGA energy consumption is 11% and 30% more energy efficient than the consumption on the integrated and discrete GPUs, respectively. Adding additional threads results in the cores participating in the computation, which increases throughput but it is more energy inefficient. When the third stage (F3) is mapped as shown in Fig. 5 both energy efficiency and throughput increase when both CPUs and accelerators participate in the computation. The combination of CPU and FPGA is the best choice for this stage for both energy and performance purposes. Now with 8 threads, the FPGA is 39% faster and 54% more energy efficient than the discrete GPU.

Finally, Fig. 6 shows the case when all the stages try to use the accelerator as its first choice. This configuration results in the higher performance achieving almost 20 fps for the embedded GPU case, 12 fps for the FPGA and 8 fps for the discrete GPU. For a single thread, performance is comparable for all the accelerators but the FPGA is the most energy efficient. The FPGA is 1.8x and 9.2x more energy efficient than the embedded and the discrete GPUs, respectively. Once the number of threads increases and the cores participate in the computation, the combination of the embedded GPU and the CPU is more energy efficient than the FPGA and CPU, but overall energy efficiency decreases because we reach the point of diminishing returns when using 4 threads. Critically, this reduction of energy efficiency takes place despite the overall increase in throughput. The fact that the embedded GPU is more energy efficient than the FPGA for the multi-threaded configuration could be explained in part due to the overheads of the data movements over the PCIe bus compared with the tighter integration between CPUs and embedded GPUs that share the L3 cache. In the case of the discrete accelerators the presence of the PCIe bus can quickly become a performance bottleneck especially when computation is shared between cores and accelerators. Other factor that explains the higher performance of the integrated GPU is that the OpenCL compiler generates a very efficient binary for the first kernel/stage, as we saw in Fig. 2.

In any case further work is necessary to understand how the tighter integration results in better performance and energy efficiency. Overall, the discrete GPU results cannot match the results observed with the embedded GPU and FPGA configurations, mainly due to the less efficient third kernel (see Fig. 2). Let's keep in mind that we use the same OpenCL source code of the kernels for all accelerators. This was done on purpose to evaluate performance portability of the same code version on the different devices. As a future work we plan to study which OpenCL optimizations work well for each accelerator.

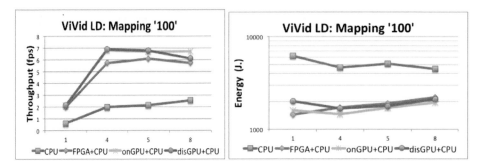

Figure 4. Stage 1 acceleration with different hardware configurations.

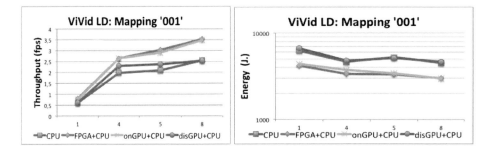

Figure 5. Stage 3 acceleration with different hardware configurations

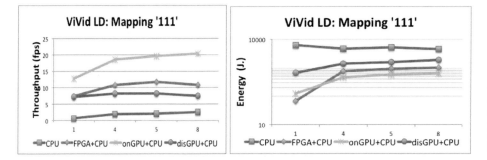

Figure 6. Stages 1+2+3 acceleration with different hardware configurations.

5. Conclusions

This paper has investigated the effects of distributing the workload between accelerators consisting of GPUs, FPGAs and CPU cores. From the conducted experiments a number of conclusions can be drawn. The first conclusion is that the FPGA device programmed with OpenCL is competitive with other accelerator types and shows good performance portability characteristics. It obtains the most energy efficient configuration superior to both embedded and discrete GPUs as seen in Fig. 6.

This takes place despite that the OpenCL code has not been optimized for the FPGA device and is essentially the same code used to program the GPU devices. The second conclusion is that the single thread configurations in which the CPU cores do not participate in the computation are more energy efficient. On the other hand Fig. 6 also shows that if the objective is to obtain raw performance the additional deployment of the cores is beneficial and it can double throughput. Future work involves optimizing the code for the FPGA device focusing on reducing the number of pixels that must be fetched from device memory by reusing pixels shared by the filter operations and also increasing hardware occupancy by activating all kernels simultaneously instead of serially as done in these experiments. We also plan to develop a system that will allow to use the GPU and FPGA cores simultaneously with the CPU cores, deploying all the computation resources at the same time.

Acknowledgments

This work was partly founded by Universidad de Málaga:"Ayudas para el fomento de la internacionalización" funded by ERDF and by the following Spanish projects: TIN 2013-42253-P and P11-TIC-08144. We also aknowledge the support from the EPSRC, UK to perform this research thanks to the ENPOWER EP/L00321X/1 award.

References

[1] AMeit Dikmen, Derek Hoiem, and Thomas S Huang. A data driven method for feature transformation. In Proc. of CVPR, pages 3314{3321, 2012.
[2] Michael Jones and Paul Viola. Fast multi-view face detection. Mitsubishi Electric Research Lab TR-20003-96, 3, 2003.
[3] Czajkowski, et. Al. "From opencl to high-performance hardware on FPGAS," Field Programmable Logic and Applications (FPL), 2012 22nd International Conference on , vol., no., pp.531,534, 29-31 Aug. 2012
[4] Altera SDK for OpenCL Programming Guide, available at: http://www.altera.co.uk/literature/hb/opencl-sdk/aocl_programming_guide.pdf
[5] OpenCL on FPGAs for GPU Programmers, available at:
http://www.altera.co.uk/products/ software/opencl/opencl-index.html
[6] Prasanna Pandit and R. Govindarajan. 2014. Fluidic Kernels: Cooperative Execution of OpenCL Programs on Multiple Heterogeneous Devices. Annual IEEE/ACM International Symposium on Code Generation and Optimization.
[7] Dolbeau, R.; Bodin, F.; de Verdiere, G.C., "One OpenCL to rule them all?," Multi-/Many-core Computing Systems (MuCoCoS), 2013 IEEE 6th International Workshop on , vol., no., pp.1,6, 7-7 Sept. 2013
[8] A. Vilches, A. Navarro, R. Asenjo, F. Corbera, R. Gran, and M. Garzaran *Mapping streaming applications on commodity multi-CPU and GPU on-chip processors*, IEEE Tranactions on Parallel and Distributed Systems, DOI: 10.1109/TPDS.2015.2432809, May 2015.
[9] Takizawa, H.; Sato, K.; Kobayashi, H., "SPRAT: Runtime processor selection for energy-aware computing," Cluster Computing, 2008 IEEE International Conference on , vol., no., pp.386,393, Sept. 29 2008-Oct. 1 2008
[10] Joshua Auerbach, et. Al. "A compiler and runtime for heterogeneous computing". In Proceedings of the 49th Annual Design Automation Conference (DAC '12). ACM, New York, NY, USA, 271-276.

Parallel Computing: On the Road to Exascale
G.R. Joubert et al. (Eds.)
IOS Press, 2016

doi:10.3233/978-1-61499-621-7-553

A Run-Time System for Partially Reconfigurable FPGAs: The case of STMicroelectronics SPEAr board

George CHARITOPOULOS [a,b,1], Dionisios PNEVMATIKATOS [a,b],
Marco D. SANTAMBROGIO [c], Kyprianos PAPADIMITRIOU [a,b] and Danillo PAU [d]

[a] *Institute of Computer Science, Foundation for Research and Technology, Hellas, Greece*
[b] *Technical University of Crete, Greece*
[c] *Politecnico di Milano, Dipartimento di Elettronica e Informazione, Italy*
[d] *STMicroelectronics, Italy*

Abstract

During recent years much research focused on making Partial Reconfiguration (PR) more widespread. The FASTER project aimed at realizing an integrated toolchain that assists the designer in the steps of the design flow that are necessary to port a given application onto an FPGA device. The novelty of the framework lies in the use of partial dynamic reconfiguration seen as a first class citizen throughout the entire design flow in order to exploit FPGA device potential.

The STMicroelectronics SPEAr development platform combines an ARM processor alongside with a Virtex-5 FPGA daughter-board. While partial reconfiguration in the attached board was considered as feasible from the beginning, there was no full implementation of a hardware architecture using PR. This work describes our efforts to exploit PR on the SPEAr prototyping embedded platform. The paper discusses the implemented architecture, as well as the integration of Run-Time System Manager for scheduling (run-time reconfiogurable) hardware and software tasks. We also propose improvements that can be exploited in order to make the PR utility more easy-to-use on future projects on the SPEAr platform.

Keywords. partial reconfiguration, run-time system manager, FPGA

Introduction

Reconfiguration can dynamically adapt the functionality of hardware systems by swapping in and out hardware tasks. To select the proper resource for loading and triggering hardware task reconfiguration and execution in partially reconfigurable systems with FPGAs, efficient and flexible runtime system support is needed [1],[2]. In this work we present the realization of the Partial Reconfiguration (PR) utility on the SPEAr prototyping development platform, we integrate the Run-Time System Manager (RTSM) pre-

---

[1] Corresponding Author: George Charitopoulos: Technical University of Crete, Greece;
E-mail: gcharitopoulos@isc.tuc.gr.

sented on [3] and check the correctness of the resulting system with the use of a synthetic task graph, using hardware tasks from a RayTracer application [4] executed in parallel with a software edge detection application.

Our main contributions are: (i) an architecture that achieves partial reconfiguration (PR) on the SPEAr's FPGA daughter-board, based on a basic DMA module provided by [4], (ii) the integration of a state of the art RTSM on the SPEAr side, and (iii) concurrent execution of HW and SW applications on the SPEAr platform.

STMicroelectronics distributes the SPEAr development platforms with an optional configurable embedded logic block; this block could be configured at manufacturing time only. With our approach, the configurability can extend even after the distribution of the board to the customers with the use of PR on the FPGA daughter-board. Despite the fact that PR has been done many times before the realization on the specific SPEAr board is done for the first time.

The next section presents the specifics for the SPEAr development board and its FPGA daughterboard, and the architectural details for the realization of PR on the SPEAr platform. Section 1 offers a performance evaluation of the actual SPEAr-FPGA system and Section 2 offers insights on the limitations faced during this effort and the advantages of PR realization on the SPEAr platform. Finally Section 3 concludes our work.

1. The SPEAr Platform and Partial Reconfiguration

In this section we describe the technology specifics and induced limitations of the SPEAr platform, and its Virtex-5 FPGA daughter-board; we also present the architecture implemented for the realization of partial reconfiguration.

1.1. SPEAr Development board

The SPEAr platform is equipped with an ARM dual-core Cortex-A9@600MHz with two level of caching and 256MB DDR3 main memory connected to the ARM processors through an 64-bit AXI bus. The board also supports several external peripherals to be connected using standard interfaces such as Ethernet, USB, UART, etc. By means of the auxiliary EXPansion Interface (EXPI) present on the board, it is also possible to plug in dedicated boards to expand the SOC with customizable external hardware. The interconnection's communication is driven by the AHBLite protocol. The choice of the EXPI interface and of the AHBlite protocol lets designers attach custom acceleration boards and interface them quickly, thanks to the simplicity of the AHBLite protocol. The overall interconnection scheme of the system is summarized in Fig. 1.

The AXI bus supports two data channel transfers, where the read and write can be done simultaneously. On the other hand the AHB has only one data channel and read and write operations cannot be overlapped, leading to lower copmpared to AXI. Moreover, the internal interconnection crossbars that convert from AHB to AXI bus increase the overall transfer latency and constitute a further bottleneck to the board's performance when multiple transmissions from main memory and the external components are happening simultaneously. Specifically the measured transfer of the AHB bus is 1 MB/s.

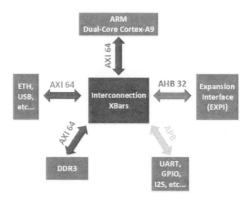

Figure 1. Interconnection scheme of the SPEAr platform.

1.2. The Xilinx Virtex-5 daughter-board

The FPGA board ships an auxiliary bidirectional interface (EXPI) to connect external peripherals. Since the SPEAr board was designed for functional prototyping, the EXPI interface provides a single AHBLite bus with both master and slave interfaces on the board side, thus requiring external components to implement these same interfaces.

The AHBLite protocol uses a single data channel for communications, so that it is impossible to receive and send data at the same time, e.g., to have a continuous stream between memory and computing cores. This is a major limitation in exploiting hardware acceleration, considering the low frequency (166 MHz) of the channel and the DMA burst size (1KByte).

The SPEAr board uses a Virtex-5 LX110 FPGA, a device series that support partial reconfiguration. A most common and efficient way to achieve PR on a Xilinx FPGA is by accessing the Internal Configuration Access Port (ICAP). While usually Virtex-5 boards provide a number of I/O peripherals (such as SD card Reader, UART interface, LEDs, switches, etc), the SPEAr board supports I/O is only through the EXPI. This poses a limitation to the designer, who has to transfer the reconfiguration data from an external memory connected to the SPEAr, e.g. a USB stick, to the FPGA, using a slow DMA interface.

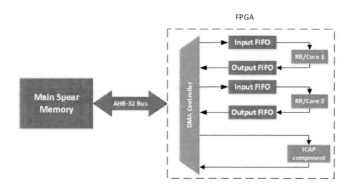

Figure 2. Main buses and components used in the communication between the SPEAr and the FPGA.

Fig. 2 shows the architecture involved in data transfer from the DMA memory to the AHB bus and finally to the reconfigurable regions (RR), which accommodate the hardware cores for the application, the ICAP component. Besides the two reconfigurable regions/cores, we also use an ICAP component for reconfiguration.

1.3. Partial Reconfiguration on the SPEAr platform

In order to perform a data transfer from the SPEAr board to the FPGA and vice versa, we need to analyze the actions performed on the two ends (SPEAr board, FPGA). On the one end is the SPEAr board, which upon booting, loads a Linux Kernel/OS and opens a bash console on the host PC, accessed by the UART port. Through this command line a software driver, that enables the communication with the AHB bus is loaded. The driver was provided to us by [4], provides the user with simple functions that initialize and perform DMA transfers functions:

- *fstart_transfer*: Used to initiate the transfer and also informs the DMA controller which RR/core the data are being transferred to or from.
- *fwait_dma*: Used to inform the OS when the dma transfer has ended.
- *fwrite_buffer* and *fread_buffer*: Used from the user write and read the buffers accommodating the dma transfer data.

The other end of the communication is the FPGA. The FPGA implements a DMA controller as well as input and output data FIFOs for the cores. In order for the different RR/cores to be able to understand whether the incoming data refers to the specific core the DMA implements a handshake master/slave protocol with valid data and not valid data signals for each RR/core. The user, through the command console initiates the transfer, deciding from which RR/core needs data, or to which RR/core data are sent. Upon initiating a transfer between the SPEAr and the FPGA the user sets an integer parameter on the *fstart_transfer* arguments, which is the selection of the core the transfer refers to.

To achieve PR the first decision made was how the reconfiguration would be done from the FPGA side. Xilinx offers several primitives in order to use PR on an FPGA. The most common, as mentioned is the ICAP controller located on the fabric's side, provides the user logic with access to the Virtex-5 configuration interface.

Then the way the ICAP will be accessed has to be determined. One option is the implementation of a MicroBlaze micro-processor, which sends the reconfiguration data to the ICAP through the PLB bus with the use of Xilinx kernel functions. The second more complex option of accessing the ICAP is via a FSM, which will control directly the ICAP input signals and the ICAP's timing diagrams. In the second case the ICAP primitive is instantiated directly inside the VHDL source code.

The first option is easier in the simple case. However in our case synchronization issues arise between the clocks of the ARM processors (SPEAr), PLB bus (FPGA), MicroBlaze (FPGA) and ICAP (FPGA). Thus the use of a MicroBlaze processor was deemed impossible. To implement the second option we implemented a FIFO that would store 15 words at a time, once this limit was reached these 15 words to the were sent to the ICAP, after applying the bitswapping technique mentioned on the Xilinx ICAP User Guide [5]. The architecture of the ICAP component we created is shown in Fig. 3.

To control the ICAP component behavior we created a custom FSM, that depending on the current state of the system, produces the correct sequence of control signals responsible for the device reconfiguration. The FSM state diagram is shown in Fig. 4.

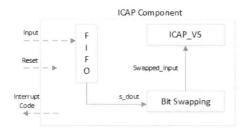

Figure 3. The ICAP component architecture.

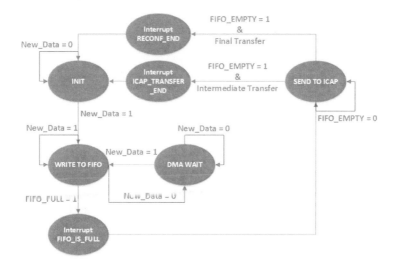

Figure 4. The FSM controlling the reconfiguration process.

During the initialization state, the system waits for new data to appear on the DMA FIFO, specifically the data have to be about the ICAP core, i.e. the *fstart_transfer* has the appropriate core selection. Once new data arrive, the FSM begins to write new data to the intermediate FIFO, upon completion the ICAP component produces an interrupt, sent directly to SPEAr. If for any reason the DMA transfer stops, the FSM enters a wait for new data state, until new data appear again in the DMA FIFO. Then the FSM begins the reconfiguration phase by sending data to the ICAP controller, as soon as all the data, residing on the intermediate FIFO have been transferred, the ICAP component produces another interrupt. The value of this interrupt depends on whether or not this reconfiguration data transfer is the last or not. If it is the interrupt produced informs the SPEAr for the reconfiguration ending point, if not, the interrupt denotes the ending of an intermediate data transfer. While the reconfiguration process is active, this FSM prohibits other cores on the FPGA to perform a data transfer through the DMA, this is necessary to ensure the validity of the reconfiguration process. Finally, when the reconfiguration ends the ICAP component resets the newly reconfigured region, as dictated by the Xilinx user guides. The interrupt codes for the three interrupts are:

- Interrupt FIFO_IS_FULL=15
- Interrupt ICAP_TRANSFER_END=13

• Interrupt RECONFIGURATION_END=12

By implementing all the above, the PR utility was enabled on the Virtex 5 FPGA daughter-board, via the SPEAr board. Also due to the fact that we do not use the slow software functions that perform reconfiguration when using the MicroBlaze micro-processor, we can achieve high reconfiguration speed. However this advantage is hindered by the slow DMA transfers necessary for transferring the bitstream, containing the reconfiguration data from the USB memory to the FPGA.

2. Performance Evaluation: A realistic scenario

To provide a performance evaluation for the PR design we have created, we use two different applications from the field of image processing. The first application is a simple Edge Detection application, run exclusively on SW, the second is a RayTracer application [4] that runs also in software but switching its operation to hardware accelerators implemented on the FPGA. The point of using both this applications is to observe how the RTSM would cope with the increasing workload, of having to manage a hardware and a software application.

The Edge Detection application is rather simple and consists of 5 (sub)tasks: Gray Scale (GS), Gaussian Blur (GB), Edge Detection (ED), Threshold (TH) and a final Write Image (WR) task. Tasks execute in succession, and each task passes its results to the next one. In order to achieve some level of parallelism we split the processed image in 4 quadrants that can be processed independently. This way each Edge Detection task must run 4 times before the task is considered as complete.

The RayTracer application starts from a description of the scene as a composition of 2D/3D geometric primitives. The basic primitives that are supported by the algorithm are the following: triangles, spheres, cylinders, cones, toruses, and polygons. Each of these primitives is described by a set of geometric properties such as, for example, the position in the scene, the height of the primitive or the rays of the circles composing the primitive. In our case we consider only three of the available primitives, the sphere, the torus, and the triangle, because for these primitives we had available the HW implementation. The logic utilized by each of the three HW cores is shown at Table 1, the results shown here are the produced by the PlanAhead Suite.

Table 1.: Summary of the logic resources used by the HW cores.

Core	LUT	FF	DSP	BRAM
Sphere	7,051	4,763	15	2
Torus	5,466	3,372	18	2
Triangle	6,168	3,432	24	4

It is clear that the critical resource are the DSPs. In order to have regions that can accommodate all the application cores we have to have at least 24 DSP modules present at each region. However Virtex 5 LX110 has only 64 available DSPs, which limits our design to just two Reconfigurable Regions. The RayTracer application does not solely run on hardware, it has a software part that runs on the SPEAr board. In order to display Partial Reconfiguration we created hardware implementations for the Sphere and

Triangle. This was done in order to place-and-swap these two tasks in the two different regions, while parallel execution takes place.

Another choice would be to create partial bitstreams for all the RayTracer primitives and have only one RR. Another static region could be present according to the DSPs limitation. This static region could accommodate one of the primitives while the reconfigurable one could swap between the other two. We choose to run the experiment with two regions instead of one in order to so how the management of multiple hardware regions is handled better by the RTSM deployed.

The RTSM used to test the offloading of hardware tasks on the FPGA is also able to manage and schedule SW tasks [3], with the use of thread create functions. The threads run in parallel accessing different parts of the processed data. While this works perfectly for the Edge Detection application, the RayTracer application access same data throughout the SW part of the application, hence the RTSM had to be extended.

To achieve the desired functionality we replaced the thread creation functions by fork operations that create copy image of the RTSM application. This way we can create images of the RTSM and then switch the execution to another thread/application, thus enabling the parallel access of the data. The penalty of forking the application is non-observable, since it is masked, with the execution of hardware tasks on the FPGA and partial bitstreams transfers. Once the fork is completed the application immediately begins its hardware execution. In total we perform 4 fork operations.

One more alteration we had to make was to synchronize the access of the different processes/threads on the DMA engine. It is easy to understand that any attempt of parallel execution is hindered by the fact that only one process at any time can have access on the DMA transfer engine. To achieve that a semaphore was created that the different RayTracer tasks must hold in order to access the DMA. This semaphored locks only the critical section of the RayTracer code, i.e. the DMA transfers achieved with the *fstart_transfer*, *fwrite/fread_buffer* and *fwait_dma* instructions. This operation from the hardware side is quite simple, since each core has its own input and output FIFOs then no mixing of input/output data would occur.

However the same fast switch between processes accessing the DMA engine cannot be done while reconfiguration is in progress. This is because the reconfigured region while it undergoes reconfiguration could produce garbage results that could override other valid results the other region produces. The *scheduling structure* contains the scheduling decision made by the RTSM, such as all the needed information for the placement and the type of the task executed. It is an argument to the reconfiguration function in order to denote the correct bitstream to be reconfigured.

The executable of the RayTracer is customized in order to offer the all the possible combinations of task/region a task can be executed into. The arguments passed to the execvp() function through the args[] array specify the core we want to execute -*s* for the sphere, and -*t* for the triangle, and an integer specifying the reconfigurable region the core will be executed into. Algorithm 1 shows the pseudo-code used to fork different processes. This code is added in the RTSM task creation section.

Since the SPEAr's resources are quite limited, we could not exploit all the abilities and the fine grain resource management offered by the RTSM deployed. Thus the built-in Linux scheduler that perform time-slicing scheduling was also used. In order to execute in parallel the two applications we created a merged task graph. For the RayTracer ap-

---

Algorithm 1 Spawn new RayTracer Task

Require: *Scheduling structure*
  sem_wait(sem);   //P operation
  reconfiguration(st);
  sem_post(sem);   //V operation
  char *args[]= "./stRayTracer"," − s", 1, (char∗)0;
  child_pid1 = fork();

  if $child\_pid1 < 0$ **then**
    $print f$("Fork error");
  else $\{child\_pid1 = 0\}$
    execvp("./stRayTracer_sphere_RR1_triangle_RR2", args);
  end if

---

plication we created a synthetic graph consisting of four tasks, each task corresponding to a different HW core. The resulting task graph is shown in Fig. 5.

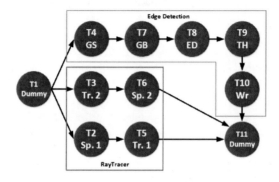

Figure 5. The application's merged task graph. Edge Detection tasks are executed in SW, RayTracer tasks are executed in HW.

The first and last tasks are dummy tasks that synchronize the start and finish of the two applications. The RayTracer tasks are either an **Sp.** or a **Tr.**, corresponding to either a sphere primitive or a triangle primitive. Each RayTracer task produces a different image with the name of a primitive and the region the task was executed in, e.g. sphere_RR1.ppm. In order to display better the advantages offer by PR we consider the tasks Sp.1 and Sp.2, which are two instances of the same sphere task that **must** run on region 1 and region 2 respectively, thus forcing a reconfiguration process to swap the placed tasks. If this differentiation was not done then the RTSM would reuse the already present on the FPGA, sphere bitstream, without the use of reconfiguration.

The experiments verified the correctness of the PR architecture from section 1 and the scheduling decisions made by the RTSM, were in accordance with the simulations made before the actual experiment. The limited resources in terms of processor cores offered by the SPEAr board forced us to use the Linux time-slicing scheduler. If more cores were available then the applications could run in truely parallel fashion: the 4 instances of the Edge Detection task are independent from each other and the two RayTracer tasks run in parallel with a semaphore protecting the critical DMA resource.

Our PR design was compared with a static implementation of the two RayTracer cores. The static design executes only the RayTracer part of the task graph in Fig. 5, without the use of reconfiguration. Also the static design is not optimized to perform the exchange of the DMA engine between different processes. The overall execution of four RayTracer tasks (2 spheres, 2 triangles) is approximately 2 minutes and 8 seconds. Our design with the use of PR and the RTSM scheduling offers the same execution time. However the Edge Detection application finished its execution much earlier than the Ray-Tracer one, the separate measured execution time for the Edge Detection application was 26.721 ms. The reconfiguration overhead is masked with the SW execution of the Edge Detection application, also in compared to the application execution time the overhead is negligible. The measured throughput for the reconfiguration process through the slow DMA bus was measured at 1.66MB/s.

3. Limitations & PR Advantages

Despite the use of hardware accelerators and partial reconfiguration, no speed-up was achieved; this is due to the specific application used coupled with the limitations of the SPEAr and FPGA boards.

- No external memory directly connected to the FPGA. This was a huge limitation we had to overcome. An external memory could limit the communication needed between the SPEAr and the FPGA, thus making the reconfiguration and the execution of HW tasks, much faster. Given the example of a Zynq Board the rate, for transferring data from an external DDR memory is 400MB/s which is 400x [6] compared to the current solution offered by SPEAr.
- The SPEAr board can connect to several peripherals, which makes it extremely useful. Data received from these peripherals can be used by the FPGA but the DMA creates a huge bottleneck with its low speed, also the one way transfer limits the access read or write operations.
- The RayTracer application used cannot achieve high execution parallelism. Applications that have two or more regions processing data in parallel and then transfer results to the SPEAr board can mask the DMA overhead.

Despite the limitations introduced by the two boards it is important to note that enabling partial reconfiguration offers many advantages:

- **Increased System Performance:** PR provides the ability, to the user, to use more efficient implementations of a design for different situations.
- **Reduced Power Consumption:** In power-constrained designs the user can simply download a more power- efficient version of a module, or a blank bitstream when the particular region of the device is not needed, thus reducing power consumption.
- **Adaptability:** Designs with the use of PR can adapt to changes in their environment, their input data or even their functionality.
- **Hardware Upgrade and Self Test:** The ability to change hardware. Xilinx FPGAs can be updated at any time, locally or remotely. Partial reconfiguration allows the end user to easily support, service and update hardware in the field.

4. Conclusion

This paper presents the work done in order to enable PR with the STMicroelectronics SPEAr development board. After making critical decisions regarding the development of the desired architecture, we tested our design with the parallel execution of two image applications. Due to severe limitations, on the transfer of data from the SPEAr to the FPGA, set by the device's architecture and due to the specifics of the chosen application, no speed-up was measured between the static and the PR design, both executing at 3 minutes. However the user can work around the DMA transfer issue, with the use of large memory blocks residing on the FPGA to store the input data and then perform true parallel execution between the regions.

The bottleneck of the device is the DMA engine which is extremely slow. However, the SPEAR platform is a development board intended for feasibility studies, in particular to evaluate software systems developed for embedded platforms and how they could benefit from external hardware acceleration. Towards that goal, the support for PR can be very beneficial. The architecture created is fairly generic and easy to be used in other R&D projects currently being developed on the STMicroelectronics SPEAr platform.

In order to achieve better results with the applications used here and also future R&D projects a change should be made on the micro-electronic development of the board. Results show that the AHB-32 bus is extremely slow, plus the access to that bus is one way. A faster two way, concurrent read-write operations, on the DMA bus could offer better results and a better parallel solution than the one offered. Also another solution could be the integration of the FPGA on the SPEAr board itself, without the use of the EXPI interface, following the paradigm of Zynq ZedBoard platforms[3].

Acknowledgement

This work was partially supported by the FP7 HiPEAC Network of Excellence under grant agreement 287759, and FASTER (#287804).

References

[1] J. Burns, A. Donlin, J. Hogg, S. Singh, M. de Wit (1997): A Dynamic Reconfiguration Run-Time System. In: Proc. of the 5th Annual IEEE Symposium on Field-Programmable Custom Computing Machines.

[2] G. Durelli, C. Pilato, A. Cazzaniga, D. Sciuto and M. D. Santambrogio (2012): Automatic Run-Time Manager Generation for Reconfigurable MPSoC Architectures. In: 7th International Workshop on Reconfigurable Communication-centric Systems-onChip (ReCoSoC).

[3] G. Charitopoulos, I. Koidis, K. Papadimitriou and D. Pnevmatikatos (2015): Hardware Task Scheduling for Partially Reconfigurable FPGAs. In: Applied Reconfigurable Computing (ARC 2015) Lecture Notes in Computer Science Volume 9040, 2015, pp 487-498 .

[4] Spada, F.; Scolari, A.; Durelli, G.C.; Cattaneo, R.; Santambrogio, M.D.; Sciuto, D.; Pnevmatikatos, D.N.; Gaydadjiev, G.N.; Pell, O.; Brokalakis, A.; Luk, W.; Stroobandt, D.; Pau, D. (2014): FPGA-Based Design Using the FASTER Toolchain: The Case of STM SPEAr Development Board. In: Parallel and Distributed Processing with Applications (ISPA), 2014 IEEE International Symposium on , vol., no., pp.134,141, 26-28 Aug. 2014

[5] http://www.xilinx.com/support/documentation/user_guides/ug191.pdf (Oct. 2012)

[6] http://www.xilinx.com/support/documentation/user_guides/ug585-Zynq a-7000-TRM.pdf (Feb. 2015)

Parallel Computing: On the Road to Exascale
G.R. Joubert et al. (Eds.)
IOS Press, 2016
doi:10.3233/978-1-61499-621-7-563

Exploring Automatically Generated Platforms in High Performance FPGAs

Panagiotis Skrimponis[b], Georgios Zindros[a], Ioannis Parnassos[a], Muhsen Owaida[b], Nikolaos Bellas[a], and Paolo Ienne[b]

[a] *Electrical and Computer Engineering Department, University of Thessaly, Greece*
[b] *Ecole Polytechnique Federale de Lausanne, Switzerland*

Abstract. Incorporating FPGA-based acceleration in high performance systems demands efficient generation of complete system architecture with multiple accelerators, memory hierarchies, bus structures and interfaces. In this work we explore a set of heuristics for complete system generation, with the objective of developing automatable methodology for system level architectural exploration and generation. Our experimental analysis on two test cases demonstrates that applying a set of system optimization heuristics incrementally on a baseline system configuration, we can converge to efficient system designs and reach target performance.

Keywords. FPGA, High Level Synthesis

Introduction

Recent advances in FPGA technology and High Level Synthesis (HLS) methodologies have placed reconfigurable systems on the roadmap of heterogeneous High Performance Computing (HPC). FPGA accelerators offer superior performance, power and cost characteristics compared to a homogeneous CPU-based platform, and are more energy efficient than GPU platforms.

However, the biggest obstacle for adoption of FPGA technology in HPC platforms is that FPGA programming still requires intimate knowledge of low-level hardware design and long development cycles. These characteristics make HDLs an unsuitable technology to implement an HPC application on an FPGA.

On the other hand, HLS tools allow designers to use high-level languages and programming models such as C/C++ and OpenCL [4][5]. By elevating the hardware design process at the level of software development, HLS not only allows quick prototyping, but also enables architectural exploration. Most of the HLS tools offer optimization directives to inform the HLS synthesis engine about how to optimize parts of the source code. The HLS synthesizer implements hardware accelerators optimized for performance or area according to these directives.

This approach does not exploit the capability of modern FPGAs to implement architectures that may include multiple hardware accelerators, memory hierarchies, bus structures and interfaces. What is really needed is a methodology to automatically realize and evaluate multiple-accelerator architectures implementing complex software applications. The complexity of such a methodology is high owing to the fact that reconfigurable platforms offer multiple degrees of design freedom and a potential large set of pareto-optimal designs.

In this paper we introduce a systematic architectural evaluation of application mapping onto High Performance FPGAs that operate as accelerators to a Linux box. The focus is to exploit all the interesting system-level architectural scenarios, in order to build a tool flow that can choose automatically the best system-level architecture for each application. Based on the experimental evaluation, we want to gain insight of optimal application-dependent architectures so that we later automate this process. We compare the performance of all hardware solutions with the performance of the software code running on a high performance CPU (the Host Unit).

Several research efforts studied the problem of Host-FPGA interface and on-chip communication channels. Vipin et al. [1], developed a framework for using PCIe communication between Host CPU and FPGA. He also used HLS standard bus interfaces for on chip communications. However, it overlooked the customization of the bus interfaces, as well as custom memory hierarchies. Other recent works considered generating latency insensitive channels [2] and shared memories [3] between multiple FPGA accelerators. In this work we seek further level of customization for the system component.

1. Design Space Exploration

Listing 1 shows the pseudocode of the *Blur* filter, one of the applications under evaluation. The algorithm first applies a horizontal and then a vertical 3-tap low pass filter to an incoming image, temporarily storing the output of the horizontal filter to the memory. This pseudo code is optimized for a CPU execution, not for a hardware design, which leads to drawbacks when it is processed by HLS tools. This code results into two hardware accelerators, which have to communicate via a large memory implemented either as an external DRAM or as an on-chip BRAM (if there is enough BRAM in the FPGA). In order to incorporate FPGAs as part of a modern heterogeneous system, we exploited the standardization of communication abstractions provided by modern high-level synthesis tools like Vivado HLS to create our adaptive system.

The dark shaded logic of Fig. 1 is generated by the Vivado toolset, based on instructions by the system developer. Two accelerators are instantiated and are connected with a BRAM memory through an AXI4-master interconnect. This baseline

```
blur_hor:
  for (i = 0; i < Height; i++)
    for (j = 0; j < Width; j++)
      tmp(i,j)=(inp(i,j-
1)+inp(i,j)+inp(i,j+1)/3

blur_ver:
  for (i = 0; i < Height; i++)
    for (j = 0; j < Width; j++)
      out(i,j)=(tmp(i-
1,j)+tmp(i,j)+tmp(i+1,j)/3
```

Listing 1. Horizontal and Vertical Blur filter

architecture is extended by automatically exploring the number and type of the various resources. Such resources include the accelerators in terms of throughput, area, latency and number. It also includes the bus structure and number of separate buses, the number and type of memories, and the interface to the Host unit.

In addition to the customizable part of the architecture, extra resources are required for communication with the Host unit. We use an open-source framework, RIFFA to provide an abstraction for software developers to access the FPGA as a PCIe-based accelerator [6].

The RIFFA hardware implements the PCIe Endpoint protocol so that the user does not need to get involved with the connectivity details of the accelerator. From the accelerator side, RIFFA provides a set of streaming channel interfaces that send and receive data between the CPU main memory and the customizable logic. On the Host unit, the RIFFA 2.0 architecture is a combination of a kernel device driver and a set of language bindings. RIFFA provides a very simple API to the user that allows for accessing individual channels for communicating data to the accelerator logic.

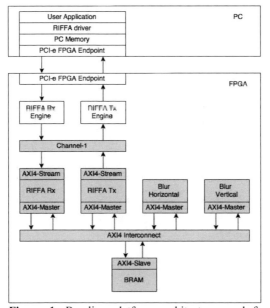

Figure 1. Baseline platform architecture used for our experimental evaluation. The dark shaded area shows the customizable logic.

Figure 2 shows two indicative architectural scenarios, expanding the baseline architecture of Fig. 1. We can effectively duplicate the customizable logic using an extra RIFFA channel (Figure 2i). Even better, the streaming, point-to-point nature of the *Blur* application allows us to use the AXI4-Stream protocol to channel data between consumer and producers (Figure 2ii). Some configurations may use external DDR3 memory (which includes an FPGA DDR3 memory controller) to be able to accommodate larger images at the cost of increasing latency and worse performance. To navigate through the large design space smartly, we devised a set of heuristics for making design decisions:

1. Keep data local as close as possible to the accelerator. The goal here is to minimize read/write latency between the accelerator and data memory.
2. Minimize shared resources between independent accelerators. Following this guideline helps eliminating collisions between multiple accelerators while accessing communication channels and memory ports.
3. Overlap data transfers with accelerators execution. The objective here is to minimize accelerators idle time waiting for data to be available.

Our design space exploration approach starts from the baseline architecture of Fig. 1. We then incrementally make design decisions while considering the aforementioned heuristics and evaluating the effects of the taken decisions on overall system performance.

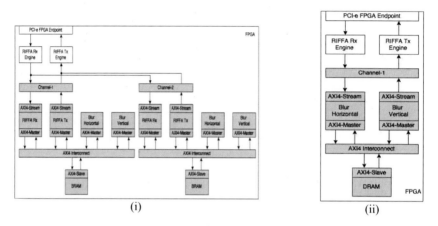

(i)   (ii)

Figure 2. Two interesting architectural scenarios. (i) Duplication of the baseline architecture using two RIFFA channels. (ii) Using AXI streaming interface between RIFFA channels, the two accelerators and the DRAM.

2. Experimental Evaluation

2.1. Methodology

In this section, we present our architectural exploration study for two applications shown in **Table 1**. For each application, we have laid out a multitude of architectural scenarios spanning different points at the area versus performance space. Software code is optimized with HLS pragmas (e.g., pipeline) with minimal code changes. We use Vivado HLS 2014.4 for hardware implementations on the VC707 evaluation board (XC7VX485T FPGA device). All results are reported after placement and routing. The same C code is executed in an E5520 Intel Xeon quad-core processor running at 2.27 GHz and the performance results are compared. Besides the *Blur* filter already described in the previous section, we have evaluated a Monte Carlo simulation application.

Table 1. Applications used for architectural exploration

App.	Description	Input Set
Monte Carlo	Monte Carlo simulations in a 2D space	120 Points, 5000 Walks per point
Blur	Blur 2D filter	4096×4096 image

Monte Carlo (MC) was developed to provide an alternative method of approaching multi-domain, multi-physics problems. It breaks down a single Partial Differential Equation (PDE) problem to produce a set of intermediate problems. The core kernel of this application performs random walks from initial points in a 2D grid to estimate the boundary conditions of the intermediate problems. MC is a heavily compute bound application with double precision arithmetic operations and calls to mathematical libraries for FP arithmetic, trigonometric and logarithmic computations, etc. It has minimal bandwidth requirements.

2.2. Results

Figure 3 presents the performance results for the two test cases each with different implementation scenarios. Table 2 shows the area requirements of each platform.

Blur. Six implementation scenarios are studied for the Blur application. The first scenario represents the baseline architecture in Fig. 1 (*bram_naive_1_chnl*). The host CPU sends a single row for the horizontal blur kernel for processing and waits for the result from the accelerator before sending the next row until the entire image is processed. The same is done for the vertical blur, but here 3 rows are needed for the vertical blur to start. This scenario is reasonable when there is not enough on-chip or off-chip memory to save the whole image, then we partition the image into smaller partitions that fit on the available memory resources. Another version of this scenario (*bram_naive_2_chnl*) replicates the hardware of a single RIFFA channel on 2 channels to exploit parallelism in the Blur application. While the second scenario

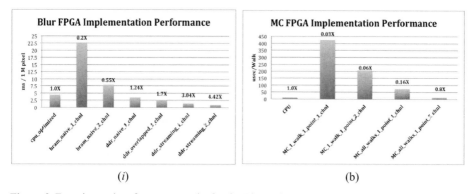

(i)   (b)

Figure 3. Experimental performance results for the Blur and Monte-Carlo applications. The numbers above the bars are improvement over the optimized CPU implementation.

improves on the performance of the BRAM naive implementation it is still worse than that of the optimized CPU implementation. Sending small chunks of data over the PCIe is not efficient because we pay the overhead of initiating a PCIe read/write transaction many times. As a result, the PCIe transactions occupy two thirds of the total execution time.

Scenario three of the Blur (`ddr_naive_1_chnl`) makes use of the off-chip DDR to store the whole image instead of partitioning it into multiple portions. Using a DDR provides few benefits; The PCIe read/write transactions consume less time compared to the first scenarios because we eliminate the overhead of initiating PCIe transactions. The second benefit of the DDR is that we do not need to send the horizontal blur output back to the host CPU, but keep it in the DDR for the vertical blur to process it, then write back to the host CPU the result of the vertical blur. As such, the third scenario achieves improvement over optimized CPU time.

To improve performance of scenario #3, we allow the horizontal blur to start as soon as the first row of the image is stored in the DDR and not wait for the whole image to be loaded. We also allow writing data back to the host CPU even before the vertical blur accelerator finishes execution. This is demonstrated in the fourth scenario (`ddr_overlapped_1_chnl`). The overlapping of accelerators execution with FPGA-

Table 2. Area results for the various configurations in terms of resource utilization for the XC7VX485T FPGA

Benchmark	LUT	FF	BRAM	DSP48
BLUR				
bram_naive_1_chnl	15%	10%	5%	11%
bram_naive_2_chnl	28%	20%	10%	23%
ddr_naive_1_chnl	20%	15%	6%	5%
ddr_overlapped_1_chnl	20%	15%	6%	5%
ddr_streaming_1_chnl	13%	9%	4%	3%
ddr_streaming_2_chnl	21%	14%	6%	6%
Monte-Carlo (MC)				
MC_1_walk_1_point_1_chnl	8%	5%	2%	5%
MC_1_walk_1_point_2_chnl	13%	9%	3%	9%
MC_all_walks_1_point_1_chnl	9%	7%	2%	5%
MC_all_walks_1_point_2_chnl	16%	12%	3%	9%

Host data transfers is possible because of the regular access patterns of the blur kernels. While this scenario eliminates most data transfers overhead, moving data between DDR and the accelerators introduces a non-negligible overhead.

To improve further and minimize the DDR-Accelerator communication overhead, we use AXI-stream interfaces for horizontal and vertical blur accelerators (`ddr_streaming_1_chnl, ddr_streaming_2_chnl`). Instead of storing the image in the DDR, the horizontal blur accelerator uses AXI-stream interface to read data from the channel FIFOs and write result to the DDR. The vertical blur will read data from the DDR, process it and send the results directly to the RIFFA channel through an AXI-stream interface. In this scenario we eliminate 60% of the DDR-Accelerator data movements. This is possible because of the streaming nature of the blur kernels. This scenario achieves the best performance compared to the CPU implementation. Moreover, this scenario consumes less area (see Table 2) than the DDR naive and overlapped implementations, which allows allocating more replicas of the accelerators to exploit parallelism and improve performance as the case in *ddr_streaming_2_chnl*.

Monte-Carlo simulation. MC is a compute intensive kernel with minimal memory accesses. Hence the different implementation scenarios are made of different accelerator configurations and by instantiating multiple instances of the accelerator. In the baseline scenario, the accelerator is configured to perform a single walk of a single point per invocation, and a single accelerator is allocated (*MC_1_walk_1_point_1_chnl*). This scenario performs much worse than the CPU implementation. Double precision operations have larger latency on FPGAs than a CPU. Also, Vivado HLS libraries of trigonometric operators (sin, cos) are not pipelined and less efficient than their CPU counterparts. The strength of the FPGA is to perform more computations in parallel. Unfortunately, the MC kernel computations of a single walk are sequential and cannot be parallelized. As such, the FPGA baseline implementation performs badly. To improve performance we need to exploit coarser-grain parallelism across multiple points and walks. The second scenario allocates two accelerator instances to parallelize the computations of walks for a single point (*MC_1_walk_1_point_2_chnl*). It reduces the execution time to half, but still worse than the CPU. We need to allocate around 40 accelerator replicas to reach the CPU performance.

Another aspect to improve on is to minimize the accelerator invocation overhead by coarsening the computations granularity per a single accelerator instance. This allows for pipelining computations of multiple walks, which will have a strong impact on performance. The third scenario minimizes accelerator invocation overhead by configuring the accelerator to perform all the walks of a single point per invocation (*MC_all_walks_1_point_1_chnl*). The fourth scenario allocates five accelerators to parallelize computations (*MC_all_walks_1_point_5_chnl*) across multiple points. The last scenario saturates the FPGA resources and almost achieves near CPU performance.

3. Conclusion

Reaching target performance does not have a trivial solution. Customizing the accelerator configuration while using a fixed system architecture is not enough to compete with state-of-the-art CPUs. It is essential to customize the system architecture to reach this goal, especially in applications where data movement overhead dominates overall performance. In this effort we studied few directions in system-level architectural exploration to orchestrate an approach for customizing system-level components, such as number and type of bus interfaces, memory hierarchies, and number of accelerators. We considered different data transfer protocols as a way to minimize data movement overhead. We intend to study other types of applications to extract more efficient ways of system customization as a preliminary for building an automatable methodology for custom system generation.

4. Acknowledgments

This research has been co-financed by the European Union (European Social Fund - ESF) and Greek national funds through the Operational Program "Education and Lifelong Learning" of the National Strategic Reference Framework (NSRF) – Research Funding Program: THALES grant number MIS 379416.

References

[1]   K. Vipin, S. Shreejith, D. Gunasekera, S. A. Fahmy, N. Kapre. System-Level FPGA Device Driver with High-Level Synthesis Support. International Conference on Field Programmable Technology (FPT), Kyoto, Japan, December 9-11, 2013.

[2]   K. Fleming, H. J. Yang, M. Adler, J. Emer. The LEAP FPGA Operating System. 24th International Conference on Field Programmable Logic and Applications (FPL). Munich, Germany, September 2-4, 2014.

[3]   H. J. Yang, K. Fleming, M. Adler, J. Emer. LEAP Shared Memories: Automating the Construction of FPGA Coherent Memories. 22nd International Symposium on Field Programmable Custom Computing Machines (FCCM). Boston, USA, May 11-13, 2014.

[4]   *Vivado Design Suite User Guide: High Level Synthesis.* Online at www.xilinx.com.

[5]   *Altera OpenCL SDK Programming Guide.* Online at www.altera.com.

[6]   M. Jacobsen, R. Kastner. *RIFFA 2.0: A reusable integration framework for FPGA accelerators.* 23rd International Conference on Field programmable Logic and Applications (FPL). Porto, Portugal, September 2-4, 2013.

Mini-Symposium:
Experiences of Porting and Optimising Code for Xeon Phi Processors

Parallel Computing: On the Road to Exascale
G.R. Joubert et al. (Eds.)
IOS Press, 2016
doi:10.3233/978-1-61499-621-7-573

Symposium on Experiences of Porting and Optimising Code for Xeon Phi Processors

Adrian JACKSON [a], Michèle WEILAND [a], Mark PARSONS [a],
Simon MCINTOSH-SMITH [b]
[a] *EPCC, The University of Edinburgh;* [b] *University of Bristol*

The flop-to-watt performance potentially available from Intel's Xeon Phi co-processor makes it very attractive for computational simulation. With its full x86 instruction set, cache-coherent architecture, and support for MPI and OpenMP parallelisations, it is in theory relatively straight-forward to port applications to the platform. However, a number of factors can make it difficult to obtain good performance for many codes. These factors include the relatively high core count, the low clock speed of the cores, the in-order instruction restrictions, 512-bit wide vector units, and low memory per core.

This mini-symposium, organised by the Intel Parallel Computing Centres at EPCC and the University of Bristol, provided a forum for those working on porting and optimising codes for this architecture to present the challenges and successes they have experienced when working with the Xeon Phi, and how these also apply to standard parallel computing hardware.

The papers presented in these proceedings highlight some of the challenges that researchers have faced exploiting the Xeon Phi co-processor, and some of the potential time to solution benefits that can be achieved from this hardware.

Parallel Computing: On the Road to Exascale
G.R. Joubert et al. (Eds.)
IOS Press, 2016

doi:10.3233/978-1-61499-621-7-575

Experiences Porting Production Codes to Xeon Phi Processors

Emmanouil FARSARAKIS[a], Adrian JACKSON[a,1], Fiona REID [a], David SCOTT[a],
Michèle WEILAND[a]

[a] *EPCC, The University of Edinburgh*

Abstract. This paper outlines our experiences with porting a number of production simulation codes to the Xeon Phi co-processor. Large scale production simulation codes present a challenge for optimisation on any platform, and can be even more problematic for accelerator hardware as the codes contain language operations or functionality that are hard to get good performance from on novel hardware. We present the challenges we have experienced porting two large FORTRAN production codes: GS2 and CP2K. We discuss the strategies, which have proven useful or otherwise, for obtaining good performance on Xeon Phi. We also discuss the reasons why achieving good performance for large-scale codes is problematic.

Keywords. Xeon Phi, Porting, GS2, CP2K, Parallelisation, Optimisation, MPI, OpenMP

Introduction

The Xeon Phi co-processor, with its large number of simple processing cores with wide vector units and multi-threading functionality, offers the potential for high performance for computational simulation. However, the simplistic nature of the cores, with in-order instruction issuing and low clock speed, can be challenging for a range of real world codes, as this can reduce the performance of any part of the code that cannot be parallelised or vectorised.

We have investigated the performance that can be achieved when porting the production codes GS2 and CP2K, both of which are large-scale FORTRAN parallel codes, parallelised with MPI for distributed memory parallelism.

Whilst there have been demonstrations of the performance of Xeon Phi co-processor with kernel benchmarks or embarrassingly parallel code, there has been much less evidence of efficient ports of large simulation codes. This paper discusses some of the challenges that we have experienced, work we have undertaken, and performance benefits or impacts that have arisen from that work.

---

[1] Corresponding Author: adrianj@epcc.ed.ac.uk, @adrianjhpc

1. Related Work

There has been a wide range of work investigating the use of accelerators for scientific computing. One example of such work is TargetDP[1], that highlights the benefits of abstracting hardware issues away from the programmer so that programmers do not spend excessive time on developing porting patterns instead of solving the actual problem at hand. The emergence of various different GPUs and accelerators has resulted in this problem becoming even more prevalent, when different systems require different methods of porting.

Others have investigated the hardware performance of Xeon Phi[2][3], and outlined the performance constraints and possibilities of the underlying hardware. One area of research that has been explored is refactoring code to convert array of structure data types into structure of array data types to improve memory access performance and enable vectorisation[4]. This has been shown to significantly improve performance for some codes on hardware such as the Xeon Phi.

EPCC has previously worked on a native Xeon Phi port [5] and also on optimising CP2K for Xeon Phi [6]. Our initial work found that the performance of the Xeon Phi version was generally around 3 times slower than what could be obtained using a 16-processor Xeon host. This earlier work helped to identify a number of vectorisation targets.

GS2 has also been previously optimised to improve communication performance by introducing unbalanced data decompositions to reduce overall communication costs[7]. This work highlights the potential performance benefits that can be achieved, even optimising already matured and previously optimised codes, with the researchers able to increase performance by up to 20% through restructuring the data decomposition.

2. Hardware

The investigations documented in this paper were undertaken on a two Xeon Phi system at EPCC comprising 2 x 5110P Xeon Phi processors and 2 x Intel Xeon E5-2650 8-core processors running at 2 GHz. We also made use of the ARCHER[8] computer, a 118,080 core Cray XC30 system made up of 4920 nodes, each with 2 x Intel Xeon E5-2697v2 12-core processors running at 2.7 GHz.

3. CP2K

CP2K[9] is a freely available and widely used program for atomistic simulation in the fields of Computational Chemistry, Materials Science, Condensed Matter Physics and Biochemistry, amongst others. It is currently the second most heavily used code on the UK National Supercomputing Service, ARCHER. CP2K has close to 1 million lines of code, written using modern FORTRAN. Both MPI and hybrid parallelisations using OpenMP are available.

Profiling of the code showed that over 25% of the runtime was spent in the libgrid part of CP2K inside integrate and collocate routines. These routines are involved in mapping between the sparse matrix representation of the electron density and the real space grid. The integrate routines carry out integration of the Gaussian products whereas the collocate routines carry out the inverse operation.

A number of approaches were investigated for optimising these routines. Compiler directives for improving vectorisation, such as !DIR$ IVDEP, !DIR$ VECTOR ALWAYS, !DIR$ SIMD were tried, along with re-writing code using array syntax, ensuring data was correctly aligned and using the OpenMP 4.0 !DIR$ OMP SIMD directive. We also tried re-writing the innermost loop to ensure that all iterations were contiguous. This enabled the loop to vectorise but unfortunately, the overheads involved in re-ordering the iterations more than negated any benefit. Ultimately the amount of work carried out inside the inner most loop inside the collocate and integrate routines is simply too small. It was decided that it was not possible to re-write CP2K to restructure the code in a way that would make these loops larger. This is because these loops operate on data that has been mapped from one co-ordinate system to another, using FFTs, and it is simply too costly to restructure all the co-ordinate systems to improve the vectorisation in one part of the code as it would make calculations in other areas of the code more costly.

When running CP2K on 16 OpenMP threads we found that the cost of allocating and deallocating arrays within threaded code blocks was unusually high. We investigated the impact of replacing the allocatable arrays with static arrays and benchmarked CP2K using both the pure MPI (POPT) and pure OpenMP (SSMP) versions of the code comparing the original code (dynamic allocations) and optimised (static allocations). Both the Intel and GNU compilers were tested, as it was important to ensure that our changes did not adversely affect the performance[2]. Figure 1 shows the performance obtained when running the code on the host (left) and Xeon Phi (right).

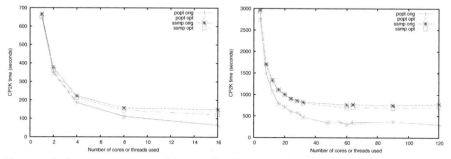

Figure 1: Performance comparison of dynamically allocated (orig) and statically allocated (opt) arrays on single 16 core host node (left) and Xeon Phi card (right). All results were obtained using ifort version 14.0.4. The host results were 2-3% faster for the POPT version and up to 18% faster for the SSMP version. The Xeon Phi results show little change for the POPT version and up to 8% faster for the SSMP version.

On the host, we found the POPT version to be 2-3% faster for both compiler suites. The SSMP version was up to 18% faster for the Intel compiler and 2-3% faster for the GNU compiler. On the Xeon Phi we found little change for the POPT version and up to

---

[2] The majority of CP2K users use the GNU compiler suite and thus changes to the code should not adversely affect the performance of the GNU version.

8% improvement for the SSMP version with the benefit increasing with the number of threads. Our original code optimisations were specific to the H2O-64 benchmark, and basically involved fixing the array sizes specific to that problem so that we could quickly test the concept. As these changes gave us a significant performance improvement we are now working on a way to generalise them such that all users of CP2K may benefit in future.

The second area we investigated was the diagonalisation involving ScaLAPACK calls only running on a subset of the available processes. When using 24 processes only 8 of them called the ScaLAPACK routines (see Figure 2). It transpires that the code manually limits the number of processes involved in ScaLAPACK operations due to performance issues in the past. The number of processes allowed to enter ScaLAPACK is dependent on the number of electronic orbitals, which means that using the H2O-64 benchmark CP2K would never run the diagonalisations on more than 8 processes.

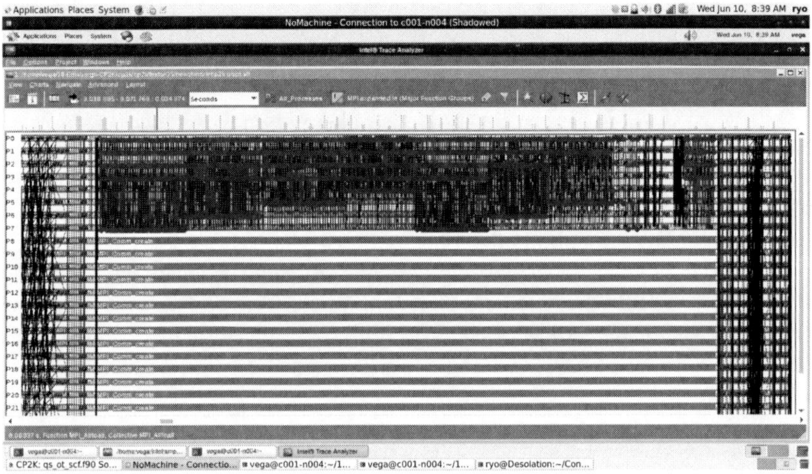

Figure 2: Intel ITAC profile running the POPT version of CP2K with the H2O-64 benchmark on 24 processes. The profile shows that only 8 of the 24 processes perform the ScaLAPACK computations.

To investigate whether this restriction of the number of processes for ScaLAPACK calls impacts performance significantly we use used the nm_pbed3_bench benchmark, which spends around 25% of its runtime in ScaLAPACK routines. This benchmark has 13034 orbitals meaning that the maximum number of processes that can be used for the ScaLAPACK computation is 220^3. We altered the code to allow all available processes to be used and re-ran the benchmark. Figure 3 shows the performance of the POPT version of CP2K running nm_pbed3_bench obtained on the ARCHER machine for both the original and modified code.

---

[3] The maximum number of processors used for the ScaLAPACK computations is throttled back according to $((n+60*4-1)/(60*4))$, where, n, is the number of electronic orbitals.

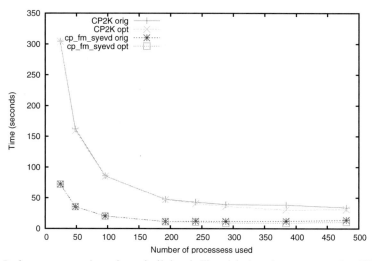

Figure 3: Performance comparison of nm_pbed3_bench. The original results use no more than 220 processes for the ScaLAPACK computation. The opt results are able to use all available processes. The CP2K time is the total runtime of the code, the cp_fm_syevd time is the time spent in the diagonalisation.

We can see that allowing all available processors to run the diagonalisation improves the performance when using more than 220 processes and thus the restricting ScaLAPACK processes may not be appropriate for this benchmark. We did a similar test with H2O-64 and found the performance to be worse when all processes were used. H2O-64 spends only a small amount of its total runtime in the diagonalisation and thus by using all the processors we simply increased the MPI overheads. However, if a benchmark, e.g. like nm_pbed3_bench, spends a significant time in the diagonalisation, then it will improve performance to use all the available processes.

It has proved difficult to improve the vectorisation of CP2K as the data structures required for the FFT computations prevent us from being able to restructure the loops used within the collocate and integrate routines within libgrid. However, we have found that replacing dynamically allocated arrays with statically allocated arrays can provide up to 18% improvement on the Xeon host processors and up to 8% improvement on the Xeon Phi using the H2O-64 benchmark. We are now working to generalise these changes.

4. GS2

GS2[10] is a gyrokinetic flux tube initial value and eigenvalue solver for fusion plasmas. It solves the gyrokinetic system of equations for the evolution of the perturbed distribution function, g, and the electromagnetic fields, Φ. GS2 is parallelised with MPI and has been demonstrated to scale efficiently to thousands of cores on large scale HPC systems.

We evaluated the performance of GS2 on Xeon Phi by using a standard benchmark case and running with up to 236 MPI processes on the Xeon Phi and up to 16 MPI processes on the host machine. As GS2 does not have any offloading functionality, it was benchmarked in native mode (i.e. compiled for, and run directly on, the co-processors) on the Xeon Phi. The performance of GS2 on the Xeon Phi was around

40% slower than the host (when run in the optimal configuration for host and Xeon Phi), with the host taking 4.64 minutes to finish and the Xeon Phi taking 6.77 minutes.

Our first approach at optimising for GS2 was to implement a hybrid parallelisation (MPI with OpenMP), to enable better scaling on large scale HPC systems and also to reduce the process count and increase the thread count on Xeon Phi processors. This new version of GS2 provided performance benefits at scale on large scale HPC systems like ARCHER, with up to 30% reduced runtime at 1000 cores when running with 4 threads per MPI process compared to the pure MPI implementation.

Unfortunately, the hybrid implementation did not improve performance on the Xeon Phi, primarily because not all the code has been parallelised with OpenMP. There are some areas that will require significant re-writing to allow an efficient OpenMP parallelisation to be implemented, and that has not yet been done. The lack of OpenMP functionality for some parts of the code reduces the number of threads running on the Xeon Phi to a sub-optimal level at some points in the simulation.

Using CrayPat on ARCHER as well as Intel's VTune, Vectorization Advisor and compiler optimisation reports on the Xeon Phi system, we investigated performance gains through vectorisation. A similar strategy to that described above for CP2K was followed, using compiler flags and directives, as well as loop restructuring on dominant subroutines and loops to optimise alignment and access patterns. The results observed however were similar to those of CP2K, showing little or no performance benefit.

The existence of poor data access patterns was identified as one of the main factors hindering performance on GS2. To address this issue, further investigation was carried out on how to optimise the data structures GS2 uses. GS2 makes extensive use of FORTRAN's primitive complex type variables in large arrays. The layout for an array of complex numbers in memory using FORTRAN is that of an array of structures, each structure consisting of two real variables for the real and imaginary part of each complex number to be represented.

Complex-complex array multiplication using this layout is not optimal for consecutive memory access. The separation of a single array of complex variables into two arrays of real variables, one array for the real parts and one for the imaginary, should benefit complex-complex array multiplications when using wide vector units, while at the same time not affecting the performance of other computations carried out such as multiplications of complex number arrays with real number arrays.

This approach was first tested on a small part of GS2. Changes were introduced to part of the `get_source_term` subroutine. The subroutine was altered ("noCmplx" version) to incorporate copies of the original array of structures variables GS2 uses into newly introduced variables which follow the layout described above. Computation is carried out on these new variables and results are then copied back to the original arrays.

A third version of the code ("control") was also tested to investigate the impact of the copy operations themselves as well as the allocation of these temporary arrays. This version carried out computations on the original GS2 arrays but also implemented the allocation and copy operations of the noCmplx version. Though useful for a rough estimate of the impact these operations have on execution time, it should be noted that these tests cannot determine the side effects these operations may have on cache access patterns and register use.

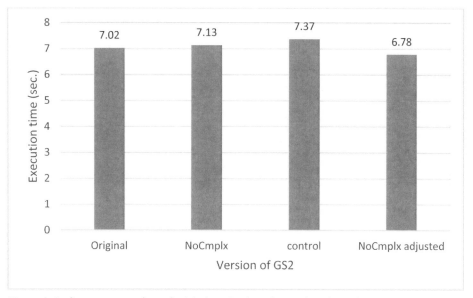

Figure 4: Performance comparison of original, noCmplx and control versions of GS2 on a single 5110P Xeon Phi using 120 MPI processes, each with 2 OpenMP threads. The last column shows the estimated execution time of noCmplx version after adjusting it to exclude the estimated time for new array allocations as well as the copy-in and copy-out operations required for test.

Results (see **Figure 4**) from these tests indicated speedup potential along with the need for generalisation of the introduced changes. While the noCmplx version of GS2 is slower than the original on the Xeon Phi system, the control version suggests that the copy-in and copy-out operations required for our test strategy more than compensate for this increase in execution time. After adjustments to factor in this artificial cost of our strategy, our tests suggest a potential speedup in the order of 3.5% from the effect of the new data layout on a part of a single function of GS2 alone. Similar tests carried out on ARCHER were inconclusive, which was to be expected given that the vector units on the Xeon Phi are much wider.

The partial transformation of complex number arrays in GS2 has therefore shown promising results. The true benefits of this strategy, however, can only be determined by implementing this data restructuring globally, which in turn would require significant changes to the GS2 code.

In addition to these tests, a mini-app was developed to mirror GS2 functionality to investigate the impact of these alternative data structures on performance. The mini-app implements similar functionality to that of GS2's `integrate_moment_lec` subroutine. It consists of a triple loop, the innermost of which contains the majority of computations carried out; a reduction on a complex number array, which requires complex-complex array multiplications.

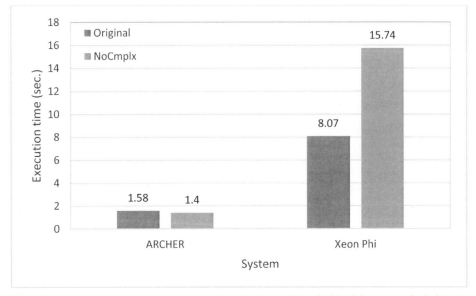

Figure 5: Performance comparison of original and noCmplx versions of GS2 mini-app on a single 24-core node on ARCHER using 24 OpenMP threads and on a single 5110P Xeon Phi using 120 threads. New complex number layout results in 1.13 and 0.51 speedups on the ARCHER and Xeon Phi systems respectively.

Tests on this mini-app are ongoing and results (see **Figure 5**) have been inconclusive thus far. Initial tests on ARCHER showed significant speedup of the optimised complex number array layout, in the order of 13%. However, the new layout proved detrimental to performance on the Xeon Phi, with tests indicating an increase in execution time in the order of 95% for the new layout compared to FORTRAN's native complex number array structures. The cause of this significant increase in execution time on the Xeon Phi is currently being investigated. Compiler vectorisation reports indicate similar levels of vectorisation and expected speedups. Changes in array size have shown no impact on this behavior.

Optimising GS2 for the Xeon Phi has proven challenging. Given the partially promising results of the structure of arrays approach to complex number arrays, we intend to continue to investigate the potential benefits of the new complex number array layout on the performance of GS2. The hybrid implementation has been demonstrated to give good performance benefits for the code on standard HPC computers but, like the complex number restructuring, has yet to translate into improved performance on the Xeon Phi

5. Summary

The optimisation work we have carried out has provided good performance improvements for the large simulation codes we have been working on, GS2 and CP2K, on standard HPC systems, like ARCHER. Unfortunately, that has not translated into having the same impact on Xeon Phi co-processors, with both codes still running slower on the Xeon Phi when compared to a running on a comparable standard node.

However, the fact that our optimisation work is beneficial for current users, and will enable simulations to be completed more efficiently for the wide user base these codes have, and thereby mean that computing resources are utilised more efficiently, means that this work has been very useful and rewarding.

The next steps are now to investigate in more detail the performance issues with the Xeon Phi and continue trying to optimise the performance on these co-processors.

6. Acknowledgements

This work has been supported by Intel through EPCC's Intel Parallel Computing Centre.

References

[1] Gray, A.; Stratford, K., "targetDP: an Abstraction of Lattice Based Parallelism with Portable Performance," in *High Performance Computing and Communications, 2014 IEEE 6th Intl Symp on Cyberspace Safety and Security, 2014 IEEE 11th Intl Conf on Embedded Software and Syst (HPCC,CSS,ICESS), 2014 IEEE Intl Conf on* , vol., no., pp.312-315, 20-22 Aug. 2014

[2] Jianbin Fang, Henk Sips, LiLun Zhang, Chuanfu Xu, Yonggang Che, and Ana Lucia Varbanescu. 2014. Test-driving Intel Xeon Phi. In *Proceedings of the 5th ACM/SPEC international conference on Performance engineering* (ICPE '14). ACM, New York, NY, USA, 137-148.

[3] A Quantitative Evaluation and Analysis on CPU and MIC, Weizhu Wang & Qingbo Wu & Yusong Tan, College of Computer, National University of Defense Technology, Changsha, China

[4] A. Sarje, X.S. Li, A. Hexemer, "Tuning HipGISAXS on Multi and Many Core Supercomputers," Performance Modeling, Benchmarking and Simulation of High Performance Computer Systems at Supercomputing (SC13), November, 2013.

[5] F. Reid and I. Bethune, Evaluating CP2K on Exascale Hardware: Intel Xeon Phi, PRACE White Paper, 2013.

[6] F. Reid and I. Bethune, Optimising CP2K for the Intel Xeon Phi, PRACE White Paper, 2013.

[7] Optimising Performance Through Unbalanced Decompositions. / Jackson, Adrian; Hein, Joachim; Roach, Colin. In: IEEE Transactions on Parallel and Distributed Systems, No. 99, 2014.

[8] ARCHER: http://www.archer.ac.uk

[9] CP2K: Open Source Molecular Dynamics, http://www.cp2k.org

[10] M. Kotschenreuther, "Comparison of initial value and eigenvalue codes for kinetic toroidal plasma instabilities," Computer Physics Communications, vol. 88, no. 2-3, pp. 128–140, 1995

Parallel Computing: On the Road to Exascale
G.R. Joubert et al. (Eds.)
IOS Press, 2016
doi:10.3233/978-1-61499-621-7-585

Preparing a Seismic Imaging Code for the Intel Knights Landing Xeon Phi processor

Gilles CIVARIO[a,1] Seán DELANEY[b] and Michael LYSAGHT[a]

[a]Intel Parallel Computing Center, ICHEC
[b]Tullow Oil plc.

Abstract. We report on how we are preparing a seismic imaging code for the Intel Knight's Landing (KNL) Xeon Phi processor. The seismic imaging code in question is a Reverse Time Migration (RTM) code based on an unconventional rotated staggered grid (RSG) method and has undergone a significant amount of Xeon/Xeon Phi-focused re-engineering at ICHEC. The code uses an explicit finite difference (FD) scheme of variable spatial order, and second order in time, to model wave propagation in three isotropy cases. The code is parallelized with MPI and OpenMP, for wide hardware compatibility. Vectorization and efficient cache utilization were carefully considered in the kernel design, while attempting to maintain portability and maintainability. The stencil-based kernels of the code have low arithmetic intensity and are bound by the main memory bandwidth of the Xeon/Xeon Phi which we have successfully alleviated by making highly efficient use of shared last level cache (LLC) on Xeon. The latter optimization is one that throws up some interesting challenges for achieving optimal performance on Xeon Phi, which we discuss further in this report.

Keywords. Xeon, Xeon Phi, Vectorization, Optimization, Finite Difference

Introduction

The TORTIA (Tullow Oil Reverse Time Imaging Application) code is proprietary software owned by Tullow Oil plc. This code implements Reverse Time Migration (RTM), which is a 'depth migration' technique for seismic imaging [1]. Migration is the process of taking the seismic wave signals recorded in a survey and 'migrating' the wave energy they represent to its origin (a collection of seismic reflectors). In this physical model, a prominent artifact in the seismic signal can be thought of as the coherent arrival of reflected energy from such a reflection event. The accuracy with which the physical model for wave propagation can represent the subsurface is limited by the underlying approximations required to make the problem computationally tractable in a reasonable time.

The variety of models available provides some control over that trade-off. In RTM, the existence and nature of isotropy in the chosen earth model is commonly used for this purpose. Common isotropy models include full isotropic, Vertically Transverse Isotropic (VTI) and Tilted Transverse Isotropic (TTI), and a number of more complex (and computationally costly) models (elastic, etc.).

---

[1] Corresponding Author: gilles.civario@ichec.ie

The TORTIA code uses an explicit finite difference (FD) scheme of variable spatial order, and second order in time, to model wave propagation in the three isotropy cases mentioned above. RTM requires that two wavefields be modeled and correlated at regular intervals. One of the correlated wavefields is accessed in reverse order of computation, requiring that the temporal evolution of one wavefield be (partially) recorded. This is achieved by storing snapshots of the wavefield at the required interval, using the most efficiently accessible storage available.

The code is parallelized with MPI and OpenMP, for wide hardware compatibility. Vectorization and efficient cache utilization were carefully considered in the kernel design, while attempting to maintain reasonable portability and maintainability.

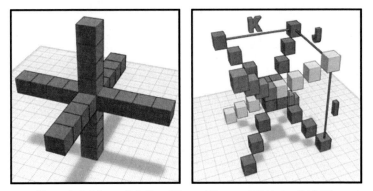

Figure 1. Axial stencil (left) and Rotated Staggered Grid stencil (right).

The Tullow-RTM code adopts a rotated staggered grid (RSG) approach, which requires a non-traditional stencil (see fig. 1), in which very few elements are contiguous, and which has significantly more elements (*4n*) than a traditional stencil (*3n+1*) of the same order (*n*). While this has a cost, we avoid the expense of interpolating variables, and can simplify the boundary conditions. It should also be pointed out that the RSG method compares well with the alternatives for anisotropic modeling, with comparable accuracy for fixed computational cost [2].

1. Initial optimizations targeting Xeon/Xeon Phi

Achieving high performance with such a non-traditional stencil requires some alterations to the optimization methodology. In particular, an approach was adopted that has very significant performance benefits by simultaneously simplifying the data access pattern and exposing additional parallelism, while also facilitating variable order of accuracy, and simplifying the kernel code. As a result, the code achieves very similar performance figures to those recently published in [3]. The optimizations carried out to date at ICHEC were conducted in unison, but, for explanatory purposes, we will attempt to isolate them for individual analysis.

The initial kernel was dominated by multi-dimensional array access code, which did not expose the inherent pattern (and some potential parallelism) of the calculation. To address this, an incrementing 'pivot' pointer was combined with an array of fixed offsets to address the elements of the stencil for each variable (see fig. 2). This yielded a simpler, reduced code, with an additional loop over the stencil elements (potential parallelism).

In addition, the progress of the 'pivot' pointer (and associated stencil) through the array was exposed, greatly facilitating the introduction of SIMD operations. To that end, OpenMP was used to deliver portable, robust vectorisation directives with minimal code footprint. OpenMP directives were also inserted to leverage shared memory (and cache), while increasing code scalability by reducing the required number of MPI processes. This also facilitated the use of OpenMP to ensure efficient overlapping of MPI communications with computations, using OpenMP nested parallelism.

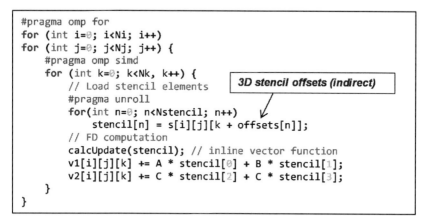

```
#pragma omp for
for (int i=0; i<Ni; i++)
for (int j=0; j<Nj; j++) {
    #pragma omp simd
    for (int k=0; k<Nk, k++) {
        // Load stencil elements       3D stencil offsets (indirect)
        #pragma unroll
        for(int n=0; n<Nstencil; n++)
            stencil[n] = s[i][j][k + offsets[n]];
        // FD computation
        calcUpdate(stencil); // inline vector function
        v1[i][j][k] += A * stencil[0] + B * stencil[1];
        v2[i][j][k] += C * stencil[2] + C * stencil[3];
    }
}
```

Figure 2. Pseudo code of kernels used in the TORTIA code.

In order to reduce the number of simultaneous streams of data required to service the kernel (bandwidth reduction), a transformation of the loop structure of the kernel was performed. This transformation had the parallel goal of accommodating variable order of accuracy in the kernel, which yields flexibility in obtaining a trade-off between performance and computational accuracy. This was achieved by parameterization of the RSG stencil, which was only possible following the introduction of a stencil offset array, as seen in fig. 2. While a similar trade-off may be accessible through control of the grid resolution and time step, such control is often limited by other factors (e.g. spectral content of results, numerical stability, etc.). Finally, the loop transformation has the added benefit of reducing register pressure arising from large stencils, which may be of particular concern on many-core architectures.

2. Theoretical analysis of attainable performance

To aid in our investigations and theoretical analysis of attainable performance on our evaluation platforms we employ the "roofline" model [4], a visually intuitive performance model used to place bounds on the performance of algorithms running on multicore, many core, or accelerator processor architectures. Rather than simply using percent-of-peak estimates, the model can be used to assess the quality of attained performance on each platform by combining locality, bandwidth, and different parallelization paradigms into a single performance figure.

To that end, we have measured the peak memory bandwidth and peak throughput characterizing our evaluations platforms, and report them on a graph with arithmetic intensity on the horizontal axis and throughput (GFlops) on the vertical axis. Estimating the arithmetic intensity of each of our kernels allows us to estimate the theoretical maximum achievable performance on each of the platforms. Estimating the arithmetic intensity of our kernels is non-trivial due to compiler optimizations and the level of data caching achieved at run time. As such, we bound the arithmetic intensity between a 'zero cache' model (where no data caching is achieved) and an 'infinite cache' model, where all data remains in cache during the execution of the kernel. The corresponding graphs, along with initial code performance are presented in fig. 3.

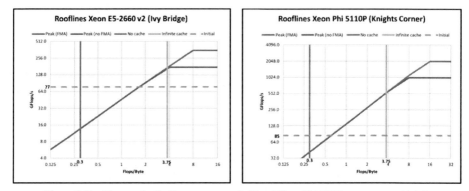

Figure 3. Roofline graphs for Xeon processor (left) and Xeon Phi KNC co-processor (right).

The roofline graphs clearly show that our kernels will remain memory bound on both platforms, even if we were to achieve perfect caching. Furthermore we can see that our initial performance on the Xeon platform is already 45% of absolute peak performance while it is only 16.5% of absolute peak performance on the Xeon Phi.

3. New approach for data reuse

An initial implementation of the kernels using conventional tiling methods proved ineffective on both the Xeon and Xeon Phi, as such methods were found to significantly hinder effective vectorization. We found that any benefit we gained from conventional tiling was overcompensated by a reduced efficiency of the vectorization of the innermost loop, leading to an overall slow-down of the code.

We have therefore implemented a different approach: since our loops are parallelized with OpenMP, we investigated the potential for taking full advantage of the shared aspect of the last level caches (LLC) on each of the platforms to mutualize the benefit of data caching across the threads. For our RSG grid, this inter-thread potential data reuse is exemplified in fig. 4.

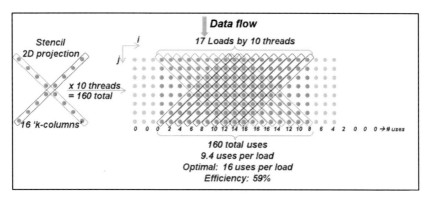

Figure 4. Example of potential inter-thread data reuse with shared LLC for our RSG stencil.

For this method to be effective, we needed to ensure that the various threads compute on nearby data in a sufficiently synchronized manner. Fortunately, this can be achieved through the thread scheduling policies supported by OpenMP. By selecting a *"static,1"* scheduling of the *"i"* loop (as seen in fig. 2), we maximize the inter-thread reuse of the data loaded into the cache by whichever thread first accesses it.

The shared aspect of the LLC cache on Xeon processors makes this approach extremely effective, to the point where, in effect, each thread appears to have full use of the LLC for itself. However, the situation is quite different on the current KNC version of the Xeon Phi platform, where the LLC is effectively private to each core and is only genuinely shared among the 4 hardware threads available per core. Since our approach relies heavily on an efficient shared LLC, the effectiveness of the method is, for the moment, more limited on the current KNC version of Xeon Phi, but is expected to improve on the future KNL Xeon Phi platform. It is also worth noting that, although data is indeed effectively cached on the LLC on the KNC chip, we traded some transactions between the main memory for L2-L2 cache exchanges which have been found to be as costly as off-chip transactions on that platform. Nevertheless, the final performance achieved as part of this work on both the Xeon and Xeon Phi platforms, as reported in table 1, is substantial.

Table 1. Performance improvements on Xeon E5-2660 v2 Ivy Bridge and Xeon Phi 5110P KNC, with a final percentage of peak performance corresponding to an unrealistic "infinite cache" hypothesis

Platform	Initial performance	Final performance	Improvement	Ratio of peak for infinite cache
Xeon Ivy Bridge	77 GFlops	94 GFlops	22%	55%
Xeon Phi KNC	85 GFlops	144 GFlops	70%	28%

4. Preparing for Xeon Phi Knights Landing processor

Now that our code has been optimized for both Xeon and Xeon Phi KNC platforms, we are in a position to further prepare the code for the forthcoming Xeon Phi Knights Landing (KNL) processor. To this end, we have pursued three goals:

- We have compiled the code with the *"-xMIC-AVX512"* KNL compiler switch and checked the levels of optimization and vectorization reported. We obtained that the vectorization intensity is predicted to be even higher than that on the

KNC platform, with a value of 16 (out of 16) for KNL relative to a value of 15 (out of 16) on the current KNC platform.

- We have run the code on the Intel Software Development Emulator (SDE) which allows for code validation, with all correctness checks fully validated.
- And finally, we have utilized the information publicly released by Intel on KNL, and have assessed how effective our optimizations could be on this platform. Knowing that LLC will be shared by 2 cores and 8 threads instead of just 1 core and 4 threads, and that the main memory bandwidth and inter-core traffic will be greatly improved, we expect our optimizations to be much more effective on KNL than on KNC. We also take note that all of the data for our current evaluation simulations will fit comfortably within the reported capacity of the on-package High Bandwidth Memory (HBM) available on the KNL and account for this in our performance modeling.

With the limited information on KNL currently at our disposal, we have nevertheless projected the performance of the code running on a future KNL chip, using the roofline methodology. In fig. 5, it can be seen that with a very conservative projection, we can make the confident claim that our RTM code should achieve a performance throughput of at least 700 GFlops on a KNL platform, indicating that the Intel Xeon Phi KNL should be extremely well suited for our RTM application.

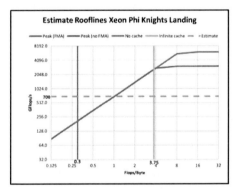

Figure 5. Estimate roofline graph for Xeon Phi KNL processor.

References

[1] Baysal, E., Kosloff D. D. and Sherwood J. W. C., Reverse time migration, *Geophysics*, **48** (1983), 1514–1524.

[2] O'Brien G. S., 3D rotated and standard staggered finite-difference solutions to Biot's poroelastic wave equations: Stability condition and dispersion analysis, *Geophysics*, **75** (2010), T111-T119.

[3] Teixeira T., Souza P., Borges L., Neto A., Philippe T. and Andreolli C., *Reverse Time Migration with Manycore Coprocessors*, 76th EAGE Conference and Exhibition (2014), DOI: 10.3997/2214-4609.20141138

[4] Williams S., Waterman A. and Patterson D., Roofline: An insightful visual performance model for multicore architectures, *Commun. ACM*, **52** (2009), 65–76

Parallel Computing: On the Road to Exascale
G.R. Joubert et al. (Eds.)
IOS Press, 2016
doi:10.3233/978-1-61499-621-7-591

LU Factorisation on Xeon and Xeon Phi Processors

Adrian JACKSON[a,1] and Mateusz Iwo DUBANIOWSKI[a]

[a] *EPCC, The University of Edinburgh*

Abstract. This paper outlines the parallelisation and vectorisation methods we have used to port a LU decomposition library to the Xeon Phi co-processor. We ported a LU factorisation algorithm, which utilizes the Gaussian elimination method to perform the decomposition, using Intel LEO directives, OpenMP 4.0 directives, Intel's Cilk array notation, and vectorisation directives. We compare the performance achieved with these different methods, investigate the cost of data transfer on the overall time to solution, and analyse the impact of these optimization and parallelisation techniques on code running on the host processors as well. The results show that performance can be improved on the Xeon Phi by optimising the memory operations, and that Cilk array notation can benefit this benchmark on standard processors but do not have the same impact on the Xeon Phi co-processor. We have also demonstrated cases where the Xeon Phi will compute our implementations faster than we can run them on a node of a HPC system, and that our implementations are not as efficient as the LU factorisation implemented in the mkl library.

Keywords. Xeon Phi, LU Factorisation, Parallelisation, OpenMP, Cilk, mkl

Introduction

Xeon Phi is Intel's many-core co-processor which provides a large number of simple cores to enable parallel execution of applications. The cores are multi-threaded, enabling up to four threads to be run on each physical core, and have large, FMA (fused multiply add) enabled, vector units, supporting 512-bit vector operations. Xeon Phi co-processors have around 60 physical cores (the exact number depends on the processor model), meaning up to 240 threads can be run on a single co-processor. The Xeon Phi cores run at ~1GHz, and offer only in-order instruction execution. As such, the serial performance of programs that don't vectorise or use FMA instructions is generally much slower than on modern processors.

As the Xeon Phi is a co-processor, attached to a host processor over the PCI Express (PCIe) bus, it can be used in the same manner as other co-processors, such as GPUs; i.e. by offloading computational kernels onto the Xeon Phi and copying results back to the host memory after computation has completed. However, it can also be used in a native mode where users can log into the co-processor and run programs directly on the hardware rather than via offloading of computational kernels.

---

[1] Corresponding Author: adrianj@epcc.ed.ac.uk, @adrianjhpc

LU factorisation or decomposition is a mathematical operation on matrices, which is widely used in solving linear algebra, deriving inverse or determinant of a matrix. These operations have wide industrial applications among others in design automation, machine learning, and signals processing. Since the implementations of LU decomposition tend to contain many loops and operations on rows of matrices, LU factorisation is highly parallelisable and potentially can be vectorised.

In this paper we outline work that we undertook to implement and port an LU factorisation library to Xeon Phi co-processors. However, the aim was not to produce an active LU factorisation library, rather it was to evaluate different optimisation and parallelisation strategies for Xeon and Xeon Phi processors. We cannot expect to obtain as good performance as existing LU factorisation libraries, such as LAPACK[1] or mkl[2], but we can use the process of implementing this library to evaluate software development and optimisation approaches for Xeon Phi, and that is what is discussed in this paper.

1. Related Work

There has been a wide range of research on the performance of co-processors and accelerators in recent years, and it is of particular interest for future HPC systems as they potentially offer a good FLOP to watt ratio. This research activity has focussed both on establishing the most beneficial architectures for use in accelerators, as well as researching the most efficient methods for exploiting accelerators for computational simulation. Furthermore, there is ongoing research into the applications that could benefit from being offloaded, or into localising parts of applications that are suitable candidates for offloading

In this work we implemented and ported a LU factorisation library to Xeon Phi and subsequently explored its performance using various parallelisation, vectorisation, and offloading methods. Similar research has been conducted in climate dynamics [3], astrophysics [4], or indeed in LU factorization algorithms [5] [6] [7]. These works primarily explore the performance of Xeon Phi by optimising the code for Xeon Phi and often compare the performance on Xeon Phi to other accelerators in order to understand which accelerators offer the best performance for the respective applications.

There is also a wealth of research into exploring kernels that could be offloaded to accelerators and GPUs[8] [9] [10]. These focus on kernels that could be offloaded and ported to co-processors, and on exploring their performance. There exists a set of problems, which are considered to be highly parallelisable and of significant importance to exploring performance of co-processors, the Berkley dwarfs[9]. The Berkley dwarfs consist of 13 problem categories considered to be of significant importance to high performance computing community. These are highly scalable and can be executed with the use of computational kernels. Consequently, they are often used to benchmark HPC solutions. LU factorization is one of the Berkley dwarfs.

Similar issues exist with porting the code to Xeon Phi. The placement of threads on the cores of Xeon Phi to exploit performance becomes crucial. A case study of porting CP2K code to Xeon Phi by Iain Bethune and Fiona Reid explored some of these issues emerging in the code ported to Xeon Phi[11] [12]. Porting the code to Xeon Phi proved to be relatively easy if the source code is parallelised. However, the work showed that efficient placement of threads on cores is important to ensure good performance results. Finding enough parallelism to fill the threads sufficiently also turned out to be a significant issue. Overall, the ported CP2K without additional optimisations performed around 4 times slower on Xeon Phi in comparison to 16 cores of the Intel Xeon E5-2670 Sandy Bridge host node.

Finally, there is ongoing work into the comparison of various methods available for optimising and parallelising code on accelerators and GPUs. A comparison of different methods for porting code to GPUs on a Cray XK7 was performed by Berry et al[13]. They focus on analysing the benefits and issues of different methods, when porting a molecular dynamics library to NVIDIA Kepler K20 GPUs, comparing CUDA[14], OpenACC[15], and OpenMP+MPI[16][17] implementations. In the molecular dynamics application, the use of OpenACC on the GPU resulted in a speed-up factor of 13 times over 32 threads of OpenMP run on AMD Interlagos processors.

The above examples of work undertaken in the field of accelerators and GPUs show that there is a significant potential in utilising these devices. However, accelerators, including Xeon Phi, are still not straight forward to exploit efficiently and their optimal programming models are far from defined. Therefore, ongoing research in this area is important to better understand the nature of programming such devices, and what can be achieved by them. Furthermore, we notice that not all applications benefit equally from the use of accelerators.

2. LU Factorisation

LU factorization is a method of decomposing a single matrix into two matrices. In doing so, we express the original matrix as a product of two triangular matrices. One of these matrices is an upper triangular matrix, while the other is a lower triangular matrix. This means that one of the matrices has only "zero" entries below the main diagonal, while the other has such entries only above the main diagonal.

For this research we implemented Gaussian elimination with partial pivoting using a number of different optimisation approaches, namely compiler assisted vectorisations, OpenMP SIMD vectorisation directive, and Cilk[18] array notation. The code was parallelised using OpenMP to distributed available work over threads on the processor or co-processor. The OpenMP `parallel for` construct was the primary method for implementing parallelism, and Intel LEO directives were used to offload computation kernels to the Xeon Phi from the host processors.

2.1. Intel "ivdep" pragma and compiler auto-vectorisation

`ivdep` is a non-binding pragma that can be used by the Intel compiler to aid the process of auto-vectorisation. It prevents the compiler from treating assumed dependencies as proven and therefore helps the compiler in deciding whether code can be vectorised.

2.2. OpenMP SIMD

In OpenMP 4.0 there is a `simd` pragma that informs the compiler that the code enclosed by the pragma can be safely vectorised, and does not contain any dependencies. Moreover, it is not bound to a specific implementation or compiler, with GNU and Intel compilers, amongst other, available that implement this functionality.

Table 1. simd example

OpenMP simd notation	Original loop

`#pragma omp simd`
`for(j = k + 1; j < n; j++)`
`  a[i][j] -= aik * a[k][j];`
	`for(j = k + 1; j < n; j++)`
	`  a[i][j] -= aik * a[k][j];`

2.3. Intel Cilk array notation

Intel Cilk array notation is an extension to C language, which allows for better expression of SIMD parallelism. It enables the transformations of loop statements is into a single line statement, which can enable the compiler to recognise vectorisation opportunities more effectively.

Table 2. Cilk example

Cilk array notation	Original loop
`a[i][k+1:n-(k+1)] -= aik *` `     a[k][ k+1:n-(k+1)];`	`for(j = k + 1; j < n; j++)` `  a[i][j] -= aik * a[k][j];`

3. Performance Results

3.1. Hardware

The investigations documented in this paper were undertaken on a Xeon Phi system at EPCC comprising 2 x 5110P Xeon Phi processors and 2 x Intel Xeon E5-2650 8-core processors running at 2 GHz. We also made use of the ARCHER[19] computer, a 118,080 core Cray XC30 system made up of 4920 nodes, each with 2 x Intel Xeon E5-2697v2 12-core processors running at 2.7 GHz.

3.2. Software

The implementation of the Gaussian elimination algorithm was written in C and compiled with the Intel C compiler. We used version 14.0.4 of the compiler and version 11.1.4 of the `mkl` library on ARCHER. On the Xeon Phi machine we used version 16.0.0 of the compiler and 11.3.0 of the `mkl` library. All code was compiled using the `-O3` compiler flag.

3.3. Benchmarks

The University of Florida sparse matrix collection[20] contains a large number of matrices that relate to a wide range of problems, such as route optimisation, circuit design, and mathematics. A set of sparse matrices from this collection were used to evaluate the performance of our LU factorisation implementation, along with some self-generated dense matrices (filled with random values). The characteristics of these matrices are presented in Table 3.

Table 3. Benchmark matrices characteristics

Name	Dimensions	None-zero elements	Sparsity ratio[2]
add32	4960 x 4960	19,848	8.07E-04
circuit_1	2624 x 2624	35,823	5.20E-03
circuit_2	4510 x 4510	21,199	1.04E-03
coupled	11341 x 11341	97,193	7.56E-04
init_adder1	1813 x 1813	11,156	3.38E-03
meg4	5860 x 5860	25,258	7.36E-04
rajat01	6833 x 6833	43,250	9.26E-04
rajat03	7602 x 7602	32,653	5.65E-04
ranmat1000	1000 x 1000	1,000,000	1
ranmat2000	2000 x 2000	4,000,000	1
ranmat3000	3000 x 3000	9,000,000	1
ranmat4000	4000 x 4000	16,000,000	1
ranmat5000	5000 x 5000	25,000,000	1
ranmat6000	6000 x 6000	36,000,000	1

Benchmarks were run 6 times and the fastest observed time for each set of runs is reported in the following sections. The time to read input datasets was not measured,

As well as the versions of the code we developed using the `ivdep` pragmas, OpenMP `simd` pragmas, and Cilk array notation; we implemented the LU factorisation operation directly using the LAPACK `dgetrf` routine (implemented in `mkl`) for performance comparison to our code. When timing the `mkl` version we included the cost of converting the matrix data from the two dimensional data structure the data is stored in for the rest of the benchmarks and the one dimensional array that this routine requires. The `mkl` benchmarks had Xeon Phi functionality enabled (using the `MKL_MIC_ENABLE` environment variable), but were not forced to use the Xeon Phi. This means that some of the results are actually benchmarking the host processors rather than the Xeon Phi, depending on whether the `mkl` library decided that using the accelerator was necessary or not for that particular benchmark.

3.4. Xeon Phi performance

Figure 1 shows the performance of our implementations, and `mkl`, on a single Xeon Phi co-processor using 236 threads (a range of thread counts was experimented with and 236 gave the best performance across the benchmarks). We can see that the `ivdep` version gives the best performance of our implementations, although there is not a large difference between the different versions. It is also obvious that we the `mkl` implementation is far superior to our code, in all but the smallest benchmarks demonstrating performance an order of magnitude better than our best implementation.

---

[2]Sparsity ratio is calculated as the number of none-zero elements divided by the total number of elements in the matrix.

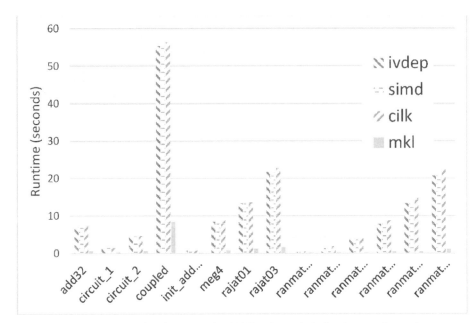

Figure 1. Xeon Phi Performance using 236 threads (not including data transfer costs)

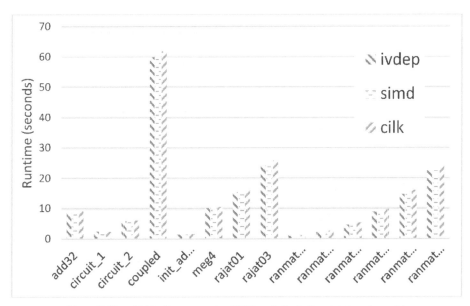

Figure 2. Xeon Phi Performance using 236 threads (including data transfer costs)

Figure 1 does not include the cost of offloading and retrieving the data used in the calculations on the Xeon Phi. These have been included in Figure 2, which shows that there is an overhead associated with this, generally around 1 second, that has a significant impact for the small benchmarks where the overall runtime is small, but is negligible for the large benchmarks.

We were also aware that altering how memory is allocated on the Xeon Phi can impact performance, specifically choosing when to allocate data in 2MB pages (using the MIC_USE_2MB_BUFFERS environment variable). We set this variable to 64K and re-ran the benchmarks, with the results presented in Figure 3.

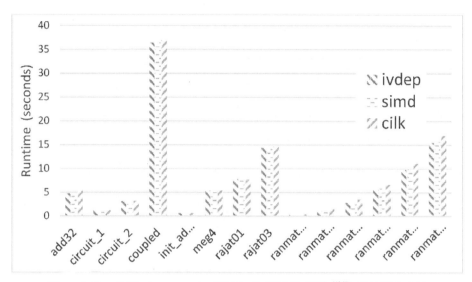

Figure 3. Xeon Phi Performance using 236 threads and MIC_USE_2MB_BUFFERS=64K

We can see that this variable has significantly improved performance, with all versions of the code running at between 20-40% faster than before. This shows that there is scope for optimisation of our codes if memory management and operation can be rationalised and optimised.

3.5. ARCHER performance

Figure 4 shows the performance that we achieved using our codes on a single node of the ARCHER computer (24 threads). We tested a range of thread counts, with 24 threads giving the best performance for the benchmarks.

We can see from the graph that for our implementations the Cilk version, on the majority of the benchmarks, gives the best performance, with ivdep often not far behind. As with the Xeon Phi results, mkl is still far faster than any of the versions we have implemented.

3.6. Performance Summary

Comparing the performance on Xeon Phi to the performance we see on ARCHER it is evident that that our ARCHER implementations are generally faster than our Xeon Phi implementations for the sparse matrix benchmarks (with the exception of the coupled test case), but slower on the dense benchmarks.

The work also demonstrates that Cilk can have performance benefits on standard processors like those in ARCHER, but those benefits do not necessarily transfer to the Xeon Phi.

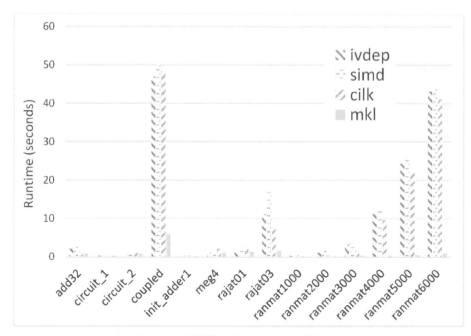

Figure 4. ARCHER performance using 24 threads

4. Summary

We have evaluated a number of approaches to optimising code on Xeon and Xeon Phi processors. We have shown that Cilk can bring significant benefits on standard processors, and tuning the memory model on the Xeon Phi can also significantly improve code performance.

Whilst we have not achieved better performance on Xeon Phi than on ARCHER across the whole range of benchmarks we have used, we have, nevertheless, demonstrated that Xeon Phi can outperform standard processors, even including offloading costs. Furthermore, as it is possible to run offload kernels asynchronously, it is possible to run these calculations whilst also using the host CPUs to run other calculations, thereby exploiting both co-processor and host processors to gain performance for applications.

It is clear that the library version of LU factorisation significantly outperforms our simplistic algorithm. However, as we do not know what algorithm is being used by `mkl` it is very possible that we are not comparing the performance of the same algorithms.

There is scope for further optimisation of our host and Xeon Phi codes, including looking in more depth at the vectorisation achieved in the code.

5. Acknowledgements

This work has been supported by Intel through EPCC's Intel Parallel Computing Centre.

References

[1] LAPACK: http://www.netlib.org/lapack/
[2] mkl: https://software.intel.com/en-us/intel-mkl
[3] C. S. Pelissier, "Climate Dynamics on the Intel Xeon Phi," in NASA@SC13, Denver, 2013.
[4] Institute for Computational Cosmology, "Institute of Advanced Research Computing: Intel Parallel Computing Center," Durham University, 27 May 2015. [Online]. Available: https://www.dur.ac.uk/iarc/intel/. [Accessed 30 July 2015].
[5] A. Haidar, P. Luszczek, S. Tomov and J. Dongarra, "Heterogenous Acceleration for Linear Algebra in Mulit-Coprocessor Environments," Lecture Notes in Computer Science, vol. 8969, pp. 31-42, 2014. 58
[6] P. Sao, X. Liu, R. Vuduc and X. Li, "A Sparse Direct Solver for Distributed Memory Xeon Phi-accelerated Systems," in 29th IEEE International Parallel & Distributed Processing Symposium (IPDPS), Hyderabad, 2015.
[7] J. Fang, A. L. Varbanescu, H. Sips, L. Zhang, Y. Che and C. Xu, "Benchmarking Intel Xeon Phi to Guide Kernel Design," Delft University of Technology, Delft, 2013.
[8] K. Asanovic, R. Bodik, B. Catanzaro, J. Gebis, P. Husbands, K. Keutzer, D. Patterson, W. Plishker, J. Shalf and S. Williams et.al., "The landscape of parallel computing research: A view from berkeley.," Citeseer, Berkley, 2006.
[9] M. Bordawekar and R. Baskaran, "Optimizing sparse matrix-vector multiplication on gpus," IBM, 2009.
[10] A. Gray, "Performance Portability," in GPU Computing Seminar, Sheffield, 2105.
[11] I. Bethune and F. Reid, "Evaluating CP2K on Exascale Hardware: Intel Xeon Phi," PRACE, Edinburgh, 2014.
[12] I. Bethune and F. Reid, "Optimising CP2K for the Intel Xeon Phi," PRACE, Edinburgh, 2014.
[13] D. K. Berry, J. Schuchart and R. Henschel, "Experiences Porting a Molecular Dynamics Code to GPUs on a Cray XK7," in Cray User Group, Napa Valley, 2013.
[14] https://developer.nvidia.com/about-cuda
[15] http://www.openacc.org/
[16] http://openmp.org
[17] http://www.mpi-forum.org/
[18] A. D. Robison, "SIMD Parallelism using Array Notation," Intel Developer Zone, 3 September 2010. [Online]. Available: https://software.intel.com/en-us/blogs/2010/09/03/simd-parallelism-using-array-notation/?wapkw=array+notation. [Accessed 30 July 2015].
[19] http://www.archer.ac.uk
[20] T. A. Davis and Y. Hu, "The University of Florida Sparse Matrix Collection," ACM Transactions on Mathematical Software, vol. 38, no. 1, pp. 1:1-1:25, 2011.

Mini-Symposium:
Coordination Programming

Parallel Computing: On the Road to Exascale
G.R. Joubert et al. (Eds.)
IOS Press, 2016
© *2016 The authors and IOS Press. All rights reserved.*
doi:10.3233/978-1-61499-621-7-603

603

Mini-Symposium on Coordination Programming
— Preface —

Clemens GRELCK [a] and Alex SHAFARENKO [b]

[a] *System and Network Engineering Lab*
University of Amsterdam, Amsterdam, Netherlands
[b] *School of Computer Science*
University of Hertfordshire, Hatfield, United Kingdom

Coordination programming is a term that everybody seems to have a vague idea about, but only a few have a definite view on. And among those there is a great deal of divergence in understanding what coordination is all about. In this mini-symposium we interpreted the term coordination programming in the broadest possible sense and invited researchers from all interpretations of and approaches to coordination: from conventional tuple-space, Linda-inspired constructions to CnC, from behavioural models, such as Reo, to approaches that focus on extra-functional properties of resource consumption and performance.

In the true tradition of workshops the focus of our mini-symposium was on lively discussions and scientific exchange, not on formalities. All participants were invited and encouraged to share their views, experiences and ambitions beyond and in between the formal presentations. Our medium to long-term goal is to help shaping a community geared towards all aspects of coordination programming. The following questions were phrased to guide discussion during the mini-symposium:

- Why does coordination require a coordination language? Is there a kind of analysis that is impeded by the lack of specific coordination-language constructs?
- What can be inferred and how should the coordination program adapt to the resource situation in parallel and distributed systems?
- What kind of tuning or self-tuning facilities should/can coordination programming approaches require/possess?
- What is the relationship between control-coordination and data-coordination? Are both needed indeed or can one be expressed by the other?
- How can coordination programming address the challenges of cloud computing, big data processing/analysis and mixed-criticality cyberphysical systems?
- What are recent success stories in applying coordination programming to real-life applications?

The Mini-Symposium on Coordination Programming received a total of five submissions that were invited for presentation:

1. Kathleen Knobe and Zoran Budlimic:
   Dependence Programming and Coordination Programming
2. Jossekin Beilharz, Frank Feinbube, Felix Eberhardt, Max Plauth and Andreas Polze:
   Claud: Coordination, Locality And Universal Distribution
3. Raimund Kirner and Simon Maurer:
   Coordination with Structured Composition for Cyberphysical Systems
4. Clemens Grelck:
   Coordination Programming in S-Net: A Critical Assessment of Design Choices and Implementation Techniques
5. Maksim Kuznetsov and Alex Shafarenko:
   AstraKahn: A Coordination Language for Streaming Networks

Following a formal reviewing process, submissions 2 and 3 from the above list were seelcted for inclusion in the ParCo conference proceedings.

Last not least, we would like to thank the additional members of our programme committee: Farhad Arbab (Centrum Wiskunde & Informatica, Netherlands) and Kath Knobe (Rice University, USA).

Amsterdam, October 2015   Clemens Grelck
Hatfield, October 2015   Alex Shafarenko

Parallel Computing: On the Road to Exascale
G.R. Joubert et al. (Eds.)
IOS Press, 2016
doi:10.3233/978-1-61499-621-7-605

Claud:
Coordination, Locality And Universal Distribution

Jossekin BEILHARZ and Frank FEINBUBE [1] and Felix EBERHARDT and
Max PLAUTH and Andreas POLZE

Hasso Plattner Institute for Software Systems Engineering
University of Potsdam, Germany

Abstract. Due to the increasing heterogeneity of parallel and distributed systems, coordination of data (placement) and tasks (scheduling) becomes increasingly complex. Many traditional solutions do not take into account the details of modern system topologies and consequently experience unacceptable performance penalties with modern hierarchical interconnect technologies and memory architectures. Others offload the coordination of tasks and data to the programmer by requiring explicit information about thread and data creation and placement. While allowing full control of the system, explicit coordination severely decreases programming productivity and disallows implementing best practices in a reusable layer.

In this paper we introduce Claud, a locality-preserving latency-aware hierarchical object space. Claud is based on the understanding that productivity-oriented programmers prefer simple programming constructs for data access (like key-value stores) and task coordination (like parallel loops). Instead of providing explicit facilities for coordination, our approach places and moves data and tasks implicitly based on a detailed topology model of the system relying on best performance practices like hierarchical task queues, concurrent data structures, and similarity-based placement.

Keywords. Distributed Object Space, Hierarchical NUMA, Federated Cloud

Introduction

With the introduction of clouds and cloud federations, computer systems have reached a new layer of complexity. Globally distributed, clouds offer easy access to vast resources at low cost enabling all kinds of parallel and distributed applications. Moreover, cloud federations promise adaptive region-aware service execution policies and load balancing, specialization, strong replication and fault-tolerance, vendor-independence, and much more [1]. In order to make good use of these resources, applications running in a cloud environment need to be capable of scaling from a single compute node to several thousands. Cloud-ready scaling can only be achieved by putting a strong focus on parallelism and locality: data and threads need to be placed in such a way that access latencies are minimal. In contrast to classical HPC-clusters, federated clouds can have arbitrary inter- and intra-connection networks of nodes resulting in heavy latency and bandwidth varia-

[1]Frank.Feinbube@hpi.de

tions. Since these characteristics are load-sensitive and thus can change during runtime, a static mapping as described by a programmer has limited feasibility. Competitive applications need to use sophisticated thread and data placement strategies that dynamically adapt the resource usage to their needs and the system topology.

The severe performance impact of threads and data coordination with respect to latencies and locality can be found in all layers of state-of-the-art system topologies. A prominent example are non-uniform memory access (NUMA) systems that are the foundation of modern server systems, especially the ones that are tailored for Big Data Analytics. Built around sophisticated interconnect technologies, NUMA systems can be regarded as a mix of parallel and distributed shared memory systems. Therefore, they share many similarities with cluster and cloud architectures: in modern hierarchical NUMA systems, access latencies vary severely depending on the distance of the NUMA nodes and the current load on the interconnects [2]. The performance impacts have become so predominant that a parallel implementation that regards a NUMA system as a conventional shared memory system runs longer with more resources than a serial implementation. Purely distributed implementations perform well, but do not benefit from the shared access capabilities of NUMA. As of today, it is unclear which programming model is best suited for parallel-distributed hybrids such as hierarchical NUMA systems. The de facto standard is a combination of message passing with MPI [3] for distribution and OpenMP [4] constructs for intra-node parallelization. In federated clouds, developers not only have to consider all the layers of it, but also use separate technologies to express and coordinate tasks and data on each level. We find that distinguishing between distributed and parallel systems is neither realistic nor helpful in modern computer architectures, where even single processors are essentially networks-on-chip.

In this paper we introduce our approach for a framework that allows developers to express tasks and data in a consistent way without the need for a detailed understanding of the underlying system topology. As in Google's MapReduce framework, the fundamental idea is to provide a programming model that is simple enough to allow for productivity while being powerful enough to allow for large-scale parallelism. We are convinced that the metaphor of a Tuple / Object Space combined with the application of performance optimization best practices to preserve locality and hide latencies provide us with a rich basis for our approach. Following the tradition of Ada and Linda, we name our framework after Claud Lovelace.

1. Related Work

Coordination Languages   As described in the introduction, the intelligent coordination of tasks and data is crucial for application performance and scalability. Consequently the effort that is required from developers to instruct the coordination frame to make good use of the topology of the target system, is a major productivity factor. When we studied different approaches to create a framework that has a concise interface while providing enough information for efficient placements, we identified Tuple Spaces [5] as one of the most promising designs. The applicability of tuple spaces all the way up to large-scale architectures such as cloud was already emphasized in the original vision [6]. Furthermore, the interface required to work with a tuple space is understandable and can easily be adapted to reflect the expectations of contemporary programmers. Before presenting our application of tuple space concepts in the design of Claud in Section 2, we discuss interesting tuple space implementations as depicted in Figure 1.

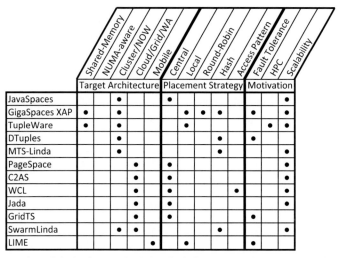

	Shared-Memory	NUMA-aware	Cluster/NOW	Cloud/Grid/WA	Mobile	Central	Local	Round-Robin	Hash	Access Pattern	Fault Tolerance	HPC	Scalability
	Target Architecture					Placement Strategy					Motivation		
JavaSpaces		•				•							•
GigaSpaces XAP	•	•					•	•	•		•		•
TupleWare	•	•				•						•	•
DTuples		•							•		•		
MTS-Linda		•							•				•
PageSpace			•			•							•
C2AS			•			•							•
WCL			•			•				•			•
Jada			•			•							•
GridTS			•			•						•	
SwarmLinda			•	•					•				•
LIME					•	•					•		

Figure 1. An overview of the landscape of existing Tuple Space research. The selection is not intended to be complete, but rather to demonstrate the variety of existing implementations. We classify implementations based on our understanding of the system architecture they target, the placement strategy that they employ and the main motivation for their development. ("NOW" stands for "network of workstations", "WA" for "wide area", "HPC" for "high performance computing")

1.1. Tuple Space Classification

Target Architecture   The computer system architecture that the tuple space was designed for or is predominantly being used with. *Shared-Memory* if the system is optimized for local accesses; *NUMA-aware* if the system is taking into account the non-uniform topology of hierarchical shared memory systems. Systems that would benefit from the topology-awareness of the underlying execution system (such as a NUMA-aware Java Virtual Machine) are not considered NUMA-aware; *Cluster/Network of Workstations* if the system mainly aims at (homogeneous) clusters with a fast network; *Cloud/Grid/Wide Area* if the system aims at multiple computers with a slow network; *Mobile* if the system is designed for mobile devices with sporadic connections.

Placement Strategy   The strategy that is applied to place the tuples within the system. *Central* where the tuple space is placed on a single node and all the other nodes are accessing it remotely; *Local* where tuples are placed on the node of the process that created them; *Round-Robin* where tuples are distributed evenly around the system; *Hash* where tuples are placed using a hash based algorithm on either the full tuple or parts of the tuple; *Access Pattern* where the run-time system monitors the tuple access patterns and migrates them accordingly. We found the access pattern placement strategy only in WCL where it is applied not to tuple, but to tuple space placement.

One of the hardest challenges placement strategies have to face is tuple retrieval overhead. While the *Central* and the *Hash* placement strategies allow for straight-forward tuple identification, the other three strategies have to either use multicast or implement a more sophisticated tuple retrieval mechanism as discussed for the respective implementations. There are two variations of tuple hashing: *Cryptographic Hashing, Random Hashing*, or *Avalanche Effect Hashing* produce a balanced distribution throughout the network and are therefore beneficial for systems that experience a high rate of random tuple reads. The alternative of *Similarity Preserving Hashing* algorithms are a powerful strategy to ensure that tuples with similar characteristics reside on the same node. If an application is structured in such a way that computations are focussed on closely related tuples, similarity preserving hashing is an efficient means to ensure locality and thus circumvent the access penalties in high-latency system topologies.

Motivation   The main driving factor for the tuple space implementation as emphasized in the original paper and the envisioned use cases. *Fault Tolerance* for tuple spaces that explicitly replicate data to tolerate node failures; *HPC* for tuple spaces that are designed for applications in high performance computing; *Scalability* for tuple spaces that are designed to improve scalability regarding their respective target architecture. The investigated systems achieve this by either distributing the tuple space across the nodes or by explicitly distinguishing between multiple tuple spaces and requiring programmers to address them correctly.

1.1.1. Coordination Language Implementations

A prominent representative of the Tuple Space landscape is JavaSpaces [7], where tuple space concepts were applied to objects, coining the term Object Spaces, and the interface was enriched with the concept of transactions. It was integrated with Sun Jini, which is now named Apache River. GigaSpaces XAP [8] is a commercialized version of JavaSpaces that offers a distributed object space with tuple redundancy that supports different placement strategies including hash-based tuple distribution. Tupleware [9] is an implementation aimed at computationally intensive applications running in a cluster. It includes a decentralized search algorithm where each node asks other nodes one by one based on a success factor of previous searches. DTuples [10] uses a distributed hash table for tuple placement and retrieval. Each tuple has to begin with a name which is then used for the hashing, resembling a key-value-store. MTS-Linda [11] was of the earliest attempts using multiple tuple spaces. It uses a tuple-to-node hash for placement.

There have been different attempts to scale the tuple space model to what we would today call a cloud architecture. PageSpace [12] is using a tuple space to coordinate distributed applications on the web. Rowstron et al. extended this notion first with C2AS [13], adding multiple tuple spaces, later with WCL [14] where a "control system" that monitors tuple space usage and migrates tuple spaces to the right location was added. Analogous to Linda, C2AS and WCL can be embedded in any host language. Jada (Java+Linda) [15] similarly implements multiple distributed but disjoint tuple spaces for Java. GridTS [16] uses a replicated tuple space for fault-tolerant scheduling.

In addition to these cloud-scale implementations still relying on the programmer to specify which tuple space (and thus which node) she wants to access, there are two interesting implementations providing one distributed, or transparently shared tuple space. SwarmLinda [17] is an attempt to transfer the ideas from the field of swarm intelligence to distributed tuple spaces. Natural multi-agent systems – such as ant colonies – show intelligent behavior, while coordinating only with local interactions in their neighborhood. This transfer results in an adaptive system that can react to changes in topology and is highly scalable while retaining some locality of similar tuples. LIME: Linda in a mobile environment [18] implements "transiently shared tuple spaces" that span multiple physical ones. The disconnection of nodes is viewed as a normal operation which results in the tuples on that node being removed from the transiently shared tuple space. The placement strategy defaults to local but can also be specified.

CnC [19] is a coordination model strongly influenced by Linda, which further allows to declaratively express data and control dependences between computational steps.

We miss two things in the systems described above, which we will describe in greater detail in section 1.3. Firstly, we want to investigate the implementation of tuple spaces at the two ends of the hierarchy: NUMA-awareness and federated clouds. Secondly, we want to be guided by the minimal set of information from a programmer needed to achieve good performance, sticking closely to modern programming models.

1.2. Hierarchical NUMA systems

Additional cores in modern business servers are either introduced by increasing the amount of cores per processor or by adding additional processors. In both cases all cores need to have access to other cores, processors and memory. These interconnects constitute the von-Neumann bottleneck, and have become one of the most crucial recent performance design challenges. Modern processor architectures, such as Intel's Haswell processors, facilitate an on-chip ring interconnection network with two opposing rings to connect cores, memory controller and processor interconnect. [20] One level higher, the reference architecture for processor interconnects provided by the processor vendors is usually a point-to-point interconnect between all processor sockets that is designed to support systems up to a certain size. (Intel for example supports up to eight processor sockets.) These systems are called glue-less systems, because the processors and the interconnection technology are provided by the same vendor. The alternative are glued systems, where third party interconnection technologies are used to build systems that support more sockets than the reference architecture. [2,21,22] In addition to the increased processor count, glued systems usually also facilitate special caching and pre-fetching solutions to compensate for the latencies and improve the overall system performance. Besides all-to-all interconnects between the processor sockets, glued architectures can realize various other popular topologies such as hypercubes and cross-bar switches.

Hierarchical NUMA systems combining multiple layers of interconnect technologies are programmed using a combination of message passing (usually with MPI [3]) and shared memory task parallelism (usually with OpenMP [4]). The application of both programming models allows programmers to account for the distributed as well as the parallel nature of hierarchical NUMA systems. Shared memory task parallelism is used on the intra-processor level where performance bottlenecks are often introduced by task and data access synchronization. Due to the significant latencies on the inter-processor level, considering the system a fully distributed one and using the message passing programming model for task and data coordination excels. The message passing model requires developers to structure their algorithm in a way that allows for the computation of independent tasks on local data and the explicit exchange of data updates via messages. The application of local data access and data duplication in form of messages reduces the load on the interconnect, while the explicit distribution ensures that the characteristics of the interconnect can be respected by the message passing framework implementation.

While allowing to achieve close to optimal application performance, the current approach restricts productivity due to the fact that programmers need to develop a detailed understanding of two programming models and their complex interplay with the systems hardware. Learning from both approaches, we designed Claud to encapsulate the best practices for parallel and distributed models into a layer that allows programmers to reuse them, while simplifying the programming model to improve productivity without sacrificing much of the performance.

1.3. Research Gap

When we set out to evaluate the design space for programming models that would allow us to coordinate task and data from the core of parallel systems up to distributed cloud federations, we assessed possible approaches based on the following question: What is the minimal set of constructs, that we need the programmer to use to express the algorithm in a way that allows for correct and efficient execution? We found tuple spaces to be a promising answer to that question. No only do they provide a very concise interface, their suitability has also been proven for both, the parallel and the distributed domain.

To apply tuple space concepts to our objective of a coherent performance framework for the whole system topology we identified some research gaps to be filled (Figure 1):

While existing tuple space implementations have a strong focus on scalability and fault tolerance, we want to evaluate how best practices for performance can be incorporated into a framework to make them reusable. Since different problems demand different optimization strategies, we want to start with a limited subset and extend our framework iteratively to support techniques for additional problem classes. The problem class of graph based algorithms possesses inherent locality characteristics which is why it is particularly well suited for a mapping onto the hierarchical system topology of modern computer systems. In this paper we describe how Claud can support developers with the coordination of tasks and data of graph problems.

Existing tuple space implementations mastered parallel shared memory systems, clusters and cloud systems. While they are probably also very well suited for both, hierarchical NUMA systems (Section 1.2) and federated clouds [23], we find that it is important to evaluate this with a number of real-world examples. We intend to study the potential and possible opportunities for improvement in the SSICLOPS [23] project.

Finally, we want to identify a minimal set of programming constructs that is required to allow a coordination framework like Claud to perform efficient data placement and task scheduling. We hope to identify programming constructs that allow programmers to express parallelism and locality without understanding the target topology in detail, while enabling us to achieve portable performance with adaptive mappings.

2. Approach

The objective of Claud is to allow task and data coordination throughout the whole system topology (from core to cloud federation) with a single coherent programming model. The overhead that the programming model imposes should to be low enough to allow productive development while allowing Claud to enable acceptable performance.

2.1. Assumptions and Design Decisions

We assume that programmers do not know the hardware topology upfront, and that the characteristics of the topology change during runtime. These assumptions are based on the fact that there is a huge variety of possible topologies and the fact that the characteristics of the topology are load dependent. Since the programmer does not know the topology, she cannot specify the data placement and task distribution statically beforehand. Since the topology changes, Claud needs to adapt to the current system characteristics by using auto-balancing and fault-tolerance techniques to provide portable performance.

We assume that programmers are more productive, if they do not need to explicitly specify coordination and dependence. Consequently, coordination should be inferred from the system topology and the logical representation of the algorithm and its data structures to make coordination as implicit as possible.

We assume that besides homogeneous tasks of similar compute intensity, there are also task sets containing a mix of compute intensive and light-weight tasks. Furthermore, we assume that programmers do not want to specify compute intensity of tasks. In contrast to the common approach of either distributing all tasks or none, we want to integrate heuristics that account for varying task profiles. The heuristics will be based on the computation-to-communication ratio of a task, resulting in appropriate task coordination. One extreme coordination decision would be to execute a set of tasks serially on one processor if the computer is very cheap and the distribution would be relative expensive.

From our experience we assume that programmers have a better intuition for the *read* and *write* programming constructs than the notion of *in* and *out* as proposed by Linda. Therefore, we provide primitives such as barriers and NUMA-aware reader-writer locks for data access synchronization, allowing programmers to see Claud as a distributed shared memory framework mimicking a familiar execution environment.

We assume that latency and bandwidth limitations are the predominant bottlenecks, and that as a consequence locality is beneficial to performance. Preserving locality means that a task working on data should executed at the subgraph of the topology (preferably on the same node) where the respective memory is located.

Since the layers of the topology have differing characteristics, we do not assume that an optimal distribution can be derived simply based on the programmer's input. Instead we want to incorporate multiple distribution modules in Claud as described in Section 2.2. These modules allow us to add constructs to Claud's interface, presenting a concise and familiar interface to programmers while providing Claud with all the information that is required for effective coordination. When evaluating Claud with real-life applications, we will iteratively integrate additional distribution modules.

2.2. Architecture and Implementation

Figure 2 shows the interfaces that Claud provides to algorithm programmers as well as the associated techniques used for the coordination of task and data on the present system. As a basis for the coordination of data and tasks, Claud comprises an extensible set of Distribution Modules. Each module may imply an extension of the interface for the programmer, as well as, a more sophisticated mapping strategy to the topology. Distribution Modules have to be designed so that they can be used in unison with the other modules or so that a module is explicitly overwriting the policies of another module. As an example, the Concurrent Data Structures Module (number III in the picture) may overwrite the policies of the Hierarchical Task Queues Module (number I), but can still be improved by the Run-Time-Analysis Module (number II).

Distributed Module I	Object/Data access is presented using the usual shared memory metaphor: memory can be read and written. Write accesses automatically allocate or update data in the Object Space, read accesses retrieve data from the Object Space. The mental model of the Object Space that the programmer can use is similar to a Key-Value Store. As our objective is to support all topology levels, we need to provide a software-managed cache for distributed levels, that integrates with the hardware caches on the parallel levels. Since reading will basically result in a local copy of the data, coherency needs to be guaranteed by invalidating all copies if data is written. The coherency requirements of the algorithm can be enforced by either by implicit synchronization barriers or by explicit synchronization with synchronization primitives like Reader/Writer Locks. Internally we have a hierarchical structure that keeps track of the data locations

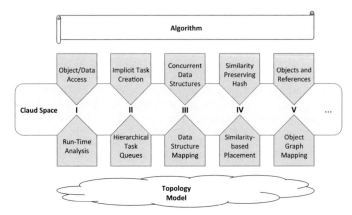

Figure 2. Architecture Overview: Claud acts as a mediator between the logical domain of the programmer and the topology model derived from the current system configuration. Currently Claud comprises five Distribution Models, each providing a distinct set of programming constructs and extended mechanisms for coordination.

and is closely modeled after the system topology allowing us to assess the distance to the data. We employ Run-Time Analysis methods to assess data access patterns, which allows us to prefetch data and migrate tuple responsibility based on auto-tuned heuristics.

Distributed Module II   Claud offers several ways to create tasks implicitly such as parallel loops and recursive task creation. [4] If no other module provides a more intelligent algorithm for the task distribution, we utilize hierarchical task queues and work-stealing. [4] Each core in the topology will have its own local queue and can also access an additional queue that it shares with its neighbors. Hierarchical task queues with work stealing provide a pretty good distribution scheme for average algorithms, but can easily be outperformed by modules exploiting additional information about the data and the algorithm like III and IV.

Distribution Module III   Another module provides Concurrent Data Structures. If programmers use our arrays, lists, trees, etc. they provide us with insight about the way their data is supposed to be structured and accessed. From this information, Claud can infer the inherent notion of locality and distribute data and tasks accordingly. As described before this module can benefit from other modules like the run-time analysis. Furthermore, if the tasks have varying complexities, work stealing can help to balance the work.

Distribution Module IV   Similarity (or Bonding-) preserving multi-dimensional hashing allows the programmer to provide a similarity measure for the data in form of a multi-dimensional vector. In a two dimensional index space (think matrix-matrix multiplication) this could be a vector describing the horizontal and vertical coordinate of the cell. Based on these vectors, Claud can determine the similarity of tuples and put similar tuples in the same place or closely together.

Distribution Module V   Another way to gather information about the data structures and presumed access patterns is by looking at the object graph. If this module is used, we map the graph that is accessible from the current context (e.g. loop body) onto the topology at the beginning of each code block and transfer data and tasks if necessary. As with all the other modules, this can improve the performance significantly or produce an additional overhead. Consequently, using heuristics and auto-tuning to find the right balance between the modules is essential.

2.3. Restrictions

In large scale scenarios such as federated clouds, some traditional operating system functionalities become increasingly challenging to provide. Hence, cloud providers usually implement such features as a part of their Infrastructure as a Service offer. The same restrictions apply to Claud: an application being executed in a distributed fashion using Claud is expected not to work with its own operating system handles. This means: no access to file handles, socket, I/O, operating system synchronization primitives, etc. To compensate for this, Claud provides its own synchronization primitives such as barriers and NUMA-aware reader-writer locks. The set of features is currently restricted, but will be extended to meet the requirements of further use cases.

3. Conclusion

We have shown that the modular design of Claud is a suitable approach to coordinate complex graph problems on hierachical system topologies. We have demonstrated several coordination techniques that are integrated into our hierarchical object space, which maximize locality and thus minimize latency penalties. We found that additional programming constructs to realize such a coordination are not only concise, but can also be tailored to fit the expectations of the programmer.

In the future, we want to implement all presented ideas and thoroughly evaluate Claud on hierarchical NUMA systems and in federated clouds. To demonstrate the applicability of the approach to real-world scenarios, we plan to evaluate it in the context of the SSICLOPS [23] and the sHiFT [24] project. The *Scalable and Secure Infrastructures for Cloud Operations (SSICLOPS)* [23] project tackles the challenge of managing federated private cloud infrastructures. We are particularly interested in is the aspect of workload scheduling: In cloud systems, data can be scattered across different datacenters. Since even modern wide area datacenter interconnections such as rented dark fibers or the public internet come with severely constrained connectivity compared to intra-datacenter connectivity, ignoring the lack of locality results in degraded performance and is not an economic option. Therefore, either data needs to move close to the processing resources or vice versa. At a much lower level on the intra-system scale, the same issues apply to modern NUMA architectures, where remote memory access caused by improper workload placement limits performance. Hence, our goal for Claud is to enable developers to benefit from versatile workload placement strategies on various scales ranging from groups of CPU cores to entire datacenter federations. The sHiFT [24] project aims at creating a high performance framework for business process analysis. Business processes can be represented as graphs annotated with natural language artifacts. Various algorithms work with these graphs to extract business information: process matching, reference model and process mining, identification of isomorphic subgraphs, and natural language processing. Most of these algorithms can be parallelized, making the mapping of the process graphs to the system topology and the efficient coordination of computations the core performance challenges of the project. We see this project as an opportunity to identify potential for further improvements in Claud's capabilities.

Acknowledgement

This paper has received funding from the European Union's Horizon 2020 research and innovation programme 2014-2018 under grant agreement No. 644866.

Disclaimer

This paper reflects only the authors' views and the European Commission is not responsible for any use that may be made of the information it contains.

References

[1] J. Costa-Requena, M. Kimmerlin, F. Eberhardt, M. Plauth, A. Polze, S. Klauck, and M. Uflacker, "Use-case scenarios for the evaluation of federated private clouds," Scalable and Secure Infrastructures for Cloud Operations, Tech. Rep., 2015, to be published.

[2] Silicon Graphics International Corp., "Technical Advances in the SGI© UV™ Architecture," Tech. Rep., June 2012.

[3] Message Passing Interface Forum, "MPI: A Message-Passing Interface Standard Version 3.1," June 2015.

[4] OpenMP Architecture Review Board, "OpenMP Application Program Interface Version 4.0," July 2013.

[5] D. Gelernter, "Generative communication in Linda," *ACM Transactions on Programming Languages and Systems*, vol. 7, no. 1, pp. 80–112, 1985.

[6] ——, *Mirror worlds: Or the day software puts the universe in a shoebox... How it will happen and what it will mean.* Oxford University Press, 1992.

[7] E. Freeman, S. Hupfer, and K. Arnold, *JavaSpaces principles, patterns, and practice.* Addison-Wesley Professional, 1999.

[8] Gigaspaces. (2015, Jun.) Gigaspaces xap. [Online]. Available: http://www.gigaspaces.com/xap

[9] A. Atkinson, "Tupleware: A distributed tuple space for cluster computing," *Parallel and Distributed Computing, Applications and Technologies, PDCAT Proceedings*, pp. 121–126, 2008.

[10] Y. Jiang, G. Xue, Z. Jia, and J. You, "DTuples: A distributed hash table based tuple space service for distributed coordination," *Proceedings - Fifth International Conference on Grid and Cooperative Computing, GCC 2006*, pp. 101–106, 2006.

[11] B. Nielsen and T. Sørensen, "Distributed Programming with Multiple Tuple Space Linda," 1994.

[12] P. Ciancarini, A. Knoche, R. Tolksdorf, and F. Vitali, "PageSpace: An architecture to coordinate distributed applications on the Web," *Computer Networks and ISDN Systems*, vol. 28, 1996.

[13] A. Rowstron, S. Li, and R. Stefanova, "C2AS: a system supporting distributed Web applications composed of collaborating agents," *Journal of Engineering and Applied Science*, pp. 127–132, 1997.

[14] A. Rowstron, "WCL: A co-ordination language for geographically distributed agents," *World Wide Web*, vol. 1, no. 3, pp. 167–179–179, 1998.

[15] P. Ciancarini and D. Rossi, "Jada: Coordination and Communication for Java Agents," *Mobile Object Systems Towards the Programmable Internet*, vol. 1222, pp. 213–228, 1997.

[16] F. Favarim, J. Fraga, L. C. Lung, M. Correia, and J. a. F. Santos, "GridTS: Tuple spaces to support fault tolerant scheduling on computational grids," pp. 1–24, 2006.

[17] R. Tolksdorf and R. Tolksdorf, "A New Approach to Scalable Linda-systems Based on Swarms," *Computing*, no. March, pp. 375–379, 2003.

[18] G. Picco, a.L. Murphy, and G.-C. Roman, "LIME: Linda meets mobility," *Proceedings of the 1999 International Conference on Software Engineering (IEEE Cat. No.99CB37002)*, pp. 368–377, 1999.

[19] Z. Budimlić, M. Burke, V. Cavé, K. Knobe, G. Lowney, R. Newton, J. Palsberg, D. Peixotto, V. Sarkar, F. Schlimbach *et al.*, "Concurrent collections," *Scientific Programming*, vol. 18, 2010.

[20] P. Hammarlund, R. Kumar, R. B. Osborne, R. Rajwar, R. Singhal, R. D'Sa, R. Chappell, S. Kaushik *et al.*, "Haswell: The fourth-generation Intel core processor," *IEEE Micro*, no. 2, 2014.

[21] Hewlett-Packard Development Company, L.P, "HP Integrity Superdome 2 - The ultimate mission-critical platform," Tech. Rep., July 2013.

[22] T. P. Morgan, "Balancing Scale And Simplicity In Shared Memory Systems," *http://www.theplatform.net*, March 2015.

[23] Scalable and Secure Infrastructures for Cloud Operations (SSICLOPS) Project. [Online]. Available: https://ssiclops.eu/

[24] DFKI GmbH, Hasso-Plattner-Institut and Software AG. sHiFT Project. In German, application to a bidding, unpublished. [Online]. Available: http://www.bmbf.de/foerderungen/26683.php

Parallel Computing: On the Road to Exascale
G.R. Joubert et al. (Eds.)
IOS Press, 2016
doi:10.3233/978-1-61499-621-7-615

Coordination with Structured Composition for Cyber-physical Systems [1]

Simon MAURER [a,2], Raimund KIRNER [a]

[a] *School of Computer Science, University of Hertfordshire, Hatfield, UK*

Abstract. Structured programming has become a very successful programming paradigm as it provides locality of a program's control flow. Similar concepts of locality are desired for the specification and development of concurrent and parallel systems. In the domain of cyber-physical systems or embedded computing it is challenging to identify such structured compositions since control flow tends to be driven by concurrently acting reactive components with often circular dataflow relations.

In this paper we discuss foundations for a structured coordination language for cyber-physical systems. We study car platooning as a use case, exhibiting typical challenges of cyber physical systems. Based on that use case we show a possible structured composition pattern and outline coordination network construction mechanisms.

Keywords. cyber-physical systems, coordination languages, structured programming

Introduction

The increasing system complexity of cyber-physical systems (CPS) drives a high pressure on software engineering methodologies to assure an effective and predictable control of resources. Coordination languages have been proposed as a solution to tackle this problem by decomposing application software into coordination and algorithmic programming [1]. In this paper we present coordination language constructs, based on streaming networks, suitable for CPS where complex interaction patterns pose a challenge for structured system composition.

As described by Arbab in [2], coordination models can be classified into endogenous and exogenous coordination, describing whether coordination is done from within a behavioural component or from the outside respectively. We further relate to the aspect of structured programming and focus on the ability of coordination languages to describe networks in a structured manner.

With respect to application aspects, we classify systems to either process data in transformative or reactive manner where CPS often fall into the latter

---

[1]The research leading to these results has received funding from the FP7 ARTEMIS-JU research project "ConstRaint and Application driven Framework for Tailoring Embedded Real-time Systems" (CRAFTERS).

[2]Corresponding Author: Simon Maurer, E-mail: s.maurer@herts.ac.uk

class. Additionally, we distinguish between systems relying on persistent state or systems following a functional behaviour.

Our aim is to provide exogenous language constructs that enforce structure, support reactive data processing, and allow persistent state within behavioural components. The proposed constructs are based on streaming networks where the topology of the network imposes dependencies between components and where message streams are coordinated within the network.

The reminder of this paper is structured as follows: In Section 1 we discuss classification aspects of coordination languages and relate them to the challenges of cyber-physical systems (CPS). In Section 2 we introduce the underlying coordination model and in Section 3 we describe network operators. Section 4 presents an example of a CPS where we apply the presented coordination concepts. Section 5 discusses related work and Section 6 concludes the paper.

1. Coordination of Cyber-physical Systems

The underlying model of the language constructs presented in this paper consists of three conceptual elements: the *computational components*, the *routing network*, and the *extra-functional requirements layer*. A computational component contains a part of the behavioural description of the application. Multiple computational components are connected and coordinated by the routing network which itself is composed of coordination components. The extra-functional requirements layer serves to annotate boxes and network elements with extra-functional requirements such as location information for distributed systems or real-time requirements in CPS.

The following Subsections discuss properties of coordination languages and requirements of languages targeting CPS.

1.1. Transformative vs. Reactive Data Processing

In contrast to a transformative system that takes inputs, performs computation, and produces outputs, CPS are often reactive systems where inputs are coupled to outputs via the environment. The output of a tansformative system can be formulated as a function of the state of the system and its input: $out = f(state, in)$. Reactive systems, on the other hand, additionally, have a relation where the input of the system is a function of its output and an unknown variable imposed by the environment: $out = f(state, in) \land in = f'(x, out)$.

The implications of a reactive system with respect to the presented coordination concepts are: support for bidirectional communication between computational components, a data-flow direction that can not be defined clearly on an application level, and computational components with a persistent internal state.

1.2. Exogenous vs. Endogenous Coordination Model

An exogenous coordination model assures a clear separation between coordination and behaviour by leaving the behavioural components oblivious of the coordination constructs that exert coordination upon them. An endogenous coordination model, on the other hand, has no such separation and the coordination is done from within a behavioural component which makes the component aware of the coordination exert on it.

An exogenous model assures clear separation of concerns which is of great importance to simplify development, integration, and verification processes. In the domain of CPS where systems are often safety critical, this is a property we need to enforce.

1.3. Persistent State vs. Non-persistent State

The design of new applications in the domain of CPS often relies on legacy code. For this reason, state must be allowed in computational components and they cannot be restricted to purely functional behaviour. Reactive data processing needs state in general but with an exogenous coordination model the coordinated components can be kept free of persistent state. However, this comes at the price of efficiency because state information has to be communicated through the streaming network.

1.4. Structured vs. Non-structured Connectivity

A structured network provides a sense of locality and can be helpful to provide composability and compositionality of sub networks by keeping port-to-port connections local. In contrast to this, a non-structured network would rather be created with global port-to-port connection tables which are hard to read and understand.

For a modular development it is important to understand the behaviour of an isolated sub-entity, independent of where it is going to be integrated, which is why a structured approach is key.

1.5. Real-time Constraints and Analysability of Cyber-pysical Systems

Due to their interaction with the physical environment, some of the services of CPS do have real-time requirements. The specification of real-time properties of streaming networks is discussed by Kirner and Maurer in [3]. Further, the application domain of CPS is often strongly regulated and requires extensive verification of the design and implementation. To enable such verification processes, the system must be made analysable by the underlying design model.

The above mentioned extra-functional requirements layer aims to serve this purpose by introducing an abstraction between the application and the timing requirements. An example of such an abstraction is the Ptides [4] language. This aspect of the model will be comprised in future work and is not further discussed in this paper.

2. Components and Coordination Elements

In the presented coordination concepts, the computational components are not part of the coordination language and are written in a separate programming language. The coordination components form the routing network which is used to connect multiple computational components and build a streaming network. In order to interface the coordination components, computational components are surrounded by a construct which is called *box* throughout this paper. A streaming network consists of *nets*, *channels*, and *synchronizers* which are either implicit or explicit instances of computational components or coordination components.

Nets and synchronizers have, possibly, multiple input or output ports. The most basic net is the instance of a box declaration. A box declaration assigns the input and output parameters of the computational component with the input and output ports of the net and links the box to the source code of the computational component. A box can be annotated as stateless if the computational component is purely functional. Inside a box declaration, ports can be merged with a *merge-synchronizer* as described in Subsection 2.1.

Nets are hierarchical and can include other nets and networks of nets. By connecting ports of nets together with directed channels a network is created. The connection semantics of nets is explained in Section 3 where network operators are described. The following Subsections describe synchronizers and discuss the problem of flow direction ambiguities.

2.1. Synchronizers

We distinguish between two types of synchronizers: the *copy-synchronizer* (Figure 2) and the *merge-synchronizer* (Figure 3).

The copy synchronizer has no explicit language element but is spawned implicitly whenever more than two ports are connected. It copies messages from its inputs to all of its outputs. The messages are made available at each output port simultaneously and thus, are synchronizing the earliest possible processing. Messages are read in arbitrary order and are processed non-deterministically. A copy-synchronizer allows a one-to-one, one-to-many, many-to-one, and many-to-many mapping of ports.

A merge-synchronizer is spawned explicitly but is only allowed inside a box declaration. It has multiple input ports and only one output port. The merge-synchronizer collects messages at its inputs and as soon as on all input ports a message is available it produces a tuple, containing a message from each input, at its output. This tuple of messages is forwarded to the computational component input where it is interpreted as an ordered set of input parameters. Inputs of the merge synchronizer can be *decoupled*, allowing the synchronizer to trigger, even if no new message is available on such a port. The necessary buffers and triggering semantics for such interfaces are described by the work of Maurer and Kirner in [5].

2.2. Flow Direction Ambiguities

As described in the beginning of this section, channels are directed. As nets and synchronizers can have multiple input and output ports, a connection between two components can be composed out of multiple channels with different directions. This results in a network where the flow-direction is not clearly defined and channel directions may become ambiguous. Lets assume the box F with the following box declaration:

```
box F (in a, out a, in b, out b) on func_f
```

If this box is instantiated twice, say as the nets H and G, the connection of the two nets would be ambiguous as there are four possible ways to connect them. This is depicted in Figure 1.

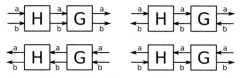

Figure 1. An example of an ambiguous flow direction. The two nets H and G can be connected in four different ways.

Note that the connection of H and G is only ambiguous when inspected locally. By unfolding the complete network and assuming that all ports are connected (this is a requirement for a network to be valid), the direction of each channel is clearly defined. However, this is not sufficient because in a structured program all parts of the program need to be unambiguous, independent of their surrounding elements.

In order to achieve an unambiguous flow direction or to help the programmer to structure the code, ports can be grouped into two separate collections: An *Up-Stream (US)* or a *Down-Stream (DS)* collection. The grouping of the ports into the two collections depends on the context of the program and each collection can hold any number of input or output ports or can be empty. The grouping provides a logical flow-direction due to the constraint that ports in an up-stream of one net can only connect to ports in a down-stream of another net and vice versa. The logical flow-direction is unrelated to the real flow-direction of messages as channels can be of arbitrary direction.

A third collection, called *Side-Ports (SP)*, exists but is explained in more detail in Section 3.4. Figure 4 depicts a schematic representation of a box declaration where ports are grouped into the three different collections.

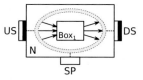

Figure 2. Copy-synchronizer

Figure 3. Merge-synchronizer with one decoupled input

Figure 4. *Box* declaration

3. Network Operators and Port Connections

This section describes the operators that allow to interconnect components in a structured manner. We propose two basic grouping operators that allow to combine two nets by either forcing a connection or preventing a connection. The connective grouping is called *serial composition* and the non-connective grouping is called *parallel composition*. Additionally, an explicit connection of nets via side-ports allows to either, connect a signal to most nets in the network (e.g. clock, reset, or logger), or to realise connections that cannot be achieved with the available network operators.

The main focus of the network operators is twofold: 1. the operators aim at structuring the network by providing a sense of locality, meaning that information necessary to understand a local part of the network is kept local. 2. connections between nets are to be kept explicit and not hidden by an implicit connection semantics of the operators.

A net N can be a single box in the simplest case or a combination of networks via network combinators. The communication interface of each net N consists of a set of ports: $\mathcal{P}(N)$. Each port $p_i \in \mathcal{P}(N)$ is either an input or output port, specified by a mode attribute: $p_i.mode \in \{input, output\}$. Based on that we define predicates for input and output ports as: $\mathcal{I}(N) = \{ p_i \mid p_i \in \mathcal{P}(N) \land (p_i.mode = input) \}$ and $\mathcal{O}(N) = \{ p_i \mid p_i \in \mathcal{P}(N) \land (p_i.mode = output) \}$.

A port p_i is identified by two parts: its signal name $p_i.signal$ and a location identifier $p_i.id$ where the latter is derived from the identifier of the net or box. Ports also have a field that indicates their belonging to a port collection, which can be either up-stream (US), down-stream (DS), or side-port (SP): $p_i.col \in \{US, DS, SP\}$. We use the following predicates for port collections: $\mathcal{US}(N) = \{ p_i \mid p_i \in \mathcal{P}(N) \land (p_i.col = US) \}$, $\mathcal{DS}(N) = \{ p_i \mid p_i \in \mathcal{P}(N) \land (p_i.col = DS) \}$, and $\mathcal{SP}(N) = \{ p_i \mid p_i \in \mathcal{P}(N) \land (p_i.col = SP) \}$.

3.1. Parallel Composition

The parallel composition uses the operator '|'. The definition of a network N as the parallel composition of networks N_1 and N_2 is written as: '$N = N_1 \mid N_2$'.

No implicit port connection is performed with the parallel composition. Instead, the set of ports of the resulting net $N_1|N_2$ is the union of the set of ports of the two operators N_1 and N_2 with preserving their mode: $\mathcal{P}(N_1|N_2) = \mathcal{P}(N_1) \cup \mathcal{P}(N_1)$. Ports that are grouped in a port collection in the operands N_1 or N_2 are grouped in the same collection in the resulting net $N_1|N_2$: $\mathcal{US}(N_1|N_2) = \mathcal{US}(N_1) \cup \mathcal{US}(N_2)$, $\mathcal{DS}(N_1|N_2) = \mathcal{DS}(N_1) \cup \mathcal{DS}(N_2)$, and $\mathcal{SP}(N_1|N_2) = \mathcal{SP}(N_1) \cup \mathcal{SP}(N_2)$. The parallel composition is schematically represented in Figure 6.

3.2. Serial Composition

The serial composition uses the operator '.'. The definition of a network N as the serial composition of networks N_1 and N_2 is written as: '$N = N_1 . N_2$'.

The down-stream ports of N_1 and the up-stream ports of N_2 of a serial composition $N_1.N_2$ are internally connected: $IntConn(\mathcal{DS}(N_1), \mathcal{US}(N_2))$. However, to be a valid internal connection and thus valid serial composition, the following properties of $\mathcal{DS}(N_1)$ and $\mathcal{US}(N_2)$ must hold:

$$\forall p_i \in \mathcal{DS}(N_1) \; \exists p_j \in \mathcal{US}(N_2). \; (p_i.signal = p_j.signal) \land IsCMode(p_i, p_j) \land$$

$$\forall p_j \in \mathcal{US}(N_2) \; \exists p_i \in \mathcal{DS}(N_1). \; (p_i.signal = p_j.signal) \land IsCMode(p_i, p_j)$$

where the predicate $IsCMode(p, p')$ ensures that input/output are connected:

$$IsCMode(p, p') : (p.mode = input \ \wedge \ p'.mode = output) \ \vee$$
$$(p.mode = output \ \wedge \ p'.mode = input)$$

Knowing which ports are internally connected, the resulting externally visible port sets of $N_1.N_2$ are defined as follows:

- Side-ports of N_1 or N_2 are grouped in the side-port collection of $N_1.N_2$: $\mathcal{SP}(N_1.N_2) = \mathcal{SP}(N_1) \cup \mathcal{SP}(N_2)$.
- Ports in the down-stream collection of N_1 are grouped in the down-stream collection of $N_1.N_2$ and ports in the up-stream collection of N_2 are grouped in the up-stream collection of $N_1.N_2$: $\mathcal{DS}(N_1.N_2) = \mathcal{DS}(N_1)$ and $\mathcal{US}(N_1.N_2) = \mathcal{US}(N_2)$.

For a network expression formed out of network operators to be valid, all ports that are not grouped in the side-port collection must be connected. For a network to be valid, all ports (including ports grouped in the side-port collection) must be connected. The schematic representation of a serial composition is shown in Figure 7.

3.3. Operator Precedence

The order of precedence of the operators is defined as follows: The serial composition precedes the parallel composition.

An example where the precedence is applied is shown in Figure 5. On the left side two sequences $A_1.B_1.C_1$ and $A_2.B_2.C_2$ are created which are then joined by the parallel composition. On the right side the parallel compositions are enforced by the parentheses, resulting in a serial composition with full connectivity.

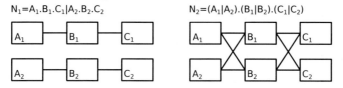

Figure 5. Two examples of connection graphs where the operator precedence is illustrated.

3.4. Side-port Connections

Side-port connections are explicit connections between matching ports in multiple side-port collections of different nets. Lets assume the box declarations

```
1   box F(out a, side in clk)
2   box G(in a, out a, side in clk)
3   box H(in a)
4   box Clk(side out clk)
```

and the two independent nets $F.G.H$ and Clk. An explicit connection of the signal clk can now be declared, connecting all ports in the side-port collections of the nets listed in the declaration block:

```
connect clk {*} // equivalent to 'connect clk {F, G, Clk}'
```

The symbol '*' is used to connect the signal to all nets that have matching ports in their side-port collection but ignores those that have not.

3.5. Scopes

Scoping of network structures is performed by explicit net declarations. A net declaration can contain box declarations, other net declarations, explicit connections, nets, and networks of nets. All elements declared inside a net declaration are not accessible from the outside. A net declaration is instantiated as a net when it is used in a network expression, equivalent to the instantiation of box declarations. A net declaration links, similar to a box declaration, ports available from elements inside the net to ports that are made available on the outside. The ports can optionally be grouped in different collections and can be renamed. A schematic representation is depicted in Figure 8.

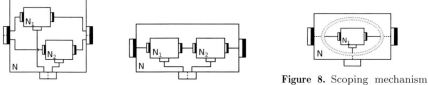

Figure 6. *Parallel composition*   **Figure 7.** *Serial composition*   **Figure 8.** Scoping mechanism of a *Net*

4. Cyber-physical Systems - An Example

In this section we demonstrate vehicle platooning as an example of cyber-physical systems with different interactions of components. The basic idea of vehicle platooning is to coordinate the cruising speed of, in series driving, vehicles to achieve a more resourceful driving. Bergenhem et al. describe different types of platooning systems [6]. In Figure 9 we show a possible interaction scenario of different car components, relevant to vehicle platooning, with a particular focus on the braking mechanism only.

The three horizontally aligned boxes represent different cars driving in series. For Car_i further internals of the braking control are shown. The *anti-lock braking system* (ABS) receives a control signal for a desired braking action but the ABS then decides on its own when to assert and release braking pressure (B) based on feedback over the revolution sensors of the wheels (RS). Besides the manual braking control (MB) we assume an automatic distance control system which uses distance sensors (DS) to measure the distance to its front vehicle and starts automatic braking requests to keep a certain minimal distance.

What we see from this example is that communication between components is bi-directional and individual components act as reactive systems on their own. Such communication patterns cannot be mapped to acyclic directed computation graphs. Figure 10 depicts the car-platooning example with a compositional structure and Figures 11 and 12 show the code describing the problem. The network

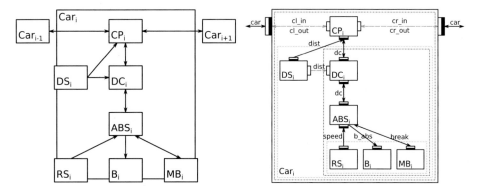

Figure 9. The car platooning example with port-to-port connections.

Figure 10. Structured representation of the car platooning example.

operators achieve a structuring of the network by implicitly grouping components together and keeping port connections local. A net declaration *Car* allows to group networks together and create local port-to-port assignments.

```
1  box DC ( side in dist, up down in dc,
              up down out dc)
2    on func_dc
3  box ABS ( in speed, in break, up in
              dc, up out dc, out b_abs, out
              breack)
4    on func_abs
5  stateless box DS (up side out dist)
6     on func_ds
7  stateless box RS (out speed)
8    on func_rs
9  stateless box B (in b_abs)
10   on func_b
11 box MB (in break, out break)
12   on func_mb
```

Figure 11. Global box declarations for the car platooning example.

```
1  net Car { up in car (cl_in), up out
              car (cl_out), down in car (cr_in
              ), down out car (cr_out) }
2  {
3    connect dist {DS, DC}
4
5    box CP ( down in dist, down in l,
              down out dc, side in cl_in, side
              out cl_out, side in cr_in, side
              out cr_out)
6      on func_cp
7
8    ((RS|B|MB).ABS.DC|DS).CP
9  }
```

Figure 12. The net description for one car.

5. Related Work

A first approach of coordinating streaming applications was introduced with StreaMIT [7], a language that allows to create a loosely structured streaming network by interconnecting computational components, called Filters, with network constructors such as split-join, feedback, or simple one-to-one streams. The fully fledged coordination language S-Net [8] is also based on streaming networks but unlike StreMIT, S-Net is exogenous and achieves a tighter structuring with network operators similar to the operators presented in this paper.

Other than the coordination languages listed above, the concepts presented in this paper target reactive systems with persistent state. Other approaches with the focus on the design of CPS are the language Giotto [9] and the Ptolemy [10] framework. Giotto is based on a time-triggered paradigm and targets applications with periodic behaviour, while the presented coordination model supports mixed timing semantics. The focus of the Ptolemy project lies on providing a unified modelling framework that allows to integrate and compose heterogeneous real-time systems but does not enforce separation of concerns.

6. Summary and Conclusion

In this paper we discussed coordination concepts based on streaming networks suitable for cyber-physical systems. One aspect of the language concepts is to make network structures locally visible to the reader of a coordination program and not to hide connectivity information through implicit connection processes. Another aspect is the enforcement of structure in networks by using a structured programming approach. We showed that this approach, designed for transformational and functional systems, can also be applied for reactive systems where components have persistent state. We applied the language on a car platooning application and presented a concise way of modelling the coordination aspect of the application.

The future work consist of defining a fully fledged coordination language, adding a layer with extra-functional requirement specifications to the model, and building a runtime system for the language.

References

[1]   Edward A. Lee. Cyber Physical Systems: Design Challenges. In *2008 11th IEEE International Symposium on Object Oriented Real-Time Distributed Computing (ISORC)*, pages 363–369. IEEE, May 2008.

[2]   Farhad Arbab. Composition of Interacting Computations. In Dina Goldin, Scott A. Smolka, and Peter Wegner, editors, *Interactive Computation*, pages 277–321. Springer Berlin Heidelberg, January 2006.

[3]   Raimund Kirner and Simon Maurer. On the Specification of Real-time Properties of Streaming Networks. In *18. Kolloquium Programmiersprachen und Grundlagen der Programmierung*, Kärnten, Austria, October 2015.

[4]   Patricia Derler, Thomas Huining Feng, Edward A. Lee, Slobodan Matic, Hiren D. Patel, Yang Zhao, and Jia Zou. PTIDES: A Programming Model for Distributed Real-Time Embedded Systems. Technical Report UCB/EECS-2008-72, EECS Department, University of California, Berkeley, May 2008.

[5]   Simon Maurer and Raimund Kirner. Cross-criticality Interfaces for Cyber-physical Systems. In *Proc. 1st IEEE Int'l Conference on Event-based Control, Communication, and Signal Processing*, Krakow, Poland, June 2015.

[6]   Carl Bergenhem, Steven Shladover, Erik Coelingh, Christoffer Englund, and Sadayuki Tsugawa. Overview of Platooning Systems. In *Proceedings of the 19th ITS World Congress, Oct 22-26, Vienna, Austria (2012)*, 2012.

[7]   William Thies, Michal Karczmarek, and Saman Amarasinghe. StreamIt: A Language for Streaming Applications. In *Compiler Construction*, number 2304 in Lecture Notes in Computer Science, pages 179–196. Springer Berlin Heidelberg, January 2002.

[8]   Clemens Grelck, Sven-Bodo Scholz, and Alex Shafarenko. Asynchronous Stream Processing with S-Net. *International Journal of Parallel Programming*, 38(1):38–67, February 2010.

[9]   Thomas A. Henzinger, Benjamin Horowitz, and Christoph Meyer Kirsch. Giotto: A Time-Triggered Language for Embedded Programming. In *Embedded Software*, number 2211 in Lecture Notes in Computer Science, pages 166–184. Springer Berlin Heidelberg, January 2001.

[10]   J. Eker, J.W. Janneck, E.A Lee, Jie Liu, Xiaojun Liu, J. Ludvig, S. Neuendorffer, S. Sachs, and Yuhong Xiong. Taming Heterogeneity - The Ptolemy Approach. *Proceedings of the IEEE*, 91(1):127–144, January 2003.

Mini-Symposium:
Symposium on Parallel Solvers for Very Large PDE Based Systems in the Earth- and Atmospheric Sciences

Parallel Computing: On the Road to Exascale
G.R. Joubert et al. (Eds.)
IOS Press, 2016
doi:10.3233/978-1-61499-621-7-627

On Efficient Time Stepping using the Discontinuous Galerkin Method for Numerical Weather Prediction

Andreas DEDNER, [a,1] Robert KLÖFKORN [b]

[a] *Mathematics Department, University of Warwick, Conventry, UK*
[b] *International Research Institute of Stavanger, Stavanger, Norway*

Abstract. We present a preconditioned matrix-free Newton Krylov method for solving meteorological problems with an implicit Runge-Kutta Discontinuous Galerkin scheme. First we report on an explicit version of the scheme, briefly studying serial and parallel efficiency of our code and present a comparison of our scheme with the dynamical core COSMO developed at the German Weather Service. On isotropic grids our code is shown to be competitive, while on grids with smaller spacing in the vertical than horizontal, the stability restrictions on the time step make this approach unsuitable. We then present new work on an implicit version which is shown to bring the run time back within the range of COSMO on the anisotropic grids more normally used in numerical weather prediction.

Keywords. Compressible flow, Euler, Navier-Stokes, Discontinuous Galerkin, Explicit Runge-Kutta, Implicit Runge-Kutta, Preconditioning, Density current, Parallelization, Code generation, DUNE

Introduction

Dynamical cores for weather prediction or climate models, i.e. numerical solvers for the compressible Euler equations or similar models, are increasingly based on higher order finite-volume type discretisations. These schemes have often been mandatory in other areas of fluid dynamic simulations due to their property to locally conserve the prognostic variables and therefore to treat shocks and other discontinuities correctly. During recent years discontinuous Galerkin (DG) methods, combining ideas from finite-volumes with finite-elements have become popular in the fluid dynamics community, resulting in locally conserving schemes while allowing discretisations of almost arbitrary order with small stencils [1]. These compact stencils facilitate implementation on massively parallel computing architectures. Consequently, several groups have started to investigate the DG method for usability in numerical models for the atmosphere. For example, [2] implemented the DG method for three different sets of budget equations and compared them with respect to their conservation properties, accuracy and efficiency. In the fluid dynamics community these methods for solving the compressible Euler equations have mostly been combined with explicit methods in time, e.g., using strong sta-

---

[1]Corresponding Author: E-mail: a.s.dedner@warwick.ac.uk

bility preserving (SSP) Runge-Kutta methods [3]. While these methods can be very efficiently implemented some characteristics of meteorological simulations which will be discussed in this paper, make fully explicit methods unsuitable. Implementing implicit methods efficiently is challenging for non-linear hyperbolic system. Often efficiency is achieved by reducing the linearized problem to a scalar elliptic equation for the pressure (Schur complement form). Due to the form of the numerical viscosity in the DG method this is not easily obtainable in this case. In this paper we suggest a different approach based on a special preconditioner combined with a matrix-free Newton Krylov solver. We implement this method within the Dune-Fem-Dg module ([4,5]) and present some tests showing a substantial speedup compared to the explicit discretization making the implicit scheme competitive to implementations used in production codes.

The starting point for our scheme are the compressible, non-hydrostatic Euler equations for a dry atmosphere formulated in Cartesian coordinates:

$$\frac{\partial \rho}{\partial t} + \nabla \cdot \mathbf{m} = 0, \quad \frac{\partial \mathbf{m}}{\partial t} + \nabla \cdot \left(\frac{1}{\rho} \mathbf{m} \otimes \mathbf{m} + pI \right) = -\rho g \mathbf{z}, \quad \frac{\partial \Theta}{\partial t} + \nabla \cdot \left(\frac{1}{\rho} \mathbf{m} \Theta \right) = 0,$$

(1)

in which $\otimes$ is the dyadic product, I is the unit matrix, g is the gravitational acceleration, and $\mathbf{z} = (0,0,1)^T$ is the vertical unit base vector. The conserved quantities are density ρ, momentum $\mathbf{m}$, and potential temperature density Θ. The pressure p is given by the ideal gas law as function of the conserved quantities. For the meteorological application studied in this paper we assume that the unknown functions are small fluctuations around a given reference atmosphere of the form $(\rho_0, 0, \Theta_0)$ depending only on height z. This reference state fulfills the hydrostatic equation $\nabla p_0 = -g\rho_0 \mathbf{z}$ and the dry ideal gas law. Note that this implies that $(\rho_0, 0, \Theta_0)$ is in fact itself a solution of the Euler equations.

To simplify notation we will use $\mathbf{U}$ to denote the vector of conserved quantities $(\rho, \mathbf{m}, \Theta)^T$ and abbreviate all spatial terms in the Euler equations using the operator notation $\mathscr{L}[\mathbf{U}]$. In this form the full system takes the form

$$\frac{\partial \mathbf{U}}{\partial t} = \mathscr{L}[\mathbf{U}].$$

(2)

For the discretization of this system we use a *method of lines* approach. The spatial operator $\mathscr{L}$ is discretized using the Discontinuous Galerkin (DG) method of order q ($q = 4$ or $q = 5$ in the following). The DG method is fully described by the flux implementation which in this case is the CDG2 method for the viscous terms, if present, and the Local Lax-Friedrichs flux for the advective terms (cf. [6,7]). This spatial discretization leads to a system of ordinary differential equations for the degrees of freedom in the DG method. To simplify notation, we will not distinguish between the analytic operator $\mathscr{L}$ and its discrete version. We will also use the same notational inaccuracy when referring to the vector of functions $\mathbf{U}$ so that in most cases (2) will refer to the semi-discrete system of ODEs. We will discuss in detail how we deal with this ODE system in the remaining paper: In Section 1 we discuss an explicit time discretization of the scheme while in Section 2 a fully implicit method is discussed. We can not present a full comparison of the methods here but will instead concentrate on a single test case. In [8] the density current test case was proposed simulating the evolution of a cold bubble in a neutrally stratified atmosphere. The bubble is positioned at a certain height and it will start to fall and eventually hit the ground. It will then slide along the ground level and create Kelvin-Helmholtz vortices. Approximately every 300 s a new Kelvin-Helmholtz vortex appears. In order to obtain a grid-convergent solution some viscosity should be added to the Euler equation. We add the viscosity terms from the compressible Navier-Stokes equations for this purpose. The solution at time $T = 900s$ is shown in Figure 1. In the following we will show 1d slices of the solution along the line $z = 1.2km$.

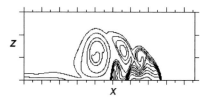

Figure 1. Potential temperature perturbation for density current test in the xz plane after 900s.

1. Explicit Time Stepping

We will first investigate the efficiency and effectiveness of an explicit time stepping method for (2). We use an SSP-RK method of order three with three stages in the following. These method can be written as linear combinations of forward Euler steps of the form

$$\mathbf{W} = \mathbf{U} + \lambda \tau \mathscr{L}[\mathbf{U}] \tag{3}$$

where $\mathbf{W}$ is the computed stage update, τ denotes the time step size, and λ is some constant depending on the stage of the RK method used. Since the time evolution is explicit the time step size τ will be restricted by the CFL condition and the order of the scheme. The actual time step will be chosen a-priori as a given fraction of the maximum timestep allowed.

We first study the parallel efficiency of the method and then will investigate how well it performs with respect to accuracy and efficiency for standard meterological benchmark problems. To get a realistic picture we compare the method with the well established operational model *COSMO* [9] developed at the *German Weather Service* (DWD). A detailed investigation was published in [7,10] and only a brief summary is presented here.

1.1. Parallel Efficiency

An explicit method does not require the assembly and solving of any linear system of equations and since the time step is assumed to be fixed no global communication is required. This makes these methods very attractive for large parallel simulations. The main computational work is in the evaluation of the discrete operator $\mathscr{L}$ in each stage of the RK method. Since the DG method requires the computation of inter element fluxes, halo cells have to be added at process boundaries and the values on these cells have to be communicated in each stage of the RK method. This communication can be overlapped with the computation in the interior leading to very little parallel overhead. So mainly the efficiency of the overall code is determined by the *serial* efficiency of the evaluation of the discrete operator $\mathcal{L}[\mathbf{U}]$ for a given vector of discrete functions $\mathbf{U}$. To evaluate the scaling behavior of the DG code we ran a 3D version of the density current test case on a fixed grid with about 243 000 grid cells on the super computer JUGENE. The size of the experiment is such that it could possibly also run on a desktop machine with about 8GB memory. As we see in Table 1 it is possible to scale the DG code for the same experiment to 65 536 cores with an efficiency of 72% in comparison to a run with only 512 cores on the same machine.

Table 1. Strong scaling and efficiency of the DG code ($q = 4$) on the supercomputer JUGENE (Jülich, Germany) **without** and **with** asynchronous communication. P denotes the number of cores, $G := |\mathscr{G}|$ the overall number of grid elements, and $N := |V_{\mathscr{G}}|$ denotes the number of degrees of freedom. $\bar{\eta}$ is the average run time in milliseconds needed to compute one timestep. $S_{512 \to P} := \bar{\eta}_{512}/\bar{\eta}_P$ denotes the speed-up from 512 to P cores with respect to $\bar{\eta}$ and $E_{512 \to P} := \frac{512}{P} S_{512 \to P}$ being the efficiency.

			synchronous comm.			asynchronous comm.		
P	G/P	N/P	$\bar{\eta}$	$S_{512 \to P}$	$E_{512 \to P}$	$\bar{\eta}$	$S_{512 \to P}$	$E_{512 \to P}$
512	474.6	296 630.8	68 579	—	—	46 216	—	—
4 096	59.3	37 324.9	14 575	4.71	0.59	6 294	7.34	0.91
32 768	7.4	4 634.8	5 034	13.62	0.21	949	48.71	0.76
65 536	3.7	2 317.4	—	—	—	504	91.70	0.72

For efficient evaluation of $\mathcal{L}$ the DG module DUNE-FEM-DG contains an automated code generator that creates optimal code for a given number of basis functions and quadrature points and a user chosen SIMD width. The code is generated based on the occurring combinations of basis functions and quadrature points during the evaluation of the operator for one time step. Then the code is recompiled using the optimized evaluation methods based on the previously discovered combinations. In Table 2 we present the measured GFLOPS for a 3D density current test case and different polynomial orders. We can see that the automated code generation increases the performance by almost a factor of two. Experiments on more recent computer architectures show even better results. A more detailed discussion of these results is given in [11].

1.2. Comparison with COSMO

For a better indication of the accuracy and the efficiency of the method described so far, we carry out a direct comparison with the COSMO dynamical core using the density current test case as benchmark problem. In Figure 2 the error vs. runtime of the DG

Table 2. Performance measurement of the DG code for $q = 1, 2, 3, 4$ using a Cartesian grid. In addition to the notation from Table 1 we introduce GFLOPS as the measured performance of the DG code ($q = 1, 2, 3, 4$) in GFLOPS and *PERF%* denotes the ratio between the measured performance and the theoretical peak performance of the Intel Core i7 (Nehalem) at hand is about 27.728 GLFOPS .

		without code generation			with code generation		
q	N/G	$\bar{\eta}$	GFLOPS	PERF %	$\bar{\eta}$	GFLOPS	PERF %
1	40	136	3.08	11.1	127	3.35	12.08
2	135	526	3.90	14.06	431	4.89	17.63
3	320	1805	4.35	15.68	1241	6.45	23.26
4	625	5261	4.58	16.51	3592	6.8	24.52

method with polynomial order $q = 4, 5$ is shown together with the results using COSMO. As can be seen in the right figure a resolution of $100m$ is still not quite enough to resolve the Kelvin-Helmholtz instabilities (especially the third one) with the COSMO core. Due to the subscale resolution of the DG method this method performs better here, leading to an overall smaller error with fewer degrees of freedom and as shown in the left figure with a comparable computational cost. For this type of problem the explicit RK-DG method is shown to be competitive. However, it should be noted that the COSMO core uses an implicit time stepping method based on a time step size $\tau = 3s$ while the CFL restriction of the Dune core leads to time steps of $\tau = 0.08s$. While for this test case the high efficiency of the explicit method allows a fast simulation not withstanding the difference in the time step size, other experiments show that this is not the case for all test problems. For a mountain overflow test case for example the difference in time step is $0.09s$ (Dune) vs. $12.5s$ (COSMO) leading to CPU times of $6724m$ and $290m$, respectively (assuming as shown above an increase in resolution of the DG core of one grid level).

The main difference between these two test cases is the spacing of the grid in the horizontal (dx) and the vertical (dz). While for the density current $dx = dz$ the grid used to simulate the mountain overflow is chosen highly anisotropic with $dx = 15dz$. This is much closer to the situation found in meteorological simulations, making the CFL restriction caused by the vertical grid resolution too restrictive for fully explicit methods.

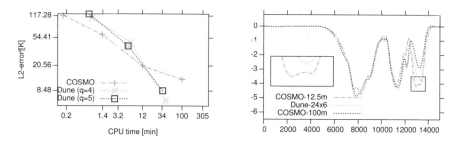

Figure 2. Density current. Comparison of run time vs error of Dune and COSMO (left) and final solution at $z = 1.2km$ with reference solution computed using a high resolution computation.

2. Implicit Time Stepping

We again employ RK methods but now fully implicit versions. We focus on the special class of *diagonally implicit* methods. In this case the main building block are backward Euler steps of the form

$$\mathbf{W} - \lambda\tau\mathscr{L}[\mathbf{W}] = \mathbf{U} \tag{4}$$

where the constant λ only depends on the method used but not on each stage of the RK method. We use a two stage method matching the order three accuracy of our explicit method but requiring one stage less. Again τ is assumed to be constant throughout the simulation and we will present our results always giving τ as a multiple $\mu \geq 1$ of the corresponding time step required by the explicit method. Given a discrete state $\mathbf{U}$ the computation of $\mathbf{W}$ requires solving a non-linear system of equations for example using a Newton type method combined with a Krylov iterative solver for the linear systems. Since the resulting dynamical core will have to be coupled to other modules (i.e. moisture and radiation computations and closure relations for turbulence modelling) the factor μ can not be taken arbitrarily large. Therefore, we expect that the scheme will require only around four or five Newton steps and in each Newton step only a few iteration in the Krylov solver will be required. Therefore, a full matrix assembly will lead to an unacceptable computational overhead. To avoid this step we use a *matrix-free* Newton-Krylov solver [12]. In this approach a finite difference approximation is used to solve the linear system

$$(I - \lambda \tau \mathcal{L}'[\mathbf{W}^k])\delta^k = \mathcal{L}[\mathbf{W}^k] \tag{5}$$

denoting with $\mathcal{L}'[\mathbf{W}^k]$ the linearization of $\mathcal{L}$ around the iterate $\mathbf{W}^k$. Noting that for the Krylov method only the matrix vector multiplication $(I - \lambda \tau \mathcal{L}'[\mathbf{W}^k])\mathbf{x}$ with given vector $\mathbf{x}$ is required, this multiplication is replaced by

$$\mathbf{x} - \lambda \tau \frac{1}{\varepsilon} \left(\mathcal{L}[\mathbf{W}^k + \varepsilon \mathbf{x}] - \mathcal{L}[\mathbf{W}^k] \right) . \tag{6}$$

Similar to the explicit method described previously, the computational cost of the resulting scheme is dominated by the remaining single evaluation of the discrete operator $\mathcal{L}$ required in each iteration of the Krylov solver (we use a GMRes method in the following).

2.1. Parallel Efficiency

Due to the matrix free solver, the computational cost in a serial computation is dominated by the evaluation of the spatial operator $\mathcal{L}$ and thus the measures discussed in the previous section to guarantee an efficient execution of the code will directly result in an efficient execution of the matrix-free implicit solver as well. In addition to the parallel overhead caused by the halo exchange required for computing $\mathcal{L}$, the implicit method also requires a number of global communication steps mostly global summations for the computation of scalar products. Especially for large core counts these global communication steps will reduce the parallel efficiency of the code. In Table 3 we show the strong scaling of the implicit solver (without preconditioning) for the 3D density current experiment with polynomial order $q = 4$ on a grid with 243000 cells. On 32768 we have between 7 and 8 cells per core on average. In this example we make use of the previously mentioned communication hiding technique. In addition we make sure that the load is equally divided onto the available number of cores by applying a space filling curve approach. Otherwise, the scaling deteriorates as the number of cores grows.

Table 3. Strong scaling for the implicit DG solver. The same notation as in Table 1 is used.

P	G/P	N/P	$\bar{\eta}$	S_{512}	E_{512}
512	474.6	296630.8	367483	—	—
4096	59.3	37324.9	51892	7.08	0.89
32768	7.4	4634.8	7666	47.94	0.75

2.2. Preconditioning

Without preconditioning, the number of iterations N required for the implicit solver, will in general be too large, so that the explicit method will be more efficient. In the following we suggest a simple approach for preconditioning the solver which leads to a significant reduction of N for the meteorological problems studied here.

In general, (right) preconditioning for $Au = b$, requires constructing a matrix R which is a good approximation to the inverse of A. Then instead of solving $Ax = b$ one applies the method to $ARw = b$ and $u = Rw$. In a Krylov solver the matrix vector multiplication Az is thus replaced with ARz requiring in addition to the matrix multiplication with A also the application of the matrix $R \approx A^{-1}$. In our case we need to find a linear operator $\mathscr{R}$ approximating the inverse of $I - \lambda \tau \mathscr{L}'[\mathbf{W}^k]$ for a given state $\mathbf{W}^k$ or more to the point we need to be able to define the action on a given $\mathbf{x}$, i.e., implement $\mathscr{R}\mathbf{x}$.

The effectiveness of our preconditioner is based on two important characteristics of the meteorological problems studied here, both already mentioned in previous sections: (i) the unknown solution $\mathbf{U} = (\rho, \mathbf{m}, \Theta)$ is in most regions only a small perturbation of a known background state $\mathbf{U}_0 = (\rho_0, 0, \Theta_0)$; (ii) the grid is anisotropic in the vertical direction so that the size of the explicit timestep is mainly restricted by the processes in the vertical direction. The first point implies that for any intermediate step in the Newton solver $\mathbf{W}^k - \mathbf{U}_0$ is of magnitude $\nu \ll 1$. Defining the linear operator

$$\mathscr{R} = (I - \tau\lambda\mathscr{L}'[\mathbf{U}_0])^{-1} \tag{7}$$

a simple calculation shows that for any intermediate state $\mathbf{W}^k$ where the magnitude of $\mathbf{W}^k - \mathbf{U}_0$ is of size ν we have

$$(I - \tau\lambda\mathscr{L}'[\mathbf{W}^k])(\mathscr{R}\mathbf{x}) \approx \mathscr{R}\mathbf{x} - \frac{\lambda\tau}{\varepsilon}\left(\mathscr{L}[\mathbf{W}^k + \varepsilon(I - \tau\lambda\mathscr{L}'[\mathbf{U}_0])^{-1}\mathbf{x}] - \mathscr{L}[\mathbf{W}^k]\right) \tag{8}$$

$$= (I - \tau\lambda\mathscr{L}'[\mathbf{U}_0])^{-1}\mathbf{x} - (I - \tau\lambda\mathscr{L}'[\mathbf{U}_0])^{-1}\tau\lambda\mathscr{L}'[\mathbf{U}_0]\mathbf{x} + O(\nu^2) = \mathbf{x} + O(\nu^2) .$$

Therefore, $\mathscr{R}$ will be a good approximation to the inverse of $I - \tau\lambda\mathscr{L}'[\mathbf{W}^k]$ for state close to $\mathbf{U}_0$. Note that since $\mathbf{U}_0$, τ, and λ are assumed to be known a priori, we can use a fixed preconditioner throughout the simulation so that any set up cost associated with $\mathscr{R}$ is not a concern. Therefore, a feasible approach would be to assemble the linearization of $\mathscr{L}$ around the background state once at the beginning. Storing the matrix $I - \tau\lambda\mathscr{L}'[\mathbf{U}_0]$ then allows us to use standard matrix based preconditioners to perform the inversion required to compute $\mathscr{R}\mathbf{x}$. The issue with this approach is the large memory consumption caused by storing the matrix (even if it is block sparse). Furthermore, even when using a good preconditioner for inverting this matrix this step could be too costly.

To reduce the memory footprint while not compromising too much on the properties of the preconditioner we make use of the second characteristic mentioned above. First note that due to the local structure of the DG discretization, the matrix representing $\mathscr{L}'[\mathbf{U}_0]$ is a sparse block matrix. For each element E of the grid one obtains one row in this block matrix with an entry on the diagonal and a block for each neighbour of E. The implication of the problem characteristic (ii) mentioned previously is that the coupling in the linearized operator $\mathscr{L}'[\mathbf{U}_0]$ is far stronger between vertically neighboring cells than between horizontal neighbors. Thus assuming that elements are indexed so that vertically neighboring cells have consecutive indices, the main entries in the matrix will be on the three main (block) diagonals. Thus, as we will show, replacing $\mathscr{R}$ by the inverse of corresponding block tridiagonal matrix, already results in an excellent preconditioner in the case that the anisotropy in the grid is sufficiently large. Furthermore, since the background state $\mathbf{U}_0$ does not depend on the horizontal coordinate, the inverse of this tridiagonal block matrix needs to be computed and stored for only one vertical column of the grid. Using *Thomas*'s algorithm we can easily precompute all required entries resulting in an efficient and not too memory intensive preconditioner. Note that we are concentrating on local area models here. For global models using a single background profile depending only on z will not be sufficient for preconditioning the system. We plan to extend our approach to this setting in future work, either introducing more than one profile and locally choosing one of these for the preconditioner. Alternatively, the preconditioner could be recomputed every few hundred time steps using the computed solution. But this would greatly increase the memory footprint and the efficiency will have to be investigated thoroughly for this setting. However, this is outside the scope of this paper.

2.3. Comparison with Explicit Time Stepping

As is generally the case with implicit methods based on iterative solvers an important parameter is the tolerance TOL used to determine when to terminate the iteration. Taking this tolerance too small increases the number of iterations N leading to an inefficient scheme while taking the value too large reduces the accuracy of the approximation. A further parameter influencing the efficiency of the scheme is the time step factor μ. Values for TOL and μ leading to an optimal speedup factor ω of the implicit scheme depend mainly on the anisotropy, i.e., the relation between the horizontal grid spacing dx and the vertical dz. We again focus on the density current test case to numerically investigate the dependents of ω on TOL, μ. Note that the original problem is formulated on a grid with dx = dz and that in this case our explicit method was competitive to the COSMO core. Since the implicit method is designed to lead to an improvement in the case of dz < dx, we solve this problem on a grid with dx = 20dz similar to the grid used for the mountain overflow simulations mentioned in the previous section. The results are shown in Table 4 - the difference between the explicit and the implicit method is measured here in the number of evaluations of the operator $\mathscr{L}$ during the full simulation. Note that this measure of the efficiency of the scheme ignores the overhead of the implicit solver and the cost of the matrix vector multiply required for the tridiagonal preconditioner. The table clearly shows that the number of required operator calls is reduced by more than a factor of 10 for any combination of μ, TOL and in the case of the highest values of TOL, μ more than a factor of 60.

To investigate how the parameters μ, TOL influence the accuracy of the method, we compare the solution of the explicit method (assumed to be an accurate reference solution) with the solution of the implicit method for varying values of μ, TOL in Figure 3. It is clear that TOL = 1 does not lead to accurate results and that furthermore $\mu = 800$ is too large independent of the tolerance used. For $\mu = 100$ any value TOL ≤ 0.1 results in an accurate representation of the solution which hardly differs from the results obtained with the explicit scheme. The same holds for $\mu = 200$. With $\mu = 400$ both TOL = 1 and TOL = 0.1 do not produce accurate solutions so that a tolerance TOL ≤ 0.01 has to be

Table 4. Dependency of number of operator calls for implicit method on time step factor μ and stopping tolerance TOL for dx $= 20$dz. Operator calls required for the explicit scheme on this grid is 540 003.

	$\mu = 100$				$\mu = 200$			
TOL	1	10^{-1}	10^{-2}	10^{-3}	1	10^{-1}	10^{-2}	10^{-3}
impl. op calls	23219	23327	22834		13711	13645	17433	

	$\mu = 400$				$\mu = 800$			
TOL	1	10^{-1}	10^{-2}	10^{-3}	1	10^{-1}	10^{-2}	10^{-3}
impl. op calls	9552	9863	16041	23469	8570	11096	10326	27433

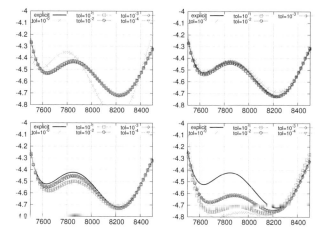

Figure 3. Solution at $z = 1.2km$ in region of first Kelvin-Helmholtz vortex. Top: $\mu = 100, 200$, bottom: $400, 800$

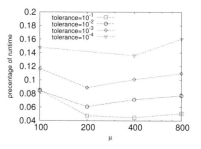

Figure 4. Percentage of run time of implicit code compared to explicit code depending on tolerance and time step factor μ.

chosen. Taking all of the above into account an acceptable accuracy with the least number of operator calls is achieved with a time step $\mu = 200$ times larger than required by the explicit scheme combined with a tolerance TOL $= 0.1$. Taking a tolerance TOL $= 0.01$ with either $\mu = 200$ or (slightly more efficient) $\mu = 400$ leads to $20 - 25\%$ more operator evaluations.

As already mentioned, while the number of operator calls is a good first indicator for the efficiency of the method, this measure does not include the full computational overhead of the implicit solver - most importantly it does not include the evaluation of the preconditioner. We thus conclude this study with an evaluation of the actual run time of the implicit solver compared to its explicit counterpart. The conclusion we have reached so far are confirmed when studying the run time for different values of μ, TOL as shown in Figure 4. The combination $\mu = 200$, TOL $= 0.1$ results in an implicit scheme requiring only 7% of the runtime required by the explicit method. The resulting time step is $\tau = 18s$ comparable to the $\tau = 12.5$ used in the mountain overflow test case by COSMO.

3. Conclusions

We compared explicit and implicit time stepping methods for use in meteorological applications. In both cases the efficient evaluation of the discrete spatial operator is a crucial building block of the scheme and we detailed how this is achieved using code generation in the Dune-Fem-DG module. Parallel efficiency of both explicit and implicit method was then demonstrated. Our previous studies indicated that the explicit method is competitive with production codes such as COSMO on isotropic grids. In meteorological applications grids with smaller spacing in the vertical are common and in this case the CFL restriction is too severe. On such a grid the run time of COSMO was about 5% of the corresponding run time of our code. COSMO uses an implicit time stepper to overcome the stability restriction. In this paper we suggest a fully implicit approach based on a preconditioned matrix-free Newton-Krylov solver. The resulting scheme required $5 - 10\%$ of the run time of the explicit method bringing it into the range of the COSMO core.

In future work we will add more test cases e.g. mountain overflow simulations and make direct comparisons with the COSMO code with respect to run time vs. error.

References

[1]   B. Cockburn. Discontinuous Galerkin methods. *ZAMM, Z. Angew. Math. Mech.*, 83(11):731–754, 2003.

[2]   F. X. Giraldo and M. Restelli. A study of spectral element and discontinuous Galerkin methods for the Navier-Stokes equations in nonhydrostatic mesoscale armospheric modeling: Equation sets and test cases. *J. Comp. Phys.*, 227:3849–3877, 2008.

[3]   S. Gottlieb, C.-W. Shu, and E. Tadmor. Strong stability preserving high-order time discretization methods. *SIAM Rev.*, 43:89–112, 2001.

[4]   P. Bastian, M. Blatt, A. Dedner, C. Engwer, R. Klöfkorn, R. Kornhuber, M. Ohlberger, and O. Sander. A generic grid interface for parallel and adaptive scientific computing. part II. *Computing*, 82, 2008.

[5]   A. Dedner, R. Klöfkorn, M. Nolte, and M. Ohlberger. A generic interface for parallel and adaptive scientific computing: Abstraction principles and the DUNE-FEM module. *Computing*, 90, 2010.

[6]   S. Brdar, A. Dedner, and R. Klöfkorn. Compact and stable discontinuous Galerkin methods for convection-diffusion problems. *SIAM J. Sci. Comput.*, 34:263–282, 2012.

[7]   S. Brdar, M. Baldauf, A. Dedner, and R. Klöfkorn. Comparison of dynamical cores for NWP models. *Theor. Comput. Fluid Dyn.*, 27:453–472, 2013.

[8]   J. M. Straka, R. B. Wilhelmson, L. J. Wicker, J. R. Anderson, and K. K. Droegemeier. Numerical solutions of a non-linear density current: A benchmark solution and comparisons. *Int. J. Num. Meth. Fluids*, 17:1–22, 1993.

[9]   M. Baldauf, A. Seifert, J. Förstner, D. Majewski, M. Raschendorfer, and T. Reinhardt. Operational convective-scale numerical weather prediction with the COSMO model: Description and sensitivities. *Mon. Wea. Rev.*, 139:3887–3905, 2011.

[10]   D. Schuster, S. Brdar, M. Baldauf, A. Dedner, R. Klöfkorn, and D. Kröner. On discontinuous Galerkin approach for atmospheric flow in the mesoscale with and without moisture. *Meteorologische Zeitschrift*, 23(4):449–464, 2014.

[11]   R. Klöfkorn. Efficient Matrix-Free Implementation of Discontinuous Galerkin Methods for Compressible Flow Problems. In A. Handlovicova et al., editor, *Proceedings of the ALGORITMY 2012*, 2012.

[12]   P. R. McHugh and D. A. Knoll. Comparison of standard and matrix-free implementations of several Newton-Krylov solvers. *AIAA J.*, 32(12):2394–2400, 1994.

Parallel Computing: On the Road to Exascale
G.R. Joubert et al. (Eds.)
IOS Press, 2016
doi:10.3233/978-1-61499-621-7-637

Porting the COSMO dynamical core to heterogeneous platforms using STELLA Library

Carlos Osuna [a,1] and Oliver Fuhrer [b] and Tobias Gysi [c,d] and Thomas C. Schulthess [e,f,g]

[a] *Center for Climate Systems Modeling, ETH Zurich*
[b] *Federal Office of Meteorology and Climatology, Meteoswiss*
[c] *Department of Computer Science, ETH Zurich*
[d] *Supercomputing Systems AG*
[e] *Institute for Theoretical Physics, ETH Zurich*
[f] *CSCS, ETH Zurich*
[g] *CSMD, Oak Ridge National Laboratory*

Abstract. Numerical weather prediction and climate models like COSMO solve a large set of Partial Differential Equations using stencil computations on structured grids. STELLA (Stencil Loop Language) is a DSL in C++ for finite difference methods on structured grids that abstracts the underlying programming model and optimization techniques used for multiple architectures. The STELLA language allows to describe stencils with a unique source code in a concise way, close to the discretized mathematical description of the PDEs, increasing its readability by hiding the complexity of loops and hardware dependent optimizations. STELLA has been used to port the COSMO dynamical core to GPUs while retaining a single source code for multiple computing architectures. We present the STELLA syntax and focus on new, advanced syntax elements for some of the algorithmic motifs present in the dynamical core of COSMO. Namely, the new features improve strong scalability, increase the conciseness of the STELLA DSL, and significantly improve the performance of the COSMO dynamical core. Performance comparisons on GPU are presented.

Introduction

The COSMO model is a non-hydrostatic limited area atmospheric model developed by a consortium and used for operational weather prediction at over 10 national weather services and over 70 universities for climate research. Recent work to provide a portable implementation of COSMO that performs optimally on different architectures was reported in [1,2]. Different porting approaches were considered for the physical parametrizations and data assimilation and the dynamical core.

The dynamical core of COSMO solves a large set of PDEs derived from the Euler equations on a curvilinear grid, which are discretized using finite difference methods. As

---

[1]Corresponding Author: ETH, Universitatstrasse 16, Zurich; E-mail: carlos.osuna@env.ethz.ch

a consequence, the main algorithmic motifs are stencil computations which typically exhibit a low arithmetic intensity. Modern supercomputers incorporating massively parallel accelerators are attractive computing platforms for such atmospheric models due to the energy efficient high throughput provided by the accelerators.

However porting atmospheric models that typically comprise hundreds of thousands of lines of Fortran code to hybrid programming models that can leverage all the capabilities of accelerators in a parallel supercomputer is a formidable challenge. Moreover the porting approach for the COSMO model should retain a single source code while being able to efficiently run on multiple architectures.

A full rewrite of the dynamical core of COSMO using the STELLA library was reported in [3]. STELLA is a domain-specific language for stencil codes on structured grids which hides the implementation details and hardware dependent optimizations for stencil codes. Using the STELLA syntax, the user can describe PDEs on structured grids such as the COSMO dynamical core in a performance portable way by describing (only) the operation to be executed at each grid point at each phase of a stencil. The library relies on C++ template metaprogramming techniques to generate an optimal parallel implementation of the loop nests at compile time for different computing architectures.

Work presented in [3] describes two backends, for x86 CPU and NVIDIA GPU architectures and reports a speedup factor for the whole dynamical core of 1.8x and 5.6x (CPU and GPU respectively) compared to the Fortran legacy code.

Numerous DSLs for stencil codes generated from finite difference or finite element discretizations have been proposed and differ significantly in terms of their application domain and feature set (see [3] for a comprehensive related work). For example, OP2[4] compiler for stencils and Firedrake[5] are frameworks widely used as code generator DSLs for finite elements on unstructured grid codes. While code generators provide a great flexibility, they rely on a custom tool chain. As opposed to these solutions, the STELLA DSL is embedded in the C++ language and relies only on the well-established boost libraries. This provides a high interoperability with other parts of a code that can make use of algorithmic patterns not supported by the DSL, and access to debugger and profiling tools in the user code.

The main contributions in this paper are a) the presentation of new advanced syntax features provided by STELLA which go well beyond of what other available DSLs provide and b) analysis of the performance of the new features on GPU focusing on improved strong scalability and increase in data-locality of operators which are applied multiple times to independent inputs and outputs, using however some common additional input fields.

STELLA

STELLA emerged from an effort to port and optimize the dynamical core of COSMO to both multi-core and hybrid CPU-GPU architectures. It is designed as a DSL for finite difference methods (or stencil methods in general) on curvilinear grids and targets mainly atmospheric codes. The DSL allows to describe the user-code for finite difference applications without exposing implementation details of the stencils like memory layout of the storages, nested loops, tiling strategies or traversal and parallelization over the grid.

This high level of abstraction provided by the STELLA DSL reduces the interdependency between the user code describing the discretized PDE operators and the hardware specific implementation of the stencil code. This allows to retain a single source code describing the domain specific implementation of the discretized form of the equations to be solved. STELLA was implemented in a modular way with the capability to adapt multiple backends that expand the specific implementation optimized for each computing architecture. A current version of the library supports two backends, for multi-core CPU and GPU architectures. A third backend targeting Intel Xeon Phi architectures is being developed.

In STELLA, a stencil is described by providing two components: a function object that implements a stencil operation at each grid point (STELLA refers to them as *stencil stages*) and the assembly of multiple of these *stencil stages* including a specification of the loop logic in the vertical dimension.

An example of a *stencil stage* is shown in Figure 1 for the computation of the divergence of the fluxes of a fourth order horizontal diffusion operator on a C-grid [6].

$$\frac{\partial \phi}{\partial t} = -\alpha \nabla^4 \phi = -\alpha \left(\frac{\partial F_x}{\partial x} + \frac{\partial F_y}{\partial y} \right) \tag{1}$$

```
1    template<typename TEnv>
2    struct Divergence {
3      STENCIL_STAGE(TEnv)
4      STAGE_PARAMETER(FullDomain, phi) //declare stencil parameters
5      STAGE_PARAMETER(FullDomain, lan)
6      STAGE_PARAMETER(FullDomain, flx)
7      STAGE_PARAMETER(FullDomain, fly)
8
9      static void Do(Context ctx, FullDomain) { //do method defines the update function
10        ctx[div::Center()] = ctx[phi::Center()] − ctx[alpha::Center()] ∗
11        (ctx[flx::Center()] − ctx[flx::At(iminus1)] + ctx[fly::Center()] − ctx[fly::At(jminus1)] )
12      }
13    };
```

Figure 1. Example stencil stage that implements the divergence of the fluxes of a fourth order horizontal diffusion operator, Equation (1). Fluxes must be computed in previous stencil stages.

The STELLA syntax to assemble multiple *stencil stages* and define the loop logic in the vertical dimension is illustrated in Figure 4 of [1] for the same operator and further examples in this work.

Multi-field Operators

Applying the same numerical operators to multiple fields is common in atmospheric and combustion codes. A prominent example is the advective transport of multiple chemical species in the atmosphere [7]. The current dynamical core of COSMO implements the transport of multiple species using STELLA via a single advection stencil, being sequentially applied to all the fields representing the concentrations of the chemical species.

However, grouping the advection of several of these species into a single stencil can increase data locality of additional fields required for the advection operator (e.g. velocity, density). If stencils are applied to multiple fields simultaneously, these additional fields can be cached in fast on-chip memory. Moreover simultaneously applying the advection stencil to multiple fields will increase the instruction level parallelism (ILP) of the kernel. Increasing the ILP helps maximizing the memory throughput for those architectures with high memory latency (like GPUs). This technique can be used to increase performance of memory bound applications when the kernel does not run at high occupancy of the device.

A naive approach in order to implement this optimization is to write stencil stages (like Figure 1) in STELLA that perform the update of multiple fields. However this introduces code redundancy, and forces the user to implement multiple versions of the same operator.

STELLA provides a new functionality to efficiently generate stencils for applying a numerical operator to multiple fields, by introducing the expandable parameters and buffer syntax elements. The fields associated to different chemical species must be packed as a expandable parameter, providing the iterators over a container that holds all the fields. Figure 2 provides an example of the assembly of an horizontal diffusion operator applied to multiple fields.

STELLA uses the syntax of the expandable parameters to generate different implementations of the same operator that updates multiples of these fields at a time. It iterates over the fields in the container in order to apply the operator to all chemical species. An arbitrary number of chemical species can be supplied at runtime.

```
1    #define NTracerPerStencil 4
2
3    Stencil stencil;
4    StencilCompiler::Build(
5      stencil,
6      StencilConfiguration<Real, block_size, NTracerPerStencil>(),
7      pack_parameters(           //associate stencil parameters with the address of memory of the fields
8        //ExpandableParam are internally expanded generating NTracerPerStencil parameters
9        ExpandableParam<res, cInOut>(dataOut.begin(), dataOut.end()),
10       ExpandableParam<phi, cIn>(dataIn.begin(), dataIn.end())
11       Param<alpha, cIn>(dataAlpha)
12     ),
13     define_temporaries(           //declare temporary buffers (storage managed by the library)
14       //StencilExpandableParam are internally expanded generating NTracerPerStencil buffers
15       StencilExpandableBuffer<lap, double, KRange<FullDomain,0,0> >(),
16       StencilExpandableBuffer<flx, double, KRange<FullDomain,0,0> >(),
17       StencilExpandableBuffer<fly, double, KRange<FullDomain,0,0> >()
18     ),
19     define_loops(           //declare multiple sequential loops
20       define_sweep<cKIncrement>(  // vertical sweep loop
21         define_stages(           // declare multiple stages (parallelized over IJ plane)
22           StencilStage<Lap, IJRange<cIndented,-1,1,-1,1>, KRange<FullDomain,0,0> >(),
23           StencilStage<Flx, IJRange<cIndented,-1,0,0,0>, KRange<FullDomain,0,0> >(),
24           StencilStage<Fly, IJRange<cIndented,0,0,-1,0>, KRange<FullDomain,0,0> >(),
25           StencilStage<Divergence, IJRange<cComplete,0,0,0,0>, KRange<FullDomain,0,0> >()
26   ) ) ) );
```

Figure 2. An implementation of smoothing example within STELLA using multi-field operators.

It makes use of the special syntax elements *ExpandableParam* and *StencilExpandableBuffer* in order to expand the update of the stencil stage to multiple fields from the container.

Performance results using the multi-field operators functionality are shown in Figure 3 (for an NVIDIA GPU) for two of the operators in the dynamical core of COSMO: advection and vertical diffusion. The optimal number of fields updated per stencil will depend on the amount of resources available on-chip (registers, shared memory, etc) and

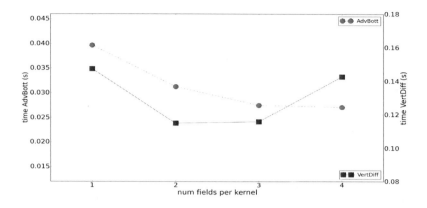

Figure 3. Computation time of an operator applied to 20 chemical species, using multi-field operators, for a domain size of 128x128x60 for a K20c NVIDIA GPU. Results are shown for advection and vertical diffusion operators.

the amount of data reuse of common fields in the operator. Results in Figure 3 show up to a factor 1.6x speedup. Increasing the number of fields updated per stencil will increment the resources required for on-chip memory, decreasing the occupancy on the device. This can limit the performance, as shown in Figure 3 for the vertical diffusion operator where the performance does no longer significantly improve with respect to the reference when applying the operator to four species simultaneously.

Strong Scalability

The dynamical core of COSMO contains contains two main algorithmic motifs: *compact stencil computations* corresponding to the finite difference discretization of the differential operators (see for example Figure 1) and *tridiagonal solvers* from operators which use an implicit discretization in the vertical. The latter is typically done in atmospheric model in order to avoid limitations of the time step due to the vertical grid spacing. Examples of vertically implicit operators are vertical advection or vertical turbulent diffusion.

Due to the vertical data-dependencies of the stencils derived from the implicitly discretized operators in the vertical dimension, the default parallelization mode of STELLA parallelizes only in the horizontal plane. As a result, the massive amount of cores available in current GPU chips cannot be fully utilized for small horizontal grid sizes [1]. Since the computational domain of atmospheric models is often decomposed only in the horizontal direction, this can lead to severe strong scalability constraints.

In order to further exploit the massive parallelism of GPUs, a new functionality of the STELLA library allows to select other parallelization modes (via new syntax elements) for each stencil individually, according to its data dependencies. This increases parallelism and therefore the occupancy of GPU devices, which may significantly improve the performance at strong scaling regime.

STELLA supports two new parallelization modes:

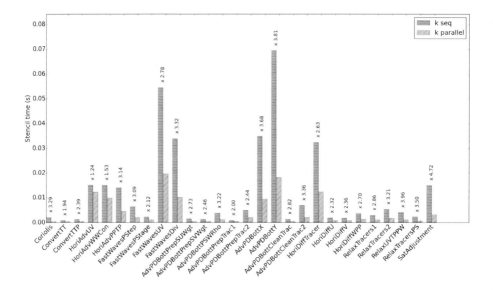

Figure 4. Performance comparison of k-parallel and default parallelization modes, for all the stencils of the dynamical core of COSMO that can be parallelized in the vertical dimension. Times are measured on K20c GPU for domain sizes of 32x32x60 and 10 time steps. Numbers above the bars show achieved speedup using k parallelization.

- a *k-parallel* mode which parallelizes over the vertical dimension that can be applied for stencils with data dependencies in the horizontal plane only and
- a parallel tridiagonal solver which results from vertically-implicit discretizations.

K-Parallel Mode

The k-parallel mode splits each vertical column of the domain into n tiles (n being a configurable parameter in STELLA), where each tile is processed by a different CUDA thread. No synchronization is required among the threads executing different tiles, as the stencils should not have vertical data dependencies. This split of the vertical domain into multiples tiles is performed at compile time (with metaprogramming algorithms), without introducing extra overheads into the logic of the loops and index calculations of the kernels. The k-parallel mode is activated for a stencil using the k-parallel syntax element as shown in the following example:

```
1   define_loops(
2     define_sweep<cKParallel>(
3       define_stages(
4         StencilStage<Lap, IJRange<cIndented,-1,1,-1,1>, KRange<FullDomain,0,0> >()
5   )))
```

Performance improvements are significant for small domain sizes, where the k-parallel mode increases the occupancy in the GPU device compared to the default parallelization. Figure 4 shows the performance comparison of the two modes for domain sizes of 32x32x60. The speedup obtained varies according to the characteristics and resources utilized by each stencil.

Parallel Tridiagonal Solvers Mode

Vertical PDE operators in the dynamical core of COSMO are discretized implicitly, which results in tridiagonal linear systems of equations of a size equal to the number of vertical levels used for the computational grid. The dynamical core of COSMO solves them using the sequential (in the vertical dimension) Thomas algorithm, with a forward and a backward sweep. Although efficient for medium to large domain sizes in the horizontal plane, when the number of horizontal grid points is smaller than the number of cores available on a GPU, the computational resources of the GPU can not be fully exploited. As a result the code executes at low occupancy on the GPU, and the latency of accesses to memory can not be hidden and therefore and the bandwidth achieved decreases with small domain sizes.

This results in the scalability problems at small domain sizes evident from Figure 7 (right panel) in [1]. In order to improve the strong scaling behavior a new STELLA feature leverages a parallel tridiagonal solver based on a hybrid parallel cyclic reduction (PCR) algorithm [8].

In a traditional implementation, the matrix coefficients (i.e. the bands of the tridiagonal matrix) are computed in a preparatory step and then passed to the PCR algorithm. However, due to performance reasons the dynamical core of COSMO often computes these coefficients in the same kernel as the tridiagonal solver from prognostic variables of the state of the atmosphere.

STELLA provides the possibility to connect the parallel tridiagonal solver with user-defined stages which compute the coefficients of the matrix and are directly passed to the PCR algorithm in a high level of the memory hierarchy. An additional user-defined stage can be supplied to process the solution of the system. An example of the STELLA syntax using the parallel tridiagonal solvers is provided in Figure 5.

```
 1    template<typename TEnv>
 2    struct SetupStage
 3    {
 4      STENCIL_STAGE(TEnv)
 5      static void Do(Context ctx, FullDomain) {
 6        ctx[ hpcr_acol ::Center()] = ...; ctx[ hpcr_bcol ::Center()] = ...;
 7        ctx[ hpcr_ccol ::Center()] = ...; ctx[ hpcr_dcol ::Center()] = ...;
 8      }
 9    };
10    //... code of ResultStage struct to process the solution stored in hpcr_xcol
11    StencilCompiler::Build(
12      StencilConfiguration<...>(), pack_parameters(...),
13      define_loops(
14        define_sweep<cTridiagonalSolve>(
15          define_stages(
16            StencilStage<SetupStage, IJRange<cIndented,0,0,0,0>, KRange<FullDomain,0,0> >(),
17            StencilStage<TridiagonalSolveFBStage, IJRange<cIndented,0,0,0,0>, KRange<FullDomain,0,0> >(),
18            StencilStage<WriteOutputStage, IJRange<cIndented,0,0,0,0>, KRange<FullDomain,0,0> >()
19    ) ) ) );
```

Figure 5. Example of a vertical operator solved using a parallel tridiagonal solver. Special syntax elements are highlighted in bold characters, which are defined by the STELLA library.

The PCR algorithm decomposes each tridiagonal system into N subsystems in a forward reduction phase which can be performed in parallel. The reduction phase is completed in $log_2 N$ steps. If the size of the system is a multiple of the warp size, all the threads on a GPU device will be active during the parallel reduction phase. Otherwise,

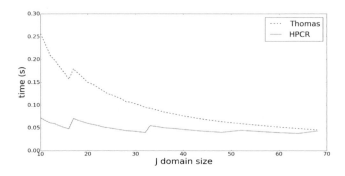

Figure 6. Time per tridiagonal system of HPCR and Thomas solvers, on a K20c GPU, vs the size of the domain in J dimension (for a fixed value of I size of 32 and 64 vertical layers) for a vertical advection operator of the dynamical core of COSMO. Times include the preparation of the coefficients of the matrix and right hand side, solving the tridiagonal system and final processing of the solution and store into a field.

the PCR algorithm computed by a warp will result in a set of N subsystems (where N is the warp size) of size larger than 1. The last phase of the hybrid parallel reduction algorithm solves in a final phase each of the subsystems, result of the PCR algorithm, using a sequential Thomas algorithm.

The default parallelization of STELLA requires a data layout of storages where data accesses are coalescing along the first of the horizontal grid axis (the i-direction) [1]. As the HPCR algorithm aligns the warp along the tridiagonal system in the vertical dimension, a transpose operation is performed before and after the TridiagonalSolveFBStage. The coefficients of the matrix and the right hand side are stored by the library in shared memory. Performance results of the parallel tridiagonal solver for a vertical advection operator on a GPU are shown in Figure 6.

Software Managed Caching

Leveraging data locality is of key importance for memory bound stencil codes. The STELLA DSL provides syntax elements to explicitly control data-locality. It supports two kind of caches for: 1) caching a buffer in the i-j plane and 2) caching buffer in the k dimension. As the i-j plane corresponds to the default parallelization plane for the GPU backend of STELLA, the i-j cache will require an on-chip memory with synchronization capabilities. Therefore i-j caches are stored in shared memory while the k caches are stored in registers (private resources to each thread).

Figure 7 shows the performance improvements achieved with the use of i-j caches and k caches for some of the operators of the dynamical core of COSMO.

In addition to i-j and k caches, STELLA supports in a new feature a cache syntax for a three-dimensional buffer. The following example illustrates the use of the different cache syntax elements of STELLA:

```
1    define_caches(
2        IJCache<lap, KRange<FullDomain,0,0> >(),
3        KCache<acol, cFlush, KWindow<-1,0>, KRange<FullDomain,0,0> >(),
4        IJKCache<div, cFill, IJKWindow<-1,1,-1,1,-2,0>, KRange<FullDomain,0,0> >()
5    )
```

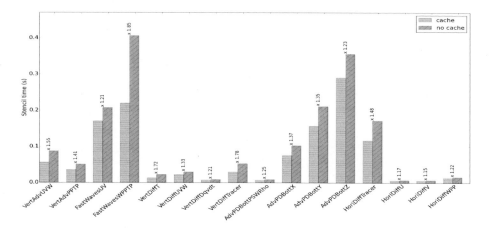

Figure 7. Time per stencil (for 10 time steps and domain sizes of 128x128x60) on a K20c GPU, for all the operators in the dynamical core that make use of the cache syntax. Numbers above the bars show achieved speedup using software manage caching.

Stencil	cache policy	no Cache (s)	IJK cache (s) (shared mem)	speedup
AdvPDBottY	fill from mem	0.15	0.14	1.07
AdvPDBottX	fill from mem	0.077	0.044	1.75
FastWavesDiv	local buffer	0.088	0.069	1.28

Table 1. Performance improvement obtained using caches in shared memory as buffers synchronized with fields in GPU memory (read only fields are loaded by the library into the shared memory buffers from GPU memory before they are accessed by the user code) and full 3D buffers (local buffer) without synchronization policy for a K20c GPU.

In addition a new functionality of STELLA allows to use multiple policies for synchronizing the data of buffer of the (shared memory) cache with the corresponding fields in the off-chip memory. This allows to also cache in fast on-chip memory read only fields which are reuse multiple times in the stencil. Significant performance improvements obtained for some of the stencils of the dynamical core of COSMO are reported in Table 1.

Conclusions

STELLA is a domain and data structure specific tool for structured grid methods, which separates the domain-logic (user code) from its hardware architecture dependent implementation and optimization. In this paper we present several extensions to STELLA which have not previously been published and represent a significant step forward in terms of usability and performance of STELLA.

The first extension allows the application of an discretized partial differential operator (for example the advection operator) to multiple data fields. This is achieved using an concise and compact syntax extension to the DSL exposed by STELLA which avoids code redundancy but at the same time allows for an implementation strategy that increases data-locality and instruction level parallelism. Results on an NVIDIA GPU indicate significant performance benefits (up to a factor 1.6x), which depend both on the details of the operator as well as the specific of the hardware architecture.

The second extension is driven by the fact that STELLA typically exhibit limited strong scalability on GPUs for atmospheric models. Since the first version of STELLA was mapping only the horizontal direction onto GPU threads the amount of parallelism in the strong scaling regime was not sufficient to efficiently utilize the available computational resources. STELLA now supports three different parallelization modes in the vertical direction: 1) sequential 2) fully parallel and 3) parallel tridiagonal solve. These modes can be specified per stencil computation and thus take account of the specific data dependencies imposed by different discretized partial differential operators. Results show that for a grid size of 32x32x60 grid points, the new parallelization modes can result in a significant performance improvement (with a speedup of up to 3.8x for certain stencils).

Finally the software managed cache functionality was extended to cover three dimensional buffers and synchronization capabilities with memory broadening the spectrum of operators that can increase the data locality property of the stencil by making use of the software manage cache.

These extensions indicate that the implementation approach chosen for STELLA (template metaprogramming in C++) is both flexible and extensible for rapidly providing new DSL syntax elements required by the users. Due to the high level of abstraction in the user code new features can be integrated rapidly into a large code base without a major refactoring effort. Further development of STELLA is ongoing in the direction of making it applicable also to block-structured codes with a focus on global simulation codes in climate and earth science.

References

[1] Oliver Fuhrer, Carlos Osuna, Xavier Lapillonne, Tobias Gysi, Ben Cumming, Mauro Bianco, Andrea Arteaga, and Thomas Schulthess. Towards a performance portable, architecture agnostic implementation strategy for weather and climate models. *Supercomputing frontiers and innovations*, 1(1), 2014.

[2] Xavier Lapillonne and Oliver Fuhrer. Using compiler directives to port large scientific applications to GPUs: An example from atmospheric science. *Parallel Processing Letters*, 24(1):1450003, 2014.

[3] Tobias Gysi, Carlos Osuna, Oliver Fuhrer, Mauro Bianco, and Thomas Shulthess. Stella: A domain-specific tool for structured grid methods in weather and climate models. *Submitted to Supercomputing 2015*.

[4] MB Giles, R Mudalige, Z Sharif, G Markall, and PHJ Kelly. Performance analysis and optimization of the op2 framework on many-core architectures. *COMPUTER JOURNAL*, 55:168–180, 2012.

[5] Florian Rathgeber, David A Ham, Lawrence Mitchell, Michael Lange, Fabio Luporini, Andrew TT McRae, Gheorghe-Teodor Bercea, Graham R Markall, and Paul HJ Kelly. Firedrake: automating the finite element method by composing abstractions. *Submitted to ACM TOMS*, 2015.

[6] Ming Xue. High-order monotonic numerical diffusion and smoothing. *Monthly Weather Review*, 128(8):2853–2864, 1999.

[7] B. Vogel, H. Vogel, D. Bäumer, M. Bangert, K. Lundgren, R. Rinke, and T. Stanelle. The comprehensive model system cosmo-art radiative impact of aerosol on the state of the atmosphere on the regional scale. *Atmospheric Chemistry and Physics*, 9(22):8661–8680, 2009.

[8] Mike Giles, Endre László, István Reguly, Jeremy Appleyard, and Julien Demouth. Gpu implementation of finite difference solvers. In *Proceedings of the 7th Workshop on High Performance Computational Finance*, WHPCF '14, pages 1–8, Piscataway, NJ, USA, 2014. IEEE Press.

Parallel Computing: On the Road to Exascale
G.R. Joubert et al. (Eds.)
IOS Press, 2016
doi:10.3233/978-1-61499-621-7-647

Towards Compiler-Agnostic Performance in Finite-Difference Codes

A. R. PORTER [a,1], R. W. FORD [a], M. ASHWORTH [a], G. D. RILEY [b] and
M. MODANI [c]

[a] *STFC Daresbury Laboratory, Warrington, WA4 4AD, UK*
[b] *The University of Manchester, UK*
[c] *STFC Hartree Centre*

Abstract. In this paper we evaluate the performance implications of applying a technique which we call PSyKAl to finite difference Ocean models. In PSyKAl the code related to the underlying science is formally separated from code related to parallelisation and single core optimisations. This separation of concerns allows scientists to code their science independently of the underlying hardware architecture (thereby keeping a single code base) and for optimisation specialists to be able to tailor the code for a particular machine independently of the science code. A finite difference shallow water benchmark optimised for cache-based architectures is taken as the starting point. A vanilla PSyKAl version is written and the performance of the two compared. The optimisations that were applied to the original benchmark (loop fusion *etc.*) are then manually applied to the PSyKAl version as a set of code modifications to the optimisation layer. Performance results are presented for the Cray, Intel and GNU compilers on Intel Ivybridge and Haswell processors and for the IBM compiler on Power8. Results show that the combined set of code modifications obtain performance that is within a few percent of the original code for all compiler and architecture combinations on all tested problem sizes. The only exception to this (other than where we see performance improvement) is the Gnu compiler on Haswell for one problem size. Our tests indicate that this may be due to immature support for that architecture in the Gnu compiler – no such problem is seen on the Ivy Bridge system. Further, the original code performed poorly using the IBM compiler on Power8 and needed to be modified to obtain performant code. Therefore, the PSyKAl approach can be used with negligible performance loss and sometimes small performance gains compared to the original optimised code. We also find that there is no single best hand-optimised implementation of the code for all of the compilers tested.

Keywords. Performance, Code-generation, Finite-difference

Introduction

The challenge presented to the developers of scientific software by the drive towards Exascale computing is considerable. With power consumption becoming the overriding design constraint, CPU clock speeds are falling and the complex, multi-purpose compute

---

[1] Corresponding Author: Andrew Porter, STFC Daresbury Laboratory, Warrington, WA4 4AD, UK; E-mail: andrew.porter@stfc.ac.uk.

core is being replaced by multiple, simpler cores. This philosophy can be seen at work in the rise of so-called accelerator based machines in the Top 500 List [1] of supercomputers: five of the top-ten machines in the November 2014 list make use of Intel Xeon Phi's or NVIDIA GPUs. Four of the remaining five machines in the top ten are IBM BlueGene/Qs, the CPU of which has hardware support for running 64 threads.

Achieving good performance on large numbers of light-weight cores requires exploiting as much parallelism in an application as possible and this results in increased complexity in the programming models that must be used. This in turn increases the burden of code maintenance and code development, in part because two specialisms are required: that of the scientific domain which a code is modelling (*e.g.* oceanography) and that of computational science. The situation is currently complicated still further by the existence of competing hardware technology; if one were to begin writing a major scientific application today it is unclear whether one would target GPU, Xeon Phi, traditional CPU, FPGA or something else entirely. This is a problem because, generally speaking, these different technologies require different programming approaches.

The PSyKAl Approach

The PSyKAl approach attempts to address the problems described in the previous section. It separates code into three layers; the Algorithm layer, the PSy layer and the Kernel layer. The approach has been developed in the GungHo project [2], which is creating a new Dynamical core for the Met Office, and its design has been influenced by earlier work on OP2 [3,4].

In common with OP2, the PSyKAl approach separates out the science code and the performance-related code into distinct layers. The calls that specify parallelism in both approaches are similar in terms of where they are placed in the code and in their semantics. However, the PSyKAl approach supports the specification of more than one kernel in a parallel region of code, compared with one for OP2, giving more scope for optimisation. Another difference is that the description metadata is provided with a kernel in the PSyKAl approach whereas it is provided as part of the kernel call in OP2.

While the PSyKAl approach is general, we are currently applying it to Atmosphere and Ocean models written in Fortran where domain decomposition is typically performed in the latitude-longitude direction, leaving columns of elements on each domain-decomposed partition.

The top layer, in terms of calling hierarchy, is the Algorithm layer. This layer specifies the algorithm that the scientist would like to perform (in terms of calls to kernel and infrastructure routines) and logically operates on full fields. We say logically here as the fields may be domain decomposed, however the Algorithm layer is not aware of this. It is the scientist's responsibility to write this Algorithm layer.

The bottom layer, in terms of calling hierarchy, is the Kernel layer. The Kernel layer implements the science that the Algorithm layer calls, as a set of subroutines. These kernels operate on fields that are local to the process doing the computation. (Depending on the type of kernel, these may be a set of elements, a single column of elements, or a set of columns.). Again the scientist is responsible for writing this layer and there is no parallelism specified here, but, depending on the complexity of the Kernels, there may be input from an HPC expert and/or some coding rules to help ensure the kernels compile into efficient code. In an alternative approach, kernels are generated from a high-level specification [5,6], potentially allowing them to be optimised automatically [7].

The PSy layer sits in-between the Algorithm and Kernel layers and its functional role is to link the algorithm calls to the associated kernel subroutines. As the Algorithm layer works on logically global fields and Kernel layer works on local fields, the PSy layer is responsible for iterating over columns. It is also responsible for including any distributed-memory operations resulting from the decomposition of the simulation domain, such as halo swaps and reductions.

As the PSy layer iterates over columns, the single core performance can be optimised by applying transformations such as loop fusion and loop blocking. Additionally, the potential parallelism within this iteration space can also be exploited and optimised. The PSy layer can therefore be tailored for a particular hardware (such as multi-core, many-core, GPGPUs, or some combination thereof) and software (such as compiler, operating system, MPI implementation) configuration with no change to the Algorithm or Kernel layer code. This approach therefore offers the potential for portable performance. In this work we apply optimisations to the PSy layer manually. The development of a tool to automate this process will be the subject of a future paper.

Clearly the separation of code into distinct layers may have an effect on performance. This overhead, how to get back to the performance of a hand-optimised code, and potentially improve on it, will be discussed in the remainder of this paper.

The 'Shallow' Program

For this work we use a benchmark called Shallow which solves the shallow-water equations on a bi-periodic plane following the finite-difference scheme introduced by Sadourny [8]. This software was originally written in 1984 by Paul Swarztrauber of the National Center for Atmospheric Research, US. However, in common with many scientific codes, it has subsequently undergone some sort of evolutionary development with subsequent people making various changes and optimising it for previous generations of hardware. There is no complete record of the people involved and the precise hardware they were targeting. In describing our work, we term the version of the Shallow program obtained at the beginning of this project the 'original' version. This code is available as part of version 1.0 of the GOcean benchmark (`https://puma.nerc.ac.uk/trac/GOcean`).

Shallow is a very good test case for our purposes since the original version is short (some 600 lines) and contained within a single source file. This makes it relatively straightforward for a compiler to optimise. Its performance is thus quite a demanding target for our modified versions of the code to reproduce.

Since any real oceanographic computational model must output results, we ensure that any PSyKAl version of Shallow retains the Input/Output capability of the original (it reads the problem specification from a namelist and outputs the solution fields every n timesteps). This aids in limiting the optimisations that can be performed on the PSyKAl version to those that should also be applicable to full oceanographic models. Note that although we retain the I/O functionality, all of the results presented in this work carefully exclude the effects of I/O since it is compute performance that interests us here.

In order to maximise the flexibility (and thus potential for optimisation) of the PSyKAl version of Shallow, we made the kernels as fine-grained as possible. In this case, this resulted in eight distinct kernels, each of which operated on a single field at a single point (since we have chosen to use point-wise kernels). With a little bit of tidying/re-

Algorithm Layer	PSy Layer	Kernel Layer

DO timesteps
 	
    CALL invoke_tstep(...)
 	
    CALL write_data(...)
END DO
	SUBROUTINE invoke_tstep(...)
	
	    DO grid-points
	        CALL kernel1(...)
	    END DO
	
	    DO grid-points
	        CALL kernel2(...)
	    END DO
	
	    ...
	
	END invoke_tstep
		SUBROUTINE kernel1(i,j,fld,...)
		    fld(i,j) = ...
		END kernel1
		
		SUBROUTINE kernel2(i,j,fld,...)
		    fld(i,j) = ...
		END kernel2

Figure 1. A schematic of the vanilla PSyKAl version of the Shallow code.

structuring, we found it was possible to express the contents of the main time-stepping loop as a single invoke (a call to the PSy layer) and a call to the I/O system (Figure 1). The single PSy layer routine then consists of applying each of the kernels to all of the points on the model mesh requiring an update. In its basic, unoptimised ('vanilla') form, this PSy layer routine then contains a doubly-nested loop around each kernel call, as indicated by the pseudo-code in Figure 1.

As with any full oceanographic model, boundary conditions must be applied at the edges of the model domain. In the case of Shallow we have periodic boundary conditions in both the *x*- and *y*-directions. These are simply implemented by having additional ('halo') rows/columns at the edges of the domain and ensuring the data in them is up-to-date before it is read. These rows/columns are updated by copying data from the corresponding row/column on the opposite side of the domain. In the current work, the lines of code to do these copies are manually inserted in the PSy layer routine as required.

Excluding the application of boundary conditions, the code has three main sections: computation of mass fluxes, vorticity and sea-surface height; computation of the pressure and velocity components; and finally, smoothing of the fields in time and copying of the field values at the next time-step to be those at the current time-step. Profiling the original code showed that these sections each account for around one third of the run-time.

1. Methodology

The primary aim of this work is to determine whether any performance loss due to the PSyKAl separation of concerns can be negated by optimising the PSy layer and if so, what the key transformations are (for a given system). To evaluate this we perform tests on a range of hardware and a range of compilers. The hardware and compilers are listed in Table 1. Where a compiler is available on a given piece of hardware, the version number used in this work is specified. The Intel Haswell-based system (Xeon E5-1620 v2) has a clock speed of 3.7 GHz and 10 MB of last-level cache (LLC). The Intel Ivy Bridge-based system (Xeon E5-2697) has a clock speed of 2.7 GHz and a LLC of 30 MB. The CPU in the IBM Power-8 system is built around 12 'chiplets'. Each chiplet has a single core with 64 KB of L1 cache, 512 KB of L2 cache and 8 MB of L3 cache. The L3 cache of each chiplet is shared with all other chiplets so that there is a total of 96 MB of LLC. The cores on the system we used had a clock speed of 3.3 GHz.

Table 1. The matrix of compilers and CPUs used in this work. The use of a compiler on a given CPU is indicated by the specification of the version of the compiler in the relevant element. No entry indicates that a compiler was not available/used on that CPU.

	Compiler			
	Gnu	Intel	Cray	IBM
Intel Haswell	4.9.3	14.0.0		
Intel Ivy Bridge	4.9.1	14.0.1.106	8.3.3	
IBM Power 8				15.1.2

Table 2. The compiler flags used in this work.

Compiler	Flags
Gnu	-Ofast -mtune=native -finline-limit=50000
Intel	-O3 -fast -fno-inline-factor
Cray	-O3 -O ipa5 -h wp
IBM	-O5 -qinline=auto:level=10 -qprefetch=dscr=0x1D7

In Table 2 we give the optimisation flags used with each compiler. These flags are particularly important for the PSyKAl versions of the code. The performance of the original version of the code is much less sensitive to the compiler options. This is because it consists of a single source file containing effectively a single routine (excluding those for I/O). For all compilers apart from Cray it was important to use flags that encourage in-lining. With the Cray compiler some benefit was obtained by increasing the level of Inter-Procedural Analysis and using 'whole-program optimisation'. In order to get performant code from the IBM compiler it was found essential to make the pre-fetching considerably more aggressive than the default.

Before applying any code transformations, we benchmark the original version of the code. We also benchmark the vanilla, unoptimised version after it has been re-structured following the PSyKAl approach. These two versions of the code effectively provide upper and lower bounds, respectively, on the performance we expect to achieve.

Beginning with the vanilla PSyKAl version, we then manually apply a series of (cumulative) code transformations while obeying the PSyKAl separation of concerns, *i.e.* optimisation is restricted to the middle, PSy layer and leaves the Kernel and Algorithm layers unchanged. The aim of these optimisations is to recover, as much as is possible, the structure and thus performance of the original version of the code. We began with two transformations that affect all of the kernels. After this, we determined the transformations to perform by comparing the timing profiles of the PSyKAl and original versions of the code. We then tackled the sections responsible for the largest slowdowns and iterated this process. While doing this we also made heavy use of the optimisation reports produced by the compilers and how these changed when moving from the original to the PSyKAl version of the code. The transformations we have performed are as follows:

T1. No optimisation: the vanilla PSyKAl version of the code;
T2. Specify array bounds in the middle layer using module variables (rather than using assumed-size array arguments);
T3. Move all kernel subroutines into the same module as that containing the middle/PSy layer ('module inlining');

T4. Loop fusion: all neighbouring loop nests were fully fused (where possible) with the exception of the first loop nest where it was found that fusing only the outer loop was more performant.

T5. Manually in-line ('kernel inline') the three field-copy operations performed as part of the time-update section;

T6. Loop fuse the three field-copy operations with the time-smoothing loop nest;

T7. Manually in-line all kernel bodies into the middle layer subroutine (kernel inlining);

T8. Fully fuse the first loop nest (only the outer loop of this loop nest was fused in the first pass);

T9. Make the array/loop bounds explicitly constant for the duration of the time-stepping loop (pass as arguments to the middle layer rather than using module variables);

T10. Un-roll the outer loop of the time-smoothing loop nest using a blocking factor of four (IBM supplied);

T11. Fission the first loop nest back into three separate loop nests (IBM supplied).

As indicated above, transformations T10 and T11 were suggested by the IBM compiler team. The second of these effectively undoes transformation four by fissioning the first loop nest back into three separate loop nests. Note that this sequence of transformations is specific to Shallow: we are currently working upon a code-generation system that will allow a user to choose from a menu of transformations when optimising a PSy layer and this will be the subject of a future paper.

We shall see that the transformations T1–T11 do not always result in improved performance. Whether or not they do so depends both on the compiler and the problem size. We also emphasise that the aim of these optimisations is typically to recover, as far as is possible, the structure of the original version of the code. Therefore this sequence of transformations is specific to Shallow. It may well be that transforming the code into some other structure would result in better performance on a particular architecture. However, exploring this optimisation space is beyond the scope of the present work. We are currently developing a code-generation system that will allow a user to choose from a menu of transformations when optimising a PSy layer and this will be the subject of a future paper.

We explore the extent to which performance depends upon the problem size by using square domains with side lengths of 64, 128, 256, 512 and 1024. This range allows us to investigate what happens when cache is exhausted as well as giving us some insight into the decisions that different compilers make when optimising the code.

2. Results

In this section we first discuss the performance of the original version of the code with the various compiler/CPU combinations. We then investigate the different code transformations that are required to recover good performance from the PSyKAl version of Shallow. Finally, we compare the most performant PSyKAl version with the original version of Shallow for each compiler/CPU combination.

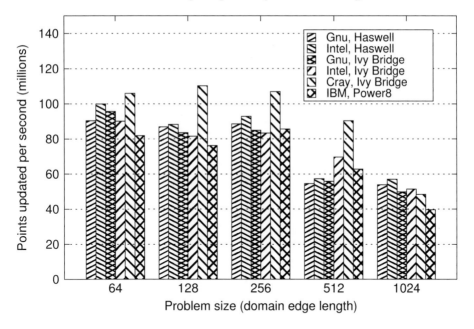

Figure 2. Summary of the performance of the original Shallow code on the range of compilers and hardware under consideration.

2.1. Performance of the Original Version of Shallow

In Figure 2 we plot the performance of the original version of the Shallow code for the range of compilers and hardware considered here. This summary demonstrates the effect of the larger LLC of the Intel Ivy Bridge system compared to that of the Haswell system; note the drop in performance in going from a problem size of 256^2 to a problem size of 512^2 for the first two bars. The performance of the Ivy Bridge system with the Cray or Intel compiler (penultimate two bars) only drops to this level when the domain size is increased to 1024^2. At this point, the working set no longer fits within cache and performance is dominated by the bandwidth to main memory, making it relatively insensitive to the choice of compiler.

Strangely, the third bar (Gnu compiler) in Figure 2 shows the same drop in performance in moving from the 256^2 case to the 512^2 case, despite the larger LLC of the Ivy Bridge system. In order to investigate this, we profiled the application to obtain hardware performance counter data for the Gnu- and Intel-compiled executables. This revealed that the Gnu-compiled executable made more references to memory and had a higher LLC miss-rate compared with the Intel binary. We conclude that the Gnu compiler is not utilising registers as efficiently as the Intel compiler and that this results in greater memory traffic.

For this compiler-friendly form of the code, there is generally little performance difference between the executables produced by the Gnu and Intel compilers on both the Haswell and Ivy Bridge CPUs (with the exception of the 512^2 case noted above). However, the executable produced by the Cray compiler generally performs significantly better for all but the largest domain size. Analysis of the optimisation reports produced

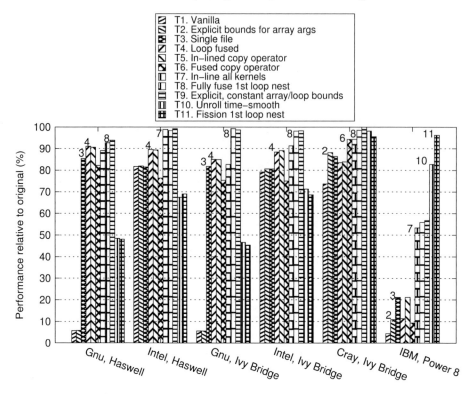

Figure 3. The performance of the PSyKAl version of Shallow for the 256^2 domain at each stage of optimisation. Results are given as a percentage of the performance of the original code for each compiler/CPU combination. As an aid to understanding, significant performance jumps are labelled with the corresponding transformation number.

by the Cray and Intel compilers did not give any clues as to the cause of this difference and an in-depth investigation is outside the scope of this paper.

2.2. Optimisations of the PSyKAl Version to Recover Performance

We now examine the performance of the PSyKAl version of Shallow and the code transformations that are required to reach the levels obtained by the original. We do this for the 256^2 problem size since this fits within LLC on all of the CPUs we are using here. The performance of the PSyKAl version after each transformation has been manually applied to the code is plotted in Figure 3. Results for a given compiler/CPU are presented relative to the performance of the original version of Shallow with the same compiler/CPU.

With the Gnu compiler (first and third clusters in Figure 3), the vanilla PSyKAl version of Shallow only achieves 5-6% of the performance of the original. Simply copying the code for each of the kernel subroutines into the module from which they are called (module in-lining, T3) has the most dramatic effect on the performance of the compiled code; it now achieves more than 80% of the performance of the original. The transformation(s) required to get more than 90% then become architecture dependent: on Haswell it is just loop fusion (T4) while on Ivy Bridge we do not exceed 90% until we have applied all of the steps up to and including T8; fully fusing (fusing the inner loops of) the first

```
! Time smoothing
DO J=1,N+1
  DO I=1,M+1
    CALL time_smooth_code(i,j,ufld,unew,uold)
!     uold(i,j) = ufld(i,j) + alpha* &
!       (unew(i,j) - 2.*ufld(i,j) + uold(i,j))
  END DO
END DO

! Copy new fields into current fields
DO J=1,N+1
  DO I=1,M+1
    Ufld(I,J) = UNEW(I,J)
  END DO
END DO
```

Figure 4. Example of the coding structure that required manual in-lining of the kernel body (as indicated by commented-out lines) to retrieve the performance of the original version of Shallow with the Intel compiler.

loop nest. The dramatic performance improvement obtained from the module-inlining (T3) demonstrates that the Gnu compiler is unable to optimise over separate source files.

With the Intel compiler, the key transformations to recover performance are different (second and fourth clusters in Figure 3). Even the vanilla PSyKAl version of Shallow achieves some 80% of the performance of the original version. Only two code transformations were required to increase this to ∼100%. The first of these was T4, the fusion of the computational loops. However, we found that performance suffered (T6) when this was extended to include the loop required for field copies at the end of a time-step (Figure 4). Further investigation of this slow-down revealed that the compiler was unable to SIMD vectorise the newly-fused loop after it had in-lined the body of the kernel called from within it. Once this in-lining was done by hand (T7), the compiler was able to vectorise the loop and the performance of the original version of Shallow was recovered on the Haswell system. On Ivy Bridge the first loop nest also had to be fully fused (T8) to recover ∼100% of the performance.

The fifth cluster in Figure 3 shows the evolution of the performance of the PSyKAl version of Shallow with the Cray compiler. Again, this has significant differences from the behaviour seen with the Gnu and Intel compilers. As with the Intel compiler, the performance of the Vanilla PSyKAl version, T1, is fairly good at 74% of that of the original. In contrast to the other compilers considered so far, the first significant transformation is simply to specify the bounds of the arrays being used within the middle layer using module variables (as opposed to specifying them as assumed size). This tells the compiler that all of the arrays used in the middle layer have the same extent and also that all of the computational loops are over almost all elements of these arrays. This simple change gives a PSyKAl version that achieves 88% of the performance of the original.

Subsequent transformations actually harm performance until T6 where the field-copy operation (lower loop in Figure 4) is fused with the preceding loop. The resulting PSyKAl version now achieves 94% of the original performance. Two further steps are required to match the latter: the first loop nest is fully fused (T8 - both inner and outer loops fused) and second, the array/loop bounds are passed as an argument to the middle layer (T9). This is done in order to indicate to the compiler that these bounds remain constant for the duration of each iteration of the time-stepping loop.

Moving to the IBM compiler on the Power 8 system (sixth cluster in Figure 3) we see that performance of the vanilla PSyKAl version is only 5% of the original and several transformations are required to achieve comparable performance. As with the Cray compiler, specifying array bounds explicitly, T2, improves performance. Module-inlining, T3, also has a significant effect; doubling the performance from 10 to 20% of the original. However, fusing loop nests actually harms performance, just as it did for the Cray compiler. Kernel inlining (T7) takes performance to over 50% and it is the IBM-supplied transformations of T10 (loop unrolling) and T11 (fissioning of the first loop) that finally recovers 96% of the performance of the original. (*i.e.* we must undo some of transformations three and seven). We note that this final pair of transformations significantly reduce the performance obtained with the Intel and Gnu compilers although they do not much perturb that obtained by the Cray compiler.

2.3. Performance Comparison of the Original and PSyKAl Versions

Finally, we compare the performance of the best PSyKAl version of Shallow with that of the original for different problem sizes. In Figure 5 we plot the percentage difference between the performance of the original and the (best) PSyKAl versions of Shallow for each compiler/CPU combination. The most important feature of this plot is that the performance penalty incurred by the PSyKAl version is less than four percent with only one exception where it is 6.6%. In fact, for the Intel and Cray compilers, the PSyKAl version of Shallow is never more than 2% slower than the original and in some cases is faster. This demonstrates that we can reliably recover the performance of the original version of the code, despite the significant restructuring required by the PSyKAl approach.

The exceptional case is that of the Gnu-compiled binary on the Haswell CPU for a problem size of 256^2. This is strange since the performance difference for the same case on the Ivy Bridge CPU is just 0.8%. We investigated this further by compiling and running this case with versions 4.8.3, 4.9.1 and 4.9.3 of the Gnu compiler on the Haswell system. These gave slow-downs of 7.8%, 7.3% and 6.6%, respectively. From these results we conclude that the Gnu compiler's support for/ability to exploit the newer Haswell architecture is still maturing.

Turning to the cases where the PSyKAl version is significantly *faster* than the original, we see from Figure 5 that, with the exception of Power 8, this only occurs for the smallest domain size. This is no doubt due in part to the fact that the problem executes very quickly and therefore a small reduction in run-time will show as a large percentage. Since this problem is well contained in L2 cache, its performance will also be more sensitive to small differences, *e.g.* in the way that CPU registers are used.

The performance of the Power 8 system with the 512^2 domain size is somewhat anomalous: the PSyKAl version of the code performs significantly better than the original and in addition, this problem size is also the only one where the Power 8 out-performs the Haswell system (see Figure 2) for the original version. The results in Figure 2 indicate that the 512^2 case marks a transition from the working set being in cache (sizes $\leq 256^2$) to spilling out of cache (size 1024^2). We therefore suggest that cache is being used more efficiently on the Power 8 system and this is further enhanced by the IBM-supplied transformations in the PSyKAl version.

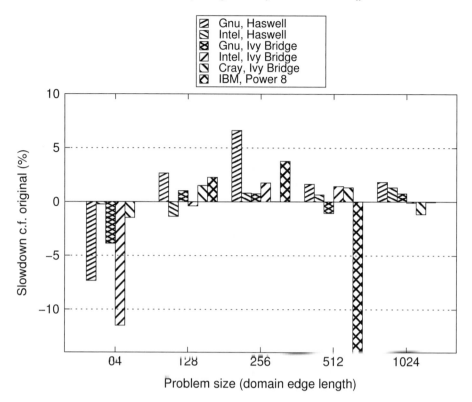

Figure 5. Comparison of the performance of the best PSyKAl version with that of the original version of the code. A negative value indicates that the PSyKAl version is faster than the original.

The main conclusion of all this analysis is that while we can employ a separation of concerns and recover performance, doing so is not straightforward. Determining how best to optimise even a simple code such as Shallow is highly compiler- and CPU-dependent. Decisions that are good on one platform may be bad for another and if these are written into the source code then they will accumulate over time and will almost certainly result in a code that does not perform optimally on any system. For instance, loop fusion benefits performance for the Gnu and Intel compilers and yet hurts performance with the Cray and IBM compilers.

3. Conclusions

We have investigated the application of the PSyKAl separation of concerns approach to the domain of finite-difference ocean models. This approach enables the computational science (performance) related aspects of a computer model to be kept separate from the natural (oceanographic) science aspects.

As expected, applying this separation of concerns does reduce performance significantly when compared with an existing, optimised code. However, the application of code transformations to the performance/PSy layer and the use of appropriate compiler flags can recover any performance losses to within a few percent and in some cases, despite limiting ourselves to transformations which replicate the structure of the optimised code, result in slightly improved performance.

More unpredictably, the code structure required to obtain good performance for different architecture and/or compiler combinations differs, even for this relatively simple benchmark code. For hand optimised codes this implies the need to support multiple code bases in order to achieve portable performance. The PSyKAl approach directly addresses the problem of requiring different optimisations for different architectures and/or compilers by limiting these differences to a separate performance layer, thereby allowing the natural science code base to remain unchanged.

In future work we will extend our performance portability analysis of the PSyKAl approach to shared memory parallelisation optimisations on different architectures using different parallelisation techniques (in particular OpenMP on multi/many-core and OpenACC on GPU's). We will then analyse the performance of a domain-specific compiler that is currently under development. This compiler will generate optimised PSy layer code by following a user-provided recipe of transformations, thereby removing the need for optimisation experts to manually write the PSy layer.

Acknowledgements

This work made use of the ARCHER UK National Supercomputing Service (http://www.archer.ac.uk) and the Hartree Centre IBM Power 8 system. The STFC Hartree Centre is a research collaboratory in association with IBM providing HPC platforms funded by the UK's investment in e-Infrastructure. The Centre aims to develop and demonstrate next generation software, optimised for the move towards exa-scale computing. This work was funded by the NERC 'GOcean' project, grant number NE/L012111/1.

References

[1] The Top 500 List, November 2014.
[2] Rupert W. Ford, Maff J. Glover, David A. Ham, Chris M. Maynard, Stephen M. Pickles, Graham D. Riley, and Nigel Wood. Gung ho: A code design for weather and climate prediction on exascale machines. *Journal of Advances in Engineering Software*, Accepted for publication, 2015.
[3] Carlo Bertolli, Adam Betts, Gihan Mudalige, Mike Giles, and Paul Kelly. Design and performance of the op2 library for unstructured mesh applications. In Michael et al. Alexander, editor, *Euro-Par 2011: Parallel Processing Workshops*, volume 7155 of *Lecture Notes in Computer Science*, pages 191–200. Springer Berlin Heidelberg, 2012.
[4] F. Rathgeber, G. R. Markall, L. Mitchell, N. Loriant, D. A. Ham, C. Bertolli, and P. H. J. Kelly. Pyop2: A high-level framework for performance-portable simulations on unstructured meshes. In *Proceedings of the 2012 SC Companion: High Performance Computing, Networking Storage and Analysis*, SCC '12, pages 1116–1123, Washington, DC, USA, 2012. IEEE Computer Society.
[5] Florian Rathgeber, David A Ham, Lawrence Mitchell, Michael Lange, Fabio Luporini, Andrew TT McRae, Gheorghe-Teodor Bercea, Graham R Markall, and Paul HJ Kelly. Firedrake: automating the finite element method by composing abstractions. *Submitted to ACM TOMS*, 2015.
[6] Anders Logg, Kent-Andre Mardal, Garth N. Wells, et al. *Automated Solution of Differential Equations by the Finite Element Method*. Springer, 2012.
[7] F. Luporini, A. L. Varbanescu, F. Rathgeber, G.-T. Bercea, J. Ramanujam, D. A. Ham, and P. H. J. Kelly. COFFEE: an Optimizing Compiler for Finite Element Local Assembly. *ArXiv e-prints*, July 2014.
[8] Robert Sadourny. The Dynamics of Finite-Difference Models of the Shallow-Water Equations. *Journal of the Atmospheric Sciences*, 32(4):680–689, 1975.

Mini-Symposium:
Is the Programming Environment Ready for Hybrid Supercomputers?

Parallel Computing: On the Road to Exascale
G.R. Joubert et al. (Eds.)
IOS Press, 2016
© 2016 The authors and IOS Press. All rights reserved.
doi:10.3233/978-1-61499-621-7-661

661

Is the Programming Environment ready for hybrid supercomputers?

Alistair HART [a] Harvey RICHARDSON [a]

[a] *Cray UK Ltd., EPCC, JCMB, King's Buildings, Edinburgh EH9 3FD*

Abstract. We introduce the Mini Symposium, placing the contributions in context and detail points made during the talks and discussion sessions.

High Performance Computing (HPC) node architectures are becoming increasingly complex as systems evolve towards exascale performance. There are many more cores per node, more threads and wider "single instruction multiple data" (SIMD) vectors.

Heterogeneous (or "hybrid") node designs are also now common, with nearly 20% of the June 2015 Top500 list using accelerators (e.g. Nvidia or AMD GPUs or Intel Xeon Phi coprocessors). Future lists are likely to include significantly more hybrid systems with the expected release of new products from Nvidia and Intel (the current lead accelerator vendors in HPC) in 2016.

It is, however, difficult to achieve an acceptable fraction of the available performance of hybrid nodes. More importantly, it is also difficult to develop (and maintain) applications that are performance portable, i.e. that can be built and executed with acceptable efficiency on a wide variety of HPC architectures with only minimal changes. This is important, as large applications are typically run on a variety of HPC platforms, and the codes often outlive many generations of HPC procurements (and even developers).

Hybrid node architectures offer two significant programming challenges. First, developers must use a "secondary" programming model (on top of the base language) that targets the accelerator. Secondly, hybrid nodes introduce a diverse memory space with, typically, a node's CPU and accelerator(s) having separate memories. Given the relatively slow (high latency, low bandwidth) connection between the memory spaces and the (consequent) lack of automatic synchronisation between them, developers are forced (for the moment, at least) to explicitly manage the memory spaces and data transfers.

The situation is more complicated in HPC, where the size or complexity of the simulated problem requires the use of parallel programming techniques to distribute work across, and then communicate between, multiple nodes. Efficient use of accelerators in this context requires tight integration between the parallel programming (MPI or PGAS) and secondary programming models, to allow streamlined communication of data between the secondary memory spaces of the accelerators on different nodes.

At a minimum, the Programming Environment (PE) on such hybrid systems must provide compiler support to allow use, and integration, of these various programming models. A good PE should, however, go further than this including and, where applicable, integrating additional tools that assist in code development, debugging, performance measurement and application tuning. Such PEs can be provided by hardware vendors, system integrators or third parties using open or closed source products. For "traditional"

HPC systems, there is (anecdotally) a rich ecosystem of PE components. For hybrid supercomputers, however, the complexity and rate of change of the platforms means there is a much smaller set of tools available.

The purpose of this Mini-Symposium was to bring vendors and application developers together to understand the programming models being used and the suitability of the Programming Environments. The format was a series of invited talks:

- Michael Neff (Cray UK), who presented a strategy for developing a performance portable hybrid application highligting PE tools used
- Timothy Lanfear (Nvidia), who concentrated on hardware architecture developments
- Andrew Mallinson (Intel), who addressed preparation for the Knights Landing products and network technologies
- William Sawyer (CSCS), who shared experience with a range of hybrid applications

These were interspersed with papers selected from the Call for Abstracts:

- Alan Gray (EPCC), described a performance portable single-source approach to programming accelerators (TargetDP)
- Aidan Chalk (Durham University), described the Quicksched tasking framework
- Rayman Reyes (Codeplay Software), described the SYCL single-source C++ accelerator programming framework
- Christos Margiolas (Edinburgh University), described Hexe, A Heterogeneous execution engine for LLVM

The workshop finished with a panel discussion with the invited speakers which fostered discussion of the state-of-the art of the hybrid programming environments and highlighted the aspirations and concerns of those present. This session and other discussions throughout the Mini-Symposium touched on various requirements and concerns.

A good PE should clearly provide efficient implementations of the relevant programming models. This might include programming models used primarily as a runtime layer (as with OpenCL for some speakers).

Performance portability from a single source application was also felt to be an important (if perhaps unachievable) goal. Directive-based programming was seen as one route to this, but with concern that current standards and compiler implementations do not fully support modern language features (e.g. Fortran derived types or C++ templates). Domain specific languages (DSLs) offered another approach, but had problems gaining traction (and critical mass) beyond one group or application area, and of maintaining these beyond an initial project. There was also concern that DSLs were not well supported in PE tools, perhaps because of their individual lack of mainstream visibility.

It was noted that there are relatively few accelerator-aware tools. Simple tools were generally favoured, as more complex tools are often harder to configure and less robust for large codes. A particular HPC problem was that advanced hardware features (e.g. multiple MPI ranks per accelerator or GPUdirect MPI communication) were not well supported. Some gaps in the current PEs were highlighted, notably in tools to help code porting and to validate accelerator results.

Co-design was viewed as important, where large codes are accelerated by teams with diverse skill sets, including PE developers. A shortage of suitably-skilled developers was an issue. For smaller codes, hackathons were raised as providing similar interactions.

The workshop was organised as a joint venture between the Cray Archer Centre of Excellence and the EPiGRAM project. This work was supported in part by the European Commission through the EPiGRAM project (grant agreement no. 610598).

Parallel Computing: On the Road to Exascale
G.R. Joubert et al. (Eds.)
IOS Press, 2016
© 2016 The authors and IOS Press. All rights reserved.
doi:10.3233/978-1-61499-621-7-663

Utilizing Hybrid Programming Environments: CSCS Case Studies

William SAWYER [a,1], Anton KOZHEVNIKOV [a] and Raffaele SOLCÀ [b]

[a] *Swiss National Supercomputing Centre (CSCS), ETH Zurich, CH-6900 Lugano, Switzerland*
[b] *Institute for Theoretical Physics, ETH Zurich, CH-8093 Zurich, Switzerland*

Abstract. Hybrid platforms — those combining multicore and many-core processors — have made extensive inroads into high performance computing, with 101 of the top 500 supercomputers being based on such technology. The addition of coprocessors ensures higher memory bandwidth and peak performance at the price of special programming or meticulous optimization. But how effective is hybrid multicore in increasing productivity of real applications? The answer depends to no small extent on the efficacy of the programming environment — compilers, debuggers, profilers, as well as black-box components, such as platform-specific numerical libraries — to port applications correctly and with good performance to the underlying hardware.

In this paper, we recount several use cases of production applications being porting to CSCS hybrid architectures, explain the challenges and strengths / weaknesses of various tools employed. Admittedly some of our conclusions are subjective, but our hope is that our experiences will lead to improvement of the PE's deficiencies, and will inform the HPC community of what worked well and what did not. This paper arises from the PARCO15 mini-symposium entitled *"Is the programming environment ready for hybrid supercomputers?"*

Keywords. high performance computing, programming environments, hybrid computing, climate and NWP modeling, density functional theory

Introduction

The main computing platform at Swiss National Supercomputing Centre (CSCS) is a Cray XC30 with 5,272 nodes, each containing one Intel SandyBridge CPU (Intel® Xeon® E5-2670) and one NVIDIA® Tesla K20X. CSCS has made a large commitment to port applications from the areas of climate / weather prediction and density functional theory, among others. In the subsequent sections we give a brief overview of the these areas and discuss the computational challenges in both.

Climate and Numerical Weather Prediction: the ICON Model

Although most scientists agree [1] that the current observed global warming is induced to a large part by human activity, quantitative projections of the magnitude, feedbacks,

---

[1]Corresponding Author: Swiss National Supercomputing Centre (CSCS), Via Trevano 131, Lugano, Switzerland; E-mail: wsawyer@cscs.ch

manifestations and the associated risk are subject to deep uncertainty. Projections can be generated by climate system models. Based on their cousins, the numerical weather prediction (NWP) models, climate models take into account long-term interactions of ocean, land, and atmosphere, as well as human and natural influences (e.g. the increase in greenhouse gases). The central limiting factor to the efficacy of a climate model is its resolution, which is ultimately determined by available computing resources. At higher resolution more physical phenomena are explicitly simulated, increasing the information content of the result. Climate modeling is compute-intensive, and new and emerging high-performance computing technologies will thus be decisive in answering important scientific questions. And yet, climate models have been slow to exploit massively parallel architectures and often run at a small fraction of peak performance.

In NWP and climate models the solution of the equations describing atmospheric *dynamics* (essentially the fully-compressible 3D Euler equations on the sphere) can take the majority of the overall model execution time, depending on the type of algorithm used and the model resolution. The collective effects of physical phenomena which cannot be resolved in the dynamics grid scale are calculated by so-called physical parameterizations or *physics* on a vertical atmospheric profile of one horizontal grid "box". Together the dynamics and physics form the crux of climate / NWP models. It is ultimately necessary to port both the hybrid multicore: Offloading just one or the other would necessitate large data transfers of the prognostic and diagnostic fields as they are updated, and this traffic would negate any performance gains from the many-core processors.

The application under consideration is the Icosahedral Non-hydrostatic (*ICON*) application [2], which is a global and/or regional climate / NWP model currently under development at the German Weather Service (DWD) and the Max Planck Institute for Meteorology. It is being ported to heterogeneous platforms by CSCS using a directive-based approach. This port and the associated PE issues will be discussed at length in Section 1.

DFT Electronic Structure Applications

Density functional theory has proved to be an extremely efficient tool in studying physical properties of molecules and bulk solids as well as chemical reactions and molecular dynamics. For instance, the Materials Project (https://www.materialsproject.org) initiative uses DFT total energy calculations as a baseline for materials screening. Time-dependent extension to DFT provides access to the dynamical properties of materials and gives a valuable information about their excited states.

The material science community has developed a large number of electronic structure codes based on the Kohn-Sham DFT method. Most of the codes make use of the same principle of expanding wave-functions in terms of a fixed number of basis functions and converting a set of second-order differential Kohn-Sham equations into a generalized eigenvalue problem of a square matrix. Thus, we have an odd situation where i) all electronic structure codes are based on the same DFT foundations, ii) each of the electronic structure codes uses one of the well-known basis sets (such as plane waves, augmented plane waves, localized orbitals, and a few other) to expand Kohn-Sham wave-functions, but iii) the particular implementation of each code solely depends on the personal tastes of the developers or the corresponding community, making it hard for external contributors to commit changes.

Clearly, it is not viable for a computing center to port each community code to hybrid platforms. A better approach is to separate concerns of the scientific community and

HPC centers, where the former takes care of the high-level physics and the latter focuses on the performance optimization on various platforms. In this paper we present a case study of a full-potential linearized augmented plane wave (LAPW) code *Exciting* [3] ported to GPUs using the domain specific library SIRIUS [4]. This family of LAPW basis sets is known as one of the most precise numerical scheme to solve the Kohn-Sham equations of density-functional theory (DFT). It can be applied to all kinds of materials, irrespective of the atomic species involved, and also allows for exploring the physics of core electrons. Exciting is written in Fortran90 and has a moderate level of MPI parallelization. Like most of the electronic structure codes, Exciting heavily relies on the linear algebra subroutines, and especially on the generalized eigenvalue solver.

1. Case study: Icosahedral Non-hydrostatic (ICON) Climate/NWP Model

In this section we focus on the port to heterogeneous multicore of the ICON model. Three different prototypes of the dynamics were written to illustrate the comparative advantages of different programming paradigms: OpenCL [5], CUDAfortran [6] and OpenACC directives [7]. In spite of technical problems and bugs with all three paradigms, it turned out that paradigm was less significant for development time than the tools to support validation of the hybrid code, and here we encountered a significant deficiency in the programming environment. Finally the code productivity was closely related to time-to-solution and thus code optimization on the hybrid platform.

1.1. Comparison of OpenCL and CUDAfortran Paradigms

Initial development encompassed two prototype single-node implementations in OpenCL and CUDAFortran[2], which are conceptually very similar (see Figure 1). However, Table 1 makes clear there were considerable differences in performance depending on the underlying accelerator architecture.

Thus the OpenCL version performed better on K20x, but CUDAFortran on older GPUs, e.g., GTX480, C2070, M2090, sometime dramatically so. The profiling information, e.g., nvprof, reflected the performances differences, but did not give hints about its cause. We attribute these differences to the corresponding device drivers. Our experiences from these two prototypes were:

- OpenCL has the distinct advantage of being a vendor-neutral standard. OpenCL code also runs on CPU (performance not shown), though much slower than the baseline CPU code, suggesting that it is still not a performance-portable way to write software.
- OpenCL required C-language wrappers, which added to the complexity of the build system.
- OpenCL's reputation for requiring more code is largely unwarranted: there was only more boilerplate for kernel invocation, which, once developed, could be reused for all of the 60-some kernels.
- CUDAFortran was easier to integrate into the existing Fortran code base.
- CUDAFortran, like CUDA, is proprietary (NVIDIA/PGI) and thus highly bound to NVIDIA GPUs.

---

[2]CUDA Fortran is a NVIDIA/PGI compiler implementing the CUDA language with Fortran syntax.

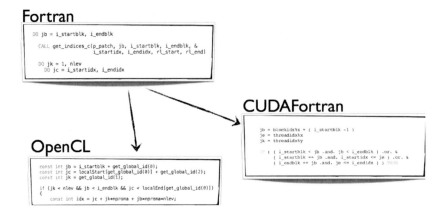

Figure 1. *The OpenCL and CUDAFortran implementations of typical ICON dycore triply-nested loops, prove to be similar. The inlined function* `get_indices` *simply adjusts the loop index range, and can be incorporated into each SIMD thread in an IF statement.*

Table 1. *Comparative single-node performance of OpenCL, CUDAFortran and baseline Fortran/OpenMP implementations for three different resolutions. The number of cells in the grid quadruples in each step R2B03 → R2B04 → R2B05. The OpenMP baseline increases consistently by a factor of four or more with increasing resolution level, a reflexion of reduced cache performance. The GPU implementations are consistently less than four, reflecting that higher occupancy is crucial for good performance.*

Architecture	R2B03 (s.)	R2B04 (s.)	R2B05 (s.)
NVIDIA K20x (OpenCL)	17.2	47.6	168
NVIDIA K20x (CUDAFortran)	53.8	82.4	201
NVIDIA GTX 480 (OpenCL)	27.6	101	N/A
NVIDIA GTX 480 (CUDAFortran)	13.3	38.6	N/A
NVIDIA C2070 (OpenCL)	36.3	120	450
NVIDIA C2070 (CUDAFortran)	27.8	60.4	192
NVIDIA M2090 (OpenCL)	21.5	65.7	241
NVIDIA M2090 (CUDAFotran)	31.6	56.8	159
Intel 2xSandybridge node, 16 threads	11.3	47.5	207
Intel 1xSandybridge node, 8 threads	13.9	59.3	240
Intel Sandybridge, 1 thread	66.3	273	1089
Intel Westmere node, 12 threads	21.1	89.7	326
Intel Westmere socket, 6 threads	26.9	114	457
Intel Westmere core, 1 thread	81.1	327	1492
AMD 2xInterlagos, 30 threads	23.1	112	472
AMD 1xInterlagos, 16 threads	39.8	158	639
AMD Interlagos, 1 thread	151	579	2424

1.2. OpenACC dycore implementation

ICON developers were not amenable to either an OpenCL or CUDAFortran implementation, since they are not transparent to the existing MPI/OpenMP implementation and would detract from the maintainability. OpenACC directives are, in fact, largely transparent to the CPU implementation, and we thus concentrated on an OpenACC prototype of a later domain-decomposed (MPI/OpenMP) dycore version. This was more complex than the single node dycore and thus not immediately comparable with the OpenCL/CUDAFortran results. This prototype performed adequately, and the decision was made to incorporate OpenACC into the main development with the constraint that no code duplication or extensive refactoring be made.

Listing 1. *The gradient calculation in the ICON shared utilities represents a typical triply-nested loop in the dycore. Note that while compilers allow compilation with both OpenMP and OpenACC, parallel regions from the two paradigms cannot overlap. Compilers are capable of inlining the* get_indices_e *routine. The calculation is only performed on the MPI processes associated with GPUs (*i_am_accel_node*), and only if accelaration has been turned on at runtime (*acc_on*). At the end, a call to* check_patch_array *illustrates the online validation check with the CPU sequential code (running on a thread with* .NOT. i_am_accel_node*), which would not appear in the final code.*

```
#ifdef _OPENACC
!$ACC DATA PCOPYIN( psi_c ), PCOPYOUT( grad_norm_psi_e ), IF( i_am_accel_node .AND. acc_on )
!$ACC PARALLEL, PRESENT( ptr_patch, iidx, iblk, psi_c, grad_norm_psi_e ), IF( i_am_accel_node .AND. acc_on )
!$ACC LOOP GANG
#else
!$OMP PARALLEL
!$OMP DO PRIVATE(jb,i_startidx,i_endidx,je,jk) SCHEDULE(runtime)
#endif
  DO jb = i_startblk, i_endblk
    CALL get_indices_e(ptr_patch, jb, i_startblk, i_endblk, i_startidx, i_endidx, rl_start, rl_end)
!$ACC LOOP VECTOR COLLAPSE(2)
#ifdef __LOOP_EXCHANGE
    DO je = i_startidx, i_endidx
      DO jk = slev, elev
#else
    DO jk = slev, elev
      DO je = i_startidx, i_endidx
#endif
! compute the normal derivative by the finite difference approximation
      grad_norm_psi_e(je,jk,jb) = ( psi_c(iidx(je,jb,2),jk,iblk(je,jb,2)) - &
        &    psi_c(iidx(je,jb,1),jk,iblk(je,jb,1)) ) * ptr_patch%edges%inv_dual_edge_length(je,jb)
      ENDDO
      ENDDO
    ENDDO
#ifdef _OPENACC
!$ACC END PARALLEL
#ifdef DEBUG_MATH_GRADIENT
!$ACC UPDATE HOST( ptr_delp_mc_new ), IF( i_am_accel_node )
    CALL check_patch_array(SYNC_E,p_patch, grad_norm_psi_e), "grad_norm_psi_e")
#endif
!$ACC END DATA
#else
!$OMP END DO NOWAIT
!$OMP END PARALLEL
#endif
```

The step into mainstream code development revealed numerous weaknesses in OpenACC, which would tend to bring its efficacy as a viable heterogeneous multicore programming paradigm into question. Listing 1 reveals that instances of derived types are used in the innermost loops which need to be vectorized on the GPU. This implies that these instances need to be deep-copied to the GPU at the beginning of the time integration loop. Support for full deep copy of derived types was not available in OpenACC 2.0 [7], and, despite extensive lobbying, was not included in OpenACC 2.5 [8], though it is envisaged for OpenACC 3.0. We have relied on a preliminary and unsupported implementation of full deep copy, part of the Cray CCE 8.3.x compiler.

Next, OpenACC compilers are not currently capable of locating subtle dependencies, and the resulting errors cannot be located with debuggers such DDT [11], whose OpenACC support proved insufficient for debugging ICON. There is currently no PE support for online validation; the only way to locate such bugs was to implement our own mechanism (Listing 1) to compare results from multiple MPI process GPU execution with single-threaded sequential execution.

Finally, the success of OpenACC is completely dependent on the expression of sufficient multi-level parallelism in the code. As Listing 1 reveals, ICON developers had the foresight to implement a blocking factor nproma (je loop, $1 \leq$ i_startidx $\leq$ i_endidx $\leq$ nproma) and array indexing (local index, level, block id) which performs adequately on both CPU and GPU, albeit with different values of nproma (CPU optimum 8 – 32, GPU optimum 128 – 1024, depending on resolution). Moreover, most intern loop pairs (je, jk) can be exchanged by setting a compiler flag. With the appropriate compilation and proper nproma values, the single-socket Intel Sandybridge + NVIDIA K20x nodes outperform dual-socket Intel Haswell nodes (Figure 2) by a factor commensurate to the ratio of obtainable memory bandwidth, typical for such bandwidth-limited calculations.

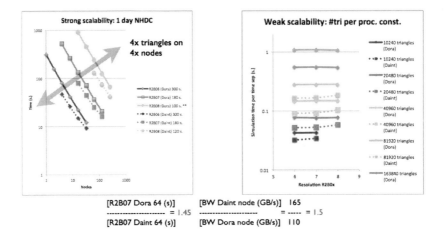

Figure 2. *The strong (left) and weak (right) scalability of the ICON dycore is compared for dual-socket Haswell nodes (solid lines) vs. hybrid Sandybridge/K20x nodes (dashed lines) for three different global resolutions. GPU strong scalability is worse than for CPU, but when the global grid just fits into GPU memory, e.g., 64 nodes for R2B05, the timings ratio is comparable to the ratio of achievable bandwidths from the stream benchmark (bottom).*

Thus the underlying message the alleged "ease" of using directives port to hybrid platforms will only yield performance if the underlying algorithm exhibits proper parallelism. If not, it is more effective to rewrite or change the algorithm entirely, probably using different paradigms, such as the domain-specific languages discussed in [12].

2. Case Study: Full-potential Linearized Augmented Plane Wave Method in Exciting

Early analysis of Exciting revealed a considerable code change was needed to scale it to a larger number of MPI ranks (by switching to ScaLAPACK) and then port it to a hybrid architecture. Furthermore, similar refactoring would have to be repeated for other LAPW codes. Thus, a decision in favor of the low-level domain-specific LAPW library was made. Since we were starting a new project we had the liberty to choose a convenient programming environment and programming model for the hybrid architectures. We selected C++ in combination with CUDA for the following reasons:

- C++ is a very rich and powerful language that provides both a low-level support such as pointer arithmetics and type casting, as well as a high-level abstractions such as classes and template meta-programming,

- easy interoperability between C++ and Fortran,
- access to the standard template library (STL),
- smooth integration with CUDA `nvcc` compiler,
- possibility to develop, debug and profile GPU code on a workstation or a laptop equipped with a GPU card using free tools (GCC, GDB, CUDA SDK, etc.),
- full control on the CUDA kernels and data offloading.

Figure 3 shows the configuration of Exciting code before and after refactoring. We kept the original Fortran90 implementation of LAPW intact and added calls to the new SIRIUS API. We think that this is a reasonable code contamination that the Exciting community can accept. Besides, we needed the canonical LAPW implementation to validate the new code.

Now we turn to the most important part of the discussion: scientific libraries. The bare minimum functionality necessary for Exciting code consists of distributed complex matrix-matrix multiplication (**pzgemm**) and distributed generalized eigenvalue problem solver (**pzhegvx**). Both functions are implemented in Cray's accelerated version of scientific library (LibSci_acc) and in theory should provide an optimal performance on the hybrid Cray XC30 platform. In practice, however, only the PBLAS part of the LibSci_acc performed well, and the ScaLAPACK part required a further improvement. A considerable effort to re-write the two-stage generalized eigenvalue solver targeting the hybrid CPU-GPU nodes was made.

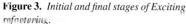

Figure 3. *Initial and final stages of Exciting refactoring.*

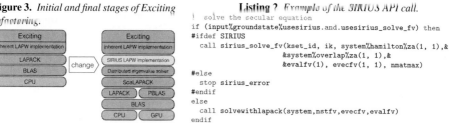

Listing 2. *Example of the SIRIUS API call.*

```
! solve the secular equation
if (input%groundstate%usesirius.and.usesirius_solve_fv) then
#ifdef SIRIUS
   call sirius_solve_fv(kset_id, ik, system%hamilton%za(1, 1),&
                        &system%overlap%za(1, 1),&
                        &evalfv(1), evecfv(1, 1), nmatmax)
#else
   stop sirius_error
#endif
else
   call solvewithlapack(system,nstfv,evecfv,evalfv)
endif
```

The Hybrid generalized eigensolver

Most of the electronic structure codes rely on the generalized eigenvalue solver. The reference distributed implementation of the Hermitian generalized eigenvalue solver is provided by ScaLAPACK. Since the eigensolver was encapsulated in a separate library we were free to select the programming paradigm. We chose C++ in combination with CUDA for the same reasons argued in the case of the SIRIUS library.

The implementation of the distributed GPU-enabled eigensolver is presented in [13]. The main challenge of GPU-enabled single node implementation was to hide the communication between the host memory and the device memory. This was achieved using the possibility to overlap the host-device communication with the computation. The distributed implementation introduced an extra level of communication — the communication between MPI ranks — which had to be overlapped to achieve good performance.

For instance during the eigenvectors back-transformation with the matrix Q_2 generated by the bulge-chasing, the communication cannot be hidden completely. In fact the

(a) Householder reflectors of the first group   (b) Householder reflectors of the second group

Figure 4. nvvp trace of the application of Householder reflector blocks.

diamond-shaped block of Householder vectors can be divided into two groups. The first group contains the blocks which affect only the part of the eigenvectors stored in only one row of the MPI communicator. In this case the implementation is straightforward. The Householder reflector block is prepared and distributed to the corresponding nodes, when the GPUs performs the application of the previous block. Figure 4a shows a trace produced by the Nvidia nvvp tool indicating that the CPU part (communication and the CPU operations) are overlapped with the GPU computation. On the other hand, the second group of Householder reflectors affect the part of the eigenvectors which are distributed on two different rows of the MPI communicator. In this case an extra reduction between the columns is required. Figure 4b shows the nvvp trace for the first implementation of this case. It is easy to notice that the performance is bad in this case, since the GPU is idle during most of the time. To solve this problem, the communication and the CPU part were optimized, and the number of blocks which belong to the second group was reduced.

The validation of linear algebra implementations was straightforward, since most of the routines had their own stand-alone tests. A different validation test was the comparison of the results of the new implementation with the reference implementation, e.g. ScaLAPACK. In the case of the generalized eigensolver, each subroutine can be tested separately. Moreover, generalized eigensolver results were easily validated, since each eigenvalue λ and eigenvector $\mathbf{x}$ pair has to fulfill the equation $A\mathbf{x} = \lambda B\mathbf{x}$.

3. Subjective Evaluation of the CSCS Hybrid Programming Environment

Experiences with the ICON and EXCITING applications have revealed many things about the underlying programming environment available on Cray hybrid systems. In the subsequent sections we recount some of the lessons learned and point to deficiencies we believe need to be addressed.

3.1. Compiler Support

The compiler support for hybrid platforms varies with the paradigm. While we found NVIDIA® CUDA-C++ to be robust, it lacks the full support of the C++ 11.[3] OpenCL implementations we used were also robust, but NVIDIA only supported OpenCL version 1.0 (rather than 1.1 or 1.2) at the time, limiting the functionality which could be used.[4] OpenACC support is limited to the PGI, Cray and ENZO-PathScale compilers.[5] Implementation deficiencies often caused compiler crashes, and CSCS reported numer-

---

[3]This deficiency was an issue in another CSCS-lead porting project[12]. CUDA 7 will support C++ 11.
[4]NVIDIA currently support OpenCL 1.2, but not yet 2.0.
[5]GCC 5 has preliminary OpenACC support.

ous bugs. Cray CCE is the only compiler that can perform full-deep copies of derived types used in ICON, and this functionality is not officially supported.

When considering the viability of using GPUs for production software, one must consider the added *programming and optimization overhead*. In our experience, adding OpenACC directives was much faster than formulating code in CUDA(fortran) or OpenCL, but the larger overhead by far was developing validation frameworks and unit tests. This implies that the alleged ease of directives is much less significant in the overall picture, particularly in view of the current limited OpenACC functionality and the lack of robustness of the compiler implementations.

3.2. Profiling and Debugging

Profiling tools such as ScoreP, Scalasca and TAU [9] have support for accelerators. But in our experience it was difficult to get these tools to work with large applications and often hard to properly interpret the traces and profiles. We have had more fortune with simpler tools such as NVIDIA `nvprof`, `nvvp`, and `cuda-memcheck`.

Proprietary debuggers, e.g., RogueWave TotalView [10] and Allinea DDT [11] have support for CUDA and OpenACC, but did not prove useful for the two use cases. There were numerous technical problems in compiling OpenACC-enabled modules in ICON with the Cray CCE compiler (8.3.12 and 8.4.0) in debugging mode. In the two use cases the built-in Cray debugging information activated by the `CRAY_ACC_DEBUG` environment variable proved invaluable, with reports on kernel execution and variable transfer between host and device. Indeed, we feel debugging of the Cray CCE OpenACC full deep copy was only possible thanks to this debugging mode.

Listing 3. *Off-line validation code for ICON. A source-to-source translator can expand the following* `savepoint` *code, adding calls to the serialization framework (roughly five times the number of lines of code). The fields* `pt` *and* `pq` *are both input and output of the* `PARALLEL` *region, and the corresponding serialization file contains* `test_counter` *as a suffix to indicate the call instance. Depending on* `ser_test_mode`, *values before the region are either written (e.g., for CPU-only reference execution) or read in to overwrite the fields. The latter is helpful in distinguishing GPU roundoff differences in the local time step from bugs creating larger errors which might get lost in the local error accumulation.*

```
!$ser init directory='.' prefix='Field'
!$ser savepoint cuadjtq.DoStep-in iteration=test_counter
!$ser mode ser_test_mode
!$ser data pt=pt(:,kk) pq=pq(:,kk)
!$ACC PARALLEL, IF (i_am_accel_node)
    :
!$ACC END PARALLEL
!$ser savepoint cuadjtq.DoStep-out iteration=test_counter
!$ser mode write
!$ser data pt=pt(:,kk) pq=pq(:,kk)
```

Still no debugger offers the functionality needed to validate results on the accelerator against those on the CPU. Until debuggers can provide this, developers are obligated to implement it themselves, for example with unit tests as in Exciting, or in the on-line ICON validation framework (`check_patch_array`) illustrated in Section 1.2. Moreover, we constructed an *off-line* testing framework which serializes fields from both CPU or GPU time-step execution. Since round-off errors quickly cause the trajectories of this highly non-linear problem to diverge, a facility is also available to overwrite intermediate device data with the "correct" host data. Thus GPU execution only yields round-off errors for the local time step. A source-to-source translator written in Python is needed to turn serialization directives (Listing 3) into the corresponding debugging code, as the former are acceptable in the development trunk while the latter is not.

4. Conclusions

We have gained extensive experiences with the Cray XC30 hybrid programming environment through the ICON and Exciting applications, and can say with certainty that it can be used successfully for real applications, albeit with considerable development overhead. Simpler but more crude tools such as nvprof for profiling or CRAY_ACC_DEBUG for debugging have proved more effectives with these non-trivial applications than more exotic ones. In addition, cruder programming paradigms (e.g., CUDA(fortran) or OpenCL) may be as effective as sophisticated ones, such as directives, because the underlying complexity of the latter detracts from the robustness of the compiler. In either case, we view the biggest development hurdle is to create a framework for validation of application components, and feel that more generic tools need to developed to support validation. We believe in the separation of concerns of science from the optimization of code for hybrid platforms, for which domain specific languages such as SIRIUS and numerical libraries such as MAGMA seem very promising.

References

[1]   W. R. L. Anderegg, J. W. Prall, J. Harold, and S. H. Schneider, *Expert credibility in climate change.* PNAS **107** (27), 12107–12109 (2010).
[2]   G. Zängl, D. Reinert, P. Ripodas, and M. Baldauf, *The ICON (ICOsahedral Non-hydrostatic) modelling framework of DWD and MPI-M: Description of the non-hydrostatic dynamical core.* QJRMS **141** (687), 563–579 (2015).
[3]   A. Gulans, S. Kontur, C. Meisenbichler, D. Nabok, P. Pavone, S. Rigamonti, S. Sagmeister, U. Werner, and C. Draxl, *Exciting: a full-potential all-electron package implementing density-functional theory and many-body perturbation theory.* Journal of Physics: Condensed Matter **26** (36) 363202, 2014.
[4]   https://github.com/electronic-structure/sirius
[5]   J. E. Stone, D. Ghoara, and G. Shi, *OpenCL: A Parallel Programming Standard for Heterogeneous Computing Systems.* IEEE Des. Test **12** (3), 66–73 (2010).
[6]   *CUDA Fortran Programming Guide and Reference.* https://www.pgroup.com/doc/pgicudaforug.pdf. 2015.
[7]   *The OpenACC Application Programming Interface, Version 2.0 (corrected).* http://www.openacc.org/sites/default/files/OpenACC.2.0a_1.pdf. August, 2013.
[8]   *The OpenACC Application Programming Interface, Version 2.5 (public comment version).* http://www.openacc.org/sites/default/files/OpenACC_2dot5_draft_for_public_comment_0.pdf. August, 2015.
[9]   W. Collins, D. T. Martinez, M. Monahan, and A. A. Munishkin, *Comparison of Performance Analysis Tools for Parallel Programs Applied to CombBLAS.* Technical Report HPCF-2015-28, hpcf.umbc.edu.
[10] http://www.roguewave.com/products-services/totalview
[11] *Allinea Forge User Guide Version 5.1.* http://content.allinea.com/downloads/userguide.pdf. August, 2015.
[12] O. Fuhrer, C. Osuna, X. Lapillonne, T. Gysi, B. Cumming, M. Bianco, A. Arteaga, and T. C. Schulthess, *Towards a performance portable, architecture agnostic implementation strategy for weather and climate models* Supercomputing Frontiers and Innovations **1** (1), 45–62 (2014).
[13] R. Solcà, A. Kozhevnikov, A. Haidar, S. Tomov, and T. C. Schulthess, *Efficient Implementation of Quantum Materials Simulations on Distributed CPU-GPU Systems*, in High Performance Computing, Networking, Storage and Analysis, SC15: in press.

Parallel Computing: On the Road to Exascale
G.R. Joubert et al. (Eds.)
IOS Press, 2016
© 2016 The authors and IOS Press. All rights reserved.
doi:10.3233/978-1-61499-621-7-673

673

SYCL: Single-source C++ accelerator programming

Ruyman REYES [1] Victor LOMÜLLER [2]

Codeplay Software Ltd
Level C, Argyle House
3 Lady Lawson Street,
Edinburgh, EH3 9DR, UK

Abstract. Hybrid systems have been massively adopted in high performance clusters and scientific applications. The latest Top500 [1] HPC list shows an increased number of heterogeneous processing elements in the latest systems. This trend continues to grow, and it is expected that future Exascale systems will include a number of hybrid cores (GPUs, FPGAs and others). In order to face these new complex architectures, scientists and engineers need more powerful and flexible programming environments. New programming environments have been designed to program these new hybrid systems. However existing libraries and scientific applications are yet to be ported, and the effort of doing so is noticeable. Members of the heterogeneous programming community, including both academia and industry, are working under the umbrella of the Khronos Group to design new programming environments for these platforms. One of the outcomes of this work has been SYCL [2]: A C++ cross-platform abstraction layer that builds on the underlying concepts, portability and efficiency of OpenCL. SYCL offers intuitive single-source development for accelerators using C++ templated functions, and can greatly facilitate porting existing C++ code to heterogeneous architectures. In this work we present the main features of the SYCL interface that had been added to complement OpenCL [3] towards the usage on more complex and high-level codes.

Keywords. OpenCL, Programmability, GPU, Exascale, C++

Introduction

When the first OpenCL specification became available, it was welcomed by application and driver developers as a standard and portable interface that would greatly facilitate the usage of accelerators for general purpose computation in multiple platforms. However, the C interface of OpenCL still requires a noticeable programming effort. In particular, there are two aspects of OpenCL that reduces its programmability: (1) Kernels are written as C strings and (2) The host interface requires several calls to multiple low-level set-up functions.

Both (1) and (2) have been a barrier for the usage of OpenCL in C++ code bases, where application developers are used to a high-level abstraction to the resources. Al-

---

[1] ruyman@codeplay.com
[2] victor@codeplay.com

though it is possible to encapsulate low-level OpenCL host API calls into user-created objects or libraries, this continues to demand development effort, and contributes to the creation of a disparate collection of C++ interfaces for OpenCL that are normally tied up to certain usage pattern, limiting reusability. In addition, (1) forces developer to rely on online compilation to detect errors on their code, and reduces the ability of developers to write type-safe code between host and device.

Due to this limitations, the Khronos Group decided to start working on a High Level Model (HLM) for OpenCL that would facilitate the usage of OpenCL in high-level environments, with C++ developers as the main target group. The work of the HLM subgroup of the OpenCL lead to the publication of the first SYCL provisional specification in 2014, based on the OpenCL 1.2 specification. Positive feedback from users, and some recommendations from implementors lead to a final specification in May 2015 that featured improved C++ integration, such as Allocators, Smart Pointers and many more.

SYCL has been designed to integrate seamlessly on C++ code-bases, by relying on many concepts familiar to C++ developers, such as Object Oriented programing, RAII (Resource Acquisition Is Initialization) or Template meta-programming. In this work we detail SYCL features that simplify programming in hybrid systems. Section 1 presents other existing C++-based programming models for accelerators and they are compared with SYCL features. Section 2 illustrates the basic capabilities of SYCL to reduce the programming effort, such as the single-source programming or the implicit generation of a task graph. Section 3 focuses on the SYCL design aspects that improves its resilience on hardware or software errors. Section 4 presents the Hierarchical Parallelism, a simplified way of expressing workgroup-level parallelism using C++ constructs. To wrap-up, Section 5 presents some final remarks, along with potential lines of work by the SYCL group.

1. Related Work

The existing literature describes many attempts at improving the programmability of accelerators. In this short review we focus on those with industrial and production-ready approaches.

One of the first popular approaches of programming GPU accelerators was CUDA [4] (Compute Unified Device Architecture). CUDA is a parallel computing platform and programming model that enables developers to harness the power of GPU devices. It has been developed by NVIDIA, and is available only on their GPUs. CUDA facilitates the development of GPU programs by supporting a C/C++ programming environment. C++ functions can be called from inside kernels, but must be annotated with a specific keyword. SYCL does not require non-standard annotations of the code, and SYCL programs can be executed without the use of a GPU device.

In High Performance Computing (HPC) environments, OpenACC [5] and OpenMP [6] are two popular standards that use pragmas/sentinels in C/C++ and Fortran to automatically generate task or loop-level parallelism. OpenACC specifically aims to produce kernels for accelerators. The latest revision of the OpenMP standard offers a set of directives to enable the generation of code to accelerators. Both standards are particularly useful to adapt legacy code. The code to parallelize is annotated using pragma directives to express parallelism or data movement. SYCL is a completely integrated modern C++

approach that does not rely on compiler extensions, integrating easier with development workflows.

Microsoft presented C++ AMP [7] (C++ Accelerated Massive Parallelism) as an open specification that allows the implementation of data parallelism directly in C++. It has been designed to facilitate the programming of accelerators. Although the programming model is open, the specification is highly tied to their initial approach based on DirectX and requires the compiler to support the programming model, whereas SYCL allow developers to use standard C++ compiler for the host code and interact with a specific device compiler.

Finally, the C++ community has presented many approaches to high-level interfaces for OpenCL. In particular, Boost.Compute [8] is a high-level C++ library that facilitates the integration of OpenCL into C++ codebases. It offers a set of containers and algorithms, together with the functionality of write partially customized functions for those algorithms. Boost.Compute relies on string manipulation to generate OpenCL kernels and the interface is limited to the algorithms and iterators provided. On the other hand, SYCL does not provide iterators or containers, but provides a flexible interface that directly produces binary device code from C++ without any additional restrictions than the hardware limitations. A separate project, Khronos Parallel STL [9] offers an STL-like interface built on top of SYCL.

2. Improved programmability

A SYCL program is based around the idea of command groups, atomic entities that define the data requirements of an accelerator kernel, alongside with the kernel itself in the form of a C++ functor. Listing 1 shows an excerpt of a simple vector addition program written in SYCL. The equivalent OpenCL code, assuming a completely blocking behaviour, would require around 57 lines of code, including the kernel. An asynchronous OpenCL implementation would require more lines of code in order to deal with the synchronization events.

Data is handled via SYCL memory objects, `buffer` and `image`. Users can provide an existing host pointer when constructing the memory object, or can rely on the host runtime to allocate data on the host. The pointer is managed by the runtime for the lifetime of the memory object. When the destructor of the memory object is called, data is synchronized to the host if requested by the user. The API also allows setting a specific pointer to copy data back via the `set_final_data` pointer. Standard C++ allocators can be used on SYCL buffers, enabling the SYCL runtime to take advantage of NUMA-aware allocators or advanced shared memory mechanisms.

The *command group* defined in line 7 contains all the dependencies for the data used in the kernel in the form of a wrapper class called accessors. Accessors are used to get access to the data inside the kernel, effectively adding compile-time checking of the correct access mode (i.e. trying to write a read only variable will cause a compile-time error).

The SYCL runtime will transparently make data available for the kernel in the most optimal way for the platform (copying data, mapping memory regions or using implementation-specific mechanisms), keeping coherence between host and the accelerator(s) whenever is required. Dependencies alongside queues, command groups and

Listing 1: Excerpt of a vector addition in SYCL

```
1   queue myQueue; // Creation of a default SYCL queue
2   {
3     buffer<float, 1> d_a(h_a, range<1>(LENGTH));
4     buffer<float, 1> d_b(h_b, range<1>(LENGTH));
5     buffer<float, 1> d_r(h_r, range<1>(LENGTH));
6     // Definition of a command group functor
7     auto command_group = [&](handler& cgh) {
8       auto a = d_a.get_access<access::mode::read>(cgh);
9       auto b = d_b.get_access<access::mode::read>(cgh);
10      auto r = d_r.get_access<access::mode::read_write>(cgh);
11      cgh.parallel_for<class vec_add> (range<1>(count),
12                   [=](id<1> i) { r[i] = a[i] + b[i]; });
13    });
14    myQueue.submit(cg);
15  } // Buffer destruction implies host synchronization
```

devices are automatically handled by the runtime, simplifying the creation of libraries and potentially enabling distant parallelism (e.g. two separate libraries using SYCL can synchronize their kernels without user intervention).

Given that accelerators are separate devices with their own instruction set, they need to execute separate programs from the host machine that holds them. This typically requires programmers to write separate source codes for the accelerator and the host: the kernel(s) source and the host source. SYCL simplifies accelerator programmability by offering a single-source programming mechanism. The functor defined as a lambda in line 11 gets passed into the `parallel_for` SYCL API call. This functor is the device-side kernel, written as standard C++ code. Apart from the usual restrictions due to hardware limitations (i.e, no recursion or dynamic memory allocation), the user can write standard C++ code, calling any existing defined functions. Any standard C++ compiler can produce a binary for the host platform, whereas a SYCL-enabled compiler will generate device code from the body of the `parallel_for`.

Generic programming in traditional OpenCL programs was restricted to using a string manipulation mechanism, where the program was constructed as a string at runtime, and then passed to the OpenCL driver fronted, that will finally compile and build the kernel at runtime. However, when using SYCL, device-kernels are represented by standard-layout C++ functors. That allows developers to use powerful C++ generic programming techniques to write generic device-kernels. In Listing 2 we illustrate a generic axpy kernel, that can be instantiated to any valid type. Note that this allow also user-specified types that overload the appropriate operators (multiplication and addition in this case).

Command groups that call kernels can also be templated, allowing for complex composition of functors and types, as shown in Listing 3. Using command group functors facilitates code *composability*. Command group functors can be re-used to repeat the same operation on multiple input data. Since dependencies are extracted at runtime, code can be re-ordered without the need of manually handling data synchronization operations.

Listing 4 shows how the previously defined command group and kernel can be re-used for several calls with different input data. The code creates two queues in two separate devices that are on the same context (such a device with integrated CPU/GPU).

Listing 2: A templated kernel functor for AXPY

```
1   template<typename T>
2   using ro_acc = accessor<T, 1, access::mode::read,
3                           access::target::global_buffer>;
4
5   template<typename T>
6   using wo_acc = accessor<T, 1, access::mode::write,
7                           access::target::global_buffer>;
8
9   template<typename T>
10  struct axpy_kernel {
11    T alpha;
12    ro_acc<T> ptrA, ptrB;
13    wo_acc<T> ptrC;
14
15    axpy_kernel(T alpha, ro_acc<T> ptrA_,
16              ro_acc<T> ptrB_, wo_acc<T> ptrC_)
17    : ptrA(ptrA_), ptrB(ptrB_), ptrC(ptrC_) { }
18
19    void operator()(id<1> id) {
20        ptrC[id] = (alpha * ptrA[id]) + ptrB[id];
21    };
22  };
```

Listing 3: A templated command group for axpy

```
1   template<class T, class B1, class B2, class B3, class nElemsT>
2   struct axpy_functor {
3     B1 bA; B2 bB; B3 bC;
4     nElemsT nElems;
5     T scalar;
6
7     axpy_functor(T scalar_, B1 bA_,
8               B2 bB_, B3 bC_, nElemsT nElems_)
9     : scalar(scalar_), bA(bA_), bB(bB_),
10       bC(bC_), nElems(nElems_) { }
11
12    void operator()(handler& cgh) {
13       auto ptrA = bA.template get_access<access::mode::read>(cgh);
14       auto ptrB = bB.template get_access<access::mode::read>(cgh);
15       auto ptrC = bC.template get_access<access::mode::write>(cgh);
16
17       cgh.parallel_for(range<1>(nElems),
18                  axpy_kernel<T>(scalar, ptrA, ptrB, ptrC));
19    }
20  };
```

initQueue will be used to initialize data, whereas runQueue will be used to execute the *saxpy* kernels. For simplicity, the creation of the buffers and constant is not shown. make_saxpy_functor is a trivial function that forwards the parameters to the call of the constructor.

The SYCL API allows users to trivially instantiate a *saxpy* command group, and

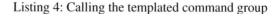

Listing 4: Calling the templated command group

```
1    ...
2    context ctxt;
3    queue initQueue(cxt, ctxt.get_devices()[0]);
4    queue runQueue(cxt, ctxt.get_devices()[1]);
5    initQueue.submit(initialize<float>(bufA));
6    initQueue.submit(initialize<float>(bufB));
7    initQueue.submit(initialize<float>(bufE));
8    initQueue.submit(initialize<float>(bufG));
9    runQueue.submit(make_saxpy_functor<float>(ALPHA, bufA, bufB, bufC,
         NELEMS));
10   runQueue.submit(make_saxpy_functor<float>(ALPHA, bufE, bufC, bufD,
         NELEMS));
11   runQueue.submit(make_saxpy_functor<float>(BETA, bufG, bufD, bufF,
         NELEMS));
12   runQueue.wait();
13   ...
```

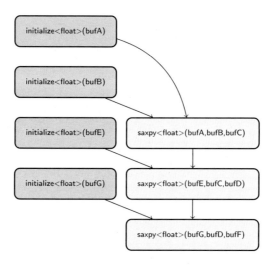

Figure 1. Nodes of the graph represent Kernels, and the lines its dependencies. A line from Node A to Node B indicates that Kernel B needs the result of Kernel A to finish. The colors represent the user-defined SYCL queues. SYCL command groups are executed in the order given by its dependencies independently of the queues they were submitted to without the user intervention.

apply the operation to the different buffers she is using in her code. When a command group is submitted to the queue, the SYCL runtime extracts the dependencies w.r.t the command groups already enqueued *in any other SYCL queue*. The ability of track inter-queue dependencies enables the SYCL runtime to interleave the initialization of data with the execution of kernels. The command groups enqueued to both `initQueue` and `runQueue` will be executed in the order given by their input/output dependencies, as shown in Figure 1. Note that potential memory operations are automatically performed by the runtime if/when required.

Listing 5: Calling the templated command group

```
1    ...
2    host_selector hS;
3    queue mainQueue;    // Default queue
4    queue fallback(hS);    // Host queue
5    mainQueue.submit(initialize<double>(bufA), fallback);
6    mainQueue.submit(initialize<double>(bufB), fallback);
7    mainQueue.submit(
8        make_saxpy_functor<double>(ALPHA, bufA, bufB, bufC, NELEMS),
9        fallback);
```

3. Resilience to accelerator failures

One of the main goals of the SYCL group while working on the specification was to improve the resilience of applications built on top of OpenCL. A SYCL implementation will always have a host-fallback version of the kernel that is generated for the GPU (simply by internally preserving the user-given C++ functor). A host executor can be used to run the user-given kernel directly on the host if no OpenCL platform is available. Queues can be created from host-only devices, and command groups can be enqueued on queues created from the host device without requiring any change. This also facilitates debugging of kernels, since they can be executed on a host queue as normal C++ code, which can be debugged using traditional CPU tools.

In addition to the host queues, when submitting a command group to a queue, it is possible to specify a secondary *fall-back* queue. If the command-group fails to execute on the primary queue, the runtime will automatically execute the command group in the *fall-back* queue. Any memory copy operation or dependency resolution is transparently resolved by the runtime. An example call is shown in Listing 5, where a host queue is used as a *fall-back* queue for the kernels. If the default device where the kernel is executed does not support double-precision computation, the runtime will automatically switch back to the fallback queue in the host and continue to compute the result.

Error handling in SYCL is exposed via exceptions. A hierarchy of exception classes is defined and users can catch the specific ones their are interested on. Asynchronous exceptions (i.e. exceptions produced by the accelerator device asynchronously from the host) are captured by the SYCL runtime and stored internally. An asynchronous exception can be thrown if there was no *fall-back* queue for a failed command group, or if the command-group failed while already on the fall-back. Users can define per-queue asynchronous error handling functions. These functions receive a list of exceptions captured by the runtime as a parameter, and enable fine-grain control to developers to decide what and when to react to asynchronous errors. The asynchronous error handler is called when the user calls the *wait_and_throw* method on the queue. Listing 6 illustrates the usage of the Async Handler. Developers can submit multiple kernels to the same queue with the guarantee that no asynchronous exceptions will be thrown until the call to wait and throw in line 18. The *asyncHandler* lambda is called then and all the asynchronous exceptions that have been captured by the runtime will provided to the user via the *exception_list* object.

The usage of asynchronous handlers for asynchronous errors guarantees developers that applications will not be stopped randomly by errors on accelerators. Develop-

Listing 6: Calling the templated command group

```
1     ...
2     auto asyncHandler = [=](cl::sycl::exception_list eL) {
3         for (auto& ePtr : eL) {
4             try {
5                 std::rethrow_exception(ePtr);
6             } catch (cl::sycl::feature_not_supported& fN) {
7                 error("The Accelerator does not support the required
                        feature");
8             } catch (cl::sycl::exception sE) {
9                 handle_internal_sycl_error(sE);
10            }
11        }
12    };
13    queue mainQueue(device, asyncHandler);
14    mainQueue.submit(initialize<double>(bufA));
15    mainQueue.submit(initialize<double>(bufB));
16    mainQueue.submit(
17        make_saxpy_functor<double>(ALPHA, bufA, bufB, bufC, NELEMS));
18    mainQueue.wait_and_throw();
```

ers can write customized asynchronous handlers for different situations. Note that non-asynchronous exceptions are thrown normally by the runtime, and can be captured by traditional *try/catch* blocks.

4. Hierarchical Parallelism

SYCL introduces a specific API to work with the workgroup and the workitem hierarchy. Some algorithms work by selecting one thread that performs data transfers form the global memory to the local one or to perform a reduction. To deal with such algorithms, SYCL exposes `parallel_for_work_group` and `parallel_for_work_item` to work at workgroup and workitem level respectively.

Instead of manually introducing guards to select the actual working thread, a user can invoke a kernel by calling `parallel_for_work_group` from a command group handler. Listing 7 presents a simple example using this API. The lambda or functor called by this method will only be executed once per workgroup and all variables declared inside this scope has the semantic of a local variable. To execute code per workitem, the user calls the `parallel_for_work_item function`. The lambda or functor provided to this function will be executed per workitem. To ensure memory coherence, there is an implicit thread synchronization for each `parallel_for_work_item` calls.

The kernel is invoked using `parallel_for_work_group`. The code in the given lambda will be executed once per workgroup and all variables declared inside this scope will store the value in the local memory. This means that on line 6, the integer array `local_sums` is allocated in the local memory and so its values are shared across workitems of the workgroup. On line 8, we make a call to `parallel_for_work_item`. The code in the lambda will be executed per workitem (like a standard `parallel_for`) and all declared variables are private. At the end of this call, all threads are implicitly synchronized. Finally, the last loop perform the final reduction at a workgroup level. An

Listing 7: Excerpt of a vector reduction in SYCL using the Hierarchical API

```
1   auto input_ptr = input_buf.get_access<access::mode::read>(cgh);
2   auto sum_ptr = sum_buf.get_access<access::mode::write>(cgh);
3
4   cgh.parallel_for_work_group<class Kernel0>(
5       range<1>(GROUP_RANGE), range<1>(LOCAL_RANGE), [=](group<1>
            groupID) {
6           int local_sums[LOCAL_RANGE];
7
8           parallel_for_work_item(groupID, [&](item<1> itemID) {
9               int global_id = itemID.get_range().size() * groupID.
                    get_linear() +
10                              itemID.get_linear_id();
11              int values_per_item =
12                  (input_ptr.get_size() / groupID.get_group_range().size())
                      /
13                  itemID.get_range().size();
14              int id_start = values_per_item * global_id;
15              int id_end = min(id_start + values_per_item, input_ptr.
                    get_size());
16
17              int sum = 0;
18              for (int i = id_start; i < id_end; i++)
19                  sum += input_ptr[i];
20              local_sums[itemID.get_linear_id()] = sum;
21          });
22
23          int sum = 0;
24          for (int i = 0; i < LOCAL_RANGE; i++) sum += local_sums[i];
25          sum_ptr[groupID.get_linear()] = sum;
26      });
```

important point optimization point on lines 23 and 24 is that the specification allow the compiler to allocate variables sum and i in the private space. As those variable are not captured by a lambda used in a parallel_for_work_item, it is the equivalent of allocating them in the private or in the local memory.

This API (enabled by the C++11 features) aims to provide a simple abstraction to work with the multi-level parallelism of the OpenCL API.

5. Conclusions and Future Work

We have shown how SYCL offers many interesting features for Hybrid Supercomputers. Built on top of existing OpenCL, SYCL eases the integration of accelerators on C++ applications and libraries.

With the announcement of the SYCL specification and the announcements of the first vendor implementations, there are plenty of opportunities to grow an ecosystem of SYCL applications for hybrid platforms. The Khronos Group has announced a Parallel STL implementation [9] based on SYCL aimed to support the future C++17 standard.

The SYCL group is continuing to move forward, working in the next SYCL specification that will be built on top of the next version of the OpenCL standard, adding features such as shared virtual memory or enqueuing kernels from inside the device itself.

There are several research lines being explored at Codeplay based on SYCL, with particular focus on large-scale image processing and computer vision, and the integration with other programming models, such as mixing SYCL with MPI or SHMEM to completely take advantage of modern large scale HPC systems. Furthermore, the SYCL API can be extended to cover distributed memory platforms, or integrate with existing approaches such as C++ Coarrays [10] or UPC++ [11].

References

[1] Top 500, *Top 500 Supercomputer list*, http://www.top500.org
[2] SYCL, *SYCL: C++ Single-Source Heterogeneous programming for OpenCL*, http://www.khronos.org/sycl
[3] OpenCL, *OpenCL : The Open Standard for parallel programming on heterogeneous systems*, http://www.khronos.org/opencl
[4] CUDA, *Scalable Parallel Programming with CUDA* http://doi.acm.org/10.1145/1365490.1365500
[5] OpenACC, *The OpenACC Application Programming Interface* http://www.openacc.org/sites/default/files/OpenACC.2.0a_1.pdf
[6] OpenMP, *OpenMP Application Program Interface* http://www.openmp.org/mp-documents/OpenMP4.0.0.pdf
[7] C++AMP, *C++ Accelerated Massive Parallelism* https://msdn.microsoft.com/en-us/library/hh265137.aspx
[8] Boost.Compute, *The Boost Compute library* http://boostorg.github.io/compute/
[9] SYCL Parallel STL, *A C++17 Parallel STL implementation using SYCL*, https://github.com/KhronosGroup/SyclParallelSTL
[10] Johnson, T.A., *Coarray C++*, Proceedings of the 7th International Conference on PGAS Programming Models
[11] Zheng, Y., Kamil, A., Driscoll, M.B., Shan, H., Yelick, K., *UPC++: A PGAS Extension for C++*, 2014 IEEE 28th International Parallel and Distributed Processing Symposium

Parallel Computing: On the Road to Exascale
G.R. Joubert et al. (Eds.)
IOS Press, 2016
© 2016 The authors and IOS Press. All rights reserved.
doi:10.3233/978-1-61499-621-7-683

Using Task-Based Parallelism Directly on the GPU for Automated Asynchronous Data Transfer

Aidan B G CHALK [a], Pedro GONNET [a,b] and Matthieu SCHALLER [c]

[a] *School of Engineering and Computing Sciences, Durham University, United Kingdom*
[b] *Google Switzerland GmbH, Brandschenkestrasse 110, 8002 Zurich, Switzerland*
[c] *Institute for Cosmological Cosmology, Durham University, United Kingdom*

Abstract We present a framework, based on the QuickSched[1] library, that implements priority-aware task-based parallelism directly on CUDA GPUs. This allows large computations with complex data dependencies to be executed in a single GPU kernel call, removing any synchronisation points that might otherwise be required between kernel calls. Using this paradigm, data transfers to and from the GPU are modelled as load and unload tasks. These tasks are automatically generated and executed alongside the rest of the computational tasks, allowing fully asynchronous and concurrent data transfers. We implemented a tiled-QR decomposition, and a Barnes-Hut gravity calculation, both of which show significant improvement when utilising the task-based setup, effectively eliminating any latencies due to data transfers between the GPU and the CPU. This shows that task-based parallelism is a valid alternative programming paradigm on GPUs, and can provide significant gains from both a data transfer and ease-of-use perspective.

Keywords. Task-based parallelism, general-purpose GPU computing, Asynchronous data transfer

Introduction

Task-based parallelism is a method for shared memory parallel programming in which a program is split into a series of tasks, which are picked up and executed by a set of cores in parallel until the computation is completed. To avoid concurrency issues, the *dependencies* between tasks need to be considered, i.e. given two tasks, A and B, where task A produces a result needed to compute task B, B is dependent on A, or A *unlocks* B. The tasks and their dependencies form a Directed Acyclic Graph (DAG).

Emails for each author: aidan.chalk@durham.ac.uk, pedro.gonnet@durham.ac.uk, matthieu.schaller@durham.ac.uk

Task-based parallelism has two major advantages over traditional parallel processing techniques: Firstly, since the tasks are assigned to the cores dynamically, the work is automatically load balanced, i.e. no core will run idle if there are still tasks to be computed. Secondly, the task dependencies avoid the necessity of any explicit synchronization between the cores, i.e. no core will sit idly waiting on data being computed by another core if any other work is available.

Projects such as QUARK [2], Cilk [3], SMPSuperscalar [4], StarPU [5], OpenMP 3.0 [6], OmpSs [7] and Intel TBB [8] all implement various forms of task-based parallelism on multi-core CPUs. Additionally, StarPU and OmpSs can use the GPU to execute individual tasks, although these are scheduled by the CPU. To our knowledge, no library currently implements task-based parallelism directly on the GPU.

In this paper we introduce an extension to our own task scheduling library, QuickSched[1], providing general-purpose task-based parallelism implemented directly on the GPU using CUDA [9]. We also introduce the automatic generation of tasks that automatically move data needed for the computation between the GPU and the host. Executing these tasks alongside the rest of the computation allows fully asynchronous and concurrent data transfers between the CPU and the GPU. Finally, we briefly describe two test problems to illustrate the method, and its advantages are compared to more traditional GPU computing techniques.

1. The QuickSched Programming Model

There are two main paradigms for generating task dependencies:

- Implicitly by spawning and waiting, such as in Cilk[3]
- Automatic Extraction from data dependencies, as done in OmpSs[7].

These setups both have advantages, but are both limited with respect to the dependency structures they can accurately represent.

Using QuickSched, the user specifies a number of *tasks*, and tells the library the task type, the data required to decode the task, plus an estimate of the task cost. Once these have been specified, the library must be informed of any dependencies between tasks. Additionally, the user specifies *resources*, which usually represent an area in memory. The tasks will normally *use* and/or *lock* a number of resources, which usually represents read or read/write access to a resource. Before a task is executed by the scheduler, the scheduler attempts to lock any resources required by the task. If this locking is successful, then the task is executed. If the locking is unsuccessful, then a *conflicting* task must be being executed, so any acquired locks are released and the task is returned to the queue.

Whilst the programmer is required to provide more information to the scheduler than in other programming models, we believe there are two advantages to this setup:

- It gives the user full flexibility with regards to the structure of the task graph generated.
- Knowing the complete structure of the task graph before execution allows the task scheduler to make more informed decisions as to which tasks should be prioritized.

2. Task-Based Parallelism on CUDA GPUs

The predominant programming paradigm for CUDA[2] GPUs has been to treat them as large vector machines, repeating the same set of instructions known as *kernels*, on large datasets in lock-step, i.e. "Single Instruction, Multiple Thread" (SIMT) parallelism. This approach is effective for problems that vectorize easily. Unfortunately, many problems cannot be easily vectorized and thus currently cannot be efficiently ported to these devices.

GPUs have a number of significant differences compared to regular shared memory parallel systems. A CUDA GPU consists of many *streaming multiprocessors* (SMs), which each currently contain up to 192 cores. The computation is split into *blocks* of up to 512 threads each. Each block is assigned to an SM when created, and run only on that SM during its lifetime. These blocks are then further broken down into *warps* of 32 threads each. The GPU executes each warp of threads in *strict* lock-step parallelism, i.e. all 32 threads execute the same instruction simultaneously.

Individual blocks have no explicit mechanisms to communicate with each other, yet synchronization between blocks can nevertheless be achieved by using atomic operations on values in global memory.

Despite the vectorized programming model, the hardware itself can be viewed as a multithreaded multi-core computer, where every block is conceptually equivalent to a single core executing with a small number of threads in parallel. In principle we could use task-based parallelism directly on the GPU by launching a set of blocks and letting each block dynamically select and execute tasks in parallel. The tasks themselves are executed in SIMT parallelism using only the threads within each block. Doing so requires implementing the infrastructure for dynamic task allocation and requires tasks that efficiently exploit SIMT parallelism, albeit for a small number of threads.

We implement task-based parallelism on CUDA GPUs as follows. The main GPU kernel that is executed is given below in CUDA-like pseudocode:

```
1   __global__ task_based_kernel(struct scheduler *s,
2                                 function *task_func) {
3     __shared__ int tid;
4     while(scheduler.stillHasTasks){
5       if(threadIdx.x == 0){
6         tid = scheduler_gettask(s);
7       }
8       __syncthreads();
9       task_func(tid);
10      schduler_unlockdependencies(s,tid);
11    }
12  }
```

In lines 5-7, the first thread in each block retrieves a task from the scheduler. The rest of the block waits at the barrier in line 8 until this process completes. In

---

[2]OpenCL uses a similar programming paradigm, however this paper focuses only on CUDA.

line 9 the task is then decoded and executed by the user-supplied task function
using all the threads of that block in parallel. After the task has been executed,
dependent tasks are unlocked in line 10. This process is repeated until all of the
tasks are complete (line 4).

The scheduler itself relies on task queues which allow exclusive access to each
task, i.e. prevent any task being assigned to more than one block for execution.
In a multi-core system, operations on task queues can be wrapped in mutual
exclusion operators (*mutexes*), meaning only one processor can access a task queue
at a time. On GPUs, this strategy can be expensive, since locking and unlocking
mutexes via atmoic operations on global variable is relatively expensive, and many
more blocks than there are cores on a CPU will access the queues simultaneously,
causing more frequent blockages. We therefore use *lock-free* double-ended queues
(DEQs). The code used to retrieve a task as well as the queue struct is given
below, in CUDA-like pseudocode:

```
1   struct queue{
2       int first, last;
3       volatile int count;
4       volatile int *data;
5       volatile int nr_avail_tasks;
6   }
7
8   __device__ gettask(struct queue *q) {
9     int ind;
10    if( atomicAdd((int*)&q->nr_avail_tasks, -1) <= 0)
11      {
12        atomicAdd((int*)&q->nr_avail_tasks, 1);
13        return -1;
14      }
15    ind = atomicAdd(&q->first, 1);
16    ind %= qsize;
17    tid = q->data[ind];
18    if ( tid >= 0 )
19      {
20        q->data[ind] = -1;
21        atomicAdd((int*) &tot_num_tasks, -1);
22      }
23    return tid;
24  }
```

The queues have two counters, `first` and `last` (line 2). These counters are
used to keep track of where the task indices are in the DEQ. The `nr_avail_tasks`
variable (line 5) keeps a count of how many tasks are in the queue, and is atomically incremented whenever a task is added, and atomically decremented whenever a task is removed (line 10). To ensure correctness, the value is marked as
`volatile` so it is always read from global memory. Before a block tries to retrieve
a task from a queue, it first checks whether the queue is empty (line 10). If it is,
the check is reverted in line 12 and a null task index (-1) is returned in line 13.

To retrieve a task, `first` is incremented atomically (which gives the index
of the first task in the queue, shown in line 15). Since the queue acts as a circular buffer, the index is then wrapped in line 16. The process then pulls out

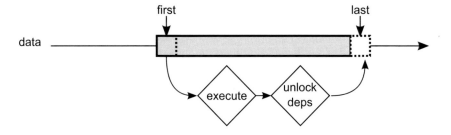

Figure 1. Schematic of the queue data structure. The indices of unexecuted tasks are stored in data, between first and last-1.

the task index (line 17). We know this is populated by a valid task index, as `nr_avail_tasks` is only incremented after an index is added to the queue. Finally, if a valid task index was found (line 18) the task index is overwritten by a -1 (line 20), and the global counter of tasks that need to be executed is decremented (line 21). The task index is then returned (line 23).

A similar operation is performed to add a task to a queue:

```
1  __device__ puttask(struct queue *q, int tid) {
2      ind - atomicAdd(&q->last, 1);
3      ind %= qsize;
4      while ( q->data[ind] != -1 );
5      q->data[ind] = tid;
6      atomicAdd(nr_avail_tasks, 1);
7  }
```

The `last` counter is incremented (line 2) and wrapped (line 3). In line 4, the scheduler may have to wait for the slot to be empty, so may wait here. The task index is then added to the queue (line 5) and finally the `nr_avail_tasks` counter is incremented in line 6.

Additionally, the GPU scheduler supports discrete levels of task priorities. There are n task queues which each represent a distinct priority level for all tasks assigned to them. The function `scheduler_gettask` tries to obtain a task index from the first queue, and if unsuccessful (due to that queue being empty) then tries the queue of next highest priority. This is repeated until it retrieves a valid task index.

2.1. Automated asynchronous data transfer between the GPU and the CPU

One weakness of the current GPU programming model is the requirement to move data to and from the device over the PCI-Express bus. The standard method is to use `cudaMemcpy` calls before and after kernels, meaning the data needed for the entire computation is copied before any work can be done, even with

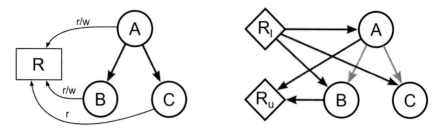

Figure 2. Tasks A, B and C all access the resource R. A and B read and write to it, while C only reads the data (as shown by the thin arrows in the left diagram). In QuickSched, two tasks R_l and R_u are generated which load and unload the resource R to and from the GPU. Since all the tasks A, B and C read from the resource, dependencies from the load task R_l are added automatically. As only A and B write to the resource, the associated unload task R_u is dependent on only A and B.

streaming and multiple kernels[3]. Newer versions of CUDA do allow access to CPU memory directly from device kernels, however these accesses are no faster than using `cudaMemcpy` directly.

Using the task-based scheme we can model the reading and writing of data to and from the GPU as individual tasks, with the necessary dependencies, and execute them during the computation. Assuming that the data required for each computational task is known, the load and unload tasks can be generated automatically.

Recall that in QuickSched, the data used by each task is represented by hierarchical *resources*. The user also specifies whether a task writes to the memory, or only reads from it.

Once the resources and tasks are specified, and the scheduler is aware of how the resources are used by the tasks, the scheduler creates tasks to load and unload each resource's data. To ensure that no resource is used before it is has been loaded, we generate a dependency from each load task to each task reading from the corresponding resource, and each unload task is dependent on every task that writes to the corresponding resource. This is shown in Figure 2. Some of the dependencies generated by the system are redundant, e.g. in Figure 2 it is not necessary for R_l to unlock B, as A depends on R_l and B depends on A. Detecting and removing these redundant dependencies is significantly more costly than the overheads incurred by leaving them in the system.

In the presence of hierarchical tasks, we don't create load and unload tasks for every resource. If a hierarchical resource has a large amount of data associated with it, we instead create load and unload tasks for its children. The resource is then made dependent on its children for loading and unloading data.

To balance the utilization of the GPU-CPU memory bandwidth with the amount of work that can be done in parallel to data movement, only a limited number of blocks are allowed to execute load tasks concurrently. To get good bandwidth usage, i.e. loading as much data as possible using a small number of

---

[3]The cycle of load/compute/unload can be parallelized in CUDA by making use of streams. This allows some amount of asynchronous data transfer to happen concurrently with computation, however this needs to be coarse-grained as there is a limit to the number of streams that perform well in parallel.

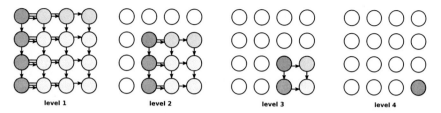

Figure 3. Task-based QR decomposition of a matrix consisting of 4×4 tiles. Each circle represents a tile, and its colour represents the type of task on that tile at that level. Empty circles have no task associated with them. The arrows represent dependencies at each level, and tasks at each level also implicitly depend on the task at the same location in the previous level.

blocks, we use Instruction Level Parallelism[10] in the implementation of the load and unload tasks. Experimenting on the GeForce GTX690 card, we found that only allowing 12 blocks to run load tasks and using 4-way ILP gave the best results, i.e. there is no need to let all the blocks load data simultaneously as we can almost completely saturate the bandwidth with only 12 blocks doing so.

The current setup contains 2 hidden queues for the system-generated tasks, which contain either the load or unload tasks. The queue containing unload tasks has the highest priority, and both have higher priority than any of the queues containing user-defined tasks. Data movement works efficiently in parallel with the computation, so prioritising these tasks is important. Additionally, moving data to the device early in the computation unlocks more tasks, allowing the scheduler to make better choices when assigning tasks.

3. Test Cases

To show our methodology is effective on CUDA GPUs, we have implemented two example problems, the Tiled QR Decomposition described in [11], and a task-based implementation of the Barnes-Hut algorithm[12] for N-body problems. This subsection presents these and the algorithms we have used to implement them. We have chosen two algorithms that do not directly translate to the GPU architecture as they don't easily vectorise to thousands of threads.

3.1. The Tiled QR Decomposition

[11] introduced the concept of using task-based parallelism for tiled algorithms in numerical linear algebra, presenting parallel codes for the Cholesky, LU, and QR decompositions. These algorithms are now part of the PLASMA and MAGMA libraries for parallel linear algebra [13]. The former uses the QUARK task scheduler, which was originally designed for this specific function, while the latter currently uses the StarPU task scheduler [14] and offloads parts of the computation to the GPU.

The tiled QR factorization is based on four basic tasks as shown in Figure 3. For a matrix consisting of $N \times N$ tiles, N passes, or levels, are computed, each computing a column and row of the QR decomposition. The tasks can be defined in terms of the tuples (i, j, k), where i and j are the row and column of the tile, respectively, and k is its level. The task names are the BLAS-like operation performed on the given tiles. Every task depends on the task at the same position and the previous level, i.e. the task (i, j, k) always depends on $(i, j, k-1)$ for $k > 1$. Each task also modifies its own tile (i, j), and the DTSQRF task additionally modifies the lower triangular part of the (j, j)th tile (see Table 1).

Task	where	depends on task(s)	locks tile(s)
⬤ SGEQRF	$i = j = k$	$(i, j, k - 1)$	(i, j)
◯ SLARFT	$i = k, j > k$	$(i, j, k-1), (k, k, k)$	(i, j)
⬤ STSQRF	$i > k, j = k$	$(i, j, k - 1), (i - 1, j, k)$	$(i, j), (j, j)$
◯ SSSRFT	$i > k, j > k$	$(i, j, k - 1), (i - 1, j, k), (i, k, k)$	(i, j)

Table 1. The task structure for the Tiled QR-decomposition.

3.2. Barnes-Hut Simulation on GPUs

The Barnes-Hut tree-code [12] is an algorithm to approximate the solution of an N-body problem, i.e. computing all the pairwise interactions between a set of N particles, in $\mathcal{O}(N \log N)$ operations, as opposed to the $\mathcal{O}(N^2)$ naive direct computation. The algorithm is based on a recursive octree decomposition: Starting from a cubic cell containing all the particles, the cell is recursively bisected along all three spatial dimensions, resulting in eight sub-cells, until the number of particles per cell is smaller than some limit n_{max}. The particle interactions can then be formulated recursively: Given a particle and a set of particles in a cell, if the particle and cell are sufficiently well separated, the particle-cell interactions are approximated by interacting the particle with the cell's centre of mass. If the particle and the cell are too close, and the cell has sub-cells, i.e. it contained more than n_{max} particles and was split in the recursive octree decomposition, then the particle is interacted with each of the sub-cells recursively. Finally, if the cell is not split, i.e. it is a leaf cell in the octree, then the particle is interacted with all particles in the cell, except for the particle itself if it is in the same cell. This operation is performed for each particle, starting with the root-level cell containing all the particles.

The GPU task-based implementation consists of three types of tasks:

- *Self*-interactions, in which all particles in a single cell interact with all other particles in the same cell,
- *Particle-particle* pair interactions, in which all particles in a cell interact with all particles in another cell,
- *Particle-cell* pair interactions, in which all particles in one cell are interacted with the monopoles of up to 8 other cells. On the GPU the particle-cell tasks are significantly more expensive than the other types of task.

This example uses the hierarchical resources. As the Barnes-Hut algorithm is based on a recursive octree decomposition, every cell in the tree is represented by a resource and the hierarchy of cells is recorded in the scheduler. This allows the system to create the load tasks for the smallest cells, meaning we can perform the first cell pair interactions early in the computation, instead of waiting to load the large cells at the top of the tree that contain thousands of particles.

The algorithms for the GPU and CPU versions in QuickSched are the same, but the task code uses SIMT parallelism of the loops on the GPU.

4. Results

We ran both test-cases using the two following variants:

- The full task-based setup with fully asynchronous load and unloads.
- A non-asynchronous version using `cudaMemcpy` to move data to and from the device before and after the computation. This version has the same task-based setup, but has no load or unload tasks in the system, and the queues that would contain them are removed from the system (so no time is spent checking them for tasks).

For the Barnes-Hut test case we also have a third variant with user-defined priorities. These variants allow us to directly show the advantages of the full task-based method with, thanks to the removal of synchronization points between memory movement and computation. The Barnes-Hut test case uses atomic operations to update the accelerations of the particles which avoids any concurrency issues.

All of our results were run with CUDA version 7.0 on one GPU of a Geforce GTX 090 (which is a dual-GPU card), or on a Tesla K40c. The source code of our implementation can be downloaded at `https://sourceforge.net/projects/quicksched/`

4.1. Tiled QR-decomposition

Figure 4 shows our code's execution on a 1536×1536 matrix (48×48 tiles of size 32). Each rectangle in the plot represents the execution of a single task. The magenta rectangles are the load tasks, whilst the cyan rectangles are unload tasks. The remainder of the tasks in the plot are coloured as in Table 1. The start and end of the plots have a lot of fraying, as the number of tasks that are available to be executed is low, which is due to structure of the QR calculation. The overall execution time with load and unload tasks is 5% faster than with `cudaMemcpy` (188.1ms with load and unload tasks, 195.4ms with `cudaMemcpy`).

The full task-based setup performs better than the version using `cudaMemcpy` as the computation starts almost immediately when the kernel is launched, after the first load tasks have completed. This means the heavy section of the computation has started before `cudaMemcpy` has even finished copying data to the device. Additionally the data movement back to the CPU is almost entirely hidden within the computation.

We also compared the speed of our code to that of CULA. CULA is a production linear algebra code that primarily utilises NVidia GPUs. Its QR routine also utilises the CPU in parallel with the GPU to achieve maximum performance. Our code is roughly 6× slower than CULA, as the underlying kernels were in no way optimised for computational efficiency.

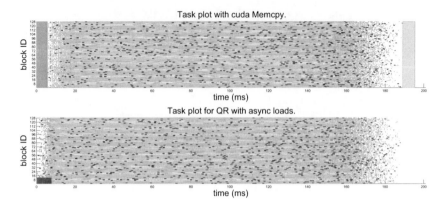

Figure 4. Task plots with and without the load/unload tasks. Each rectangle represents a single task that is executed on each block in the GPU. The full task-based setup performs significantly better than the version using `cudaMemcpy` as the computation can start almost immediately after the first load tasks (magenta) have completed. This means the heavy section of the computation has started before `cudaMemcpy` has even finished copying data to the device. Additionally, the data unloading (cyan tasks) is hidden almost entirely within the computation.

4.2. Barnes-Hut Simulation

Figure 5 shows the execution of our Barnes-Hut code on a uniform random distribution of 150k particles, with the three variants described above. We obtained a 10% speedup by replacing `cudaMemcpy` calls with asynchronous task-based data transfers (70.1ms with task-based data transfer and 77.1ms with `cudaMemcpy`), and a further 5% from adding the priority awareness to the setup (66.9ms), an overall 1.15× speedup.

We again have the advantage of the computation beginning sooner with the full-task based version, but we gain a further advantage from the priority awareness, as it allows us to execute the heavy tasks which write to large sections of memory early in the computation. These tasks often unlock many unload tasks, so if they are left until the end of the computation most of the unload tasks have to wait before they can be executed, resulting in the middle task plot in Figure 5

5. Conclusions

Our results show that Task-Based Parallelism directly on CUDA GPUs works, allowing us to port task-based algorithms that would otherwise not vectorize well without much effort. Furthermore, the Task-Based setup allows us to integrate data movement into the kernel easily and is generated automatically by the system. We also show how much speedup can be gained simply by reordering the computation and using fully asynchronous loads and stores. Our Barnes-Hut simulation code performs similarly to Bonsai-2 when using single precision (the same as Bonsai), though the latter uses higher degree multipoles and does more computation (timestepping and quadrupole calculation) on the GPU. However, the timings for Bonsai-2 do not include the data transfer time to and from the device.

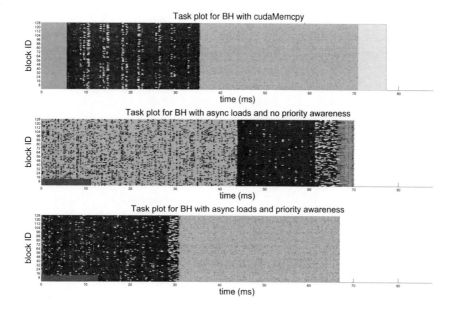

Figure 5. Task plots with/without load and unload tasks, and with/without priority awareness on 150k particles. Each rectangle represents a single task that is executed. The full task-based setup performs better than the versions using `cudaMemcpy` due to starting the computation sooner. Without priority awareness of user-specified tasks, we don't get as much of an advantage due to the apparent synchronisation of the unload tasks. This occurs as data is being written to large resources at the end of the computation, meaning any children of those resources have to wait until this is completed before they can be unloaded. Adding further priority awareness allows us to specify that these tasks should be executed first, so the unload costs become fully integrated within the computation.

Simulation type	1M parts	3M parts	10M parts
1 CPU with QuickSched	15.9s	50.5s	174.5s
16 CPUs with QuickSched	1.217s	3.489s	12.0s
GTX690 GPU	0.239s	0.677s	2.636 s
GTX690 GPU Single precision	0.116s	0.344s	1.414s
Tesla K40c GPU	0.099s	0.271s	2.025s
Gadget-2, 16 CPUs	2.25s	6.59s	47.91s
Bonsai-2 GTX690	0.069s	0.228s	Error.

Table 2. Average time taken to compute the accelerations for a single timestep of a cosmological simulation. The CPU code run is our own test case[1] run on a single node of the DiRAC Data Centric system at Durham University, with up to 16 processors (2 Intel E5-2670 0 @ 2.60GHz per node). Gadget-2 is a commonly used cosmology code that contains a similar gravity solver. Bonsai-2 is a GPU only Barnes-Hut simulation software. Bonsai-2 [15] timings also include any other work done on the GPU during a timestep, but does not account for data transfer to and from the device. Bonsai-2 is fully single precision, and ran out of memory when we attempted to run it on the 10 million particle test case. Our GPU code uses mixed precision unless otherwise stated, and is primarily double precision.

Our code for the QR decomposition does not perform as well as the heavily optimised CULA library, however our example is a proof of concept, that can be improved by optimising the kernels themselves. Additionally CULA makes use of both the CPU and GPU while our code only uses the GPU.

Figures 4 and 5 show the advantage and speedup from removing `cudaMemcpy` calls and the synchronization points they introduce from the computation. The traditional use of streams and small kernels still requires some initial chunk of data to be moved to the device before the first kernel can begin, and no data can be moved back until any kernel that writes to it has finished. Our load and unload tasks are similar in concept, but are much more fine-grained. This allows computation to begin as soon as any tiny chunk has been moved to the device, and asynchronous movement of data back to the host as soon all computation writing to that data is complete. Further, Figure 5 shows the advantage of having priority awareness, as it allows users to specify some ordering of the tasks that can avoid a large number of unlocks being left until the end of the computation. Additionally it allows heavy tasks to be prioritised, which can avoid large amounts of load imbalance at the end of the task-based kernel.

A final advantage of the Task-Based setup is that it can open the GPU up to a new set of problems that do not typically vectorise well and are thus not easily adaptable to GPUs. For example Bonsai had to reinvent the algorithm to get a setup that worked efficiently on the GPU. Our Barnes-Hut GPU code is almost identical to the CPU code, but with SIMT parallelism of the innermost loops, and we get speeds comparable to the heavily optimised Bonsai-2. The dependencies also allow launching a single kernel to do all the work, instead of potentially having to pick an order to execute multiple kernels. We have also created a Molecular Dynamics library using a similar setup [16] which can use task-based CPU algorithms with SIMT parallelism and achieves excellent speedup.

In summary, we have presented a method to use Task-Based parallelism directly on the GPU. We have also introduced the automatic generation of load and unload tasks, which allows fully asynchronous data transfer to and from the GPU inside the kernel. These tasks are shown to significantly improve the performance of the code, as the time before computation is reduced and the time required to move data back to the host is almost completely hidden inside the computation.

6. Acknowledgements

This work was supported by the UK Engineering and Physical Sciences Research Council.

This work used facilities provided as a part of the Durham University NVidia CUDA Research Centre. This work also used the DiRAC Data Centric system at Durham University, operated by the Institute for Computational Cosmology on behalf of the STFC DiRAC HPC Facility (www.dirac.ac.uk). This equipment was funded by BIS National E-infrastructure capital grant ST/K00042X/1, STFC capital grant ST/H008519/1, and STFC DiRAC Operations grant ST/K003267/1 and Durham University. DiRAC is part of the National E-Infrastructure.

This work was supported by the Science and Technology Facilities Council [ST/F001166/1] and the European Research Council under the European Union's ERC Grant agreements 267291 Cosmiway.

We would also like to thank Professor Tom Theuns of the Institute for Computation Cosmology for his expertise regarding the Barnes-Hut N-body code. We also thank Dr Evghenii Gaburov and Jeroen Bédorf for their help using Bonsai-2.

References

[1] Pedro Gonnet, Aidan B. G. Chalk, and Matthieu Schaller. Quicksched: Task-based parallelism with dependencies and conflicts. *Parallel Computing*, Submitted 2014.

[2] Asim Yarkhan, Jakub Kurzak, and Jack Dongarra. QUARK users guide. Technical report, Technical Report April, Electrical Engineering and Computer Science, Innovative Computing Laboratory, University of Tenessee, 2011.

[3] Keith H Randall. *Cilk: Efficient Multithreaded Computing*. PhD thesis, Massachusetts Institute of Technology, 1998.

[4] Josep M Pérez, Rosa M Badia, and Jesús Labarta. A flexible and portable programming model for smp and multi-cores. Technical report, 2007.

[5] C. Augonnet and R Namyst. A unified runtime system for heterogeneous multicore architectures. In *Proceedings of the International Euro-Par Workshops 2008, HPPC'08*, volume 5415 of *LNCS*, 2008.

[6] OAR Board. OpenMP application program interface version 3.0. In *The OpenMP Forum, Tech. Rep*, 2008.

[7] Alejandro Duran, Eduard Ayguadé, Rosa M Badia, Jesús Labarta, Luis Martinell, Xavier Martorell, and Judit Planas. Ompss: a proposal for programming heterogeneous multi-core architectures. *Parallel Processing Letters*, 21(02):173–193, 2011.

[8] James Reinders. *Intel Threading Building Blocks: outfitting C++ for multicore processor parallelism*. O'Reilly Media, 2010.

[9] NVidia. CUDA C programming guide. *NVIDIA Corporation, July*, 2012.

[10] Vasily Volkov. Better performance at lower occupancy. 2010.

[11] Alfredo Buttari, Julien Langou, Jakub Kurzak, and Jack Dongarra. A class of parallel tiled linear algebra algorithms for multicore architectures. *Parallel Computing*, 35(1):38–53, 2009.

[12] Josh Barnes and Piet Hut. A hierarchical o (n log n) force-calculation algorithm. *Nature*, 1986.

[13] Emmanuel Agullo, Jim Demmel, Jack Dongarra, Bilel Hadri, Jakub Kurzak, Julien Langou, Hatem Ltaief, Piotr Luszczek, and Stanimire Tomov. Numerical linear algebra on emerging architectures: The plasma and magma projects. In *Journal of Physics: Conference Series*, volume 180, page 012037. IOP Publishing, 2009.

[14] Emmanuel Agullo, Cédric Augonnet, Jack Dongarra, Mathieu Faverge, Hatem Ltaief, Samuel Thibault, and Stanimire Tomov. Qr factorization on a multicore node enhanced with multiple gpu accelerators. In *Parallel & Distributed Processing Symposium (IPDPS), 2011 IEEE International*, pages 932–943. IEEE, 2011.

[15] Jeroen Bédorf, Evghenii Gaburov, and Simon Portegies Zwart. Bonsai: A gpu tree-code. *arXiv preprint arXiv:1204.2280*, 2012.

[16] Pedro Gonnet and A. B. G. Chalk. `mdcore`, http://mdcore.sourceforge.net, 2013.

Parallel Computing: On the Road to Exascale
G.R. Joubert et al. (Eds.)
IOS Press, 2016

doi:10.3233/978-1-61499-621-7-697

A Strategy for Developing a Performance Portable Highly Scalable Application

Michael NEFF [a,1], Stefan ANDERSSON [a], Aaron VOSE [a] and John LEVESQUE [a]

[a] *Cray Inc., 901 Fifth Avenue, Suite 1000, Seattle, WA 98164, Phone: +1 206-701-2000, Fax: +1 206-701-2500*

Abstract. Over the last years Cray has gained extensive experience scaling real-world applications to hundreds of thousands of cores, as in the Titan project at ORNL Based on this experience, we look into what is needed to scale to next generations of HPC computers with millions of cores where increased performance is not only coming from more nodes but from more powerful nodes.

Keywords. Cray, extreme scaling, vectorization, hybridization, IO

Introduction

Over the last years Cray has gained extensive experience scaling real-world applications to hundreds of thousands of cores, as in the Titan project at ORNL.

The challenges for the application developer are based on the increase of parallelism and complexity of the processors. The need for vectorization of CPU intensive kernels is important. Also, compared to the increase in the peak performance of a core and node, slow bandwidth development both in memory and in the interconnect has to be taken into account when developing an application.

- Threading
  As the number of cores per node increases and the injection bandwidth stays about the same, the importance of threading becomes apparent.
- Vectorization
  Modern CPUs are using specific instructions and registers for increasing the number of floating point operations (FLOPs) it can execute per cycle. These are basically vector registers working in SIMD mode. As shown in table 1, these vector registers will not only grow in size over time but also be able to do more FLOPs per cycle.
- Must avoid scalar code
  Scalar code will either induce more memory traffic from accelerator to host on co-processor systems or will run 3-4 times slower than the fastest Xeon processor on a self-hosted system like KNL.

---

[1]Corresponding Author: Michael Neff, Cray Inc., 901 Fifth Avenue, Suite 1000, Seattle, WA 98164, USA; E-mail:mneff@cray.com

- Data placement
  Most systems will have close, relatively small high bandwidth memory supplemented by a larger slower main memory. Application developers must manage data placement and movement to assure that parallel or vector execution is not waiting for data which is not stored in local high bandwidth memory.

In order to be able to deal with all these complex topics, the developer has to have tools, which not only display information about the application but are able to scale to hundreds of thousands cores. These tools also need to actively help the developer by either pointing to relevant issues or, even better, make direct suggestions of what to improve. Also the ability to work directly on the source code is getting more and more important.

	CPU Familiy			
	AVX	AVX2	AVX512	Intel Xeon Phi
Cores per socket	8	16	16+	60+
Vector length in DP	2	4	8	8
FP Ops per cycle	4	16	32	32

Table 1. performance related changes on sockets

1. Site

Configuration of system used:

Titan, the Cray XK7 system at the Oak Ridge Leadership Computing facility (*OLCF*, https://www.olcf.ornl.gov/), has a hybrid architecture with a theoretical peak performance of 27 Pflops (17.59 Pflops by LINPACK) and 40 PB of Lustre storage with a transfer rate of 1.4 TB/s. Titan nodes have 16-core 2.2 GHz AMD Opteron 6274 (Interlagos) processors and 32 GB of RAM. Each pair of nodes share a *Gemini* high-speed interconnect router in a 3D torus topology. The system contains 299,008 cores with 598 TB of memory. Each of Titan's 18,688 physical compute nodes contains an NVIDIA Tesla K20X GPU computing accelerator with 6 GB of GDDR5 memory, 2.6 GHz memory clock speed, and 250 GB/sec of maximum memory bandwidth. Each GPU contains up to 2,688 single-precision cores with a GPU clock rate of 732 MHz.

2. Cray tools

Cray develops several tools for the XC and CS lines of computers. Most of the tools are 'stand-alone' solutions which are developed for solving a specific problem, and others combine the information generated by other tools into one single place.

2.1. Cray compiler Environment (CCE)

CCE has been used in HPC for over 35 years starting with the Cray-1. For 10 years now it has supported the x86 processors from AMD and Intel. It provides support for the Fortran, C and C++ languages and also supports OpenMP and OpenACC directives. Having their own compiler in the tool portfolio allows Cray to not only react quickly to user demands but also to implement features which can be used by other Cray tools.

2.2. Cray Profiling tools

The Cray Performance Measurement and Analysis Tools (CrayPAT) is a suite of utilities that enables the developer to capture and analyze performance data generated during the execution of the application on a Cray system. The information collected and analysis produced by use of these tools can help one find answers to two fundamental programming questions: How fast is my program running? And how can I make it run faster? CrayPAT helps the developer by not only displaying information like time, hardware performance counters and call-tree but also makes direct suggestions on where the application has potential to improve. This is displayed at the processor level when a kernel shows many cache misses and on the communication level, where a reordering of the ranks might take advantage of the faster intra-node communication.

Another tool in the Cray Performance Tool suite is Reveal. Reveal looks like a basic source code navigator; however, it uses information from both CCE (vectorization, loopmark) and CrayPAT to give the application developer a convenient way of not only browsing the source code, but also to see exactly where the hot-spots of the program are. In a second step Reveal will helps the developer in scoping the variables and can create OpenMP directives in the application. This greatly reduces the time for hybridization of an application.

2.3. Cray Debugging Tools

In addition Cray also provides some tools which are needed in certain cases during application development and are not profiling tools. We will not go into details in this paper but instead list the most important ones here:

2.3.1. Stack Trace Analysis Tool (STAT)

is a highly scalable, lightweight tool that gathers and merges stack traces from all of the processes of a running parallel application. After running the STAT command, it writes an output file with the merged stack traces in DOT format. This tools makes it easy to analyze a running program which at scale experience issues like communication deadlocks.

2.3.2. Abnormal Termination Processing (ATP)

is a system that monitors Cray system user applications. If an application takes a system trap, ATP performs analysis on the dying application. All stack backtraces of the application processes are gathered into a merged stack backtrace tree and written to disk as the file. The stack backtrace tree for the first process to die is sent to stderr as is the number of the signal that caused the application to fail. If Linux core dumping is enabled, a heuristically selected set of processes also dump their cores. The output file can be viewed with *statview*. This allows the developer to analyze a failing program without having to deal with hundreds or thousand large core dumps.

3. Threading

Threading on the node is extremely important and nontrivial. It is not a matter of just parallelizing the lower level loops, one must have significant granularity and pay attention to the NUMA characteristics of the node. Arrays are allocated on the memory that is closest to the processor that initializes the data, so on the many-core systems the application developer should make sure that the loops that initialize the arrays are performed with OpenMP in the same manner as the computational loops are parallelized. In this way the processor that will access that portion of the arrays in the computational loop will work on the memory closest to it.

High level looping structures promise the best granularity to overcome the overhead of OpenMP and give the developer better control over the scheduling to address any load imbalance in the parallel loop. Variable scoping high level loops is extremely difficult.

A few years ago, Cray started addressing this problem by developing a set of tools to assist the user in identifying and scoping high level loops. The Cray Perftools, together with Cray Compiler Environment (CCE), allows the developer automatically to instrument loops to obtain, min, max, average iteration count and granularity of loops.

With Reveal, Cray helps the developer to answer the question if OpenMP can be employed on a certain loop and how the variables accessed in these loops can be scooped.

3.1. Example : TACOMA

In the following section we are going to show the hybridization and vectorization done on GE's in-house CFD solver is named "TACOMA". This work is described in more details in the paper "Tri-Hybrid Computational Fluid Dynamics on DOE's Cray XK7, Titan." presented at the CUG 2014 in Lugano, Switzerland.

TACOMA is a 2nd order accurate (in time and space), finite-volume, block-structured, compressible flow solver, implemented in Fortran 90. Stability is achieved via the JST scheme [1] and convergence is accelerated using pseudo-time marching and multi-grid techniques. The Reynolds Averaged Navier-Stokes (RANS) equations are closed via the k-ω model of Wilcox [6]. TACOMA achieves a high degree of parallel scalability with MPI. For example, GE demonstrated a large scale calculation at Oak Ridge National Laboratory on the "Jaguar" Cray XT5 supercomputer utilizing 87K MPI ranks in 2011.

A number of programming paradigms exist for porting codes to the GPU, the most important of which are CUDA [2], OpenCL [5], and OpenACC [3]. For TACOMA, it was decided that the most straightforward porting path was to use OpenACC since it could build on previous work porting TACOMA to OpenMP [4].

Towards this end, General Electric and Cray have collaborated to create a tri-hybrid parallel version of TACOMA that combines three parallelization technologies, namely MPI, OpenMP, and OpenACC. Combining all three of these technologies is critical to extracting maximum performance. We highlight the following key "lessons learned" during the OpenMP and OpenACC porting and optimization process.

3.2. Porting to OpenMP

3.2.1. Loop Parallelization for Host CPUs

In 2013, GE extended TACOMA's parallelization to include OpenMP. This was accomplished by carefully porting significant loops that are executed during a multi-grid iteration. Approximately 250 loops were ported by adding appropriate OpenMP parallel directives and data clauses. The motivations for this port were three fold. First, GE wanted the ability to exploit the shared memory on a given compute node. Second, GE wanted to reduce the amount of additional block splitting that was required to ensure adequately parallel decomposition, since the additional blocks consume extra memory and incur computational overhead. Third, GE understood OpenMP to be a gateway for a future OpenACC port.

Given the block-structured nature of the solver, typical loops consist of a triple loop over i, j, and k. Three general types of these triple loops were encountered which are distinguished by the locality of the operations done inside the loop:

1. Loops with strong locality, e.g.
   ```
   q(i,j,k) = q0(i,j,k) +
                 dt(i,j,k) * R(i,j,k)
   ```
2. Loops that involve storing to neighbors, e.g.
   ```
   dflux = q(i+1,j,k) - q(i,j,k)
   R(i+1,j,k) = R(i+1,j,k) + dflux
   R(i,  j,k) = R(i+1,j,k) - dtlux
   ```
3. Loops that involved reductions, e.g.
   ```
   l2norm = l2norm + R(i,j,k)**2
   ```

Loops of type (1) can be ported to OpenMP in a straightforward manner. Loops of type (3) are also easily managed with reduction clauses; however this is not always possible due to the use of Fortran 90 complex data structures, thus custom reduction loops were hand crafted as required.

Loops of type (2) require special attention, since the form shown above contains a recurrence, which becomes a race condition when naively parallelized. Loops of this type account for approximately 50% of the CPU time in TACOMA. What these loops are doing is computing the flux (mass, momentum, and energy) dflux on the cell face between two cell volumes (i,j,k and i+1,j,k in the example above), and then accumulating this flux into the net residual R stored at the cell centers.

There are two ways to address the race condition. The approach used by GE was to color the cell volumes and then assign a thread to each color. Each thread is then responsible for computing dflux on all faces associated with the cell centers of the assigned color, and accumulating the residual. The downside of this approach is a small amount of redundant calculations of dflux for faces between nodes with different colors. The second method, which is used in the OpenACC port and discussed in more detail later, is to split each of these loops into two. The first loop computes and stores dflux and the second loop accumulates it.

With these three primary loop types successfully parallelized, GE demonstrated the use of hybrid MPI and OpenMP at scale on computations using in excess of 100K total threads (total threads = MPI ranks × OpenMP threads per rank).

3.2.2. Lessons Learned from OpenMP Porting

The hybrid MPI–OpenMP port of TACOMA serves as a good starting point for the addition of OpenACC directives, enabling TACOMA to run efficiently on accelerator devices such as GPUs. A key lesson learned in this process is that OpenMP should be added before OpenACC. Not only is OpenMP easier as it doesn't require as much analysis of data location, but the scoping performed when adding OpenMP can be largely reused when adding OpenACC as well.

4. Vectorization

With OpenMP additions completed by GE, work on a GPU accelerated port began in earnest. First, the most time-consuming routines are identified using the Cray Performance Analysis Tool (CrayPAT). In addition to finding the top routines, CrayPAT collects and reports loop-level statistics including min, max, and average iteration counts. The number of loop iterations is critical information to have when attempting to optimize for OpenACC, as each iteration typically forms one thread on the GPU. If there are not enough iterations in a loop, there will be a paucity of threads, resulting in poor performance. In cases where a number of nested loops are to be parallelized, being limited by the number of iterations in an individual loop can be avoided by collapsing the loop nest with the OpenACC `collapse` directive. For the reason just mentioned this directive was used frequently while porting TACOMA.

Once candidate loops have been identified with help from the CrayPAT tool, OpenACC directives can be added to the source code to express the existing loop-level parallelism. During this process, the scoping information from the previous OpenMP work can be largely reused. In particular, variables with `private` scope in OpenMP almost always remain so scoped in OpenACC. The OpenMP reductions will usually be the same as well. However, the variables with `shared` scope in OpenMP are typically those which will require data motion between host and device in OpenACC. These variables can be given a specific OpenACC data motion directive or be left unscoped, leaving the data motion responsibility to the compiler toolchain. Cray's compiler makes very good decisions here, but additional hand optimization of data motion is required to get optimal performance from the vast majority of real-world codes.

While on the topic of real-world codes, it should be mentioned that it is often the case — and certainly was for TACOMA — that expressing the *existing* loop-level parallelism with OpenMP and OpenACC is not enough to achieve good performance. Often, the underlying algorithm contains more parallelism than is available in a given implementation of that algorithm. Thus, in addition to expressing the parallelism in the original code, one often needs to change the implementation so more of the algorithm's inherent parallelism is expressed. An example of this can be seen in the pseudocode in Figure 1, where the original code contains a recurrence - preventing parallelization. The first solution to this limitation was created by GE during porting to OpenMP. GE introduced a coloring scheme, whereby each OpenMP thread would be responsible for a region in the result array having a particular color. While the coloring method worked well for the case of OpenMP, it prevented proper vectorization on the GPU with OpenACC. Thus, we devised a solution compatible with OpenACC, as depicted in Figure 2. First, the loop is split into two parts: the computation of `dflux` and its accumulation into the net

```
do k=1,n3
  do j=1,n2
    do i=1,n1
      df(1:3) = comp_dflux(i,j,k)
      R(i,j,k)    += df(1) + df(2) + df(3)
      R(i-1,j,k) -= df(1)
      R(i,j-1,k) -= df(2)
      R(i,j,k-1) -= df(3)
    end do
  end do
end do
```

Figure 1. Pseudocode showing the original code with the recurrence

```
do k=1,n3
  do j=1,n2
    do i=1,n1
      df(i,j,k,1:3) = comp_dflux(i,j,k)
    end do
  end do
end do
do k=1,n3
  do j=1,n2
    do i=1,n1
      R(i,j,k) += df(i,  j,k,1) + df(i,j,  k,2) + df(i,j,k,  3)
      R(i,j,k) -= df(i+1,j,k,1) + df(i,j+1,k,2) + df(i,j,k+1,3)
    end do
  end do
end do
```

Figure 2. Pseudocode showing the recurrence resolved. — *Cray's OpenACC port uses a two-loop, two-kernel solution with index translation. The first computes all the fluxes, and the second applies them. As no two iterations assign to the same location, there is no recurrence in either of these loops. The edge cases don't matter here, as the surface elements of the result array are never actually read later on in the code. While this approach does require the use of more memory to store the intermediary fluxes as well as the overhead of two kernel launches, it can run efficiently on the GPU due to the large amount of parallelism available in the loop nests.*

residual array. With this split, the computation of dflux no longer contains a recurrence and can be parallelized. The remaining recurrence in the accumulation is removed by an index translation: that is, $(a[i]-=b[i]; a[i-1]+=b[i]) \implies a[i]+=b[i+1]-b[i]$. Thus, the loop no longer has multiple iterations assign to the same index in the result array a, and the recurrence is removed. Normally such an index translation would introduce some edge cases, but in the case of TACOMA, the surface cells of the output array are never read and don't need to be fully computed.

When adding OpenACC directives to the source code, care must be taken to ensure the compiler is parallelizing the loops properly. Depending on the target compiler and accelerator device, there are a number of levels of parallelism available. In particular, the Cray compiler will by default partition a loop across thread blocks, across the threads within a block, or both. In code with non-trivial loop structures, there can be many ways to perform the partitioning, so care must be taken to ensure the compiler is partitioning in a reasonable way. Cray's compiler provides detailed output in the form of "compiler listing" files, which consist of annotated versions of the source code with ASCII art as well as textual messages. These listing files can be examined to ensure proper loop partitioning.

Finally, the resulting code with OpenACC directives can be executed and profiled. At this early stage, data motion should be mostly ignored when profiling and optimizing OpenACC kernels. Optimization of data motion will require examination of the inter-actions among multiple kernels. This inter-kernel examination is best performed later, when the kernels involved are completed and have known data requirements. The opti-mization that can most frequently and most easily produce a large improvement in per-formance is the tuning of the number of threads per thread block for a given loop with the OpenACC `vector` clause. Compilers differ in the default vector size, with the Cray compiler utilizing 128 threads per thread block. In the case of TACOMA, a number of loops show nearly double the performance when using a vector size of 256, while some loops perform worse.

It should be noted that this version of the kernel will most likely perform worse than the original version on a *CPU only* based machine due to the increased need of memory bandwidth.

5. Data placement

5.1. OpenACC Data Motion Optimization

Once good kernel performance is achieved, data motion can be examined. To reduce the amount of data that is transferred between host and device, OpenACC data regions are created around adjacent kernels to keep data used by more than one kernel on the device. This first step is depicted by the small light blue data regions in Figure 3. Ideally, the data regions can be merged and moved up the call tree to the primary timestep loop. There, a data region with relatively few lines can wrap all the kernels further down the call tree. This placement in the call-tree can be seen by the location of the large blue data region in Figure 3. However, the ideal of merging all or most of the data regions into a larger one isn't always realistic due to I/O, communication, or serial code. In the more pragmatic case, the data regions can be nested hierarchically. In the case of TACOMA, a large data region is created as depicted by data region F in Figure 3. Here, data with a lifetime of at least a timestep can be loaded into GPU memory upon entry and stay on the device for the lifetime of many kernel executions.

With loop-level parallelism expressed and host/device data motion optimized, par-allelism among data transfers and kernels is expressed with the OpenACC `async` clause. This allows data to be prefetched before a dependent kernel is launched, and allows mul-tiple kernels from a rank to run on a node's GPU in different streams concurrently. Fi-nally, the CUDA-proxy feature is used, allowing sharing of each GPU among multiple MPI ranks. This allows different MPI to OpenMP ratios and improves OpenACC per-formance by hiding data transfer latency; a kernel from one rank can execute while data motion for another rank takes place.

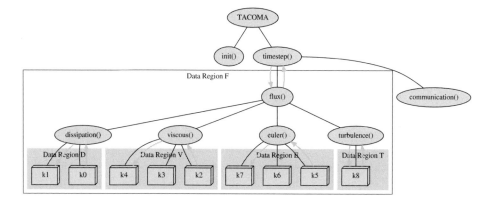

Figure 3. call-tree highlighting OpenACC data regions. — *A large data region (big blue box) can be seen at the level just below the primary timestep loop, where all the kernels in the routines further down the call tree are encompassed. In this region of the code, data that is only needed by the GPU and data that is constant for at least a timestep can be loaded into GPU memory once and be reused for the duration of the timestep. This transfer of data to GPU memory upon entry to data regions and of results to the host upon exit from data regions is represented by the orange arrows in the figure.*

5.2. Lessons Learned from OpenACC Porting

A key lesson is to ignore data motion and to focus on bare kernel performance during this stage. Optimization of data motion will likely require examination of the interactions among multiple kernels. This inter-kernel examination is best performed a single time, after the kernels involved are completed and have known data requirements. Another key lesson learned is that expressing the parallelism of the underlying algorithm is critical to achieving good performance. At times the code does need to be restructured to allow this. Additionally, some techniques that work well with today's OpenMP (cell coloring algorithm) may not work well with OpenACC and GPUs.

During the porting effort, a number of limitations with the OpenACC 2.0 standard were encountered. The most important of which is the lack of support for Fortran derived data types in the regions of code turned into kernels for the accelerator. Working around this issue results in a moderate amount of extra coding, as sections using derived types must be "sanitized". This is typically achieved by acquiring a pointer to the desired data member within the derived type, and passing this pointer to the OpenACC directives instead of the original data member. There is a feature called deep copy in the cray compiler solving this issue. Adding this feature is one of the main topics in discussions about the new OpenACC standard.

In addition to the issues with derived data types, OpenACC has restrictions with subroutine and function calls. OpenACC relies heavily on the compiler's ability to inline function calls within GPU accelerated regions. While the OpenACC 2.0 standard does provide some support for the calling of routines, there are many limitations. In particular, each routine to be called needs to have directives added describing what combination of the three levels of available OpenACC parallelism to use: gang, worker, and vector. To avoid this additional coding work, we make use of as much automatic inlining as possible. Fortunately, the Cray compiler does a very good job of inlining huge routines without issue. For the few cases where a routine was unable to be inlined due to I/O or similar issues, a sanitized version able to be inlined could be constructed.

5.3. Summary of the Lessons learned

As originally implemented, TACOMA utilized a loop structure which contained a recurrence in each of the three dimensions of the result array as seen in figure 1.

1. OpenMP directives should be added before OpenACC because OpenMP scoping work can be largely reused when porting to OpenACC. Additionally, OpenMP is easier due a lack of data motion concerns.
2. OpenACC data motion should be mostly ignored in the beginning, with focus instead on bare kernel performance. Optimization of data motion will likely require examination of the interactions of multiple kernels. This inter-kernel examination is best performed after the kernels involved are completed and have known data requirements.
3. Real world codes often do not express enough of the underlying algorithms' parallelism. Expressing this parallelism is key to achieving good performance. Additionally, some techniques that work well for OpenMP (cell coloring algorithm) are not adequate in the case of OpenACC (a loop fissure and index translation was required).

6. Conclusions

Today's tools do offer the developers help so they can optimize their application to take advantage of the features of the used hardware, both for hybridization and vectorization, but it also clear that the developer is responsible for selecting the best algorithm for solving the problem, knowing that it will different for different architectures.

References

[1]   JAMES, A., SCHMIDT, W., AND TURKEL, E. Numerical solution of the euler equations by finite volume methods using runge-kutta time-stepping schemes. *AIAA* (1981).
[2]   NVIDIA. *NVIDIA CUDA Programming Guide 2.0*. 2008.
[3]   OPENACC ARCHITECTURE REVIEW BOARD. OpenACC application program interface version 2.0a, Aug. 2013.
[4]   OPENMP ARCHITECTURE REVIEW BOARD. OpenMP application program interface version 3.0, May 2008.
[5]   STONE, J. E., GOHARA, D., AND SHI, G. Opencl: A parallel programming standard for heterogeneous computing systems. *IEEE Des. Test 12*, 3 (May 2010), 66–73.
[6]   WILCOX, D. C. Reassessment of the scale determining equations for advanced turbulence models. *AIAA 26(11)*.

Mini-Symposium:
Symposium on Energy and Resilience in Parallel Programming

Parallel Computing: On the Road to Exascale
G.R. Joubert et al. (Eds.)
IOS Press, 2016
© 2016 The authors and IOS Press. All rights reserved.
doi:10.3233/978-1-61499-621-7-709

Mini-Symposium on Energy and Resilience in Parallel Programming

Dimitrios S. Nikolopoulos [a] and Christos D. Antonopoulos [b,1]

[a] *Queen's University of Belfast*
[b] *IRETETH/CERTH & University of Thessaly, Greece*

Computing systems now expose power and reliability indicators to software. These indicators are in turn used to develop new energy-aware optimizations and new approaches to resilience that span all layers of the software stack, from firmware and operating systems, to compilers, runtime systems, languages and application software. Awareness of power and resilience are essential in large-scale parallel computing systems and datacenters, where mean time to failure rates are deteriorating and software executes under power caps that often manifest as non-deterministic performance variation. Power and resilience are perennially important for many-core embedded systems, where emerging applications push for higher performance and data processing ability on a limited energy budget, while component density and feature sizes compromise reliability.

The mini-symposium on Energy and Resilience in Parallel Programming (ERPP 2015) explored the implications of energy and resilience on the principles and practice of parallel programming. The mini-symposium focused on research that uses energy and resilience as first-class resources in parallel programming languages, libraries and models and demonstrates how parallel programming can improve energy-efficiency and resilience of large-scale computing systems or many-core embedded systems. The mini-symposium also explored how energy and resilience management in hardware or system software affect the performance of existing parallel programming environments.

We would like to thank all authors for their contributions. We would also like to thank the members of the Program Committee for their effort and insightful comments on both the short and the extended versions of the submitted manuscripts.

The organizers of this mini-symposium have been supported by (a) The European Commission (grant agreements FP7-323872 Project "SCoRPiO" and FP7-610509 Project "NanoStreams"), (b) The Aristeia II action of the operational program Education and Lifelong Learning which is co-funded by the European Social Fund and Greek national resources (grant agreement 5211, project "Centaurus"), and (c) The UK Engineering and Physical Sciences Research Council (grant agreements EP/L000055/1 Project "ALEA", and EP/L004232/1 Project "Enpower").

---

[1]Corresponding Author: Prof. Christos D. Antonopoulos, Department of Electrical and Computer Engineering, University of Thessaly, Greece; E-mail: cda@inf.uth.gr

Parallel Computing: On the Road to Exascale
G.R. Joubert et al. (Eds.)
IOS Press, 2016
doi:10.3233/978-1-61499-621-7-711

Performance and Fault Tolerance of Preconditioned Iterative Solvers on Low-Power ARM Architectures

José I. ALIAGA, [a,1] Sandra CATALÁN, [a] Charalampos CHALIOS, [b]
Dimitrios S. NIKOLOPOULOS, [b] Enrique S. QUINTANA-ORTÍ [a]

[a] Dpto. Ingeniería Ciencia de Computadores, Universidad Jaume I, Castellón (Spain)
[b] School of EEECS, Queen's University of Belfast (United Kingdom)

Abstract. As the complexity of computing systems grows, reliability and energy are two crucial challenges that will demand holistic solutions. In this paper, we investigate the interplay among concurrency, power dissipation, energy consumption and voltage-frequency scaling for a key numerical kernel for the solution of sparse linear systems. Concretely, we leverage a task-parallel implementation of the Conjugate Gradient method, equipped with an state-of-the-art preconditioner embedded in the ILUPACK software, and target a low-power multicore processor from ARM. In addition, we perform a theoretical analysis on the impact of a technique like Near Threshold Voltage Computing (NTVC) from the points of view of increased hardware concurrency and error rate.

Keywords. Sparse linear systems, iterative solvers, ILUPACK, low power multicore processors, high performance, energy efficiency, convergence

1. Introduction

As we move along the scaling projection for computing systems predicted by Moore's law, some of the technologies that have fuelled this exponential growth seem to be heading for serious walls enforced by physical constraints [7]. Concretely, a system with billions of components will experience multiple faults and, therefore, the software has to be made resilient in order to deal with this scenario. In addition, with the end of Dennard's scaling [5], the fraction of silicon that can be active (at the nominal operating voltage) for a target thermal design power (TDP) rapidly decays. As a consequence, computer architectures have turned towards dark silicon and heterogeneous designs [8], and Near Threshold Voltage Computing (NTVC) has arisen as an appealing technology to reduce energy consumption at the cost of increasing error rates.

The *High Performance Conjugate Gradients (HPCG) benchmark* [6] has been recently introduced in an effort to create a relevant metric for ranking HPC systems using a benchmark with data access patterns that mimic those present in crucial HPC applications. In the reference implementation of HPCG, parallelism is extracted via MPI

---

[1]Corresponding Author: Dpto. de Ingeniería y Ciencia de Computadores, Universidad Jaume I, 12.071–
Castellón (Spain); E-mail: aliaga@icc.uji.es.

and OpenMP [6]. However, in an era where general-purpose processors (CPUs) contain dozens of cores, the concurrency that is targeted by this legacy implementation may be too fine-grain.

In this paper we investigate the scalability, energy efficiency and fault resilience of low-power multicore ARM processors using our task-parallel version [1] of ILUPACK[2] (Incomplete LU PACKage). This is a multi-threaded CG solver for sparse linear systems furnished with a sophisticated algebraic multilevel factorization preconditioner. Compared with the HPCG benchmark, our implementation of ILUPACK exhibits analogous data access patterns and arithmetic-to-memory operation ratios. On the other hand, our version is likely better suited to exploit the hardware concurrency of current multicore processors [1,2]. This paper is an extension of previous work [4], with the following major differences:

- First, we target a much more sophisticated iterative solver, with a complex preconditioner based on ILUPACK, instead of the simple CG iteration in [4].
- Second, we employ a task-parallel version of the solver, in lieu of the simple loop-based parallelization of the numerical kernels integrated into CG that was leveraged in [4].
- As a result, our task-parallel solver exhibits fair scalability even when the data resides off-chip, a property that is not present for the simple CG targeted in our previous work.

The rest of the paper is structured as follows. In Sections 2 and 3 we briefly describe the task-parallel version of ILUPACK and the target architecture, respectively. In Section 4 we experimentally analyze the scalability of the solver and the impact of voltage-frequency scaling on the execution time. In Section 5, we repeat this analysis from the perspectives of power and energy consumption, so as to obtain an estimation of the energy gains (or losses) that would result from an execution that employed increasing levels of hardware concurrency. In Section 6 we link error corruption with degradation of convergence for the iterative solver, and we discuss its impact under two different scenarios. Finally, in Section 7 we offer a few concluding remarks.

2. Task-Parallel Implementation of ILUPACK

Consider the linear system $Ax = b$, where $A \in \mathbb{R}^{n \times n}$ is sparse, $b \in \mathbb{R}^n$, and $x \in \mathbb{R}^n$ is the sought-after solution. ILUPACK integrates an "inverse-based approach" to compute and apply an algebraic multilevel preconditioner in order to accelerate the iterative solution of the system [3]. In analogy with the HPCG benchmark, we consider hereafter that A is symmetric positive definite (s.p.d.), and we study the (preconditioned) iterative solution stage only, dismissing the computation of the preconditioner. The solve procedure involves a sparse matrix-vector product (SPMV), the application of the preconditioner, and a few vector operations (basically DOT products, AXPY-like updates and vector norms) per iteration [13]; see Figure 1. We emphasize that a similar PCG iteration underlies the HPCG benchmark.

Our task-parallel version of ILUPACK decomposes the solver into tasks, and abides to the existing inter-task dependencies in order to produce a "correct" (i.e., dependency-

---

[2]http://ilupack.tu-bs.de

$A \rightarrow M$	O0. Preconditioner computation
Initialize $x_0, r_0, z_0, d_0, \beta_0, \tau_0; k := 0$	
while $(\tau_k > \tau_{max})$	Loop for iterative PCG solver
$w_k := A d_k$	O1. SPMV
$\rho_k := \beta_k / d_k^T w_k$	O2. DOT product
$x_{k+1} := x_k + \rho_k d_k$	O3. AXPY
$r_{k+1} := r_k - \rho_k w_k$	O4. AXPY
$z_{k+1} := M^{-1} r_{k+1}$	O5. Apply preconditioner
$\beta_{k+1} := r_{k+1}^T z_{k+1}$	O6. DOT product
$d_{k+1} := z_{k+1} + (\beta_{k+1}/\beta_k) d_k$	O7. AXPY-like
$\tau_{k+1} := \| r_{k+1} \|_2$	O8. vector 2-norm
$k := k + 1$	
endwhile	

Figure 1. Algorithmic formulation of the preconditioned CG method. Here, τ_{max} is an upper bound on the relative residual for the computed approximation to the solution.

aware) execution, while exploiting the task parallelism implicit to the operation. Concretely, each iteration of the PCG solve is decomposed into 8 macro-tasks, say O1–O8, related by a partial order which enforces an almost strict serial execution. Specifically, O1 $\rightarrow$ O2 $\rightarrow$ O4 $\rightarrow$ O5 $\rightarrow$ O6 $\rightarrow$ O7, but O3 and O8 can be computed any time once O2 and O4 are respectively available. Here, each macro-task corresponds to one of the basic operations that compose the iteration: SPMV, application of preconditioner, DOT, AXPY and norms. The application of the preconditioner, performed inside O5, is decomposed into two groups of micro-tasks, both organized as binary trees, with bottom up dependencies in the first one and top-down in the second, and a number of leaves l controlled by the user. The remaining macro-tasks are decomposed into l independent micro-tasks each, with the two dot products and vector 2-norm introducing a synchronization point each. For further details, see [2].

3. Setup

All the experiments in the paper were performed using IEEE double-precision arithmetic on an Exynos5 Odroid-XU development board assembled by Samsung. The Exynos5 contains an ARM Cortex-A15 quad-core cluster plus an ARM Cortex-A7 quad-core cluster integrated into a single big.LITTLE system-on-chip (SoC). Each Cortex-A7 core has a (32+32)–KByte L1 cache (data+instruction) and shares a 512–KByte L2 cache with its siblings. The system has 2 Gbytes of DRAM. In order to target low-power scenarios, we only employ the ARM Cortex-A7 cores during the experimentation, with frequencies that vary in the range of $\{250, \ldots, 600\}$ MHz with step changes of 50 MHz.[3] All codes were compiled using gcc version 4.8.1 with the appropriate optimization flags.

For the analysis, we employed a s.p.d. linear system arising from the finite difference discretization of a 3D Laplace problem, for a particular instance of size $n=1,000,000$ and $nnz=6,940,000$ nonzero entries in the coefficient matrix A. Thus, the data clearly resides

---

[3]The actual frequencies of the Cortex-A7 double those reported by the cpufreq driver and the real range is in [500, 1200] MHz. The driver exposes these values (half of the actual) to make it easier to activate one of the clusters/deactivate the other by just re-setting the frequency. Otherwise, the ranges of Cortex-A15 and Cortex-A7 cores would overlap, and a different mechanism would be needed to change frequency across clusters.

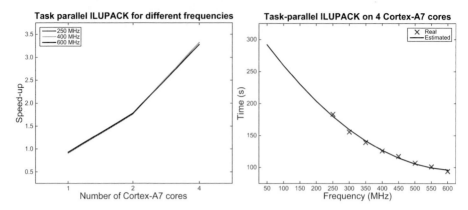

Figure 2. Computational performance using 1–4 (left) and 4 (right) ARM Cortex-A7 cores and a problem instance consisting of l=8 leaves.

off-chip. In the experiments, we always set $l = 8$, which offers enough parallelism for the four ARM Cortex-A7 cores available in the system.

4. Computational Performance vs Frequency-Voltage Scaling

In this section we analyze the scalability of our task-parallel solver based on ILUPACK, and the effect of frequency on performance.

The left hand-side plot in Figure 2 reports the speed-up of the solver with respect to the sequential version of ILUPACK, operating on the same problem instance, but with only one leaf. (Similar acceleration factors were observed when the sequential code was applied to the same problem with the data partitioned into 8 leaves, as done in the parallel case.) The results show fair speed-ups, close to 2× for 2 Cortex-A7 cores and slightly below 3.5× when the full quad-core Cortex-A7 cluster is employed. Furthermore, the acceleration is mostly independent of the operating (voltage-)frequency (pair). At this point, it is worth mentioning that our experiments with this code and a slightly larger instance of the same problem, on an Intel Xeon Phi, reveal accelerations factors of 15.5× and 27.7× with 16 and 32 x86 cores, respectively, providing additional evidence of the scalability of the solver [1].

The right-hand side plot in Figure 2 relates execution time vs frequency when the number of cores is fixed to 4; see also the columns labeled as "Time" in Table 1. In principle, we could expect that a variation of the operating frequency rendered an inversely proportional variation of the execution time. However, the interplay between frequency and time is more subtle and strongly depends on whether the code is compute- or memory-bound (i.e., dominated by the performance of the floating-point units or the access to memory, respectively) as well as the effect of frequency on the memory bandwidth. For example, in some x86 architectures, this bandwidth is independent of the frequency while in others, and specifically for the Cortex-A7 cluster, it is mildly governed by it. For example, in our experiments with the stream benchmark [12] on this architecture, we observed decreases in the memory bandwidth by factors 0.86 and 0.70 when the frequency was reduced in factors of 0.66 and 0.41.

Freq. (MHz)	Time (in s) $T(f_i)$		Power (in W)				Energy (in J)			
			Total, $P_T(f_i)$		A7, $P_{A7}(f_i)$		Total, $P_T(f_i)$		A7, $P_{A7}(f_i)$	
f_i	Real	Estim.	Real	Estim.	Real	Estim.	Real	Estim.	Real	Estim.
50	–	291.8	–	0.215	–	0.118	–	62.5	–	30.9
100	–	259.5	–	0.214	–	0.111	–	55.8	–	27.2
150	–	230.1	–	0.217	–	0.109	–	50.3	–	24.4
200	–	203.6	–	0.225	–	0.112	–	46.1	–	22.6
250	183.4	180.0	0.237	0.239	0.120	0.121	43.5	43.0	21.9	21.7
300	155.8	159.3	0.263	0.259	0.141	0.137	40.9	41.2	21.0	21.7
350	139.6	141.5	0.287	0.287	0.161	0.161	40.1	40.6	22.5	22.6
400	125.7	126.6	0.324	0.325	0.193	0.194	40.7	41.2	24.3	24.5
450	117.4	114.6	0.368	0.372	0.235	0.238	43.2	43.1	27.5	27.3
500	106.7	105.5	0.436	0.431	0.297	0.292	46.6	46.1	31.7	31.1
550	100.6	99.3	0.502	0.502	0.359	0.359	50.5	50.4	36.1	35.7
600	94.0	96.0	0.587	0.587	0.438	0.438	55.2	55.8	41.2	41.3
Error	1.63e-2		6.29e-2		1.10e-2		9.20e-3		8.83e-3	

Table 1. Experimental results and estimations collected with the task-parallel version of ILUPACK using 4 ARM Cortex-A7 cores and a problem instance consisting of l=8 leaves. The last row ("Error") displays the average relative error $(\sum_i |r_i - e_i|/r_i)/n$, where r_i and e_i respectively denote the real and estimated values, $i \in \{50, 100, 150, \ldots, 600\}$, and n is the number of samples.

A major observation from this evaluation is that, for a complex code such as our task-parallel version of ILUPACK, there are fragments of the code that are compute-bound while others are memory-bound, making a prediction for the global behaviour of the application is difficult. Nevertheless, the plot shows that it is possible to apply linear regression in order to fit a quadratic polynomial that estimates the execution time T, as a function of the frequency f (in MHz): $T(f) = 5.80\text{E-}4 f^2 - 7.33\text{E-}1 f + 3.27\text{E+}2$ s. Moreover, the validity of this regression is quantitatively demonstrated by the coefficient of determination, $1 - r2 = 6.69\text{E-}3$, and the small relative differences between the real measures and the polynomial approximation shown in the row labeled as "Error" of Table 1. Using this polynomial to extrapolate the data, we observe an asymptotic lower bound on the execution time, independent of the operating frequency, close to 100 s.

5. Power and Energy Efficiency vs Frequency-Voltage Scaling

This section considers the following iso-power[4] scenario: Given the power dissipated by the system when operating at its highest frequency, what is the number of cores/clusters that can be crammed within the same power budget? In addition, given the variation of hardware concurrency that is possible under iso-power conditions, how this affects the execution time and, therefore, the energy efficiency of the alternative configurations?

The left-hand side plot in Figure 3 and (the columns labeled as "Power" in) Table 1 show the total power dissipated by the Exynos5 SoC plus the memory DIMMs as well as that of the Cortex-A7 cluster only when executing the task-parallel version of ILUPACK using 4 cores. For this metric, it is also possible to fit a precise linear regression curve.

---

[4]An analysis via a given *iso-metric* aims to obtain a metric-invariant set of analysis or design solutions.

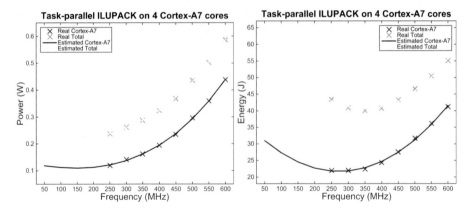

Figure 3. Power and energy efficiency vs frequency-voltage scaling using 4 ARM Cortex-A7 cores and a problem instance consisting of l=8 leaves.

For this purpose, we take into account that the power is cubically dependent on the frequency.[5] Thus, for example, the total power is accurately estimated by $P_T(f) = 1.46\text{E-}9\,f^3 + 2.76\text{E-}7\,f^2 - 7.60\text{E-}5\,f + 2.18\text{E-}1$ W, as $1 - r2 = 5.72\text{E-}4$. The regression curves expose asymptotic lower bounds on the power dissipation rates, at 0.21 W and 0.11 W respectively for the total and Cortex-A7 cluster, which can be attributed to the static power of this board/CPU.

To conclude this initial analysis, the right-hand side plot in Figure 3 and (the columns labeled as "Energy" in) Table 1 illustrate the behaviour of the code/architecture from the point of view of total and Cortex-A7 energy consumption. The former can be approximated by the quadratic polynomial $E_T(f) = 2.43\text{E-}4\,f^2 - 1.70\text{E-}1\,f + 7.04\text{E+}1$, with $1 - r2 = 7.36\text{E-}3$. (Alternatively, we could have used $E_T(f) = T(f)P_T(f)$.) This plot reveals a "sweet spot" (optimal) from the point of view of total energy at 350 MHz, which is shifted to 250 MHz if we consider the energy consumed by the Cortex-A7 cluster only.

For simplicity, let us work hereafter with the approximations to power and energy obtained via linear regression. Table 1 reports that the Exynos5 SoC plus the memory DIMMs, operating at the highest frequency ($f_M = 600$ MHz), dissipate $P_T(f_M) = 0.587$ W, with the Cortex-A7 cluster itself being responsible for a large fraction of this: $P_{A7}(f_M) = 0.438$ W. However, from the point of view of energy, the optimal configuration is attained when the application is executed with the cores at $f = 350$ MHz or 250–300 MHz, depending respectively on whether we consider the consumption by the complete SoC+DIMMs or the Cortex-A7 only.

Let us examine the intermediate case $f_{opt} = 300$ MHz. At this frequency, the Exynos5+DIMMs dissipate $P_T(f_{opt}) = 0.259$ W while the Cortex-A7 cluster is responsible for $P_{A7}(f_{opt}) = 0.137$ W. This implies that, with the same power (*isopower*) dissipated by the system operating at f_M, we can feed an ideal configuration, which operates at f_{opt}, and consists of $P_T(f_M)/P_T(f_{opt}) = 0.587/0.259 = 2.26\times$ or $P_{A7}(f_M)/P_{A7}(f_{opt}) = 0.438/0.137 = 3.19\times$ more Cortex-A7 clusters/cores, depending

---

[5]We can identify two components in the power: static and dynamic. In practice, the static power depends on the square of the voltage V while the dynamic power depends on $V^2 f$, with the voltage itself depending linearly on the frequency [9].

respectively on whether we account for the full Exynos5+DIMMs or the Cortex-A7 cores only. Given that it is not possible to build a fragment of a cluster, we now approximate these numbers to $C_T(f_M, f_{opt}) = \lfloor 2.26 \rfloor = 2$ and $C_{A7}(f_M, f_{opt}) = \lfloor 3.19 \rfloor = 3$.

Let us analyze the energy efficiency of these options. At f_M, the system consumes $E_T(f_M) = 55.8$ J to solve the problem, with $E_{A7}(f_M) = 41.3$ J corresponding to the Cortex-A7 cluster. Assuming perfect scalability (see Section 4), we can expect that 2 Cortex-A7 clusters, operating at f_{opt}, obtain the solution in $\bar{T}(f_{opt}, 2) = T(f_{opt})/2 = 159.3/2 = 79.6$ s and 3 clusters in $\bar{T}(f_{opt}, 3) = T(f_{opt})/3 = 159.3/3 = 53.1$ s. For these configurations, we can therefore estimate total and Cortex-A7 energy consumption of $\bar{E}_T(f_{opt}, 2) = \bar{T}(f_{opt}, 2) \cdot P_T(f_M) = 79.6 \cdot 0.587 = 46.7$ J and $\bar{E}_{A7}(f_{opt}, 3) = \bar{T}(f_{opt}, 3) \cdot P_{A7}(f_M) = 53.1 \cdot 0.438 = 23.2$ J, respectively. This represents a gain in energy efficiency of $E_T(f_M)/\bar{E}_T(f_{opt}, 2) = 55.8/46.7 = 1.19\times$ compared with the SoC+DIMMs; and $E_{A7}(f_M)/\bar{E}_{A7}(f_{opt}, 3) = 41.3/23.2 = 1.77\times$ with respect to the Cortex-A7.

We recognize that our assumption of perfect scalability may be slightly too optimistic (tough we could experimentally observe a speed-up higher than 15 when executing the same code on 16 Intel Xeon cores). On the other hand, we point out that we considered that a system consisting of 2 (or 3) clusters dissipated the same instantaneous power as one composed of 2.26 (or 3.19) clusters. This partially compensates for the scalability approximation. Table 2 collects the results from this analysis for all possible frequencies, exposing the largest energy saving factors to be at $1.77\times$, for $f_i = 300$ MHz, if we consider only the Cortex-A7; and $1.34\times$, for $f_i = 350$ MHz, if we take into account the SoC+DIMMs.

Freq. (MHz) f_i	$P(f_M)/P(f_i) =$		$C_i = C(f_M, f_i) = \lfloor P(f_M)/P(f_i) \rfloor$		$\bar{T}(f_i, C_i) = T(f_i)/C(f_i)$		$\bar{E}(f_i, C_i) = \bar{T}(f_i, C_i) \cdot P(f_M)$		Gain/loss= $E(f_M)/\bar{E}(f_i, C_i)$	
	Total	A7	Total	A7	Total	A7	Total	A7	Total	A7
50	2.73	3.71	2	3	145.9	97.2	85.6	42.6	0.65	0.96
100	2.74	3.94	2	3	129.7	86.5	76.1	37.8	0.73	1.09
150	2.70	4.01	2	4	115.0	57.5	67.5	25.1	0.82	1.63
200	2.60	3.91	2	3	101.8	67.8	59.7	29.7	0.93	1.38
250	2.45	3.61	2	3	90.0	60.0	52.8	26.2	1.05	1.57
300	2.26	3.19	2	3	79.6	53.1	46.7	23.2	1.19	1.77
350	2.04	2.72	2	2	70.7	70.7	41.5	30.9	1.34	1.33
400	1.80	2.25	1	2	126.6	63.3	74.3	27.7	0.75	1.48
450	1.57	1.84	1	1	114.6	114.6	67.2	50.1	0.82	0.82
500	1.36	1.50	1	1	105.5	105.5	61.9	46.2	0.90	0.89
550	1.16	1.22	1	1	99.3	99.3	58.2	43.4	0.95	0.94
600	1.00	1.00	1	1	96.0	96.0	55.8	41.3	1.00	1.00

Table 2. Potential energy savings (or losses) within an iso-power budget scenario determined using 4 ARM Cortex-A7 cores and a problem instance consisting of $l=8$ leaves.

To summarize the analysis in this section, our experiments show that there exist some "sweet points" from the perspective of frequency, which could allow to leverage a larger number of cores that match the power budget of a full Cortex-A7 cluster operating at the highest frequency (iso-power), solve the problem in less time, and increase energy efficiency with respect to that configuration.

6. Energy Efficiency and Fault Tolerance

NTVC is a technology that promises important power/energy reductions by lowering the voltage while keeping the frequency mostly constant [11]. While this decrease of power can, in principle, be leveraged to integrate additional core concurrency, the potential negative effect is that these hardware becomes less reliable and additional mechanisms (e.g., in software) need to compensate for it.

In this section we study the error rate that can be accommodated into an iterative solver such as ILUPACK, running on a "faulty" architecture, while still being more efficient from the point of view of energy consumption than the same code executed on a reliable system. For this purpose, we consider that an unreliable hardware, operating under NTVC, only corrupts the results from the floating-point arithmetic operations, degrading the convergence rate of the PCG iteration. In practice, faults can occur anywhere, producing an ample variety of effects: from catastrophic crashes in the program (which are easy to detect) to soft errors exerting no visible impact on the application (e.g., a fault that corrupts the result of a branch prediction may affect performance, but not the numerical results) [15].

As argued earlier, we can decompose the power into its static and dynamic components, where the global consumption depends on $V^2 f$ and, for safety, current technology sets V proportionally to f. Assume that NTVC can lower the voltage while maintaining the frequency. (In practice, even with NTVC, the frequency would need to be slightly reduced as the voltage is diminished.) In an ideal situation where no errors occur, we can therefore expect that the execution time of the solver does not vary, but its power dissipation rate rapidly decays (indeed, quadratically with the reduction of voltage) and, therefore, so does energy (in the same proportion). In other words, scaling the voltage as V/σ changes the power to P/σ^2, but preserves the execution time T, hence reducing the energy by E/σ^2. Let us analyze next the trade-offs in two configurations where errors are present:

- **Improve power/energy at the expense of time-to-solution (TTS).** Given a decrease of power $\hat{P} = P/s$ (produced by a reduction of voltage by $\sigma = \sqrt{s}$), we can afford an error rate $\hat{e}$ which degrades convergence by a factor of up to $\hat{d}$, with $\hat{d} \leq s$, with an analogous increase in execution time $\hat{T} = T \cdot \hat{d}$, and still save energy by a factor $\hat{d}/s$, as $\hat{E} = \hat{T} \cdot \hat{P} = T \cdot \hat{d} \cdot P/s = (\hat{d}/s)E \leq E$.

- **Improve TTS/energy using additional hardware.** Alternatively, we can leverage a reduction of power in P/s to increase the number of computational resources (i.e., hardware) by a factor of s, and thus confront an iso-power scenario with a dissipation rate $\tilde{P} \approx P$. This approach would benefit from the near perfect scalability of ILUPACK, in order to reduce the execution time to T/s (when no errors are present). In addition, we require that the increase in the error rate induced by the use of additional hardware, likely from e to $\tilde{e} = e \cdot s$, does not produce an analogous raise the degradation rate by a factor of s as, otherwise, the advantages of increasing the amount of hardware will be blurred. Our only hope in this sense is to introduce a low-cost mechanism in the solver, in the form of a detection+correction or a prevention strategy [10,14] which, for a cost $\tilde{c}$ that depends on the iteration number, limits the effect of the errors on the convergence degradation.

Under these ideal conditions, with a convergence degradation factor of $\tilde{d} \leq s$, the execution is completed in $\tilde{T} = (T/s + \tilde{c}) \cdot \tilde{d} = (\tilde{d}/s)T + \tilde{c}\tilde{d} \leq T$; and the energy consumed by the new configuration is given by $\tilde{E} = \tilde{T} \cdot \tilde{P} = (T/s + \tilde{c}) \cdot \tilde{d} \cdot P = (\tilde{d}/s)E + \tilde{c}\tilde{d}P \leq E$. The factor $\tilde{c}\tilde{d}$ in the time and energy expressions represents the cost of the fault tolerance mechanism, which initially increases time by $\tilde{c}$ units, but in total raises the cost to $\tilde{c}\tilde{d}$ because of the convergence degradation. For simplicity, for the energy expression we assume that this mechanism dissipates the same power rate as the solver, though the formula can be easily adapted otherwise.

7. Concluding Remarks

We have conducted an experimental analysis of the effect of voltage-frequency scaling on the scalability, power dissipation and energy consumption of an efficient multi-threaded version of the preconditioned CG method on a low-power ARM multicore SoC. Our results show a remarkable scalability for the solver, independent of the operating frequency f, but a lower bound on the execution time as f grows. Combined with the cubic relation between power and frequency, this determines an optimal operating frequency from the point of view of energy consumption which is in the low band, much below the highest possible in this chip. Using linear regression to interpolate the experimental data, we have exposed the potential gains that can be obtained by leveraging the power budget available by running at a lower frequency to execute the code with an increased number of cores. For example, under certain conditions, the execution of the solver using 2 ARM Cortex-A7 clusters at a very low frequency can report energy savings around 16% with respect to an execution on a single cluster running at the highest frequency while matching the iso-power of the global SoC+DIMMs. If we consider the power budget for the Cortex-A7 cluster, though, it is possible to employ 3 ARM Cortex-A7 clusters instead of 1, and the savings boost to 43%.

NTVC promises important reductions in the power consumption that allow the exploitation of Moore's law to build multicore processors with increased numbers of cores (or wider SIMD units) at the expense, possibly, of higher error rates. For an iterative numerical solver like ILUPACK, we can expect that many of these errors occur during the floating-point arithmetic, affecting the convergence rate of the method. In this sense, it is important that the convergence degradation of the method does not grow at the same pace as the error rate/number of computational resources enabled by NTVC. Otherwise, benefits are cancelled, and we can only trade lower energy consumption for increased execution time while keeping constant the number of computational resources.

Acknowledgments

The researchers from *Universidad Jaume I* (UJI) were supported by projects TIN2011-23283 and TIN2014-53495-R of the Spanish *Ministerio de Economía y Competitividad*. We thank Maria Barreda from UJI for her support with the power measurement system on the Exynos5 SoC. This research has also been partially supported by the UK Engineering and Physical Sciences Research Council (grants EP/L000055/1,

EP/L004232/1, EP/M01147X/1, EP/M015742/1, EP/K017594/1), the Royal Society (grant WM150009), and the European Commission (grants 644312, 610509, 323872).

References

[1]   J. I. Aliaga, R. M. Badia, M. Barreda, M. Bollhöfer, and E. S. Quintana-Ortí. Leveraging task-parallelism with OmpSs in ILUPACK's preconditioned CG method. In *26th Int. Symp. on Computer Architecture and High Performance Computing (SBAC-PAD)*, pages 262–269, 2014.

[2]   J. I. Aliaga, M. Bollhöfer, A. F. Martín, and E. S. Quintana-Ortí. Exploiting thread-level parallelism in the iterative solution of sparse linear systems. *Parallel Computing*, 37(3):183–202, 2011.

[3]   Matthias Bollhöfer and Yousef Saad. Multilevel preconditioners constructed from inverse-based ILUs. *SIAM Journal on Scientific Computing*, 27(5):1627–1650, 2006.

[4]   C. Chalios, D. S. Nikolopoulos, S. Catalán, and E. S. Quintana-Ortí. Evaluating asymmetric multicore systems-on-chip and the cost of fault tolerance using iso-metrics. *IET Computers & Digital Techniques*, 2015. To appear.

[5]   R.H. Dennard, F.H. Gaensslen, V.L. Rideout, E. Bassous, and A.R. LeBlanc. Design of ion-implanted MOSFET's with very small physical dimensions. *IEEE J. Solid-State Circuits*, 9(5):256–268, 1974.

[6]   J. Dongarra and M. A. Heroux. Toward a new metric for ranking high performance computing systems. Sandia Report SAND2013-4744, Sandia National Laboratories, June 2013.

[7]   M. Duranton, K. De Bosschere, A. Cohen, J. Maebe, and H. Munk. HiPEAC vision 2015, 2015. https://www.hipeac.org/assets/public/publications/vision/hipeac-vision-2015_DqOboL8.pdf.

[8]   H. Esmaeilzadeh, E. Blem, R. St. Amant, K. Sankaralingam, and D. Burger. Dark silicon and the end of multicore scaling. In *Proc. 38th Annual Int. Symp. Computer Arch.*, ISCA'11, pages 365–376, 2011.

[9]   J. L. Hennessy and D. A. Patterson. *Computer Architecture: A Quantitative Approach*. Morgan Kaufmann Pub., 5th edition, 2012.

[10] M. Hoemmen and M. A. Heroux. Fault-tolerant iterative methods via selective reliability. In *Proceedings of the 2011 International Conference for High Performance Computing, Networking, Storage and Analysis (SC)*, 2011.

[11] U.R. Karpuzcu, Nam Sung Kim, and J. Torrellas. Coping with parametric variation at near-threshold voltages. *Micro, IEEE*, 33(4):6–14, 2013.

[12] J. D. McCalpin. STREAM: sustainable memory bandwidth in high performance computers.

[13] Y. Saad. *Iterative methods for sparse linear systems*. Society for Industrial and Applied Mathematics, Philadelphia, PA, USA, 3rd edition, 2003.

[14] P. Sao and R. Vuduc. Self-stabilizing iterative solvers. In *Workshop Latest Advances in Scalable Algorithms for Large-Scale Systems*, pages 4:1–4:8, 2013.

[15] Daniel J. Sorin. *Fault Tolerant Computer Architecture*. Morgan & Claypool Pub., 2009.

Parallel Computing: On the Road to Exascale
G.R. Joubert et al. (Eds.)
IOS Press, 2016
© *2016 The authors and IOS Press. All rights reserved.*
doi:10.3233/978-1-61499-621-7-721

Compiling for Resilience: the Performance Gap

Norman A. RINK[1], Dmitrii KUVAISKII, Jeronimo CASTRILLON, and
Christof FETZER

Technische Universität Dresden, Dresden, Germany
Center for Advancing Electronics Dresden (cfaed)

Abstract. In order to perform reliable computations on unreliable hardware, software-based protection mechanisms have been proposed. In this paper we present a compiler infrastructure for software-based code hardening based on *encoding*. We analyze the trade-off between performance and fault coverage. We look at different code generation strategies that improve the performance of hardened programs by up to $2x$ while incurring little fault coverage degradation.

Keywords. AN enoding, resilient code generation, optimization, LLVM

Introduction

Nowadays there are many safety-critical applications, e.g. automotive applications, that pose serious challenges to reliability since a program bug or a hardware fault can have catastrophic consequences. Lately, advances in technology have further reduced systems reliability, with non-negligible failure probabilities in processors [9] and memories [14]. Hardware-based protection is costly and inexistent in commodity hardware. To enable resilient computations on unreliable hardware, several software-based fault detection techniques have been proposed [3]. These techniques harden programs against hardware faults by adding instructions to detect and potentially recover from faults at run-time. A prominent software protection mechanism works by *encoding* the values and operations of the program and inserting checks to detect transient and permanent faults.

Several encoding strategies have been proposed and analyzed in the literature [2,13, 12,6]. Fault coverage increases with the number of encoding and checking instructions added by these strategies, but so too does the slow-down. Typical slow-downs for achieving a high fault coverage are in the range of $10x$-$100x$. Previous work has focused on analyzing the slow-down and coverage characteristics of different encoding techniques, which usually follow ad-hoc strategies when inserting checks into the code. We believe that a more careful placement of checks based on code analysis can lead to considerable performance improvements with a low coverage penalty.

In this paper, we introduce a compiler infrastructure for the generation of resilient code which allows us to implement and analyze different check-insertion strategies. We

---

[1] norman.rink@tu-dresden.de

focus on AN encoding [12] and perform a thorough analysis of the trade-off between fault coverage and performance degradation for simple check-insertion strategies. Our analysis provides insights into the performance gap which could be further reduced by clever encoding-specific compiler optimizations in the future.

The rest of this paper is organized as follows. In Section 1 we introduce AN encoding and look into implementation details related to it. Section 2 discusses related work. Our compilation framework and tool flow are introduced in Section 3. In Section 4 we analyze fault coverage and perfomance characteristics of our implementation of AN encoding. Section 5 concludes the paper and gives an outlook towards future work.

1. Background: AN Encoding

AN encoding is a fault detection technique that changes the representation of data. Let n be an integer variable. The AN-encoded version of n is $\hat{n} = n \cdot A$, with a constant integer A. Decoding amounts to $n = \hat{n}/A$. One can test whether a variable is correctly encoded by checking if $\hat{n} \bmod A = 0$. If $\hat{n}$ is corrupted, then, with high probability, $\hat{n} \bmod A \neq 0$. Encoding, decoding, and checking are implemented by the functions in Listing 1.

The ability of AN encoding to detect faults efficiently varies with A. In our work we use one of the recommended values from [4], namely $A = 58659$. To avoid overflow due to encoding, programs must only use integer values that fit into 32 bits but must declare integer variables with 64-bit data types.

When AN-encoding a program, operations on encoded values must be replaced with encoded versions. Since addition and subtraction operations preserve multiples of A, their encoded versions are identical to the standard operations. In the encoded versions of bitwise operations, arguments are decoded first, then the unencoded operation is applied, and finally the result is encoded, as shown in Listing 2 (see [12] for more details). Note that while operating on decoded values (variables xp and yp in Listing 2), AN encoding cannot give any protection.

Listing 1. Basic AN encoding functions.

```
int64_t encode (int64_t x) {
    return x * A;
}
int64_t decode (int64_t x) {
    return x / A;
}
int64_t check (int64_t x) {
    return x % A;
}
```

Listing 2. Encoded bitwise operations.

```
int64_t and_enc (int64_t x,
                 int64_t y) {
    int64_t xp = decode (x);
    int64_t yp = decode (y);
    return encode (xp & yp);
}
```

A subtlety occurs for multiplication: if two encoded values are multiplied, a factor of A^2 is picked up, which may cause overflow even if 64-bit integers are used. Hence the encoded version of multiplication should be performed on 128-bit data types. Since this is expensive, we implement multiplication by operating on partially decoded values: in Listing 3 we use the fact that $58659 = 278 * 211 + 1$. This ensures that none of the intermediate values in Listing 3 are greater than A times the respective decoded values. Note that despite the fact that decoded values are used in Listing 3, operations are never performed exclusively on decoded values (unlike in Listing 2). Hence partially encoded multiplication is not as vulnerable to faults as bitwise operations.

Listing 3. Partially encoded multiplication.

```
int64_t mul_enc(int64_t x, int64_t y) {
   int64_t xp = decode(x);
   int64_t yp = decode(y);
   return ((x - xp)/278)*((y - yp)/211) + xp*yp;
}
```

The encoded version of division also requires special treatment. We omit a detailed discussion here since the test cases we look at in Section 4 do not use integer division. The interested reader is again referred to [12].

AN encoding does not offer direct protection for control-flow. However, illegal control-flow is detected if it leads to incorrectly encoded data. Memories, including caches and register files, are immediately protected by AN encoding: if a value that is stored in memory is corrupted, this will be detected the next time the value is used in a computation.

2. Related Work

Increasing fault coverage and reducing the overhead of encoding have been the focus of many research projects in the past. Improvements of AN encoding, namely ANB and ANBD, were first proposed in [2], with further work in [13,12], where slow-downs of over $250x$ due to improved fault coverage were reported. Δ-encoding [6] improves performance and fault coverage by coupling AN encoding with code duplication. By introducing ad-hoc optimizations Δ-encoding achieves average slow-downs of $3x$-$5x$. The impact of the encoding factor A on fault coverage and performance has been analyzed in [4] and [5] respectively.

Optimization-driven research has been conducted on fault detection techniques other than AN encoding. Partly similar to our approach, ESoftCheck [15] aims to reduce the number of checks in the SWIFT [11] fault detection approach. Shoestring [1] investigates selective hardening of programs. Both ESoftCheck and Shoestring differ from our work since AN encoding is amenable to substantially different optimization strategies.

3. The Encoding Compilation Flow

Figure 1 gives an overview of our compilation flow, which can be summarized as follows. After the *Manual refactoring* and *IR generation* stages the code portion to be AN-encoded is transformed by the encoding compiler passes at the level of LLVM [7] intermediate representation (IR). The AN-encoded IR is linked and compiled together with the rest of the application. In the *Testing* stage the binary is fed to our fault injection and

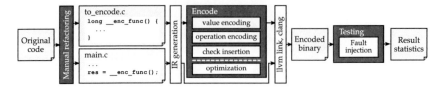

Figure 1. Tool flow for the encoding compiler.

testing framework. The following subsections discuss the compilation flow in detail. The testing framework will be introduced in Section 4.

3.1. Restrictions and Manual Refactoring

In our flow one must manually identify parts of the original code to which AN encoding is to be applied (to_encode.c in Figure 1). Since AN encoding is not applied to main.c, a calling convention must be defined and adhered to when calling encoded functions. Whenever Encode sees a function that is prefixed with ___enc_, it assumes that this function is only called from non-encoded parts of the application. It then encodes function arguments before emitting the function body and decodes return values before emitting return statements.

As explained in Section 1, to avoid overflow due to encoding of values, functions to be encoded must only use integer values that fit into 32 bits but must declare integer variables with 64-bit data types. The Encode stage expects all integer data types to be 64 bits wide. Optimizations are therefore not applied at the *IR generation* stage since they may introduce smaller data types.

3.2. Compiler Passes for AN Encoding

AN encoding is achieved in three passes: (a) value encoding, (b) operation encoding, (c) check insertion (see Figure 1). Each pass operates on a data-flow graph corresponding to a basic block in the input program. The data-flow graph in Figure 2a serves to illustrate the actions of these passes.

Value encoding identifies two kinds of nodes in the data-flow graph: *entry* and *exit* nodes. An entry node represents unencoded values that enter the data-flow graph, e.g. constants or return values from external functions. An *exit* node is where an encoded value leaves the encoded region, e.g. arguments to external functions or return values from functions prefixed with ___enc_. This pass places encode operations on data-flow edges from entry nodes and decode operations on edges to exit nodes (see Figure 2b).

Operation encoding replaces arithmetic and bitwise operations with their respective encoded versions (see and_enc node in Figure 2b).

Check insertion inserts check placeholders for every argument of an encoded operation, as depicted in Figure 2c. How placeholders are later filled in is explained in Section 3.3. We do not emit checks for results of encoded operations since they are checked again when they appear as arguments of subsequent operations. We also do not emit checks for compile-time constants; such checks would be redundant since constants have been encoded by the value encoding pass.

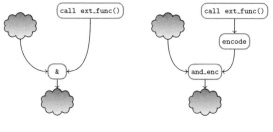
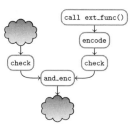

Figure 2a. Original data-flow graph.

Figure 2b. Data-flow graph after encoding.

Figure 2c. Data-flow graph after encoding and check insertion.

3.3. Optimization strategies for AN-encoding

Naively, every placeholder that has been added by the check insertion pass must be expanded into the code sequence in Listing 4. AN-encoding-specific optimization strategies are aimed at reducing the number of expensive modulo operations used in checks, which can be achieved by two orthogonal approaches: (a) avoidance of the emission of code for redundant checks and (b) replacement of modulo operations by instructions of lower latency. Based on these approaches we implement different strategies for filling in the check placeholders.

In our first strategy, every placeholder is expanded into the code in Listing 4. This serves as the baseline for comparisons with other strategies. We refer to this strategy as *comprehensive checking* (*COMPCHK*) since it inserts the largest number of checks.

In the second strategy, every placeholder is expanded into an accumulation operation which adds the value to be checked to the local variable acc. Since AN encoding is preserved under addition, it then suffices to check that acc mod $A = 0$ before exiting the function, thus requiring only a single modulo operation per function. However, since overflow does not preserve AN encoding, placeholders are expanded into the code in Listing 5. Since overflow happens rarely, the if-body adds little overhead at run-time.[2] We refer to this second strategy as *accumulation of checks* (*ACCUCHK*), more details of which can be found in [6].

The third strategy is a relaxation of the previous one: only every other placeholder is expanded. The check that acc mod $A = 0$ is still performed at the end of each function. We refer to this strategy as *omission of accumulations* (*OMIACCU*). This strategy serves as a model for future optimization strategies that should omit checks based on the structure and vulnerabilities of the data-flow graph.

Listing 4. Expansion of a check placeholder.

```
if  (x % A)
    exit (AN_ERROR_CODE);
```

Listing 5. Check with accumulator.

```
_acc  =  acc ;
acc  +=  x ;
if  (/* overflow has occured */) {
    if  (_acc % A)  exit (AN_ERROR_CODE);
    acc  =  x ;
}
```

---

[2]Checking for overflow is implemented in the x86 instruction set as follows:
```
add acc, x
jno end of if-body
```

The resulting LLVM IR is subjected to LLVM's standard optimizations at level -O2. During these standard optimizations, the compiler may want to remove check instructions if it can statically infer that the value is a multiple of A. Since faults happen dynamically, check instructions should not be removed. Therefore we *pin* check instructions by first applying an opaque copy instruction to the check's argument. The opaque copy is removed only immediately before register allocation. This way the register allocator can delete unnecessary move instructions that may have been introduced due to the opaque copy, and further optimizations can be applied post register allocation.

4. Fault Injection, Benchmarking, and Results

For measuring performance and fault coverage we have selected five representative benchmarks. **Array Reduction** and **Matrix-Vector Multiplication** are common linear algebra tasks, featuring a large number of arithmetic operations. **Array Copy** serves to assess the impact of AN encoding on pointer arithmetic. Since our implementation of AN encoding does not encode pointers, this benchmark uses integer arithmetic on addresses to access the elements of the source and target array. The **DES**[3] benchmark is a simplified version of the Data Encryption Standard algorithm, which contains a large basic block with many bitwise operations. **CRC** (cyclic redundancy check) also features many bitwise operations but has smaller basic blocks.

Recall that in our AN encoder we use $A = 58659$. All data reported in this paper was obtained on an Intel Core i7 CPU running at 3.60GHz with 32GB of RAM. It should be noted that all benchmarks listed above are implemented as single-threaded programs.

4.1. Performance Benchmarking

The above benchmarks have been implemented in separate source files which are valid input to the Encode stage in Figure 1. Each benchmark is called from a main program and cycles spent are counted, following the procedure in [10]. For each benchmark we report the slow-downs of the three AN-encoded versions, obtained by applying the strategies *COMPCHK*, *ACCUCHK*, and *OMIACCU*, over the original program.

4.2. Fault Injection and Fault Coverage

We use the same fault model and fault injection mechanism as in [6]. Specifically, faults are injected at run-time using the Pin tool [8] in conjunction with the BFI plug-in[4]. During program run-time these tools introduce transient bit-flips into a single one of the following places: memory (during read and write), registers (during read and write), address bus (during read and write to memory), and instruction opcodes.

For every benchmark and each of our strategies we execute the benchmark program 36,000 times. During each execution a single fault is injected at random and the program's exit code and output are used to detect one of five events. If the program completes with its expected exit code and correct output, we say that a **CORRECT** event has occurred. If AN encoding detects a fault, then the program is exited prematurely

---

[3]http://csrc.nist.gov/publications/fips/fips46-3/fips46-3.pdf
[4]https://bitbucket.org/db7/bfi

with exit code AN_ERROR_CODE. This is called an **ANCRASH** event. If the injected fault causes the operating system to terminate the program, e.g. due to a segmentation fault, an **OSCRASH** event has occured. If the program does not finish within $10x$ of its execution time without fault injection, the program is deemed to hang and is terminated. This is a **HANG** event. Finally, if the program completes with its expected exit code but produces incorrect output, *silent data corruption* has happened, i.e. an **SDC** event.

The goal of any error detection strategy is to reduce the frequency of silent data corruption. For evaluation purposes, we define *fault coverage* as the proportion of fault injection experiments that did not lead to silent data corruption. This is reasonable since for non-SDC events the program either behaved correctly or it terminated abnormally, which serves to indicate to the user that the program's output cannot be relied on.[5]

4.3. Results

Figure 3 contains the fault coverage results. The sets of bars on the left of each plot show the proportion of all events listed above. Given that we only encode and check a limited number of operations, it is remarkable that three of the benchmarks, namely Array Reduction, Matrix-Vector Mult., and CRC, exhibit a fault coverage of around 80%. For DES this is also the case in the *COMPCHK* strategy. Unsurprisingly, the fault coverage is much lower for Array Copy, which uses few arithmetic operations.

The sets of bars on the right of each plot refer only to those fault injections that led to incorrect program completion. This eases the comparison of ANCRASH events between the different strategies. The bars on the right are based on the same data as the ones on the left. Figure 3 clearly shows that the *COMPCHK* strategy produces the highest number of ANCRASH events, with *ACCUCHK* in second place and *OMIACCU* in third, as one would expect. However, an important observation is that the overall fault coverage does not always vary greatly between different strategies.

It is easy to understand why there should be little difference in the fault coverage of the *COMPCHK* and *ACCUCHK* strategies: precisely the same intermediate values contribute to the checks performed in these strategies. Since the *ACCUCHK* strategy performs checks later, there is a possibility that an OSCRASH event occurs before the ANCRASH can be triggered. This will lead to a shift of proportions away from AN-CRASH and towards OSCRASH, which is indeed observed for the Array Reduction, Matrix-Vector Mult., and Array Copy benchmarks.

An analogous argument explains the large proportion of CORRECT events for the CRC benchmark in the *OMIACCU* strategy. In the *COMPCHK* and *ACCUCHK* strategies the AN encoder apparently detects many *masked* faults. These are faults which do not affect the program's output. Since in the *OMIACCU* strategy only every other check is performed, many masked faults will not cause an ANCRASH but will instead lead to correct program behaviour.

For the Matrix-Vector Mult. benchmark the fault coverage has an unexpected peak at the *ACCUCHK* strategy (Figure 3b). To understand this, one has to bear in mind that different code is generated for the different strategies. Specifically, the code that is generated for the Matrix-Vector Mult. benchmark in the *ACCUCHK* strategy exhibits more register spilling than in the *COMPCHK* strategy. One of the spilled values is the base address of the result vector. If a fault is injected into the address bus while the vector's

---

[5]Here we regard a HANG event, namely the program's failure to terminate, also as an abnormal termination.

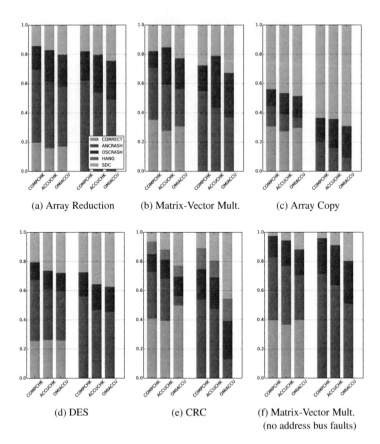

(a) Array Reduction   (b) Matrix-Vector Mult.   (c) Array Copy

(d) DES   (e) CRC   (f) Matrix-Vector Mult.
(no address bus faults)

Figure 3. Fault coverage. Bars on the left show event frequencies. Bars on the right show frequencies of non-CORRECT events.

base address is being restored from the stack, a subsequent write to the result vector will take place at an invalid address. This will trigger a segmentation fault, i.e. an OSCRASH occurs. This behaviour is responsible for the significant increase in the proportion of OSCRASH events in the *ACCUCHK* strategy compared with *COMPCHK*. If we ignore faults injected into the address bus, Figure 3f, then we obtain the expected degradation of fault coverage between *COMPCHK* and *ACCUCHK*.

In Figure 4, the vertical axes show the slow-downs incurred by different benchmarks due to AN encoding. The horizontal axes denote the size of the input array in units of 64-bit words. The slow-downs are roughly constant across different parts of the depicted ranges. Where jumps occur, they are due to reaching the end of a cache level. There are significant improvements in the slow-downs for Array Reduction, Matrix-Vector Mult., and Array Copy when moving to the *ACCUCHK* and the *OMIACCU* strategies. This is remarkable since there is only a moderate difference in the fault coverage, especially for the Array Reduction and Array Copy benchmarks. The speed-ups of *OMIACCU* over the *COMPCHK* strategy for Array Reduction and Array Copy are 2.09x and 2.21x respectively. For Matrix-Vector Mult. this speed-up is 1.59x.

In Table 1 we give the slow-downs for the DES and CRC benchmarks, with fixed input length. For the DES benchmark there is only a small difference between the slow-

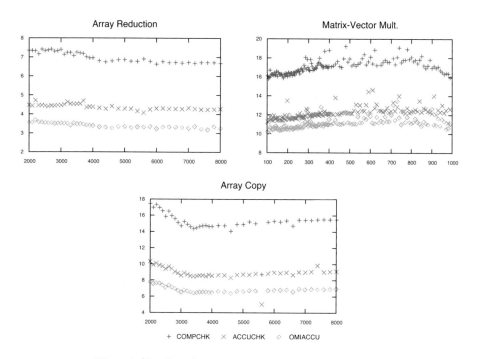

Figure 4. Slow-down due to AN encoding, variable input length.

down in the *ACCUCHK* and the *OMIACCU* scheme. This is nicely aligned with the fact that the respective fault coverages are almost identical (cf. Figure 3d). However, for the CRC benchmark little variation in the slow-downs between the different strategies is accompanied by noticeable drops in the fault coverages (Figure 3e). The speed-ups in going from the *COMPCHK* to the *OMIACCU* strategy are $1.34x$ for DES and $1.11x$ for CRC.

5. Summary and Outlook

Our analysis has identified essentially two ways in which the omission of checks or accumulations can influence the AN-encoded versions of programs: (1) performance improves significantly while fault coverage hardly decreases and (2) performance remains approximately the same while fault coverage drops. Where performance improves, our strategies have reduced the performance gap we mentioned in the introduction by half.

A smart generator of resilient code should be able to determine when it is beneficial to omit checks or accumulations. In the future we would like to look at more sophisticated

	COMPCHK	ACCUCHK	OMIACCU	input length
DES	6.08	4.89	4.55	256KB
CRC	5.36	4.98	4.85	1.4MB

Table 1. Slow-down due to AN encoding, fixed input length.

models of program vulnerability to faults. Such models should take into account the program or data-flow structure when deciding where to place checks.

Since not all programs benefit from the omission of checks, one must also study different approaches to generate fast and resilient code. Feeding coverage data back to our encoding compiler could be one such approach.

Acknowledgements

This work is partly supported by the German Research Foundation (DFG) within the Cluster of Excellence 'Center for Advancing Electronics Dresden' (cfaed). The authors thank Sven Karol for useful discussions and proof-reading the manuscript of this paper.

References

[1]   S. Feng, S. Gupta, A. Ansari, and S. Mahlke. Shoestring: Probabilistic soft error reliability on the cheap. In *Architectural Support for Programming Languages and Operating Systems*, ASPLOS, pages 385–396. ACM, 2010.

[2]   P. Forin. Vital coded microprocessor principles and application for various transit systems. *IFAC/IFIP/I-FORS*, 1989.

[3]   O. Goloubeva, M. Rebaudengo, M. Sonza Reorda, and M. Violante. *Software-Implemented Hardware Fault Tolerance*. Springer, 2006.

[4]   M. Hoffmann, P. Ulbrich, C. Dietrich, H. Schirmeier, D. Lohmann, and W. Schroder-Preikschat. A practitioner's guide to software-based soft-error mitigation using AN-codes. In *High-Assurance Systems Engineering*, pages 33–40, Jan 2014.

[5]   T. Kolditz, D. Habich, P. Damme, W. Lehner, D. Kuvaiskii, O. Oleksenko, and C. Fetzer. Resiliency-aware data compression for in-memory database systems. In *Data Management Technologies and Applications*, DATA, 2015.

[6]   D. Kuvaiskii and C. Fetzer. Δ-encoding: Practical encoded processing. In *Dependable Systems and Networks (DSN'15)*. IEEE Comp. Soc., June 2015.

[7]   C. Lattner and V. Adve. LLVM: A compilation framework for lifelong program analysis & transformation. In *Code Generation and Optimization (CGO)*, pages 75–86. IEEE, 2004.

[8]   C.-K. Luk, R. Cohn, R. Muth, H. Patil, A. Klauser, G. Lowney, S. Wallace, V. J. Reddi, and K. Hazelwood. Pin: Building customized program analysis tools with dynamic instrumentation. In *Programming Language Design and Implementation*, PLDI, pages 190–200. ACM, 2005.

[9]   E. B. Nightingale, J. R. Douceur, and V. Orgovan. Cycles, cells and platters: An empirical analysis of hardware failures on a million consumer PCs. *EuroSys 2011*, April 2011.

[10] G. Paoloni. How to benchmark code execution times on Intel IA-32 and IA-64 instruction set architectures, 2010.

[11] G. A. Reis, J. Chang, N. Vachharajani, R. Rangan, and D. I. August. SWIFT: Software implemented fault tolerance. In *Code generation and optimization (CGO)*, pages 243–254. IEEE Comp. Soc., 2005.

[12] U. Schiffel. *Hardware Error Detection Using AN-Codes*. PhD thesis, TU Dresden, 2011.

[13] U. Schiffel, A. Schmitt, M. Süßkraut, and C. Fetzer. ANB- and ANBDmem-encoding: Detecting hardware errors in software. In E. Schoitsch, editor, *Computer Safety, Reliability, and Security*, volume 6351 of *Lecture Notes in Computer Science*, pages 169–182. Springer Berlin / Heidelberg, 2010.

[14] B. Schroeder, E. Pinheiro, and W.-D. Weber. DRAM errors in the wild: A large-scale field study. In *easurement and Modeling of Computer Systems*, SIGMETRICS, pages 193–204. ACM, 2009.

[15] J. Yu, M. J. Garzaran, and M. Snir. ESoftCheck: Removal of non-vital checks for fault tolerance. In *Code Generation and Optimization (CGO)*, pages 35–46. IEEE Comp. Soc., 2009.

Parallel Computing: On the Road to Exascale   731
G.R. Joubert et al. (Eds.)
IOS Press, 2016
doi:10.3233/978-1-61499-621-7-731

Automation of Significance Analyses with Interval Splitting

Deussen, J. [a,1], Riehme, J. [a] and Naumann, U. [a]

[a] *LuFG Informatik 12, RWTH Aachen University*
Software and Tools for Computational Engineering

Abstract. In the SCoRPiO project we are interested in the significance of program code with regard to its outputs in order to compute less significant parts for instance on less reliable but power saving hardware. Multiple approaches can be taken including pure interval arithmetics [1], Monte Carlo methods, and a tool chain for interval derivative based significance analysis. The tool chain $\texttt{dco/scorpio}$ [2,3] was introduced in the SCoRPiO project. In this paper we propose to automate the process of interval derivative based significance analysis to widen input domains. We present an interval splitting approach to handle difficulties introduced by the interval evaluation, e.g. unfeasible relational operators or the *wrapping effect*. Each split will result in multiple scenarios which can be computed in parallel. The presented approach is a step forward towards a fully automatic significance analysis of computer code.

Keywords. Significance Analysis, Energy Efficient Algorithm, Approximate Computing, Green Computing, Interval Arithmetic, Algorithmic Differentiation, Significance Based Hardware Development

Introduction

The aim of the SCoRPiO project[2] is to exploit the fact that not all computations of an application are equally important for the quality of the result. Therefore automatic code characterization techniques which use compile- and run-time analyses have to be developed to classify computations and data structures. By defining a significance for the computations it is possible to reduce the energy consumption by steering insignificant computations to a low-power, yet unreliable hardware. Furthermore the significance can be used on a software level to save computing time by replacing insignificant computations by representative expressions or constants. For that reason, the significance analysis is executed at compile time such that a high computational effort can be tolerated.

The main idea of the analysis is to define significance based on user given input intervals and an interval evaluation of function values and first-order derivatives. For this significance analysis we developed $\texttt{dco/scorpio}$ [3] which is a SCoRPiO specific ex-

---

[1]Corresponding Author: Researcher, LuFG Informatik 12, RWTH Aachen, 52062 Aachen, Germany; E-mail: deussen@stce.rwth-aachen.de.

[2]$\texttt{http://www.scorpio-project.eu/outline/}$

tension of our tool dco/c++ [4,5] for Algorithmic Differentiation (AD) [6,7]. To handle difficulties introduced by the interval evaluation, e.g. unfeasible relational operators or the *wrapping effect*, an additional approach is required. Therefore we will use interval splitting for the affected variables which will result in multiple scenarios that can be computed in parallel.

In this paper we will give an overview of dco/scorpio for the significance analysis and we will introduce an approach for the interval splitting that will be part of this tool chain. The significance analysis with the splitting approach is first applied on a minimal example and a discrete cosine transformation. It will be extended to bigger kernels to automatically generate statements about black box computer code later.

The document is organized as follows: Section 1 gives an overview of the methodology which is used to assess the significances of computer code and data. Subsequently, in section 2 we give applications for the significance analysis by dco/scorpio. Finally, section 3 contains a summary and an outlook.

1. Methodology

In this section we describe the basics of the tool chain dco/scorpio which is used for the not yet fully automatic significance analysis developed in the context of the SCoR-PiO project. Furthermore we introduce the interval splitting to extend our tool chain for unfeasible significance analyses with interval evaluation.

1.1. Significance Analysis by dco/scorpio

Significance analysis developed in SCoRPiO is based on the forward propagation of intervals by interval arithmetics (IA) [1,8] and backwards propagation of adjoints by AD [6,7].

For a given function $F : \mathbb{R}^n \to \mathbb{R}^m$ with $y = F(x)$ IA computes a set $[y] = F[x]$ with $F[x] \supseteq \{F(x) | x \in [x]\}$, that contains all possible function values of $F(x)$ for $x \in [x] = [\underline{x}, \overline{x}]$. The lower bounds $\underline{x}$ and upper bounds $\overline{x}$ of the input intervals $[x]$ need to be defined by the user. For the implementation of interval arithmetics in the tool chain of dco/scorpio the interval library filib++ [9,10] is used.

AD is a technique which uses the chain rule to compute additionally to the function value the derivative of that function with respect to its input variables. Therefore it is assumed that a given implementation of the function can be decomposed into single assignment code

$$v_{j-n+1} = x_j, \qquad\qquad j = 0, \dots, n-1, \qquad (1)$$

$$v_j = \varphi_j(v_i)_{i \prec j}, \qquad\qquad j = 1, \dots, p, \qquad (2)$$

$$y_j = v_{j+p-m+1}, \qquad\qquad j = 0, \dots, m-1, \qquad (3)$$

where φ_j denotes an elemental function (binary operations and intrinsic functions), p is the number of intermediate variables and $i \prec j$ describes a direct dependency of v_j on v_i. The adjoint mode propagates output adjoints $v_{(1),j}$ for intermediate variable v_j backwards through the single assignment code to the adjoints of the inputs, as in

$$v_{(1),i+p-m+1} = y_{(1),i}, \qquad\qquad i = m-1,\ldots,0, \qquad\qquad (4)$$

$$v_{(1),i} = \sum_{j:i \prec j} \frac{\partial \varphi_j(v_i)}{\partial v_i} \cdot v_{(1),j}, \qquad\qquad i = p-m, \ldots, 1-n, \qquad (5)$$

$$x_{(1),i} = v_{(1),i-n+1}, \qquad\qquad i = n-1, \ldots, 0. \qquad\qquad (6)$$

The advantage of this mode is that the derivatives of an output with respect to all inputs and intermediates can be obtained with a single evaluation of the adjoint model.

Our C++ implementation of AD is the template class library dco/c++ [4,5]. The dco/scorpio tool is a specific extension of dco/c++ that allows to apply AD to interval functions. It can compute the interval derivative $\nabla_{[v_i]}[y]$ of the function result $[y]$ with respect to input and intermediate intervals $[v_i]$.

Eq. (7) gives the significance definition for all intermediate and input variables v_i, in which $w([x]) = \overline{x} - \underline{x}$ is the width of interval $[x]$. This definition was also developed in the scope of the SCoRPiO project [3].

$$S_{[y]}[v_i] = w([v_i] \cdot \nabla_{[v_i]}[y]) , \; i = 1, \ldots, n \qquad\qquad (7)$$

The significance for each input and intermediate variable can be obtained by the combination of IA and AD. While IA yields $[v_i]$ by forward propagation of the input intervals, $\nabla_{[v_i]}[y]$ is derived by the backwards propagation of adjoint AD.

A variable v_i is called significant if its significance value greater than a user defined bound, $S_{[y]}[v_i] > \epsilon$, otherwise it is insignificant. Insignificant variables can be exploited by calculating their corresponding computations on unreliable hardware, by computing in lower precision, by using a representative constant or by reusing a previous value.

Evaluating a function in IA might lead to certain problems: Overestimation of value and adjoint intervals by the *wrapping effect* and unfeasible relational operators (e.g. $[x] > 1$ is not defined if $1 \in [x]$), such that we want to use a divide and conquer algorithm. Therefore we introduce the interval splitting approach described in the following section.

1.2. Interval Splitting

The interval splitting approach divides value or adjoint intervals into subintervals. After the divide the significance analysis is continued or restarted with the subintervals of the variables. The splitting can be applied recursively, such that this procedure can be very expensive in terms of computational costs. Nevertheless this approach is embarrassingly parallel and it can be considered as a compile-time analysis since the analysis is a preprocessing step leading to a code, that will be evaluated later.

The interval splitting is used to ensure

- **control flow feasibility**: Due to the interval evaluation conditional constructs such as *if*- or *switch*-statements are not necessarily well-defined for intervals. Therefore we split the interval at the corresponding points. Assuming we have a condition $[x] < c$ with $c \in [x] = [\underline{x}, \overline{x}]$, we split the interval into $[\underline{x}, c)$ and $[c, \overline{x}]$.
- **value feasibility**: If a forward propagated interval v_i is larger than a predefined bound, $w([v_i]) \geq \beta$, the corresponding interval is divided into k predefined subintervals.

- **adjoint feasibility**: If a backward propagated adjoint interval $\nabla_{[v_i]}[y]$ is larger than a predefined bound, $w(\nabla_{[v_i]}[y]) \geq \gamma$, the adjoint interval of v_i will be split into l predefined subintervals.

The bounds β and γ need to be chosen carefully, because a too fine grained interval splitting leads potentially to a lot of exceptions which influence the accuracy and performance of the function. An analysis of those parameters is beyond the scope of this article and is part of the future work.

2. Examples

In this section two examples of the significance analysis are presented. The analysis is applied to a simple function to illustrate the methodology of the significance analysis with interval splitting. The second example is the analysis of a discrete cosine transformation and includes a small case study on the influence of the modified code on the accuracy of the result.

2.1. Basic Example

We assume the scalar function f given in Eq. (8) with a single input and the corresponding implementation in Listing 1.

$$f(x) = \frac{\sin(x)}{2} + \exp\left(\frac{x}{2}\right) \tag{8}$$

Furthermore it is assumed that the user-defined input interval of x is set to $[-5, 5]$.

Listing 1: Implementation of function f

```
1 template<typename A> void f( A &x, A &y ) {
2    y = 0.5 * sin( x ) + exp( x/2 );
3 }
```

By applying a code flattener to the implementation of f the single assignment code in Listing 2 is generated. Additional macros of the significance analysis tool dco/scorpio are inserted for the registration of the intermediate variables.

Listing 2: Generated single assignment code of function f with macros for the significance analysis

```
1 template <typename ADTYPE>
2 void flat( scorpio_info &si, ADTYPE& x, ADTYPE& y ) {
3    ADTYPE v0 = x;            SIADDM(si, v0, 1, 0);
4    ADTYPE v1 = sin( v0 );    SIADDM(si, v1, 1, 1);
5    ADTYPE v2 = 0.5 * v1;     SIADDM(si, v2, 1, 2);
6    ADTYPE v3 = v0 / 2;       SIADDM(si, v3, 1, 3);
7    ADTYPE v4 = exp( v3 );    SIADDM(si, v4, 1, 4);
8    ADTYPE v5 = v2 + v4;      SIADDM(si, v5, 1, 5);
9    y = v5;
10 } // void flat( )
```

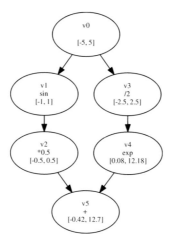

Figure 1. Directed acyclic graph of the single assignment code of f with the forward propagated inputs

Table 1. Significances obtained by dco/scorpio with the significance definition from Eq. (7) and $\epsilon = 0.5$

[x]	v0 = x	v1 = sin(v0)	v2 = 0.5*v1	v3 = v0/2	v4 = exp(v3)	v5 = v2+v4
$[-5, 5]$	65.91	1.00	1.00	60.91	12.10	13.10
$[-5, -2.5]$	3.72	0.80	0.80	0.61	**0.20**	1.00
$[-2.5, 0]$	3.14	**0.50**	**0.50**	1.25	0.71	1.21
$[0, 2.5]$	5.61	**0.50**	**0.50**	4.36	2.49	2.99
$[2.5, 5]$	28.05	0.80	0.80	26.09	8.69	9.49

The implementation can be visualized as a directed acyclic graph that contains a node for each assignment (see Figure 1). The nodes are labeled with three attributes, the variable name, the operation and the interval range which is propagated from the given input intervals respectively.

Table 1 lists the significances for the particular intermediate variables. For the significance analysis with dco/scorpio we assume here the following user-defined bounds and parameters: $\epsilon = 0.5$, $\beta = 10$, $\gamma = 10$, $k = 4$, $l = 4$. It can be seen, that all of the variables are marked as significant for the specified input interval and significance bound. Because the input interval of variable x is larger than the defined bound β it is split into four subintervals to ensure value feasibility and the significance analysis is reapplied on those subintervals. The results are also given in Table 1, in which the insignificant variables are in bold print. For this example the applied split additionally ensures adjoint feasibility. In the scenario with an input interval of $[-5, -2.5]$ $v4$ is marked as insignificant. Furthermore the variables $v1$ and $v2$ are insignificant for the scenarios with the input intervals $[-2.5, 0]$ and $[0, 2.5]$.

By assuming that all values of an interval have the same expectation value, we approximate the insignificant variables by constants equal to the center of their interval. The optimized variant of the code with four scenarios is given in Listing 3 and the computational graphs for these scenarios are visualized in Figure 2.

For this basic example we can save 30% of the computations on average with a significance bound of $\epsilon = 0.5$. The approximated function is shown in Figure 3.

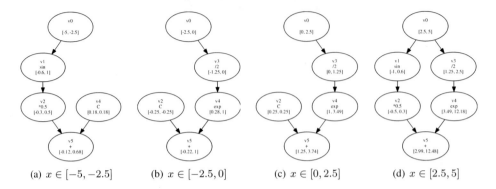

(a) $x \in [-5, -2.5]$ (b) $x \in [-2.5, 0]$ (c) $x \in [0, 2.5]$ (d) $x \in [2.5, 5]$

Figure 2. Modified DAGs for the different scenarios. Some of the nodes are eliminated, due to the fact that they are unused after the replacement.

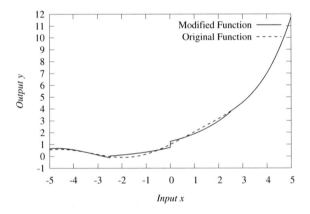

Figure 3. Comparison of the optimized code variant with the original function for the basic example

Listing 3: Optimized code variant of function f

```
1  void f_opt( double &x, double &y ) {
2    if ( x >= −5 && x < −2.5 )
3      y = 0.5 * sin( x ) + 0.18;
4    else if ( x >= −2.5 && x < 0 )
5      y = −0.25 + exp( x/2 );
6    else if ( x >= 0 && x < 2.5 )
7      y = 0.25 + exp( x/2 );
8    else
9      y = 0.5 * sin( x ) + exp( x/2 );
10 }
```

2.2. Discrete Cosine Transformation

The algorithm which is analyzed consists of the discrete cosine transformation, the quantization, the inverse discrete cosine transformation and an error computation. Input of this code is a 64×64 pixel grayscale picture in raw image format. In a first step this

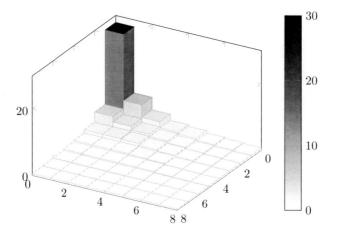

Figure 4. Significance values for the frequency coefficients mapped to an 8×8 matrix

picture is divided into 8×8 blocks and for each block the pixel values are transformed into frequency coefficients. After that the quantization is applied, in which reduction of the file size of the picture takes place. In this function the frequency coefficients are divided by a constant element of the quantization matrix, rounded to integers and multiplied by the element of the quantization matrix. In the next step the resultant frequencies are transformed back to pixel values and those are compared to the original pixel values by using the mean square error. This error can be interpreted as a measurement for the error introduced by the transformations and the quantization.

Each of the 4096 pixels of the grayscale test image is registered as an input. By adding the interval [-5,5] to the actual pixel values the input intervals are artificially generated. Therefore the result of the significance analysis is valid for all test images out of the test space. As an output for the analysis the mean square error of the created and the original image is registered.

For this example the code flattener generates single assignment code with fixed control flow. The 1,347,585 operations make a visualization of the code and the computational graph infeasible. Instead of giving the significance results for all intermediates, we will focus on the frequency coefficients. Those coefficients are mapped to an 8×8 matrix by using the euclidean norm.

High significance values are assigned to the low frequency coefficients in the top left corner while the significance drops towards the high frequencies in the bottom right corner (see Figure 4). This matches directly the knowledge of human experts: Frequencies in the upper left corner are more important for the human eye than frequencies in the lower right region of each 8×8 block.

The ratio of insignificant and the ratio of the saved computations are increasing for an increasing significance bound, as shown in Figure 5. By replacing insignificant computations with constant values one can additionally save those computations which just depends on constants or which are no longer required for the output of the algorithm. This explains why the ratio of saved computations is always larger or equal to the ration of insignificant computations. The resultant code is evaluated for the original test image to obtain the peak signal-to-noise ratio (PSNR). This value is used as an indicator of the quality of the output image. A PSNR of 35 db or greater usually indicates acceptable

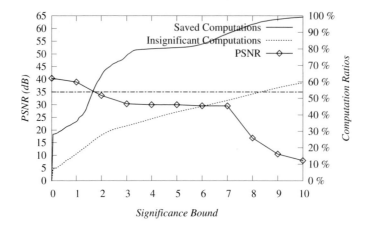

Figure 5. Insignificant nodes (dashed) and saved computations of the implementation of the discrete cosine transformation after dead code elimination for varying significance bounds. The PSNR is given for evaluations of the resultant codes. A PSNR value of at least 35 db indicates acceptable results.

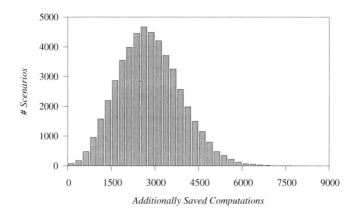

Figure 6. Number of scenarios that save the particular number of computations by

quality. Figure 5 also shows the expected result: The quality of the output image drops for higher significance bounds. For the given input ranges and a significance bound of approximately $\epsilon = 1.74$ about 50% of the computations can be saved by keeping the quality of the result acceptable.

Although there are already a lot of computations that can be saved, we will apply the interval splitting to this example as well. Interval splitting of all input variables into two parts would result in 2^{4096} scenarios. Due to this high combinatorial complexity of the interval splitting we pick 50000 random scenarios. The assumed significance bound is $\epsilon = 1$, the bound to ensure value feasibility is $\beta = 5$ and the splitting parameter $k = 2$. Adjoint feasibility is not be considered in this example.

In Figure 6 a histogram shows the number of scenarios that additionally save the particular number of computations. The maximal number of additionally saved computations for the 50000 random scenarios is 8585 for 47 random splits. One can almost save further 0.6% of the total number of computations. Due to the fact that those scenarios do not cover the whole input space, we would only create special code variants for those 19 scenarios that save at least 7250 computations for a significance bound of $\epsilon = 1$. If a given test image is not covered by the chosen scenarios the original algorithm is computed as default. A resulting sketch of the code is given in Listing 4.

Listing 4: Structure of the optimized code by applying an interval splitting

```
1  void dct_opt( vector<vector<double> > pic , vector<vector<double> > &
      new_pic ) {
2    switch ( pic ) {
3      case pic ∈ scenario 1:
4        // Code for scenario 1
5        break ;
6                :
7      case pic ∈ scenario 19:
8        // Code for scenario 19
9        break ;
10     default :
11       dct ( pic , new_pic );
12   }
13 }
```

The significance analysis without interval splitting can already save more than 30% for an significance bound of $\epsilon = 1$. The saving found by the interval splitting are small compared to the original analysis. Unfortunately, this is a result which cannot be predicted and can just be identified after the analysis with interval splitting is done. We believe that the potential of the interval splitting approach will be revealed by other applications in the future. At least, the example illustrates the procedure of input interval splitting for more complex codes and shows its capability to generate specialized code for a few scenarios only.

3. Summary and Outlook

An interval splitting approach for the significance analysis was introduced and we applied it to two examples. The approach enables the application of the tool chain to more complex functions and computer programs. We will automate this process and improve the interval splitting. By looking for appropriate splitting parameters we want to obtain a trade-off between too much details and not enough information. Therefore, a heuristic is required to decide which variables should be split and how many subintervals should be used. Besides the interval splitting of inputs, we also want to split intermediates in the forward as well as in the backward propagation. Due to the possibly high computational costs of this approach, parallelization is necessary to run the significance analysis on a cluster.

Moreover, a Monte Carlo approach as a backup for non-differentiable programs or as a verification of the significance results obtained by dco/scorpio is under development.

References

[1]   Moore, R. E., Kearfott, R. B., and Cloud, M. J. (2009). *Introduction to interval analysis.* Siam.

[2]   Riehme, J., and Naumann, U. (2014). *D1.1: Significance Based Computing Modeling.* RWTH Aachen, Tech. Rep. [Online]. Available: `www.scorpio-project.eu/wp-content/uploads/2014/07/Scorpio_D1.1.pdf`.

[3]   Riehme, J., and Naumann, U. (2015). *Significance Analysis for Numerical Models.* WAPCO Available: `http://wapco.inf.uth.gr/papers/SESSION3/WAPCO_3_1.pdf`

[4]   Software and Tools for Scientific Engineering, RWTH Aachen University, Germany. *Derivative Code by Overloading in C++ (dco/c++).* `http://www.stce.rwth-aachen.de/software/dco_cpp.html`.

[5]   Lotz, J., Leppkes, K., and Naumann, U. (2011). *dco/c++-derivative code by overloading in C++.* Aachener Informatik Berichte (AIB-2011-06). [Online]. Available: `http://sunsite.informatik.rwth-aachen.de/Publications/AIB/2011/2011-06.pdf`

[6]   Griewank, A., and Walther, A. (2008). *Evaluating derivatives: principles and techniques of algorithmic differentiation.* Siam.

[7]   Naumann, U. (2012). *The Art of Differentiating Computer Programs. An Introduction to Algorithmic Differentiation* (Vol. 24). SIAM.

[8]   Moore, R. E. (1966). *Interval analysis* (Vol. 4). Englewood Cliffs: Prentice-Hall.

[9]   Lerch, M., Tischler, G., Wolff von Gudenberg, J., Hofschuster, W., and Krämer, W. . *FILIB++ interval library.* `www2.math.uni-wuppertal.de/~xsc/software/filib.html`.

[10] Lerch, M., Tischler, G., Wolff von Gudenberg, J., Hofschuster, W., and Krämer, W. (2001). *The interval library filib++ 2.0 - design, features and sample programs.* Preprint 2001/4, Universität Wuppertal.

Parallel Computing: On the Road to Exascale
G.R. Joubert et al. (Eds.)
IOS Press, 2016
doi:10.3233/978-1-61499-621-7-741

Energy Minimization on Heterogeneous Systems through Approximate Computing

Michalis Spyrou, Christos Kalogirou, Christos Konstantas, Panos Koutsovasilis,
Manolis Maroudas, Christos D. Antonopoulos [1] and Nikolaos Bellas
Centre for Research and Technology Hellas - CERTH
Department of Electrical and Computer Engineering, University of Thessaly
e-mail: {mispyrou, hrkalogi, hriskons, pkoutsovasilis, emmmarou, cda,
nbellas}@uth.gr

Abstract. Energy efficiency is a prime concern for both HPC and conventional workloads. Heterogeneous systems typically improve energy efficiency at the expense of increased programmer effort. A novel, complementary approach is approximating selected computations in order to minimize the energy footprint of applications. Not all applications or application components are amenable to this method, as approximations may be detrimental to the quality of the end result. Therefore the programmer should be able to express algorithmic wisdom on the importance of specific computations for the quality of the end-result and thus their tolerance to approximations.

We introduce a framework comprising of a parallel meta-programming model based on OpenCL, a compiler which supports this programming model, and a runtime system which serves as the compiler backend. The proposed framework: (a) allows the programmer to express the relative importance of different computations for the quality of the output, thus facilitating the dynamic exploration of energy / quality tradeoffs in a disciplined way, and (b) simplifies the development of parallel algorithms on heterogeneous systems, relieving the programmer from tasks such as work scheduling and data manipulation across address spaces.

We evaluate our approach using a number of real-world applications, beyond kernels, with diverse characteristics. Our results indicate that significant energy savings can be achieved by combining the execution on heterogeneous systems with approximations, with graceful degradation of output quality.

Keywords. Energy Saving, Approximate Computing, Programming Model, Controlled Quality Degradation, Heterogeneous Systems

Introduction

Energy efficiency is a primary concern when designing modern computing systems. Moving to the multicore era allowed architects to exploit increasing transis-

---

[1] Corresponding Author: Christos D. Antonopoulos, Assistant Professor, Department of Electrical and Computer Engineering, University of Thessaly, Greece; E-mail: cda@inf.uth.gr URL: http://www.inf.uth.gr/~cda

tor counts by implementing additional cores. However, the end of Dennard scaling [3] limits expectations for energy efficiency improvements in future devices by manufacturing processors in lower geometries and lowering supply voltage. Traditional hardware / system software techniques, such as DFS and DVFS also have their limitations when it comes to CPU intensive workloads.

Heterogeneous systems appeared as a promising alternative to multicores and multiprocessors and dominate the Top500 [10] and Green500 [4] HPC lists. They offer unprecedented performance and energy efficiency for certain classes of workloads, however at significantly increased development effort: programmers have to spend significant effort reasoning on code mapping and optimization, synchronization, and data transfers among different devices and address spaces.

One contributing factor to the energy footprint of current software is that all parts of the program are considered equally important for the quality of the final result, thus all are executed at full accuracy. However, as shown by previous work on approximate computing [2,16,19], several classes of applications include blocks of computations that do not affect the output quality significantly. Non-significant computations can often tolerate approximations or even substitution by a default value.

In this paper we introduce a directive-, task-based meta-programming model on top of OpenCL [20], which allows programmers to: (a) express their insight on the importance of different parts of the computation for the quality of the end-result, (b) provide alternative, approximate versions of selected computations, (c) control the ratio of approximate / accurate computations executed, and thus the energy / quality tradeoff using a single knob, and (d) exploit heterogeneous, accelerator-based systems, without many of the development overheads typically associated with such systems. To the best of our knowledge this is the first time a single programming model offers support for approximate execution on heterogeneous, accelerator-based systems. For our experiments we use a number of real-world applications from different domains, with diverse characteristics. We discuss approximation techniques that fit each application, and we apply appropriate metrics to evaluate the output quality. We find that, by exploiting application specific high level information among proper device and ratio selection, we can approximate the output with acceptable quality, while considerably reducing the energy footprint of the application.

The rest of this paper is organized as follows: Section 1 presents the key features of our programming model and Section 2 discusses the runtime implementation, highlighting its fundamental design decisions. Section 3 presents the applications used to evaluate our programming model and the heterogeneous platform we used for the evaluation, whereas in Section 4 we present and discuss evaluation results. Related work is discussed in Section 5 and Section 6 concludes the paper.

1. Programming Model

The programming model we introduce adopts a task-based paradigm, using *#pragma* directives to annotate parallelism and approximations. Tasks are implemented as OpenCL kernels [20], facilitating execution on heterogeneous systems.

The main objectives of the programming model are to allow (a) flexible execution on heterogeneous systems, without overwhelming the programmer with low-level concerns, such as inter-task synchronization, scheduling and data manipulation, and (b) flexible exploration by the user of the quality / energy tradeoff at runtime, using a single knob and exploiting developer wisdom on the importance of different parts of the code for the quality of the end-result.

Listing 1 summarizes the *#pragma* task and taskwait directives used for task manipulation. Listing 2 outlines the implementation of Discrete Cosine Transform (DCT), which serves as a minimal example to illustrate the use of the main programming model concepts. Below we explain each directive and clause referring to this DCT example as appropriate.

```
1 #pragma acl task [approxfun( function )] [significant( expr )] [label("name")] \
2                  [in( varlist )] [out( varlist )] [inout( varlist )] \
3                  [device_in( varlist )] [device_out( varlist )] \
4                  [device_inout( varlist )] [bind( device_type )] \
5                  [workers( int_expr_list )] [groups( int_expr_list)] \
6 accurate_task_impl( ... );
7 #pragma acl taskwait [label("name")] [ratio( double )]
```

Listing 1 Pragma directives for task creation/completion.

```
1 __kernel void dctAccurate(double *image,double *result,int subblock) { }
2 __kernel void dctApprox(double *image, double *result, int subblock) { }
3
4 int subblocks=2*4, subblockSize=4*2, blockSize=32, imgW=1920, imgH=1080;
5 /*DCT block to 2x4 subblocks with different significance, image dimensions*/
6 double sgnf_lut[] = {   1,   .9,  .7,  .3,
7                        .8,   .4,  .3,  .1};
8 void DCT(double *image, double *result, double sgnf_ratio) {/* entry point */
9     for (int id = 0; id < subblocks; id++) {   /*spawn dct task group*/
10        #pragma acl task in(image) out(&result[id*subblockSize]) \
11               label("dct") \
12               significant(sgnf_lut[id]) approxfun(dctApprox) \
13               workers(blockSize, blockSize) groups(imgW, imgH)
14        dctAccurate(image, result, id);
15    }
16    #pragma acl taskwait ratio(sgnf_ratio) label("dct") /*execution barrier*/
17 }
```

Listing 2 Programming model use case: Discrete Cosine Transform (DCT) on blocks of an image.

The *task* directive (lines 10-13) defines a new task. It annotates the following function call (line 14) as the task body which corresponds to an OpenCL kernel (*dctAccurate()*, line 1) and specifies the accurate implementation of the task.

The *approxfun()* clause (line 12) allows the programmer to provide an alternative, approximate implementation of the task. This is generally simpler and less accurate (may even return a default value in the extreme case), however has a lower energy footprint than its accurate counterpart. For example, *dctApprox()*, also defined as OpenCL kernel at line 2, sets all coefficient values equal to zero. The actual call to the accurate version may be replaced at execution time by a call to the approximate version, if present.

The *significant()* clause quantifies the relative significance of the computation implemented by the task for the quality of the output, with a value (or expression) in the range [0.0, 1.0]. If set to 1.0 or omitted, the runtime will always execute the task accurately. If set to 0.0, the runtime will execute the task approximately, or even discard it if an approximation is not available.

The DCT example defines each task's significance at line 12, using values from a lookup table (array *sgnf_lut[]*, line 6). Notice that tasks calculating coefficients near the upper left corner of each block (low spatial frequencies) are more significant (values in the *sgnf_lut[]* array which are used to assign significance to tasks) than those calculating coefficients which correspond to higher spatial frequencies. This is due to the fact that the human eye is less sensitive to higher frequencies.

The programmer explicitly specifies the input and output arguments of each task with the *in()*, *out()* and *inout()* data clauses (line 10). The corresponding information is exploited by the runtime system for dependence analysis and scheduling, as well as for data management, as explained in Section 2. The *device_in()*, *device_out()* and *device_inout()* data clauses extend the above clauses by forcing data transfers from/to device. We also support a subarray notation to express data dependencies, in the form of *array[i:i+size]* in the spirit of OpenACC [14]. Expressing arguments in data clauses as subarrays further reduces unnecessary data transfers.

The programmer can explicitly annotate a task for execution on a specific device, using the *bind()* clause. This limits the flexibility of the programming model, however it proves useful in case an implementation is optimized for a specific device. To specify the work-items and work-groups geometry for kernel execution, the programmer uses the *workers()* and *groups()* clauses as shown at line 13, which follow the semantics of local- and global workgroup size of OpenCL, respectively. Finally, the *label()* clause associates tasks with named task groups. Each group is characterized by a unique string identifier. In our DCT example, line 11 adds the newly created task to the "*dct*" task group.

The *taskwait* directive specifies an explicit synchronization point, acting as a computation and memory barrier. By default, taskwait waits on all issued tasks so far, unless the *label()* clause is present, which limits the barrier to tasks of the specific task group.

The *ratio()* clause accepts a value (or expression) ranging in [0.0, 1.0] as an argument. It specifies the minimum percentage of tasks of the specific group that the runtime should execute accurately. *ratio* is a single knob which allows the programmer or the user to control the energy footprint / quality tradeoff. If ratio is 0.0, the runtime does not need to execute any task accurately. Similarly, if ratio is 1.0, all tasks need to be executed accurately regardless of their significance. In our DCT example, line 16 waits for all tasks inside the "*dct*" task group with a user defined ratio.

The programming model is implemented in the context of a source-to-source compiler, based on LLVM/Clang [8] and the LibTooling library. The compiler lowers the *#pragma* directives to the corresponding runtime API calls.

2. Runtime Support

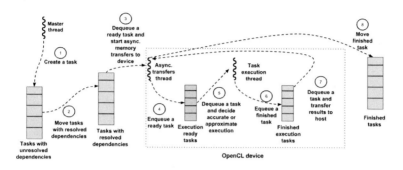

Figure 1. Runtime system architecture and typical task life cycle

Fig. 1 outlines the architecture of our runtime system. It is organized as a master/slave work-sharing scheduler. For each device on the system, two threads are created: (a) a memory transfers thread, responsible for transparent data transfers between the host and the device, and (b) a task issue thread, responsible for issuing tasks (implemented as OpenCL kernels) for execution to the corresponding device. Our runtime reuses the underlying vendor OpenCL implementation for each device for data transfers, code execution, as well as to extract system configuration information. The master thread executes the main program sequentially and every task created is stored into a global pool (Fig. 1, step 1).

2.1. Data Flow Analysis - Scheduling & Memory Transfers

The runtime system can perform automatic data flow analysis at the granularity of tasks, exploiting the information provided by the programmer via the data clauses of each task. More specifically, upon task creation the runtime system tracks the memory ranges read and written by each task. The results of this analysis are exploited in two different ways: (a) to detect data dependencies among tasks and enforce execution in the correct order, and (b) to automate memory transfers among different address spaces of the heterogeneous system.

All task scheduling and data manipulation are transparent to the programmer. Overlaps between data ranges from data clauses of different tasks coexisting in the system at any time, indicate potential WaW, RaW or WaR data dependencies. The runtime identifies these dependencies and enforces execution of inter-dependent tasks in the order they were spawned. Once all its dependencies are resolved, a task is transferred to the ready queue (Fig. 1, step 2) and can be selected for execution.

Devices can execute tasks from the global pool whenever they have resources (execution units and memory) available, even if there are other tasks concurrently executing on the device (Fig. 1, step 3). The runtime respects potential limitations for task execution on specific devices specified by the programmer. If input data for the task does not already reside in the device address space, they have to be transferred before the task can be executed. The runtime system includes a simple memory manager which tracks the location of each named object used as an argument in any data clause, as well as the amount of available memory on each device. The corresponding data structures are updated by the memory transfers threads. When input data for a task are on the device memory, they can be issued for execution (Fig. 1, step 5). Similarly, *out()* and *device_out()* data are transferred to the respective device when they are required as input for another task, or to the host either at synchronization points, or whenever the memory manager needs to reuse memory on the device (Fig. 1, step 7). The runtime tries to overlap data transfers with computations when possible by prefetching data for tasks to be executed while other tasks still keep the computational units of the device busy. Given that data transfers typically incur significant overhead, the scheduler associates tasks with devices according to data locality (beyond resource availability). If a device, despite data affinity, has no free memory or computational resources, the next available device is used.

2.2. Accurate / Approximate Task Execution

A newly created task includes the binaries of both accurate and approximate versions of the OpenCL kernels. When issuing the task for execution, the runtime decides whether it will execute the approximate or the accurate version. More specifically, the runtime observes the distribution of significance values assigned to spawned tasks and heuristically and dynamically adjusts the significance threshold beyond which tasks are executed accurately, with the target of achieving the user-specified ratio of accurate/approximate tasks. Whenever a task is issued for execution the runtime compares its significance to the current threshold and executes the appropriate implementation (accurate/approximate) accordingly.

2.3. Performance and Energy Monitoring

Information about energy, power and performance is collected during execution by periodically polling the interfaces (hardware counters and libraries) offered by each device. For example, for Intel CPUs, power is calculated by sampling energy measurements using the RAPL [7] interface whereas for NVIDIA GPUs we use the NVML [13] library. In order to monitor task execution times and the overhead of memory transfers we exploit OpenCL events.

3. Applications - Approximation and Quality Estimation Case Studies

In order to validate our framework and quantify the quality / energy footprint tradeoff on heterogeneous systems using realistic codes, we ported and evaluated a number of real-world applications to our programming model. In the following paragraphs we introduce these applications.

PBPI [5] is a high performance implementation of the Bayesian phylogenetic inference method for DNA sequence data. It starts from random phylogenetic trees and estimates the likelihood of them being realistic. The trees are then modified and re-evaluated in an iterative evolutionary process. The tree with the maximum likelihood is the output of the application. PBPI is quite sensitive to errors and applying approximations is not a straightforward task. We introduce an implementation where we randomly drop calculations for mutations with low probabilities. We validate the approximate version by comparing the similarity of the produced trees to those of the accurate version, using an algorithm for tree comparison [12]. This quality metric takes into consideration both tree topology and branch lengths.

Conjugate gradient (CG) is an iterative numerical solver for systems of linear equations. The matrix form of these systems has to be symmetric and positive-definite. The algorithm stops when it reaches convergence within a tolerance value, or executes the maximum number of iterations requested by the user. In order to approximate CG we used mixed precision: we perform computations of low significance in single precision, while the rest are executed in double precision. Given that the application is iterative, the number of iterations to convergence depends on the method and degree of approximation. To quantify the quality of the solution we use the relative error w.r.t. the result of the fully accurate execution.

The SPStereo Disparity [22] application calculates a dense depth estimate image from a stereo pair camera input. It consists of two parts: the first produces an initial disparity image; the second exploits shape regularization in the form of boundary length, while preserving connectivity of image segments to produce the depth estimate image. The hotspot of the algorithm is the computation of the initial disparity image. We approximate the disparity image computation by relaxing synchronization between consecutive rows of pixels in the image. We compare the image quality using the PSNR metric, with respect to the disparity image produced by a fully accurate execution.

Bonds [6] is part of the QuantLib [1] library used in computational finance. The application calculates the dirty price, clean price, accrued amount on a date and the forward value of a bond[2]. We apply two different approximation techniques. The first one uses mixed precision and fast-math functions for the calculation of exponentials, while the second drops computations of the iterative algorithm that computes the bond yield. The quality metric we use is the relative error of the computed forward price of the bond with respect to the value computed by a fully accurate execution.

HOG [15] is a computer vision application for pedestrian detection using machine learning techniques. The input image is divided into independent blocks that can be analyzed in parallel. A set of kernels is applied iteratively, in a pipeline manner on each block. The first kernel creates a histogram of the gradients orientation. Then it combines them into a descriptor and finally feeds it on a Support Vector Machine (SVM) which classifies each block. We use an approximation approach that skips the histogram and SVM computations on some image blocks in a round robin manner. We ensure that neighboring tasks have different significance values, allowing the runtime to apply approximations uniformly to the image. To assess quality, we calculate the percentage of overlap between bounding

---

[2]A bond is a loan that exists between an issuer and a holder. The issuer is obligated to pay the holder the initial loan augmented by an interest.

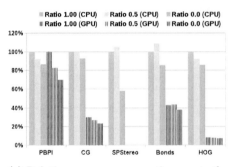

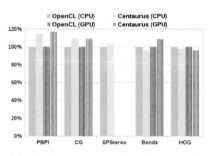

(a) Relative energy consumption w.r.t. the accurate CPU run.

(b) Performance overhead w.r.t. the corresponding accurate OpenCL implementation.

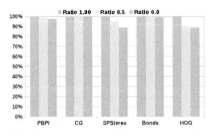

(c) Relative quality of output w.r.t the fully accurate execution.

	Device	Time (s)	Energy (J)	Quality metric
PBPI	CPU	72.20	11811	Tree similarity
	GPU	104.00	11065	(topology & branch length)
CG	CPU	83.00	16157	Relative error
	GPU	48.00	4814	wrt correct execution (%)
BONDS	CPU	2.02	471	Relative error
	GPU	1.97	201	wrt correct execution (%)
HOG	CPU	15.43	3820	Windows overlapping (%)
	GPU	3.80	312	
SPStereo	MIXED	5.12	935	PSNR (dB)

(d) Baseline execution time and energy consumption of fully accurate executions. We also report the quality metric used for each application.

Figure 2.

windows of recognized pedestrians produced by the accurate and the approximate versions.

4. Experimental Evaluation

The experimental evaluation was carried out on a dual-socket system equipped with two Intel XEON E5 2695 processors, clocked at 2.3 GHz, with 128 GB DRAM and an NVIDIA Tesla K80 GPU. The operating system is Ubuntu 14.04 server, using the 3.16 Linux kernel. The combination of two CPUs results to more energy consumption than a single GPU in some applications despite comparable execution times. The GPU power monitoring interface returns the instantaneous power consumption polled every 2 ms. To estimate energy on GPU, we calculate the integral of power in this time window of 2 ms, assuming constant power within the window. On CPU, in order to calculate power, we monitor energy consumption using the Running Average Power Limit (RAPL) [7] interface. Although our evaluation system and runtime can handle execution on multiple GPUs, we limit our profiling benchmarks only to one GPU chip of the K80, as most of the applications we use do not offer enough parallelism to exploit both GPU chips.

We evaluate each application on different devices (CPU/GPU) and degrees of approximation (fully accurate (ratio 1.0), fully approximate (ratio 0.0) and mixed (ratio 0.5)). In the literature, approximation techniques have been typically evaluated at the granularity of computational kernels, and not on end-to-end applications. We focus on the energy efficiency and the total execution time of each application, including data transfers between host and device. Fig. 2a depicts the relative energy consumption of all cases compared with the energy consumption of the accurate CPU execution for each application. Fig. 2c shows the quality loss due to approximations. Note that the quality between different device types for the same approximation degree remains the same for all applications in our evaluation. Also the energy consumption of the fully accurate, pure OpenCL implementation and the accurate run using our programming model is the same for all applications, for both CPU and GPU executions. Table 2d outlines CPU/GPU execution time and energy consumption for a fully accurate execution of each application.

All applications exploit the features of our programming model such as dependency analysis and automated data manipulation. We observe measurable energy gains in all applications ranging from 12% up to 43% due to approximations only. Considering also the proper device selection, these percentages become 30% and 90% respectively. We also observe that properly adjusting the ratio that controls the degree of approximation, we can control the energy/quality tradeoff in a controlled and straightforward manner. Both observations validate our approach. On average our runtime adds a minimal performance overhead about 0.28% on all applications except for PBPI and CG which are discussed below.

We notice that our runtime introduces an overhead of 15.7% (Fig. 2b) on average for PBPI when compared with the pure OpenCL version. The reason is the fine task granularity: PBPI creates about 100,000 tasks with an average execution time of 1 ms each. The overhead is due to both the latency of the underlying OpenCL implementation which notifies our runtime for task completion, and the frequent calls to the data dependency resolver. Another interesting observation for PBPI is that although GPU is slower than the CPU execution, the approximate version consumes 30.2% and 19.2% less energy than the accurate and approximate CPU execution respectively.

Our runtime also introduces an overhead of 9.1% on average in CG, again due to the number and granularity of tasks (which are however coarser than in the case of PBPI). GPU seems to gain more performance and saves more energy because these devices are designed to execute single precision calculations – as those used by the approximate version of the implementation – efficiently. CG has an energy gain of 76.9% on the approximate GPU execution.

The SPStereo Disparity accurate version suffers from sequential dependencies across consecutive rows of the image, limiting parallelism. In contrast, the approximate version due to the alleviation of dependencies is highly parallel and can easily benefit from running on GPU. Thus this application makes appropriate use of both GPU and CPU task bindings, a feature our programming model offers out of the box. The PSNR of the images produced by the approximate execution is in the range of 36 dB, indicating extremely high quality. Therefore, the approximate version offers an excellent trade-off between performance, energy efficiency (up to 43%) and quality of output. Although the PSNR value of the accurate run is – by definition – infinity, for visualization purposes in Fig. 2c we limit it to 41 dB.

In Bonds, we run a number of experiments with different input sets, using combinations of the available input variables such as issue date, maturity data and coupon rate for the bond. The application appears to benefit from execution on a GPU, facilitated by our programming model, although the difference with CPU is quite small. Bonds uses demanding operations (like exponential) in which CPU thrives against GPU. Using both approximation techniques, we introduce a quality loss of 1%, in favor of energy gains up to 14.7% in CPU and 11.8% in GPU w.r.t the accurate CPU and GPU executions respectively.

In HOG approximations result to some quality loss, which is mainly due to unrecognized pedestrians when they are smaller than the block size. Energy gains correlate with image sizes and not with the content. The highest energy gain with respect to the CPU accurate version is 90% and comes from the GPU approximate version. Our programming model results to a better execution time on both CPU and GPU than pure OpenCL, because it automatically exploits all opportunities for minimization of data transfers and their overlap with computations. The energy gain from running the approximate versions is 13% for GPU and 14% for CPU compared with the corresponding GPU and CPU accurate executions.

5. Related work

Green [2] supports energy-conscious programming using controlled approximation while providing guaranteed QoS. Ringenburg et al. [17] propose an architecture and tools for autotuning applications, that enable trading quality of results and energy efficiency. They assume, however, approximations at the hardware level. EnerJ [19] introduces an approximate type system using code annotations without defining a specific programming and execution model. ApproxIt [23] approximates iterative methods at the granularity of one solver iteration. Variability-aware OpenMP [16] also follows a *#pragma*-based notation and correlates parallelism with approximate computing. Quickstep [11] is a tool that parallelizes sequential code. It approximates the semantics of the code by altering data and control dependencies. SAGE [18] is a domain-specific environment with a compiler and a runtime component that automatically generates approximate kernels for image processing and machine learning applications. GreenGPU [9] dynamically splits and distributes workloads on a CPU-GPU heterogeneous system, aiming to keep busy both sides all the time, thus minimizing idle energy consumption. It also applies DFS for the GPU core and memory for maximizing energy savings. Tsoi and Luk [21] estimate performance and power efficiency tradeoffs to identify optimal workload distribution on a heterogeneous system.

Our work introduces the concept of computation significance as a means to express programmer wisdom and facilitate the controlled, graceful quality degradation of results in the interest of energy efficiency. We support approximate computing in a unified, straightforward way on different devices of accelerator-based systems, thus exploiting and combining energy efficiency benefits from both heterogeneity and approximation. Our approach does not require hardware support apart from what is already available on commodity processors and accelerators.

6. Conclusions

We introduced a framework which allows the programmer to express her wisdom on the importance of different computations for the quality of the end result, to provide approximate, more energy efficient implementations of computations and to control the quality / energy efficiency tradeoff at execution time, using a single, simple knob. In addition, our framework allows execution on heterogeneous systems and alleviates some technical concerns, such as computation scheduling and data management, which limit the programmer productivity. We evaluated our approach using a number of real-world applications and found that exploiting the concept of significance at the application level enables measurable energy gains through approximations, while the programmer maintains control of the quality of the output.

It should be noted that software-level approximate computing, as discussed in this paper, is orthogonal to energy efficiency optimizations at the hardware-level. Therefore, our approach can be applied on a wide range of existing and future systems, spanning the range from HPC architectures to embedded systems.

Acknowledgements

This work has been supported by the "Aristeia II" action (Project "Centaurus") of the operational program Education and Lifelong Learning and is co-funded by the European Social Fund and Greek national resources.

References

[1] F. Ametrano and L. Ballabio. Quantlib-a free/open-source library for quantitative finance. *Availabl e: http://quantlib. org/(visited on 04/29/2014)*, 2003.

[2] W. Baek and T. M. Chilimbi. Green: A framework for supporting energy-conscious programming using controlled approximation. In *Proceedings of the 2010 ACM SIGPLAN Conference on Programming Language Design and Implementation*, PLDI '10, pages 198–209, New York, NY, USA, 2010. ACM.

[3] M. Bohr. A 30 year retrospective on dennard's mosfet scaling paper. *Solid-State Circuits Society Newsletter, IEEE*, 12(1):11–13, Winter 2007.

[4] W.-c. Feng and K. W. Cameron. The green500 list: Encouraging sustainable supercomputing. *Computer*, 40(12):50–55, 2007.

[5] X. Feng, K. W. Cameron, and D. A. Buell. Pbpi: A high performance implementation of bayesian phylogenetic inference. In *Proceedings of the 2006 ACM/IEEE Conference on Supercomputing*, SC '06, New York, NY, USA, 2006. ACM.

[6] S. Grauer-Gray, W. Killian, R. Searles, and J. Cavazos. Accelerating financial applications on the gpu. In *Proceedings of the 6th Workshop on General Purpose Processor Using Graphics Processing Units*, pages 127–136. ACM, 2013.

[7] Intel. Intel 64 and ia-32 architectures software developer manual, 2010. Chapter 14.9.1.

[8] C. Lattner and V. Adve. LLVM: A Compilation Framework for Lifelong Program Analysis & Transformation. In *Proceedings of the International Symposium on Code Generation and Optimization: Feedback-directed and Runtime Optimization*, CGO '04, pages 75–, Washington, DC, USA, 2004. IEEE Computer Society.

[9] X. Li. Power Management for GPU-CPU Heterogeneous Systems. Master's thesis, University of Tennessee, 12 2011.

[10] H. Meuer, E. Strohmaier, J. Dongarra, and H. Simon. Top 500 list. *Electronically published at http://www. top500. org*, 2010.

[11] S. Misailovic, D. Kim, and M. Rinard. Parallelizing sequential programs with statistical accuracy tests. *ACM Trans. Embed. Comput. Syst.*, 12(2s):88:1–88:26, May 2013.

[12] T. Munzner, F. Guimbretière, S. Tasiran, L. Zhang, and Y. Zhou. Treejuxtaposer: Scalable tree comparison using focus+context with guaranteed visibility. *ACM Trans. Graph.*, 22(3):453–462, July 2003.

[13] NVIDIA. NVML API Reference. http://docs.nvidia.com/deploy/nvml-api/index.html.

[14] OpenACC standard committee. The OpenACC Application Programming Interface, v2.0, June 2013.

[15] V. Prisacariu and I. Reid. fastHOG-a real-time GPU implementation of HOG. Technical Report 2310/9, Department of Engineering Science, Cambridge University, 2009.

[16] A. Rahimi, A. Marongiu, R. K. Gupta, and L. Benini. A variability-aware openmp environment for efficient execution of accuracy-configurable computation on shared-fpu processor clusters. In *Proceedings of the Ninth IEEE/ACM/IFIP International Conference on Hardware/Software Codesign and System Synthesis*, CODES+ISSS '13, pages 35:1–35:10, Piscataway, NJ, USA, 2013. IEEE Press.

[17] M. Ringenburg, A. Sampson, I. Ackerman, and L. C. D. Grossman. Monitoring and debugging the quality of results in approximate programs. In *Proceedings of the 20th International Conference on Architectural Support for Programming Languages and Operating Systems (ASPLOS 2015)*, Istanbul, Turkey, March 2015.

[18] M. Samadi, J. Lee, D. A. Jamshidi, A. Hormati, and S. Mahlke. Sage: Self-tuning approximation for graphics engines. In *Proceedings of the 46th Annual IEEE/ACM International Symposium on Microarchitecture*, MICRO-46, pages 13–24, New York, NY, USA, 2013. ACM.

[19] A. Sampson, W. Dietl, E. Fortuna, D. Gnanapragasam, L. Ceze, and D. Grossman. Enerj: Approximate data types for safe and general low-power computation. In *Proceedings of the 32Nd ACM SIGPLAN Conference on Programming Language Design and Implementation*, PLDI '11, pages 164–174, New York, NY, USA, 2011. ACM.

[20] J. E. Stone, D. Gohara, and G. Shi. Opencl: A parallel programming standard for heterogeneous computing systems. *IEEE Des. Test*, 12(3):66–73, May 2010.

[21] K. H. Tsoi and W. Luk. Power profiling and optimization for heterogeneous multi-core systems. *SIGARCH Comput. Archit. News*, 39(4):8–13, Dec. 2011.

[22] K. Yamaguchi, D. McAllester, and R. Urtasun. Efficient joint segmentation, occlusion labeling, stereo and flow estimation. In *ECCV*, 2014.

[23] Q. Zhang, F. Yuan, R. Ye, and Q. Xu. Approxit: An approximate computing framework for iterative methods. In *Proceedings of the The 51st Annual Design Automation Conference on Design Automation Conference*, DAC '14, pages 97:1–97:6, New York, NY, USA, 2014. ACM.

Parallel Computing: On the Road to Exascale
G.R. Joubert et al. (Eds.)
IOS Press, 2016
doi:10.3233/978-1-61499-621-7-753

Landing Containment Domains on SWARM: Toward a Robust Resiliency Solution on a Dynamic Adaptive Runtime Machine

Sam Kaplan[1] Sergio Pino[2] Aaron M. Landwehr[3] Guang R. Gao[4]

ET International, Inc.

Abstract. Software and hardware errors are expected to be a much larger issue on exascale systems than current hardware. For this reason, resilience must be a major component of the design of an exascale system. By using containment domains, we propose a resilience scheme that works with the type of codelet-based runtimes expected to be utilized on exascale systems. We implemented a prototype of our containment domain framework in SWARM (SWift Adaptive Runtime Machine), and adapted a Cholesky decomposition program written in SWARM to use this framework. We will demonstrate the feasibility of this approach by showing the low overhead and high adaptability of our framework.

Keywords. reliability, resiliency, program execution models, fine-grain tasks, runtimes, containment domains, codelet model

Introduction

Exascale systems are expected to exhibit a much higher rate of faults than current systems, for a few reasons. Given identical hardware, failure rate will increase at least linearly with number of nodes in a system. In addition, exascale hardware will include more intricate pieces, including smaller transistors, which will be less reliable due to manufacturing tolerances and cosmic rays. Software will also have increased complexity, which again results in more errors [3]. The combination of the above factors indicates that resilience will be incredibly important for exascale systems, to a higher degree than it has for any preceding generation of hardware.

On current systems, most resilience methods take the form of checkpointing. Common types of checkpointing exhibit flaws that limit their scalability to exascale, due to the larger amount of state needing to be saved, and the lower mean time between failures. For this reason, it is desirable to have a resilience scheme that requires no coordination and can scale to any workload size. To this end, we leverage ideas from contain-

---

[1] stkaplan@gmail.com
[2] sergiop@udel.edu
[3] aron@udel.edu
[4] ggao.capsl@gmail.com

ment domain research performed by Mattan Erez and his team at University of Texas at Austin[5]. Similar to codelet model used in SWARM, containment domains exhibit a distributed, fine-grained, hierarchical nature. For this reason, we expect the impact of containment domains to be well realized when mapping onto a codelet model.

SWARM is a codelet-based runtime created at ETI [14]. We have previously adapted applications to use fine-grained, distributed, low-overhead SWARM codelets, and have demonstrated positive results in both performance and scalability. Because of its efficiency, maturity, and programmability, as well as our own familiarity with it, SWARM was chosen as the underlying runtime for our resilience research.

By implementing a prototype containment domain framework in SWARM, we show the feasibility of utilizing containment domains in a codelet-based runtime. Specifically, we created a continuation-based API to allow containment domains to conform to the requirements of the codelet model: fine-grained, non-blocking, and largely self-contained. We adapt a Cholesky decomposition program written in SWARM to use this API, showing that the necessary functionality is implemented and performs correctly. We also benchmarked this program to show that our implementation of containment domains has a very low overhead.

1. Background

At a high-level, a containment domain contains four components: data preservation, to save any necessary input data; a body function which performs algorithmic work; a detection function to identify hardware and software errors; and a recovery method, to restore preserved data and re-execute the body function. The detection function is a user-defined function that will be run after the body. It may check for hardware faults by reading error counters, or for software errors by examining output data (e.g. using a checksum function). Since containment domains can be nested, the recovery function may also escalate the error to its parent. Since no coordination is needed, any number of containment domains may be in existence, with multiple preserves and recoveries taking place simultaneously.

An initial prototype implementation of containment domains was developed by Cray [11]. In addition, a more fully-featured containment domain runtime is in currently in development by Mattan Erez and his team. However, none of these implementations support a continuation-based model. If exascale hardware is to use a codelet-based runtime, it is necessary to adapt these ideas to support such a model. For this reason, it is important that we demonstrate use of a codelet-based runtime.

2. Containment Domains in SWARM

We have developed a containment domain API as a feature of the SWARM runtime. This allows us to leverage existing runtime features and internal structures in order to support the hierarchical nature of containment domains. The main features include data preservation, user-defined fault detection functions, and re-execution of failed body functions. This feature set is realized by implementing a number of functions as follows:

swarm_ContainmentDomain_create(parent): Create a new containment domain as a child of the specified *parent* domain.

swarm_ContainmentDomain_begin(THIS, body, body_ctxt, check, check_cxt, done, done_ctxt): Begin execution of the current containment domain denoted by *THIS* by scheduling the codelet denoted by *body_ctxt*. When the codelet finishes execution, the codelet denoted by *check_ctxt* is scheduled to verify results. If the result of the execution is *TRUE* then the codelet denoted by *done_cxt* is scheduled.

swarm_ContainmentDomain_preserve(THIS, data, length, id, type): In the containment domain denoted by *THIS*, do a memory copy of length bytes from data into a temporary location inside the CD. We support multiple preservations per CD (e.g. to allow preservation of tiles within a larger array, such that the individual tiles are non-contiguous in memory), by adding a user-selected *id* field. For each containment domain in SWARM, a boolean value is set based on its execution status. On the first execution, data is preserved normally. On subsequent executions, data is copied in reverse (i.e. from the internal preservation into the data pointer). The CD in which the data is preserved is denoted by type. This can either be the currently activated CD or the parent CD.

swarm_ContainmentDomain_finish(THIS): Close the current containment domain denoted by *THIS*, discard any preserved data, and make the parent domain active.

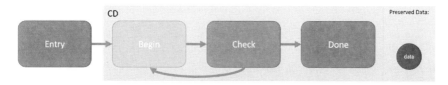

Figure 1. Simple Containment Domains Graph.

Figure 1 shows a graph of a very simple program using containment domains. This example shows a small program that multiplies two integers, and uses a single containment domain. The entry codelet initializes the containment domain, and enters it. The begin codelet multiplies its two inputs, and stores the result in C. The check codelet performs the same multiplication, and compares with the original result in C. If the results are not the same, an error has occurred and must be corrected. The begin codelet is re-executed, and the inputs are recovered from their saved locations. This continues until the begin and check codelets achieve the same result, in which case the done codelet is called, and the runtime is terminated. Figure 2 shows the accompanying code for the graph.

```
1    #include <swarm/ContainmentDomain.h>
2    #include <eti/swarm_convenience.h>
3    #include <stdio.h>
4    #include <stdlib.h>
5
6    CODELET_DECL(entry); CODELET_DECL(begin); CODELET_DECL(check); CODELET_DECL(done);
7
8    swarm_ContainmentDomain_t cd;
9    int gA = 17; int gB = 100;
10
11   typedef struct {
12       int *A; int *B; int *C;
13   } mult_t;
14
15   CODELET_IMPL_BEGIN_NOCANCEL(entry)
16       int *C = malloc(sizeof(int));
17       mult_t *ctxt = malloc(sizeof(mult_t));
18       ctxt->A = &gA; ctxt->B = &gB; ctxt->C = C;
19
20       swarm_ContainmentDomain_init(&cd);
21       swarm_ContainmentDomain_begin(&cd, &CODELET(begin), ctxt, &CODELET(check), ctxt,
              &CODELET(done), ctxt);
22   CODELET_IMPL_END;
23
24   CODELET_IMPL_BEGIN_NOCANCEL(begin)
25       mult_t *ctxt = THIS;
26       swarm_ContainmentDomain_preserve(&cd, &gA, sizeof(int), 0,
              swarm_CONTAINMENT_DOMAIN_COPY);
27       swarm_ContainmentDomain_preserve(&cd, &gB, sizeof(int), 1,
              swarm_CONTAINMENT_DOMAIN_COPY);
28       *ctxt->C = *ctxt->A * *ctxt->B;
29       swarm_dispatch(NEXT, NEXT_THIS, NULL, NULL, NULL);
30   CODELET_IMPL_END;
31
32   CODELET_IMPL_BEGIN_NOCANCEL(check)
33       mult_t *ctxt = THIS;
34       swarm_bool_t success = (*ctxt->C == *ctxt->A * *ctxt->B);
35       swarm_dispatch(NEXT, NEXT_THIS, (void*)success, NULL, NULL);
36   CODELET_IMPL_END;
37
38   CODELET_IMPL_BEGIN_NOCANCEL(done)
39       mult_t *ctxt = THIS;
40       printf("done, result = %d\n", *ctxt->C);
41       swarm_shutdownRuntime(NULL);
42   CODELET_IMPL_END;
43
44   int main() {
45       return swarm_posix_enterRuntime(NULL, &CODELET(entry), NULL, NULL);
46   }
```

Figure 2. Simple Containment Domains Code

3. Experimental Results

We evaluate our approach through three primary means: feasibility, efficiency, and re-silience and make a number of key observations. To show that our prototype implemen-

Figure 3. The execution time for Cholesky with different tile sizes.

tation has sufficient functionality, we instrument a Cholesky decomposition program in SWARM to use containment domains. For the experiments, the program was run on a dual-processor Intel Xeon system, using 12 threads. The workload sizes were confirmed to not exhaust the physical memory of the machine. Though we found insignificant variance between runs, we have averaged all times over 5 program runs due to the natural variation in run time due to extraneous system factors (such as scheduling differences).

The Cholesky program has three main codelets, one for each linear algebra routine run on a tile (POTRF, TRSM, and GEMM/SYRK), and each of these is called a number of times for each tile. For our purposes, each of these is considered a containment domain. In our model, we only considered faults similar to arithmetic errors; that is, incorrectly calculated results. For this reason, we did not need to preserve input data unless it would be overwritten by an operation (e.g. the input/output tile for a POTRF operation). In order to simulate arithmetic errors, rather than relying on error counters from actual faulty hardware, a probabilistic random number generator is used. If a random number is below the specified configurable threshold, a fault is deemed to have occurred. Fault generation occurs within the *check* codelets causing checks to fail at random and the subsequent re-execution of the entire failed containment domain.

Firstly, through the implementation of our framework in SWARM, and the working Cholesky application using said framework, we observe that it is feasible to adapt a codelet-based application to use containment domains. Secondly, Our implementation shows very low overhead. Figure 3 shows the execution time for various tile sizes executing Cholesky of size 40000x40000. Base denotes the Cholesky kernel runtime without containment domains or data preservation. CD denotes the time spent within CD related API calls without preservation. *Preserve* denotes the time spent preserving data. One can see that the API itself adds negligible overhead and that the only significant overhead comes from actual preservation of data. As with many tile based approaches to computation, choosing an inappropriate tile size will cause performance degradation due to inefficient use of caches or by limiting parallelism. In this particular case, tile sizes

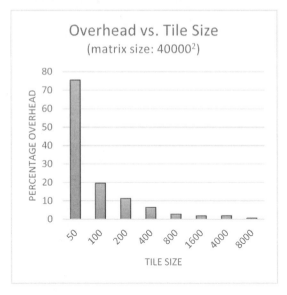

Figure 4. Percentage overhead versus tile size.

above 1600 limit the core utilization to 10 or 5 threads respectfully, yielding the U-shape shown in the graph. Figure 4 shows the total overhead (preservation + API calls) relative to the base cholesky code without containment domains. The trends indicate that as tile sizes (workload per codelet) increase the overhead is mitigated and eventually becomes negligible. This trend is unsurprising given that the runtime overhead per API call is relatively constant and as the tile size increases less and increasingly larger data sized preservation calls are made to the runtime. Additionally, the cost of preservation (i.e. for data movement) increases at a much slower rate than the cost of the Cholesky computation as tile sizes are increased. Overall, this trend shows that there is a sweet spot in terms of granularity and that proper decomposition is key to mitigate preservation overheads and maximize performance.

Figure 5 shows simulated injected failures that result in codelet re-execution within the SWARM framework. The *idealized* case is computed by taking the average execution time without faults for a Cholesky of size 40000x40000 and tile size of 200x200, and computing the expected execution time for various fault rates using the geometric distribution. In order to accurately access the overhead of our implementation, this projected base execution time includes neither CD or preservation overhead. The *actual* case shows the execution times actually obtained from running SWARM with injected failures. We note that there is around 11% overhead without failures and that this overhead decreases to 6% at a failure rate of 75%. This is because some allocation and API overheads are not present upon re-execution. Trend wise, we note that maximal overhead occurs when faults are not present in the system. We additionally note that the execution time follows reasonably well to that of the idealized case and that it is possible to project with reasonable accuracy the execution time in the event of failures using data from actual runs without failure.

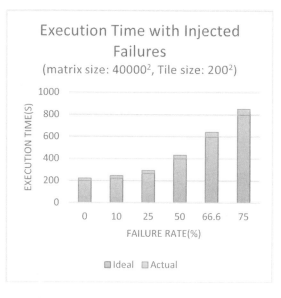

Figure 5. Execution time with simulated errors.

4. Related Work

As systems have become larger and larger, reliability has become an exceedingly active area of research over the last decade. Containment domains provide a flexible mechanism to ensure reliability at varying granularities. Additionally, CDs provide a novel bridge between reliability and programming models that facilitates reliability-aware or fault-aware application development, thus, giving the application programmer the ability to dynamically provide the runtime with the information needed to ensure reliability at the right granularities in terms of costs and benefits.

Much work in the field focuses on providing similar preservation and restoration capabilities, but generally lacks a programmer centric view of reliability. Some examples include global or local checkpointing [15] approaches, combining local and global checkpointing [21,18], as well as, multi-level [16,6] and hierarchical checkpointing [20].

There has been work to incorporate fault tolerance at the programmer level into MPI (Message Passing Interface) in the form of user-level failure mitigation (ULFM) [1]. ULFM provides mechanisms to inform and allow users to handle failed MPI processes on a per operation basis. Another approach, FA-MPI [10] seeks to provide fault-awareness to applications without significantly impacting the MPI interface. Similar to CDs, FA-MPI incorporates transactional semantics to provide a less ad-hoc approach to reliability.

Still other work focuses on enhancing reliability through specialized scheduling techniques. Static approaches use offline analysis to provide fault tolerance scheduling for a fixed number of faults [12,7], however, these lack the flexibility to adapt to changing system resources or workloads. Dynamic approaches use system level monitoring to adapt to faults that occur during execution. These can put into several subcategories including system reconfiguration [2], workload assignment [8,4,9], or providing automatic or semi-automatic replication of tasks[17].

Containment domains address several weaknesses to prior forms for fault-tolerance. One fundamental difference between CDs and generic checkpointing is that CDs are not interval or time dependent [19]. This gives a flexibility and control lacking in prior fault-tolerant schemes by allowing the programmer and system software to tune the location and method of preservation and the recovery to a desired level of reliability while also maximizing performance of the system. Furthermore due to the transactional characteristics of CDs, they are not susceptible to domino effect [13] that can cause full system rollback in the event of faults.

5. Acknowledgment

This material is based upon work supported by the Department of Energy [Office of Science] under Award Number DE-SC0008716.

6. Conclusion and Future Work

In conclusion, we demonstrate that containment domains can be adapted to the codelet model. Our Cholesky application shows that containment domains can be used in a decentralized, continuation-based manner, to provide a fine-grained, low-overhead framework for resilience. Although the best method for adapting individual applications is still an open problem, we show that this is an approach worth pursuing. Due to the Cholesky programs very decentralized call graph, it was not feasible to add nested containment domains. Another example would provide additional insight. For future work, we plan to implement a Self-Consistent Field (SCF) program to evaluate nested containment domains.

References

[1] W. Bland, K. Raffenetti, and P. Balaji. Simplifying the recovery model of user-level failure mitigation. In *Proceedings of the 2014 Workshop on Exascale MPI*, ExaMPI '14, pages 20–25, Piscataway, NJ, USA, 2014. IEEE Press.

[2] C. Bolchini, A. Miele, and D. Sciuto. An adaptive approach for online fault management in many-core architectures. In *Design, Automation Test in Europe Conference Exhibition (DATE), 2012*, pages 1429–1432, March 2012.

[3] F. Cappello, A. Geist, W. Gropp, S. Kale, B. Kramer, and M. Snir. Toward exascale resilience: 2014 update. *Supercomputing frontiers and innovations*, 1(1), 2014.

[4] T. Chantem, Y. Xiang, X. Hu, and R. P. Dick. Enhancing multicore reliability through wear compensation in online assignment and scheduling. In *Design, Automation Test in Europe Conference Exhibition (DATE), 2013*, pages 1373–1378, March 2013.

[5] J. Chung, I. Lee, M. Sullivan, J. H. Ryoo, D. W. Kim, D. H. Yoon, L. Kaplan, and M. Erez. Containment domains: A scalable, efficient, and flexible resilience scheme for exascale systems. In *the Proceedings of SC12*, November 2012.

[6] S. Di, L. Bautista-Gomez, and F. Cappello. Optimization of a multilevel checkpoint model with uncertain execution scales. In *Proceedings of the International Conference for High Performance Computing, Networking, Storage and Analysis*, SC '14, pages 907–918, Piscataway, NJ, USA, 2014. IEEE Press.

[7] L. Duque and C. Yang. Guiding fault-driven adaption in multicore systems through a reliability-aware static task schedule. In *Design Automation Conference (ASP-DAC), 2015 20th Asia and South Pacific*, pages 612–617, Jan 2015.

[8] L. A. R. Duque, J. M. M. Diaz, and C. Yang. Improving mpsoc reliability through adapting runtime task schedule based on time-correlated fault behavior. In *Proceedings of the 2015 Design, Automation*

& Test in Europe Conference & Exhibition, DATE '15, pages 818–823, San Jose, CA, USA, 2015. EDA Consortium.

[9] N. Fisher, J.-J. Chen, S. Wang, and L. Thiele. Thermal-aware global real-time scheduling on multicore systems. In *Real-Time and Embedded Technology and Applications Symposium, 2009. RTAS 2009. 15th IEEE*, pages 131–140, April 2009.

[10] A. Hassani, A. Skjellum, and R. Brightwell. Design and evaluation of fa-mpi, a transactional resilience scheme for non-blocking mpi. In *Dependable Systems and Networks (DSN), 2014 44th Annual IEEE/IFIP International Conference on*, pages 750–755, June 2014.

[11] C. Inc. Containment domains api. lph.ece.utexas.edu/public/CDs, April 2012.

[12] V. Izosimov, P. Pop, P. Eles, and Z. Peng. Scheduling and optimization of fault-tolerant embedded systems with transparency/performance trade-offs. *ACM Trans. Embed. Comput. Syst.*, 11(3):61:1–61:35, Sept. 2012.

[13] R. Koo and S. Toueg. Checkpointing and rollback-recovery for distributed systems. *Software Engineering, IEEE Transactions on*, SE-13(1):23–31, Jan 1987.

[14] C. Lauderdale and R. Khan. Towards a codelet-based runtime for exascale computing: Position paper. In *Proceedings of the 2Nd International Workshop on Adaptive Self-Tuning Computing Systems for the Exaflop Era*, EXADAPT '12, pages 21–26, New York, NY, USA, 2012. ACM.

[15] Z. Luo. Checkpointing for workflow recovery. In *Proceedings of the 38th Annual on Southeast Regional Conference*, ACM-SE 38, pages 79–80, New York, NY, USA, 2000. ACM.

[16] A. Moody, G. Bronevetsky, K. Mohror, and B. R. d. Supinski. Design, modeling, and evaluation of a scalable multi-level checkpointing system. In *Proceedings of the 2010 ACM/IEEE International Conference for High Performance Computing, Networking, Storage and Analysis*, SC '10, pages 1–11, Washington, DC, USA, 2010. IEEE Computer Society.

[17] X. Ni, E. Meneses, N. Jain, and L. V. Kalé. Acr: Automatic checkpoint/restart for soft and hard error protection. In *Proceedings of the International Conference on High Performance Computing, Networking, Storage and Analysis*, SC '13, pages 7:1–7:12, New York, NY, USA, 2013. ACM.

[18] B. Panda and S. Das. Performance evaluation of a two level error recovery scheme for distributed systems. In S. Das and S. Bhattacharya, editors, *Distributed Computing*, volume 2571 of *Lecture Notes in Computer Science*, pages 88–97. Springer Berlin Heidelberg, 2002.

[19] J. S. Plank and M. G. Thomason. Processor allocation and checkpoint interval selection in cluster computing systems. *Journal of Parallel and Distributed Computing*, 61(11):1570 – 1590, 2001.

[20] T. Ropars, T. V. Martsinkevich, A. Guermouche, A. Schiper, and F. Cappello. Spbc: Leveraging the characteristics of mpi hpc applications for scalable checkpointing. In *Proceedings of the International Conference on High Performance Computing, Networking, Storage and Analysis*, SC '13, pages 8:1–8:12, New York, NY, USA, 2013. ACM.

[21] N. H. Vaidya. A case for two-level distributed recovery schemes. In *Proceedings of the 1995 ACM SIGMETRICS Joint International Conference on Measurement and Modeling of Computer Systems*, SIGMETRICS '95/PERFORMANCE '95, pages 64–73, New York, NY, USA, 1995. ACM.

Mini-Symposium:
Symposium on Multi-System Application Extreme-Scaling Imperative

Parallel Computing: On the Road to Exascale
G.R. Joubert et al. (Eds.)
IOS Press, 2016
doi:10.3233/978-1-61499-621-7-765

MAXI – Multi-System
Application Extreme-Scaling Imperative

Dirk BRÖMMEL [a], Wolfgang FRINGS [a], Brian J. N. WYLIE [a]

[a] *Jülich Supercomputing Centre, Forschungszentrum Jülich GmbH, Germany*

Future supercomputer systems are expected to employ very large numbers of processors/cores and possibly to become more heterogeneous. Application scalability has therefore become a critical requirement, and with significant differences between supercomputer architectures experience with multiple computer systems is imperative.

In preparation, research is done on how to make the coming resources more accessible to users, e.g. new programming models, performance and debugging tools, and algorithmic improvements are developed. At the same time, numerous application code teams have already demonstrated the ability to exploit massive process/thread parallelism or adapt to limited compute-node memory.

While workshop and conference contributions from the aforementioned more theoretical research side are abundant, the view of application developers is scarce in comparison. The goal of this mini-symposium was to alleviate this situation and give application code teams a venue to report their outstanding achievements in both strong and weak scalability. In particular, we encouraged the participants to also report on the tools they used to get insight into performance, the issues encountered which needed to be resolved, and open issues that still need to be addressed. Special focus on application performance on multiple state-of-the-art systems and a comparison between those systems was desired.

Ten presentations were accepted for this mini-symposium — seven from code developers on experience scaling their applications from the fields of Earth modelling, computational fluid dynamics, engineering and neuroscience, complemented by three from supercomputer centres surveying highly-scaling applications on their systems — from which eight contributed papers for the proceedings.

In his presentation "Earthquake simulations at Petascale – Optimizing high-order ADER-BG in SeisSol," Michael Bader from the Technical University of Munich gave a comprehensive overview of the end-to-end optimisation of the SeisSol earthquake simulation code, which performs multiphysics simulations of the dynamic rupture process cess couples to seismic wave propagation, reporting on experience and scalability tests on *Tianhe-2*, *Stampede* and *SuperMUC*. SeisSol was a finalist for the 2014 Gordon Bell Prize reaching 8.6 PFLOPS on 8192 compute nodes of *Tianhe-2* based on Intel Xeon Phi processors.

Computational fluid dynamics on IBM Blue Gene/Q systems was addressed by two codes. Panagiotis Hadjidoukas of ETH Zürich presented "High throughput simulations of two-phase flows on Blue Gene/Q" with the CUBISM-MPCF code which won the 2013 ACM Gordon Bell Prize for peak performance, used to simulate cavitation collapse dynamics with 13 trillion finite-volume cells on 1.6M cores of *Sequoia* at 14.4 PFLOPS.

Jens Henrik Göbbert from the Jülich Aachen Research Alliance presented "Direct numerical simulation of fluid turbulence at extreme scale with `psOpen`" featuring scalability results on the 458,752 cores of *JUQUEEN* obtained from the 2015 JUQUEEN Extreme Scaling Workshop.

Two other workshop participants also presented their successful scaling to 458,752 cores of *JUQUEEN*. Aleksandr Ovcharenko of the EPFL Blue Brain Project presented "Simulating morphologically detailed neuronal networks at extreme scale" with up to 155 million neurons using `CoreNeuron` software isolated from the NEURON simulator and optimized with reduced memory footprint and three-level node, thread and vector parallelisation. Martin Lanser from the University of Cologne presented "FE2TI: Computational scale bridging for dual-phase steels," including recent scaling results with up to 786,432 cores on the *Mira* BG/Q at ANL of simulations of two- and three-dimensional nonlinear and micro-heterogeneous hyperelasticity problems.

The performance of two codes with different simulation capabilities using Lattice Boltzmann methods were compared on the three German tier-0 computer systems *JUQUEEN*, *Hermit/Hornet* and *SuperMUC* phases 1 & 2 at the largest scales. "`waLBerla`, an ultra-scalable multi-physics simulation framework for piecewise regular grids" was presented by Christian Godenschwager from the University of Erlangen-Nuremberg. "Performance of a Lattice Boltzman solver `Musubi` on various HPC systems" presented by Jiaxing Qi from the University of Siegen additionally included comparison with the *Kabuki* NEC SX-ACE multi-core vector supercomputer at HLRS which achieved the best single node performance.

The results of the seven international application code teams that participated in the 2015 *JUQUEEN* Extreme Scaling Workshop, and which were all successful within 24 hours in scaling to its full 458,752 cores, were reviewed by Dirk Brömmel of JSC in his presentation "Extreme-scaling applications 24/7 on *JUQUEEN* Blue Gene/Q." The associated High-Q Club now has a wide variety of over 24 codes (five in the mini-symposium) demonstrating extreme scalability.

Nicolay Hammer of Leibniz-Rechenzentrum (LRZ) presented "Extreme scale-out of *SuperMUC* phase 2, lessons learned," showing that of the 14 code teams given a month of early access to the phase 2 of *SuperMUC* at LRZ, most were able to improve scalability achieved in prior years' scaling workshops to successfully run on its 86,016 Intel Haswell cores, including `SeisSol` and three High-Q Club codes. Comparison of this form of scaling activity with that of short dedicated extreme scaling workshops was discussed, identifying its benefits when a new system is installed with a significant existing community of scalable applications.

Finally, in the presentation "K-scale applications on the *K* computer and co-design effort for the design and development of post-K" by Miwako Tsuji of RIKEN AICS, initial access to the *K* computer was similarly dedicated to selected code teams with scalable applications, two of which became ACM Gordon Bell Prize winners and were examined in detail. Experience with applications from nine priority research areas resulted in the selection of nine application codes which are now being used to co-design the successor to the *K* computer.

The organisers want to thank all who contributed a presentation and paper as well as everyone taking part in the discussions during the mini-symposium.

Parallel Computing: On the Road to Exascale
G.R. Joubert et al. (Eds.)
IOS Press, 2016
doi:10.3233/978-1-61499-621-7-767

High throughput simulations of two-phase flows on Blue Gene/Q

Panagiotis HADJIDOUKAS, Diego ROSSINELLI, Fabian WERMELINGER,
Jonas SUKYS, Ursula RASTHOFER, Christian CONTI,
Babak HEJAZIALHOSSEINI, and Petros KOUMOUTSAKOS [1]
*Chair of Computational Science, Department of Mechanical and Process Engineering,
ETH Zürich, Switzerland*

Abstract. CUBISM-MPCF is a high throughput software for two-phase flow simulations that has demonstrated unprecedented performance in terms of floating point operations, memory traffic and storage. The software has been optimized to take advantage of the features of the IBM Blue Gene/Q (BGQ) platform to simulate cavitation collapse dynamics using up to 13 Trillion computational elements. The performance of the software has been shown to reach an unprecedented 14.4 PFLOP/s on 1.6 Million cores corresponding to 72% of the peak on the 20 PFLOP/s Sequoia supercomputer. It is important to note that, to the best of our knowledge, no flow simulations have ever been reported exceeding 1 Trillion elements and reaching more than 1 PFLOP/s or more than 15% of peak. In this work, we first extend CUBISM-MPCF with a more accurate numerical flux and then summarize and evaluate the most important software optimization techniques that allowed us to reach 72% of the theoretical peak performance on BGQ systems. Finally, we show recent simulation results from cloud cavitation comprising 50000 vapor bubbles.

Keywords. Petaflop computing, Flow simulations, Cavitation

Introduction

Modern supercomputers enable engineers to design effective solutions for the energy and the environment where fluid flows play a key role. Cloud cavitation collapse can induce pressure peaks up to two orders of magnitude larger than the ambient pressure [1]. It is detrimental to the lifetime of high pressure injection engines and ship propellers and instrumental to kidney lithotripsy and drug delivery [2]. The simulation of cavitation requires two-phase flow solvers capable of capturing interactions between deforming bubbles, formation of shocks and their impact on solid walls, over a multitude of spatiotemporal scales. Moreover, simulations of bubble cloud collapse are very demanding in terms of numbers of operations, system size and memory traffic.

CUBISM-MPCF [3] is a compressible, two-phase finite volume solver capable of simulating and study cavitation collapse of clouds composed of up to 50000 bubbles. It is designed for multi-core clusters and highly optimized on Blue Gene/Q (BGQ) platforms, where it has managed to achieve up to 72% of the peak performance, to date the

---

[1]Corresponding Author: petros@ethz.ch

best performance for flow simulations in supercomputer architectures. A set of software techniques take advantage of the underlying hardware capabilities and concern all levels in the software abstraction aiming at full exploitation of the inherent instruction/data-, thread- and cluster-level parallelism.

1. Models and numerical approach

Cavitation dynamics are mainly governed by the compressibility of the flow while viscous dissipation and capillary effects take place at orders of magnitude larger time scales. We therefore solve inviscid, compressible, two-phase flows by discretizing the corresponding Euler equations. The system of equations describing the evolution of density, momentum and total energy of the flow reads:

$$\frac{\partial \rho}{\partial t} + \nabla \cdot (\rho \mathbf{u}) = 0,$$

$$\frac{\partial (\rho \mathbf{u})}{\partial t} + \nabla \cdot (\rho \mathbf{u}\mathbf{u}^T + p\mathbb{I}) = \mathbf{0}, \tag{1}$$

$$\frac{\partial E}{\partial t} + \nabla \cdot ((E + p)\mathbf{u}) = 0.$$

The evolution of the vapor and liquid phases is determined by another set of advection equations:

$$\frac{\partial \phi}{\partial t} + \mathbf{u} \cdot \nabla \phi = 0, \tag{2}$$

where $\phi = (\Gamma, \Pi)$ with $\Gamma = 1/(\gamma - 1)$ and $\Pi = \gamma p_c/(\gamma - 1)$. The specific heat ratio γ and the correction pressure of the mixture p_c are coupled to the system of equations (1) through a stiffened equation of state of the form $\Gamma p + \Pi = E - 1/2\rho |\mathbf{u}|^2$. We discretize these equations using a finite volume method in space and evolving the cell averages in time with an explicit time discretization.

Finite Volume Method. The governing system (1) and (2) can be recast into the conservative form

$$\frac{\partial \mathbf{Q}}{\partial t} + \frac{\partial \mathbf{F}}{\partial x} + \frac{\partial \mathbf{G}}{\partial y} + \frac{\partial \mathbf{H}}{\partial z} = \mathbf{R}, \tag{3}$$

where $\mathbf{Q} = (\rho, \rho \mathbf{u}, E, \phi)^T$ is the vector of conserved variables and $\mathbf{F}, \mathbf{G}, \mathbf{H}$ are vectors of flux functions

$$\mathbf{F} = \begin{pmatrix} \rho u_x \\ \rho u_x^2 + p \\ \rho u_y u_x \\ \rho u_z u_x \\ (E + p)u_x \\ \phi u_x \end{pmatrix}, \quad \mathbf{G} = \begin{pmatrix} \rho u_y \\ \rho u_x u_y \\ \rho u_y^2 + p \\ \rho u_z u_y \\ (E + p)u_y \\ \phi u_y \end{pmatrix}, \quad \mathbf{H} = \begin{pmatrix} \rho u_z \\ \rho u_x u_z \\ \rho u_y u_z \\ \rho u_z^2 + p \\ (E + p)u_z \\ \phi u_z \end{pmatrix}, \quad \mathbf{R} = \begin{pmatrix} 0 \\ 0 \\ 0 \\ 0 \\ 0 \\ \phi(\nabla \cdot \mathbf{u}) \end{pmatrix}.$$

The last term in R is due to rewriting (2) in conservative form [4]. The method of lines is applied to obtain a semi-discrete representation of (3), where space continuous operators are approximated using the finite volume method. The time continuous system of ordinary differential equations

$$\frac{d\mathbf{V}(t)}{dt} = \mathcal{L}(\mathbf{V}(t)), \tag{4}$$

is then solved using a low-storage third-order Runge-Kutta scheme [5]. $\mathbf{V} \in \mathbb{R}^{7N}$ is a vector of conserved cell average values at each center of the N cells in the domain. The evaluation of the discrete operator $\mathcal{L}: \mathbb{R}^{7N} \to \mathbb{R}^{7N}$ requires the solution of a Riemann problem at each cell face in the computational domain.

Three computational kernels are considered to perform one step. First, the admissible time step, Δt, is determined by adhering to the CFL condition. We call this kernel "DT" and execute it once per step. The second stage requires the evaluation of the right-hand side in (4). The explicit third order time integration requires the evaluation of $\mathcal{L}$ three times per step. The computational kernel for this task is called "RHS". Finally, updating the state of each of the solution variables in the domain is performed by calling the kernel "UP" once each step. RHS is bounded by the maximum performance of a BGQ node, while the DT and UP are memory bound [3]. In addition, RHS, DT and UP correspond approximately to 90%, 2% and 8% of the total simulation time, respectively (with I/O disabled).

Improved Numerical Flux. The RHS solves a Riemann problem on each cell interface in order to determine the numerical flux $\mathscr{F}^n(\mathbf{W}^-, \mathbf{W}^+)$ at discrete time t^n. Here $\mathbf{W} = (\rho, \mathbf{u}, p, \phi)^T$ is a vector of primitive variables. The two states $\mathbf{W}^-$ and $\mathbf{W}^+$ are the initial states for the Riemann problem. They are reconstructed from cell center values to the cell faces, using a third- or fifth-order weighted essentially non-oscillatory (WENO) scheme [6]. We use primitive variables for reconstruction to prevent numerical instabilities at interfaces [4]. The Riemann problem is then approximated at each cell face by assuming a single constant state $\mathbf{W}^*$ instead of the state $\mathbf{W}^1$, obtained from the exact wave structure, cf. Figure 1. This approximate Riemann solver is due to Harten, Lax and van Leer [7] and known as HLLE, where the wave speed estimates, s_L and s_R in Figure 1(b) are computed based on the work of Einfeldt [8].

In the context of this work, the accuracy of the approximate Riemann problem has been improved by explicitly modeling the contact discontinuity, labeled by "c" in Figure 1(a), by implementing the HLLC numerical flux [9]. The HLLC approximation assumes two constant intermediate states, separated by a contact discontinuity, propagating with a speed s^*, cf. Figure 1(c). Separating the contact discontinuity by two states allows for sharper resolution of material interfaces, which is important for multicomponent flows. The single state in the HLLE approximation is diffusive over the whole wave structure and consequently produces larger amounts of numerical viscosity in flow regions with multiple components. Estimates for s_L and s_R are again obtained from Einfeldt [8], which results in comparable approximations for shock and expansion waves for both, HLLE and HLLC solvers.

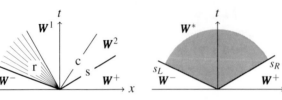
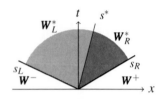

(a) Wave patterns for a specific exact solution to the Riemann problem.

(b) HLLE approximation to the exact solution of (a).

(c) HLLC approximation to the exact solution of (a).

Figure 1. (a) Exact solution of the Riemann problem for the $1D$ Euler equations with intermediate states W^j for $j = 1, 2$. "r" denotes a continuous rarefaction wave, "c" a contact discontinuity and "s" a shock wave. The initial states W^- and W^+ are obtained from a WENO reconstruction. (b) HLLE approximation to the exact solution (a) using a single intermediate state W^*. (c) HLLC approximation to (a) using two intermediate states W_L^* and W_R^*.

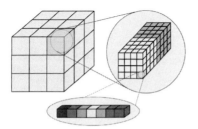
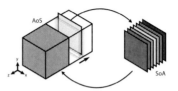

(a) Array of structures hierarchy for a memory block.

(b) Conversion to structure of arrays for the evaluation of RHS on the core layer.

Figure 2. (a) Memory layout for a computational block in CUBISM-MPCF. The data is stored in an array of structures (AoS) format in memory. Each cell provides enough space to store the vector of conserved variables Q, illustrated by the different colors. (b) At the core layer, the AoS layout is reformatted into a structure of arrays (SoA) layout to exploit data parallelism. Note that a second copy of each block (gray) is stored in memory due to the low-storage time integrator.

2. Optimization techniques and software

CUBISM-MPCF is decomposed into three layers: *cluster*, *node* and *core* to maximize the reusability. The *cluster layer* is responsible for the domain decomposition and the inter-rank information exchange. We divide the data into blocks that are formed by 32^3 cells. Each cell is represented by the vector of conserved variables Q, which we consecutively store in memory. The 3D block structure is represented in linear memory by V for a total of N computational cells. This results in an array of structures (AoS) format for the data in main memory. A second copy for each block is required due to the low-storage Runge-Kutta scheme. See Figure 2(a) for a visualization of a block.

The data is further decomposed into subdomains across the ranks in a cartesian topology with a constant subdomain size. The cluster layer dispatches the blocks for computation to the *node layer*, which is responsible for coordinating the work within each rank. The work associated to each block is exclusively assigned to one thread. To evaluate the RHS of a block, the assigned thread loads the block data and ghosts into a per-thread dedicated buffer. For a given block, the intra-rank ghosts are obtained by loading fractions of the surrounding blocks, whereas for the inter-rank ghosts data is

Table 1. Performance in fraction of the peak as well as time-to-solution (TtS) for the two accuracy levels on 96 BGQ nodes [10].

Accuracy	ALL	RHS	DT	UP	TtS (sec)
1 NR iteration	61.1%	68.5%	10.2%	2.3%	15.2
2 NR iterations	64.8%	71.7%	13.2%	2.3%	17.0

fetched from a global buffer. The node layer relies on the *core layer* for the execution of the compute kernels on each block. In order to exploit the data parallelism, the AoS layout is reformatted into a structure of arrays (SoA) layout, expressed by $2D$ slices suited for the required stencil computations in RHS, see Figure 2(b) for a visualization. The data conversion is a substage of RHS with about 1% execution time relative to the execution time of RHS (cf. Table 8 in [3]). The conservative variables stored in each block are read once by DT, UP and RHS, where the same number is written back by UP and RHS. Further micro-kernels are called within RHS, requiring further memory accesses that correspond mostly to cache hits due to the design of the blocks to fit the cache. A roofline plot of the three kernels on BGQ is shown in Figure 9 in [3].

CUBISM-MPCF employs a number of optimization techniques such as data re-ordering, vectorization by using QPX intrinsics, computation reordering and code fusion. These techniques are applied to increase the FLOP/Byte and FLOP/instruction ratios [3]. In addition, the code exploits mechanisms supported by the BGQ hardware, such as data prefetching, optimized memory copy functions and computation-transfer overlap using asynchronous progress communication. Finally, the software implements two levels of accuracy for floating point divisions by employing one or two iterations in the Newton-Raphson (NR) scheme. A detailed description of these techniques can be found in [10].

3. Results

In this section we present for the first time, performance results that concern the strong scaling efficiency of our code. We also demonstrate the effect of asynchronous progress communication and discuss, in detail, about the different levels of code fusion. Finally, we evaluate the performance of the improved approximate Riemann solver.

We compiled our code with the IBM XL C/C++ compiler (v12.1) and used the IBM Hardware Performance Monitor (HPM) Toolkit for measuring performance figures. We use $16^3 = 4096$ blocks per compute node with 32^3 computational elements in each block. Performance measurements from a previous publication are presented in Table 1. It is important to note that due to the efficient computation/transfer overlap employed in CUBISM-MPCF, these results are valid for practically any number of BGQ nodes [10].

Strong scaling.   Figure 3(a) depicts the strong scaling efficiency of the cluster layer from 256 to 2048 BG/Q nodes, ranging the number of blocks per node from 4096 to 512. We observe an efficiency of 89% on 2048 nodes and that both metrics, overall time/step and achieved performance of RHS, exhibit similar scaling results.

Figure 3(b) shows how the cluster layer scales with respect to the number of blocks per node. In this case, we range the number of blocks from 64 to 4096, running our experiments on 512 BGQ nodes. For down to 512 blocks, the results coincide with those in Figure 3(a). The efficiency remains above 82% for 256 blocks and drops down to 63%

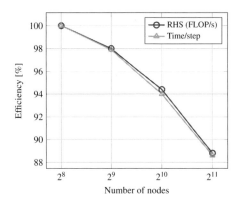
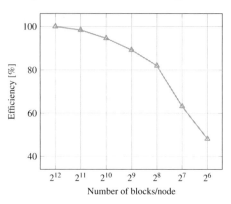

(a) Efficiency with respect to achieved performance of RHS and time required per simulation step.

(b) Efficiency on 512 nodes for decreasing number of blocks per node.

Figure 3. (a) Strong scaling efficiency of the cluster layer of CUBISM-MPCF. The efficiency is illustrated for both floating point operations of RHS and time per Runge-Kutta step. (b) Efficiency for fixed number of nodes (512) and decreasing number of blocks that are processed by each node.

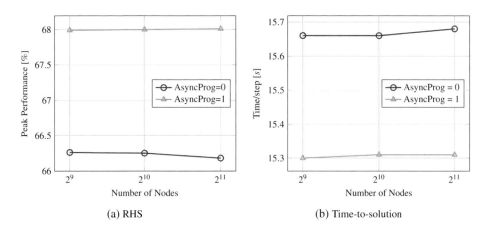

(a) RHS

(b) Time-to-solution

Figure 4. Effect of asynchronous progress communication on (a) peak performance and (b) time-to-solution.

and 48% for 128 and 64 blocks per node, due to underutilization of processor cores and inefficient computation/communication overlap. For instance, the 64 blocks, arranged in a 4x4x4 subdomain, correspond to 27 inner and 37 halo blocks that are processed in two phases by the 64 total OpenMP threads of each node. Therefore, the majority of threads remains idle.

Computation/transfer overlap. To overlap communication with computation, we use non-blocking point-to-point communications to exchange ghost information for the halo blocks and then process the inner blocks before calling `MPI_Waitall()`. To take full advantage of this mechanism and eliminate communication overheads, however, we had to activate the asynchronous progress communication at the PAMID layer. In addition, we had to modify the workflow in the RHS kernel as follows: after issuing the MPI calls for the ghost data, we create an OpenMP parallel region with 63 threads, each processing a single inner block. After this parallel region, we call `MPI_Waitall()` and then process

Table 2. Levels of micro-kernel fusion.

Level	Description
0	No fusion, 8 micro-kernels.
1	As Level 0 with reduced accuracy of WENO smoothness indicators.
2	Fusion of energy flux with wave speed estimator, as well as fusion of mass flux with the diagonal entry of the momentum flux, 6 micro-kernels.
3	As Level 2 with reduced accuracy of WENO smoothness indicators.
4	Aggressive fusion of all micro-kernels into a single macro-kernel with code transformations and reduced accuracy of WENO smoothness indicators.

the rest of the blocks using 64 threads [10]. In Figure 4 we observe the gain in achieved performance (left) and time-to-solution (right) on up to 2 BGQ racks, attributed to the negligible communication time of `MPI_Waitall()` due to the available hardware thread that advances MPI communications.

Effect of code fusion.   The evaluation of RHS requires the computation of the numerical flux $\mathscr{F}^n(\boldsymbol{W}^-, \boldsymbol{W}^+) \in \mathbb{R}^7$ for each of the 7 components of the conserved variables $\boldsymbol{Q}$ based on the HLLE or HLLC scheme. In addition, wave speed estimates for s_L and s_R must be computed based on [8]. This results in 8 micro-kernels for each spatial direction in $3D$ space.

We have implemented and tested several depths of code fusion, which are summarized in Table 2. Code fusion reduces redundant accesses to main memory and increases instruction level parallelism. On the other hand, pressure on the register file increases, which might cause register spills. In addition to fusing the low-level micro-kernels of RHS, reduction of complexity for the WENO smoothness indicators allows for further code optimizations.

We assess the performance of these optimizations at the node layer by performing simulations on a single BGQ chip. Although this layer performs ghost reconstruction across the blocks, it completely avoids explicit communication and synchronization overheads due to MPI. In contrast to the cluster layer, the 4096 blocks are dynamically scheduled to the 64 OpenMP threads using a single parallel for loop.

Figure 5 shows the results for the different levels of code fusion on a single BGQ node, where we further distinguish between the IBM `SWDIV` intrinsic and our NR implementation for floating point divisions. Figure 5(a) illustrates the achieved peak performance, which we managed to increase by **8%** in absolute value when going from the initial version to the one with the most aggressive optimizations. Figure 5(b) shows time-to-solution based on our optimizations.

Improved numerical flux.   The increased complexity of the HLLC algorithm further improves the fraction of the peak for RHS to **69.5%** and **72.8%** for one and two NR iterations, respectively, on a single BGQ node. Despite the additional logic required to distinguish between the two constant states $\boldsymbol{W}_L^*$ and $\boldsymbol{W}_R^*$ in the HLLC algorithm, we observe an improvement of about 1% in the achieved performance using the HLLC approximate Riemann solver over HLLE. The improvement is due to a slightly better density of FMA instructions in the QPX implementation of HLLC. This, however, at the expense of higher execution time, which is increased by 9% compared to the version that uses the HLLE scheme, due to the increased number of floating point operations. Table 3 com-

Table 3. Measurements for time to solution and RHS performance on a single BGQ node for one and two NR iterations, respectively, for the HLLE and HLLC solvers. On 2048 BGQ nodes, RHS using the HLLC solver achieves 68.8% and 72.1% of peak performance for one and two NR iterations, respectively.

	One NR iteration		Two NR iterations	
	HLLE	HLLC	HLLE	HLLC
Time/step [s]	15.0	16.4	16.8	18.4
RHS [% peak]	68.7%	69.5%	72.0%	72.8%

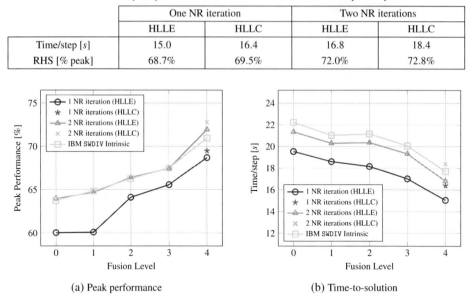

(a) Peak performance   (b) Time-to-solution

Figure 5. Achieved peak performance (a) and time-to-solution (b) for different code fusion levels on a single BGQ node. The plots compare three variants for the computation of floating point divisions. We distinguish between the NR scheme for floating point divisions with either one or two iterations, as well as the IBM intrinsic SWDIV. See Table 2 for a description of the different fusion levels.

pares measurements for time to solution and RHS performance on a single BGQ node for the HLLE and HLLC solvers.

4. Simulations

We present recent results from cloud cavitation comprising 50000 vapor bubbles. Figure 6(a) displays a random spherical cloud of vapor bubbles with an initial radius of $r_c = 8$ mm and cloud interaction parameter of $\beta = 120$ at time $t = 0$. The bubble radii range from $50\,\mu$m to $200\,\mu$m. The domain is discretized using 4096^3 cells. The simulation was scheduled on 2 BGQ racks and required 25000 time steps.

The collapse of bubbles is initiated at the most outer shell of the cloud and further propagates towards the cloud center. Instantaneous bubble shapes of these initial collapses are depicted in Figure 6(b). At the final stage of the collapse, a strong pressure shock is emitted from the center of the cloud, see Figure 6(c). The maximum pressure, an indicator for the damage potential, exceeds the ambient pressure by a factor of 25 for this particular cloud. The pressure amplification relative to the ambient pressure p_∞ is shown in Figure 7(a). Highest Mach numbers are observed prior to the final collapse of the cloud. During that time, the collapsing bubbles are located at the outer shells of the spherical cloud with re-entrant micro-jets focused towards the cloud center. The non-spherical collapse generates high velocity jets, which penetrate through the bubbles. These jets are associated with large kinetic energy, which in turn cause high Mach num-

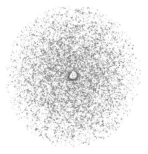

(a)   Spherical   cloud   with   50000 bubbles at time $t = 0$.

(b) Close-up of the first collapsing bubbles at the most outer shell.

(c) Peak pressure in the cloud center at the final stage of the collapse.

Figure 6. (a) Initial state of the cloud. (b) Close-up view of the outer bubbles during the collapse process. (c) Emerging pressure wave after the final collapse of the cloud. Pressure regions are depicted in yellow (15–25 times larger than the initial ambient pressure) and blue (10–15 times larger). Refer to the online version for colors.

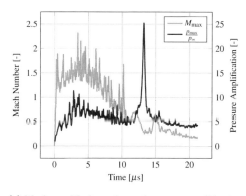

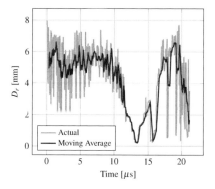

(a) Maximum Mach number and pressure amplification factor.

(b) Radial distance of maximum pressure from the cloud center.

Figure 7. (a) Maximum Mach number and pressure amplification during the simulation. (b) Occurrence of maximum pressure measured by radial distance from the cloud center.

bers. As the bubble collapse propagates closer towards the cloud center, the jet velocities become weaker and concentrate at the center of the cloud. As the total kinetic energy decreases, the potential energy increases due to conservation of energy. Hence the sharp decline of the maximum Mach number just prior to the emission of the strong pressure shock from the cloud center, cf. Figure 7(a).

Figure 7(b) illustrates the radial distance, D_r, of the maximum pressure, measured from the cloud center. For the first collapsing bubbles, the maximum pressure randomly jumps to radial distances further away from the cloud center. As collapses progress, the maximum pressure obeys a structured information propagation with a signal velocity of approximately 1405 m/s, which is lower than the speed of sound in water at standard conditions due to the disruptive vapor cavities. The minimum radial distance of the maximum pressure is observed when the pressure is found to be the global maximum, see Figure 7(a) and 7(b). The emission of a strong pressure shock at the final collapse stage causes the radial distance of the maximum pressure to increase. As the radial distance increases, the structure in the information propagation is lost and maximum pressure locations continue to jump randomly between spherical shells. A notable difference to the initial phase of the collapse is that the pressure maximum in the post cloud collapse regime rapidly jumps back somewhere close to the cloud center. Similar pressure rebounds are observed in spherical collapse of a single bubble.

5. Conclusions

The employment of algorithmic and software techniques and the exploitation of underlying hardware capabilities have enabled CUBISM-MPCF to reach 72% of the theoretical peak performance of BGQ platforms, allowing us to perform simulation studies of cloud cavitation collapse at unprecedented scale. Our approach is generally applicable and can be adopted to enhance the performance of all uniform grid based solvers [2]. We are currently enhancing our software with wavelet adapted grids for multiresolution flow simulations.

Acknowledgements.   We wish to thank Dr. R. Walkup (IBM Watson) for providing us the HPM toolkit. We acknowledge support by the DOE INCITE project CloudPredict and the PRACE projects PRA091 and Pra09_2376.

References

[1]   D. P. Schmidt and M. L. Corradini.   The internal flow of Diesel fuel injector nozzles: A review. International Journal of Engine Research, 2(1):1–22, 2001.
[2]   Tetsuya Kodama and Kazuyoshi Takayama. Dynamic behavior of bubbles during extracorporeal shockwave lithotripsy. Ultrasound in medicine & biology, 24(5):723–738, 1998.
[3]   Diego Rossinelli, Babak Hejazialhosseini, Panagiotis Hadjidoukas, Costas Bekas, Alessandro Curioni, Adam Bertsch, Scott Futral, Steffen J Schmidt, Nikolaus Adams, Petros Koumoutsakos, et al. 11 pflop/s simulations of cloud cavitation collapse. In High Performance Computing, Networking, Storage and Analysis (SC), 2013 International Conference for, pages 1–13. IEEE, 2013.
[4]   Eric Johnsen and Tim Colonius. Implementation of WENO schemes in compressible multicomponent flow problems. Journal of Computational Physics, 219(2):715 – 732, 2006.
[5]   JH Williamson. Low-storage Runge-Kutta schemes. Journal of Computational Physics, 35(1):48–56, 1980.
[6]   Xu-Dong Liu, Stanley Osher, and Tony Chan. Weighted essentially non-oscillatory schemes. Journal of computational physics, 115(1):200–212, 1994.
[7]   A. Harten, P. Lax, and B. van Leer. On upstream differencing and Godunov-type schemes for hyperbolic conservation laws. SIAM Review, 25(1):35–61, 1983.
[8]   B. Einfeldt.   On Godunov-type methods for gas dynamics.   SIAM Journal on Numerical Analysis, 25(2):294–318, 1988.
[9]   E. F. Toro, M. Spruce, and W. Speares. Restoration of the contact surface in the HLL-Riemann solver. Shock Waves, 4(1):25–34, 1994.
[10]   Panagiotis Hadjidoukas, Diego Rossinelli, Babak Hejazialhosseini, and Petros Koumoutsakos. From 11 to 14.4 pflops: Performance optimization for finite volume flow solver. In 3rd International Conference on Exascale Applications and Software (EASC 2015), pages 7–12, 2015.

---

[2]The software can be downloaded from GitHub, https://github.com/cselab/CUBISM-MPCF.

Parallel Computing: On the Road to Exascale
G.R. Joubert et al. (Eds.)
IOS Press, 2016
doi:10.3233/978-1-61499-621-7-777

Direct Numerical Simulation of Fluid Turbulence at Extreme Scale with psOpen

Jens Henrik GOEBBERT [a,b,1], Michael GAUDING [c], Cedrick ANSORGE [d],
Bernd HENTSCHEL [a,b], Torsten KUHLEN [e,b] and Heinz PITSCH [f]

[a] *Virtual Reality Group, RWTH Aachen University, Germany*
[b] *Jülich Aachen Research Alliance (JARA) - High Performance Computing*
[c] *Chair of Numerical Thermo-Fluid Dynamics, TU Freiberg, Germany*
[d] *Max Planck Institute for Meteorology, Hamburg, Germany*
[e] *Jülich Supercomputing Centre - Forschungszentrum Jülich GmbH*
[f] *Institut für Technische Verbrennung, RWTH Aachen University, Germany*

Abstract. The hybrid OpenMP/MPI code psOpen has been developed at the Institute for Combustion Technology, RWTH Aachen University, to study incompressible fluid turbulence by means of direct numerical simulations (DNS). For efficiency and accuracy psOpen employs a pseudo-spectral method, where the governing equations are solved partly in Fourier space. Hence, a pseudo-spectral method requires frequent transformations between real and Fourier space which is particularly challenging for massively-parallel setups. The frequently invoked Fourier transformation is a non-local operation and requires access to all data along a global grid line for each computational process. psOpen was improved by a new inhouse-developed 3d-FFT library optimised to the special needs of pseudo-spectral DNS. For an optimal use of the hardware resources two techniques have been combined to reduce the communication time significantly. Firstly, the number of operations and the size of data to be transposed while computing a 3d-FFT has been reduced by integrating the dealiasing cut-off filter into the 3d-FFT. Secondly, the new 3d-FFT library allows to overlap communication and computation of multiple FFTs at the same time. The scaling performance of psOpen with three different grid sizes, namely 4096^3, 6144^3 and 8192^3, has been studied on JUQUEEN up to the full machine.

Keywords. turbulence, direct numerical simulation, 3d fast Fourier transformation, extreme scaling

Introduction

Over more than a century the understanding of turbulence has remained a big challenge of great importance to both science and engineering. It is involved in many natural and engineering processes like turbulent mixing, turbulent combustion, meteorology,

---

[1]Corresponding Author: Jens Henrik Goebbert, RWTH Aachen University, IT Center, Seffenter Weg 23, 52074 Aachen, Germany; E-mail: goebbert@jara.rwth-aachen.de.

oceanography, astronomy etc. As a continuum field phenomenon, turbulence is in principle infinite-dimensional and strongly non-local and non-linear. The temporal and spatial evolution of a velocity field is described by the Navier-Stokes equations, which contain all necessary information to fully characterize the motion of turbulent flows. Although the Navier-Stokes equations are formally deterministic, turbulence dynamics are by no means the same. Up to now, turbulence dynamics are still one of the unsolved problems of classical physics [1,2].

The direct numerical simulation (DNS) is an indispensable tool in turbulence research [3] and has a long tradition starting with the works of Patterson and Orszag [4,5] on a 32^3 grid at a Reynolds number (based on Taylor micro-scale) of 35. Over the last decades the possible grid size and the significance of DNS have increased rapidly. Widely used numerical methods in the industry are based on Reynolds Averaged Navier-Stokes equations (RANS) by the idea of Reynolds [6,7] or Large Eddy Simulation (LES) first proposed by Smagorinsky [8]. Both allow for simulations with complex geometries and incorporate numerous physical phenomena. Compared with DNS they are relatively cheap in terms of computational cost as they do not resolve the whole range of scales in time and space. In contrast to RANS and LES, DNS solves for all scales present in turbulent flows without any model and makes no assumptions about the physics (except the basic assumption of a Newtonian fluid being a continuum), but resolves all scales of the energy cascade down to the dissipation scale of the turbulent flow. Hence, DNS can be seen as a numerical experiment. It is meaningful especially in the sense of statistical studies. It has shown to be an important benchmarking tool for theoretical ideas and has broadened the understanding of turbulence in the past decades significantly.

The canonical case of a DNS as a numerical experiment is a fully developed stationary homogeneous isotropic turbulence without any wall effects. The algorithms used to compute these DNS have to have good performance and have to be suitable for nowadays parallel supercomputers. DNS in general is highly parallelizable even though a global task has to be solved, which cannot be split into independent sub-problems due to the non-locality of the pressure term. Contrary to applications in genetics or quantum physics the strong communication between the compute kernels cannot be avoided. This is one of the major challenges towards a highly scalable DNS.

1. Direct Numerical Simulation of Turbulent Flows

Turbulence is a strongly non-local and non-linear continuum field phenomenon and is governed by the Navier-Stokes equations. For incompressible flows the Navier-Stokes equations can be written in several equivalent formulations. The convection form is written with the velocity-pressure variables for continuity and momentum equation as

$$\nabla \cdot u = 0, \tag{1}$$

$$\frac{\partial u}{\partial t} - \nu \nabla^2 u + (u \cdot \nabla u) + \nabla p = f_u, \tag{2}$$

where $u(x,t)$, $p(x,t)$, $\nu > 0$ and f_u is the velocity, the kinematic pressure, the kinematic viscosity and an external forcing (which drives the fluid field and acts at the large scales

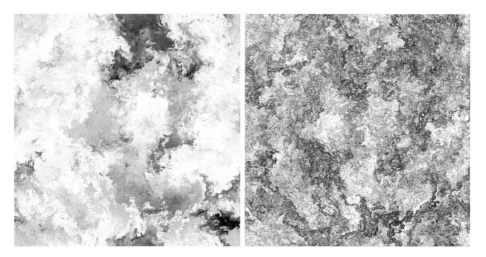

Figure 1. DNS of a passive scalar advected by a turbulent velocity field with 4096^3 grid points and a Taylor-based $Re_\lambda = 530$. Slice of scalar field (left) and scalar dissipation (right). Scalar dissipation rate exhibits very fine structures which have to be resolved by the numerical grid.

only), respectively. Incompressibility is ensured by the the continuity equation for a fluid with constant density. By these equations all necessary information is given to fully characterize the motion of turbulent flows if initial and boundary conditions are given.

The most import non-dimensional number for turbulent flows is the turbulent Reynolds number Re_t. It is defined as $Re_t = u' \cdot L_t / \nu$, where u' is the turbulent intensity and L_t the integral length scale.

The integral scale L_t describes the size of the largest structures in contrast to the Kolmogorov scale η, which is the size of the smallest structures in the flow. To fully resolve all properties of a turbulent flow, η should be larger than the grid size Δx of the calculation domain. Hence, DNS is computationally very expensive as the number of required grid points N^3 increases tremendously with the Reynolds number,

$$N^3 \propto Re_t^{9/4} \tag{3}$$

2. Pseudo-Spectral Algorithm

For efficiency and accuracy psOpen employs a pseudo-spectral method, where the governing equations are solved in Fourier space. The algorithm for DNS of isotropic homogeneous turbulence was first suggested in 1972 by Orszag and Patterson [5]. In the following, we based on the detailed description of this algorithm by Ruetsch [9]. The numerical algorithm implemented in psOpen is outlined in Alg. 1. and requires main memory for 22 scalar values per grid point and needs to compute 13 three-dimensional fast Fourier transformations (3d-FFT) in each iteration. It is based on the Navier-Stokes equations in rotational form written in Fourier space.

$$\frac{\partial \widehat{u}}{\partial t} + \underbrace{\widehat{(\omega \times u)}}_{\widehat{G}} + i\kappa \widehat{P} + \nu \kappa^2 \widehat{u} = \widehat{f}_u \tag{4}$$

Here u is the velocity, ω is the vorticity, P is the Bernoulli pressure, $v > 0$ the kinematic viscosity and an external forcing f_u applied at the large scales only.

Beside the velocity field of the turbulent flow psOpen solves a transport equation for a scalar fluctuation $\phi(x,t)$. Its Fourier transform can be written as

$$\frac{\partial \widehat{\phi}}{\partial t} + \underbrace{\widehat{(u \cdot \nabla \phi)}}_{\widehat{J}} = -\kappa^2 D \widehat{\phi} - \widehat{f}_\phi . \tag{5}$$

Here D is the molecular diffusivity and f_ϕ the forcing term. Derivatives in the transport equations turn into multiplications by the wave-number vector κ. Hence, all linear terms can be treated in Fourier Space. However, the Fourier transformation of the non-linear term $\widehat{G}$ and $\widehat{J}$ turns into a convolution in Fourier space. This operation is computationally very expensive and requires $\mathcal{O}(N^{2.3})$ operations. Therefore, instead of directly evaluating the convolution operation, the multiplication of the non-linear term is computed in real space. This approach requires only $\mathcal{O}(N^3 \log N)$ operations and is called pseudo-spectral method since only differentiation is performed in Fourier space. Hence, a pseudo-spectral method requires frequent 3d-FFT between real and Fourier space which is particularly challenging for massive-parallel setups.

psOpen solves the three-dimensional Navier-Stokes equations for the velocity field $u(x)$ and the transport equation for passive scalar fluctuations $\phi(x)$ in a triply periodic domain of size $(2\pi)^3$. The cartesian domain has $N_x \times N_y \times N_z$ grid points in real space and $\kappa_x \times \kappa_y \times \kappa_z$ wave-number modes in Fourier space. The domain can either be sliced in one dimension to slabs or in two dimensions to pencils with each slab or pencil associated to a single MPI rank.

The first proof of scalability on IBM Blue Gene/P architecture was made on JU-GENE in 2008 and the code has been further improved over the years since then. In 2012 it was ported to IBM Blue Gene/Q (JUQUEEN). psOpen has been used for multiple projects and publications, see [10,11,12,13,14,15,16,17,18,19,20].

3. 3D Fast Fourier Transformation

As the frequently invoked Fourier transformation is a non-local operation it requires access to all data along a global grid line for each computational process. psOpen was improved by the inhouse-developed 3d-FFT library nb3dfft optimized to the special needs of pseudo-spectral DNS and consuming most of the CPU time. It uses the Engineering and Scientific Subroutine Library (ESSL), which is specifically designed for the IBM BlueGene/Q processor and provides a shared memory FFT function set for best parallelization on each node. For an optimal use of the hardware resources three techniques have been combined reducing the time required for communication by a factor of more than two.

For dealiasing after each forward 3d-FFT a filter operation is required to remove energy of high wave-number modes by isotropic truncation. This operation can most easily be applied in Fourier space by an explicit $2/3$ filter. But this simple filter technique discarded 84.5% of the expensively transformed data. Only 15.5% of the transformed data is required to describe all dynamically active modes in Fourier space. Implicit $3/2$ filtering reduces the amount of operations and the size of data to be transposed significantly by in-

Table 1. Strong scaling tests of psOpen for various grid sizes. Listed are the measured configurations for the different grid sizes 2048^3, 4096^3, 6144^3 and 8192^3. Here bg_size is number of nodes, rpn is MPI ranks per node, tpp is OpenMP tasks per MPI process.

| bg_size | rpn | ranks | tpp | threads | \multicolumn{4}{c}{time per iteration in seconds} |
					2048^3	4096^3	6144^3	8192^3
2048	32	65536	2	131072	0.6295	3.0785	-	-
4096	32	131072	2	262144	0.3281	1.8815	-	-
8192	32	262144	2	524288	0.1805	0.9606	2.3276	-
16384	32	524288	2	1835008	-	0.4950	1.2132	-
24576	32	786432	2	1572864	-	-	0.9530	3.7811
28672	32	917504	2	1835008	-	-	0.9278	3.6801

tegrating the dealiasing cut-off filter into the 3d-FFT operation. It combines the separate 3d-FFT and filter operations and directly transforms between a (N_x, N_y, N_z)-domain in real space and a filtered $(\kappa_{x,flt}, \kappa_{y,flt}, \kappa_{z,flt})$-domain in Fourier space and avoids a transform to a $(\kappa_x, \kappa_y, \kappa_z)$-domain in between. Figure 2 shows the optimized 3d-FFT algorithm including the implicit filtering technique of the nb3dfft library. Its three phases are described for a forward 3d-FFT with implict $3/2$ filtering. The domain is decomposed in 2d as an (i, j) grid of pencils, one for each MPI process. Implicit filtering reduces the number of complex-to-complex 1d-FFTs by 44.4% and data to be sent for the global transposes by 44.4% as the data shrinks from real space to Fourier space by 70.4%.

A MPI-parallelized 3d-FFT is based on time-consuming collective communications. The new 3d-FFT library allows to overlap these communications with the computation of multiple FFTs at the same time. This reduces the time for each 3d-FFT by another 15-25%. This technique incorporated in nb3dfft has been also adapted for simulations of planetary boundary layer (see [21]).

All 3d-FFTs required to compute one iteration of the velocity and passive scalar are blocked in two single calls of the non-blocking 3d-FFT library nb3dfft, which therefore can overlap once six and once seven 3d-FFTs at the same time. This increases the benefit from an overlap communication and computation of 3d-FFTs and reduces the required extra time for a passive scalar by almost 50%.

4. Results

The scaling performance of psOpen with three different grid sizes, namely 4096^3, 6144^3 and 8192^3, has been studied. The chosen grid sizes are of high relevance for production runs. Production runs with up to 6144^3 grid points have been already conducted and those with 8192^3 grid points are planned in the near future. It is customary to compute DNS of homogeneous isotropic turbulent flows in a periodic box using single precision arithmetic. Therefore, all data presented in this report are based on single-precision computations. Compared to double-precision this reduces the communication amount by a factor of two, while keeping constant the computational cost on a Blue Gene/Q architecture. Figure 3 shows the speedup of psOpen for configurations between 2048^3 and 8192^3 grid points. Full machine runs were performed for 6144^3 and 8192^3 grid points. The memory requirement becomes very demanding for these grid sizes and determines the number of compute nodes that are necessary. Therefore, for only a few configurations measurements are possible.

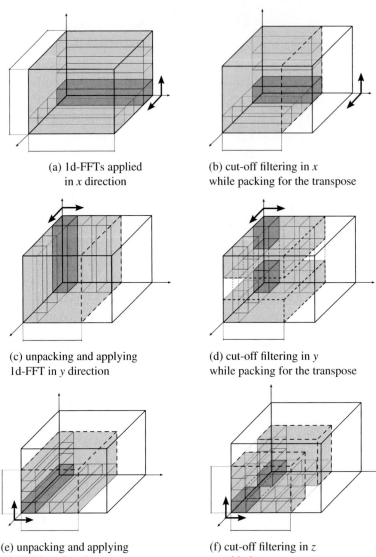

(a) 1d-FFTs applied
in *x* direction

(b) cut-off filtering in *x*
while packing for the transpose

(c) unpacking and applying
1d-FFT in *y* direction

(d) cut-off filtering in *y*
while packing for the transpose

(e) unpacking and applying
1d-FFT in *z* direction

(f) cut-off filtering in *z*
considering access patterns

Figure 2. Steps performed to apply 3d-FFT with implict ³/₂ filtering of a 2d decomposed domain (highlighting data of MPI rank 0 and skeletons of its neighbor pencils). In all figures the domain coordinates x, y, z are preserved while the MPI process grid (i, j) is moved to match the changed pencil orientation. Implicit filtering reduces the number of complex-to-complex 1d-FFTs by 44.4% and data to be sent for the global transposes by 44.4% as the data (grayed volume) shrinks from real space to Fourier space by 70.4%.

psOpen exhibits an almost linear speedup up to 16384 compute nodes for all investigated grid sizes. Runs with 24576 compute nodes exhibit a satisfactory efficiency, considering the underlying mathematical operation of solving the Poisson equation which enforces global communication. For the full-machine run with 28672 compute nodes we observe a further decline in efficiency, which might result from the large (size 7) B-dimension of the five-dimensional torus network of JUQUEEN. For reference tab. 1

Algorithm 1 Outline of the pseudo-spectral algorithm for iterating the velocity of homogeneous isotropic forced turbulence and a passive scalar in a periodic domain. It requires memory for 22 scalars values (numbered by the lower index) per grid point and computes 13 3d-FFTs in each iteration.

1: **procedure** ITERATE VELOCITY $(n \to [n+1])$, PASSIVE SCALAR $([n-1] \to n)$

2:      **input (velocity):** $\widehat{u}^n_{1|2|3}$, $\widehat{G}^{n-1}_{4|5|6}$, $\widehat{f}^{n-1}_u$

3:      **input (passive scalar):** $\widehat{\phi}^{n-1}_{17}$, J^{n-1}_{19}, $\widehat{J}^{n-2}_{18}$, $\widehat{u}^{n-1}_{16}$

4:      **for all** wave numbers (κ) **do:**   ▷ compute vorticity

5:          $\widehat{\omega}^n_{x,10} \leftarrow \kappa_z \widehat{u}^n_{y,2} - \kappa_y \widehat{u}^n_{z,3}$

6:          $\widehat{\omega}^n_{y,11} \leftarrow \kappa_x \widehat{u}^n_{z,3} - \kappa_z \widehat{u}^n_{x,1}$

7:          $\widehat{\omega}^n_{z,12} \leftarrow \kappa_y \widehat{u}^n_{x,1} - \kappa_x \widehat{u}^n_{y,2}$

8:          $\omega^n_{10|11|12} \xleftarrow{\mathscr{F}+3/2\ \text{filter}} \widehat{\omega}^n_{10|11|12}$ ▷ 3x in-place backward 3d-FFT

9:          $u^n_{7|8|9} \xleftarrow{\mathscr{F}+3/2\ \text{filter}} \widehat{u}^n_{1|2|3}$ ▷ 3x out-of-place backward 3d-FFT

10:          $\widehat{J}^{n-1}_{19} \xleftarrow{\mathscr{F}+3/2\ \text{filter}} J^{n-1}_{19}$ ▷ 1x in-place forward 3d-FFT

11:      **for all** wave numbers (κ) **do:**   ▷ advance passive scalar

12:          $\widehat{\phi}^n_{17} \leftarrow \mathrm{F}_{\mathrm{adv}}(\widehat{\phi}^{n-1}_{17}, \widehat{J}^{n-1}_{19}, \widehat{J}^{n-2}_{18}, \widehat{u}^{n-1}_{16})$

13:          $\widehat{J}^{n-1}_{19} \xrightleftharpoons{\text{zero copy}} \widehat{J}^{n-2}_{18}$ ▷ swap memory

14:      **for all** grid points (N) **do:**   ▷ compute $G^n = \omega^n \times u^n$

15:          $G^n_{x,13} \leftarrow u^n_{y,8} \cdot \omega^n_{z,12} - u^n_{z,9} \cdot \omega^n_{y,11}$

16:          $G^n_{y,14} \leftarrow u^n_{7,9} \cdot \omega^n_{x,10} - u^n_{y,7} \cdot \omega^n_{z,12}$

17:          $G^n_{z,15} \leftarrow u^n_{x,7} \cdot \omega^n_{y,11} - u^n_{y,8} \cdot \omega^n_{x,10}$

18:          $\widehat{\nabla\phi}^n_{10|11|12} \leftarrow \widehat{\phi}^n_{17}$ ▷ 3x compute derivatives

19:          $\widehat{G}^n_{13|14|15} \xleftarrow{\mathscr{F}+3/2\ \text{filter}} G^n_{13|14|15}$ ▷ 3x in-place forward 3d-FFT

20:          $\nabla\phi^n_{20|21|22} \xleftarrow{\mathscr{F}+3/2\ \text{filter}} \widehat{\nabla\phi}^n_{20|21|22}$ ▷ 3x in-place backward 3d-FFT

21:          $J^n_{19} \leftarrow u^n_{7|8|9} \cdot \nabla\phi^n_{20|21|22}$ ▷ compute convective term

22:          $\widehat{G}^n_{13|14|15} \xrightleftharpoons{\text{zero copy}} \widehat{G}^{n-1}_{4|5|6}$ ▷ swap memory

23:          $\widehat{u}^n_{16} \xrightleftharpoons{\text{zero copy}} \widehat{u}^n_2$ ▷ swap memory

24:          $\widehat{f}^n_u \leftarrow \mathrm{F}(\widehat{f}^{n-1}_u)$ ▷ compute forcing energy

25:      **for** wave numbers $(|\kappa_{ijk}| < k_f = 2\sqrt{2})$ **do:**   ▷ add forcing energy

26:          $\widehat{u}^{\mathrm{force}}_{1|2|3} \leftarrow \mathrm{F}_{\mathrm{force}}(\widehat{u}^n_{1|16|3}, \widehat{f}^n_u)$

27:      **for all** wave numbers (κ) **do:**   ▷ advance velocity

28:          $\widehat{u}^{\mathrm{step1}}_{1|2|3} \leftarrow \mathrm{F}_{\mathrm{step1}}(\widehat{u}^{\mathrm{force}}_{1|2|3}, \widehat{G}^n_{4|5|6}, \widehat{G}^{n-1}_{13|14|15})$

29:      **for all** wave numbers (κ) **do:**   ▷ apply projection tensor

30:          $\widehat{u}^{n+1}_{1|2|3} \leftarrow \mathrm{F}_{\mathrm{step2}}(\widehat{u}^{\mathrm{step1}}_{1|2|3})$

31:      $\langle \widehat{u}^{n+1}_{1|2|3} \rangle = 0$ ▷ set mean velocity to zero

32:      **output (velocity):** $\widehat{u}^{n+1}_{1|2|3}$, $\widehat{G}^n_{4|5|6}$, $u^n_{7|8|9}$, $\widehat{u}^n_{16}$

33:      **output (passive scalar):** $\widehat{\phi}^n_{17}$, J^n_{19}, $\widehat{J}^{n-1}_{18}$

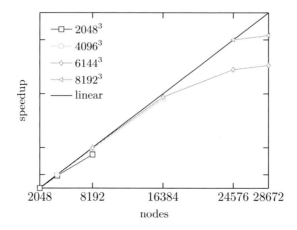

Figure 3. Scaling of `psOpen` for four grid sizes between 2048^3 and 8192^3 grid points. Linear scaling is shown for reference. `psOpen` exhibits an almost linear speedup for up to 16384 nodes.

summarizes the investigated runs and shows the time per iteration. Currently 32 MPI processes each with two OpenMP tasks are running on each compute node. As the IBM XLF compiler on JUQUEEN does not support nested OpenMP the number of MPI processes per compute node is currently rather large. Using GCC compilers and/or introducing pthreads over OpenMP might reduce this overhead in future.

File I/O is integrated into `psOpen` by means of parallel HDF5. The I/O performance depends on the number of allocated compute nodes. With 8192 compute nodes up 30.2 GB/s can be reached. For the scaling analysis `psOpen` was initialised with synthetic turbulence and file I/O was skipped.

For custom process mapping we use the Python tool Rubik [3], which was called from the jobscript and generates the map file on the fly. It provides an intuitive interface to create mappings for structured communication patterns and showed 10% performance increase for `psOpen` production runs in the past. As `psOpen` has a two-stage communication pattern with large messages in stage one and smaller message in stage two, the mapping was chosen such that in the first stage only MPI processes on the same nodeboard communicate. The communication between MPI processes on different nodeboards therefore exchange the small messages of the second stage. Even though this mapping shows good results up to 16 rack runs, `psOpen` did not seem to benefit in the full-machine run.

5. Conclusion

Extreme scaling of DNS using psOpen on JUQUEEN has been conducted with different grid sizes of 2048^3, 4096^3, 6144^3 and 8192^3 up to the full machine. It has been made possible by the inhouse-developed 3d-FFT library `nb3dfft` optimized to the special needs of massivly-parallel pseudo-spectral DNS. `psOpen` exhibits an almost linear speedup up to 16384 compute nodes and runs with 24576 compute nodes exhibit a satisfactory efficiency.

6. Acknowledgements

The authors gratefully acknowledge the computing time granted by the JARA-HPC Vergabegremium and provided on the JARA-HPC Partition part of the supercomputer JUQUEEN at Forschungszentrum Jülich. Furthermore funding from the Cluster of Excellence "Tailor-Made Fuels from Biomass", which is part of the Excellence Initiative of the German federal state governments, is gratefully acknowledged.

References

[1] Mark Nelkin. In what sense is turbulence an unsolved problem? *Science*, 255(5044):566–570, 1992.

[2] Boris I Shraiman and Eric D Siggia. Scalar turbulence. *Nature*, 405(6787):639–646, 2000.

[3] Parviz Moin and Krishnan Mahesh. Direct numerical simulation a tool in turbulence research. *Annual review of fluid mechanics*, 30(1):539–578, 1998.

[4] GS Patterson Jr and Steven A Orszag. Spectral calculations of isotropic turbulence: Efficient removal of aliasing interactions. *Physics of Fluids*, 14(11):2538–2541, 1971.

[5] Steven A Orszag and GS Patterson Jr. Numerical simulation of three-dimensional homogeneous isotropic turbulence. *Physical Review Letters*, 28(2):76, 1972.

[6] Osborne Reynolds. On the dynamical theory of incompressible viscous fluids and the determination of the criterion. *Proceedings of the Royal Society of London*, 56(336-339):40–45, 1894.

[7] David C Wilcox et al. *Turbulence modeling for CFD*, volume 2. DCW industries La Canada, CA, 1998.

[8] Joseph Smagorinsky. General circulation experiments with the primitive equations: I. the basic experiment*. *Monthly weather review*, 91(3):99–164, 1963.

[9] Gregory R Ruetsch. *The structure and dynamics of the vorticity and passive scalar fields at small scales in homogeneous isotropic turbulence*. PhD thesis, Brown University, 1992.

[10] Michael Gauding, Jens Henrik Goebbert, Christian Hasse, and Norbert Peters. Line segments in homogeneous scalar turbulence. *Physics of Fluids*, 2015.

[11] Bernd Hentschel, Jens Henrik Göbbert, Michael Klemm, Paul Springer, Andrea Schnorr, and Torsten W Kuhlen. Packet-oriented streamline tracing on modern simd architectures. In *EGPGV*, 2015.

[12] M Gampert, P Schaefer, JH Goebbert, and N Peters. Decomposition of the turbulent kinetic energy field into regions of compressive and extensive strain. *Physica Scripta*, 2013(T155):014002, 2013.

[13] Lisa Schäfer, Jens Henrik Göbbert, and Wolfgang Schröder. Dissipation element analysis in experimental and numerical shear flow. *European Journal of Mechanics-B/Fluids*, 38:85–92, 2013.

[14] Michael Gauding, Achim Wick, Heinz Pitsch, and Norbert Peters. Generalised scale-by-scale energy-budget equations and large-eddy simulations of anisotropic scalar turbulence at various schmidt numbers. *Journal of Turbulence*, 15(12):857–882, 2014.

[15] Markus Gampert, Jens Henrik Goebbert, Philip Schaefer, Michael Gauding, Norbert Peters, Fettah Aldudak, and Martin Oberlack. Extensive strain along gradient trajectories in the turbulent kinetic energy field. *New Journal of Physics*, 13(4):043012, 2011.

[16] Philip Schaefer, Markus Gampert, Jens Henrik Goebbert, Michael Gauding, and N Peters. Asymptotic analysis of homogeneous isotropic decaying turbulence with unknown initial conditions. *Journal of Turbulence*, (12), 2011.

[17] Michael Gauding, Jens Henrik Goebbert, and Norbert Peters. Scale-by-scale statistics of passive scalar mixing with uniform mean gradient in turbulent flows. In *Proceedings of the 6th AIAA Theoretical Fluid Mechanics Conference*, 2011.

[18] Jens Henrik Goebbert, Michael Gauding, Markus Gampert, Philip Schaefer, Norbert Peters, and Lipo Wang. A new view on geometry and conditional statistics in turbulence. *inSiDE*, 9(1):31–37, 2011.

[19] Philip Schaefer, Markus Gampert, Jens Henrik Goebbert, Lipo Wang, and Norbert Peters. Testing of model equations for the mean dissipation using kolmogorov flows. *Flow, turbulence and combustion*, 85(2):225–243, 2010.

[20] Norbert Peters, Lipo Wang, Juan-Pedro Mellado, Jens Henrik Goebbert, Michael Gauding, Philip Schafer, and Markus Gampert. Geometrical properties of small scale turbulence. In *John von Neumann Institute for Computing NIC Symposium*, pages 365–371, 2010.

[21] Cedrick Ansorge and Juan Pedro Mellado. Global intermittency and collapsing turbulence in the stratified planetary boundary layer. *Boundary-Layer Meteorology*, 153(1):89–116, 2014.

Parallel Computing: On the Road to Exascale
G.R. Joubert et al. (Eds.)
IOS Press, 2016
doi:10.3233/978-1-61499-621-7-787

Simulating Morphologically Detailed Neuronal Networks at Extreme Scale

Aleksandr OVCHARENKO [a,1], Pramod KUMBHAR [a], Michael HINES [b],
Francesco CREMONESI [a], Timothée EWART [a], Stuart YATES [a],
Felix SCHÜRMANN [a] and Fabien DELALONDRE [a]

[a] *Blue Brain Project, EPFL, Switzerland*
[b] *Yale University, USA*

Abstract. In order to achieve performance at very large scale, the core functionalities of the widely used NEURON simulator have been isolated and optimized into a new application *CoreNeuron*. CoreNeuron has been developed with the goal of minimizing memory footprint and maximizing scalability. This paper presents the scaling behaviour and performance of CoreNeuron on up to 28 racks of the IBM Blue Gene/Q, with one MPI process per node and 64 OpenMP threads per MPI process, comprising 458,752 cores and 1,835,008 threads at maximum.

Keywords. extreme scale, strong scaling, weak scaling, computational neuroscience, Blue Brain Project, neuronal network, IBM Blue Gene, parallel efficiency

Introduction

The computational neuroscience community has been doing considerable work over the last 20 years to implement neural simulation applications (NEURON [1], NEST [2], pGENESIS [3], SPLIT [4], NCS [5], C2 [6]) by relying mainly on MPI and MPI-threaded [7] programming models. Leveraging these developments and application-specific memory optimizations [8], the NEST application was recently able to demonstrate high scalability at very large core counts on the RIKEN K-computer [9] using point neuron models. This endeavor showed that computational neuroscientists are just a few years away from being able to simulate models of the size of the human brain using simplified neuron morphologies.

As many neuroscientific use cases require more detailed neuron models, a similar scaling and optimization effort must be made for software supporting models including detailed morphologies such as NEURON [1]. NEURON has been developed over the last 30 years and supports a very wide range of computational neuroscience use cases from single neuron to neuron networks using multiple levels of model fidelity. NEURON is implemented with a mixture of compiled (C, C++), interpreted (Python, HOC) and domain specific (NMODL) languages which allows the framework to be very flexible. The NEURON simulator has been demonstrated to scale up to 64k core counts on the

---

[1]Corresponding Author: Blue Brain Project, Chemin des Mines 9, 1201 Geneva, Switzerland; E-mail: aleksandr.ovcharenko@epfl.ch

INTREPID IBM Blue Gene/P system, but simulating models of the scale of the human brain will require further development to effectively utilize the next generation of super-computing hardware.

Joining forces, Michael Hines from Yale University and the High Performance Computing Team of the Blue Brain Project [10] from the Ecole Federale Polytechnique de Lausanne (EPFL) investigated new methods and implementations to improve NEURON's on-node performance and scalability on existing HPC systems and prepare the application for future supercomputing architectures. This paper presents the CoreNeuron simulator for the first time, which has been derived from NEURON to efficiently support a reduced set of its core functionalities at extreme scale. This application, which is intended to be re-integrated into the NEURON framework for general usage, is implemented with the goal of minimizing memory footprint and obtaining optimal time to solution performance.

This paper is organized as follows: Section 1 provides the mathematical description modeling the electrophysiology of neurons and networks of neurons. Section 2 introduces CoreNeuron design and implementation details targeting on-node performance and scalability at large core counts. Finally, Section 3 presents the results obtained on the JUQUEEN IBM Blue Gene/Q system using up to 28 racks.

1. Modeling Electrophysiology using Morphologically Detailed Neuronal Networks

Morphologically detailed models try to account for the spatial diversity of electrical and biophysical properties of a neuron and for the complex ways in which signals may interact due to their propagation through the morphology. Such models typically rely on the coupling of a set of partial differential equations modeling each branch of the dendritic tree via suitable boundary conditions at the branching points. In NEURON, each cell is modeled as a tree of connected *sections*, where a section is an unbranched part of the cell with possibly inhomogeneous biophysical properties. The electrical behaviour of each section is described by the cable Eq. (1)

$$c_m \frac{\partial v}{\partial t} = \frac{10^4}{4d(x)R_a} \frac{\partial}{\partial x} \left(d(x)^2 \frac{\partial v}{\partial x} \right) - I_{ion} + I_{syn}, \qquad (1)$$

where the unknown $v[mV]$ represents the membrane potential, $c_m[\frac{\mu F}{cm^2}]$ is the membrane capacitance, $R_a[\Omega cm]$ is the section's axial resistivity (a constant), $d(x)[\mu m]$ is the diameter of the cross section as a function of the axial coordinate, $I_{ion} [\frac{mA}{cm^2}]$ is the current due to the flow of ions through the membrane via ion channels and ion pumps and $I_{syn} [\frac{mA}{cm^2}]$ is the current due to the flow of ions through the membrane as a consequence of a synaptic event.

Currents arising from the flow of ions through the ion channels or pumps are modeled with Hodgkin-Huxley [11] formalism, which can be written in its general form as:

$$c_m \frac{\partial v}{\partial t} = \frac{10^4}{4d(x)R_a} \frac{\partial}{\partial x} \left(d(x)^2 \frac{\partial v}{\partial x} \right) - I_{ion}(v,m) + I_{syn},$$

$$\frac{\partial m}{\partial t} = \alpha_m(v)(1-m) - \beta_m(v)m, \qquad (2)$$

where $m \in [0, 1]$ is the gating state of a channel distribution over a section, α_m and β_m are channel type specific rate functions depending of voltage, the ionic current contribution I_{ion} is a linear function of v but a nonlinear function of the states of the channels. Other channel types, with similar state equations, may be included in the system of equations, in which case the term I_{ion} should be updated to include contributions from all the channels in Eq. (2).

Synaptic currents on the other hand give a discrete contribution to Eq. (2). For both excitatory and inhibitory synapses we use an in-house version of the Probabilistic Tsodyks-Markram model [12] with short term plasticity [13] and magnesium gate kinetics [14] . The excitatory model's contribution to Eq. (2), for example, uses a conductance based injection term I_{syn}, whose value is determined by four state equations coupled with an equation for vesicle release probability P_v and another for the probability that the site actually contains a vesicle U_{SE}.

$$\tau_{r,AMPA} \frac{dA_{AMPA}}{dt} = A_{AMPA},$$

$$\frac{dP_v}{dt} = \frac{1 - P_v}{\tau_{rec}} - U_{SE} P_v \delta(t - t_{sp}),$$

$$\frac{dU_{SE}}{dt} = -\frac{U_{SE}}{\tau_{facil}} + U_1(1 - U_{SE})\delta(t - t_{sp}), \tag{3}$$

$$I_{syn} = g_{max}(B_{AMPA} - A_{AMPA})(v - e)$$

$$+g_{max}(B_{NMDA} - A_{NMDA})(v - e)k_{Mg}.$$

The equations for $B_{AMPA}, B_{NMDA}, A_{NMDA}$ have the same formulation as the one for A_{AMPA}. NEURON uses a finite difference method to discretize Eq. (2); a backward Euler scheme is used in the temporal discretization, and a centered second order scheme in the 1D spatial discretization. Thanks to a staggered time scheme [15] it is possible to maintain second order accuracy in the discretisation of Eq. (2) without the need for an iterative scheme to account for such coupling. Each section is split into compartments of equal size whose centers lie at the points x_i. Let δ_t be the first order backward in time finite difference operator. Then the general discretized form of Eq. (2) for the unknown $v(t^{n+1}, x_i)$ is:

$$c_m \delta_t v(t^{n+1}, x_i) - \frac{10^4}{4d(x_i)R_a \Delta x}\left(d(x_{i+1/2})^2 \frac{v(t^{n+1}, x_{i+1}) - v(t^{n+1}, x_i)}{\Delta x}\right.$$

$$\left. +d(x_{i-1/2})^2 \frac{v(t^{n+1}, x_{i-1}) - v(t^{n+1}, x_i)}{\Delta x}\right) =$$

$$I_{ion}\left(v(t^{n+1}, x_i), m(t^{n+1/2}, x_i), \ldots\right) + I_{syn}, \tag{4}$$

$$\frac{m(t^{n+3/2}, x_i) - m(t^{n+1/2}, x_i)}{\Delta t} = \alpha\left(v(t^{n+1}, x_i)\right)\left(1 - m(t^{n+3/2}, x_i)\right)$$

$$-\beta\left(v(t^{n+1}, x_i)\right)m(t^{n+3/2}, x_i).$$

Eq. (4) gives rise to a symmetric quasi-tridiagonal system, where off-diagonal terms occur at branching points. The sparse representation of the linear algebraic system and its resolution, known as the Hines algorithm [15], allows the application of a slightly modified version of the Thomas algorithm [16].

2. CoreNeuron Design and Implementation

The rat somatosensory cortex model currently investigated by computational neuroscientists of the Blue Brain Project [10] comprises approximately two hundred thousand neurons [17], with roughly 400 compartments and 3,500 synapses per neuron, and 3 to 5 channels per compartment. Each compartment has one state variable (membrane potential) as well as all the state variables of the channels belonging to it (each channel has typically between 1 and 3 state variables), plus roughly 10 parameters including membrane capacitance, axial resistivity and channel-specific time constants. Each synapse accounts for about 6 state variables and roughly 10 parameters, as can be seen from Eq. (3).

The BBP intends to use CoreNeuron to be able to simulate very large models such as the rat, monkey or human brain. As such, we anticipate that our problem size will reach up to the order of 100 PiB as described in Table 1. The memory estimates should be regarded as approximate as on the one hand they do not include software implementation overhead, and on the other hand they may vary considerably as a consequence of future modeling efforts.

Table 1. Parameter requirements estimate for future simulations which do not include software implementation overhead.

	rat	monkey	human
number of neurons	1×10^8	1×10^9	1×10^{10}
number of synapses	5×10^{11}	1×10^{13}	1×10^{15}
number of state variables	3.3×10^{12}	6.3×10^{13}	6×10^{15}
estimated size in memory (states and parameters)	0.07 PiB	1 PiB	100 PiB

Solving these models using morphologically detailed neurons in a tractable time on available supercomputers requires the application to 1) be optimized for low memory footprint, 2) expose as much parallelism as possible to take full advantage of available hardware threads and 3) utilize the full capability of the on-node computing units using vectorization.

2.1. Support of Building and Execution of Large Scale Models: From NEURON to CoreNeuron

Simulating the electrical activity of large scale neuronal networks first requires building a representation of the network in memory. Support for building this representation was not included directly in CoreNeuron because it brings about a large memory footprint which is not necessary for the simulation phase. Instead, we rely on the NEURON [1] software, which provides flexibility thanks to both HOC and Python interpreted interfaces.

Neurodamus is another software project developed at the Blue Brain Project as an extension to NEURON. It provides additional flexibility by allowing users to specify models, algorithms and queries that are specific to the biological problem at hand.

Users can construct and simulate large neuronal networks with Neurodamus and NEURON with a memory footprint of approximately 12 MiB per neuron. To meet the memory challenges for larger scale simulations while keeping a high level of configuration flexibility, a new optimized model-building workflow relying on NEURON and Neurodamus software has been implemented (see Figure 1). In the initial phase, the model specification is decomposed into submodels, which are built independently and are written to persistent storage. Once the complete model has been built part by part in a fully embarrassingly parallel way, the entire data set is then reassembled in an efficient data structure layout by CoreNeuron at loading time of the simulation phase. As this software is implemented using memory optimized data structures, it uses 6-8 times less memory simulating the electrical activity of networks made of morphologically detailed neurons, supporting the execution of simulations which would otherwise have exceeded the memory limits under Neurodamus and NEURON.

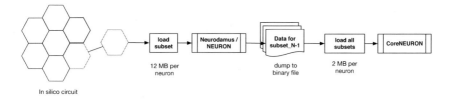

Figure 1. Neuron with Neurodamus vs CoreNeuron

2.2. CoreNeuron Workflow

The minimum network delay, denoted δ_{min}, is the smallest simulation time interval between the generation of an event and its effect [18]. Leveraging from this concept, CoreNeuron minimizes communication by calling the MPI routines that exchange spike events only every minimum network delay. Several simulation timesteps, usually around 4, are computed in between two minimum network delay intervals. Figure 2 depicts the tasks performed during a simulation loop. At the beginning of the inner loop, events whose delivery time has been reached are popped from a queue and the conductance g_{syn} of the receiving synapse is updated. Consequently the diagonal elements of the matrix are updated with the synaptic current contributions from the active synapses (in the form of the last equation of (3)) and the contributions from the ion channels and pumps, typically in the form of $I_{ion} = g_{ion}(m)(v - e_{ion})$. The linear system that represents the first equation of Eq. (4) is solved to obtain the membrane potential values at the current timestep. The state equations for channels and synapses are then integrated by solving the corresponding equations in Eq. (4). Finally, each spike source (typically neuron somas) is checked to see whether the conditions for spike generation are met. The inner loop is repeated $\frac{\delta_{min}}{\Delta t}$ times before reaching the next minimum network delay multiple. Spike communication is performed at every minimum network delay interval, consisting of an interprocess spike exchange and an event enqueueing phase.

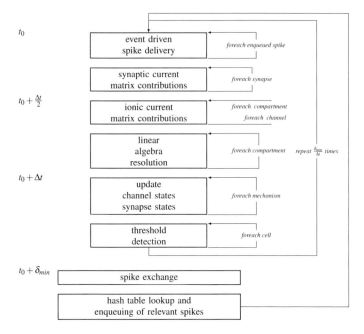

t_0

$t_0 + \frac{\Delta t}{2}$

$t_0 + \Delta t$

$t_0 + \delta_{min}$

Figure 2. Task-based representation of the minimum delay loop in the hybrid clock-event driven NEURON implementation.

2.3. CoreNeuron Implementation

CoreNeuron implements the core simulation functionality of NEURON software. As CoreNeuron does not require supporting model configuration nor adaptivity throughout the course of a simulation, data structures representing neuron discretization (like section and node) and support for both HOC and Python interpreters have been removed, leading to considerable memory footprint reduction.

The CoreNeuron parallel implementation relies on three distinct levels of parallelism. At the highest level (single MPI process per node), a set of neuron groups that have equivalent computational cost is defined and equi-distributed according to the Least Processing Time (LPT) algorithm [19]. Within a node/MPI-process, each neuron group is assigned a specific computing (OpenMP) thread to ensure data locality. As each neuron group has the same expected computational cost, thread load imbalance remains under 2%. Finally, the lowest level of parallelism vectorization is achieved by ordering the resolution of the mechanisms by type within a neuron group: all channels of the same type, for example all sodium channels, of all cells defined within a group associated to a thread are first solved before moving on to another mechanism type (and access pattern). This linear traversal of biological processes allows both cache efficiency and efficient vectorization.

As this on-node implementation requires the use of a single MPI process per node, scalability across the network fabric using the MPI stack is more easily achieved at a large core/thread count. A single thread is responsible for initiating the synchronization of neurons through the exchange of spike events at minimum network delay. This synchronization is currently implemented using a combination of MPI Allgather and Allgatherv operations which allow every neuron group to receive spiking information from all the other neuron groups. Even though such an algorithm requires extra work at spike delivery time to determine that a spike is not needed by any cell on the node, it avoids the explicit storage of memory consuming neuron network topology information. This implementation relies on the efficient implementation of MPI collectives on supercomputers, and we expect the slight loss of weak scaling at very large node counts due to the increase of MPI buffer size and hash table lookups.

3. Simulating Large Scale Networks on World-class Supercomputers

3.1. Use Case Description

The initial circuit used for the simulation of the electrical activity of realistic neuronal networks reconstructed from experimental data contained 3 million neurons and about 9 billion synapses (Figure 3). As it was not yet possible to build a larger biologically realistic circuit at the time of the publication, an additional functionality which supports the in-memory duplication of a circuit has been added to CoreNeuron. Using such functionality a circuit can be replicated in memory by a specific factor, both for cells and connections, allowing scaling studies at very large core counts.

The data is read from disk in either a "file-per-process" or "file-per-thread" manner. Replication was then performed "in-memory", whereupon all threads then received roughly the same amount of compute work. The total I/O size for 28 racks was 5 TB, comprising data in both binary and ASCII formats. Without in-memory replication, the I/O demands for the 24 million cell circuit would total 224 TB.

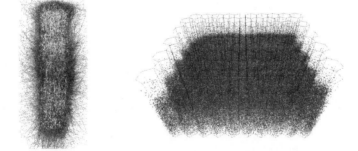

Figure 3. 3 million neurons on a single IBM Blue Gene/Q rack. On the left is the front view of a single column from the circuit, together with its spike activity. On the right is a top-side view of the full 3 million circuit, displaying the somas with a membrane voltage above a certain threshold.

3.2. Performance Analysis on an IBM Blue Gene/Q Compute Node

A detailed roofline analysis of representative kernels (Figure 4) shows that many kernels are memory bound. Even though these kernels (*ProbAM State*, *ProbGA State*, *ProbAM Current* and *SK State*) are memory bandwidth limited, kernels such as *Ih State* and *Na State* admit performance improvement opportunities through the use of vectorization.

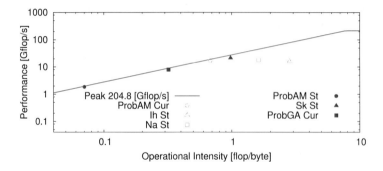

Figure 4. Roofline model for the most computationally intensive kernels.

3.3. Analysis of Performance at Extreme Scale

CoreNeuron was configured to run with 1 MPI rank and 64 OpenMP threads per node. Both strong and weak scaling results were obtained by simulating the electrical activity of circuits on 4, 8, 16, 20, 24, and 28 racks for 10 milliseconds of biological time. Simulations carried out in the strong scaling configuration were performed on a circuit of 24 million morphologically detailed neurons while 2906 neurons per MPI task (or about 45 neurons per thread) were used in the weak scaling configuration.

3.3.1. Strong Scaling

The strong scaling results shown in Figure 5 and Figure 6 indicate that while the simulation time decreases with the increased number of racks, MPI communication time (MPI_Allgather and MPI_Allgatherv) increased when using 20 or more racks, which is reflected in the overall simulation time. The simulation data set had been arranged so as to be distributable across a power of two number of racks, and consequently it was not able to be uniformly distributed across 20, 24 and 28 racks, leading to the observed increase in load imbalance past 16 racks. The authors strongly believe that such an issue will be resolved by the next implementation of parallel I/O and corresponding static load balancing functionality currently under development. It is then worthwhile to analyze the strong scaling data up to 16 racks, the largest number of racks utilisable without the load imbalance issue. Up to this scale, we see that the code loses about 10% of strong scaling efficiency and the authors are currently investigating which part of the workflow is responsible for the loss.

3.3.2. Weak Scaling

The weak scaling results presented in Figure 7 and Figure 8 show that the parallel efficiency remains nearly optimal up to 20 racks, and the time needed to complete the simulation is roughly the same. As described earlier, owing to the particular configuration of our input data, the load imbalance issue presents itself in the weak scaling runs on 24 and 28 racks, where a significant portion of the time is spent in spike exchange MPI communication.

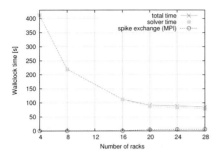

Figure 5. Simulation time for the strong scaling experiments.

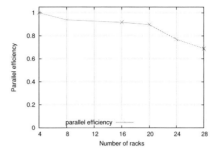

Figure 6. Parallel efficiency for the strong scaling experiments.

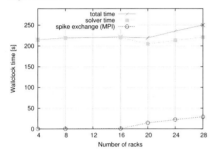

Figure 7. Simulation time for the weak scaling experiments.

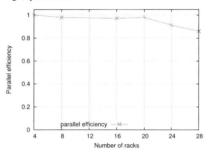

Figure 8. Parallel efficiency for the weak scaling experiments.

4. Conclusions and Future Work

CoreNeuron is an optimized simulator supporting a subset of the core functionality of NEURON. Its implementation allows the reduction of memory footprint by roughly a factor of 6, improving its on-node performance and increasing the scale of neuronal networks that can be simulated. Using a hybrid OpenMP-MPI implementation with 64 threads and a single MPI task per node, it was possible to execute a simulation on the full JUQUEEN IBM Blue Gene/Q supercomputer with a total of 1,835,008 threads. Both strong and weak scaling studies were conducted to demonstrate the usefulness of this implementation.

Several challenges remain to be addressed in future work. A more general disk-to-memory data management and file abstraction is required to allow greater flexibility in load balancing, and further reductions in the size of CoreNeuron data structures will allow the simulation of even larger networks.

5. Acknowledgments

The work was supported by the EPFL Blue Brain Project Fund, ETH Board funding to the Blue Brain Project and European Union Seventh Framework Program (FP7/2007-2013) under grant agreement no. 604102 (HBP). Calculations were performed on the JUQUEEN IBM Blue Gene/Q supercomputer hosted at the Jülich Supercomputing Centre (JSC).

References

[1]   Michele Migliore, C. Cannia, William W. Lytton, Henry Markram, and Michael L. Hines.   Parallel network simulations with NEURON. *Journal of Computational Neuroscience*, 21(2):119–129, 2006.

[2]   Hans E. Plesser, Jochen M. Eppler, Abigail Morrison, Markus Diesmann, and Marc-Oliver Gewaltig. Efficient parallel simulation of large-scale neuronal networks on clusters of multiprocessor computers. *Euro-Par 2007 Parallel Processing*, 4641:672–681, 2007.

[3]   Mark Hereld, Rick Stevens, Justin Teller, Wim van Drongelen, and Hyong Lee. Large neural simulations on large parallel computers. *International Journal of Bioelectromagnetism*, 7(1):44–46, 2005.

[4]   Mikael Djurfeldt, Mikael Lundqvist, Christopher Johansson, Martin Rehn, O Ekeberg, and Anders Lansner. Brain-scale simulation of the neocortex on the IBM Blue Gene/L supercomputer. *IBM Journal of Research and Development*, 52(1.2):31–41, 2008.

[5]   E. Courtenay Wilson, Philip H. Goodman, and Frederick C Harris Jr. Implementation of a biologically realistic parallel neocortical-neural network simulator. *Proceedings of the Tenth SIAM Conference on Parallel Processing for Scientific Computing*, 2001.

[6]   Rajagopal Ananthanarayanan, Steven K. Esser, Horst D. Simon, and Dharmendra S. Modha. The cat is out of the bag: cortical simulations with 109 neurons, 1013 synapses. *Proceedings of the Conference on High Performance Computing Networking, Storage and Analysis*, 63:1–12, 2009.

[7]   Jochen M. Eppler, Hans E. Plesser, Abigail Morrison, Markus Diesmann, and Marc-Oliver Gewaltig. Multithreaded and distributed simulation of large biological neuronal networks. *Recent Advances in Parallel Virtual Machine and Message Passing Interface*, 4757:391–392, 2007.

[8]   Susanne Kunkel, Tobias C Potjans, Jochen M Eppler, Hans Ekkehard Plesser, Abigail Morrison, and Markus Diesmann.   Meeting the memory challenges of brain-scale network simulation.   *Frontiers in Neuroinformatics*, 5(35), 2011.

[9]   Markus Diesmann.   Brain-scale neuronal network simulations on K.   In *Proceedings of the 4th Biosupercomputing Symposium: Next-Generation Integrated Simulation of Living Matter (IS-LiM) program of MEXT*, 2012.   Available online at: `http://www.csrp.riken.jp/4thbscs/4th-BSCS-proceedings.pdf`.

[10]   Henry Markram. The Blue Brain Project. *Nature Reviews Neuroscience*, 7(2):153–160, 2006.

[11]   Idan Segev and R. E. Burke. Compartmental models of complex neurons. pages 183–188. MIT press, 2nd edition, 1998.

[12]   Misha Tsodyks, Klaus Pawelzik, and Henry Markram. Neural networks with dynamic synapses. *Neural computation*, 10(4):821–835, 1998.

[13]   Galit Fuhrmann, Idan Segev, Henry Markram, and Misha Tsodyks. Coding of temporal information by activity-dependent synapses. *Journal of neurophysiology*, 87(1):140–148, 2002.

[14]   Craig E Jahr and Charles F Stevens. Voltage dependence of NMDA-activated macroscopic conductances predicted by single-channel kinetics. *The Journal of Neuroscience*, 10(9):3178–3182, 1990.

[15]   Michael Hines. Efficient computation of branched nerve equations. *International journal of bio-medical computing*, 15(1):69–76, 1984.

[16]   Llewellyn Hilleth Thomas. Elliptic problems in linear difference equations over a network. *Watson Sci. Comput. Lab. Rept., Columbia University, New York*, page 1, 1949.

[17]   Henry Markram et al. Reconstruction and simulation of neocortical microcircuitry. *Cell*, 2015. under review.

[18]   Michael Hines, Sameer Kumar, and Felix Schurmann. Comparison of neuronal spike exchange methods on a Blue Gene/P supercomputer. *Frontiers in Computational Neuroscience*, 5(49), 2011.

[19]   Richard E. Korf.   A complete anytime algorithm for number partitioning. *Artificial Intelligence*, 106:181–203, 1998.

Parallel Computing: On the Road to Exascale
G.R. Joubert et al. (Eds.)
IOS Press, 2016
doi:10.3233/978-1-61499-621-7-797

FE²TI: Computational Scale Bridging for Dual-Phase Steels

Axel KLAWONN [a], Martin LANSER [a,1], Oliver RHEINBACH [b]

[a] *Universität zu Köln, Germany*
[b] *Technische Universität Bergakademie Freiberg, Germany*

Abstract. A scale bridging approach combining the FE² method with parallel domain decomposition (FE²TI) is presented. The FE²TI approach is used in the project "EXASTEEL - Bridging Scales for Multiphase Steels" (within the German priority program "Software for Exascale Computing - SPPEXA") for the simulation of modern dual-phase steels. This approach incorporates phenomena on the microscale into the macroscopic problem by solving many independent microscopic problems on representative volume elements (RVEs). The results on the RVEs replace a phenomenological material law on the macroscale. In order to bring large micro-macro simulations to modern supercomputers, in the FE²TI approach a highly scalable implementation of the inexact reduced FETI-DP (Finite Element Tearing and Interconnecting Dual Primal) domain decomposition method (scalable up to 786 432 Mira BlueGene/Q cores) is used as a solver on the RVEs. Weak scalability results for the FE²TI method are presented, filling the complete JUQUEEN at JSC Jülich (458 752 cores) and the complete Mira at Argonne National Laboratory (786 432 cores).

Keywords. Computational Scale Bridging, Domain Decomposition, FETI-DP, FE²

Introduction

We are concerned with the computational simulation of advanced high strength steels, incorporating phase transformation phenomena at the microscale. The project "EXASTEEL - Bridging Scales for Multiphase Steels" is part of the German priority program (DFG-Schwerpunktprogramm 1648) SPPEXA (Software for Exascale Computing) and one of its goals is bringing computational scale bridging methods such as the FE² method to recent supercomputers. The FE² method, see, e.g., [1,2,3,4,5], is a computational micro-macro scale bridging approach directly incorporating micromechanics into macroscopic simulations. In this approach, a microscopic boundary value problem based on the definition of a representative volume element (RVE) is solved at each Gauß integration point of a macroscopic finite element problem. Then, volumetric averages of microscopic stress distributions are returned to the macroscopic level, which replaces a phenomenological material law at the macro scale. The microscopic problems are only coupled through the macroscopic problem; see Figures 1 and 2. On the RVEs

---

[1]Corresponding Author: Mathematisches Institut, Universität zu Köln, Weyertal 86-90, 50931 Köln, Germany; E-mail: martin.lanser@uni-koeln.de

nonlinear implicit structural mechanics problems have to be solved. We are applying the inexact reduced FETI-DP (Finite Element Tearing and Interconnecting) method as a solver on the RVEs. Nonoverlapping domain decomposition methods of the FETI type [6,7,8,9,10,11,12,13,14,15] are well established solution methods in implicit structural mechanics. A structural simulation using a FETI-DP algorithm was awarded a Gordon Bell prize already in 2002 using 4 000 processors of the then second fastest supercomputer of the world. However, the classical FETI-DP method does not scale well beyond 10K processor cores. Inexact FETI-DP methods [16], have shown a much better parallel scalability, and scalability for 65 536 cores was shown during the 2008 JUGENE scaling workshop in Jülich [17,13]. Recently, nonlinear FETI-DP and BDDC methods [18,19,20] with improved concurrency were introduced. In these methods, the nonlinear problem is decomposed into concurrent subproblems before linearization. This is opposed to standard Newton-Krylov approaches where the problem is first linearized and then decomposed. Hybrid parallelization in our context was discussed in [21]. Nonlinear nonoverlapping domain decomposition is not new. It was used, e.g., in multiphysics and fluid-structure-interaction as a coupling method in the case of a small number of subdomains. Only recently, it has attracted interest as a scalable solver approach [22,23,18,19,20]. The ASPIN method [24] is a related nonlinear overlapping domain decomposition approach as a solver.

We refer to the combination of the FE² scale bridging method with a FETI-DP method on each RVE as a FE²TI method. For our FE² method, as a solver on the RVEs, we use a Newton-Krylov-irFETI-DP method. For the first time weak scalability results for the FE²TI method for the complete Mira BlueGene/Q (rank 5 in the current TOP500 list 06/2015, Argonne National Laboratory) is presented and also scalability for the complete JUQUEEN BlueGene/Q (rank 9 in current TOP500 list 06/2015, Jülich Supercomputing Centre). This current paper is an extended version of the technical report [25] on JUQUEEN scaling results. The results on Mira have been obtained later and have benefited from the experience gained on JUQUEEN.

1. The FE²TI Method

1.1. Problem Statement and Algorithmic Description

We provide an algorithmic overview of the FE² method using FETI-DP on the RVEs in Figure 3. We proceed by discussing the steps in Figure 3. The FE² method considers a macroscopic problem and many independent microscopic finite element problems. The undeformed macroscopic body $\mathscr{B}_0$ can be discretized with relatively large finite elements neglecting the microscopic structure. We are interested in a macroscopic deformation gradient $\overline{F}$ and a macroscopic first Piola-Kirchhoff stress tensor $\overline{P}$ fulfilling the balance of momentum

$$- \int_{\mathscr{B}_0} \delta \overline{x} \cdot (\text{Div } \overline{P}(\overline{F}) + \overline{f}) \, dV = 0$$

under suitable boundary conditions, an external load $\overline{f}$, and with a variational function $\delta \overline{x}$. In order to incorporate the microstructure, a nonlinear boundary value problem resolving the microstructure is then considered in each Gauß interpolation point of the macroscopic problem.

These problems replace a phenomenological material law deriving the stress $\overline{P}$ directly from the deformation $\overline{F}$. The geometry of the microscopic problem has to represent the heterogeneity of the material effectively and is derived from the definition of a representative volume element (RVE) $\mathscr{B}_0$. Applying boundary constraints derived from the deformation gradient $\overline{F}$, we solve the microscopic problems using an inexact reduced FETI-DP type domain decomposition method; "1." and "2." in Figure 3. After convergence of the microscopic problem, the macroscopic stress $\overline{P}$ in the corresponding Gauß integration point is given as the volumetric average of the microscopic stresses $P(F)$; "3." in Figure 3. Let us remark that we assume a phenomenological law $P(F)$ on the microscale, as, e.g., a Neo-Hookean hyperelasticity model or a J2 elasticity-plasticity model. Since high peaks in the stress can lead to material failure and are typically a microscopic phenomenon, the microscopic stresses $P(F)$ have to be considered in order to predict material failure. In order to solve the macroscopic problem, the discrete macroscopic tangent modulus $\overline{\mathbb{A}}^h$ has to be computed, which can also be performed by averaging microscopic quantities; "4." in Figure 3. The term $L^T(DK)^{-1}L$ in "4." of Figure 3 requires the solution for nine right hand sides on the micro scale, i.e., we have nine additional microscopic FETI-DP solves. Here, DK is the tangential matrix of the microscopic problem in the stationary point and L contains nine different right hand sides; see [2] for more details. Using $\overline{\mathbb{A}}^h$ and $\overline{P}^h$, the macroscopic problem can be assembled and solved; "5.", "6.", and "7." in Figure 3.

Let us remark that Figure 3 describes a single macroscopic load step. The total deformation $\overline{F}$ may only be reached using many incremental load steps. In each such load step, a macroscopic Newton iteration is performed and in each macroscopic Newton step a nonlinear microscopic boundary value problem is solved in each macroscopic Gauß integration point.

1.2. Granularity and Load Balancing

Let us finally provide a short description of the parallelism of the FE2TI algorithm. First, we distribute the RVEs. Each RVE is assigned to its own MPI communicator obtained by an MPI_Comm_split. Then, the RVEs are decomposed geometrically into nonoverlapping FETI-DP subdomains. Each subdomain is assigned to one MPI rank of the RVE subcommunicator. In order to obtain an optimal load balance and properly distributed data, the sizes of all subdomains have to be similar and each MPI rank should handle the same number of subdomains. Most of the FETI-DP matrices and data structures can be created and saved locally, only using the mesh information related to a subdomain. Parallel structures, as the FETI-DP coarse space, are implemented using the parallel matrix and vector classes provided by PETSc. Thus, these structures are distributed linearly to all MPI ranks of the RVE subcommunicator. A detailed description of the parallel implementation of inexact FETI-DP methods can be found in [26].

1.3. Implementation

We have implemented the FE² method using PETSc 3.5.2 [27] using C/C++ and MPI and MPI/OpenMP. Furthermore, we rely on MUMPS [28,29], UMFPACK [30] or PARDISO [31] for sequential (or parallel) direct solves. Note that on the BlueGene/Q, when linked to the ESSL and for our setting with nine right hand sides on the micro structure,

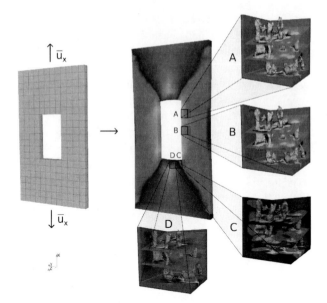

Figure 1. FE2TI computation with 1 792 RVEs and real micro structure; cf. Section 2.3. The computation was performed on all 28 racks of JUQUEEN. Left: Undeformed rectangular plate with a hole discretized by 224 Q1 finite elements with 8 Gauß points each. Right: Visualization of the von Mises stresses of the deformed macroscopic problem and four exemplary RVEs in different Gauß points (A,B,C,D). The stress peaks in the microstructures are 5-7 times higher than the peaks in the macroscopic problem.

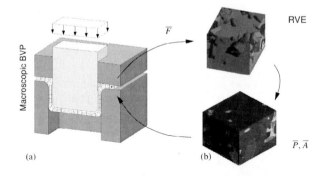

Figure 2. FE² approach with (a) macroscopic boundary value problem (BVP) and (b) microscopic BVP on an RVE. In the FE² computational scale bridging method, in each macroscopic Gauß point a microscopic problem is solved.

UMFPACK and MUMPS showed very similar performance. This is opposed to our experience on other architectures, where MUMPS often showed a better performance. The algebraic multigrid solver BoomerAMG [32] from the hypre [33] package is used in our inexact reduced FETI-DP methods as a preconditioner of the FETI-DP coarse problem. All packages are interfaced through PETSc. On Blue Gene/Q, the software environment is compiled using the IBM XL C/C++ compilers to profit from auto vectorization. Since the lion's share of the runtime is spent in IBM's ESSL library when using UMFPACK for all direct solves, the effect of (additional) auto vectorization is limited. The macroscopic problem is discretized using piecewise trilinear brick elements (Q1) in three dimensions.

Repeat until convergence:

1. Apply boundary conditions to RVE (representative volume element) based on macroscopic deformation gradient: Enforce $x = \overline{F}X$ on the boundary of the microscopic problem $\partial\mathscr{B}$ in the case of Dirichlet constraints.

2. Solve one microscopic nonlinear implicit boundary value problem for each macroscopic Gauß point using (ir)FETI-DP or related methods.

3. Compute and return macroscopic stresses as volumetric average over microscopic stresses P^h:
$$\overline{P}^h = \frac{1}{V} \sum_{T \in \tau} \int_T P^h \, dV.$$

4. Compute and return macroscopic tangent moduli as average over microscopic tangent moduli $\mathbb{A}^h$:
$$\overline{\mathbb{A}}^h = \frac{1}{V} \left(\sum_{T \in \tau} \int_T \mathbb{A}^h \, dV \right) - \frac{1}{V} L^T (DK)^{-1} L$$

5. Assemble tangent matrix and right hand side of the linearized macroscopic boundary value problem using $\overline{P}^h$ and $\overline{\mathbb{A}}^h$.

6. Solve linearized macroscopic boundary value problem.

7. Update macroscopic deformation gradient $\overline{F}$.

Figure 3. Algorithmic description of the FE²TI approach. Overlined letters denote macroscopic quantities.

2. Numerical Results

The FE²TI computational scale bridging software is member of the High-Q-Club[2] after having scaled to the complete 28 racks of the JUQUEEN BlueGene/Q in Jülich in 2015; see the JUQUEEN scaling report [25]. FE²TI also scales to the complete 48 BlueGene/Q racks of Mira. The scaling runs presented here always consist of one macroscopic load step using a heterogenous nonlinear hyperelasticity material on the microscale. In our application, we are also interested in plastification on the RVEs. We will perform corresponding numerical experiments in the near future.

2.1. Scalability of the Method on the JUQUEEN Supercomputer (JSC, Jülich)

We present our scaling results for the computational scale bridging in 2D and 3D. Most of the scaling results for the complete JUQUEEN machine were achieved on the Workshop on "Extreme Scaling on JUQUEEN" and collected in the technical report [25]. This paper builds on this report. Details on the FETI-DP iterative solver algorithm and successive improvements of the solver to enhance its scalability on JUQUEEN and other supercomputers are submitted as [26].

We first scale up the size of the macroscopic problem while keeping the size of the microscopic RVEs fixed. We also keep the number of FETI-DP subdomains for each RVE fixed and use one MPI rank per FETI-DP subdomain. As we increase the number of processor cores in proportion to the problem size (weak scalability), in the best case, for a parallel efficiency of 100%, we would expect a constant time to solution. In Tables 1 and 2, we present the weak scalability for 2D and 3D; we use one MPI rank for each BlueGene/Q processor core and threading with 4 OpenMP threads. The baseline for our parallel efficiency is the smallest meaningful macroscopic problem, i.e., with 8 Gauß points in 2D and 16 Gauß points in 3D. A parallel efficiency of approximately 98% is

---

[2]http://www.fz-juelich.de/ias/jsc/EN/Expertise/High-Q-Club/FE2TI/_node.html

Table 1. Scaling up the macro problem: FE^2 in 2D using FETI-DP on each RVE; heterogeneous hyperelasticity; P1 finite elements macro, P2 finite elements micro; 5.1 million d.o.f. on each RVE; 256 subdomains for each RVE; 4 OpenMP threads per MPI rank.

FE²TI in 2D (Weak scaling; JUQUEEN)				
Cores	MPI-ranks	#RVEs	Time to Solution	
2 048	2 048	8	158.47s	100.0%
4 096	4 096	16	159.03s	99.6%
8 192	8 192	32	159.27s	99.5%
16 384	16 384	64	159.32s	99.5%
32 768	32 768	128	159.58s	99.3%
65 536	65 536	256	159.68s	99.2%
131 072	131 072	512	159.99s	99.1%
262 144	262 144	1 024	160.62s	98.7%
393 216	393 216	1 536	161.41s	98.2%
458 752	458 752	1 792	161.78s	98.0%

achieved in Tables 1 and 2. These results confirm the assumed good weak scalability behavior of the method and the potential to scale to even larger machines. Thus, the FE^{2}TI approach is suitable and efficient for large multiscale simulations.

In our implementation, we use MPI_Comm_split to create subcommunicators for the computations on the RVEs. We use the environment variable PAMID_COLLECTIVES_MEMORY_OPTIMIZED=1 to keep the time for the communicator split short. In our computations the resulting timings for the communicator split was below 2 seconds. In Tables 1 and 2, the number of subdomains for each RVE, i.e., 256 in 2D and 512 in 3D, is still small. In Table 3, starting from the largest problem in Table 1, the size of the RVEs is increased by a factor of 4.

Next, we disable OpenMP threading and consider the effect of oversubscription using pure MPI. In Table 4, we show weak scaling but using oversubscription with up to 4 MPI ranks for each BlueGene/Q processor core. In the latter case, only 256 MB are available for each MPI rank. We use 16, 32, and 64 MPI ranks per node and the RVE size is kept constant, i.e., the total problem size is increased by a factor of 4. We, of course, cannot expect perfect scalability in this situation. But we still see that acceptable scalability is obtained when scaling from a total of 458 752 MPI ranks to 917 504 MPI ranks, i.e., the total time to solution is 266.47s instead of $2 \cdot 215.41s = 430.82s$. Using 1 835 008 MPI ranks only gives minor additional savings. From these results, when we are not using OpenMP threading, we now use 32 MPI ranks per node as a default. Of course, we then have to respect the memory constraint of 512 MB.

We see that the algorithmic approach of solving the macroscopic FE^2 problem fully redundantly is currently sufficient, given the three level structure of the algorithm with the very aggressive coarsening on the third level: In the largest case on JUQUEEN in Table 4, we have 1.8 million subdomains, 3 584 concurrent FETI-DP coarse problems, and a macroscopic problem of size 3 051. Nevertheless, we may move to a parallel solve of the macro problem in the future.

2.2. Scalability of the Method on the Mira Supercomputer (ALCF, Argonne Nat. Lab.)

We present our scaling results for the FE^{2}TI method in 3D. During the Mira Bootcamp 2015 we have achieved weak scalability up to the full Mira supercomputer, i.e., 786 432 cores using 1.5 million MPI ranks; see Table 5. These results have not been presented

Table 2. Scaling up the macro problem (small RVEs): FE² in 3D using FETI-DP on each RVE. Time for a single load step of heterogeneous hyperelasticity; Q1 finite elements macro, P2 finite elements micro; 1.6 million d.o.f. on each RVE; 512 subdomains for each RVE; 4 OpenMP threads per MPI-rank.

FE²TI in 3D (Weak scaling; JUQUEEN)				
Cores	**MPI-ranks**	**#RVEs**	**Time to Solution**	
8 192	8 192	16	184.86s	100.0%
16 384	16 384	32	185.09s	99.9%
32 768	32 768	64	185.61s	99.6%
65 536	65 536	128	185.72s	99.5%
131 072	131 072	256	186.43s	99.2%
262 144	262 144	512	186.61s	99.1%
393 216	393 216	768	187.32s	98.7%
458 752	458 752	896	187.65s	98.5%

Table 3. We increase the RVE sizes starting from the largest problem in Table 1; heterogeneous hyperelasticity; P1 finite elements macro, P2 finite elements micro.

FE²TI in 2D (Increasing RVE sizes; JUQUEEN)					
Cores	**MPI-ranks**	**#RVEs**	**RVE-size**	**RVE-size × #RVEs**	**Time to Solution**
458 752	458 752	1 792	5 126 402	9 186 512 384	161.78s
458 752	458 752	1 792	7 380 482	13 225 823 744	248.19s
458 752	458 752	1 792	13 117 442	23 506 456 064	483.68s
458 752	458 752	1 792	20 492 802	36 723 101 184	817.06s

Table 4. "Weak scaling-type" efficiency using 16 / 32 / 64 MPI-ranks per node while increasing the problem size proportionally to the number of MPI ranks. FE² in 3D using FETI-DP on each RVE (FE²TI). We use 1 594 323 d.o.f. per RVE and 512 subdomains per RVE.

FE²TI in 3D (1x, 2x, 4x MPI overcommit; JUQUEEN)					
Cores	**ranks per node**	**MPI-ranks**	**#RVEs**	**Time to Solution**	
458 752	16	458 752	896	215.41s	100%
458 752	32	917 504	1 792	266.47s	81%
458 752	64	1 835 008	3 584	522.10s	41%

elsewhere. In Table 5, weak scalability in 3D is presented where the baseline for the parallel efficiency is, again, the smallest meaningful macroscopic problem, i.e., using 16 Gauß points in 3D. A parallel efficiency of approximately 96.9% is achieved, which is remarkable. These results could only be achieved by building in the experience previously gained on the JUQUEEN supercomputer and show the potential of the method beyond today's supercomputer.

2.3. Production Runs on JUQUEEN

We were able to run for the first time large scale 3D FE² multiscale simulations with 40 load steps using the complete JUQUEEN supercomputer. The total computation used 5 hours on the full 28 racks to compute a deformation of 8%. To the best of our knowledge, no FE² simulations of this size have been carried out before. We confirmed the expected stress concentrations at the microscopic level which are significantly higher than at the macroscopic level; see Figure 1 for a visualization of the stresses.

Table 5. Scaling up the macro problem (large RVEs) on Mira using multiple subdomains per core: FE² in 3D using FETI-DP on each RVE. Time for a single load step of heterogeneous hyperelasticity; Q1 finite elements macro, P2 finite elements micro; 12.5 million d.o.f. on each RVE; 4 096 subdomains for each RVE; 1 024 MPI ranks and 512 cores per RVE.

FE²TI in 3D (Weak scaling; Mira)					
Cores	**MPI ranks**	**#RVEs**	**Total dof**	**Time to Solution**	
8 192	16 384	16	200M	914.34s	100.0%
16 384	32 768	32	401M	932.96s	98.0%
32 768	65 536	64	801M	932.48s	98.1%
65 536	131 072	128	1.6B	929.35s	98.4%
131 072	262 144	256	3.2B	935.26s	97.8%
262 144	524 288	512	6.4B	937.78s	97.5%
524 288	1 048 576	1 024	12.8B	948.91s	96.4%
786 432	1 572 864	1 536	19.3B	943.81s	96.9%

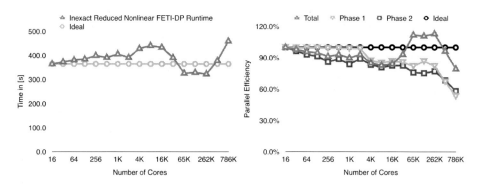

Figure 4. Left: Time to solution of inexact reduced Nonlinear-FETI-DP applied to a heterogeneous 2D Neo-Hooke hyperelasticity problem. Weak scalability from 16 up to 786 432 cores on MIRA Blue Gene/Q. The largest problem has 62.9 billion degrees of freedom. **Right:** Parallel Efficiency of the algorithm.

2.4. Scalability of the Solver on the Microscale - Inexact FETI-DP

We use a FETI-DP method to solve the nonlinear microscopic problems on the RVEs. Substantial effort has been made to obtain good scalability for our FETI-DP methods. Weak scalability results of inexact reduced Nonlinear FETI-DP is presented in Figure 4 for up to 786 432 cores of the Mira supercomputer for a model problem. Choosing the total time to solution on 16 cores as a baseline, we achieve a parallel efficiency of 79.3% on 786K cores. Here, we benefit from a decreasing number of Newton steps needed for convergence. Using a different metric to measure the scalability, i.e. the average time per Newton step, we also achieve a good efficiency of more than 53%; see Phase 1 and 2 in Figure 4 (Right). The largest problem has approximately 63 billion unknowns. These results are also part of the submitted publication [26].

2.5. Conclusion

We performed multiscale simulations using the FE² method for the first time at the full scale of the largest supercomputers currently available, both using pure MPI and (limited) hybrid OpenMP/MPI parallelization. This has been achieved by continuously improving the performance and scalability of the FE2TI implementation. Moreover, we have pushed the weak parallel scalability of implicit domain decomposition solvers to over half a million cores making these computations the largest currently known to us for a domain decomposition solver in terms of the number of cores as well as the problem size.

Acknowledgements This work was supported by the German Research Foundation (DFG) through the Priority Programme 1648 "Software for Exascale Computing" (SPPEXA) under KL2094/4-1, RH 122/2-1. The authors gratefully acknowledge the Gauss Centre for Supercomputing (GCS) for providing computing time through the John von Neumann Institute for Computing (NIC) on the GCS share of the supercomputer **JUQUEEN** at Jülich Supercomputing Centre (JSC). The authors also gratefully acknowledge the use of JUQUEEN during the Workshop on "Extreme Scaling on JUQUEEN" (Jülich, 02/05/2015 - 02/06/2015). This research used resources, i.e., **Mira**, of the Argonne Leadership Computing Facility, which is a DOE Office of Science User Facility supported under Contract DE-AC02-06CH11357.

References

[1]   R.J.M. Smit, W.A.M. Brekelmans, and H.E.H. Meijer. Prediction of the mechanical behavior of non-linear heterogeneous systems by multi-level finite element modeling. *Computer Methods in Applied Mechanics and Engineering*, 155:181–192, 1998.

[2]   C. Miehe, J. Schröder, and J. Schotte. Computational homogenization analysis in finite plasticity. Simulation of texture development in polycrystalline materials. *Computer Methods in Applied Mechanics and Engineering*, 171:387–418, 1999.

[3]   J. Schröder. *Homogenisierungsmethoden der nichtlinearen Kontinuumsmechanik unter Beachtung von Stabilitätsproblemen.* PhD thesis, Bericht aus der Forschungsreihe des Institut für Mechanik (Dauwe sen), Lehrstuhl I, Universität Stuttgart, 2000. Habilitationsschrift.

[4]   V. Kouznetsova, W.A.M. Brekelmans, and F.P.T. Baaijens. An approach to micro-macro modeling of heterogeneous materials. 27:37–48, 2001.

[5]   Frédéric Feyel. Multiscale FE² elastoviscoplastic analysis of composite structures. *Computational Materials Science*, 16(14):344 – 354, 1999.

[6]   Charbel Farhat, Jan Mandel, and Francois-Xavier Roux. Optimal convergence properties of the FETI domain decomposition method. *Comput. Methods Appl. Mech. Engrg.*, 115:367–388, 1994.

[7]   Charbel Farhat and Jan Mandel. The two-level FETI method for static and dynamic plate problems - part I: an optimal iterative solver for biharmonic systems. *Computer Methods in Applied Mechanics and Engineering*, 155:129–152, 1998.

[8]   Manoj Bhardwaj, David Day, Charbel Farhat, Michel Lesoinne, Kendall Pierson, and Daniel Rixen. Application of the FETI method to ASCI problems - scalability results on one thousand processors and discussion of highly heterogeneous problems. *Int. J. Numer. Meth. Engrg.*, 47:513–535, 2000.

[9]   Ch. Farhat, K. Pierson, and M. Lesoinne. The second generation of FETI methods and their application to the parallel solution of large-scale linear and geometrically nonlinear structural analysis problems. *Computer Meth. Appl. Mech. Eng.*, 184:333–374, 2000.

[10] Axel Klawonn and Olof B. Widlund. FETI and Neumann-Neumann iterative substructuring methods: connections and new results. *Communications on Pure and Applied Mathematics*, LIV:57–90, 2001.

[11] Ch. Farhat, M. Lesoinne, and K. Pierson. A scalable dual-primal domain decomposition method. *Numer. Lin. Alg. Appl.*, 7:687–714, 2000.

[12] Charbel Farhat, Michel Lesoinne, Patrick LeTallec, Kendall Pierson, and Daniel Rixen. FETI-DP: A dual-primal unified FETI method - part I: A faster alternative to the two-level FETI method. *Internat. J. Numer. Methods Engrg.*, 50:1523–1544, 2001.

[13] Axel Klawonn and Oliver Rheinbach. Highly scalable parallel domain decomposition methods with an application to biomechanics. *ZAMM Z. Angew. Math. Mech.*, 90(1):5–32, 2010.

[14] Axel Klawonn and Olof B. Widlund. Dual-Primal FETI Methods for Linear Elasticity. *Comm. Pure Appl. Math.*, 59(11):1523–1572, 2006.

[15] Axel Klawonn and Oliver Rheinbach. Robust FETI-DP methods for heterogeneous three dimensional elasticity problems. *Comput. Methods Appl. Mech. Engrg.*, 196(8):1400–1414, 2007.

[16]   Axel Klawonn and Oliver Rheinbach. Inexact FETI-DP methods. *Internat. J. Numer. Methods Engrg.*, 69(2):284–307, 2007.

[17]   Oliver Rheinbach. Parallel iterative substructuring in structural mechanics. *Arch. Comput. Methods Eng.*, 16(4):425–463, 2009.

[18]   Axel Klawonn, Martin Lanser, Patrick Radtke, and Oliver Rheinbach. On an adaptive coarse space and on nonlinear domain decomposition. In Jocelyne Erhel, Martin J. Gander, Laurence Halpern, Géraldine Pichot, Taoufik Sassi, and Olof B. Widlund, editors, *Domain Decomposition Methods in Science and Engineering XXI*, volume 98 of *Lect. Notes Comput. Sci. Eng.*, pages 71–83. Springer-Verlag, 2014. Proc. of the 21st Int. Conf. on Domain Decomp. Meth., Rennes, France, June 25-29, 2012. `http://dd21.inria.fr/pdf/klawonna_plenary_3.pdf`.

[19]   A. Klawonn, M. Lanser, and O. Rheinbach. Nonlinear FETI-DP and BDDC methods. *SIAM J. Sci. Comput.*, 36(2):A737–A765, 2014.

[20]   Axel Klawonn, Martin Lanser, and Oliver Rheinbach. A nonlinear FETI-DP method with an inexact coarse problem. 2014. Accepted to the proceedings of the 22nd International Conference on Domain Decomposition Methods, Sept. 16-20, 2013, Universita della Svizzera italiana, Lugano, Switzerland. Preprint: `http://www.mathe.tu-freiberg.de/files/personal/253/rheinbach-plenarytalk-dd22.pdf`.

[21]   Axel Klawonn, Martin Lanser, Oliver Rheinbach, Holger Stengel, and Gerhard Wellein. Hybrid MPI/OpenMP parallelization in FETI-DP methods. Technical Report 2015-02, Fakultät für Mathematik und Informatik, Technische Universität Bergakademie Freiberg, 2015. Submitted. `http://tu-freiberg.de/fakult1/forschung/preprints`.

[22]   Julien Pebrel, Christian Rey, and Pierre Gosselet. A nonlinear dual-domain decomposition method: Application to structural problems with damage. *Inter. J. Multiscal. Comp. Eng.*, 6(3):251–262, 2008.

[23]   Felipe Bordeu, Pierre-Alain Boucard, and Pierre Gosselet. Balancing domain decomposition with nonlinear relocalization: Parallel implementation for laminates. In B.H.V. Topping and P. Ivnyi, editors, *Proceedings of the First International Conference on Parallel, Distributed and Grid Computing for Engineering*, Stirlingshire, UK, 2009. Civil-Comp Press.

[24]   Xiao-Chuan Cai and David E. Keyes. Nonlinearly preconditioned inexact Newton algorithms. *SIAM J. Sci. Comput.*, 24(1):183–200 (electronic), 2002.

[25]   Axel Klawonn, Martin Lanser, and Oliver Rheinbach. EXASTEEL - computational scale bridging using a FE²TI approach with ex_nl/FE². Technical Report FZJ-JSC-IB-2015-01, Jülich Supercomputing Center, Germany, 2015. In: JUQUEEN Extreme Scaling Workshop 2015. Dirk Brömmel and Wolfgang Frings, and Brian J.N. Wylie (eds.).

[26]   Axel Klawonn, Martin Lanser, and Oliver Rheinbach. Towards extremely scalable nonlinear domain decomposition methods for elliptic partial differential equations. Submitted to SISC 11/2014. Revised 06/2015. Accepted 09/2015. Original version also available as Technical Report 2014-13 of Fakultät für Mathematik und Informatik, Technische Universität Bergakademie Freiberg.

[27]   Satish Balay, Jed Brown, Kris Buschelman, William D. Gropp, Dinesh Kaushik, Matthew G. Knepley, Lois Curfman McInnes, Barry F. Smith, and Hong Zhang. PETSc Web page, 2014. http://www.mcs.anl.gov/petsc.

[28]   P. R. Amestoy, I. S. Duff, J. Koster, and J.-Y. L'Excellent. A fully asynchronous multifrontal solver using distributed dynamic scheduling. *SIAM Journal on Matrix Analysis and Applications*, 23(1):15–41, 2001.

[29]   P. R. Amestoy, A. Guermouche, J.-Y. L'Excellent, and S. Pralet. Hybrid scheduling for the parallel solution of linear systems. *Parallel Computing*, 32(2):136–156, 2006.

[30]   Timothy A. Davis. *Direct Methods for Sparse Linear Systems (Fundamentals of Algorithms 2)*. Society for Industrial and Applied Mathematics, Philadelphia, PA, USA, 2006.

[31]   Olaf Schenk and Klaus Gärtner. Two-level dynamic scheduling in PARDISO: Improved scalability on shared memory multiprocessing systems. *Parallel Comput.*, 28(2):187–197, 2002.

[32]   Van E. Henson and Ulrike M. Yang. BoomerAMG: A parallel algebraic multigrid solver and preconditioner. *Applied Numerical Mathematics*, 41:155–177, 2002.

[33]   Robert D. Falgout, Jim E. Jones, and Ulrike M. Yang. The design and implementation of hypre, a library of parallel high performance preconditioners. *Chapter in Numerical solution of Partial Differential Equations on Parallel Computers, A.M. Bruaset, P. Bjorstad, and A. Tveito, eds. Springer-Verlag, to appear.*, 2004. Also available as LLNL Technical Report UCRL-JRNL-205459, 2004.

Parallel Computing: On the Road to Exascale
G.R. Joubert et al. (Eds.)
IOS Press, 2016
doi:10.3233/978-1-61499-621-7-807

807

Performance Evaluation of the LBM Solver Musubi on Various HPC Architectures

Jiaxing QI [a,1], Kartik JAIN [a], Harald KLIMACH [a] and Sabine ROLLER [a]

[a] *Simulationstechnik und Wissenschaftliches Rechnen, Universität Siegen*

Abstract. This contribution presents the performance of the Lattice Boltzmann implementation Musubi on four different High Performance Computing architectures. Musubi is maintained within the APES simulation framework that makes use of a distributed octree mesh representation and includes a mesh generation and a post-processing tool to enable end-to-end parallel simulation work flows. An unstructured representation of the mesh is used, so only fluid elements are stored and computed for any arbitrary complex geometry with minimum user interference. Elements are serialized according to a space filling curve to ensure good spatial locality. The validity of our approach is demonstrated by the good performance and scaling behavior on the four HPC systems with minimal porting efforts.

Keywords. lattice Boltzmann Method, octree, CFD, HPC

Introduction

Musubi is an incompressible fluid flow solver based on the Lattice Boltzmann Method (LBM). Instead of discretizing the Navier-Stokes equation directly, the LBM emerges from a highly simplified gas-kinetic description [1]. It operates on structured Cartesian meshes and requires information only from the nearest neighbors. Such data locality makes LBM a good candidate for parallelization. Moreover, the simple link-wise boundary treatment makes LBM very suitable to handle complex geometries [2]. Strategies and techniques for the large-scale LBM parallelization have gained significant attention in recent years, see for example [3–5].

The flow solver *Musubi* is a part of the APES simulation framework [6,7]. APES is based on a distributed octree mesh representation library *TreElM* [8]. Using a dedicated mesh representation, the common geometrical and topological operations on octree are encapsulated into the library. Together with the mesh generator and the post-processing tool, the APES framework provides users an end-to-end high performance simulation tool chain. *Musubi* has been successfully applied in complex engineering applications like flow of liquid mixtures through a complex spacer [9] as well as clinical applications like blood flow in intracranial aneurysms [10, 11].

---

[1]Corresponding Author: Jiaxing Qi, Simulationstechnik und Wissenschaftliches Rechnen, Universität Siegen, Hölderlinstr. 3, 57076 Siegen, Germany; E-Mail: qijiaxing@gmail.com

In the remainder of this work, the validity of our approach is investigated on four different HPC architectures namely:

- the IBM BlueGene/Q (PowerPC) system *JUQUEEN* at the FZJ in Jülich,
- and the NEC SX-ACE vector machine *Kabuki* at the HLRS in Stuttgart,
- the Cray XC40 (Intel x86 Haswell) system *Hornet* at the HLRS in Stuttgart,
- The *SuperMUC* petascale system installed at the Leibniz Supercomputing Center in Munich.

The intra-node and inter-node performance and scaling behavior of *Musubi* is presented and compared on these systems.

1. Lattice Boltzmann Flow Solver

1.1. Lattice Boltzmann Equation

In LBM, the state of fluid is described by the particle distribution functions (PDF) f_i, each associated with a discretized velocity $\vec{c}_i$ at a spatial position $\vec{x}$ and time t. For 3-dimensional simulations, several commonly used stencils exist and are termed as $DdQq$, e.g. D3Q15, D3Q19 and D3Q27, which means each element has q degrees of freedom (DoF). The evolution of f_i is given by the LB equation

$$f_i(\vec{x}+\vec{c}_i\Delta t, t+\Delta t) = f_i(\vec{x},t) - \Omega_i(f_i(\vec{x},t)) \tag{1}$$

where $\Omega_i(f_i(\vec{x},t))$ is the collision operator that describes the change in f_i resulting from collision. The macroscopic quantities, pressure p and momentum $\vec{m}$, are defined as particle velocity moments of the distribution function, f_i,

$$p = c_s^2 \left(\sum_{i=1}^{q} f_i \right), \qquad \vec{m} = \left(\sum_{i=1}^{q} \vec{c}_i f_i \right) \tag{2}$$

where c_s is the speed of sound. Each iteration in LBM consists of two steps: streaming and collision. Streaming only involves movement of data to neighbor elements but no computation, whereas collision is a purely local computation.

1.2. Implementation

As part of the *APES* framework [6, 7], *Musubi* is built upon the octree mesh representation provided by the *TreElM* library [8]. With the help of a space filling curve, each element in the mesh can be uniquely labeled by an 8-byte integer called *treeID*. The *treeID* implicitly embeds the spatial and topological information about the element. All the fluid elements in the mesh can be uniquely serialized according to the space filling curve by just sorting their *treeID*s. This can be done automatically for any arbitrarily complex geometry while still maintaining a good spatial locality. After serialization, all elements are equally distributed across all processes, thus resulting in an optimal load balance. The sparse matrix method [12] is used, which means only fluid elements are stored and their neighbors are recursively identified during initialization. In cases with low volume fraction of the fluid space as in porous media, this saves a lot of memory and avoids unnecessary computation. *Halo* elements are introduced at the domain interface to receive information from neighbor processes. All fluid and halo elements are stored in a sorted list and assembled for computation. This results in a 1D array containing the state variables f_i for all elements. Another 1D connectivity array provides the link-wise neighbor information required during the streaming step. Streaming f_i during computation is accomplished by memory access to this array, thus being an indirect memory access method.

The streaming and collision steps are combined together into one computing kernel, which is highly optimized and independent from the actual mesh. In the current study, the streaming step is performed before the collision step resulting in the so called *PULL* scheme. To eliminate spatial data dependencies, state variables for odd and even time steps are stored in double buffers separately. The collision-optimized *array-of-structure* (AOS) data layout, i.e. f(1:19,1:M,0:1) (Fortran style array is used here), was applied in the current study.

2. Benchmark Analysis on Four HPC Systems

We investigated *Musubi*'s performance on four different HPC architectures. A fully periodic cubic geometry without any boundary conditions was selected as the test bed. Performances under various scenarios (intra-node and inter-nodes) were examined. The million lattice updates per second (MLUPS) was chosen as the performance metric. For a given compute kernel, this number can be converted directly into the number of floating point operations. The BGK relaxation scheme of the LBM and the D3Q19 layout were chosen throughout for the performance comparisons. The use of the D3Q19 layout implies 19 8-byte real numbers for each cell. With a double buffer data structure and another 1D 4-byte integer array providing adjacency information, this leads to a total of ($8 \times 3 \times 19 + 4 \times 19$=) 532 bytes data volume per element per time step to be transferred over the memory interface, assuming a write allocate cache strategy. After compiler optimization, we measured that the BGK kernel requires 160 floating point operations (FLOPS) per element at every time step. The resulting code balance B_{code} (Byte to FLOPS ratio) is 3.325, which indicates the performance is limited by main memory bandwidth.

2.1. The Blue Gene/Q (IBM PowerPC) System - Juqueen

The *JUQUEEN* supercomputer installed at the Jülich Research Centre is an IBM Blue Gene/Q system that consists of 458,752 PowerPC A2 processor cores with each core capable of 4-way multi-threading. These cores are based on Power Instruction Set Architecture (ISA) and are designed to achieve low power consumption. Each node of Blue Gene/Q consists of 16-core nodes which run at 1.6 GHz and achieve a peak performance of 204.8 GFLOPS, and 16 GB of main memory. *JUQUEEN* uses a 5-dimensional torus network topology capable of achieving up to 40 GB/s transfer rate, with a latency up to 2.6 μs. Our software was compiled using the IBM XL Fortran 12.1 compiler together with IBM MPI library. The compiler optimization flag -O3 was turned on for performance tests.

Figure 1(a) shows the single node performance for problem sizes of 8^3, 16^3 and 32^3, utilizing different numbers of cores where each MPI task has 2 OpenMP threads spawned. Larger problem sizes could not be completed due to the abnormal long time taken by the not optimized recursive element identification during initialization. For the the problem sizes of 8^3 and 16^3, the non-computation overheads are dominating so that the performance hardly increases with more cores. For the problem size of 32^3, the performance increases with more cores within a node. When looking at the figure vertically, one can clearly observe that performance increases greatly with larger problem sizes, especially for 8 and 16 cores. In summary, to exploit the maximum performance within a single node, one has to employ all cores on a 32^3 or larger mesh.

The inter-node performance using up to 14336 nodes is shown in Figure 2, in which performance per node (MLUPS/node) is plotted against the problem size within each node (nElems/node). All the 16 cores within a node have been utilized and each task has 2 OpenMP threads spawned. The strong scaling behavior as seen from the internode performance map depicts that the performance increases steadily as the problem size is increased. One can also obtain the weak scaling behavior by looking at the figure vertically. The performance lines from 16 nodes to 4096 nodes (4 racks) coincide with each other closely over the problem size range 10^3–10^5 which indicates a very good weak scaling. Starting from 8192 and 14336 nodes (8 and 14 racks, respectively), these two performance lines drop slightly as compared to the others. The largest problem size that fits on a single node is $\sim 2 \times 10^5$ elements.

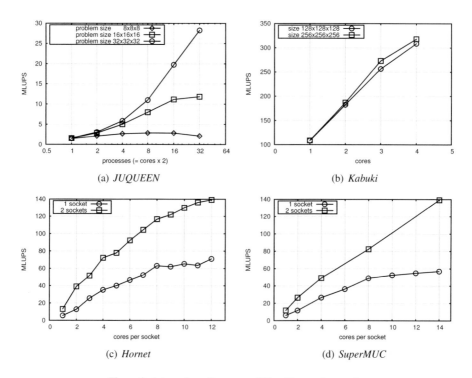

Figure 1. Intranode performance of *Musubi* on various systems

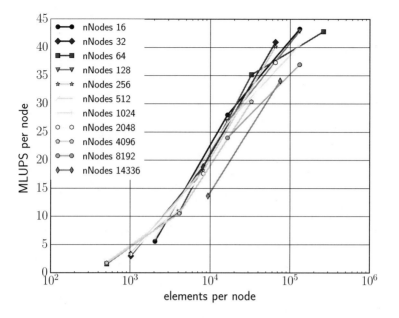

Figure 2. *Musubi*'s inter node performance on *JUQUEEN*

2.2. The NEC SX-ACE System - Kabuki

Kabuki is the NEC SX-ACE vector system installed at the High Performance Computing Center (HLRS), Stuttgart, Germany. The whole system consists of 64 4-core nodes and 64 GB total memory in each node. With 4 cores, each node can deliver a peak performance of 256 GFLOPS along with a peak memory bandwidth of 256 GB/s, thus resulting in a high machine balance B_m (Byte to FLOPS ratio) of 1. The SX-ACE CPU also has a cache similar design called Assignable Data Buffer (ADB). But its size is very small, only 1 MB. The NEC `sxf03 rev.020` Fortran compiler was used to compile our code. The compiler directive `!CDIR NODEP` was added before the compute loop for compiler assisted vectorization of the code.

Figure 1(b) depicts the single node performance for 2 different problem sizes 128^3 and 256^3. The SX-ACE CPU has less cores but each core behaves like a strong core: a single core achieves a performance of more than 100 MLUPS, far better than the CPUs on other system. The maximum performance within a single node is ~ 310 MLUPS, which corresponds to a memory bandwidth of 165 GB/s, i.e. 64.4% of the theoretical peak memory bandwidth.

Figure 3 shows *Musubi*'s inter-node performance on *Kabuki* when all the 4 cores within a node are utilized. For small problem sizes, the non-computation overheads dominate the simulation, resulting in low performance. Consequently the performance gets better upon increasing the problem sizes as the computation to communication ratio increases. This figure depicts a rough weak scaling from 1 to 8 nodes. The performance curves for 8 up to 64 nodes are closer to each other portraying an improved scaling behavior. Additionally, due to the very small size cache, we can't notice its effects on the performance map.

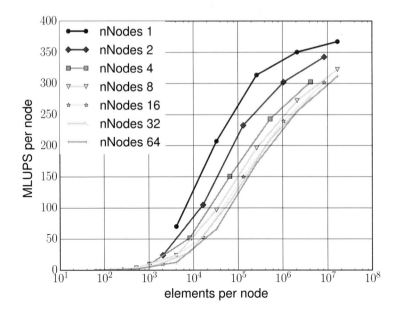

Figure 3. *Musubi*'s inter node performance on *Kabuki*

2.3. The Cray XC40 (Intel x86 Haswell) System - Hornet

The *Hornet* supercomputer is a Cray XC40 system based on the 12 cores Intel Xeon E5-2680 v3 Haswell processors, located at HLRS, Stuttgart Germany. The system consists of 3944 nodes where each node has 2 sockets and 128 GB total memory, and a peak memory bandwidth of 114 GB/s. The network of *Hornet* deploys the Cray XC Dragonfly topology. *Musubi* was compiled on *Hornet* using the Intel Fortran 15 compiler together with the Cray MPI library. Compiler optimization level was set to the highest. The compiler directive !DIR$ NOVECTOR was added before the compute loop to explicitly avoid vectorization, because each individual memory reference in the compute loop exhibits a non-unit stride, which adversely affects vector performance.

Figure 1(c) shows the intra-node performance using various number of cores within a single node. The performance scales well from 1 socket to 2 sockets for all number of cores. The maximum performance is obtained by using all the 24 cores within a node. However, we do not observe a memory bandwidth saturation pattern even with all cores within a single socket.

The inter-node performance using up to 2048 nodes is shown in Figure 4. Besides the drastic cache effect for problem size between 10^4–10^5 (cache region), the performances of other number of nodes increase steadily as problem size become large. After the cache region (problem size 10^6–10^8), most performance curves coincide with each other and finally converge to about 148 MLUPS per node, which indicates little communication thus very good weak scaling behavior. The maximum performance - 148 MLUPS per node, corresponds to a data transfer rate of 78.7 GB/s.

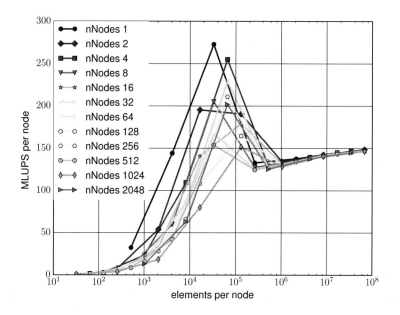

Figure 4. *Musubi*'s inter node performance on Cray XC40

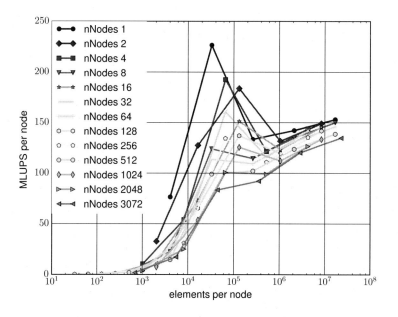

Figure 5. *Musubi*'s inter node performance on *SuperMUC*

2.4. *The* SuperMUC *Petascale System*

SuperMUC phase 2 provides 86016 cores of Intel Xeon E5-2697 v3 Haswell processors. Each node has 64 GB total momery with a theoretical peak bandwidth of 137 GB/s. Performance of *Musubi* on the first phase of SuperMUC has been discussed in [7]. *Musubi*

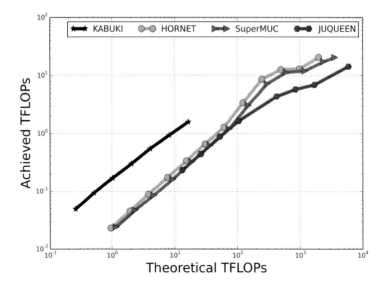

Figure 6. Achieved TFLOPs by *Musubi* against theoretical TFLOPs performance of particular system

was compiled with the Intel 15.0 Fortran compiler using -03 $-x$CORE$-$AVX2 optimization flags.

Figure 1(d) depicts the single node performance on this system which is, due to the similarity in the processor architecture, qualitatively similar to that on *Hornet* (Figure 1(c)). The performance keeps increasing with more cores within a single socket. To obtain the max performance from a node, one has to use all the 28 cores.

The internode performance shown in Figure 5 depicts similar internode behavior as that on *Hornet*. The maximum single node performance on *SuperMUC* is ~ 155 MLUPS, which is slightly better than that of obtained on *Hornet*. However, the weak scaling, though reasonable, is not so good as on *Hornet*, which can be explained by the standard network tree deployed in *SuperMUC*, while *Hornet* makes use of the Cray Dragonfly network.

3. Performance Comparison

It is clear from the preceding sections that *Musubi* scales reasonably in the weak sense with a fixed problem size per node on all four discussed HPC architectures. Now we compare the strong scaling over these systems, by which the decreased performance for smaller problems per node is taken into account, which especially affects *Kabuki* and *JUQUEEN*, as can be seen from the strong gradient in the performance maps shown in Figures 2 and 3. Figure 6 portrays the performance achieved by *Musubi* in TFLOP/s against the theoretical peak performance for various fractions of the four systems. It captures the strong scaling behavior and compares the scale-up from the smallest fraction of the machine where the fixe problem size fits up to the full machine or some limit of scalability. A fixed problem size of 8^8 elements is chosen for this plot comparison, which fits on a single node of the machines except for *JUQUEEN*. Double logarithmic axes are used to capture the wide scaling range. Whereas nearly 20% of peak performance is achieved by *Musubi* on a single node of *Kabuki*, it achieves around 4% of the peak performance on the other systems. For the scalar systems a superlinear speed-up can be observed with a large number of nodes, where the problem size per node fits into the cache.

4. Conclusions

With a single implementation and thus little porting effort, *Musubi* can efficiently make use of the computing resources on the four different HPC systems that were studied in this article. To further improve the performance, i.e. memory bandwidth in the LBM context, it seems necessary to deploy an appropriate data layout (e.g. Structure-of-Array) with dedicated SIMD instruction set on target platform (e.g. SSE or AVX on Intel and QPX on IBM PowerPC) [3, 5]. A complex streaming technique that requires only one copy of state variables has been shown being able to improve the performance significantly [13], and is part of our ongoing research efforts. We found the NEC SX-ACE system to be highly competitive to current scalar architectures for such memory intensive applications like LBM.

Acknowledgements

We are thankful to the Research Center Julich (FZJ), the High Performance Computing Center (HLRS), Stuttgart and the Leibniz Supercomputing Center (LRZ) in Munich for the compute resources used in this study, and for their encouraging support. Especially we would like to thank Uwe Küster for his advices on using the systems efficiently, and Holger Berger for his support to port our software to the SX-ACE.

References

[1] Shiyi Chen and Gary D Doolen. Lattice boltzmann method for fluid flows. *Annual review of fluid mechanics*, 30(1):329–364, 1998.

[2] Manuel Hasert, Joerg Bernsdorf, and Sabine Roller. Towards aeroacoustic sound generation by flow through porous media. *Philosophical Transactions of the Royal Society A: Mathematical, Physical and Engineering Sciences*, 369(1945):2467–2475, 2011.

[3] Christian Godenschwager, Florian Schornbaum, Martin Bauer, Harald Köstler, and Ulrich Rüde. A framework for hybrid parallel flow simulations with a trillion cells in complex geometries. In *Proceedings of the International Conference on High Performance Computing, Networking, Storage and Analysis*, page 35. ACM, 2013.

[4] Manuel Hasert, Kannan Masilamani, Simon Zimny, Harald Klimach, Jiaxing Qi, Jörg Bernsdorf, and Sabine Roller. Complex fluid simulations with the parallel tree-based lattice boltzmann solver musubi. *Journal of Computational Science*, 2013.

[5] Markus Wittmann, Georg Hager, Thomas Zeiser, Jan Treibig, and Gerhard Wellein. Chip-level and multi-node analysis of energy-optimized lattice boltzmann cfd simulations. *Concurrency and Computation: Practice and Experience*, 2015.

[6] Sabine Roller, Jörg Bernsdorf, Harald Klimach, Manuel Hasert, Daniel Harlacher, Metin Cakircali, Simon Zimny, Kannan Masilamani, Laura Didinger, and Jens Zudrop. An adaptable simulation framework based on a linearized octree. In *High Performance Computing on Vector Systems 2011*, pages 93–105. Springer, 2012.

[7]   Harald Klimach, Kartik Jain, and Sabine Roller. End-to-end parallel simulations with apes. In Michael Bader, Arndt Bode, Hans-Joachim Bungartz, Michael Gerndt, Gerhard R. Joubert, and Frans Peters, editors, *Parallel Computing: Accelerating Computational Science and Engineering (CSE)*, volume 25 of *Advances in Parallel Computing*, pages 703–711, Munich, Germany, September 2014. IOS Press.

[8]   Harald G. Klimach, Manuel Hasert, Jens Zudrop, and Sabine P. Roller. Distributed octree mesh infrastructure for flow simulations. In Josef Eberhardsteiner, Helmut J. Böhm, and Franz G. Rammerstorfer, editors, *Proceedings of the 6th European Congress on Computational Methods in Applied Sciences and Engineering*, page 3390, Oct 2012.

[9]   Kannan Masilamani, Jens Zudrop, and Sabine Roller. Towards simulation of electrodialytic sea water desalination. In *Sustained Simulation Performance 2013*, pages 137–146. Springer, 2013.

[10] Kartik Jain and Kent-André Mardal. Exploring the critical reynolds number for transition in intracranial aneurysms - highly resolved simulations below kolmogorov scales. (0):560 – 563, 2015. 2015 Computational and Mathematical Biomedical Engineering.

[11] Kartik Jain, Simon Zimny, Harald Klimach, and Sabine Roller. Thrombosis modeling in stented cerebral aneurysms with lattice boltzmann method. In *Nordic Seminar on Computational Mechanics*, pages 206–209, 2013.

[12] M. Schulz, M. Krafczyk, J. Tölke, and E. Rank. Parallelization strategies and efficiency of cfd computations in complex geometries using lattice boltzmann methods on high-performance computers. In Michael Breuer, Franz Durst, and Christoph Zenger, editors, *High performance scientific and engineering computing*, volume 21, pages 115–122. Springer, 2002.

[13] Markus Wittmann, Thomas Zeiser, Georg Hager, and Gerhard Wellein. Comparison of different propagation steps for lattice boltzmann methods. *Computers & Mathematics with Applications*, 65(6):924–935, 2013.

Parallel Computing: On the Road to Exascale
G.R. Joubert et al. (Eds.)
IOS Press, 2016

doi:10.3233/978-1-61499-621-7-817

Extreme-scaling Applications 24/7 on *JUQUEEN* Blue Gene/Q

Dirk BRÖMMEL [a,1], Wolfgang FRINGS [a], Brian J. N. WYLIE [a]

[a] *Jülich Supercomputing Centre, Forschungszentrum Jülich GmbH, Germany*

Abstract.

Jülich Supercomputing Centre has offered Extreme Scaling Workshops since 2009, with the latest edition in February 2015 giving seven international code teams an opportunity to (im)prove the scaling of their applications to all 458 752 cores of the *JUQUEEN* IBM Blue Gene/Q. Each of them successfully adapted their application codes and datasets to the restricted compute-node memory and exploit the massive parallelism with up to 1.8 million processes or threads. They thereby qualified to become members of the *High-Q Club* which now has over 24 codes demonstrating extreme scalability. Achievements in both strong and weak scaling are compared, and complemented with a review of program languages and parallelisation paradigms, exploitation of hardware threads, and file I/O requirements.

Keywords. HPC applications, *JUQUEEN*, Blue Gene/Q, extreme scaling workshop, High-Q Club.

Introduction

From 5 to 6 February 2015, Jülich Supercomputing Centre (JSC) organised the latest edition of its series of Blue Gene Extreme Scaling Workshops [1]. These workshops started with the 2006 Blue Gene/L Scaling Workshop using JUBL (16 384 cores) and moved to JUGENE for the 2008 Blue Gene/P Porting, Tuning & Scaling Workshop [2], then followed by dedicated Extreme Scaling Workshops in 2009 [3], 2010 [4] and 2011 [5]. These latter three workshops attracted 28 teams selected from around the world to investigate scalability on the most massively-parallel supercomputer at the time with its 294 912 cores. 26 of their codes were successfully executed at that scale, three became ACM Gordon Bell prize finalists, and one participant was awarded an ACM/IEEE-CS George Michael Memorial HPC fellowship. The Leibniz Supercomputing Centre (LRZ) adopted a similar format for workshops in 2013 [6] and 2014 [7] to scale applications on the SuperMUC IBM iDataPlex system, and from 22 participating code teams three succeeded in running on all 14 "thin node" islands (147 456 cores in total).

The focus for the current workshop was on application codes likely to be able to scale during the workshop to run on the full JUQUEEN system [8]. This 28-rack IBM Blue Gene/Q (Figure 1) with 28 672 compute nodes, consisting of 1.6 GHz PowerPC A2 processors each with 16 cores (64 hardware threads) and 16 GB of node memory, has a total of 458 752 cores capable of running 1 835 008 processes or threads. A broad va-

---

[1]Corresponding author: d.broemmel@fz-juelich.de

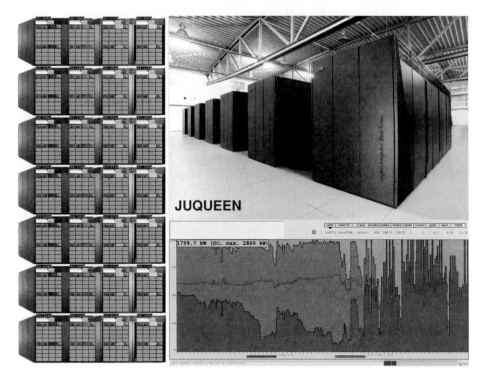

Figure 1. *JUQUEEN* Blue Gene/Q as presented by the *LLview* system monitor when running a single job on the full configuration of 4×7 racks during the workshop, where the lower-right chart shows the mix of jobs changing to dedicated large jobs (shown darker).

riety of application codes which have demonstrated that they can productively exploit the entire JUQUEEN resources have already been recognised as members of the High-Q Club [9]. The High-Q Club is a collection of the highest scaling codes on JUQUEEN and as such requires the codes to run on all 28 racks. Codes also have to demonstrate that they profit from each additional rack of JUQUEEN in reduced time to solution when strong scaling a fixed problem size or a tolerable increase in runtime when weak scaling progressively larger problems. Furthermore the application configurations should be beyond toy examples and we encourage use of all available hardware threads which is often best achieved via mixed-mode programming combining message-passing with multithreading. Each code is then individually evaluated based on its weak or strong scaling results with no strict limit on efficiency. The workshop thus provided an opportunity for additional candidates to prove their scalability and qualify for membership, or – as was the case for one of the codes – improve on the scaling and efficiency that they had already achieved.

1. Workshop Overview

Seven application teams were invited to work on the scalability of their codes, with dedicated access to the entire JUQUEEN system for a period of 30 hours. Most of the teams' codes had thematic overlap with JSC Simulation Laboratories or were part of an ongoing collaboration with one of the SimLabs. Following earlier tradition, the 2015 Extreme Scaling Workshop was directly preceded by a Porting and Tuning Workshop, offered by JSC as part of the PRACE Advanced Training Centre (PATC) curriculum. Hence most of the application teams were among the 25 new and more experienced users of JUQUEEN who were also present for the prior three days and used the opportunity for initial preparations, performance analyses and tuning tips. Pre-workshop preparations had already made sure that suitable datasets and execution configuration were ready. During both workshops the code teams were supported by JSC Cross-sectional teams and Climate Science, Fluids & Solids Engineering and Neuroscience SimLabs, along with IBM and JUQUEEN technical support.

The seven participating code teams (attendees marked in **bold**) were:

- CoreNeuron *electrical activity of neuronal networks with morphologically-detailed neurons*
  Fabien Delalondre, Pramod Kumbhar, **Aleksandr Ovcharenko** (Blue Brain Project, EPFL), and Michael Hines (Yale University)
- FE^{2}TI *scale-bridging approach incorporating micro-mechanics in macroscopic simulations of multi-phase steels*
  Axel Klawonn and **Martin Lanser** (University of Cologne), **Oliver Rheinbach** (TU Freiberg), Jörg Schröder (University Duisburg-Essen), Daniel Balzani (TU Dresden), and Gerhard Wellein (University Erlangen-Nürnberg)
- FEMPAR *massively-parallel finite-element simulation of multi-physics problems governed by PDEs* — High-Q Club member since Dec. 2014
  Santiago Badia, **Alberto F. Martín**, and Javier Principe (Centre Internacional de Mètodes Numèrics a l'Enginyeria (CIMNE), Universitat Politècnica de Catalunya)
- ICON *icosahedral non-hydrostatic atmospheric model*
  Catrin Meyer (Forschungszentrum Jülich GmbH, JSC) and **Thomas Jahns** (Deutsches Klimarechenzentrum GmbH)
- MPAS-A *multi-scale non-hydrostatic atmospheric model for global, convection-resolving climate simulations*
  Dominikus Heinzeller (Karlsruhe Inst. of Technology, Inst. of Meteorology and Climate Research) and Michael Duda (National Center for Atmospheric Research, Earth System Laboratory)
- psOpen *direct numerical simulation of fine-scale turbulence*
  Jens Henrik Goebbert (Jülich Aachen Research Alliance) and **Michael Gauding** (TU Freiberg)
- SHOCK *structured high-order finite-difference computational kernel for direct numerical simulation of compressible flow*
  Manuel Gageik and Igor Klioutchnikov (Shock Wave Laboratory, RWTH Aachen University)

A total of 370 'large' jobs were executed (58 on 28 racks, 19 on 24 racks, 6 on 20 racks and 105 on 16 racks) using 12 of the 15 million core-hours reserved for the extreme scaling workshop. Most of the familiar LoadLeveler job scheduling quirks were avoided by deft sysadmin intervention, and a single nodeboard failure requiring a reset resulted in only a short outage when smaller jobs could be executed on the remaining racks.

Table 1. Characteristics of workshop application codes: main programming languages (excluding external libraries), parallelisation including maximal process/thread concurrency (per compute node and overall), and file I/O implementation. (Supported capabilities unused for scaling runs on *JUQUEEN* in parenthesis.)

Code	Programming Languages		MPI	OMP	Concurrency	File I/O
CoreNeuron	C	C++	1	64	64: 1 835 008	MPI-IO
FE²TI	C	C++	16	4	64: 1 835 008	
FEMPAR		F08	64		64: 1 756 001	
ICON	C	Ftn	1	64	64: 1 835 008	(netCDF)
MPAS-A	C	Ftn	16		16: 458 752	PIO,pNetCDF
psOpen		F90	32	2	64: 1 835 008	pHDF5
SHOCK	C		64		64: 1 835 008	(cgns/HDF5)

2. Parallel Program & Execution Configuration Characteristics

Characteristics of the workshop application codes are summarised in Table 1 and discussed in this section, with scaling performance compared in the following section.

Since Blue Gene/Q offers lower-level function calls for some hardware-specific features that are sometimes not available for all programming languages, a starting point is looking at the languages used. Of the workshop codes, two combine Fortran with C, two use C and C++, and the remaining three exclusively use only either Fortran or C, indicating that all three major programming languages are equally popular (without considering lines of code) as seen with the other High-Q Club codes.

The four hardware threads per core of the Blue Gene/Q chip in conjunction with the limited amount of memory suggest to make use of multi-threaded programming. It is therefore interesting to see whether this is indeed the preferred programming model and whether the available memory is an issue. As a basis, all seven workshop codes used MPI, which is almost ubiquitous for portable distributed-memory parallelisation – for example only one High-Q Club application employs lower-level machine-specific SPI for maximum performance. Three of the workshop codes exclusively used MPI for their scaling runs, both between and within compute nodes. A memory fragmentation issue in a third-party library currently inhibits the use of OpenMP by FEMPAR. On the other hand MPAS-A just started to include OpenMP multi-threading, whereas an earlier investigation with the SHOCK code found this not to be beneficial. The remaining four workshop codes employ OpenMP multi-threading to exploit compute node shared memory in conjunction with MPI. In addition, CoreNeuron has an ongoing effort investigating use of OpenMP-3 tasking and new MPI-3 capabilities (e.g. non-blocking collectives), so these are generally expected to become increasingly important. CoreNeuron is also reorganising data structures to be able to exploit vectorisation. To address MPI overhead, psOpen exploited their own three-dimensional FFT library using non-blocking communication to more than halve communication time by overlapping multiple FFT instances.

The decision for a specific programming model had other implications. ICON needed MPI to be initialised with `MPI_THREAD_MULTIPLE` multi-threading support for an external library, which was determined to result in prohibitive time during model initialisation for `MPI_Allreduce` calls with user-defined reductions of `MPI_IN_PLACE` arguments on communicators derived from `MPI_COMM_WORLD`: the code was therefore

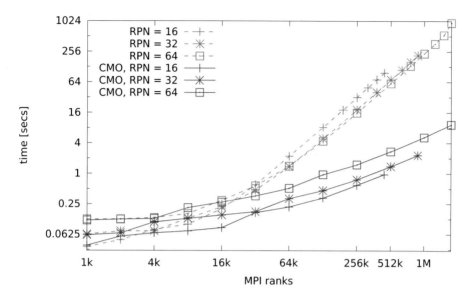

Figure 2. Scaling of wallclock execution time for MPI_Comm_split sub-communicator creation on *JUQUEEN* Blue Gene/Q: default and less memory-optimised alternative (CMO).

changed to circumvent this. MPAS-A bootstrapping to set up the grid and neighbourhood halo/ghost cells during its model initialisation was also found to take almost 30 minutes.

Using only MPI means accommodating to the restricted per-process memory. However, two codes in addition had to trade somewhat higher memory requirements for much faster MPI communicator management, a consequence of the vast number of MPI processes possible on JUQUEEN. For FEMPAR and FE^{2}TI the PAMID_COLLECTIVES_MEMORY_OPTIMIZED environment variable was critical to reduce the time of MPI_Comm_split from 15 minutes down to under 10 seconds. Figure 2 shows the benefit of this as well as different optimisation strategies within the MPI library for different numbers of MPI ranks.

Codes employing shared memory parallelisation also struggled with memory. For CoreNeuron available memory is the limiting factor for larger simulations, with the current limit being 155 million neurons using 15.9 GB of RAM. ICON was able to benefit from a recent reworking to substantially reduce the memory that it needed for large-scale executions, whereas SHOCK started to investigate using single-precision datatypes to reduce its memory requirements. MPAS-A required 1 GB of memory on each process for its regular 3 km mesh simulation (over 65 million grid cells with 41 vertical levels), and could therefore only use a single hardware thread per core, limiting its effective performance.

The other six workshop codes were able to use all four hardware threads of each processor core. FEMPAR and SHOCK used all 64 hardware threads for MPI processes, and in this way FEMPAR was able to increase its efficiency and scalability to 1.75 million processes using $27\frac{1}{2}$ racks of JUQUEEN when employing an additional (fourth-)level of domain decomposition. The other five codes exploited mixed-mode parallelisation with each MPI process having 64 OpenMP threads for CoreNeuron and ICON or only a few OpenMP threads in the case of FE^{2}TI and psOpen.

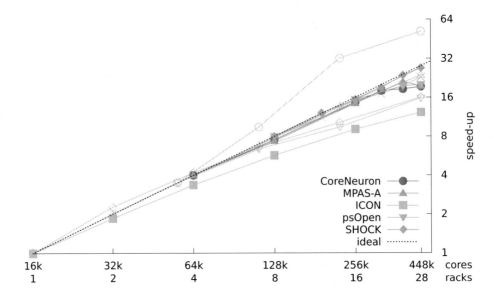

Figure 3. Strong scaling results of the workshop codes with results from existing High-Q Club members included in light grey.

3. Strong and Weak Scaling and Performance

An overview of the results of a scaling workshop entails some form of comparison of achievements in *strong* (fixed total problem size) and *weak* (fixed problem size per process or thread) scaling, put in context of the scalability results from other codes in the High-Q Club.

Figures 3 and 4 show strong and weak scaling results of the workshop codes, including in grey results from a selection of High-Q Club codes. This indicates the spread in execution results and diverse scaling characteristics of the codes. The figures show that the workshop codes not only managed to run on the full JUQUEEN system, but they also achieved very nice scalability and five new codes therefore qualified for High-Q Club status as an outcome of the workshop. Note that in many cases the graphs do not have a common baseline of one rack since datasets sometimes did not fit available memory or no data was provided for 1024 compute nodes: for strong scaling an execution with a minimum of seven racks (one quarter of JUQUEEN) is accepted for a baseline measurement, with perfect-scaling assumed from a single rack to the baseline.

In Figure 3 almost ideal strong-scaling speed-up of 27× on 28 racks is achieved by SHOCK, whereas ICON only achieved a modest 12× speed-up and with the other workshop codes in between.

Even with its heroic dataset of over 65 million grid-points, MPAS-A suffered a performance breakdown in strong scaling going from 24 to 28 racks due to growing communication costs overwhelming diminishing per-rank computation. A similar breakdown was also found with SHOCK when strong scaling with 64 MPI ranks per compute node (but not evident with only 32 rpn). In both cases, larger datasets are expected to avoid this breakdown.

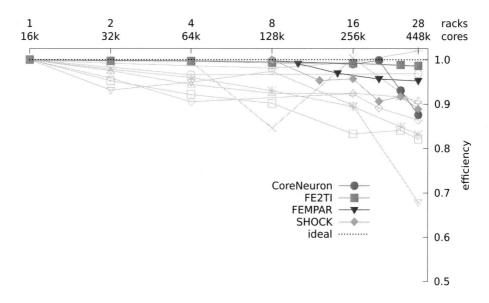

Figure 4. Weak scaling results of the workshop codes with results from existing High-Q Club members included in light grey.

In Figure 4 FE^{2}TI is able to sustain weak scaling efficiency of 99% with 28 racks, whereas for CoreNeuron efficiency drops to a still respectable 88% due to a load-balancing artifact of the input data configuration. Various codes show erratic scaling performance, most likely due to topological effects. SHOCK is characterised by particularly poorly performing configurations with an odd number of racks in one dimension (i.e. 4×3, 4×5 and 4×7 as seen in Figure 1).

4. Parallel Performance Utilities

Managing I/O   A critical point attracting increasing attention is performance of file I/O, which is often a scalability constraint for codes which need to read and write huge datasets or open a large number of files. MPAS-A file reading was tuned via environment variables and employing 128 ranks to read and distribute data for the 16 384 tasks in each rack, however, it still needed 20 minutes to load its 1.2 TB of initial condition data using PIO/NetCDF — after taking the better part of a week to transfer this single file from KIT (due to the source institution policy limiting outgoing transfer bandwidth) — while simulation output was disabled for these tests to avoid similar writing inefficiency. Large-scale executions of ICON, psOpen and SHOCK (and various High-Q member codes) using the popular HDF5 and pNetCDF libraries needed to disable file I/O and synthesise initialisation data, whereas CoreNeuron replicated a small dataset to fill memory to 15.9 GB.

SIONlib [10], which was developed to address file I/O scalability limitations, has been used effectively by three High-Q codes and several others are currently migrating to adopt it.

Tools at scale   Darshan [11] was engaged with SHOCK and various other codes to investigate I/O performance on JUQUEEN and identify copious reads of small numbers of bytes. The Score-P instrumentation and measurement infrastructure [12] employed by the latest release of Scalasca [13] was used to profile file I/O performance of MPAS-A, however, only MPI call count and timing is currently supported and not measurement of bytes read or written. While Score-P profiles have been produced for applications with one million threads, the largest trace collection configuration currently handled with OTF2 is approximately 655 360 threads (or processes). SIONlib needs to be employed for such traces to avoid file creation limitations and have managable numbers of files.

Custom mappings of MPI process ranks to JUQUEEN compute nodes generated by the Rubik [14] tool were investigated with psOpen and found to deliver some benefits, however, for the largest machine partitions these did not provide the expected reduction in communication times yet suffered from increased application launch/initialisation time.

5. Conclusions

The 2015 JUQUEEN Extreme Scaling Workshop surpassed our expectations and completely achieved its goal: all seven teams succeeded in running and validating their codes on 28 racks within the first 24 hours of access to the full JUQUEEN system. They also demonstrated excellent strong and/or weak scaling which qualified five new members for the High-Q Club: unfortunately, MPAS-A scaling was limited to only 24 racks (393 216 cores). In this case, the dataset used was insufficient to have a performance benefit with 28 racks.

Most optimisations employed by the codes are not specific to Blue Gene (or BG/Q) systems, but can also be exploited on other highly-parallel computer systems. High-Q Club codes have also run at scale on various Cray supercomputers, K computer, MareNostrum-3, SuperMUC and other x86-based computers, as well as on systems with GPGPUs.

Feedback from participants confirmed that the workshop facilitated exchange of ideas that empowered them to identify additional optimisation opportunities that they could exploit. Detailed results for each code are found in chapters contributed to the workshop report [1] by each of the participating teams. These present and discuss more execution configurations and scaling results achieved by the application codes during the workshop.

Acknowledgments

Particular thanks are due to Sandra Diaz, Markus Geimer, Klaus Görgen, Sabine Grießbach, Lars Hoffmann, Michael Knobloch, Alex Peyser, Christoph Pospiech, Michael Rambadt, Michael Schlottke, Michael Stephan, Alexandre Strube and Kay Thust, and the workshop participants themselves who openly shared their own knowledge and expertise.

References

[1] Dirk Brömmel, Wolfgang Frings & Brian J. N. Wylie, JUQUEEN Extreme Scaling Workshop 2015, Technical Report FZJ-JSC-IB-2015-01, Forschungszentrum Jülich, Feb. 2015.
     http://juser.fz-juelich.de/record/188191
[2] Bernd Mohr & Wolfgang Frings, Jülich Blue Gene/P Porting, Tuning & Scaling Workshop 2008, Innovatives Supercomputing in Deutschland, inSiDE 6(2), 2008.
[3] Bernd Mohr & Wolfgang Frings, Jülich Blue Gene/P Extreme Scaling Workshop 2009, Technical Report FZJ-JSC-IB-2010-02, Forschungszentrum Jülich, Feb. 2010.
     http://juser.fz-juelich.de/record/8924
[4] Bernd Mohr & Wolfgang Frings, Jülich Blue Gene/P Extreme Scaling Workshop 2010, Technical Report FZJ-JSC-IB-2010-03, Forschungszentrum Jülich, May 2010.
     http://juser.fz-juelich.de/record/9600
[5] Bernd Mohr & Wolfgang Frings, Jülich Blue Gene/P Extreme Scaling Workshop 2011, Technical Report FZJ-JSC-IB-2011-02, Forschungszentrum Jülich, Apr. 2011.
     http://juser.fz-juelich.de/record/15866
[6] Helmut Satzger et al, Extreme Scaling of Real World Applications to >130,000 Cores on SuperMUC, Poster, Int'l Conf. for High Performance Computing, Networking, Storage and Analysis (SC13, Denver, CO, USA), Nov. 2013.
[7] Ferdinand Jamitzky & Helmut Satzger, 2nd Extreme Scaling Workshop on SuperMUC, Innovatives Supercomputing in Deutschland, inSiDE 12(2), 2014.
[8] Michael Stephan & Jutta Docter, JUQUEEN: IBM Blue Gene/Q supercomputer system at the Jülich Supercomputing Centre. Journal of Large-scale Research Facilities (1), A1, 2015. http://dx.doi.org/10.17815/jlsrf-1-18
[9] The High-Q Club at JSC. http://www.fz-juelich.de/ias/jsc/high-q-club
[10] SIONlib: Scalable I/O library for parallel access to task-local files.
     http://www.fz-juelich.de/jsc/sionlib
[11] Darshan: HPC I/O characterisation tool, Argonne National Laboratory.
     http://www.mcs.anl.gov/research/projects/darshan/
[12] Score-P: Community-developed scalable instrumentation and measurement infrastructure.
     http://www.score-p.org/
[13] Scalasca: Toolset for scalable performance analysis of large-scale parallel applications.
     http://www.scalasca.org/
[14] Rubik tool for generating structured Cartesian communication mappings, Lawrence Livermore National Laboratory. https://computation.llnl.gov/project/performance-analysis-through-visualization/software.php

High-Q Club codes

The full description of the High-Q Club codes along with developer and contact information can be found on the web page [9]. The current list also includes:

CIAO *advanced reactive turbulent simulations with overset*
RWTH Aachen University ITV and Sogang University
dynQCD *lattice quantum chromodynamics with dynamical fermions*
JSC SimLab Nuclear and Particle Physics & Universität Wuppertal
Gysela *gyrokinetic semi-Lagrangian code for plasma turbulence simulations*
CEA-IRFM Cadarache
IMD *classical molecular dynamics simulations*
Ruhr-Universität Bochum & JSC SimLab Molecular Systems
JURASSIC *solver for infrared radiative transfer in the Earth's atmosphere*
JSC SimLab Climate Science
JuSPIC *relativistic particle-in-cell code for plasmas and laser-plasma interaction*
JSC SimLab Plasma Physics
KKRnano *Korringa-Kohn-Rostoker Green function code for quantum description of nano-materials in all-electron density-functional calculations*
FZJ-IAS
LAMMPS(DCM) *molecular dynamics simulation with dynamic cutoff method*
Aachen Inst. for Advanced Study in Computational Engineering Science
MP2C *massively-parallel multi-particle collision dynamics for soft matter physics and mesoscopic hydrodynamics*
JSC SimLab Molecular Systems
$\mu\phi$ (muPhi) *water flow and solute transport in porous media, algebraic multi-grid*
Universität Heidelberg
Musubi *multi-component Lattice Boltzmann solver for flow simulations*
Universität Siegen
NEST *large-scale simulations of biological neuronal networks*
FZJ/INM-6 & IAS-6
OpenTBL *direct numerical simulation of turbulent flows*
Universidad Politécnica de Madrid
PEPC *tree code for N-body simulations, beam-plasma interaction, vortex dynamics, gravitational interaction, molecular dynamics simulations*
JSC SimLab Plasma Physics
PMG+PFASST *space-time parallel solver for ODE systems with linear stiff terms*
LBNL, Universität Wuppertal, Università della Svizzera italiana & JSC
PP-Code *simulations of relativistic and non-relativistic astrophysical plasmas*
University of Copenhagen
TERRA-NEO *modeling and simulation of Earth mantle dynamics*
Universität Erlangen-Nürnberg, LMU & TUM
waLBerla *Lattice-Boltzmann method for the simulation of fluid scenarios*
Universität Erlangen-Nürnberg
ZFS *multiphysics framework for flows, aero-acoustics and combustion*
RWTH Aachen AIA and JSC SimLab Fluids & Solids Engineering

Parallel Computing: On the Road to Exascale
G.R. Joubert et al. (Eds.)
IOS Press, 2016
827
doi:10.3233/978-1-61499-621-7-827

Extreme Scale-out SuperMUC Phase 2 - lessons learned

Nicolay HAMMER [a,1], Ferdinand JAMITZKY [a], Helmut SATZGER [a],
Momme ALLALEN [a], Alexander BLOCK [a], Anupam KARMAKAR [a],
Matthias BREHM [a], Reinhold BADER [a], Luigi IAPICHINO [a], Antonio RAGAGNIN [a],
Vasilios KARAKASIS [a], Dieter KRANZLMÜLLER [a], Arndt BODE [a],
Herbert HUBER [a], Martin KÜHN [b], Rui MACHADO [b], Daniel GRÜNEWALD [b],
Philipp V. F. EDELMANN [c], Friedrich K. RÖPKE [c], Markus WITTMANN [d],
Thomas ZEISER [d], Gerhard WELLEIN [e], Gerald MATHIAS [f], Magnus SCHWÖRER [f],
Konstantin LORENZEN [f], Christoph FEDERRATH [g], Ralf KLESSEN [h],
Karl-Ulrich BAMBERG [i], Hartmut RUHL [i], Florian SCHORNBAUM [j],
Martin BAUER [k], Anand NIKHIL [k], Jiaxing QI [k], Harald KLIMACH [k],
Hinnerk STÜBEN [l], Abhishek DESHMUKH [m], Tobias FALKENSTEIN [m],
Klaus DOLAG [n], and Margarita PETKOVA [n]

[a] *Leibniz-Rechenzentrum, Garching*
[b] *CCHPC - Fraunhofer ITWM, Kaiserslautern*
[c] *Heidelberger Institut für Theoretische Studien, Heidelberg*
[d] *Erlangen Regional Computer Center (RRZE), University of Erlangen-Nürnberg, Erlangen*
[e] *Department of Computer Science, University of Erlangen-Nürnberg*
[f] *Lehrstuhl für Biomolekulare Optik, Ludwig-Maximilians-Universität München, München*
[g] *Research School of Astronomy and Astrophysics, The Australian National University, Canberra*
[h] *Universität Heidelberg, Zentrum für Astronomie, Institut für Theoretische Astrophysik, Heidelberg*
[i] *Chair for Computational and Plasma Physics at the LMU, Munich*
[j] *Chair for System Simulation, University of Erlangen-Nürnberg, Erlangen*
[k] *Chair of Simulation Techniques & Scientific Computing, University Siegen*
[l] *Universität Hamburg, Zentrale Dienste, Hamburg*
[m] *Fakultät für Maschinenwesen, Institut für Technische Verbrennung, RWTH Aachen University, Templergraben 64, Aachen*
[n] *Universitäts-Sternwarte München, München*

Abstract. We report lessons learned during the friendly user block operation period of the new system at the Leibniz Supercomputing Centre (SuperMUC Phase 2).

Keywords. Supercomputing, HPC, Extreme Scaling, MPI, Application Scaling

---

[1] Corresponding Author. E-mail: nicolay.hammer@lrz.de.

Introduction

In spring 2015, the Leibniz Supercomputing Centre (Leibniz-Rechenzentrum, LRZ), installed their new Peta-Scale System SuperMUC Phase2. Selected users were invited for a 28 day extreme scale-out block operation during which they were allowed to use the full system for their applications.

The following projects participated in the extreme scale-out workshop: BQCD (Quantum Physics; M. Allalen), SeisSol (Geophysics, Seismics; S. Rettenberger, A. Breuer), GPI-2/GASPI (Toolkit for HPC; M. Kühn, R. Machado, D. Grünewald), Seven-League Hydro (Computational Fluid Dynamics; P. Edelmann), ILBDC (Lattice Boltzmann CFD; M. Wittmann, T. Zeiser), Iphigenie (Molecular Dynamics; G. Mathias, M. Schwörer, K. Lorenzen), FLASH (CFD; C. Federrath, L. Iapichino), GADGET (Cosmological Dynamics; K. Dolag, M. Petkova), PSC (Plasma Physics; K. Bamberg), waLBerla (Lattice Boltzmann CFD; F. Schornbaum, M. Bauer), Musubi (Lattice Boltzmann CFD; A. Nikhil, J. Qi, H. Klimach), Vertex3D (Stellar Astrophysik; T. Melson, A. Marek), CIAO (CFD; A. Deshmukh, T. Falkenstein), and LS1-Mardyn (Material Science; N. Tchipev).

The projects were allowed to use the machine exclusively during the 28 day period, which corresponds to a total of 63.4 million core-hours, of which 43.8 million core-hours were used by the applications, resulting in a utilization of 69%. The top 3 users were using 15.2, 6.4, and 4.7 million core-hours, respectively.

1. System Description

The new PetaScale System SuperMUC Phase2 consists of 6 Islands of Lenovos NeXtScale nx360M5 WCT system each with 512 nodes. Each node contains 2 Intel Haswell Xeon E5-2697v3 processors with 28 cores and 64 GB RAM . The compute nodes are connected via an Infiniband FDR14 network with a non-blocking intra-island and a pruned 4:1 inter-island tree topology. The complete system contains 86,016 cores and 194 TB RAM. The double precision LINPACK Performance was measured as 2.81 PetaFlop/s. Attached to the compute nodes is a parallel filesystem based on IBMs GPFS with 15 PetaBytes. The system runs Novells SUSE Linux Enterprise Edition 11, IBMs LoadLeveler is used as batch system, Intel's C and Fortran compiler, Intel and IBM MPI and is in operation for selected users since May 12th 2015. For an extensive system description, please see www.lrz.de/services/compute/supermuc/system_description.

2. Overall Observations

During the extreme scale-out workshop the performance and system monitoring were already active and therefore some statistics can be calculated.

Each Haswell node contains 28 cores which can also be used with hyperthreading activated, resulting in a maximum of 56 tasks per node. This maximum number of 56 tasks per node was only tested by a single software package. Most of the projects were using 28 tasks per node. However, a significant amount of projects was using a hybrid approach with varying numbers of OpenMP threads on each node. The two main cases for

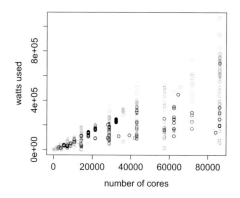

Figure 1. Scaling of the total power consumption of the system versus job size, measured by the number of cores used for each job. Different colors decode the different software packages used.

mixed OpenMP/MPI usage was 1, 2, or 4 MPI tasks per node and 28, 14, or 7 OpenMP threads, respectively. For some codes the factors of 7 instead of powers of 2 were a challenge and required some re-adjustment.

The schedule of the workshop was dominated by two modes of operation: special-time and general-time operation. During special-time operation mode the system was exclusivly available for a single user who could then run large jobs filling the whole system. During general-time operation mode the general queue was available where all participants of the workshop had the opportunity to submit jobs with a maximum size of half of the system. Also this operating time could be used for testing and debugging the code.

Figure 1 shows the watts used for each run versus the number of cores used by this run for all jobs during the workshop. One can see that the power consumption scales nearly linear with the job size. For the largest jobs a maximum watts power of more than 1.2 MW was measured. It is crucial for the power consumption of large jobs that the node level performance is optimized. More than a relative factor of 10 in the variation of power consumption was observed for the largest jobs with 86,016 cores which is not only important for the layout of the electrical infrastructure but also determines the power bill.

The most power hungry compute intensive simulation code SeisSol (more than 1 PFlops sustained, cyan circles) used several times more energy in comparison to the memory bound Lattice Boltzmann Code ILBDC (red circles).

3. FLASH

FLASH is a public, modular grid-based hydrodynamical code for the simulation of astrophysical flows. In the framework of the SuperMUC Phase 2 scale-out workshop, the current version (Flash4) has been optimised to reduce the memory and MPI communication requirements. In particular, non-critical operations are now performed in single precision, without causing any significant impact on the accuracy of the results. In this way, the code runs with a factor of 4.1 less memory and 3.6 times faster than the version

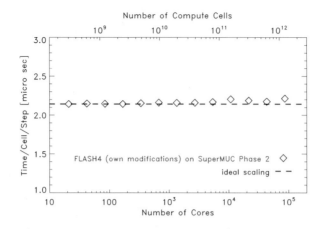

Figure 2. Weak scaling of the FLASH code.

used for the previous large-scale project at LRZ [2], and scales remarkably well up to the whole Phase 2 system (Figure 2).

This scale-out workshop has been used for the preparation of a simulation of super-sonic, isothermal turbulence with an unprecedented resolution exceeding $10,000^3$ grid elements. The simulation is expected to require several million core-hours; it will use about 155 TB of memory, and every data dump will be 19 TB in size. This simulation is devoted to studying the complex flow pattern in the interstellar medium, with the aim of fully resolving the sonic length. It marks the transition scale between compressible and incompressible turbulence where the turbulent cascade crosses from the supersonic into the subsonic regime.

4. Seven-League Hydro

The SLH (Seven-League Hydro) code is an astrophysical hydrodynamics code that solves the compressible Euler equations using a finite-volume method including source terms for gravity, nuclear reactions and thermal conduction, focusing on the simulation of the interior of stars. As these generally involve flows at very low Mach numbers, SLH includes special discretizations that reduce the excessive artificial dissipation which usu-ally occurs in this regime (see [3]). It also uses implicit time-stepping to overcome the CFL criterion, which is exceedingly restrictive at low Mach numbers, leading to an over-all more efficient scheme. The most time-consuming part of the computation is solving very large sparse Jacobian matrices using iterative linear solvers (e.g. BiCGstab or multi-grid). This is mostly memory bandwidth limited. The code is parallelized with MPI and OpenMP, allowing pure MPI and hybrid MPI+OpenMP configurations.

For the scaling tests on SuperMUC Phase 2 we chose the Taylor–Green vortex, which is commonly used as a benchmark for the capability of codes to simulate turbu-lence. It can easily be scaled to an arbitrary number of grid cells, has a very homoge-neous flow pattern and does not involve any source terms. We tested strong scaling on a $2,016^3$ grid up to the full machine. The minimum number of cores needed to store the sparse Jacobian matrix in memory is 21,504, using ~ 2.3 GiB/core. The code shows

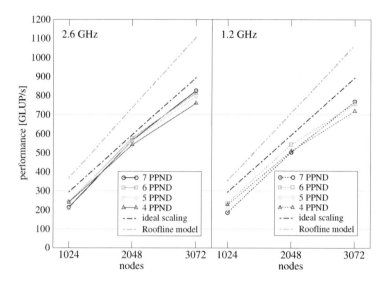

Figure 3. Strong scaling of the ILBDC code with a fixed bed reactor geometry with $17500 \times 3500 \times 3500$ nodes at two clock frequencies (ca. 10^{11} fluid nodes $\approx 19,6\,\text{TiB}$).

more than ideal scaling behavior in the step from 21,504 to 43,008 cores. This is very likely due to cache effects. Similar behavior was observed on SuperMUC Phase 1. It does not show with smaller grid sizes that use less memory per core. Hybrid and pure MPI parallelization behave very similarly using the IBM MPI library. Acceptable scaling is possible even with 86,016 processes using IBM MPI. Intel MPI could not be tested with a high number of MPI tasks due to limitations in the library at the time.

5. ILBDC

ILBDC [5] is a D3Q19-TRT lattice Boltzmann flow solver. Figure 3 (right panel) shows the *strong scaling* behavior of ILBDC from two to six islands for 2.6 GHz (left panel). Despite the 19 concurrent memory streams and indirect access, ILBDC sustains 87 % of the memory bandwidth achieved with the simple STREAM copy benchmark. Typically 5 PPND (processes per NUMA domain) saturate the memory bandwidth and thus already sustained the same performance up to 7 PPND. In the large-scale case communication partially effects this behaviour. With the Haswell-EP architecture, the sustained memory bandwidth of a node is almost independent of the core frequency. Consequently ILBDC at 1.2 GHz still reaches 93% of the performance at 2.6 GHz (Fig. 3, right panel). For memory-bound codes reducing the core frequency and the number of cores used per NUMA domain has only minimal performance impact. This bears the potential to drastically save energy on SuperMUC phase 2.

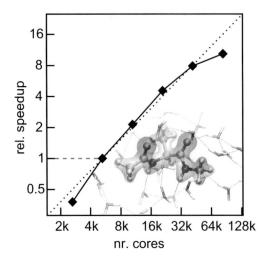

Figure 4. Strong scaling of a IPHIGENIE/CPMD generalized ensemble MD simulation on SuperMUC Phase II for an Alanine dipeptide (DFT) in polarizable water (MM) as sketched in the inset.

6. Iphigenie

The MPI/OpenMP-parallel molecular dynamics (MD) package IPHIGENIE/CPMD[4] links the molecular mechanics (MM) C-code IPHIGENIE (which can be downloaded from www.sourceforge.net/projects/iphigenie) with the quantum–mechanical (QM) density functional theory (DFT) Fortran-implementation CPMD (www.cpmd.org). It is designed for highly accurate and efficient hybrid QM/MM–MD simulations of biomolecules in their native solvent environment. In particular, the use of polarizable MM force fields for the aqueous solution set it apart from related approaches. Efficient sampling of biomolecular conformations is achieved by employing generalized ensemble techniques, which jointly simulate multiple replicas of a system and require only sparse and infrequent communication between the replicas.

The setup for the scaling test comprises the Alanine dipeptide (Ac-ALA-NHMe) molecule as the DFT fragment at a plane wave cutoff of 100 Ry. It is solvated in 4500 water molecules described by a complex polarizable water model. A total of 128 replicas of the system span the generalized ensemble. Every node hosted 4 MPI processes each using 7 OpenMP threads.

Figure 4 (left panel) shows the speedup of the calculation achieved on Phase 2 of the SuperMUC system vs. the number of cores employed. Choosing the reference speed at 5376 cores, we find perfect scaling up to half the machine and good scaling on the full machine (86016 cores). The graph even hints at some super-scaling effects. Based on this excellent scaling fundamental questions related to protein folding and vibrational spectroscopy are now targeted on SuperMUC Phase 2 with unprecedented accuracy.

7. The Plasma Simulation Code (PSC)

The Plasma Simulation Code (PSC) is a general purpose framework to solve the extended Maxwell-Vlasov and extended Maxwell-Vlasov-Boltzmann equations via the Particle-

In-Cell (PIC) approach. Recent extensions comprise the self-field effects of radiation and electron-positron pair production in strong fields. The PSC is a well-tested, widely-recognized and reliable Particle-in-Cell Code that has also been fundamental to other codes, e.g. the EPOCH code. The code was ported to a modern modularized C simulation framework supporting bindings to FORTRAN and C/CUDA that features selectable field and particle pushers. The framework allows the simulation of a large set of problems ranging from ultra-thin foils as light sources and proton-driven wake fields to QED effects in extreme laser fields. The PSC enables the simulation of large-scale, three-dimensional problems, e.g. ELI and AWAKE (CERN).

8. GASPI

The framework for reverse time migration (FRTM) was chosen as showcase for GPI-2. This code is used in exploration for oil and gas (seismic imaging). It fully respects the two-way wave equation and provides high quality imaging also in regions with complex geological structures, e.g. regions composed of steep flanks and/or high velocity contrasts. RTM has high demands on the underlying compute resources. Complex physical modeling, large target output domains, large migration aperture and/or high frequency content require efficient parallelization on the algorithmic side.

In FRTM, the parallelization is based on a fine granular domain decomposition on a regular grid. It is supplemented by a fully asynchronous data dependency driven task based execution. Remote completion is used to take the data dependency driven execution from the process local to the inter- process level. The underlying halo exchange is implemented efficiently with GPI 2.0 (next generation Global address space Programming Interface) which perfectly fits into this concept. GPI 2.0 is a scalable communication API for one-sided, truly asynchronous communication primitives with remote completion. It is the reference implementation of the GASPI specification and is released under GPLv3 (www.gpi-site.com).

For the workshop, the strong scalability of a 15Hz single shot migration of the SEAM dataset achieved by FRTM was analyzed. The SEAM dataset is a well established synthetic benchmark data set used to evaluate the quality of seismic imaging algorithms. The computational cost for a single shot migration is dominated by the finite difference modeling of the wave equation.

The underlying physical model is given by a tilted transverse isotropic (TTI) medium. The finite difference approximation order of the temporal discretization is second order, the spatial part is an 8-th order discretization.

Up to 512 nodes, the achieved scalability is almost perfect resulting in a parallel efficiency of 94% at 512 nodes. Beyond 512 nodes, one observes a drop in the parallel efficiency to 75% at 1,024 nodes and to 70% at 1,536 nodes, respectively. This drop could be explained by the reduced inter-island network bandwidth or by the transition from a 2D to a full 3D domain decomposition beyond 512 nodes. The absolute FRTM run time for a single shot migration at 1,536 nodes is 54.5 seconds (absolute single precision floating point performance of 210 TFlop/s), enabling interactive velocity model building based on RTM as driving engine.

9. Gadget

GADGET is a widely used, publicly available cosmological N-body / Smoothed Particle Magnetohydrodynamics (TreePM-MHD-SPH) simulation code. It uses an explicit communication model implemented via MPI.

For gravity, GADGET uses a TreePM algorithm, based on the fully MPI-parallelized FFTW library to perform the PM part of the gravity solver. Thereby the long range gravity part is computed by sorting the particles onto a mesh and solving Poissons equation via FFT; the short range part is determined from a Tree-walk algorithm, computing a direct sum of the forces between the particles and tree nodes (TreePM). Hydrodynamics is solved via the Smoothed Particle Hydrodynamics (SPH) method, which also make use of the Tree-walk algorithm to perform the neighbor search needed. Additional processes rely on various different numerical methods, for example transport processes are solved by a conjugated gradient method. These different physical modules are already optimized for mixed shared/distributed memory architectures, making use of OpenMP. In addition most of the physics modules – for example star formation, thermal conduction, black hole treatment and on-the-fly post-processing, which are essential for modern cosmological applications – have been prepared for the latest architectures, resulting in a 30% performance improvement and efficient scalability up to 131,072 cores on SuperMUC.

During the workshop, GADGET was used to perform one of the largest cosmological hydrodynamical simulations (in terms of resolution elements and covered cosmological volume) to date. The simulation followed $2 \times 4,526^3$ particles and contained a detailed description of various, complex, non-gravitational, physical processes which determine the evolution of the cosmic baryons and impact their observational properties (for details, see www.magneticum.org). Amongst them are the star formation and related feedback; chemical pollution by SN Ia (Supernova Type Ia), SN II (Supernova Type II) and asymptotic giant branch (AGB) winds; transport processes like the thermal conduction as well as the evolution of black holes and their related active galactic nucleus (AGN) feedback. All these processes are self-consistently coupled with the underlying hydrodynamics. GADGET also uses a new optimization of the tree walk (GreenTree) as well as OpenMP lock improvements.

Including hyper-threading, GADGET was running with 172,032 threads in an OpenMP/MPI hybrid configuration. GADGET showed an extremely good I/O performance and reached 130Gbyte/s writing and 150Gbyte/sec reading for the regular check pointing every 2h (each having a total size of 66 TB). Overall, more than 4 Pbyte of data were produced.

10. BQCD

BQCD (Berlin Quantum Chromodynamics) has implemented various communication methods [1]: MPI, OpenMP, MPI+OpenMP, as well as SHMEM (single sided communication). The pronounced kernel is an iterative solver of a large system of linear equations (conjugate gradient). Depending on the physical parameters, more than 95% of the execution time is spent in the solver. The dominant operation in the solver is a matrix-vector multiplication of a large and sparse hopping matrix. The entries in a row are the eight nearest neighbours of one side of the four-dimensional lattice. The conjugate gradient

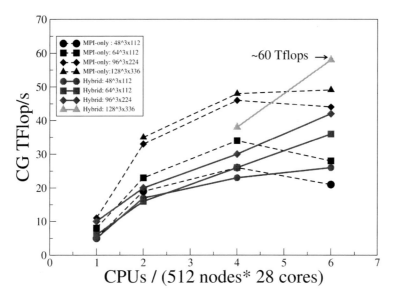

Figure 5. Strong scaling results of conjugate gradient solver for BQCD using MPI only and combination of MPI + 7 OpenMP threads per task, for different lattice sizes on SuperMUC Phase 2 system.

solver is communication intensive and represents the overall performance of the program in practical simulations. It serves as a good test to check the latency and resulting communication overhead.

Several strong and weak scaling runs were performed. One difficulty is to find the right lattice size to fit in to the data cache, another is to describe the full system with a local lattice which fits the Infiniband network. Figure 5 shows the performance results of the conjugate gradient solver for the pure MPI versus the hybrid version, using lattice sizes of $48^3 \times 112$, $64^3 \times 112$, $96^3 \times 224$, and $128^3 \times 336$. Up to 4 islands (57,344 cores), the best performance is achieved using MPI only. On the full system, the hybrid version of the code delivers the best performance for all the lattice sizes using 7 OpenMP threads per MPI task.

11. CIAO

CIAO is an in-house code developed in collaboration between the Institute for Combustion Technology at RWTH Aachen University and Sogang University. Depending on the physical nature of the problem, the Navier-Stokes equations are solved for either fully compressible flows or the low Mach limit. Various models for complex multi-physics flow configurations are available. For local mesh refinement or very stiff problems, a compressible multi-domain solver has been developed. CIAO is a structured, arbitrary order, finite difference code, which is parallelized with MPI. Use of spatial and temporal staggering of flow variables increases the accuracy of stencils with given size. The low Mach solver uses Crank-Nicolson time advancement and an iterative predictor corrector scheme. The compressible solver uses a low-storage five- stage explicit Runge-Kutta time advancement scheme. Scalar equations are discretized with a higher order WENO scheme, while momentum equations are spatially discretized with an arbitrary order central scheme. For Large-Eddy simulations, all of the subfilter stresses and scalar fluxes are modeled with dynamic Smagorinsky-type models using Lagrangian averaging along fluid particle trajectories. For the scale-out tests, a large-eddy simulation of a periodic channel with 20 additional scalars was performed using the compressible Navier-Stokes solver of CIAO which does not use any third-party libraries. The code shows good strong scaling behaviour from 7,168 up to 86,0168 cores.

12. Results and Conclusions

The workshop at LRZ showed that preparation of a simulation campaign is crucial for the success of the project. All aspects like scaling tests, choice of OpenMP/MPI balance, interval for checkpoint and restart files, good preparation of input files, I/O strategy, and risk management have to be addressed. Under these conditions it was possible to use a brand new system like SuperMUC Phase 2 directly after installation and obtain scientific results right from the start.

One big advantage of the extreme scale-out workshop was that only one code was running at a time and this code was filling up the whole system. Thus, hardware bugs were much easier to detect and resolve. One especially hard to find bug was a combination of two timeouts and a hardware problem. During normal user operation this error would have been close to impossible to detect because of the low probability of three errors occurring simultaneously for smaller jobs.

It also became obvious that MPI is at its limits. The size of the MPI stack is growing on each node and for a system of almost 100,000 cores it occupies a significant amount of memory. The startup time can exceed the range of minutes and become a significant part of the overall run time. One way to overcome this bottleneck is the use of hybrid OpenMP/MPI programming models. However, this implies very deep system knowledge on the user side, since process pinning and the choice of the OpenMP/MPI balance has to be evaluated and decided by the user. Furthermore, I/O strategies have to be developed and tested before the complete system can be used. In the future, I/O libraries which can mediate this task become more and more important. Even for hybrid OpenMP/MPI set-ups with a single MPI-task per node, problems arise due to internal limit of the MPI send/receive buffer. This limit is caused by the Integer*4 Byte implementation of the MPI index values. Such problems can be overcome by using application internal buffering.

References

[1] M. Allalen, M. Brehm, and H. Stüben. Performance of quantum chromodynamics (qcd) simulations on the sgi altix 4700. *Computational Methods in Science and Technology*, 14(2):69–75, 2008.

[2] C. Federrath. On the universality of supersonic turbulence. *Monthly Notices of the Royal Astronomical Society*, 436:1245–1257, December 2013.

[3] F. Miczek, F. K. Röpke, and P. V. F. Edelmann. New numerical solver for flows at various mach numbers. *Astronomy and Astrophysics*, 576:A50, April 2015.

[4] Magnus Schwörer, Konstantin Lorenzen, Gerald Mathias, and Paul Tavan. Utilizing Fast Multipole Expansions for Efficient and Accurate Quantum-Classical Molecular Dynamics Simulations. *J. Chem. Phys.*, 142:104108, 2015.

[5] Markus Wittmann, Georg Hager, Thomas Zeiser, Jan Treibig, and Gerhard Wellein. Chip-level and multi-node analysis of energy-optimized lattice boltzmann cfd simulations. *Concurrency and Computation: Practice and Experience*, 2015.

Parallel Computing: On the Road to Exascale
G.R. Joubert et al. (Eds.)
IOS Press, 2016
doi:10.3233/978-1-61499-621-7-837

837

"K-scale" applications on the K computer and co-design effort for the development of "post-K"

Miwako TSUJI [a,1]

[a] *RIKEN Advanced Institute for Computational Science, JAPAN*

Abstract. K computer is the first supercomputer to achieve a LINPACK benchmark performance for 10 PFLOPS in the world. The K computer shows sustained performance in real world applications as well as the LINPACK benchmark. In this paper, through describing a wide range of applications, we present problems and solutions in porting and scaling applications on the K computer. Additionally, we briefly introduce our approach to develop the post K computer.

Keywords. HPC, applications

Introduction

"K", in Japanese (京), stands for 10^{16} (10-peta). The K computer is the first supercomputer in the world to achieve a LINPACK benchmark performance of 10 PFLOPS. The K computer shows sustained PFLOPS performance in real world applications as well as the LINPACK benchmark. In this paper, we describe a wide range of applications on the K computer and present issues and resolutions in porting and scaling those applications on the K computer. At the second part of this paper, we briefly show our approach to design and develop the successor of the K computer.

1. Overview of K Computer

The K computer was developed by RIKEN and Fujitsu Co. Ltd, and is installed at RIKEN Advanced Institute for Computational Science (AICS), Kobe-city, JAPAN. The project to develop the K computer, which was called next-generation supercomputer project, was launched in 2005 [1]. The objectives of the project were

- provide a computer infrastructure for a wide range of scientific, technological, academic and industrial areas
- contribute to society in multiple areas such as materials and medical services.

Additionally, the project aimed to maintain and enhance the technology to develop supercomputers in Japan.

Table 1. Specification of K computer

		K computer
SYSTEM	Number of Nodes	88,218 (inc. IO nodes)
		82,944
	Total Memory	1.26 PB
	Total Storage	30 PB (global file system)
		11 PB (local file system)
	Peak FLOPS	11.28 PFLOPS (inc. IO nodes)
		10.62 PFLOPS
	LINPACK FLOPS	10.51 PFLOPS (inc. IO nodes)
	LINPACK efficiency	93.2%
	Performance Per Watt	0.8 GFLOPS/W (LINPACK)
NODE	CPU Technology	SPARC64 VIIIfx
	# of Cores in CPU	8 cores
	Peak FLOPS	128 GFLOPS
	CPU Clock	2 GHz
	Cache	L1: 32 KB/core
		L2: 6 MB/node
	Memory Technology	DDR3
	Memory Capacity	16 GB
	Memory Bandwidth	64 GB/s
NETWORK	Topology	6 dimensional mesh/torus
		(Tofu)
	Peak bandwidth	5GB/s x 2
	Bisection bandwidth	30 TB/s

The development of the K computer was completed in June 2012 and the full service for shared use was started on 28th September 2012. Table 1 shows the specification of the K computer.

The interconnect of the K computer is called "Tofu" (Torus Fusion), 6 dimensional (6D) mesh/torus network. Users can run multiple topology-aware applications in Tofu because each cubic fragment of the 6D mesh/torus network has the embeddability of a 3D torus graph. As shown in Figure 1, a Tofu network router provides 10 links to construct the 6D network: six in three scalable axes (XYZ) and four in three fixed size axes (ABC). Each of Tofu units consists of 12 (2x3x2) nodes. 4 chips (4 chips are on a single boards) are interconnected with A,C axes and three boards are interconnected with B-axis. The Tofu units are interconnected with XYZ-axes to form a 3D torus[2].

2. K-scale applications on K computer

In this section, we show a wide range of K-scale applications. The word "K-scale" applications, which is an off-the-cuff coined term, does not mean that the performance of

[1] E-mail:miwako.tsuji@riken.jp

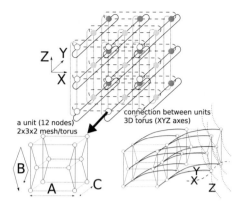

Figure 1. Tofu topology. 12 nodes in a unit form 3D mesh/torus and units form 3D torus.

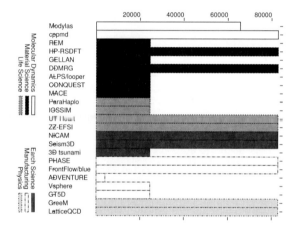

Figure 2. List of applications on the K computer as of September 2012 in 6 categories. X-axis shows the maximum number of nodes used by the application. (up to full 82,944. Provided by Operations and Computer Technologies Division, AICS

the applications is 10 PFLOPS, but the applications can exploit the full performance capacity of the K computer. Additionally, we illustrate how we have tuned applications by showing two examples.

2.1. Supporting a Wide Range of Applications

Figure 2 shows a list of applications on K computer as of September 2012, i.e. before the full service for shared use was started. The X-axis of the figure shows the number of nodes used by the application. As shown in the figure, even in the early days of the K computer, many applications from various fields had already exploited the massively parallel architecture. During 28th September 2012 to 3rd June 2015, there were 2706 jobs using more than 36864 nodes and 1172 jobs using more than 80000 nodes.

Table 2 shows some examples of applications on the K computer. As shown here, while some of them use structured grids, others use unstructured grids. While some ap-

Table 2. Effective applications on the K computer [3][4][5][6][7][8]. The effectiveness (%) is calculated based on the peak performance for the number of nodes used.

Code Name	Characteristics and keywords for the app	Performance (efficiency)	# of nodes
HP-RSDFT	First principles calculation DGEMM (dense matrix calculation)	3.08PFLOPS (44%) 5.43PFLOPS (52%)	55,296 82,944
	Astrophysical N-body FFT	4.45PFLOPS (43%) 5.67PFLOPS (56%)	82,944 82,944
GAMERA	Earthquake simulation Unstructured finite element Space matrix computation	0.8PFLOPS (7.9%)	82,944
NICAM	Global could resolving model Stencil on structured grids	0.87PFLOPS (8.3%)	81,944
SCALE-LES	Regional climate Model Stencil on structures grids	0.7PFLOPS (7%)	82,944
CCS-QCD	Lattice QCD multi-denominational structured grids	0.14PFLOPS (26%)	4096

plications perform dense matrix multiplication, other applications perform sparse matrix multiplication. The K computer can satisfy different requirements from applications.

Most of applications in the K computer are parallelized using MPI and OpenMP, and are written mainly in Fortran.

2.2. Case study 1: First-Principles Calculations

First-principles electronic structure calculations based on a real space density functional theory (RSDFT) [3,4] is one successful application on the K computer. RSDFT calculated electron states of a silicon nanowire with 100,000 atoms, that is close to the actual size of the material. In 2011, RSDFT used 55296 nodes of the K computer and achieved 3.08 PFLOPS. Later, it used 82944 nodes and achieved 5.48 PFLOPS, which is 51.67% of the K computer's peak performance.

RSDFT had been developed to be executed on large scale PC clusters such as PACS-CS and T2K-Tsukuba (installed in 2006 and 2008 respectively). The RSDFT works on 4-dimensional arrays of 3-dimensional space and one-dimension which represents electron orbitals. The 3-dimensional real space had been partitioned into sub-spaces and distributed over the nodes. To execute RSDFT on the K computer, which has more nodes than PACS-CS and T2K-Tsukuba, the Gram Schmidt orthogonalization was further optimized. We adopted 4-dimensional partitioning by parallelizing orbitals as well as the 3-dimensional real space. Moreover, the partitioned 3-dimensional real sub-spaces were mapped onto appropriate nodes of the Tofu network (Fig. 3).

The first breakthrough to achieve effective performance in RSDFT was that Gram Schmidt orthogonalization had been transformed into matrix-matrix products with BLAS Level3 DGEMM (Figure 4). As shown in the equations in Figure 4, DGEMMs of square

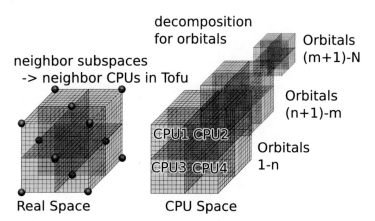

Figure 3. Sub-spaces are mapped onto Tofu network appropriately. Orbitals are decomposed as well

$$\Psi_1' = \Psi_1$$
$$\Psi_2' = \Psi_2 - \Psi_1 \langle \Psi_1 | \Psi_2 \rangle$$
$$\Psi_3' = \Psi_3 - \Psi_1 \langle \Psi_1 | \Psi_3 \rangle - \Psi_2 \langle \Psi_2 | \Psi_3 \rangle$$
$$\Psi_4' = \Psi_4 - \Psi_1 \langle \Psi_1 | \Psi_4 \rangle - \Psi_2 \langle \Psi_2 | \Psi_4 \rangle - \Psi_3 \langle \Psi_3 | \Psi_4 \rangle$$
$$\Psi_5' = \Psi_5 - \Psi_1 \langle \Psi_1 | \Psi_5 \rangle - \Psi_2 \langle \Psi_2 | \Psi_5 \rangle - \Psi_3 \langle \Psi_3 | \Psi_5 \rangle - \Psi_4 \langle \Psi_4 | \Psi_5 \rangle$$
$$\Psi_6' = \Psi_6 - \Psi_1 \langle \Psi_1 | \Psi_6 \rangle - \Psi_2 \langle \Psi_2 | \Psi_6 \rangle - \Psi_3 \langle \Psi_3 | \Psi_6 \rangle - \Psi_4 \langle \Psi_4 | \Psi_6 \rangle - \Psi_5 \langle \Psi_5 | \Psi_6 \rangle$$
$$\Psi_7' = \Psi_7 - \Psi_1 \langle \Psi_1 | \Psi_7 \rangle - \Psi_2 \langle \Psi_2 | \Psi_7 \rangle - \Psi_3 \langle \Psi_3 | \Psi_7 \rangle - \Psi_4 \langle \Psi_4 | \Psi_7 \rangle - \Psi_5 \langle \Psi_5 | \Psi_7 \rangle - \Psi_6 \langle \Psi_6 | \Psi_7 \rangle$$
$$\Psi_8' = \Psi_8 - \Psi_1 \langle \Psi_1 | \Psi_8 \rangle - \Psi_2 \langle \Psi_2 | \Psi_8 \rangle - \Psi_3 \langle \Psi_3 | \Psi_8 \rangle - \Psi_4 \langle \Psi_4 | \Psi_8 \rangle - \Psi_5 \langle \Psi_5 | \Psi_8 \rangle - \Psi_6 \langle \Psi_6 | \Psi_8 \rangle - \Psi_7 \langle \Psi_7 | \Psi_8 \rangle$$

Figure 4. Gram Schmidt orthogonalization was transformed into matrix-matrix products with BLAS Level3 DGEMM. The square areas show the matrix-matrix products. Above them, you can find the triangular areas which can not be transformed into DGEMM

areas in a same column can be computed in parallel after the result of the top triangle area has been computed.

Figure 5 (a) shows the parallel Gram Schmidt orthogonalization over the spatial parallel and orbital parallel node groups. DGEMM can be parallelized and decomposed in a standard way over a group of spatial nodes. For the orbital nodes, we have assigned blocks of calculations in a block-cyclic manner. Figure 5 (b) shows the time line of the Gram Schmidt orthogonalization. In Figure 5 (a) and (b), the squares 2 to 8 can be calculated in parallel after the the result of triangle 1 is broadcast. Apparent in Figure 5 (b), CPUs must wait for the results of the triangle areas. Therefore, in order to avoid the idling CPU times, we have overlapped the calculations of square areas and triangular areas of different columns as shown in the Figure 5 (c). The performance evaluations for the optimized and the original codes are shown in Figure 6. The scalability of the Gram Schmidt orthogonalization is shown in Figure 7.

2.3. Case study 2: Astrophysical N-body Simulation

In 2012, astrophysical N-body simulation had also achieved more than 50% of the peak performance of the K computer [5]. This simulation was the first gravitational N-body simulation with one trillion particles, therefore, it contributed to understand the evolution

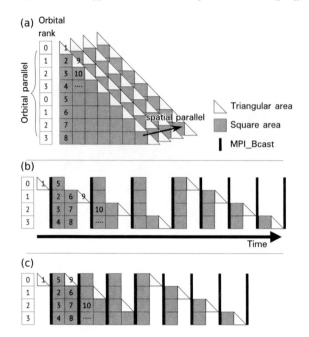

Figure 5. Overlapping calculations of triangular areas and square areas over orbital parallel nodes

of dark matter to reveal the structure of the Universe. It used 82944 nodes and achieved 5.67 PFLOPS, which is 56% of the peak performance [2].

The kernel part of the astrophysical N-body simulation which calculates short-range force had been highly optimized:

- function transformation
  - * branching is reduced
  - * optimized for a SIMD hardware with FMA (multiply-add)
- Implemented with SIMD built-in functions
- Unrolled 8 times by hand
- Unrolled 10 times by compiler (software pipelining)

Owing to the hihgly skilled optimization, the kernel part achieved 97% of theoretical limit of the performance: While the peak performance of a core is 16 GFLOPS, the theoretical limit of the peak performance is 12 GFLOPS since there are 17 FMAs and 17 non-FMAs in an iteration. The optimized kernel code achieved 11.65 GFLOPS/core.

A 3-D multi-section decomposition, where the shape of a domain is rectangular, had been used. In astrophysical N-body simulation, while the initial particles are distributed uniformly, a number of high density dark matter structures should be formed as the simulation progresses. The calculation cost of a high density domain and low density domain are extremely different. Therefore, they adopt the sampling method to determine the ge-

---

[2] 4.45 PFLOPS when the article was submitted. After the submission, authors continued to tune their code and achieved 5.67 PFLOPS

ometries of domains for load balancing. As shown in Figure 8, the geometry of domains are adjusted based on the calculation time for the domains.

Figure 9 shows the scalability of the astrophysical N-body simulations with 2048^3 to 10240^3 particles. As shown in the figure, 10240^3 particles simulation is well scaled from 24576 to 82944 nodes of the K computer.

2.4. Summary

In the previous section, we have briefly introduced different applications on the K computer and focused on two specific applications. As shown in two cases, the successful applications had been tuned based on various view points such as load balancing, communication overhead, and intra-node performance. In addition to such efforts in algorithms, 6D torus/mesh topology of the Tofu had reduced the communication overhead since the network topology had been designed to meet the needs of many distributed real-world simulations. The design of applications seen as being as imporant as the design of architecture. Therefore, we consider the "co-design" for post K computer. In the next section, we briefly show the co-design effort for the "post-K" computer.

3. Project for Post K Computer

On April 1, 2014, RIKEN AICS has launched a new project to create a successor of the K computer. The key concept of the development of the post K computer is "co-design" in which benefits to cover many applications should be maximized.

The co-design is one of the collaborative works between computer science and computational science. The co-design has a bidirectional approach: although a system would be designed on demand from applications, the applications must be optimized to the system. Both of sysmtem and application sides must cope with technical limits and resource constraints. The elements to be co-designed include hardware, system software, algorithms, mathematical libraries and applications (Table 3).

In order to identify target applications used in the co-design process, a committee was organized by the Japanese government to identify 9 priority research areas and 4 exploratory challenges (Table 4). From 9 priority research areas, projects had been selected and typical applications in their areas were provided for the co-design of the post K computer.

In October 2014, Fujitsu Ltd. was selected to work with RIKEN to develop the basic design for the post K computer. In the basic design phase, we decide basic system configurations and parameters by taking the estimated performance of the applications into account. Fujitsu provides (1) a performance estimation tool based on the profiling data obtained from an existing system and (2) a simulator. By using these tools, we evaluate the performance of target applications and will decide basic architecture parameters such as the number of cores, memory and cache hierarchies, and network configuration. At the same time, production costs and electric power have to be taken into account as constraint conditions. We consider a power control method for each application. In order to develop environments with programming languages and compilers, profiling tools, mathematical libraries, we are interacting with application developers to reflect their requests to the basic design.

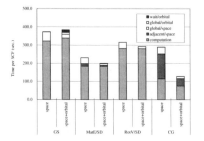

Figure 6. Performance evaluations for the "3D space" and "3D space + orbital" partitionings. Shown is the execution time for SiNW 19,848 atoms on 1536 nodes (12,288 cores). (cited from the presentation slide by Hasegawa et. al [3])

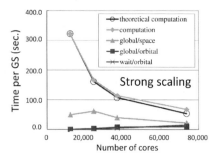

Figure 7. Scalability of Gram Schmidt in grid spaces and orbitals for SiNW 19,848 atoms (cited from the presentation slide by Hasegawa et. al [3])

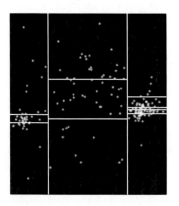

Figure 8. Dynamic load balancing based on the sampling method

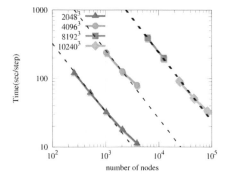

Figure 9. Scalability of the astrophysical N-body simulations with 2048^3 to 10240^3 particles (cited from the presentation slide by Ishiyama et. al [5])

Table 3. The elements to be co-designed

Hardware/Architecture	System Software
Node architecture	OS for many core architecture
(# of cores, SIMD, etc)	Communication and file I/O libraries
Cache	Programming model and languages
(size and bandwidth)	Algorithms and Mathematics libraries
Network	Dense and sparse solvers
(topology, latency and bandwidth)	Eigen solvers
Memory technologies	Domain specific languages
Specialized hardware	Applications
The number of nodes	applications
Storage and file systems	
System configurations	

Table 4. Priority research areas and exploratory challenges for the post K computer

Category	9 Priority Research areas
Health and Longevity	(1) Innovative drug discovery infrastructure ugh functional control of biomolecular systems (2) Integrated computational life science to support personalized and preventive medicine
Disaster prevention and global climate problem	(3) Development of integrated simulation systems for hazard and disaster induced by earthquake and tsunami (4) Advancement of meteorological and global environmental predictions utilizing observational "Big Data"
Energy problem	(5) Development of new fundamental technologies for high efficiency energy creation conversion/storage and use (6) Accelerated development of innovative clean energy systems
Enhancement of industrial competitiveness	(7) Creation of new functional devices and high performance materials to support next-generation industries (8) Development of innovative design and production processes that lead the way for the manufacturing industry in the near future
Development of basic science	(9) Elucidation of the fundamental laws and evolution of the universe
Exploratory challenges	

(1) Frontiers of basic science: challenge to the limits
(2) Construction of models for interaction among multiple socioeconomic
(3) Elucidation of the birth of exoplanets (second earths) and the environmental variations of planets in the solar system
(4) Elucidation of how neural networks realize thinking and its application to artificial intelligence

4. Conclusion

In this paper, we have described applications on K computer and focused on two applications illustrating how to improve their performance. In these applications, kernels and algorithms had been changed to optimize performance for K computer. In addition to the efforts of applications, system features, such as Tofu topology, well-tuned mathmatical libraries, have enhanced the efficiency of applications.

We also have shown the effort to design the post K computer. Our keyword to develop the post K computer is "co-design" which means while a system would be designed on demand from applications, the applications must be optimized to the system.

Acknowledgments.

Authors would like to thank everyone provides information and data about applications on the K computer.

References

[1] Ministry of Education, Culture, Sports, Science and Technology.   K computer project (in Japanse) http://www.mext.go.jp/b_menu/shingi/chousa/ shinkou/031/shiryo/__icsfiles/afieldfile/2013/01/24/1330285_01.pdf.

[2] Yuichiro Ajima, Tomohiro Inoue, Shinya Hiramoto, Toshiyuki Shimizu, and Yuzo Takagi. The tofu interconnect. *IEEE Micro*, 32(1):21–31, 2012.

[3] Yukihiro Hasegawa, Jun-Ichi Iwata, Miwako Tsuji, Daisuke Takahashi, Atsushi Oshiyama, Kazuo Minami, Taisuke Boku, Fumiyoshi Shoji, Atsuya Uno, Motoyoshi Kurokawa, Hikaru Inoue, Ikuo Miyoshi, and Mitsuo Yokokawa. First-principles calculations of electron states of a silicon nanowire with 100,000 atoms on the K computer. In *Proceedings of 2011 International Conference for High Performance Computing, Networking, Storage and Analysis (SC 2011)*, 2011.

[4] Yukihiro Hasegawa, Jun-Ichi Iwata, Miwako Tsuji, Daisuke Takahashi, Atsushi Oshiyama, Kazuo Minami, Taisuke Boku, Hikaru Inoue, Yoshito Kitazawa, Ikuo Miyoshi, and Mitsuo Yokokawa. Performance evaluation of ultra-large-scale first-principles electronic structure calculation code on the K computer. *International Jornal of High Performance Computing Applications*, 28(3):335–355, 2014.

[5] Tomoaki Ishiyama, Keigo Nitadori, and Junichiro Makino. 4.45 Pflops astrophysical N-body simulation on K computer – the gravitational trillion-body problem. In *Proceedings of 2012 International Conference for High Performance Computing, Networking, Storage and Analysis (SC 2012)*, 2012.

[6] Tsuyoshi Ichimura, Kohei Fujita, Seizo Tanaka, Muneo Hori, Maddegedara Lalith, Yoshihisa Shizawa, and Hiroshi Kobayashi. Physics-based urban earthquake simulation enhanced by 10.7 blndof x 30 k time-step unstructured fe non-linear seismic wave simulation. In *Proceedings of 2014 International Conference for High Performance Computing, Networking, Storage and Analysis (SC 2014)*, 2014.

[7] Masaaki Terai, Hisashi Yashiro, Kiyotaka Sakamoto, Shin ichi Iga, Hirofumi Tomita, Masaki Satoh, and Kazuo Minami. Performance optimization and evaluation of a global climate application using a 440m horizontal mesh on the K computer.

[8] Taisuke Boku, Kenichi Ishikawa, Kazuo Minami, Yoshifumi Nakamura, Fujiyoshi Shoji, Daisuke Takahasi, Masaaki Terai, Akira Ukawa, and Tomoaki Yosie. Multi-block/multi-core SSOR preconditioner for the QCD quark solver for K computer. In *Proceedings of The 30th International Symposium on Lattice Field Theory*, 2012.

Parallel Computing: On the Road to Exascale
G.R. Joubert et al. (Eds.)
IOS Press, 2016
847

Author Index